THE BOOK OF WORLD RANKINGS

THE BOOK OF WORLD RANKINGS

By GEORGE THOMAS KURIAN

Facts On File

119 West 57th Street, New York, N.Y. 10019

THE BOOK OF WORLD RANKINGS

Copyright © 1979 by Facts On File, Inc.

Published by Facts on File, Inc.,
119 West 57th Street, New York, N.Y. 10019.

Library of Congress Cataloging in Publication Data

Kurian, George Thomas
  The book of world rankings.

  Bibliography: p.
  Includes index.
  1. Social indicators.   I. Title.
HN25.K87   309'.07'2   79-10452
ISBN 0-87196-394-9

9 8 7 6 5 4 3 2
PRINTED IN
THE UNITED STATES OF AMERICA

Indexed by Laura Soifer

TABLE OF CONTENTS

VI BOOK OF WORLD RANKINGS

INTRODUCTION

THE BOOK OF WORLD RANKINGS is designed as an international scorecard that compares and ranks over 190 nations of the world according to their performance in some 300 key areas.

The output and refinement of international statistics have reached a level where it now seems possible, timely and logical to convert this raw data into indicators of comparative performance. Such rankings are widely used in business and industry—the *Fortune* 500 list is perhaps the most familiar American example. Nation-states function within an environment as competitive as corporations, and an evaluation of their track records is vastly more significant.

THE BOOK OF WORLD RANKINGS includes over 50,000 variables that measure national achievement in 23 broad areas by using no less than 300 specific performance yardsticks, making it one of the most comprehensive data bases ever attempted in the field of international affairs. Interpreted sensibly, the organization of the data in these rankings will help not only to explain and evaluate national behavior but sometimes even to predict it.

Numbers may be used to terrify as well as to comfort; to inform as well as to amuse; to encourage as well as to edify; to accuse as well as to honor; and the numbers in this book do all of these. Perhaps one of the most important contributions of these rankings is to test popular perceptions of national performance and environments. Most of us hold on to perceived notions of alien cultures, notions that are often stereotyped and embedded in prejudice. We may believe that Icelanders are the best read, Americans the most productive, Germans the most ingenious, Indians the poorest and so on. While the rankings bear out these perceptions in a number of cases, they disprove them even more often. Some of these rankings can also tell us what makes the nations tick; why some of them are rich, while others are poor; why some are powerful, while others are powerless and dependent; why some are cauldrons of change, while others are mired in inertia. An effort has been made in each ranking to briefly analyze and interpret the data, but the analyses hew closely to the framework of facts; there has been no attempt to predict trends or force conclusions, although the temptation to do so has frequently been very great.

THE BOOK OF WORLD RANKINGS is not simply concerned with superlatives (although it in-

directly measures excellence) but with establishing the proper rung on which each nation stands. All nations for which comparable data are available are represented in the ranklists, even those that are not currently independent. Only in the rhetoric of the United Nations General Assembly are all nations equal; but in the real world of nations inequality is the rule, and this work underscores just how unequal the nations are in each area of performance.

The selection of data to be included was based on five concepts: availability; comparability; usability; reliability and rankability. Much of the available data was derived from the publications of the United Nations, the World Bank, the International Monetary Fund and the U.S. Agency for International Development, the four principal agencies engaged in the collection of international statistics. Despite the efforts of these agencies, there are a number of subjects on which there are no data for any country and others for which available data are fragmentary. In the *U. N. Statistical Yearbook* there is only one complete table—"Population"—for which data have been provided for each country. Even in this table the figures for many countries represent estimates and conjectures based on sample surveys.

From this pool of available data my first task was to select comparable data, i.e., series where information exists on at least 20 countries. The problems of comparability are discussed in detail below.

The third element is usability. Do the figures really tell us something? Does the ranking add to our knowledge or give us some new insight? Does it provide a backdrop to some emerging trend or a clue to some problem or solution?

The fourth element is reliability. Have the statistics been collected by an international organization without any revealed bias? If they were collected by national organizations, have they been checked for reliability and verified through independent sources?

The fifth element is rankability. Not all valid data are rankable; the spread between the highest and the lowest units may be too small in some cases to be statistically significant. For example, the age of suffrage varies only by a few years among countries. As emphasized earlier we are treating inequalities, and where there are no discernible inequalities, ranking becomes pointless.

One significant feature of the work is that the geographical coverage is as complete as the sources permit. Another is the broad-spectrum characteristic of the indicators themselves. With so many rankings, every important segment of national acitvity has been included. Some crucial subjects, such as defense spending, have been examined from different angles: per capita, per soldier, as percentage of GNP, and so on. The comprehensiveness of the list of rankings is essential since what may be considered of minor importance in large industrialized countries may indeed be critical for small countries. The production of phosphates, for example, is more important for Nauru than even GNP or population. Indeed, with the growing web of interdependence, some apparently trivial indicators can affect the economies of superpowers. The effect of the disappearance of anchovies off the Peruvian coast on beef prices in the United States in the early 1970s—to give just one example—demonstrated vividly how even the citizens of powerful nations can have their daily habits changed by seemingly minor events in distant nations.

One source of unending despair in international statistics is the comparability of data. Strictly, data used in rankings should: be based on identical definitions; relate to the same calendar year or other base period; use the same techniques of collection; and be presented in the same form. Few, if any, of these conditions are ideally met in the rankings in this book. First of all, definitions vary from country to country even for terms that one might imagine could be defined only in one way, such as birth, death, marriage, household, etc. * Secondly, the year or base period varies even more widely. Agricultural or housing censuses are held only once in every 20 or 30 years, and sometimes censuses are begun but never completed because of lack of funds or because of a change of government in the intervening period. There are also discontinuities in the publication of collected data resulting from political instability or civil war, as most recently in Lebanon. Thirdly, the methodology and techniques of data collection vary from country to country.

Only a few countries have the necessary personnel skilled in data-gathering and data analysis procedures. Small countries, faced with the constant demand for statistics beyond the resources of their trained personnel to collect, may find ingenious ways of reporting fabricated data. Given these circumstances, I have invariably taken *the best available data for the latest available year* for each country. In practice this means that data for varying years have been used together and some of the information may go back to the 1960s. If some readers feel this method offends scientific requirements, they should remember that these rankings can only reflect the state of the art in international statistics; the rankings are no better and no worse than the sources from which they are derived.

A further caveat must be entered here about the quality and reliability of data on developing countries. In general there is a direct relationship between the quality and availability of data and the level of economic development. This is attributable not only to the lack of resources and expertise in developing countries but also to deliberate distortion of facts. Many of the developing countries manipulate data to suit their self-image. Because the appearance of economic might, or of rapid development or of a literate and healthy population are important national assets, data in these areas may be modified to back up the official claims. (In one recent case with an ironic twist, Singapore, which has had phenomenal economic growth in recent years, has been accused of doctoring or at the very least misinterpreting various economic indicators to prove that it was poorer than it is in order to continue to qualify for the special concessions granted developing countries by the international financial agencies.) In addition, there is a prohibition against collection and publication of data in some developing countries. There are at least three countries where the publication of national statistics is considered a punishable criminal offense: Equatorial Guinea, Guinea and Cambodia. There are many more countries that consider dissemination of data about their failing economies undesirable for political reasons. Data on developing countries are therefore subject to more serious qualifications and should be used with greater caution.

It must be pointed out here that in most cases only the aggregate or total figures have been derived from the sources cited and that per capita figures or share of total figures are based on my own calculations. In general an effort has been made to present the rankings in their most meaningful form, particularly by minimizing the impact of sheer physical size on national performance. Because the book is aimed at a general rather than specialized audience, I have also tried to avoid, perhaps not always successfully, the scholarly trappings and buzz words that may turn off the lay reader. Technical notes are also limited to the bare minimum. Scholars who need more information on the vintage and quality of the data and the methodology used for collecting data in each case are advised to consult the source or sources cited at the end of each ranking. For more detailed information on data relating to U.S. states they are also advised to consult *THE BOOK OF U.S. RANKINGS* by Clark Judge (Facts On File, 1979).

The second part of this work presents country profiles, describing each country briefly in the light of the rankings. Since countries are not listed alphabetically in the rankings in the first part, I hope that these profiles will add to the usefulness of the book for those engaged in area studies.

The work may be properly described as a beginning, the first of a series. As we refine our techniques of collection and presentation of data and expand the range of our sources, we may be enabled to plot more accurately the progress of each country up and down the rankings. Furthermore, with the second volume in the series the validity of the rankings as barometers of political, economic and social change will become even more apparent.

In the compilation of this work, I have drawn liberally on the resources of a number of persons and organizations, and their assistance is acknowledged separately. But my principal obligation is to Edward W. Knappman, vice-president of Facts On File; every page of this book bears the impress of his editorial skills, lucid thinking, and constructive ideas.

Every effort has been made to make the work as comprehensive, up to date and accurate as possible. However, errors and inadequacies (for which the author assumes full responsibility) are inevitable in a work of such a large scope, and the author welcomes criticisms, corrections and suggestions for inclusion in future editions.

April 1979   GEORGE THOMAS KURIAN

* The U.N. definition of birth illustrates how a simple word can be transformed into a terminological monstrosity: "Live Birth is the complete expulsion or extraction from its mother of a product of conception, irrespective of the duration of pregnancy, which after such separation, breathes or shows any other evidence of life, such as beating of heart, pulsation of the umbilical cord, or definite movement of voluntary muscles, whether or not the umbilical cord has been cut or the placenta is attached; each product of such a birth is considered live-born regardless of gestational age."

Acknowledgments

- Dr. Arthur Banks, Center for Social Analysis, University of Binghamton
- Dr. Hunt Howell, Economic & Social Data Services, Agency for International Development
- Juan Gonzalez, U.N. Dag Hammarskjold Library
- Louis B. Sims, Director, U.S. National Central Bureau, INTERPOL
- Elliott R. Rosenberg, Vice-President, Starch INRA Hooper
- John E. Merriam, Director, Information & Public Affairs, World Bank
- Dr. Ray Cline, Executive Director, The Center for Strategic and International Studies, Georgetown University

Note on
Format & Entry Order

Each ranking begins with an introduction discussing the data in general terms. Entry order following the introduction is as follows:

1. Number of Countries
2. Midpoint (also known as Median)
3. Period Covered: Usually the Year; Sometimes, Latest Available Year
4. Type of Table: Description of Table; Structure of Table, whether Ascending or Descending
5. Highlights & Findings: Discussion of Peculiarities in the Data; General Conclusions; Regional Totals; Degree of Concentration
6. Regional top-ranked and bottom-ranked Countries: Africa, Asia & Oceania, Europe and Western Hemisphere
7. Table: The Rank Order on the Left and the Aggregate on the Right of the Countries. In addition to numerical order the countries are divided into four categories: top 10, upper middle, lower middle and bottom 10.
8. Sources

GEOGRAPHY & CLIMATE

Geography is the gateway to the study of nations. The earth's 135 million sq km (52 million sq mi), excluding Antarctica's 16 million sq km (6 million sq mi), are divided so unevenly among nations that it could be described as the original inequality, as theologians might describe original sin. Geographers, historians, politicians and military strategists group these countries differently according to the conceptual bases or biases of their respective disciplines. The United Nations has adopted a scheme described in *World Population Prospects, 1970-2000* that refers to eight macro regions on the basis of demographic characteristics. Six of these macro regions are further subdivided into 22 regions. Using a broader approach that takes into account geographic and political features as well as demographic ones, we can discern at least 10 zones. In descending order of size they are:

1) Soviet Union, Eastern Europe & Mongolia	24.8 million sq km
2) North America	24.0 million sq km
3) Middle East & North Africa	18.1 million sq km
4) South America	17.6 million sq km
5) Africa South of the Sahara	17.0 million sq km
6) East Asia	10.8 million sq km
7) Oceania	7.7 million sq km
8) South Asia	5.1 million sq km
9) Europe	3.9 million sq km
10) South East Asia	3.9 million sq km

Physical size is the most important equation in the calculus of power. Not only does size determine *Lebensraum* (a perfectly valid word that got into disrepute because of misuse by the Nazis) but it also affects our perceptions of national strength. It is true that many small nations because of their strategic location or financial clout (Israel, Singapore and Switzerland are obvious examples) have a disproportionately large impact, but by and large the so-called superpowers hog the stage of world affairs.

This chapter also deals with five other areas that are purely geographical in character and content: the coldest, the warmest, the wettest and the highest as well as coastline. The last one ranks countries by the length of their international borders. A long coastline and a long border may confer some advantages, but, as the United States is discovering, they also pose problems of surveillance against smugglers and illegal migrants.

1. Total Land Area

There are approximately 150 million sq km (58 million sq mi) of land surface in the world divided among 188 nations. Of these, the top 17 nations occupy nearly two-thirds of the total land mass and the top 71 occupy nearly 80%. But many of the biggest countries have enormous areas of desert and wasteland; only about 26% of the Soviet Union is arable, cultivated or natural pastureland and much of the rest is permafrost. Canada has much less arable or cultivated land (6%) and China a little more (11%). This factor scales these giants down in size considerably so that they roughly match the United States, which has 46% of its territory in arable land or cultivated pasture. Farther down the scale, Australia,

India and Argentina have almost half or more of their land cultivated or arable. Perceptions of territorial extent must therefore be qualified by the determining factor of usable or inhabitable land area.

Territorial extent is based on de facto political sovereignty and does not reflect border disputes or border claims. But following U.N. and U.S. State Department usage, territories under Turkish occupation in Cyprus, under Israeli occupation in the West Bank, and under Moroccan and Mauritanian occupation in the former Western Sahara have been excluded from the national territories of Turkey, Israel, and Morocco and Mauritania respectively.

Number of Countries: 188
Midpoint: 114,478 sq km (44,200 sq mi)
Period Covered: 1978
Type of Ranking: Area in Sq Km and Sq Mi; Share of Total Land Area for Top 10; Highest to Lowest

Highlights & Findings: The first six countries—the Soviet Union, Canada, China, the United States, Brazil and Australia—must be considered in a class by themselves, being giants in every sense of the term. On the next level, taking the top 50 countries, African nations predominate accounting for 23. European countries are relatively smaller; the largest, France, ranks only 46th on the scale.

Regions	Africa	Asia	Europe	Western Hemisphere
Most	Sudan (9)	China (3)	France (46)	Canada (2)
Least	Seychelles (171)	Macao (185)	Vatican City (188)	Bermuda (182)

Rank	Country	Share of Total Land Area %	Sq Km	Sq Mi
		TOP 10		
1.	Soviet Union	14.84	22,274,000	8,599,991
2.	Canada	6.64	9,971,500	3,849,996
3.	China	6.40	9,600,000	3,706,650
4.	United States	6.24	9,363,396	3,615,207
5.	Brazil	5.68	8,521,000	3,289,958
6.	Australia	5.12	7,692,000	2,969,881
7.	India	2.09	3,136,500	1,211,002
8.	Argentina	1.84	2,771,300	1,069,998
9.	Sudan	1.66	2,504,530	967,000
10.	Algeria	1.64	2,460,500	950,000
		UPPER MIDDLE		
11.	Zaire		2,343,950	905,000
12.	Saudi Arabia		2,331,000	900,000
13.	Greenland		2,175,600	840,000
14.	Mexico		1,978,800	764,014
15.	Indonesia		1,906,240	736,000
16.	Libya		1,758,610	679,000
17.	Iran		1,647,240	636,000
18.	Mongolia		1,564,610	604,095
19.	Chad		1,284,640	496,000
20.	Peru		1,284,640	496,000
21.	Niger		1,266,510	489,000
22.	Angola		1,245,790	481,000
23.	Mali		1,204,350	465,000
24.	South Africa		1,178,480	455,011
25.	Ethiopia		1,178,450	455,000
26.	Colombia		1,139,600	440,000
27.	Bolivia		1,098,160	424,000
28.	Mauritania		1,085,210	419,000
29.	Egypt		1,000,258	386,200
30.	Tanzania		939,652	362,800
31.	Nigeria		924,630	357,000
32.	Venezuela		911,680	352,000
33.	Namibia		823,620	318,000
34.	Pakistan		803,000	310,038
35.	Mozambique		786,762	303,768
36.	Turkey		766,640	296,000
37.	Zambia		745,920	288,000
38.	Chile		740,740	286,000
39.	Burma		678,600	262,007
40.	Afghanistan		647,500	250,000
41.	Somalia		637,140	246,000
42.	Central African Empire		626,780	242,000
43.	Madagascar		595,700	230,000
44.	Kenya		582,750	225,000
45.	Botswana		569,800	220,000
46.	France		551,670	212,000
47.	Thailand		512,820	198,000
48.	Spain		505,050	195,000
49.	Cameroon		475,400	183,551
50.	Papua New Guinea		475,369	183,540
51.	Sweden		448,070	173,000
52.	Iraq		445,480	172,000

Rank	Country	Share of Total Land Area %	Sq Km	Sq Mi
53.	Morocco		409,200	157,992
54.	Paraguay		406,630	157,000
55.	Rhodesia (Zimbabwe)		391,090	151,000
56.	Japan		370,370	143,000
57.	Congo		349,650	135,000
58.	Finland		336,700	130,000
59.	Vietnam		329,707	127,300
60.	Ivory Coast		323,750	125,000
61.	Norway		323,750	125,000
62.	Poland		312,354	120,600
63.	Italy		301,217	116,300
64.	Philippines		300,440	116,000
65.	South Yemen		287,490	111,000
66.	Ecuador		274,540	106,000
66.	Upper Volta		274,540	106,000
68.	New Zealand		268,276	103,581
69.	Gabon		264,180	102,000
70.	Yugoslavia		255,892	98,800
71.	West Germany		248,640	96,000
72.	Guinea		246,050	95,000
73.	United Kingdom		243,978	94,200
74.	Ghana		238,280	92,000
75.	Rumania		237,503	91,700
76.	Laos		236,804	91,430
77.	Uganda		235,690	91,000
78.	Guyana		214,970	83,000
79.	Oman		212,380	82,000
80.	Senegal		196,840	76,000
81.	Yemen Arab Republic		194,250	75,000
82.	Uruguay		186,998	72,200
83.	Syria		186,480	72,000
84.	Cambodia		181,300	70,000
85.	Tunisia		164,206	63,400
86.	Nicaragua		147,900	57,104
87.	Surinam		142,709	55,100
88.	Bangladesh		142,500	55,020
		LOWER MIDDLE		
89.	Nepal		141,400	54,594
90.	Greece		132,608	51,200
91.	Czechoslovakia		127,946	49,400
92.	North Korea		121,730	47,000
93.	Benin		115,773	44,700
94.	Cuba		114,478	44,200
95.	Honduras		112,150	43,301
96.	Bulgaria		111,852	43,186
97.	Liberia		111,370	43,000
98.	Guatemala		108,880	42,038
99.	East Germany		108,262	41,800
100.	Iceland		102,952	39,750
101.	South Korea		98,400	37,992
102.	Jordan (1)		96,089	37,100
103.	Malawi		95,053	36,700
104.	Portugal		94,276	36,400
105.	Hungary		92,981	35,900

Rank	Country	Share of Total Land Area %	Sq Km	Sq Mi
106.	French Guiana		90,909	35,100
107.	Austria		83,916	32,400
108.	United Arab Emirates		82,880	32,000
109.	Panama		75,650	29,208
110.	Sierra Leone		72,261	27,900
111.	Ireland		68,894	26,600
112.	Sri Lanka		65,500	25,290
113.	Togo		56,980	22,000
114.	Costa Rica		51,000	19,691
115.	Dominican Republic		48,692	18,800
116.	Bhutan		46,600	17,992
117.	Transkei		44,000	16,988
118.	Denmark		42,994	16,600
119.	Switzerland		41,440	16,000
120.	Guinea-Bissau		36,260	14,000
121.	Netherlands		33,929	13,100
122.	Taiwan		32,260	12,455
123.	Belgium		30,562	11,800
124.	Lesotho		30,303	11,700
125.	Solomon Islands		29,785	11,500
126.	Albania		28,749	11,100
127.	Burundi		28,490	11,000
128.	Equatorial Guinea		27,972	10,800
129.	Haiti		27,713	10,700
130.	Rwanda		25,900	10,000
131.	Djibouti		23,310	9,000
132.	Belize		22,973	8,870
133.	New Caledonia		22,015	8,500
134.	El Salvador		21,400	8,262
135.	Israel		20,720	8,000
136.	Fiji		18,272	7,055
137.	Swaziland		17,364	6,704
138.	Kuwait		16,058	6,200
139.	New Hebrides		14,763	5,700
140.	Malaysia		13,313	5,140
141.	Falkland Islands		12,168	4,698
142.	Jamaica		11,422	4,410
143.	Bahamas		11,396	4,400
144.	Gambia		10,360	4,000
145.	Lebanon		10,360	4,000
146.	Qatar		10,360	4,000
147.	Cyprus		9,251	3,572
148.	Brunei		5,776	2,230
149.	Trinidad & Tobago		5,128	1,980
150.	Cape Verde		4,040	1,560
151.	French Polynesia (e)		4,000	1,544
152.	Western Samoa		2,849	1,100
153.	Luxembourg		2,590	1,000
154.	Reunion		2,512	970
155.	Comoros		2,170	838
156.	Mauritius		1,856	717
157.	Guadeloupe		1,779	687
158.	Faroe Islands		1,340	517
159.	Martinique		1,100	425
160.	Hong Kong		1,036	400

Rank	Country	Share of Total Land Area %	Sq Km	Sq Mi
161.	Netherlands Antilles		1,020	394
162.	Tonga		997	385
163.	Sao Tome & Principe		964	372
164.	Dominica		790	305
165.	Gilbert Islands (e)		684	264
166.	St. Lucia		616	238
167.	Bahrain		596	230
168.	Singapore		583	225
169.	Andorra		466	180
170.	Barbados		430	166
171.	Seychelles		404	156

Rank	Country	Share of Total Land Area %	Sq Km	Sq Mi
172.	St. Kitts-Nevis-Anguilla		389	150
173.	St. Vincent		389	150
174.	Grenada		344	132
175.	Malta		313	121
176.	Maldives		298	115
177.	Antigua		280	108
178.	Cook Islands		240	93
	BOTTOM 10			
179.	Wallis & Futuna		207	80
180.	Liechtenstein		168	65

Rank	Country	Share of Total Land Area %	Sq Km	Sq Mi
181.	San Marino		62	24
182.	Bermuda		54	21
183.	Tuvalu		26	10
184.	Nauru		21	8
185.	Macao		15	6
186.	Gibraltar		6	2
187.	Monaco		1.5	0.5
188.	Vatican City		0.4	0.1

(1) Includes territory under Israeli occupation
(e) Estimates

Source: *U.N. Demographic Yearbook.*

2. Coldest Places

Outside of Antarctica and the Arctic regions, there are very few cold regions where some form of human activity cannot be carried on. Yet, human settlements do not thrive in places where the temperatures are consistently below zero in winter because of the extra burdens imposed on the economy in terms of heating, warm clothing, snow removal, etc. The following ranking rates countries by the lowest temperatures recorded in each. Winters are notably erratic, with cycles of warm winters alternating with cycles of cold ones. The figures therefore represent outer limits recorded over a period of time rather than regular temperatures. They are also for cities; therefore lower temperatures have undoubtedly been reached in more remote or mountainous regions in most of the countries included in this ranking.

Number of Countries: 160
Midpoint: 1.1°C (34°F)
Period Covered: 1977
Type of Ranking: Lowest Recorded Temperatures in Centigrade (Celsius) and Fahrenheit; Highest to Lowest

Highlights & Findings: There are only 30 countries where subzero temperatures are regularly recorded on the Fahrenheit scale. Of these, the most intense cold has been experienced only in Siberia, Alaska, the Northwest Territories of Canada and Greenland.

Region	Africa	Asia & Oceania	Europe	Western Hemisphere
Most	Tsabong (45)	Yakutsk (2)	Kuusamo (7)	Eismitte (1)
Least	Seychelles (157)	Brunei (160)	Gibraltar (83)	Cayenne (153)

Rank	Country	Lowest Recorded Temperature °C	°F
	TOP 10		
1	Eismitte, Greenland	−64.8	−85
2	Yakutsk, Soviet Union	−64.3	−84
3	Fairbanks, U.S.	−54.4	−66
4	Aklavik, Canada	−52.2	−62
5	Ulan Bator, Mongolia	−44.4	−48
6	Harbin, China	−41.7	−43
7	Kuusamo, Finland	−40.0	−40
8	Haparanda, Sweden	−36.7	−34
9	Krakow, Poland	−33.3	−28
10	Cluj, Rumania	−32.2	−26
	UPPER MIDDLE		
11	Prerov, Czechoslovakia	−30.6	−23

Rank	Country	Lowest Recorded Temperature °C	°F
12	Debrecen, Hungary	−30.0	−22
13	Trondheim, Norway	−30.0	−22
14	Erzurum, Turkey	−30.0	−22
15	Kushiro, Japan	−28.3	−19
16	Pyongyang, North Korea	−28.3	−19
17	Nurnberg, West Germany	−27.8	−18
18	Sofia, Bulgaria	−27.2	−17
19	Innsbruck, Austria	−26.7	−16
20	Belgrade, Yugoslavia	−25.6	−14
21	Lyon, France	−25.0	−13
22	Kermanshah, Iran	−25.0	−13
23	Aarhus, Denmark	−24.4	−12
24	Seoul, South Korea	−24.4	−12
25	Zurich, Switzerland	−24.4	−12
26	Luxembourg	−23.3	−10

Rank	Country	Lowest Recorded Temperature °C	°F
27	Akureyri, Iceland	−22.2	−8
28	Kabul, Afghanistan	−21.1	−6
29	Ushuaia, Argentina	−21.1	−6
30	Srinagar, India	−20.0	−4
31	Les Escaldes, Andorra	−17.8	0
32	Burgos, Spain	−17.8	0
33	Perth, United Kingdom	−17.8	0
34	Amsterdam, Netherlands	−16.1	3
35	Thorshavn, Faroe Islands	−13.3	8
36	Dublin, Ireland	−13.3	8
37	Aleppo, Syria	−12.8	9
38	Braganca, Portugal	−12.2	10
39	Punta Arenas, Chile	−11.7	11
40	Stanley, Falkland Islands	−11.1	12
41	Mosul, Iraq	−11.1	12

Rank	Country	Lowest Recorded Temperature °C	°F
42	Chihuahua, Mexico	−11.1	12
43	Canberra, Australia	−10.0	14
44	Venice, Italy	−10.0	14
45	Tsabong, Botswana	−9.4	15
46	Thessaloniki, Greece	−9.4	15
47	Cusco, Peru	−8.9	16
48	Fort Flatters, Algeria	−7.2	19
49	Riyadh, Saudi Arabia	−7.2	19
50	Cangamba, Angola	−6.7	20
51	Bela Vista, Brazil	−6.7	20
52	Kimberley, South Africa	−6.7	20
53	Durres, Albania	−6.1	21
54	Amman, Jordan	−6.1	21
55	Christchurch, New Zealand	−6.1	21
56	Nicosia, Cyprus	−5.0	23
57	Sabhah, Libya	−4.4	24
58	Artigas, Uruguay	−4.4	24
59	Sucre, Bolivia	−3.9	25
60	Quito, Ecuador	−3.9	25
61	Windhoek, Namibia	−3.9	25
62	Rawalpindi, Pakistan	−3.9	25
63	Jerusalem, Israel	−3.3	26
64	Monaco	−2.8	27
65	Marrakech, Morocco	−2.8	27
66	Katmandu, Nepal	−2.8	27
67	Gabes, Tunisia	−2.8	27
68	Bulawayo, Rhodesia (Zimbabwe)	−2.2	28
69	Wadi Halfa, Sudan	−2.2	28
70	Bilma, Niger	−1.7	29
71	Asuncion, Paraguay	−1.7	29
72	Bogota, Colombia	−1.1	30
73	Beirut, Lebanon	−1.1	30
74	Asmara, Ethiopia	−0.6	31
75	Hong Kong	0.0	32
76	Chicoa, Mozambique	0.0	32
77	Taipei, Taiwan	0.0	32
78	Vientiane, Laos	0.0	32
79	Kuwait	0.6	33
LOWER MIDDLE			
80	Cairo, Egypt	1.1	34

Rank	Country	Lowest Recorded Temperature °C	°F
81	Antananarive, Madagascar	1.1	34
82	Valetta, Malta	1.1	34
83	Gibraltar	1.7	35
84	Faya, Chad	2.8	37
85	Araouane, Mali	2.8	37
86	Balovale, United Arab Emirates	2.8	37
87	Balovale, Zambia	3.3	38
88	Kouroussa, Guinea	3.9	39
89	Atar, Mauritania	3.9	39
90	Hamilton, Bermuda	4.4	40
91	Reunion	4.4	40
92	Nassau, Bahamas	5.0	41
93	Guatemala City, Guatemala	5.0	41
94	Nairobi, Kenya	5.0	41
95	Zomba, Malawi	5.0	41
96	Hanoi, Vietnam	5.0	41
97	Iringa, Tanzania	5.6	42
98	Havana, Cuba	6.1	43
99	Dacca, Bangladesh	6.1	43
100	Maiduguri, Nigeria	6.1	43
101	Mandalay, Burma	6.7	44
102	San Salvador, El Salvador	7.2	45
103	Bathurst, Gambia	7.2	45
104	Ngaoundere, Cameroon	7.8	46
105	Bobo Dioulasso, Upper Volta	7.8	46
106	Kaolack, Senegal	8.9	48
107	Merida, Venezuela	8.9	48
108	Belize	9.4	49
109	San Jose, Costa Rica	9.4	49
110	Mauritius	10.0	50
111	St. Helena	10.0	50
112	Bangkok, Thailand	10.0	50
113	Lira, Uganda	10.0	50
114	Kalemi, Zaire	10.0	50
115	Kumasi, Ghana	10.6	51
116	Muscat, Oman	10.6	51
117	Noumea, New Caledonia	11.1	52
118	St. Clair, Trinidad & Tobago	11.1	52
119	Brazzaville, Congo	12.2	54
120	Camp Jacob, Guadeloupe	12.2	54
121	Phnom Penh, Cambodia	12.8	55

Rank	Country	Lowest Recorded Temperature °C	°F
122	Suva, Fiji	12.8	55
123	Porto de Praia, Cape Verde	13.3	56
124	Kingston, Jamaica	13.3	56
125	Martinique	13.3	56
127	Sao Tome, Sao Tome & Principe	13.3	56
128	Bangui, Central African Empire	13.9	57
129	Bouake, Ivory Coast	13.9	57
130	Aden, South Yemen	13.9	57
131	Port-au-Prince, Haiti	14.4	58
132	Tela, Honduras	14.4	58
133	Penfui, Indonesia	14.4	58
134	Manila, Philippines	14.4	58
135	Berbera, Somalia	14.4	58
136	Lome, Togo	14.4	58
137	Santo Domingo, Dominican Rep.	15.0	59
138	Bolama, Guinea-Bissau	15.0	59
139	Colombo, Sri Lanka	15.0	59
140	Mayoumba, Gabon	15.6	60
141	San Juan, Puerto Rico	15.6	60
142	Barbados	16.1	61
143	Santa Isabel, Equatorial Guinea	16.1	61
144	St. Kitts-Nevis-Anguilla	16.1	61
145	Monrovia, Liberia	16.7	62
146	Madang, Papua New Guinea	16.7	62
147	Freetown, Sierra Leone	16.7	62
148	Paramaribo, Surinam	16.7	62
149	Lethem, Guyana	17.2	63
150	Djibouti	17.2	63
BOTTOM 10			
151	Kuala Lumpur, Malaysia	17.8	64
152	Benin	18.3	65
153	Cayenne, French Guyana	18.3	65
154	Singapore	18.9	66
155	Kamaran, Yemen Arab Republic	18.9	66
156	Pago Pago, Samoa	19.4	67
157	Seychelles	19.4	67
158	Cocos (Keeling) Islands	20.0	68
159	Tulagi, Solomon Islands	20.0	68
160	Brunei	21.1	70

Source: Library of Congress.

3. Warmest Places

One of summer's worst ordeals is to watch the mercury climbing inexorably past the 100s until the air crackles with the heat and the earth becomes a scorching hot plate. In 43 countries of the world temperatures over 43.3°C (110°F) have been recorded, and these places are considered as among the most inhospitable to man. Scientists have concluded that the human body can withstand cold better than heat, and it is difficult to imagine that man can survive in these places for any length of time. The rank-ing is by no means conclusive because it is limited to places with metereological stations. It is conceivable that in the forbidding Rub al-Khali in Saudi Arabia, the kavirs of the Central Plateau in Iran and in the Sahara where there are no recording stations, temperatures soar above 60°C (140°F) in the summer. Desert winds such as the harmattan in the Sahara also tend to intensify the heat and shrivel all living things.

Number of Countries: 159
Midpoint: 38.3°C (101°F)
Period Covered: 1976
Type of Ranking: Highest Recorded Temperatures in Centigrade and Fahrenheit; Highest to Lowest

Highlights & Findings: The highest recorded temperature in the world is a sizzling 54.4°C (130° F) in Arouane in Mali, which must therefore be regarded as earth's closest competitor to Hades. Generally, countries with long coastlines as well as island countries have lower temperatures on the average, while interiors and desert regions are hotter.

Region	Africa	Asia & Oceania	Europe	Western Hemisphere
Most	Arouane (1)	Abadan (3)	Seville (24)	Phoenix (18)
Least	St. Helena (157)	Cocos (Keeling) Islands (140)	Thorshavn (159)	Stanley (158)

Highest Recorded Temperature

Rank	Country	°C	°F
	TOP 10		
1	Arouane, Mali	54.4	130
2	Cloncurry, Australia	52.8	127
3	Abadan, Iran	52.8	127
4	Wadi Halfa, Sudan	52.8	127
5	Fort Flatters, Algeria	51.1	124
6	Aswan, Egypt	51.1	124
7	Mosul, Iraq	51.1	124
8	Cufra, Libya	50.0	122
9	Multan, Pakistan	50.0	122
10	Gabes, Tunisia	50.0	122
	UPPER MIDDLE		
11	Faya, Chad	49.4	121
12	Nema, Mauritania	48.9	120
13	Marrakech, Morocco	48.9	120
14	Dhahran, Saudi Arabia	48.9	120
15	Lucknow, India	48.3	119
16	Kuwait	48.3	119
17	Sharjah, United Arab Emirates	47.8	118
18	Phoenix, United States	47.8	118
19	Ouagadougou, Upper Volta	47.8	118
20	Djibouti	47.2	117
21	Guaymas, Mexico	47.2	117
22	Chicao, Mozambique	47.2	117
23	Berbera, Somalia	47.2	117
24	Sevilla, Spain	47.2	117
25	Aleppo, Syria	47.2	117
26	Santiago del Estero, Argentina	46.7	116
27	Nicosia, Cyprus	46.7	116
28	Bilma, Niger	46.7	116
29	Muscat, Oman	46.7	116
30	Iraklion, Crete, Greece	45.6	114
31	Kaolack, Senegal	45.6	114
32	Palermo, Italy	45.0	113
33	Urumchi, China	44.4	112
34	Haifa, Israel	44.4	112
35	Maiduguri, Nigeria	44.4	112
36	Kandahar, Afghanistan	43.9	111
37	Mandalay, Burma	43.9	111
38	Gambela, Ethiopia	43.9	111
39	Toulouse, France	43.9	111
40	Aden, South Yemen	43.9	111
41	Regina, Canada	43.3	110
42	Asuncion, Paraguay	43.3	110
43	Maun, Botswana	43.3	110
44	Cangamba, Angola	42.8	109
45	Ndele, Central African Empire	42.8	109
46	Kouroussa, Guinea	42.8	109
47	Amman, Jordan	42.8	109
48	Adana, Turkey	42.8	109
49	Montevideo, Uruguay	42.8	109
50	Bangladesh, Dacca	42.2	108
51	Uruguaiana, Brazil	42.2	108
52	Vientiane, Laos	42.2	108
53	Tulear, Madagascar	42.2	108
54	Keetmanshoop, Namibia	42.2	108
55	Kazalinsk, Soviet Union	42.2	108
56	Hanoi, Vietnam	42.2	108
57	Balovale, Zambia	42.2	108
58	Varna, Bulgaria	41.7	107
59	Beirut, Lebanon	41.7	107
60	Lagos, Portugal	41.7	107
61	Durban, South Africa	41.7	107
62	Belgrade, Yugoslavia	41.7	107
63	Oursso, Congo	41.1	106
64	Bathurst, Gambia	41.1	106
65	Bolama, Guinea-Bissau	41.1	106
66	Phnom Penh, Cambodia	40.6	105
67	San Salvador, El Salvador	40.6	105
68	Valetta, Malta	40.6	105
69	Bucharest, Rumania	40.6	105
70	Kamaran, Yemen Arab Republic	40.6	105
71	Havana, Cuba	40.0	104
72	Bouake, Ivory Coast	40.0	104
73	Bangkok, Thailand	40.0	104
74	Budapest, Hungary	39.4	103
75	Ngaoundere, Cameroon	38.9	102
76	Santa Isabel, Equatorial Guinea	38.9	102
77	Osaka, Japan	38.9	102
78	Maracaibo, Venezuela	38.9	102
	LOWER MIDDLE		
79	Concepcion, Bolivai	38.3	101
80	Taipei, Taiwan	38.3	101
81	Port-au-Prince, Haiti	38.3	101
82	Penfui, Indonesia	38.3	101
83	Manila, Philippines	38.3	101
84	Geneva, Switzerland	38.3	101
85	St. Clair, Trinidad & Tobago	38.3	101
86	Prerov, Czechoslovakia	37.8	100
87	Frankfurt, West Germany	37.8	100
88	Accra, Ghana	37.8	100
89	Pyongyang, North Korea	37.8	100
90	Rabaul, Papua New Guinea	37.8	100
91	Iquitos, Peru	37.8	100
92	Kigoma, Tanzania	37.8	100
93	Lira, Uganda	37.8	100
94	Hamilton, Bermuda	37.2	99
95	Brunei	37.2	99
96	Santiago, Chile	37.2	99
97	Libreville, Gabon	37.2	99
98	Seoul, South Korea	37.2	99
99	Luxembourg	37.2	99
100	Karonga, Malawi	37.2	99
101	Kuala Lumpur, Malaysia	37.2	99
102	Katmandu, Nepal	37.2	99
103	Noumea, New Caledonia	37.2	99
104	Bulawayo, Rhodesia (Zimbabwe)	37.2	99
105	Colombo, Sri Lanka	37.2	99
106	Paramaribo, Surinam	37.2	99
107	London, United Kingdom	37.2	99
108	Vienna, Austria	36.7	98
109	Cartagena, Colombia	36.7	98
110	Santo Domingo, Dominican Rep.	36.7	98
111	Guayquil, Ecuador	36.7	98
112	Suva, Fiji	36.7	98
113	Warsaw, Poland	36.7	98
114	Pago Pago, Samoa	36.7	98
115	Freetown, Sierra Leone	36.7	98
116	Belize	36.1	97
117	Cayenne, French Guyana	36.1	97
118	Gibraltar	36.1	97
119	Lethem, Guyana	36.1	97
120	Hong Kong	36.1	97
121	Kingston, Jamaica	36.1	97
122	Monrovia, Liberia	36.1	97
123	Ulan Bator, Mongolia	36.1	97
124	Singapore	36.1	97
125	Stockholm, Sweden	36.1	97
126	Kinshasa, Zaire	36.1	97
127	Tela, Honduras	35.6	96
128	Mombasa, Kenya	35.6	96
129	Fort-de-France, Martinique	35.6	96
130	Christchurch, New Zealand	35.6	96
131	Tulagi, Solomon Islands	35.6	96
132	Durres, Albania	35.0	95
133	Bridgetown, Barbados	35.0	95
134	Cotonou, Benin	35.0	95
135	Mauritius	35.0	95
136	Amsterdam, Netherlands	35.0	95
137	Trondheim, Norway	35.0	95
138	Nassau, Bahamas	34.4	94
139	Cape Verde	34.4	94
140	Cocos (Keeling) Islands	34.4	94
141	San Juan, Puerto Rico	34.4	94
142	Lome, Togo	34.4	94
143	Monaco	33.9	93
144	San Jose, Costa Rica	33.3	92
145	Camp Jacob, Guadeloupe	33.3	92
146	Seychelles	33.3	92
147	Les Escaldes, Andorra	32.8	91
148	Copenhagen, Denmark	32.8	91
149	St. Kitts-Nevis-Anguilla	32.8	91
150	Sao Tome, Sao Tome & Principe	32.8	91
	BOTTOM 9		
151	Kuusamo, Finland	32.2	90
152	Guatemala City, Guatemala	32.2	90
153	Ivigtut, Greenland	30.0	86
154	Dublin, Ireland	30.0	86
155	Reunion	28.9	84
156	Akureyri, Iceland	28.3	83
157	St. Helena	27.8	82
158	Stanley, Falkland Islands	24.4	76
159	Thorshavn, Faroe Islands	21.1	70

Source: Library of Congress.

4. Wettest Places

Total annual world precipitation is estimated by the U.S. Geological Survey at 420,000 cubic km (102,000 cubic mi), of which 320,000 cubic km (78,000 cubic mi) falls on the oceans and is not of much use to man and 110,303 cubic km (24,000 cubic mi) falls on the land surface. By continents, Asia receives the most precipitation (32,690 cu km) and is followed by South America (29,355 cu km) Africa (20,780 cu km), North America (13,910 cu km), Europe (7,165 cu km) and Oceania (6,405 cu km). As with other natural resources, there is wide disparity in the distribution of rainfall. There are places in the Sahara region that receive rain only once in several years and even then only a few mm, while Cherrapunji in India receives on the average 2.95 cm (1.2 in.) every day of the year. Because precipitation ultimately determines the groundwater table, the volume of river runoff and the water balance, its absence or paucity can be critical. Nothing can be more damaging to human settlements, agriculture, livestock and indeed every form of human activity as the lack of rain, as was demonstrated so tragically in the Sahel in the early 1970s.

Number of Countries: 158
Midpoint: 124.46 cm (48.8 in.)
Period Covered: 1976
Type of Ranking: Highest Recorded Precipitation in Each Country in Cm and In.; Highest to Lowest

Highlights & Findings: The ranking compares countries by their highest recorded precipitation. Such a ranking has been constructed because in many large countries (such as the United States or Soviet Union, for example) average rainfall will be meaningless. However, there is a strong correlation between this ranking and a ranking by average rainfall because both are determined by such general characteristics as topography, wind systems and latitudes. We discover in the ranking that three regions receive the most rainfall: Southeast Asia, where the rainbearing monsoons function with almost clockwork regularity, Southern West Africa and the West Indies and Central America.

Region	Africa	Asia & Oceania	Europe	Western Hemisphere
Most	Monrovia (6)	Cherrapunji (1)	Bergen (33)	Andagoya (2)
Least	Alexandria (152)	Aden (158)	Nicosia (145)	Falkland Islands (127)

Rank	Country	Cm	In.
	TOP 10		
1	Cherrapunji, India	1,079.50	425.1
2	Andagoya, Colombia	713.74	281.1
3	Pago Pago, Samoa	492.76	193.6
4	Moulmein, Burma	482.60	190.2
5	Tabing, Indonesia	444.50	175.4
6	Monrovia, Liberia	441.96	174.9
7	Conakry, Guinea	429.26	169.0
8	Kuching, Malaysia	391.16	153.7
9	Guadeloupe	355.60	140.4
10	Freetown, Sierra Leone	350.52	137.6
	UPPER MIDDLE		
11	Madang, Papua New Guinea	347.98	137.2
12	Yakutat, United States	335.28	132.0
13	Brunei	332.74	131.0
14	Cayenne, French Guyana	320.04	126.1
15	Tulagi, Solomon Islands	312.42	123.4
16	Los Evangelistas, Chile	302.26	119.4
17	Suva, Fiji	297.18	117.1
18	Iquitos, Peru	274.32	107.7
19	Vaupes, Brazil	266.70	105.4
20	Libreville, Gabon	248.92	98.8
21	Tela, Honduras	243.84	96.1
22	Prince Rupert, Canada	241.30	95.3
23	Singapore	241.30	95.0
24	Seychelles	233.68	92.5
25	Colombo, Sri Lanka	233.68	92.3
26	Paramaribo, Surinam	231.14	91.0
27	Reunion	228.60	90.5
28	Georgetown, Guyana	226.06	88.7
29	Bolama, Guinea-Bissau	218.44	85.9
30	Hong Kong	215.90	85.1
31	Manila, Philippines	208.28	82.0
32	Martinique	203.20	80.4
33	Bergen, Norway	200.66	78.8
34	Cocos (Keeling) Islands	198.12	78.2
35	Ho Chi Minh City, Vietnam	198.12	78.1
36	Abidjan, Ivory Coast	195.58	77.1
37	Nagasaki, Japan	190.50	75.5
38	Santa Isabel, Equatorial Guinea	190.50	74.9
39	Belize	187.96	74.4
40	Dacca, Bangladesh	187.96	73.9
41	Taipei, Taiwan	185.42	72.7
42	Lagos, Nigeria	182.88	72.3
43	San Jose, Costa Rica	180.34	70.8
44	Santa Elena, Venezuela	180.34	70.7
45	San Salvador, El Salvador	177.80	70.0
46	Thursday Island, Australia	170.18	67.5
47	Vientiane, Laos	170.18	67.5
48	Kisangani, Zaire	170.18	67.1
49	Vera Cruz, Mexico	167.64	65.7
50	San Juan, Puerto Rico	162.56	64.2
51	St. Clair, Trinidad & Tobago	162.56	64.2
52	Canton, China	162.56	63.6
53	Yaounde, Cameroon	154.94	61.2
54	Bangui, Central African Empire	154.94	60.8
55	Kampala, Uganda	154.94	60.7
56	Sofala, Mozambique	152.40	59.9
57	Oursso, Congo	149.86	58.6
58	Bangkok, Thailand	147.32	57.8
59	Hamilton, Bermuda	147.32	57.6
60	Nova Lisboa, Angola	144.78	57.0
61	Faroe Islands	142.24	56.2
62	Katmandu, Nepal	142.24	56.2
63	Santo Domingo, Dominican Rep.	142.24	55.8
64	Kumasi, Ghana	139.70	55.2
65	Phnom Penh, Cambodia	139.70	54.8
66	Braganca, Portugal	137.16	53.8
67	Antananarive, Madagascar	134.62	53.4
68	Port au Prince, Haiti	134.62	53.3
69	Zomba, Malawi	134.62	52.9
70	Cotonou, Benin	132.08	52.4
71	Asuncion, Paraguay	132.08	51.8
72	Guatemala City, Guatemala	129.54	51.8
73	Bathurst, Gambia	129.54	51.0
74	La Guerite, St. Christopher-Nevis-Anguilla	129.54	50.9
75	Mauritius	129.54	50.6
76	Barbados	127.0	50.3
77	Seoul, South Korea	124.46	49.2
78	Auckland, New Zealand	124.46	49.1
79	Gambela, Ethiopia	124.46	48.8
80	Artigas, Uruguay	124.46	48.6
	LOWER MIDDLE		
81	Havana, Cuba	121.92	48.2
82	Mombasa, Kenya	119.38	47.3
83	Genoa, Italy	119.38	46.6
84	Djibouti	116.84	46.0

Rank	Country	Highest Recorded Rainfall Cm	In.
85	Corrientes, Argentina	116.84	46.4
86	Nassau, Bahamas	116.84	46.4
87	Bobo Dioulasso, Upper Volta	116.84	46.4
88	Bamako, Mali	111.76	44.1
89	Quito, Ecuador	111.76	43.9
90	Noumea, New Caledonia	109.22	43.5
91	Wau, Sudan	109.22	43.3
92	Durres, Albania	109.22	42.9
93	Dar es Salaam, Tanzania	106.68	41.9
94	Cardiff, United Kingdom	106.68	41.9
95	Cork, Ireland	104.14	41.3
96	Zurich, Switzerland	104.14	40.9
97	Durban, South Africa	101.60	39.7
98	Concepcion, Bolivia	99.06	38.6
99	Balovale, Zambia	96.52	38.3
100	Sao Tome, Sao Tome & Principe	96.52	38.0
101	Cherbourg, France	93.98	37.3
102	Am Timan, Chad	93.98	37.2
103	Rawalpindi, Pakistan	91.44	36.5
104	Pyongyang, North Korea	91.44	36.4
105	Petropavlovsk, Soviet Union	91.44	35.9
106	Tangier, Morocco	88.90	35.3
107	Beirut, Lebanon	88.90	35.1
108	Split, Yugoslavia	88.90	35.1
109	Les Escaldes, Andorra	88.90	34.3
110	Munich, West Germany	86.36	34.1

Rank	Country	Highest Recorded Rainfall Cm	In.
111	Reykjavik, Iceland	86.36	33.9
112	Innsbruck, Austria	86.36	33.8
113	Salisbury, Rhodesia (Zimbabwe)	83.82	32.6
114	St. Helena	81.28	32.1
115	Kingston, Jamaica	78.74	31.5
116	Istanbul, Turkey	78.74	31.5
117	Bone, Algeria	78.74	31.0
118	Lome, Togo	78.74	31.0
119	Goteberg, Sweden	76.20	30.5
120	Kaolack, Senegal	76.20	30.3
121	Monaco	76.20	30.1
122	Gibraltar	76.20	29.7
123	Luxembourg	73.66	29.2
124	Krakow, Poland	73.66	28.6
125	Rhodes, Greece	71.12	28.5
126	Helsinki, Finland	71.12	27.6
127	Falkland Islands	68.58	26.8
128	Aarhus, Denmark	68.58	26.6
129	Haifa, Israel	66.04	26.2
130	Amsterdam, Netherlands	66.04	25.6
131	Sofia, Buigaria	63.50	25.0
132	Prerov, Czechoslovakia	63.50	24.8
133	Budapest, Hungary	60.96	24.2
134	Cluj, Rumania	60.96	24.0
135	Barcelona, Spain	58.42	23.5
136	Niamey, Niger	55.88	21.6

Rank	Country	Highest Recorded Rainfall Cm	In.
137	Valetta, Malta	50.80	20.3
138	Maun, Botswana	45.72	18.2
139	Mogadiscio, Somalia	43.18	16.9
140	Tunis, Tunisia	40.64	16.5
141	Kermanshah, Iran	40.64	16.4
142	Aleppo, Syria	38.10	15.5
143	Mosul, Iraq	38.10	15.2
144	Tripoli, Libya	38.10	15.1
145	Nicosia, Cyprus	38.10	14.6
146	Windhoek, Namibia	35.56	14.3
147	Kabul, Afghanistan	33.02	12.6
148	Nema, Mauritania	29.52	11.6
	BOTTOM 10		
149	Amman, Jordan	27.46	10.9
150	Porto da Praia, Cape Verde	26.03	10.2
151	Ulan Bator, Mongolia	19.05	7.7
152	Alexandria, Egypt	17.78	7.0
153	Kuwait	12.85	5.1
154	Sharjah, United Arab Emirates	10.47	4.2
155	Muscat, Oman	10.00	3.9
156	Dhahran, Saudi Arabia	8.89	3.5
157	Kamaran, Yemen Arab Republic	8.25	3.4
158	Aden, South Yemen	6.35	2.5

Source: Library of Congress.

5. Highest Elevation

This ranking rates countries by the elevation of their highest point, often the highest national peak. Although the percentage of mountainous terrain in each country's land area would have been more meaningful, such statistics have never been compiled. Elevation might, however, give us a clue in this direction because the countries with the highest elevations are also very often the most mountainous.

Number of Countries: 148
Midpoint: 2,620 meters (8,595 ft)
Period Covered: 1977
Type of Ranking: Elevation of Highest Point in Meters and Ft; Highest to Lowest

Highlights & Findings: The top seven countries are those that share the majestic Himalayas, whose serried ranges stretch from Afghanistan to Burma. Immediately following are the five countries that share the Andes. It might be interesting to note here that many geographers believe (because the earth is shaped not entirely as a sphere but as an irregular oval) the Andes reach higher into the sky than the Himalayas. There are at least 30 countries with no prominent mountainous feature.

Regions	Africa	Asia & Oceania	Europe	Western Hemisphere
Most	Tanzania (16)	China (1)	Soviet Union (6)	Argentina (8)
Least	Guinea-Bissau (144)	Maldives (148)	Denmark (145)	Bahamas (147)

Rank	Country	Elevation of Highest Point Meters	Ft
	TOP 10		
1	China	8,848	29,028
2	Nepal	8,848	29,028
3	Pakistan	8,611	28,250
4	India	7,817	25,645

Rank	Country	Elevation of Highest Point Meters	Ft
5	Bhutan	7,541	24,740
6	Soviet Union	7,495	24,590
7	Afghanistan	7,485	24,557
8	Argentina	6,958	22,831
9	Chile	6,880	22,572

Rank	Country	Elevation of Highest Point Meters	Ft
10	Peru	6,768	22,205
	UPPER MIDDLE		
11	Bolivia	6,400	21,000
12	Ecuador	6,267	20,561

Rank	Country	Elevation of Highest Point Meters	Ft
13	United States	6,194	20,320
14	Burma	6,096	20,000
15	Canada	5,950	19,520
16	Tanzania	5,894	19,340
17	Colombia	5,775	18,947
18	Iran	5,771	18,934
19	Mexico	5,700	18,701
20	Kenya	5,199	17,058
21	Turkey	5,185	17,011
22	Zaire	5,109	16,762
23	Indonesia	5,030	16,503
24	Venezuela	5,002	16,411
25	Uganda	4,876	16,000
26	France	4,807	15,771
27	Italy	4,731	15,521
28	Switzerland	4,634	15,203
29	Ethiopia	4,618	15,153
30	Rwanda	4,532	14,870
31	Papua New Guinea	4,509	14,793
32	Mongolia	4,362	14,311
33	Guatemala	4,220	13,845
34	Morocco	4,165	13,665
35	Malaysia	4,101	13,455
36	Taiwan	3,997	13,113
37	Costa Rica	3,819	12,530
38	Austria	3,797	12,457
39	Japan	3,776	12,388
40	New Zealand	3,764	12,349
41	Yemen Arab Republic	3,760	12,336
42	Greenland	3,700	12,139
43	Iraq	3,609	11,840
44	Lesotho	3,482	11,425
45	Spain	3,478	11,411
46	Panama	3,477	11,410
47	South Africa	3,377	11,081
48	Dominican Republic	3,175	10,417
49	Libya	3,150	10,335
50	Chad	3,145	10,318
51	Vietnam	3,143	10,312
52	Saudi Arabia	3,133	10,279
53	Lebanon	3,083	10,115
54	Malawi	3,048	10,000
55	Brazil	3,014	9,888
56	Algeria	3,003	9,852
57	West Germany	2,963	9,721
58	Philippines	2,954	9,690
59	Andorra	2,946	9,665

Rank	Country	Elevation of Highest Point Meters	Ft
60	Bulgaria	2,925	9,596
61	Greece	2,917	9,570
62	Madagascar	2,880	9,450
63	Honduras	2,870	9,400
64	Yugoslavia	2,863	9,393
65	Guyana	2,835	9,304
66	Cape Verde	2,829	9,281
67	Laos	2,816	9,242
68	Syria	2,814	9,232
69	Albania	2,750	9,023
70	North Korea	2,744	9,003
71	Haiti	2,677	8,783
72	Czechoslovakia	2,654	8,707
73	Egypt	2,642	8,668
74	Angola	2,620	8,595
	LOWER MIDDLE		
75	Liechtenstein	2,599	8,527
76	Rhodesia (Zimbabwe)	2,595	8,517
77	Thailand	2,595	8,514
78	Rumania	2,543	8,343
79	Sri Lanka	2,524	8,281
80	South Yemen	2,513	8,245
81	Poland	2,499	8,199
82	Norway	2,470	8,104
83	Cameroon	2,438	8,000
84	Nicaragua	2,438	8,000
85	Mozambique	2,436	7,992
86	El Salvador	2,417	7,933
87	Somalia	2,406	7,894
88	Comoros	2,361	7,746
89	Jamaica	2,256	7,402
90	Australia	2,228	7,310
91	Sudan	2,133	7,000
92	Zambia	2,133	7,000
93	Iceland	2,119	6,952
94	Sweden	2,111	6,926
95	Nigeria	2,042	6,699
96	Sao Tome & Principe	2,024	6,640
97	Cuba	1,994	6,552
98	Portugal	1,993	6,539
99	Cyprus	1,952	6,406
100	South Korea	1,950	6,398
101	Sierra Leone	1,947	6,390
102	Swaziland	1,862	6,109
103	Guinea	1,828	6,000
104	Niger	1,798	5,900

Rank	Country	Elevation of Highest Point Meters	Ft
105	Jordan	1,754	5,755
106	Ivory Coast	1,752	5,748
107	Burundi	1,706	5,600
108	Gabon	1,574	5,165
109	Tunisia	1,544	5,065
110	United Arab Emirates	1,527	5,010
111	Congo	1,500	4,921
112	Liberia	1,380	4,528
113	United Kingdom	1,343	4,406
114	Finland	1,324	4,344
115	Fiji	1,323	4,341
116	Surinam	1,286	4,218
117	Central African Empire	1,280	4,200
118	Bangladesh	1,229	4,034
119	Botswana	1,219	4,000
120	East Germany	1,214	3,983
121	Israel	1,208	3,963
122	Equatorial Guinea	1,200	3,937
123	Ireland	1,041	3,414
124	Tonga	1,030	3,380
125	Hungary	1,015	3,330
126	Togo	986	3,235
127	Trinidad & Tobago	940	3,085
128	Belize	914	3,000
129	Seychelles	912	2,993
130	Ghana	884	2,900
131	Grenada	840	2,757
132	Mauritius	826	2,711
133	Cambodia	762	2,500
134	Upper Volta	717	2,352
135	Mali	701	2,300
136	Belgium	694	2,277
137	Benin	610	2,001
138	Paraguay	609	1,998
139	Uruguay	609	1,998
	BOTTOM 9		
140	Luxembourg	559	1,835
141	Senegal	487	1,600
142	Mauritania	457	1,500
143	Netherlands	322	1,051
144	Guinea-Bissau	300	1,000
145	Denmark	173	568
146	Bahrain	135	443
147	Bahamas	63	206
148	Maldives	24	80

Source: *WorldBook Encyclopedia.*

6. National Coastlines

A coastline is one of the most strategic advantages and natural resources of a nation. It ensures free and unfettered participation in world commerce, provides access to coastal fishing grounds and extends territorial sovereignty over offshore mineral deposits. It may also promote the development of a strong navy and the creation of urban settlements and free trade zones around ports and harbors. Attractive beaches often bring in additional tourist revenues.

The problem of nations without coastlines has engaged the attention of the United Nations and has been the subject of many international conferences. There are 30 such landlocked nations in the world, nine in Europe, two in Latin America, five in Asia and 14 in Africa. They are: Bolivia and Paraguay in Latin America; Czechoslovakia, Hungary, Switzerland, Austria, Liechtenstein, San Marino, Andorra,

Luxembourg and the Vatican in Europe; Afghanistan, Bhutan, Nepal, Laos and Mongolia in Asia; and Malawi, Rhodesia (Zimbabwe), Botswana, Zambia, Swaziland, Lesotho, Central African Empire, Mali, Niger, Chad, Upper Volta, Uganda, Rwanda and Burundi in Africa.

Number of Countries: 157
Midpoint: 901 km (560 mi)
Period Covered: 1978
Type of Ranking: Length of Coastline in Km and Mi; Most to Least

Highlights & Findings: Of the total length of 599,653 km (372,384 mi) of coastline, half is accounted for by the top seven countries. Canada alone has 15% of the world's total coastline.

Regions	Africa	Asia & Oceania	Europe	Western Hemisphere
Longest	Madagascar (25)	Indonesia (2)	Soviet Union (3)	Canada (1)
Shortest	Zaire (152)	Naura (155)	Monaco (157)	St. Vincent (146)

Rank	Country	Coastline in km	Coastline in mi		Rank	Country	Coastline in km	Coastline in mi		Rank	Country	Coastline in km	Coastline in mi
	TOP 10				50	Ecuador	2,237	1,389		100	Seychelles	491	305
1	Canada	90,908	56,453		51	Oman	2,092	1,299		101	Guyana	459	285
2	Indonesia	54,716	33,978		52	Morocco	1,835	1,139		102	Netherlands	451	280
3	Soviet Union	46,670	28,982		53	Portugal	1,793	1,113		103	Cambodia	443	275
4	Greenland	44,087	27,378		54	Haiti	1,771	1,099		104	Tonga	419	260
5	Australia	25,760	15,997		55	Libya	1,770	1,099		105	Albania	418	260
6	Philippines	22,540	13,997		56	Angola	1,600	993		106	Western Samoa	403	250
7	United States	19,924	12,372		57	Yugoslavia	1,521	944		107	Cameroon	402	249
8	Norway	16,093	9,993		58	Namibia	1,489	924		108	Sierra Leone	402	249
9	New Zealand	15,134	9,398		59	West Germany	1,488	924		109	Guatemala	400	248
10	China	14,500	9,004		60	Taiwan	1,449	900		110	Belize	386	240
	UPPER MIDDLE				61	Ireland	1,448	899		111	Surinam	386	240
11	Greece	13,676	8,492		62	United Arab Emirates	1,448	899		112	French Guyana	378	235
12	United Kingdom	12,429	7,718		63	Tanzania	1,424	884		113	Netherlands Antilles	364	226
13	Japan	12,075	7,498		64	South Yemen	1,383	858		114	Trinidad & Tobago	362	225
14	Mexico	9,330	5,794		65	Sri Lanka	1,340	832		115	Bulgaria	354	220
15	Brazil	7,491	4,652		66	Costa Rica	1,290	801		116	Guinea	346	215
16	Turkey	7,200	4,471		67	Dominican Republic	1,288	800		117	Comoros	340	211
17	India	7,000	4,347		68	Falkland Islands	1,288	800		118	Djibouti	314	195
18	Chile	6,435	3,996		69	Algeria	1,183	735		119	El Salvador	307	190
19	Solomon Islands	5,313	3,299		70	Gilbert Islands	1,143	710		120	Guadeloupe	306	190
20	Papua New Guinea	5,152	3,200		71	Tunisia	1,143	710		121	Equatorial Guinea	296	183
21	Italy	4,996	3,102		72	Fiji	1,129	701		122	Martinique	290	180
22	Argentina	4,989	3,098		73	Finland	1,126	700		123	Guinea-Bissau	274	170
23	Iceland	4,988	3,097		74	Ethiopia	1,094	679		124	Israel	273	170
24	Spain	4,964	3,082		75	Pakistan	1,046	650		125	Lebanon	225	140
25	Madagascar	4,828	2,998		76	Jamaica	1,022	634		126	Rumania	225	140
26	Malaysia	4,675	2,903		77	Cape Verde	965	606		127	Sao Tome & Principe	209	130
27	Cuba	3,735	2,319		78	Nicaragua	910	565		128	Reunion	201	125
28	Bahamas	3,542	2,199		79	East Germany	901	560		129	St. Christopher-Nevis-Anguilla	193	120
29	Vietnam	3,444	2,138			*LOWER MIDDLE*				130	Singapore	193	120
30	France	3,427	2,128		80	Gabon	885	550		131	Syria	193	120
31	Denmark	3,379	2,098		81	Nigeria	853	530		132	Mauritius	177	110
32	Thailand	3,219	1,999		82	Sudan	853	530		133	Congo	169	105
33	Sweden	3,218	1,998		83	Honduras	820	509		134	Bahrain	161	100
34	Iran	3,180	1,974		84	Faroe Islands	764	474		135	Brunei	161	100
35	Burma	3,060	1,900		85	Mauritania	754	468		136	St. Lucia	158	98
36	Somalia	3,025	1,878		86	Hong Kong	733	455		137	Antigua	153	95
37	South Africa	2,881	1,789		87	Uruguay	660	410		138	Dominica	148	92
38	Venezuela	2,800	1,738		88	Cyprus	644	400		139	Malta	140	87
39	New Hebrides	2,528	1,570		89	Maldives	644	400		140	Wallis & Futuna	129	80
40	French Polynesia	2,525	1,568		90	Bangladesh	580	360		141	Grenada	121	75
41	Saudi Arabia	2,510	1,558		91	Liberia	579	360		142	Benin	121	75
42	North Korea	2,495	1,549		92	Qatar	563	350		143	Cook Islands	120	74
43	Panama	2,490	1,546		93	Ghana	539	334		144	Bermuda	103	64
44	Mozambique	2,470	1,534		94	Kenya	536	332		145	Barbados	97	60
45	Egypt	2,450	1,521		95	Senegal	531	330		146	St. Vincent	84	52
46	Colombia	2,414	1,499		96	Yemen Arab Republic	523	325		147	Gambia	80	50
47	Peru	2,414	1,499		97	Ivory Coast	515	320			*BOTTOM 10*		
48	South Korea	2,413	1,498		98	Kuwait	499	310		148	Belgium	64	40
49	New Caledonia	2,254	1,400		99	Poland	491	305		149	Iraq	58	36

Rank	Country	Coastline in km	Coastline in mi	Rank	Country	Coastline in km	Coastline in mi	Rank	Country	Coastline in km	Coastline in mi
150	Togo	56	34	153	Jordan	26	16	156	Gibraltar	12	7
151	Macao	40	25	154	Tuvalu	26	16	157	Monaco	4	2
152	Zaire	37	23	155	Nauru	24	15				

Source: *National Basic Intelligence Factbook.*

7. International Borders

Among the principal responsibilities of a sovereign nation is the defense of its frontiers. Because most national boundaries were determined by historical accidents or were settled through warfare or by colonialization, many borders appear as arbitrary lines drawn across maps. The length of the borders, the number of neighbors, the political compatibility of these neighbors and the pressures of irredentist claims or territorial ambitions are among the more crucial determinants of foreign policy. Although a long border may require more customs and immigration checkpoints and surveillance, some of the longest borders are among the most peaceful in the world; the U.S.-Canadian border is a case in point. On the other hand, the sensitivity of the frontier is often inversely related to the homogeneity of the neighbors. Two of the most heavily armed borders are those that divide South and North Korea and East and West Germany. Also, frontiers are more important for landlocked nations than for those with access to the sea. In the following section an effort has been made to identify those nations with border disputes, either active or quiescent, with an asterisk.

Number of Countries: 138
Midpoint: 2,309 km; 1,434 mi
Period Covered: 1978
Type of Ranking: Length of Land Border in Km and Mi (Nations with disputed borders identified with an asterisk); Most to Least

Highlights & Findings: Since the length of a country's border is related to its land area, this ranking bears a rough correspondence to the ranking by land area. But there are significant variations. Of the first 10 nations in this ranking, two do not appear among the top 10 in the ranking by land area and all countries appear in different order.

Regions	Africa	Asia	Europe	Western Hemisphere
Most	Zaire (6)	China (1)	Soviet Union (2)	Brazil (3)
Least	Swaziland (121)	Hong Kong (135)	Gibraltar (138)	Haiti (124)

Rank Country (Disputed Border *)	Land Border in km	Land Border in mi	Rank Country (Disputed Border *)	Land Border in km	Land Border in mi	Rank Country (Disputed Border *)	Land Border in km	Land Border in mi
TOP 10			18 Chad*	5,987	3,718	38 Venezuela*	4,181	2,596
1 China*	24,000	14,904	19 Pakistan*	5,900	3,664	39 Nigeria*	4,034	2,505
2 Soviet Union*	20,619	12,804	20 Burma	5,850	3,633	40 Tanzania*	3,883	2,411
3 Brazil*	13,076	8,120	21 Niger	5,745	3,568	41 Namibia	3,798	2,358
4 India*	12,700	7,886	22 Afghanistan*	5,510	3,421	42 Botswana	3,774	2,343
5 United States	12,002	7,453	23 Iran*	5,318	3,302	43 Iraq*	3,668	2,278
6 Zaire*	9,902	6,149	24 Ethiopia*	5,198	3,228	44 Czechoslovakia	3,540	2,198
7 Argentina*	9,414	5,846	25 Mauritania*	5,118	3,178	45 Guinea	3,476	2,158
8 Canada	9,010	5,595	26 Angola*	5,070	3,148	46 Paraguay*	3,444	2,139
9 Mongolia	8,000	4,968	27 Laos	5,053	3,138	47 Kenya*	3,368	2,091
10 Sudan*	7,805	4,847	28 Central African Empire	4,981	3,093	48 Upper Volta*	3,307	2,053
			29 Thailand*	4,868	3,023	49 Ivory Coast	3,227	2,004
UPPER MIDDLE			30 Mozambique	4,627	2,873	50 Poland	3,090	1,919
11 Mali*	7,459	4,632	31 Vietnam*	4,562	2,833	51 Rhodesia (Zimbabwe)	3,017	1,873
12 Chile*	6,325	3,928	32 Cameroon	4,554	2,828	52 Yugoslavia	3,001	1,863
13 Algeria*	6,260	3,887	33 Saudi Arabia*	4,537	2,817	53 Rumania	2,969	1,844
14 Peru*	6,131	3,807	34 Congo	4,514	2,803	54 France	2,888	1,793
15 Bolivia*	6,083	3,777	35 Libya*	4,345	2,698	55 Malawi*	2,881	1,789
16 Colombia*	6,035	3,747	36 West Germany	4,232	2,628	56 Nepal	2,800	1,739
17 Zambia	6,003	3,728	37 Mexico*	4,220	2,620	57 Indonesia	2,736	1,699

Rank Country (Disputed Border *)	Land Border in km	Land Border in mi	Rank Country (Disputed Border *)	Land Border in km	Land Border in mi	Rank Country (Disputed Border *)	Land Border in km	Land Border in mi
58 Senegal	2,680	1,664	85 North Korea	1,675	1,040	114 Panama	630	391
59 Uganda*	2,680	1,664	86 Togo	1,646	1,022	115 Equatorial Guinea	539	335
60 Austria	2,582	1,603	87 Guatemala*	1,625	1,009	116 Lebanon	531	330
61 Norway	2,579	1,601	88 Surinam*	1,561	969	117 Djibouti	517	321
62 Guyana*	2,575	1,599	89 Honduras*	1,530	950	118 Belize	515	320
63 Turkey*	2,574	1,598	90 Yemen Arab Republic	1,528	949	119 El Salvador	515	320
64 Bangladesh	2,535	1,574	91 Tunisia*	1,408	874	120 Kuwait	459	285
65 Finland	2,534	1,574	92 Oman*	1,384	859	121 Swaziland	435	270
66 Egypt*	2,527	1,569	93 South Yemen	1,383	859	122 Brunei	381	236
67 Cambodia*	2,438	1,514	94 Belgium	1,377	855	123 Dominican Republic	361	224
68 Gabon	2,422	1,504	95 Uruguay	1,352	839	124 Haiti	361	224
69 East Germany	2,309	1,434	96 Liberia	1,336	829	125 Ireland	360	223
70 Malaysia	2,295	1,425	97 Nicaragua	1,220	758	126 United Kingdom	360	223
71 Ghana	2,285	1,419	98 Portugal	1,207	750	127 Luxembourg	356	221
72 Somalia*	2,263	1,405	99 Greece	1,191	739	128 South Korea	241	150
73 Hungary	2,245	1,394	100 French Guiana	1,183	735			
74 Sweden	2,196	1,364	101 United Arab Emirates	1,094	679			
75 Syria*	2,196	1,364	102 Israel	1,036	643	*BOTTOM 10*		
76 South Africa	2,044	1,269	103 Netherlands	1,022	635	129 Macao	201	125
77 Morocco*	1,996	1,240	104 Burundi	974	605	130 Andorra	105	65
			105 Papua New Guinea	966	600	131 Liechtenstein	76	47
LOWER MIDDLE			106 Sierra Leone	933	579	132 Denmark	68	42
78 Benin	1,963	1,219	107 Rwanda	877	545	133 Qatar	56	35
79 Ecuador*	1,931	1,199	108 Bhutan	870	540	134 San Marino	34	21
80 Spain	1,899	1,179	109 Lesotho	805	500	135 Hong Kong	24	15
81 Switzerland	1,884	1,170	110 Gambia	740	460	136 Monaco	3.7	2
82 Bulgaria	1,883	1,169	111 Guinea-Bissau	740	460	137 Vatican	3	1.8
83 Jordan	1,770	1,099	112 Albania	716	444	138 Gibraltar	1.6	1
84 Italy	1,702	1,057	113 Costa Rica	670	416			

Source: U.S. Central Intelligence Agency.

VITAL STATISTICS

Population is the key indicator in this book, determining all other indicators. (Because population data are available for all countries, these rankings are also the most comprehensive). Although national censuses are still uneven in quality and sporadic in occurrence, the United Nations has refined its techniques for collecting population data to such a degree that the error range is only 1.0% in censuses taken at least decennially. In countries where no censuses have been held regularly, the United Nations estimates the outer limits of the size of population through sample surveys and even unconventional counts and conjectures. The error range in the case of sample surveys is 5.0%, in the case of unconventional counts 10.0% and in the case of conjectures 20.0%. Size of population is presented for two periods, Current and 2000, the latter representing an estimate.

Demographers are concerned not only with the size of population but also with growth rates or trends. Growth rates are determined on the basis of three indicators, all of which are presented here: Crude Birth Rates, Crude Death Rates and Fertility Rates. The reverse correlation between population growth and economic development is generally acknowledged, and in many of the poorer countries a rising birth rate is watched with the same alarm as a rising crime rate. It is interesting to recall that in Indira Gandhi's India people were jailed and their ration cards confiscated for begetting more than the statutorily permitted quota of children. It is not inconceivable that in a *Clockwork Orange* society procreation itself could become the ultimate crime.

8. Current Population

The total population of the globe was estimated by the U.N. in 1977 at 4.124 billion. Nearly 90% of this total live in countries with populations of 15 million or more. Approximately one-half of the population resides in the four largest countries: China, India, the Soviet Union and the United States. Altogether the 42 most populated states have within their borders more than nine-tenths of the world's inhabitants. Although a large population is a mixed blessing in countries like Bangladesh, the size of population remains an important—if far from the exclusive—determinant of national power and economic development.

Population figures for each country are based partly on national censuses and partly on U.N. estimates. Both are subject to wide margins of error. A serious source of inaccuracy is the practice in some countries of excluding jungle tribes, aborigines, nomadic peoples, displaced persons and refugees. In some undeveloped countries censuses are hampered by opposition to the enumeration of women and children. In other countries, including Saudi Arabia and Afghanistan, an official census has never been conducted.

Number of Countries: 188
Midpoint: 3,988,000
Period Covered: 1978
Type of Ranking: Total population; Share of World Population for top 10 only; Highest to Lowest

Highlights & Findings: Of the 50 most populous countries, 19 are in Asia and 10 are in Africa. Of the top 10, only one is in Europe and one in Africa. Of the 10 demographic zones, the most populous is the East Asian zone, which accounts for 28.7% of the world population. It is followed by the South Asian zone with 19.9% of the world population, the Soviet Union and East European zone with 9.0%, the West European zone with 8.8%, the North American zone with 8.0%, Africa south of the Sahara with 7.3%, the South East Asian zone with 6.5%, the Middle Eastern and North African Zone with 5.4%, the South American zone with 5.2% and Oceania with 0.4%. (Figures may not add up to 100 because of rounding).

Region	Africa	Asia	Europe	Western Hemisphere
Most	Nigeria (10)	China (1)	Soviet Union (3)	United States (4)
Least	Seychelles (172)	Tuvalu (186)	Vatican City (188)	Falkland Island (187)

Rank	Country	Total population	Share of World % Population
	TOP 10		
1	China	973,334,000	23.6
2	India	649,354,000	15.7
3	Soviet Union	260,178,000	6.3
4	United States	217,799,000	5.2
5	Indonesia	139,075,000	3.3
6	Japan	114,595,000	2.7
7	Brazil	113,859,000	2.7
8	Bangladesh	78,750,000	1.9
9	Pakistan	75,657,000	1.8
10	Nigeria	67,520,000	1.6
	UPPER MIDDLE		
11	Mexico	65,487,000	
12	West Germany	61,520,000	
13	Italy	56,722,000	
14	United Kingdom	55,925,000	
15	France	53,352,000	
16	Vietnam	50,569,000	
17	Philippines	45,690,000	
18	Thailand	44,790,000	
19	Turkey	42,518,000	
20	Egypt	39,396,000	
21	South Korea	36,921,000	
22	Spain	36,542,000	
23	Poland	34,875,000	
24	Iran	34,769,000	
25	Burma	31,859,000	
26	Ethiopia	29,789,000	
27	Zaire	26,724,000	
28	Argentina	26,224,000	
29	Colombia	25,473,000	
30	South Africa	25,003,000	
31	Canada	23,623,000	
32	Yugoslavia	21,855,000	
33	Rumania	21,760,000	
34	Morocco	18,644,000	
35	Algeria	18,120,000	
36	North Korea	17,847,000	
37	Afghanistan	17,642,000	
38	Taiwan	16,835,000	
39	Peru	16,832,000	
40	Sudan	16,740,000	
41	East Germany	16,736,000	
42	Tanzania	16,259,000	
43	Czechoslovakia	15,109,000	
44	Kenya	14,578,000	
45	Sri Lanka	14,122,000	
46	Australia	13,973,000	
47	Netherlands	13,891,000	
48	Nepal	13,348,000	
49	Venezuela	12,929,000	
50	Malaysia	12,736,000	
51	Uganda	12,566,000	
52	Iraq	11,977,000	
53	Ghana	10,790,000	
54	Chile	10,742,000	
55	Hungary	10,695,000	
56	Belgium	9,831,000	
57	Portugal	9,830,000	
58	Mozambique	9,798,000	
59	Cuba	9,720,000	
60	Greece	9,251,000	
61	Bulgaria	8,848,000	
62	Sweden	8,254,000	
63	Cambodia	8,060,000	
64	Madagascar	7,990,000	
65	Syria	7,973,000	
66	Saudi Arabia	7,746,000	
67	Ecuador	7,686,000	
68	Austria	7,522,000	
69	Ivory Coast	7,278,000	
70	Rhodesia (Zimbabwe)	6,876,000	
71	Cameroon	6,722,000	
72	Guatemala	6,531,000	
73	Upper Volta	6,446,000	
74	Angola	6,346,000	
75	Switzerland	6,307,000	
76	Mali	6,205,000	
77	Tunisia	5,936,000	
78	Guinea	5,882,000	
79	Yemen Arab Republic	5,721,000	
80	Zambia	5,383,000	
81	Malawi	5,378,000	
82	Senegal	5,301,000	
83	Denmark	5,096,000	
84	Dominican Republic	5,051,000	
85	Niger	4,925,000	
86	Bolivia	4,845,000	
87	Haiti	4,777,000	
88	Finland	4,746,000	
89	Hong Kong	4,563,000	
90	Rwanda	4,457,000	
91	El Salvador	4,310,000	
92	Chad	4,245,000	
93	Norway	4,054,000	
94	Burundi	3,988,000	
	LOWER MIDDLE		
95	Israel	3,631,000	
96	Laos	3,538,000	
97	Somalia	3,342,000	
98	Benin	3,330,000	
99	Singapore	3,323,000	
100	Sierra Leone	3,219,000	
101	Ireland	3,199,000	
102	New Zealand	3,168,000	
103	Honduras	2,954,000	
104	Papua New Guinea	2,941,000	
105	Jordan	2,899,000	
106	Paraguay	2,846,000	
107	Uruguay	2,803,000	
108	Libya	2,708,000	
109	Albania	2,560,000	
110	Lebanon	2,510,000	
111	Togo	2,371,000	
112	Nicaragua	2,346,000	
113	Transkei	2,185,000	
114	Jamaica	2,130,000	
115	Costa Rica	2,079,000	
116	Central African Empire	1,891,000	
117	South Yemen	1,831,000	
118	Panama	1,798,000	
119	Liberia	1,682,000	
120	Mongolia	1,561,000	
121	Mauritania	1,522,000	
122	Congo	1,450,000	
123	Bhutan	1,247,000	
124	Kuwait	1,119,000	
125	Lesotho	1,098,000	
126	Trinidad & Tobago	1,038,000	
127	Namibia	951,000	
128	Mauritius	917,000	
129	Guyana	804,000	
130	Botswana	740,000	
131	United Arab Emirates	656,000	
132	Cyprus	640,000	
133	Fiji	597,000	
134	Gabon	566,000	
135	Gambia	559,000	
136	Oman	541,000	
137	Guinea-Bissau	527,000	
138	Swaziland	518,000	
139	Reunion	504,000	
140	Surinam	429,000	
141	Luxembourg	362,000	
142	Equatorial Guinea	333,000	
143	Guadeloupe	330,000	
144	Martinique	327,000	
145	Comoros	326,000	
146	Malta	322,000	
147	Cape Verde	312,000	
148	Bahrain	278,000	
149	Macao	251,000	
150	Barbados	249,000	
151	Netherlands Antilles	246,000	
152	Iceland	223,000	
153	Bahamas	221,000	
154	Solomon Islands	210,000	
155	Djibouti	180,000	
156	Brunei	177,000	
157	Qatar	165,000	
158	Western Samoa	152,000	
159	Belize	149,000	
160	French Polynesia	142,000	
161	New Caledonia	140,000	
162	Maldives	137,000	
163	St. Lucia	114,000	
164	Grenada	108,000	
165	St. Vincent	104,000	
166	New Hebrides	101,000	
167	Tonga	92,000	
168	Dominica	80,000	
169	Sao Tome & Principe	75,000	
170	Antigua	72,000	
171	French Guiana	61,000	
172	Seychelles	61,000	
173	Bermuda	58,000	
174	St. Kitts-Nevis-Anguilla	55,000	
175	Gilbert Islands	52,000	
176	Greenland	51,000	
177	Faroe Islands	42,000	
178	Gibraltar	30,000	
	BOTTOM 10		
179	Andorra	29,000	
180	Liechtenstein	25,000	
181	Monaco	25,000	
182	San Marino	20,000	
183	Cook Islands	18,000	
184	Wallis & Futuna	9,000	
185	Nauru	7,000	
186	Tuvalu	6,000	
187	Falkland Islands	2,000	
188	Vatican City	1,000	

Source: *U.N. Demographic Yearbook.*

9. Estimated Population in 2000

World population is estimated to grow by nearly 2 billion between 1976 and 2000 reaching 5.916 billion by that year. This means that more people will be born in these 24 years than were born during all the millennia up to around the year 1920. Assumptions about future growth are based on analyses of recent fertility and mortality trends in each country. It is assumed that life expectancy rates will continue to rise for both males and females, while fertility rates will decline until a stationary population is reached. These are highly speculative assumptions and should not be regarded as predictions. Through extrapolation of these same assumptions, it is estimated that world population will reach an ultimate size of about 10 billion in about 200 years, when Malthusian constraints will begin to operate forcing it to decline until the net replacement level reaches 1:1.

Number of Countries: 125
Midpoint: 14 million
Period Covered: 2000
Type of Ranking: Estimated Population in Year 2000; Year When Stationary Population Will Be Reached; Highest to Lowest

Highlights & Findings: There are no significant differences in the rankings between this table and the table on current population. It may be noted that in several industrialized countries the fertility rate is at present below replacement level and this is reflected in the rank order.

Regions	Africa	Asia & Oceania	Europe	Western Hemisphere
Most	Nigeria (7)	China (1)	Soviet Union (3)	United States (4)
Least	Mauritania (123)	Mongolia (124)	Norway (110)	Trinidad & Tobago (125)

Rank	Country	Estimated Population in Year 2000 (million)	Year When Stationary Population Will Be Reached
	TOP 10		
1	China	1,093	2090
2	India	958	2150
3	Soviet Union	320	2065
4	United States	254	2035
5	Brazil	205	2070
6	Indonesia	198	2165
7	Nigeria	154	2155
8	Bangladesh	146	2165
9	Pakistan	135	2155
10	Japan	133	2045
	UPPER MIDDLE		
11	Mexico	126	2075
12	Vietnam	86	2125
13	Thailand	76	2080
14	Philippines	75	2080
15	West Germany	63	2005
16	Italy	63	2065
17	Turkey	63	2095
18	United Kingdom	61	2040
19	France	60	2055
20	Iran	60	2100
21	Egypt	59	2100
22	Ethiopia	54	2175
23	South Korea	53	2070
24	Burma	50	2145
25	Zaire	47	2165
26	South Africa	46	2075
27	Spain	45	2065
28	Poland	41	2060
29	Colombia	37	2065
30	Algeria	35	2100
31	Morocco	35	2115
32	Argentina	33	2070
33	Tanzania	32	2160
34	Kenya	31	2120
35	Sudan	30	2115

Rank	Country	Estimated Population in Year 2000 (million)	Year When Stationary Population Will Be Reached
36	Peru	29	2085
37	Canada	28	2040
38	North Korea	26	2095
39	Rumania	26	2075
40	Yugoslavia	26	2095
41	Taiwan	25	2065
42	Iraq	25	2090
43	Afghanistan	24	2175
44	Venezuela	24	2070
45	Uganda	23	2150
46	Nepal	22	2160
47	Sri Lanka	21	2095
48	Ghana	20	2135
49	Madagascar	19	2165
50	Malaysia	19	2095
51	Saudi Arabia	19	2120
52	Australia	17	2070
53	Czechoslovakia	17	2075
54	East Germany	17	2010
55	Mozambique	17	2135
56	Netherlands	16	2030
57	Cambodia	15	2160
58	Chile	15	2065
59	Ecuador	15	2080
60	Rhodesia (Zimbabwe)	15	2105
61	Syria	15	2085
62	Cuba	14	2070
63	Ivory Coast	14	2135
	LOWER MIDDLE		
64	Cameroon	13	2155
65	Angola	12	2160
66	Guatemala	12	2090
67	Portugal	12	2090
68	Hungary	11	2030
69	Mali	11	2175
70	Zambia	11	2135
71	Belgium	10	2030

Rank	Country	Estimated Population in Year 2000 (million)	Year When Stationary Population Will Be Reached
72	Bulgaria	10	2075
73	Greece	10	2065
74	Guinea	10	2170
75	Bolivia	9	2100
76	Dominican Republic	9	2075
77	Haiti	9	2130
78	Malawi	9	2175
79	Niger	9	2175
80	Senegal	9	2155
81	Tunisia	9	2095
82	Upper Volta	9	2175
83	Yemen Arab Republic	9	2145
84	Austria	8	2035
85	Rwanda	8	2170
86	Sweden	8	2015
87	Burundi	7	2175
88	El Salvador	7	2075
89	Honduras	7	2100
90	Somalia	7	2170
91	Switzerland	7	2015
92	Chad	6	2180
93	Denmark	6	2030
94	Hong Kong	6	2060
95	Finland	5	2015
96	Israel	5	2060
97	Jordan	5	2110
98	Laos	5	2180
99	Lebanon	5	2070
100	Libya	5	2090
101	Benin	5	2170
102	Nicaragua	5	2110
103	Papua New Guinea	5	2120
104	Paraguay	5	2075
105	Sierra Leone	5	2160
106	Albania	4	2065
107	Ireland	4	2095
108	Jamaica	4	2065
109	New Zealand	4	2070

Rank	Country	Estimated Population in Year 2000 (million)	Year When Stationary Population Will Be Reached	Rank	Country	Estimated Population in Year 2000 (million)	Year When Stationary Population Will Be Reached	Rank	Country	Estimated Population in Year 2000 (million)	Year When Stationary Population Will Be Reached
110	Norway	4	2045	114	Congo	3	2135	120	Bhutan	2	2165
111	Togo	4	2150	115	Costa Rica	3	2065	121	Kuwait	2	2090
112	Uruguay	4	2065	116	Liberia	3	2135	122	Lesotho	2	2160
	BOTTOM 13			117	Panama	3	2070	123	Mauritania	2	2155
				118	Singapore	3	2060	124	Mongolia	2	2070
113	Central African Empire	3	2175	119	South Yemen	3	2130	125	Trinidad & Tobago	2	2065

Sources: United Nations; World Bank.

10. Annual Population Growth Rate

The annual growth rate of population has become one of the most critical factors influencing a nation's strategy for achieving economic prosperity and in some cases for staving off disaster. Although population experts in industrialized countries have been talking of zero population growth as the ideal for a stable society, developing countries have been experiencing uncontrolled growth rates as high as 6% annually. Another way of looking at the problem is to determine in how many years a national population will double itself. With a 4% growth rate a population could easily double itself in 20 years. Percentages are, however, deceptive and may not reveal the full enormity of the problems some countries face. In India, for example, each 0.1% growth rate means another 600,000 additional mouths to feed. At the same time, all growth is not undesirable. A country like Kuwait may find a higher population growth rate necessary to utilize effectively its vast economic resources and to allow its native population to outnumber aliens.

Number of Countries: 184
Midpoint: 2.4%
Period Covered: 1970-75
Type of Ranking: Annual Growth Rate of Population, 1970-75; Highest to Lowest

Highlights & Findings: At the head of the list are the so-called pronatalist countries, which encourage population growth as a national policy. Other countries are divided into two groups: those that have an official family planning program but have not been successful in controlling growth and those that have achieved planned growth. Paradoxically, the majority of the countries experiencing a growth rate of over 2% are also among the poorest in the world. Three of the lowest seven countries are German-speaking.

Regions	Africa	Asia & Oceania	Europe	Western Hemisphere
Most	Libya (4)	Kuwait (1)	Andorra (2)	Honduras (5)
Least	Gabon (153)	Japan (147)	Malta (184)	Grenada (175)

Rank	Country	Population Annual Growth Rate(%)	Rank	Country	Population Annual Growth Rate(%)	Rank	Country	Population Annual Growth Rate(%)
	TOP 12			*UPPER MIDDLE*		25	United Arab Emirates	3.2
1	Kuwait	6.0	13	Ecuador	3.4	26	Zambia	3.2
2	Andorra	4.9	14	French Polynesia	3.4	27	Belize	3.1
3	Pacific Islands	4.7	15	Angola	3.3	28	Israel	3.1
4	Libya	4.2	16	Cook Islands	3.3	29	Oman	3.1
5	Honduras	3.9	17	Iraq	3.3	30	Panama	3.1
6	Bahamas	3.6	18	Jordan	3.3	31	Qatar	3.1
7	Botswana	3.6	19	Nicaragua	3.3	32	Solomon Islands	3.1
8	Kenya	3.6	20	Syria	3.3	33	South Yemen	3.1
9	Bahrain	3.5	21	Uganda	3.3	34	Albania	3.0
10	French Guiana	3.5	22	Algeria	3.2	35	Brazil	3.0
11	Mexico	3.5	23	Gilbert Islands	3.2	36	Dominican Republic	3.0
12	Rhodesia (Zimbabwe)	3.5	24	Swaziland	3.2	37	El Salvador	3.0

Rank	Country	Population Annual Growth Rate(%)	Rank	Country	Population Annual Growth Rate(%)	Rank	Country	Population Annual Growth Rate(%)
38	Lebanon	3.0		*LOWER MIDDLE*		137	Greenland	1.5
39	Mongolia	3.0	88	Afghanistan	2.4	138	Guinea-Bissau	1.5
40	Morocco	3.0	89	Bangaldesh	2.4	139	Martinique	1.5
41	Pakistan	3.0	90	Brunei	2.4	140	Canada	1.4
42	Peru	3.0	91	Guinea	2.4	141	Argentina	1.3
43	Saudi Arabia	3.0	92	Liechtenstein	2.4	142	St. Lucia	1.3
44	Tonga	3.0	93	Reunion	2.4	143	Trinidad & Tobago	1.3
45	Guatemala	2.9	94	Tunisia	2.4	144	Western Samoa	1.3
46	Iran	2.9	95	Turkey	2.4	145	Antigua	1.2
47	Namibia	2.9	96	Central African Empire	2.3	146	Ireland	1.2
48	New Hebrides	2.9	97	Liberia	2.3	147	Japan	1.2
49	Philippines	2.9	98	Madagascar	2.3	148	Monaco	1.2
50	Tanzania	2.9	99	Mozambique	2.3	149	Uruguay	1.2
51	Thailand	2.9	100	Nepal	2.3	150	Dominica	1.1
52	Venezuela	2.9	101	Upper Volta	2.3	151	Faroe Islands	1.1
53	Vietnam	2.9	102	Djibouti	2.2	152	Iceland	1.1
54	Yemen Arab Republic	2.9	103	Egypt	2.2	153	Gabon	1.0
55	Cambodia	2.8	104	Guyana	2.2	154	Luxembourg	1.0
56	Colombia	2.8	105	Laos	2.2	155	Rumania	1.0
57	Malaysia	2.8	106	Lesotho	2.2	156	Spain	1.0
58	Paraguay	2.8	107	Seychelles	2.2	157	Poland	0.9
59	Zaire	2.8	108	Sri Lanka	2.2	158	Soviet Union	0.9
60	Benin	2.7	109	Bhutan	2.1	159	Yugoslavia	0.9
61	Bolivia	2.7	110	Chad	2.1	160	Cyprus	0.8
62	Gambia	2.7	111	India	2.1	161	France	0.8
63	North Korea	2.7	112	South Korea	2.1	162	Italy	0.8
64	Nauru	2.7	113	Turks & Caicos	2.1	163	Netherlands	0.8
65	Niger	2.7	114	Fiji	2.0	164	United States	0.8
66	Nigeria	2.7	115	Hong Kong	2.0	165	Norway	0.7
67	Norfolk Islands	2.7	116	Maldives	2.0	166	Switzerland	0.7
68	Rwanda	2.7	117	Papua New Guinea	2.0	167	Barbados	0.6
69	Costa Rica	2.6	118	British Virgin Islands	1.9	168	Czechoslovakia	0.6
70	Ethiopia	2.6	119	Cameroon	1.9	169	Greece	0.6
71	Indonesia	2.6	120	Cape Verde	1.9	170	St. Kitts-Nevis-Anguilla	0.6
72	Malawi	2.6	121	Cayman Islands	1.9	171	San Marino	0.6
73	Mauritius	2.6	122	New Zealand	1.9	172	Bulgaria	0.5
74	New Caledonia	2.6	123	Chile	1.8	173	Denmark	0.5
75	Puerto Rico	2.6	124	Macao	1.8			
76	Somalia	2.6	125	China	1.7		*BOTTOM 11*	
77	Surinam	2.6	126	Equatorial Guinea	1.7	174	Finland	0.4
78	Burma	2.5	127	Jamaica	1.7	175	Grenada	0.4
79	Comoros	2.5	128	Netherlands Antilles	1.7	176	Hungary	0.4
80	Congo	2.5	129	Sao Tome & Principe	1.7	177	Sweden	0.4
81	Gambia	2.5	130	Bermuda	1.6	178	West Germany	0.4
82	Ivory Coast	2.5	131	Cuba	1.6	179	Austria	0.3
83	Mali	2.5	132	Guadeloupe	1.6	180	Belgium	0.2
84	Mauritania	2.5	133	Haiti	1.6	181	Portugal	0.2
85	South Africa	2.5	134	Montserrat	1.6	182	United Kingdom	0.2
86	Sudan	2.5	135	Singapore	1.6	183	East Germany	−0.2
87	Togo	2.5	136	Australia	1.5	184	Malta	−1.6

Source: *UN Demographic Yearbook.*

11. Birth Rate

Birth rates measure gross additions to the population and, when used in combination with death rates, provide some estimate of population growth.

Statistics on live birth rates are subject to the same errors as other vital statistics. Most of the rates are based on civil registers, which in many cases are incomplete or unreliable. In other cases there is a prolonged lag between birth and registration. Some countries do not include in the statistics infants who are born alive but who die within the first 24 hours of life. The rates are also affected by the problems of underenumeration or overenumeration of the total population.

Number of Countries: 194
Midpoint: 35.5 per 1,000 inhabitants
Period Covered: 1970-75
Type of Ranking: Number of Live Births per 1,000 Inhabitants; Highest to Lowest

Highlights & Rankings: The top 10 as well as the upper middle nations are all members of the Third World, while industrialized countries predominate toward the end of the scale. Over 123 countries have birth rates exceeding the acceptable level of 25 per 1,000.

Regions	Africa	Asia & Oceania	Europe	Western Hemisphere
Most	Niger (1)	Maldives (5)	Albania (104)	Honduras (15)
Least	St. Helena (126)	Christmas Island (91)	Gibraltar (194)	United States (174)

Rank	Country	Birth Rate per 1,000 Inhabitants	Rank	Country	Birth Rate per 1,000 Inhabitants	Rank	Country	Birth Rate per 1,000 Inhabitants
	TOP 11		52	Laos	44.6	104	Albania	33.3
1	Niger	52.2	53	Bolivia	44.0	105	Gabon	32.2
2	Zambia	51.5	54	Chad	44.0	106	Nauru	32.2
3	Togo	50.6	55	Philippines	43.8	107	New Caledonia	32.2
4	Malawi	50.5	56	Bhutan	43.6	108	Malaysia	31.4
5	Maldives	50.1	57	Central African Empire	43.4	109	Jamaica	30.3
6	Mali	50.1	58	Thailand	43.4	110	Sri Lanka	29.5
7	Rwanda	50.0	59	Gambia	43.3	111	Costa Rica	29.3
8	Benin	49.9	60	Wallis & Futuna Islands	43.3	112	Cape Verde	29.2
9	Liberia	49.8	61	Mozambique	43.1	113	South Korea	28.8
10	Arab Republic Yemen	49.6	62	Indonesia	42.9	114	French Guiana	28.3
11	South Yemen	49.6	63	Nepal	42.9	115	Israel	28.2
			64	South Africa	42.9	116	Reunion	28.1
	UPPER MIDDLE		65	Guatemala	42.8	117	Guadeloupe	20.0
			66	Burundi	42.0	118	Seychelles	27.7
12	Bangladesh	49.5	67	Djibouti	42.0	119	Grenada	27.4
13	Saudi Arabia	49.5	68	Mexico	42.0	120	China	26.9
14	Ethiopia	49.4	69	Ecuador	41.8	121	Guyana	26.7
15	Honduras	49.3	70	Vietnam	41.5	122	Mauritius	25.6
16	Nigeria	49.3	71	Peru	41.0	123	Cook Islands	25.2
17	Afghanistan	49.2	72	St. Lucia	40.9	124	Chile	25.0
18	Swaziland	49.0	73	Surinam	40.9	125	Fiji	25.0
19	Ghana	48.8	74	Colombia	40.6	126	St. Helena	24.9
20	Algeria	48.7	75	Papua New Guinea	40.6	127	Cayman Islands	24.7
21	Kenya	48.7	76	Cameroon	40.4	128	Tokelau	24.5
22	Upper Volta	48.5	77	El Salvador	40.1	129	Montserrat	24.3
23	Nicaragua	48.3	78	Guinea-Bissau	40.1	130	Niue Island	23.9
24	Iraq	48.1	79	Tunisia	40.0	131	Puerto Rico	23.3
25	Rhodesia	47.9	80	Lebanon	39.8	132	Trinidad & Tobago	23.0
26	Sudan	47.8	81	Paraguay	39.8	133	Argentina	22.9
27	Jordan	47.6	82	Turkey	39.6	134	St. Kitts-Nevis-Anguilla	22.9
28	Senegal	47.6	83	Burma	39.5	135	Martinique	22.4
29	Angola	47.2	84	Lesotho	39.0	136	Gilbert Islands	22.3
30	Somalia	47.2	85	Mongolia	38.8	137	Cyprus	22.2
31	Kuwait	47.1	86	Belize	38.7	138	Ireland	21.6
32	Tanzania	47.0	87	Brazil	37.1	139	British Virgin Islands	21.5
33	Cambodia	46.7	88	Samoa	36.9	140	Falkland Islands	21.5
34	Comoros	46.6	89	Equatorial Guinea	36.8	141	Cuba	20.7
35	Guinea	46.6	90	Dominica	36.4	142	Iceland	20.1
36	Morocco	46.2	91	Panama	36.2	143	Netherlands Antilles	20.0
37	Madagascar	46.0	92	Solomon Islands	36.1	144	Faroe Islands	19.9
38	Dominican Republic	45.8	93	Venezuela	36.1	145	Bahamas	19.8
39	Botswana	45.6	94	Pakistan	36.0	146	Rumania	19.7
40	Ivory Coast	45.6	95	Haiti	35.8	147	Portugal	19.6
41	Syria	45.4	96	North Korea	35.7	148	Czechoslovakia	19.5
42	Iran	45.3	97	Egypt	35.5	149	Poland	19.5
43	Uganda	45.2				150	Uruguay	19.3
44	Zaire	45.2		*LOWER MIDDLE*		151	Malta	19.1
45	Congo	45.1				152	Singapore	18.8
46	Libya	45.0	98	Pacific Islands	34.9	153	Barbados	18.6
47	Namibia	45.0	99	India	34.5	154	New Zealand	18.5
48	New Hebrides	45.0	100	St. Vincent	34.4	155	Antigua	18.3
49	Sao Tome & Principe	45.0	101	Turks & Caicos	34.3	156	Hong Kong	18.3
50	Mauritania	44.8	102	French Polynesia	33.7	157	Soviet Union	18.1
51	Sierra Leone	44.7	103	Brunei	33.4	158	Yugoslavia	18.0

Rank	Country	Birth Rate per 1,000 Inhabitants	Rank	Country	Birth Rate per 1,000 Inhabitants	Rank	Country	Birth Rate per 1,000 Inhabitants
							BOTTOM 10	
159	Spain	17.7	172	Cocos Islands	14.8	185	Sweden	11.9
160	Greenland	17.5	173	Italy	14.8	186	Austria	11.6
161	Hungary	17.5	174	United States	14.7	187	Luxembourg	10.9
162	San Marino	17.4	175	Denmark	14.2	188	East Germany	10.8
163	Australia	17.3	176	Norway	14.1	189	Macao	10.8
164	Japan	17.2	177	Finland	14.1	190	Norfolk Island	10.2
165	St. Pierre & Miquelon	16.6	178	France	13.6	191	Christmas Island	10.1
166	Andorra	16.5	179	Tonga	13.0	192	West Germany	9.8
167	Belgium	16.5	180	Netherlands	12.9	193	Monaco	8.2
168	Pitcairn Island	16.4	181	Liechtenstein	12.8	194	Gibraltar	7.7
169	Bermuda	16.3	182	Switzerland	12.3			
170	Canada	15.7	183	Belgium	12.2			
171	Greece	15.7	184	United Kingdom	12.1			

Source: *UN Demographic Yearbook.*

12. Death Rate

Death is defined as the permanent disappearance of all evidence of life at any time after live birth has taken place. Death statistics are subject to the same qualifications as other vital statistics and are obtained mostly from civil registers, the reliability of which varies from country to country.

Number of Countries: 192
Midpoint: 10.5 per 1,000 inhabitants
Period Covered: 1970-75
Type of Ranking: Number of deaths per 1,000 Inhabitants; Highest to Lowest

Highlights & Findings: Death rates are generally highest in Africa and lowest in small island countries with the exception of Pitcairn Island. There are only 10 countries with death rates exceeding 25 per 1,000; the majority of the countries fall in the under 15 bracket.

Regions	Africa	Asia & Oceania	Europe	Western Hemisphere
Most	Malawi (4)	Pitcairn Island (1)	East Germany (71)	Bolivia (50)
Least	Reunion (158)	Tonga (192)	Andorra (184)	Netherlands Antilles (187)

Rank	Country	Death Rate per 1,000 Inhabitants	Rank	Country	Death Rate per 1,000 Inhabitants	Rank	Country	Death Rate per 1,000 Inhabitants
	TOP 10		21	Guinea	22.9	44	Zambia	20.3
1	Pitcairn Island	50.0	22	Maldives	22.9	45	Saudi Arabia	20.2
2	Brunei	43.0	23	Laos	22.8	46	Mozambique	20.1
3	Bangladesh	28.1	24	Nigeria	22.7	47	New Hebrides	20.0
4	Malawi	26.5	25	Central African Empire	22.5	48	Equatorial Guinea	19.7
5	Mali	25.9	26	Gabon	22.2	49	Lesotho	19.7
6	Ethiopia	25.8	27	Cameroon	22.0	50	Bolivia	19.1
7	Upper Volta	25.8	28	Tanzania	22.0	51	Cambodia	19.0
8	Niger	25.5	29	Ghana	21.9	52	Sudan	17.5
9	Guinea-Bissau	25.1	30	Swaziland	21.8	53	Papua New Guinea	17.1
10	Madagascar	25.0	31	Comoros	21.7	54	Indonesia	16.9
			32	Somalia	21.7	55	Namibia	16.7
	UPPER MIDDLE		33	Liberia	20.9	56	Haiti	16.3
11	Mauritania	24.9	34	Congo	20.8	57	Kenya	16.0
12	Angola	24.5	35	Sierra Leone	20.7	58	Uganda	15.9
13	Gambia	24.1	36	Ivory Coast	20.6	59	Burma	15.8
14	Chad	24.0	37	Yemen Arab Republic	20.6	60	Morocco	15.7
15	Senegal	23.9	38	South Yemen	20.6	61	Iran	15.6
16	Afghanistan	23.8	39	Bhutan	20.5	62	South Africa	15.5
17	Rwanda	23.6	40	Vietnam	20.5	63	Algeria	15.4
18	Togo	23.3	41	Zaire	20.5	64	Jordan	14.7
19	Benin	23.0	42	Burundi	20.4	65	Libya	14.7
20	Botswana	23.0	43	Nepal	20.3	66	Honduras	14.6

Rank	Country	Death Rate per 1,000 Inhabitants	Rank	Country	Death Rate per 1,000 Inhabitants	Rank	Country	Death Rate per 1,000 Inhabitants
67	Iraq	14.6	109	Argentina	9.4	153	French Polynesia	7.2
68	Turkey	14.6	110	Finland	9.4	154	Surinam	7.2
69	India	14.4	111	North Korea	9.4	155	Antigua	7.1
70	Rhodesia	14.4	112	Mongolia	9.3	156	Guyana	7.1
71	East Germany	14.3	113	Rumania	9.3	157	Panama	7.1
72	Nicaragua	13.9	114	Soviet Union	9.3	158	Reunion	7.1
73	Falkland Islands	13.8	115	Barbados	9.2	159	Venezuela	7.0
74	Tunisia	13.8	116	Uruguay	9.2	160	Jamaica	6.9
75	Solomon Islands	13.0	117	St. Pierre & Miquelon	9.1	161	Cyprus	6.8
76	Austria	12.6	118	Greece	8.9	162	Martinique	6.8
77	Luxembourg	12.6	119	South Korea	8.9	163	Samoa	6.7
78	Hungary	12.5	120	Paraguay	8.9	164	British Virgin Islands	6.5
79	Egypt	12.4	121	Poland	8.9	165	Gilbert Islands	6.5
80	Monaco	12.3	122	St. Kitts-Nevis-Anguilla	8.9	166	Iceland	6.5
81	Belgium	12.2	123	United States	8.9	167	Puerto Rico	6.5
82	United Kingdom	12.2	124	Brazil	8.8	168	Trinidad & Tobago	6.5
83	Pakistan	12.0	125	Cape Verde	8.8	169	Bermuda	6.4
84	West Germany	11.9	126	Colombia	8.8	170	Japan	6.4
85	Peru	11.9	127	Switzerland	8.7	171	Malaysia	6.4
86	Guatemala	11.8	128	Mexico	8.6	172	Greenland	6.2
87	Czechoslovakia	11.5	129	Nauru	8.3	173	Belize	6.1
88	Sao Tome & Principe	11.2	130	Netherlands	8.3	174	Niue Islands	6.1
89	Dominican Republic	11.0	131	New Zealand	8.2	175	Cayman Islands	6.0
90	Portugal	11.0	132	Yugoslavia	8.2	176	Grenada	5.9
91	Sweden	11.0	133	Albania	8.1	177	Cook Islands	5.9
92	Thailand	10.8	134	Australia	8.1	178	Bahamas	5.4
93	Ireland	10.7	135	St. Helena	8.1	179	Cuba	5.4
94	Wallis & Futuna	10.6	136	El Salvador	8.0	180	Norfolk Island	5.4
95	France	10.5	137	Spain	8.0	181	Kuwait	5.3
96	Montserrat	10.5	138	New Caledonia	7.9			
97	Philippines	10.5	139	Seychelles	7.9		*BOTTOM 11*	
98	Turks & Caicos	10.4	140	French Guyana	7.8	182	Pacific Islands	5.1
			141	Gibraltar	7.8	183	Singapore	5.1
	LOWER MIDDLE		142	Mauritius	7.8	184	Andorra	5.0
99	China	10.3	143	St. Lucia	7.8	185	Costa Rica	4.9
100	Bulgaria	10.1	144	San Marino	7.7	186	Hong Kong	4.9
101	Dominica	10.1	145	Sri Lanka	7.7	187	Netherlands Antilles	4.8
102	Denmark	10.0	146	Djibouti	7.6	188	Syria	4.8
103	Norway	10.0	147	Liechtenstein	7.5	189	Tokelau	4.5
104	St. Vincent	10.0	148	Canada	7.3	190	Fiji	4.3
105	Italy	9.9	149	Faroe Islands	7.3	191	Christmas Island	2.1
106	Lebanon	9.9	150	Guadeloupe	7.3	192	Tonga	1.9
107	Malta	9.8	151	Israel	7.3			
108	Ecuador	9.5	152	Chile	7.2			

Source: *UN Demographic Yearbook.*

13. Fertility Rate

Fertility rates are the number of live births reported in a calendar year per 1,000 females aged 15 to 49. When used together with birth rates, they provide a useful tool for the measurement of population growth rates.

Number of Countries: 188
Midpoint: 156.6 per 1,000 females
Period Covered: 1970-75
Type of Ranking: Number of Live Births per 1,000 Females Aged 15 to 49; Highest to Lowest

Highlights & Findings: Fertility rates reflect in addition to birth rates the percentage of females of child-bearing age in the population. Thus, although the rank order may vary for each country, the basic pattern in both birth rates and fertility rates remains the same. The differences between the two rates are most striking in those countries where the sex ratio is skewed in favor of males.

Regions	Africa	Asia & Oceania	Europe	Western Hemisphere
Most	Mali (1)	Kuwait (2)	Albania (37)	St. Vincent (5)
Least	Mauritius (135)	Macao (185)	Monaco (188)	United States (173)

Rank	Country	Fertility Rate per 1,000 Females	Rank	Country	Fertility Rate per 1,000 Females	Rank	Country	Fertility Rate per 1,000 Females
	TOP 10		56	Egypt	189.3	112	Cambodia	143.1
1	Mali	262.7	57	Bolivia	188.6	113	Montserrat	142.3
2	Kuwait	240.3	58	Uganda	187.0	114	Martinique	140.8
3	Nauru	237.1	59	Lebanon	184.3	115	St. Helena	140.2
4	Sudan	234.3	60	Papua New Guinea	183.8	116	Sao Tome & Principe	140.0
5	St. Vincent	232.9	61	Vietnam	183.3	117	St. Kitts-Nevis-Anguilla	138.4
6	Bangladesh	231.7	62	Nepal	182.5	118	India	136.7
7	Togo	228.0	63	Colombia	181.7	119	Guyana	136.2
8	Guinea	227.8	64	Zambia	181.0	120	Malaysia	135.8
9	Benin	226.9	65	Peru	180.7	121	Tonga	135.6
10	Algeria	225.2	66	South Africa	180.2	122	Cayman Islands	134.1
			67	Paraguay	179.8	123	St. Lucia	133.5
	UPPER MIDDLE		68	Congo	178.5	124	Costa Rica	124.9
11	Honduras	224.6	69	Grenada	177.6	125	South Korea	117.4
12	Ghana	224.0	70	British Virgin Islands	177.1	126	Israel	117.3
13	Jordan	221.3	71	Jamaica	175.9	127	Gabon	115.6
14	Saudi Arabia	220.8	72	Indonesia	175.7	128	Greenland	115.0
15	South Yemen	220.7	73	Reunion	175.3	129	Fiji	114.0
16	Yemen Arab Republic	220.7	74	Turkey	175.0	130	China	112.5
17	Nicaragua	220.4	75	Pakistan	174.8	131	Bahamas	112.0
18	Ivory Coast	220.0	76	Cook Islands	174.0	132	Trinidad & Tobago	106.6
19	Iraq	219.8	77	Senegal	174.0	133	Gilbert Islands	104.9
20	Rwanda	218.7	78	Mozambique	173.5	134	Puerto Rico	102.0
21	Kenya	218.0	79	Mauritania	173.0	135	Mauritius	101.9
22	Afghanistan	217.9	80	French Polynesia	171.9	136	Faroe Islands	100.5
23	Nigeria	217.8	81	Cape Verde	171.4	137	Chile	99.8
24	Tanzania	217.0	82	Burundi	171.0	138	Netherlands Antilles	95.6
25	Morocco	215.7	83	Mongolia	170.2	139	Argentina	94.2
26	Ethiopia	215.0	84	Pacific Islands	167.3	140	Falkland Islands	93.8
27	Syria	213.7	85	Guinea-Bissau	165.8	141	Ireland	93.8
28	Swaziland	213.3	86	Burma	165.3	142	Gibraltar	92.0
29	Dominican Republic	212.7	87	Cameroon	164.0	143	Spain	91.5
30	Dominica	211.5	88	Seychelles	163.2	144	Cuba	89.6
31	Iran	209.7	89	Venezuela	163.1	145	Cyprus	87.6
32	Libya	209.3	90	Lesotho	161.3	146	Iceland	84.2
33	Rhodesia	207.0	91	Central African Empire	160.3	147	Barbados	84.1
34	Angola	206.5	92	Tunisia	160.1	148	Bermuda	81.2
35	Malawi	203.7	93	Brunei	159.5	149	Portugal	78.2
36	Madagascar	203.6	94	Brazil	158.6	150	Liechtenstein	77.9
37	Albania	202.8	95	Turks & Caicos	156.6	151	Uruguay	77.6
38	Somalia	201.0	96	Niue Island	156.3	152	Rumania	77.5
39	Philippines	200.4	97	Sri Lanka	155.8	153	Hong Kong	77.3
40	Niger	200.0	98	Equatorial Guinea	155.2	154	New Zealand	76.5
41	Mexico	198.8	99	North Korea	152.5	155	Australia	76.4
42	Comoros	197.4	100	Gambia	151.3	156	Singapore	76.2
43	Guatemala	197.3	101	Surinam	150.9	157	Czechoslovakia	75.8
44	Upper Volta	197.0	102	Wallis & Futuna	150.9	158	St. Pierre & Miquelon	73.0
45	Namibia	195.4				159	Hungary	72.9
46	El Salvador	194.5		*LOWER MIDDLE*		160	France	72.0
47	Thailand	194.1	103	Antigua	149.0	161	Poland	71.3
48	Botswana	192.7	104	Guadeloupe	148.1	162	Christmas Island	70.0
49	Belize	191.7	105	Chad	147.7	163	Yugoslavia	68.1
50	Liberia	191.7	106	French Guiana	146.8	164	Bulgaria	67.9
51	Laos	190.4	107	New Caledonia	146.0	165	Malta	65.8
52	Sierra Leone	190.4	108	Zaire	145.7	166	Italy	65.7
53	Ecuador	190.3	109	Panama	144.4	167	Norway	64.1
54	Bhutan	189.7	110	Tokelau	143.7	168	Greece	63.5
55	Samoa	189.7	111	Haiti	143.3	169	Japan	62.6

Rank	Country	Fertility Rate per 1,000 Females	Rank	Country	Fertility Rate per 1,000 Females	Rank	Country	Fertility Rate per 1,000 Females
170	San Marino	62.5	177	Soviet Union	55.5	182	Switzerland	50.2
171	Denmark	61.6	178	Austria	54.5	183	Cocos (Keeling) Islands	49.7
172	Canada	61.5				184	Luxembourg	45.6
173	United States	58.5		**BOTTOM 10**		185	Macao	45.5
174	Norfolk Island	58.0				186	East Germany	45.3
175	Sweden	56.4	179	Belgium	54.2	187	West Germany	41.2
176	United Kingdom	55.7	180	Netherlands	53.9	188	Monaco	40.6
			181	Finland	52.2			

Source: *UN Demographic Yearbook.*

POPULATION DYNAMICS & THE FAMILY

This section deals with four key areas of population dynamics: density, urbanization, marriage and divorce and family planning. The density rankings reflect dispersion and concentration of population within national borders. Of the two rankings, the density per sq km/sq mi of agricultural land is the more reliable because it is the effective density measured against usable land area. There are three rankings dealing with urbanization. In addition to the overall ratio of urban population, the ratio of population in cities over 50,000 has been also ranked. The threshold of urbanization has not been determined (it is perhaps not determinable) and 50,-000 is as good a cutoff point as any other. The rise of megalopolises is making the traditional dichotomy between rural and urban less viable. A person could live within 100 miles of New York City or London and still lead an urban and unrural existence because of the availability of fast transport, electronic media and other conveniences.

The central themes of the marriage and divorce rankings are those that concern every sociologist. They may not answer the question: will the family survive as an institution. But they point to some significant trends. Two related rankings are provided here: Illegitimate Births and the Average Size of Household. Two rankings are presented on family planning. Although family planning has been accepted as official policy in 33 countries, statistics are available only on the developing countries, but it is difficult to determine how much these resemble Potemkin Villages, facades created not to inform but to mislead.

The quality of the data in these rankings are among the most deficient in the book. The reasons are obvious. There is a lack of comparability even in definitions of such terms as marriage or household. Many countries do not have the capability to collect such specialized data, and even where such capability exists, there is no national provision for registration of events such as marriage or divorce but only municipal or state ordinances, which vary in force and sanction. The comparability of the data is further undermined by the differing periods or time frames to which they refer. Thus, considerable caution should be exercised in interpreting the data in the rankings or in attempting analyses or comparisons.

14. Population Density

Population density is the most common indicator of the relation of population to available land. However, since overall density figures obscure unequal distribution within countries, this ranking should be read in light of the ranking for density in agricultural areas. In many countries with a moderate overall density (Egypt is a good example), virtually the entire population is concentrated along rivers or other productive areas. Density of population is both a cause and a result of economic development. A thinly spread population, for example, often requires greater investment in transportation and infrastructure.

The average worldwide density is 20 per sq km (75 per sq mi) with significant variations among continents. It is 13 per sq km (33.6 per sq mi) in Africa, 11 per sq km (28.4 per sq mi) in North America, 13 per sq km (33.6 per sq mi) in South America, 82 per sq km (212 per sq mi) in Asia, 96 per sq km (248.6 per sq mi) in Europe and 3 per sq km (7.7 per sq mi) in Oceania.

Number of Countries: 162
Midpoint: 37 per sq km (97 per sq mi)
Period Covered: 1976
Type of Ranking: Densest to the Least Dense

Highlights & Findings: The density of population is highest among small city-states and urbanized islands. Among true nation-states, Bangladesh has the highest density. Density is uniformly low in Africa and high in Europe.

Regions	Africa	Asia & Oceania	Europe	Western Hemisphere
Most	Mauritius (10)	Hong Kong (3)	Monaco (1)	Barbados (7)
Least	Namibia (161)	Mongolia (162)	Iceland (155)	Surinam (150)

Ranking	Country	Density per sq km	Density per sq mi	Ranking	Country	Density per sq km	Density per sq mi	Ranking	Country	Density per sq km	Density per sq mi
		TOP 10		55	Yugoslavia	82	213	110	Guinea	17	45
1	Monaco	16,671	43,179	56	Sao Tome & Principe	81	212	111	Uruguay	16	42
2	Gibraltar	5,004	12,960	57	Seychelles	80	208	112	Nicaragua	15	41
3	Hong Kong	4,179	10,823	58	Thailand	80	207	113	Rhodesia	15	40
4	Singapore	3,824	9,906	59	Cuba	79	206	114	Tanzania	15	40
5	Vatican City	1,589	4,117	60	Bulgaria	78	202	115	Liberia	14	38
6	Malta	1,022	2,647	61	Cape Verde	77	201	116	Ivory Coast	14	38
7	Barbados	567	1,469	62	Spain	69	180	117	Guinea-Bissau	13	37
8	Bangladesh	526	1,363	63	Cyprus	69	179	118	Bahamas	13	36
9	Taiwan	437	1,132	64	Greece	67	175	119	Finland	13	36
10	Mauritius	426	1,103	65	Nigeria	66	171	120	Laos	13	35
				66	Andorra	61	160	121	Chile	13	35
		UPPER MIDDLE		67	Western Samoa	54	141	122	Cameroon	13	34
11	Netherlands	402	1,041	68	Kuwait	52	135	123	Venezuela	12	33
12	Bahrain	391	1,012	69	Turkey	49	127	124	Norway	12	31
13	South Korea	339	880	70	Guatemala	47	123	125	Brazil	12	31
14	Nauru	338	875	71	Uganda	47	122	126	Madagascar	12	31
15	Belgium	315	817	72	Gambia	45	117	127	Peru	12	31
16	San Marino	306	792	73	Burma	44	115	128	Mozambique	11	29
17	Japan	296	767	74	Ireland	44	114	129	New Zealand	11	29
18	Grenada	280	727	75	Cambodia	43	112	130	Soviet Union	11	29
19	Lebanon	267	693	76	Maldives	42	111	131	Equatorial Guinea	10	27
20	West Germany	249	646	77	Malawi	41	106	132	Zaire	10	26
21	United Kingdom	230	596	78	Ghana	40	104	133	Argentina	9	23
22	Sri Lanka	211	547	79	Syria	38	100	134	Qatar	8	21
23	Trinidad & Tobago	208	540	80	Togo	37	98	135	Sudan	7	18
24	El Salvador	185	481	81	Morocco	37	98	136	Algeria	6	17
25	Italy	184	477	82	Sierra Leone	37	97	137	Paraguay	6	16
26	Jamaica	182	472	83	Costa Rica	37	96	138	Zambia	6	16
27	India	179	464					139	Papua New Guinea	5	14
28	Israel	159	412			*LOWER MIDDLE*		140	South Yemen	5	14
29	Rwanda	159	412	84	Egypt	36	94	141	Bolivia	5	13
30	Haiti	158	410	85	Malaysia	35	92	142	Angola	5	12
31	East Germany	157	408	86	Tunisia	34	89	143	Somalia	4	12
32	Switzerland	156	405	87	Yemen Arab Republic	33	86	144	Mali	4	11
33	Liechtenstein	154	400	88	Lesotho	32	84	145	Saudi Arabia	3	10
34	Tonga	140	362	89	Fiji	30	79	146	Congo	3	10
35	Philippines	138	357	90	Mexico	29	76	147	Guyana	3	9
36	Comoros	133	345	91	Afghanistan	29	75	148	Niger	3	9
37	Luxembourg	132	342	92	Brunei	27	72	149	Chad	3	8
38	Burundi	129	334	93	Swaziland	27	71				
39	Vietnam	128	333	94	Jordan	26	69			*BOTTOM 13*	
40	North Korea	126	328	95	Benin	26	68	150	Surinam	2	6
41	Czechoslovakia	115	299	96	Iraq	24	64	151	Central African Empire	2	6
42	Denmark	114	296	97	Bhutan	24	63	152	United Arab Emirates	2	6
43	Hungary	112	290	98	Honduras	23	61	153	Oman	2	6
44	Poland	108	280	99	Ecuador	22	59	154	Canada	2	5
45	Portugal	96	249	100	United States	22	58	155	Iceland	2	5
46	France	95	248	101	Ethiopia	22	57	156	Gabon	2	5
47	Dominican Republic	92	240	102	Kenya	22	57	157	Australia	1.5	4
48	Austria	90	235	103	Senegal	21	56	158	Libya	1.3	3
49	Rumania	88	228	104	Panama	21	56	159	Mauritania	1.2	3
50	Nepal	88	228	105	Upper Volta	21	55	160	Botswana	1	2
51	China	86	223	106	Colombia	20	54	161	Namibia	1	2
52	Indonesia	86	223	107	South Africa	20	53	162	Mongolia	1	2
53	Albania	84	219	108	Iran	19	50				
54	Pakistan	84	219	109	Sweden	18	47				

Source. *U.N. Demographic Yearbook.*

15. Population Density in Agricultural Areas

The old demographic concept of living space perhaps may be expressed best through a ranking of population density in agricultural areas. By restricting consideration to areas that are capable of supporting human life, we can devise a more accurate ratio of man to land. Agricultural land is defined by the Food and Agriculture Organization as covering arable land, land under permanent crops, and permanent meadows and pastures. It also includes lands temporarily fallow, land under market and kitchen gardens, plantations, and land under trees, vines and shrubs. Potentially productive land is sometimes excluded, and in any case, it is difficult to determine accurately what land is potentially productive and what is not.

Number of Countries: 98
Midpoint: 108 per sq km (279.7 per sq mi)
Period Covered: Mid-1970s
Type of Ranking: Population Density per Sq Km and Sq Mi of Agricultural Area; Highest to Lowest

Highlights & Findings: The highest density in agricultural areas is found in East Asia, where it is 501.6 per sq km (1,291.1 per sq mi), and the lowest is in Africa, where it is 34.8 per sq km (90.1 per sq mi). Industrialized countries have an average density of 239.5 per sq km (620.3 per sq mi). It is 43.2 per sq km (111.6 per sq mi) in the Western Hemisphere, 121.4 per sq km (314.4 per sq mi) in the Middle East and 126.0 per sq km (326.3 per sq mi) in Southern Europe.

Regions	Africa	Asia & Oceania	Europe	Western Hemisphere
Most	Egypt (5)	China (2)	Malta (1)	Bahamas (6)
Least	Botswana (97)	Australia (96)	Iceland (92)	Bolivia (95)

Rank	Country	Population Density per sq km	Population Density per sq mi
	TOP 11		
1	Malta	2,060	5,335.4
2	China	1,610	4,169.9
3	Japan	1,610	4,169.9
4	South Korea	1,337	3,462.8
5	Egypt	1,172	3,035.4
6	Bahamas	1,025	2,654.7
7	Lebanon	836	2,165.2
8	Mauritius	746	1,932.1
9	Belgium	609	1,577.3
10	Netherlands	594	1,538.4
11	Sri Lanka	520	1,346.8
	UPPER MIDDLE		
12	Haiti	486	1,258.7
13	Papua New Guinea	470	1,217.3
14	Trinidad & Tobago	454	1,175.8
15	West Germany	453	1,173.2
16	Indonesia	426	1,103.3
17	Norway	407	1,054.1
18	Philippines	369	955.7
19	Jamaica	330	854.7
20	Malaysia	304	787.3
21	India	301	779.5
22	United Kingdom	294	761.4
23	Switzerland	284	735.5
24	El Salvador	276	714.8
25	Nepal	276	714.8
26	Italy	265	686.3
27	Pakistan	258	668.2
28	Rwanda	235	608.6
29	Ireland	234	606.0
30	Thailand	234	606.0
31	Nigeria	229	593.1
32	Sweden	216	559.4
33	Portugal	215	556.8
34	Burundi	206	533.5
35	Austria	190	492.1
36	Guatemala	172	445.4
37	Denmark	166	429.9
38	Dominican Republic	166	429.9
39	Jordan	165	427.3
40	Finland	164	424.7
41	France	153	396.2
42	Gambia	152	393.6
43	Malawi	150	388.5
44	Kenya	148	383.3
45	Burma	143	370.3
46	Yugoslavia	140	362.6
47	Rumania	136	352.2
48	Cyprus	121	313.3
49	Chile	116	300.4
50	Iran	108	279.7
	LOWER MIDDLE		
51	Afghanistan	102	264.1
52	Greece	99	256.4
53	Colombia	98	253.8
54	Spain	97	251.2
55	Iraq	92	238.2
56	Panama	88	227.9
57	Nicaragua	84	217.5
58	Costa Rica	73	189.0
59	Togo	72	186.4
60	Turkey	66	170.9
61	Ghana	61	157.9
62	Syria	56	145.0
63	Brazil	50	129.5
64	Honduras	49	126.9
65	Morocco	48	124.3
66	Sudan	47	121.7
67	United States	47	121.7
68	Peru	46	119.1
69	Venezuela	38	98.4
70	Cameroon	37	95.8
71	Sierra Leone	37	95.8
72	Lesotho	36	93.2
73	Mexico	35	90.6
74	Senegal	34	88.0
75	Canada	31	80.2
76	Ethiopia	31	80.2
77	Liberia	31	80.2
78	Algeria	30	77.7
79	Ivory Coast	30	77.7
80	Upper Volta	28	72.5
81	Tanzania	23	59.5
82	Guyana	22	56.9
83	Niger	22	56.9
84	New Zealand	21	54.3
85	Madagascar	19	49.2
86	Paraguay	19	49.2
87	Zaire	19	49.2
88	Uruguay	18	46.6
	BOTTOM 10		
89	Argentina	14	36.2
90	South Yemen	14	36.2
91	Mali	12	31.0
92	Somalia	10	25.9
93	Iceland	9	23.3
94	Zambia	9	23.3
95	Chad	7	18.1
96	Bolivia	5	12.9
97	Australia	3	7.7
98	Botswana	2	5.1

Source: Food & Agriculture Organization.

16. Urbanization

Urbanization is a universal phenomenon; in some countries it has assumed alarming proportions leading to the depletion of the rural population and the overcrowding of towns. However, urban statistics are impaired by serious limitations. The first question is at what point does a concentration of people become urban? The distinction between urban and rural areas is made in different ways in different countries. The urban status is granted to places with as few as 400 inhabitants in Albania, while in Austria the lower limit is 5,000 persons. In Bulgaria urban denotes places with urban status regardless of size, while in Israel it implies predominantly nonagricultural localities. In Sweden it is built-up areas with less than 200 meters between houses, in Peru populated centers with 100 or more occupied dwellings, in Iceland localities of 200 or more inhabitants, in Australia 250 or more dwellings of which at least 100 are occupied, in Senegal agglomerations of 15,000 or more inhabitants, in South Africa areas of less than 500 inhabitants if 100 of such inhabitants are white, in India places having a density of not less than 1,000 persons per square mile or 390 persons per square kilometer where at least three-fourths of the adult male population are employed in nonagricultural pursuits, in Yugoslavia localities of 15,-000 or more inhabitants, and in Japan areas (called shis) having 50,000 or more inhabitants.

Other countries define towns not so much in terms of inhabitants but in terms of urban characteristics such as streets, plazas, water supply, and sewerage systems and electric light. In still others the distinction is based on administrative divisions with headquarters of civil divisions being gazetted as towns. The differences in definition are so bound up with historical, cultural and administrative considerations that it is difficult to discern a uniform pattern. Further, because these definitions change over time, they become inapplicable for statistical comparisons even within the same country. If the threshhold of urbanization cannot be determined by size of population alone, it is more difficult to determine it on the basis of facilities of urban life. Many of the rural areas in the United States are relatively more modernized than the largest towns in Africa. Another potential source of error is the difficulty of estimating internal migration into the cities, which is changing the population balance in almost every country. Because of these shortcomings the data presented in the following ranking should be used with caution and are useful only for attempting broad comparisons.

Number of Countries: 144 **Midpoint:** 39.9% **Period Covered:** 1976 **Type of Ranking:** Percentage of Population Living in Localities Officially Defined as Urban; Highest to Lowest	**Highlights & Findings:** Urbanization is related to the process of modernization; at the top of the list are small city-states and industrialized countries. At the bottom are the least developed countries without an industrial base. Only two countries of significant size are in the top 10: Chile and Australia.

Regions	Africa	Asia & Oceania	Europe	Western Hemisphere
Most	Mozambique (44)	Nauru (2)	Monaco (1)	Chile (8)
Least	Lesotho (143)	Bhutan (144)	Portugal (94)	Barbados (141)

Rank	Country	Percentage of Urban Population	Rank	Country	Percentage of Urban Population	Rank	Country	Percentage of Urban Population
	TOP 10		15	United Arab Emirates	80.0	32	Czechoslovakia	61.0
1	Monaco	100	16	West Germany	79.0	33	Iraq	61.0
2	Nauru	100	17	Bahrain	78.1	34	Lebanon	60.1
3	Singapore	100	18	New Zealand	77.3	35	Cuba	60.0
4	Malta	94.3	19	United Kingdom	77.1	36	Brazil	59.1
5	Kuwait	88.0	20	Netherlands	77.0	37	Spain	59.1
6	Qatar	85.0	21	Canada	76.0	38	Taiwan	59.0
7	Australia	83.0	22	France	76.0	39	Bulgaria	58.8
8	Chile	83.0	23	Venezuela	75.7	40	Bahamas	57.9
9	Israel	82.0	24	East Germany	74.2	41	Switzerland	57.4
10	Sweden	81.4	25	United States	74.0	42	Soviet Union	56.0
			26	Belgium	71.8	43	Peru	55.3
	UPPER MIDDLE		27	Colombia	70.0	44	Mozambique	55.0
11	Andorra	81.0	28	Iceland	70.0	45	Poland	54.6
12	Uruguay	80.6	29	Luxembourg	68.0	46	China	51.1
13	Argentina	80.0	30	Greece	64.8	47	Finland	50.9
14	Denmark	80.0	31	Mexico	63.3	48	Tonga	50.0

Rank	Country	Percentage of Urban Population	Rank	Country	Percentage of Urban Population	Rank	Country	Percentage of Urban Population
49	Panama	49.6	81	Zambia	36.3	115	Thailand	16.5
50	Ireland	49.2	82	Central African Empire	35.9	116	Laos	15.0
51	South Korea	48.5	83	South Yemen	35.3	117	Sierra Leone	15.0
52	Mauritius	48.3	84	Ivory Coast	34.3	118	Togo	15.0
53	Italy	48.0	85	Albania	34.0	119	Madagascar	14.5
54	Nicaragua	48.0	86	Bolivia	34.0	120	Afghanistan	14.3
55	South Africa	47.0	87	North Korea	34.0	121	Swaziland	14.3
56	Tunisia	47.0	88	Ghana	32.4	122	Gambia	14.0
57	Syria	46.2	89	Gabon	32.0	123	Chad	13.9
58	Austria	46.0	90	Honduras	31.4	124	Mali	13.4
59	Dominican Republic	45.9	91	Malaysia	30.2	125	Sudan	13.2
60	Hungary	45.1	92	Libya	30.0	126	Benin	13.1
61	Norway	44.7	93	Philippines	29.8	127	Papua New Guinea	12.9
62	Egypt	44.6	94	Portugal	28.8	128	Upper Volta	12.1
63	Iran	43.0	95	Cameroon	28.5	129	Kenya	11.3
64	Jordan	43.0	96	Somalia	28.3	130	Ethiopia	11.2
65	Rumania	43.0	97	Liberia	27.6	131	Botswana	10.7
66	Turkey	42.6	98	Zaire	26.4	132	Niger	9.4
67	Cyprus	42.2	99	Nigeria	26.0	133	Bangladesh	8.8
68	Ecuador	41.6	100	Pakistan	26.0	134	Uganda	8.4
69	Costa Rica	40.6	101	Trinidad & Tobago	25.1			
70	Morocco	40.1	102	Mongolia	25.0		*BOTTOM 10*	
71	Guyana	40.0	103	Sri Lanka	24.3	135	Tanzania	7.3
72	Algeria	39.9	104	Haiti	23.1	136	Yemen Arab Republic	7.0
			105	Burma	22.3	137	Malawi	6.4
	LOWER MIDDLE		106	Mauritania	21.7	138	Oman	5.0
73	El Salvador	39.4	107	India	20.6	139	Nepal	4.8
74	Senegal	38.8	108	Western Samoa	20.3	140	Rwanda	3.8
75	Yugoslavia	38.7	109	Vietnam	20.0	141	Barbados	3.7
76	Fiji	38.5	110	Guinea	19.5	142	Burundi	3.7
77	Congo	38.0	111	Indonesia	18.2	143	Lesotho	3.1
78	Paraguay	37.4	112	Angola	18.0	144	Bhutan	0.0
79	Guatemala	37.3	113	Rhodesia	18.0			
80	Jamaica	37.1	114	Saudi Arabia	17.9			

Source: *World Bank Atlas.*

17. Population in Cities over 50,000

The urban percentage of national populations has been treated in another ranking. However, demographers are dissatisfied with the current definitions of the word urban. At what point does a settlement become urban? Often a town of 2,500 or even 5,000 may have more buildings and more people than a village, but it may lack the environment and quality of life normally associated with large metropolises. The threshold is not determined by size alone and varies from country to country. A reasonably reliable ranking is the percentage of population living in cities over 50,000, although many social scientists use 100,000 as the cutoff point. (The lower figure has been adopted in this ranking in order to do justice to smaller developing countries). But such an approach is also subject to numerous qualifications.

The true limits of urbanized areas are constantly changing and governments have neither the inclination nor the capability to adapt their census procedures to these changes. Also, the ranking does not take into account disparities in distribution or concentration within a country. For example, Thailand has only one large metropolis—Bangkok/Thonburi—with a population of over 2.5 million, and all other towns have less than 75,000 inhabitants each. The one constant in urbanology is that larger cities are always gaining at the expense of smaller ones. Obviously, therefore, the best that can be expected with the present data sets is some indication of the total size of the urban population on the basis of crude and unrefined criteria.

Number of Countries: 128	**Highlights & Findings:** There are 14 countries where the majority of the population live in cities over 50,000. In 43 of the smaller developing countries there are no cities over this limit.
Midpoint: 25.5%	
Period Covered: 1976	

	Africa	Asia & Oceania	Europe	Western Hemisphere
Type of Ranking: Percentage of Population Living in Cities over 50,000; Highest to Lowest	**Region**			
	Most Gabon (2)	Australia (1)	Sweden (11)	Argentina (8)
	Least Uganda (128)	Papua New Guinea (126)	Albania (94)	Jamaica (117)

Rank	Country	Percentage of Population in Cities over 50,000	Rank	Country	Percentage of Population in Cities over 50,000	Rank	Country	Percentage of Population in Cities over 50,000
	TOP 10		43	East Germany	34.9	86	Trinidad & Tobago	14.7
1	Australia	77.6	44	Ireland	34.6	87	Guatemala	14.5
2	Gabon	75.9	45	Philippines	34.6	88	Liberia	14.3
3	Singapore	70.7	46	Finland	33.4	89	Yugoslavia	14.3
4	Japan	66.5	47	Tunisia	33.3	90	Nigeria	14.1
5	Jordan	62.9	48	Dominican Republic	32.8	91	Algeria	14.0
6	New Zealand	60.7	49	Bolivia	32.6	92	Central African Empire	14.0
7	North Korea	59.3	50	Austria	32.0	93	Indonesia	13.7
8	Argentina	59.2	51	Hungary	31.7	94	Albania	13.6
9	United Arab Emirates	58.0	52	Cyprus	31.6	95	India	12.9
10	Chile	55.0	53	France	31.3	96	Guinea-Bissau	12.3
			54	Lebanon	30.7	97	Burma	12.0
	UPPER MIDDLE		55	Nicaragua	30.6	98	Somalia	11.8
11	Sweden	54.8	56	Iran	30.3	99	Costa Rica	11.2
12	Uruguay	51.5	57	Greece	28.9	100	Fiji	10.8
13	Spain	51.4	58	Norway	27.7	101	Benin	10.1
14	United Kingdom	51.1	59	Ecuador	26.6	102	Togo	10.0
15	Libya	46.1	60	Ghana	26.3	103	Haiti	9.9
16	Taiwan	45.5	61	Mongolia	26.1	104	Yemen Arab Republic	9.5
17	Denmark	45.0	62	Honduras	25.7	105	Mauritania	9.3
18	Israel	44.7	63	Switzerland	25.7	106	Sudan	9.2
19	Venezuela	43.7				107	Cameroon	8.7
20	Colombia	43.1		*LOWER MIDDLE*		108	Kenya	8.5
21	Saudi Arabia	42.7	64	South Africa	25.5	109	Cambodia	8.2
22	Iraq	42.6	65	Turkey	25.5	110	Sierra Leone	7.9
23	Mauritius	42.2	66	Rumania	25.3	111	Laos	7.4
24	Netherlands	41.3	67	Senegal	25.3	112	Madagascar	7.4
25	Peru	40.7	68	Czechoslovakia	25.0	113	Thailand	7.2
26	Italy	40.5	69	Kuwait	24.5	114	Mali	7.1
27	Soviet Union	40.1	70	El Salvador	24.0	115	Sri Lanka	6.6
28	Canada	39.4	71	Luxembourg	23.6	116	Malawi	6.4
29	Brazil	39.0	72	Morocco	23.4	117	Jamaica	6.2
30	Panama	39.0	73	Zaire	21.5	118	Chad	6.1
31	West Germany	38.8	74	Zambia	19.9			
32	Egypt	38.7	75	Belgium	19.7		*BOTTOM 10*	
33	Iceland	38.2	76	Qatar	18.8	119	Ethiopia	5.9
34	Poland	38.0	77	Guyana	18.3	120	Afghanistan	5.6
35	Bahrain	37.3	78	Equatorial Guinea	16.8	121	Upper Volta	5.0
36	United States	36.6	79	Rhodesia (Zimbabwe)	16.8	122	Nepal	4.5
37	Syria	36.3	80	Paraguay	16.6	123	Tanzania	4.5
38	Cuba	36.1	81	Ivory Coast	16.2	124	Burundi	3.9
39	Surinam	36.0	82	Guinea	15.8	125	Niger	3.9
40	Congo	35.8	83	Portugal	15.3	126	Papua New Guinea	2.8
41	Mexico	35.6	84	Vietnam	15.0	127	Rwanda	2.1
42	Bulgaria	35.3	85	South Yemen	15.0	128	Uganda	0.9

Source: Cross-National Data Archive, Center for Social Analysis, Binghamton, N.Y.

18. Annual Urban Population Growth Rate

Urban population growth rates are calculated from U.N. estimates. Because these estimates reflect differing definitions of the term urban, cross-country comparisons should be attempted only with caution.

Number of Countries: 125
Midpoint: 4.5%
Period Covered: 1970-75
Type of Ranking: Annual Growth Rate of Urban Population; Highest to Lowest

Highlights & Findings: Urban population growth seems to be particularly explosive in the newly independent developing countries that had overwhelmingly rural populations before World War II. All countries at the bottom of the table are, significantly, industrialized nations of Europe and North America. Although the concentration of population in urban areas can, and in many cases does, promote economic development (by reducing costs of transportation and expanding availability of social and medical services, for instance), the experience of most developing countries has been almost uniformly adverse. Rapid urban growth rate has led to an increase of crime, unemployment, political unrest, social anomie, breakup of traditional family structures and overload on available public services. The urban growth rate was 5.5% in low-income countries, 4.5% in middle-income countries, 1.8% in industrialized countries, 6.3% in oil-exporting countries and 3.2% in Communist countries. (See the introduction for a definition of these country categories.)

Regions	Africa	Asia & Oceania	Europe	Western Hemisphere
Most	Rwanda (4)	Papua New Guinea (1)	Albania (48)	Dominican Republic (29)
Least	South Africa (86)	Hong Kong (112)	United Kingdom (125)	United States (116)

Rank	Country	Annual Urban Population Growth Rate (%)
	TOP 11	
1	Papua New Guinea	10.1
2	Kuwait	8.2
3	Yemen Arab Republic	8.0
4	Rwanda	7.7
5	Tanzania	7.5
6	Nigeria	7.0
7	Uganda	6.8
8	Zambia	6.8
9	Lesotho	6.7
10	Benin	6.6
11	Guinea	6.6
	UPPER MIDDLE	
12	Ivory Coast	6.5
13	Zaire	6.4
14	Chad	6.3
15	Kenya	6.3
16	Saudi Arabia	6.3
17	Angola	6.2
18	Burundi	6.1
19	Cambodia	6.1
20	Mozambique	6.1
21	Madagascar	6.0
22	Rhodesia (Zimbabwe)	5.9
23	Central African Empire	5.8
24	Liberia	5.8
25	Algeria	5.7
26	Taiwan	5.6
27	Ethiopia	5.6
28	Nepal	5.6
29	Dominican Republic	5.5
30	Ghana	5.5
31	Sudan	5.5
32	Afghanistan	5.4
33	Lebanon	5.4
34	Mongolia	5.4
35	Niger	5.4
36	South Yemen	5.4
37	Malawi	5.3
38	Pakistan	5.3
39	Thailand	5.3
40	Cameroon	5.2
41	Upper Volta	5.2

Rank	Country	Annual Urban Population Growth Rate (%)
42	North Korea	5.1
43	Morocco	5.1
44	Iraq	5.0
45	Libya	5.0
46	Mauritania	5.0
47	Togo	5.0
48	Albania	4.9
49	Colombia	4.9
50	Jordan	4.9
51	South Korea	4.9
52	Laos	4.9
53	Burma	4.8
54	Philippines	4.8
55	Indonesia	4.7
56	Iran	4.7
57	Malaysia	4.7
58	Somalia	4.7
59	Bhutan	4.6
60	Mali	4.6
61	Mexico	4.6
62	Vietnam	4.6
	LOWER MIDDLE	
63	Brazil	4.5
64	Congo	4.5
65	Honduras	4.5
66	Nicaragua	4.5
67	Sierra Leone	4.4
68	Sri Lanka	4.3
69	Panama	4.2
70	Peru	4.2
71	Syria	4.2
72	Tunisia	4.2
73	Turkey	4.2
74	Senegal	4.1
75	Bolivia	4.0
76	Guatemala	4.0
77	Ecuador	3.9
78	Egypt	3.9
79	El Salvador	3.9
80	Venezuela	3.9
81	Bangladesh	3.8
82	Costa Rica	3.8
83	India	3.8

Rank	Country	Annual Urban Population Growth Rate (%)
84	Jamaica	3.8
85	Paraguay	3.7
86	South Africa	3.7
87	Haiti	3.6
88	Israel	3.4
89	China	3.3
90	Cuba	2.9
91	Yugoslavia	2.9
92	Bulgaria	2.8
93	Rumania	2.8
94	Chile	2.7
95	Singapore	2.5
96	Soviet Union	2.4
97	Ireland	2.3
98	Japan	2.3
99	Australia	2.2
100	Poland	2.2
101	Argentina	2.0
102	Canada	2.0
103	Norway	2.0
104	Finland	1.9
105	New Zealand	1.9
106	Spain	1.9
107	Switzerland	1.9
108	Trinidad & Tobago	1.9
109	France	1.8
110	Czechoslovakia	1.7
111	Greece	1.7
112	Hong Kong	1.7
113	Portugal	1.7
114	Uruguay	1.7
	BOTTOM 11	
115	Hungary	1.5
116	United States	1.5
117	Italy	1.3
118	Netherlands	1.2
119	Sweden	1.2
120	Belgium	1.0
121	Denmark	1.0
122	Austria	0.8
123	West Germany	0.8
124	East Germany	0.5
125	United Kingdom	0.5

Source: United Nations Population Division.

19. Marriage Rate

Marriage is defined in most countries of the world as the legal union of husband and wife through civil, religious or other means. Because marriage is a legal event, unlike birth and death which are biological events, it is affected by the laws of the individual countries. In some countries statistics are compiled only for civil marriages and in others only for religious marriages as recorded in church registers. Although the legal requirements vary, some form of registration is required in all countries, and there-fore marriage statistics tend to be more reliable than those on births and deaths. However, customary unions and consensual unions (where unmarried couples live together) are universally excluded from these statistics, and the recent decline in marriage rates may in some cases only reflect a rise in such de facto unions. Marriage rates are also seriously affected by the age and sex structure of the populations to which they relate.

Number of Countries: 132
Midpoint: 6.6 per 1,000
Period Covered: 1970-75
Type of Ranking: Number of Reported Marriages per 1,000 persons; Highest to Lowest

Highlights & Findings: A chart of this ranking (such as a frequency distribution or Lorenz curve) would be interesting because the rates fall precipitously in the beginning and become stable thereafter. The low marriage rates in some African countries reflect the prevailing practice of customary union. Higher marriage rates in industrialized countries are partly the result of a greater number of persons marrying while still in their teens.

Regions	Africa	Asia & Oceania	Europe	Western Hemisphere
Most	Liberia (1)	Guam (2)	Gibraltar (3)	Falkland Islands (4)
Least	Guinea-Bissau (132)	Cook Islands (131)	Andorra (91)	Colombia (123)

Rank	Country	Number of Marriages per 1,000	Rank	Country	Number of Marriages per 1,000	Rank	Country	Number of Marriages per 1,000
	TOP 10		36	Yugoslavia	8.2	72	Denmark	6.2
1	Liberia	39.4	37	Greece	8.1	73	Austria	6.1
2	Guam	17.9	38	New Zealand	8.0	74	Lebanon	6.1
3	Gibraltar	16.6	39	Spain	8.0	75	West Germany	6.0
4	Falkland Islands	13.2	40	Jordan	7.9	76	New Caledonia	6.0
5	South Korea	12.0	41	Australia	7.8	77	Norway	5.9
6	Cayman Islands	10.9	42	Iceland	7.7	78	Belize	5.8
7	St. Pierre & Miquelon	10.9	43	United Kingdom	7.7	79	Brunei	5.8
8	Syria	10.8	44	French Polynesia	7.5	80	Libya	5.8
9	Soviet Union	10.7	45	Iraq	7.5	81	Ecuador	5.6
10	Indonesia	10.6	46	Belgium	7.4	82	Sweden	5.5
			47	Costa Rica	7.4	83	Switzerland	5.5
			48	Argentina	7.3	84	Faroe Islands	5.4
	UPPER MIDDLE		49	Liechtenstein	7.2	85	Bahamas	5.2
11	Malta	10.1	50	France	7.1	86	Kuwait	5.2
12	Puerto Rico	10.1	51	Monaco	7.1	87	Gilbert Islands	5.0
13	United States	9.9	52	Netherlands Antilles	7.1	88	Guadeloupe	5.0
14	Egypt	9.8	53	Venezuela	7.1	89	Jamaica	5.0
15	Czechoslovakia	9.5	54	Albania	7.0	90	Paraguay	4.9
16	Hungary	9.5	55	Cuba	7.0	91	Andorra	4.8
17	Mauritius	9.5	56	Cyprus	7.0	92	Nicaragua	4.8
18	Norfolk Island	9.5	57	Finland	7.0	93	Seychelles	4.8
19	Poland	9.5	58	Netherlands	7.0	94	Algeria	4.7
20	Singapore	9.4	59	Ireland	6.9	95	Martinique	4.7
21	British Virgin Islands	9.3	60	Mexico	6.9	96	Western Samoa	4.7
22	Portugal	9.3	61	Philippines	6.9	97	French Guyana	4.6
23	Bermuda	9.2	62	Sri Lanka	6.9	98	Angola	4.5
24	San Marino	9.2	63	Trinidad & Tobago	6.8	99	Bolivia	4.5
25	Rumania	8.9	64	Italy	6.7	100	Dominican Republic	4.3
26	Chile	8.8	65	Reunion	6.7	101	Greenland	4.3
27	Fiji	8.8				102	Niue Island	4.3
28	Japan	8.5				103	Panama	4.3
29	Bulgaria	8.4		*LOWER MIDDLE*		104	El Salvador	4.1
30	East Germany	8.4	66	Iran	6.6	105	Guatemala	4.1
31	Canada	8.3	67	Isle of Man	6.6	106	Montserrat	4.1
32	Hong Kong	8.3	68	St. Helena	6.5	107	Thailand	4.1
33	Israel	8.3	69	Wallis & Funtuna	6.5	108	Nauru	4.0
34	Uruguay	8.3	70	Luxembourg	6.3	109	St. Kitts-Nevis-Anguilla	4.0
35	Tunisia	8.2	71	Tonga	6.3			

Rank	Country	Number of Marriages per 1,000	Rank	Country	Number of Marriages per 1,000	Rank	Country	Number of Marriages per 1,000
110	Barbados	3.9	119	Rwanda	3.1	126	Cocos (Keeling) Islands	1.7
111	Guyana	3.8	120	Surinam	3.0	127	Malaysia	1.7
112	Honduras	3.8	121	Grenada	2.8	128	Pacific Islands	1.5
113	Antigua	3.7	122	Turks & Caicos	2.7	129	Equatorial Guinea	0.8
114	Christmas Island	3.5				130	Mozambique	0.7
115	Cape Verde	3.4		*BOTTOM 10*		131	Cook Islands	0.4
116	Peru	3.4	123	Colombia	2.4	132	Guinea-Bissau	0.2
117	Dominica	3.2	124	Tokelau	2.0			
118	St. Lucia	3.2	125	Sao Tome & Principe	1.9			

Source: *UN Demographic Yearbook.*

20. Divorce Rate

Divorce is defined as the final legal dissolution of a marriage conferring on the parties the right to remarry in accordance with the laws of each country. Divorce is a legal event and the laws pertaining to divorce vary from one country to another. The incidence of divorce is affected by the relative ease or difficulty in obtaining a divorce and the ability of individuals to meet the financial and other costs of court procedures. Another influential factor is the authority of the prevailing religious system. In most Catholic countries, such as Chile, Argentina, Brazil, Ireland, Malta, Paraguay, the Philippines, St. Lucia and Spain, divorce is still illegal, and it became legal in Italy and Colombia only in the 1970s. For these reasons divorce statistics are not strictly comparable, particularly when there are other legal means of family dissolution, such as separation. Divorce statistics are obtained from court records and civil registers. These registers refer to the number of divorces granted and not to the persons obtaining them. Divorce rates—like birth, death and marriage rates—are also affected by the age-sex structure of the population to which they relate.

Number of Countries: 103
Midpoint: 0.7 per 1,000
Period Covered: Latest Available Year 1957-76
Type of Ranking: Number of Divorces Reported per 1,000 Persons; Highest to Lowest

Highlights & Findings: Divorce rates seem to follow recognizable geographical or social patterns. Although the highest rate in Djibouti is 6.9, the spread between the highest and the lowest is only 6.8 and most of the countries fall toward the lower end of the scale.

Regions	Africa	Asia & Oceania	Europe	Western Hemisphere
Most	Djibouti (1)	New Zealand (24)	Soviet Union (5)	United States (2)
Least	St. Helena (94)	Vietnam (103)	Portugal (101)	St. Kitts-Nevis-Anguilla (102)

Rank	Country	Number of Divorces per 1,000	Rank	Country	Number of Divorces per 1,000	Rank	Country	Number of Divorces per 1,000
	TOP 9		16	Canada	2.0	34	Australia	1.3
1	Dijibouti	6.9	17	Egypt	2.0	35	Bulgaria	1.3
2	United States	5.0	18	Liberia	2.0	36	Comoros	1.3
3	Puerto Rico	4.3	19	Libya	2.0	37	West Germany	1.3
4	Falkland Islands	3.9	20	Monaco	2.0	38	French Polynesia	1.2
5	Soviet Union	3.1	21	United Kingdom	2.0	39	Poland	1.2
6	Bermuda	2.8	22	Iceland	1.8	40	Yugoslavia	1.2
7	Sweden	2.7	23	Netherlands Antilles	1.6	41	Belgium	1.1
8	Cayman Islands	2.6	24	New Zealand	1.6	42	Japan	1.1
9	Denmark	2.6	25	Rumania	1.6	43	Tonga	1.1
			26	Netherlands	1.5	44	Tunisia	1.1
	UPPER MIDDLE		27	Austria	1.4	45	France	1.0
10	East Germany	2.5	28	Jordan	1.4	46	Israel	0.9
11	Hungary	2.5	29	Kuwait	1.4	47	Montserrat	0.9
12	Cuba	2.4	30	Norway	1.4	48	Albania	0.8
13	Czechoslovakia	2.2	31	Switzerland	1.4	49	Liechtenstein	0.8
14	Dominican Republic	2.1	32	Turks & Caicos Islands	1.4	50	Luxembourg	0.8
15	Finland	2.1	33	Uruguay	1.4	51	Surinam	0.8

Rank	Country	Number of Divorces per 1,000	Rank	Country	Number of Divorces per 1,000	Rank	Country	Number of Divorces per 1,000
52	Cook Islands	0.7	69	Antigua	0.4	88	Cyprus	0.2
53	Greenland	0.7	70	Barbados	0.4	89	Ecuador	0.2
			71	Faroe Islands	0.4	90	French Guiana	0.2
	LOWER MIDDLE		72	Greece	0.4	91	Honduras	0.2
54	Guyana	0.6	73	Grenada	0.4	92	Nicaragua	0.2
55	Iran	0.6	74	Pacific Islands	0.4	93	Mauritius	0.2
56	New Caledonia	0.6	75	Reunion	0.4	94	St. Helena	0.2
57	St. Vincent	0.6	76	Seychelles	0.4	95	St. Pierre & Miquelon	0.2
58	Syria	0.6	77	Trinidad & Tobago	0.4	96	Thailand	0.2
59	Algeria	0.5	78	Christmas Island	0.3			
60	British Virgin Islands	0.5	79	El Salvador	0.3		*BOTTOM 7*	
61	Brunei	0.5	80	Italy	0.3	97	Bahamas	0.1
62	Fiji	0.5	81	Jamaica	0.3	98	Belize	0.1
63	Guadeloupe	0.5	82	Mexico	0.3	99	Guatemala	0.1
64	Iraq	0.5	83	Niue Island	0.3	100	Peru	0.1
65	South Korea	0.5	84	Samoa	0.3	101	Portugal	0.1
66	Lebanon	0.5	85	Turkey	0.3	102	St.Kitts-Nevis-Anguilla	0.1
67	Martinique	0.5	86	Venezuela	0.3	103	Vietnam	0.1
68	Panama	0.5	87	Costa Rica	0.2			

Source: *UN Demographic Yearbook.*

21. Divorced Persons as Proportion of Population

Divorce is so often thought of as a transitional stage between one marriage and the next that it has not been adequately examined as an independent marital phenomenon. Divorce is also subject to the same terminological confusion that affects marriage. In simple societies divorce is just physical separation, while in more advanced and complex societies divorce is a legal event with a formidable array of regulations and obligations. In addition, there are religious sanctions, which may explain differences in divorce rates as well as social attitudes toward divorce. In orthodox Christian societies, where the family is regarded as a divinely ordained institution, divorce is both illegal and immoral, but in societies where plurality of wives is permitted, as in Islam, Hinduism and animism, there is no stigma against divorce and consequently few legal restraints. In fact, in these societies divorce is considered as normal as marriage, a notion gaining ground in the most secular Western societies.

Number of Countries: 117
Midpoint: 3.19 per 100 married persons
Period Covered: 1975 or Latest Available Year
Type of Ranking: Number of Divorced Persons per 100 Married Persons: Highest to Lowest

Highlights & Findings: Traditionally, African countries have had the highest percentage of divorced persons in their adult populations. Western countries, such as the United States, are relative newcomers among the top 10, and their presence high up the scale reflects the widespread breakdown in moral values and the relative ease of obtaining a divorce. Although divorce is illegal in only a few Catholic countries (Italy, one of the last holdouts, legalized it in the mid-1970s), they generally have the lowest divorce rates. Paradoxically, Islamic countries also have low rates; this may be explained by the fact that divorce is a kind of safety valve more necessary in monogamous rather than polygamous societies.

Region	Africa	Asia & Oceania	Europe	Western Hemisphere
Most	Tanzania (Zanzibar) (2)	Samoa (19)	Sweden (8)	Panama (1)
Least	St. Helena (100)	Nepal (115)	San Marino (117)	Costa Rica (101)

Rank	Country	Divorced Persons per 100 Married Persons	Rank	Country	Divorced Persons per 100 Married Persons	Rank	Country	Divorced Persons per 100 Married Persons
	TOP 10		41	Dominican Republic *	4.47	82	Tunisia	1.92
1	Panama	30.74	42	Morocco	4.46	83	El Salvador	1.89
2	Tanzania (Zanzibar)	20.56	43	Czechoslovakia	4.39	84	Canada **	1.79
3	Puerto Rico *	19.26	44	Kenya	4.22	85	Tonga	1.74
4	Botswana	13.21	45	Gilbert Islands	4.17	86	Christmas Island	1.55
5	United States *	11.28	46	United Arab Emirates	4.12	87	Kuwait	1.52
6	Uganda	10.72	47	France	4.09	88	Italy *	1.47
7	Zambia	9.82	48	Chile	4.06	89	Faroe Islands	1.45
8	Sweden	9.69	49	Colombia	4.06	90	Greece	1.45
9	Madagascar	9.35	50	Mexico	3.97	91	Bahamas	1.30
10	Seychelles	9.04	51	New Caledonia	3.78	92	Belize	1.26
			52	Lesotho	3.70	93	Cyprus *	1.25
	UPPER MIDDLE		53	Nauru	3.66	94	Haiti	1.24
11	Denmark *	8.78	54	Peru *	3.61	95	Fiji	1.14
12	Cuba	8.20	55	Thailand *	3.53	96	Solomon Islands	1.13
13	Ethiopia	8.18	56	Togo	3.51	97	South Korea	1.11
14	Greenland	8.13	57	Rwanda	3.42	98	New Hebrides	1.09
15	Switzerland *	7.58	58	Poland *	3.29	99	Iran	1.06
16	Antigua	7.46	59	British Virgin Islands	3.19	100	St. Helena	1.06
17	Bermuda	7.19	60	Netherlands	3.18	101	Costa Rica	1.05
18	East Germany	7.18				102	Singapore	1.02
19	Samoa	6.70		**LOWER MIDDLE**		103	Jordan	0.98
20	Netherlands Antilles	6.55	61	Guadeloupe	3.14	104	Philippines *	0.98
21	Monaco	6.54	62	Argentina	3.13	105	Syria	0.93
22	Tanzania (Tanganyika)	6.35	63	Bahrain	3.12	106	Turkey	0.93
23	Liberia	6.26	64	New Zealand *	3.06	107	Portugal	0.90
24	Norfolk Island	6.25	65	Liechtenstein	3.03			
25	Austria	6.22	66	Paraguay	2.93		**BOTTOM 10**	
26	Finland	6.20	67	England & Wales	2.89	108	Malaysia	0.84
27	Hungary	5.96	68	Burma	2.88	109	Tokelau	0.78
28	Ecuador *	5.79	69	Rumania	2.88	110	Macao *	0.64
29	Norway *	5.57	70	Martinique	2.86	111	India	0.59
30	Mauritius *	5.45	71	Algeria	2.84	112	Pakistan	0.57
31	Australia	5.41	72	Reunion	2.80	113	Hong Kong	0.55
32	Iceland	5.38	73	Yugoslavia	2.74	114	Spain	0.54
33	Rhodesia (Zimbabwe)	5.23	74	Cook Islands *	2.48	115	Nepal	0.41
34	Luxembourg *	5.17	75	South Africa	2.46	116	Northern Ireland	0.31
35	Pacific Islands	5.11	76	Scotland	2.45	117	San Marino	0.04
36	Brazil *	4.96	77	Venezuela	2.39			
37	West Germany	4.91	78	Japan	2.33	* Includes divorced and separated persons		
38	Cocos (Keeling) Islands	4.70	79	Israel	2.08	** Per 100 married and separated persons combined in		
39	French Guyana	4.70	80	Belgium	2.05	Canadian statistics		
40	Indonesia	4.56	81	Niue Island	2.05			

Source: *U.N. Demographic Yearbook.*

22. Singles (Male)

Demographers often talk of the intensity of marriage, meaning all those who have been married, divorced, or widowed at least once in their life. Outside of this circle are those described as never-marrieds, or singles. Although the percentage of such singles in the population is available for a number of age groups, the 45 to 49 age group has been selected for the following two rankings because it represents a group that will in all probability never marry. The stigma attached to nonmarrieds in the past has dissipated in the current sexual revolution, and the state of being nonmarried may become quite acceptable in the emerging social milieu.

Number of Countries: 118
Midpoint: 7.7%
Period Covered: Early 1970s
Type of Ranking: Percentage of Non-Married Males, Ages 45 to 49; Highest to Lowest

Highlights & Findings: There is only one country in the world where non-married males constitute a majority: French Guyana. Similarly there is one country where all males are married by this age: Pitcairn Island. Interestingly, all Pitcairnese, or Pitcairnians, (the proper form has never been determined) are married by the age of 19. In what is conventionally known as the developed world, Ireland is first on the list, a position it has historically occupied for a number of centuries.

Region	Africa	Asia & Oceania	Europe	Western Hemisphere
Most	Kenya (2)	Norfolk Island (9)	Ireland (4)	French Guyana (1)
Least	Rwanda (115)	Pitcairn Island (118)	East Germany (110)	United States (77)

Rank	Country	Percentage of Bachelors (45-49)
	TOP 10	
1	French Guyana	53.2
2	Kenya	32.1
3	Seychelles	30.3
4	Ireland	28.3
5	Martinique	27.3
6	Guadeloupe	27.2
7	Dominican Republic	23.8
8	British Virgin Islands	22.5
9	Norfolk Island	20.5
10	Faroe Islands	18.0
	UPPER MIDDLE	
11	Northern Ireland	17.8
12	Malta	17.6
13	Greenland	16.3
14	Netherlands Antilles	16.0
15	New Caledonia	16.0
16	Venezuela	15.2
17	Iceland	15.1
18	Cuba	14.7
19	El Salvador	14.5
20	Haiti	13.8
21	St. Helena	13.8
22	Finland	13.5
23	Sweden	13.5
24	Bahamas	13.1
25	Argentina	12.7
26	Cook Islands	12.6
27	Uganda	12.1
28	Botswana	12.0
29	Norway	12.0
30	Panama	12.0
31	Colombia	11.9
32	Rumania	11.9
33	Monaco	11.4
34	Paraguay	11.3
35	Chile	11.1
36	Italy	11.1
37	France	10.9
38	Scotland	10.9
39	Christmas Island	10.8

Rank	Country	Percentage of Bachelors (45-49)
40	Costa Rica	10.4
41	England & Wales	10.1
42	Ecuador	9.8
43	Puerto Rico	9.7
44	Switzerland	9.7
45	Tokelau	9.7
46	Cocos (Keeling) Islands	9.5
47	Rhodesia (Zimbabwe) (Blacks Only)	9.5
48	Denmark	9.4
49	Canada	9.1
50	St. Pierre & Miquelon	9.1
51	Australia	9.0
52	New Zealand	8.8
53	Spain	8.8
54	Peru	8.5
55	Belgium	8.3
56	Luxembourg	8.2
57	Guatemala	7.9
58	Bahrain	7.8
59	Netherlands	7.7
	LOWER MIDDLE	
60	Portugal	7.6
61	Solomon Islands	7.6
62	Austria	7.5
63	Gibraltar	7.5
64	Macao	7.5
65	Hong Kong	7.2
66	Brazil	7.0
67	Tanzania (Zanzibar)	7.0
68	Mexico	6.4
69	Tonga	6.3
70	Greece	6.0
71	Singapore	5.9
72	Czechoslovakia	5.7
73	Pacific Islands	5.7
74	San Marino	5.7
75	West Germany	5.6
76	New Hebrides	5.6
77	United States	5.6
78	Brunei	5.5

Rank	Country	Percentage of Bachelors (45-49)
79	Mauritius	5.4
80	Niue Islands	5.3
81	Sabah	5.1
82	Kuwait	4.8
83	Liberia	4.6
84	Togo	4.6
85	Hungary	4.5
86	Tanzania (Tanganyika)	4.4
87	Lesotho	4.3
88	Samoa	4.3
89	Fiji	4.2
90	Sarawak	4.2
91	Algeria	4.1
92	Gilbert Islands	3.9
93	Poland	3.9
94	Israel	3.8
95	Jordan	3.7
96	Pakistan	3.7
97	Philippines	3.7
98	Tunisia	3.7
99	Yugoslavia	3.7
100	Burma	3.6
101	Thailand	3.2
102	Malaysia	3.1
103	Morocco	3.1
104	Madagascar	3.0
105	Zambia	3.0
106	India	2.9
107	Cyprus	2.7
108	Rumania	2.7
109	Syria	2.7
	BOTTOM 9	
110	East Germany	2.4
111	Japan	2.4
112	Indonesia	1.8
113	Turkey	1.8
114	Nepal	1.6
115	Rwanda	0.8
116	Iran	0.7
117	South Korea	0.2
118	Pitcairn Island	0.0

Source: *UN Demographic Yearbook.*

23. Singles (Female)

Number of Countries: 116 **Midpoint:** 6.7% **Period Covered:** Early 1970s **Type of Ranking:** Percentage of Non-Married Females, Ages 45 to 49; Highest to Lowest	**Highlights & Findings:** In almost every country there are more nonmarried males than females, as this ranking shows. There are also significant variations in the rank order, although French Guyana remains at the top and Pitcairn Island is at the bottom. There are nine Caribbean or Latin American countries in the top 12.

Region	Africa	Asia & Oceania	Europe	Western Hemisphere
Most	Kenya (4)	New Caledonia (29)	Malta (9)	French Guyana (1)
Least	Rwanda (115)	Pitcairn Island (116)	Rumania (81)	United States (79)

Rank	Country	Percentage of Singles (45-49)	Rank	Country	Percentage of Singles (45-49)	Rank	Country	Percentage of Singles (45-49)
	TOP 10		39	Cuba	10.0	78	Macao	4.4
1	French Guyana	46.7	40	Austria	9.8	79	United States	4.4
2	Martinique	33.3	41	Iceland	9.8	80	Cook Islands	4.3
3	Guadeloupe	32.1	42	Scotland	9.8	81	Rumania	4.3
4	Kenya	28.0	43	Brazil	8.8	82	Niue Island	4.2
5	Seychelles	28.0	44	St. Pierre & Miquelon	8.6	83	Solomon Islands	4.1
6	British Virgin Islands	24.4	45	West Germany	8.3	84	Pacific Islands	3.9
7	El Salvador	22.3	46	East Germany	8.2	85	Hong Kong	3.8
8	Netherlands Antilles	21.1	47	France	8.0	86	Mauritius	3.7
9	Malta	20.9	48	Belgium	7.7	87	Kuwait	3.4
10	Venezuela	20.9	49	Netherlands	7.3	88	Sarawak	3.4
			50	Rhodesia (Zimbabwe) (Blacks Only)	7.3	89	Fiji	3.2
	UPPER MIDDLE		51	Greece	7.2	90	Singapore	3.1
11	Paraguay	20.0	52	England & Wales	7.2	91	Thailand	3.0
12	Haiti	19.7	53	Mexico	7.1	92	Jordan	2.8
13	Ireland	18.2	54	Sweden	7.1	93	Sabah	2.8
14	Dominican Republic	17.0	55	Canada	7.0	94	Samoa	2.8
15	Reunion	16.5	56	Panama	6.9	95	Lesotho	2.6
16	Northern Ireland	16.2	57	Faroe Islands	6.7	96	New Hebrides	2.5
17	Colombia	14.8	58	New Zealand	6.7	97	Syria	2.5
18	Costa Rica	14.6	59	Philippines	6.7	98	Israel	2.3
19	Bahamas	14.4				99	Morocco	2.3
20	St. Helena	14.2		*LOWER MIDDLE*		100	Zambia	2.2
21	Monaco	13.9	60	Tonga	6.6	101	Togo	2.0
22	Italy	13.5	61	Puerto Rico	6.5	102	Algeria	1.9
23	Botswana	13.3	62	Norway	6.4	103	Bahrain	1.9
24	Greenland	13.3	63	Poland	6.4	104	Liberia	1.7
25	Tokelau	13.3	64	Denmark	6.3	105	Turkey	1.7
26	Chile	12.5	65	Yugoslavia	6.3	106	Tunisia	1.5
27	Switzerland	12.2	66	Uganda	5.8			
28	Spain	12.1	67	Burma	5.7		*BOTTOM 10*	
29	New Caledonia	11.9	68	Gilbert Islands	5.2	107	Malaysia (West)	1.3
30	Portugal	11.7	69	San Marino	5.2	108	Tanzania	1.3
31	Finland	11.4	70	Norfolk Island	5.1	109	Indonesia	1.0
32	Cocos (Keeling) Islands	11.1	71	Madagascar	5.0	110	Nepal	0.8
33	Ecuador	11.0	72	Cyprus	5.0	111	Pakistan	0.8
34	Argentina	10.9	73	Czechoslovakia	5.0	112	Iran	0.6
35	Gibraltar	10.5	74	Australia	4.9	113	India	0.4
36	Guatemala	10.5	75	Japan	4.8	114	South Korea	0.1
37	Luxembourg	10.4	76	Brunei	4.5	115	Rwanda	0.1
38	Peru	10.2	77	Hungary	4.4	116	Pitcairn Island	0.0

Source: *UN Demographic Yearbook.*

24. Male/Female Ratio

One of the most remarkable biological phenomena in the world is the parity between males and females. The world's total reported population of 4.1 billion is amost evenly divided between males and females, the 7 million more males than females being statistically insignificant. It is not known what biological laws are at work ensuring this parity so necessary for the survival of the race considering the odds against it. (One particularly gruesome sci-fi scenario is the destruction of the human species through the mutation of the genes leading to the procreation of males or females alone.) But although the overall ratio reveals near-total parity, there are significant differences within age groups, within regions and within nations. Barring Bulgaria, where the ratio is a remarkable 50,00: 50.00, there is no nation where the ratio is not skewed in favor of either the males or females; in 66 countries males form the majority, and in 87 countries females constitute the majority. The differences within age groups and within regions are striking as the following table shows:

Africa	49.7103	50.2839	49.4725	45.2916
North America	48.9070	51.0130	49.2932	41.1808
Latin America	50.0536	50.6610	49.8720	45.9487
Asia	50.9740	51.1351	51.1371	47.2991
Europe	48.7460	51.1348	49.4691	40.3741
Oceania	50.7415	51.1860	51.3202	44.1269
Soviet Union	46.4432	50.9315	46.8504	30.7762

One impressive constant in the above table is the numerical superiority of males in the under-15 age group and of females in the over-65 age group in every region. Particularly in the over 65-age group, females outnumber males by a substantial margin in every region—in the Soviet Union by over 2 to 1. Note: The ratios are based on the latest available national censuses and not on current U.N. population estimates, because the latter do not include breakdown by sex.

	Percentage of Males in Total Population	Age Group Under 15	Age Group 15-64	Age Group Over 65
World	50.0893	50.9697	50.2425	42.9810

Number of Countries: 153
Midpoint: 49.7824%
Period Covered: 1976 or Latest Available Year
Type of Ranking: Percentage of Males in the Total Population (also known as Masculinity Coefficient); Highest to Lowest

Highlights & Findings: Barring a few countries, such as Ireland, Israel, Canada and Australia (in the last three of which immigrants tend to alter the ratio in favor of males), all developed countries have a female majority. There are six countries where the percentage of males is over 54% as a result of abnormal immigration or special circumstances (as in the Vatican).

Region	Africa	Asia & Oceania	Europe	Western Hemisphere
Most	Equatorial Guinea (8)	Christmas Island (1)	Vatican City (3)	Falkland Islands (5)
Least	Gabon (147)	Tokelau (150)	Monaco (153)	Montserrat (148)

Rank	Country	Percentage of Males in Population
	TOP 10	
1	Christmas Island	64.3626
2	United Arab Emirates	61.8592
3	Vatican City	61.5730
4	Nauru	61.1358
5	Falkland Islands	55.2376
6	Kuwait	54.6590
7	Bahrain	53.8296
8	Equatorial Guinea	53.7800
9	Brunei	53.4082
10	British Virgin Islands	53.1806
	UPPER MIDDLE	
11	Libya	53.1779
12	Maldives	53.0711
13	New Hebrides	53.0440
14	Pakistan	52.9657
15	Solomon Islands	52.9068
16	Greenland	52.4725
17	Faroe Islands	52.1884
18	Angola	52.1411
19	New Caledonia	52.0141
20	Papua New Guinea	51.9648
21	Bangladesh	51.8637
22	India	51.8187
23	Pacific Islands	51.6759
24	Macao	51.3614
25	Albania	51.3611
26	Sri Lanka	51.3403
27	Syria	51.2810
28	Cook Islands	51.2753
29	Singapore	51.1990

Rank	Country	Percentage of Males in Population
30	Cuba	51.1265
31	Tonga	51.0706
32	Egypt	51.0116
33	Iraq	50.9792
34	Fiji	50.9194
35	Jordan	50.8488
36	Tunisia	50.8376
37	Lebanon	50.7925
38	Turkey	50.7919
39	Sao Tome & Principe	50.7756
40	Gambia	50.7368
41	Panama	50.6769
42	Hong Kong	50.6715
43	Iceland	50.5640
44	Nigeria	50.4972
45	Liberia	50.4938
46	Cocos (Keeling) Islands	50.4854
47	Uganda	50.4610
48	China	50.4161
49	Malaysia	50.3755
50	Rhodesia (Zimbabwe)	50.3448
51	Nepal	50.3393
52	Gibraltar	50.3149
53	Bermuda	50.2862
54	Australia	50.2735
55	Israel	50.2532
56	Niue Island	50.2404
57	Ireland	50.2228
58	Belize	50.2224
59	Guatemala	50.1773
60	Costa Rica	50.1413
61	Peru	50.1139

Rank	Country	Percentage of Males in Population
62	Kenya	50.1007
63	Mauritius	50.0581
64	Canada	50.0519
65	Surinam	50.0126
66	Bulgaria	50.0028
67	Cambodia	49.9747
68	Ecuador	49.9625
69	Seychelles	49.9133
70	Bahamas	49.9069
71	Mexico	49.9025
72	Venezuela	49.8969
73	Dominican Republic	49.8948
74	Mongolia	49.8830
75	South Korea	49.8450
76	Thailand	49.7824
	MIDDLE	
77	Guyana	49.7564
78	Sweden	49.7264
79	Liechtenstein	49.7236
80	Norway	49.7181
81	Burma	49.7016
82	Argentina	49.6577
83	Denmark	49.6477
84	El Salvador	49.6023
85	Paraguay	49.5815
86	Brazil	49.5493
87	Honduras	49.5378
88	Trinidad & Tobago	49.5213
89	South Yemen	49.4893
90	Cyprus	49.4740
91	St. Pierre & Miquelon	49.4349

Rank	Country	Percentage of Males in Population		Rank	Country	Percentage of Males in Population		Rank	Country	Percentage of Males in Population
92	San Marino	49.3305		114	Spain	48.8131		136	West Germany	47.5951
93	Indonesia	49.3093		115	Greece	48.8109		137	Guinea	47.5950
94	Congo	49.3076		116	Tanzania	48.7749		138	Cayman Islands	47.5430
95	South Africa	49.3068		117	Colombia	48.7727		139	Turks & Caicos Islands	47.4585
96	Switzerland	49.2732		118	Czechoslovakia	48.7188		140	Antigua	47.3925
97	Japan	49.2391		119	Guinea-Bissau	48.6806		141	Malawi	47.3628
98	Algeria	49.2074		120	United States	48.6688		142	St. Lucia	47.3402
99	Rwanda	49.1909		121	Italy	48.6470		143	St. Vincent	47.3340
100	Madagascar	49.1774		122	Poland	48.5677				
101	Comoros	49.1535		123	United Kingdom	48.5497			*BOTTOM 10*	
102	Yugoslavia	49.1024		124	Niger	48.5402		144	Portugal	47.3130
103	Nicaragua	49.0717		125	Hungary	48.4751		145	Grenada	47.1957
104	Puerto Rico	49.0388		126	Benin	48.4595		146	Barbados	47.1323
105	Luxembourg	49.0082		127	Zaire	48.4176		147	Gabon	47.1170
106	Gilbert Islands	49.0011		128	Cape Verde	48.3488		148	Montserrat	47.0336
107	Zambia	48.9774		129	Finland	48.2780		149	Austria	46.9625
108	Norfolk Island	48.9601		130	Haiti	48.2644		150	Tokelau	46.0913
109	Rumania	48.9504		131	Togo	48.0322		151	Soviet Union	46.0860
110	Belgium	48.9264		132	St. Helena	48.0300		152	East Germany	46.0810
111	Chile	48.8871		133	Jamaica	47.9282		153	Monaco	45.2528
112	Wallis & Futuna Islands	48.8532		134	Malta	47.6930				
113	Netherlands Antilles	48.8319		135	Dominica	47.6238				

Source: *U.N. Demographic Yearbook.*

25. Senior Citizens (65 and over) in the Population

Every solution, it has been said, has a problem. Developed countries that congratulate themselves on reducing birth and death rates are soon confronted with a problem of a different, if equally serious, dimension: the growing proportion of senior citizens in the population. The economic costs of this phenomenon are enormous, especially in countries with social security, medicare and other support systems. Eventually, fewer and fewer people who are economically productive are supporting more and more retirees. In addition, there are social and psychological costs of aging that are paid by the elderly alone, such as victimization, loneliness, dependence, etc.

Number of Countries: 117
Midpoint: 4%
Period Covered: 1975
Type of Ranking: Percentage of Senior Citizens (65 and over) in the Population; Highest to Lowest

Highlights & Findings: The proportion of senior citizens varies inversely with the birthrate. Accordingly, the lowest percentage is noted in South Asia (3.0%) and the highest in industrialized countries (11.8%). In between, it is 3.4% in East Asia, 3.6% in Africa, 4% in the Middle East and the Western Hemisphere and 8.8% in Southern Europe.

Regions	Africa	Asia & Oceania	Europe	Western Hemisphere
Most	Gambia (9)	New Zealand (24)	Austria (1)	United States (16)
Least	Somalia (117)	Papua New Guinea (116)	Yugoslavia (30)	Venezuela (109)

Rank	Country	Percentage of Senior Citizens in the Population		Rank	Country	Percentage of Senior Citizens in the Population		Rank	Country	Percentage of Senior Citizens in the Population
	TOP 10			4	Belgium	13.3		8	Luxembourg	12.7
1	Austria	14.2		5	United Kingdom	13.3		9	Gambia	12.0
2	Sweden	13.7		6	West Germany	13.2		10	Denmark	11.9
3	France	13.4		7	Norway	12.9				

Rank	Country	Percentage of Senior Citizens in the Population	Rank	Country	Percentage of Senior Citizens in the Population	Rank	Country	Percentage of Senior Citizens in the Population
	UPPER MIDDLE		48	Botswana	4.0	84	India	3.0
11	Switzerland	11.4	49	Chad	4.0	85	Iran	3.0
12	Greece	11.1	50	Costa Rica	4.0	86	Ivory Coast	3.0
13	Italy	10.8	51	Egypt	4.0	87	Jordan	3.0
14	Ireland	10.3	52	Ethiopia	4.0	88	Liberia	3.0
15	Netherlands	10.1	53	Ghana	4.0	89	Madagascar	3.0
16	United States	9.9	54	Iraq	4.0	90	Mauritania	3.0
17	Iceland	9.7	55	Kenya	4.0	91	Nepal	3.0
18	Portugal	9.7	56	South Korea	4.0	92	Nicaragua	3.0
19	Finland	9.0	57	Malawi	4.0	93	Niger	3.0
20	Malta	9.0	58	Malaysia	4.0	94	Oman	3.0
21	Rumania	9.0	59	Mauritius	4.0	95	Pakistan	3.0
22	Spain	9.0	60	Mexico	4.0	96	Paraguay	3.0
23	Uruguay	9.0	61	Panama	4.0	97	Peru	3.0
24	New Zealand	8.5	62	Philippines	4.0	98	Sierra Leone	3.0
25	Australia	8.4	63	Senegal	4.0	99	Singapore	3.0
26	Argentina	8.0	64	Syria	4.0	100	Sudan	3.0
27	Barbados	8.0	65	Trinidad & Tobago	4.0	101	Swaziland	3.0
28	Canada	8.0	66	Tunisia	4.0	102	Tanzania	3.0
29	Cyprus	8.0				103	Thailand	3.0
30	Yugoslavia	8.0		**LOWER MIDDLE**		104	Togo	3.0
31	Japan	7.1	67	Afghanistan	3.0	105	United Arab Emirates	3.0
32	Israel	6.5	68	Bahamas	3.0	106	Upper Volta	3.0
33	Chile	6.0	69	Bangladesh	3.0	107	Zaire	3.0
34	Lesotho	6.0	70	Benin	3.0	108	Zambia	3.0
35	Sri Lanka	6.0	71	Bolivia	3.0			
36	Soviet Union	5.2	72	Brazil	3.0		**BOTTOM 9**	
37	Algeria	5.0	73	Burma	3.0	109	Venezuela	2.5
38	Congo	5.0	74	Burundi	3.0	110	Abu Dhabi	2.0
39	Gabon	5.0	75	Cameroon	3.0	111	Honduras	2.0
40	Haiti	5.0	76	Taiwan	3.0	112	Indonesia	2.0
41	Jamaica	5.0	77	Colombia	3.0	113	Kuwait	2.0
42	Lebanon	5.0	78	Domincan Republic	3.0	114	Mali	2.0
43	Libya	5.0	79	Ecuador	3.0	115	Nigeria	2.0
44	Morocco	5.0	80	El Salvador	3.0	116	Papua New Guinea	2.0
45	Rwanda	5.0	81	Fiji	3.0	117	Somalia	2.0
46	South Yemen	5.0	82	Guatemala	3.0			
47	Turkey	4.3	83	Guyana	3.0			

Source: United Nations Population Division.

26. Widowed Proportion of Population

Demographers have long treated widowed persons as the least significant segment of the population, although in many countries they outnumber both singles and divorced persons. However, recently there has been a flurry of interest in the emotional and psychological problems of being widowed, and the following ranking underscores the statistical dimensions of those problems. In almost every country widows are more numerous than widowers for the simple reason that women outlive men as the expectation of life rankings prove. The ratio of widows to widowers is as high as 10:1, as in Botswana, but more commonly it is 5:1. The ratio of widowed persons in the population is therefore greater in those countries where the differences in the expectations of life for males and females are more than normal.

Number of Countries: 121
Midpoint: 11.77 per 100 married persons
Period Covered: 1975 or Latest Available Year
Type of Ranking: Widowed Persons per 100 Married Persons; Highest to Lowest

Highlights & Findings: African and European countries share the top ranks, and Asian countries enter the picture only toward the middle. The presence of East and West Germany as well as other European countries in the top 20 is a tragic reminder of the continuing effect of the loss of millions of young men in World War II. No data are available for the Soviet Union, but if they were, the figures undoubtedly would have revealed a similar high percentage of widows in the population. Lesotho's number one ranking is due to its incredibly high rate of domestic violence.

Region	Africa	Asia & Oceania	Europe	Western Hemisphere
Most	Lesotho (1)	Norfolk Island (10)	Monaco (2)	Haiti (3)
Least	Tanzania (Zanzibar) (116)	Nauru (119)	Cyprus (97)	Guadeloupe (121)

Rank	Country	Widowed Persons per 100 Married Persons	Rank	Country	Widowed Persons per 100 Married Persons	Rank	Country	Widowed Persons per 100 Married Persons
	TOP 10		41	Burma	13.18	82	Bahrain	10.01
1	Lesotho	25.06	42	Solomon Islands	13.16	83	Bermuda	9.91
2	Monaco	20.20	43	Denmark	13.08	84	Jordan	9.90
3	Haiti	19.12	44	Greece	12.96	85	Venezuela	9.86
4	Austria	19.73	45	Cook Islands	12.82	86	Thailand	9.80
5	East Germany	18.77	46	Singapore	12.63	87	Kenya	9.74
6	West Germany	17.53	47	Norway	12.57	88	New Caledonia	9.73
7	Botswana	17.30	48	South Africa	12.49	89	Canada	9.65
8	Ireland	16.27	49	Chile	12.39	90	Syria	9.60
9	St. Helena	16.24	50	Rumania	12.39	91	Pitcairn Island	9.52
10	Norfolk Island	16.17	51	Puerto Rico	12.38	92	Uganda	9.42
			52	Yugoslavia	12.32	93	Pacific Islands	9.39
	UPPER MIDDLE		53	Argentina	12.31	94	Iran	9.35
11	Panama	15.98	54	Morocco	12.24	95	Tonga	9.33
12	Luxembourg	15.72	55	Pakistan	12.16	96	Madagascar	9.12
13	France	15.33	56	United States	12.16	97	Cyprus	9.07
14	Seychelles	15.31	57	Portugal	12.11	98	Rhodesia (Zimbabwe)	8.91
15	Niue Island	15.14	58	Colombia	12.07	99	Mexico	8.73
16	Martinque	15.05	59	Japan	11.87	100	Turkey	8.53
17	Mauritius	14.98	60	Tokelau	11.78	101	Hong Kong	8.48
18	South Korea	14.95	61	Antigua	11.77	102	Netherlands Antilles	8.43
19	Czechoslovakia	14.80	62	Switzerland	11.68	103	Philippines	8.39
20	Scotland	14.80	63	United Arab Emirates	11.52	104	Nepal	8.38
21	Hungary	14.78				105	Samoa	8.36
22	Tunisia	14.66		*LOWER MIDDLE*		106	Paraguay	8.35
23	Indonesia	14.63	64	Bahamas	11.40	107	Tanzania (Zanzibar)	8.25
24	Belgium	14.62	65	New Hebrides	11.32	108	Liberia	8.22
25	Algeria	14.44	66	Australia	11.05	109	Tanzania (Tanganyika)	8.22
26	Gilbert Islands	14.37	67	Liechtenstein	10.92	110	Fiji	8.12
27	French Guyana	14.21	68	Israel	10.83	111	Ethiopia	7.86
28	Northern Ireland	14.20	69	Cuba	10.82			
29	Finland	14.18	70	Faroe Islands	10.74		*BOTTOM 10*	
30	England & Wales	13.94	71	Belize	10.72	112	Costa Rica	7.76
31	Italy	13.91	72	Togo	10.68	113	British Virgin Islands	7.46
32	Sweden	13.91	73	Rwanda	10.65	114	Cocos (Keeling) Islands	7.26
33	El Salvador	13.79	74	New Zealand	10.64	115	Kuwait	6.73
34	Peru	13.66	75	San Marino	10.61	116	Zambia	6.25
35	Spain	13.49	76	Ecuador	10.58	117	Christmas Island	5.08
36	Poland	13.45	77	Dominican Republic	10.47	118	Malaysia	4.67
37	Malta	13.41	78	Brazil	10.43	119	Nauru	4.44
38	Macao	13.42	79	Netherlands	10.36	120	St. Pierre & Miquelon	1.84
39	India	13.30	80	Iceland	10.25	121	Guadeloupe	1.49
40	Reunion	13.22	81	Greenland	10.19			

Source: *U.N. Demographic Yearbook.*

27. Average Household Size

The concept of household is based on the arrangements made by persons, either individually or in groups, for providing themselves with food or other essentials of living. When it consists of more than one person, members of a household may pool their incomes and have a common budget and may occupy a whole, a part of or more than one housing unit. The members of a household may be related or unrelated or may consist of extended families with a common head. Couples living in consensual unions are also regarded as households. Although the United Nations defines a household on the basis of common

housekeeping arrangements, some countries simply define a household as the entire group of persons, jointly occupying a housing unit or as a person living alone in a separate unit. Such differing definitions of households limit the international comparability of data. Aside from the definition of a household, national practices in collecting and compiling statistics of households also differ according to certain differences in enumeration practices. In some countries persons are counted only where physically present, but in others physical presence is not required for enumeration.

Number of Countries: 96
Midpoint: 4.5
Period Covered: 1975
Type of Ranking: Average Size of Household; Highest to Lowest

Highlights & Findings: The size of household is directly related to population policies. It is therefore highest in those countries where a large family is regarded as a social blessing or where population growth is actively encouraged.

Regions	Africa	Asia & Oceania	Europe	Western Hemisphere
Most	Gambia (1)	Tonga (2)	Cyprus (64)	Colombia (10)
Least	Mali (40)	Norfolk Island (82)	Sweden (96)	United States (87)

Rank	Country	Average Size of Household	Rank	Country	Average Size of Household	Rank	Country	Average Size of Household
	TOP 9		33	Tunisia	5.1	66	Argentina	3.8
			34	Iran	5.0	67	Israel	3.8
1	Gambia	8.3	35	Macao	5.0	68	Liechtenstein	3.8
2	Tonga	6.9	36	New Hebrides	5.0	69	Spain	3.8
3	Nauru	6.6	37	Mexico	4.9	70	Yugoslavia	3.8
4	Bahrain	6.4	38	Panama	4.9	71	Christmas Island	3.7
5	Cocos (Keeling) Islands	6.3	39	Reunion	4.9	72	New Zealand	3.7
6	Fiji	6.3	40	Mali	4.8	73	Soviet Union	3.7
7	Kuwait	6.2	41	Peru	4.8	74	Canada	3.5
8	Niue Island	6.2	42	Trinidad & Tobago	4.8	75	Montserrat	3.5
9	Gilbert Islands	6.0	43	Seychelles	4.7	76	Bermuda	3.4
			44	Zambia	4.6	77	French Guiana	3.4
	UPPER MIDDLE		45	Cuba	4.5	78	Japan	3.4
			46	Greenland	4.5	79	Poland	3.4
10	Colombia	5.9	47	Hong Kong	4.5	80	Australia	3.3
11	Philippines	5.9	48	St. Helena	4.5	81	Italy	3.3
12	Samoa	5.9				82	Norfolk Island	3.3
13	Syria	5.9		*LOWER MIDDLE*		83	Rumania	3.2
14	Brunei	5.8				84	Czechoslovakia	3.1
15	Thailand	5.8	49	Guadeloupe	4.4	85	France	3.1
16	Pakistan	5.7	50	Martinique	4.4	86	Luxembourg	3.1
17	Costa Rica	5.6	51	Mongolia	4.4	87	United States	3.1
18	India	5.6	52	Tanzania	4.4			
19	Kenya	5.6	53	Antigua	4.3		*BOTTOM 9*	
20	Nepal	5.5	54	Jamaica	4.3			
21	Guyana	5.4	55	Turks & Caicos	4.3	88	Finland	3.0
22	Morocco	5.4	56	Rhodesia (Zimbabwe)	4.2	89	Hungary	3.0
23	Dominican Republic	5.3	57	Bahamas	4.1	90	Austria	2.9
24	Mauritius	5.3	58	Cayman Islands	4.1	91	Belgium	2.9
25	Singapore	5.3	59	St. Pierre & Miquelon	4.1	92	Switzerland	2.9
26	Belize	5.2	60	Barbados	4.0	93	United Kingdom	2.9
27	El Salvador	5.2	61	Malta	4.0	94	West Germany	2.7
28	South Korea	5.2	62	St. Kitts-Nevis-Anguilla	4.0	95	East Germany	2.6
29	Brazil	5.1	63	St. Vincent	4.0	96	Sweden	2.6
30	Chile	5.1	64	Cyprus	3.9			
31	Netherlands Antilles	5.1	65	Ireland	3.9			
32	Solomon Islands	5.1						

Source: *UN Demographic Yearbook.*

28. Illegitimate Births

Illegitimacy is almost as old as the human family. Despite the many contributions that bastards have made to civilization (Leonardo da Vinci and Willy Brandt are two of the more familiar names), social stigma, religious anathema and legal sanctions have combined to give illegitimacy a sinister reputation. Under English common law an illegitimate child is an outlaw with no legal rights to his or her father's property except by specific designation, as in a will. Recently the condition of illegitimate offsprings has been somewhat improved. In about half the states of the United States, the union of the parents in marriage after the birth of a child makes that child legitimate. The figures are, of course, significantly distorted by the informality of marriage rituals and legal registration in many countries.

Number of Countries: 102
Midpoint: 15.4%
Period Covered: Early 1970s
Type of Ranking: Illegitimate Births as a Percentage of Total Births; Highest to Lowest

Highlights & Findings: It is surprising that despite the growing promiscuity and permissiveness in Western societies, they place relatively low in the ranking. The pill and abortion may be responsible for keeping these rates low. In 18 countries the majority of the births are illegitimate. Most of these countries are in Latin America, and the others are in Africa. The rates are lowest in Asia; Hong Kong is the highest in this region ranking 71st.

Region	Africa	Asia & Oceania	Europe	Western Hemisphere
Most	Guinea-Bissau (1)	French Polynesia (15)	Iceland (33)	St. Kitts-Nevis-Anguilla (2)
Least	Tunisia (102)	Macao (98)	Cyprus (101)	Bolivia (47)

Illegitimate Births as Percentage of Total Births

Rank	Country	
	TOP 10	
1	Guinea-Bissau	88.7
2	St. Kitts-Nevis-Anguilla	82.8
3	Sao Tome & Principe	82.4
4	Antigua	77.3
5	Montserrat	76.6
6	Barbados	73.3
7	Grenada	72.8
8	Panama	71.6
9	El Salvador	69.7
10	Domincan Republic	66.6
	UPPER MIDDLE	
11	Guatemala	65.2
12	Dominica	65.0
13	French Guyana	63.1
14	Cape Verde	56.6
15	French Polynesia	54.9
16	Venezuela	53.0
17	Seychelles	51.8
18	Martinique	50.9
19	British Virgin Islands	49.8
20	Greenland	48.1
21	Peru	46.8
22	Belize	44.6
23	Paraguay	43.0
24	Guadeloupe	42.9
25	Bahamas	42.3
26	Trinidad & Tobago	41.5
27	Guyana	38.6
28	St. Helena	38.1
29	South Africa (Blacks Only)	35.4
30	Costa Rica	34.7
31	Mozambique	34.3
32	Uruguay	34.2
33	Iceland	34.0
34	Cayman Islands	33.2

Rank	Country	
35	Ecuador	32.1
36	Sweden	31.4
37	Bermuda	28.9
38	Netherlands Antilles	26.6
39	Argentina	26.4
40	Colombia	24.8
41	Reunion	24.0
42	Faroe Islands	23.8
43	Wallis & Futuna Islands	21.7
44	Mexico	21.4
45	Chile	19.9
46	Puerto Rico	19.2
47	Bolivia	19.1
48	Denmark	17.1
49	East Germany	16.3
50	New Zealand	15.8
51	St. Pierre & Miquelon	15.4
	LOWER MIDDLE	
52	Austria	13.8
53	Guam	13.0
54	American Samoa	12.8
55	United States	12.4
56	Canada	12.1
57	Falkland Islands	10.3
58	Australia	9.8
59	Bulgaria	9.6
60	Norway	9.3
61	Scotland	9.1
62	England & Wales	8.6
63	Channel Islands	8.5
64	Isle of Man	8.2
65	Jersey	8.1
66	Finland	7.9
67	South Africa (Asiatics only)	7.9
68	France	7.8
69	Yugoslavia	7.7

Rank	Country	
70	Portugal	7.3
71	Hong Kong	6.9
72	West Germany	6.3
73	Hungary	5.7
74	Cocos (Keeling) Islands	5.6
75	Czechoslovakia	5.2
76	Norfolk Island	4.8
77	Northern Ireland	4.8
78	Poland	4.8
79	Luxembourg	4.4
80	Philippines	3.7
81	Switzerland	3.7
82	Djibouti	3.2
83	Liechtenstein	3.2
84	Monaco	3.2
85	Belgium	3.0
86	Christmas Island	2.9
87	Ireland	2.9
88	South Africa (Whites Only)	2.9
89	Gibraltar	2.8
90	Mauritius	2.8
91	Italy	2.5
92	Netherlands	2.0
	BOTTOM 10	
93	Spain	1.5
94	Greece	1.2
95	Malta	1.2
96	Rhodesia (Zimbabwe) (Whites Only)	1.2
97	Japan	0.8
98	Macao	0.7
99	San Marino	0.7
100	Israel	0.6
101	Cyprus	0.5
102	Tunisia	0.4

Source: *UN Demographic Yearbook.*

29. Legally Induced Abortions

Abortion is defined in most countries of the world as an interruption of pregnancy before 28 weeks of gestation with a dead fetus. Abortions are either spontaneous or induced, and the latter are subject to government regulations in almost all countries of the world. These regulations vary from complete prohibition to abortion on request by or under the supervision of authorized medical professionals.

Abortion is currently legal in only 26 countries of the world. The following ranking is restricted to these countries. The data suffer from serious limitations because in almost all countries of the world, including countries where abortion is legal, many abortions are performed illegally or are not reported at all due to fear of social consequences.

Number of Countries: 26
Midpoint: 23,362
Period Covered: 1975 or Latest Available Year
Type of Ranking: Abortions as a Percentage of Live Births; Total Number of Legal and Reported Induced Abortions; Highest to Lowest

Highlights & Findings: Only four Third World countries appear on the list. The only African and Muslim country represented is Tunisia.

Regions	Africa	Asia & Oceania	Europe	Western Hemisphere
Most	Tunisia (17)	Japan (3)	Hungary (1)	United States (13)
Least	N.A.	Singapore (5)	Greece (26)	Panama (25)

Rank	Country	Legal Abortions as a Percentage of Live Births	Total	Rank	Country	Legal Abortions as a Percentage of Live Births	Total	Rank	Country	Legal Abortions as a Percentage of Live Births	Total
	TOP 5			9	Australia	26.0	60,000	20	Ireland	3.0	1,800
1	Hungary	51.89	96,212	10	Norway	25.4	15,171	21	Spain	2.0	15,100
2	Finland	41.1	23,362	11	France	18.0	133,600				
3	Japan	35.9	739,674	12	United Kingdom	15.7	106,224		*BOTTOM 5*		
4	Denmark	34.8	24,868	13	United States	14.7	480,259	22	Venezuela	0.7	3,085
5	Singapore	32.2	12,873	14	Canada	13.9	48,136	23	Yugoslavia	0.6	2,519
				15	Netherlands	9.0	16,000	24	New Zealand	0.5	313
	MIDDLE			16	Iceland	7.0	308	25	Panama	0.02	14
6	Poland	31.6	212,101	17	Tunisia	6.3	12,427	26	Greece	0.04	59
7	Sweden	31.3	32,526	18	Faroe Islands	3.7	30				
8	Czechoslovakia	28.7	83,604	19	West Germany	3.0	17,800				

Source: *U.N. Demographic Yearbook.*

30. Users of Contraceptives

Estimates of contraceptive users come from what are known as KAP (Knowledge, Attitude and Practice) surveys. Because many acceptors are serviced more than once, duplications in count can easily arise and therefore the number of acceptors is often an educated estimate made by program administrators and evaluators. The main family planning methods covered are intrauterine devices, oral contraceptives, sterilization and abortion.

Number of Countries: 23
Midpoint: 17%
Period Covered: 1976
Type of Ranking: Users of Contraceptive Methods as a Percentage of Married Women of Child-Bearing Age (15-44); Total Number of Such Users; Highest to Lowest

Highlights & Findings: Demographers have suggested that unless family planning methods are accepted by at least 40% of the age cohort to which they are directed, they do not have a significant impact. Using this guideline, we find that only four countries included in this ranking have reached that level.

Regions	Africa	Asia	Europe	Western Hemisphere
Most	Mauritius (6)	Singapore (1)	N.A.	Costa Rica (8)
Least	Ghana (23)	Bangladesh (22)	N.A.	Ecuador (21)

Rank	Country	Contraceptive Users as a Percentage of Married Women	Total	Rank	Country	Contraceptive Users as a Percentage of Married Women	Total	Rank	Country	Contraceptive Users as a Percentage of Married Women	Total
		TOP 5		8	Costa Rica	33.7	78,800	18	El Salvador	10.4	87,000
1	Singapore	77.1	212,300	9	Thailand	32.0	1,731,000				
2	Hong Kong	61.0	290,000	10	Dominican Republic	24.0	142,200			*BOTTOM 5*	
3	Taiwan	55.0	880,00	11	Philippines	21.7	1,129,000	19	Paraguay	10.0	49,000
4	Malaysia	43.0	662,000	12	Nepal	17.0	375,000	20	Morocco	6.7	177,000
5	Turkey	38.0	2,262,000	13	India	16.9	17,554,000	21	Ecuador	6.3	51,700
				14	Iran	16.5	854,000	22	Bangladesh	4.7	742,000
		MIDDLE		15	Indonesia	14.8	3,037,000	23	Ghana	2.0	33,600
6	Mauritius	36.9	43,500	16	Mexico	14.0	1,716,000				
7	South Korea	34.2	1,670,000	17	Tunisia	13.7	110,300				

Source: Population Council.

31. Family Planning Expenditures

The Population Council reports only 30 countries in the world have official family planning programs and budgetary allotments for family planning either separately or as part of the public health budget. Data on funds for family planning are difficult to compile. De jure allocations may not always be de facto; grants approved in one year are often made available at some later date and actually spent several years later. Further it is often difficult to distinguish between funds strictly earmarked for family planning and those for related services. Foreign governments and private organizations provide a substantial percentage of the funding in developing countries. However, in many countries, including Ghana, Hong Kong, Indonesia, Iran, South Korea, Mauritius, Nepal, the Philippines, Rhodesia, Singapore, Taiwan and Turkey, 50% or more of the program is financed from domestic funds. Per capita expenditures are based on both domestic and foreign, official and private funds expended on family planning programs within a country.

Number of Countries 30
Midpoint: $0.19
Period Covered: 1976
Type of Ranking: Per Capita Expenditures on Family Planning in Dollars; Total expenditures in Dollars; Highest to Lowest

Highlights & Findings: The ranking illustrates the contention of many family planning experts that governments in developing countries are not spending adequately on programs in this field even where they subscribe to the general philosophy of reducing population levels. Only two countries spend over $1.0 per capita and others spend only a fraction of a dollar.

Regions	Africa	Asia	Europe	Western Hemisphere
Most	Mauritius (2)	Iran (4)	N.A.	Puerto Rico (1)
Least	Uganda (29)	Turkey (26)	N.A.	Brazil (30)

Rank	Country	Family Planning Expenditures Per Capita ($)	Total ($)	Rank	Country	Family Planning Expenditures Per Capita ($)	Total ($)	Rank	Country	Family Planning Expenditures Per Capita ($)	Total ($)
		TOP 5		11	Venezuela	0.34	4,000,000	24	Sri Lanka	0.11	1,562,000
1	Puerto Rico	3.55	11,557,000	12	Malaysia	0.28	3,100,000	25	Thailand	0.088	3,686,000
2	Mauritius	1.28	1,115,000	13	Bolivia	0.27	1,590,000				
3	Costa Rica	0.86	1,695,000	14	Colombia	0.23	5,535,000			*BOTTOM 5*	
4	Iran	0.85	28,000,000	15	South Korea	0.19	6,905,000	26	Turkey	0.063	2,473,000
5	Philippines	0.58	25,258,000	16	Taiwan	0.17	2,781,000	27	Egypt	0.045	1,686,000
				17	Bangladesh	0.16	13,062,000	28	Rhodesia (Zimbabwe)	0.040	227,000
		MIDDLE		18	Ghana	0.16	1,488,000	29	Uganda	0.018	226,400
6	Kenya	0.54	7,320,000	19	Indonesia	0.15	21,007,000	30	Brazil*	0.0097	104,500
7	Tunisia	0.45	2,588,000	20	India	0.14	85,699,000				
8	Singapore	0.42	950,000	21	Hong Kong	0.14	623,000	*Government funds only			
9	Dominican Republic	0.39	1,957,000	22	Guatemala	0.12	653,000				
10	Pakistan	0.34	24,000,000	23	Nepal	0.11	1,440,000				

Source: Population Council: *Reports on Population/Family Planning*.

RACE & RELIGION

This chapter deals with race and religion, both of which are not susceptible to statistical analysis or quantification but which, nevertheless, constitute important dimensions of every society.

Historically, ethnic homogeneity has been one of the great strengths of a nation, although its contribution to social cohesiveness has also been greatly exaggerated. Ethnic diversity is more often than not a source of conflict; when coupled with language and religion, it can become a powerful and explosive force in national life. One has only to think of Cyprus, India, South Africa, Belgium, Ireland and Lebanon to perceive the destructiveness of racial, religious and linguistic rivalries as well as the tenacity of ethnic affiliations. The trend, therefore, has been to suppress ethnicity, to make it irrelevant and even to obliterate its manifestations in speech, conduct and dress. Censuses throughout the world now deliberately omit references to ethnic origin. The result, unfortunately, has been not only enforced uniformity and homogeneity but also the assimilation of the small minorities into the dominant majority. The process may be slower but the end result is the same as that which Hitler's Germany and Turkey achieved through their respective "Final Solutions." The dangers inherent in such a policy are best illustrated by the experience of the plant geneticists who during the Green Revolution attempted to eliminate weaker strains of rice and wheat in favor of the high-yielding ones only to discover that such homogenization increased the vulnerability of the chosen strain to diseases and ultimate extinction. In plants as well as races there is safety in variety. Current thinking thus favors ethnic diversity. In countries such as the United States, Canada and Australia the melting pot is being transformed into the mixing pot.

Religion is the subject of the next three rankings. The problems of collecting and interpreting religious statistics are discussed in the introduction to the ranking of Christians. The quality and intensity of religious beliefs vary so greatly from individual to individual that a head count becomes a futile exercise. Nevertheless, if we adopt the usual precautions, the rankings can give some insights into the composition of the religious mosaic. The lead ranking is on Christianity, which is not only the world's largest religion but the one that had the greatest impact on the course of human history. The only other religion whose adherents constitute a majority in at least 10 countries is Islam. The medieval and even draconian character of Muslim ethics and jurisprudence (stoning for adultery, amputation for stealing and prohibition of music) has not prevented it from growing in Asia and Africa, and its propagation has been helped by the grace of both Allah and petrodollars. Judaism is included not so much because of but in spite of the size of its membership; there are few countries in the world that the Jews have not enriched with their contributions and fewer countries where they have escaped persecution and prejudice.

The other religions have been excluded for valid reasons. Hindus form the majority in only two countries (India and Nepal), although they command a plurality in a number of small countries, such as Guyana, Fiji and Mauritius. Hinduism is not essentially different from the animist religions of Africa, which have not been included either because they are too amorphous and indiscrete for statistical purposes. Buddhism is the majority and official religion in Sri Lanka and Thailand and, in a more muted fashion, Burma; its present status in Vietnam, Laos, Cambodia, China and North Korea is uncertain. In China, Korea and Japan Buddhism is mixed with Confucianism and Taoism; in fact, in these countries a man may belong to all of these religions at the same time. In addition to these organized religions, the world is full of cults ranging from Scientology to Jim Jones-type suicide squads, but statistics on these cults are as unreliable as their doctrines.

32. Homogeneity Index

Political stability is often associated with linguistic and ethnic homogeneity. While developed societies in the West are moving toward pluralism and multiculturalism, traditional societies in Asia and Africa are moving toward monocultures. Many governments are striving to create nations from heterogeneous populations and finding the task difficult. Because the primary loyalty of an individual in traditional societies is to his race, language and religion, ethnicity becomes the basis for factional and separatist tendencies. More civil wars have been fought in Asia and Africa in modern times on the issue of race, language or religion than on that of political ideology. Unfortunately, in the process of achieving ethnic cohesiveness minorities are brutally suppressed and even—as in Turkey in the after-math of World War I—exterminated or driven into exile.

The Ethnic and Linguistic Homogeneity Index was devised by the Department of Geodesy and Cartography of the State Geological Committee of the USSR Academy of Sciences in Moscow and published in *Atlas Narodov Mira*. The index which originally measured lack of homogeneity has been slightly modified for use in this section.

Number of Countries: 135
Midpoint: 67%
Period Covered: 1960-65
Type of Ranking: Percentage of Homogeneity; Most Homogeneous to Least Homogeneous

Highlights & Findings: Ethnic diversity is most marked in Africa where political borders, drawn artificially by Western colonial powers, often cut across ethnic boundaries. It has been estimated that if Africa were to be redivided on the basis of significant ethnic cleavages, there would be more than 300 nations on the continent. Outside of Africa, India has the most complex ethnic configuration, but common adherence to Hinduism by the vast majority of Indians is a moderating influence. As a result of the influx of immigrants from alien societies, Western countries are likely to move down the scale in the future as they face the challenges of ethnic, linguistic and religious fractionalization.

Regions	Africa	Asia & Oceania	Europe	Western Hemisphere
Most	Burundi (14)	North & South Korea (1 & 2)	Portugal (4)	Puerto Rico (7)
Least	Tanzania (135)	India (131)	Yugoslavia (118)	Bolivia (102)

Rank	Country	Percentage of Homogeneity	Rank	Country	Percentage of Homogeneity	Rank	Country	Percentage of Homogeneity
	TOP 9		37	China	88	74	Singapore	58
1	North Korea	100	38	Austria	87	75	Taiwan	58
2	South Korea	100	39	Lebanon	87	76	Algeria	57
3	South Yemen	99	40	Chile	86	77	Spain	56
4	Portugal	99	41	Paraguay	86	78	Burma	53
5	Japan	99	42	Rwanda	86	79	Sri Lanka	53
6	Haiti	99	43	Luxembourg	85	80	Czechoslovakia	51
7	Puerto Rico	98	44	Finland	84	81	Switzerland	50
8	Hong Kong	98	45	Honduras	84	82	United States	50
9	East Germany	98	46	Tunisia	84	83	Botswana	49
			47	El Salvador	83	84	Ecuador	47
	UPPER MIDDLE		48	Nicaragua	82	85	Morocco	47
10	West Germany	97	49	Kuwait	82	86	Rhodesia	46
11	Poland	97	50	Maldives	82	87	Belgium	45
12	Yemen Arab Republic	96	51	Vietnam	81	88	Trinidad & Tobago	44
13	Egypt	96	52	Israel	80	89	Guyana	42
14	Burundi	96	53	Uruguay	80	90	Mauritius	42
15	Cuba	96	54	Barbados	78	91	Peru	41
16	Dominican Republic	96	55	Bulgaria	78	92	Laos	40
17	Ireland	96	56	Lesotho	78	93	Benin	38
18	Italy	96	57	Syria	78	94	Malawi	38
19	Norway	96	58	Libya	77	95	Guatemala	36
20	Denmark	95	59	Rumania	75	96	Pakistan	36
21	Iceland	95	60	Turkey	75	97	Mozambique	35
22	Jamaica	95	61	France	74	98	Afghanistan	34
23	Jordan	95	62	Panama	72	99	Congo	34
24	Colombia	94	63	Cambodia	70	100	Thailand	34
25	Madagascar	94	64	Mexico	70	101	Soviet Union	33
26	Saudi Arabia	94	65	Argentina	69	102	Bolivia	32
27	Brazil	93	66	United Kingdom	68	103	Upper Volta	32
28	Costa Rica	93	67	Australia	68	104	Central African Empire	31
29	Malta	92				105	Ethiopia	31
30	Somalia	92		*LOWER MIDDLE*		106	Gabon	31
31	Sweden	92	68	Mauritania	67	107	Nepal	30
32	Albania	91	69	Cyprus	65	108	Ghana	29
33	Greece	90	70	Iraq	64	109	Togo	29
34	Hungary	90	71	New Zealand	63	110	Malaysia	28
35	Netherlands	90	72	Mongolia	62	111	Senegal	28
36	Venezuela	89	73	Papua New Guinea	58	112	Niger	27

Rank	Country	Percentage of Homogeneity	Rank	Country	Percentage of Homogeneity	Rank	Country	Percentage of Homogeneity
113	Sudan	27	122	Angola	22	128	Ivory Coast	14
114	Gambia	27	123	Mali	22	129	Nigeria	13
115	Philippines	26	124	Zambia	18	130	South Africa	12
116	Canada	25				131	India	11
117	Guinea	25				132	Cameroon	11
118	Yugoslavia	25		*BOTTOM 11*		133	Zaire	10
119	Indonesia	24	125	Liberia	17	134	Uganda	10
120	Iran	24	126	Chad	17	135	Tanzania	7
121	Sierra Leone	23	127	Kenya	17			

Source: *Atlas Narodov Mira.*

33. Christians

Christianity is perhaps the only true world religion in the sense of having adherents and churches in virtually every country in the world. Out of 188 countries there are only six countries—Afghanistan, Saudi Arabia, Maldives, Yemen Arab Republic, Mongolia and Nepal—where there are no native or permanent resident Christians. Taking the larger countries only, Christians form the majority of the population in 63 countries.

Religious statistics are available only for 2.5 billion of the earth's total population of 4 billion. Of this 2.5 billion, close to 1 billion are Christians, although Protestants and Catholics employ different methods for counting members. The Roman Catholic Church claims a membership of 542 million, which makes it the largest single religious organization in the world. Nearly 36% of the world's Christian population lives in Europe, 23% in North America, 16% in South America, 9% in Asia and 10% in Africa.

Number of Countries: 129
Midpoint: 48%
Period Covered: Mid-1970s
Type of Ranking: Percentage of Christians in National Populations; Most to Least

Highlights & Findings: In absolute terms the United States has the largest Christian population in the world, with 127 million reported in the *Yearbook of American and Canadian Churches, 1977,* or approximately 12% of the world total. There are six countries, led by Brazil, where the entire native population is officially classifed as Christian. Religious statistics tend to be relatively stable except in Africa, where dramatic increases are reported in the membership of Christian churches; usually at the expense of traditional religions.

Religious statistics present serious problems affecting their reliability in the conventional sense. Very few governments include religious affiliations in their census questionnaires, and often the only sources of information in this field are the religious organizations themselves; their figures, more often than not, tend to be self-serving. Again, there are problems of definition of membership varying from denomination to denomination. Many Christian churches, including the Anglican Church, accept the fact of baptism as indicating lifelong membership and do not acknowledge the constant erosion of membership through backsliding and even apostasy. Other Christian denominations, such as the Evangelical churches, go to the other extreme and count as members only those who meet their strict standards of faith and conduct. A headcount is therefore nothing more than an educated guess when used as a tool for estimating religious membership and may be accepted only because of the lack of a better method.

A problem of a different kind is hidden church membership in Communist countries where people may not openly avow their membership because of fear of official persecution. The governments in these countries may also depress actual membership figures for propaganda purposes. It is the author's belief that church membership in the Soviet Union, for example, has been seriously underestimated even in the West and may run as high as 30% and the percentage of core believers as high as 10%, both of which are higher figures than those of many Western countries. As has been demonstrated in Poland, the fact that a country is officially Communist does not eliminate religion as a force in its national life, although this is what the Soviet government would like us to believe.

Some of these difficulties are clearly illustrated in the following ranking, which is taken from the *World Christian Handbook.* A 100% Christian population in a large country such as Brazil where there are known minorities following Judaism, Shintoism and African cults and Spiritualists who follow Allen Kardec, strains credulity and so does a 100% membership in Communist Rumania.

These figures have been allowed to stand as they are since I cannot doctor figures borrowed from recognized sources, but readers should bear in mind that they do not correspond to reality in a mathematical sense and should be treated as only approximations with a very wide margin of error.

Regions	Africa	Asia & Oceania	Europe	Western Hemisphere
Most	Lesotho (51)	Philippines (44)	Ireland (3)	Brazil (1)
Least	Somalia (129)	Iran (127)	Soviet Union (80)	Jamaica (64)

Rank	Country	Orthodox or Protestant (%)	Roman Catholic (%)	Total Christian (%)
		TOP 10		
1	Brazil	10	90	100
2	El Salvador	3	97	100
3	Ireland	5	95	100
4	Rumania	87	13	100
5	Norway	100	0	100
6	Spain	0	100	100
7	Sweden	100	0	100
8	Barbados	99	0	99
9	Bolivia	2	97	99
10	Malta	0	99	99
		UPPER MIDDLE		
11	Dominican Republic	2	96	98
12	Finland	98	0	98
13	Guatemala	3	95	98
14	Austria	8	89	97
15	Denmark	97	1	98
16	Puerto Rico	8	89	97
17	West Germany	52	45	97
18	Luxembourg	2	94	96
19	Argentina	2	93	95
20	Belgium	2	93	95
21	Iceland	94	1	95
22	Panama	5	90	95
23	Paraguay	1	94	95
24	Portugal	1	94	95
25	Greece	93	1	94
26	Peru	1	93	94
27	East Germany	82	11	93
28	Poland	3	90	93
29	Italy	0	91	91
30	Chile	10	80	90
31	United States	52	38	90
32	Venezuela	1	89	90
33	Yugoslavia	59	31	90
34	Ecuador	1	88	89
35	Nicaragua	3	85	88
36	Colombia	1	86	87
37	Mexico	2	85	87
38	Switzerland	44	43	87
39	Australia	63	23	86
40	Bulgaria	86	0	86
41	Hungary	27	59	86
42	Cuba	4	81	85
43	France	2	82	84

Rank	Country	Orthodox or Protestant (%)	Roman Catholic (%)	Total Christian (%)
44	Philippines	10	74	84
45	Uruguay	1	83	84
46	Canada	40	41	81
47	New Zealand	66	15	81
48	Haiti	12	67	79
49	Netherlands	38	40	78
50	Cyprus	75	1	76
51	Lesotho	35	40	75
52	Trinidad & Tobago	39	36	75
53	Costa Rica	4	67	71
54	Honduras	3	68	71
55	United Kingdom	62	9	71
56	Gabon	19	51	70
57	Czechoslovakia	16	50	66
58	Congo	20	42	62
59	South Africa	56	6	62
60	Zaire	20	39	59
61	Burundi	8	50	58
62	Guyana	42	15	57
63	Uganda	21	33	54
64	Jamaica	43	8	51
65	Papua New Guinea	27	21	48
		LOWER MIDDLE		
66	Lebanon	17	28	45
67	Angola	7	36	43
68	Madagascar	21	20	41
69	Mauritius	2	35	37
70	Ethiopia	35	0	35
71	Rhodesia (Zimbabwe)	27	8	35
72	Rwanda	6	29	35
73	Cameroon	15	19	34
74	Malawi	18	16	34
75	Albania	29	4	33
76	Kenya	15	12	27
77	Tanzania	10	17	27
78	Central African Empire	11	14	25
79	Togo	6	19	25
80	Soviet Union	23	1	24
81	Zambia	9	15	24
82	Botswana	20	2	22
83	Ghana	10	12	22
84	Ivory Coast	7	10	17
85	Liberia	14	2	16
86	Benin	1	14	15

Rank	Country	Orthodox or Protestant (%)	Roman Catholic (%)	Total Christian (%)
87	Mozambique	3	12	15
88	Egypt	14	1	15
89	Hong Kong	5	6	11
90	Vietnam	1	10	11
91	Nigeria	5	5	10
92	Syria	5	5	10
93	South Korea	7	2	9
94	Singapore	2	6	8
95	Sri Lanka	1	6	7
96	Chad	3	3	6
97	Indonesia	4	2	6
98	North Korea	4	2	6
99	Taiwan	4	2	6
100	Jordan	4	1	5
101	Malaysia	2	3	5
102	Senegal	0	5	5
103	Sierra Leone	3	2	5
104	South Yemen	1	4	5
105	Upper Volta	1	4	5
106	Algeria	0	4	4
107	Burma	3	1	5
108	Iraq	2	2	4
109	Israel	1	3	4
110	Sudan	2	2	4
111	Gambia	2	2	4
112	India	2	1	3
113	Morocco	0	3	3
114	Kuwait	1	1	2
115	Libya	0	2	2
		BOTTOM 14		
116	Cambodia	0	1	1
117	China	0.5	0.5	1
118	Guinea	0	1	1
119	Japan	1	0	1
120	Laos	0	1	1
121	Mali	0	1	1
122	Mauritania	0	1	1
123	Pakistan	1	0	1
124	Thailand	0.5	0.5	1
125	Tunisia	0	1	1
126	Turkey	1	0	1
127	Iran	1	0	1
128	Niger	0	1	1
129	Somalia	0	1	1

Source: *World Christian Handbook.*

34. Muslims

Islam is the second largest religion in the world both in the number of adherents and in the number of countries where it is professed by the majority of the population. The total number of Muslims in the world is estimated at close to 550 million, or 19% of all religious membership. Of this membership, 71% is in Asia and 24% in Africa. Islam is an expansionary religion and backed by petrodollars, it has been making gains in Africa, a continent that had been ravaged by Arab slave raiders until the 20th century. (Islam is one of the few religions that expressly sanction slavery.) Islam's appeal is enhanced by a number of factors, particularly its approval of polygamy (Muhammad himself had 13 concubines), its easy divorce laws and its simple theology, almost entirely borrowed from Judaism.

Number of Countries: 67
Midpoint: 40%
Period Covered: Early 1970s
Type of Ranking: Percentage of Muslims in the Population: Highest to Lowest

Highlights & Findings: There are three countries where the population is entirely Muslim. Of these, Saudi Arabia prohibits the exercise of any religion other than Islam. There are 26 countries where Muslims form a majority of the population (excluding Albania, which describes itself as the world's first atheist state). Muslims may also form a majority in Lebanon, although the legal fiction of a Christian majority is maintained by the government. The influx of Muslim immigrants into European countries, such as the United Kingdom, France and West Germany, may have altered the percentage of Muslims in the population of these countries.

Regions	Africa	Asia & Oceania	Europe	Western Hemisphere
Most	Somalia (4)	Maldives (1)	Albania (27)	Guyana (49)
Least	South Africa (67)	Australia (62)	France (65)	N.A.

Rank	Country	Percentage of Muslims in National Population
	TOP 10	
1	Maldives	100
2	Saudi Arabia	100
3	Yemen Arab Republic	100
4	Somalia	96
5	Iraq	95
6	Kuwait	95
7	South Yemen	95
8	Afghanistan	92
9	Libya	92
10	Turkey	90
	UPPER MIDDLE	
11	Mauritania	87
12	Pakistan	87
13	Algeria	85
14	Indonesia	85
15	Egypt	85
16	Iran	84
17	Morocco	81
18	Jordan	79
19	Tunisia	78
20	Niger	75
21	Senegal	75
22	Syria	68
23	Guinea	65

Rank	Country	Percentage of Muslims in National Population
24	Mali	62
25	Chad	58
26	Sudan	58
27	Albania	52
28	Gambia	46
29	Nigeria	45
30	Malaysia	44
31	Lebanon	42
32	Ethiopia	40
	LOWER MIDDLE	
33	Liberia	25
34	Tanzania	25
35	Upper Volta	25
36	Ivory Coast	23
37	Sierra Leone	23
38	Cameroon	18
39	Cyprus	18
40	Benin	17
41	Mozambique	12
42	Bulgaria	11
43	Singapore	11
44	Soviet Union	11
45	Ghana	10

Rank	Country	Percentage of Muslims in National Population
46	India	10
47	Kenya	10
48	Yugoslavia	10
49	Guyana	9
50	Malawi	8
51	Israel	7
52	Sri Lanka	5
53	Madagascar	5
54	Togo	5
55	Uganda	5
56	Central African Empire	4
57	Thailand	4
	BOTTOM 10	
58	Burma	3
59	Greece	3
60	Philippines	3
61	China	2
62	Australia	1
63	Burundi	1
64	Zaire	1
65	France	1
66	Rwanda	1
67	South Africa	1

Source: *World Christian Handbook.*

35. Jews

Jews are among the most widely dispersed communities in the world, and the word diaspora has been applied most properly to their dispersion. They are also among the few communities in the world that have succeeded in maintaining their nationhood without a nation. The Jewish diaspora began in A.D. 70, following the destruction of the Temple by Emperor Titus, and in succeeding waves, known as *galut* in Hebrew, reached first North Africa and Spain, then Russia and Northern Europe and finally the New World where the first Sephardic Jews are believed to have arrived soon after the Spaniards. Isolated groups of Jews are also believed to have migrated to Cochin in India and even as far as China, where their presence was recorded by medieval travelers. Their present concentration in North America and Israel is a much later phenomenon and is the product of what might be described as remigration. The impact of the Jewish presence in a country cannot be adequately measured by numbers alone, because the drive and intellectual vigor of this people have left a vastly disproportionate imprint in almost every country where they have resided. Their remarkable resilience is attested by many instances, such as a Jew becoming the chancellor of Catholic Austria within a few decades of the virtual extermination of the Jews in the Holocaust.

Number of Countries: 87
Midpoint: 2,000
Period Covered: 1977
Type of Ranking: Number of Jews; Highest to Lowest (Percentage of Jews for Top 9 Countries only)

Highlights & Findings: The total Jewish population in the world is estimated at 14,342,920, distributed as follows: North America, 6,142,500; Europe, 4,050,325; Asia, 3,130,910; South and Central America, 758,595; Africa, 184,390; and Oceania, 76,200. Interestingly, the largest concentration of Jews is found not in Israel but in New York, particularly New York City.

Region	Africa	Asia & Oceania	Europe	Western Hemisphere
Most	South Africa (9)	Israel (2)	Soviet Union (3)	United States (1)
Least	Libya (86)	China (87)	Cyprus (88)	Barbados (84)

Rank	Country	Number of Jews	Percentage of Total
	TOP 9		
1	United States	5,800,000	40.43
2	Israel	3,000,000	20.91
3	Soviet Union	2,680,000	18.68
4	France	550,000	3.83
5	Argentina	475,000	3.31
6	United Kingdom	410,000	2.85
7	Canada	305,000	2.12
8	Brazil	155,000	1.08
9	South Africa	118,000	0.82
	UPPER MIDDLE		
10	Iran***	80,000	
11	Hungary	80,000	
12	Rumania	80,000	
13	Australia	72,000	
14	Uruguay	50,000	
15	Belgium	40,000	
16	Mexico	37,500	
17	Italy	35,000	
18	Morocco	31,000	
19	West Germany	30,500	
20	Turkey	30,000	
21	Chile	30,000	
22	Netherlands	30,000	
23	Switzerland	21,000	
24	Ethiopia****	20,000	

Rank	Country	Number of Jews	Percentage of Total
25	Sweden	15,000	
26	Venezuela	15,000	
27	Czechoslovakia	14,000	
28	Austria	12,000	
29	Colombia	12,000	
30	India	12,000	
31	Spain	9,000	
32	Poland	8,000	
33	Tunisia	8,000	
34	Bulgaria	7,000	
35	Denmark	7,000	
36	Yugoslavia	6,000	
37	Peru	5,300	
38	Greece	5,000	
39	Rhodesia (Zimbabwe)	4,800	
40	New Zealand	4,200	
41	Ireland	3,000	
42	Syria	2,500	
	LOWER MIDDLE		
43	Bolivia	2,000	
44	Panama	2,000	
45	Puerto Rico	2,000	
46	Guatemala	1,900	
47	Costa Rica	1,500	
48	Cuba	1,500	
49	East Germany	1,500	
50	Finland	1,320	
51	Lebanon	1,200	
52	Paraguay	1,200	
53	Algeria	1,000	
54	Ecuador	1,000	
55	Luxembourg	1,000	
56	Norway	950	

Rank	Country	Number of Jews	Percentage of Total
57	Curacao	700	
58	Gibraltar	625	
59	Portugal	580	
60	Egypt	500	
61	Iraq	500	
62	Jamaica	500	
63	Japan	500	
64	Singapore	500	
65	Surinam	500	
66	Yemen Arab Republic	500	
67	Kenya	400	
68	Zambia	400	
69	Trinidad & Tobago	350	
70	El Salvador	310	
71	Albania	300	
72	Pakistan	250	
73	Zaire	250	
	BOTTOM 14		
74	Afghanistan	200	
75	Burma	200	
76	Dominican Republic	200	
77	Honduras	200	
78	Hong Kong	200	
79	Nicaragua	200	
80	Philippines	200	
81	Haiti	150	
82	Indonesia	100	
83	Barbados	85	
84	Malta	50	
85	Libya	40	
86	China	30	
87	Cyprus	30	

***An undetermined number of Iranian Jews are believed to have fled Iran following the establishment of an Islamic Republic in 1979.
****These are the Falasha (also known as Beta Israel or Black Jews) who are racially distinct from Jews. They claim descent from followers of the Queen of Sheba and observe a primitive form of Judaism based on the Torah.

Source: *World Zionist Handbook,* Jewish Information Center, New York.

POLITICS

It is unfortunate that politics, although one of the critical areas of national life, has been subjected to so little statistical study and analysis. The central theme of politics is power; power gained, power used, power transferred and power opposed. While power is the universal given in politics, the power structure and the political behavior of the masses vary sharply from nation to nation. It is possible, therefore, only to rank countries on the basis of the relative capabilities and stabilities of political systems. The resulting profile would enable us to discern patterns in what would otherwise appear to be a mere concatenation of political events. Professor Ray Cline has attempted in the first ranking in this chapter to scale the world's nations on the basis of perceived power, combining economic, military and geopolitical factors.

The subsequent rankings examine both positive and negative features of political systems. Voter registration helps us to ascertain the degree of mass participation in organized politics. The percentage of registered voters is affected by a number of variables such as the minimum voting age (ranging, on the average, between 17 and 21) and qualifications sub-tly designed to reduce the voting population, such as literacy and payment of property taxes. The age of nations may provide a clue to the quality of each nation's self-image. Other political mechanisms describe the power structure; these include the size of the executive or cabinet and the size of the legislative opposition. Order and stability are measured through the civil disorder and violence ranking. Just as with individuals, some nations seem more prone to violence than others. Not all violence is negative or deviant or even illegitimate. In a broader sense it can represent a different kind of participation within the political system by those who had been excluded from it. The frequency with which violent events occur in a country may be a useful indicator of political health regardless of the scope or severity of these events.

Communist Party membership forms the subject of another ranking. Communism is perhaps the only worldwide political organization, and although riven by pro-Moscow and pro-Peking factionalism, it still retains enough ideological appeal to pose a threat to democratic governments.

36. Most Powerful Nations

Power is an intriguing subject. Decisions affecting foreign policy and international conflicts are usually made by national leaders on the basis of projections of what they perceive their own power to be or what they think is the power of others. Although the perceptions of power are thus often blurred or diffuse, they contain concrete elements and ingredients that can be identified and even measured broadly. One of the most successful attempts to do so is that by Professor Ray Cline in *World Power Assessment,* in which he presents an overall conceptual methodology that incorporates military, economic, geopolitical and psychological factors. He has also devised a calibrated scale of perceived power on which the rank of each nation can be determined. There are five basic elements in Dr. Cline's scale of perceived power: (1) Critical Mass (Population plus Territory), (2) Economic Capability, (3) Military Capability, (4) Strategic Purpose and (5) Will to Pursue National Strategy. National power is a mix of all these factors. It is determined by its potential for the deterrence of war, and even more so by the size and strategic location of territory, the nature of its frontiers, size of population, political and economic alliances, technological development, raw material resources, economic structure, financial strength, ethnic mix, social cohesiveness, stability of political processes and above all that intangible quality generally described as national will. The index numbers used by Dr. Cline convey easily and manipulate arithemetically estimates of comparative strengths and weaknesses among nations. Because these elements are being measured in a broad context, precise details may not significantly vary the rank order.

Number of Countries: 76
Midpoint: 31
Period Covered: 1977
Type of Ranking: Total Power; Elements of Power (Critical Mass; Economic Capability; Military Capability-Strategic Weapons; Military Capability-Conventional Weapons; National Strategy; National Will); Highest to Lowest

Highlights & Findings: The ranking demonstrates the concentration of great power in the hands of a small number of nations. The 76 nations in the ranking include over 85% of the peoples of the world. The total number of weighted values is 3,778. Of this, the United States and the Soviet Union alone have 870. The majority of the nations have little impact on international affairs or on their own regions. In the words of Dr. Cline, they serve as the political equivalent of iron filings which automatically arrange themselves around magnetic fields of force constituted by the 40 or so nations that determine the pattern of world balance of power at any given time.

Regions	Africa	Asia & Oceania	Europe	Western Hemisphere
Most	Nigeria (17)	China (3)	Soviet Union (2)	United States (1)
Least	Guinea (58)	Singapore (75)	Albania (73)	Surinam (76)

Rank	Country	Total	Critical Mass	Economic Capability	Military Capability-Strategic	Military Capability-Conventional	National Strategy*	National Will*
				TOP 10				
1	United States	468	100	174	100	94	(0.4)	(0.5)
2	Soviet Union	402	100	105	100	97	(0.8)	(0.5)
3	China	171	100	29	10	32	(0.5)	(0.2)
4	France	112	55	36	10	11	(0.4)	(0.5)
5	West Germany	112	50	48	–	14	(0.7)	(0.8)
6	Japan	111	60	46	–	5	(0.5)	(0.8)
7	United Kingdom	99	55	26	10	8	(0.6)	(0.4)
8	Canada	97	70	26	–	1	(0.2)	(0.4)
9	India	97	90	4	–	3	(0.3)	(0.3)
10	Brazil	94	85	7	–	2	(0.5)	(0.8)
				UPPER MIDDLE				
11	Indonesia	85	80	4	–	1	(0.5)	(0.5)
12	Iran	80	60	12	–	8	(0.9)	(0.7)
13	Mexico	74	70	4	–	–	(0.2)	(0.4)
14	Argentina	71	65	5	–	1	(0.3)	(0.2)
15	Italy	71	50	16	–	5	(0.5)	(0.3)
16	Egypt	65	55	1	–	9	(0.5)	(0.6)
17	Nigeria	65	60	5	–	–	(0.4)	(0.4)
18	Turkey	65	55	3	–	7	(0.2)	(0.4)
19	Pakistan	62	60	1	–	1	(0.5)	(0.5)
20	Australia	60	40	20	–	–	(0.4)	(0.7)
21	South Africa	60	50	7	–	3	(0.6)	(0.4)
22	Spain	59	45	9	–	5	(0.5)	(0.4)
23	Zaire	55	55	–	–	–	(0.5)	(0.5)
24	Burma	50	50	–	–	–	(0.2)	(0.1)
25	Poland	48	35	9	–	4	(0.5)	(0.2)
26	Vietnam	48	40	–	–	8	(0.8)	(0.4)
27	Thailand	47	45	1	–	1	(0.5)	(0.3)
28	Ethiopia	45	45	–	–	–	(0.1)	(0.2)
29	Saudi Arabia	43	30	13	–	–	(0.7)	(0.7)
30	Algeria	41	40	1	–	–	(0.5)	(0.5)
31	Colombia	41	40	1	–	–	(0.5)	(0.5)
32	Philippines	41	40	1	–	–	(0.5)	(0.3)
33	Bangladesh	40	40	–	–	–	(0.3)	(0.2)
34	Sudan	40	40	–	–	–	(0.2)	(0.3)
35	South Korea	38	30	2	–	6	(0.7)	(0.7)
36	Yugoslavia	36	30	3	–	3	(0.5)	(0.2)
37	Libya	33	30	3	–	3	(0.5)	(0.6)
38	Peru	31	30	1	–	–	(0.5)	(0.5)

Rank	Country	Total	Critical Mass	Economic Capability	Military Capability-Strategic	Military Capability-Conventional	National Strategy*	National Will*
				LOWER MIDDLE				
39	Afghanistan	30	30	–	–	–	(0.5)	(0.3)
40	Mongolia	30	30	–	–	–	(0.3)	(0.1)
41	Morocco	30	30	–	–	–	(0.5)	(0.5)
42	Tanzania	30	30	–	–	–	(0.5)	(0.5)
43	Sweden	29	15	10	–	4	(0.5)	(0.7)
44	Venezuela	26	20	6	–	–	(0.5)	(0.5)
45	Iraq	25	15	4	–	6	(0.3)	(0.5)
46	Rumania	24	20	3	–	1	(0.5)	(0.5)
47	Taiwan	23	10	2	–	11	(0.7)	(0.9)
48	Chile	22	20	2	–	–	(0.5)	(0.7)
49	East Germany	22	10	7	–	5	(0.8)	(0.2)
50	Israel	22	–	1	–	21	(0.9)	(0.8)
51	North Korea	22	10	–	–	12	(0.8)	(0.6)
52	Zambia	22	20	2	–	22	(0.5)	(0.5)
53	Norway	20	15	4	–	1	(0.5)	(0.5)
54	Finland	17	15	2	–	–	–	–
55	Rhodesia	16	15	1	–	–	–	–
56	Netherlands	15	–	12	–	3	–	–
57	Belgium	12	–	10	–	2	–	–
58	Guinea	12	10	2	–	–	–	–
59	New Zealand	11	10	1	–	–	(0.5)	(0.5)
60	Czechoslovakia	10	–	6	–	4	–	–
61	Switzerland	8	–	6	–	2	–	–
62	Syria	7	–	–	–	7	–	–
63	Denmark	5	–	4	–	1	–	–
64	Hungary	5	–	3	–	2	–	–
65	Austria	4	–	4	–	–	–	–
66	Kuwait	4	–	4	–	–	–	–
				BOTTOM 10				
67	Bulgaria	3	–	1	–	2	–	–
68	Greece	3	–	1	–	2	–	–
69	Cuba	2	–	–	–	2	(0.7)	(0.6)
70	Jamaica	2	–	2	–	2	–	–
71	Portugal	2	–	1	–	1	–	–
72	United Arab Emirates	2	–	2	–	–	–	–
73	Albania	1	–	1	–	–	–	–
74	Guyana	1	–	1	–	–	–	–
75	Singapore	1	–	1	–	–	(0.5)	(0.5)
76	Surinam	1	–	1	–	–	–	–

* Not included in total column.

Source: Ray Cline, *World Power Assessment* © Ray Cline By Permission.

37. Registered Voters

In a legitimate parliamentary democracy the size of the electorate, particularly in relation to the population, is more than just another statistic. It shows how concerned the citizens are in the working of their democratic political institutions, the degree of their participation in the electoral processes and the number of people to whom each representative is answerable. In most countries where the universal franchise is guaranteed by a constitution, every native-born citizen who reaches a certain age automatically becomes eligible to vote. In other countries the franchise is hedged in with many restrictions, such as literacy, property qualifications, proof of sanity, freedom from criminal record, etc. In some Latin American countries married persons receive the franchise earlier than unmarried people. Registration is still more difficult in countries where the governments view the electorate with suspicion. There are numerous laws, such as residence for a number of years, designed to make it almost impossible for members of the opposition to register as voters.

Number of Countries: 30
Midpoint: 64.4%
Period Covered: 1975-78
Type of Ranking: Percentage of Registered Voters; Total Number of Registered Voters; Highest to Lowest

Highlights & Findings: The ranking is limited to countries where voter lists are maintained properly and revised periodically. South Africa, at the bottom, needs an explanation. Since blacks are excluded from the political process and are not permitted to register or vote, registered voters constitute less than 10% of the population. The percentage is also low in India—which incidentally has the largest electorate in the world—because of the relative youth of the population. In some Latin American countries it is evident that large numbers of eligible persons simply do not bother to register.

Region	Africa	Asia	Europe	Western Hemisphere
Most	South Africa (30)	Japan (6)	Finland (1)	United States (9)
Least	N.A.	Turkey (27)	Switzerland (23)	Brazil (29)

Rank	Country	Percentage of Registered Voters	Total Number of Registered Voters	Rank	Country	Percentage of Registered Voters	Total Number of Registered Voters	Rank	Country	Percentage of Registered Voters	Total Number of Registered Voters
		TOP 10				*MIDDLE*				*BOTTOM 10*	
1	Finland	80.6	3,798,000	11	Italy	68.3	38,143,000	21	Iceland	59.1	129,000
2	United Kingdom	72.0	40,257,000	12	East Germany	68.0	11,461,000	22	Ireland	58.5	1,832,000
3	West Germany	71.7	44,215,000	13	Austria	66.7	5,019,000	23	Switzerland	58.2	3,687,000
4	Norway	71.1	2,850,000	14	Belgium	65.0	6,406,000	24	India	54.8	327,758,000
5	Greece	70.7	6,400,000	15	Soviet Union	64.4	163,845,000	25	Mexico	48.2	29,009,000
6	Japan	70.6	79,038,000	16	Malta	64.2	198,000	26	Chile	47.7	4,894,000
7	Sweden	69.9	5,736,000	17	Canada	63.6	14,451,000	27	Turkey	45.4	17,803,000
8	Netherlands	69.3	9,470,000	18	Luxembourg	61.7	208,000	28	Venezuela	41.2	4,898,000
9	United States	69.2	147,571,000	19	Israel	61.4	2,171,000	29	Brazil	35.3	37,828,000
10	Denmark	68.3	3,458,000	20	France	59.3	31,269,000	30	South Africa	9.7	2,486,000

Source: Cross-National Data Archive, Center for Social Analysis, Binghamton, N.Y.

---

38. Age of Nations

It was Henry Kissinger who in the early 1970s raised the interesting question of the legitimacy of nations. One determinant of legitimacy is of course age. A nation-state that has been around for a long time acquires the patina of legitimacy and becomes accepted more easily into the community of nations. Pursuing this line of argument, it becomes obvious that not many nations have been around for longer than a century. (We are considering here nations and not countries). The relative youth of nations is a major factor in the conduct of international affairs. It might explain their immaturity, sibling rivalries and frequent alternations between assertiveness and dependence. This raises the question: how do we determine the age of nations. It is easy in the case of countries that were under colonial rule until the mid-20th century and therefore can point to a particular year as the year of independence. It becomes more difficult in the case of nations that have no such clearly demarcated watershed. In their case it is necessary to establish a point in time when they became accepted political entities within their present borders and in their present form. Using this formula, countries such as Egypt, China and India with a long history behind them must be regarded as comparatively young nations. In other words the age of nations has been determined on the basis of unbroken independence and systemic continuity.

Number of Countries: 160
Midpoint: 32
Period Covered: 1980
Type of Ranking: Age of Nations in 1980; Year of Independence or Year of Establishment in Present Form; Highest to Lowest

Highlights & Findings: There are 45 nations out of over 160 independent countries in the world that can claim birth before the 20th century. More than half are post-World War II nations. It is interesting to note that more nations were born in 1960 than in any other year in human history. The early 1800s was another period that saw the birth of many nations following the end of the Napoleonic wars and the breakup of Spain's South American empire.

Region	Africa	Asia & Oceania	Europe	Western Hemisphere
Earliest	Ethiopia (1)	Japan (4)	San Marino (2)	United States (16)
Latest	Djibouti (159)	Solomon Islands (160)	Malta (126)	Surinam (158)

Rank	Country	Age in 1980	Year of Independence or Year of Establishment	Rank	Country	Age in 1980	Year of Independence or Year of Establishment	Rank	Country	Age in 1980	Year of Independence or Year of Establishment
		TOP 10		37	Greece	150	1830	77	New Zealand	33	1947
1	Ethiopia	over 4,900	3000 B.C.	38	Belgium	149	1831	78	Pakistan	33	1947
2	San Marino	Over 1,500	400s	39	Dominican Republic	136	1844	79	Burma	32	1948
3	France	Over 1,400	486	40	Liberia	133	1847	80	Israel	32	1948
4	Japan	Over 1,400	500s	41	Denmark	131	1849				
5	United Kingdom	914	1066	42	Haiti	121	1859				
6	Hungary	879	1101	43	Italy	119	1861			*LOWER MIDDLE*	
7	Andorra	702	1278	44	Luxembourg	113	1867	81	North Korea	32	1948
8	Switzerland	689	1291	45	Rumania	102	1878	82	South Korea	32	1948
9	Monaco	642	1338	46	Australia	80	1900	83	Sri Lanka	32	1948
10	Spain	488	1492	47	Cuba	78	1902	84	Bhutan	31	1949
				48	Norway	75	1905	85	Taiwan	31	1949
		UPPER MIDDLE		49	Iran	74	1906	86	West Germany	31	1949
11	Portugal	340	1640	50	Bulgaria	72	1908	87	East Germany	31	1949
12	Oman	330	1650	51	Albania	68	1912	88	Libya	29	1951
13	Liechtenstein	261	1719	52	China	68	1912	89	Cambodia	27	1953
14	Afghanistan	233	1747	53	Finland	63	1917	90	Laos	27	1953
15	Nepal	211	1769	54	Soviet Union	63	1917	91	Morocco	24	1956
16	United States	204	1776	55	Austria	62	1918	92	Sudan	24	1956
17	Thailand	198	1782	56	Czechoslovakia	62	1918	93	Tunisia	24	1956
18	Sweden	171	1809	57	Poland	62	1918	94	Ghana	23	1957
19	Mexico	170	1810	58	Yemen Arab Republic	62	1918	95	Malaysia	23	1957
20	Paraguay	169	1811	59	Yugoslavia	62	1918	96	Guinea	22	1958
21	Venezuela	169	1811	60	Mongolia	59	1921	97	Benin	20	1960
22	Netherlands	166	1814	61	Ireland	59	1921	98	Cameroon	20	1960
23	Argentina	164	1816	62	Egypt	58	1922	99	Central African Empire	20	1960
24	Chile	162	1818	63	Turkey	57	1923	100	Chad	20	1960
25	Colombia	161	1819	64	Vatican	51	1929	101	Congo	20	1960
26	Panama	161	1819	65	Canada	49	1931	102	Cyprus	20	1960
27	Costa Rica	159	1821	66	Iraq	48	1932	103	Gabon	20	1960
28	El Salvador	159	1821	67	Saudi Arabia	48	1932	104	Ivory Coast	20	1960
29	Guatemala	159	1821	68	South Africa	46	1934	105	Madagascar	20	1960
30	Honduras	159	1821	69	Iceland	36	1944	106	Mali	20	1960
31	Nicaragua	159	1821	70	Indonesia	35	1945	107	Mauritania	20	1960
32	Peru	159	1821	71	Vietnam	35	1945	108	Niger	20	1960
33	Brazil	158	1822	72	Jordan	34	1946	109	Nigeria	20	1960
34	Ecuador	158	1822	73	Lebanon	34	1946	110	Senegal	20	1960
35	Bolivia	155	1825	74	Philippines	34	1946	111	Somalia	20	1960
36	Uruguay	155	1825	75	Syria	34	1946	112	Togo	20	1960
				76	India	33	1947	113	Upper Volta	20	1960

Rank	Country	Age in 1980	Year of Independence or Year of Establishment	Rank	Country	Age in 1980	Year of Independence or Year of Establishment	Rank	Country	Age in 1980	Year of Independence or Year of Establishment
114	Zaire	20	1960	131	Rhodesia (Zimbabwe)	15	1965	148	Bahamas	7	1973
115	Kuwait	19	1961	132	Singapore	15	1965	149	Grenada	6	1974
116	Sierra Leone	19	1961	133	Barbados	14	1966	150	Guinea-Bissau	6	1974
117	Algeria	18	1962	134	Botswana	14	1966				
118	Burundi	18	1962	135	Guyana	14	1966		*BOTTOM 10*		
119	Jamaica	18	1962	136	Lesotho	14	1966				
120	Rwanda	18	1962	137	South Yemen	13	1967	151	Angola	5	1975
121	Trinidad & Tobago	18	1962	138	Equatorial Guinea	12	1968	152	Cape Verde	5	1975
122	Uganda	18	1962	139	Mauritius	12	1968	153	Comoros	5	1975
123	Western Samoa	18	1962	140	Nauru	12	1968	154	Mozambique	5	1975
124	Kenya	17	1963	141	Swaziland	12	1968	155	Papua New Guinea	5	1975
125	Malawi	16	1964	142	Fiji	10	1970	156	Sao Tome & Principe	5	1975
126	Malta	16	1964	143	Tonga	10	1970	157	Surinam	5	1975
127	Tanzania	16	1964	144	Bahrain	9	1971	158	Seychelles	4	1976
128	Zambia	16	1964	145	Bangladesh	9	1971	159	Djibouti	3	1977
129	Gambia	15	1965	146	Qatar	9	1971	160	Solomon Islands	2	1978
130	Maldives	15	1965	147	United Arab Emirates	9	1971				

Source: Library of Congress.

39. Size of Cabinet

"Not I but 10,000 clerks rule Russia," said Peter the Great. Productivity is constantly evaluated in almost every field of endeavor but public administration and government. What is the optimum size of a cabinet or bureaucracy has never been determined and there are few studies on the subject. The 12 members of the Soviet Presidium preside over the largest country in the world, yet it requires 36 cabinet members to rule Guinea. In many states the size of the cabinet is evidently determined by the spoils system, whereby the plums of office are shared by as many of the ruling party hierarchy as possible. There is safety in numbers and the more the merrier.

Number of Countries: 151	**Highlights & Findings:** All countries in the top 11, with the exception of New Zealand, are dictatorships. In relation to size of population, the most compact cabinets are found in the Soviet Union, the United States, Japan and Argentina.
Midpoint: 18	
Period Covered: 1976	
Type of Ranking: Number of Cabinet Members; Highest to Lowest	

Region	Africa	Asia & Oceania	Europe	Western Hemisphere
Most	Guinea (5)	China (1)	East Germany (2)	Cuba (12)
Least	Mauritania (147)	Bhutan (151)	Luxembourg (146)	Argentina (143)

Rank	Country	Number of Cabinet Members	Rank	Country	Number of Cabinet Members	Rank	Country	Number of Cabinet Members
	TOP 11			*UPPER MIDDLE*		23	Malaysia	26
1	China	42	12	Cuba	30	24	Nigeria	26
2	East Germany	42	13	Bulgaria	29	25	Sri Lanka	26
3	New Zealand	40	14	India	29	26	Mauritius	25
4	Yugoslavia	39	15	Italy	29	27	Zaire	25
5	Guinea	36	16	Australia	28	28	Iraq	24
6	Poland	36	17	Gabon	28	29	Somalia	24
7	Bangladesh	34	18	Syria	28	30	Algeria	23
8	Egypt	33	19	Canada	27	31	Hungary	23
9	North Korea	31	20	Mongolia	27	32	Saudi Arabia	23
10	Rumania	31	21	Pakistan	27	33	United Kingdom	23
11	Vietnam	31	22	Czechoslovakia	26	34	Iran	22

Rank	Country	Number of Cabinet Members	Rank	Country	Number of Cabinet Members	Rank	Country	Number of Cabinet Members
35	Ivory Coast	22	76	South Yemen	18	115	El Salvador	14
36	Kenya	22				116	Gambia	14
37	United Arab Emirates	22		*LOWER MIDDLE*		117	Japan	14
38	Belgium	21	77	Chile	17	118	Lesotho	14
39	Burma	21	78	Taiwan	17	119	Niger	14
40	Central African Empire	21	79	Costa Rica	17	120	Thailand	14
41	Ghana	21	80	Denmark	17	121	Upper Volta	14
42	Guyana	21	81	Finland	17	122	Venezuela	14
43	Israel	21	82	West Germany	17	123	Maldives	13
44	Laos	21	83	Grenada	17	124	Malta	13
45	Libya	21	84	Ireland	17	125	Panama	13
46	Papua New Guinea	21	85	Kuwait	17	126	United States	13
47	Rhodesia (Zimbabwe)	21	86	Netherlands	17	127	Uruguay	13
48	Sierra Leone	21	87	Senegal	17	128	Cyprus	12
49	South Africa	21	88	Swaziland	17	129	Benin	12
50	Sudan	21	89	Turkey	17	130	Ecuador	12
51	Tanzania	21	90	Bahrain	16	131	Guatemala	12
52	Uganda	21	91	Fiji	16	132	Haiti	12
53	Cameroon	20	92	France	16	133	Honduras	12
54	Jamaica	20	93	Malawi	16	134	Iceland	12
55	Jordan	20	94	Mali	16	135	Nicaragua	12
56	South Korea	20	95	Norway	16	136	Soviet Union	12
57	Lebanon	20	96	Portugal	16	137	Cape Verde	11
58	Yemen Arab Republic	20	97	Qatar	16	138	Paraguay	11
59	Ethiopia	19	98	Rwanda	16	139	Sao Tome & Principe	11
60	Greece	19	99	Singapore	16	140	Samoa	11
61	Guinea-Bissau	19	100	Austria	15			
62	Indonesia	19	101	Bahamas	15		*BOTTOM 11*	
63	Mexico	19	102	Bolivia	15	141	Equatorial Guinea	9
64	Morocco	19	103	Chad	15	142	Switzerland	9
65	Philippines	19	104	Colombia	15	143	Argentina	8
66	Sweden	19	105	Madagascar	15	144	Congo	8
67	Zambia	19	106	Mozambique	15	145	Comoros	8
68	Afghanistan	18	107	Surinam	15	146	Luxembourg	8
69	Albania	18	108	Togo	15	147	Mauritania	8
70	Brazil	18	109	Tunisia	15	148	Nepal	7
71	Liberia	18	110	Barbados	14	149	Tonga	6
72	Oman	18	111	Botswana	14	150	Nauru	5
73	Peru	18	112	Burundi	14	151	Bhutan	4
74	Spain	18	113	Cambodia	14			
75	Trinidad & Tobago	18	114	Dominican Republic	14			

Source: Cross-National Data Archive, Center for Social Analysis, Binghamton, N.Y.

40. Political Opposition Index

One characteristic of parliamentary democracy is pluralism as expressed in the legislative participation of a healthy opposition. The proportion of seats held by the majority party and the opposition is thus an index of the degree of pluralism within the political system. In the following ranking countries are scaled by the size of the opposition within the legislature. The index is calculated by dividing the seats held by the majority party by the total seats in the legislature. The principal reason for calculating the index in this manner (rather than as a percentage of seats held) is to ensure that countries with no political parties or no legislatures and countries with one-party systems will be adjacent rather than at opposite extremes of the array. Thus, a country with no parties has a score of zero, a country with a one-party system has a score of 1, a country with 40 out of 100 seats held by the majority party has a score of 2.5 and so on.

Number of Countries: 59
Midpoint: 1.84
Period Covered: 1977
Type of Ranking: Index of Political Opposition; Seats Held by the Majority Party; Total Number of Seats in the Legislature; Highest to Lowest

Highlights & Findings: One of the anomalies in this index is that political systems with a large opposition are not necessarily the most democratic. In fact, a strong or widely fragmented opposition may sometimes create conditions of instability leading to eventual dictatorship. This is what happened to Thailand, which had the top ranking (3.74) until the military takeover in the mid-1970s. The most stable democracies are generally found in the middle of the ranking. The United States, for example, with an index of 1.49 seems to have the optimum conditions for a workable democracy. Of course, some countries at the top of the ranking have long traditions of stable coalition governments, e.g. Switzerland.

Region	Africa	Asia & Oceania	Europe	Western Hemisphere
Most	Lesotho (9)	Lebanon (7)	Finland (1)	Guatemala (3)
Least	Sierra Leone (59)	Syria (58)	Greece (46)	Trinidad & Tobago (57)

Rank	Country	Opposition Index	Seats Held by Majority Party	Total Seats in Legislature	Rank	Country	Opposition Index	Seats Held by Majority Party	Total Seats in Legislature	Rank	Country	Opposition Index	Seats Held by Majority Party	Total Seats in Legislature
	TOP 10				20	Costa Rica	2.11	27	57	40	South Korea	1.50	146	219
1	Finland	3.70	54	200	21	Ireland	2.09	69	144	41	Paraguay	1.50	46	60
2	Switzerland	3.64	55	200	22	United Kingdom	1.99	319	635	42	India	1.49	352	526
3	Guatemala	3.59	17	61	23	Venezuela	1.99	102	203	43	United States	1.49	291	435
4	Netherlands	3.49	43	150	24	Austria	1.97	93	183	44	Guyana	1.43	37	53
5	Denmark	3.38	53	179	25	Malta	1.96	28	55	45	Jamaica	1.43	37	53
6	Cyprus	3.33	15	50	26	Surinam	1.95	20	39	46	Greece	1.38	216	300
7	Lebanon	3.30	30	99	27	Canada	1.88	140	264	47	South Africa	1.38	123	170
8	Belgium	2.94	72	212	28	Australia	1.86	68	127	48	Barbados	1.33	18	24
9	Lesotho	2.74	34	93	29	Brazil	1.84	198	364	49	Botswana	1.33	27	36
10	Luxembourg	2.67	18	59	30	Mauritius	1.84	38	70		**BOTTOM 10**			
	UPPER MIDDLE					**LOWER MIDDLE**				50	Rhodesia (Zimbabwe)	1.32	50	66
11	France	2.65	185	490	31	Japan	1.81	271	491	51	Bahamas	1.27	30	38
12	Norway	2.50	62	155	32	Colombia	1.76	113	199	52	Mexico	1.17	189	222
13	Turkey	2.43	185	450	33	Indonesia	1.76	261	460	53	Gambia	1.14	28	32
14	Iceland	2.40	25	60	34	Sri Lanka	1.74	90	157	54	Malaysia	1.14	135	154
15	Italy	2.36	267	630	35	Nicaragua	1.67	42	70	55	Grenada	1.07	14	15
16	Israel	2.35	51	120	36	New Zealand	1.64	53	87	56	Dominican Republic	1.06	86	91
17	Sweden	2.24	156	350	37	Pakistan	1.64	89	146	57	Trinidad & Tobago	1.06	34	36
18	Portugal	2.17	115	250	38	El Salvador	1.63	32	52	58	Syria	1.02	182	186
19	West Germany	2.16	230	496	39	Fiji	1.58	33	52	59	Sierra Leone	1.01	84	85

Source: Cross-National Data Archive, Center for Social Analysis, Binghamton, N.Y.

41. Civil Disorder Index

The study of disorder in national and international affairs, just as the study of entropy in physics, is becoming quite a discipline in itself. What this study needs most is something like the Richter scale on which to measure those rumblings, convulsions, cataclysms, tremors and explosions that periodically hit nations and send shock waves throughout the world. Such a scale would enable us to determine which countries are most unstable, measure the intensity and severity of the upheavals and even establish predictable cycles of unrest in political and social life. In the absence of such a scale, the best that can be done is to keep count of incidents of civil disorder in each country. The Center for Social Analysis at Binghamton, N. Y., where such a count is being maintained, identifies eight common manifestations of civil disorder: (1) assassinations, (2) general strikes, (3) guerrilla incidents, (4) government crises, (5) purges, (6) riots, (7) revolutions and (8) antigovernment demonstrations. In the following ranking all these elements have been combined and countries are ranked according to their combined value.

Number of Countries: 99
Midpoint: 5
Period Covered: 1975 Through 1978
Type of Ranking: Total Number of Incidents of Civil Disorder; Highest to Lowest

Highlights & Findings: The ranking establishes that instability is not related to the size of a country, its political system, or its economic or military strength. Because unrest springs from many sources—racial, religious, political, economic or a combination of all these—no country is totally exempt, although some countries are more disorder-prone than others. However, a word of caution is in order. The absence of civil disorder may be simply an indication that repression is complete and total, as in the Soviet Union. In some cases disorder may be—paradoxical as it may sound—a sign of political and social health and may often be a catalyst for change.

Region	Africa	Asia & Oceania	Europe	Western Hemisphere
Most	South Africa (3)	Iran (4)	Spain (1)	Argentina (5)
Least	Somalia (97)	South Yemen (99)	Ireland (89)	Haiti (88)

Rank	Country	Incidents of Civil Disorder, 1975-78	Rank	Country	Incidents of Civil Disorder, 1975-78	Rank	Country	Incidents of Civil Disorder, 1975-78
	TOP 10		34	Cambodia	9	67	Soviet Union	3
1	Spain	83	35	Greece	9	68	Venezuela	3
2	Italy	58	36	Nigeria	8	69	Finland	2
3	South Africa	56	37	Uganda	8	70	West Germany	2
4	Iran	51	38	Bangladesh	7	71	Ghana	2
5	Argentina	50	39	Kenya	7	72	Kuwait	2
6	Portugal	41	40	Malaysia	7	73	Mozambique	2
7	Turkey	37	41	Vietnam	7	74	Saudi Arabia	2
8	Ethiopia	33	42	Chad	6	75	Sierra Leone	2
9	Pakistan	33	43	Iraq	6	76	Sudan	2
10	United States	32	44	Oman	6	77	Uruguay	2
			45	Cyprus	5			
	UPPER MIDDLE		46	Ecuador	5		*BOTTOM 22*	
11	India	30	47	Egypt	5	78	Albania	1
12	China	25	48	Honduras	5	79	Algeria	1
13	Colombia	23	49	Indonesia	5	80	Austria	1
14	France	23	50	Yemen Arab Republic	5	81	Benin	1
15	Israel	23				82	Central African Empire	1
16	Peru	23		*LOWER MIDDLE*		83	Taiwan	1
17	El Salvador	21	51	Afghanistan	4	84	Czechoslovakia	1
18	Thailand	20	52	Canada	4	85	Denmark	1
19	Lebanon	19	53	Congo	4	86	Equatorial Guinea	1
20	South Korea	17	54	Mauritania	4	87	Guinea	1
21	Nicaragua	17	55	Panama	4	88	Haiti	1
22	Philippines	16	56	Yugoslavia	4	89	Ireland	1
23	Guatemala	15	57	Zaire	4	90	Madagascar	1
24	Japan	15	58	Australia	3	91	Malawi	1
25	United Kingdom	14	59	Belgium	3	92	Maldives	1
26	Rhodesia (Zimbabwe)	13	60	Brazil	3	93	Morocco	1
27	Burma	12	61	Comoros	3	94	New Zealand	1
28	Sri Lanka	12	62	Libya	3	95	Niger	1
29	Angola	11	63	Netherlands	3	96	Seychelles	1
30	Laos	11	64	Poland	3	97	Somalia	1
31	Mexico	11	65	Rumania	3	98	Syria	1
32	Bolivia	10	66	Tunisia	3	99	South Yemen	1
33	Jamaica	10						

Source: Cross-National Data Archive, Center for Social Analysis, Binghamton, N.Y.

42. Communist Party Membership

Although the international Communist movement is no longer the monolithic force that it once was and has shed much of its former ideological mystique, it remains the single most important and the best organized international political group in the world. The party officially claims a membership of over 70 million, or just 1.75% of the world's population, but it holds power in 14 countries comprising nearly one-third of the world's population and slightly more of its land area. Worldwide membership is divided almost equally between the Soviet and Chinese factions, although the Soviet faction has an edge in the number of countries. Soviet influence has also been steadily growing as a result of diplomatic victories in Africa and Asia, including countries like Ethiopia, Angola and Mozambique. This has not necessarily meant more party members in those countries. In Ethiopia, for example, the official Communist party is apparently opposed to the Soviet-backed Dergue government.

Data on party membership suffer from numerous deficiencies. In countries where the party is in power, membership figures are generally bloated, and even official sources concede that the majority of the members join the party involuntarily to advance their careers. In democratic countries where the party is legal, membership is limited to card-carrying members, but this is only the tip of the iceberg and the hidden membership of fellow travelers and sympathizers becomes visible only at election times. In countries where the party is illegal, membership figures represent only rough estimates, often limited to the core of hardened militants. In many cases the Central Intelligence Agency furnishes only a range rather than a precise figure, but in such cases the upper limit has been selected for the purpose of this ranking.

Number of Countries: 88
Midpoint: 5,000
Period Covered: 1977
Type of Ranking: Total Number of Communist Party Members; Highest to Lowest

Highlights & Findings: The largest party outside of countries ruled by Communists is in Italy, where the movement has been particularly dynamic and militant. Other countries where the party wields significant influence on the course of national affairs are France, Japan and India. Within the Communist world, the Sino-Soviet rift is reflected in every country with only one country—Albania—openly pro-Chinese outside of Southeast Asia. However, since Mao's death, there has been a widening rift between China and Albania.

Region	Africa	Asia & Oceania	Europe	Western Hemisphere
Most	Sudan (48)	China (1)	Soviet Union (2)	Cuba (16)
Least	Réunion (88)	New Zealand (82)	Malta (87)	Guyana (86)

Rank	Country	Communist Party Membership	Status	Stand in Sino-Soviet Dispute
		TOP 10		
1	China	35,000,000	In Power	–
2	Soviet Union	16,000,000	In Power	–
3	Rumania	2,577,534	In Power	Independent
4	Poland	2,573,000	In Power	Pro-Soviet
5	North Korea	2,000,000	In Power	Neutral
6	East Germany	1,900,000	In Power	Pro-Soviet
7	Italy	1,712,084	Legal	Open Split
8	Yugoslavia	1,500,000	In Power	Independent
9	Czechoslovakia	1,380,000	In Power	Pro-Soviet
10	Vietnam	900,000	In Power	Pro-Soviet
		UPPER MIDDLE		
11	Bulgaria	781,000	In Power	Pro-Soviet
12	Hungary	754,000	In Power	Pro-Soviet
13	France	600,000	Legal	Open Split
14	Japan	350,000	Legal	Independent
15	Spain	300,000	Legal	Open Split
16	Cuba	200,000	In Power	Pro-Soviet
17	India	175,000	Legal	Open Split
18	Portugal	120,000	Legal	Open Split
19	Sri Lanka	107,000	Legal	Open Split
20	Albania	101,500	In Power	Pro-Chinese
21	Argentina	70,000	Illegal	Pro-Soviet
22	Mongolia	67,000	In Power	Pro-Soviet
23	South Korea	50,000	Illegal	Open Split
24	Finland	43,000	Legal	Pro-Soviet
25	West Germany	40,000	Legal	Open Split
26	Uruguay	40,000	Illegal	Pro-Soviet
27	Greece	30,000	Legal	Pro-Soviet
28	United Kingdom	29,000	Legal	Pro-Soviet
29	Austria	25,000	Legal	Open Split
30	Chile	20,000	Illegal	Neutral
31	Sweden	17,000	Legal	Open Split
32	Laos	13,000	In Power	Neutral
33	Netherlands	13,000	Legal	Independent
34	Colombia	12,000	Legal	Pro-Soviet
35	Cyprus	12,000	Legal	Pro-Soviet
36	Belgium	10,000	Legal	Open Split
37	United States	10,000	Legal	Pro-Soviet
38	Burma	8,000	Illegal	Pro-Chinese
39	Denmark	8,000	Legal	Pro-Soviet
40	Nepal	6,500	Illegal	Open Split
41	Brazil	6,000	Illegal	Open Split
42	Venezuela	6,000	Legal	Pro-Soviet
43	Mexico	5,000	Legal	Independent
44	Switzerland	5,000	Legal	Open Split
45	Syria	5,000	Illegal	Open Split
		LOWER MIDDLE		
46	Paraguay	4,000	Illegal	Pro-Soviet
47	Australia	3,900	Legal	Open Split
48	Sudan	3,500	Illegal	Pro-Soviet
49	Costa Rica	3,200	Illegal	Pro-Soviet
50	Peru	3,200	Illegal	Open Split
51	Malaysia	3,125	Illegal	Pro-Chinese
52	Guadeloupe	3,000	Legal	Pro-Soviet
53	Lebanon	3,000	Legal	Open Split
54	Bangladesh	2,500	Legal	Pro-Soviet
55	Norway	2,250	Legal	Independent
56	Iceland	2,200	Legal	Pro-Soviet
57	Canada	2,000	Legal	Open Split
58	Hong Kong	2,000	Legal	Pro-Chinese
59	Iran	2,000	Illegal *	Pro-Soviet

* Illegal until the establishment of Islamic Republic; present status unknown.
Note: Cambodia has not been included although it is still a Communist country. Country's present status has not been determined.

Rank	Country	Communist Party Membership	Status	Stand in Sino-Soviet Dispute	Rank	Country	Communist Party Membership	Status	Stand in Sino-Soviet Dispute	Rank	Country	Communist Party Membership	Status	Stand in Sino-Soviet Dispute
60	Iraq	2,000	Illegal	Open Split	71	Honduras	600	Illegal	Open Split	80	Algeria	400	Illegal	Pro-Soviet
61	Mauritius	2,000	Legal	Pro-Soviet	72	Ireland	600	Legal	Pro-Soviet	81	Morocco	300	Illegal	Pro-Soviet
62	Dominican Republic	1,800	Illegal	Open Split	73	Bolivia	500	Illegal	Open Split	82	New Zealand	300	Legal	Neutral
63	Philippines	1,600	Illegal	Open Split	74	Egypt	500	Illegal	Open Split	83	San Marino	300	Legal	Pro-Soviet
64	Israel	1,500	Legal	Pro-Soviet	75	Jordan	500	Illegal	Pro-Soviet	84	Nicaragua	250	Illegal	Open Split
65	Turkey	1,250	Illegal	Pro-Soviet	76	Luxembourg	500	Legal	Pro-Soviet	85	El Salvador	200	Illegal	Pro-Soviet
66	Thailand	1,200	Illegal	Pro-Chinese	77	Panama	500	Illegal	Pro-Soviet	86	Guyana	100	Legal	Pro-Soviet
67	Indonesia	1,000	Illegal	Not Known	78	Singapore	500	Illegal	Pro-Chinese	87	Malta	100	Legal	Pro-Soviet
68	Martinique	1,000	Legal	Pro-Soviet						88	Reunion	20	Legal	Pro-Chinese
69	Ecuador	800	Illegal	Open Split		*BOTTOM 10*								
70	Guatemala	750	Illegal	Pro-Soviet	79	Afghanistan	400	Legal	Pro-Soviet					

Source: Central Intelligence Agency. *Yearbook on International Communist Affairs.*

FOREIGN AID

In the 19th century von Clausewitz defined war as diplomacy by other means. Foreign aid in the 20th century might be similarly defined. Large-scale aid to poorer nations is a comparatively recent phenomenon that exists on four fronts:

● From Western nations, especially the United States, to developing nations that are within their sphere of influence;

● From Communist nations, especially the Soviet Union and China, to pro-Communist as well as fellow traveling nations;

● From oil-rich Arab nations to poorer Muslim nations as well as to nations that extend moral support to the Arabs in their struggle with Israel;

● From the United Nations and other international agencies, such as the World Bank, to all developing countries.

In addition there are specific bodies, such as the Development Assistance Committee of the OECD or consortia such as the Aid to Bangladesh Club, that meet regularly and determine the quantum and nature of aid and monitor repayment schedules. Currently much of foreign aid is nonconcessional in nature and the grant element has been decreasing for years. (On the other hand, Sweden set a remarkable example to other developed nations by writing off all loans to developing nations in 1977.) Information about foreign aid from Western nations and international agencies is accurate, but information about the transfer of resources from centrally planned economies is available only as reported by official sources and may represent commitments rather than disbursements.

43. Foreign Aid per Capita

Foreign aid is broadly defined as the flow of financial resources from developed market economies to developing countries expressly intended for the economic and social development of the latter and which is concessional in character. Developing countries include all countries and territories in Africa except South Africa; in the Western Hemisphere, all except the United States, Canada, Greenland and Puerto Rico; in Asia, all except China, North Korea, Vietnam, Japan, Mongolia and Turkey; and in Oceania, all except Australia, New Zealand and U.S. possessions. Developed market economies comprise the 17 members of the Development Assistance Committee of the Organization for Economic Cooperation and Development: Australia, Austria, Belgium, Canada, Denmark, Finland, West Germany, France, Italy, Japan, the Netherlands, New Zealand, Norway, Sweden, Switzerland, the United Kingdom and the United States and also Iceland, Ireland, Luxembourg, Portugal and South Africa. The centrally

planned economies with foreign aid programs include Bulgaria, China, Czechoslovakia, East Germany, Hungary, Poland, Rumania and the Soviet Union. Multilateral institutions extending aid to developing countries include the World Bank, regional banks and financial institutions of the European Community and a number of U.N. agencies and funds.

The following rankings relate to the disbursements from developed market economies, centrally planned economies and multilateral institutions during the years 1973 through 1975. (Because of pipeline effects some of these disbursements may reflect earlier commitments.) The total aid for the period was $10.646 billion, or $5.26 per capita. By regions, Africa received $3.027 billion, or $8.10 per capita; the Western Hemisphere $1.465 billion, or $4.45 per capita; Asia $4.790 billion, or $3.97 per capita; and Oceania $521.6 million, or $122.93 per capita.

Number of Countries: 132
Midpoint: $9.01
Period Covered: 1973-75
Type of Ranking: Per Capita Aid in U.S. Dollars (with Total Aid in U.S. Dollars); Highest to Lowest

Highlights & Findings: Because most aid from developed market economies and centrally planned economies are tied to political, ideological and diplomatic factors, it bears little relation to the actual development needs of receiving countries. Nonaligned and nationalistic countries therefore receive less aid than those that are aligned or are able to play off rival donors in an effort to maximize benefits. Countries with small populations dominate the top of the list. St. Pierre & Miquelon's position in first place is a result of enormous French subsidies to preserve French culture on these islands in the Gulf of St. Lawrence.

Regions	Africa	Asia & Oceania	Western Hemisphere
Highest	St. Helena (5)	Pacific Islands (3)	St. Pierre & Miquelon (1)
Lowest	Sao Tome & Principe (131)	Qatar (132)	Bermuda (126)

Rank	Country	Per Capita Aid ($)	Total Aid ($ million)
	TOP 10		
1	St. Pierre & Miquelon	1,721.70	10.3
2	French Guyana	747.59	43.4
3	Pacific Islands	649.65	74.1
4	New Caledonia	504.74	67.1
5	St. Helena	480.00	2.4
6	Niue Island	454.00	2.3
7	Reunion	442.14	216.7
8	French Polynesia	429.44	53.3
9	Martinique	347.20	124.30
10	Guadeloupe	319.66	111.6
	UPPER MIDDLE		
11	Wallis & Futuna Islands	274.44	2.5
12	Djibouti	273.76	27.7
13	Cook Islands	272.63	5.2
14	Takelau Islands	255.00	0.5
15	Seychelles	132.83	8.0
16	New Hebrides	128.93	12.0
17	Congo	128.88	40.3
18	Netherlands Antilles	117.77	28.0
19	Surinam	106.18	43.6
20	Papua New Guinea	96.01	254.6
21	Gilbert Islands	89.75	5.8
22	Solomon Islands	82.22	15.2
23	Israel	76.35	256.9
24	Comoros	75.45	22.0
25	West Indies (Undistributed)	68.51	37.2
26	Gabon	62.87	32.7
27	Botswana	60.58	40.0
28	Western Samoa	48.34	7.3
29	Belize	47.65	6.5
30	Jordan	39.32	103.0
31	Swaziland	31.79	14.7
32	Mauritania	29.73	38.4
33	Fiji	28.61	16.0
34	Tonga	25.50	2.5
35	Mauritius	25.43	21.5
36	Tunisia	24.95	140.8
37	Senegal	24.41	103.1
38	Cambodia	22.65	178.7
39	Central African Empire	22.19	38.1
40	Niger	22.19	99.3
41	Lesotho	19.57	19.9
42	Nicaragua	19.39	40.4
43	Laos	17.70	57.6
44	Barbados	17.66	4.3
45	Panama	17.44	28.2
46	Ivory Coast	16.98	80.9
47	Mali	16.81	93.5
48	Togo	15.82	34.4
49	Somalia	14.80	45.7
50	Chad	13.93	55.0
51	Rwanda	13.32	54.9
52	Gambia	13.22	7.9
53	Costa Rica	13.20	25.4
54	Upper Volta	13.15	77.5
55	Guyana	12.82	9.9
56	Zambia	12.75	60.0
57	Paraguay	12.43	32.0
58	Benin	12.19	36.9
59	Tanzania	12.18	179.7
60	Cameroon	12.14	76.3
61	Jamaica	11.63	23.2
62	Maldives	10.34	1.2
63	Honduras	10.24	30.0
64	Burundi	9.55	35.1
65	Malawi	9.07	44.6
66	Bolivia	9.01	49.3
	LOWER MIDDLE		
67	Singapore	8.90	19.8
68	Liberia	8.72	14.6
69	Kenya	8.70	112.8
70	Madagascar	8.65	67.4
71	Guinea-Bissau	8.55	4.4
72	South Yemen	8.50	13.8
73	Bangladesh	8.14	610.1
74	South Korea	7.72	258.2
75	Morocco	7.60	128.2
76	El Salvador	7.37	29.3
77	Algeria	7.35	119.6
78	Ecuador	7.14	49.6
79	Zaire	7.11	172.3
80	Ghana	6.94	66.7
81	Sri Lanka	6.72	92.0
82	Chile	6.61	66.6
83	Malaysia	6.05	70.5
84	Dominican Republic	5.69	25.9
85	Haiti	5.66	25.4
86	Peru	5.47	82.9
87	Yemen Arab Republic	5.25	34.0
88	Guatemala	5.19	30.7
89	Lebanon	5.19	14.5
90	Pakistan	5.17	352.6
91	Egypt	5.16	188.2
92	Indonesia	5.11	652.3
93	Colombia	5.07	116.0
94	Bahrain	4.90	1.2
95	Sierra Leone	4.78	13.0
96	Trinidad & Tobago	4.75	5.1
97	Philippines	4.55	187.8
98	Uruguay	4.50	13.6
99	Sudan	4.49	77.8
100	Libya	4.38	10.3
101	Cape Verde	4.12	1.2
102	Ethiopia	3.80	10.35
103	Bahamas	3.00	0.6
104	Syria	3.00	21.4
105	Nepal	2.97	36.6
106	Equatorial Guinea	2.79	0.9
107	Burma	2.51	76.1
108	Afghanistan	2.41	45.4
109	United Arab Emirates	2.33	0.5
110	Guinea	2.21	9.5
111	India	1.87	1,097.1
112	Thailand	1.76	72.2
113	Iraq	1.61	17.3
114	Brazil	1.44	148.4
115	Kuwait	1.42	1.3
116	Argentina	1.41	35.2
117	Cuba	1.38	13.7
118	Oman	1.28	1.0
119	Uganda	1.27	14.1
120	Venezuela	1.26	14.7
121	Mexico	0.98	55.3
122	Brunei	0.93	0.1
	BOTTOM 10		
123	Bhutan	0.54	0.6
124	Saudi Arabia	0.53	4.6
125	Mozambique	0.47	4.3
126	Bermuda	0.36	N.A.
127	Rhodesia (Zimbabwe)	0.35	2.1
128	Angola	0.25	1.6
129	Macao	0.23	0.1
130	Hong Kong	0.16	0.7
131	Sao Tome & Principe	0.13	N.A.
132	Qatar	0.06	0.5

Source: *U.N. Statistical Yearbook 1977.*

44. Development Assistance

Development assistance is defined by the United Nations as financial and technical aid from developed market economies (or donor countries) to developing countries expressly intended for the economic and social development of the latter when the financial terms are concessional in character. At least 25% of the assistance must be in the form of grants. Only 17 nations are officially classified as donor countries and all of them are members of the Development Assistance Committee of the Organization for Economic Cooperation and Development. In 1976, $36.793 billion was disbursed by these 17 countries (as well as five other countries that are not members of the Development Assistance Committee: Iceland, Ireland, Portugal, Luxembourg and South Africa). This figure was slightly less than the 1975 figure of $37.087 billion but two and a half times more than the 1970 figure of $14.08 billion. Donor countries are ranked in terms of their financial assistance as a percentage of GNP in 1976.

Number of Countries: 17
Midpoint: 2.8%
Period Covered: Percentage of GNP in 1976; Total, 1973-76
Type of Ranking: Development Assistance from Donor Countries as a Percentage of Their Respective GNP; Total Development Assistance, 1973-76; Highest to Lowest

Highlights & Findings: Although a variety of considerations determine the extent and type of development assistance (historical links, trade relations, political affinities, as well as financial capacity), the United Nations recommends 2.5% of GNP as a guideline for donor countries in budgeting their annual disbursements. Only six countries fall short of this recommendation. The ranking, however, does not reveal the terms of the assistance but only its size. Aid in an easily convertible currency or one that is long-term and concessional is more desirable for developing countries even when the amount is limited.

Rank	Country	Development Assistance 1976 as a Percentage of GNP	Total Assistance 1973-76 ($ million)	Rank	Country	Development Assistance 1976 as a Percentage of GNP	Total Assistance 1973-76 ($ million)	Rank	Country	Development Assistance 1976 as a Percentage of GNP	Total Assistance 1973-76 ($ million)
1	Netherlands	4.9	4,222	7	United Kingdom	3.5	8,018	13	Italy	2.3	3,999
2	Belgium	4.4	2,968	8	Norway	3.3	990	14	Australia	2.2	1,913
3	Switzerland	4.2	2,413	9	Denmark	2.8	1,062	15	Austria	1.8	751
4	France	4.1	14,478	10	Japan	2.7	15,417	16	New Zealand	1.6	212
5	Canada	3.8	6,768	11	West Germany	2.6	12,107	17	Finland	0.8	229
6	Sweden	3.7	2,686	12	United States	2.4	41,584				

Sources: U.N. Center for Development Planning; *Projections and Policies.*

45. Aid from International Organizations

A major source of assistance to both developed and developing countries has been international organizations. These organizations include the World Bank Group (International Bank for Reconstruction and Development, International Development Association, International Finance Corporation) Asian Development Bank, African Development Bank, Inter-American Development Bank, the United Nations Development Program and the related technical assistance programs of U.N. specialized agencies and the European Economic Community. The data presented cover the period 1946 through 1977. Total worldwide disbursements during this period were $72.216 billion divided as follows:

Near East and South Asia	$17,368.1 million
Latin America	$23,302.8 million
East Asia	$11,983.8 million
Africa	$13,429.5 million
Oceania	$770.1 million
Interregional	$476.0 million

Number of Countries: 135
Midpoint: $232.7 million
Period Covered: 1946 through 1977
Type of Ranking: Disbursements from International Organizations in U.S. Dollars; Highest to Lowest

Highlights & Findings: Over the years international organizations have tried to achieve a regional balance in their expenditures that takes into account development needs, population, internal resources and aid through bilateral agreements. This effort has been so successful that the rank order in this table reflects as accurately as possible the size and importance of developing nations within each region.

Regions	Africa	Asia & Oceania	Europe	Western Hemisphere
Most	Egypt (15)	India (1)	Yugoslavia (11)	Brazil (2)
Least	Sao Tome & Principe (130)	Brunei (132)	Soviet Union (135)	Canada (133)

Rank	Country	Aid from International Organizations 1946-77 ($ million)	Rank	Country	Aid from International Organizations 1946-77 ($ million)	Rank	Country	Aid from International Organizations 1946-77 ($ million)
	TOP 10		46	Italy	399.6	92	Jordan	110.5
1	India	7,030.4	47	Burma	380.5	93	Austria	105.2
2	Brazil	5,760.9	48	Nicaragua	377.4	94	New Zealand	102.1
3	Mexico	4,143.6	49	Uruguay	368.9	95	Mauritius	95.9
4	Indonesia	2,527.9	50	Ghana	364.3	96	Uganda	95.9
5	South Korea	2,450.7	51	El Salvador	360.3	97	Rhodesia	88.5
6	Colombia	2,393.5	52	Paraguay	353.8	98	Denmark	85.2
7	Pakistan	2,139.3	53	Dominican Republic	339.3	99	Sierra Leone	77.1
8	Turkey	2,064.2	54	Sri Lanka	332.8	100	Vietnam	74.5
9	Argentina	2,045.2	55	Singapore	326.3	101	Guyana	69.4
10	Philippines	1,988.4	56	Finland	320.2	102	Swaziland	65.8
			57	Mali	314.4	103	Hong Kong	62.9
	UPPER MIDDLE		58	Israel	311.3	104	South Yemen	61.2
11	Yugoslavia	1,813.3	59	Nepal	266.2	105	Belgium	58.0
12	Thailand	1,482.7	60	Portugal	258.0	106	Surinam	56.6
13	Iran	1,251.5	61	Jamaica	254.9	107	Lesotho	49.7
14	Malaysia	1,198.9	62	France	250.3	108	Iceland	48.7
15	Egypt	1,130.5	63	Rumania	243.1	109	Barbados	35.6
16	Bangladesh	1,089.3	64	South Africa	242.3	110	Cuba	28.2
17	Peru	1,001.6	65	Afghanistan	239.6	111	Oman	27.6
18	Nigeria	945.0	66	Netherlands	236.7	112	Libya	25.6
19	Chile	941.5	67	Somalia	232.7	113	Cambodia	24.6
20	Morocco	920.1				114	Laos	24.4
21	Japan	860.4		*LOWER MIDDLE*		115	Western Samoa	22.4
22	Kenya	733.3	68	Upper Volta	223.0	116	Gambia	21.6
23	Algeria	719.3	69	Mauritania	216.7	117	Saudi Arabia	21.0
24	Zaire	667.5	70	Malawi	208.5	118	Poland	16.8
25	Ecuador	657.3	71	Congo	208.1	119	Mozambique	15.5
26	Venezuela	633.8	72	Niger	198.3	120	Guinea-Bissau	12.8
27	Bolivia	612.5	73	Haiti	195.1	121	Bahamas	12.1
28	Ivory Coast	593.5	74	Chad	193.9	122	Malta	12.0
29	Greece	567.0	75	Togo	174.9	123	Angola	5.7
30	Tunisia	561.2	76	Gabon	166.3	124	St. Pierre & Miquelon	4.0
31	Ethiopia	557.5	77	Papua New Guinea	156.6	125	Namibia	3.8
32	Tanzania	556.9	78	Rwanda	153.7			
33	Zambia	546.9	79	Ireland	153.3		*BOTTOM 10*	
34	Cameroon	527.0	80	Iraq	150.7	126	Kuwait	3.2
35	Costa Rica	517.2	81	Benin	150.5	127	Belize	2.4
36	Guatemala	507.8	82	Lebanon	150.3	128	Cape Verde	1.6
37	Honduras	502.9	83	Norway	145.1	129	Seychelles	1.3
38	Sudan	463.1	84	Liberia	142.9	130	Sao Tome & Principe	0.3
39	Taiwan	451.3	85	Burundi	137.4	131	Sweden	0.2
40	Spain	435.7	86	Guinea	135.7	132	Brunei	0.1
41	Panama	429.0	87	Trinidad & Tobago	135.6	133	Canada	0.1
42	Australia	418.9	88	Yemen Arab Republic	130.2	134	West Germany	0.1
43	Senegal	404.4	89	Botswana	115.0	135	Soviet Union	0.1
44	Madagascar	402.8	90	Cyprus	114.1			
45	Syria	401.8	91	Central African Empire	112.2			

Sources: World Bank, U.S. Agency for International Development

46. U.S. Economic Aid

Economic aid in the form of loans and grants was initiated by the United States soon after World War II and has been continued ever since. The major economic assistance programs are carried out under the Agency for International Development, Food For Peace, the Peace Corps and similar organizations. Short-term credits, emergency relief and donations, paid-in contributions to international lending organizations and assistance to refugees are also included in the data. Currently 54 countries are receiving aid through the Agency for International Development and 10 countries from other supporting organi-

zations. Seventy-seven countries receive PL480 funds (also known as Food For Peace), and the Peace Corps is active in 52 countries.

From 1946 through 1977 U.S. economic aid totaled $100.565 billion distributed as follows:

Near East and South Asia	$23.768 billion
Latin America	$12.748 billion
East Asia	$23.087 billion
Africa	$5.588 billion
Europe	$20.070 billion
Oceania	$841 million
Inter-regional	$14.461 billion

Number of Countries: 135
Midpoint: $128.5 million
Period Covered: 1946 through 1977
Type of Ranking: Total U.S. Economic Aid Received from 1946 through 1977; Highest to Lowest

Highlights & Findings: The top 10 countries have received 40% of all U.S. aid. Of these, Vietnam, South Korea and Israel received aid as part of a package that included military assistance as well. The United Kingdom, France, Italy and West Germany owe their position in the top 10 to the Marshall Plan and its successors. Much of the aid to India and Pakistan was in the form of PL480 funds repayable in rupees, which were later written off as outright grants. Aid to Egypt is a more recent (and continuing) phenomenon dating from 1975 and is related to U.S. efforts to secure peace in the Mideast.

Regions	Africa	Asia & Oceania	Europe	Western Hemisphere
Most	Egypt (7)	Vietnam (1)	United Kingdom (4)	Brazil (12)
Least	Angola (135)	Papua New Guinea (133)	East Germany (130)	Bahamas (132)

Rank	Country	U.S. Economic Aid 1946-77 ($ million)	Rank	Country	U.S. Economic Aid 1946-77 ($ million)	Rank	Country	U.S. Economic Aid 1946-77 ($ million)
	TOP 10		26	Pacific Islands	823.2	59	Haiti	197.5
1	South Vietnam	6,457.1	27	Netherlands	789.9	60	Tanzania	190.0
2	South Korea	5,550.0	28	Spain	772.8	61	Czechoslovakia	189.5
3	India	5,436.9	29	Cambodia	768.2	62	Algeria	188.6
4	United Kingdom	4,600.0	30	Morocco	674.4	63	Soviet Union	186.4
5	Pakistan	4,123.2	31	Tunisia	670.6	64	Kenya	163.1
6	France	3,132.2	32	Bolivia	655.2	65	El Salvador	144.8
7	Egypt	2,924.7	33	Thailand	618.7	66	Lebanon	135.2
8	Italy	2,822.5	34	Afghanistan	496.4	67	Jamaica	131.7
9	Israel	2,664.7	35	Zaire	489.1	68	Paraguay	128.5
10	West Germany	2,555.8 (excluding $131.9 million for West Berlin)	36	Belgium & Luxembourg	472.1			
			37	Dominican Republic	457.7		**LOWER MIDDLE**	
			38	Iran	457.1	69	Sudan	120.9
	UPPER MIDDLE		39	Poland	408.2	70	Uruguay	119.4
11	Turkey	2,061.2	40	Peru	393.2	71	Guinea	112.0
12	Brazil	2,049.2	41	Nigeria	392.9	72	Cyprus	102.3
13	China, Nationalist & Taiwan	1,936.5	42	Syria	361.2	73	Venezuela	100.5
14	Indonesia	1,838.0	43	Guatemala	351.4	74	Mali	89.7
15	Japan	1,685.4	44	Panama	326.3	75	Yemen Arab Republic	83.0
16	Philippines	1,652.0	45	Ethiopia	310.1	76	Somalia	82.2
17	Greece	1,617.8	46	Portugal	300.3	77	Guyana	82.1
18	Yugoslavia	1,464.2	47	Sri Lanka	292.4	78	Sweden	82.0
19	Jordan	1,131.1	48	Liberia	248.5	79	Senegal	81.8
20	Austria	1,104.3	49	Denmark	246.1	80	Niger	79.8
21	Bangladesh	1,098.6	50	Nicaragua	244.0	81	Argentina	78.9
22	Colombia	1,078.6	51	Ghana	236.7	82	Malta	75.9
23	Laos	899.4	52	Norway	227.6	83	Upper Volta	65.3
24	Chile	893.0	53	Ecuador	212.9	84	Malaysia	61.2
25	Indochina (undistributed)	825.6 (represents regional aid programs)	54	Mexico	210.8	85	Sierra Leone	57.2
			55	Nepal	205.8	86	Burma	53.6
			56	Honduras	205.1	87	Botswana	45.7
			57	Libya	204.1	88	Hong Kong	43.8
			58	Costa Rica	198.2	89	Cameroon	43.7

Rank	Country	U.S. Economic Aid 1946-77 ($ million)	Rank	Country	U.S. Economic Aid 1946-77 ($ million)	Rank	Country	U.S. Economic Aid 1946-77 ($ million)
90	Chad	42.2	106	Rwanda	15.7	122	South Yemen	4.5
91	Uganda	42.2	107	Burundi	13.9	123	Cuba	4.0
92	Trinidad & Tobago	40.5	108	Cape Verde	12.7	124	Guinea-Bissau	3.6
93	Ivory Coast	36.0	109	Swaziland	12.3	125	Singapore	2.8
94	Lesotho	35.9	110	Gambia	11.7			
95	Togo	34.0	111	Central African Empire	11.6		*BOTTOM 10*	
96	Iraq	33.6	112	Hungary	10.9	126	Barbados	2.2
97	Iceland	33.0	113	Rumania	10.1	127	Bahrain	2.0
98	Mauritania	31.7	114	Gabon	9.8	128	Oman	1.4
99	Malawi	31.2	115	Ireland	8.6	129	Seychelles	1.0
100	Saudi Arabia	27.5	116	Belize	8.1	130	East Germany	0.8
101	Albania	20.4	117	Zambia	7.9	131	Rhodesia (Zimbabwe)	0.6
102	Benin	19.2	118	Congo	7.8	132	Bahamas	0.3
103	Mozambique	17.5	119	Western Samoa	6.9	133	Papua New Guinea	0.3
104	Madagascar	17.2	120	Finland	6.4	134	Sao Tome & Principe	0.3
105	Mauritius	16.5	121	Surinam	5.0	135	Angola	0.2

Source: U.S. Agency for International Development.

47. Soviet Economic Aid

Soviet economic aid to developing countries is primarily commercial in orientation: its purpose is to ensure return flows of raw materials. It therefore emphasizes flexible accords and long-term supply relationships. In many cases the Soviets are using open-ended agreements, which do not specify the amount of the aid. Soviet credit usually carries liberal terms (up to 20 years' repayment with 2.5% interest). Total Soviet aid during 1954-77 was $12.932 billion, which is nearly 50% of all Communist aid to the developing world. The Soviets tend to concentrate on a few countries rather than spread out their aid; while the agreements are in force, the assistance is often massive and substantial. Soviet aid is particularly strong in North Africa with $939 million and the Middle East and South Asia with $9.446 billion. It is weakest in sub-Saharan Africa, where the Soviets have yet to find the right allies or recipients.

Number of Countries: 54
Midpoint: $39 million
Period Covered: 1954-77
Type of Ranking: Total Soviet Aid in U.S. Dollars, 1954-77; Highest to Lowest

Highlights & Findings: The showpieces of Soviet aid have been India, Algeria and Afghanistan, but aid to Ethiopia and Vietnam is likely to dominate the thinking of Soviet foreign policymakers in the future. Aid to India, which has very liberal terms, is particularly significant. It accounted for 85% of aid extensions in 1977. The Middle East is another area where the Soviets are using aid as an effective political tool.

Regions	Africa	Asia	Europe	Western Hemisphere
Most	Egypt (2)	India (1)	N.A.	Argentina (11)
Least	Upper Volta (54)	Laos (52)	N.A.	Colombia (40)

Rank	Country	Total Soviet Aid, 1954-77 ($ million)	Rank	Country	Total Soviet Aid, 1954-77 ($ million)	Rank	Country	Total Soviet Aid, 1954-77 ($ million)
	TOP 10		7	Iraq	699	12	Chile	238
1	India	1,943	8	Pakistan	652	13	Guinea	201
2	Egypt	1,300	9	Syria	467	14	Somalia	154
3	Afghanistan	1,251	10	Bangladesh	300	15	Indonesia	114
4	Turkey	1,180				16	Ethiopia	105
5	Iran	750		*UPPER MIDDLE*		17	Morocco	98
6	Algeria	715	11	Argentina	245	18	Yemen Arab Republic	98

Rank	Country	Total Soviet Aid, 1954-77 ($ million)	Rank	Country	Total Soviet Aid, 1954-77 ($ million)	Rank	Country	Total Soviet Aid, 1954-77 ($ million)
19	Sri Lanka	95	31	Cambodia	25		*BOTTOM 10*	
20	Ghana	93	32	Nepal	20	45	Benin	5
21	Mali	86	33	Tanzania	20	46	Mauritania	5
22	Greece	84	34	Uruguay	20	47	Mozambique	3
23	Brazil	83	35	Burma	16	48	Central African Empire	2
24	Tunisia	82	36	Uganda	16	49	Chad	2
25	Sudan	64	37	Congo	14	50	Niger	2
26	Kenya	48	38	Guinea-Bissau	14	51	Equatorial Guinea	1
27	South Yemen	39	39	Angola	10	52	Laos	1
			40	Colombia	10	53	Rwanda	1
	LOWER MIDDLE		41	Senegal	9	54	Upper Volta	1
28	Bolivia	31	42	Cameroon	8			
29	Peru	28	43	Nigeria	7			
30	Sierra Leone	28	44	Zambia	6			

Source: U.S. Central Intelligence Agency.

48.   Chinese Economic Aid

Chinese aid is primarily designed to further Peking's international political ambitions and has never had the commercial orientation of other Communist programs. While there has been some stimulation of Chinese domestic industries and some nominal repayments, Peking has never considered the program as having commercial advantages. The aid programs have been sharply deemphasized in the period of turbulence that followed Mao's death. The fact that extensions in 1977 were for only $160 million—almost all for agricultural products, for which China is noted—reflects continuing domestic restraints. Total Chinese aid from 1954 to 1977 amounted to $4.49 billion (about one-third of total Soviet aid). It is far more evenly spread out than Soviet aid, and the Chinese have avoided the costly blunders such as the Russians made in aid to Egypt. Chinese aid is particularly strong in sub-Saharan Africa with $2.036 billion (compared to the Soviet $939 million) and East Asia with $307 million (compared to the Soviet $156 million). Although Albania received considerable Chinese aid during the 1960s, no precise figures are available.

Number of Countries: 51 **Midpoint:** $56 million **Period Covered:** 1954-77 **Type of Ranking:** Total Chinese aid in U.S. Dollars, 1954-77; Highest to Lowest	**Highlights & Findings:** The showpieces of Chinese aid have been Pakistan, Sri Lanka and Tanzania (where the TanZam Railway is its most enduring—if at the moment somewhat rundown—monument), but few Third World countries (with the notable exception of a hostile India) have not been included the program. The Chinese lose no opportunity to compete with the Soviets, especially where the Soviet influence appears to be weakening.

Regions	Africa	Asia	Europe	Western Hemisphere
Most	Tanzania (2)	Pakistan (1)	Malta (31)	Chile (22)
Least	Central African Empire (51)	Bangladesh (49)	N.A.	Jamaica (50)

Rank	Country	Total Chinese Aid, 1954-77 ($ million)	Rank	Country	Total Chinese Aid, 1954-77 ($ million)	Rank	Country	Total Chinese Aid, 1954-77 ($ million)
	TOP 10		7	Somalia	133	12	Cambodia	92
1	Pakistan	405	8	Yemen Arab Republic	106	13	Ethiopia	85
2	Tanzania	359	9	Indonesia	105	14	Mauritania	85
3	Zambia	307	10	Zaire	100	15	Burma	84
4	Nepal	179				16	Sudan	82
5	Sri Lanka	158		*UPPER MIDDLE*		17	Guinea	77
6	Egypt	134	11	Algeria	92	18	Afghanistan	73

Rank	Country	Total Chinese Aid, 1954-77 ($ million)	Rank	Country	Total Chinese Aid, 1954-77 ($ million)	Rank	Country	Total Chinese Aid, 1954-77 ($ million)
19	Cameroon	71	31	Malta	45	43	Rwanda	22
20	Mali	68	32	Togo	45	44	Burundi	20
21	Madagascar	66	33	Benin	44	45	Kenya	18
22	Chile	65	34	Ghana	42	46	Gambia	17
23	Syria	61	35	Peru	42	47	Guinea-Bissau	17
24	Upper Volta	60	36	Tunisia	40	48	Uganda	15
25	Mozambique	59	37	Guyana	36	49	Bangladesh	11
26	South Yemen	56	38	Mauritius	35	50	Jamaica	10
			39	Morocco	32	51	Central African Empire	4
	LOWER MIDDLE		40	Sierra Leone	30			
27	Niger	51	41	Laos	26			
28	Chad	50						
29	Senegal	49		**BOTTOM 10**				
30	Iraq	45	42	Congo	25			

Source: U.S. Central Intelligence Agency.

DEFENSE

"How many divisions has the Pope?" Stalin's probably apocryphal question illustrates one aspect of military power: its relatively easy measurability. The general problems of measuring military strength are discussed in the introduction to the ranking of military power. But it seems pertinent to mention here that military strength ideally should be measured not on a general scale but only against that of neighboring countries. Except for the Soviet Union and the United States, no nation today has the reach or capacity to wage intercontinental warfare or for that matter any type of warfare against nations other than its neighbors. One cannot conceive of Bolivia being attacked by Ethiopia; the relative military rankings of these two nations are irrelevant because one is not a threat to the other. On the other hand, the military power of Ethiopia is best evaluated against those of say Somalia or Sudan, its hostile neighbors. This brings us to the concept of usable military power, which is vastly different from actual military power. Usable military power may be defined in terms of its effectiveness against hostile neighbors, its credibility and its state of readiness. The United States discovered in the 1960s that the very awesome military power at its command inhibited it from taking appropriate measures in certain situations, thus making its power useless in short-of-war confrontations.

A second disturbing element on the world military scene is the indiscriminate arms transfers from developed countries to smaller and more irresponsible nations. The smaller the country and the less responsible its leadership the greater and the more credible its military posture becomes. The proliferation of arms is in itself an invitation to promiscuous use of weapons. In this sense there is considerable logic behind the efforts to limit the size of the nuclear club. The moral is that the powerful may be trusted with power but the powerless may not be. To rephrase Lord Acton, power corrupts, but powerlessness corrupts absolutely.

The third element is the folly of alliances and treaties. With U.S. withdrawal from Taiwan and Vietnam, we may have reached the end of the age of alliances. The dynamics of international affairs are such that there is no longer any guarantee that one nation will rush to the aid of the other for fear of enlarging the area of conflict. Within weeks of solemnly promising to do so, the Soviet Union failed to move militarily against China during the 1979 Sino-Vietnam war. The old theory that the military strength of a nation is in its alliances no longer holds true.

The rankings focus on four areas: total military strength; personnel strength of the armed forces per capita; defense expenditures (total, as a percentage of GNP, per capita and per soldier) and U.S. military aid.

49. Most Powerful Military Nations

Assessments of military power are highly subjective but generally take into account two concrete and critical elements: nuclear deterrence (total in the case of the United States and the Soviet Union and limited in the case of other members of the "nuclear club") and conventional capability. The dominant fact of the military scene since World War II has been the overwhelming preponderance of U.S. and Soviet nuclear forces. But because of the awesome and unthinkable nature of nuclear weapons, they have only a psychological advantage, either as a nuclear form of a blackmail or a nuclear shield. Their use is circumscribed in actual situations of conflict. Only in the most desperate life-or-death struggles is it conceivable that these weapons would be rationally employed as military weapons. Conventional military strength is therefore the key to confrontations short of war. Such military capability not only enables smaller nations to defend themselves until help arrives from more powerful allies but also helps to prevent the conflict from escalating into nuclear war.

Since the end of World War II, all military combat has involved only conventional weapons. The main advantage of conventional forces is that they can be used in small doses, and they can be recalled before much damage has been done. They can also be used in situations where only limited response is required. Thus, despite the development of nuclear weapons on a large scale, military power must still be perceived in terms of the "old-fashioned" conventional armed forces.

Standard assessments of military capability have been based mainly on manpower or percentage of GNP expended on armed forces—both of which are highly misleading because they do not take into account such intangibles as morale, organization, leadership, skill and strategy. In most wars, as demonstrated most dramatically in Vietnam and the Middle East, these intangibles count more than numbers of men or quantity of equipment. If these intangibles are to be evaluated, some subjective judgments have to be made. Professor Ray Cline has devised a scale in his *World Power Assessment* that translates these intangibles into internationally comparable estimates of military power. The scale consists of five elements:

(1) manpower quality, including morale and leadership under conditions of actual combat;

(2) weapon effectiveness, distinguished from the efficiency of the weapons themselves as illustrated in the case of oil-rich Arab countries whose armies are equipped with sophisticated military equipment (bought with petrodollars) that they do not really know how to use;

(3) infrastructure and logistic support, which covers internal production of military equipment, adequate stockpiles of strategic materials, radar surveillance, airport and port installations and maintenance systems, and adequate communications systems;

(4) organizational quality, comprising fighting qualities and leadership of the officer corps, recent combat experience and tactical planning; and

(5) strategic reach and mobility.

Number of Countries: 46
Midpoint: 128 units of combat capability
Period Covered 1977
Type of Ranking: Combat Capability; Elements of Combat Capability (Manpower Quality, Weapon Effectiveness, Infrastructure & Logistics, Organizational Quality and Strategic Reach); Highest to Lowest

Highlights & Findings: Only 46 of the 170 or so independent nations of the world have true military capability. Other armies are mainly equipped with light weapons and are in reality only glorified police forces designed primarily to control their own populations. Of these 46 powers, the Soviet Union and the Warsaw Pact countries have a total gross military manpower of 5,582,000 and 3,842 units of combat capability; the United States and its NATO allies have a gross military manpower of 4,922,000 and 3,788 units of combat capability; and East and South Asian countries, including China, have a gross military manpower of 9,144,000 and 3,252 units of combat capability.

Regions	Africa	Asia	Europe	Western Hemisphere
Most	Egypt (21)	China (3)	Soviet Union (1)	United States (2)
Least	Nigeria (43)	Burma (46)	Denmark (44)	Argentina (40)

Rank	Country	Combat Capability	Manpower (000)	Manpower Quality	Weapon Effectiveness	Infrastructure & Logistics	Organizational Quality	Strategic Reach
	Top 10							
1	Soviet Union	3,080	4,400	0.7	0.9	0.7	0.5	0.03
2	United States	1,877	2,086	1.0	1.0	0.9	0.8	0.05
3	China	1,357	4,525	0.4	0.2	0.2	0.3	0.02
4	West Germany	464	515	1.0	0.9	0.9	0.7	0.03
5	Israel	360	400	0.9	0.8	0.8	1.0	0.03
6	France	359	513	0.8	0.7	0.8	0.6	0.03
7	India	317	1,055	0.2	0.4	0.3	0.3	0.01
8	Vietnam	308	615	0.5	0.4	0.3	0.9	0.01
9	South Korea	298	595	0.5	0.4	0.6	0.5	0.02
10	Taiwan	282	470	0.6	0.5	0.6	0.6	0.02
	UPPER MIDDLE							
11	United Kingdom	275	344	1.0	0.8	0.8	0.7	0.03
12	North Korea	248	495	0.4	0.6	0.6	0.5	0.03

Rank	Country	Combat Capability	Manpower (000)	Manpower Quality	Weapon Effectiveness	Infrastructure & Logistics	Organizational Quality	Strategic Reach
13	Turkey	245	490	0.7	0.5	0.4	0.5	0.03
14	Italy	181	362	0.6	0.5	0.5	0.4	0.03
15	Poland	180	300	0.6	0.7	0.6	0.5	0.02
16	Sweden	180	200	1.0	1.0	1.0	0.6	0.02
17	Switzerland	173	247	0.9	0.5	0.6	0.5	0.01
18	Japan	165	235	0.8	0.6	0.7	0.8	0.03
19	East Germany	163	204	0.9	0.8	0.6	0.7	0.03
20	Spain	151	302	0.7	0.5	0.5	0.4	0.03
21	Egypt	137	343	0.3	0.6	0.3	0.4	0.03
22	Czechoslovakia	133	190	0.8	0.8	0.6	0.4	0.03
23	Pakistan	128	428	0.3	0.4	0.2	0.3	0.01
	LOWER MIDDLE							
24	Yugoslavia	125	250	0.7	0.5	0.5	0.4	0.02
25	South Africa	114	190	0.6	0.7	0.6	0.5	0.03

Rank	Country	Combat Capability	Manpower (000)	Manpower Quality	Weapon Effectiveness	Infrastructure & Logistics	Organizational Quality	Strategic Reach
26	Bulgaria	106	177	0.6	0.7	0.6	0.5	0.02
27	Greece	100	200	0.7	0.5	0.4	0.5	0.02
28	Rumania	96	191	0.5	0.6	0.6	0.4	0.01
29	Syria	91	227	0.3	0.6	0.3	0.3	0.02
30	Iran	90	300	0.2	0.5	0.3	0.2	0.03
31	Netherlands	90	112	0.9	0.8	0.8	0.6	0.03
32	Hungary	84	120	0.8	0.7	0.6	0.5	0.02
33	Brazil	77	257	0.2	0.4	0.4	0.2	0.02
34	Belgium	70	88	0.9	0.8	0.8	0.6	0.03
35	Thailand	63	210	0.3	0.3	0.2	0.2	0.01
36	Canada	55	78	0.9	0.6	0.6	0.6	0.02

Rank	Country	Combat Capability	Manpower (000)	Manpower Quality	Weapon Effectiveness	Infrastructure & Logistics	Organizational Quality	Strategic Reach
			BOTTOM 10					
37	Cuba	53	175	0.2	0.5	0.2	0.3	0.03
38	Indonesia	49	246	0.2	0.1	0.2	0.1	0.02
39	Iraq	47	158	0.2	0.5	0.2	0.2	0.03
40	Argentina	40	133	0.4	0.3	0.4	0.2	0.01
41	Norway	27	39	0.9	0.8	0.6	0.6	0.03
42	Portugal	24	60	0.7	0.2	0.2	0.6	0.02
43	Nigeria	23	230	0.1	0.1	0.1	0.2	0.01
44	Denmark	21	35	0.8	0.6	0.6	0.4	0.03
45	Afghanistan	20	100	0.2	0.2	0.1	0.1	0.01
46	Burma	17	170	0.1	0.1	0.1	0.1	0.01

Source: Ray Cline, *World Power Assessment.*

50. Men and Women Under Arms

Historically, a standing army is one of the most visible expressions of national sovereignty. This explains why one of the first acts of a newly independent nation almost always is to create its own military establishment, even when there is no external threat to its existence.

In 1976 there were 22,127,380 men and women under arms in 132 standing armies throughout the world, accounting for 0.55% of the world's population. Excluding civilian women and children, there was one person under arms for every 45 civilians. The most militarized nations on a per capita basis are the 14 nations with Communist regimes, whose armies have an aggregate personnel strength of 9.3 million, or 42% of the world total.

Number of Countries: 132
Midpoint: 32,000
Period Covered: 1976
Type of Rankings: Total Strength of Armed Forces: Highest to Lowest

Highlights & Findings: What is staggering about world military power is its concentration in about a dozen nations. The top 10 nations account for 60% of the world's armed forces. Furthermore, these are among the best trained and the best armed in the world, whereas the troops of nations lower down the scale are wholly dependent on the big powers for their supplies, equipment and training.

Regions	Africa	Asia	Europe	Western Hemisphere
Most	Egypt (15)	China (2)	Soviet Union (1)	United States (3)
Least	Sao Tome & Principe (132)	Bahrain (128)	Luxembourg (130)	Trinidad & Tobago (126)

Rank	Country	Men & Women Under Arms
	TOP 10	
1	Soviet Union	3,575,000
2	China	3,250,000
3	United States	2,130,000
4	India	956,000
5	South Korea	625,000
6	France	599,531
7	Vietnam	583,000
8	West Germany	500,500
9	Taiwan	494,000

Rank	Country	Men & Women Under Arms
10	North Korea	468,000
	UPPER MIDDLE	
11	Turkey	435,000
12	Italy	421,000
13	Pakistan	393,000
14	United Kingdom	333,600
15	Egypt	322,500
16	Spain	302,300
17	Poland	293,000

Rank	Country	Men & Women Under Arms
18	Iran	281,500
19	Indonesia	266,000
20	Brazil	254,000
21	Japan	236,000
22	Yugoslavia	230,000
23	Czechoslovakia	220,000
24	Portugal	216,500
25	Nigeria	208,000
26	Thailand	204,000
27	East Germany	201,000

Rank	Country	Men & Women Under Arms	Rank	Country	Men & Women Under Arms	Rank	Country	Men & Women Under Arms
28	Syria	177,500	69	Singapore	30,000	112	Rwanda	4,280
29	Cambodia	177,000	70	Bolivia	27,000	113	Chad	4,200
30	Rumania	170,000	71	Tunisia	24,000	114	Mali	4,200
31	Burma	167,000	72	Somalia	23,000	115	Ivory Coast	4,100
32	Greece	161,000	73	Ecuador	22,300	116	Bhutan	4,000
33	Bulgaria	152,000	74	Uruguay	22,000	117	Qatar	2,200
34	Iraq	135,000	75	Uganda	21,000	118	Sierra Leone	2,125
35	Argentina	133,500	76	United Arab Emirates	20,550	119	Niger	2,100
36	Cuba	121,000	77	Nepal	20,000	120	Upper Volta	2,050
37	Netherlands	112,500	78	Ghana	18,600	121	Guyana	2,000
38	Hungary	105,000	79	Sweden	18,100	122	Burundi	1,950
39	Morocco	90,000	80	South Yemen	18,000			
40	Afghanistan	88,000	81	Austria	17,000		**BOTTOM 10**	
41	Belgium	87,000	82	Dominican Republic	15,800	123	Togo	1,750
42	Mexico	82,500	83	Lebanon	15,300	124	Benin	1,650
43	Jordan	80,250	84	Cyprus (2)	15,000	125	Malawi	1,600
44	Canada	77,000	85	Tanzania	14,600	126	Costa Rica (3)	1,200
45	Chile	76,000	86	Paraguay	14,400	127	Trinidad & Tobago	1,200
46	Australia	69,100	87	Oman	14,100	128	Bahrain	1,100
47	Philippines	67,200	88	Sri Lanka	13,500	129	Equatorial Guinea	1,000
48	Colombia	64,300	89	Ireland	13,000	130	Luxembourg	900
49	Algeria	63,000	90	New Zealand	12,685	131	Gabon	750
50	Malaysia	61,100	91	Guatemala	11,400	132	Sao Tome & Principe	200
51	Peru	60,000	92	Honduras	11,200			
52	Laos	52,000	93	Mauritania	10,350			
53	Saudi Arabia	52,000	94	Kuwait	10,200			
54	South Africa	50,750	95	Mozambique	10,000			
55	Sudan	48,600	96	Kenya	7,550			
56	Venezuela	44,000	97	Nicaragua	7,100			
57	Zaire	43,500	98	Haiti	6,550			
58	Switzerland	42,500	99	Senegal	6,550			
59	Ethiopia	41,000	100	Guinea-Bissau	6,000			
60	Finland	40,000	101	Zambia	5,800			
61	Albania	38,000	102	Rhodesia (Zimbabwe)	5,700			
62	Bangladesh	36,000	103	Guinea	5,650			
63	Norway	35,400	104	Cameroon	5,600			
64	Denmark	34,000	105	Congo	5,500			
65	Israel (1)	34,000	106	Liberia	5,220			
66	Libya	32,000	107	El Salvador	5,130			
			108	Panama	4,800			
	LOWER MIDDLE		109	Madagascar	4,760			
67	Yemen Arab Republic	32,000	110	Jamaica	4,600			
68	Mongolia	30,000	111	Djibouti	4,400			

Notes: (1) Excluding mobilized and semimobilized reserves.
(2) Including 5,000 Turkish troops in the Turkish Sector.
(3) Strictly a national guard. The constitution proscribes a standing army.
No figures are available for Angola and Central African Empire.
The following independent and semi-independent countries maintain no standing army: Andorra, Antigua, Bahamas, Comoros, Dominica, Faroe Islands, Barbados, Belize, Bermuda, Botswana, Solomon Islands, Brunei, Cape Verde, Fiji, Gambia, Gilbert Islands, Grenada, Guadeloupe, Iceland, Lesotho, Liechtenstein, Maldives, Malta, Mauritius, Nauru, Papua New Guinea, San Marino, Seychelles, Surinam, Swaziland, Tonga, Vatican City and Western Samoa.

Source: U.S. Central Intelligence Agency.

51. Soldier/Civilian Ratio

The size of a nation's defense force is determined by many factors, such as martial traditions, existence of hostile neighbors, extent of national territory and degree of civilian unemployment. Theoretically, in times of war every citizen should bear arms; most countries consider enlistment of all able-bodied males between certain ages as a constitutional obligation, although in practice they may not be required to so enlist; in advanced countries this requirement is being extended to women as a concession to the equal rights movement. Barring Israel, where a continuous military emergency has existed for over 30 years and whose defense forces operate at near-maximum manpower levels, there is no country today with total conscription in force. The practice is to maintain a sufficiently large reserve in case of emergency, and for many countries it is unlikely that such an emergency will ever arise.

Some countries are also experimenting with all-volunteer armies, a concept that poses many dangers, as the United States is discovering. Not the least of these dangers is the purely mercenary motivation of those who may be called upon to defend not only the country but also its political, social and economic institutions. The practice may also under-mine the very underpinnings of a modern state—the equal stake that every citizen should have in its defense and survival. In Asia, Africa and Latin America the armed forces have become power bases or virtual sixth estates bent on destroying the other five. The moral is that a large army is not only a nation's security blanket but an ever-present threat to its freedoms.

Number of Countries: 135
Midpoint: 239 civilians per one soldier
Period Covered: 1975
Type of Ranking: Population per Soldier (the Term Soldier Being Defined as Including All Members of the Armed Forces); Lowest to Highest

Highlights & Findings: Worldwide there are 186 civilians for every soldier. In developing countries the ratio is 1:248, more than twice as high as that in developed countries, 1:106. The ratio is smallest in Warsaw Pact countries (1:77) and largest in South Asia (1:533). In between, the ratios are 1:92 in the Middle East, 1:107 in North America, 1:110 in the NATO countries of Europe, 1:116 in nonaligned Europe, 1:214 in the Far East, 1:240 in Oceania, 1:325 in Latin America and 1:454 in Africa.

Region	Africa	Asia & Oceania	Europe	Western Hemisphere
Most	Libya (19)	Israel (1)	Portugal (5)	Cuba (20)
Least	Niger (135)	Bangladesh (134)	Ireland (74)	Costa Rica (120)

Rank	Country	Soldier-Civilian Ratio; Number of Inhabitants per Soldier
	TOP 10	
1	Israel	22
2	Taiwan	32
3	Jordan	33
4	North Korea	35
5	Portugal	40
6	Syria	41
7	United Arab Emirates	41
8	Mongolia	48
9	South Korea	55
10	Oman	55
	UPPER MIDDLE	
11	Greece	56
12	Bulgaria	57
13	Albania	63
14	Vietnam	64
15	Laos	65
16	Soviet Union	71
17	Czechoslovakia	74
18	Singapore	75
19	Libya	76
20	Cuba	79
21	Iraq	82
22	Turkey	88
23	Yugoslavia	93
24	South Yemen	94
25	Hungary	100
26	Qatar	100
27	United States	100
28	Kuwait	100
29	France	105
30	Cambodia	106
31	Belgium	112
32	Norway	115
33	Egypt	116
34	Poland	116
35	Sweden	117
36	East Germany	118
37	Spain	118
38	Netherlands	122

Rank	Country	Soldier-Civilian Ratio: Number of Inhabitants per Soldier
39	Rumania	124
40	West Germany	125
41	Finland	131
42	Italy	133
43	Somalia	137
44	Uruguay	139
45	Iran	140
46	Chile	145
47	Denmark	149
48	Afghanistan	153
49	Saudi Arabia	153
50	Switzerland	154
51	Cyprus	160
52	Equatorial Guinea	160
53	Malta	162
54	United Kingdom	162
55	Lebanon	177
56	Pakistan	177
57	Paraguay	183
58	Bolivia	187
59	Burma	187
60	Argentina	193
61	Austria	198
62	Malaysia	199
63	Thailand	207
64	Yemen Arab Republic	207
65	Angola	215
66	Congo	225
67	Australia	229
68	New Zealand	239
69	Tunisia	241
	LOWER MIDDLE	
70	Bahrain	243
71	Barbados	245
72	Algeria	249
73	Gabon	259
74	Ireland	259
75	Peru	276
76	China	287
77	Morocco	287

Rank	Country	Soldier-Civilian Ratio; Number of Inhabitants per Soldier
78	Honduras	288
79	Venezuela	291
80	Canada	296
81	Nigeria	303
82	Dominican Republic	306
83	Liberia	313
84	Ecuador	320
85	Nicaragua	323
86	Luxembourg	358
87	Sudan	374
88	Guyana	393
89	Colombia	403
90	Brazil	421
91	Japan	470
92	Swaziland	493
93	South Africa	510
94	Indonesia	524
95	Jamaica	527
96	Uganda	550
97	Guatemala	553
98	Central African Empire	571
99	Zaire	579
100	Fiji	580
101	Mauritania	620
102	Botswana	626
103	Philippines	628
104	Nepal	635
105	Ethiopia	642
106	India	642
107	Ghana	687
108	Mexico	722
109	Senegal	730
110	Guinea	730
111	Ivory Coast	813
112	Rhodesia (Zimbabwe)	821
113	Zambia	823
114	El Salvador	820
115	Haiti	842
116	Mozambique	906
117	Madagascar	940
118	Trinidad & Tobago	974

Rank	Country	Soldier-Civilian Ratio: Number of Inhabitants per Soldier	Rank	Country	Soldier-Civilian Ratio: Number of Inhabitants per Soldier	Rank	Country	Soldier-Civilian Ratio: Number of Inhabitants per Soldier
119	Sri Lanka	980		BOTTOM 10		132	Mali	1,407
120	Costa Rica	988	126	Rwanda	1,060	133	Kenya	1,701
121	Sierra Leone	993	127	Cameroon	1,080	134	Bangladesh	2,199
122	Benin	1,025	128	Togo	1,115	135	Niger	2,275
123	Tanzania	1,034	129	Upper Volta	1,192			
124	Lesotho	1,038	130	Malawi	1,253			
125	Chad	1,044	131	Burundi	1,348			

Source: U.S. Central Intelligence Agency.

52. Defense Expenditures

National military expenditures include current and capital expenditures on the armed forces, military assistance to foreign countries, and military components of military, space, and research and development programs. Standard definitions of military expenditures do not include expenditures on veterans' benefits, interest on war debts, civil defense and outlays for strategic stockpiling. There are also substantial social costs that are not reflected in defense budgets, such as tax exemptions extended to military properties and cheap manpower made available through conscription.

The figures relating to the Soviet Union and Warsaw Pact countries are highly speculative. The official Soviet budget of $25 billion in 1975 is obviously unreal and deliberately understated. Analysts differ widely in their estimates of actual expenditures: $61 billion, according to the Stockholm Peace Research Institute; $114 billion, according to the Central Intelligence Agency; $124 billion, according to the International Institute for Strategic Studies of London and $94 billion according to the World Military and Social Expenditures, which is adopted in this ranking. In the last estimate all identifiable items in the Soviet defense programs are priced at U.S. dollar costs and then converted into rubles on a ratio derived from an estimated average purchasing power of the ruble. Because of the uncertainties involved in such a calculation, the estimate must be viewed as highly tentative.

World military expenditures, climbing steadily since the end of World War II, have reached $1 billion a day, or close to $400 billion a year. This outlay has risen 15% above the 1970 level and 60% above the 1960 level. Public military expenditures on military R & D are approaching $30 billion a year, bringing the total since 1960 to $336 billion. One result of this explosive advance in military technology has been the manufacture, stockpiling, and sale of sophisticated arms and weaponry on an unprecedented scale. From 1970 to 1976 arms transfers from the United States, the Soviet Union, France, the United Kingdom, West Germany, Italy and China have been valued at $44.9 billion and have included over 12,000 aircraft and 30,000 missiles. Strategic nuclear stockpiles of the two superpowers have risen to 14,000 warheads, a gain of 8,000 since 1970. With a procurement budget of $80 billion, the armament industry is one of the largest and richest in the world, and its power and influence is felt on political power structures as well as on economic systems. Although military spending accounts for only 5% of global GNP, its real burden on the world economy is much greater. In many limited national budgets, military spending competes with civilian expenditures on education and health and social services. In other countries it feeds the inflationary spiral and damages prospects for long-term economic development.

There are a number of countries that do not maintain standing armies and hence do not have a defense budget. These include Iceland, Papua New Guinea, Swaziland, Lesotho, the Gambia and Botswana.

Number of Countries: 133
Midpoint: $137 million
Period Covered: 1975
Type of Ranking: Military Expenditures in Dollars; Highest to Lowest

Highlights & Findings: Of the world total of $331.6 billion, the Soviet Union and the United States account for 54%; between them they control 80% of all research on new weapons and have over 95% of the world's stock of nuclear weapons. Military expenditures have also recorded spectacular increases in developing countries; such spending increased by three times in East Asia, four times in South Asia, six times in Africa and 14 times in the Middle East. Even the poorest 20% spend 3.2% of their GNP on military programs. By regions and categories, the military spending in millions of dollars was:

Developed Countries:	262,819		Other European Countries	8,431
Developing Countries:	68,781		Middle East	25,184
North America	94,022		South Asia	3,874
Latin America	5,510		East Asia	28,805
NATO	55,248		Oceania	2,203
Warsaw Pact	102,917		Africa	5,406

Regions	Africa	Asia & Oceania	Europe	Western Hemisphere
Most	Egypt (8)	China (3)	Soviet Union (1)	United States (2)
Least	Mauritius (133)	Fiji (132)	Malta (130)	Barbados (131)

Rank	Country	Military Expenditures (million $)	Rank	Country	Military Expenditures (million $)	Rank	Country	Military Expenditures (million $)
	TOP 10		45	Venezuela	569	90	Kenya	43
1	Soviet Union	94,000	46	Bulgaria	565	91	Guatemala	40
2	United States	90,948	47	Vietnam	500	92	Afghanistan	35
3	China	18,000	48	Malaysia	457	93	Cameroon	34
4	West Germany	15,299	49	Austria	439	94	Senegal	32
5	France	13,093	50	Thailand	434	95	Madagascar	28
6	United Kingdom	11,477	51	Peru	422	96	Nicaragua	27
7	Iran	7,742	52	Philippines	404	97	Sri Lanka	27
8	Egypt	5,368	53	Finland	396	98	Laos	26
9	Italy	4,656	54	Cuba	380	99	Congo	25
10	Japan	4,640	55	Kuwait	380	100	Paraguay	25
			56	Chile	300	101	Luxembourg	23
	UPPER MIDDLE		57	Singapore	300	102	Somalia	23
11	Saudi Arabia	4,260	58	Morocco	272	103	Chad	22
12	Israel	3,517	59	Algeria	262	104	Cyprus	20
13	Canada	3,074	60	New Zealand	234	105	El Salvador	20
14	India	3,008	61	Libya	203	106	Guinea	20
15	Netherlands	2,869	62	Jordan	150	107	Jamaica	18
16	East Germany	2,644	63	Zaire	150	108	Gabon	17
17	Poland	2,384	64	Burma	141	109	Honduras	17
18	Sweden	2,344	65	Lebanon	140	110	Bahrain	14
19	Spain	2,200	66	Albania	137	111	Upper Volta	12
20	Turkey	1,971	67	Colombia	137	112	Mali	11
21	Australia	1,968				113	Mauritania	11
22	Czechoslovakia	1,904		*LOWER MIDDLE*		114	Guyana	10
23	Belgium	1,888	68	Sudan	123	115	Haiti	10
24	Nigeria	1,875	69	Ireland	111	116	Burundi	9
25	Brazil	1,872	70	Rhodesia (Zimbabwe)	101	117	Nepal	9
26	Iraq	1,854	71	Angola	100	118	Togo	9
27	Yugoslavia	1,711	72	Qatar	100	119	Central African Empire	8
28	South Africa	1,441	73	Mongolia	90	120	Rwanda	8
29	Greece	1,361	74	Zambia	90	121	Benin	7
30	Indonesia	1,104	75	Ethiopia	89	122	Costa Rica	7
31	Switzerland	1,091	76	Uganda	85	123	Trinidad & Tobago	6
32	Taiwan	988	77	Uruguay	85			
33	South Korea	961	78	Tanzania	84		*BOTTOM 10*	
34	Denmark	919	79	Ecuador	77	124	Equatorial Guinea	5
35	Norway	916	80	United Arab Emirates	75	125	Liberia	5
36	Rumania	806	81	Tunisia	68	126	Malawi	5
37	Argentina	800	82	Bangladesh	67	127	Sierra Leone	5
38	Portugal	776	83	Ghana	61	128	Niger	4
39	Syria	760	84	Cambodia	60	129	Panama	4
40	Pakistan	728	85	Bolivia	58	130	Malta	2
41	North Korea	700	86	Ivory Coast	58	131	Barbados	1
42	Oman	698	87	Yemen Arab Republic	56	132	Fiji	1
43	Hungary	614	88	South Yemen	50	133	Mauritius	1
44	Mexico	581	89	Dominican Republic	46			

Source: *World Military & Social Expenditures.*

53. Defense Expenditures as Percentage of GNP

In terms of global gross product, military expenditures not only constitute a relatively small element but have actually decreased from 7.06% in 1960 to 5.21% in 1976. Although this might seem to belie reports of an escalating arms race, the decrease is restricted to the heavily industrialized nations (which are overmilitarized in any case), and defense expenditures as percentage of GNP have increased 300% from 1.78% to 5.38% during the same period for developing countries. The implications of military growth are therefore most damaging for countries in their early stages of development and may permanently inhibit their economic potential. Because of their ripple effects, the long-term adverse consequences of large military expenditures may exert a significant impact not only on the economy but also on the political structure, environment, education and infrastructure. The military competes with the civilian sector for scarce scientific and management talents, raw materials and transportation facilities. Ultimately military expenditures intensify existing economic problems, while diluting the efforts to solve them.

Number of Countries: 133
Midpoint: 2.63%
Period Covered: 1975
Type of Ranking: Defense Expenditures as Percentage of GNP; Highest to Lowest

Highlights & Findings: The highest level of military expenditures—to no one's surprise—is found in the Middle East (15.26%); above-average expenditures are also reported in Warsaw Pact countries (9.5%) and in North America (5.63%). There are four regions with middle-level expenditures: NATO Europe (3.83%); Africa (3.48%); South Asia (3.47%); and the Far East (3.18%). The lowest levels of military preparedness are found in Europe outside of the Warsaw Pact and NATO countries (2.54%), Oceania (2.41%) and Latin America (1.68%).

Differences in military spending may best be illustrated by comparing the expenditures of traditional enemies or hostile neighbors. For example: Israel 27.6% vs. Syria 12.8%; Iraq 14.4%, Saudi Arabia 12.8% and Jordan 12.3%; Somalia 6.6% vs. Ethiopia 3.3%; Pakistan 6.5% vs. India 3.%; Greece 6.3% vs. Turkey 5.4%; Soviet Union 11.9% vs. United States 5.9%; North Korea 10.3% vs. South Korea 5.0%; Tanzania 3.3% vs. Uganda 3.2%.

In most of these cases the poorer nation is forced to spend more of its GNP on the military in order to sustain a credible defense posture.

Region	Africa	Asia & Oceania	Europe	Western Hemisphere
Most	Egypt (1)	Oman (2)	Soviet Union (10)	United States (23)
Least	Mauritius (130)	Fiji (132)	Malta (127)	Barbados (133)

Rank	Country	Defense Expenditures as Percentage of GNP	Rank	Country	Defense Expenditures as Percentage of GNP	Rank	Country	Defense Expenditures as Percentage of GNP
	TOP 10		20	Pakistan	6.50	42	France	3.87
1	Egypt	44.29	21	Greece	6.33	43	Zambia	3.82
2	Oman	39.41	22	China	6.29	44	Chile	3.70
3	Israel	27.69	23	United States	5.99	45	West Germany	3.60
4	Iran	14.19	24	Qatar	5.95	46	Czechoslovakia	3.55
5	Iraq	14.04	25	Turkey	5.40	47	Netherlands	3.54
6	Saudi Arabia	12.83	26	Singapore	5.37	48	India	3.49
7	Syria	12.82	27	Cuba	5.11	49	Congo	3.41
8	South Yemen	12.19	28	Yugoslavia	5.09	50	Sweden	3.38
9	Jordan	12.13	29	Malaysia	5.05	51	Ethiopia	3.37
10	Soviet Union	11.94	30	South Korea	5.03	52	Tanzania	3.35
			31	United Kingdom	5.02	53	Uganda	3.29
	UPPER MIDDLE		32	Portugal	5.01	54	Norway	3.26
11	Albania	11.22	33	Equatorial Guinea	4.90	55	Morocco	3.24
12	North Korea	10.30	34	Chad	4.36	56	Bulgaria	3.06
13	Cambodia	10.00	35	Burma	4.35	57	Thailand	3.03
14	Mongolia	9.00	36	South Africa	4.27	58	Belgium	3.01
15	Laos	8.66	37	Zaire	4.17	59	Peru	3.00
16	Nigeria	7.38	38	East Germany	4.01	60	Rhodesia (Zimbabwe)	2.97
17	Vietnam	7.04	39	Indonesia	4.01	61	Bolivia	2.90
18	Taiwan	6.82	40	Yemen Arab Republic	4.00	62	Angola	2.88
19	Somalia	6.64	41	Lebanon	3.88	63	Sudan	2.86

Rank	Country	Defense Expenditures as Percentage of GNP	Rank	Country	Defense Expenditures as Percentage of GNP	Rank	Country	Defense Expenditures as Percentage of GNP
64	Italy	2.79	87	Algeria	1.89	112	Guatemala	1.13
65	Hungary	2.70	88	Nicaragua	1.82	113	El Salvador	1.11
66	Poland	2.69	89	New Zealand	1.77	114	United Arab Emirates	1.09
67	Guinea	2.63	90	Brazil	1.73	115	Luxembourg	1.07
			91	Paraguay	1.73	116	Colombia	0.97
	LOWER MIDDLE		92	Upper Volta	1.73	117	Japan	0.94
68	Australia	2.58	93	Rumania	1.72	118	Bangladesh	0.90
69	Denmark	2.58	94	Afghanistan	1.69	119	Sri Lanka	0.80
70	Philippines	2.58	95	Benin	1.65	120	Sierra Leone	0.77
71	Kuwait	2.54	96	Libya	1.65	121	Liberia	0.75
72	Cyprus	2.49	97	Honduras	1.64	122	Mexico	0.75
73	Mauritania	2.47	98	Senegal	1.59	123	Malawi	0.74
74	Bahrain	2.43	99	Ivory Coast	1.58			
75	Uruguay	2.42	100	Tunisia	1.57		*BOTTOM 10*	
76	Spain	2.23	101	Togo	1.53			
77	Venezuela	2.17	102	Finland	1.51	124	Nepal	0.66
78	Burundi	2.14	103	Madagascar	1.51	125	Jamaica	0.64
79	Guyana	2.06	104	Cameroon	1.50	126	Niger	0.62
80	Canada	2.02	105	Ireland	1.41	127	Malta	0.41
81	Argentina	2.00	106	Kenya	1.39	128	Costa Rica	0.37
82	Switzerland	1.94	107	Dominican Republic	1.30	129	Trinidad & Tobago	0.26
83	Rwanda	1.92	108	Gabon	1.17	130	Mauritius	0.18
84	Ecuador	1.91	109	Ghana	1.16	131	Panama	0.18
85	Mali	1.91	110	Austria	1.15	132	Fiji	0.15
86	Central African Empire	1.90	111	Haiti	1.14	133	Barbados	0.002

Source: *World Military & Social Expenditures.*

54. Defense Expenditures per Capita

Defense expenditures per capita reveal the burden of military spending in relation to a nation's human resources. This ranking confirms the conclusion that the average family the world over pays more in taxes to support the arms race than to educate its children or to fight diseases.

Number of Countries: 133
Midpoint: $17
Period Covered: 1975
Type of Ranking: Defense Expenditures per Capita in Dollars; Highest to Lowest

Highlights & Findings: Per capita defense expenditures worldwide are estimated at $81. Developed nations spend $258 on national security per capita and developing nations $23. The highest per capita expenditures are reported by North America with $398 and Warsaw Pact countries with $285. Because of the Arab-Israeli conflict the figure for the Middle East is a high $213. The next highest group consists of the NATO countries, with $174 taken together. Following in a descending order are: Oceania with $111, non-NATO Western and Southern European countries with $94, East Asia with $20, Latin America with $17, Africa with $15 and South Asia with $5.

Regions	Africa	Asia & Oceania	Europe	Western Hemisphere
Most	Egypt (22)	Israel (1)	Soviet Union (7)	United States (5)
Least	Niger (133)	Nepal (132)	Malta (98)	Panama (124)

Rank	Country	Defense Expenditures per Capita ($)	Rank	Country	Defense Expenditures per Capita ($)	Rank	Country	Defense Expenditures per Capita ($)
	TOP 10		5	United States	426	10	West Germany	247
1	Israel	1,018	6	Kuwait	378			
2	Oman	911	7	Soviet Union	370		*UPPER MIDDLE*	
3	Saudi Arabia	593	8	Sweden	286	11	Norway	228
4	Qatar	500	9	France	249	12	Iran	221

Rank Country	Defense Expenditures per Capita ($)	Rank Country	Defense Expenditures per Capita ($)	Rank Country	Defense Expenditures per Capita ($)
13 Netherlands	210	55 Gabon	33	95 Sudan	7
14 United Kingdom	205	56 Argentina	31	96 Uganda	7
15 Belgium	193	57 Cyprus	31	97 Ghana	6
16 Denmark	181	58 Nigeria	30	98 Malta	6
17 Iraq	168	59 South Yemen	30	99 Trinidad & Tobago	6
18 Switzerland	168	60 Chile	28	100 Zaire	6
19 East Germany	157	61 South Korea	28	101 Burma	5
20 Greece	151	62 Uruguay	28	102 Cameroon	5
21 Australia	146	63 Peru	27	103 Central African Empire	5
22 Egypt	144	64 China	19	104 Chad	5
23 Canada	135	65 Congo	19	105 Colombia	5
24 Singapore	133	66 Zambia	18	106 El Salvador	5
25 Czechoslovakia	129			107 Guinea	5
26 United Arab Emirates	115	**LOWER MIDDLE**		108 Honduras	5
27 Syria	103	67 Algeria	17	109 India	5
28 Portugal	88	68 Brazil	17	110 Tanzania	5
29 Finland	84	69 Equatorial Guinea	16	111 Barbados	4
30 Italy	83	70 Morocco	16	112 Costa Rica	4
31 Libya	83	71 Angola	15	113 Madagascar	4
32 Yugoslavia	80	72 Rhodesia (Zimbabwe)	15	114 Togo	4
33 New Zealand	75	73 Guyana	13	115 Afghanistan	3
34 Poland	70	74 Ivory Coast	12	116 Ethiopia	3
35 Bulgaria	65	75 Nicaragua	12	117 Kenya	3
36 Luxembourg	64	76 Tunisia	12	118 Liberia	3
37 Mongolia	62	77 Bolivia	11		
38 Spain	62	78 Ecuador	11	**BOTTOM 15**	
39 Taiwan	61	79 Pakistan	11	119 Benin	2
40 Austria	59	80 Vietnam	11	120 Burundi	2
41 Bahrain	58	81 Mexico	10	121 Fiji	2
42 Hungary	58	82 Paraguay	10	122 Haiti	2
43 Albania	57	83 Philippines	10	123 Mali	2
44 Jordan	57	84 Thailand	10	124 Panama	2
45 South Africa	57	85 Dominican Republic	9	125 Rwanda	2
46 Lebanon	53	86 Jamaica	9	126 Sierra Leone	2
47 Turkey	49	87 Mauritania	9	127 Sri Lanka	2
48 Venezuela	44	88 Indonesia	8	128 Upper Volta	2
49 Japan	42	89 Laos	8	129 Bangladesh	1
50 North Korea	42	90 Yemen Arab Republic	8	130 Malawi	1
51 Cuba	41	91 Cambodia	7	131 Mauritius	1
52 Malaysia	38	92 Guatemala	7	132 Nepal	1
53 Rumania	38	93 Senegal	7	133 Niger	1
54 Ireland	36	94 Somalia	7		

Source: *World Military & Social Expenditures.*

55. Defense Expenditures per Soldier

Because of the importance of defense spending in assessing a nation's military preparedness and its impact on the economy as a whole, it is necessary to use a number of indicators, each gauging the military budget from a different perspective. One not so commonly used is defense expenditures per soldier. (The term soldier is used to cover all members of the armed forces, male and female). In other words, how much does it cost to place one soldier in the field fully equipped and trained? Although combatworthiness and financial capability are not directly related, there is enough correlation between them to make this indicator an important consideration. Future wars may become prohibitively costly, and they may eventually be won not by the military generals but by the auditor generals. To paraphrase an old saying, God is on the side of not only the big battalions but also the big budgets.

Number of Countries: 131
Midpoint: $4,500
Period Covered: 1976
Type of Ranking: Defense Expenditures per Soldier in U.S. Dollars; Highest to Lowest

Highlights & Findings: The average defense expenditure per soldier worldwide is $15,174, but it is $27,520 in developed countries and only $5,591 in developing countries. To break it down by other categories, it is $42,602 in North America, $5,561 in Latin America, $19,297 in NATO countries, $22,185 in Warsaw Pact countries, $10,949 in other European countries, $19,675 in the Middle East, $2,572 in South Asia, $4,281 in East Asia, $26,542 in Oceania and $6,751 in Africa.

Regions	Africa	Asia & Oceania	Europe	Western Hemisphere
Most	Egypt (25)	Saudi Arabia (1)	Sweden (7)	United States (4)
Least	Somalia (125)	Afghanistan (131)	Malta (124)	Barbados (121)

Rank	Country	Defense Expenditures per Soldier ($)	Rank	Country	Defense Expenditures per Soldier ($)	Rank	Country	Defense Expenditures per Soldier ($)
	TOP 10		44	Yugoslavia	7,439	88	Guinea	3,333
1	Saudi Arabia	90,638	45	Brazil	7,370	89	Cuba	3,248
2	Qatar	50,000	46	Lebanon	7,333	90	India	3,146
3	Oman	49,857	47	Spain	7,285	91	Burundi	3,000
4	United States	42,699	48	Mexico	7,085	92	Mongolia	3,000
5	Canada	39,922	49	Libya	6,344	93	Dominican Republic	2,875
6	Kuwait	38,000	50	Philippines	6,030	94	Tunisia	2,833
7	Sweden	33,486	51	Trinidad & Tobago	6,000	95	South Yemen	2,778
8	United Kingdom	33,267	52	Argentina	5,970	96	Mali	2,750
9	Iran	30,968	53	Hungary	5,848	97	Central African Empire	2,667
10	West Germany	30,907	54	Cameroon	5,667	98	Sudan	2,510
			55	Tanzania	5,600	99	Equatorial Guinea	2,500
	UPPER MIDDLE		56	Chad	5,550	100	Upper Volta	2,400
11	South Africa	28,820	57	China	5,538	101	Benin	2,333
12	Australia	28,522	58	Mauritania	5,500	102	Bolivia	2,148
13	Denmark	27,029	59	Kenya	5,375	103	Thailand	2,127
14	Soviet Union	26,294	60	Senegal	5,333	104	Colombia	2,078
15	Norway	26,171	61	Cyprus	5,000	105	Taiwan	2,000
16	France	26,082	62	Guyana	5,000	106	Niger	2,000
17	Switzerland	25,976	63	Rumania	4,713	107	Rwanda	2,000
18	Netherlands	25,616	64	United Arab Emirates	4,688	108	Ethiopia	1,978
19	Luxembourg	23,000	65	Jamaica	4,500	109	Sri Lanka	1,929
20	Israel	22,545	66	Togo	4,500	110	Jordan	1,875
21	Belguim	21,701				111	Bangladesh	1,861
22	Japan	19,661		*LOWER MIDDLE*		112	Pakistan	1,857
23	East Germany	18,490	67	Morocco	4,459	113	Paraguay	1,786
24	New Zealand	18,000	68	Turkey	4,351	114	Yemen Arab Republic	1,750
25	Egypt	16,671	69	Syria	4,270	115	Haiti	1,667
26	Zambia	15,000	70	Congo	4,167	116	Sierra Leone	1,667
27	Bahrain	14,000	71	Algeria	4,159	117	Honduras	1,545
28	Iraq	13,733	72	Indonesia	4,150	118	South Korea	1,538
29	Venezuela	12,932	73	Chile	4,110	119	North Korea	1,499
30	Rhodesia (Zimbabwe)	12,625	74	Ghana	4,067	120	Malawi	1,250
31	Austria	11,553	75	Uganda	4,048			
32	Italy	11,059	76	El Salvador	4,000		*BOTTOM 11*	
33	Finland	11,000	77	Uruguay	3,864	121	Barbados	1,000
34	Singapore	10,000	78	Nicaragua	3,857	122	Fiji	1,000
35	Ivory Coast	9,667	79	Bulgaria	3,717	123	Liberia	1,000
36	Czechoslovakia	9,520	80	Guatemala	3,636	124	Malta	1,000
37	Ireland	9,250	81	Albania	3,605	125	Somalia	1,000
38	Nigeria	9,014	82	Ecuador	3,591	126	Burma	844
39	Gabon	8,500	83	Portugal	3,576	127	Cambodia	750
40	Greece	8,453	84	Costa Rica	3,500	128	Vietnam	714
41	Poland	8,137	85	Madagascar	3,500	129	Laos	500
42	Peru	7,536	86	Zaire	3,488	130	Nepal	450
43	Malaysia	7,492	87	Angola	3,333	131	Afghanistan	398

Source: *World Military & Social Expenditures.*

56. U.S. Military Aid

From the end of World War II to the end of 1977, military aid to allies has been a bulwark of the foreign policy of the United States. During this period such aid totaled $75.727 billion, distributed as follows:

Near East and South Asia	$16.403 billion
Latin America	$ 1.782 billion
East Asia	$35.442 billion
Africa	$ 752 million
Europe	$15.686 billion
Canada	$ 13 million
Inter-regional	$ 5.647 billion

The figures represent primarily grants of military equipment, supplies and services, including military education and training. They include direct cash and credit sales of military equipment under the Military Assistance Program (MAP), Foreign Military Sales Act (FMS) and Foreign Assistance Act (FAA), defense articles and services transferred to foreign countries under Military Assistance Service-Funded Grants and transfers from excess stocks of military equipment and supplies granted to countries without charge. In 1977, 48 countries were receiving MAP grants and 27 countries Foreign Military Credit Sales.

Number of Countries: 84
Midpoint: $84.7 million
Period Covered: 1946 Through 1977
Type of Ranking: Total U.S. Military Aid 1946 Through 1977; Highest to Lowest

Highlights & Findings: Three countries account for nearly 40% of U.S. military aid during the period covered: South Vietnam, South Korea and Israel. This concentration of aid reflects the degree of U.S. involvement in the defense of these countries. Five other countries in the top 10 are allies in NATO; aid extended to them is part of U.S. commitments to the defense of Western Europe.

Regions	Africa	Asia & Oceania	Europe	Western Hemisphere
Most	Ethiopia (29)	South Vietnam (1)	France (5)	Brazil (26)
Least	Upper Volta (84)	Syria (83)	Finland (79)	Jamaica (72)

Rank	Country	U.S. Military Aid ($ million)	Rank	Country	U.S. Military Aid ($ million)	Rank	Country	U.S. Military Aid ($ million)
	TOP 10		28	Indonesia	307.3	57	Liberia	14.1
1	South Vietnam	16,424.1	29	Ethiopia	285.3	58	Panama	13.1
2	South Korea	6,933.7	30	Peru	197.0	59	Canada	13.0
3	Israel	6,102.0	31	Argentina	190.3	60	Singapore	11.4
4	Turkey	4,756.7	32	Chile	172.7	61	Senegal	10.9
5	France	4,468.2	33	Colombia	159.5	62	Mexico	9.9
6	China, Nationalist & Taiwan	4,101.2	34	Morocco	136.3	63	Costa Rica	7.0
7	Greece	3,023.5	35	India	127.2	64	Afghanistan	5.4
8	Italy	2,535.0	36	Zaire	118.5	65	Haiti	4.9
9	Laos	1,606.8	37	Tunisia	106.0	66	Gabon	4.0
10	Thailand	1,557.4	38	Austria	105.3	67	Mali	3.5
			39	Ecuador	94.5	68	Sri Lanka	3.2
	UPPER MIDDLE		40	Bolivia	92.6	69	New Zealand	2.8
11	Netherlands	1,282.5	41	Burma	88.7	70	Nepal	2.0
12	Cambodia	1,281.6	42	Uruguay	84.7	71	Nigeria	1.5
13	Belgium-Luxembourg	1,267.2				72	Jamaica	1.1
14	Japan	1,204.9		*LOWER MIDDLE*		73	Sudan	1.1
15	United Kingdom	1,107.5	43	Malaysia	78.6	74	Guinea	1.0
16	Spain	1,055.6	44	Kenya	50.7			
17	Norway	943.8	45	Iraq	50.0		*BOTTOM 10*	
18	West Germany	939.3	46	Lebanon	49.0	75	Ghana	0.6
19	Iran	896.2	47	Saudi Arabia	41.6	76	Malta	0.5
20	Philippines	866.6	48	Dominican Republic	41.0	77	Yemen Arab Republic	0.5
21	Indochina (undistributed)	731.5	49	Venezuela	36.1	78	Cameroon	0.3
	(represents regional aid programs)		50	Guatemala	34.4	79	Finland	0.2
22	Yugoslavia	721.4	51	Nicaragua	30.6	80	Ivory Coast	0.2
23	Pakistan	704.7	52	Paraguay	30.0	81	Benin	0.1
24	Denmark	640.0	53	Honduras	22.7	82	Niger	0.1
25	Jordan	621.3	54	Libya	17.6	83	Syria	0.1
26	Brazil	511.8	55	Cuba	16.1	84	Upper Volta	0.1
27	Portugal	398.1	56	El Salvador	15.1			

Source: U.S. Agency for International Development.

ECONOMY

Rankings in this section deal with economic performance—not resources. Here—unlike in politics—the statistician is at home, and there is such a wealth of data that it becomes positively embarrassing. But considering the many levels of economic activity, the abundance of data is more apparent than real. GNP (gross national product) for example is perhaps the world's best known and widely used economic indicator; it is also the most overrated. Although presented in three rankings below (total, per capita and annual growth rate), it fails to reflect the disparities in income within a nation. Its usefulness is further vitiated by the need to convert national currencies into dollars—a conversion that may actually serve to introduce new distortions into the calculation.

Centrally planned economies do not use GNP as a statistical indicator but have an equivalent called the net material product (NMP) which, because it is based on different factors, can be converted only approximately into GNP. Economists often supplement the GNP with another indicator called the GDP (gross domestic product); the GDP is not included in this section because it is too specialized and might easily confuse the layman. What is required is a composite indicator that will measure total and per capita national wealth and at the same time

factor in data on income distribution and use weighted scores for the stage of economic development that each country has reached. In the absence of such an indicator, four more rankings have been added to supplement the GNP: one on income received by the top 5%, one on income received by the bottom 10%, one on percentage of population subsisting on absolute poverty levels and a recently published index devised by three University of Pennsylvania economists that measures the real wealth of nations with the United States as 100. There are five price indices: two consumer price indices, the wholesale price index and two special indices. Other themes dealt with in this chapter's rankings are the inflation rate, consumption, and revenues and expenditures.

These rankings may not answer the question—and there is no attempt to do so—of whether free-market or centrally planned economies are superior. The question is purely academic because all countries in our opinion have a mixed economy. No country today has a pure capitalist or pure communist economic system. Many areas of U.S. economy, for example, are closely regulated by the state, and there are clearly discernible elements of capitalism in the Soviet economy.

57. Gross National Product

The most frequently employed measure of the production and total wealth and resources of a country is the gross national product. The GNP is the measure of total domestic and foreign output claimed by residents of a country. The gross domestic product measures the total final output of a country's economy—that is, all goods produced and services rendered within its territory by residents and nonresidents—without regard to its allocation among domestic and foreign claims. GDP and GNP are commonly valued either at factor cost or at market prices. At factor cost they comprise compensa-

tion of employees, operating surplus and provision for the consumption of fixed capital. At market prices they include indirect taxes less subsidies to producers. The difference between GNP and GDP consists in the addition or substraction of the value of return on foreign investment. GDP equals GNP plus income earned in the country but sent abroad minus income earned abroad but sent into the country. GDP thus tends to exceed GNP in debtor countries with the reverse true in creditor countries.

GNP does not reflect income disparities in a country and is frequently unreliable when employed as a measure of comfort or well-being Variations in accuracy are related to the extent of income disparities, which exist not merely in developing countries, as is commonly supposed, but also in developed countries.

Number of Countries: 145
Midpoint: $ 3.75 billion
Period Covered: 1976
Type of Ranking: GNP in U.S. Dollars; Highest to Lowest

Highlights & Findings: What emerges from a quick examination of the GNP data is that most of the world's economic activity takes place in a relatively small number of countries. The total value of economic goods and services in the whole world (in 1975 dollars) was about $6 trillion. Of this the United States alone produced and consumed about one-fourth, and its GNP is rapidly approaching $2 trillion. The Soviet economy has been producing for a number of years about one-half of the GNP of the United States. The two superpowers thus account for nearly 40% of the world's GNP. If we add Japan and West Germany, the share of the four nations is over one-half. France, the United Kingdom, Italy, Canada and China produce another $1 trillion and the collective share of these nine nations is two-thirds. The top 46 nations account for 90% of the GNP, leaving the other 10% to be shared by 142 nations.

No Black African country appears among the top 40. Despite a low per capita income, both India and China appear among the top 20 by virtue of their sheer size of population. More than half of the top 20 countries are in Europe. If *Fortune's* list of the top 1,000 corporations in the world were to be superimposed on this list, number one General Motors will rank around 23rd.

Region	Africa	Asia & Oceania	Europe	Western Hemisphere
Most	Nigeria (34)	Japan (3)	Soviet Union (2)	United States (1)
Least	Sao Tome & Principe (145)	Western Samoa (144)	Cyprus (109)	Grenada (143)

Rank	Country	Aggregate (million $) (Market Prices, 1976)	Rank	Country	Aggregate (million $) (Market Prices, 1976)	Rank	Country	Aggregate (million $) (Market Prices, 1976)
	TOP 10		39	Bulgaria	20,270	79	Uganda	2,820
1	United States	1,698,060	40	Philippines	17,810	80	Sri Lanka	2,750
2	Soviet Union	708,170	41	Taiwan	17,500	81	Tanzania	2,700
3	Japan	553,140	42	Kuwait	16,480	82	Trinidad & Tobago	2,450
4	West Germany	457,540	43	Portugal	16,480	83	Qatar	2,390
5	France	346,730	44	Thailand	16,230	84	Luxembourg	2,330
6	China	343,090	45	Algeria	16,060	85	Afghanistan	2,300
7	United Kingdom	225,150	46	Libya	16,000	86	Bolivia	2,280
8	Canada	174,120	47	Iraq	15,940	87	Panama	2,260
9	Italy	171,250	48	Colombia	15,400	88	Cameroon	2,240
10	Brazil	125,570	49	Israel	13,980	89	Jamaica	2,230
			50	New Zealand	13,120	90	Zambia	2,200
	UPPER MIDDLE		51	Peru	12,610	91	Oman	2,130
11	Spain	104,090	52	Pakistan	12,190	92	Costa Rica	2,090
12	Poland	98,130	53	Chile	10,980	93	El Salvador	2,030
13	India	95,880	54	Malaysia	10,900	94	Senegal	1,980
14	Netherlands	85,320	55	Egypt	10,530	95	Madagascar	1,870
15	Australia	83,380	56	United Arab Emirates	9,710	96	Angola	1,830
16	Sweden	71,290	57	Hong Kong	9,410	97	Nicaragua	1,760
17	East Germany	70,880	58	Morocco	9,220	98	Jordan	1,710
18	Mexico	67,640	59	Bangladesh	8,470	99	Paraguay	1,680
19	Belgium	66,660	60	Cuba	8,120	100	Mozambique	1,600
20	Iran	66,250	61	Ireland	8,090	101	Yemen Arab Republic	1,540
21	Czechoslovakia	57,250	62	Puerto Rico	7,670	102	Nepal	1,490
22	Switzerland	56,900	63	North Korea	7,610	103	Gabon	1,410
23	Turkey	40,960	64	Singapore	6,150	104	Papua New Guinea	1,400
24	Austria	40,080	65	Syria	5,970	105	Iceland	1,380
25	Argentina	39,920	66	Ghana	5,920	106	Albania	1,330
26	Saudi Arabia	38,510	67	Tunisia	4,790	107	Mongolia	1,280
27	Denmark	37,770	68	Ecuador	4,690	108	Honduras	1,160
28	Yugoslavia	36,170	69	Sudan	4,610	109	Cyprus	930
29	South Africa	34,850	70	Ivory Coast	4,280	110	Haiti	930
30	Indonesia	32,440	71	Guatemala	4,070	111	Guinea	880
31	Venezuela	31,750	72	Uruguay	3,900	112	Niger	740
32	Rumania	31,070	73	Dominican Republic	3,750	113	Liberia	720
33	Norway	29,920	74	Burma	3,730	114	Upper Volta	710
34	Nigeria	29,320	75	Rhodesia (Zimbabwe)	3,560	115	Bahamas	700
35	Finland	26,570	76	Zaire	3,510	116	Congo	700
36	Hungary	24,140	77	Kenya	3,280	117	Malawi	700
37	South Korea	24,050		*LOWER MIDDLE*		118	Fiji	670
38	Greece	23,600	78	Ethiopia	2,960	119	Bahrain	660

Rank	Country	Aggregate (million $) (Market Prices, 1976)
120	Sierra Leone	610
121	Mauritius	600
122	Togo	600
123	Mali	590
124	Chad	510
125	Rwanda	480
126	South Yemen	480
127	Burundi	460
128	Mauritania	460
129	Benin	430

Rank	Country	Aggregate (million $) (Market Prices, 1976)
130	Guyana	430
131	Central African Empire	420
132	Barbados	380
133	Somalia	370
134	Laos	310
135	Botswana	280
	BOTTOM 10	
136	Swaziland	240

Rank	Country	Aggregate (million $) (Market Prices, 1976)
137	Lesotho	210
138	Equatorial Guinea	110
139	Gambia	100
140	Bhutan	90
141	Guinea-Bissau	70
142	Comoros	60
143	Grenada	50
144	Western Samoa	50
145	Sao Tome & Principe	40

Source: World Bank.

58. GNP per Capita

The inadequacies of GNP as an economic indicator are pointed out in the introduction to GNP ranking. It has been humorously suggested that what is wrong with GNP is that it is gross. As a derived indicator, per capita GNP suffers from all these inadequacies; in addition, it has deficiencies of its own. It fails to reflect the distributional inequalities of income and it is easily affected by differences in population estimates. However, despite all these shortcomings it is still the best known and most widely used indicator in the world. Furthermore, in dealing with macroeconomics it is questionable whether any indicator can ever be devised that does not have some kind of bias. In fact, in the context in which per capita GNP is generally used, the trends and patterns are more important than details and this indicator can reveal them more satisfactorily than any other known indicator.

Number of Countries: 145
Midpoint: $670
Period Covered: 1976
Type of Ranking: GNP per Capita in Dollars; Highest to Lowest

Highlights & Findings: Of the bottom 20 nations, 13 are African. Of the top 10 nations, three are oil exporters and five are European. It is significant that the top 20 countries are all free-market economies, and the first country with a centrally planned economy is only 23rd.

Region	Africa	Asia & Oceania	Europe	Western Hemisphere
Most	Libya (14)	Kuwait (1)	Switzerland (4)	United States (6)
Least	Mali (143)	Bhutan (145)	Albania (82)	Haiti (116)

Rank	Country	GNP per Capita ($)
	TOP 10	
1	Kuwait	15,480
2	United Arab Emirates	13,990
3	Qatar	11,400
4	Switzerland	8,880
5	Sweden	8,670
6	United States	7,890
7	Canada	7,510
8	Denmark	7,450
9	Norway	7,420
10	West Germany	7,380
	UPPER MIDDLE	
11	Belgium	6,780

Rank	Country	GNP per Capita ($)
12	France	6,550
13	Luxembourg	6,460
14	Libya	6,310
15	Netherlands	6,200
16	Australia	6,100
17	Iceland	6,100
18	Finland	5,620
19	Austria	5,330
20	Japan	4,910
21	Saudi Arabia	4,480
22	New Zealand	4,250
23	East Germany	4,220
24	United Kingdom	4,020
25	Israel	3,920

Rank	Country	GNP per Capita ($)
26	Czechoslovakia	3,840
27	Bahamas	3,310
28	Italy	3,050
29	Spain	2,920
30	Poland	2,860
31	Soviet Union	2,760
32	Singapore	2,700
33	Oman	2,680
34	Gabon	2,590
35	Greece	2,590
36	Venezuela	2,570
37	Ireland	2,560
38	Puerto Rico	2,430
39	Bahrain	2,410

Rank	Country	GNP per Capita ($)	Rank	Country	GNP per Capita ($)	Rank	Country	GNP per Capita ($)
40	Bulgaria	2,310	77	Guatemala	630	112	Indonesia	240
41	Hungary	2,280	78	Ivory Coast	610	113	Kenya	240
42	Trinidad & Tobago	2,240	79	Jordan	610	114	Uganda	240
43	Hong Kong	2,110	80	Ghana	580	115	Central African Empire	230
44	Iran	1,930	81	Rhodesia (Zimbabwe)	550	116	Haiti	200
45	Portugal	1,690	82	Albania	540	117	Madagascar	200
46	Yugoslavia	1,680	83	Guyana	540	118	Sierra Leone	200
47	Argentina	1,550	84	Morocco	540	119	Sri Lanka	200
48	Barbados	1,550	85	Congo	520	120	Comoros	180
49	Cyprus	1,480				121	Gambia	180
50	Rumania	1,450		**LOWER MIDDLE**		122	Tanzania	180
51	Iraq	1,390	86	El Salvador	490	123	Lesotho	170
52	Uruguay	1,390	87	Papua New Guinea	490	124	Mozambique	170
53	South Africa	1,340	88	Sao Tome & Principe	490	125	Pakistan	170
54	Panama	1,310	89	North Korea	470	126	Afghanistan	160
55	Fiji	1,150	90	Swaziland	470	127	Niger	160
56	Brazil	1,140	91	Liberia	450	128	Guinea	150
57	Mexico	1,090	92	Zambia	440	129	India	150
58	Taiwan	1,070	93	Grenada	420	130	Guinea-Bissau	140
59	Jamaica	1,070	94	Botswana	410	131	Malawi	140
60	Chile	1,050	95	China	410	132	Zaire	140
61	Costa Rica	1,040	96	Philippines	410	133	Benin	130
62	Algeria	990	97	Bolivia	390			
63	Turkey	990	98	Honduras	390		**BOTTOM 12**	
64	Cuba	860	99	Senegal	390	134	Burma	120
65	Malaysia	860	100	Nigeria	380	135	Burundi	120
66	Mongolia	860	101	Thailand	380	136	Chad	120
67	Tunisia	840	102	Western Samoa	350	137	Nepal	120
68	Peru	800	103	Mauritania	340	138	Bangladesh	110
69	Dominican Republic	780	104	Angola	330	139	Rwanda	110
70	Syria	780	105	Equatorial Guinea	330	140	Somalia	110
71	Nicaragua	750	106	Cameroon	290	141	Upper Volta	110
72	Mauritius	680	107	Sudan	290	142	Ethiopia	100
73	South Korea	670	108	Egypt	280	143	Mali	100
74	Ecuador	640	109	South Yemen	280	144	Laos	90
75	Paraguay	640	110	Togo	260	145	Bhutan	70
76	Colombia	630	111	Yemen Arab Republic	250			

Source: World Bank.

59. Per Capita GNP Annual Growth Rate

The principal indicator of economic change is the annual growth rate of per capita GNP. The pace of growth in GNP per capita must be positive if a nation is not to suffer a decrease in its absolute level of income. Unfortunately, GNP per capita growth rates do not reflect inequalities inherent in the economy, particularly inequalities among sectors and among income groups. In some cases growth in absolute or per capita terms may accentuate and even perpetuate these inequalities. If wealth is concentrated in the hands of a small minority, a higher average income reflects only the greater welfare of this small minority. What is important, therefore, is balanced growth, although no indicator has yet been devised to measure such a balanced growth.

Number of Countries: 122
Midpoint: 2.4%
Period Covered: 1970-75
Type of Ranking: Annual Growth Rates of per Capita Income, 1970-75; Highest to Lowest

Highlights & Findings: Some countries achieve phenomenal growth rates over short terms because of a sudden spurt in the price of one or more of their natural resources, but these rates tend to decline just as sharply after a plateau is reached. The 1970-75 period was one in which aberrations in the price mechanisms tended to favor a few countries producing primary raw materials. During the same period industrialized countries were able to maintain their growth rates only with difficulty, and the majority of the Third World countries failed to achieve adequate growth rates or experienced negative growth rates on a per capita basis.

Regions	Africa	Asia & Oceania	Europe	Western Hemisphere
Most	Lesotho (4)	Iran (1)	Rumania (2)	Dominican Republic (9)
Least	Uganda (120)	Laos (122)	Switzerland (99)	Chile (117)

Rank	Country	Annual Growth Rate of Per Capita GNP (%)
	TOP 10	
1	Iran	13.3
2	Rumania	10.2
3	South Korea	8.2
4	Lesotho	7.3
5	Singapore	7.3
6	Malawi	7.0
7	Tunisia	6.9
8	Iraq	6.7
9	Dominican Republic	6.6
10	Brazil	6.2
	UPPER MIDDLE	
11	Ecuador	6.1
12	Yugoslavia	5.9
13	Poland	5.8
14	Yemen Arab Republic	5.8
15	Taiwan	5.7
16	China	5.3
17	Malaysia	5.3
18	Nigeria	5.3
19	Spain	5.1
20	Turkey	4.9
21	Portugal	4.5
22	Algeria	4.3
23	Congo	4.3
24	Greece	4.2
25	Hong Kong	4.2
26	Finland	4.1
27	Saudi Arabia	4.1
28	Austria	4.0
29	Israel	4.0
30	Jamaica	4.0
31	Japan	4.0
32	Belgium	3.9
33	Bulgaria	3.9
34	Colombia	3.9
35	Libya	3.9
36	Albania	3.8
37	Sudan	3.8
38	Costa Rica	3.7
39	East Germany	3.7
40	Philippines	3.7

Rank	Country	Annual Growth Rate of per Capita GNP (%)
41	Thailand	3.6
42	Indonesia	3.5
43	Bolivia	3.4
44	France	3.4
45	Peru	3.4
46	Canada	3.3
47	Norway	3.3
48	Paraguay	3.3
49	Angola	3.2
50	Hungary	3.2
51	Soviet Union	3.1
52	Czechoslovakia	3.0
53	Morocco	3.0
54	Argentina	2.9
55	Tanzania	2.9
56	Guatemala	2.8
57	Rhodesia (Zimbabwe)	2.8
58	Mauritania	2.6
59	Nicaragua	2.5
60	Trinidad & Tobago	2.5
61	Australia	2.4
	LOWER MIDDLE	
62	Kenya	2.4
63	Mexico	2.3
64	Mongolia	2.3
65	Papua New Guinea	2.3
66	Sweden	2.3
67	Netherlands	2.2
68	Panama	2.2
69	Afghanistan	2.1
70	Togo	2.0
71	United Kingdom	2.0
72	Ivory Coast	1.9
73	El Salvador	1.9
74	Jordan	1.9
75	West Germany	1.9
76	Syria	1.8
77	Denmark	1.7
78	Italy	1.7
79	South Africa	1.7
80	United States	1.6
81	Haiti	1.5

Rank	Country	Annual Growth Rate of per Capita GNP (%)
82	New Zealand	1.5
83	Venezuela	1.5
84	Zaire	1.5
85	Egypt	1.3
86	Guinea	1.3
87	Ireland	1.3
88	Sri Lanka	1.1
89	Upper Volta	1.1
90	Cuba	1.0
91	Burma	0.9
92	North Korea	0.9
93	Liberia	0.9
94	Zambia	0.9
95	Honduras	0.8
96	Pakistan	0.8
97	Puerto Rico	0.8
98	Nepal	0.7
99	Switzerland	0.7
100	Cameroon	0.5
101	India	0.5
102	Ethiopia	0.4
103	Rwanda	0.2
104	Mali	−0.1
105	Somalia	−0.2
106	Ghana	−0.3
107	Uruguay	−0.3
108	Sierra Leone	−0.5
109	Central African Empire	−0.7
110	Benin	−1.1
111	Burundi	−1.1
112	Senegal	−1.1
	BOTTOM 10	
113	Chad	−2.0
114	Madagascar	−2.2
115	Bangladesh	−2.3
116	Mozambique	−2.6
117	Chile	−2.7
118	Niger	−2.8
119	Kuwait	−3.3
120	Uganda	−4.5
121	South Yemen	−5.8
122	Laos	−15.9

Source: *World Bank Atlas.*

60. Percentage of National Income Received by Richest 5%

The percentage of national income received by the richest 5% presents a reliable index of the concentration of wealth in a country. Even in countries traditionally regarded as bastions of capitalism, this percentage is being whittled down by a combination of political and economic forces. In many countries the wealthy are simply being dispossessed by revolutions or near-revolutions; in others they are strangled by taxes, weakened by regulations and deprived of their privileges.

Number of Countries: 65
Midpoint: 23%
Period Covered: Mid-1970s
Type of Ranking: Percentage of National Income Received by the Richest 5%; Highest to Lowest

Highlights & Findings: While the poor may be growing poorer in developed countries, the rich are growing poorer too. No developed country appears among the top 10, but Mexico is a surprising inclusion because social justice has been an overriding concern of the ruling party in Mexico for over 60 years. It is also surprising that the United States appears to fare better than some professed socialist countries in this regard.

Regions	Africa	Asia & Oceania	Europe	Western Hemisphere
Most	Liberia (1)	Iraq (12)	West Germany (11)	Ecuador (3)
Least	Libya (65)	Israel (64)	Cyprus (62)	United States (63)

Rank	Country	Percentage of National Income Received by Richest 5%.	Rank	Country	Percentage of National Income Received by Richest 5%.	Rank	Country	Percentage of National Income Received by Richest 5%.
	TOP 10		22	Paraguay	30.0	44	Barbados	20.0
1	Liberia	60.0	23	Honduras	29.0	45	Egypt	20.0
2	Gabon	45.0	24	Malaysia	28.0	46	El Salvador	20.0
3	Ecuador	42.0	25	Brazil	27.0	47	Fiji	20.0
4	Venezuela	40.0	26	Malawi	27.0	48	Japan	20.0
5	Madagascar	39.0	27	Dominican Republic	26.0	49	Spain	20.0
6	Zambia	38.0	28	Lebanon	26.0	50	Guyana	19.0
7	Bolivia	36.0	29	France	25.0	51	Sri Lanka	19.0
8	Mexico	36.0	30	India	25.0	52	Pakistan	18.0
9	Senegal	36.0	31	Iran	25.0	53	Sweden	17.6
10	Sierra Leone	36.0	32	Philippines	25.0	54	Bangladesh	17.0
						55	Burma	17.0
	UPPER MIDDLE			*LOWER MIDDLE*			*BOTTOM 10*	
11	West Germany	35.7	33	Chad	23.0	56	Norway	15.4
12	Iraq	34.4	34	Costa Rica	23.0	57	South Korea	15.0
13	Tanzania	34.0	35	Greece	23.0	58	New Zealand	15.0
14	Peru	34.0	36	Niger	23.0	59	United Kingdom	15.0
15	Colombia	33.0	37	Denmark	22.0	60	Yugoslavia	15.0
16	Panama	33.0	38	Netherlands	22.0	61	Canada	14.0
17	Benin	32.0	39	Argentina	21.0	62	Cyprus	14.0
18	Turkey	32.0	40	Bahamas	21.0	63	United States	13.3
19	Chile	30.0	41	Finland	21.0	64	Israel	13.0
20	Ivory Coast	30.0	42	Sudan	21.0	65	Libya	13.0
21	Jamaica	30.0	43	Uruguay	21.0			

Source: World Bank.

61. Percentage of National Income Received by Poorest 20%

Estimates of national income per capita have been under fire for a number of years because they conceal rather than reveal income disparities among sectors, especially between the poorest and the richest. A number of efforts, therefore, have been made to measure these disparities; the most widely adopted one is the percentage of national income as received by the lowest and poorest 20%. This ranking should be read together with the preceding ranking on percentage of national income received by the richest 5% to determine the patterns of income distributions within a country.

Number of Countries: 65
Midpoint: 5%
Period Covered: Mid-1970s
Type of Ranking: Percentage of National Income Received by the Poorest 20%; Highest to Lowest

Highlights & Findings: The most striking revelation is that the poor receive much less than their share of national wealth not only in developing countries, as is commonly supposed, but also in highly developed countries, such as the United States and Sweden. In fact, included among the bottom 10 are such countries as France and Finland. Many reasons have been advanced to explain why the poor remain poor and even grow poorer, but obviously there are built-in mechanisms in almost all monetary economies that, in the absence of state intervention, tend to favor the rich and depress the poor. Yet, paradoxically, the countries at the upper end of the scale are not particularly socialist in their orientation. In fact, some of the European social democracies, such as Sweden, fall far below more free-wheeling capitalist states, such as the United States.

Regions	Africa	Asia & Oceania	Europe	Western Hemisphere
Most	Liberia (1)	South Korea (2)	Greece (6)	Barbados (12)
Least	Sierra Leone (65)	Iraq (61)	France (60)	Venezuela (64)

Rank	Country	Percentage of National Income Received by Poorest 20%	Rank	Country	Percentage of National Income Received by Poorest 20%	Rank	Country	Percentage of National Income Received by Poorest 20%
	TOP 11		22	Zambia	6.0	44	Ivory Coast	4.0
1	Liberia	13.0	23	Spain	6.0	45	Lebanon	4.0
2	South Korea	10.0	24	Argentina	5.0	46	Mexico	4.0
3	Libya	10.0	25	Benin	5.0	47	Paraguay	4.0
4	Malawi	10.0	26	Brazil	5.0	48	Philippines	4.0
5	Bangladesh	9.0	27	Chile	5.0	49	Uruguay	4.0
6	Greece	9.0	28	Costa Rica	5.0	50	Malaysia	3.4
7	New Zealand	9.0	29	Dominican Republic	5.0	51	Netherlands	3.1
8	Chad	8.0	30	West Germany	5.0	52	Bahamas	3.0
9	Cyprus	8.0	31	India	5.0	53	Ecuador	3.0
10	Israel	8.0	32	Iran	5.0	54	Gabon	3.0
11	Pakistan	8.0	33	Sudan	5.0	55	Honduras	3.0
			34	Tanzania	5.0	56	Panama	3.0
	UPPER MIDDLE					57	Senegal	3.0
12	Barbados	7.0		*LOWER MIDDLE*		58	Turkey	3.0
13	Sri Lanka	7.0	35	Japan	4.7			
14	Yugoslavia	7.0	36	Norway	4.5			
15	United States	6.7	37	Sweden	4.4		*BOTTOM 7*	
16	Canada	6.4	38	Bolivia	4.0	59	Finland	2.0
17	Burma	6.0	39	Colombia	4.0	60	France	2.0
18	Fiji	6.0	40	Denmark	4.0	61	Iraq	2.0
19	Madagascar	6.0	41	Egypt	4.0	62	Jamaica	2.0
20	Niger	6.0	42	El Salvador	4.0	63	Peru	2.0
21	United Kingdom	6.0	43	Guyana	4.0	64	Venezuela	2.0
						65	Sierra Leone	1.0

Source: World Bank.

62. Percentage of Population Living in Absolute Poverty

Poverty is relative and therefore defies definition; yet, everyone knows it when he sees it, as U.S. Justice Byron White said of another social evil. One-fourth of the planet's population—some one billion human beings—live in poverty so stark and dehumanizing that it is inconceivable for most people living in Western societies. The upper limits of absolute poverty, so described to distinguish it from the kind of poverty with which we are familiar, are low- er than the poverty levels fixed by governments in the developed world. By thus excluding the developed world, the characteristics and extent of poverty in the developing world emerge into startling focus.

Number of Countries: 83
Midpoint: 19%
Period Covered: 1977
Type of Ranking: Percentage of Population Living in Absolute Poverty; Highest to Lowest

Highlights & Findings: In 21 countries the majority of the population live in absolute poverty. These include two of the most populous countries in the world, Indonesia and Bangladesh. The presence of many of the impoverished countries on the list is self-explanatory; what is surprising is the presence of oil-rich countries, such as Saudi Arabia and Iran.

Region	Africa	Asia & Oceania	Europe	Western Hemisphere
Most	Benin (2)	Bangladesh (1)	N.A.	Bolivia (39)
Least	Gabon (74)	Iran (82)	Portugal (79)	Venezuela (83)

Rank	Country	Percentage of Population Living in Absolute Poverty	Rank	Country	Percentage of Population Living in Absolute Poverty	Rank	Country	Percentage of Population Living in Absolute Poverty
	TOP 10		28	Senegal	36	56	Nicaragua	12
1	Bangladesh	75	29	Mauritania	34	57	Peru	12
2	Benin	75	30	Pakistan	34	58	Iraq	11
3	Burundi	75	31	Cameroon	33	59	South Korea	11
4	Chad	75	32	Botswana	31	60	Turkey	11
5	Ethiopia	75	33	Nigeria	30	61	Colombia	10
6	Mali	75	34	Thailand	27	62	Dominican Republic	10
7	Rwanda	75	35	Ghana	25	63	Malaysia	10
8	Somalia	75	36	Congo	23	64	Mexico	10
9	Upper Volta	75	37	Sri Lanka	22	65	Saudi Arabia	10
10	Guinea	70	38	Morocco	21	66	Syria	10
			39	Bolivia	20	67	Tunisia	10
	UPPER MIDDLE		40	Liberia		68	Fiji	9
11	Lesotho	68				69	Jamaica	9
12	Niger	67		*LOWER MIDDLE*		70	Brazil	8
13	Uganda	64	41	El Salvador	19	71	Chile	8
14	Afghanistan	63	42	Honduras	19	72	Costa Rica	8
15	Malawi	62	43	Jordan	19			
16	Zaire	60	44	Mauritius	19		*BOTTOM 11*	
17	Burma	55	45	Guyana	17	73	Cyprus	7
18	Tanzania	54	46	Swaziland	17	74	Gabon	7
19	Central African Empire	53	47	Ivory Coast	16	75	Hong Kong	7
20	Madagascar	52	48	Philippines	16	76	Panama	7
21	Indonesia	51	49	Algeria	15	77	Trinidad & Tobago	7
22	Gambia	45	50	Papua New Guinea	15	78	Argentina	6
23	Kenya	43	51	Zambia	15	79	Portugal	6
24	Sudan	43	52	Oman	14	80	Singapore	6
25	Togo	43	53	Paraguay	14	81	Uruguay	6
26	Sierra Leone	39	54	Ecuador	12	82	Iran	5
27	India	36	55	Guatemala	12	83	Venezuela	5

Source: Overseas Development Council, Washington, D.C.

63. Real GDP per Capita

The most widely used yardstick of wealth is per capita GNP or GDP, but these indicators have often proved to be unsatisfactory because exchange rate conversions to a common currency such as that of the United States dollar does not yield a reliable basis for international comparisons. It is generally appreciated that the purchasing power of low-income countries is systematically greater than their exchange rates as compared to high-income countries. Correspondingly, the real income of low-income countries is relatively higher than is indicated by simple exchange rate conversions to the U.S. dollar. Several attempts have therefore been made to present real income based on careful comparisons of purchasing power. The United Nations International Comparison Project (ICP) was one. Another was

the work of Professors Irving B. Kravis, Alan W. Heston and Robert Summers of the University of Pennsylvania, on which the following ranking is based. These estimates are derived from careful studies on purchasing power comparisons (called purchasing power parities by the authors) of a selected basket of goods. A further advantage is that the data are presented with the United States as the benchmark for comparison, with a value of 100.

Number of Countries 95
Midpoint: 20.8
Period Covered: 1974
Type of Ranking: Real GDP per Capita
with U.S. as 100; Highest to Lowest

Highlights & Findings: The ranking reveals that Kuwait and the United States lead the world in per capita GDP. Because the survey is not affected by the impacts of erratic fluctuations of monetary exchange, many European countries that lead the per capita GNP ranking are found lower down the scale. But there is still concentration at the top. The most productive 10% of the population produces nearly 33% of the world product, while the highest fifth accounts for over one-half. The least productive half of the world produces only 12% of the world's goods. The real per capita output of North America is 3.4 times the world average, while that of Asia and Africa is only one-fourth to one-third of the world average.

Region	Africa	Asia & Oceania	Europe	Western Hemisphere
Most	Libya (3)	Kuwait (1)	Sweden (5)	United States (2)
Least	Rwanda (95)	Bangladesh (94)	Cyprus (36)	Bolivia (72)

Rank	Country	Real Per Capita GDP	Rank	Country	Real Per Capita GDP	Rank	Country	Real Per Capita GDP
	TOP 10		32	Uruguay	31.1	64	Ghana	12.7
1	Kuwait	161.0	33	Hong Kong	30.7	65	Vietnam	12.2
2	United States	100.0	34	Malta	30.2	66	Swaziland	12.1
3	Libya	92.5	35	Brazil	29.4	67	Honduras	11.6
4	Canada	90.4	36	Cyprus	28.8	68	Botswana	11.4
5	Sweden	86.0	37	Chile	28.4	69	Morocco	11.3
6	France	77.0	38	South Africa	28.3	70	Liberia	11.1
7	Iceland	76.8	39	Jamaica	28.2	71	Philippines	10.3
8	West Germany	75.7	40	Panama	27.7	72	Bolivia	10.2
9	Denmark	73.1	41	Iraq	27.5	73	Egypt	10.1
10	Norway	72.7	42	Mexico	26.5	74	Sri Lanka	10.0
			43	Costa Rica	23.9	75	Nigeria	9.8
	UPPER MIDDLE		44	Fiji	22.6	76	Thailand	9.7
11	Australia	71.5	45	Dominican Republic	21.8	77	Senegal	9.6
12	Finland	68.9	46	Nicaragua	21.8	78	Cameroon	8.8
13	Belgium	68.4	47	Malaysia	21.2	79	Sierra Leone	8.8
14	Saudi Arabia	66.1	48	Turkey	20.8	80	Pakistan	8.5
15	Netherlands	64.5	49	Algeria	20.4	81	Mauritania	8.3
16	Israel	63.7	50	Colombia	19.2	82	Togo	7.8
17	Japan	62.6				83	Kenya	6.7
18	United Kingdom	61.4		*LOWER MIDDLE*		84	Indonesia	6.4
19	Austria	59.5	51	Guatemala	18.0	85	Madagascar	5.7
20	Oman	58.4	52	Tunisia	17.9			
21	Venezuela	50.6	53	Peru	17.6		*BOTTOM 10*	
22	Italy	48.0	54	South Korea	17.0	86	India	5.4
23	Gabon	47.2	55	Zambia	17.0	87	Tanzania	5.4
24	Argentina	46.4	56	Mauritius	16.9	88	Malawi	4.6
25	Spain	45.1	57	Syria	16.5	89	Lesotho	4.5
26	Ireland	42.3	58	Ecuador	15.6	90	Zaire	4.4
27	Greece	42.2	59	El Salvador	14.5	91	Burma	4.0
28	Singapore	40.2	60	Guyana	14.5	92	Benin	4.0
29	Trinidad & Tobago	39.8	61	Ivory Coast	13.9	93	Ethiopia	3.8
30	Portugal	33.8	62	Paraguay	13.9	94	Bangladesh	3.2
31	Iran	33.3	63	Papua New Guinea	12.9	95	Rwanda	3.0

Source: Irving B. Kravis, Alan W. Heston and Robert Summers. "Real GDP Per Capita." *The Economic Journal.* June 1978.

64. Average Annual Rate of Inflation

Inflation may be the single most important fact of life in the 1980s and therefore bears careful watching. Even normal and healthy economic systems experience a slow but constant escalation in prices given the push of population growth and the pull of finite and depleting resources. But this process is accelerated in times of internal and external stress, as for instance in Chile and Cambodia in the mid-1970s. Economists sometimes distinguish between creeping inflation and galloping inflation and have introduced various terms such as stagflation to characterize peculiar types of inflation. But these distinctions are purely academic because every form of inflation represents a threat to the stability of economic and, ultimately, political systems.

Number of Countries: 109
Midpoint: 11%
Period Covered: 1970-76
Type of Ranking: Average Annual Rate of Inflation (%); Highest to Lowest

Highlights & Findings: The ranking is based on World Bank figures, which are derived from what is known as the implicit GDP deflator. This is calculated by dividing for each year of the six-year period the value of the GDP in current market prices by the value of the GDP in constant market prices. On this scale the highest rate of inflation is experienced by oil-exporting countries at 33.3% and the lowest by industrialized countries at 9.3%. In between, middle-income countries had a rate of 12.5% and low-income countries 9.8%. Sixty-three nations had what is generally described as double-digit inflation and one had triple-digit inflation.

Regions	Africa	Asia & Oceania	Europe	Western Hemisphere
Most	Ghana (11)	Cambodia (2)	Yugoslavia (24)	Chile (1)
Least	Niger (109)	Afghanistan (107)	West Germany (100)	Honduras (102)

Rank	Country	Average Annual Rate of Inflation (%)	Rank	Country	Average Annual Rate of Inflation (%)	Rank	Country	Average Annual Rate of Inflation (%)
	TOP 10		35	Ecuador	13.6	70	France	9.3
1	Chile	273.6	36	Finland	13.6	71	Morocco	9.3
2	Cambodia	98.6	37	Paraguay	13.6	72	Canada	9.2
3	Argentina	88.7	38	Angola	13.5	73	India	9.2
4	Uruguay	70.5	39	Australia	13.5	74	Dominican Republic	8.9
5	Kuwait	35.6	40	Haiti	13.5	75	Netherlands	8.9
6	Saudi Arabia	33.3	41	Venezuela	13.4	76	Somalia	8.9
7	Brazil	26.1	42	Greece	13.3	77	Belgium	8.8
8	Bolivia	25.9	43	United Kingdom	13.3	78	Lesotho	8.8
9	Iran	25.2	44	Italy	12.9	79	Sweden	8.8
10	Israel	23.7	45	Spain	12.8	80	Burundi	8.7
			46	Senegal	12.1	81	Hong Kong	8.6
	UPPER MIDDLE		47	Taiwan	11.9	82	Norway	8.6
11	Ghana	23.5	48	Portugal	11.9	83	Togo	8.6
12	Indonesia	22.7	49	Tanzania	11.7	84	Nepal	8.4
13	Laos	22.3	50	New Zealand	11.6	85	Benin	8.3
14	Bangladesh	20.7	51	Sri Lanka	11.5	86	Central African Empire	8.3
15	Colombia	20.7	52	South Africa	11.3	87	Singapore	8.1
16	Turkey	19.8	53	Panama	11.2	88	Japan	7.9
17	Syria	18.8	54	Kenya	11.1	89	Papua New Guinea	7.8
18	Trinidad & Tobago	18.8	55	Ivory Coast	11.0	90	Tunisia	7.7
19	Iraq	17.5				91	Rhodesia (Zimbabwe)	7.5
20	Jamaica	17.5		*LOWER MIDDLE*		92	Switzerland	7.4
21	South Korea	17.5				93	Guinea	7.2
22	Uganda	17.1	56	Nicaragua	10.8	94	El Salvador	7.1
23	Libya	16.5	57	Rwanda	10.6	95	Mali	7.1
24	Yugoslavia	16.3	58	Liberia	10.3	96	Malaysia	7.0
25	Burma	16.1	59	Mauritania	10.3	97	Mozambique	6.9
26	Niger	16.1	60	Thailand	10.3	98	United States	6.8
27	Zaire	15.7	61	Madagascar	10.2	99	Chad	6.6
28	Peru	15.6	62	Sierra Leone	10.2			
29	Pakistan	15.2	63	Japan	10.1		*BOTTOM 10*	
30	Philippines	15.1	64	Denmark	9.8	100	West Germany	6.4
31	Algeria	14.8	65	Malawi	9.8	101	Upper Volta	6.3
32	Mexico	14.2	66	Cameroon	9.7	102	Honduras	5.5
33	Ireland	13.9	67	Jordan	9.6	103	Egypt	5.2
34	Costa Rica	13.7	68	Guatemala	9.4	104	Lebanon	4.4
			69	Congo	9.3			

Rank	Country	Average Annual Rate of Inflation (%)	Rank	Country	Average Annual Rate of Inflation (%)	Rank	Country	Average Annual Rate of Inflation (%)
105	Zambia	3.8	107	Afghanistan	3.1	109	Niger	1.7
106	Sudan	3.5	108	Ethiopia	2.3			

Source: World Bank.

65. Consumer Price Index: All Items

The index numbers shown in this ranking are based on 1970=100 for most countries and reflect the cost of a typical basket of goods and services purchased by a representative group of consumers in a representative city. Also known as the cost of living index, this index is used by the United Nations to determine cost-of-living allowances for its officials stationed in various regions and countries.

Number of Countries: 153
Midpoint: 170
Period Covered: 1976
Type of Ranking: Consumer Price Index, 1976 (1970=100), All Items; Highest to Lowest

Highlights & Findings: A comparison between food prices and prices of all items in the consumer price index is interesting. By and large, food prices tend to rise and fall more steeply than prices of other commodities because they are more sensitive to the push and pull of supply and demand. The presence of many Communist countries at the bottom of the list may be explained by the fact that different price mechanisms operate in centrally planned economies.

Regions	Africa	Asia & Oceania	Europe	Western Hemisphere
Most	Uganda (6)	Cambodia (4)	Iceland (7)	Chile (1)
Least	Morocco (142)	New Hebrides (148)	East Germany (153)	Nicaragua (145)

Rank	Country	Consumer Price Index, (1970=100)	Rank	Country	Consumer Price Index (1970=100)	Rank	Country	Consumer Price Index (1970=100)
	TOP 10		26	St. Lucia	230	54	Fiji	186
1	Chile	86,565	27	Nigeria	227	55	Australia	185
2	Argentina	6,539	28	Ireland	220	56	St. Kitts-Nevis-Anguilla	185
3	Uruguay	2,086	29	Cook Islands	217	57	Martinique	184
4	Cambodia	1,819	30	Dominica	215	58	Cameroon	182
5	Laos	457	31	United Kingdom	215	59	Philippines	182
6	Uganda	434	32	Jamaica	214	60	Guadeloupe	181
7	Iceland	404	33	Pakistan	212	61	Paraguay	180
8	Israel	388	34	Gibraltar	211	62	Reunion	180
9	Ghana	352	35	Sudan	211	63	Liberia	179
10	Vietnam	332	36	Ecuador	208	64	Niger	178
			37	Spain	208	65	Tonga	178
	UPPER MIDDLE		38	Antigua	205	66	Greenland	177
11	Indonesia	292	39	Trinidad & Tobago	205	67	Togo	177
12	Burma	285	40	Mexico	204	68	French Guyana	176
13	Cape Verde	284	41	Finland	202	69	Sierra Leone	176
14	Colombia	281	42	Greece	202	70	Iran	175
15	Seychelles	279	43	Mauritius	202	71	South Africa	174
16	Yugoslavia	271	44	Tanzania	201	72	Dominican Republic	173
17	Bolivia	267	45	Haiti	200	73	French Polynesia	172
18	Brazil	254	46	Italy	200	74	Mozambique	172
19	Bangladesh	252	47	Costa Rica	196	75	Botswana	171
20	Turkey	252	48	Syria	195	76	Bermuda	170
21	Barbados	246	49	Gambia	193	77	Central African Empire	170
22	Portugal	244	50	Senegal	193	78	Denmark	170
23	Peru	242	51	Jordan	192			
24	South Korea	235	52	New Zealand	190		*LOWER MIDDLE*	
25	Zaire	232	53	Japan	188	79	France	168

Rank	Country	Consumer Price Index (1970=100)	Rank	Country	Consumer Price Index (1970=100)	Rank	Country	Consumer Price Index (1970=100)
80	Papua New Guinea	168	106	Chad	153	132	Tunisia	136
81	Zambia	168	107	Ethiopia	153	133	Malta	134
82	New Caledonia	166	108	Puerto Rico	153	134	Lebanon	130
83	Swaziland	166	109	Solomon Islands	151	135	Libya	130
84	Netherlands	165	110	Iraq	150	136	Guam	129
85	Somalia	165	111	Nepal	150	137	Singapore	123
86	Burundi	164	112	Rwanda	150	138	Afghanistan	122
87	Madagascar	164	113	Cyprus	148	139	Mauritania	121
88	Malawi	164	114	Egypt	147	140	Hungary	120
89	Netherlands Antilles	164	115	Switzerland	147	141	Poland	118
90	Belgium	163	116	United States	147	142	Morocco	117
91	Falkland Islands	163	117	Brunei	146	143	Hong Kong	112
92	Norway	163	118	Malaysia (West)	146			
93	Surinam	163	119	Lesotho	145		*BOTTOM 10*	
94	El Salvador	162	120	Panama	145	144	Guatemala	111
95	Ivory Coast	162	121	Sri Lanka	145	145	Nicaragua	111
96	Sweden	162	122	Rhodesia (Zimbabwe)	143	146	Gilbert Islands	110
97	India	161	123	Samoa	143	147	Faroe Islands	100
98	Kenya	160	124	Honduras	142	148	New Hebrides	103
99	Thailand	160	125	Venezuela	142	149	Rumania	103
100	Gabon	158	126	West Germany	141	150	Czechoslovakia	102
101	Guyana	158	127	Algeria	140	151	Bulgaria	101
102	Congo	157	128	Sarawak	140	152	Soviet Union	100
103	Luxembourg	156	129	Kuwait	139	153	East Germany	97
104	Austria	153	130	Sabah	139			
105	Canada	153	131	Bahamas	137			

Source: International Labor Organization.

66. Consumer Price Index: Food

The index numbers shown in this ranking are based on 1970=100 for most countries and are calculated on the price of a representative food basket purchased by a representative group of consumers in a representative city. Because it represents average food prices, it may not reflect the cost of living for the well-to-do or for those with a better standard of living than the majority of a country's inhabitants.

Number of Countries: 153
Midpoint: 175
Period Covered: 1976
Type of Ranking: Consumer Price Index, 1976 (1970=100), Food only; Highest to Lowest

Highlights & Findings: Because food claims the largest share in low-income family budgets, a rise in food prices is often accompanied by widespread human distress. Governments throughout the world constantly initiate programs to keep food prices down. These include food stamps, rationing, subsidies and fair-price shops. Nevertheless, food prices have jumped over three times in 13 countries and have also tended to push up prices of other commodities as well. A number of Communist countries report below average increases in food prices, but it must be remembered that these are artificial prices set by the state without reference to actual costs of production and marketing.

Regions	Africa	Asia	Europe	Western Hemisphere
Most	Uganda (6)	Cambodia (3)	Iceland (7)	Chile (1)
Least	Libya (153)	New Hebrides (149)	East Germany (152)	Nicaragua (144)

Rank	Country	Consumer Price Index: Food	Rank	Country	Consumer Price Index: Food	Rank	Country	Consumer Price Index: Food
	TOP 10		5	Laos	545	10	Indonesia	338
1	Chile	112,040	6	Uganda	490			
2	Argentina	6,632	7	Iceland	460		*UPPER MIDDLE*	
3	Cambodia	2,278	8	Ghana	414	11	Colombia	329
4	Uruguay	2,128	9	Israel	402	12	Vietnam	321

Rank	Country	Consumer Price Index: Food	Rank	Country	Consumer Price Index: Food	Rank	Country	Consumer Price Index: Food
13	Cape Verde	301	62	Greenland	191	109	Sarawak	160
14	Burma	300	63	Guadeloupe	189	110	Solomon Islands	160
15	Bolivia	292	64	Mozambique	188	111	Sabah	159
16	Yugoslavia	278	65	Reunion	188	112	Congo	158
17	Turkey	277	66	Tonga	188	113	United States	157
18	Barbados	274	67	New Zealand	186	114	India	156
19	South Korea	274	68	South Africa	184	115	Panama	156
20	Nigeria	268	69	Somalia	183	116	Honduras	154
21	Brazil	267	70	Bermuda	181	117	Iraq	153
22	Jordan	266	71	Denmark	181	118	Netherlands	152
23	Portugal	264	72	Martinique	181	119	Nepal	151
24	Peru	263	73	Philippines	178	120	Rwanda	151
25	St. Lucia	261	74	Zambia	177	121	Brunei	150
26	Zaire	261	75	Madagascar	176	122	Lesotho	149
27	Gibraltar	252	76	Malawi	176	123	Samoa	149
28	United Kingdom	247	77	French Guyana	175	124	Lebanon	148
29	Ecuador	245				125	Sri Lanka	148
30	Antigua	244		*LOWER MIDDLE*		126	Chad	145
31	Bangladesh	242	78	Egypt	174	127	Austria	144
32	Jamaica	231	79	France	174	128	Bahamas	144
33	Cook Islands	227	80	New Caledonia	174	129	Rhodesia (Zimbabwe)	144
34	Ireland	227	81	Papua New Guinea	174	130	South Yemen	144
35	Tanzania	226	82	Surinam	174	131	Seychelles	142
36	Trinidad & Tobago	226	83	Australia	173	132	Tunisia	142
37	Pakistan	222	84	Puerto Rico	173	133	Switzerland	139
38	St. Kitts-Nevis-Anguilla	222	85	Thailand	173	134	West Germany	137
39	Netherlands Antilles	219	86	Central African Empire	172	135	Malta	137
40	Gambia	218	87	Iran	172	136	Guam	136
41	Greece	215	88	Burundi	171	137	Falkland Islands	131
42	Senegal	214	89	Lebanon	171	138	Mauritania	127
43	Dominica	213	90	Dominican Republic	169	139	Hungary	121
44	Haiti	213	91	Swaziland	169	140	Morocco	119
45	Spain	210	92	Sweden	169	141	Singapore	119
46	Finland	209	93	Canada	168	142	Poland	118
47	Mexico	208	94	Norway	167	143	Guatemala	110
48	Italy	202	95	Botswana	166			
49	Mauritius	201	96	El Salvador	165		*BOTTOM 10*	
50	Niger	201	97	Cyprus	164	144	Nicaragua	109
51	Sudan	201	98	French Polynesia	164	145	Gilbert Islands	108
52	Paraguay	200	99	Kuwait	164	146	Hong Kong	107
53	Togo	199	100	Venezuela	164	147	Rumania	106
54	Syria	198	101	Algeria	162	148	Bulgaria	103
55	Fiji	196	102	Gabon	162	149	New Hebrides	103
56	Japan	196	103	Malaysia (West)	162	150	Czechoslovakia	101
57	Mali	196	104	Luxembourg	161	151	Soviet Union	101
58	Sierra Leone	195	105	Belgium	160	152	East Germany	100
59	Costa Rica	192	106	Ethiopia	160	153	Libya	96
60	Guyana	192	107	Ivory Coast	160			
61	Cameroon	191	108	Kenya	160			

Source: International Labor Organization.

67. Wholesale Price Index

A wholesale price index refers to a representative basket of commodities priced at the wholesale stage of distribution. They are based on such prices as those charged by representative manufacturers or producers to wholesalers, prices charged by wholesalers to retailers and prices paid by importers to producers. There are two principal types of wholesale price indices: the first reflects the price movements of the flow of goods into and out of various sectors of the economy; the second type is those weighted by the total value of sales or the value of home-consumed goods.

Number of Countries: 57 **Midpoint:** 180 **Period Covered:** 1976 **Type of Ranking:** Wholesale Price Index, 1970=100, General Index Only; Highest to Lowest	**Highlights & Findings:** Except for Chile and, to a lesser extent, Argentina and Uruguay, where the wholesale price mechanisms seem to have collapsed under inflationary pressures, the index does not reveal any abnormalities during the year under review. Most of the countries in the ranking are the developed and industrialized nations, where prices generally edged upward steadily reflecting the changes in the prices of primary commodities imported from developing countries. The Soviet Union appears to be the only country in which the wholesale prices have declined, but the weights used in constructing the Soviet index are not comparable to those used in the West.

Regions	Africa	Asia & Oceania	Europe	Western Hemisphere
Most	Ghana (9)	Israel (4)	United Kingdom (7)	Chile (1)
Least	Zambia (55)	Singapore (56)	Soviet Union (57)	Venezuela (43)

Rank	Country	Wholesale Price Index	Rank	Country	Wholesale Price Index	Rank	Country	Wholesale Price Index
	TOP 10		20	El Salvador	208	40	Japan	165
1	Chile	258,663	21	Portugal	208	41	Gabon	164
2	Argentina	7,770	22	Mexico	205	42	Norway	163
3	Uruguay	2,281	23	South Africa	204	43	Venezuela	163
4	Israel	405	24	Panama	202	44	Central African Empire	159
5	Brazil	372	25	New Zealand	200	45	France	159
6	Colombia	354	26	Spain	191	46	Tunisia	154
7	United Kingdom	299	27	Syria	191	47	Iraq	148
8	Indonesia	286	28	Thailand	185			
9	Ghana	278	29	Sudan	180		*BOTTOM 10*	
10	Turkey	272				48	Belgium	147
				LOWER MIDDLE		49	Netherlands	146
	UPPER MIDDLE		30	Canada	179	50	Austria	143
11	Philippines	270	31	India	177	51	Egypt	142
12	South Korea	267	32	Guatemala	176	52	West Germany	141
13	Pakistan	243	33	Denmark	175	53	Switzerland	132
14	Costa Rica	242	34	Sweden	172	54	Hungary	127
15	Yugoslavia	242	35	Morocco	168	55	Zambia	127
16	Italy	236	36	Iran	167	56	Singapore	105
17	Ireland	231	37	Australia	166	57	Soviet Union	97
18	Greece	220	38	United States	166			
19	Finland	210	39	Dominican Republic	165			

Source: *U.N. Monthly Bulletin of Statistics.*

68. Rent Index

This and the following two rankings rate countries by the indexes of three essential goods and services —rent, clothing, and fuel and light—selected as representative of the general consumption patterns and the standard of living. Although the indexes vary in reliability, they may be accepted as a useful measure of the deflation of wages and real purchasing power in each country.

Number of Countries: 122 **Midpoint:** 148.9 **Period Covered:** 1976 **Type of Ranking:** Rent Index (1970=100); Highest to Lowest	**Highlights & Findings:** Over 62 countries reported abnormal increases in rents with Latin American countries in the lead. Twelve countries report no hikes in rent at all during this period and four report a decline. The conclusion is that rents are susceptible not only to normal inflationary pressures but, in accordance with the law of supply and demand, to overcrowded conditions in the cities, mortgage rates and other factors.

Regions	Africa	Asia & Oceania	Europe	Western Hemisphere
Most	Sudan (6)	Israel (4)	Iceland (5)	Chile (1)
Least	Somalia (119)	South Yemen (122)	Soviet Union (117)	Puerto Rico (108)

Rank	Country	Consumer's Rent Index	Rank	Country	Consumer's Rent Index	Rank	Country	Consumer's Rent Index
	TOP 10		42	Denmark	171.1	84	Cyprus	121.1
1	Chile	49,461.0	43	Netherlands	169.4	85	Sabah	120.9
2	Argentina	5,029.0	44	Reunion	169.1	86	Canada	120.8
3	Uruguay	563.0	45	Cameroon	166.3	87	Zambia	120.1
4	Israel	417.0	46	Japan	164.8	88	Sarawak	119.5
5	Iceland	304.7	47	South Africa	164.0	89	Nigeria	118.4
6	Sudan	289.4	48	Liberia	162.5	90	Surinam	118.2
7	Colombia	263.9	49	Kenya	156.8	91	Gambia	115.8
8	Portugal	247.1	50	Paraguay	156.7	92	Morocco	115.5
9	Laos	246.1	51	Italy	155.5	93	Panama	115.2
10	Bangladesh	241.7	52	Switzerland	154.6	94	Hong Kong	114.0
			53	France	153.9	95	Guyana	113.4
	UPPER MIDDLE		54	French Guyana	153.9	96	Iraq	113.3
11	Jamaica	237.9	55	Iran	153.8	97	Netherlands Antilles	112.1
12	Vietnam	234.2	56	Norway	152.8	98	Nicaragua	112.1
13	Indonesia	231.9	57	Ivory Coast	151.7	99	Tunisia	111.4
14	Dominica	229.3	58	Antigua	151.4	100	Rumania	111.1
15	Libya	220.6	59	Dominican Republic	151.1	101	Guatemala	109.7
16	St. Lucia	218.2	60	Burundi	150.3	102	Venezuela	109.6
17	Hungary	215.0	61	French Polynesia	148.9	103	Malta	109.3
18	Brazil	211.3				104	Algeria	108.8
19	Yugoslavia	207.8		*LOWER MIDDLE*		105	Gilbert Islands	108.2
20	Austria	204.9	62	El Salvador	147.3	106	Mozambique	107.9
21	United Kingdom	203.9	63	Greece	146.5	107	Tanzania	104.9
22	Pakistan	200.6	64	Sweden	146.1	108	Puerto Rico	104.1
23	Australia	198.8	65	New Caledonia	144.7	109	Gibraltar	103.8
24	Finland	196.0	66	Zaire	141.1	110	Kuwait	103.3
25	New Zealand	193.3	67	Ecuador	141.0			
26	Barbados	193.2	68	West Germany	140.0			
27	Fiji	189.1	69	Jordan	139.4		*BOTTOM 12*	
28	Burma	188.7	70	Nepal	139.1	111	Egypt	100.0
29	Cook Islands	188.7	71	Bermuda	133.1	112	East Germany	100.0
30	Peru	187.9	72	Sierra Leone	131.5	113	Ghana	100.0
31	Greenland	187.0	73	United States	131.4	114	Lebanon	100.0
32	Martinique	183.6	74	Trinidad & Tobago	131.3	115	Mauritius	100.0
33	Ireland	181.8	75	Senegal	130.1	116	Samoa	100.0
34	Philippines	181.2	76	India	129.5	117	Soviet Union	100.0
35	Mexico	180.7	77	Singapore	125.4	118	Sri Lanka	100.0
36	Costa Rica	177.8	78	Seychelles	124.5	119	Somalia	85.3
37	Spain	174.4	79	Honduras	124.3	120	Guam	84.4
38	Haiti	173.5	80	Malaysia	124.2	121	Solomon Islands	83.3
39	South Korea	172.8	81	Thailand	123.5	122	South Yemen	75.0
40	Guadeloupe	172.5	82	Bahamas	123.3			
41	Cambodia	172.0	83	Lesotho	122.2			

Source: International Labor Organization, *Yearbook of Labor Statistics.*

69. Clothing Price Index

This ranking compares the national clothing price indexes, one of the constituents of the consumer price index. Increases in the price of textiles are not due to inherent costs but to add-on costs. There is no reason why their costs should go up abnormally if only the cost of production and raw materials were taken into consideration; however, they cost more because of higher transporation costs, taxation, merchandising and warehousing costs, etc.

Number of Countries: 148
Midpoint: 162.5
Period Covered: 1976
Type of Ranking: Clothing Price Index (1970=100); Highest to Lowest

Highlights & Findings: The clothing price index has climbed steeply by over 10% a year in at least 30 countries. In four countries it has remained stable or has declined. As in all essential commodities, clothing prices are generally inelastic, i.e., demand does not change according to the price structure.

Regions	Africa	Asia & Oceania	Europe	Western Hemisphere
Most	Ghana (8)	Cambodia (4)	Iceland (5)	Chile (1)
Least	Gambia (133)	Hong Kong (147)	East Germany (148)	Falkland Islands (134)

Rank	Country	Clothing Price Index	Rank	Country	Clothing Price Index	Rank	Country	Clothing Price Index
	TOP 10		50	St. Lucia	184.1	100	Thailand	146.9
1	Chile	47,418.0	51	Ecuador	182.9	101	Zambia	145.2
2	Argentina	6,785.0	52	Venezuela	182.3	102	Solomon Islands	144.7
3	Uruguay	1,582.0	53	Martinique	181.5	103	Lebanon	143.8
4	Cambodia	507.5	54	Rwanda	181.0	104	Malaysia (West)	143.6
5	Iceland	420.0	55	Syria	180.5	105	Nepal	143.4
6	Laos	333.8	56	Somalia	179.6	106	South Yemen	143.3
7	Israel	324.7	57	Botswana	179.1	107	Bahamas	143.1
8	Ghana	323.2	58	Greenland	179.0	108	Austria	142.3
9	Bolivia	296.7	59	Haiti	178.3	109	Egypt	142.0
10	Colombia	285.4	60	Finland	176.8	110	Madagascar	142.0
			61	Cameroon	176.6	111	Sierra Leone	141.0
	UPPER MIDDLE		62	Reunion	175.8	112	West Germany	140.9
11	Turkey	272.8	63	Netherlands	175.3	113	Honduras	140.5
12	Yugoslavia	261.5	64	Trinidad & Tobago	175.1	114	Guam	139.4
13	Nigeria	257.5	65	Vietnam	174.6	115	Central African Empire	139.3
14	Cook Islands	233.6	66	Mauritius	173.1	116	Malawi	137.2
15	Barbados	232.7	67	El Salvador	170.5	117	Seychelles	135.9
16	French Guyana	232.4	68	Costa Rica	169.2	118	Kuwait	135.6
17	Peru	232.1	69	Swaziland	164.4	119	Cyprus	135.0
18	Bangladesh	228.6	70	France	164.2	120	Canada	134.3
19	Indonesia	226.9	71	Surinam	163.9	121	Sabah	134.3
20	Burma	226.8	72	Papua New Guinea	163.6	122	Netherlands Antilles	133.0
21	Pakistan	224.8	73	Bermuda	163.5	123	Sarawak	132.4
22	Mozambique	222.6	74	Guyana	162.5	124	Tunisia	132.2
23	Sudan	219.4				125	Panama	131.9
24	Mexico	214.5		*LOWER MIDDLE*		126	Lesotho	128.4
25	Ireland	214.3	75	Tonga	162.0	127	United States	127.1
26	Antigua	213.2	76	Ivory Coast	162.0	128	Gabon	126.6
27	Brazil	212.3	77	South Africa	161.8	129	Mauritania	126.1
28	Tanzania	212.1	78	Senegal	161.7	130	Guatemala	124.7
29	Portugal	211.9	79	French Polynesia	161.4	131	British Virgin Islands	123.2
30	Spain	211.5	80	Jordan	161.3	132	Hungary	121.8
31	Chad	207.7	81	Uganda	161.1	133	Puerto Rico	120.1
32	Dominican Republic	207.4	82	Congo	159.6	134	Libya	119.6
33	South Korea	205.3	83	Paraguay	159.6	135	Malta	117.7
34	Zaire	205.2	84	Iraq	158.7	136	Algeria	114.3
35	Dominica	204.6	85	Samoa	158.7	137	Morocco	112.2
36	Italy	204.1	86	Norway	158.1	138	Nicaragua	109.6
37	Liberia	199.8	87	Iran	154.2			
38	India	198.7	88	Sri Lanka	154.2		*BOTTOM 10*	
39	Australia	198.5	89	Togo	153.3	139	Singapore	109.4
40	Japan	196.5	90	Burundi	152.7	140	Gilbert Islands	109.3
41	Philippines	195.2	91	Belgium	151.3	141	Niger	107.7
42	Jamaica	194.5	92	Niue Island	150.4	142	Gambia	107.2
43	Fiji	193.0	93	Sweden	150.2	143	Falkland Islands	104.9
44	Kenya	192.6	94	Guadeloupe	149.9	144	New Hebrides	100.8
45	St. Kitts-Nevis-Anguilla	191.5	95	Ethiopia	149.8	145	Rumania	100.0
46	New Zealand	189.4	96	Denmark	148.8	146	Soviet Union	98.6
47	United Kingdom	187.6	97	New Caledonia	148.3	147	Hong Kong	98.0
48	Gibraltar	184.9	98	Luxembourg	147.8	148	East Germany	81.2
49	Greece	184.8	99	Switzerland	147.8			

Source: International Labor Organization, *Yearbook of Labor Statistics.*

70. Fuel & Light Price Index

Fuel and light, treated as a single item by economists though not by producers, is described as the pacesetter of inflation. In many countries they fuel—to employ a light but legitimate wordplay—the rise in the cost of living. Both fuel and light are primary human needs and are therefore price-inelastic, i.e., demand is not influenced by price. Colder countries are particularly susceptible to variations in the availability and cost of fuel and light.

Number of Countries: 108
Midpoint: 165.7
Period Covered: 1976
Type of Ranking: Fuel & Light Price Index (1970=100); Highest to Lowest

Highlights & Findings: Increases in the fuel and light price index have been severe in the majority of the countries of the world. In 26 countries the index rose to over 200, and in only four countries did it decline. Much of this increase was accounted for by the quantum jump in the prices of heating oil and gasoline.

Regions	Africa	Asia & Oceania	Europe	Western Hemisphere
Most	Ghana (5)	Israel (2)	Iceland (3)	Argentina (1)
Least	Somalia (108)	Iraq (107)	East Germany (104)	Venezuela (102)

Rank	Country	Fuel & Light Price Index	Rank	Country	Fuel & Light Price Index	Rank	Country	Fuel & Light Price Index
	TOP 10		37	Netherlands	178.5	74	New Hebrides	140.8
1	Argentina	9,143.0	38	West Germany	176.4	75	Seychelles	138.8
2	Israel	543.1	39	Botswana	175.8	76	Mauritius	138.0
3	Iceland	385.9	40	Guatemala	175.5	77	Hong Kong	132.0
4	Yugoslavia	382.7	41	Dominica	175.3	78	Madagascar	131.1
5	Ghana	294.7	42	Belgium	174.9	79	Syria	129.2
6	Burma	292.1	43	Mozambique	174.7	80	Solomon Islands	128.1
7	El Salvador	269.7	44	Japan	172.9	81	Brazil	125.9
8	Ireland	262.0	45	Chad	172.5	82	Uganda	125.4
9	Costa Rica	248.3	46	Norway	172.4	83	Malta	124.1
10	Bermuda	245.9	47	Tanzania	172.2	84	Netherlands Antilles	122.4
			48	Malawi	171.0	85	Puerto Rico	121.2
	UPPER MIDDLE		49	Portugal	170.3	86	Samoa	121.0
11	Swaziland	241.6	50	Togo	169.2	87	Rumania	120.8
12	Finland	239.9	51	Fiji	168.6	88	Niger	116.9
13	Sweden	239.5	52	Peru	166.7	89	Jordan	116.8
14	Denmark	238.1	53	Austria	165.7	90	Ecuador	116.2
15	United Kingdom	236.1	54	New Zealand	165.7	91	Mauritania	115.9
16	Bangladesh	233.9				92	Iran	115.8
17	United States	227.8		*LOWER MIDDLE*		93	Zaire	114.4
18	Cape Verde	226.5	55	Senegal	165.6	94	Tunisia	113.4
19	Jamaica	222.8	56	Trinidad & Tobago	165.4	95	Gibraltar	111.4
20	Greenland	222.0	57	Switzerland	164.9	96	Gabon	111.1
21	St. Lucia	217.9	58	Surinam	161.9	97	Bahamas	107.5
22	St. Kitts-Nevis-Anguilla	213.8	59	Dominican Republic	161.6	98	Hungary	107.2
23	Lesotho	211.4	60	Australia	161.3			
24	South Korea	208.0	61	Gambia	160.4		*BOTTOM 10*	
25	Spain	205.2	62	New Caledonia	159.3	99	Congo	106.1
26	Honduras	203.3	63	Panama	157.5	100	Falkland Islands	105.3
27	Greece	196.7	64	Cyprus	156.4	101	Algeria	101.6
28	India	195.2	65	Ethiopia	155.9	102	Venezuela	101.3
29	Sri Lanka	194.9	66	South Yemen	155.6	103	Lebanon	101.0
30	Philippines	189.2	67	Kenya	155.5	104	East Germany	100.0
31	France	187.3	68	Sierra Leone	154.2	105	Egypt	99.1
32	Ivory Coast	183.7	69	Central African Empire	152.9	106	Libya	93.8
33	Liberia	183.7	70	Nigeria	151.4	107	Iraq	85.3
34	Canada	183.6	71	Luxembourg	150.8	108	Somalia	79.1
35	South Africa	181.8	72	Nepal	148.3			
36	Italy	179.1	73	Singapore	144.2			

Source: International Labor Organization, *Yearbook of Labor Statistics.*

71. Retail Trade Index

Retail trade, as distinguished from wholesale trade, is the resale of used and new goods to the general public, including the sale from displayed merchandise of such products as lumber and station-ery, which may not be for household or personal consumption in the strict sense. The base period of the index is 1970.

Number of Countries: 35 **Midpoint:** 197 **Period Covered:** 1976 **Type of Ranking:** Index of Retail Trade, 1970-100; Highest to Lowest	**Highlights & Rankings:** Retail trade is highly susceptible to inflationary pressures and reflects the general state of the economy more accurately than any other segment. Where there are no price controls, retail prices have a natural tendency to surge upwards and more so in times of scarcity or shortage. Argentina, which leads the ranking, is a classic case of a retail trade system gone wild.

Regions	Africa	Asia and Oceania	Europe	Western Hemisphere
Most	South Africa (12)	Israel (2)	Yugoslavia (4)	Argentina (1)
Least	Rhodesia (21)	Japan (18)	Switzerland (35)	United States (25)

Rank Country	Index of Retail Trade	Rank Country	Index of Retail Trade	Rank Country	Index of Retail Trade
TOP 10		12 South Africa	223	*BOTTOM 10*	
1 Argentina	5,184	13 New Zealand	219	26 Netherlands	177
2 Israel	799	14 Australia	218	27 Hungary	171
3 Colombia	567	15 United Kingdom	218	28 West Germany	160
4 Yugoslavia	393	16 Canada	204	29 Bulgaria	157
5 South Korea	278	17 Poland	204	30 France	156
6 Venezuela	277	18 Japan	197	31 Rumania	151
7 Mexico	265	19 Norway	197	32 Soviet Union	141
8 Finland	250	20 Denmark	190	33 Czechoslovakia	135
9 Ireland	235	21 Rhodesia (Zimbabwe)	190	34 East Germany	134
10 Greece	229	22 Belgium	188	35 Switzerland	129
		23 Austria	184		
MIDDLE		24 Sweden	181		
11 Italy	224	25 United States	179		

Source: *U.N. Statistical Yearbook.*

72. Public Revenues per Capita

In the following ranking and the ranking on public expenditures per capita, an attempt is made to present government receipts and expenditures in the most meaningful form possible, that is, per capita. International comparisons of government expenditures and receipts are rendered extremely difficult as a result of many circumstances. First, the level of total expenditures and receipts depends on the structure of the state's organization and on the scope of the government's economic activities. Many governments own and operate railways, power plants, and telephone and telegraph systems, which in other states are private enterprises. Second, budgetary systems and accounting practices vary from country to country. In many countries closed accounts represent only cash payments and cash collections, while in others pay orders, liabilities and commitments are also included.

Revenues or receipts generally comprise three broad categories: (1) direct taxes, including taxes on income and wealth, taxes on personal and corporate income, death and gift duties and social security taxes; (2) indirect taxes, i.e., taxes that take no account of the personal circumstances of the taxpayer and are therefore regressive, including general sales or turnover taxes, customs duties, entertainment duties, stamp duties, motor vehicle duties, real estate and land taxes and the profits of fiscal monopolies; and (3) nontax revenues, covering all current revenues not included in the above two categories, particularly noncompulsory receipts, such as those derived from government enterprises, sale of assets, rents and royalties.

Number of Countries: 143
Midpoint: $163.81
Period Covered: 1976
Type of Ranking: Government Revenues per Capita in Dollars; Highest to Lowest

Highlights & Findings: Six of the top 10 nations are oil producers and the impact of oil revenues is felt on the rank order throughout. Leaving aside the oil exporters, the per capita public revenues are highest in the Western European countries generally described as welfare states, where the tax scales on income and wealth are highest.

Regions	Africa	Asia & Oceania	Europe	Western Hemisphere
Most	Libya (16)	Qatar (1)	Luxembourg (5)	Canada (17)
Least	Rwanda (141)	Nepal (143)	Albania (105)	Haiti (123)

Rank	Country	Revenues per Capita ($)
	TOP 10	
1	Qatar	23,427.98
2	Kuwait	15,518.91
3	Nauru	6,371.50
4	Saudi Arabia	4,350.87
5	Luxembourg	3,207.67
6	United Arab Emirates	3,050.54
7	Sweden	2,696.36
8	Denmark	2,279.32
9	Netherlands	2,274.73
10.	Iraq	2,073.51
	UPPER MIDDLE	
11	Norway	1,984.40
12	Israel	1,970.35
13	Belgium	1,869.68
14	Oman	1,849.42
15	Bahrain	1,766.32
16	Libya	1,738.83
17	Canada	1,723.36
18	Finland	1,695.21
19	Australia	1,490.01
20	United States	1,476.44
21	Gabon	1,466.31
22	Iceland	1,445.88
23	United Kingdom	1,334.00
24	France	1,330.91
25	New Zealand	1,304.01
26	Soviet Union	1,205.89
27	Austria	1,095.28
28	West Germany	974.40
29	Switzerland	886.18
30	Hungary	853.32
31	Ireland	835.00
32	Venezuela	801.33
33	Czechoslovakia	772.57
34	Iran	768.52
35	East Germany	704.03
36	Trinidad & Tobago	698.67
37	Malta	681.26
38	Italy	649.68
39	Bahamas	636.06
40	Singapore	622.70
41	Mongolia	597.53
42	Syria	552.05
43	Greece	504.28
44	Surinam	456.67
45	Portugal	437.86
46	Egypt	416.51
47	Barbados	410.23

Rank	Country	Revenues per Capita ($)
48	Japan	406.10
49	Bulgaria	375.25
50	Spain	359.87
51	Rumania	349.06
52	Jamaica	333.49
53	Algeria	308.70
54	Yugoslavia	301.48
55	Cyprus	290.77
56	Grenada	287.07
57	South Africa	277.87
58	Taiwan	272.13
59	Tunisia	259.29
60	Seychelles	254.23
61	Morocco	251.39
62	Costa Rica	233.59
63	Fiji	232.62
64	North Korea	229.03
65	Guyana	226.41
66	Turkey	208.74
67	Poland	199.61
68	Papua New Guinea	196.92
69	Chile	189.94
70	Mauritius	185.09
71	Mexico	184.16
	LOWER MIDDLE	
72	Panama	163.81
73	Malaysia	163.56
74	Swaziland	161.32
75	South Korea	158.54
76	Congo	156.33
77	Uruguay	152.47
78	Nigeria	135.23
79	Western Samoa	134.77
80	Botswana	131.61
81	Brazil	123.32
82	Dominican Republic	120.93
83	Jordan	120.17
84	Lebanon	117.29
85	Zambia	112.03
86	Peru	109.25
87	Rhodesia (Zimbabwe)	107.20
88	Liberia	97.70
89	Nicaragua	96.47
90	Bolivia	89.80
91	Togo	88.16
92	Ecuador	85.49
93	Ivory Coast	82.43
94	Burma	79.90
95	El Salvador	78.11

Rank	Country	Revenues per Capita ($)
96	Guatemala	76.12
97	Senegal	75.52
98	Ghana	71.88
99	Tonga	69.85
100	Vietnam	67.68
101	Philippines	64.60
102	Guinea	64.53
103	Madagascar	63.68
104	Honduras	63.13
105	Albania	60.99
106	Sudan	60.06
107	Argentina	59.68
108	Cameroon	59.15
109	Paraguay	58.25
110	Colombia	58.16
111	Somalia	54.37
112	Indonesia	52.40
113	Thailand	49.65
114	Mauritania	49.07
115	Central African Empire	45.85
116	Sri Lanka	45.55
117	Kenya	43.77
118	Yemen Arab Republic	32.33
119	Uganda	31.67
120	Tanzania	31.27
121	Gambia	29.38
122	Sierra Leone	28.65
123	Haiti	28.52
124	Lesotho	27.75
125	South Yemen	27.44
126	Pakistan	24.67
127	Ethiopia	24.54
128	Zaire	23.00
129	Niger	20.57
130	Benin	20.24
131	Mozambique	19.89
132	Malawi	17.49
133	Chad	16.36
	BOTTOM 10	
134	Upper Volta	15.27
135	India	15.00
136	Bhutan	14.55
137	Afghanistan	13.49
138	Mali	13.37
139	Burundi	13.29
140	Comoros	12.81
141	Rwanda	11.41
142	Bangladesh	7.93
143	Nepal	6.94

Source: Cross-National Data Archive, Center for Social Analysis, Binghampton, N.Y.

73. Public Expenditures per Capita

Because of the diversity and complexity of public expenditures, it is not possible to describe the main categories under which they are presented in national budgets. However, considerable progress has been made in recent years in classifying government transactions according to rational functional headings. Such a classification usually distinguishes between current expenditures and capital expenditures and includes grants to foreign governments and net results of current operations of state trading enterprises. The percentages of public expenditures on some of the major functions, such as education, defense and social services, are given in other rankings.

Number of Countries: 143
Midpoint: $197.12
Period Covered: 1976
Type of Ranking: Public Expenditures per Capita, 1976, in Dollars; Status of the Budget (S=Surplus; B=Balanced; D=Deficit); Highest to Lowest

Highlights & Findings: Since public expenditures represent a compromise between expectations and needs on the one hand and resources on the other, it is interesting to note how many countries have managed to balance their budget or achieve a surplus. The count shows 28 countries with a surplus, 33 countries with a balanced budget and 78 countries with a deficit budget. The ranking also reveals that a balanced or surplus budget is the product of deliberate fiscal policy and is not directly related to the extent of resources. There are almost as many nations with balanced or surplus budgets at the bottom of the scale as there are at the top.

Regions	Africa	Asia	Europe	Western Hemisphere
Most	Libya (16)	Qatar (1)	Luxembourg (5)	Canada (17)
Least	Rwanda (142)	Bangladesh (143)	Albania (108)	Haiti (124)

Rank	Country	Per Capita Public Expenditures ($)	Status (S=Surplus; B=Balanced; D=Deficit)
	TOP 10		
1	Qatar	15,671.83	S
2	Saudi Arabia	4,350.87	B
3	Nauru	3,734.25	S
4	Kuwait	3,588.74	S
5	Luxembourg	3,271.26	D
6	United Arab Emirates	3,050.54	B
7	Denmark	2,697.36	D
8	Sweden	2,629.78	S
9	Netherlands	2,524.02	D
10	Belgium	2,243.73	D
	UPPER MIDDLE		
11	Oman	2,100.13	D
12	Norway	2,089.50	D
13	Iraq	2,073.51	B
14	Israel	1,969.03	S
15	Australia	1,823.59	D
16	Libya	1,789.31	D
17	Canada	1,781.54	D
18	Bahrain	1,766.32	B
19	United States	1,739.55	D
20	Finland	1,531.95	S
21	Gabon	1,466.31	B
22	United Kingdom	1,451.80	D
23	Iceland	1,410.29	S
24	France	1,378.87	D
25	Austria	1,362.51	D
26	New Zealand	1,304.01	B
27	West Germany	1,181.50	D
28	Soviet Union	1,172.99	S
29	Ireland	1,099.51	D
30	Switzerland	976.47	D
31	Italy	861.72	D
32	Hungary	860.96	D
33	Venezuela	838.81	D
34	Iran	789.03	D
35	Czechoslovakia	767.03	S
36	Trinidad & Tobago	739.28	D
37	Malta	725.12	D
38	East Germany	701.27	S
39	Bahamas	668.00	D
40	Greece	596.27	D
41	Mongolia	594.53	S
42	Syria	552.05	B
43	Jamaica	547.94	D
44	Surinam	521.45	D
45	Japan	505.74	D
46	Barbados	479.72	D
47	Singapore	478.70	S
48	Portugal	437.86	B
49	Egypt	416.51	B
50	Bulgaria	374.40	S
51	Spain	371.43	D
52	South Africa	364.97	D
53	Rumania	343.06	S
54	Guyana	334.23	D
55	Yugoslavia	329.31	D
56	Algeria	308.70	B
57	Morocco	294.67	D
58	Grenada	287.07	B
59	Taiwan	272.02	S
60	Cyprus	263.45	S
61	Panama	259.33	D
62	Tunisia	259.29	B
63	Seychelles	254.23	B
64	Mauritius	248.31	D
65	Mexico	247.26	D
66	Jordan	243.46	D
67	Fiji	234.21	D
68	Malaysia	233.25	D
69	Costa Rica	230.73	D
70	Turkey	229.54	D
71	North Korea	229.03	B
72	Papua New Guinea	197.12	D
	LOWER MIDDLE		
73	Poland	190.72	S
74	Chile	187.70	S
75	Uruguay	180.26	D
76	Lebanon	174.15	D
77	Swaziland	172.84	D
78	Peru	172.54	D
79	Nigeria	170.52	D
80	Zambia	162.90	D
81	Congo	156.33	B
82	South Korea	155.56	S
83	Western Samoa	135.31	D
84	Brazil	123.00	S
85	Argentina	145.89	D
86	Botswana	121.59	S
87	Nicaragua	116.33	D
88	Dominican Republic	114.82	S
89	Rhodesia (Zimbabwe)	105.87	S
90	Ghana	101.12	D
91	Ecuador	98.09	D
92	Guatemala	93.31	D
93	Bolivia	89.80	B
94	Liberia	88.19	S
95	Togo	88.16	B
96	Madagascar	83.78	D
97	Burma	82.97	D
98	Ivory Coast	82.43	B
99	El Salvador	80.19	D
100	Tonga	78.36	D
101	Senegal	75.52	B
102	Philippines	71.49	D
103	Honduras	68.72	D
104	Sri Lanka	68.68	D
105	Thailand	68.07	D
106	Vietnam	67.68	B

Rank	Country	Per Capita Public Expenditures ($)	Status (S=Surplus; B=Balanced; D=Deficit)	Rank	Country	Per Capita Public Expenditures ($)	Status (S=Surplus; B=Balanced; D=Deficit)	Rank	Country	Per Capita Public Expenditures ($)	Status (S=Surplus; B=Balanced; D=Deficit)
107	Guinea	64.53	B	120	Zaire	40.18	D	133	India	18.99	D
108	Albania	60.99	B	121	South Yemen	40.02	D				
109	Cameroon	59.15	B	122	Uganda	37.97	D		*BOTTOM 10*		
110	Kenya	57.47	D	123	Gambia	31.61	D	134	Mali	16.73	D
111	Indonesia	56.61	D	124	Haiti	31.25	D	135	Chad	16.36	B
112	Paraguay	55.48	S	125	Pakistan	31.15	D	136	Upper Volta	15.27	B
113	Somalia	54.37	B	126	Sierra Leone	30.80	D	137	Bhutan	14.55	B
114	Sudan	54.20	S	127	Ethiopia	29.14	D	138	Afghanistan	14.52	D
115	Colombia	52.53	S	128	Lesotho	27.75	B	139	Comoros	12.81	B
116	Mauritania	49.07	B	129	Malawi	26.35	D	140	Nepal	11.90	D
117	Yemen Arab Republic	46.31	D	130	Mozambique	26.05	D	141	Burundi	11.56	S
118	Central African Empire	45.85	B	131	Niger	20.57	B	142	Rwanda	11.45	D
119	Tanzania	43.68	D	132	Benin	20.24	B	143	Bangladesh	6.14	D

Source: Cross-National Data Archive, Center for Social Analysis, Binghampton, N.Y.

74. Expenditures on Civil Service as Percentage of Total Budget

An important element in determining the cost-benefit of public administration is the proportion of the national budget spent on wages and salaries. Ideally, this proportion should not exceed the ceiling of 10% recommended by public administration experts. But in the following ranking only three countries conform to this standard. The reason lies not so much in the level of civil service salaries—in fact, in most countries civil servants are not as well paid as their counterparts in business and industry—but in the proliferation of government agencies, red tape, low productivity, nepotism and patronage. Information is not available from any Communist countries for this ranking.

Number of Countries: 55
Midpoint: 25.46%
Period Covered: 1976
Type of Ranking: Expenditures on Civil Service Salaries as Percentage of Total Budget; Highest to Lowest

Highlights & Findings: Almost all countries at the top of the ranking are developing countries. Wages and salaries represent about 29% of total government outlays in nonoil-exporting developing countries (32% in the Western Hemisphere, 28% in Africa, 21% in Asia) but only 12% in industrialized countries.

Regions	Africa	Asia & Oceania	Europe	Western Hemisphere
Most	Ethiopia (6)	Yemen Arab Republic (1)	Greece (4)	Bahamas (2)
Least	Zambia (35)	Indonesia (48)	Switzerland (55)	Canada (47)

Rank	Country	Expenditures on Civil Service as Percentage of Total Budget	Rank	Country	Expenditures on Civil Service as Percentage of Total Budget	Rank	Country	Expenditures on Civil Service as Percentage of Total Budget
	TOP 10		9	Honduras	33.65	16	Mauritius	29.99
1	Yemen Arab Republic	52.16	10	Paraguay	33.32	17	Botswana	29.33
2	Bahamas	48.12				18	Cyprus	29.05
3	Bolivia	46.52		*UPPER MIDDLE*		19	Malta	28.83
4	Greece	42.37	11	Turkey	33.26	20	Nicaragua	27.55
5	Costa Rica	41.45	12	Dominican Republic	32.50	21	Peru	27.14
6	Ethiopia	38.43	13	Uruguay	31.29	22	Spain	26.62
7	Zaire	36.13	14	Guatemala	30.45	23	Singapore	26.55
8	Barbados	34.66	15	Tunisia	30.29	24	Syria	26.38

Rank	Country	Expenditures on Civil Service as Percentage of Total Budget	Rank	Country	Expenditures on Civil Service as Percentage of Total Budget	Rank	Country	Expenditures on Civil Service as Percentage of Total Budget
25	Philippines	26.19	35	Zambia	19.22		*BOTTOM 10*	
26	Venezuela	25.88	36	Denmark	18.69	46	India	12.98
27	Tanzania	25.73	37	Kuwait	17.84	47	Canada	12.85
28	Chile	25.46	38	South Korea	17.47	48	Indonesia	12.54
			39	Iceland	16.67	49	Italy	12.13
	LOWER MIDDLE		40	France	16.33	50	Austria	10.75
29	Morocco	25.29	41	United Kingdom	15.71	51	Netherlands	10.56
30	Mexico	23.57	42	United States	14.34	52	Finland	10.49
31	Thailand	21.81	43	Ireland	13.71	53	West Germany	9.99
32	Sri Lanka	21.20	44	Brazil	13.69	54	Sweden	9.03
33	Gambia	20.65	45	Israel	13.30	55	Switzerland	6.50
34	Nigeria	19.37						

Source: International Monetary Fund.

75. Public Expenditures on Social Welfare

Governmental expenditures on social security and welfare provide an important yardstick for measuring social progress. Because social welfare programs must compete with other sectors for funds and for their share of finite national revenues, such expenditures can reveal the extent of a government's commitment to general welfare and the satisfaction of human needs.

Number of Countries: 53
Midpoint: 11.85%
Period Covered: 1976
Type of Ranking: Percentage of Funds Allocated for Social Security and Welfare in Public Budgets; Highest to Lowest

Highlights & Findings: The ratio is highest in industrialized countries and lowest in developing countries, where, ironically, the need for social services is most critical and acute. Nineteen countries included in this ranking spend less than 5% of their national budgets on social welfare, while 18 countries spend over 25%.

Regions	Africa	Asia & Oceania	Europe	Western Hemisphere
Most	Chad (18)	New Zealand (17)	Sweden (2)	Uruguay (1)
Least	Botswana (53)	Nepal (50)	Rumania (24)	Peru (52)

Rank	Country	Funds for Social Security & Welfare as Percentage of National Budgets	Rank	Country	Funds for Social Security & Welfare as Percentage of National Budget	Rank	Country	Funds for Social Security & Welfare as Percentage of National Budget
	TOP 10		18	Chad	25.80	36	Tunisia	4.57
1	Uruguay	51.76	19	Sri Lanka	24.22	37	Bahamas	4.16
2	Sweden	49.11	20	United Kingdom	22.99	38	Turkey	3.93
3	West Germany	48.84	21	Mexico	21.93	39	South Korea	3.78
4	Switzerland	46.66	22	Nicaragua	19.90	40	Thailand	3.64
5	Denmark	44.53	23	Morocco	15.47	41	Iran	3.55
6	Brazil	42.59	24	Rumania	12.37	42	Kuwait	3.37
7	Austria	40.37	25	Tanzania	12.01	43	Philippines	2.75
8	United States	36.09	26	Barbados	11.96			
9	Canada	35.36	27	Kenya	11.85		*BOTTOM 10*	
10	Yugoslavia	34.73				44	Bolivia	2.70
				LOWER MIDDLE		45	Malaysia	2.55
	UPPER MIDDLE		28	Israel	11.68	46	Pakistan	1.56
11	Malta	31.25	29	Taiwan	10.64	47	Singapore	1.45
12	Cyprus	30.63	30	Zaire	9.86	48	Syria	1.43
13	Norway	30.59	31	Guatemala	8.65	49	Ecuador	1.38
14	Iceland	29.95	32	Venezuela	7.31	50	Nepal	0.66
15	Finland	29.27	33	Dominican Republic	6.25	51	Mauritius	0.62
16	Greece	27.66	34	Burma	5.64	52	Peru	0.21
17	New Zealand	27.47	35	Honduras	4.73	53	Botswana	0.16

Source: International Monetary Fund.

FINANCE & BANKING

There is a strange, mysterious quality about financial rankings that brings to mind the smoke-filled boardrooms of high finance peopled by the gnomes of Zurich. The fact is that finance is not merely another facet of economic activity; it is the pilot of the economy determining its direction, speed, and thrust and manipulating its controls. If the economy tends to pitch and roll or if it goes into a nosedive, it must be maneuvered back into safety with a few simple and crude mechanisms, such as higher interest rate, devaluation or large-scale borrowing. In no sector is there such a heavy concentration of power as in finance. The economy of the free world is probably controlled by fewer than 500 men who guide the surging flow of money through the invisible financial pipelines.

This section deals with four key areas of finance. The first determines the wealth of nations through rankings of their currency per capita, gold holdings and SDR (special drawing rights) allocations. The second group examines public debt and public debt service. The third group ranks countries by private investment flows, market prices of industrial shares and rates of discount of central banks. The final group ranks countries by their rate of savings and savings per capita.

76. Currency per Capita

Currency in circulation is a widely used economic indicator, but its comparability is limited unless, as in the following ranking, it is converted into a common currency and expressed in per capita terms. Because currency in circulation is closely regulated by central banks and is often used as an instrument of fiscal policy, it has considerable economic significance. Used with other indicators, such as per capita GNP, it can provide a reliable guide to the health of the monetary system.

Number of Countries: 107	
Midpoint: $37.00	
Period Covered: 1977	
Type of Ranking: Currency in Circulation per Capita in U.S. Dollars; Highest to Lowest	

Highlights & Findings: The ranking reveals vast disparities in currency in circulation per capita; Switzerland at the top of the list has 2,163 times more currency in circulation per capita than Sri Lanka at the bottom. Thirty-one countries have less than $25 and only 28 countries have more than $150.

Regions	Africa	Asia & Oceania	Europe	Western Hemisphere
Most	Libya (13)	Qatar (6)	Switzerland (1)	United States (10)
Least	Uganda (104)	Sri Lanka (107)	Poland (69)	Haiti (97)

Rank	Country	Currency in Circulation per Capita ($)	Rank	Country	Currency in Circulation per Capita ($)	Rank	Country	Currency in Circulation per Capita ($)
	TOP 10		12	West Germany	354.10	26	Ireland	191.17
1	Switzerland	1,168.18	13	Libya	350.00	27	Jordan	172.82
2	Belgium	690.00	14	Singapore	331.98	28	Syria	160.88
3	Sweden	618.99	15	Canada	319.37	29	Finland	147.73
4	Norway	591.66	16	Italy	312.28	30	Iraq	134.33
5	France	484.42	17	Portugal	304.63	31	Algeria	133.53
6	Qatar	450.10	18	Lebanon	300.00	32	Cyprus	131.57
7	Austria	435.65	19	Greece	280.00	33	Venezuela	120.00
8	Netherlands	410.64	20	Australia	276.25	34	New Zealand	112.21
9	Kuwait	399.57	21	Spain	265.79	35	Yugoslavia	110.45
10	United States	372.89	22	Bahrain	255.51	36	Israel	100.00
			23	Denmark	250.00	37	Hungary	95.00
	UPPER MIDDLE		24	Saudi Arabia	250.00	38	Surinam	89.00
11	Japan	356.42	25	United Kingdom	213.03	39	Mexico	79.25

Rank	Country	Currency in Circulation per Capita ($)	Rank	Country	Currency in Circulation per Capita ($)	Rank	Country	Currency in Circulation per Capita ($)
40	Malaysia	72.10	62	Gabon	31.06	86	Pakistan	15.37
41	Czechoslovakia	72.00	63	Ivory Coast	31.06	87	Angola	14.69
42	Iran	70.00	64	Niger	31.06	88	Nigeria	14.50
43	Tunisia	69.75	65	Senegal	31.06	89	Indonesia	13.27
44	Morocco	66.30	66	Togo	31.06	90	Philippines	13.00
45	Taiwan	64.80	67	Upper Volta	31.06	91	Afghanistan	12.00
46	East Germany	57.00	68	Ecuador	31.00	92	Zambia	12.00
47	Iceland	54.00	69	Poland	29.00	93	Kenya	10.66
48	Turkey	50.61	70	Thailand	28.10	94	India	10.50
49	Egypt	49.22	71	Ghana	28.07	95	Sudan	9.74
50	Costa Rica	48.00	72	Cuba	28.03	96	Rhodesia (Zimbabwe)	9.00
51	South Africa	42.00	73	Bolivia	27.79	97	Haiti	7.21
52	Peru	39.98	74	Dominican Republic	27.26			
53	Uruguay	38.80	75	Colombia	26.15		*BOTTOM 10*	
54	South Korea	37.00	76	Paraguay	25.77	98	Burma	6.18
			77	Nicaragua	24.00	99	Ethiopia	4.00
	LOWER MIDDLE		78	China	22.76	100	Tanzania	4.00
55	Guatemala	33.00	79	Honduras	21.38	101	Nepal	3.80
56	Argentina	32.00	80	El Salvador	21.15	102	Malawi	3.53
57	Benin	31.06	81	Brazil	20.00	103	Mozambique	3.00
58	Cameroon	31.06	82	Chile	19.53	104	Uganda	1.66
59	Chad	31.06	83	Western Samoa	18.24	105	Bangladesh	1.50
60	Central African Empire	31.06	84	Mali	16.95	106	Laos	1.00
61	Congo	31.06	85	Zaire	15.54	107	Sri Lanka	0.54

Source: Cross-National Data Archive, Center for Social Analysis, Binghampton, N.Y.

77. Strongest Currency

A nation's currency is not only a unit of monetary transactions within national borders but also an index of economic performance and strength and a tool of international trade and finance. Its latter two functions have become critical in the post-World War II years as the international monetary system has wrestled with the task of regulating the gyrations and fluctuations of exchange rates. The International Monetary Fund, as the policeman of the world's monetary system, has choreographed for the past 30 years the intricate movements, the tumbles, the jetes and the glissades of national currencies across the stage of the world money markets.

The fund must be credited with some of the most successful innovations in monetary history: special drawing rights, or paper gold; the floating currency, or currency without a fixed exchange rate tied to a weighted basket of commodity prices; the crawling peg, or the regulation of exchange rates by frequent but small adjustments to reflect trading values on the exchange markets; and even the snake, the joint Eurocurrency float. Its constant monitioring of monetary systems has made it possible to trace the progress of national currencies over a period of 30 years and to identify those that have consistently moved upward as well as those that have lost ground, both measured against the United States dollar, which, until its recent setbacks, was universally accepted as a fixed point of reference, a kind of financial North Star. Despite the numerous charges that exchange rates are manipulated by the gnomes of Zurich, the rates by and large reflect the inherent strength of a currency in terms of national resources, economic policies, trading strategies and international reserves, especially when considering a span of some nine years and not a few seasons or months.

Number of Countries: 144
Midpoint: 0.00%
Period Covered: 1969 to 1977
Type of Ranking: Gain (+) or Loss (−) in Exchange Rate per U.S. Dollar, 1969 to 1977; Highest to Lowest

Highlights & Findings: Sixty-six countries have gained in value against the dollar during the period under review. These include the currencies of almost all oil-producing countries, EEC members other than the United Kingdom, and Japan. Because the decline of the U.S. dollar in 1978 has introduced new complications that may diminish its usefulness as a standard, the survey is limited to the period ending in 1977. If anything the dollar's convulsions may have served to strengthen the EEC currencies as well as the Japanese yen.

Regions	Africa	Asia & Oceania	Europe	Western Hemisphere
Most	Tunisia (17)	Japan (5)	Switzerland (1)	Cuba (19)
Least	Gambia (143)	Cambodia (144)	Iceland (138)	Brazil (142)

Rank	Country (Currency)	Gain/Loss Against the U.S. Dollar, 1969-1977 (%)
	TOP 10	
1	Switzerland (Franc)	+49.86
2	West Germany (Deutsche Mark)	+39.62
3	Austria (Schilling)	+38.34
4	Netherlands (Guilder)	+33.58
5	Japan (Yen)	+31.33
6	Belgium (Franc)	+29.33
7	Luxembourg (Franc)	+29.33
8	Hungary (Forint)	+27.51
9	Norway (Krone)	+24.36
10	Singapore (Dollar)	+22.97
	UPPER MIDDLE	
11	Malaysia (Ringgit)	+22.72
12	Saudi Arabia (Riyal)	+22.00
13	Kuwait (Dinar)	+20.58
14	Mongolia (Tughrik)	+20.50
15	Soviet Union (Rouble)	+18.88
16	United Arab Emirates (Dirham)	+18.14
17	Tunisia (Dinar)	+18.04
18	Albania (Lek)	+18.00
19	Cuba (Peso)	+18.00
20	Denmark (Krone)	+17.92
21	Rumania (Leu)	+17.16
22	East Germany (Mark)	+17.11
23	Oman (Rial)	+17.11
24	South Yemen (Dinar)	+17.11
25	Bulgaria (Lev)	+17.09
26	Czechoslovakia (Koruna)	+17.08
27	Iraq (Dinar)	+17.08
28	Libya (Dinar)	+17.08
29	China (Yuan)	+17.07
30	Yemen Arab Republic (Rial)	+17.05
31	Poland (Zloty)	+17.00
32	Bahrain (Dinar)	+16.92
33	Qatar (Riyal)	+16.90
34	Algeria (Dinar)	+16.73
35	Ethiopia (Birr)	+16.40
36	Benin (CFAF)	+12.59
37	Cameroon (CFAF)	+12.59
38	Central African Empire (CFAF)	+12.59
39	Chad (CFAF)	+12.59
40	Congo (CFAF)	+12.59
41	France (Franc)	+12.59
42	Gabon (CFAF)	+12.59
43	Ivory Coast (CFAF)	+12.59
44	Madagascar (Franc)	+12.59
45	Mali (Franc)	+12.59
46	Niger (CFAF)	+12.59
47	Senegal (CFAF)	+12.59
48	Togo (CFAF)	+12.59
49	Upper Volta (CFAF)	+12.59
50	Somalia (Shilling)	+11.87
51	Morocco (Dirham)	+11.66
52	Egypt (Pound)	+10.00
53	Jordan (Dinar)	+9.26
54	Guinea (Syli)	+8.35
55	Iran (Rial)	+7.54
56	Rwanda (Franc)	+7.16
57	Sweden (Krona)	+6.59
58	Lebanon (Pound)	+5.23
59	Surinam (Guilder)	+4.74
60	Venezuela (Bolivar)	+3.59
61	Cyprus (Pound)	+3.55
62	Thailand (Baht)	+2.53
63	Bahamas (Dollar)	+1.96
64	Mauritania (Ouguiya)	+1.93
65	Malta (Pound)	+1.22
66	Australia (Dollar)	+0.83
	LOWER MIDDLE	
67	Afghanistan (Afghani)	0.00
68	Dominican Republic (Peso)	0.00
69	El Salvador (Colon)	0.00
70	Guatemala (Quetzal)	0.00
71	Haiti (Gourde)	0.00
72	Honduras (Lempira)	0.00
73	Liberia (Dollar)	0.00
74	Nicaragua (Cordoba)	0.00
75	Panama (Balboa)	0.00
76	Paraguay (Guarani)	0.00
77	Sudan (Pound)	0.00
78	Barbados (Dollar)	−0.05
79	Finland (Markka)	−0.23
80	Fiji (Dollar)	−1.96
81	Burundi (Franc)	−2.85
82	Canada (Dollar)	−3.22
83	Syria (Pound)	−3.40
84	Samoa (Tala)	−6.42
85	Jamaica (Dollar)	−9.09
86	Angola (Kwanza)	−9.73
87	Mozambique (Escudo)	−10.12
88	Zambia (Kwacha)	−11.10
89	Papua New Guinea (Kina)	−12.04
90	New Zealand (Dollar)	−12.54
91	Ghana (Cedi)	−12.70
92	Kenya (Shilling)	−14.06
93	Uganda (Shilling)	−14.60
94	Tanzania (Shilling)	−15.20
95	India (Rupee)	−15.48
96	Seychelles (Rupee)	−16.66
97	Mauritius (Rupee)	−17.08
98	Equatorial Guinea (Ekuele)	−18.06
99	Spain (Peseta)	−18.06
100	Grenada (Dollar)	−20.00
101	Trinidad & Tobago (Dollar)	−20.00
102	Greece (Drachma)	−20.50
103	Botswana (Pula)	−21.63
104	Lesotho (Rand)	−21.63
105	Swaziland (Lilangeni)	−21.63
106	South Africa (Rand)	−21.63
107	Nepal (Rupee)	−23.45
108	Indonesia (Rupiah)	−27.30
109	Guyana (Dollar)	−27.50
110	Costa Rica (Colon)	−29.06
111	United Kingdom (Pound)	−32.26
112	Ireland (Pound)	−32.29
113	Sierra Leone (Leone)	−32.29
114	Ecuador (Sucre)	−38.88
115	Italy (Lira)	−40.33
116	Cape Verde (Escudo)	−42.37
117	Guinea-Bissau (Escudo)	−42.37
118	Portugal (Escudo)	−42.37
119	Sao Tome & Principe (Escudo)	−42.37
120	Sri Lanka (Rupee)	−44.64
121	Maldives (Rupee)	−45.22
122	Yugoslavia (Dinar)	−46.60
123	Burma (Kyat)	−54.90
124	South Korea (Won)	−59.21
125	Argentina (Peso)	−59.28
126	Bolivia (Peso)	−68.35
127	Zaire (Zaire)	−70.00
128	Mexico (Peso)	−81.20
129	Uruguay (Peso)	−82.05
130	Nigeria (Naira)	−82.41
131	Philippines (Peso)	−89.74
132	Bangladesh (Taka)	−102.71
133	Pakistan (Rupee)	−107.28
134	Colombia (Peso)	−107.97
	BOTTOM 10	
135	Malawi (Kwacha)	−113.27
136	Turkey (Lira)	−115.04
137	Peru (Sol)	−122.63
138	Iceland (Krona)	−141.18
139	Laos (Kip)	−150.00
140	Chile (Peso)	−152.10
141	Israel (Pound)	−196.00
142	Brazil (Cruzeiro)	−251.14
143	Gambia (Dalasi)	−428.89
144	Cambodia (Riel)	−2,872.77

Source: International Monetary Fund.

78. Gold Holdings

Much of the world's gold is held not by private individuals but by governments. Until SDRs, or paper gold, were devised by the IMF, these holdings guaranteed the convertibility of national currencies. Of the total world gold reserves of $47.33 billion, $6.265 billion is held by institutions. Gold was valued at $35 per fine troy ounce through 1971, at $38 from 1971 through 1973 and at $42.22 from 1973 through 1974. Since 1974 gold has been valued at 35 SDRs and then converted into U.S. dollars at the prevailing exchange rate. The Soviet Union, China, Cuba and Eastern European countries are not members of IMF, and their gold holdings are not reported to that body. The gold holdings of the Soviet Union are reported to be considerable, but estimates vary widely.

Number of Countries: 82
Midpoint: $43 million
Period Covered: 1976
Type of Ranking: Gold Holdings in Million Dollars; Highest to Lowest

Highlights & Findings: The United States alone accounts for 27.2% of the world's reported gold reserves and the top five countries account for 65.2%. However, it is significant that the U.S. gold holdings have declined by 7.4% since 1967, while those of oil-exporting countries have risen by 481% since 1970.

Regions	Africa	Asia & Oceania	Europe	Western Hemisphere
Most	South Africa (14)	Japan (10)	West Germany (2)	United States (1)
Least	Zambia (78)	South Yemen (77)	Iceland (75)	Paraguay (82)

Rank	Country	Gold Holdings ($ million)	Rank	Country	Gold Holdings ($ million)	Rank	Country	Gold Holdings ($ million)
	TOP 10		28	Saudi Arabia	125	56	Ecuador	16
1	United States	11,171	29	Egypt	99	57	Malta	14
2	West Germany	4,782	30	Libya	99	58	Morocco	12
3	France	4,108	31	Thailand	95	59	Ethiopia	11
4	Switzerland	3,387	32	Denmark	74	60	Zaire	11
5	Italy	3,354	33	Malaysia	68	61	Burma	8
6	Netherlands	2,209	34	Pakistan	66	62	Qatar	7.8
7	Belgium	1,715	35	Mexico	65	63	Ghana	7
8	Portugal	1,126	36	Yugoslavia	59	64	Bahamas	6
9	Canada	879	37	Colombia	57	65	Bahrain	6
10	Japan	859	38	Chile	54	66	Surinam	6
			39	Brazil	53	67	Nepal	5.3
	UPPER MIDDLE		40	Israel	45	68	Benin	5.2
11	United Kingdom	853	41	Philippines	43	69	Tunsia	5
12	Austria	849				70	Dominican Republic	4
13	Spain	580		*LOWER MIDDLE*		71	South Korea	4
14	South Africa	515	42	Peru	41	72	Barbados	3
15	Venezuela	454	43	Norway	40			
16	Lebanon	375	44	Afghanistan	38		*BOTTOM 10*	
17	Australia	300	45	Finland	34	73	Indonesia	2
18	India	282	46	Syria	33	74	Costa Rica	1.4
19	Sweden	236	47	Jordan	32	75	Iceland	1.3
20	Kuwait	227	48	Nigeria	23	76	New Zealand	1
21	Algeria	223	49	United Arab Emirates	22	77	South Yemen	1
22	Iraq	167	50	El Salvador	20	78	Zambia	1
23	Argentina	163	51	Guatemala	20	79	Nicaragua	0.7
24	Iran	152	52	Bangladesh	19	80	Haiti	0.1
25	Greece	149	53	Ireland	19	81	Honduras	0.1
26	Turkey	145	54	Cyprus	17	82	Paraguay	0.1
27	Uruguay	144	55	Bolivia	16.8			

Source: International Monetary Fund.

79. SDR Quotas

SDRs, or special drawing rights, designate a monetary reserve of the International Monetary Fund from which member nations may draw credit in proportion to their contribution to the fund. Originally intended to supplement rather than supplant gold and foreign exchange, they have become increasingly effective in stabilizing international financial transactions and in easing temporary shortages in foreign currencies experienced by most nations. The interest rate on SDR withdrawals is about 60 to 80% of a combined market rate, which is the weighted average of short-term interest rates in the United States, West Germany, the United Kingdom, France and Japan. The quotas are reviewed annually; the latest on December 13, 1978, increased the total allocations to SDR 58.6 billion.

Number of Countries: 137
Midpoint: SDR 82.5 million
Period Covered: 1978
Type of Ranking: SDR Quotas in the IMF; Highest to Lowest

Highlights & Findings: Since the quotas are fixed in proportion to members' contributions to the IMF, five nations—France, West Germany, Japan, the United Kingdom and the United States—hold 43.68% of the quotas. There are only 16 other nations—Argentina, Australia, Belgium, Brazil, Canada, India, Indonesia, Iran, Italy, Mexico, Netherlands, Saudi Arabia, South Africa, Spain, Sweden and Venezuela—with more than 1% each of the total. These 21 nations together may thus be considered the most powerful nations in the financial world.

Regions	Africa	Asia & Oceania	Europe	Western Hemisphere
Most	South Africa (21)	Japan (5)	United Kingdom (2)	United States (1)
Least	Seychelles (136)	Maldives (137)	Malta (106)	Dominica (134)

Rank	Country	Quota (SDR million)
	TOP 10	
1	United States	12,607.5
2	United Kingdom	4,387.5
3	West Germany	3,234.0
4	France	2,878.5
5	Japan	2,488.5
6	Canada	2,035.5
7	Italy	1,860.0
8	India	1,717.5
9	Netherlands	1,422.0
10	Belgium	1,335.0
	UPPER MIDDLE	
11	Australia	1,185.0
12	Iran	1,075.0
13	Saudi Arabia	1,040.1
14	Brazil	997.5
15	Venezuela	990.0
16	Spain	835.5
17	Argentina	802.5
18	Mexico	802.5
19	Indonesia	720.0
20	Sweden	675.0
21	South Africa	636.0
22	Taiwan	550.0
23	Nigeria	540.0
24	Austria	495.0
25	Denmark	465.0
26	Norway	442.5
27	Algeria	427.5
28	Pakistan	427.5
29	Yugoslavia	415.5
30	Kuwait	393.3
31	Finland	393.0
32	Malaysia	379.5
33	Rumania	367.5
34	New Zealand	348.0
35	Egypt	342.0
36	Chile	325.5

Rank	Country	Quota (SDR million)
37	Philippines	315.0
38	Israel	307.5
39	Turkey	300.0
40	Libya	298.4
41	Colombia	289.5
42	Greece	277.5
43	Thailand	271.5
44	Portugal	258.0
45	South Korea	255.9
46	Peru	246.0
47	Iraq	234.1
48	Ireland	232.5
49	Bangladesh	228.0
50	Zaire	228.0
51	Morocco	225.0
52	Zambia	211.5
53	United Arab Emirates	202.6
54	Sri Lanka	178.5
55	Ghana	159.0
56	Vietnam	135.0
57	Sudan	132.0
58	Uruguay	126.0
59	Trinidad & Tobago	123.0
60	Ivory Coast	114.0
61	Jamaica	111.0
62	Burma	109.5
63	Ecuador	105.0
64	Kenya	103.5
65	Syria	94.5
66	Tunisia	94.5
67	Singapore	92.4
68	Dominican Republic	82.5
69	Tanzania	82.5
	LOWER MIDDLE	
70	Guatemala	76.5
71	Uganda	75.0
72	Afghanistan	67.5
73	Bolivia	67.5

Rank	Country	Quota (SDR million)
74	Cameroon	67.5
75	Panama	67.5
76	Qatar	66.2
77	El Salvador	64.5
78	Senegal	63.0
79	Costa Rica	61.5
80	South Yemen	61.5
81	Liberia	55.5
82	Ethiopia	54.0
83	Cyprus	51.0
84	Honduras	51.0
85	Madagascar	51.0
86	Nicaragua	51.0
87	Bahamas	49.5
88	Luxembourg	46.5
89	Sierra Leone	46.5
90	Gabon	45.0
91	Guinea	45.0
92	Jordan	45.0
93	Papua New Guinea	45.0
94	Iceland	43.5
95	Mali	40.5
96	Mauritius	40.5
97	Guyana	37.5
98	Surinam	37.5
99	Oman	35.1
100	Burundi	34.5
101	Haiti	34.5
102	Paraguay	34.5
103	Rwanda	34.5
104	Somalia	34.5
105	Bahrain	30.0
106	Malta	30.0
107	Malawi	28.5
108	Nepal	28.5
109	Togo	28.5
110	Lebanon	27.9
111	Fiji	27.0
112	Barbados	25.5

Rank	Country	Quota (SDR million)	Rank	Country	Quota (SDR million)	Rank	Country	Quota (SDR million)
113	Congo	25.5	122	Yemen Arab Republic	19.5	129	Grenada	4.5
114	Mauritania	25.5	123	Swaziland	18.0	130	Western Samoa	4.5
115	Cambodia	25.0	124	Equatorial Guinea	15.0	131	Comoros	3.5
116	Benin	24.0	125	Botswana	13.5	132	Solomon Islands	3.2
117	Central African Empire	24.0	126	Gambia	13.5	133	Sao Tome & Principe	3.0
118	Chad	24.0	127	Lesotho	10.5	134	Dominica	2.9
119	Laos	24.0				135	Cape Verde	2.0
120	Niger	24.0		BOTTOM 10		136	Seychelles	2.0
121	Upper Volta	24.0	128	Guinea-Bissau	5.9	137	Maldives	1.4

Source: International Monetary Fund

80. External Public Debt as Percentage of GNP

External public debt represents outstanding publicly guaranteed loans that have been disbursed less canceled loan commitments and repayments of principal. Because disbursements of loans and grants are made on differing financial terms, the burden of the external public debt may vary from country to country. Concessional loans are those with an interest rate of 3% or less and are usually extended by governments or international organizations. The average interest rate of loan commitments from official creditors in 1975 was 5.1%, the maturity period 24.3 years and the grant element 35%. In the case of suppliers, the interest rate was 7.9% and the maturity period 10.1 years, while in the case of the private creditors and private banks the interest rate was 8.1% and the maturity periods were 7.6 years and 6.9 years respectively.

Total outstanding external public debt for 84 developing countries in 1979 was $120.2 billion, including undisbursed amounts. Of this amount, private lenders accounted for $32.1 billion.

Number of Countries: 84
Midpoint: 19%
Period Covered: 1976
Type of Ranking: External Public Debt as Percentage of GNP; Total External Public Debt in million Dollars; Highest to Lowest

Highlights & Findings: Average external public debt is 20.9% of GNP in low-income countries and 17% in middle-income countries.

Regions	Africa	Asia & Oceania	Europe	Western Hemisphere
Most	Guinea (1)	Israel (7)	Greece (60)	Panama (11)
Least	Nigeria (81)	Hong Kong (84)	Spain (77)	Trinidad & Tobago (80)

Rank	Country	External Public Debt as Percentage of GNP	Total External Public Debt ($ million)	Rank	Country	External Public Debt as Percentage of GNP	Total External Public Debt ($ million)	Rank	Country	External Public Debt as Percentage of GNP	Total External Public Debt ($ million)
	TOP 10			12	Pakistan	45.1	5,968	26	Jordan	28.7	447
1	Guinea	99.1	872	13	Bolivia	41.4	1,000	27	Togo	28.5	167
2	Mauritania	76.7	354	14	Chile	39.1	3,527	28	Sierra Leone	27.7	159
3	Somalia	70.9	277	15	Bangladesh	39.0	1,943	29	Sudan	27.4	1,268
4	Zaire	63.8	2,002	16	Nicaragua	37.8	642	30	Ivory Coast	27.2	1,183
5	Congo	56.5	405	17	Malawi	37.5	258	31	South Korea	26.7	6,690
6	Zambia	53.7	1,184	18	Algeria	37.4	5,853	32	Liberia	25.7	191
7	Israel	51.1	6,828	19	Afghanistan	37.2	911	33	Morocco	24.6	2,131
8	Mali	49.5	376	20	Jamaica	36.6	855	34	Costa Rica	24.0	534
9	South Yemen	48.8	226	21	Tanzania	35.7	914	35	Cameroon	23.3	529
10	Egypt	48.1	5,043	22	Peru	31.3	3,379	36	Papua New Guinea	23.3	289
				23	Tunisia	30.3	1,356	37	Benin	23.2	95
	UPPER MIDDLE			24	Honduras	29.1	335	38	Kenya	22.2	688
11	Panama	46.9	1,091	25	Indonesia	29.1	10,141	39	Sri Lanka	22.1	682

Rank	Country	External Public Debt as Percentage of GNP	Total External Public Debt ($ million)	Rank	Country	External Public Debt as Percentage of GNP	Total External Public Debt ($ million)	Rank	Country	External Public Debt as Percentage of GNP	Total External Public Debt ($ million)
40	Mexico	20.8	15,547	55	Upper Volta	12.4	84	72	Portugal	5.4	875
41	Chad	19.7	94	56	Philippines	12.3	2,126	73	Thailand	5.2	822
42	Uruguay	19.0	688	57	Malaya	12.1	1,619	74	Burundi	5.1	24
				58	Singapore	11.8	687				
	LOWER MIDDLE			59	Brazil	11.7	14,852		*BOTTOM 10*		
43	Central African Empire	18.7	79	60	Greece	10.4	2,377	75	Guatemala	5.0	212
44	Senegal	17.0	336	61	Madagascar	10.2	181	76	Argentina	4.6	4,255
45	Niger	16.1	112	62	Burma	9.7	321	77	Spain	4.6	4,761
46	Colombia	15.6	2,449	63	Haiti	9.5	92	78	Rhodesia (Zimbabwe)	4.5	156
47	Syria	15.2	968	64	Venezuela	9.4	2,970	79	Lebanon	4.2	64
48	Ethiopia	14.9	431	65	Turkey	8.8	3,569	80	Trinidad & Tobago	4.1	99
49	India	14.6	12,392	66	Lesotho	8.5	15	81	Nigeria	3.3	954
50	Dominican Republic	14.1	528	67	Rwanda	8.1	35	82	Nepal	3.2	44
51	Paraguay	13.1	222	68	Ghana	7.5	594	83	Iraq	2.4	391
52	Taiwan	13.0	2,236	69	Uganda	6.8	212	84	Hong Kong	0.7	62
53	Ecuador	13.0	639	70	Yugoslavia	6.8	2,488				
54	El Salvador	12.9	272	71	Iran	6.5	4,271				

Source: World Bank Debt Reporting Service.

81. Debt Service as Percentage of GNP

Debt service is the sum of interest payments and repayments of principal on external public and publicly guaranteed debt. Debt-servicing capacity is commonly assessed as a percentage of either the GNP or total exports of goods. It is important to note that the ratio does not cover private debt, which for some countries is substantial. It should also be noted that debt contracted for the purchase of military equipment is not usually reported.

Number of Countries: 80
Midpoint: 1.7%
Period Covered: 1976
Type of Ranking: Debt Service as Percentage of GNP; Total Debt Service in Million Dollars; Highest to Lowest

Highlights & Findings: The debt service ratio for low-income countries is 1.1% and that for middle-income countries is 2.0%. Since 1970 the ratio has risen by 0.1% for low-income countries and by 0.6% for middle-income countries. Variations in the ratio are determined not only by the capacity to repay but also the fiscal policies of the governments and the nature of the creditors.

Regions	Africa	Asia & Oceania	Europe	Western Hemisphere
Most	Mauritania (1)	Sri Lanka (11)	Greece (28)	Chile (2)
Least	Uganda (78)	Nepal (80)	Spain (73)	Guatemala (74)

Rank	Country	Debt Service as Percentage of GNP	Interest Payments on External Debt (million $)	Rank	Country	Debt Service as Percentage of GNP	Interest Payments on External Debt (million $)	Rank	Country	Debt Service as Percentage of GNP	Interest Payments on External Debt (million $)
	TOP 10			9	Bolivia	4.3	35	16	Peru	3.5	178
1	Mauritania	14.7	3	10	Panama	4.2	60	17	Mexico	3.1	1,070
2	Chile	8.4	209					18	Costa Rica	3.0	28
3	Guinea	6.1	16.7		*UPPER MIDDLE*			19	Trinidad & Tobago	3.0	10
4	Egypt	6.0	77	11	Sri Lanka	4.1	23	20	Liberia	2.7	6
5	Algeria	5.7	341	12	Israel	4.0	196	21	Sudan	2.6	55
6	Uruguay	5.7	57	13	Ivory Coast	4.0	66	22	Honduras	2.5	15
7	Nicaragua	4.6	44	14	South Korea	3.8	345	23	Morocco	2.5	89
8	Jamaica	4.5	54	15	Sierra Leone	3.7	4	24	Tunisia	2.4	41

Rank	Country	Debt Service as Percentage of GNP	Interest Payments on External Debt (million $)	Rank	Country	Debt Service as Percentage of GNP	Interest Payments on External Debt (million $)	Rank	Country	Debt Service as Percentage of GNP	Interest Payments on External Debt (million $)
25	Zambia	2.4	52	44	Zaire	1.6	35	65	Madagascar	0.7	5
26	Congo	2.3	6	45	Iran	1.5	332	66	Portugal	0.7	41
27	Indonesia	2.3	354	46	Chad	1.4	2	67	Turkey	0.7	114
28	Greece	2.2	177	47	Dominican Republic	1.4	12	68	Upper Volta	0.7	1
29	Malaysia	2.2	120	48	Kenya	1.4	23	69	Burundi	0.6	1
30	Papua New Guinea	2.2	19	49	Yugoslavia	1.4	141	70	Thailand	0.6	44
31	Senegal	2.1	18	50	Bangladesh	1.3	29				
32	Pakistan	2.0	129	51	Brazil	1.3	734		*BOTTOM 10*		
33	Togo	2.0	4	52	Philippines	1.3	87	71	Ghana	0.5	17
34	Taiwan	1.9	145	53	Singapore	1.3	35	72	Mali	0.5	9
35	Malawi	1.9	6	54	Venezuela	1.3	122	73	Spain	0.5	267
36	Cameroon	1.8	19	55	Haiti	1.2	–	74	Guatemala	0.4	13
37	Central African Empire	1.8	2	56	Afghanistan	1.1	–	75	Iraq	0.4	13
38	Colombia	1.8	125	57	Paraguay	1.1	7	76	Lesotho	0.2	–
39	Jordan	1.8	8	58	Tanzania	1.1	13	77	Rhodesia		
				59	Burma	1.0	8		(Zimbabwe)	0.2	2
	LOWER MIDDLE			60	Argentina	0.9	258	78	Uganda	0.2	2
40	Benin	1.7	1	61	Ethiopia	0.9	11	79	Hong Kong	0.1	2
41	Ecuador	1.7	25	62	India	0.9	253	80	Nepal	0.1	1
42	El Salvador	1.7	12	63	Niger	0.9	2				
43	Syria	1.7	27	64	Nigeria	0.9	39				

Source: World Bank Debt Reporting Service.

82. Net Direct Foreign Private Investment

Net direct foreign private investment is the net amount invested by nonresidents in enterprises over which they exercise a significant degree of managerial control. The bottom end of the same scale, where the quantities are negative, in effect measures the outflow of capital from developed countries, especially in the form of direct investments.

Number of Countries: 63
Midpoint: $27 million
Period Covered: 1976
Type of Ranking: Net Direct Private Investment in Million Dollars; Highest to Lowest

Highlights & Findings: This ranking provides a clue to the favorite destinations of private investment capital from developed countries. These are the so-called safe countries, where the risk of nationalization is low, political conditions are at least apparently stable and investment laws are relatively liberal.

Regions	Africa	Asia & Oceania	Europe	Western Hemisphere
Most	Nigeria (6)	Australia (2)	Belgium (5)	Brazil (1)
Least	Libya (56)	Japan (61)	United Kingdom (62)	United States (63)

Rank	Country	Net Direct Private Investment ($ million)	Rank	Country	Net Direct Private Investment ($ million)	Rank	Country	Net Direct Private Investment ($ million)
	TOP 10		9	South Korea	173	16	Ecuador	80
1	Brazil	1,009	10	Peru	170	17	Thailand	79
2	Australia	784				18	Taiwan	69
3	Singapore	722		*UPPER MIDDLE*		19	Costa Rica	55
4	Mexico	689	11	Spain	165	20	Portugal	55
5	Belgium	473	12	Philippines	127	21	Austria	50
6	Nigeria	387	13	Guatemala	96	22	Ivory Coast	50
7	Norway	185	14	Denmark	92	23	Mauritania	50
8	New Zealand	179	15	Trinidad & Tobago	82	24	Colombia	49

Rank	Country	Net Direct Private Investment ($ million)	Rank	Country	Net Direct Private Investment ($ million)	Rank	Country	Net Direct Private Investment ($ million)
25	Egypt	42	38	Honduras	8	53	France	−391
26	Kenya	42	39	Pakistan	8			
27	Morocco	38	40	Jordan	7		*BOTTOM 10*	
28	Israel	35	41	Haiti	5	54	Saudi Arabia	−401
29	Cameroon	31	42	Central African Empire	4	55	Sweden	−495
30	Turkey	28	43	Ethiopia	4	56	Libya	−523
31	Chad	27	44	Rwanda	4	57	Netherlands	−645
32	Finland	27	45	Mali	3	58	Venezuela	−828
			46	Somalia	2	59	West Germany	−927
	LOWER MIDDLE		47	Jamaica	−1	60	Canada	−965
33	Ghana	13	48	Chile	−5	61	Japan	−1,786
34	Bolivia	12	49	Uganda	−7	62	United Kingdom	−2,026
35	Nicaragua	12	50	Paraguay	−32	63	United States	−7,335
36	El Salvador	10	51	Italy	−60			
37	Greece	10	52	South Africa	−95			

Source: World Bank.

83. Stock Market Performance (Industrial Shares)

Index numbers of market prices for industrial shares are based primarily on common shares traded on the leading exchange or exchanges of each country and are intended to cover a representative sample of industrial companies. In some cases where an industrial index was not available, a general index including shares of companies in the utilities, transportation, distribution and finance fields has been used. The indices are designed to show the increase in value accruing to an investor who bought in the base period and who retained the proceeds of all rights, warrants and share dividends made available since that period.

Number of Countries: 29	
Midpoint: 104	**Highlights & Findings:** Eleven countries report a decline in the index during the period covered. Five countries reported gains of over 100% but these were evidently inflationary.
Period Covered: January 1, 1977	
Type of Ranking: Market Price Index of Industrial Shares, 1977 (1970=100); Highest to Lowest	

Regions	Africa	Asia & Oceania	Europe	Western Hemisphere
Most	South Africa (21)	Israel (2)	Denmark (5)	Chile (1)
Least	N.A.	Australia (28)	Italy (29)	Colombia (16)

Rank	Country	Market Price Index of Industrial Shares (1970=100)	Rank	Country	Market Price Index of Industrial Shares (1970=100)	Rank	Country	Market Price Index of Industrial Shares (1970=100)
	TOP 10			*MIDDLE*			*BOTTOM 10*	
1	Chile	487	11	United States	124	20	Pakistan	92
2	Israel	336	12	Ireland	120	21	South Africa	92
3	Venezuela	250	13	Peru	116	22	Philippines	91
4	Japan	232	14	Canada	105	23	Netherlands	89
5	Denmark	218	15	Belgium	104	24	New Zealand	89
6	Mexico	182	16	Colombia	103	25	Norway	88
7	Finland	161	17	Spain	102	26	Switzerland	80
8	Sweden	159	18	India	101	27	France	78
9	Austria	130	19	West Germany	95	28	Australia	76
10	United Kingdom	127				29	Italy	47

Source: International Monetary Fund.

84. Discount Rates of Central Banks

The rate of discount of central banks—also known as the minimum lending rate—is the crucial figure that bankers watch all the time. Upon it depends the rates at which banks can borrow and lend money. It generally fluctuates in accordance with fiscal policy, with higher rates during times when there is a heavy deficit in the balance of payments or when a nation wants to attract foreign capital. Thus, it is one of the most reliable indicators of the general health of a country's monetary system.

Number of Countries: 59
Midpoint: 8%
Period Covered: 1977
Type of Ranking: Rate of Discount of Central Banks; Highest to Lowest

Highlights & Findings: Because many governments are using interest rates as a monetary tool for controlling inflation, interest rates are highest in countries with runaway inflation. An interesting sidelight is the case of Switzerland, which actually discourages the inflow of foreign money with an interest rate of 1.5%. Any rate over 5% is generally an indication of considerable inflationary pressures in the economy.

Regions	Africa	Asia & Oceania	Europe	Western Hemisphere
Most	South Africa (16)	South Korea (4)	Italy (7)	Chile (1)
Least	Rwanda (58)	Japan (53)	Switzerland (59)	Honduras (54)

Rank	Country	Rates of Discount of Central Banks (%)	Rank	Country	Rates of Discount of Central Banks (%)	Rank	Country	Rates of Discount of Central Banks (%)
	TOP 11		20	Benin	8.00	40	Norway	6.00
1	Chile	75.00	21	Ecuador	8.00	41	Philippines	6.00
2	Brazil	30.00	22	Ghana	8.00	42	United States	6.00
3	Colombia	20.00	23	Iran	8.00	43	Tunisia	5.75
4	South Korea	14.00	24	Ivory Coast	8.00	44	Austria	5.50
5	Peru	12.50	25	Niger	8.00	45	Jordan	5.50
6	New Zealand	12.00	26	Senegal	8.00	46	United Kingdom	5.50
7	Italy	11.50	27	Spain	8.00	47	Ireland	5.10
8	Greece	11.00	28	Sweden	8.00	48	Libya	5.00
9	Iceland	10.00	29	Togo	8.00	49	Mauritania	5.00
10	Pakistan	10.00	30	Upper Volta	8.00	50	Syria	5.00
11	Sri Lanka	10.00				51	Venezuela	5.00
				LOWER MIDDLE				
	UPPER MIDDLE		31	Canada	7.50		*BOTTOM 8*	
12	France	9.50	32	Costa Rica	7.00	52	Mexico	4.50
13	Denmark	9.00	33	Egypt	7.00	53	Japan	4.25
14	India	9.00	34	Guyana	6.50	54	Honduras	4.00
15	Jamaica	9.00	35	Portugal	6.50	55	West Germany	3.50
16	South Africa	9.00	36	El Salvador	6.10	56	Netherlands	3.50
17	Thailand	9.00	37	Belgium	6.00	57	Nigeria	3.50
18	Turkey	9.00	38	Mauritius	6.00	58	Rwanda	3.00
19	Finland	8.25	39	Nicaragua	6.00	59	Switzerland	1.50

Source: *U.N. Monthly Bulletin of Statistics.*

85. National Saving Rate

The average national saving rate—an important element in domestic investment capacity—is calculated from national accounts data by dividing the sum of gross national savings by the sum of the annual GNP and converting the resulting ratios into percentages. The ratio varies from 23.8% for industrialized countries to 19.5% for developing countries. Within developing countries themselves, the rate varies from 22.3% for South Europe, 32.5% for the Middle East, 20.8% for Africa, 13.8% for South Asia, 22.3% for East Asia and 19.0% for Latin America.

Number of Countries: 120
Midpoint: 18.2%
Period Covered: Early 1970s
Type of Ranking: Average National Saving Rate in Percentage; Highest to Lowest

Highlights & Findings: Six of the top 10 are oil producers, a not surprising conclusion. At the bottom of the scale eight countries—six of them African—have a negative saving rate. Much of the saving by countries like Kuwait, Saudi Arabia and Hong Kong is channeled into other countries.

Regions	Africa	Asia & Oceania	Europe	Western Hemisphere
Most	Libya (3)	Kuwait (1)	Austria (9)	Venezuela (7)
Least	Lesotho (120)	Vietnam (117)	Malta (82)	Barbados (118)

Rank	Country	Average National Saving Rate (%)	Rank	Country	Average National Saving Rate (%)	Rank	Country	Average National Saving Rate (%)
	TOP 10		41	Turkey	22.4	82	Malta	12.4
1	Kuwait	66.8	42	Canada	22.3	83	Cameroon	12.3
2	Saudi Arabia	54.8	43	South Korea	22.1	84	Sudan	11.9
3	Libya	49.4	44	Rhodesia (Zimbabwe)	21.9	85	Pakistan	11.7
4	Japan	40.1	45	Swaziland	21.9	86	Senegal	11.6
5	Iran	37.0	46	Spain	21.8	87	Bolivia	11.3
6	Zambia	35.5	47	Greece	21.6	88	Ghana	11.3
7	Venezuela	34.4	48	Argentina	21.4	89	Chile	11.1
8	Algeria	32.6	49	Italy	21.1	90	Madagascar	9.9
9	Austria	32.6	50	Denmark	20.8	91	Central African Empire	9.8
10	Finland	32.0	51	Portugal	20.6	92	Uruguay	9.8
			52	Ireland	20.3	93	Malawi	9.7
	UPPER MIDDLE		53	Mozambique	20.3	94	Burma	8.9
11	Switzerland	31.9	54	Ivory Coast	19.8	95	Jamaica	8.8
12	Nigeria	31.4	55	United Kingdom	19.6	96	Sierra Leone	8.6
13	Singapore	30.9	56	Colombia	19.1	97	Benin	8.0
14	Luxembourg	30.6	57	Syria	19.0	98	Somalia	7.9
15	Hong Kong	30.2	58	United States	18.9	99	Guyana	7.2
16	Oman	29.8	59	Paraguay	18.3	100	Egypt	6.4
17	Norway	29.6	60	Brazil	18.2	101	Bangladesh	6.2
18	Netherlands	28.7	61	Mexico	18.1	102	Israel	5.4
19	France	28.6				103	Rwanda	5.1
20	West Germany	28.1		*LOWER MIDDLE*		104	Fiji	4.4
21	Gabon	27.1	62	Liberia	17.4	105	Mali	4.4
22	South Africa	26.8	63	Tunisia	17.1	106	Gambia	4.1
23	New Zealand	26.6	64	Costa Rica	17.0	107	Afghanistan	3.5
24	Iraq	26.3	65	Zaire	16.7	108	Togo	3.2
25	Australia	26.2	66	Ethiopia	16.4	109	Burundi	2.8
26	Iceland	26.2	67	Cyprus	16.1	110	Niger	1.5
27	Yugoslavia	25.4	68	Tanzania	16.1			
28	Belgium	25.2	69	Sri Lanka	15.7		*BOTTOM 10*	
29	Trinidad & Tobago	24.6	70	Ecuador	15.3	111	Haiti	1.4
30	Papua New Guinea	24.4	71	Lebanon	15.2	112	Jordan	0.2
31	China	24.3	72	India	15.0	113	Mauritania	−0.9
32	Angola	23.3	73	Dominican Republic	14.8	114	Congo	−2.0
33	Sweden	23.1	74	Guatemala	14.5	115	Upper Volta	−2.2
34	Mauritius	23.0	75	Morocco	14.2	116	Chad	−2.4
35	Malaysia	22.8	76	Peru	14.1	117	Vietnam	−2.4
36	Philippines	22.7	77	Honduras	13.8	118	Barbados	−4.6
37	Kenya	22.6	78	Indonesia	13.8	119	Guinea	−9.3
38	Panama	22.5	79	El Salvador	13.2	120	Lesotho	−17.3
39	Thailand	22.5	80	Uganda	13.1			
40	Botswana	22.4	81	Nicaragua	12.5			

Source: World Bank.

86. Savings per Capita

The rate of savings is accepted by economists as a key indicator of the health of an economy. Paradoxi-cally, the rate is often greater in times of inflation, as people tend to salt away their savings as a hedge against the anticipated rainy days and become more wary of investments. The rate is also influenced by what is called disposable income, i.e., personal in-come left after deduction of taxes. Lower taxes, therefore, generally encourage savings.

Number of Countries: 25
Midpoint: 1,788 SDR
Period Covered: 1977
Type of Ranking: Savings per Capita in SDRs and National Currency; Highest to Lowest

Highlights & Findings: Continued inflation in all free-market economies has led to pronounced swelling of the savings accounts in these countries. In 1976 the growth rate for savings accounts was more than 200% in Argentina—the country highest hit by inflation—and 5% in Sweden. In poorer countries postal and state savings accounts absorbed most of the increased savings. Switzerland remains the most thrifty nation, a position it has occupied for a number of years.

Regions	Africa	Asia & Oceania	Europe	Western Hemisphere
Most	N.A.	Japan (2)	Switzerland (1)	United States (4)
Least	N.A.	Sri Lanka (23)	Portugal (20)	Colombia (25)

Rank	Country	Savings per Capita in SDRs	National Currency		Rank	Country	Savings per Capita SDRs	National Currency		Rank	Country	Savings per Capita SDRs	National Currency	
		TOP 5			8	Norway	2,602	15,678	krone	18	Hungary	968	8,237	forint
1	Switzerland	7,269	20,696	franc	9	Austria	2,567	50,009	schilling	19	Greece	783	33,677	drachma
2	Japan	4,906	1,668,811	yen	10	France	2,374	13,706	franc	20	Portugal	704	25,812	escudo
3	Belgium	3,552	148,511	franc	11	Australia	1,868	1,997	dollar					
4	United States	3,254	3,781	dollar	12	Finland	1,802	7,888	markka			*BOTTOM 5*		
5	Sweden	3,120	14,957	krona	13	Netherlands	1,788	5,104	guilder	21	Singapore	313	894	dollar
					14	United Kingdom	1,668	1,138	pound	22	Sri Lanka	312	30	rupee
		MIDDLE			15	Spain	1,420	112,703	peseta	23	Thailand	101	2,385	baht
6	West Germany	2,689	7,382	mark	16	Italy	1,303	1,324,441	lira	24	Argentina	25	8,074	peso
7	Denmark	2,659	17,879	kroner	17	New Zealand	1,043	1,276	dollar	25	Colombia	13	566	peso

Source: International Savings Bank Institute, Zurich, Switzerland.

TRADE

International trade passed the $2 trillion mark for the first time in history in 1976, marking the recovery of the world economy from the recession of the early 1970s. Imports passed the trillion mark with $1.026 trillion, while exports nudged that mark with $989 billion. For the period 1973-76 world exports expanded at an average yearly rate of 4%, as compared with 8.5% in the preceding decade. One of the more striking features of this recovery was the behavior of trade relative to production. During the downswing in 1975 the volume of world trade fell by twice the decline in world output (4% versus 2%), while during the recovery it expanded at nearly twice the rate of production.

In industrial countries the recovery of demand stimulated more imports than exports; the volume of the former increased by 14% and that of the latter by 11%. In terms of value, exports from industrial countries represented about 63% of the world total as compared to 69% in the years preceding the 1973 hike in the price of petroleum. Exports by oil-exporting countries rose by about one-fifth in value and about 12% in volume to reach a new peak of $132 billion, representing more than 13% of world exports. The combined exports of oil-importing developing countries rose by 17% to $120 billion (about 12% of world exports), but because of growing balance of payments problems, imports declined by 5% in value and even more markedly in volume. Exports from the Eastern Communist countries rose by 11% to $95 billion, or 9.5% of world exports. In commodities, world trade in primary products climbed in value by nearly 14%, agricultural products by nearly 11.5%, primary products of mineral origin by 15% and manufactured products by 12%. The largest increases were reported for automobiles (19%), household equipment (22%) and clothing (17%). Machinery increased by only 5.5% (reflecting the weakness of investment demand in industrial countries) and steel actually declined.

The first group of rankings in this section presents exports and imports per capita. A series of indices follows: the import price index, export price index, terms of trade, ratio of exports to imports and the ratio of international reserves to imports. The third group focuses on the share of primary commodities in exports and the share of food in imports. The last group examines the annual growth rates of imports and exports.

87. Balance of Trade

Although the balance of trade may vary for each country from year to year, certain patterns persist over long periods. Thus, 1976 may be taken as a representative year for the mid-1970s. Because a nation's gold holdings and international reserves are the sum total of the balances of trade, there is a direct relation between this ranking and that of international reserves and gold holdings.

Number of Countries: 125
Midpoint: −$111 million
Period Covered: 1976
Type of Ranking: Total Balance of Trade in U.S. Dollars; Highest to Lowest

Highlights & Findings: Only 32 nations had a favorable balance of trade in 1976. Of these, 10 are oil-producers. Saudi Arabia, the leader, accounts for 28.7% of the balance of trade in these 32 nations and West Germany for 16.8%. At the end of the scale is the United States with a whopping negative balance of $15.5 billion; nine of the bottom 10 are the industrialized nations of the West. Nothing illustrates more dramatically the growing fault lines in international economy.

Regions	Africa	Asia & Oceania	Europe	Western Hemisphere
Most	Libya (5)	Saudi Arabia (1)	West Germany (2)	Venezuela (7)
Least	South Africa (115)	Turkey (117)	United Kingdom (124)	United States (125)

Rank	Country	Balance of Trade 1976 ($ million)	Rank	Country	Balance of Trade 1976 ($ million)	Rank	Country	Balance of Trade 1976 ($ million)
	TOP 10		42	Sierra Leone	−44	84	Reunion	−356
1	Saudi Arabia	24,360	43	Dominican Republic	−48	85	Sudan	−426
2	West Germany	14,250	44	Guatemala	−48	86	Netherlands Antilles	−430
3	Iran	9,737	45	Togo	−48	87	New Zealand	−459
4	Kuwait	6,522	46	Mali	−53	88	Jordan	−578
5	Libya	4,488	47	Chad	−55	89	Thailand	−592
6	Iraq	4,072	48	Malawi	−57	90	Panama	−611
7	Venezuela	3,126	49	Ghana	−61	91	Czechoslovakia	−671
8	Austria	3,016	50	Zaire	−61	92	Bahamas	−681
9	Indonesia	2,874	51	Uruguay	−63	93	Lebanon	−727
10	Japan	2,426	52	Iceland	−66	94	Tunisia	−740
			53	Somalia	−69	95	Ireland	−879
	UPPER MIDDLE		54	Madagascar	−71	96	Sweden	−894
11	Nigeria	2,368	55	Ethiopia	−75	97	Syria	−921
12	Australia	1,784	56	Mauritius	−85	98	Soviet Union	−969
13	Argentina	883	57	India	−91	99	Pakistan	−990
14	Brunei	754	58	Guyana	−94	100	Finland	−1,051
15	Gabon	639	59	Bolivia	−97	101	South Korea	−1,058
16	Angola	602	60	Cameroon	−98	102	Hungary	−1,085
17	Netherlands	593	61	Benin	−104	103	Morocco	−1,356
18	Chile	387	62	Upper Volta	−107	104	Philippines	−1,507
19	Ivory Coast	324				105	Peru	−1,687
20	Trinidad & Tobago	286				106	Israel	−1,742
21	Malaysia	284		*LOWER MIDDLE*		107	East Germany	−1,835
22	Uganda	280	63	Honduras	−111	108	Egypt	−2,286
23	Canada	218	64	Tanzania	−111	109	Singapore	−2,485
24	Papua New Guinea	143	65	Senegal	−115	110	Yugoslavia	−2,489
25	Ecuador	134	66	South Yemen	−125	111	Portugal	−2,497
26	Liberia	77	67	Afghanistan	−127	112	Belgium-Luxembourg	−2,521
27	Switzerland	71	68	Zambia	−127	113	Mexico	−2,732
28	New Caledonia	25	69	Barbados	−133	114	Poland	−2,850
29	El Salvador	16	70	Fiji	−136	115	South Africa	−3,042
30	Congo	14	71	Cyprus	−173			
31	Mauritania	14	72	Malta	−192		*BOTTOM 10*	
32	Nicaragua	10	73	Costa Rica	−201	116	Norway	−3,192
33	Rumania	−1	74	Cuba	−203	117	Turkey	−3,239
34	Burundi	−3	75	Mozambique	−215	118	Denmark	−3,306
35	Niger	−7	76	Bulgaria	−244	119	Greece	−3,470
36	Burma	−12	77	Algeria	−251	120	Brazil	−3,494
37	Sri Lanka	−21	78	Yemen Arab Republic	−283	121	Italy	−6,459
38	Rwanda	−22	79	Kenya	−285	122	France	−8,587
39	Colombia	−30	80	Jamaica	−308	123	Spain	−8,736
40	Paraguay	−41	81	Bahrain	−318	124	United Kingdom	−9,715
41	Haiti	−42	82	Bangladesh	−350	125	United States	−15,549
			83	Hong Kong	−356			

Source: *Yearbook of International Trade Statistics.*

88. Exports Per Capita

Export or perish is the catch phrase that describes the mercantile strategy of most nations of the world. Success in this strategy is best measured in terms of exports per capita.

Number of Countries: 125
Midpoint: $187
Period Covered: Latest Available Year, 1974-76
Type of Ranking: Exports per Capita in U.S. Dollars; Highest to Lowest

Highlights & Findings: The top seven nations are either oil-producing or oil-refining nations, reflecting the price advantage of petroleum in world markets. The next 10 nations are small nations with surplus export capacity and moderate domestic demand. As usual, African nations dominate the bottom 10.

Regions	Africa	Asia & Oceania	Europe	Western Hemisphere
Most	Gabon (14)	Kuwait (2)	Belgium-Luxembourg (8)	Bahamas (1)
Least	Upper Volta (122)	Yemen Arab Republic (125)	Soviet Union (77)	Haiti (113)

Rank	Country	Exports Per Capita ($)	Rank	Country	Exports Per Capita ($)	Rank	Country	Exports Per Capita ($)
	TOP 10		42	Cyprus	402	84	Peru	83
1	Bahamas	13,709	43	Jamaica	400	85	Bolivia	82
2	Kuwait	10,138	44	Cuba	394	86	Cameroon	78
3	Netherlands Antilles	9,988	45	Guyana	345	87	Ghana	77
4	Brunei	6,394	46	Ivory Coast	323	88	Angola	75
5	Bahrain	4,985	47	Malaysia	322	89	Morocco	71
6	Saudi Arabia	3,909	48	Poland	321	90	Thailand	69
7	Libya	3,322	49	Mauritius	305	91	Paraguay	64
8	Belgium-Luxembourg	3,220	50	Algeria	292	92	Colombia	62
9	Netherlands	2,917	51	Greece	277	93	Indonesia	61
10	Singapore	2,888	52	Liberia	272	94	Jordan	57
			53	Rumania	251	95	Philippines	56
	UPPER MIDDLE		54	Costa Rica	250	96	Togo	55
11	Switzerland	2,338	55	Nicaragua	243	97	Mexico	53
12	New Caledonia	2,315	56	Spain	243	98	Kenya	47
13	Sweden	2,243	57	Yugoslavia	226	99	Egypt	40
14	Gabon	2,143	58	Fiji	219	100	Sri Lanka	38
15	Norway	1,965	59	South Korea	215	101	Madagascar	36
16	Hong Kong	1,947	60	Papua New Guinea	202	102	Sierra Leone	36
17	Iceland	1,836	61	Chile	198	103	Turkey	36
18	Denmark	1,797	62	Uruguay	191	104	Zaire	35
19	West Germany	1,659	63	Portugal	187	105	Sudan	34
20	Canada	1,648				106	Uganda	30
21	Trinidad & Tobago	1,627		*LOWER MIDDLE*		107	Malawi	29
22	Finland	1,341	64	Lebanon	184	108	Tanzania	29
23	Austria	1,133	65	Reunion	184	109	Somalia	27
24	France	1,055	66	El Salvador	175	110	Mozambique	22
25	Ireland	1,048	67	Nigeria	163	111	Rwanda	19
26	Australia	943	68	Zambia	163	112	Niger	18
27	New Zealand	890	69	Ecuador	154	113	Haiti	17
28	United Kingdom	827	70	Argentina	152	114	Mali	17
29	Iraq	744	71	Dominican Republic	148	115	Pakistan	16
30	Venezuela	740	72	Syria	140			
31	Malta	694	73	Tunisia	137		*BOTTOM 10*	
32	East Germany	677	74	Mauritania	133	116	Benin	15
33	Israel	668	75	Congo	132	117	Burundi	14
34	Italy	658	76	Panama	132	118	Afghanistan	12
35	Bulgaria	614	77	Soviet Union	131	119	Ethiopia	10
36	Iran	608	78	South Africa	125	120	Chad	9
37	Czechoslovakia	606	79	Guatemala	121	121	India	9
38	Japan	598	80	Senegal	111	122	Upper Volta	7
39	Hungary	578	81	South Yemen	111	123	Bangladesh	5
40	United States	527	82	Honduras	107	124	Burma	5
41	Barbados	416	83	Brazil	93	125	Yemen Arab Republic	2

Source: *Yearbook of International Trade Statistics.*

89. Imports Per Capita

Imports per capita is a useful measure of two factors: the success of import-substitution efforts and the degree of economic self-dependence. Both goals can be pursued only to a limited degree without affecting development efforts adversely. Most nations that impose import controls and high tariffs also classify imports into various classes ranging from essential to prohibited. Others permit imports only through state agencies or through a rigorous system of licenses. The efficiency of such controls and licensing varies from country to country. In many countries they only tend to encourage smuggling, an activity which is not reflected in the statistics presented below.

Number of Countries: 135
Midpoint: $298.00
Period Covered: Latest Available Year, 1974-76
Type of Ranking: Imports per Capita in U.S. Dollars; Highest to Lowest

Highlights & Findings: Imports are highest in countries experiencing a rapid rate of development or in countries that serve as entrepots engaged in processing and re-exporting, such as the Bahamas. Northern European countries also have a high import rate per capita.

Regions	Africa	Asia	Europe	Western Hemisphere
Most	Libya (18)	Bahrain (3)	Netherlands (2)	Bahamas (1)
Least	Uganda (134)	Burma (135)	Rumania (73)	Haiti (123)

Rank	Country	Imports Per Capita (U.S.$)	Rank	Country	Imports Per Capita (U.S. $)	Rank	Country	Imports Per Capita (U.S. $)
	TOP 10		42	Jamaica	550	94	Maritius	122
1	Bahamas	16,952	43	Panama	487	95	Congo	121
2	Netherlands	11,779	44	Venezuela	487	96	Argentina	118
3	Bahrain	6,163	45	Spain	485	97	Turkey	118
4	Singapore	3,978	46	Guyana	465	98	Egypt	100
5	Belgium-Luxembourg	3,467	47	Fiji	453	99	Bolivia	99
6	Kuwait	3,224	48	Lebanon	453	100	Mexico	97
7	Netherlands	2,874	49	Portugal	443	101	Cameroon	93
8	Norway	2,757	50	Cuba	416	102	Philippines	90
9	Denmark	2,450	61	Poland	404	103	Ghana	83
10	Sweden	2,352	62	Mauritius	402	104	Thailand	83
			63	Iraq	378	105	Paraguay	79
	UPPER MIDDLE		64	Costa Rica	352	106	Togo	76
11	Switzerland	2,327	65	Yugoslavia	342	107	Kenya	68
12	Iceland	2,136	66	Iran	313	108	Angola	65
13	New Caledonia	2,123	67	Algeria	307	109	Colombia	63
14	Hong Kong	2,028				110	Sudan	60
15	Brunei	1,681		*LOWER MIDDLE*		111	Sierra Leone	50
16	Canada	1,638	68	Malaysia	298	112	Somalia	49
17	Finland	1,563	69	Jordan	271	113	Benin	48
18	Libya	1,555	70	Tunisia	266	114	Madagascar	45
19	Austria	1,534	71	Syria	261	115	Mozambique	45
20	West Germany	1,427	72	Ivory Coast	258	116	Yemen Arab Republic	44
21	Trinidad & Tobago	1,362	73	Rumania	251	117	Indonesia	41
22	Ireland	1,327	74	South Korea	245	118	Malawi	40
23	Malta	1,276	75	Nicaragua	239	119	Sri Lanka	40
24	Saudi Arabia	1,273	76	Liberia	228	120	Tanzania	37
25	France	1,217	77	Uruguay	214	121	Zaire	37
26	Israel	1,171	78	Peru	191	122	Pakistan	29
27	New Zealand	1,036	79	Zambia	188	123	Haiti	26
28	United Kingdom	1,001	80	South Yemen	185	124	Mali	26
29	Barbados	948	81	South Africa	174	125	Upper Volta	25
30	Gabon	938	82	El Salvador	171			
31	Reunion	882	83	Chile	161		*BOTTOM 10*	
32	Australia	813	84	Dominican Republic	158	126	Rwanda	24
33	East Germany	786	89	Papua New Guinea	152	127	Chad	23
34	Italy	773	86	Honduras	147	128	Niger	20
35	Hungary	681	87	Morocco	147	129	Afghanistan	18
36	Cyprus	672	88	Soviet Union	145	130	Burundi	15
37	Greece	656	89	Senegal	139	131	Ethiopia	12
38	Czechoslovakia	651	90	Ecuador	136	132	Bangladesh	9.5
39	Bulgaria	642	91	Guatemala	129	133	India	9
40	United States	599	92	Nigeria	127	134	Uganda	7
41	Japan	576	93	Brazil	125	135	Burma	6

Source: *Yearbook of International Trade Statistics.*

90. Import Price Index

One of the anomalies of international trade is the differing growth rates of import prices and export prices. Many nations trying hard to increase exports find that their goods are fetching less and less while they continue to pay more and more for their imports. Since the price structure of exports and imports (rather than their volume) is ultimately the critical factor for creating and maintaining a healthy balance of trade, the import price index has become a key indicator in measuring the real growth rates in external trade. The import price index is based on 1970=100 and reflects unit values. The coverage of the index is often limited in the case of developing countries to a small number of primary products.

Number of Countries: 59
Midpoint: 209
Period Covered: Latest Available Year, 1974-76
Type of Ranking: Import Price Index (1970 =100) in National Currency; Highest to Lowest

Highlights & Findings: At the top of the ranking are those nations most deficient in vital natural resources, which command the highest prices in international markets. These include the developed nations of Europe and North America as well as the less-developed nations of other continents.

The presence of many Eastern European countries in the bottom 10 needs explanation. Most of their external trade is with other COMECON countries, and the prices of their imports are not the ruling world prices but artificial rates set through negotiations among these countries. All centrally planned economies enjoy the advantage of such price stability, as reflected in other rankings as well.

Regions	Africa	Asia & Oceania	Europe	Western Hemisphere
Most	Kenya (8)	Pakistan (1)	Iceland (3)	Trinidad & Tobago (2)
Least	Morocco (39)	Hong Kong (46)	Switzerland (59)	Canada (47)

Rank	Country	Import Price Index	Rank	Country	Import Price Index	Rank	Country	Import Price Index
	TOP 10		20	New Zealand	237	40	Australia	183
1	Pakistan	554	21	South Africa	235	41	France	180
2	Trinidad & Tobago	437	22	Thailand	234	42	Colombia	178
3	Iceland	418	23	Fiji	231	43	Denmark	178
4	Turkey	352	24	United States	223	44	Cyprus	173
5	Italy	320	25	Malta	221	45	Netherlands	171
6	Sri Lanka	309	26	Egypt	218	46	Hong Kong	164
7	Philippines	307	27	Finland	214	47	Canada	161
8	Kenya	290	28	South Korea	212	48	Norway	161
9	United Kingdom	289	29	Brazil	209	49	Belgium-Luxembourg	158
10	Uganda	288		*LOWER MIDDLE*			*BOTTOM 10*	
	UPPER MIDDLE		30	Japan	207	50	Mexico	153
11	Spain	280	31	Yugoslavia	207	51	Czechoslovakia	149
12	Jamaica	273	32	Syria	203	52	Soviet Union	147
13	India	272	33	Israel	196	53	East Germany	144
14	Ireland	263	34	Zambia	195	54	Poland	142
15	Ecuador	262	35	El Salvador	191	55	Hungary	138
16	Greece	260	36	Jordan	189	56	Austria	137
17	Portugal	251	37	Sweden	186	57	Bulgaria	134
18	Panama	249	38	Tunisia	186	58	West Germany	133
19	Malawi	243	39	Morocco	185	59	Switzerland	119

Source: *U.N. Statistical Yearbook.*

91. Export Price Index

Although only a few nations in the world have the ability to regulate the export prices of their commodities (other than in near-monopoly situations), the formation of cartels is an attempt in that direction. Such cartels are advantageous to exporting nations where there is heavy commodity concentration, i.e., where the exporting country depends for its receipts on one or a few commodities. But apart from cartels, the export prices on which the export price index is based reflect the free interplay of market forces, as well as inflationary effects. In such a situa-

tion the smaller exporting countries have an advantage and therefore top the list, while developed nations fill out the bottom. Of course, countries dependent entirely on one or two commodities subject to volatile price swings may be up one year and down the next.

Number of Countries: 58
Midpoint: 192
Period Covered: 1976
Type of Ranking: Export Price Index, 1970 =100; Highest to Lowest

Highlights & Findings: Since the exports of one nation are the imports of another, export and import price indices theoretically should have similar patterns; but because of the complexities of international trade, these similarities are not readily apparent. In any case, the 1970s have witnessed a steady attrition in the commercial bargaining position of developed nations and a proportionate rise in the export prices of smaller nations, especially those possessing vital resources such as petroleum.

Regions	Africa	Asia & Oceania	Europe	Western Hemisphere
Most	Tunisia (8)	Pakistan (3)	Iceland (2)	Trinidad & Tobago (1)
Least	Zambia (58)	Japan (49)	Hungary (57)	Jamaica (42)

Rank Country	Export Price Index	Rank Country	Export Price Index	Rank Country	Export Price Index
TOP 10		20 Brazil	206	40 Sri Lanka	169
1 Trinidad & Tobago	547	21 South Africa	206	41 Denmark	167
2 Iceland	451	22 Thailand	205	42 Jamaica	166
3 Pakistan	407	23 Colombia	199	43 South Korea	166
4 Syria	406	24 India	199	44 Norway	165
5 Ecuador	344	25 Morocco	196	45 Cyprus	160
6 Turkey	290	26 Malawi	192	46 Soviet Union	160
7 Ireland	270	27 Panama	192	47 Netherlands	156
8 Tunisia	268	28 Spain	192	48 Belgium-Luxembourg	147
9 Kenya	264	29 Yugoslavia	192		
10 Fiji	252			*BOTTOM 10*	
		LOWER MIDDLE		49 Japan	147
UPPER MIDDLE		30 Sweden	190	50 Poland	147
11 Jordan	248	31 Mexico	186	51 Austria	134
12 Italy	246	32 Portugal	186	52 West Germany	134
13 El Salvador	242	33 United States	183	53 Czechoslovakia	131
14 United Kingdom	240	34 Malta	182	54 Switzerland	129
15 Uganda	229	35 Canada	178	55 East Germany	126
16 Philippines	225	36 Australia	173	56 Bulgaria	122
17 Finland	216	37 Israel	173	57 Hungary	117
18 Greece	215	38 Hong Kong	172	58 Zambia	83
19 New Zealand	214	39 France	171		

Source: *Yearbook of International Trade Statistics.*

92. Terms of Trade

Terms of trade indicates changes in the level of export prices expressed as a percentage of import prices. It is calculated by dividing export prices by import prices x 100. A country's ranking on this scale shows the profitability of its international

trade if it were conducted under barter arrangements. The unit values of the index are derived from the *Handbook of International Trade & Development Statistics* compiled by the United Nations Conference on Trade and Development (UNCTAD).

Number of Countries: 105
Midpoint: 101
Period Covered: 1976 (Base Period = 1970).
Type of Ranking: Terms of Trade for 1976 with 1970 as 100; Highest to Lowest

Highlights & Findings: The index favors two types of countries: oil-exporting countries where export prices took a quantum jump in 1973 and countries where imports were severely curtailed. Over 46% of the countries had a negative terms of trade.

Regions	Africa	Asia & Oceania	Europe	Western Hemisphere
Most	Libya (5)	Kuwait (1)	Switzerland (37)	Venezuela (6)
Least	Zambia (104)	Philippines (101)	Spain (102)	Chile (105)

Rank	Country	Terms of Trade	Rank	Country	Terms of Trade	Rank	Country	Terms of Trade
	TOP 10		36	Mali	109	72	New Zealand	90
1	Kuwait	462	37	Switzerland	108	73	Paraguay	90
2	Iraq	451	38	Guatemala	107	74	Israel	88
3	Saudi Arabia	432	39	Ivory Coast	107	75	South Africa	88
4	Iran	406	40	Ireland	106	76	Ethiopia	87
5	Libya	337	41	Jamaica	106	77	Malaysia	87
6	Venezuela	323	42	Hong Kong	105	78	Rhodesia (Zimbabwe)	87
7	Nigeria	322	43	Morocco	105	79	Australia	86
8	Algeria	308	44	Poland	104	80	Honduras	86
9	Indonesia	238	45	Mozambique	103	81	Lebanon	86
10	Cambodia	178	46	Upper Volta	103	82	Hungary	85
			47	Kenya	102	83	Greece	83
	UPPER MIDDLE		48	Norway	102	84	Somalia	83
11	Angola	169	49	Singapore	102	85	United Kingdom	83
12	Syria	154	50	Sweden	102	86	Thailand	82
13	Togo	154				87	Turkey	82
14	Tunisia	152		**LOWER MIDDLE**		88	Uruguay	82
15	Chad	148	51	Finland	101	89	United States	82
16	Ecuador	143	52	West Germany	101	90	Burma	81
17	Bolivia	133	53	Ghana	101	91	Sierra Leone	81
18	Afghanistan	128	54	Madagascar	101	92	Peru	80
19	Guatemala	128	55	Nicaragua	101	93	South Korea	78
20	Uganda	127	56	Colombia	100	94	Liberia	78
21	Sudan	125	57	Jordan	100	95	Italy	77
22	Congo	124	58	Brazil	99			
23	Cameroon	118	59	Benin	97		**BOTTOM 10**	
24	Dominican Republic	118	60	Costa Rica	97	96	Mauritania	74
25	Cuba	116	61	Niger	97	97	India	73
26	Rwanda	116	62	Argentina	96	98	Bangladesh	72
27	Tanzania	114	63	France	95	99	Panama	72
28	Central African Empire	113	64	Austria	95	100	Japan	71
29	El Salvador	113	65	Portugal	95	101	Philippines	69
30	Canada	111	66	Denmark	94	102	Spain	69
31	Pakistan	111	67	Belgium	93	103	Zaire	56
32	Trinidad & Tobago	111	68	Yugoslavia	93	104	Zambia	47
33	Malawi	110	69	Sri Lanka	92	105	Chile	43
34	Senegal	110	70	Mexico	91			
35	Egypt	109	71	Netherlands	91			

Source: United Nations Conference on Trade and Development.

93. Ratio of Exports to Imports

Because a nation's capacity to import goods is based on export receipts, the ratio of exports to imports is one of the prime indicators determining the flow of external trade. The ratio expresses how successful a nation has been in maximizing exports and reducing imports and in balancing the push and pull forces of supply and demand.

Number of Countries: 125
Midpoint: 84.8
Period Covered: Latest Available Year, 1974-76
Type of Ranking: Ratio of Exports to Imports; Highest to Lowest

Highlights & Findings: Oil-exporting nations feature prominently in the top 10. It is also remarkable that the top 18 nations are Third World countries, many of them producers of primary commodities. The ratio demonstrates the growing disadvantage of consuming nations, only seven of which have a ratio of over 100.

Regions	Africa	Asia	Europe	Western Hemisphere
Most	Uganda (1)	Brunei (2)	West Germany (19)	Venezuela (10)
Least	Reunion (124)	Yemen Arab Republic (125)	Portugal (115)	Panama (122)

Rank	Country	Ratio of Exports & Imports	Rank	Country	Ratio of Exports & Imports	Rank	Country	Ratio of Exports & Imports
	TOP 10		42	Guatemala	94.1	84	Honduras	72.5
1	Uganda	446.9	43	Dominican Republic	93.7	85	Togo	72.4
2	Brunei	380.2	44	Zaire	93.4	86	Malawi	72.2
3	Saudi Arabia	307.2	45	Czechoslovakia	93.1	87	Sierra Leone	71.8
4	Kuwait	296.4	46	Burma	92.9	88	Norway	71.3
5	Gabon	228.6	47	Belgium-Luxembourg	92.8	89	Costa Rica	71.0
6	Libya	213.6	48	Ghana	92.6	90	Kenya	69.7
7	Iraq	203.2	49	Niger	92.4	91	Yugoslavia	66.2
8	Angola	196.3	50	Soviet Union	90.1	92	Haiti	65.3
9	Iran	194.2	51	Uruguay	89.5	93	Mali	64.7
10	Venezuela	151.9	52	South Korea	87.9	94	Afghanistan	63.7
			53	United States	87.9	95	Philippines	61.8
	UPPER MIDDLE		54	France	86.7	96	South Yemen	59.9
11	Indonesia	150.7	55	Zambia	86.4	97	Cyprus	59.8
12	Papua New Guinea	133.3	56	East Germany	86.1	98	South Africa	59.8
13	Argentina	129.1	57	Iceland	86.0	99	Israel	57.0
14	Nigeria	128.9	58	New Zealand	85.9	100	Sudan	56.5
15	Ivory Coast	125.0	59	Finland	85.8	101	Somalia	55.5
16	Chile	122.9	60	Italy	85.1	102	Mexico	54.7
17	Trinidad & Tobago	119.4	61	Hungary	84.9	103	Malta	54.4
18	Liberia	119.3	62	Netherlands Antilles	84.8	104	Bangladesh	54.1
19	West Germany	116.2				105	Pakistan	53.6
20	Australia	116.0				106	Syria	53.6
21	Ecuador	113.5		*LOWER MIDDLE*		107	Tunisia	51.6
22	New Caledonia	109.1	63	Cameroon	83.9	108	Spain	49.9
23	Mauritania	108.7	64	Thailand	83.4	109	Mozambique	48.4
24	Congo	108.5	65	Bolivia	82.6	110	Fiji	48.2
25	Malaysia	108.0	66	United Kingdom	82.6	111	Morocco	48.2
26	Japan	103.7	67	Paraguay	81.4	112	Barbados	43.9
27	El Salvador	102.2	68	Bahamas	80.8	113	Peru	43.5
28	Nicaragua	101.9	69	Bahrain	80.8	114	Greece	42.3
29	Netherlands	101.5	70	Tanzania	80.5	115	Portugal	42.2
30	Canada	100.5	71	Madagascar	80.4			
31	Switzerland	100.4	72	Senegal	80.0			
32	Rumania	100.0	73	Poland	79.4		*BOTTOM 10*	
33	India	98.3	74	Ireland	79.0	116	Lebanon	40.6
34	Colombia	98.0	75	Ethiopia	78.7	117	Chad	40.2
35	Sri Lanka	96.1	76	Rwanda	78.6	118	Egypt	39.9
36	Hong Kong	96.0	77	Mauritius	75.7	119	Benin	30.7
37	Bulgaria	95.7	78	Brazil	74.3	120	Turkey	30.2
38	Sweden	95.4	79	Guyana	74.1	121	Upper Volta	29.1
39	Algeria	95.2	80	Austria	73.8	122	Panama	27.1
40	Burundi	94.8	81	Denmark	73.4	123	Jordan	20.9
41	Cuba	94.8	82	Jamaica	72.6	124	Reunion	20.9
			83	Singapore	72.6	125	Yemen Arab Republic	2.7

Source: General Agreement on Tariffs & Trade; *U.N. Statistical Yearbook.*

94. Ratio of International Reserves to Imports

Economists generally measure a nation's solvency by a number of indicators, but one of the most common is international reserves expressed as the value of imports, i.e., for how many months will the international reserves be sufficient to meet the cost of imports. The ratio, however, does not take into account the export receipts during the same period; it only provides a gross yardstick of a nation's ability to meet future trading obligations given the current level of its international reserves.

Number of Countries: 104
Midpoint: 3.2 months
Period Covered: 1976
Type of Ranking: International Reserves Divided by Average Monthly Value of Imports and Expressed as Number of Months; Highest to Lowest

Highlights & Rankings: The ratio favors those countries with small populations and consequently low demand for imports. Only 27 countries have international reserves adequate to cover imports for six months and over. Seven of these are oil-producing countries.

Regions	Africa	Asia & Oceania	Europe	Western Hemisphere
Most	Ethiopia (5)	Saudi Arabia (1)	Malta (2)	Venezuela (3)
Least	Sudan (103)	Sri Lanka (71)	Finland (97)	Bahamas (104)

Rank	Country	Number of Months of Imports	Rank	Country	Number of Months of Imports	Rank	Country	Number of Months of Imports
	TOP 10		35	West Germany	4.8	70	Dominican Republic	2.0
1	Saudi Arabia	27.6	36	Austria	4.6	71	Sri Lanka	2.0
2	Malta	17.7	37	Algeria	4.4	72	Peru	1.9
3	Venezuela	17.0	38	Singapore	4.4	73	Sierra Leone	1.9
4	Switzerland	10.5	39	Afghanistan	4.2	74	South Africa	1.9
5	Ethiopia	10.4	40	Israel	4.1	75	Zambia	1.9
6	Burundi	10.2	41	South Korea	4.0	76	Canada	1.8
7	Iran	10.1	42	Mauritania	3.6	77	France	1.8
8	Burma	9.9	43	Portugal	3.6	78	Greece	1.8
9	Libya	9.7	44	Spain	3.6	79	Italy	1.8
10	Colombia	8.8	45	El Salvador	3.5	80	New Zealand	1.8
			46	Kenya	3.5	81	Belgium-Luxembourg	1.7
	UPPER MIDDLE		47	Australia	3.4	82	United States	1.7
11	Paraguay	8.6	48	Bolivia	3.3	83	Malawi	1.5
12	Lebanon	8.5	49	Nicaragua	3.3	84	Sweden	1.5
13	Cyprus	8.0	50	Yugoslavia	3.3	85	Barbados	1.4
14	Iraq	8.0	51	Chile	3.2	86	Jamaica	1.3
15	Jordan	8.0	52	Indonesia	3.2	87	Benin	1.2
16	Guatemala	7.6				88	Haiti	1.2
17	Nigeria	7.6		**LOWER MIDDLE**		89	Madagascar	1.2
18	Rwanda	7.4	53	Japan	3.1	90	Egypt	1.1
19	Kuwait	7.0	54	Mauritius	3.1	91	Congo	1.0
20	India	6.7	55	South Yemen	3.1	92	Panama	1.0
21	Niger	6.5	56	Pakistan	3.0			
22	Thailand	6.4	57	Honduras	2.9		**BOTTOM 12**	
23	Argentina	6.3	58	Tunisia	2.9	93	Cameroon	0.9
24	Uruguay	6.3	59	Togo	2.8	94	Costa Rica	0.9
25	Ecuador	6.2	60	Turkey	2.7	95	Denmark	0.9
26	Trinidad & Tobago	6.1	61	Mexico	2.5	96	United Kingdom	0.9
27	Upper Volta	6.0	62	Norway	2.4	97	Finland	0.8
28	Brazil	5.7	63	Tanzania	2.4	98	Zaire	0.8
29	Uganda	5.6	64	Morocco	2.3	99	Ivory Coast	0.7
30	Fiji	5.4	65	Ghana	2.2	100	Mali	0.6
31	Ireland	5.3	66	Netherlands	2.2	101	Senegal	0.6
32	Somalia	5.3	67	Syria	2.2	102	Liberia	0.5
33	Malaysia	5.2	68	Iceland	2.1	103	Sudan	0.3
34	Philippines	5.0	69	Chad	2.0	104	Bahamas	0.2

Sources: *U.N. Statistical Yearbook, Yearbook of International Trade Statistics.*

95. Percentage of Primary Products in Exports

Exports are generally categorized into two broad classes: manufactures and primary products. The latter comprise food and live animals, beverages and tobacco, inedible crude materials, fuels, oils, fats and waxes. Generally, developing countries are exporters of primary products as raw materials to developed countries. The prices of these raw materials are determined by the consuming countries except in a few cases, as in petroleum, where the producers have been successful in forming cartels. The relative weakness of exporters of primary products is intensified when there is commodity concentration, i.e., when a nation derives almost all of its export receipts from one or two products.

Number of Countries: 109
Midpoint: 82%
Period Covered: 1975
Type of Ranking: Percentage of Primary Commodities in Exports; Highest to Lowest

Highlights & Findings: Primary commodities make up over 50% of exports in 79 countries. The ratio is 99% for oil-exporting countries, 94% for low-income countries, 82% for middle-income countries, 47% for Communist countries and 24% for industrialized countries.

Regions	Africa	Asia	Europe	Western Hemisphere
Most	Benin (1)	Iraq (3)	Soviet Union (60)	Cuba (6)
Least	Sierra Leone (88)	Hong Kong (109)	Switzerland (107)	United States (93)

Rank	Country	Percentage of Primary Commodities in Exports	Rank	Country	Percentage of Primary Commodities in Exports	Rank	Country	Percentage of Primary Commodities in Exports
	TOP 14		37	Syria	91	74	Singapore	57
1	Benin	100	38	Mozambique	90	75	India	55
2	Chad	100	39	Paraguay	90	76	Iceland	54
3	Iraq	100	40	Cameroon	89	77	Canada	53
4	Libya	100	41	Honduras	89	78	Lebanon	53
5	Uganda	100	42	Sri Lanka	89	79	Greece	52
6	Cuba	99	43	Congo	88	80	Bulgaria	48
7	Guinea	99	44	Ivory Coast	88	81	Mexico	48
8	Indonesia	99	45	Tanzania	88	82	Poland	47
9	Iran	99	46	Kenya	87	83	Netherlands	46
10	Nigeria	99	47	Morocco	87	84	Jamaica	45
11	Saudia Arabia	99	48	New Zealand	86	85	Pakistan	45
12	Sudan	99	49	Afghanistan	85	86	Denmark	43
13	Venezuela	99	50	Australia	83	87	Hungary	43
14	Zambia	99	51	Dominican Republic	83	88	Sierra Leone	42
			52	Nicaragua	83	89	Norway	38
	UPPER MIDDLE		53	Philippines	83	90	Bangladesh	37
15	Algeria	98	54	Chile	82	91	East Germany	35
16	Ethiopia	98	55	Malaysia	82	92	Czechoslovakia	34
17	Ghana	98				93	United States	31
18	Liberia	98		*LOWER MIDDLE*		94	Spain	30
19	Bolivia	97	56	Jordan	80	95	Portugal	29
20	Burma	97	57	Tunisia	80	96	Yugoslavia	28
21	Ecuador	97	58	Colombia	79	97	France	24
22	Rwanda	97	59	Senegal	78	98	Finland	23
23	Somalia	97	60	Soviet Union	77			
24	Zaire	97	61	Thailand	77		*BOTTOM 11*	
25	Mauritania	96	62	Central African Empire	76	99	Belgium	22
26	Madagascar	95	63	South Africa	76	100	Sweden	22
27	Peru	95	64	Argentina	75	101	South Korea	18
28	Malawi	94	65	Guatemala	75	102	Israel	17
29	Togo	94	66	Costa Rica	74	103	Italy	17
30	Trinidad & Tobago	94	67	Brazil	73	104	United Kingdom	17
31	Upper Volta	94	68	El Salvador	71	105	Austria	15
32	Angola	93	69	Uruguay	70	106	West Germany	11
33	Yemen Arab Republic	93	70	Egypt	66	107	Switzerland	8
34	Kuwait	92	71	Haiti	66	108	Japan	4
35	Mali	92	72	Turkey	64	109	Hong Kong	3
36	Niger	91	73	Rumania	59			

Source: United Nations Trade Data System.

96. Share of Food in Imports

Many nations have to import a large percentage of their food because they do not grow enough food to feed their inhabitants. These are the nations that would be the most affected by global food shortages. However, poor weather conditions during the single year covered by this ranking may have produced distortions in the ranking.

Number of Countries: 80
Midpoint: 14%
Period Covered: 1975
Type of Ranking: Percentage of Food Imports in Total Imports; Highest to Lowest

Highlights & Findings: Food imports make up 21% of total imports in low-income countries, 14% in middle-income countries and 11% in industrialized countries. The Soviet Union's place as number 11 is noteworthy; the other countries with a high ranking are among the most underdeveloped in the world.

Regions	Africa	Asia	Europe	Western Hemisphere
Most	Egypt (4)	Bangladesh (1)	Portugal (10)	Haiti (6)
Least	South Africa (79)	Thailand (80)	Yugoslavia (72)	Argentina (75)

Rank	Country	Percentage of Food Imports in Total Imports	Rank	Country	Percentage of Food Imports in Total Imports	Rank	Country	Percentage of Food Imports in Total Imports
	TOP 11		27	Kuwait	17	54	Costa Rica	10
1	Bangladesh	51	28	Libya	17	55	Denmark	10
2	Sri Lanka	50	29	Spain	17	56	Greece	10
3	Yemen Arab Republic	45	30	Zaire	17	57	Nigeria	10
4	Egypt	36	31	Central African Empire	16	58	Poland	10
5	Morocco	30	32	Congo	16	59	Trinidad & Tobago	10
6	Haiti	29	33	West Germany	16	60	Colombia	9
7	India	26	34	Iran	16	61	Nicaragua	9
8	Jordan	25	35	Israel	16	62	Austria	8
9	Pakistan	24	36	Netherlands	16	63	Canada	8
10	Portugal	23	37	Ivory Coast	15	64	Finland	8
11	Soviet Union	23	38	Ghana	14	65	Hungary	8
			39	Ireland	14	66	Sweden	8
	UPPER MIDDLE		40	South Korea	14	67	Zambia	8
12	Niger	22	41	Liberia	14	68	New Zealand	7
13	Hong Kong	21	42	Togo	14	69	Norway	7
14	Syria	21				70	Panama	7
15	Upper Volta	21		*LOWER MIDDLE*		71	Turkey	7
16	Jamaica	20				72	Yugoslavia	7
17	Tanzania	20	43	Belgium	13			
18	Italy	19	44	France	13			
19	Rwanda	19	45	Honduras	13		*BOTTOM 8*	
20	Sudan	19	46	Indonesia	13	73	Brazil	6
21	Tunisia	19	47	Switzerland	13	74	Kenya	6
22	United Kingdom	19	48	Venezuela	12	75	Argentina	5
23	Iraq	18	49	Cameroon	11	76	Australia	5
24	Japan	18	50	Czechoslovakia	11	77	Ethiopia	5
25	Malaysia	18	51	Philippines	11	78	Uganda	5
26	Senegal	18	52	Singapore	11	79	South Africa	4
			53	United States	11	80	Thailand	4

Source: United Nations Trade Data Systems.

97. Import Growth Rate

Although the growth rates of both imports and exports vary from year to year because of fluctuations in production or price, certain patterns persist and the growth rates may be accepted as a fairly reliable indicator of the state of a nation's external trade. Because the ranking is based on the growth factor rather than on size, even minute variations can affect a small country's growth rate more sharply than a large increment can affect a developed country's relative rate. This should be borne in mind when viewing the apparent anomaly of smaller countries enjoying higher average growth rates than developed countries.

Number of Countries: 125
Midpoint: 21.1%
Period Covered: Latest Available Year,1973-76
Type of Ranking: Annual Import Growth Rate as Percentages; Highest to Lowest

Highlights & Findings: The top three countries as well as a number of countries in the upper middle are oil producers whose sudden spurt in imports is related to the strategy of recycling petrodollars on a massive program of internal development. Toward the end of the scale are the oil-poor developing countries who have been forced to cut back on their imports as part of a program of fiscal restraint and austerity. Four countries have negative growth rates; of these Uganda, Mozambique and Cyprus had their imports reduced because of political unrest or instability. In general, all healthy, stable economies had a moderate growth rate in imports.

Regions	Africa	Asia & Oceania	Europe	Western Hemisphere
Most	Nigeria (6)	Iraq (1)	Soviet Union (25)	Bahamas (5)
Least	Uganda (125)	Bangladesh (120)	Cyprus (123)	Argentina (109)

Rank	Country	Import Growth Rate (%)	Rank	Country	Import Growth Rate (%)	Rank	Country	Import Growth Rate (%)
	TOP 10		42	Senegal	26.7	84	Canada	17.6
1	Iraq	115.4	43	South Africa	26.6	85	Austria	17.4
2	Saudi Arabia	81.2	44	Brunei	26.5	86	West Germany	17.2
3	Iran	74.6	45	Haiti	25.4	87	Belgium & Luxembourg	17.0
4	Peru	71.1	46	Brazil	24.9	88	Denmark	16.8
5	Bahamas	67.0	47	El Salvador	24.3	89	Kenya	16.8
6	Nigeria	63.8	48	Upper Volta	24.1	90	Czechoslovakia	16.5
7	Egypt	60.7	49	Costa Rica	23.5	91	Mexico	16.5
8	Yemen Arab Republic	54.6	50	United States	23.4	92	Hong Kong	16.2
9	Rwanda	49.2	51	Guatemala	23.3	93	Reunion	16.0
10	Jordan	48.6	52	Burundi	23.2	94	Italy	15.8
			53	Trinidad & Tobago	23.2	95	Angola	15.3
	UPPER MIDDLE		54	Honduras	23.0	96	Chile	15.3
11	Syria	48.0	55	Ivory Coast	22.2	97	Somalia	14.6
12	Cuba	47.2	56	South Yemen	22.2	98	Ireland	14.5
13	Kuwait	46.7	57	Ghana	22.1	99	New Zealand	14.3
14	Bahrain	46.2	58	Sweden	22.1	100	Malawi	13.0
15	Gabon	42.4	59	Cameroon	22.0	101	Papua New Guinea	13.0
16	Bolivia	41.7	60	Spain	22.0	102	United Kingdom	13.0
17	Afghanistan	38.3	61	Dominican Republic	21.9	103	Barbados	12.2
18	Ecuador	35.7	62	Norway	21.2	104	Chad	12.2
19	Hungary	35.3	63	Poland	21.1	105	Mauritania	12.2
20	Tunisia	34.2				106	Portugal	12.0
21	Madagascar	33.7		*LOWER MIDDLE*		107	Israel	11.3
22	Venezuela	33.7	64	Singapore	20.8	108	Mali	10.9
23	Netherlands Antilles	33.2	65	Rumania	20.7	109	Argentina	10.7
24	Algeria	33.0	66	Malta	20.6	110	Benin	10.2
25	Soviet Union	32.3	67	Malaysia	20.4	111	Iceland	9.5
26	Zambia	32.3	68	Thailand	20.4	112	Sri Lanka	9.1
27	Morocco	31.8	69	Greece	20.0	113	Zaire	8.8
28	Turkey	31.3	70	Bulgaria	19.9	114	Congo	8.6
29	Sudan	31.0	71	Togo	19.9	115	Switzerland	8.3
30	Philippines	30.2	72	France	19.8	116	Tanzania	8.3
31	Pakistan	30.1	73	India	19.8			
32	Jamaica	29.7	74	Finland	19.3		*BOTTOM 9*	
33	Libya	29.6	75	Japan	19.1	117	New Caledonia	8.0
34	Lebanon	29.2	76	East Germany	18.9	118	Fiji	6.1
35	Uruguay	28.1	77	Colombia	18.6	119	Burma	5.9
36	Paraguay	28.0	78	Panama	18.6	120	Bangladesh	5.4
37	Mauritius	27.7	79	Ethiopia	18.3	121	Niger	3.4
38	Indonesia	27.6	80	Netherlands	18.2	122	Sierra Leone	−0.4
39	Guyana	27.5	81	Yugoslavia	17.8	123	Cyprus	−1.4
40	South Korea	27.4	82	Australia	17.7	124	Mozambique	−5.5
41	Liberia	27.2	83	Nicaragua	17.7	125	Uganda	−6.5

Source: *Yearbook of International Trade Statistics.*

98. Export Growth Rate

The export growth rate ranking should be read together with the import growth rate ranking, and the general remarks in that section also apply to export growth rates.

Number of Countries: 125
Midpoint: 18.6%
Period Covered: Latest Available Year, 1973-76
Type of Ranking: Annual Export Growth Rate as Percentages; Highest to Lowest

Highlights & Findings: Oil-producing nations dominate the top of the list. Growth rates in exports are sustained only with difficulty over long periods, although most nations stimulate them through subsidies, tax rebates and other incentives. There are six nations with negative growth rates, five of them in Africa, three of which suffered major political or economic crises during the period covered.

Regions	Africa	Asia & Oceania	Europe	Western Hemisphere
Most	Congo (5)	Iraq (1)	Malta (23)	Bahamas (3)
Least	Zambia (125)	Turkey (118)	Portugal (120)	Argentina (111)

Rank	Country	Export Growth Rate (%)	Rank	Country	Export Growth Rate (%)	Rank	Country	Export Growth Rate (%)
	TOP 10		42	Japan	22.1	84	East Germany	14.7
1	Iraq	94.2	43	Singapore	21.6	85	Canada	14.5
2	Iran	80.6	44	Kenya	21.3	86	Czechoslovakia	14.4
3	Bahamas	75.8	45	Burundi	21.1	87	Cyprus	14.1
4	Brunei	71.0	46	Bolivia	21.0	88	Liberia	13.7
5	Congo	69.4	47	Greece	20.5	89	Belgium	13.5
6	Jordan	62.4	48	Poland	20.0	90	Denmark	13.4
7	Cuba	61.6	49	Afghanistan	19.9	91	Fiji	13.4
8	Saudi Arabia	58.4	50	Madagascar	19.9	92	Cameroon	13.1
9	Gabon	57.8	51	Yugoslavia	19.6	93	Malawi	13.0
10	Angola	57.5	52	Costa Rica	19.5	94	Malaysia	12.1
			53	Guatemala	19.5	95	Paraguay	12.1
	UPPER MIDDLE		54	Panama	19.5	96	Colombia	11.6
11	Senegal	53.8	55	Norway	19.1	97	Iceland	11.6
12	Bahrain	49.0	56	Chile	18.9	98	Morocco	11.5
13	Nigeria	45.0	57	Hong Kong	18.9	99	Australia	11.3
14	Syria	44.8	58	Mexico	18.8	100	Honduras	11.2
15	Jamaica	44.6	59	Spain	18.8	101	Peru	11.2
16	Rwanda	39.2	60	Mali	18.7	102	Egypt	10.7
17	Indonesia	38.6	61	Israel	18.6	103	Uganda	10.3
18	Algeria	38.5	62	Netherlands	18.6	104	Tanzania	10.2
19	Kuwait	37.1				105	Ghana	10.1
20	Trinidad & Tobago	36.3		*LOWER MIDDLE*		106	Philippines	10.0
21	Lebanon	35.9	63	Uruguay	18.5	107	Sri Lanka	8.8
22	South Korea	33.7	64	Italy	18.4	108	Sudan	8.5
23	Malta	32.7	65	Rumania	18.4	109	Bangladesh	8.3
24	Upper Volta	32.7	66	South Yemen	18.3	110	Pakistan	6.4
25	Netherlands Antilles	32.3	67	Finland	18.2	111	Argentina	6.2
26	Ecuador	28.4	68	Brazil	17.8	112	Mauritania	5.9
27	Libya	28.1	69	Bulgaria	17.7	113	Ethiopia	5.3
28	Togo	27.4	70	Dominican Republic	17.4	114	Reunion	4.2
29	El Salvador	26.2	71	New Caledonia	17.4	115	Burma	3.9
30	Tunisia	25.7	72	Yemen Arab Republic	17.3			
31	Nicaragua	25.4	73	United States	17.3		*BOTTOM 10*	
32	Guyana	25.2	74	Austria	17.2	116	Papua New Guinea	3.8
33	Mauritius	24.6	75	Hungary	17.2	117	New Zealand	2.5
34	Soviet Union	24.6	76	Niger	16.2	118	Turkey	2.1
35	Haiti	24.5	77	Switzerland	15.9	119	Benin	1.5
36	Barbados	24.4	78	Ireland	15.8	120	Portugal	−0.8
37	Thailand	24.0	79	France	15.7	121	Chad	−2.6
38	Ivory Coast	23.6	80	South Africa	15.3	122	Sierra Leone	−5.3
39	Venezuela	23.2	81	United Kingdom	14.9	123	Mozambique	−5.7
40	India	22.9	82	West Germany	14.8	124	Zaire	−7.6
41	Somalia	22.3	83	Sweden	14.8	125	Zambia	−16.0

Source: *Yearbook of International Trade Statistics.*

AGRICULTURE

This is the largest section in the book with 37 rankings, because agriculture is a truly universal economic activity. (There are nations without any industries and without any mines but hardly any without farms and farmers). Agriculture is also the world's largest economic sector in terms of employment, although its share of the GDP and its budgetary allocations have been declining in most countries of the world. Agricultural data are generally reliable because governments consider the collection of statistics relating to land one of their traditional and prime responsibilities.

Agriculture is characterized by many dichotomies: between modern and traditional, between rain-fed and irrigated, between subsistence and commercial, between owner-operated and rented, between large and small, and between mechanized and labor-intensive. In almost all countries agriculture is the least efficient and least productive sector of the economy and the sector that receives the smallest share of investment capital and credit. In some countries, such as the United States, inefficiency is perpetuated by government intervention to maintain higher prices for farmers. It is conceded by agricultural experts that few countries of the world have reached their full agricultural potential; with proper land use, soil management, mechanization, use of improved seeds and application of fertilizers, present agricultural production rates can be quadrupled and decupled as was demonstrated by the Green Revolution.

Over 100 countries in the world have what are generally described as agricultural economies. In these countries agriculture employs the bulk of the labor force, contributes most of the GNP and accounts for the lion's share of production. Agricultural economies operate on three levels: a subsistence level consisting of small farms that provide little more than food for their owners; a more advanced level including truck farms that supply surplus crops for domestic markets, and an export level consisting of cash crops for exports. In most countries the third level is dominated by estates and plantations; as a result of mechanization and scientific application of fertilizers, this sector is generally the most efficient and productive of the three.

The Food and Agriculture Organization publishes production statistics on all major crops grown in the world. Of these, 11 have been selected and presented in this section: rice, wheat, tobacco, soybeans, potatoes, oats, corn, peanuts (groundnuts), cotton, coffee and barley. Three related livestock products are also included: eggs, milk and wool. Interestingly, agricultural production is or appears to be unrelated to the size of the country; few countries, except perhaps for the United States, have managed to achieve a commanding position in more than one or two crops. Farmers are universally conservative, sticking to their traditional crops, resisting large-scale introduction of new crops (the failure of the peanut plantation scheme in Kenya in the 1940s provides a classic moral for agricultural innovators) and receiving only limited official encouragement in the form of capital, credit and marketing services.

There is no country in the world that is totally self-sufficient in agricultural commodities; many of the developing countries are chronically dependent on imports for their basic food grains. The patterns of agricultural production illustrate not only the state of agriculture in each country but also their global implications. In an interdependent world if the wheat crop fails in Iowa, the shortage will be felt not only in the United States but also in the Soviet Union, India and Saudi Arabia.

As it stands now, the majority of the countries of the world that are not self-sufficient in food have to spend hard-earned foreign currency for food imports. (See "Food Imports as Percentage of Total Imports" in the chapter on Trade). Exporters of agricultural products and foodgrains are bound to acquire considerable leverage in international trade in the coming years as the problem of feeding the world's growing population becomes critical. Called agripower, it was demonstrated most dramatically in 1972 when the Soviet Union was forced to purchase millions of tons of grain from the United States to offset its bad harvests.

The rankings in this chapter may be grouped under seven headings. The first group, an overview of agriculture, presents five rankings: annual growth rate, agricultural share of GDP, area under cultivation as a percentage of total land area and agricultural production and food production indices. The second group, also consisting of five rankings, deals with the average size of farms, percentage of owner-operated farms, percentage of cultivated area owned by the top 10% and the bottom 10% of farmers and per capita agricultural indebtedness. The third group of three rankings deals with tractors, fertilizers and irrigated land, all related to the modernization of agriculture. The fourth deals with forestland as a percentage of total land area and production of roundwood; the fifth with fish catch; the sixth, consisting of four rankings, with livestock; and the final group with the production of 17 commodities.

99. Annual Growth Rate of Agriculture

The agricultural sector covers agriculture, forestry, hunting, and fishing. Growth rates in agriculture are determined by mechanization, application of fertilizers, development of improved seeds, irrigation, sustained favorable weather conditions, soil conservation and related factors. Figures for the Soviet Union and most Communist countries are not available.

Number of Countries: 97
Midpoint: 2%
Period Covered: 1970-76
Type of Ranking: Average Annual Growth Rate in Agriculture; Highest to Lowest

Highlights & Findings: Average annual growth rates during the period covered were highest in middle-income countries at 3.2% and lowest in low-income countries at 1.6%. The rate in industrialized countries was 1.8%. Seventeen countries had negative growth rates, while 16 countries had abnormal growth rates over 5%.

Regions	Africa	Asia & Oceania	Europe	Western Hemisphere
Most	Libya (1)	Israel (6)	Rumania (4)	Paraguay (10)
Least	Algeria (97)	Hong Kong (95)	Belgium (84)	Uruguay (87)

Rank	Country	Annual Growth Rate of Agriculture (%)
	TOP 10	
1	Libya	23.5
2	Guinea	10.2
3	Tunisia	9.2
4	Rumania	8.9
5	Sudan	8.8
6	Israel	6.6
7	Malaysia	6.4
8	Syria	6.4
9	South Yemen	6.2
10	Paraguay	5.9
	UPPER MIDDLE	
11	Iran	5.8
12	Ecuador	5.7
13	Nicaragua	5.7
14	Bolivia	5.6
15	Brazil	5.5
16	Malawi	5.5
17	Liberia	4.9
18	Netherlands	4.9
19	Turkey	4.9
20	South Korea	4.8
21	Philippines	4.6
22	Colombia	4.5
23	Thailand	4.3
24	El Salvador	4.2
25	Indonesia	4.0
26	Costa Rica	3.8
27	Saudi Arabia	3.6
28	Ivory Coast	3.5
29	Cameroon	3.4
30	Senegal	3.4
31	Yugoslavia	3.4
32	Rwanda	3.3

Rank	Country	Annual Growth Rate of Agriculture (%)
33	Upper Volta	3.2
34	Zambia	3.2
35	Venezuela	3.1
36	Dominican Republic	3.0
37	Egypt	3.0
38	Togo	3.0
39	Austria	2.7
40	Greece	2.7
41	Jordan	2.6
42	Spain	2.6
43	Burma	2.5
44	Finland	2.5
45	Japan	2.5
46	Tanzania	2.5
47	Argentina	2.4
48	Mozambique	2.1
	LOWER MIDDLE	
49	West Germany	2.0
50	Ireland	2.0
51	Norway	2.0
52	Sierra Leone	2.0
53	United States	2.0
54	Central African Empire	1.9
55	Nepal	1.9
56	Zaire	1.9
57	Haiti	1.6
58	Italy	1.6
59	Kenya	1.6
60	Pakistan	1.6
61	United Kingdom	1.6
62	China	1.5
63	Portugal	1.5
64	India	1.4
65	Denmark	1.4

Rank	Country	Annual Growth Rate of Agriculture (%)
66	Mexico	1.4
67	Ghana	1.3
68	Jamaica	1.3
69	Uganda	1.3
70	Madagascar	1.2
71	Sri Lanka	1.2
72	Burundi	1.0
73	Ethiopia	0.9
74	Morocco	0.6
75	Peru	0.6
76	Bangladesh	0.5
77	Chile	0.5
78	Canada	0.4
79	France	0.3
80	Singapore	0.3
81	Nigeria	−0.2
82	Sweden	−0.2
83	Benin	−0.3
84	Belgium	−0.4
85	Honduras	−0.6
86	Angola	−0.7
87	Uruguay	−0.7
	BOTTOM 10	
88	Mali	−0.8
89	Somalia	−1.2
90	Chad	−1.3
91	Iraq	−2.0
92	Australia	−2.1
93	Mauritania	−2.1
94	Niger	−4.0
95	Hong Kong	−5.1
96	Congo	−7.2
97	Algeria	−8.7

Source: World Bank.

100. Agriculture's Share of the GDP

Despite the importance of food production in a hungry world, agriculture remains labor intensive, agricultural products are subject to price fluctuations and agricultural pursuits are characterized by low productivity. As a result, agriculture's share of the GDP is highest in the least-developed countries, and in most countries of the world it has been declining in relation to other sectors. National policy in almost all countries deliberately favors industry over agriculture and even short-term growth prospects in this sector are depressed by the irreversible migration of manpower to the towns and cities and consequent depletion of the agricultural labor force.

Number of Countries: 102
Midpoint: 23%
Period Covered: 1976
Type of Ranking: Agriculture's Percentage Share of the GDP; Highest to Lowest

Highlights & Findings: Agriculture's share of the GDP is highest in low-income countries at 45% and lowest in industrialized countries at 6%. Middle-income countries reported a figure of 21%, which is close to the median. In eight countries the share is over 50%, while in both oil-exporting and industrialized countries it is so negligible as to be insignificant.

Regions	Africa	Asia & Oceania	Europe	Western Hemisphere
Most	Burundi (2)	Nepal (1)	Greece (58)	Paraguay (25)
Least	Libya (98)	Saudi Arabia (102)	West Germany (97)	United States (99)

Rank	Country	Agriculture's Share of GDP (%)	Rank	Country	Agriculture's Share of GDP (%)	Rank	Country	Agriculture's Share of GDP (%)
	TOP 9		35	Honduras	29	70	Zambia	14
1	Nepal	65	36	Indonesia	29	71	Rumania	13
2	Burundi	64	37	Liberia	29	72	China	12
3	Bangladesh	59	38	Madagascar	29	73	Chile	10
4	Afghanistan	55	39	Malaysia	29	74	Finland	10
5	Uganda	55	40	Philippines	29	75	Mexico	10
6	Chad	52	41	Turkey	29	76	Austria	9
7	Rwanda	52	42	Bolivia	28	77	Iran	9
8	Ethiopia	50	43	Papua New Guinea	28	78	South Africa	9
9	Ghana	49	44	Senegal	28	79	Spain	9
			45	Colombia	27	80	Brazil	8
	UPPER MIDDLE		46	South Korea	27	81	Iraq	8
10	Burma	47	47	El Salvador	26	82	Israel	8
11	India	47	48	Ivory Coast	25	83	Italy	8
12	Niger	47	49	Togo	25	84	Jamaica	8
13	Haiti	45	50	Nicaragua	23	85	Algeria	7
14	Malawi	45	51	Nigeria	23	86	Australia	7
15	Mozambique	45	52	South Yemen	23	87	Denmark	7
16	Tanzania	45	53	Ecuador	23	88	Netherlands	7
17	Guinea	43				89	France	6
18	Sudan	41		**LOWER MIDDLE**		90	Norway	6
19	Benin	39	54	Costa Rica	21	91	Venezuela	6
20	Lesotho	38	55	Dominican Republic	21	92	Japan	5
21	Mali	38	56	Morocco	21			
22	Central African Empire	37	57	Tunisia	21		**BOTTOM 10**	
23	Sri Lanka	37	58	Greece	18	93	Canada	4
24	Mauritania	35	59	Portugal	18	94	Sweden	4
25	Paraguay	35	60	Syria	17	95	United Kingdom	4
26	Upper Volta	34	61	Ireland	16	96	Belgium	3
27	Cameroon	33	62	Peru	16	97	West Germany	3
28	Pakistan	32	63	Rhodesia (Zimbabwe)	16	98	Libya	3
29	Sierra Leone	32	64	Zaire	16	99	United States	3
30	Somalia	31	65	Argentina	15	100	Hong Kong	2
31	Kenya	30	66	Congo	15	101	Singapore	2
32	Thailand	30	67	Uruguay	15	102	Saudi Arabia	1
33	Angola	29	68	Yugoslavia	15			
34	Egypt	29	69	Jordan	14			

Source: World Bank.

101. Land Under Cultivation

The effective land area of a country includes land under cultivation, arable land, fallow, pastures and built-up areas. In many countries the classification agricultural land is used to denote land under cultivation, pastures and fallow land, without separate figures given for each of these categories. Land under cultivation must be further qualified by the practice in countries such as Bangladesh of double and even triple cropping, which results in increased yields per hectare.

Number of Countries: 157
Midpoint: 15%
Period Covered: 1976
Type of Ranking: Percentage of Land Area Under Actual Cultivation; Highest to Lowest

Highlights & Findings: There are only 17 nations with over 50% of their land area under cultivation. Because the application of fertilizers and mechanization can have a greater impact on productivity than land area, the natural advantage these nations possess is seriously reduced. There are 10 nations with only a negligible percentage of land (under 0.01%) under cultivation. These are Greenland, Iceland, Kuwait, Mali, Namibia, Nauru, Oman, Qatar, Surinam and United Arab Emirates.

Regions	Africa	Asia & Oceania	Europe	Western Hemisphere
Most	Gambia (8)	Tonga (1)	San Marino (2)	Barbados (6)
Least	Somalia (155)	South Yemen (156)	Norway (136)	French Guyana (157)

Rank	Country	Percentage of Land Under Cultivation
	TOP 10	
1	Tonga	77
2	San Marino	74
3	Netherlands	70
4	Bangladesh	66
5	Denmark	64
6	Barbados	60
7	Hungary	60
8	Gambia	55
9	Antigua	54
10	Seychelles	54
	UPPER MIDDLE	
11	India	50
12	Italy	50
13	Mauritius	50
14	St. Lucia	50
15	St. Vincent	50
16	Swaziland	50
17	Poland	49
18	Portugal	48
19	Syria	48
20	Cyprus	47
21	Malta	45
22	Grenada	44
23	Rumania	44
24	East Germany	43
25	Czechoslovakia	42
26	Bulgaria	41
27	Spain	41
28	St. Kitts-Nevis-Anguilla	40
29	Cuba	35
30	France	35
31	Turkey	35
32	West Germany	33
33	Rwanda	33
34	El Salvador	32
35	Morocco	32
36	Yugoslavia	32
37	Haiti	31
38	Martinique	31
39	Fiji	30
40	Philippines	30
41	United Kingdom	30

Rank	Country	Percentage of Land Under Cultivation
42	Greece	29
43	Belgium	28
44	Tunisia	28
45	Lebanon	27
46	Trinidad & Tobago	25
47	Burundi	25
48	Luxembourg	25
49	Sri Lanka	25
50	China	24
51	Dominica	24
52	Guadeloupe	24
53	Pakistan	24
54	Thailand	24
55	Western Samoa	24
56	South Korea	22
57	Singapore	22
58	Jamaica	21
59	Uganda	21
60	Austria	20
61	Israel	20
62	Liberia	20
63	Reunion	20
64	Yemen Arab Republic	20
65	Albania	19
66	Ghana	19
67	United States	19
68	Iraq	18
69	Chad	17
70	Ireland	17
71	North Korea	17
72	Malaysia	17
73	Cambodia	16
74	Japan	16
75	Nepal	16
76	Bhutan	15
77	Central African Empire	15
78	Lesotho	15
79	Malawi	15
80	Tanzania	15
81	Togo	15
	LOWER MIDDLE	
82	Dominican Republic	14
83	Guatemala	14

Rank	Country	Percentage of Land Under Cultivation
84	Hong Kong	14
85	Iran	14
86	Vietnam	14
87	Kenya	13
88	Nigeria	13
89	Afghanistan	12
90	Burma	12
91	Indonesia	12
92	Mexico	12
93	Senegal	12
94	South Africa	12
95	Argentina	11
96	Benin	11
97	China	11
98	Ecuador	11
99	Jordan	11
100	Uruguay	11
101	Ethiopia	10
102	Macao	10
103	Switzerland	10
104	Upper Volta	10
105	Soviet Union	9.3
106	Bermuda	8
107	Costa Rica	8
108	Finland	8
109	Ivory Coast	8
110	Laos	8
111	Sweden	8
112	Comoros	7
113	Honduras	7
114	Nicaragua	7
115	Australia	6
116	Libya	6
117	New Caledonia	6
118	Rhodesia (Zimbabwe)	6
119	Sierra Leone	6
120	Bahrain	5
121	Belize	5
122	Colombia	5
123	Madagascar	5
124	Netherlands	5
125	Zambia	5
126	Brazil	4
127	Cameroon	4

Rank	Country	Percentage of Land Under Cultivation	Rank	Country	Percentage of Land Under Cultivation	Rank	Country	Percentage of Land Under Cultivation
128	Canada	4	139	Bolivia	2	148	Gabon	1
129	Panama	4	140	Chile	2	149	Guyana	1
130	Venezuela	4	141	Congo	2	150	Mauritania	1
131	Algeria	3	142	Paraguay	2	151	Mongolia	1
132	Brunei	3	143	Peru	2	152	Mozambique	1
133	Guinea	3				153	Saudi Arabia	1
134	New Zealand	3		*BOTTOM 14*		154	Zaire	1
135	Niger	3	144	Angola	1	155	Somalia	0.3
136	Norway	3	145	Bahamas	1	156	South Yemen	0.2
137	Sudan	3	146	Botswana	1	157	French Guyana	0.05
138	Egypt	2.8	147	Djibouti	1			

Source: U.S. Central Intelligence Agency.

102. Agricultural Land Per Capita

How many hectares of land are needed to feed a person for a whole year? This question asked often at food conferences has never been satisfactorily answered because food requirements and diet patterns vary as well as per hectare yields. But it is certain that agricultural land per capita has been shrinking the world over and will continue to shrink in all countries other than those that achieve zero population growth. In the not too distant future, this ranking may have to be recast using square meters rather than hectares—so drastic is this irreversible shrinkage.

Number of Countries: 142
Midpoint: 0.80 hectare (2.0 acres)
Period Covered: 1976
Type of Ranking: Agricultural Land per Capita in Hectares and Acres; Highest to Lowest

Highlights & Findings: Significantly per capita agricultural area is less than one hectare in the majority of countries around the world. This is the case not only in the overpopulated Asian countries, as would be expected, but also in European countries, where much agricultural land has been diverted for other uses. Agricultural land is plentiful only in about 20 countries; of these, 16 are in Africa. Unfortunately, these are also among the least productive agricultural economies with the poorest per hectare yields. If efficiency of land use and availability of land are combined on a single scale, Argentina would clearly be the leader.

Regions	Africa	Asia & Oceania	Europe	Western Hemisphere
Most	Namibia (1)	Australia (3)	Iceland (8)	Argentina (13)
Least	Egypt (135)	Singapore (142)	Malta (140)	Surinam (133)

Rank	Country	Agricultural Land per Capita Hectares	Acres	Rank	Country	Agricultural Land per Capita Hectares	Acres	Rank	Country	Agricultural Land per Capita Hectares	Acres
	TOP 10			13	Argentina	6.47	16.0	28	Tanzania	3.64	9.0
1	Namibia	85.79	212.0	14	Paraguay	6.07	15.0	29	Upper Volta	3.23	8.0
2	Botswana	66.37	164.0	15	Bolivia	5.66	14.0	30	Zaire	3.23	8.0
3	Australia	35.03	86.5	16	South Yemen	5.38	13.3	31	Algeria	2.83	7.0
4	Mauritania	31.97	79.0	17	Mozambique	5.26	13.0	32	Ethiopia	2.83	7.0
5	Congo	14.97	37.0	18	South Africa	5.09	12.6	33	Lesotho	2.83	7.0
6	Chad	12.14	30.0	19	Madagascar	4.85	12.0	34	Senegal	2.83	7.0
7	Saudi Arabia	11.65	28.8	20	Uruguay	4.85	12.0	35	Swaziland	2.83	7.0
8	Iceland	11.12	27.5	21	Angola	4.45	11.0	36	Cameroon	2.42	6.0
9	Gabon	10.11	25.0	22	New Zealand	4.30	10.6	37	Liberia	2.42	6.0
10	Zambia	7.68	19.0	23	Guyana	4.04	10.0	38	Soviet Union	2.29	5.6
				24	Libya	4.04	10.0	39	Canada	2.02	5.0
	UPPER MIDDLE			25	Niger	4.04	10.0	40	Peru	2.02	5.0
11	Mali	7.28	18.0	26	Central African Empire	3.64	9.0	41	Sierra Leone	2.02	5.0
12	Somalia	6.87	17.0	27	Ivory Coast	3.64	9.0	42	United States	2.02	5.0

Rank	Country	Agricultural Land per Capita Hectares	Acres
43	Ghana	1.61	4.0
44	Ireland	1.61	4.0
45	Mexico	1.61	4.0
46	Sudan	1.61	4.0
47	Syria	1.61	4.0
48	Brazil	1.49	3.7
49	Chile	1.49	3.7
50	Yemen Arab Republic	1.49	3.7
51	Venezuela	1.45	3.6
52	Turkey	1.37	3.4
53	Honduras	1.33	3.3
54	Costa Rica	1.21	3.0
55	Gambia	1.21	3.0
56	Guinea	1.21	3.0
57	Rhodesia (Zimbabwe)	1.21	3.0
58	Togo	1.21	3.0
59	Tunisia	1.21	3.0
60	Equatorial Guinea	1.13	2.8
61	Spain	1.09	2.7
62	Greece	0.97	2.4
63	Panama	0.97	2.4
64	Colombia	0.89	2.2
65	Ecuador	0.84	2.1
66	Benin	0.80	2.0
67	Cyprus	0.80	2.0
68	Iraq	0.80	2.0
69	Malawi	0.80	2.0
70	Morocco	0.80	2.0
71	Nigeria	0.80	2.0
72	Uganda	0.80	2.0

LOWER MIDDLE

73	Iran	0.76	1.9
74	Nicaragua	0.76	1.9
75	Afghanistan	0.72	1.8

Rank	Country	Hectares	Acres
76	Yugoslavia	0.72	1.8
77	Belize	0.68	1.7
78	Rumania	0.68	1.6
79	Bulgaria	0.66	1.6
80	Finland	0.64	1.6
81	France	0.64	1.6
82	Hungary	0.64	1.6
83	Laos	0.64	1.6
84	Cuba	0.62	1.5
85	Denmark	0.60	1.5
86	Austria	0.52	1.3
87	Cambodia	0.52	1.3
88	Jordan	0.52	1.3
89	Portugal	0.52	1.3
90	Poland	0.51	1.2
91	Albania	0.48	1.1
92	Dominican Republic	0.48	1.1
93	Fiji	0.48	1.1
94	Malaysia	0.48	1.1
95	Czechoslovakia	0.47	1.1
96	Sweden	0.44	1.1
97	Burundi	0.40	1.0
98	Guatemala	0.40	1.0
99	Israel	0.40	1.0
100	Kenya	0.40	1.0
101	Luxembourg	0.40	1.0
102	Rwanda	0.40	1.0
103	East Germany	0.38	0.9
104	Burma	0.36	0.9
105	Italy	0.36	0.9
106	Mongolia	0.36	0.9
107	Switzerland	0.36	0.9
108	United Kingdom	0.36	0.9
109	El Salvador	0.32	0.8
110	Nepal	0.32	0.8

Rank	Country	Hectares	Acres
111	Pakistan	0.32	0.8
112	Thailand	0.32	0.8
113	India	0.28	0.7
114	Norway	0.24	0.6
115	Philippines	0.24	0.6
116	West Germany	0.20	0.5
117	Indonesia	0.20	0.5
118	Jamaica	0.20	0.5
119	Reunion	0.20	0.5
120	Vietnam	0.20	0.5
121	Barbados	0.16	0.4
122	Belgium	0.16	0.4
123	Haiti	0.16	0.4
124	Netherlands	0.16	0.4
125	Sri Lanka	0.16	0.4
126	Trinidad & Tobago	0.16	0.4
127	China	0.13	0.3
128	Bangladesh	0.12	0.3
129	Brunei	0.12	0.3
130	Kuwait	0.12	0.3
131	Lebanon	0.12	0.3
132	Mauritius	0.12	0.3
133	Surinam	0.12	0.3

BOTTOM 9

134	North Korea	0.10	0.2
135	Egypt	0.08	0.2
136	South Korea	0.08	0.2
137	Papua New Guinea	0.05	0.1
138	Taiwan	0.04	0.1
139	Japan	0.04	0.1
140	Malta	0.04	0.1
141	Hong Kong	0.004	0.01
142	Singapore	0.004	0.01

Source: Library of Congress.

103. Agricultural Production Index

The agricultural production index is issued by the Food and Agriculture Organization and is based on the volume of agricultural output using 1961-65 as the base period. It includes the following commodity groups: cereals, starchy roots, sugar, pulses, edible oil crops, nuts, fruit, vegetables, wine, cocoa, tea, coffee, livestock and livestock products, fibers, rubber, industrial oilseeds and tobacco. The food production index, which follows, excludes fibers, rubber, industrial oilseeds and tobacco. Deductions are made for commodities used within agricultural processes themselves, such as seeds and livestock feed. In 1975 the agricultural production index worldwide was 134 and the regional index numbers were as follows: North America, 129; Western Europe, 128; Oceania 129; Africa, 137; Latin America, 123; Middle East, 136; Far East, 148; and centrally planned (Communist) economies, 136.

Number of Countries: 107
Midpoint: 131
Period Covered: 1975
Type of Ranking: Agricultural Production Index, 1975 (1961-65=100); Highest to Lowest

Highlights & Findings: In terms of population developing countries suffered a decline in agricultural production. The decline was most severe in Africa, where the per capita agricultural production dropped to 91 and in Latin America where the relative number was 98. Other regions registered minor gains, and the global index number in the same year was 107 per capita. Singapore's first place ranking is somewhat misleading (or at least unimportant) given that small city-state's tiny agricultural sector.

Regions	Africa	Asia & Oceania	Europe	Western Hemisphere
Most	Libya (2)	Singapore (1)	Rumania (8)	Venezuela (10)
Least	Angola (106)	Hong Kong (107)	Denmark (100)	Trinidad & Tobago (105)

Rank	Country	Agricultural Production Index	Rank	Country	Agricultural Production Index	Rank	Country	Agricultural Production Index
	TOP 10		36	Sudan	144	72	Nigeria	124
1	Singapore	267	37	Indonesia	143	73	South Africa	124
2	Libya	223	38	Zaire	142	74	Belgium	123
3	Malaysia	211	39	Kenya	141	75	Argentina	122
4	Tunisia	211	40	Iraq	140	76	Chile	122
5	Malawi	199	41	Soviet Union	140	77	France	122
6	Israel	197	42	Nicaragua	139	78	Nepal	122
7	Iran	189	43	Czechoslovakia	137	79	Austria	121
8	Rumania	180	44	India	137	80	Morocco	121
9	South Korea	175	45	Madagascar	137	81	Paraguay	121
10	Venezuela	174	46	Mexico	137	82	Sweden	119
			47	Australia	136	83	Cyprus	118
	UPPER MIDDLE		48	Finland	136	84	West Germany	118
11	Costa Rica	172	49	Ireland	136	85	United Kingdom	118
12	Philippines	171	50	Syria	133	86	Senegal	117
13	Ivory Coast	169	51	South Yemen	133	87	Burma	116
14	Guatemala	168	52	Benin	132	88	Uganda	112
15	Turkey	167	53	Poland	132	89	Sri Lanka	111
16	Thailand	166	54	El Salvador	131	90	Japan	109
17	Greece	165	55	East Germany	131	91	Jordan	109
18	Albania	164				92	Honduras	106
19	Zambia	163		*LOWER MIDDLE*		93	Guyana	105
20	Taiwan	161	56	New Zealand	130	94	Norway	105
21	Netherlands	159	57	Guinea	129	95	Haiti	104
22	Pakistan	159	58	Niger	129	96	Mali	104
23	Brazil	155	59	Togo	129	97	Peru	103
24	Liberia	155	60	Burundi	128			
25	Saudi Arabia	154	61	Cameroon	128		*BOTTOM 10*	
26	Yugoslavia	154	62	Bolivia	127	98	Ethiopia	98
27	Lebanon	151	63	Sierra Leone	127	99	Portugal	98
28	Spain	150	64	Afghanistan	126	100	Denmark	97
29	Yemen Arab Republic	150	65	Bangladesh	125	101	Algeria	93
30	Colombia	146	66	Italy	125	102	Uruguay	93
31	Panama	145	67	Tanzania	125	103	Upper Volta	92
32	Bulgaria	144	68	Switzerland	124	104	Jamaica	86
33	Ecuador	144	69	Dominican Republic	124	105	Trinidad & Tobago	80
34	Hungary	144	70	Egypt	124	106	Angola	73
35	Rwanda	144	71	Ghana	124	107	Hong Kong	66

Source: Food and Agriculture Organization.

104. Food Production Index

The food production index is a useful indicator of a nation's improved ability to feed its population, especially when the index is read with the population growth index. Based on the 1961-65 period, the world food production index in 1975 was 136; regionally, it was 136 for North America, 147 for Latin America, 128 for Africa, 151 for Asia (excluding Japan), 128 for Western Europe, 139 for South Asia and 164 for the Middle East. It is notable that the real gains in food production (after allowances for population growth) are unimpressive and that in many countries food production is outpaced by population growth.

Number of Countries: 120
Midpoint: 104
Period Covered: 1974-76
Type of Ranking: Per Capita Food Production Index, 1965-67=100; Highest to Lowest

Highlights & Findings: By the mid-1970s the Green Revolution that had transformed agriculture in developing countries had more or less spent itself, and some of the negative consequences of the miracle strains of rice and wheat were becoming apparent. This explains the absence of many of the developing countries from the top ranks. However, because food production tends to vary from year to year, these statistics must be interpreted with caution. The two lowest countries rankings were affected by special circumstances—war in the case of Cambodia and the loss of the West Bank in Jordan's case.

Regions	Africa	Asia & Oceania	Europe	Western Hemisphere
Most	Tunisia (4)	Singapore (1)	Netherlands (3)	Costa Rica (7)
Least	Togo (118)	Jordan (120)	Denmark (78)	Jamaica (106)

Rank	Country	Per Capita Food Production Index	Rank	Country	Per Capita Food Production Index	Rank	Country	Per Capita Food Production Index
	TOP 10		41	United Kingdom	110	82	Mexico	98
1	Singapore	208	42	Uruguay	110	83	Nepal	98
2	Malaysia	146	43	Iran	109	84	Ecuador	97
3	Netherlands	136	44	Cameroon	108	85	Sierra Leone	97
4	Tunisia	134	45	China	108	86	South Yemen	97
5	Hungary	133	46	El Salvador	108	87	Libya	96
6	Greece	131	47	Liberia	108	88	Senegal	96
7	Costa Rica	130	48	Philippines	108	89	Bangladesh	95
8	Ireland	126	49	France	107	90	Cuba	95
9	Israel	126	50	India	107	91	Lebanon	95
10	Spain	125	51	Italy	107	92	Mozambique	95
			52	Japan	107	93	Afghanistan	94
	UPPER MIDDLE		53	Malawi	107	94	Canada	94
11	Ivory Coast	124	54	Rhodesia (Zimbabwe)	107	95	Guinea	94
12	Czechoslovakia	123	55	Colombia	106	96	Paraguay	94
13	East Germany	120	56	Thailand	106	97	Congo	93
14	Yugoslavia	120	57	Norway	105	98	Ghana	93
15	Belgium	119	58	Argentina	104	99	Zaire	93
16	Bolivia	119	59	Egypt	104	100	Angola	92
17	Austria	117	60	South Korea	104	101	Chile	92
18	Indonesia	117	61	Zambia	104	102	Trinidad & Tobago	92
19	Rumania	117				103	Somalia	91
20	Sudan	117		*LOWER MIDDLE*		104	Madagascar	90
21	Poland	115	62	Central African Empire	103	105	Iraq	89
22	Albania	114	63	Haiti	103	106	Jamaica	89
23	Brazil	114	64	Laos	103	107	Nigeria	89
24	Guatemala	114	65	Morocco	103	108	Uganda	89
25	Pakistan	114	66	Nicaragua	103	109	Kenya	88
26	Panama	114	67	Portugal	103			
27	Rwanda	114	68	Honduras	102			
28	Turkey	114	69	Lesotho	102		*BOTTOM 11*	
29	United States	114	70	New Zealand	102	110	Hong Kong	84
30	Finland	113	71	Saudi Arabia	102	111	Upper Volta	84
31	Soviet Union	113	72	South Africa	102	112	Benin	83
32	Syria	113	73	Switzerland	102	113	Ethiopia	83
33	Tanzania	113	74	Burundi	101	114	Chad	76
34	Venezuela	113	75	Yemen Arab Republic	101	115	Mali	71
35	Australia	112	76	Algeria	100	116	Mauritania	68
36	Dominican Republic	111	77	Bulgaria	100	117	Niger	67
37	West Germany	111	78	Denmark	99	118	Togo	59
38	North Korea	110	79	Papua New Guinea	99	119	Cambodia	53
39	Sri Lanka	110	80	Peru	99	120	Jordan	47
40	Sweden	110	81	Burma	98			

Source: Food and Agriculture Organization.

105. Average Size of Farms

Next to land tenure, the most important factor in agricultural economics is the average size of farms. The size of farms is determined by land colonization practices. In Latin America, for example, the ease with which the conquistadores could establish large estates called latifundios or haciendas led to a system in which large farms were the rule rather than the exception. On the other hand, in countries where Muslim or Hindu inheritance laws prevail, the division of farms among all male heirs has led to fragmentation of holdings into minute parcels. In Asia and Africa the current trend is to consolidate individual holdings into contiguous blocks of land without actually changing the distribution of land ownership. It is now generally conceded that although smaller farms are worked more intensively, larger farms are more efficient in terms of mechanization and application of fertilizers. Figures for the USSR, whose agriculture is dominated by enormous collective farms, are not available.

Number of Countries: 41
Midpoint: 4.75 hectares (11.73 acres)
Period Covered: Early 1970s
Type of Ranking: Average Farm Size in Hectares and Acres; Highest to Lowest

Highlights & Findings: The Food and Agriculture Organization (FAO) World Census of Agriculture revealed that there are 138.3 million farms in 83 of the larger countries of the world. Of these, 53.9 million, or 39% of the total, are less than one hectare in size and occupy 1.1% of the land area and 3.4% of the cropland. About 109 million farms, or 78.8% of the total, are less than five hectares in size and occupy 6.8% of the total land area and 20.7% of the cropland. One million holdings of 200 hectares or more represent less than 0.8% of all holdings, but they account for 66% of the total land area and 25% of all cropland. This pattern is even more skewed in the developing countries of Asia and Africa. In Asia, for example, 40% of the land is comprised of farms (accounting for 80% of the holdings) less than five hectares in size.

Regions	Africa	Asia & Oceania	Europe	Western Hemisphere
Most	Tunisia (14)	India (19)	United Kingdom (11)	Argentina (1)
Least	Madagascar (40)	South Korea (41)	Greece (30)	El Salvador(18)

Rank	Country	Average Farm Size Hectares	Acres	Rank	Country	Average Farm Size Hectares	Acres	Rank	Country	Average Farm Size Hectares	Acres
	TOP 10			14	Tunisia	15.41	38.07	30	Greece	3.18	7.85
1	Argentina	270.10	667.41	15	Spain	14.85	36.69	31	Togo	2.62	6.47
2	Uruguay	208.80	515.94	16	Dominican Republic	8.64	21.34				
3	United States	157.83	390.00	17	Guatemala	8.17	20.18		*BOTTOM 10*		
4	Mexico	123.90	306.15	18	El Salvador	6.95	17.17	32	Pakistan	2.35	5.80
5	Chile	118.50	292.81	19	India	6.52	16.11	33	Sri Lanka	1.61	3.97
6	Paraguay	108.70	268.59	20	Iran	6.05	14.94	34	Egypt	1.59	3.92
7	Venezuela	81.24	200.74	21	Turkey	5.03	12.42	35	Vietnam	1.33	3.28
8	Brazil	79.25	195.82	22	Botswana	4.75	11.73	36	China	1.27	3.13
9	Costa Rica	40.70	100.56	23	Morocco	4.62	11.41	37	Nepal	1.23	3.03
10	Nicaragua	37.34	92.26	24	Mali	4.35	10.74	38	Japan	1.18	2.91
				25	Kenya	4.20	10.37	39	Indonesia	1.05	2.59
	MIDDLE			26	Senegal	3.62	8.94	40	Madagascar	1.04	2.57
11	United Kingdom	24.74	61.15	27	Philippines	3.59	8.87	41	South Korea	0.85	2.10
12	Colombia	22.60	55.84	28	Thailand	3.47	8.57				
13	Peru	20.37	50.33	29	Uganda	3.29	8.12				

Sources: World Bank, U.S. Data: U.S. Census of Agriculture.

106. Farm Ownership

More revolutions have been caused by inequities in land ownership than by any other single reason in history. The owners of land have traditionally been the privileged class, while the renters have been the hewers of wood and the drawers of water. The most glaring inequities have been corrected in most countries through a combination of reform and revolt to the point that, as revealed in the following ranking, farm operators constitute the majority of farm owners in the majority of the reporting countries.

Number of Countries: 59
Midpoint: 62.72%
Period Covered: Early 1970s
Type of Ranking: Percentage of Farms Operated by Owners; Total Number of Holdings; Highest to Lowest

Highlights & Findings: The ranking attests to the success of the land reform movements in this century. Although data are limited to those countries where agricultural censuses have been held (and even in these, data are fragmentary), they are adequate to permit extrapolation about trends in nonreporting countries. Only in 12 countries do owner-operator farms constitute less than 40% of the total. In fact, only in a handful of countries does land reform remain a live issue.

Regions	Africa	Asia & Oceania	Europe	Western Hemisphere
Most	Mali (3)	Sarawak (10)	Northern Ireland (1)	Mexico (4)
Least	Senegal (40)	Iran (52)	Malta (59)	Surinam (58)

Rank	Country	Percentage of Owner-Operated Holdings	Total Number of Holdings	Rank	Country	Percentage of Owner-Operated Holdings	Total Number of Holdings	Rank	Country	Percentage of Owner-Operated Holdings	Total Number of Holdings
	TOP 10			20	Jamaica	75.96	158,941	40	Senegal	48.78	295,400
1	Northern Ireland	100.00	86,827	21	Japan	75.38	6,038,953	41	England & Wales	47.31	333,180
2	Denmark	96.47	206,635	22	Italy	73.85	4,279,175	42	Guatemala	47.01	274,400
3	Mali	94.50	280,260	23	South Korea	73.63	2,331,874	43	Trinidad & Tobago	46.07	30,511
4	Mexico	94.49	1,365,141	24	Canada	72.86	480,903	44	Israel	43.05	17,363
5	Finland	90.37	261,750	25	Portugal	72.82	853,568	45	West Germany	41.77	2,011,992
6	Puerto Rico	90.02	45,792	26	Sweden	68.89	232,920	46	Venezuela	41.33	248,738
7	Austria	89.28	421,433	27	Ecuador	67.94	344,234	47	Argentina	41.12	546,698
8	Norway	86.80	198,315	28	Peru	66.85	851,957	48	El Salvador	39.28	224,289
9	Mozambique	86.45	N.A.	29	Egypt	65.60	1,003,023	49	Netherlands	37.12	290,723
10	Sarawak	85.89	44,712	30	Malaysia (West)	62.72	449,650				
	UPPER MIDDLE				*LOWER MIDDLE*				*BOTTOM 10*		
11	Sabah	85.46	42,974	31	New Zealand	62.48	79,628	50	Hong Kong	35.35	26,088
12	Thailand	82.38	2,119,287	32	Colombia	62.43	1,209,672	51	Iran	33.25	1,877,299
13	Rhodesia (Zimbabwe)	82.22	N.A.	33	Dominican Republic	60.19	276,848	52	Paraguay	32.51	149,614
14	Luxembourg	81.17	13,578	34	Barbados	58.02	4,881	53	Scotland	30.06	62,490
15	Jordan	80.51	92,068	35	United States	57.08	3,707,973	54	Guyana	27.42	28,187
16	Brazil	79.29	2,064,278	36	France	53.65	2,229,957	55	Belgium	26.81	267,861
17	South Africa	77.47	110,317	37	Philippines	52.55	1,638,624	56	Panama	24.60	95,505
18	Tunisia	76.78	325,700	38	Pakistan	52.08	10,999,463	57	Honduras	21.32	156,135
19	Costa Rica	76.34	64,621	39	Uruguay	49.86	86,928	58	Surinam	18.23	16,231
								59	Malta	7.72	11,747

Source: Food and Agriculture Organization.

107. Landownership: Bottom 10%

Disparities in landownership are best illustrated in two types of rankings: the percentage of land owned by the bottom 10% of landowners in relation to total land area and the percentage of land owned by the top 10% of landowners in relation to total land area. It must be borne in mind that such disparities are being progressively reduced in many countries of the world; nevertheless, they continue to exist in hidden forms even in developed countries.

Number of Countries: 22
Midpoint: 1.0%
Period Covered: Latest Available Year
Type of Ranking: Percentage of Total Land Area Owned by the Bottom 10% of Landowners; Highest to Lowest

Highlights & Findings: Because of the small number of countries in the ranking, no valid conclusions may be drawn.

Regions	Africa	Asia	Europe	Western Hemisphere
Most	Lesotho (2)	Indonesia (1)	Greece (3)	Dominican Republic (5)
Least	Tunisia (16)	Pakistan (18)	N.A.	Peru (22)

Rank Country	Percentage of Total Land Area Owned by Bottom 10% of Landowners	Rank Country	Percentage of Total Land Area Owned by Bottom 10% of Landowners	Rank Country	Percentage of Total Land Area Owned by Bottom 10% of Landowners
TOP 5		7 Jamaica	1.6	16 Tunisia	0.5
1 Indonesia	3.0	8 Brazil	1.5		
2 Lesotho	3.0	9 Bangladesh	1.0	**BOTTOM 6**	
3 Greece	2.6	10 Lebanon	1.0	17 El Salvador	0.4
4 South Korea	2.0	11 Morocco	1.0	18 Pakistan	0.4
5 Dominican Republic	2.0	12 Panama	1.0	19 Mexico	0.3
		13 Turkey	0.9	20 Colombia	0.2
MIDDLE		14 Barbados	0.5	21 Nicaragua	0.1
6 Mauritius	1.8	15 Guatemala	0.5	22 Peru	0.1

Source: U.S. Agency for International Development.

108. Landownership: Top 10%

Number of Countries: 22
Midpoint: 53%
Period Covered: Latest Available Year
Type of Ranking: Percentage of Total Land Area Owned by the Top 10% of Landowners; Highest to Lowest

Highlights & Findings: Because of the small number of countries in the ranking, no valid conclusions may be drawn.

Regions	Africa	Asia	Europe	Western Hemisphere
Most	Mauritius (4)	Lebanon (10)	Greece (21)	Barbados (1)
Least	Lesotho (22)	South Korea (20)	N.A.	Mexico (18)

Rank Country	Percentage of Total Land Area Owned by the Top 10% of Landowners	Rank Country	Percentage of Total Land Area Owned by the Top 10% of Landowners	Rank Country	Percentage of Total Land Area Owned by the Top 10% of Landowners
TOP 5		7 Jamaica	74.6	16 Brazil	45.0
1 Barbados	95.0	8 Nicaragua	67.0	17 Panama	45.0
2 Peru	93.0	9 Dominican Republic	62.7		
3 Colombia	80.0	10 Lebanon	57.0	**BOTTOM 5**	
4 Mauritius	80.0	11 Tunisia	53.0	18 Mexico	37.0
5 El Salvador	78.0	12 Turkey	53.0	19 Bangladesh	34.0
		13 Morocco	49.0	20 South Korea	28.0
MIDDLE		14 Indonesia	48.0	21 Greece	27.5
6 Guatemala	76.6	15 Pakistan	46.2	22 Lesotho	22.0

Source: U.S. Agency for International Development.

109. Per Capita Rural Indebtedness

Credit is the key element in the modernization of agriculture. Outstanding institutional loans for agriculture in developing countries are estimated at approximately $15 billion. Another $75 billion in credit is outstanding in the so-called informal or noninstitutional sector which consists mostly of private moneylenders. The percentage of farmers receiving institutional credit varies widely from around 5% in Africa to about 15% in South Asia and Latin America and 100% in Taiwan. Most of the loans are short-term usually for one season and only rarely for over a year or two. The nominal interest rates fall between 5% and 30% per year with the mean around 9% and 12%. In the informal sector interest rates up to 150% are not unknown. Although data on defaults are scanty, they rarely exceed 5% of outstanding loans.

Number of Countries: 37 **Midpoint:** $20 **Period Covered:** Early 1970s **Type of Ranking:** Per Capita Rural Indebtedness in Dollars; Highest to Lowest	**Highlights & Findings:** Higher indebtedness among Latin American countries indicates the easier availability of credit and the larger size of the farms that serve as collateral. Eight of the 10 countries at the bottom are in Asia.

Regions	Africa	Asia	Europe	Western Hemisphere
Most	Tunisia (20)	Sri Lanka (7)	N.A.	Venezuela (1)
Least	Ethiopia (35)	Malaysia (37)	N.A.	Bolivia (27)

Rank	Country	Debt per Capita of Rural Population ($)	Rank	Country	Debt per Capita of Rural Population ($)	Rank	Country	Debt per Capita of Rural Population ($)
	TOP 10		12	Uruguay	36	26	Iran	9
1	Venezuela	179	13	Honduras	35	27	Bolivia	8
2	Costa Rica	126	14	Panama	31			
3	Argentina	111	15	Pakistan	26		*BOTTOM 10*	
4	Chile	106	16	Peru	25			
5	Mexico	84	17	Dominican Republic	24	28	Ghana	4
6	Nicaragua	77	18	Paraguay	22	29	Philippines	4
7	Sri Lanka	74	19	Thailand	20	30	India	3
8	South Korea	55	20	Tunisia	20	31	Taiwan	3
9	Colombia	52	21	Guatemala	18	32	Turkey	2
10	Brazil	40	22	Jordan	17	33	Afghanistan	1
			23	Ecuador	13	34	Bangladesh	1
	MIDDLE		24	Morocco	13	35	Ethiopia	1
11	El Salvador	36	25	Kenya	12	36	Indonesia	1
						37	Malaysia	0.2

Source: World Bank.

110. Tractors Per Hectare

Agriculture is generally divided into two sectors: modern and traditional. The traditional sector is characterized by intensive labor and the law of diminishing returns. As a result, traditional agriculture is one of the least productive of all economic activities. The modern sector, on the other hand, is characterized by large-scale mechanization, application of fertilizers, soil conservation, irrigation and the use of improved seeds, among other things. Mechanization is best measured by the number of tractors in use per hectare of land actually under cultivation.

Number of Countries: 172 **Midpoint:** 3.59 tractors per 1,000 hectares **Period Covered:** 1976 **Type of Ranking:** Number of Tractors in Use per 1,000 Hectares of Cultivated Land; Total number of Tractors in Use; Highest to Lowest	**Highlights & Findings:** Worldwide there are 18,324,674 tractors in use distributed as follows: Africa, 407,929; North America, 5,262,396; South America, 601,126; Asia, 1,798,374; Europe, 7,417,645; Oceania, 435,203; and the Soviet Union, 2,402,000. The United States, whose agriculture is perhaps among the most mechanized in the world, accounts for 24% of all tractors in use, while the Soviet Union, whose agricultural sector has been operating below capacity for a number of decades, accounts for another 12%.

Regions	Africa	Asia & Oceania	Europe	Western Hemisphere
Most	Djibouti (19)	Japan (6)	Iceland (1)	Bermuda (11)
Least	Upper Volta (172)	Afghanistan (157)	Hungary (52)	Falkland Islands (155)

Rank	Country	Tractors per 1,000 Hectares (2,471 Acres)	Total Number of Tractors	Rank	Country	Tractors per 1,000 Hectares (2,471 Acres)	Total Number of Tractors	Rank	Country	Tractors per 1,000 Hectares (2,471 Acres)	Total Number of Tractors
	TOP 10			4	Austria	175.83	294,000	8	New Zealand	126.59	99,000
1	Iceland	1,159.00	10,200	5	Netherlands	174.15	159,000	9	Belgium	122.80	108,801
2	Switzerland	210.39	85,000	6	Japan	140.74	800,000	10	Ireland	98.82	118,000
3	West Germany	177.60	1,452,661	7	Norway	130.48	109,999				

Rank	Country	Tractors per 1,000 Hectares (2,471 Acres)	Total Number of Tractors
	UPPER MIDDLE		
11	Bermuda	78.16	34
12	France	69.64	1,380,000
13	Finland	69.54	192,000
14	Denmark	67.41	182,618
15	United Kingdom	65.41	482,871
16	Sweden	63.51	192,500
17	Israel	58.41	24,010
18	Italy	56.97	865,715
19	Djibouti	47.00	47
20	Yugoslavia	31.63	260,831
21	Poland	28.01	434,043
22	East Germany	27.68	137,718
23	Surinam	26.66	1,200
24	Czechoslovakia	26.36	141,123
25	Martinique	26.25	840
26	French Guyana	26.00	52
27	Greece	25.18	97,000
28	United States	24.82	4,380,000
29	Liechtenstein*	24.80	418
30	Netherlands Antilles	24.40	122
31	Cuba	23.97	49,000
32	Malta	23.92	335
33	Cyprus	23.14	10,000
34	Dominican Republic	20.00	4,886
35	Spain	19.57	400,928
36	Barbados	19.37	500
37	Guyana	19.23	3,750
38	Albania	18.36	9,200
39	Trinidad & Tobago	15.46	2,150
40	Antigua	15.33	230
41	Guadeloupe	15.30	750
42	Canada	14.97	650,000
43	South Africa	14.92	180,000
44	Bulgaria	14.37	65,500
45	Uruguay	14.07	27,550
46	North Korea	13.72	26,000
47	St. Kitts-Nevis-Anguilla	13.54	210
48	Rumania	12.12	128,024
49	Portugal	11.36	49,660
50	Jamaica	10.78	2,600
51	Soviet Union	10.70	2,402,000
52	Hungary	10.60	59,500
53	Turkey	10.58	281,479
54	Rhodesia (Zimbabwe)	10.50	19,300
55	Papua New Guinea	10.27	1,500
56	Lebanon	9.49	3,000
57	Costa Rica	9.16	5,700
58	Brazil	9.07	270,000
59	Gabon	8.26	1,050
60	Sri Lanka	8.08	16,000
61	Australia	8.00	332,000
62	Egypt	7.85	22,000
63	Swaziland	7.67	1,950
64	Algeria	7.66	52,000
65	New Caledonia	7.62	610
66	Panama	6.73	3,800
67	Tunisia	6.65	30,000
68	Fiji	6.44	1,450
69	Colombia	6.34	32,000
70	Chile	6.31	28,500
71	Mexico	6.08	145,000
72	Singapore	5.76	75
73	Argentina	5.75	190,000
74	Belize	5.74	270
75	Dominican Republic	5.43	5,800
76	Venezuela	5.37	28,000
77	Cook Islands	5.29	127
78	Reunion	5.24	325
79	Dominica	5.17	88
80	Bahamas	5.00	65
81	Peru	4.83	12,700
82	South Yemen	4.76	1,200
82	Botswana	4.43	1,900
84	St. Vincent	3.86	75
85	Namibia	3.66	2,350
86	Kenya	3.59	6,000
	LOWER MIDDLE		
87	Jordan	3.43	3,914
88	Syria	3.16	18,567
89	Norfolk Island*	3.05	11
90	French Polynesia	2.96	190
91	Paraguay	2.95	2,800
92	Mauritius	2.93	305
93	Lesotho	2.83	1,000
94	Iraq	2.80	21,000
95	Morocco	2.72	21,500
96	Iran	2.58	30,000
97	Guatemala	2.50	3,750
98	Mongolia	2.42	8,500
99	Mozambique	2.09	5,550
100	Malaysia	1.99	7,120
101	Thailand	1.92	22,000
102	Pakistan	1.91	37,000
103	China	1.82	200,000
104	Saudi Arabia	1.79	830
105	St. Lucia	1.76	37
106	Libya	1.73	4,350
107	India	1.53	250,884
108	Nicaragua	1.50	1,316
109	Grenada	1.45	22
110	Ecuador	1.42	3,700
111	Angola	1.39	9,500
112	Greenland	1.37	3,000
113	Seychelles	1.37	30
114	Somalia	1.35	1,300
115	Honduras	1.27	1,050
116	Sao Tome & Principe*	1.26	122
117	Sudan	1.26	9,000
118	Montserrat*	1.22	12
119	Haiti	1.21	450
120	Tonga	1.21	67
121	Ghana	1.14	3,250
122	Congo	1.03	655
123	Kuwait	1.00	16
124	Vietnam	0.94	600
125	Pacific Islands	0.90	48
126	Zambia	0.87	4,200
127	Indonesia	0.85	10,800
128	Madagascar	0.84	2,400
129	Philippines	0.76	6,500
130	New Hebrides	0.74	52
131	Tanzania	0.63	7,400
132	Laos	0.50	400
133	Burma	0.49	8,000
134	Hong Kong	0.46	6
135	Cambodia	0.45	1,350
136	El Salvador	0.42	275
137	Equatorial Guinea	0.42	95
138	Gilbert Islands	0.39	16
139	Gambia	0.35	70
140	Nigeria	0.35	7,700
141	South Korea	0.34	790
142	Malawi	0.34	1,000
143	Uganda	0.33	1,656
144	Brunei	0.30	20
145	Ethiopia	0.29	3,700
146	Niue Island*	0.27	7
147	British Virgin Islands*	0.26	4
148	Ivory Coast	0.25	2,300
149	Bangladesh	0.24	2,350
150	Bolivia	0.24	760
151	Samoa	0.22	20
152	Nepal	0.20	460
153	Zaire	0.18	1,300
154	Yemen Arab Republic	0.17	690
155	Falkland Islands*	0.09	114
156	Guinea	0.09	70
157	Afghanistan	0.08	700
158	Mali	0.08	600
159	Rwanda	0.08	80
160	Cameroon	0.07	300
161	Cape Verde	0.07	30
	BOTTOM 11		
162	Benin	0.06	92
163	Liberia	0.06	260
164	Senegal	0.06	380
165	Sierra Leone	0.06	255
166	Togo	0.05	120
167	Central African Empire	0.02	130
168	Chad	0.02	140
169	Burundi	0.006	7
170	Guinea-Bissau*	0.006	24
171	Niger	0.006	70
172	Upper Volta	0.005	55

* Because no reliable estimates of cropland are available, calculation is based on rough estimates of agricultural land.

Source: Food and Agriculture Organization.

111. Fertilizer Consumption

The contribution that fertilizers make to agricultural production has never been determined precisely, but it is bound to be enormous, particularly in countries where the soil is being constantly impoverished through poor soil management practices and intensive cultivation techniques. Three types of fertilizers are used, sometimes in combination, according to the needs of the soil: nitrogenous fertilizers, phosphate fertilizers (such as superphosphates and ammonium phosphates) and potash fertilizers (such as muriate, nitrate and sulfate of potash). In addition to these inorganics, various organic fertilizers are being added to the soil, but no statistics are available on them. In the following ranking all three types of inorganic fertilizers have been combined and presented in terms of hectares of cultivated land.

Number of Countries: 140
Midpoint: 38.42 kg (84.71 lb)
Period Covered: 1976
Type of Ranking: Amount of Fertilizers per Hectare/2.471 Acres in Kg and Lb; Total Amount of Fertilizer Consumption in Metric Tons; Highest to Lowest

Highlights & Findings: Total worldwide consumption of fertilizers in 1976 was 94.645 million metric tons. Of this, total consumption was 23.064 million tons for potash fertilizers, 26.493 million tons for phosphate fertilizers and 45.088 million tons for nitrogenous fertilizers. The regional distribution is as follows (in 000 tons):

Region	Nitrogenous	Phosphate	Potash
Africa	1,428	910	350
North America	11,595	6,036	5,818
South America	943	1,489	825
Asia	11,167	4,449	2,002
Europe	12,455	8,415	8,241
Oceania	247	1,131	251
Soviet Union	7,252	4,063	5,577

In interpreting fertilizer application patterns, it should be remembered that some soils are naturally so rich that they require only relatively low levels of artificial replenishment of nutrients. The low ranking of countries such as Argentina and Uruguay may be better understood in the light of this qualification. Total worldwide consumption of fertilizers has been steadily increasing since the end of World War II and has grown by over 300% since 1966. But it is difficult to predict how long this upward thrust can be maintained because many fertilizers are oil-based or require vast amounts of energy to produce, and the energy shortage is bound to have a negative impact on their availability and price.

Regions	Africa	Asia & Oceania	Europe	Western Hemisphere
Most	Mauritius (12)	New Zealand (2)	Netherlands (1)	Martinique (3)
Least	Niger (140)	Laos (138)	Iceland (92)	Haiti (131)

Rank	Country	Kg	Lb	Total Consumption 000 Metric Tons
	TOP 10			
1	Netherlands	699.89	1,543.25	639.0
2	New Zealand	698.97	1,541.22	546.6
3	Martinique	453.12	999.12	14.5
4	West Germany	416.38	918.11	3,405.6
5	Belgium-Luxembourg	413.09	910.86	366.0
6	Ireland	406.95	897.32	485.9
7	Japan	380.94	839.97	2,165.3
8	Switzerland	375.99	829.05	151.9
9	East Germany	354.60	781.89	1,763.8
10	Czechoslovakia	314.06	692.50	1,681.2
	UPPER MIDDLE			
11	South Korea	277.31	611.46	643.1
12	Mauritius	276.92	610.60	288.0
13	Norway	264.29	582.75	222.8
14	United Kingdom	258.73	570.49	1,910.0
15	France	254.35	560.84	5,040.3
16	Hungary	247.28	544.25	1,388.0
17	Denmark	240.53	530.36	651.6
18	Poland	231.96	511.47	3,594.1
19	Singapore	230.76	508.82	3.0
20	North Korea	229.51	506.06	434.7
21	Austria	219.79	484.63	367.5
22	Egypt	211.99	467.43	593.8
23	Guadeloupe	195.91	431.98	9.6
24	St. Lucia	195.23	430.48	4.1
25	Reunion	182.25	401.86	11.3
26	Israel	181.26	399.67	74.5
27	St. Vincent	180.41	397.80	3.5
28	Sweden	175.51	386.99	532.0
29	El Salvador	157.71	347.75	102.2
30	Finland	152.73	336.76	421.7
31	Bulgaria	144.33	318.24	657.9
32	Albania	143.71	316.88	72.0
33	Surinam	133.33	293.99	6.0
34	Greece	131.00	288.85	504.5
35	St. Kitts-Nevis-Anguilla	129.03	284.51	2.0
36	Cuba	127.44	281.00	260.5
37	United States	113.66	250.62	20,055.9
38	Rumania	108.37	238.95	1,144.4
39	Barbados	100.77	222.19	2.6
40	Lebanon	95.25	210.02	30.1
41	Costa Rica	89.54	197.43	55.7
42	Yugoslavia	89.49	197.32	738.0
43	Italy	85.68	188.92	1,302.0
44	Rhodesia (Zimbabwe)	84.92	187.24	156.0
45	Spain	82.76	182.48	1,695.1
46	Brazil	79.65	175.63	2,370.6
47	Vietnam	79.44	175.16	385.7
48	Bahamas	76.92	169.60	1.0

Rank	Country	Consumption of Fertilizers per Hectare/ 2.471 Acres of Cultivated Land Kg	Lb	Total Consumption 000 Metric Tons	Rank	Country	Consumption of Fertilizers per Hectare/ 2.471 Acres of Cultivated Land Kg	Lb	Total Consumption 000 Metric Tons	Rank	Country	Consumption of Fertilizers per Hectare/ 2.471 Acres of Cultivated Land Kg	Lb	Total Consumption 000 Metric Tons
49	Soviet Union	75.30	166.03	16,892.0	79	Ecuador	29.81	65.73	77.4	111	Equatorial Guinea	3.61	7.96	0.8
50	Malaysia	74.80	164.93	266.9	80	Belize	29.78	65.66	1.4	112	Madagascar	3.22	7.10	9.2
51	Dominican Republic	71.04	156.64	75.8	81	Algeria	28.31	62.42	192.2	113	Burma	3.17	6.98	51.1
52	Papua New Guinea	67.64	149.14	6.9	82	Saudi Arabia	25.75	56.77	11.9	114	Lesotho	2.83	6.24	1.0
53	South Africa	66.19	145.94	798.2	83	Chile	25.71	56.69	116.0	115	Tanzania	2.53	5.57	29.7
54	Cyprus	65.04	143.41	28.1	84	Bangladesh	25.66	56.58	241.4	116	Angola	2.33	5.13	2.1
55	Trinidad & Tobago	61.87	136.42	8.6	85	Australia	25.64	56.53	1,063.3	117	Argentina	2.17	4.78	71.8
56	Guyana	59.48	131.15	11.6	86	Morocco	23.30	51.37	184.1	118	Guinea	1.76	3.88	1.3
57	Jamaica	59.33	130.82	14.3	87	India	20.83	45.93	3,411.0	119	Zaire	1.76	3.88	12.7
58	China	57.93	127.73	6,335.0	88	Thailand	20.71	45.66	236.5	120	Benin	1.68	3.70	2.6
59	Guatemala	57.61	127.03	86.3	89	Libya	17.28	38.10	43.4	121	Ethiopia	1.67	3.68	21.0
60	Portugal	56.70	125.02	247.8	90	Sudan	14.80	32.60	105.1	122	Sierra Leone	1.67	3.68	1.6
61	Fiji	56.00	123.48	12.6	91	Zambia	13.29	29.30	63.8	123	Mali	1.63	3.59	11.8
62	Nicaragua	52.23	115.16	45.6	92	Iceland	12.67	27.93	28.7	124	Liberia	1.53	3.37	5.9
63	Peru	49.10	108.26	128.9	93	Tunisia	12.52	27.60	56.5	125	Togo	1.29	2.84	2.8
64	Colombia	49.05	108.15	247.6	94	Syria	11.26	24.82	66.0	126	Paraguay	0.95	2.09	0.9
65	Mexico	48.90	107.82	1,164.8	95	Malawi	8.57	18.89	25.1	127	Bolivia	0.93	2.05	2.9
66	Turkey	48.24	106.36	1,283.4	96	Gambia	8.00	17.64	1.6	128	Chad	0.80	1.76	5.6
67	Sri Lanka	43.63	96.20	86.4	97	Ghana	7.23	15.94	20.5	129	Mongolia	0.77	1.69	2.7
68	Panama	40.24	88.72	22.7	98	South Yemen	7.14	15.74	1.8	130	Yemen Arab Republic	0.69	1.52	2.7
69	Swaziland	38.97	85.92	9.9	99	Jordan	7.01	15.45	8.0					
70	Indonesia	38.42	84.71	487.9	100	Nepal	6.57	14.48	14.9		*BOTTOM 10*			
					101	Senegal	6.50	14.33	37.2	131	Haiti	0.54	1.19	0.2
	LOWER MIDDLE				102	Iraq	5.82	12.83	43.7	132	Upper Volta	0.49	1.08	4.8
71	Pakistan	32.32	71.26	626.9	103	Afghanistan	5.63	12.41	44.2	133	Rwanda	0.40	0.88	0.4
72	Kenya	32.27	71.15	53.9	104	Nigeria	5.15	11.35	112.3	134	Burundi	0.39	0.85	0.4
73	Canada	32.06	70.69	1,391.6	105	Congo	4.92	10.84	3.1	135	Mauritania	0.38	0.83	0.1
74	Uruguay	32.03	70.60	62.7	106	Botswana	4.67	10.29	2.0	136	Uganda	0.37	0.74	1.7
75	Philippines	31.44	69.32	268.7	107	Ivory Coast	4.67	10.29	41.4	137	Cambodia	0.26	0.57	0.8
76	Iran	30.92	68.17	358.5	108	Mozambique	4.22	9.30	11.2	138	Laos	0.25	0.55	0.2
77	Venezuela	30.89	68.11	161.1	109	Cameroon	4.11	9.06	17.7	139	Central African Empire	0.15	0.33	0.9
78	Honduras	30.86	68.04	25.4	110	Somalia	3.76	8.29	3.6	140	Niger	0.04	0.08	0.5

Note: Oman and the United Arab Emirates consumed 1,300 and 1,000 tons of fertilizers respectively but no figures are available on their cultivated areas.

Source: Food and Agriculture Organization.

112. Percentage of Irrigated Land

Irrigation is used chiefly in regions receiving an annual rainfall of less than 51 cm (20 in.) and also in areas of great rainfall to supply the high water requirements of certain crops such as rice. Methods of irrigation include free-flooding, check-flooding (in which water is guided over trips or checks of land between levees), the furrow method (in which water is run between rows of crops at distances) and the surface-pipe method (in which water is conducted through movable slip-joint pipes). The use of canals, dams, weirs and reservoirs for distribution, control and storage of water dates back to ancient Egypt. In the 20th century large-scale irrigation is commonly a part of multipurpose water projects combining irrigation, water supply, flood control and production of hydroelectric power.

Number of Countries: 111 **Midpoint:** 5.01% **Period Covered:** Early 1970s **Type of Ranking:** Percentage of Agricultural Land Under Irrigation; Total Area Under Irrigation in Hectares; Highest to Lowest	**Highlights & Findings:** More than 81 million hectares (200 million acres) of agricultural land are under some form of irrigation. Of this total, half are in the Indian subcontinent and China. Areas in Egypt and Mesopotamia have been under continuous irrigation for thousands of years.

Region	Africa	Asia & Oceania	Europe	Western Hemisphere
Most	Egypt (1)	China (2)	Albania (13)	Peru (8)
Least	Sierra Leone (111)	Brunei (87)	Denmark (110)	Canada (94)

Rank	Country	Irrigated Land as Percentage of Cropland	Total Irrigated Area (000 Hectares)	Rank	Country	Irrigated Land as Percentage of Cropland	Total Irrigated Area (000 Hectares)	Rank	Country	Irrigated Land as Percentage of Cropland	Total Irrigated Area (000 Hectares)
	TOP 10			38	Spain	10.92	2,238	76	Panama	2.48	14
1	Egypt	100.00	2,801	39	Dominican Republic	10.30	110	77	Uruguay	2.14	42
2	China	67.67	74,000	40	Sudan	10.01	711	78	Guatemala	2.13	32
3	Taiwan	61.44	553	41	Jamaica	9.95	24	79	Norway	2.13	18
4	Guyana	55.89	109	42	Reunion	9.67	6	80	Bolivia	2.07	64
5	Japan	55.78	3,171	43	Syria	9.17	538	81	Guadeloupe	2.04	1
6	Iraq	49.02	3,675	44	Malaysia (West)	8.99	236	82	Laos	1.87	15
7	Pakistan	42.68	12,043	45	Honduras	8.01	66	83	Tunisia	1.77	80
8	Peru	41.06	1,078	46	Trinidad & Tobago	7.91	11	84	Martinique	1.56	0.5
9	Iran	40.11	4,651	47	United States	7.23	12,770	85	Brazil	1.55	462
10	Israel	38.68	159	48	South Africa	6.70	808	86	United Kingdom	1.43	106
				49	Libya	6.57	165	87	Brunei	1.36	0.9
	UPPER MIDDLE			50	Turkey	5.82	1,549	88	Senegal	1.32	76
11	Surinam	33.33	15	51	Switzerland	5.69	23	89	Yugoslavia	1.32	109
12	South Korea	32.47	753	52	Netherlands	5.58	51	90	Mauritania	1.14	3
13	Albania	31.13	156	53	Hungary	5.55	312	91	Paraguay	0.95	9
14	Saudi Arabia	29.22	135	54	Jordan	5.26	60	92	Kenya	0.83	14
15	Indonesia	28.88	3,668	55	Rumania	5.01	530	93	Sweden	0.82	25
16	Chile	24.45	1,103					94	Canada	0.79	346
17	Cuba	24.11	493		*LOWER MIDDLE*			95	Rwanda	0.70	7
18	Cyprus	23.61	102	56	Sabah	4.91	12	96	Namibia	0.62	4
19	Madagascar	21.70	620	57	Burma	4.68	753	97	Botswana	0.46	2
20	Vietnam	21.60	613	58	Nepal	4.63	105	98	Ghana	0.42	12
21	Lebanon	21.51	68	59	Argentina	4.54	1,500	99	Tanzania	0.34	40
22	Bulgaria	21.00	959	60	Soviet Union	4.48	10,060	100	Austria	0.23	4
23	Sri Lanka	19.69	390	61	Colombia	4.47	226	101	Ethiopia	0.23	30
24	Ecuador	17.83	463	62	St. Lucia	4.28	0.9				
25	Somalia	17.24	165	63	Costa Rica	4.18	26		*BOTTOM 10*		
26	India	16.80	27,520	64	Venezuela	4.18	218	102	Ivory Coast	0.15	14
27	Greece	16.33	629	65	Algeria	3.97	270	103	France	0.12	25
28	Italy	16.08	2,444	66	Cambodia	3.35	100	104	Uganda	0.08	4
29	Puerto Rico	15.98	39	67	Morocco	3.35	265	105	Finland	0.07	2
30	Thailand	15.48	1,768	68	Nicaragua	3.32	29	106	Malawi	0.06	2
31	Mexico	14.75	3,515	69	West Germany	3.30	270	107	Belgium	0.05	0.5
32	Portugal	14.62	639	70	Australia	3.24	1,344	108	Niger	0.04	5
33	Mauritius	14.42	15	71	Czechoslovakia	2.98	160	109	Zambia	0.04	2
34	Haiti	11.35	42	72	Burundi	2.77	28	110	Denmark	0.02	0.6
35	New Zealand	11.25	88	73	Poland	2.64	410	111	Sierra Leone	0.02	0.8
36	Philippines	11.23	960	74	Rhodesia (Zimbabwe)	2.50	46				
37	Swaziland	11.02	28	75	East Germany	2.49	124				

Source: Food and Agriculture Organization.

113. Percentage of Forest Land

Throughout history the percentage of land under forests has been declining, and this process has been hastened in the 20th century by the requirements of industrial civilization for forest and agricultural products. Nevertheless, as conservationists have been reminding us, the ecological value of forests makes it dangerous to reduce further the present area under them. The debate on the building of the Trans-Amazonian Highway through the forests of Brazil illustrates the worldwide concern over the deforestation of the earth in the name of economic development.

Number of Countries: 140
Midpoint: 25%
Period Covered: 1977
Type of Ranking: Percentage of Land Area Under Forests; Highest to Lowest

Highlights & Findings: Only 35 countries have over 50% of their land area classified as forests. Over 30 countries have no forests or have only a negligible land area under forests. These include Guinea-Bissau, Bahrain, Botswana, Djibouti, Egypt, Fiji, Greenland, Iceland, Kuwait, Lesotho, Liechtenstein, Macao, Mali, Malta, Namibia, Mauritania, Nauru, Niger, the Netherlands Antilles, Oman, Qatar, Reunion, Rhodesia, Rwanda, Swaziland, Sao Tome and Principe, Singapore, Trinidad and Tobago, United Arab Emirates and South Yemen.

Regions	Africa	Asia & Oceania	Europe	Western Hemisphere
Most	Gabon (4)	Brunei (3)	Finland (24)	French Guyana (1)
Least	Libya (138)	Yemen Arab Republic (140)	Ireland (130)	Haiti (120)

Rank	Country	Percentage of Land Under Forests
	TOP 10	
1	French Guyana	90
2	Surinam	76
3	Brunei	75
4	Gabon	75
5	Cambodia	74
6	North Korea	74
7	Colombia	72
8	Bhutan	70
9	Equatorial Guinea	70
10	Papua New Guinea	70
	UPPER MIDDLE	
11	Japan	69
12	Dominica	67
13	South Korea	67
14	Guyana	66
15	Western Samoa	65
16	Indonesia	64
17	Congo	63
18	Burma	62
19	Bermuda	60
20	Brazil	60
21	Costa Rica	60
22	Ghana	60
23	Laos	60
24	Finland	58
25	Guatemala	57
26	Mozambique	56
27	Thailand	56
28	Taiwan	55
29	Ecuador	55
30	Peru	55
31	Sweden	55
32	Philippines	53
33	Paraguay	52
34	Cameroon	50
35	Vietnam	50
36	Tanzania	48
	(Mainly bush forest)	
37	Belize	46
38	Dominican Republic	45
39	Uganda	45
40	Zaire	45
41	Angola	44
42	Canada	44
43	St. Vincent	44
44	Sri Lanka	44
45	Albania	43
46	Bolivia	40
47	Ivory Coast	40
48	Liberia	40
49	Mauritius	39
50	Austria	38
51	Soviet Union	37
52	Czechoslovakia	35
53	Nigeria	35
54	Yugoslavia	34
55	Bulgaria	33
56	Luxembourg	33
57	Nepal	32
58	United States	32
59	Portugal	31
60	Bahamas	29
61	Chile	29
62	West Germany	29
63	Martinique	29
64	Malaysia	28
65	East Germany	27
66	Honduras	27
67	Poland	27
68	Rumania	27
	LOWER MIDDLE	
69	Argentina	25
70	France	25
71	Malawi	25
72	Togo	25
73	Switzerland	24
74	Turkey	23
75	India	22
76	Mexico	22
77	Spain	22
78	Italy	21
79	Kenya	21
80	Madagascar	21
81	Norway	21
82	Venezuela	21
83	Belgium	20
84	Greece	20
85	Panama	20
86	Benin	19
87	Jamaica	19
88	St. Lucia	19
89	Cyprus	18
90	Morocco	17
91	St. Kitts-Nevis-Anguilla	17
92	Seychelles	17
93	Bangladesh	16
94	Comoros	16
95	Guadeloupe	16
96	Hungary	16
97	New Zealand	16
98	Uruguay	16
99	Cuba	15
100	New Caledonia	15
101	Nicaragua	15
102	Sudan	15
103	Antigua	14
104	Somalia	14
105	Senegal	13
106	Tonga	13
107	Zambia	13
108	Grenada	12
109	Denmark	11
110	El Salvador	11
111	Iran	11
112	Burundi	10
113	Guinea	10
114	Hong Kong	10
115	Mongolia	10
116	Lebanon	9
117	Upper Volta	9
118	China	8
119	Netherlands	8
120	Haiti	7
121	United Kingdom	7
122	Ethiopia	6
123	Tunisia	6
124	Central African Empire	5
125	Gambia	4
126	Iraq	4
127	Israel	4
128	Sierra Leone	4
129	Afghanistan	3
130	Ireland	3
131	Pakistan	3
	BOTTOM 9	
132	Australia	2
133	Chad	2
134	South Africa	2
135	Syria	2
136	Algeria	1
137	Jordan	1
138	Libya	1
139	Saudi Arabia	1
140	Yemen Arab Republic	1

Source: Food and Agriculture Organization.

114. Production of Roundwood

Production of roundwood (wood felled and stripped of bark but not cut into logs) varies only slightly from year to year. Worldwide production of roundwood (of both coniferous and broadleaved trees) was 2.498 billion cubic meters (88.216 billion cubic feet) in 1976 as compared to 2.388 billion cubic meters (84.332 billion cubic feet) in 1970 and 2.510 billion cubic meters (88.640 billion cubic feet) in 1974. This worldwide production is distributed by continent as follows:

	Million Cubic Meters	Feet
Africa	327	11,548
North America	502	17,728
Asia	715	25,250
South America	237	8,369
Europe	303	10,700
Oceania	30	1,059
Soviet Union	384	11,371

Number of Countries: 111
Midpoint: 6.2 million cubic meters (218.9 million cubic feet)
Period Covered: 1976
Type of Ranking: Production of Roundwood in Million Cubic Meters and Million Cubic Feet; Percentage Share of World Total Output for Top 10 Countries only; Highest to Lowest

Highlights & Findings: Production of roundwood bears a rough relation to land area, with the Soviet Union alone accounting for 15% of the world total. The shares of the leading producers are also shown in the ranking. Two basic factors influence production of roundwood: the percentage of forestland that is exploitable and the varieties of timber available for such exploitation. In many countries forests are considered as national resources and may be exploited only by the state or by citizens. Countries without proper reafforestation programs are experiencing progressive declines in production.

Regions	Africa	Asia & Oceania	Europe	Western Hemisphere
Most	Nigeria (8)	China (3)	Soviet Union (1)	United States (2)
Least	Mauritania (110)	Solomon Islands (111)	Netherlands (108)	Uruguay (104)

Production of Roundwood in Million Cubic

Rank	Country	Meters	Feet	Share of World Total (%)
	TOP 10			
1	Soviet Union	384.0	13,560.0	15.3
2	United States	341.4	12,056.5	13.6
3	China	195.2	6,893.4	7.8
4	Brazil	164.0	5,791.6	6.5
5	Indonesia	129.8	4,583.8	5.1
6	India	127.5	4,502.6	5.0
7	Canada	115.3	4,071.8	4.6
8	Nigeria	68.9	2,433.0	2.7
9	Sweden	52.4	1,850.5	2.0
10	Tanzania	37.5	1,324.3	1.5
	UPPER MIDDLE			
11	Japan	36.8	1,299.5	
12	Malaysia	36.4	1,285.4	
13	Philippines	33.5	1,183.0	
14	Finland	32.0	1,130.0	
15	France	30.4	1,073.5	
16	West Germany	30.0	1,059.4	
17	Ethiopia	24.2	854.6	
18	Colombia	23.0	812.2	
19	Sudan	22.4	791.0	
20	Burma	21.7	766.3	
21	Poland	21.6	762.8	
22	Thailand	21.1	748.6	
23	Rumania	20.5	723.9	
24	Vietnam	18.8	663.9	
25	Czechoslovakia	16.9	596.8	
26	Turkey	16.9	596.8	
27	Bangladesh	14.8	522.6	
28	Uganda	14.6	515.5	
29	Mexico	14.5	512.0	
30	Yugoslavia	14.0	494.4	
31	Australia	13.9	490.8	

Production of Roundwood in Million Cubic

Rank	Country	Meters	Feet
32	Zaire	13.7	483.8
33	Austria	13.1	462.6
34	Ghana	12.6	444.9
35	Kenya	12.4	437.9
36	Spain	12.1	427.3
37	Argentina	11.5	406.1
38	South Africa	10.5	370.8
39	Ivory Coast	10.1	356.6
40	New Zealand	10.0	353.1
41	South Korea	9.5	335.4
42	Nepal	9.2	324.8
43	Mozambique	9.1	321.3
44	Norway	9.0	317.8
45	Pakistan	9.0	317.8
46	Chile	8.9	314.3
47	East Germany	8.4	296.6
48	Cameroon	8.3	293.1
49	Venezuela	8.0	282.5
50	Angola	7.8	275.4
51	Portugal	7.5	264.8
52	Peru	7.3	257.7
53	Afghanistan	7.0	247.2
54	Italy	6.6	233.0
55	Madagascar	6.4	226.0
56	Iran	6.2	218.9
	LOWER MIDDLE		
57	Papua New Guinea	5.9	208.3
58	Rhodesia (Zimbabwe)	5.9	208.3
59	Guatemala	5.7	201.2
60	Hungary	5.5	194.2
61	Sri Lanka	4.7	165.9
62	Cambodia	4.6	162.4
63	Bulgaria	4.4	155.3

Production of Roundwood in Million Cubic

Rank	Country	Meters	Feet
64	Upper Volta	4.4	155.3
65	North Korea	4.3	151.8
66	Paraguay	4.3	151.8
67	Ecuador	4.0	141.2
68	Haiti	4.0	141.2
69	Zambia	4.0	141.2
70	Bolivia	3.9	137.7
71	Chad	3.9	137.7
72	El Salvador	3.9	137.7
73	Rwanda	3.9	137.7
74	Honduras	3.8	134.1
75	Switzerland	3.6	127.1
76	Costa Rica	3.5	123.6
77	Malawi	3.3	116.5
78	United Kingdom	3.3	116.5
79	Laos	3.2	113.0
80	Somalia	3.2	113.0
81	Guinea	3.1	109.4
82	Morocco	3.1	109.4
83	Mali	3.0	105.9
84	Nicaragua	3.0	105.9
85	Greece	2.9	102.4
86	Senegal	2.7	95.3
87	Belgium	2.6	91.8
88	Gabon	2.6	91.8
89	Sierra Leone	2.6	91.8
90	Benin	2.5	88.2
91	Niger	2.5	88.2
92	Swaziland	2.5	88.2
93	Congo	2.4	84.7
94	Mongolia	2.4	84.7
95	Albania	2.3	81.2
96	Central African Empire	2.3	81.2
97	Liberia	2.1	74.1

Rank	Country	Production of Roundwood in Million Cubic Meters	Feet
98	Cuba	1.9	67.0
99	Dominican Republic	1.8	63.5
100	Tunisia	1.8	63.5
101	Denmark	1.6	56.5

Rank	Country	Production of Roundwood in Million Cubic Meters	Feet
	BOTTOM 10		
102	Algeria	1.5	52.9
103	Panama	1.5	52.9
104	Uruguay	1.3	45.9
105	Togo	1.1	38.8
106	Burundi	0.9	31.7

Rank	Country	Production of Roundwood in Million Cubic Meters	Feet
107	Equatorial Guinea	0.9	31.7
108	Netherlands	0.9	31.7
109	Botswana	0.7	24.7
110	Mauritania	0.6	21.1
111	Solomon Islands	0.4	14.1

Source: Food and Agriculture Organization.

115. Fish Catch

Fishing is not only one of the oldest human occupations but also one of the most universal. According to international law, the fish of the oceans (outside of territorial limits) are the common resources of all men, perhaps the only resource for which this claim can be made. In recent years, therefore, developing nations with limited internal resources have turned to the ocean to supplement their revenues. Despite ease of entry, fishing requires substantial long-term investments in refrigeration, vessels and equipment and marketing facilities.

Of the total 1975 world production of 69.7 million tons of fish, Africa accounted for 4.52 million, North America for 4.81 million, South America for 5.97 million, Asia for 31.69 million, Europe for 12.62 million and Oceania for 240,000 and the Soviet Union for 9.876 million.

Number of Countries: 95
Midpoint: 153,000 tons
Period Covered: 1975
Type of Ranking: Annual Fish Catch in Metric Tons; Highest to Lowest

Highlights & Findings: The top 10 nations account for 43.82 million tons, or 63% of the annual world catch. The bottom 10 nations account for 0.26% of the world catch. Despite pressures from other nations, both Japan and the Soviet Union have been increasing their share of the world fish catch. Fishing has become a sensitive political issue and has triggered a number of international incidents, such as the "cod war" between the United Kingdom and Iceland.

Regions	Africa	Asia & Oceania	Europe	Western Hemisphere
Most	Nigeria (25)	Japan (1)	Soviet Union (2)	Peru (4)
Least	Liberia (93)	Singapore (91)	Czechoslovakia (92)	Bermuda (95)

Rank	Country	Fish Catch in Metric Tons (000)
	TOP 10	
1	Japan	10,508
2	Soviet Union	9,876
3	China	6,880
4	Peru	3,447
5	United States	2,798
6	Norway	2,550
7	India	2,328
8	South Korea	2,133
9	Denmark	1,767
10	Spain	1,533
	UPPER MIDDLE	
11	Indonesia	1,390
12	Thailand	1,370
13	Philippines	1,342
14	South Africa	1,315

Rank	Country	Fish Catch in Metric Tons (000)
15	Chile	1,128
16	Canada	1,024
17	Vietnam	1,014
18	Iceland	995
19	United Kingdom	980
20	France	806
21	Poland	801
22	North Korea	800
23	Brazil	675
24	Bangladesh	640
25	Nigeria	507
26	Mexico	499
27	Burma	485
28	Malaysia	474
29	West Germany	442
30	Italy	406
31	East Germany	375

Rank	Country	Fish Catch in Metric Tons (000)
32	Portugal	369
33	Senegal	362
34	Netherlands	350
35	Faroe Islands	286
36	Turkey	259
37	Ghana	255
38	Argentina	224
39	Ecuador	223
40	Sweden	215
41	Morocco	211
42	Pakistan	195
43	Angola	184
44	Tanzania	181
45	Uganda	170
46	Cuba	165
47	Bulgaria	158
48	Venezuela	153

Rank	Country	Fish Catch in Metric Tons (000)	Rank	Country	Fish Catch in Metric Tons (000)	Rank	Country	Fish Catch in Metric Tons (000)
	LOWER MIDDLE		65	Cameroon	72	82	Hungary	31
49	Hong Kong	151	66	Malawi	71	83	Saudi Arabia	30
50	Rumania	137	67	Greece	71	84	Benin	29
51	Sri Lanka	129	68	United Arab Emirates	68	85	Maldives	28
52	South Yemen	127	69	Sierra Leone	67			
53	Zaire	125	70	Colombia	66		*BOTTOM 10*	
54	Chad	115	71	New Zealand	65	86	Kenya	27
55	Finland	114	72	Ivory Coast	63	87	Ethiopia	26
56	Egypt	107	73	Yugoslavia	57	88	Uruguay	26
57	Australia	103	74	Madagascar	56	89	Israel	24
58	Mali	100	75	Zambia	50	90	Guyana	20
59	Oman	100	76	Belgium	49	91	Singapore	18
60	Namibia	87	77	Greenland	47	92	Czechoslovakia	17
61	Ireland	85	78	Papua New Guinea	43	93	Liberia	16
62	Cambodia	84	79	Tunisia	42	94	Jamaica	10
63	Puerto Rico	81	80	Algeria	38	95	Bermuda	0.5
64	Panama	80	81	Mauritania	34			

Source: Food and Agriculture Organization, *Yearbook of Fishery Statistics.*

116. Cattle per Capita

Of all domesticated animals, cattle are the most numerous and the most productive. Worldwide there are 30 head of cattle for every 100 human beings. Throughout the world they are the principal source of meat and milk, and in the developing world they also serve as draft animals. In many places even today wealth consists chiefly of cattle (the word pecuniary is derived from the Latin word for cattle, *pecus,* and the words capital and cattle are etymologically related). Since the 18th century, new types of breeds have been developed. The principal beef breeds include the Angus and the Hereford, and the principal dairy breeds the Ayrshire, Brown Swiss, Guernsey, Holstein-Friesian and Jersey. The dual purpose breeds include Devon, Red Poll and Shorthorn.

Number of Countries: 148
Midpoint: 251.54 per 1,000
Period Covered: 1976
Type of Ranking: Cattle Per Capita; Total Cattle Population; Highest to Lowest

Highlights & Findings: The worldwide cattle population is 1,211,950,000 distributed as follows: Africa, 159,624,000; North America, 190,165,000; South America, 215,756,000; Asia, 357,836,000; Europe, 133,735,000; Oceania, 43,801,000; and the Soviet Union, 111,034,000. In the top 12 countries the cattle population exceeds the human population—by more than three to one in Uruguay, Namibia and Botswana.

Regions	Africa	Asia & Oceania	Europe	Western Hemisphere
Most	Namibia (2)	Australia (4)	Ireland (6)	Uruguay (1)
Least	Djibouti (146)	Hong Kong (148)	Cyprus (143)	Surinam (131)

Rank	Country	Cattle Population per 1,000 Inhabitants	Total (000)	Rank	Country	Cattle Population per 1,000 Inhabitants	Total (000)	Rank	Country	Cattle Population per 1,000 Inhabitants	Total (000)
	TOP 10			8	Mongolia	1,628.85	2,427	14	Colombia	954.45	23,222
1	Uruguay	3,821.78	10,701	9	Swaziland	1,260.00	630	15	Sudan	948.54	15,300
2	Namibia	3,238.63	2,850	10	Nicaragua	1,192.82	2,660	16	Rhodesia (Zimbabwe)	934.15	6,100
3	Botswana	3,188.40	2,200					17	Tanzania	920.05	14,362
4	Australia	2,451.17	33,434		*UPPER MIDDLE*			18	Costa Rica	911.38	1,841
5	Argentina	2,261.81	58,164	11	Madagascar	1,190.08	9,842	19	Ethiopia	905.26	25,963
6	Ireland	2,200.63	6,954	12	New Hebrides	1,100.00	110	20	Chad	887.86	3,658
7	Paraguay	2,047.05	5,568	13	Mauritania	984.84	1,300	21	Brazil	870.12	95,000

Rank	Country	Cattle Population per 1,000 Inhabitants	Total (000)	Rank	Country	Cattle Population per 1,000 Inhabitants	Total (000)	Rank	Country	Cattle Population per 1,000 Inhabitants	Total (000)
22	Somalia	797.54	2,600	66	India	295.58	180,328	108	Sri Lanka	127.02	1,744
23	Panama	791.27	1,361	67	Iceland	281.81	62	109	Spain	122.54	4,408
24	Venezuela	760.84	9,404	68	Rumania	275.61	5,912	110	Ivory Coast	119.52	600
25	New Caledonia	707.69	92	69	El Salvador	269.17	1,109	111	Solomon Islands	115.00	23
26	Mali	698.63	4,080	70	Fiji	268.96	156	112	Ghana	106.69	1,100
27	Honduras	636.04	1,800	71	Guatemala	267.25	1,673	113	Portugal	105.82	1,000
28	Denmark	610.45	3,095	72	Yugoslavia	266.92	5,755	114	Togo	103.07	235
29	Niger	609.09	2,881	73	Peru	259.04	4,168	115	Thailand	100.34	4,311
30	United States	594.90	127,976	74	United Kingdom	251.54	14,069	116	French Polynesia	100.00	13
31	Canada	590.27	13,659					117	Sierra Leone	98.07	305
32	Cuba	581.39	5,500		*LOWER MIDDLE*			118	Oman	96.20	76
33	Gambia	574.07	310	75	Benin	250.00	800	119	Israel	91.90	318
34	Lesotho	557.69	580	76	Guadeloupe	238.88	86	120	China	75.84	64,629
35	Kenya	541.51	7,500	77	Comoros	238.70	74	121	Syria	75.52	574
36	Bolivia	518.13	3,000	78	Burma	236.78	7,300	122	Algeria	73.41	1,270
37	Angola	517.24	3,000	79	West Germany	235.62	14,493	123	Barbados	72.00	18
38	Nepal	517.10	6,650	80	Norway	228.53	921	124	Trinidad & Tobago	67.59	73
39	Guinea-Bissau	486.79	258	81	Sweden	228.22	1,876	125	Libya	62.29	152
40	South Africa	486.03	12,700	82	Iraq	225.89	2,600	126	Mauritius	60.91	53
41	Senegal	467.58	2,380	83	Bermuda	207.25	800	127	South Yemen	58.28	102
42	Mexico	460.45	28,700	84	Cambodia	203.59	1,700	128	Papua New Guinea	54.77	155
43	France	458.18	24,247	85	Morocco	201.90	3,600	129	Egypt	54.60	2,079
44	Zambia	447.47	2,300	86	Iran	199.10	6,650	130	Philippines	52.57	2,300
45	Soviet Union	432.59	111,034	87	Pakistan	198.59	14,372	131	Surinam	52.27	23
46	Uganda	410.38	4,900	88	Bulgaria	189.04	1,656	132	North Korea	50.21	816
47	Cameroon	406.58	2,655	89	Afghanistan	186.86	3,700	133	Cape Verde	50.00	15
48	Dominican Republic	402.89	1,950	90	Albania	184.31	470	134	Reunion	49.01	25
49	Ecuador	392.47	2,869	91	Hungary	179.62	1,904	135	Indonesia	44.70	6,242
50	Finland	383.72	1,815	92	Puerto Rico	174.76	561	136	Zaire	44.63	1,144
51	Poland	374.82	12,879	93	Nigeria	174.51	11,300	137	South Korea	43.11	1,546
52	Netherlands	360.49	4,964	94	Bhutan	165.00	198	138	Congo	35.97	50
53	Guyana	358.97	280	95	Haiti	159.95	747				
54	Turkey	348.28	13,987	96	Samoa	153.33	23		*BOTTOM 10*		
55	Bangladesh	347.59	28,002	97	Tunisia	153.31	880	139	Malaysia	34.06	419
56	Belize	342.85	48	98	Italy	150.36	8,446	140	Vietnam	32.24	1,500
57	Guinea	342.16	1,550	99	Rwanda	148.71	638	141	Japan	31.13	3,500
58	Austria	332.88	2,500	100	Laos	148.22	501	142	Lebanon	28.37	84
59	East Germany	329.48	5,532	101	Yemen Arab Republic	145.56	1,000	143	Cyprus	26.56	17
60	Central African Empire	322.75	610	102	Mozambique	140.46	1,326	144	Liberia	20.00	35
61	Chile	319.23	3,336	103	St. Lucia	136.36	15	145	Saudi Arabia	18.39	170
62	Switzerland	315.74	2,005	104	Jamaica	135.92	280	146	Djibouti	12.94	18
63	Upper Volta	307.94	1,900	105	Malawi	135.13	700	147	Jordan	11.87	33
64	Czechoslovakia	305.29	4,555	106	Martinique	135.13	50	148	Hong Kong	2.28	10
65	Belgium	304.44	3,011	107	Greece	129.11	1,184				

Source: Food and Agriculture Organization.

117. Horses per Capita

The name horse is commonly applied to the domestic horse as well as to the wild, or Przewalski's, horse. Although common to both Old and New Worlds, they disappeared from the New World about 10,000 years ago with camels and mammoths and were reintroduced by European settlers only in the 16th century. The two major groups of modern horses—the light, swift southern breeds called light horses and the heavy powerful northern breeds called draft horses—are of independent origin, modified by interbreeding. As the use of horses in warfare and farm work has declined, the demand for show and sport has increased. Common draft breeds are the Belgian, Clydesdale, Percheron and Shire. Light horses are descended in part from the Arabian horse, the oldest living breed. They include the thoroughbred, the American saddle horse, the Morgan, the quarterhorse, the Standardbred, the Appaloosa and the Pinto.

Number of Countries: 90
Midpoint: 16.20 per 1,000 inhabitants
Period Covered: 1976
Type of Ranking: Horse Population per 1,000 Inhabitants; Total Horse Population; Highest to Lowest

Highlights & Findings: The total world horse population is 65,448,000, down from 66,915,000 in 1961. The regional distribution is as follows: Africa, 3,667,000; North America, 17,230,000; South America, 17,613,000; Asia, 13,696,000; Europe, 6,129,000; Oceania, 698,000; Soviet Union, 6,415,000. Mongolia is the only country in the world where horses outnumber human inhabitants.

Regions	Africa	Asia & Oceania	Europe	Western Hemisphere
Most	Lesotho (15)	Mongolia (1)	Iceland (3)	Ecuador (2)
Least	Egypt (86)	South Korea (90)	Belgium (88)	Puerto Rico (67)

Rank	Country	Horse Population per 1,000 Inhabitants	Total Horse Population (000)	Rank	Country	Horse Population per 1,000 Inhabitants	Total Horse Population (000)	Rank	Country	Horse Population per 1,000 Inhabitants	Total Horse Population (000)
	TOP 10			31	Mexico	29.16	1,818	62	Syria	7.10	54
1	Mongolia	1,513.42	2,255	32	Ireland	26.26	83	63	Finland	6.97	33
2	Ecuador	418.84	289	33	Rumania	26.20	562	64	Libya	6.14	15
3	Iceland	213.63	47	34	Mali	25.68	150	65	Pakistan	6.05	438
4	Uruguay	178.21	499	35	Soviet Union	24.99	6,415	66	Iraq	5.99	69
5	Argentina	136.08	3,500	36	New Zealand	23.56	74	67	Puerto Rico	5.91	19
6	Paraguay	119.48	325	37	Turkey	21.66	870	68	Sweden	5.83	48
7	Nicaragua	113.04	260	38	Guatemala	19.96	125	69	West Germany	5.54	341
8	Honduras	98.93	280	39	El Salvador	19.90	82	70	Austria	5.45	41
9	Panama	95.34	164	40	Afghanistan	18.68	370	71	Norway	5.45	22
10	Brazil	87.92	9,600	41	Tunisia	18.46	106	72	Italy	4.50	253
				42	Morocco	17.38	310	73	Indonesia	4.49	627
	UPPER MIDDLE			43	Greece	17.33	159	74	Netherlands	4.35	60
11	Cuba	85.72	811	44	Albania	16.47	42	75	East Germany	4.16	70
12	Haiti	82.86	387	45	Upper Volta	16.20	100	76	Czechoslovakia	4.15	62
13	Poland	62.60	2,151					77	Thailand	3.88	167
14	Bolivia	62.17	360					78	Nigeria	3.86	250
15	Lesotho	61.53	64		*LOWER MIDDLE*			79	Burma	3.24	100
16	Colombia	61.03	1,485	46	Bhutan	15.83	19				
17	Fiji	60.35	35	47	Bulgaria	15.18	133				
18	Costa Rica	56.43	114	48	Canada	14.90	345		*BOTTOM 10*		
19	Ethiopia	52.64	1,510	49	Hungary	14.71	156	80	Portugal	3.17	30
20	Namibia	47.72	42	50	Denmark	11.83	60	81	United Kingdom	2.50	140
21	Senegal	44.40	226	51	Mauritania	11.36	15	82	North Korea	2.03	33
22	Niger	43.55	206	52	Iran	10.47	350	83	Vietnam	1.50	70
23	Chile	43.06	450	53	Laos	10.35	35	84	India	1.47	900
24	Dominican Republic	41.73	202	54	Cameroon	9.03	59	85	Sudan	1.23	20
25	Australia	40.32	550	55	Algeria	8.95	155	86	Egypt	0.55	21
26	Yugoslavia	40.07	864	56	South Africa	8.80	230	87	Bangladesh	0.53	43
27	United States	39.97	8,600	57	China	8.09	6,900	88	Belgium	0.50	54
28	Peru	39.83	641	58	France	7.59	402	89	Japan	0.32	36
29	Venezuela	37.05	458	59	Spain	7.45	268	90	South Korea	0.25	9
30	Chad	35.19	145	60	Switzerland	7.40	47				
				61	Philippines	7.31	320				

Source: Food and Agriculture Organization.

118. Sheep per Capita

Sheep, first domesticated about 7,000 years ago, are found mostly in temperate climates. The present-day breeds vary because they were bred for different purposes and in different environments, but most of them are derived from the wild mouflon of Sardinia and Corsica and from the urial of Asia.

They are raised for their wool, meat (called mutton or lamb according to age) and skins; in some countries their milk is drunk and made into cheese. Among the major species of wild sheep are the argali, the Barbary sheep or aoudad of North Africa, and the North American bighorn or Rocky Mountain sheep. The more important breeds of domesticated sheep are Columbia, Cotswold, Dorset, Hampshire, Karakul, Leicester, Lincoln, Merino, Oxford, Rambouillet, Shropshire, Southdown and Suffolk.

Number of Countries: 131
Midpoint: 174.58 per 1,000 inhabitants
Period Covered: 1976
Type of Ranking: Sheep Population per 1,000 Inhabitants; Total Sheep Population; Highest to Lowest

Highlights & Findings: The total world sheep population is 1,036,000,000 only slightly less than that of cattle; until 1961 sheep outnumbered cattle in the world. Per capita there are 25 sheep for every 100 inhabitants. The regional distribution is as follows: Africa, 159,410,000; North America, 20,392,000; South America, 109,851,000; Asia, 274,668,000; Europe, 125,191,000; Oceania, 205,051,000; and the Soviet Union, 141,436,000. In 20 countries sheep outnumber human beings; in the Falkland Islands they outnumber human beings by 322 to 1 and in New Zealand by 18 to 1.

Regions	Africa	Asia & Oceania	Europe	Western Hemisphere
Most	Namibia (6)	New Zealand (2)	Iceland (7)	Falkland Islands (1)
Least	Mozambique (123)	Japan (131)	Belgium (124)	Venezuela (125)

Rank	Country	Sheep Population per 1,000 Inhabitants	Total Sheep Population (000)
		TOP 10	
1	Falkland Islands	322,500.00	645
2	New Zealand	17,961.78	56,400
3	Australia	10,897.58	148,643
4	Mongolia	9,703.35	14,458
5	Uruguay	5,705.00	15,974
6	Namibia	5,681.81	5,000
7	Iceland	3,909.09	860
8	Mauritania	3,409.09	4,500
9	Somalia	2,147.23	7,000
10	Faroe Islands	1,725.00	69
		UPPER MIDDLE	
11	Lesotho	1,576.92	1,640
12	Argentina	1,360.80	35,000
13	Bolivia	1,341.45	7,767
14	Libya	1,209.01	2,950
15	South Africa	1,186.37	31,000
16	Bulgaria	1,143.15	10.014
17	Ireland	1,099.68	3,475
18	Iran	1,056.88	35,300
19	Iraq	1,033.88	11,900
20	Turkey	1,030.05	41,367
21	Sudan	948.54	15,300
22	Peru	932.25	15,000
23	Greece	911.77	8,361
24	Afghanistan	909.09	18,000
25	Syria	853.94	6,490
26	Morocco	813.23	14,500
27	Ethiopia	804.21	23,065
28	Mali	722.43	4,219
29	Rumania	646.38	13,865
30	Botswana	615.94	425
31	Tunisia	609.75	3,500
32	Chad	588.34	2,424
33	Algeria	566.47	9,800
34	Soviet Union	551.04	141,436
35	Chile	536.55	5,607
36	Niger	533.40	2,523
37	South Yemen	531.42	930
38	United Kingdom	505.36	28,265
39	Yemen Arab Republic	465.79	3,200
40	Albania	456.07	1,163
41	Spain	437.72	15,745
42	Norway	413.64	1,667
43	Portugal	402.11	3,800
44	Greenland	400.00	20
45	Qatar	400.00	40
46	Yugoslavia	363.21	7,831
47	Cyprus	351.56	225
48	Senegal	341.84	1,740
49	Togo	328.94	750
50	Cameroon	322.35	2,105
51	Ecuador	293.70	2,147
52	Jordan	287.76	800
53	Kenya	274.36	3,800
54	Benin	265.62	850
55	Pakistan	250.53	18,131
56	Brazil	229.89	25,100
57	Upper Volta	210.69	1,300
58	France	202.32	10,707
59	St. Kitts-Nevis-Anguilla	200.00	22
60	Ivory Coast	199.20	1,000
61	Barbados	196.00	49
62	Hungary	192.35	2,039
63	Tanzania	188.98	2,950
64	Gambia	188.88	102
65	Nepal	179.62	2,310
		LOWER MIDDLE	
66	Ghana	174.58	1,800
67	Saudi Arabia	149.35	1,380
68	Bahamas	147.61	31
69	Italy	145.13	8,152
70	Guyana	138.46	108
71	Paraguay	136.02	370
72	Guinea-Bissau	132.07	70
73	Nigeria	122.00	7,900
74	Rhodesia (Zimbabwe)	117.91	770
75	Martinique	113.51	42
76	East Germany	112.15	1,883
77	Gabon	111.32	59
78	Kuwait	107.76	111
79	Liberia	100.57	176
80	Equatorial Guinea	100.00	32
81	Poland	99.82	3,430
82	Oman	96.20	76
83	Guinea	92.71	420
84	Uganda	92.12	1,100
85	China	87.42	74,500
86	Mexico	85.03	5,300
87	Madagascar	84.64	700
88	Colombia	83.27	2,026
89	Bermuda	80.56	311
90	Lebanon	79.05	234
91	Guatemala	75.07	470
92	Swaziland	70.00	35
93	Djibouti	69.78	97
94	India	65.87	40,187
95	United States	62.17	13,376
96	Switzerland	59.37	377
97	Israel	58.38	202
98	Rwanda	57.80	248
99	Netherlands	56.64	780
100	Czechoslovakia	53.95	805
101	Egypt	49.33	1,878
102	Sweden	46.47	382
103	Central African Empire	40.21	76
104	Congo	37.41	52
105	Cuba	35.94	340
106	Angola	35.34	205
107	South Korea	34.77	1,247
108	Bhutan	32.50	39
109	Zaire	27.74	711
110	Indonesia	24.16	3,374
111	Finland	23.46	111
112	Austria	22.50	169
113	Canada	22.21	514
114	Sierra Leone	21.86	68
115	West Germany	17.67	1,087
116	Haiti	17.34	81
117	Malawi	16.98	88
118	North Korea	16.49	268
119	Denmark	11.63	59
120	Dominican Republic	10.53	51
121	Zambia	9.72	50
		BOTTOM 10	
122	Bangladesh	9.64	777
123	Mozambique	9.32	88
124	Belgium	8.69	86
125	Venezuela	8.33	103
126	Burma	5.83	180
127	Malaysia	3.73	46
128	Sri Lanka	2.18	30
129	Thailand	1.16	50
130	Philippines	0.68	30
131	Japan	0.08	10

Source: Food and Agriculture Organization.

119. Pigs per Capita

Pigs, more properly known as swine and sometimes as hogs, are native to the Old World and were introduced into America by the Spanish explorers. They are commonly grouped as meat-type, lard-type and bacon-type: meat-type breeds include the Hereford and Berkshire; lard-type breeds include Poland China, Duroc and Spotted Swine; and bacon-type breeds include Tamworth, Yorkshire and American Landrace. Male domestic swines suitable for breeding are known as boars.

Number of Countries: 129
Midpoint: 100.59 per 1,000 inhabitants
Period Covered: 1976
Type of Ranking: Pigs per 1,000 Inhabitants; Total Pig Population; Highest to Lowest

Highlights & Findings: The total world population of pigs is 640,300,000, or one pig for every 16 inhabitants. The regional distribution of pigs is affected by persisting religious sanctions against raising them as well as against eating pork. Both Judaism and Islam condemn the eating of pork as an unpardonable offense; throughout Asia and Africa pigs are regarded as unclean or taboo. There is some basis for this prejudice because pigs are in fact susceptible to a greater number of diseases than any other domestic animal and many of them are transmissible to humans. The regional population of pigs is as follows: Africa, 7,894,000; North America, 74,353,000; South America, 51.630,000; Asia, 290,395,000; Europe, 153,929,000; Oceania, 4,200,000; and the Soviet Union, 57,899,000. Denmark is the only country with more pigs than human beings.

Regions	Africa	Asia & Oceania	Europe	Western Hemisphere
Most	Guinea-Bissau (22)	New Hebrides (4)	Denmark (1)	Paraguay (16)
Least	Egypt (128)	Turkey (129)	Albania (91)	Costa Rica (104)

Rank	Country	Pig Population per 1,000 Inhabitants	Total Pig Population (000)	Rank	Country	Pig Population per 1,000 Inhabitants	Total Pig Population (000)	Rank	Country	Pig Population per 1,000 Inhabitants	Total Pig Population (000)
	TOP 10			36	Soviet Union	225.57	57,899	72	Malta	83.33	25
1	Denmark	1,518.93	7,701	37	Philippines	221.71	9,700	73	Madagascar	82.22	680
2	East Germany	684.99	11,501	38	Cyprus	220.31	141	74	Greece	81.78	750
3	Hungary	655.94	6,953	39	Bolivia	204.83	1,186	75	Lesotho	81.73	85
4	New Hebrides	640.00	64	40	Reunion	201.96	103	76	Bahamas	80.95	17
5	Tonga	611.11	55	41	Mexico	194.12	12,100	77	Guatemala	80.03	501
6	Poland	548.54	18,848	42	Honduras	183.74	520	78	Brunei	77.77	14
7	Netherlands	545.17	7,507	43	Portugal	178.09	1,683	79	Colombia	76.40	1,859
8	Austria	490.44	3,683	44	Norway	173.20	698	80	Thailand	74.74	3,211
9	Belgium	481.79	4,765	45	Solomon Islands	170.00	34	81	Guadeloupe	72.22	26
10	Singapore	469.73	1,071	46	Pacific Islands	166.66	20	82	Chile	67.36	704
				47	New Zealand	160.82	505	83	Japan	66.34	7,459
	UPPER MIDDLE			48	Argentina	160.45	4,127	84	Cameroon	63.09	412
11	Czechoslovakia	447.92	6,683	49	Guyana	160.25	125	85	Angola	62.06	360
12	Bulgaria	443.94	3,889	50	Australia	159.31	2,173	86	Fiji	53.44	31
13	Laos	428.10	1,447	51	Italy	158.23	8,888	87	Liberia	53.14	93
14	Papua New Guinea	414.48	1,173	52	Cuba	154.33	1,460	88	South Africa	52.81	1,380
15	Rumania	410.86	8,813	53	Venezuela	152.10	1,880	89	Burma	48.65	1,500
16	Paraguay	405.14	1,102	54	Barbados	148.00	37	90	Bhutan	46.66	56
17	Haiti	379.22	1,771	55	Dominican Republic	145.66	705	91	Albania	45.88	117
18	Ecuador	374.00	2,734	56	Belize	142.85	20	92	Ivory Coast	41.83	210
19	Samoa	333.33	50	57	United Kingdom	142.08	7,947	93	Ghana	38.79	400
20	Brazil	325.15	35,500	58	Peru	133.18	2,143	94	Namibia	37.50	33
21	West Germany	321.98	19,805	59	Malaysia	119.34	1,468	95	Malawi	36.48	189
22	Guinea-Bissau	320.75	170	60	Togo	118.42	270	96	South Korea	34.77	1,247
23	Switzerland	315.90	2,006	61	Jamaica	114.07	235	97	Central African Empire	32.80	62
24	Yugoslavia	303.15	6,536	62	Benin	114.06	365	98	Congo	31.65	44
25	Sweden	302.31	2,485	63	Panama	104.06	179	99	Senegal	31.43	160
26	Nicaragua	300.44	670	64	El Salvador	103.15	425	100	Rhodesia (Zimbabwe)	30.62	200
27	Ireland	292.72	925	65	Cambodia	100.59	840	101	Nepal	24.88	320
28	China	279.66	238,315					102	Zaire	24.46	627
29	St. Kitts-Nevis-Anguilla	272.72	18		**LOWER MIDDLE**			103	Upper Volta	24.31	150
30	Vietnam	247.20	11,500	66	Hong Kong	100.45	440	104	Costa Rica	21.78	44
31	Spain	238.61	8,583	67	Grenada	100.00	10	105	Israel	21.67	75
32	Canada	234.44	5,425	68	North Korea	96.92	1,575	106	Zambia	20.62	106
33	Finland	231.92	1,097	69	Martinique	94.59	35	107	Indonesia	19.38	2,707
34	New Caledonia	230.76	30	70	Uruguay	92.85	260	108	Mozambique	19.38	183
35	United States	230.49	49,602	71	Puerto Rico	83.80	269	109	Rwanda	16.55	71

Rank	Country	Pig Population per 1,000 Inhabitants	Total Pig Population (000)
110	Uganda	15.91	190
111	Nigeria	13.89	900
112	Brundi	11.91	46
113	India	11.57	7,062
114	Sierra Leone	11.57	36
115	Mongolia	8.72	13
116	Lebanon	7.77	23
117	Guinea	7.72	35

Rank	Country	Pig Population per 1,000 Inhabitants	Total Pig Population (000)
118	Cape Verde	6.00	18
119	Niger	5.70	27
	BOTTOM 10		
120	Kenya	4.98	69
121	Mali	4.28	25
122	Sri Lanka	2.62	36
123	Iran	2.03	68

Rank	Country	Pig Population per 1,000 Inhabitants	Total Pig Population (000)
124	Tanzania	1.53	24
125	Pakistan	1.24	90
126	Morocco	0.61	11
127	Ethiopia	0.59	17
128	Egypt	0.39	15
129	Turkey	0.39	16

Source: Food and Agriculture Organization.

120. Barley Production

Barley is one of the earliest cereal plants cultivated by man. A special-purpose grain with many varieties, it is a valuable stock feed and is also used for malting. It has a wide range of cultivation even at high altitudes, and its growing period is short. However, it cannot withstand hot and humid climates and is subject to several diseases including rust and smut.

Number of Countries: 57
Midpoint: 0.410%
Period Covered: 1976
Type of Ranking: Production of Barley; Share of World Total and Total in Metric Tons; Highest to Lowest

Highlights & Findings: The total world production of barley is 183,910,000 tons distributed as follows: Africa, 4,759,000; North America, 19,104,000 tons; South America, 1,377,000; Asia, 29,821,000; Europe, 56,118,000; Oceania, 3,191,000; and the Soviet Union, 69,539,000. What is most notable in this ranking is the dominance of the Soviet Union, which produces one out of every three tons in the world.

Regions	Africa	Asia & Oceania	Europe	Western Hemisphere
Most	Morocco (15)	China (2)	Soviet Union (1)	Canada (3)
Least	South Africa (55)	Mongolia (56)	Cyprus (51)	Uruguay (57)

Rank	Country	Production of Barley Share of World Total (%)	Total (000 tons)
	TOP 10		
1	Soviet Union	37.811	69,539
2	China	8.374	15,401
3	Canada	5.716	10,513
4	France	4.523	8,319
5	United States	4.410	8,111
6	United Kingdom	4.158	7,648
7	West Germany	3.527	6,487
8	Spain	2.975	5,473
9	Turkey	2.664	4,900
10	Denmark	2.610	4,801
	UPPER MIDDLE		
11	Poland	1.966	3,617
12	East Germany	1.879	3,456
13	India	1.735	3,192
14	Czechoslovakia	1.577	2,901
15	Morocco	1.556	2,862
16	Australia	1.548	2,847
17	Sweden	0.992	1,825
18	Bulgaria	0.968	1,781
19	South Korea	0.956	1,759

Rank	Country	Production of Barley Share of World Total (%)	Total (000 tons)
20	Finland	0.8444	1,553
21	Iran	0.808	1,487
22	Austria	0.699	1,287
23	Rumania	0.669	1,231
24	Syria	0.575	1,059
25	Greece	0.520	957
26	Ireland	0.501	922
27	Ethiopia	0.434	800
28	Argentina	0.413	760
29	Italy	0.410	755
	LOWER MIDDLE		
30	Hungary	0.406	747
31	Yugoslavia	0.355	653
32	Belgium	0.348	641
33	Iraq	0.314	579
34	Norway	0.264	486
35	Mexico	0.260	480
36	Algeria	0.228	420
37	Afghanistan	0.217	400
38	North Korea	0.201	370
39	New Zealand	0.187	344

Rank	Country	Production of Barley Share of World Total (%)	Total (000 tons)
40	Netherlands	0.143	263
41	Tunisia	0.125	231
42	Japan	0.114	210
43	Libya	0.108	200
44	Switzerland	0.099	183
45	Peru	0.089	165
46	Pakistan	0.0706	130
47	Egypt	0.066	123
	BOTTOM 10		
48	Portugal	0.0636	117
49	Colombia	0.0543	100
50	Bolivia	0.050	92
51	Cyprus	0.048	90
52	Chile	0.048	89
53	Yemen Arab Republic	0.043	80
54	Ecuador	0.034	63
55	South Africa	0.034	63
56	Mongolia	0.029	54
57	Uruguay	0.025	47

Source: Food and Agriculture Organization.

121. Coffee Production

The bulk of the world's supply of coffee is obtained from varieties of Arabian coffee native to Ethiopia but introduced into Arabia probably during the 15th century. Coffee requires a warm, moist climate with a rainfall of at least 127 cm (50 in.) and a rich soil. It thrives particularly above 460 meters (1,500 ft), on volcanic soils and on well-drained slopes. Although the coffee tree produces its maximum yield between its fifth and 10th years, its productive life is over 35 years. Coffee is susceptible to frost and a variety of plant diseases, resulting in wide variations in production from year to year. The coffee-quota agreement of 1940 administered by the Inter-American Coffee Board attempts to stabilize the market by allocating U.S. imports from Latin America.

Number of Countries: 49
Midpoint: 1.1235%
Period Covered: 1976
Type of Ranking: Production of Coffee: Share of World Total and Total in Metric Tons; Highest to Lowest

Highlights & Findings: The total world production of coffee is 3,631,400 tons distributed as follows: Africa, 1,228,400 tons; North America, 866,400 tons; South America, 1,117,500 tons; Asia, 376,000 tons; and Oceania 42,600 tons. In terms of quality, South American coffee surpasses that of African and therefore commands higher prices in world markets.

Regions	Africa	Asia	Europe	Western Hemisphere
Most	Ivory Coast (3)	Indonesia (6)	N.A.	Colombia (1)
Least	Benin (49)	Laos (48)	N.A.	Panama (41)

Rank	Country	Production of Coffee Share of World Total (%)	Total (000 tons)	Rank	Country	Production of Coffee Share of World Total (%)	Total (000 tons)	Rank	Country	Production of Coffee Share of World Total (%)	Total (000 tons)
	TOP 10			16	Cameroon	2.2030	80.0	34	Sri Lanka	0.2450	8.9
1	Colombia	14.0441	510.0	17	Philippines	2.1974	79.8	35	Paraguay	0.2340	8.5
2	Brazil	10.7148	389.1	18	Angola	1.9827	72.0	36	Equatorial Guinea	0.1487	5.4
3	Ivory Coast	8.3934	304.8	19	Peru	1.6522	60.0	37	China	0.1404	5.1
4	Mexico	6.6696	242.2	20	Nicaragua	1.6274	59.1	38	Guinea	0.1376	5.0
5	Uganda	5.2927	192.2	21	Tanzania	1.5255	55.4	39	Malaysia	0.1321	4.8
6	Indonesia	4.9292	179.0	22	Venezuela	1.3658	49.6	40	South Yemen	0.1321	4.8
7	Ethiopia	4.6813	170.0	23	Honduras	1.2502	45.4				
8	El Salvador	4.3784	159.0	24	Dominican Republic	1.1565	42.0		*BOTTOM 9*		
9	Guatemala	4.1003	148.9	25	Papua New Guinea	1.1235	40.8	41	Panama	0.1294	4.7
10	Madagascar	2.5609	93.0	26	Haiti	0.9913	36.0	42	Sierra Leone	0.1294	4.7
				27	Cuba	0.6856	24.9	43	Vietnam	0.1239	4.5
	MIDDLE			28	Burundi	0.5782	21.0	44	Liberia	0.1211	4.4
11	Costa Rica	2.3902	86.8	29	Rwanda	0.5590	20.3	45	Ghana	0.0963	3.5
12	Zaire	2.3682	86.0	30	Bolivia	0.4406	16.0	46	Nigeria	0.0826	3.0
13	India	2.3131	84.0	31	Togo	0.3387	12.3	47	Trinidad & Tobago	0.0743	2.7
14	Ecuador	2.2938	83.3	32	Puerto Rico	0.3304	12.0	48	Laos	0.0605	2.2
15	Kenya	2.2112	80.3	33	Central African Empire	0.2726	9.9	49	Benin	0.0357	1.3

Source: Food and Agriculture Organization.

122. Corn Production

Corn, also known as maize or Indian corn, was domesticated and cultivated in the Americas long before the Spaniards reached the New World, and is probably a complex hybrid of several related New World grasses. The plant with its tassel and ears has been a motif of American art since prehistoric times. It is the basic food of Central and South Americans, who eat it either fresh or ground. It is the primary feed grain in the United States, where almost half the annual crop is so used. In Europe corn is used almost entirely as fodder. Because of its easily identifiable genetic characteristics, corn is a favorite subject for genetic experiments.

Number of Countries: 109
Midpoint: 0.0837%
Period Covered: 1976
Type of Ranking: Production of Corn; Share of World Total and Total in Metric Tons; Highest to Lowest

Highlights & Findings: The total world production of corn is 334,276,000 tons (up from 216,291,000 in 1961) distributed as follows: Africa, 24,292,000; North America, 173,449,000; South America, 27,089,000; Asia, 54,146,000; Europe, 44,793,000; Oceania, 369,000; and Soviet Union, 10,138,000. In the United States, which accounts for nearly half the world production, corn is grown in Midwestern states, commonly known as the Corn Belt.

Regions	Africa	Asia & Oceania	Europe	Western Hemisphere
Most	South Africa (8)	China (2)	Rumania (4)	United States (1)
Least	Mauritania (109)	Japan (104)	Netherlands (106)	Jamaica (103)

Rank	Country	Production of Corn Share of World Total (%)	Total (000 tons)	Rank	Country	Production of Corn Share of World Total (%)	Total (000 tons)	Rank	Country	Production of Corn Share of World Total (%)	Total (000 tons)
	TOP 10			37	Uganda	0.1881	629	74	South Korea	0.0251	84
1	United States	47.6172	159,173	38	Venezuela	0.1591	532	75	Mali	0.0242	81
2	China	9.9061	33,114	39	Czechoslovakia	0.1537	514	76	Iran	0.0239	80
3	Brazil	5.3380	17,845	40	Greece	0.1498	501	77	Cambodia	0.0224	75
4	Rumania	3.4651	11,583	41	Morocco	0.1474	493	78	Yemen Arab Republic	0.0215	72
5	Soviet Union	3.0328	10,138	42	West Germany	0.1435	480	79	Rwanda	0.0212	71
6	Yugoslavia	2.7240	9,106	43	Angola	0.1346	450	80	Burma	0.0191	64
7	Mexico	2.5107	8,393	44	Mozambique	0.1346	450	81	Panama	0.0191	64
8	South Africa	2.1874	7,312	45	Portugal	0.1283	429	82	Botswana	0.0185	62
9	India	1.8718	6,257	46	Zaire	0.1226	410	83	Bhutan	0.0167	56
10	Argentina	1.7510	5,855	47	Cameroon	0.1031	355	84	Lesotho	0.0164	55
				48	Paraguay	0.1050	351	85	Iraq	0.0152	51
	UPPER MIDDLE			49	Bolivia	0.1023	342	86	Syria	0.0152	51
11	France	1.6585	5,544	50	El Salvador	0.1023	342	87	Sudan	0.0149	50
12	Italy	1.5917	5,321	51	Guinea	0.0957	320	88	Senegal	0.0140	47
13	Hungary	1.5379	5,141	52	Vietnam	0.0957	320	89	Upper Volta	0.0137	46
14	Canada	1.1281	3,771	53	Ghana	0.0897	300	90	Central African Empire	0.0113	38
15	Egypt	0.9115	3,047	54	Honduras	0.0864	289	91	Dominican Republic	0.0104	35
16	Bulgaria	0.9067	3,031	55	Albania	0.0837	280	92	Belgium	0.0089	30
17	Philippines	0.8277	2,767					93	Laos	0.0089	30
18	Thailand	0.8002	2,675		*LOWER MIDDLE*			94	Sri Lanka	0.0080	27
19	Indonesia	0.7690	2,672	56	Haiti	0.0747	250	95	Malaysia	0.0077	26
20	North Korea	0.6282	2,100	57	Chile	0.0741	248	96	Namibia	0.0044	15
21	Tanzania	0.4843	1,619	58	New Zealand	0.0694	232	97	Congo	0.0041	14
22	Kenya	0.4636	1,550	59	Poland	0.0691	231	98	Israel	0.0041	14
23	Spain	0.4621	1,545	60	Benin	0.0661	221	99	Reunion	0.0041	14
24	Rhodesia (Zimbabwe)	0.4188	1,400	61	Ecuador	0.0646	216	100	Sierra Leone	0.0041	14
25	Turkey	0.3918	1,310	62	Uruguay	0.0628	210	101	South Yemen	0.0041	14
26	Ethiopia	0.3589	1,200	63	Nicaragua	0.0601	201				
27	Malawi	0.3290	1,100	64	Burundi	0.0478	160		*BOTTOM 8*		
28	Zambia	0.3200	1,070	65	Togo	0.0403	135	102	Belize	0.0032	11
29	Nigeria	0.3141	1,050	66	Australia	0.0391	131	103	Jamaica	0.0032	11
30	Austria	0.2800	936	67	Cuba	0.0373	125	104	Japan	0.0032	11
31	Colombia	0.2423	810	68	Madagascar	0.0367	123	105	Chad	0.0029	10
32	Afghanistan	0.2393	800	69	Somalia	0.0358	120	106	Netherlands	0.0012	5
33	Nepal	0.2354	787	70	Ivory Coast	0.0350	117	107	Gambia	0.0011	4
34	Pakistan	0.2285	764	71	Switzerland	0.0341	114	108	Cape Verde	0.0011	4
35	Guatemala	0.2052	686	72	Swaziland	0.0329	110	109	Mauritania	0.0008	3
36	Peru	0.2004	670	73	Costa Rica	0.0266	89				

Source: Food and Agriculture Organization.

123. Cotton Fiber Production

Cotton is perhaps the most important of the vegetable fibers, and has played a significant role in the history and development of world industry. The cotton industry was the pacemaker of the Industrial Revolution. In fact, the need to find markets for its cotton goods dictated much of the imperial policy of Great Britain in the 19th century. In the United States the one-crop cotton economy of the South was one of the principal economic causes of the Civil War. Cotton is of tropical origin but is most successfully cultivated in temperate climates with well-distributed rainfall. The chief cultivated species are sea island cotton, American-Egyptian cotton and upland cotton; all of them are subject to numerous pests and diseases, such as the boll weevil. Standard grades of cotton have been established by the U.S. Department of Agriculture.

Number of Countries: 80
Midpoint: 0.1223%
Period Covered: 1976
Type of Ranking: Production of Cotton Fiber (Lint); Share of World Total and Total in Metric Tons; Highest to Lowest

Highlights & Findings: Total annual world production of cotton fiber is 12,260,000 tons, down from an all-time high of 13,816,000 tons in 1973. The regional distribution is as follows: Africa, 1,080,000 tons; North America, 2,787,000 tons; South America, 824,000 tons; Asia, 4,789,000 tons; Europe, 165,000 tons; Oceania, 25,000 tons; and the Soviet Union, 2,590,000 tons. After being the leading producer for a number of decades, the United States lost its number one position to the Soviet Union beginning in 1970.

Regions	Africa	Asia & Oceania	Europe	Western Hemisphere
Most	Egypt (8)	China (2)	Soviet Union (1)	United States (3)
Least	Somalia (80)	Cambodia (74)	Italy (79)	Haiti (78)

Rank	Country	Production of Cotton Fiber Share of World Total (%)	Total (000 tons)	Rank	Country	Production of Cotton Fiber Share of World Total (%)	Total (000 tons)	Rank	Country	Production of Cotton Fiber Share of World Total (%)	Total (000 tons)
	TOP 10			27	Spain	0.3181	39	54	Swaziland	0.0489	6
1	Soviet Union	21.1256	2,590	28	Paraguay	0.2773	34	55	Ghana	0.0407	5
2	China	19.3556	2,373	29	Mozambique	0.2283	28	56	Indonesia	0.0407	5
3	United States	18.7928	2,304	30	Thailand	0.2202	27	57	Kenya	0.0407	5
4	India	8.3115	1,019	31	Ivory Coast	0.2120	26	58	Zambia	0.0326	4
5	Turkey	3.8743	475	32	Australia	0.2039	25	59	North Korea	0.0244	3
6	Pakistan	3.3605	412	33	Chad	0.2039	25	60	Niger	0.0244	3
7	Brazil	3.2381	397	34	Venezuela	0.1876	23	61	Rumania	0.0244	3
8	Egypt	3.2300	396	35	Ethiopia	0.1631	20	62	South Yemen	0.0244	3
9	Mexico	1.7210	211	36	South Africa	0.1549	19	63	Burundi	0.0163	2
10	Iran	1.3050	160	37	Cameroon	0.1468	18	64	South Korea	0.0163	2
				38	Upper Volta	0.1386	17	65	Laos	0.0163	2
	UPPER MIDDLE			39	Burma	0.1305	16	66	Sri Lanka	0.0163	2
11	Syria	1.2642	155					67	Togo	0.0163	2
12	Colombia	1.1827	145					68	Vietnam	0.0163	2
13	Argentina	1.1419	140		*LOWER MIDDLE*			69	Yugoslavia	0.0163	2
14	Sudan	1.0114	124	40	Benin	0.1223	15				
15	Greece	0.9216	113	41	Central African Empire	0.1223	15		*BOTTON 11*		
16	Guatemala	0.8075	99	42	Senegal	0.1223	15	70	Algeria	0.0081	1
17	Nicaragua	0.8075	99	43	Angola	0.1060	13	71	Bangladesh	0.0081	1
18	Tanzania	0.5628	69	44	Madagascar	0.1060	13	72	Bulgaria	0.0081	1
19	Peru	0.5301	65	45	Zaire	0.1060	13	73	Botswana	0.0081	1
20	El Salvador	0.5057	62	46	Bolivia	0.0978	12	74	Cambodia	0.0081	1
21	Nigeria	0.4975	61	47	Iraq	0.0978	12	75	Costa Rica	0.0081	1
22	Afghanistan	0.4404	54	48	Yemen Arab Republic	0.0815	10	76	Cuba	0.0081	1
23	Israel	0.4404	54	49	Ecuador	0.0652	8	77	Dominican Republic	0.0081	1
24	Mali	0.3344	41	50	Albania	0.0570	7	78	Haiti	0.0081	1
25	Uganda	0.3344	41	51	Honduras	0.0570	7	79	Italy	0.0081	1
26	Rhodesia (Zimbabwe)	0.3181	39	52	Morocco	0.0570	7	80	Somalia	0.0081	1
				53	Malawi	0.0489	6				

Source: International Cotton Advisory Committee.

124. Egg Production

Like milk, eggs play a significant role in the diet of people in all countries. Although human consumption is not limited to hen's eggs, statistics are not available for the consumption of other types of eggs. FAO presents data relating to the production of hen's eggs in tons rather than the number of eggs. Because egg weights vary markedly, it has not been possible to convert the data into number of eggs per capita, although such a presentation would have been more meaningful.

Number of Countries: 115
Midpoint: 0.1372%
Period Covered: 1976
Type of Ranking: Production of Eggs;
Share of World Total and Total in Metric
Tons; Highest to Lowest

Highlights & Findings: World production of eggs is 24,051,900 tons, up from 16,332,700 in 1961. Per capita worldwide consumption is 6 kg, or 13.2 lb. The regional distribution (with per capita production in parentheses) is as follows:
Africa: 744,600 tons (1.80 kg; 3.9 lb)
North America: 4,843,900 tons (13.91 kg; 30.67 lb)
South America: 1,118,000 tons (5.0 kg; 10.4 lb)
Asia: 7,261,400 tons (3.15 kg; 6.9 lb)
Europe: 6,782,400 tons (14.2 kg; 31.3 lb)
Oceania: 242,800 (11.18 kg; 24.6 lb)
Soviet Union: 3,059,800 (11.91 kg; 26.2 lb)

Regions	Africa	Asia & Oceania	Europe	Western Hemisphere
Most	South Africa (25)	China (2)	Soviet Union (3)	United States (1)
Least	Upper Volta (115)	Yemen Arab Republic (113)	Iceland (110)	Guyana (107)

Rank	Country	Production of Eggs Share of World Total (%)	Total (000 tons)
		TOP 10	
1	United States	15.9072	3,826.0
2	China	15.6349	3,760.5
3	Soviet Union	12.7183	3,059.0
4	Japan	7.5461	1,815.0
5	West Germany	3.6724	883.3
6	United Kingdom	3.3473	805.1
7	Italy	3.2221	775.0
8	France	3.1390	755.0
9	Spain	2.5636	616.6
10	Brazil	2.1703	522.0
		UPPER MIDDLE	
11	Poland	1.8672	449.1
12	Mexico	1.7528	421.6
13	Netherlands	1.3903	334.4
14	Canada	1.2364	297.4
15	East Germany	1.1928	286.9
16	Rumania	1.1225	270.0
17	Czechoslovakia	0.9338	224.6
18	Hungary	0.9234	222.1
19	Argentina	0.8855	213.0
20	Belgium	0.8722	209.8
21	Yugoslavia	0.7637	183.7
22	Australia	0.7604	182.9
23	Philippines	0.7068	170.0
24	South Korea	0.6984	168.0
25	South Africa	0.6740	162.3
26	Turkey	0.6431	154.7
27	Thailand	0.5812	139.8
28	Greece	0.5795	139.4
29	Iran	0.5404	130.0
30	Nigeria	0.4714	113.4
31	Vietnam	0.4573	110.0
32	Malaysia	0.4515	108.6
33	Sweden	0.4365	105.0
34	Colombia	0.4303	103.5
35	Bulgaria	0.4228	101.7
36	Venezuela	0.4091	98.4
37	Israel	0.4007	96.4
38	Austria	0.3671	88.3

Rank	Country	Production of Eggs Share of World Total (%)	Total (000 tons)
39	Finland	0.3571	85.9
40	Cuba	0.3517	84.6
41	India	0.3425	82.4
42	Egypt	0.3159	76.0
43	North Korea	0.2993	72.0
44	Burma	0.2972	71.5
45	Denmark	0.2943	70.8
46	Ethiopia	0.2918	70.2
47	Indonesia	0.2785	67.0
48	Pakistan	0.2748	66.1
49	Morocco	0.2727	65.6
50	Chile	0.2261	54.4
51	New Zealand	0.2216	53.3
52	Peru	0.2120	51.0
53	Portugal	0.1858	44.7
54	Switzerland	0.1692	40.7
55	Ireland	0.1675	40.3
56	Norway	0.1530	36.8
57	Syria	0.1455	35.0
58	Guatemala	0.1372	33.0
59	Lebanon	0.1372	33.0
		LOWER MIDDLE	
60	Nicaragua	0.1159	27.9
61	El Salvador	0.1143	27.5
62	Bangladesh	0.1035	24.9
63	Singapore	0.1018	24.5
64	Dominican Republic	0.0914	22.0
65	Laos	0.0864	20.8
66	Sudan	0.0864	20.8
67	Ecuador	0.0823	19.8
68	Puerto Rico	0.0823	19.8
69	Tanzania	0.0819	19.7
70	Honduras	0.0769	18.5
71	Paraguay	0.0765	18.4
72	Kenya	0.0752	18.1
73	Tunisia	0.0740	17.8
74	Iraq	0.0715	17.2
75	Algeria	0.0706	17.0
76	Uruguay	0.0706	17.0
77	Zaire	0.0706	17.0

Rank	Country	Production of Eggs Share of World Total (%)	Total (000 tons)
78	Sri Lanka	0.0681	16.4
79	Costa Rica	0.0673	16.2
80	Afghanistan	0.0665	16.0
81	Bolivia	0.0631	15.2
82	Uganda	0.0619	14.9
83	Saudi Arabia	0.0615	14.8
84	Panama	0.0582	14.0
85	Nepal	0.0548	13.2
86	Jamaica	0.0540	13.0
87	Zambia	0.0511	12.3
88	Ghana	0.0440	10.6
89	Madagascar	0.0411	9.9
90	Malawi	0.0399	9.6
91	Mozambique	0.0365	8.8
92	Rhodesia (Zimbabwe)	0.0349	8.4
93	Jordan	0.0340	8.2
94	Haiti	0.0332	8.0
95	Trinidad & Tobago	0.0303	7.3
96	Cameroon	0.0282	6.8
97	Hong Kong	0.0257	6.2
98	Senegal	0.0241	5.8
99	Mali	0.0228	5.5
100	Malta	0.0224	5.4
101	Cyprus	0.0216	5.2
102	Guinea	0.0216	5.2
103	Niger	0.0207	5.0
104	Ivory Coast	0.0199	4.8
105	Albania	0.0182	4.4
		BOTTOM 10	
106	Cambodia	0.0145	3.5
107	Guyana	0.0145	3.5
108	Angola	0.0141	3.4
109	Libya	0.0133	3.2
110	Iceland	0.0124	3.0
111	Reunion	0.0124	3.0
112	Benin	0.0116	2.8
113	Yemen Arab Republic	0.0116	2.8
114	Chad	0.0103	2.5
115	Upper Volta	0.0091	2.2

Source: Food and Agriculture Organization.

125. Meat Production

Meat has been a staple human food since prehistoric times, in a raw state at first and later, as man became civilized, in a dried or cooked form. At the same time it has been subject to various ritual prohibitions as well as butchering regulations, such as the Jewish tradition that distinguishes between kosher and tref. Meat consumption is related to the supply of as well as to preferences for types of meat, which vary from country to country. Lamb and mutton are preferred in the Middle East, veal in Italy, and pork and beef in Europe and the Americas. All forms of meat are taboo for the orthodox Hindu and Buddhist, a taboo common to many primitive African religions. Because meat is one of the richest sources of protein, countries with high per capita meat production also rank high in the food consumption index.

Number of Countries: 114
Midpoint: 15.31 kg (33.75 lb)
Period Covered: 1976
Type of Ranking: Production of Meat; Per Capita in Kg and Lb; Total and Share of Beef in Kg; Highest to Lowest

Highlights & Findings: The ranking figures include three types of meat: beef and veal; pork; mutton and lamb. The total world production of meat is 95,820,000 tons, consisting of 47,283,000 tons of beef and veal, 41,426,000 tons of pork, and 7,111,000 tons of lamb and mutton. Worldwide per capita production of meat is 23.9 kg, or 52.7 lb, annually. The regional distribution is as follows (000 metric tons):

Region	Total	Beef	Pork	Mutton
Africa	3,935	2,525	305	1,105
North America	21,437	14,455	6,761	221
South America	8,549	6,792	1,394	363
Asia	19,653	4,364	12,955	2,334
Europe	26,801	10,131	15,547	1,123
Oceania	3,789	2,465	236	1,088
Soviet Union	11,658	6,552	4,228	878

Regions	Africa	Asia & Oceania	Europe	Western Hemisphere
Most	Namibia (22)	New Zealand (1)	Denmark (3)	Uruguay (4)
Least	Zaire (112)	India (114)	Albania (49)	Haiti (80)

Rank	Country	Per Capita Production of Meat Kg	Lb	Total Production Kg (000 tons)	Beef Kg (000 tons)
	TOP 10				
1	New Zealand	368.78	813.15	1,158	613
2	Australia	190.02	418.99	2,592	1,840
3	Denmark	189.15	417.07	959	242
4	Uruguay	170.00	374.85	476	405
5	Ireland	145.25	320.27	459	303
6	Mongolia	124.16	273.77	185	58
7	Argentina	123.79	272.95	3,184	2,792
8	Netherlands	97.67	215.36	1,345	392
9	East Germany	91.81	201.05	1,531	417
10	Belgium	87.96	193.95	870	290
	UPPER MIDDLE				
11	Iceland	86.36	190.42	19	3
12	United States	83.51	184.13	17,965	12,166
13	Hungary	81.22	179.09	861	140
14	Czechoslovakia	72.92	160.78	1,088	382
15	Canada	71.69	158.07	1,659	1,139
16	Poland	68.16	150.29	2,342	779
17	France	67.68	149.45	3,587	1,799
18	Austria	65.51	144.44	492	183
19	Switzerland	62.83	138.54	399	149
20	West Germany	62.68	138.20	3,856	1,365
21	Paraguay	59.92	132.12	163	102
22	Namibia	59.09	130.29	52	31
23	Bulgaria	55.47	122.31	486	100
24	Sweden	54.50	120.17	448	149
25	Finland	53.06	116.99	251	114
26	Rumania	51.46	113.46	1,104	207
27	Botswana	50.72	111.83	35	30
28	Soviet Union	45.42	100.15	11,658	6,552
29	Hong Kong	39.72	87.58	174	30
30	Norway	38.21	84.25	154	62
31	United Kingdom	38.08	83.96	2,130	1,038
32	Swaziland	36.00	79.38	18	15
33	Costa Rica	35.64	78.58	72	63
34	Nicaragua	35.42	78.10	79	66
35	Yugoslavia	35.29	77.81	761	326
36	Greece	34.56	76.20	317	96
37	Spain	33.72	74.35	1,213	418
38	Italy	32.86	72.45	1,846	1,006
39	Venezuela	31.55	69.56	390	313
40	Panama	30.81	67.93	53	48
41	Cyprus	28.12	62.00	18	2
42	Brazil	27.79	61.27	3,035	2,220
43	Colombia	25.68	56.62	625	542
44	South Africa	25.37	55.94	663	400
45	Cuba	25.05	55.23	237	196
46	Rhodesia (Zimbabwe)	24.96	55.03	163	142
47	Portugal	23.49	51.79	222	86
48	Chile	23.34	51.46	244	198
49	Albania	20.78	45.81	53	19
50	Honduras	20.14	44.40	57	47
51	Bolivia	19.86	43.79	115	67
52	Somalia	19.63	43.28	64	28
53	Singapore	17.54	38.67	40	2
54	Madagascar	17.53	38.65	145	114
55	Sudan	17.04	37.57	275	158
56	Ecuador	16.82	37.08	123	68
57	Mexico	15.85	34.94	988	527
58	Turkey	15.31	33.75	615	231
	LOWER MIDDLE				
59	China	15.11	33.31	12,882	2,066
60	Guatemala	13.09	28.86	82	67
61	Dominican Republic	13.01	28.68	63	42
62	Puerto Rico	12.46	27.47	40	21
63	Central African Empire	12.16	26.81	23	20
69	Laos	12.13	26.74	41	16
65	El Salvador	11.89	26.21	49	30
66	Ethiopia	11.71	25.82	336	204
67	Ivory Coast	11.55	25.46	58	42

Rank	Country	Per Capita Production of Meat Kg	Lb	Total Production Kg (000 tons)	Beef Kg (000 tons)
68	Tunisia	11.49	25.33	66	26
69	Philippines	11.47	25.29	502	123
70	Peru	11.24	24.78	181	79
71	Japan	11.16	24.60	1,255	298
72	Angola	10.86	23.94	63	48
73	Vietnam	10.85	23.92	505	95
74	Chad	10.67	23.52	44	28
75	Jamaica	10.67	23.52	22	12
76	Iran	10.50	23.15	351	116
77	Kenya	10.46	23.06	145	117
78	Cameroon	10.41	22.95	68	44
79	Senegal	10.41	22.95	53	37
80	Haiti	10.27	22.64	48	19
81	Mali	10.10	22.27	59	30
82	Israel	9.82	21.65	34	21
83	Tanzania	9.60	21.16	150	121
84	Niger	9.51	20.96	45	26

Rank	Country	Per Capita Production of Meat Kg	Lb	Total Production Kg (000 tons)	Beef Kg (000 tons)
85	Syria	9.47	20.88	72	14
86	Morocco	9.31	20.52	166	90
87	Yemen Arab Republic	9.17	20.21	63	14
88	Iraq	8.94	19.71	103	51
89	Thailand	8.37	18.85	360	159
90	Zambia	8.36	18.43	43	37
91	Afghanistan	8.03	17.70	159	44
92	Egypt	7.72	17.02	294	243
93	Uganda	7.70	16.97	92	70
94	Lebanon	7.43	16.31	22	10
94	South Yemen	6.85	15.10	12	1
96	Cambodia	6.10	13.45	51	20
97	North Korea	5.47	12.06	89	24
98	South Korea	5.29	11.66	190	76
99	Mozambique	5.29	11.66	50	35
100	Nigeria	5.09	11.22	330	194

Rank	Country	Per Capita Production of Meat Kg	Lb	Total Production Kg (000 tons)	Beef Kg (000 tons)
101	Algeria	4.91	10.82	85	29
102	Burma	4.80	10.58	148	87
103	Saudi Arabia	4.76	10.49	44	11
104	Malaysia	4.63	10.20	57	12
	BOTTOM 10				
105	Upper Volta	4.37	9.63	27	13
106	Ghana	3.97	8.75	41	24
107	Pakistan	3.89	8.57	282	191
108	Nepal	3.34	7.36	43	21
109	Guinea	3.09	6.81	14	11
110	Bangladesh	2.71	5.97	219	166
111	Indonesia	2.29	5.04	320	180
112	Zaire	2.10	4.63	54	20
113	Sri Lanka	1.82	4.01	25	23
114	India	1.03	2.27	634	189

Source: Food and Agriculture Organization.

126. Milk Production

Milk is one of the most universal drinks, and it is also one of the most important farm products. As a commercial product it is subject to regulations regarding its composition, such as the proportion of butterfat and other solids, its nonadulteration and its purity. The following ranking is limited to the milk of the cow, buffalo, sheep and goat, but milk from many other animals is widely consumed, including that of the mare, camel, ass, zebra, reindeer, llama and yak. (See also "Milk Consumption Per Capita").

Number of Countries: 105
Midpoint: 0.1525%
Period Covered: 1976
Type of Ranking: Production of Milk; Share of World Total and Total in Metric Tons; Highest to Lowest

Highlights & Findings: World production of milk is 435,871,000 tons, of which cow milk accounts for 90.6% (394,823,000 tons), buffalo milk for 6.3% (27,092,000 tons), sheep milk for 1.6% (6,985,000 tons) and goat milk for 1.5% (6,606,000 tons). This production was distributed as follows: Africa, 12,475,000 tons; North America, 69,371,000 tons; South America, 23,592,000 tons; Asia, 59,723,000 tons; Europe, 168,618,000 tons; Oceania 13,034,000 tons; and the Soviet Union, 89,058,000. Superior breeds, such as Holsteins, Jerseys and Guernseys, enable Europe and North America to produce more milk with fewer milk cows.

Regions	Africa	Asia & Oceania	Europe	Western Hemisphere
Most	South Africa (32)	India (4)	Soviet Union (1)	United States (2)
Least	Zaire (105)	South Yemen (102)	Cyprus (100)	Jamaica (98)

Rank	Country	Production of Milk Share of World Total (%)	Total (000 tons)
	TOP 10		
1	Soviet Union	20.4321	89,058
2	United States	12.5248	54,592
3	France	7.1259	31,060
4	India	5.8379	25,446

Rank	Country	Production of Milk Share of World Total (%)	Total (000 tons)
5	West Germany	5.0907	22,189
6	Poland	3.8022	16,573
7	United Kingdom	3.3083	14,420
8	Brazil	2.4702	10,767
9	Netherlands	2.4181	10,538

Rank	Country	Production of Milk Share of World Total (%)	Total (000 tons)
10	Italy	2.2990	10,021
	UPPER MIDDLE		
11	Pakistan	2.2437	9,780
12	East Germany	1.8624	8,118

Rank	Country	Production of Milk Share of World Total (%)	Total (000 tons)	Rank	Country	Production of Milk Share of World Total (%)	Total (000 tons)	Rank	Country	Production of Milk Share of World Total (%)	Total (000 tons)
13	Canada	1.7649	7,693	46	Portugal	0.1878	819	77	Chad	0.0422	.184
14	New Zealand	1.4999	6,538	47	Kenya	0.1720	750	78	Saudi Arabia	0.0380	166
15	Australia	1.4779	6,442	48	Uruguay	0.1720	750	79	Mauritania	0.0357	156
16	Spain	1.3545	5,904	49	Israel	0.1617	705	80	Angola	0.0321	140
17	Argentina	1.3185	5,747	50	Tanzania	0.1605	700	81	South Korea	0.0293	128
18	Czechoslovakia	1.2957	5,648	51	Ethiopia	0.1601	698	82	Paraguay	0.0293	128
19	China	1.2914	5,629	52	Nepal	0.1594	695	83	Iceland	0.0289	126
20	Japan	1.2079	5,265	53	Syria	0.1525	665	84	Mali	0.0261	114
21	Denmark	1.1574	5,045					85	Senegal	0.0252	110
22	Turkey	1.1485	5,006		**LOWER MIDDLE**			86	Lebanon	0.0220	96
23	Rumania	1.0601	4,621	54	Algeria	0.1493	651	87	Bolivia	0.0213	93
24	Ireland	1.0438	4,550	55	Cuba	0.1461	637	88	Botswana	0.0178	78
25	Mexico	0.9553	4,164	56	Afghanistan	0.1385	604	89	Panama	0.0169	74
26	Yugoslavia	0.9156	3,991	57	Morocco	0.1232	537	90	Mozambique	0.0165	72
27	Belgium	0.8947	3,900	58	Iraq	0.1076	469	91	Upper Volta	0.0158	69
28	Switzerland	0.7967	3,473	59	Somalia	0.1066	465	92	Haiti	0.0151	66
29	Finland	0.7520	3,278	60	Puerto Rico	0.0936	408	93	Namibia	0.0149	65
30	Sweden	0.7449	3,247	61	Burma	0.0922	402	94	Libya	0.0137	60
31	Austria	0.7364	3,210	62	Uganda	0.0805	351	95	Burundi	0.0130	57
32	South Africa	0.5873	2,560	63	Guatemala	0.0734	320	96	Indonesia	0.0130	57
33	Colombia	0.5047	2,200	64	Nigeria	0.0724	316				
34	Hungary	0.4914	2,142	65	El Salvador	0.0674	294		**BOTTOM 9**		
35	Iran	0.4875	2,125	66	Dominican Republic	0.0672	293	97	Cameroon	0.0128	56
36	Norway	0.4345	1,894	67	Albania	0.0658	287	98	Jamaica	0.0123	54
37	Egypt	0.4175	1,820	68	Costa Rica	0.0612	267	99	Zambia	0.0114	50
38	Bulgaria	0.4168	1,817	69	Nicaragua	0.0603	263	100	Cyprus	0.0112	49
39	Greece	0.3909	1,704	70	Rhodesia (Zimbabwe)	0.0585	255	101	Jordan	0.0105	46
40	Bangladesh	0.3257	1,420	71	Tunisia	0.0562	245	102	South Yemen	0.0100	44
41	Sudan	0.3159	1,377	72	Yemen Arab Republic	0.0550	240	103	Malawi	0.0066	29
42	Venezuela	0.2737	1,193	73	Mongolia	0.0529	231	104	Madagascar	0.0066	29
43	Chile	0.2335	1,018	74	Sri Lanka	0.0449	196	105	Zaire	0.0061	27
44	Peru	0.1940	846	75	Niger	0.0447	195				
45	Ecuador	0.1904	830	76	Honduras	0.0429	187				

Source: Food and Agriculture Organization.

127. Oats Production

Oats are annuals of moist temperate regions. Of the oats now grown commercially, less than 5% is for human consumption, chiefly in the form of rolled oats or oatmeal, and the rest is used as pasturage and hay crop, especially for horses, and for various industrial purposes. They are also valuable for crop rotation, and their hay is used for animal bedding.

Number of Countries: 50
Midpoint: 0.2181%
Period Covered: 1976
Type of Ranking: Production of Oats; Share of World Total and Total in Metric Tons; Highest to Lowest

Highlights & Findings: The total world production of oats is 49,511,000 tons, down from a high of 56,811,000 tons in 1971. The regional distribution is as follows: Africa, 214,000; North America, 12,821,000; South America, 717,000; Asia, 2,446,000; Europe, 14,088,000; Oceania, 1,113,000; the Soviet Union, 18,113,000. Oats rival wheat and corn as the leading grain crop in the United States and the Soviet Union.

Regions	Africa	Asia & Oceania	Europe	Western Hemisphere
Most	South Africa (29)	China (6)	Soviet Union (1)	United States (2)
Least	Tunisia (46)	Lebanon (49)	Albania (41)	Peru (50)

Rank	Country	Production of Oats Share of World Total (%)	Total (000 tons)
		TOP 10	
1	Soviet Union	36.5837	18,113
2	United States	16.0166	7,930
3	Canada	9.7574	4,831
4	Poland	5.4430	2,695
5	West Germany	5.0433	2,497
6	China	3.8375	1,900
7	Finland	3.1770	1,573
8	France	2.8316	1,402
9	Sweden	2.5267	1,251
10	Australia	2.1651	1,072
		MIDDLE	
11	United Kingdom	1.5430	764
12	Argentina	1.0704	530
13	Spain	1.0664	528
14	East Germany	1.0219	506
15	Italy	0.8886	440
16	Turkey	0.8381	415

Rank	Country	Production of Oats Share of World Total (%)	Total (000 tons)
17	Czechoslovakia	0.7654	379
18	Yugoslavia	0.6463	320
19	Netherlands	0.5796	287
20	Austria	0.5715	283
21	Denmark	0.5311	263
22	Belgium	0.2928	145
23	Ireland	0.2625	130
24	Portugal	0.2565	127
25	Greece	0.2181	108
26	Netherlands	0.2080	103
27	Chile	0.1938	96
28	Hungary	0.1858	92
29	South Africa	0.1716	85
30	Algeria	0.1312	65
31	Bulgaria	0.1312	65
32	North Korea	0.1312	65
33	Mexico	0.1211	60
34	Rumania	0.1110	55
35	Switzerland	0.0969	48

Rank	Country	Production of Oats Share of World Total (%)	Total (000 tons)
36	Uruguay	0.0969	48
37	New Zealand	0.0828	41
38	Brazil	0.0787	39
39	Mongolia	0.0787	39
40	Morocco	0.0727	36
		BOTTOM 10	
41	Albania	0.0565	28
42	Japan	0.0444	22
43	Zaire	0.0242	12
44	Ethiopia	0.0100	5
45	Kenya	0.0100	5
46	Tunisia	0.0100	5
47	Bolivia	0.0040	2
48	Syria	0.0040	2
49	Lebanon	0.0020	1
50	Peru	0.0020	1

Source: Food and Agriculture Organization.

128. Peanut Production

Peanuts (also known as groundnuts, groundpeas and earthnuts) are among the most versatile agricultural crops because of their adaptability to a number of uses (the American botanist George Washington Carver alone developed hundreds of such uses). Usually eaten fresh or roasted, peanuts are also used in cookery, peanut butter and oil (noted for its high protein content) are used in confectionary, peanut herbage is used for hay, peanut cake is used as stock feed and the whole plant, left in the ground, is used as pasturage for swine. Usually about 20% of the peanut crop is converted into oil. Native to South America, the peanut plant is now grown mostly in tropical, subtropical and temperate regions.

Number of Countries: 97
Midpoint: 0.1300%
Period Covered: 1976
Type of Ranking: Production of Peanuts; Share of World Total and Total in Metric Tons; Highest to Lowest

Highlights & Findings: The total world production of peanuts is 17,923,100 tons distributed as follows: Africa, 5,239,700 tons; North America, 1,858,500 tons; South America, 924,600; Asia, 9,841,700; Europe, 19,700; Oceania, 37,900; and the Soviet Union 900 tons. Much of the peanut crop in Asia and Africa is exported to Europe and the United States for processing.

Regions	Africa	Asia & Oceania	Europe	Western Hemisphere
Most	Senegal (4)	India (1)	Cyprus (86)	United States (3)
Least	Reunion (93)	Tonga (97)	Yugoslavia (94)	St. Kitts-Nevis-Anguilla (96)

Rank	Country	Production of Peanuts Share of World Total (%)	Total (000 tons)
		TOP 10	
1	India	29.3611	5,262.4
2	China	16.1183	2,888.9
3	United States	9.4928	1,701.4
4	Senegal	6.6512	1,192.1
5	Sudan	4.6141	827.0
6	Nigeria	3.9055	700.0
7	Indonesia	3.0686	550.0

Rank	Country	Production of Peanuts Share of World Total (%)	Total (000 tons)
8	Burma	2.9013	520.0
9	Brazil	2.8672	513.9
10	Argentina	1.8852	337.9
		UPPER MIDDLE	
11	Zaire	1.6124	289.0
12	Mali	1.4372	257.6
13	Uganda	1.1024	197.6

Rank	Country	Production of Peanuts Share of World Total (%)	Total (000 tons)
14	Cameroon	0.9981	178.9
15	Malawi	0.9468	169.7
16	South Africa	0.8536	153.0
17	Thailand	0.8480	152.0
18	Gambia	0.7922	142.0
19	Rhodesia (Zimbabwe)	0.6695	120.0
20	Mozambique	0.5579	100.0
21	Niger	0.5328	95.5

Rank	Country	Production of Peanuts Share of World Total (%)	Total (000 tons)
22	Vietnam	0.5300	95.0
23	Upper Volta	0.4865	87.2
24	Ghana	0.4463	80.0
25	Tanzania	0.4128	74.0
26	Chad	0.3905	70.0
27	Dominican Republic	0.3794	68.0
28	Japan	0.3648	65.4
29	Pakistan	0.3576	64.1
30	Mexico	0.3459	62.0
31	Turkey	0.3051	54.7
32	Benin	0.2555	45.8
33	Guinea-Bissau	0.2510	45.0
34	Ivory Coast	0.2510	45.0
35	Madagascar	0.2159	38.7
36	Philippines	0.2047	36.7
37	Central African Empire	0.2030	36.4
38	Australia	0.1980	35.5
39	Bangladesh	0.1785	32.0
40	Guinea	0.1673	30.0
41	Zambia	0.1673	30.0
42	Egypt	0.1584	28.4
43	Ethiopia	0.1556	27.9
44	Togo	0.1478	26.5
45	Malaysia	0.1394	25.0
46	Burundi	0.1322	23.7
47	Israel	0.1311	23.5
48	Congo	0.1300	23.3

Rank	Country	Production of Peanuts Share of World Total (%)	Total (000 tons)
	LOWER MIDDLE		
49	Syria	0.1283	23.0
50	Venezuela	0.1171	21.0
51	Angola	0.1115	20.0
52	Sierra Leone	0.1060	19.0
53	Sri Lanka	0.1037	18.6
54	Paraguay	0.1064	18.0
55	Cuba	0.0836	15.0
56	Bolivia	0.0797	14.3
57	Libya	0.0781	14.0
58	Rwanda	0.0742	13.3
59	Cambodia	0.0725	13.0
60	Morocco	0.0714	12.8
61	Somalia	0.0541	9.7
62	Greece	0.0502	9.0
63	Ecuador	0.0440	7.9
64	Nicaragua	0.0424	7.6
65	North Korea	0.0418	7.5
66	Peru	0.0401	7.2
67	Botswana	0.0362	6.5
68	Spain	0.0334	6.0
69	Iran	0.0212	3.8
70	Lebanon	0.0212	3.8
71	Kenya	0.0167	3.0
72	Liberia	0.0150	2.7
73	Bulgaria	0.0145	2.6
74	Haiti	0.0122	2.2

Rank	Country	Production of Peanuts Share of World Total (%)	Total (000 tons)
75	Uruguay	0.0122	2.2
76	Gabon	0.0111	2.0
77	Italy	0.0106	1.9
78	Colombia	0.0083	1.5
79	Mauritius	0.0083	1.5
80	Papua New Guinea	0.0083	1.5
81	Laos	0.0078	1.4
82	Jamaica	0.0050	0.9
83	Soviet Union	0.0050	0.9
84	Fiji	0.0044	0.8
85	Guatemala	0.0039	0.7
86	Cyprus	0.0033	0.6
87	Mauritania	0.0033	0.6
	BOTTOM 10		
88	El Salvador	0.0022	0.4
89	Guyana	0.0016	0.3
90	Iraq	0.0016	0.3
91	St. Vincent	0.0016	0.3
92	Surinam	0.0016	0.3
93	Reunion	0.0011	0.2
94	Yugoslavia	0.0011	0.2
95	New Hebrides	0.0005	0.1
96	St. Kitts-Nevis-Anguilla	0.0005	0.1
97	Tonga	0.0005	0.1

Source: Food and Agriculture Organization.

129. Potato Production

Potatoes are among the most widely used vegetables in the world, especially in Europe and North America. Native to the Andes, where it was first cultivated by the Incas and Indians as a staple food, the potato was introduced by the Spanish explorers into Spain. From there its culture spread widely throughout Europe, and it was later reintroduced in the New World. It became a major food crop in Ireland (hence the name Irish potato), and the Irish famine of 1845–46 was the direct result of the failure of the potato crop due to blight. The potato is also believed to have kept the Germans alive during two world wars. Beside its food value, the potato is also a primary source of starch, alcohol, dextrin and fodder.

Number of Countries: 112
Midpoint: 0.0584%
Period Covered: 1976
Type of Ranking: Production of Potatoes; Share of World Total and Total in Metric Tons; Highest to Lowest

Highlights & Findings: The total world production of potatoes is 291,067,000 tons distributed as follows: Africa, 4,308,000; North America, 19,526,000; South America, 8,600,000; Asia, 59,644,000; Europe, 112,936,000; Oceania, 950,000; Soviet Union, 85,102,000. Europe accounts for 39% of world production, but the bulk of European production is used for feeding cattle.

Regions	Africa	Asia & Oceania	Europe	Western Hemisphere
Most	Egypt (32)	China (3)	Soviet Union (1)	United States (4)
Least	Reunion (109)	Saudi Arabia (112)	Faroe Islands (110)	Nicaragua (108)

Rank	Country	Production of Potatoes Share of World Total (%)	Total (000 tons)
	TOP 10		
1	Soviet Union	29.2379	85,102
2	Poland	17.1613	49,951
3	China	14.1699	41,244
4	United States	5.5753	16,228
5	West Germany	3.3696	9,808
6	India	2.5100	7,306
7	East Germany	2.3417	6,816
8	Spain	1.9442	5,659
9	United Kingdom	1.6453	4,789
10	Rumania	1.6449	4,788
	UPPER MIDDLE		
11	Netherlands	1.6432	4,783
12	France	1.6054	4,673
13	Czechoslovakia	1.4477	4,214
14	Japan	1.0994	3,200
15	Italy	1.0269	2,989
16	Yugoslavia	1.0059	2,928
17	Turkey	0.9791	2,850
18	Canada	0.8073	2,350
19	Peru	0.6630	1,930
20	Brazil	0.6239	1,816
21	Austria	0.5998	1,746
22	Argentina	0.5249	1,528
23	Hungary	0.4796	1,396
24	North Korea	0.4466	1,300
25	Ireland	0.4050	1,179
26	Colombia	0.3868	1,126
27	Sweden	0.3634	1,058
28	Portugal	0.3445	1,003
29	Greece	0.3404	991
30	Finland	0.3256	948
31	Bangladesh	0.3102	903
32	Egypt	0.3068	893
33	Belgium	0.3019	879
34	Bolivia	0.2830	824
35	Switzerland	0.2642	769
36	Australia	0.2394	697
37	Mexico	0.2387	695
38	South Africa	0.2308	672
39	South Korea	0.2030	591
40	Algeria	0.1992	580
41	Denmark	0.1975	575
42	Iran	0.1889	550
43	Chile	0.1851	539
44	Ecuador	0.1831	533
45	Norway	0.1662	484
46	Kenya	0.1271	370
47	Uganda	0.1257	366
48	Bulgaria	0.1202	350
49	Pakistan	0.1102	321
50	Nepal	0.1078	314
51	New Zealand	0.0858	250
52	Cyprus	0.0628	183
53	Israel	0.0601	175
54	Ethiopia	0.0597	174
55	Morocco	0.0584	170
56	Rwanda	0.0584	170
	LOWER MIDDLE		
57	Uruguay	0.0570	166
58	Burundi	0.0511	149
59	Venezuela	0.0463	135
60	Indonesia	0.0436	127
61	Syria	0.0432	126
62	Madagascar	0.0422	123
63	Albania	0.0419	122
64	Cuba	0.0408	119
65	Tunisia	0.0360	105
66	Malawi	0.0336	98
67	Lebanon	0.0292	85
68	Tanzania	0.0288	84
69	Libya	0.0274	80
70	Yemen Arab Republic	0.0261	76
71	Burma	0.0171	50
72	Zaire	0.0161	47
73	Iraq	0.0158	46
74	Mozambique	0.0144	42
75	Cameroon	0.0137	40
76	Bhutan	0.0127	37
77	Mongolia	0.0123	36
78	Angola	0.0120	35
79	Guatemala	0.0103	30
80	Nigeria	0.0103	30
81	Dominican Republic	0.0099	29
82	Sri Lanka	0.0096	28
83	Costa Rica	0.0085	25
84	Sudan	0.0085	25
85	Afghanistan	0.0079	23
86	Rhodesia (Zimbabwe)	0.0079	23
87	Malta	0.0068	20
88	Phillippines	0.0068	20
89	El Salvador	0.0054	16
90	Laos	0.0054	16
91	Vietnam	0.0048	14
92	Jordan	0.0044	13
93	Panama	0.0037	11
94	Liechtenstein	0.0034	10
95	Mauritius	0.0034	10
96	Thailand	0.0034	10
97	Haiti	0.0027	8
98	Jamaica	0.0027	8
99	Iceland	0.0024	7
100	Swaziland	0.0024	7
101	Honduras	0.0017	5
102	Senegal	0.0017	5
	BOTTOM 10		
103	Paraguay	0.0013	4
104	Congo	0.0010	3
105	Zambia	0.0010	3
106	Cape Verde	0.0006	2
107	Mauritania	0.0006	2
108	Nicaragua	0.0006	2
109	Reunion	0.0006	2
110	Faroe Islands	0.0003	1
111	New Caledonia	0.0003	1
112	Saudi Arabia	0.0003	1

Source: Food and Agriculture Organization.

130. Rice Production

In terms of the number of people who depend on it as their staple article of food, rice is the principal food crop in the world. It has been estimated that half the world's population subsists wholly or partly on rice. It is significant that in several Oriental languages the words for rice and food are one and the same, while in Chinese the words for rice and agriculture are the same. In the religions of the Orient, the planting and harvesting of rice are occasions of religious festivals, and the grain and the plant are the most popular traditional motifs in folk art. Rice is also the only major cereal crop that is consumed by man directly as harvested.

Thousands of rice strains are known to man and during the Green Revolution many more were added; known as miracle rices, these latter categories are richer in protein and have higher yields. The main problem with rice cultivation is its water requirement and the consequent dependence on either rain or irrigation. Rice is also used for production of rice wine, such as sake in Japan.

The statistics relate to 1976, but it should be noted

that there are wide swings in production from year to year because of the vagaries of weather, floods, storms and pests.

Number of Countries: 108
Midpoint 0.0319%
Period Covered: 1976
Type of Ranking: Production of Rice: Share of World Total and Total in Metric Tons Highest to Lowest

Highlights & Findings: World production of rice in 1976 was 350,260,000 tons distributed as follows: Africa, 7,621,000; North America, 6,987,000; South America, 13,522,000; Asia, 318,006,000; Europe, 1,679,000; Oceania, 444,000; and the Soviet Union, 2,001,000. Asia accounts for 91% of world production; this is not surprising because rice is the staple food of almost all Asians and is particularly suited to the terrain and agricultural techniques prevalent in Asia. Rice is also growing in importance in Africa and has been introduced successfully into South America.

Regions	Africa	Asia & Oceania	Europe	Western Hemisphere
Most	Egypt (16)	China (1)	Italy (24)	Brazil (8)
Least	Mauritius (108)	Syria (107)	Albania (82)	Puerto Rico (105)

Rank	Country	Production of Rice Share of World Total (%)	Total (000 tons)	Rank	Country	Production of Rice Share of World Total (%)	Total (000 tons)	Rank	Country	Production of Rice Share of World Total (%)	Total (000 tons)
	TOP 10			37	Ecuador	0.1050	368	74	Honduras	0.0074	26
1	China	36.8452	129,054	38	Argentina	0.0882	309	75	Angola	0.0071	25
2	India	18.3757	64,363	39	Venezuela	0.0790	277	76	Guatemala	0.0068	24
3	Indonesia	6.6522	23,300	40	Bhutan	0.0785	275	77	Yugoslavia	0.0065	23
4	Bangladesh	5.0325	17,627	41	Dominican Republic	0.0736	258	78	Fiji	0.0059	21
5	Thailand	4.5109	15,800	42	Turkey	0.0716	251	79	Benin	0.0057	20
6	Japan	4.3658	15,292	43	Mali	0.0676	237	80	Trinidad & Tobago	0.0057	20
7	Vietnam	3.0834	10,800	44	Liberia	0.0653	229	81	Cameroon	0.0054	19
8	Brazil	2.7294	9,560	45	Guyana	0.0648	227	82	Albania	0.0051	18
9	Burma	2.6571	9,307	46	Uruguay	0.0608	213	83	Morocco	0.0051	18
10	South Korea	2.0678	7,243	47	Zaire	0.0542	190	84	Uganda	0.0045	16
				48	Surinam	0.0493	173	85	Comoros	0.0042	15
	UPPER MIDDLE			49	Iraq	0.0465	163	86	Central African Empire	0.0034	12
11	Philippines	1.8429	6,455	50	Costa Rica	0.0428	150	87	Sudan	0.0034	12
12	United States	1.4977	5,246	51	Panama	0.0411	144	88	Brunei	0.0028	10
13	Pakistan	1.1722	4,106	52	Haiti	0.0374	131	89	Togo	0.0028	10
14	North Korea	1.0849	3,800	53	Bolivia	0.0322	113	90	Congo	0.0022	8
15	Nepal	0.6809	2,385	54	Senegal	0.0319	112	91	Belize	0.0017	6
16	Egypt	0.6566	2,300					92	Burundi	0.0017	6
17	Soviet Union	0.5712	2,001		*LOWER MIDDLE*			93	Somalia	0.0017	6
18	Malaysia	0.5290	1,853	55	Portugal	0.0276	97	94	Mauritania	0.0014	5
19	Madagascar	0.5179	1,814	56	Chile	0.0271	95	95	Rhodesia (Zimbabwe)	0.0014	5
20	Cambodia	0.5139	1,800	57	Greece	0.0234	82	96	Solomon Islands	0.0014	5
21	Iran	0.4470	1,566	58	Guinea-Bissau	0.0228	80	97	Swaziland	0.0014	5
22	Colombia	0.4453	1,560	59	Ghana	0.0191	67	98	Hong Kong	0.0008	3
23	Sri Lanka	0.3577	1,253	60	Nicaragua	0.0174	61	99	Rwanda	0.0008	3
24	Italy	0.2589	907	61	Paraguay	0.0162	57	100	South Africa	0.0008	3
25	Laos	0.2426	850	62	Chad	0.0142	50				
26	Peru	0.1627	570	63	Gambia	0.0142	50		*BOTTOM 8*		
27	Sierra Leone	0.1513	530	64	Mozambique	0.0128	45	101	Algeria	0.0005	2
28	Mexico	0.1313	460	65	Bulgaria	0.0117	41	102	Gabon	0.0005	2
29	Afghanistan	0.1279	448	66	Upper Volta	0.0117	41	103	Jamaica	0.0005	2
30	Cuba	0.1199	420	67	Kenya	0.0111	39	104	Papua New Guinea	0.0005	2
31	Ivory Coast	0.1199	420	68	Rumania	0.0105	37	105	Puerto Rico	0.0005	2
32	Australia	0.1190	417	69	El Salvador	0.0102	36	106	Zambia	0.0005	2
33	Spain	0.1159	406	70	France	0.0099	35	107	Syria	0.0002	1
34	Nigeria	0.1156	405	71	Malawi	0.0094	33	108	Mauritius	0.0002	1
35	Tanzania	0.1084	380	72	Hungary	0.0091	32				
36	Guinea	0.1070	375	73	Niger	0.0082	29				

Source: Food and Agriculture Organization.

131. Rubber Production

Natural rubber, also called caoutchouc, is obtained from the latex, or milky secretion, of various plants, the most important of which is the para rubber tree. Native to South America, especially the Amazon basin, it was harvested wild until late 19th century, when its seeds were smuggled in defiance of Brazilian legal restrictions to England. The resulting seedlings were sent to Sri Lanka, Malaysia, Java and Sumatra, where they were scientifically cultivated and managed. Today these tropical regions control the bulk of the world's output of natural rubber.

Number of Countries: 17
Midpoint: 0.9129%
Period Covered: 1976
Type of Ranking: Production of Natural Rubber; Share of World Total and Total in Metric Tons; Highest to Lowest

Highlights & Findings: World production of natural rubber is 3,560,000 tons. Of this total, South East Asian countries account for over 80%.

Regions	Africa	Asia & Oceania	Europe	Western Hemisphere
Most	Liberia (6)	Malaysia (1)	N.A.	Brazil (11)
Least	Central African Empire (17)	Burma (15)	N.A.	N.A.

Rank	Country	Production of Natural Rubber Share of World Total (%)	Total (000 tons)	Rank	Country	Production of Natural Rubber Share of World Total (%)	Total (000 tons)	Rank	Country	Production of Natural Rubber Share of World Total (%)	Total (000 tons)
	TOP 5			7	Papua New Guinea	1.6516	58.8	14	Ivory Coast	0.4915	17.5
1	Malaysia	46.0252	1,638.5	8	Nigeria	1.4466	51.5	15	Burma	0.4494	16.0
2	Indonesia	23.8061	847.5	9	Vietnam	0.9129	32.5	16	Ghana	0.0955	3.4
3	Thailand	11.0252	392.5	10	Zaire	0.8426	30.0	17	Central African Empire	0.0280	1.0
4	Sri Lanka	4.2724	152.1	11	Brazil	0.5702	20.3				
5	India	4.1516	147.8	12	Cambodia	0.5617	20.0				
	MIDDLE				*BOTTOM 5*						
6	Liberia	2.3146	82.4	13	Cameroon	0.4943	17.6				

Source: International Rubber Study Group, London.

132. Soybean Production

The soybean is a leguminous plant native to tropical and warm temperate regions of the Orient, where it has been cultivated for at least 5,000 years. There are over 2,500 varieties in cultivation, producing beans of many shapes and colors. The green crop is used as forage and hay and the cake as stock feed and as fertilizer. Recently soybeans have been recognized as a valuable source of protein for human consumption.

Number of Countries: 44
Midpoint: 0.0531%
Period Covered: 1976
Type of Ranking: Production of Soybeans: Share of World Total; Total in Metric Tons; Highest to Lowest

Highlights & Findings: The total world production of soybeans is 62,053,000 tons distributed as follows: Africa, 112,000; North America, 34,996,000; South America, 12,372,000; Asia, 13,641,000; Europe, 408,000; Oceania, 45,000; and the Soviet Union 408,000. The most dramatic growth in soybean production has been in the United States, which accounts for over half of world production.

Regions	Africa	Asia & Oceania	Europe	Western Hemisphere
Most	Nigeria (19)	China (2)	Soviet Union (6)	United States (1)
Least	Zambia (44)	Sri Lanka (41)	Spain (32)	Nicaragua (40)

Rank	Country	Production of Soybeans Share of World Total (%)	Total (000 tons)	Rank	Country	Production of Soybeans Share of World Total (%)	Total (000 tons)	Rank	Country	Production of Soybeans Share of World Total (%)	Total (000 tons)
		TOP 10		15	Colombia	0.1788	111	30	Turkey	0.0145	9
1	United States	55.4767	34,425	16	Japan	0.1772	110	31	Philippines	0.0145	9
2	China	19.4237	12,053	17	Iran	0.1643	102	32	Spain	0.0096	6
3	Brazil	18.0925	11,227	18	Bulgaria	0.1595	99	33	Uganda	0.0080	5
4	Argentina	1.1200	695	19	Nigeria	0.1128	70	34	Cambodia	0.0064	4
5	Indonesia	0.7767	482	20	Yugoslavia	0.0773	48	35	Laos	0.0064	4
6	Soviet Union	0.7735	480	21	Australia	0.0725	45	36	Rwanda	0.0064	4
7	Mexico	0.5140	319	22	Hungary	0.0676	42				
8	North Korea	0.4834	300							**BOTTOM 8**	
9	South Korea	0.4673	290			**LOWER MIDDLE**		37	Peru	0.0048	3
10	Paraguay	0.4576	284	23	Vietnam	0.0531	33	38	Iraq	0.0016	1
				24	Uruguay	0.0370	23	39	Malaysia	0.0016	1
		UPPER MIDDLE		25	South Africa	0.0306	19	40	Nicaragua	0.0016	1
11	Canada	0.4028	250	26	Bolivia	0.0241	15	41	Sri Lanka	0.0016	1
12	Rumania	0.3432	213	27	Ecuador	0.0241	15	42	Tanzania	0.0016	1
13	India	0.1933	120	28	Egypt	0.0177	11	43	Zaire	0.0016	1
14	Thailand	0.1837	114	29	Burma	0.0161	10	44	Zambia	0.0016	1

Source: Food and Agriculture Organization.

133. Sugar Production

Sugar production is important because of its central role in manufacture of a wide range of soft drinks and foods. At the same time the processing of both beet and cane sugar requires only relatively simple technology. World sugar prices and export quotas are determined by the International Sugar Organization.

Number of Countries: 104
Midpoint: 0.2769%
Period Covered: 1976
Type of Ranking: Production of Sugar; Share of World Total and Total Production in Metric Tons; Highest to Lowest

Highlights & Findings: World production of sugar is estimated at 86.513 million metric tons, up from 66.390 million tons in 1960. The top 10 nations account for 60% of world production, but outside of the top 10 production is more or less evenly distributed.

Regions	Africa	Asia & Oceania	Europe	Western Hemisphere
Most	South Africa (12)	India (5)	Soviet Union (1)	Brazil (2)
Least	Tunisia (104)	Nepal (101)	Portugal (97)	Surinam (102)

Rank	Country	Production of Sugar Share of World Total (%)	Total (000 tons)	Rank	Country	Production of Sugar Share of World Total (%)	Total (000 tons)	Rank	Country	Production of Sugar Share of World Total (%)	Total (000 tons)
		TOP 10		12	South Africa	2.4381	2,113	26	Pakistan	0.7811	677
1	Soviet Union	9.8081	8,500	13	Poland	2.0470	1,774	27	United Kingdom	0.7581	657
2	Brazil	8.3495	7,236	14	Italy	2.0285	1,758	28	Iran	0.7500	650
3	United States	7.1114	6,163	15	Thailand	2.0273	1,757	29	Czechoslovakia	0.7154	620
4	Cuba	7.0976	6,151	16	Argentina	1.7896	1,551	30	East Germany	0.7027	609
5	India	5.8075	5,033	17	Indonesia	1.5923	1,380	31	Yugoslavia	0.6692	580
6	China	4.6155	4,000	18	Dominican Republic	1.4850	1,287	32	Egypt	0.6646	576
7	Australia	3.9174	3,395	19	Spain	1.3408	1,162	33	Rumania	0.6473	561
8	Philippines	3.4432	2,984	20	Turkey	1.2577	1,090	34	Guatemala	0.5965	517
9	West Germany	3.2816	2,844	21	Netherlands	1.0927	947	35	Venezuela	0.5884	510
10	France	3.1397	2,721	22	Colombia	1.0788	935	36	Japan	0.5838	506
				23	Peru	1.0731	930	37	Denmark	0.4984	432
		UPPER MIDDLE		24	Mauritius	0.8434	731	38	Austria	0.4915	426
11	Mexico	3.1270	2,710	25	Belgium	0.8319	721	39	Hungary	0.4557	395

Rank	Country	Production of Sugar Share of World Total (%)	Total (000 tons)
40	Greece	0.4454	386
41	Jamaica	0.4246	368
42	Guyana	0.3946	342
43	Ecuador	0.3565	309
44	Fiji	0.3542	307
45	Sweden	0.3473	301
46	Puerto Rico	0.3173	275
47	El Salvador	0.3011	261
48	Morocco	0.2884	250
49	Rumania	0.2884	250
50	Nicaragua	0.2792	242
51	Bolivia	0.2769	240
52	Chile	0.2769	240
	LOWER MIDDLE		
53	Bulgaria	0.2653	230
54	Swaziland	0.2607	226
55	Mozambique	0.2538	220
56	Rhodesia (Zimbabwe)	0.2538	220
57	Trinidad & Tobago	0.2365	205
58	Costa Rica	0.2307	200
59	Kenya	0.2100	182
60	Panama	0.1857	161

Rank	Country	Production of Sugar Share of World Total (%)	Total (000 tons)
61	Canada	0.1776	156
62	Ireland	0.1730	150
63	Sudan	0.1615	140
64	Ethiopia	0.1569	136
65	Uruguay	0.1384	120
66	Madagascar	0.1315	114
67	Bangladesh	0.1269	110
68	Tanzania	0.1269	110
69	Barbados	0.1223	106
70	Malawi	0.1003	87
71	Switzerland	0.0957	83
72	Honduras	0.0934	81
73	Burma	0.0923	80
74	Zambia	0.0923	80
75	Finland	0.0888	77
76	Belize	0.0784	68
77	Zaire	0.0750	65
78	Paraguay	0.0715	62
79	Haiti	0.0692	60
80	Angola	0.0576	50
81	Malaysia	0.0576	50
82	Israel	0.0461	40
83	Somalia	0.0461	40

Rank	Country	Production of Sugar Share of World Total (%)	Total (000 tons)
84	St. Kitts-Nevis-Anguilla	0.0415	36
85	Congo	0.0392	34
86	Cameroon	0.0369	32
87	Nigeria	0.0346	30
88	Syria	0.0300	26
89	Sri Lanka	0.0276	24
90	Ivory Coast	0.0253	22
91	Albania	0.0242	21
92	Algeria	0.0230	20
93	Uganda	0.0230	20
94	Martinique	0.0161	14
	BOTTOM 10		
95	Guinea	0.0150	13
96	Ghana	0.0138	12
97	Portugal	0.0138	12
98	Iraq	0.0126	11
99	Afghanistan	0.0115	10
100	Lebanon	0.0115	10
101	Nepal	0.0115	10
102	Surinam	0.0115	10
103	Mali	0.0057	5
104	Tunisia	0.0057	5

Source: International Sugar Organization.

134. Tobacco Production

Tobacco is believed to be native to tropical America and was introduced into Spain and Portugal in the 16th century. It then spread to other European countries, where its use became popular in the 17th century. By 1619 tobacco had become the leading export of Virginia and for some time was the basis of its currency. There are many grades of tobacco depending on climate, soil and cultivation techniques.

Number of Countries: 110
Midpoint: 0.0992%
Period Covered: 1976
Type of Ranking: Production of Tobacco; Share of World Total and Total in Metric Tons; Highest to Lowest

Highlights & Findings: The total world production is 5,644,300 tons, up from 4,380,000 tons in 1961. Tobacco production has risen steadily every year since 1971. The regional distribution is as follows: Africa, 270,800 tons; North America, 1,239,700 tons; South America, 503,400 tons; Asia, 2,496,000 tons; Europe, 812,300 tons; Oceania, 18,500 tons; and the Soviet Union, 303,000 tons.

Regions	Africa	Asia & Oceania	Europe	Western Hemisphere
Most	Rhodesia (Zimbabwe) (13)	China (1)	Soviet Union (5)	United States (2)
Least	Niger (105)	Solomon Islands (109)	Cyprus (107)	Trinidad & Tobago (110)

Rank	Country	Production of Tobacco Share of World Total (%)	Total (000 tons)
	TOP 10		
1	China	17.8303	1,006.4
2	United States	17.1659	968.9
3	India	6.1974	349.8
4	Turkey	5.5613	313.9

Rank	Country	Production of Tobacco Share of World Total (%)	Total (000 tons)
5	Soviet Union	5.3682	303.0
6	Brazil	5.2885	298.5
7	Japan	2.9268	165.2
8	Bulgaria	2.9250	165.1
9	Greece	2.5391	138.8

Rank	Country	Production of Tobacco Share of World Total (%)	Total (000 tons)
10	Poland	2.2464	125.0
	UPPER MIDDLE		
11	South Korea	1.9665	111.0
12	Italy	1.9240	108.6

Rank	Country	Production of Tobacco Share of World Total (%)	Total (000 tons)
13	Rhodesia (Zimbabwe)	1.8319	103.4
14	Argentina	1.6760	94.6
15	Canada	1.4439	81.5
16	Indonesia	1.4191	80.1
17	Burma	1.3553	76.5
18	Thailand	1.2915	72.9
19	Yugoslavia	1.2738	71.9
20	Mexico	1.2047	68.0
21	France	1.0913	61.6
22	Pakistan	1.0754	60.7
23	Philippines	1.0612	59.9
24	Dominican Republic	0.8149	46.0
25	Cuba	0.8114	45.8
26	Bangladesh	0.8008	45.2
27	Rumania	0.7972	45.0
28	North Korea	0.7263	41.0
29	Colombia	0.6838	38.6
30	Paraguay	0.6821	38.5
31	Malawi	0.6218	35.1
32	South Africa	0.5279	29.8
33	Spain	0.5155	29.1
34	Hungary	0.3437	19.4
35	Tanzania	0.3383	19.1
36	Iran	0.3366	19.0
37	Vietnam	0.3189	18.0
38	Venezuela	0.2657	15.0
39	Australia	0.2639	14.9
40	Syria	0.2480	14.0
41	Nigeria	0.2462	13.9
42	Albania	0.2303	13.0
43	Lebanon	0.1895	10.7
44	Portugal	0.1807	10.2
45	Malaysia	0.1789	10.1
46	West Germany	0.1771	10.0

Rank	Country	Production of Tobacco Share of World Total (%)	Total (000 tons)
47	Iraq	0.1683	9.5
48	Guatemala	0.1364	7.7
49	Chile	0.1364	7.7
50	Cambodia	0.1293	7.3
51	Angola	0.1240	7.0
52	Sri Lanka	0.1169	6.6
53	Honduras	0.1116	6.3
54	Zambia	0.1116	6.3
55	Morocco	0.0992	5.6
56	Yemen Arab Republic	0.0992	5.6
	LOWER MIDDLE		
57	East Germany	0.0956	5.4
58	Czechoslovakia	0.0939	5.3
59	Nepal	0.0850	4.8
60	Peru	0.0797	4.5
61	Tunisia	0.0744	4.2
62	Madagascar	0.0726	4.1
63	Laos	0.0708	4.0
64	Ghana	0.0637	3.6
65	Ivory Coast	0.0620	3.5
66	Algeria	0.0602	3.4
67	New Zealand	0.0602	3.4
68	Uganda	0.0584	3.3
69	Costa Rica	0.0566	3.2
70	Cameroon	0.0531	3.0
71	Nicaragua	0.0531	3.0
72	Ethiopia	0.0496	2.8
73	Mozambique	0.0478	2.7
74	Haiti	0.0442	2.5
75	Central African Empire	0.0425	2.4
76	Ecuador	0.0407	2.3
77	Bolivia	0.0389	2.2
78	El Salvador	0.0389	2.2

Rank	Country	Production of Tobacco Share of World Total (%)	Total (000 tons)
79	Zaire	0.0389	2.2
80	Congo	0.0354	2.0
81	Togo	0.0354	2.0
82	Switzerland	0.0336	1.9
83	Puerto Rico	0.0336	1.9
84	Benin	0.0318	1.8
85	Burundi	0.0283	1.6
86	Rwanda	0.0265	1.5
87	Belgium	0.0248	1.4
88	Uruguay	0.0248	1.4
89	South Yemen	0.0248	1.4
90	Guinea	0.0230	1.3
91	Jamaica	0.0212	1.2
92	Libya	0.0194	1.1
93	Panama	0.0194	1.1
94	Israel	0.0141	0.8
95	Mauritius	0.0141	0.8
96	Bhutan	0.0124	0.7
97	Jordan	0.0124	0.7
98	Austria	0.0106	0.6
99	Kenya	0.0106	0.6
100	Upper Volta	0.0106	0.6
	BOTTOM 10		
101	Mali	0.0070	0.4
102	Oman	0.0070	0.4
103	Swaziland	0.0070	0.4
104	Singapore	0.0053	0.3
105	Niger	0.0035	0.2
106	Samoa	0.0035	0.2
107	Cyprus	0.0017	0.1
108	Guyana	0.0017	0.1
109	Solomon Islands	0.0017	0.1
110	Trinidad & Tobago	0.0017	0.1

Source: Food and Agriculture Organization.

135. Wheat Production

Wheat is one of the first grains domesticated by man and is known to have been cultivated as early as 5000 B.C. It has always been the staple food of Middle Easterners and Europeans and was introduced into the New World by the Spaniards and the English colonists. Modern wheat varieties are usually classified as winter wheats and spring wheats on the basis of planting seasons and as hard wheats and soft and white wheats on the basis of color and quality of kernels. High-yield wheat, one of the grains developed during the Green Revolution requires adequate irrigation and high concentration of fertilizers.

Number of Countries: 95
Midpoint: 0.0669%
Period Covered: 1976
Type of Ranking: Production of Wheat; Share of World Total and Total in Metric Tons: Highest to Lowest

Highlights & Findings: Total annual world production of wheat is 418,383,000 tons distributed as follows: Africa, 10,806,000 tons; North America, 85,305,000; South America, 16,142,000 tons; Asia, 111,281,000 tons; Europe, 85,809,000 tons; Oceania, 12,140,000 tons; and the Soviet Union, 96,900,000 tons. Since 1961 world production has jumped by 64%, up from 254,562,000 tons; much of this growth resulted from a 100% increase in Asian production. Elsewhere growth has been slower; it was only 50% in the Soviet Union, 63% in South America, 44% in Europe and 70% in Africa.

Regions	Africa	Asia & Oceania	Europe	Western Hemisphere
Most	South Africa (27)	China (3)	Soviet Union (1)	United States (2)
Least	Swaziland (94)	Oman (81)	Malta (80)	Venezuela (95)

Rank	Country	Production of Wheat Share of World Total (%)	Total (000 tons)
	TOP 10		
1	Soviet Union	23.1605	96,900
2	United States	13.9362	58,307
3	China	10.2779	43,001
4	India	6.8946	28,846
5	Canada	5.6376	23,587
6	Turkey	3.9623	16,578
7	France	3.8600	16,150
8	Australia	2.7995	11,713
9	Argentina	2.6769	11,200
10	Italy	2.2744	9,516
	UPPER MIDDLE		
11	Pakistan	2.0772	8,691
12	Rumania	1.6071	6,724
13	West Germany	1.6018	6,702
14	Iran	1.4446	6,044
15	Yugoslavia	1.4290	5,979
16	Poland	1.3731	5,745
17	Hungary	1.2304	5,148
18	Czechoslovakia	1.1489	4,807
19	United Kingdom	1.1329	4,740
20	Spain	1.0602	4,436
21	Mexico	0.8038	3,363
22	Brazil	0.7710	3,226
23	Bulgaria	0.7533	3,152
24	Afghanistan	0.7003	2,930
25	East Germany	0.6489	2,715
26	Greece	0.5619	2,351
27	South Africa	0.5351	2,239
28	Morocco	0.5102	2,135
29	Algeria	0.4923	2,060
30	Egypt	0.4684	1,960
31	Syria	0.4278	1,790
32	Sweden	0.4213	1,763
33	Iraq	0.3135	1,312
34	Austria	0.2949	1,234
35	Belgium	0.2227	932
36	Tunisia	0.2175	910
37	Chile	0.2069	866
38	Netherlands	0.1697	710
39	Ethiopia	0.1658	694
40	Portugal	0.1658	694
41	Finland	0.1563	654
42	Denmark	0.1414	592
43	Uruguay	0.1207	505
44	New Zealand	0.1020	427
45	Switzerland	0.0975	408
46	Albania	0.0932	390
47	Nepal	0.0924	387
48	Mongolia	0.0669	280
	LOWER MIDDLE		
49	Sudan	0.0631	264
50	Japan	0.0530	222
51	Bangladesh	0.0521	218
52	Israel	0.0492	206
53	Saudi Arabia	0.0489	205
54	Ireland	0.0478	200
55	Kenya	0.0478	200
56	Peru	0.0353	148
57	North Korea	0.0346	145
58	Rhodesia (Zimbabwe)	0.0215	90
59	South Korea	0.0195	82
60	Libya	0.0167	70
61	Bolivia	0.0164	69
62	Jordan	0.0160	67
63	Norway	0.0155	65
64	Bhutan	0.0145	61
65	Burma	0.0143	60
66	Tanzania	0.0143	60
67	Cyprus	0.0141	59
68	Colombia	0.0141	59
69	Yemen Arab Republic	0.0124	52
70	Guatemala	0.0114	48
71	Ecuador	0.0093	39
72	Lesotho	0.0093	39
73	Lebanon	0.0071	30
74	Paraguay	0.0069	29
75	Nigeria	0.0047	20
76	Uganda	0.0040	17
77	Angola	0.0031	13
78	Burundi	0.0031	13
79	South Yemen	0.0028	12
80	Malta	0.0007	3
81	Oman	0.0007	3
82	Zambia	0.0007	3
83	Mali	0.0006	3
84	Mozambique	0.0006	3
85	Rwanda	0.0006	3
	BOTTOM 10		
86	Chad	0.0004	2
87	Niger	0.0004	2
88	Zaire	0.0004	2
89	Botswana	0.0002	1
90	Honduras	0.0002	1
91	Malawi	0.0002	1
92	Namibia	0.0002	1
93	Somalia	0.0002	1
94	Swaziland	0.0002	1
95	Venezuela	0.0002	1

Source: Food and Agriculture Organization.

136. Wool Production

The data in this ranking refer to the production of raw wool covering both shorn and pulled wool together with the wool element of wooled sheep-skins. For minor countries estimates are based on sheep population.

Number of Countries: 27
Midpoint: 0.9222%
Period Covered: 1976
Type of Ranking: Production of Wool; Share of World Total and Total in Metric Tons; Highest to Lowest

Highlights & Findings: The total wool production in the world is 2,494,000 tons distributed as follows: Africa, 150,000 tons; North America, 54,000 tons; South America, 318,000 tons; Asia, 263,000 tons; Europe, 266,000 tons; Oceania, 1,012,000 tons; and the Soviet Union, 431,000. Australia and New Zealand together account for 40% of the world production

Regions	Africa	Asia & Oceania	Europe	Western Hemisphere
Most	South Africa (5)	Australia (1)	Soviet Union (2)	Argentina (4)
Least	Lesotho (26)	Iraq (17)	West Germany (25)	Canada (27)

Rank	Country	Production of Wool Share of World Total (%)	Total (000 tons)	Rank	Country	Production of Wool Share of World Total (%)	Total (000 tons)	Rank	Country	Production of Wool Share of World Total (%)	Total (000 tons)
		TOP 9		11	India	1.4033	35	22	Yugoslavia	0.4009	10
1	Australia	28.4282	709	12	Iran	1.1226	28	23	Ireland	0.3608	9
2	Soviet Union	17.2814	431	13	Spain	1.1226	28	24	Greece	0.3608	9
3	New Zealand	12.1491	303	14	Pakistan	0.9222	23	25	West Germany	0.2004	5
4	Argentina	7.0569	176	15	France	0.8821	22	26	Lesotho	0.0801	2
5	South Africa	4.1299	103	16	Morocco	0.8420	21	27	Canada	0.0400	1
6	Uruguay	2.5260	63	17	Iraq	0.7217	18				
7	Turkey	2.1651	54								
8	United States	2.1251	53			*BOTTOM 10*					
9	United Kingdom	1.9246	48	18	Chile	0.6816	17				
				19	Portugal	0.5613	14				
		MIDDLE		20	Italy	0.4811	12				
10	Brazil	1.4033	35	21	Peru	0.4410	11				

Source: Commonwealth Secretariat, London.

INDUSTRY AND MINING

Compared to agriculture, industry, particularly manufacturing, is a glamor sector, and the terms industrialize and modernize are often used as synonyms. Developing nations including the oil-rich ones are anxious to move into the industrial age and experience their own version of the Industrial Revolution. It has been observed that Karl Marx himself was similarly oriented. Communist nations tend to overstress industry thus giving rise to the term Goulash Communism, or a form of Communism that equates production of consumer goods with revolutionary success. The secret is that industrialization creates a multiplier or ripple effect; each factory leads to the establishment of satellite factories supplying parts; to the building of townships; to the construction of the infrastructure, such as roads; to increased energy consumption; to the refinement of vocational skills and to a number of other similar improvements.

Industrial strength may not always ensure economic independence, as many nations are discovering; in fact, it may have the opposite effect of reinforcing dependence because of the more critical need to find and maintain markets and suppliers of raw materials. Industrial progress is therefore a complex phenomenon, which can be measured only at certain middle levels. Technological capability, supply of raw materials, infrastructure support and downstream facilities form the base, while industrial production forms only the top of the pyramid. There are only a handful of countries where all these conditions are so ideally combined that they can be called industrial nations. The United States, already described as a postindustrial nation, leads the list, with West Germany and Japan close runners-up. The United Kingdom, France, Sweden and Italy complete the list; all the other nations are far behind.

This section is divided into three groups of rankings, the first two of which relate to manufacturing and the third to mining. The first group, an overview, ranks countries by the index of industrial production, industrial share of GDP and the annual growth rate of industry. The second group deals with industrial production in three categories; primary products (pig iron, steel, cement, ships and aluminum); consumer products (butter, cheese, cigarettes, cigars, beer, wine and salt) and consumer durables (television sets, radios and automobiles). The third group deals with the index of mineral production for five minerals (copper, silver, gold, iron ore and diamonds).

137. Industrial Production Index

The Production Index of Manufacturing Industries covers food, beverages and tobacco, textiles, chemicals, petroleum, basic metals and metal products, according to the International Standard Industrial Classification of Economic Activities. The base period is 1970.

Number of Countries: 73
Midpoint: 112
Period Covered: Latest Available Year, 1974-76
Type of Ranking: Production Index of Manufacturing Industries, 1970=100; Highest to Lowest

Highlights & Findings: As in many indices, a word of caution is in order here. Nations emerging into a period of accelerated manufacturing growth in the mid-1970s are favored in this index over nations that have an established and large industrial base but have reached a plateau in their growth rate. During the mid-1970s the quantum jump in oil prices exerted a steady downward pull on all countries but particularly on the industrialized nations of the West. Nevertheless, the index does not reveal any serious decline in industrial growth.

Regions	Africa	Asia & Oceania	Europe	Western Hemisphere
Most	Senegal (10)	Syria (4)	Rumania (6)	Bolivia (1)
Least	Mozambique (72)	Vietnam (73)	Finland (69)	Mexico (64)

Rank	Country	Production Index of Manufacturing		Rank	Country	Production Index of Manufacturing		Rank	Country	Production Index of Manufacturing
	TOP 10			25	Panama	126		50	Israel	106
1	Bolivia	297		26	Zambia	125		51	Soviet Union	106
2	Ecuador	191		27	Guatemala	122		52	United States	106
3	Brazil	183		28	Honduras	122		53	France	105
4	Syria	168		29	Paraguay	122		54	West Germany	105
5	Mongolia	167		30	Pakistan	120		55	Hungary	105
6	Rumania	167		31	Cyprus	119		56	Belgium	103
7	Malta	165		32	Spain	116		57	Canada	103
8	Turkey	158		33	South Korea	113		58	Netherlands	103
9	Nicaragua	154		34	Malaysia	113		59	Switzerland	103
10	Senegal	154		35	Portugal	112		60	Greece	102
				36	Uruguay	112		61	Norway	102
	UPPER MIDDLE			37	Yugoslavia	112		62	United Kingdom	102
11	East Germany	146						63	Argentina	101
12	Kenya	145			**LOWER MIDDLE**			64	Mexico	101
13	Peru	145		38	Chile	111				
14	Dominican Republic	143		39	Poland	110			**BOTTOM 9**	
15	Morocco	143		40	Tunisia	110				
16	Philippines	141		41	Austria	109		65	Australia	100
17	Colombia	139		42	India	109		66	Denmark	100
18	Egypt	139		43	Italy	109		67	Luxembourg	99
19	Venezuela	139		44	Singapore	109		68	Sweden	99
20	Iran	137		45	Bulgaria	108		69	Finland	96
21	New Zealand	137		46	Ireland	108		70	Rhodesia (Zimbabwe)	95
22	Costa Rica	132		47	Sri Lanka	108		71	South Africa	94
23	Ghana	129		48	Japan	107		72	Mozambique	90
24	El Salvador	128		49	Czechoslovakia	106		73	Vietnam	82

Source: *Yearbook of Industrial Statistics.*

138. Industry's Share of GDP

The industrial sector comprises mining, manufacturing, construction, electricity, water and gas. It is one of three principal sectors contributing to GDP, the other two being agriculture and services. The U.S.S.R. and many other Communist countries have no statistical data strictly comparable to the GDP.

Number of Countries: 101
Midpoint: 31%
Period Covered: 1976
Type of Ranking: Percentage of the Industrial Sector's Contribution to GDP; Highest to Lowest

Highlights & Findings: Industry's share of the GDP is highest in industrialized countries, where it is 41%, and lowest in low-income countries, where it is only 19. In middle-income countries it contributes 32% to the GDP. Apart from oil-producing countries, industry contributes over 50% of the GDP in only two countries; the United Kingdom and West Germany.

Regions	Africa	Asia & Oceania	Europe	Western Hemisphere
Most	Libya (2)	Saudi Arabia (1)	Rumania (4)	Venezuela (11)
Least	Uganda (101)	Bangladesh (98)	Greece (50)	Haiti (85)

Rank	Country	Industry's Share of the GDP (%)		Rank	Country	Industry's Share of the GDP (%)		Rank	Country	Industry's Share of the GDP (%)
	TOP 10			9	Austria	50		16	France	43
1	Saudi Arabia	86		10	Nigeria	50		17	Israel	43
2	Libya	68						18	Japan	43
3	Iraq	66			**UPPER MIDDLE**			19	Portugal	43
4	Rumania	63		11	Venezuela	48		20	Yugoslavia	43
5	Iran	59		12	Taiwan	45		21	Belgium	42
6	United Kingdom	58		13	Finland	44		22	Argentina	41
7	Algeria	57		14	Netherlands	44		23	Italy	41
8	West Germany	52		15	Congo	43		24	Zambia	41

Rank	Country	Industry's Share of the GDP (%)	Rank	Country	Industry's Share of the GDP (%)	Rank	Country	Industry's Share of the GDP (%)
25	Canada	40	51	Morocco	31	79	Sri Lanka	21
26	Jamaica	40	52	Peru	31	80	Togo	21
27	Rhodesia (Zimbabwe)	40	53	Colombia	30	81	Benin	20
28	Australia	39	54	Egypt	30	82	Cameroon	20
29	Brazil	39	55	Malaysia	30	83	Ivory Coast	20
30	Chile	39	56	Tunisia	30	84	Madagascar	20
31	Spain	39	57	Zaire	30	85	Haiti	19
32	Sweden	38	58	Honduras	28	86	Upper Volta	19
33	Ireland	37	59	Jordan	28	87	Mali	17
34	Liberia	37	60	Nicaragua	28	88	Sudan	16
35	Mauritania	37	61	Turkey	28	89	Tanzania	16
36	Norway	37	62	Angola	27	30	South Yemen	16
37	Denmark	36	63	Costa Rica	26	91	Burundi	15
38	Syria	36	64	Ecuador	26	92	Ethiopia	15
39	Mexico	35	65	Ghana	25	93	Mozambique	15
40	Singapore	35	66	Thailand	25			
41	Hong Kong	34	67	Niger	24		*BOTTOM 8*	
42	Indonesia	34	68	Pakistan	24	94	Afghanistan	14
43	South Korea	34	69	Senegal	24	95	Chad	14
44	Philippines	34	70	Central African Empire	23	96	Burma	11
45	Guinea	33	71	India	23	97	Nepal	10
46	Bolivia	32	72	Kenya	23	98	Bangladesh	8
47	Dominican Republic	32	73	Sierra Leone	23	99	Lesotho	8
48	United States	32	74	South Africa	23	100	Somalia	8
49	Uruguay	32	75	Malawi	22	101	Uganda	8
			76	Paraguay	22			
	LOWER MIDDLE		77	Rwanda	22			
50	Greece	31	78	El Salvador	21			

Source: World Bank.

139. Annual Growth Rate of Industry

The industrial sector comprises mining, manufacturing, construction, electricity, water and gas. Growth rates in industry are determined by a number of variable factors, such as availability of raw materials; an adequately large pool of skilled manpower; a supporting infrastructure, especially road and rail transport; flow of investment funds and a national policy geared to industrial growth.

Number of Countries: 96
Midpoint: 6.3%
Period Covered: 1970-76
Type of Ranking: Average Annual Growth Rate of Industry; Highest to Lowest

Highlights & Findings: Industrial growth rates are highest in middle-income countries at 7.2% and lowest in industrialized countries at 3.2%. Low-income countries fare slightly better with 4.5%. Worldwide industrial growth rates are more encouraging than corresponding rates for agriculture, and the majority of the countries covered in the ranking have growth rates exceeding 5%. Only six countries have experienced negative growth rates.

Regions	Africa	Asia & Oceania	Europe	Western Hemisphere
Most	Congo (1)	South Yemen (2)	Rumania (13)	Ecuador (7)
Least	Libya (96)	Australia (86)	West Germany (90)	Jamaica (92)

Rank	Country	Annual Growth Rate of Industry (%)	Rank	Country	Annual Growth Rate of Industry (%)	Rank	Country	Annual Growth Rate of Industry (%)
	Top 10		5	Algeria	16.4	10	Nigeria	12.6
1	Congo	22.6	6	Jordan	16.0			
2	South Yemen	17.7	7	Ecuador	14.2		*UPPER MIDDLE*	
3	South Korea	17.1	8	Taiwan	14.1	11	Indonesia	12.4
4	Saudi Arabia	16.5	9	Puerto Rico	14.1	12	Malawi	12.4

Rank	Country	Annual Growth Rate of Industry (%)	Rank	Country	Annual Growth Rate of Industry (%)	Rank	Country	Annual Growth Rate of Industry (%)
13	Rumania	12.3	42	Portugal	6.8	69	Zambia	3.4
14	Angola	11.6	43	Colombia	6.7	70	Belgium	3.3
15	Brazil	11.6	44	Mexico	6.6	71	Cameroon	3.3
16	Syria	11.1	45	Yugoslavia	6.5	72	Netherlands	3.3
17	Somalia	10.3	46	El Salvador	6.3	73	France	3.1
18	Tunisia	10.1	47	Greece	6.3	74	Sri Lanka	3.0
19	Iraq	10.0	48	Spain	6.3	75	Tanzania	2.9
20	Niger	10.0				76	Burma	2.8
21	Benin	9.8		*LOWER MIDDLE*		77	Sudan	2.8
22	Kenya	9.8				78	Sweden	2.4
23	Malaysia	9.6	49	Peru	6.2	79	Venezuela	2.4
24	Turkey	9.5	50	Iran	5.6	80	Italy	2.3
25	Singapore	9.1	51	Norway	5.4	81	Madagascar	2.0
26	Mali	8.9	52	Israel	5.3	82	Bangladesh	1.8
27	Haiti	8.8	53	Zaire	5.0	83	Uruguay	1.7
28	Philippines	8.7	54	Bolivia	4.9	84	Ethiopia	1.6
29	Rwanda	8.4	55	Japan	4.8	85	Denmark	1.2
30	Thailand	8.2	56	Canada	4.7	86	Australia	1.0
31	Chad	8.1	57	Central African Empire	4.7		*BOTTOM 10*	
32	Costa Rica	8.0	58	Burundi	4.3			
33	Ivory Coast	7.9	59	Egypt	4.3	87	United States	0.9
34	Morocco	7.8	60	Ghana	4.2	88	United Kingdom	0.5
35	Paraguay	7.7	61	Pakistan	4.1	89	Liberia	0.3
36	Nicaragua	7.3	62	Iceland	4.0	90	West Germany	0.2
37	Honduras	7.2	63	Austria	3.9	91	Chile	−2.2
38	Hong Kong	7.1	64	Guinea	3.9	92	Jamaica	−3.0
39	Mauritania	7.1	65	Senegal	3.9	93	Sierra Leone	−3.0
40	Togo	7.0	66	Finland	3.8	94	Mozambique	−3.8
41	Upper Volta	7.0	67	India	3.8	95	Uganda	−6.7
			68	Argentina	3.4	96	Libya	−7.4

Source: World Bank.

140. Pig Iron Production

Iron is the fourth most abundant element in the earth's crust, of which it constitutes about 5% by weight. Although rarely found uncombined, it is widely distributed as iron ore and is also found in the soil and groundwaters in low concentrations. Iron ores are refined in a blast furnace, and the product is called pig iron, which contains about 4% carbon and small amounts of manganese, silicon, phosphorus and sulfur. About 95 of pig iron is processed further to make steel; the balance is cast in sand molds into blocks called pigs. Pigs are further processed to make cast iron, wrought iron, gray iron and ductile iron.

Number of Countries: 45
Midpoint: 0.6567%
Period Covered: 1976
Type of Ranking: Production of Pig Iron and Ferroalloys; Share of World Total and Total in Metric Tons; Highest to Lowest

Highlights & Findings: Total annual world production of pig iron and ferroalloys is 505,200,000 tons, up from 357,900,000 in 1967. The top five nations account for 66% of total production.

Regions	Africa	Asia & Oceania	Europe	Western Hemisphere
Most	South Africa (18)	Japan (2)	Soviet Union (1)	United States (3)
Least	Morocco (44)	Thailand (45)	Switzerland (43)	Peru (41)

Rank	Country	Production of Pig Iron & Ferroalloys Share of World Total (%)	Total (000 tons)	Rank	Country	Production of Pig Iron & Ferroalloys Share of World Total (%)	Total (000 tons)	Rank	Country	Production of Pig Iron & Ferroalloys Share of World Total (%)	Total (000 tons)
	TOP 10			2	Japan	17.5344	88,584	4	West Germany	6.3515	32,088
1	Soviet Union	20.8578	105,374	3	United States	15.5985	78,804	5	China	5.9382	30,000

Rank	Country	Production of Pig Iron & Ferroalloys Share of World Total (%)	Total (000 tons)	Rank	Country	Production of Pig Iron & Ferroalloys Share of World Total (%)	Total (000 tons)	Rank	Country	Production of Pig Iron & Ferroalloys Share of World Total (%)	Total (000 tons)
6	France	3.8622	19,512	18	South Africa	1.3085	6,611	33	Argentina	0.2533	1,280
7	United Kingdom	2.7759	14,024	19	Netherlands	0.8442	4,265	34	Egypt	0.1126	569
8	Italy	2.3530	11,888	20	Luxembourg	0.7434	3,756	35	Venezuela	0.0845	427
9	Canada	1.9845	10,026	21	Mexico	0.7022	3,548				
10	India	1.9726	9,966	22	Austria	0.6567	3,318		*BOTTOM 10*		
				23	Sweden	0.6326	3,196	36	Algeria	0.0817	413
	MIDDLE			24	North Korea	0.5938	3,000	37	Chile	0.0797	403
11	Belgium	1.9526	9,865	25	East Germany	0.4986	2,519	38	Portugal	0.0704	356
12	Czechoslovakia	1.9073	9,636	26	Hungary	0.4420	2,233	39	Rhodesia (Zimbabwe)	0.0613	310
13	Brazil	1.6175	8,172	27	Yugoslavia	0.4192	2,118	40	Colombia	0.0566	286
14	Poland	1.5989	8,078	28	Turkey	0.3941	1,991	41	Peru	0.0441	223
15	Australia	1.4883	7,519	29	South Korea	0.3865	1,953	42	Tunisia	0.0203	103
16	Rumania	1.4677	7,415	30	Bulgaria	0.3190	1,612	43	Switzerland	0.0069	35
17	Spain	1.3707	6,925	31	Norway	0.2921	1,476	44	Morocco	0.0023	12
				32	Finland	0.2614	1,321	45	Thailand	0.0023	12

Source: U.S. Bureau of Mines.

141. Steel Production

Steel has long been acknowledged as the bellwether of industrial development, and its production is an indicator of the general level of industrial activity. Steel derives its importance from its status as the basic raw material of the hard-technology manufacturing sector, and its price and production levels influence those of a host of other products, appliances and vehicles. The following ranking reveals as closely as any single ranking can the degree of a nation's industrialization.

Number of Countries: 52
Midpoint: 0.44%
Period Covered: 1976
Type of Ranking: Production of Steel; Share of World Total and Total Production in Metric Tons; Highest to Lowest

Highlights & Findings: There are few surprises in this ranking. The world production in 1976 was 675 million tons, up from 493.6 million tons in 1967, yielding an annual average growth rate of 3.5%. Significantly, the U.S. share of the world total has declined from 23.48% in 1967 (when it was the world's largest steel producer), although its overall production has gained by 705,000 tons. Overall production has declined in at least five countries (the United Kingdom, Chile, Ireland, Israel and Uganda), since 1967, while production in industrialized European countries shows only moderate increases. The highest increases have been recorded by South Korea (799.33%), Rumania (162.54%), Spain (145.67%), China (145.45%), Brazil (143.49%) and Japan (72.79%). The Soviet Union, the second largest producer in 1967, has edged out the United States to become the world's number one producer with a 41.65% gain during the intervening period.

Regions	Africa	Asia & Oceania	Europe	Western Hemisphere
Most	South Africa (18)	Japan (3)	Soviet Union (1)	United States (2)
Least	Uganda (52)	Israel (49)	Ireland (50)	Uruguay (51)

Rank	Country	Production of Steel Share of World Total (%)	Total (000 tons)	Rank	Country	Production of Steel Share of World Total (%)	Total (000 tons)	Rank	Country	Production of Steel Share of World Total (%)	Total (000 tons)
	TOP 10			7	France	3.440	23,221	12	Belgium	1.799	12,145
1	Soviet Union	21.452	144,805	8	United Kingdom	3.299	22,274	13	Spain	1.642	11,085
2	United States	17.203	116,121	9	Poland	2.257	15,231	14	Rumania	1.590	10,733
3	Japan	15.910	107,399	10	Czechoslovakia	2.176	14,693	15	India	1.379	9,310
4	West Germany	6.283	42,415					16	Brazil	1.346	9,092
5	China	4.000	27,000		*UPPER MIDDLE*			17	Australia	1.175	7,937
6	Italy	3.473	23,446	11	Canada	1.946	13,137	18	South Africa	1.026	6,926

Rank	Country	Production of Steel Share of World Total (%)	Total (000 tons)
19	East Germany	0.998	6,740
20	Mexico	0.776	5,243
21	Netherlands	0.768	5,190
22	Sweden	0.765	5,168
23	Luxembourg	0.676	4,566
24	Austria	0.648	4,376
25	Hungary	0.541	3,652
26	North Korea	0.444	3,000
	LOWER MIDDLE		
27	Yugoslavia	0.407	2,751
28	South Korea	0.399	2,698
29	Bulgaria	0.364	2,460

Rank	Country	Production of Steel Share of World Total (%)	Total (000 tons)
30	Argentina	0.332	2,244
31	Finland	0.243	1,644
32	Turkey	0.215	1,457
33	Norway	0.133	898
34	Greece	0.118	800
35	Venezuela	0.111	754
36	Denmark	0.107	723
37	Switzerland	0.080	545
38	Egypt	0.067	457
39	Chile	0.067	456
40	Portugal	0.057	389
41	Peru	0.051	349
42	Rhodesia (Zimbabwe)	0.044	300

Rank	Country	Production of Steel Share of World Total (%)	Total (000 tons)
	BOTTOM 10		
43	Colombia	0.037	252
44	Cuba	0.037	250
45	Algeria	0.030	206
46	Thailand	0.024	163
47	Tunisia	0.015	103
48	Bangladesh	0.013	90
49	Israel	0.010	70
50	Ireland	0.008	58
51	Uruguay	0.002	15
52	Uganda	0.001	12

Source: *Yearbook of Industrial Statistics.*

142. Cement Production

Hydraulic cement is one of the most important building materials, and its production and consumption provide a reliable index of building activity. By far the most widely used hydraulic cement is known as portland cement, invented in 1824 by an English bricklayer, Joseph Aspdin. Other forms of cement in use are aluminous cement and natural cement.

Number of Countries: 118
Midpoint: 0.1370%
Period Covered: 1976
Type of Ranking: Production of Cement; Share of World Total and Total in Metric Tons; Highest to Lowest

Highlights & Findings: Total world production of cement is 729 million tons, up from 478 million in 1967. Production dipped slightly between 1973 and 1975 but picked up again in 1976. The regional distribution is as follows: Africa, 24 million tons; North America, 99 million tons; South America, 35 million tons; Asia, 186 million tons; Europe, 255 million tons; Oceania, 6 million tons; and the Soviet Union 124 million tons. The top five nations account for 45% of the total production.

Regions	Africa	Asia & Oceania	Europe	Western Hemisphere
Most	South Africa (23)	Japan (2)	Soviet Union (1)	United States (3)
Least	Cape Verde (118)	Cambodia (115)	Iceland (100)	Surinam (114)

Rank	Country	Production of Cement Share of World Total (%)	Total (000 tons)
	TOP 10		
1	Soviet Union	17.0433	124,246
2	Japan	9.4255	68,712
3	United States	9.3705	68,311
4	Italy	4.9831	36,327
5	China	4.8010	35,000
6	West Germany	4.6847	34,152
7	France	4.0489	29,517
8	Spain	3.4699	25,296
9	Poland	2.7165	19,804
10	Brazil	2.6264	19,147
	UPPER MIDDLE		
11	India	2.5629	18,684
12	United Kingdom	2.1646	15,780

Rank	Country	Production of Cement Share of World Total (%)	Total (000 tons)
13	Turkey	1.8043	13,154
14	Rumania	1.7953	13,088
15	Mexico	1.7408	12,691
16	South Korea	1.6286	11,873
17	East Germany	1.5560	11,344
18	Canada	1.3577	9,898
19	Czechoslovakia	1.3100	9,552
20	Greece	1.2016	8,760
21	Yugoslavia	1.0454	7,621
22	Belgium	1.0293	7,504
23	South Africa	0.9668	7,048
24	North Korea	0.8230	6,000
25	Austria	0.8065	5,880
26	Argentina	0.7842	5,717
27	Iran	0.7544	5,500

Rank	Country	Production of Cement Share of World Total (%)	Total (000 tons)
28	Australia	0.6913	5,040
29	Thailand	0.6065	4,422
30	Bulgaria	0.5983	4,362
31	Hungary	0.5895	4,298
32	Philippines	0.5801	4,229
33	Venezuela	0.5264	3,838
34	Portugal	0.5101	3,713
35	Colombia	0.4954	3,612
36	Switzerland	0.4864	3,546
37	Netherlands	0.4775	3,481
38	Egypt	0.4513	3,290
39	Pakistan	0.4384	3,196
40	Sweden	0.3838	2,798
41	Norway	0.3676	2,680
42	Cuba	0.3436	2,501

Rank	Country	Production of Cement Share of World Total (%)	Total (000 tons)	Rank	Country	Production of Cement Share of World Total (%)	Total (000 tons)	Rank	Country	Production of Cement Share of World Total (%)	Total (000 tons)
43	Iraq	0.3271	2,385	67	Vietnam	0.0960	700	94	Nicaragua	0.0286	209
44	Denmark	0.3230	2,355	68	Uruguay	0.0927	676	95	Sudan	0.0249	182
45	Morocco	0.2935	2,140	69	Angola	0.0891	650	96	Togo	0.0229	167
46	Israel	0.2742	1,999	70	Libya	0.0853	622	97	Benin	0.0224	164
47	Peru	0.2696	1,966	71	Ecuador	0.0844	616	98	Mongolia	0.0218	159
48	Finland	0.2503	1,825	72	Dominican Republic	0.0798	582	99	Paraguay	0.0212	155
49	Indonesia	0.2482	1,810	73	Rhodesia (Zimbabwe)	0.0742	541	100	Iceland	0.0197	144
50	Malaysia	0.2385	1,739	74	Jordan	0.0731	533	101	Bangladesh	0.0193	141
51	Lebanon	0.2331	1,700	75	Tunisia	0.0655	478	102	Guadeloupe	0.0178	130
52	Ireland	0.2152	1,569	76	Zambia	0.0620	452	103	Afghanistan	0.0171	125
53	Puerto Rico	0.1906	1,390	77	Sri Lanka	0.0584	426	104	Ethiopia	0.0156	117
54	Algeria	0.1823	1,329	78	Senegal	0.0521	380	105	Gabon	0.0127	93
55	Nigeria	0.1747	1,274	79	Jamaica	0.0500	365	106	Liberia	0.0123	90
56	Syria	0.1522	1,110	80	Costa Rica	0.0496	362	107	Uganda	0.0120	88
57	Saudi Arabia	0.1514	1,104	81	Guatemala	0.0467	341	108	Malawi	0.0116	85
58	Cyprus	0.1406	1,025	82	El Salvador	0.0441	322				
59	New Zealand	0.1370	999	83	Panama	0.0426	311		**BOTTOM 10**		
				84	Luxembourg	0.0410	299	109	Madagascar	0.0096	70
				85	Bahamas	0.0371	271	110	Fiji	0.0094	69
				86	Mozambique	0.0353	258	111	Yemen Arab Republic	0.0090	66
	LOWER MIDDLE			87	Tanzania	0.0334	244	112	New Caledonia	0.0074	54
60	Kenya	0.1348	983	88	Trinidad & Tobago	0.0331	242	113	Congo	0.0071	52
61	Chile	0.1322	964	89	Honduras	0.0320	234	114	Surinam	0.0069	51
62	Albania	0.1097	800	90	Burma	0.0319	233	115	Cambodia	0.0068	50
63	Zaire	0.1056	770	91	Bolivia	0.0318	232	116	Mali	0.0067	49
64	Hong Kong	0.1049	765	92	Haiti	0.0318	232	117	Niger	0.0052	38
65	Ivory Coast	0.1038	757	93	Cameroon	0.0288	210	118	Cape Verde	0.0005	4
66	Ghana	0.0960	700								

Source: *Yearbook of Industrial Statistics.*

143. Ship Production

Dominance in world shipbuilding has been held by a number of nations in the 20th century, but in each case such dominance has not lasted more than a few decades. Until World War I, Germany and the United Kingdom were the leading shipbuilders. During the interwar years the United Kingdom was the principal maritime nation. Following the passage of the U.S. Merchant Marine Act of 1936 and the huge shipbuilding program during World War II, the United States wrested the leadership briefly in the 1940s. Subsequently, the U.S. merchant marine declined again as the expense of labor and construction costs priced American ships out of the market despite the large subsidies provided to the shipping industry by the federal government. Since then Japan has become the undisputed leader in production of merchant vessels with a share estimated at 46% of the total.

Number of Countries: 30
Midpoint: 1.3721%
Period Covered: 1976
Type of Ranking: Production of Merchant Ships: Share of World Total and Total in Gross Registered Tons; Highest to Lowest

Highlights & Findings: World tonnage launched in 1976 was 31,047,000, up from 15,780,000 in 1967. Much of this increase was accounted for by oil tankers, whose production grew from 4,990,000 in 1967 to 15,420,000 in 1976, making up nearly 50% of total tonnage launched.

Regions	Africa	Asia & Oceania	Europe	Western Hemisphere
Most	Egypt (30)	Japan (1)	Sweden (2)	United States (7)
Least	N.A.	Turkey (29)	Ireland (27)	Peru (28)

Rank Country	Production of Merchant Vessels Share of World Total (%)	Total (000 GRT)	Rank Country	Production of Merchant Vessels Share of World Total (%)	Total (000 GRT)	Rank Country	Production of Merchant Vessels Share of World Total (%)	Total (000 GRT)
	TOP 5		10 South Korea	2.2192	689	22 Singapore	0.2769	86
1 Japan	46.0914	14,310	11 Italy	2.1322	662	23 Greece	0.2415	75
2 Sweden	7.6593	2,378	12 Yugoslavia	1.8906	587	24 Australia	0.2222	69
3 West Germany	5.7718	1,792	13 Netherlands	1.8488	574	25 India	0.1771	55
4 Spain	5.2114	1,618	14 Poland	1.7199	534			
5 United Kingdom	4.3192	1,341	15 Brazil	1.3721	426			
			16 Finland	1.2561	390		*BOTTOM 5*	
	MIDDLE		17 East Germany	1.1981	372	26 Agrentina	0.1127	35
6 France	3.8490	1,195	18 Portugal	0.8116	252	27 Ireland	0.0934	29
7 United States	3.4990	1,068	19 Canada	0.7633	237	28 Peru	0.0773	24
8 Denmark	3.0824	957	20 Belgium	0.5990	186	29 Turkey	0.0483	15
9 Norway	2.4382	757	21 Bulgaria	0.5539	172	30 Egypt	0.0064	2

Source: *Lloyd's Register of Shipping.*

144. Aluminum Production

Aluminum is the most abundant metal in the earth's crust, of which it constitutes about 8% by weight. It does not occur uncombined but as a constituent of many other metals such as bauxite, mica, feldspar and alum. Although aluminum compounds were used in antiquity, the metal was not isolated until the 19th century; the commercial process by which aluminum is produced today was developed only in 1886 by two metallurgists working independently: C. M. Hall, a student in Oberlin College, and Paul Heroult, a Frenchman. The Hall-Heroult process is critically dependent on the availability of cheap hydroelectric power. Because of its structural characteristics the metal is used widely in high-tension power transmission, aircraft and kitchenware.

Number of Countries: 40
Midpoint: 1.0795%
Period Covered: 1976
Type of Ranking: Production of Aluminum; Share of World Total and Total in Metric Tons; Highest to Lowest

Highlights & Findings: Total production of aluminum worldwide (including secondary or recycled aluminum) is 12,320,000 tons, up from 7,480,000 tons in 1967. The top five countries account for 75% of world production.

Regions	Africa	Asia & Oceania	Europe	Western Hemisphere
Most	Ghana (18)	Japan (3)	Soviet Union (2)	United States (1)
Least	Cameroon (30)	South Korea (36)	Portugal (40)	Mexico (33)

Rank Country	Production of Aluminum Share of World Total (%)	Total (000 tons)	Rank Country	Production of Aluminum Share of World Total (%)	Total (000 tons)	Rank Country	Production of Aluminum Share of World Total (%)	Total (000 tons)
	TOP 10		13 Spain	1.7159	211.4	28 Iceland	0.5292	65.2
1 United States	39.7962	4,902.9	14 India	1.7086	210.5	29 East Germany	0.4870	60.0
2 Soviet Union	12.9870	1,600.0	15 Rumania	1.6801	207.0	30 Cameroon	0.4407	54.3
3 Japan	11.7750	1,450.7	16 China	1.6233	200.0	31 Venezuela	0.4407	54.3
4 West Germany	5.9821	737.0	17 Yugoslavia	1.6047	197.7			
5 Canada	5.0982	628.1	18 Ghana	1.1899	146.6			
6 Norway	5.0308	619.8	19 New Zealand	1.1347	139.8		*BOTTOM 9*	
7 United Kingdom	4.3855	540.3	20 Greece	1.0795	133.0	32 Surinam	0.3652	45.0
8 France	4.2077	518.4	21 Bahrain	0.9910	122.1	33 Mexico	0.3441	42.4
9 Italy	3.2832	404.5	22 Brazil	0.9878	121.7	34 Czechoslovakia	0.2922	36.0
10 Austria	2.3620	291.0	23 Sweden	0.8709	107.3	35 Iran	0.2483	30.6
			24 Poland	0.8400	103.5	36 South Korea	0.1428	17.6
	MIDDLE		25 Switzerland	0.6347	78.2	37 Denmark	0.0876	10.8
11 Netherlands	2.0738	255.5	26 South Africa	0.6339	78.1	38 Finland	0.0495	6.1
12 Australia	2.0073	247.3	27 Hungary	0.5722	70.5	39 Belgium	0.0219	2.6
						40 Portugal	0.0137	1.7

Source: *Yearbook of Industrial Statistics.*

145. Butter Production

Butter, exclusively farm-made until about 1850, has become a factory product since the development of the centrifugal cream separator. Sweet or unsalted butter is favored in Europe, but other markets prefer at least 2% salt.

Number of Countries: 79 **Midpoint:** 0.1528% **Period Covered:** 1976 **Type of Ranking:** Production of Butter; Share of World Total and Total in Metric Tons; Highest to Lowest	**Highlights & Findings:** The world production of butter is 6,541,000 tons, of which the top five countries account for 50%. Much of the butter made in India is in the form of clarified butter, known as ghee.

Regions	Africa	Asia & Oceania	Europe	Western Hemisphere
Most	Egypt (22)	India (4)	Soviet Union (1)	United States (5)
Least	Upper Volta (79)	Saudi Arabia (77)	Iceland (73)	Puerto Rico (69)

Rank	Country	Production of Butter Share of World Total (%)	World Total (000 tons)	Rank	Country	Production of Butter Share of World Total (%)	World Total (000 tons)	Rank	Country	Production of Butter Share of World Total (%)	World Total (000 tons)
	TOP 10			27	Rumania	0.6726	44	54	Peru	0.0917	6
1	Soviet Union	20.7307	1,356	28	Japan	0.6726	44	55	Uruguay	0.0917	6
2	West Germany	8.3320	545	29	Argentina	0.6115	40	56	Afghanistan	0.0764	5
3	France	8.3167	544	30	Switzerland	0.5350	35	57	El Salvador	0.0764	5
4	India	6.8643	449	31	South Africa	0.4280	28	58	Israel	0.0764	5
5	United States	6.7879	444	32	Norway	0.3669	24	59	Mongolia	0.0764	5
6	East Germany	4.2501	278	33	Mexico	0.3516	23	60	Chad	0.0611	4
7	Poland	4.0306	264	34	Hungary	0.3057	20	61	Guatemala	0.0611	4
8	New Zealand	3.9902	261	35	Bulgaria	0.2293	15	62	Honduras	0.0611	4
9	Netherlands	3.3022	216	36	Spain	0.2293	15	63	Nicaragua	0.0611	4
10	Pakistan	3.2563	213	37	Yugoslavia	0.2293	15	64	Niger	0.0611	4
				38	Iraq	0.1681	11	65	Portugal	0.0611	4
	UPPER MIDDLE			39	Ethiopia	0.1528	10	66	Yemen Arab Republic	0.0611	4
11	Australia	2.2626	148	40	Syria	0.1528	10	67	Costa Rica	0.0458	3
12	Denmark	2.1250	139	41	Sudan	0.1528	10	68	Kenya	0.0458	3
13	Turkey	1.8345	120					69	Puerto Rico	0.0458	3
14	Canada	1.7887	117		**LOWER MIDDLE**			70	Rhodesia (Zimbabwe)	0.0458	3
15	Czechoslovakia	1.7734	116					71	Tanzania	0.0458	3
16	Belgium	1.4982	98	42	Luxembourg	0.1375	9				
17	Ireland	1.4982	98	43	Burma	0.1223	8				
18	China	1.3912	91	44	Cuba	0.1223	8		**BOTTOM 8**		
19	United Kingdom	1.3606	89	45	Morocco	0.1223	8	72	Albania	0.0305	2
20	Finland	1.2689	83	46	Nepal	0.1223	8	73	Iceland	0.0305	2
21	Brazil	1.0243	67	47	Bangladesh	0.1070	7	74	Mali	0.0305	2
22	Egypt	1.0090	66	48	Chile	0.1070	7	75	Tunisia	0.0305	2
23	Italy	0.9478	62	49	Colombia	0.1070	7	76	Oman	0.0152	1
24	Sweden	0.9325	61	50	Greece	0.1070	7	77	Saudi Arabia	0.0152	1
25	Iran	0.8561	56	51	Nigeria	0.1070	7	78	Somalia	0.0152	1
26	Austria	0.6879	45	52	Venezuela	0.1070	7	79	Upper Volta	0.0152	1
				53	Ecuador	0.0917	6				

Source: Food and Agriculture Organization.

146. Cheese Production

Cheese, made from the curd of milk separated from the whey, is one of the oldest foods. The yield of cheese is about 1 kg for every 10 kg of milk. Cheeses are often named for the place of origin and derive their distinctive qualities from the kind and condition of the milk used, the process of manufacture, and the method and extent of curing. Cheeses are generally divided into two classes: hard and soft. Hard cheeses, which improve with age, include Parmesan, Romano, Cheddar, Edam, Emmental, Gouda, Gruyere, Provolone and Swiss. Soft cheeses, which are intended for prompt consumption, include Gorgonzola, Limburger, Roquefort, Muenster, Stilton, Brie, Camembert, cottage, Neufchattel and ricotta. The best cheeses are ripened by introducing microorganisms and bacteria into the cheese and permitting them to develop.

Number of Countries: 76	**Highlights & Findings:** The total world production of cheese is 11,626,000 tons, of this amount the top five countries account for 55%.
Midpoint: 0.4214%	
Period Covered: 1976	
Type of Ranking: Production of Cheese; Share of World Total and Total in Metric Tons; Highest to Lowest	

Regions	Africa	Asia & Oceania	Europe	Western Hemisphere
Most	Egypt (10)	India (2)	Soviet Union (3)	United States (1)
Least	Mauritania (76)	South Yemen(72)	Iceland (69)	Haiti (75)

Rank	Country	Production of Cheese Share of World Total (%)	Total (000 tons)	Rank	Country	Production of Cheese Share of World Total (%)	Total (000 tons)	Rank	Country	Production of Cheese Share of World Total (%)	Total (000 tons)
	TOP 10			26	Iran	0.7483	87	52	Chile	0.1118	13
1	United States	15.7921	1,836	27	Sweden	0.7483	87	53	Guatemala	0.1118	13
2	India	13.0999	1,523	28	Mexico	0.7225	84	54	Afghanistan	0.0774	9
3	Soviet Union	11.7581	1,367	29	Austria	0.7139	83	55	Albania	0.0774	9
4	France	8.3175	967	30	Nepal	0.6365	74	56	Honduras	0.0688	8
5	West Germany	5.5995	651	31	Norway	0.5332	62	57	Uruguay	0.0688	8
6	Italy	4.4899	522	32	Finland	0.4902	57	58	Bangladesh	0.0602	7
7	Netherlands	3.2420	377	33	Japan	0.4902	57	59	Bolivia	0.0602	7
8	Poland	3.0362	353	34	Brazil	0.4644	54	60	Cuba	0.0602	7
9	Argentina	2.1331	248	35	Iraq	0.4300	50	61	Cyprus	0.0602	7
10	Egypt	1.9611	228	36	Israel	0.4300	50	62	Lebanon	0.0602	7
				37	Sudan	0.4300	50	63	Niger	0.0602	7
				38	Hungary	0.4214	49	64	Morocco	0.0516	6
	UPPER MIDDLE							65	Nigeria	0.0516	6
11	United Kingdom	1.9009	221					66	Costa Rica	0.0430	5
12	East Germany	1.6858	196		*LOWER MIDDLE*			67	Rhodesia (Zimbabwe)	0.0430	5
13	China	1.5998	186	39	Ireland	0.4128	48				
14	Greece	1.5310	178	40	Belgium	0.3612	42				
15	Denmark	1.3504	157	41	Peru	0.3440	40		*BOTTOM 9*		
16	Canada	1.2988	151	42	Syria	0.3010	35	68	Tunisia	0.0344	4
17	Czechoslovakia	1.2902	150	43	Colombia	0.2838	33	69	Iceland	0.0258	3
18	Bulgaria	1.2472	145	44	Portugal	0.2580	30	70	Jordan	0.0258	3
19	Rumania	1.1095	129	45	South Africa	0.2580	30	71	Mongolia	0.0258	3
20	Yugoslavia	1.0665	124	46	Venezuela	0.2408	28	72	South Yemen	0.0258	3
21	Spain	0.9805	114	47	Burma	0.1978	23	73	Angola	0.0172	2
22	Turkey	0.9805	114	48	El Salvador	0.1376	16	74	Dominican Republic	0.0172	2
23	Australia	0.9719	113	49	Nicaragua	0.1376	16	75	Haiti	0.0172	2
24	Switzerland	0.9547	111	50	Yemen Arab Republic	0.1376	16	76	Mauritania	0.0086	1
25	New Zealand	0.8859	103	51	Ecuador	0.1204	14				

Source: Food and Agriculture Organization.

147. Cigarette Production

The cigarette industry has grown phenomenally in recent years. In fact, it has achieved record sales every year (except 1975) since 1964, the year the U.S. Surgeon General issued a report linking lung cancer and cigarette smoking. This growth is all the more remarkable because of continuing and officially enforced deterrents in many countries, such as a ban on television advertising and warning labels on packages. The industry, however, has made serious efforts to reduce the tar and nicotine content of cigarettes.

Number of Countries: 114
Midpoint: 775 per Capita
Period Covered: 1976
Type of Ranking: Production of Cigarettes per Capita; Total Production; Highest to Lowest

Highlights & Findings: Total worldwide production of cigarettes is 3,251,960 million, or 813 per every man, woman and child per year or 2.2 per capita per day. Cigarette production has grown by 35% since 1967, when total production was 2,412,530 million. The top five countries in total population the-United States, the Soviet Union, Japan, West Germany and the United Kingdom, in that order—account for 50% of the world total.

Regions	Africa	Asia & Oceania	Europe	Western Hemisphere
Most	Sierra Leone (25)	Japan (9)	Bulgaria (1)	United States (4)
Least	Liberia (114)	Burma (111)	Norway (100)	Bolivia (106)

Rank	Country	Production of Cigarettes per Capita	Total (million)
	TOP 10		
1	Bulgaria	8,346	73,110
2	Switzerland	4,376	27,788
3	Malta	3,293	988
4	United States	3,199	688,200
5	Cyprus	3,193	2,044
6	Belgium	2,675	26,459
7	Canada	2,660	61,559
8	Poland	2,585	88,831
9	Japan	2,569	288,813
10	Greece	2,495	22,882
	UPPER MIDDLE		
11	West Germany	2,422	148,966
12	Hungary	2,348	24,896
13	Australia	2,314	31,563
14	Albania	2,274	5,800
15	United Kingdom	2,217	124,033
16	Netherlands	2,215	30,502
17	Ireland	2,186	6,910
18	New Zealand	2,081	6,535
19	Denmark	1,987	10,077
20	Yugoslavia	1,959	42,240
21	Austria	1,870	14,041
22	Macao	1,785	500
23	Spain	1,639	58,970
24	France	1,635	86,546
25	Sierra Leone	1,607	5,000
26	Israel	1,586	5,488
27	Czechoslovakia	1,557	23,232
28	South Korea	1,527	54,773
29	Cuba	1,520	14,377
30	Venezuela	1,517	18,755
31	Soviet Union	1,462	375,201
32	Sweden	1,372	11,278
33	Finland	1,348	6,378
34	Singapore	1,342	3,060
35	Portugal	1,335	12,662
36	Argentina	1,314	33,798
37	Italy	1,311	73,636
38	Rumania	1,259	27,000

Rank	Country	Production of Cigarettes per Capita	Total (million)
39	Uruguay	1,233	3,453
40	Turkey	1,193	47,918
41	East Germany	1,181	19,828
42	Philippines	1,164	50,950
43	Costa Rica	1,124	2,270
44	Libya	1,121	2,736
45	Brazil	1,027	112,101
46	Mauritius	1,021	888
47	Trinidad & Tobago	955	1,031
48	Malaysia	918	11,289
49	Hong Kong	915	4,006
50	Fiji	912	529
51	South Africa	896	23,405
52	Congo	888	1,235
53	Tunisia	877	5,035
54	Jordan	866	2,408
55	Chile	847	8,850
56	Surinam	777	342
57	Syria	775	5,888
	LOWER MIDDLE		
58	Nicaragua	760	1,695
59	Barbados	756	189
60	Colombia	754	18,344
61	Jamaica	749	1,544
62	Mexico	748	46,653
63	Guyana	717	559
64	Honduras	694	1,965
65	Rhodesia (Zimbabwe)	674	4,400
66	Dominican Republic	657	3,178
67	Gabon	626	332
68	Panama	626	1,077
69	Iraq	617	7,100
70	Belize	578	81
71	Egypt	546	20,795
72	Thailand	527	22,642
73	Ivory Coast	522	2,620
74	Morocco	507	9,043
75	Algeria	504	8,724
76	El Salvador	464	1,912

Rank	Country	Production of Cigarettes per Capita	Total (million)
77	Guatemala	437	2,737
78	Angola	431	2,500
79	Iran	420	14,045
80	Senegal	407	2,070
81	Pakistan	379	27,454
82	Seychelles	350	21
83	Lebanon	338	1,000
84	Sri Lanka	325	4,461
85	Mozambique	318	3,000
86	Cambodia	314	2,622
87	Indonesia	297	41,440
88	Ecuador	285	2,085
89	Kenya	267	3,703
90	Zambia	253	1,300
91	Paraguay	250	681
92	Cameroon	235	1,538
93	Tanzania	234	3,659
94	Peru	233	3,750
95	Ghana	227	2,339
96	Nepal	212	2,724
97	Vietnam	204	9,501
98	Nigeria	195	12,606
99	Laos	186	628
100	Norway	176	710
101	Madagascar	174	1,439
102	Haiti	160	746
103	Zaire	153	3,930
104	Uganda	151	1,800
	BOTTOM 10		
105	Bangladesh	148	11,907
106	Bolivia	124	720
107	India	110	67,094
108	Malawi	104	541
109	Chad	76	313
110	Upper Volta	74	460
111	Burma	71	2,181
112	Sudan	43	690
113	Ethiopia	42	1,207
114	Liberia	14	24

Source: *Yearbook of Industrial Statistics.*

148. Cigar Production

Cigars were introduced into Spain by conquistadores returning from the New World and rapidly spread to other European countries. Spanish words such as claro, colorado, maduro and perfecto are still used to describe the color, shape and quality of cigars. The most highly esteemed cigars are Havanas, made of fine Cuban leaf.

Number of Countries: 49
Midpoint: 4.69 per capita
Period Covered: 1976
Type of Ranking: Production of Cigars per Capita; Total Production of Cigars; Highest to Lowest

Highlights & Findings: Total annual production of cigars in the world is 22.597 billion, or 5.64 cigars for every man, woman and child. The top four producing countries—the United States, the Netherlands, the United Kingdom and West Germany—account for 60% of world production.

Regions	Africa	Asia & Oceania	Europe	Western Hemisphere
Most	Ivory Coast (18)	Malaysia (8)	Netherlands (1)	United States (9)
Least	Egypt (49)	Indonesia (48)	Poland (40)	Peru (47)

Rank	Country	Production of Cigars per Capita	Total Production (millions)
	TOP 10		
1	Netherlands	176.47	2,430
2	Switzerland	77.63	493
3	Belgium	72.19	714
4	East Germany	57.95	973
5	Denmark	47.73	242
6	United Kingdom	43.32	2,423
7	West Germany	39.29	2,417
8	Malaysia	37.72	464
9	United States	31.15	6,701
10	Sweden	30.04	247
	UPPER MIDDLE		
11	Finland	30.02	142
12	Spain	29.05	1,045
13	Cuba	27.37	259
14	Argentina	25.34	652
15	Canada	24.20	560
16	France	23.37	1,237

Rank	Country	Production of Cigars per Capita	Total Production (million)
17	Guatemala	19.96	125
18	Ivory Coast	14.54	73
19	Italy	9.29	522
20	Jamaica	7.76	16
21	South Africa	7.00	183
22	Austria	6.92	52
23	Venezuela	6.71	83
24	Colombia	5.67	138
25	Czechoslovakia	4.69	70
26	Singapore	4.38	10
27	Paraguay	3.30	9
	LOWER MIDDLE		
28	Hungary	2.54	27
29	Sri Lanka	2.47	34
30	Yugoslavia	2.31	50
31	Dominican Republic	1.85	9
32	Israel	1.15	4
33	Libya	0.81	2

Rank	Country	Production of Cigars per Capita	Total Production (million)
34	Brazil	0.76	84
35	Greece	0.76	7
36	Algeria	0.69	12
37	Philippines	0.50	22
38	Portugal	0.31	3
39	Japan	0.30	34
	BOTTOM 10		
40	Poland	0.26	9
41	Tunisia	0.17	1
42	Morocco	0.16	3
43	Ecuador	0.13	1
44	Burma	0.09	3
45	Chile	0.09	1
46	Turkey	0.09	4
47	Peru	0.06	1
48	Indonesia	0.03	5
49	Egypt	0.02	1

Source: Food and Agriculture Organization.

149. Beer Production

Beer is one of the oldest of alcoholic beverages, but it became a commercial product only in the Middle Ages. Modern beers contain about 3% to 6% alcohol, although stout and porter, heavier and darker types of beer, have a higher alcohol content. British, American and German beers differ markedly in flavor and content, but the brewing processes are similar. The most common type of beer is lager beer, so called because it is stored for weeks or months in a lager, or storage place. The term ale is applied in the United Kingdom to any light-colored beer and in the United States to a pale, strongly hopped malt beverage.

Number of Countries: 124
Midpoint: 13.70 Liters (3.61 Gallons) per Capita
Period Covered: 1976
Type of Ranking: Production of Beer per Capita in Liters and Gallons; Total Production in Hectoliters; Highest to Lowest

Highlights & Findings: World production of beer is 804,790,000 hectoliters, up from 553,920,000 hectoliters in 1967. The production has risen steadily every year since 1967. The top five producing nations—the United States, West Germany, the United Kingdom, the Soviet Union and Japan, in that order—account for 54% of world production.

Regions	Africa	Asia & Oceania	Europe	Western Hemisphere
Most	Gabon (18)	Australia (7)	Luxembourg (1)	Canada (13)
Least	Mali (119)	Pakistan (124)	Albania (87)	Nicaragua (83)

Rank	Country	Production of Beer per Capita		Total Prod. (000 Hecto-liters)
		Liter	Gallon	
	TOP 10			
1	Luxembourg	219.16	57.90	789
2	Denmark	164.26	43.39	8,328
3	Czechoslovakia	151.66	40.06	22,629
4	West Germany	148.57	39.25	91,391
5	Belgium	147.05	38.85	14,544
6	Ireland	145.37	38.40	4,492
7	Australia	140.45	37.10	19,158
8	New Zealand	130.44	34.46	4,096
9	East Germany	126.27	33.36	21,202
10	United Kingdom	117.35	31.00	65.635
	UPPER MIDDLE			
11	Austria	103.63	27.37	7,783
12	Netherlands	100.66	26.59	13,862
13	Canada	88.63	23.41	20,511
14	United States	86.75	22.91	185,257
15	French Polynesia	73.07	19.30	95
16	Switzerland	66.85	17.66	4,245
17	Hungary	63.82	16.86	6,765
18	Gabon	61.69	16.29	327
19	Zambia	60.40	15.95	2,670
20	Finland	56.21	14.85	2,659
21	Sweden	55.70	14.71	4,562
22	Seychelles	55.00	14.53	33
23	Bulgaria	53.59	14.15	4,695
24	Spain	47.62	12.58	17,130
25	Norway	46.75	12.35	1,875
26	France	46.45	12.27	24,585
27	Venezuela	41.17	10.87	4,504
28	Yugoslavia	40.28	10.64	8,685
29	Poland	35.93	9.49	12,347
30	Colombia	35.65	9.41	8,194
31	Rumania	35.54	9.38	7,625
32	Malta	33.33	8.80	100
33	Japan	33.12	8.75	37,236
34	Portugal	32.31	8.53	3,054
35	Peru	31.33	8.27	5,041
36	Mexico	31.05	8.20	19,357
37	Jamaica	29.41	7.77	606
38	Congo	28.34	7.48	394
39	Trinidad & Tobago	27.96	7.38	302
40	Fiji	27.75	7.33	161
41	Netherlands Antilles	25.21	6.66	58
42	Panama	25.17	6.64	433
43	Barbados	24.00	6.34	60
44	Cuba	23.25	6.14	2,200
45	Soviet Union	23.04	6.08	59,152
46	Uruguay	21.42	5.65	600
47	Surinam	21.36	5.64	94
48	South Africa	20.62	5.44	5,389
49	Singapore	20.53	5.42	462
50	Botswana	20.00	5.28	130
51	Zaire	19.12	5.05	4,762
52	Guyana	17.82	4.70	139
53	Cameroon	17.54	4.63	1,146
54	Cyprus	17.18	4.53	110
55	Puerto Rico	16.91	4.46	543
56	Ivory Coast	16.23	4.28	815
57	Greece	15.70	4.14	1,440
58	Ecuador	15.01	3.96	1,060
59	Namibia	14.77	3.90	130
60	Rhodesia (Zimbabwe)	13.78	3.64	900
61	Philippines	13.71	3.62	6,000
62	Costa Rica	13.70	3.61	270
	LOWER MIDDLE			
63	Burundi	13.34	3.52	515
64	Iceland	13.18	3.48	29
65	Italy	13.13	3.46	7,377
66	Brazil	12.80	3.38	13,980
67	Mauritius	12.64	3.33	110
68	Kenya	11.85	3.13	1,642
69	El Salvador	11.74	3.10	484
70	Bolivia	11.61	3.06	654
71	Argentina	11.03	2.91	2,839
72	Hong Kong	10.27	2.71	450
73	Chile	10.22	2.70	1,069
74	Israel	10.14	2.67	351
75	New Caledonia	10.00	2.64	13
76	Paraguay	9.84	2.59	253
77	Dominican Republic	9.46	2.49	445
78	Guatemala	9.13	2.41	572
79	Togo	9.00	2.37	200
80	Malawi	8.84	2.33	458
81	Honduras	8.76	2.31	248
82	Central African Empire	7.61	2.01	144
83	Nicaragua	7.60	2.00	144
84	Mozambique	6.93	1.83	655
85	Sierra Leone	6.67	1.76	181
86	Rwanda	6.33	1.67	266
87	Albania	6.12	1.61	144
88	South Korea	5.28	1.39	1,896
89	Mongolia	5.00	1.32	72
90	Nigeria	4.88	1.28	3,161
91	Ghana	4.84	1.27	500
92	Tunisia	4.84	1.27	278
93	Benin	4.53	1.19	145
94	Tanzania	4.45	1.17	695
95	Senegal	4.40	1.16	224
96	Turkey	4.25	1.12	1,709
97	Algeria	4.23	1.11	711
98	Chad	3.69	0.97	149
99	Uganda	3.36	0.88	389
100	Vietnam	3.18	0.84	1,362
101	Madagascar	3.10	0.81	257
102	Upper Volta	2.00	0.52	121
103	Jordan	1.79	0.47	50
104	Morocco	1.77	0.46	316
105	Thailand	1.74	0.45	750
106	Iraq	1.73	0.45	193
107	Ethiopia	1.51	0.39	422
108	Iran	1.21	0.32	370
109	Angola	1.12	0.29	650
110	Lebanon	1.01	0.26	30
111	Syria	0.89	0.23	68
112	Niger	0.84	0.22	38
113	Egypt	0.73	0.19	286
114	Sudan	0.60	0.15	93
	BOTTOM 10			
115	Liberia	0.45	0.11	8
116	Indonesia	0.33	0.08	470
117	Cambodia	0.23	0.06	18
118	Sri Lanka	0.21	0.05	30
119	China	0.20	0.05	1,750
120	Mali	0.20	0.05	12
121	India	0.15	0.03	941
122	Burma	0.09	0.02	30
123	Nepal	0.06	0.01	8
124	Pakistan	0.04	0.01	35

Source: Food and Agriculture Organization.

150. Wine Production

Wine is such an ancient human drink that its origin is unknown. But its modern development is associated with the mechanical extraction of juice from grapes, a process that has almost entirely replaced treading. Wines are generally divided into three main types: still or natural wines, fortified wines (such as sherry, port, Madeira and Malaga), and sparkling wines (such as champagne). The best and superfine natural wines are made in good vintage years from perfect grapes of the better varieties grown in the Bordeaux and Burgundy regions in France, the Rhine Valley in Germany and around   Tokaj in Hungary.

Number of Countries: 42
Midpoint: 10.156 Liters (2.68 Gallons)
Period Covered: 1976
Type of Ranking: Production of Wine Per Capita in Liters & Gallons; Total Production in Hectoliters; Highest to Lowest

Highlights & Findings: Annual world production of wine is 314,675,000 hectoliters, of which the top five nations account for 70%. The Food and Agriculture Organization reports only 43 nations as producers of wine, although Frank Schoonmaker's *Encyclopedia of Wine* states that more countries are engaged in its cultivation.

Regions	Africa	Asia & Oceania	Europe	Western Hemisphere
Most	Algeria (15)	Australia (16)	France (1)	Argentina (3)
Least	Egypt (41)	Japan (40)	Belgium (32)	Panama (42)

Rank	Country	Production of Wine per Capita Liter	Gallon	Total Production (000 hectoliters)	Rank	Country	Production of Wine per Capita Liter	Gallon	Total Production (000 hectoliters)	Rank	Country	Production of Wine per Capita Liter	Gallon	Total Production (000 hectoliters)
		TOP 10			14	Yugoslavia	29.591	7.81	6,380	30	Brazil	3.205	0.84	3,500
1	France	135.700	35.85	71,813	15	Algeria	28.901	7.63	5,000	31	Paraguay	3.125	0.82	85
2	Italy	117.233	30.97	65,850	16	Australia	24.633	6.50	3,360	32	Belgium	1.658	0.43	164
3	Argentina	103.032	27.22	26,500	17	South Africa	24.110	6.36	6,300					
4	Portugal	86.031	22.73	8,130	18	Switzerland	18.803	4.96	1,194			*BOTTOM 10*		
5	Cyprus	82.812	21.87	530	19	West Germany	12.950	3.42	7,966	33	Turkey	1.578	0.41	634
6	Spain	68.804	18.17	24,749	20	Soviet Union	12.272	3.24	31,500	34	Lebanon	1.452	0.38	43
7	Bulgaria	58.401	15.42	5,116	21	Tunisia	10.156	2.68	583	35	Canada	1.210	0.31	280
8	Greece	49.400	13.05	4,530	22	Israel	9.537	2.47	330	36	Peru	0.509	0.13	82
9	Chile	47.846	12.63	5,000	23	Macao	9.285	2.45	26	37	Mexico	0.505	0.13	315
10	Rumania	41.790	11.04	8,964	24	New Zealand	8.598	2.26	270	38	Bolivia	0.276	0.07	16
					25	Czechoslovakia	7.372	1.94	1,100	39	Madagascar	0.241	0.06	20
		MIDDLE			26	Albania	7.333	1.93	187	40	Japan	0.225	0.05	254
11	Hungary	40.283	10.64	4,270	27	United States	6.969	1.83	14,992	41	Egypt	0.181	0.04	69
12	Austria	38.628	10.20	2,901	28	Malta	6.000	1.58	18	42	Panama	0.174	0.04	3
13	Uruguay	33.928	8.96	950	29	Morocco	3.925	1.03	700					

Source: Food and Agriculture Organization.

---

151. Salt Production

This ranking covers the production of common salt (technically known as sodium chloride) irrespec-   tive of the source from which it is obtained and the degree of purity or concentration.

Number of Countries: 90
Midpoint: 12.38 Kg (27.29 Lb) per 1,000 Inhabitants
Period Covered: 1976
Type of Ranking: Production of Common Salt per 1,000 Inhabitants in Kg and Lb; Total Production in Metric Tons; Highest to Lowest

Highlights & Findings: The total world production of salt is 171,900,000 tons, of which the top four nations account for 56%. The presence of the Bahamas at the top of the ranking is explained by the Inagua salt complex, one of the largest facilities producing solar-evaporated salt in the world. In industrialized countries the bulk of the consumption is for industrial purposes—the manufacture of glass, textiles, soap and the preservation of foods—whereas in Asian countries salt is more important as an ingredient of human diet.

Regions	Africa	Asia & Oceania	Europe	Western Hemisphere
Most	Namibia (6)	Australia (4)	Netherlands (7)	Bahamas (1)
Least	Niger (90)	Indonesia (87)	Czechoslovakia (78)	Nicaragua (89)

Rank	Country	Production of Salt per 1,000 Kg	Lb	Total Prod. (000 tons)	Rank	Country	Production of Salt per 1,000 Kg	Lb	Total Prod. (000 tons)	Rank	Country	Production of Salt per 1,000 Kg	Lb	Total Prod. (000 tons)
		TOP 10			3	Martinique	440.54	971.39	163	6	Namibia	238.63	526.17	210
1	Bahamas	5,280.95	11,644.49	1,109	4	Australia	392.22	864.84	5,350	7	Netherlands	219.75	484.54	3,026
2	Netherlands Antilles	2,000.00	4,410.00	480	5	Canada	259.03	571.16	5,994	8	Rumania	196.27	432.77	4,210

Rank	Country	Production of Salt per 1,000 Kg	Lb	Total Prod. (000 tons)	Rank	Country	Production of Salt per 1,000 Kg	Lb	Total Prod. (000 tons)	Rank	Country	Production of Salt per 1,000 Kg	Lb	Total Prod. (000 tons)
9	West Germany	188.61	415.88	11,602	36	Turkey	19.92	43.92	800	63	Bangladesh	6.92	15.25	558
10	United States	186.36	410.92	40,091	37	Peru	18.89	41.65	304	64	Mauritius	6.89	15.19	6
					38	South Korea	17.84	39.33	640	65	Malta	6.66	14.68	2
	UPPER MIDDLE				39	Kuwait	17.47	38.52	18	66	El Salvador	5.58	12.30	23
11	Poland	159.19	351.01	5,470	40	Angola	17.24	38.01	100	67	Iraq	5.56	12.25	64
12	East Germany	152.47	336.19	2,560	41	Greece	16.24	35.80	149	68	Ghana	5.04	11.11	52
13	United Kingdom	143.14	315.62	8,006	42	Cuba	15.85	34.94	150	69	Cyprus	4.68	10.31	3
14	France	105.34	232.27	5,575	43	New Zealand	13.69	30.18	43	70	Philippines	4.66	10.27	204
15	Austria	88.54	195.23	665	44	Egypt	13.34	29.41	508	71	Sudan	4.64	10.23	75
16	Spain	87.07	191.98	3,132	45	Yugoslavia	12.38	27.29	267	72	Burma	4.28	9.43	132
17	Italy	71.44	157.52	4,013						73	Libya	4.09	9.01	10
18	Mexico	70.44	155.32	4,391		*LOWER MIDDLE*				74	Thailand	3.72	8.20	160
19	Denmark	68.83	151.77	349	46	Lebanon	11.82	26.06	35	75	Afghanistan	3.68	8.11	73
20	Soviet Union	55.39	122.13	14,219	47	Honduras	10.60	23.37	30	76	Cambodia	3.59	7.91	30
21	Portugal	55.34	122.02	523	48	Sri Lanka	10.19	22.46	140	77	Madagascar	3.26	7.18	27
22	Tunisia	50.17	110.62	288	49	Jordan	10.07	22.20	28	78	Czechoslovakia	3.21	7.07	48
23	Switzerland	49.13	108.33	312	50	Costa Rica	9.90	21.82	20	79	Ethiopia	3.06	6.74	88
24	Cape Verde	46.66	102.88	14	51	India	9.57	21.10	5,843	80	Mozambique	2.96	6.52	28
25	Argentina	46.65	102.86	1,200	52	Japan	9.08	20.02	1,021					
26	Colombia	45.70	100.76	1,112	53	Algeria	8.67	19.11	150		*BOTTOM 10*			
27	South Yemen	42.85	94.48	75	54	South Africa	8.57	18.89	224	81	Guatemala	1.75	3.85	11
28	Chile	40.95	90.29	428	55	Bulgaria	8.56	18.87	75	82	Tanzania	1.40	3.08	22
29	China	35.20	77.61	30,000	56	Dominican Republic	8.26	18.21	40	83	Kenya	1.01	2.22	14
30	North Korea	33.23	73.27	540	57	Pakistan	7.71	17.00	558	84	Mali	0.85	1.87	5
31	Senegal	27.89	61.49	142	58	Vietnam	7.52	16.58	350	85	Morocco	0.84	1.85	15
32	Israel	25.14	55.43	87	59	Puerto Rico	7.47	16.47	24	86	Somali	0.61	1.34	2
33	Venezuela	24.27	53.51	300	60	Mongolia	7.38	16.27	11	87	Indonesia	0.37	0.81	52
34	Iran	20.95	46.19	700	61	Syria	7.10	15.65	54	88	Uganda	0.25	0.55	3
35	Brazil	20.15	44.43	2,200	62	Panama	6.97	15.36	12	89	Nicaragua	0.23	0.50	15
										90	Niger	0.21	0.46	1

Source: U. S. Bureau of Mines.

152. Television Set Production

The data in this ranking refer to the production of television sets but make no distinction between sets made from domestically produced parts and those merely assembled from imported parts. Although manufacturing operations are widely dispersed, the industry exhibits such a high degree of concentration and specialization that only a handful of countries possess a full range of production capability.

Number of Countries: 54
Midpoint: 0.2965%
Period Covered: 1976
Type of Ranking: Production of Television Sets; Share of World Total and Total; Highest to Lowest

Highlights & Findings: Total world production of television sets is 56,990,000, up from 33,270,000 in 1967. The top five producing nations account for 67% of the total production.

Regions	Africa	Asia & Oceania	Europe	Western Hemisphere
Most	Egypt (40)	Japan (1)	Soviet Union (3)	United States (2)
Least	Ghana (53)	Hong Kong (54)	Bulgaria (43)	Ecuador (52)

Rank	Country	Production of Television Sets Share of World Total (%)	Total (000)	Rank	Country	Production of Television Sets Share of World Total (%)	Total (000)	Rank	Country	Production of Television Sets. Share of World Total (%)	Total (000)
	TOP 10			5	South Korea	4.0200	2,291	10	Poland	1.6897	963
1	Japan	30.0140	17,105	6	United Kingdom	3.6988	2,108				
2	United States	13.7217	7,820	7	France	3.1180	1,777		*UPPER MIDDLE*		
3	Soviet Union	13.3409	7,603	8	Brazil	2.8706	1,636	11	Mexico	1.2791	729
4	West Germany	6.5397	3,727	9	Italy	2.7987	1.595	12	Spain	1.2668	722

Rank	Country	Production of Television Sets Share of World Total (%)	Total (000)
13	Turkey	1.0861	619
14	East Germany	0.9843	561
15	Belgium	0.9791	558
16	Australia	0.9370	534
17	Rumania	0.8984	512
18	Czechoslovakia	0.8001	450
19	Canada	0.7703	439
20	Austria	0.7422	423
21	Hungary	0.7229	412
22	Yugoslavia	0.7053	402
23	Sweden	0.5965	340
24	Portugal	0.5351	305
25	Iran	0.4246	242
26	Finland	0.3965	226
27	Greece	0.3035	173
28	Argentina	0.2965	169

Rank	Country	Production of Television Sets Share of World Total (%)	Total (000)
	LOWER MIDDLE		
29	Indonesia	0.2912	166
30	New Zealand	0.2754	157
31	Malaysia	0.1895	108
32	Norway	0.1895	108
33	Philippines	0.1877	107
34	Ireland	0.1859	106
35	Chile	0.1807	103
36	Peru	0.1754	100
37	Venezuela	0.1509	86
38	Colombia	0.1333	76
39	Denmark	0.1245	71
40	Egypt	0.1245	71
41	Thailand	0.1228	70
42	El Salvador	0.1193	68
43	Bulgaria	0.1017	58

Rank	Country	Production of Television Sets Share of World Total (%)	Total (000)
44	Syria	0.1017	58
	BOTTOM 10		
45	Algeria	0.0842	48
46	Israel	0.0842	48
47	Tunisia	0.0789	45
48	Iraq	0.0438	25
49	Nigeria	0.0245	14
50	Trinidad & Tobago	0.0228	13
51	Jamaica	0.0105	6
52	Ecuador	0.0087	5
53	Ghana	0.0035	2
54	Hong Kong	0.0035	2

Source: *Yearbook of Industrial Statistics.*

153. Radio Receiver Production

The data in this ranking relate to the production of radio receivers. Because of severe competition and increased labor costs in developed countries, the industry has been gravitating toward Asia and is now heavily concentrated in Hong Kong, Japan and South Korea.

Number of Countries: 62
Midpoint: 0.1281%
Period Covered: 1976
Type of Ranking: Production of Radio Receivers; Share of World Total and Total; Highest to Lowest

Highlights & Findings: The total world production of radio receivers is 122,540,000, up from 87,500,000 in 1967. The top five countries account for 78% of the total production. The production figures ascribed to Hong Kong and South Korea relate to receivers assembled in the country and not units actually produced in the strict sense of the term.

Regions	Africa	Asia & Oceania	Europe	Western Hemisphere
Most	South Africa (21)	Hong Kong (1)	Soviet Union (4)	United States (3)
Least	Rwanda (59)	Israel (60)	Ireland (49)	Ecuador (62)

Rank	Country	Production of Radio Receivers Share of World Total (%)	Total (000)
	TOP 10		
1	Hong Kong	41.2036	50,491
2	Japan	13.6853	16,770
3	United States	10.4512	12,807
4	Soviet Union	6.9006	8,456
5	South Korea	5.3680	6,578
6	West Germany	4.4418	5,443
7	France	2.8219	3,485
8	Poland	1.6631	2,038
9	Belgium	1.4085	1,726
10	India	1.3677	1,676
	UPPER MIDDLE		
11	Mexico	0.9262	1,135
12	East Germany	0.9156	1,122
13	Indonesia	0.8976	1,100

Rank	Country	Production of Radio Receivers Share of World Total (%)	Total (000)
14	Italy	0.6455	791
15	Rumania	0.6455	791
16	Brazil	0.6193	759
17	United Kingdom	0.5900	723
18	Canada	0.5842	712
19	Portugal	0.4063	498
20	Spain	0.3133	384
21	South Africa	0.2554	313
22	Iran	0.2293	281
23	Hungary	0.2040	250
24	Czechoslovakia	0.1819	223
25	Finland	0.1517	186
26	Sweden	0.1517	186
27	Turkey	0.1460	179
28	Tanzania	0.1444	177
29	Bulgaria	0.1379	169
30	New Zealand	0.1289	158

Rank	Country	Production of Radio Recievers Share of World Total (%)	Total (000)
31	Egypt	0.1281	157
32	Morocco	0.1281	157
	LOWER MIDDLE		
33	Denmark	0.1175	144
34	Australia	0.1085	133
35	Philippines	0.1011	124
36	Cuba	0.0922	113
37	Nigeria	0.0913	112
38	Norway	0.0905	111
39	Yugoslavia	0.0889	109
40	Cameroon	0.0734	90
41	Ghana	0.0734	90
42	Tunisia	0.0726	89
43	Peru	0.0718	88
44	Vietnam	0.0709	87
45	Chile	0.0701	86

Rank	Country	Production of Radio Receivers Share of World Total (%)	Total (000)		Rank	Country	Production of Radio Receivers Share of World Total (%)	Total (000)		Rank	Country	Production of Radio Receivers Share of World Total (%)	Total (000)
46	Austria	0.0669	82		52	Zambia	0.0326	40		57	Trinidad & Tobago	0.0146	18
47	Ivory Coast	0.0652	80			BOTTOM 10				58	Central African Empire	0.0106	13
48	Venezuela	0.0603	74		53	Burma	0.0269	33		59	Rwanda	0.0097	12
49	Ireland	0.0587	72		54	Malawi	0.0261	32		60	Israel	0.0089	11
50	Sri Lanka	0.0448	55		55	Angola	0.0212	26		61	Jamaica	0.0057	7
51	Algeria	0.0359	44		56	Mozambique	0.0195	24		62	Ecuador	0.0016	2

Source: *U.N. Statistical Yearbook.*

154. Passenger Car Production

Production of passenger cars is almost entirely confined to the developed world and is therefore one of the true indices of industrial development. The data include units shipped in knocked-down form for local assembly in other countries.

Number of Countries: 23	**Highlights & Findings:** The total production of passenger cars worldwide was 29.22 million, up
Midpoint: 1.0506%	from 18.34 million in 1967 but slightly lower than the peak of 30 million units produced in 1973.
Period Covered: 1976	
Type of Ranking: Production of Passenger Cars; Share of World Total and Total; Highest to Lowest	

	Regions	Africa	Asia & Oceania	Europe	Western Hemisphere
	Most	N.A.	Japan (2)	West Germany (3)	United States (1)
	Least	N.A.	India (21)	Bulgaria (23)	Argentina (17)

Rank	Country	Production of Passenger Cars Share of World Total (%)	Total (000)		Rank	Country	Production of Passenger Cars Share of World Total (%)	Total (000)		Rank	Country	Production of Passenger Cars Share of World Total (%)	Total (000)
		TOP 5			8	Canada	3.8921	1,137.3		18	Yugoslavia	0.4757	139.0
1	United States	29.9541	8,752.6		9	Spain	2.6317	769.0					
2	Japan	17.2067	5,027.8		10	Brazil	1.9383	566.4			BOTTOM 5		
3	West Germany	12.1386	3,546.9		11	Australia	1.2628	369.0		19	Netherlands	0.2539	74.2
4	France	11.5947	3,388.0		12	Sweden	1.0506	307.0		20	Rumania	0.2429	71.0
5	Italy	5.0352	1,471.3		13	Mexico	0.7837	229.0		21	India	0.1300	38.0
					14	Poland	0.7837	229.0		22	Finland	0.0934	27.3
		MIDDLE			15	Czechoslovakia	0.6098	178.2		23	Bulgaria	0.0513	15.0
6	United Kingdom	4.5636	1,333.5		16	East Germany	0.5612	164.0					
7	Soviet Union	4.2402	1,239.0		17	Argentina	0.4863	142.1					

Source: *Yearbook of Industrial Statistics.*

155. Mineral Production Index

The Index of Mineral Production is constructed on the same basis as the Production Index of Manufacturing Industries (1970=100) and covers both mining and quarrying.

Number of Countries: 53
Midpoint: 107
Period Covered: Latest Available Year, 1974-76
Type of Ranking: Index of Mineral Production, 1970=100; Highest to Lowest

Highlights & Findings: Because minerals are depleting resources, mineral production is subject to slower growth rates than either manufacturing or agriculture. Where the index records unusual growth, as in Syria, on this ranking, it is the result of some new find, and the growth curve usually flattens out in the course of a few years. Although almost every country has some mineral deposits, only in about 50 countries does mineral production contribute a significant portion of the GDP.

Regions	Africa	Asia & Oceania	Europe	Western Hemisphere
Most	Egypt (2)	Syria (1)	Italy (3)	Brazil (20)
Least	Zambia (35)	Malaysia (47)	Portugal (52)	Venezuela (53)

Rank	Country	Index of Mineral Production	Rank	Country	Index of Mineral Production	Rank	Country	Index of Mineral Production
	TOP 10		18	Norway	112	36	Chile	102
1	Syria	345	19	Tunisia	112	37	India	102
2	Egypt	196	20	Brazil	109	38	Japan	101
3	Italy	192	21	South Korea	109	39	Czechoslovakia	100
4	Senegal	159	22	East Germany	108	40	Hungary	100
5	Iran	143	23	Ghana	108	41	Belgium	99
6	Turkey	136	24	Soviet Union	108	42	France	98
7	New Zealand	135	25	Canada	107	43	West Germany	98
8	Philippines	134	26	Finland	107			
9	Kenya	127	27	Mexico	107		*BOTTOM 10*	
10	Mozambique	124				44	Israel	97
				LOWER MIDDLE		45	Rhodesia (Zimbabwe)	96
	UPPER MIDDLE		28	Argentina	106	46	Malta	94
11	Morocco	120	29	Greece	106	47	Malaysia	93
12	Rumania	119	30	Yugoslavia	105	48	Sweden	91
13	United Kingdom	118	31	United States	104	49	Colombia	90
14	Spain	116	32	Netherlands	103	50	Luxembourg	89
15	Pakistan	115	33	Poland	103	51	Austria	83
16	Cyprus	114	34	South Africa	103	52	Portugal	81
17	Ireland	113	35	Zambia	103	53	Venezuela	61

Source: U.N. Statistical Yearbook.

156. Copper Production

Copper, one of the first metals known to man, was named after Cyprus, where it was mined in the ancient world. The chief commercial use of copper is derived from its electrical conductivity, and about half of the annual output of copper is used in the manufacture of electrical apparatus and wire. Copper is also used widely in roofing, plumbing, heat-exchanging devices such as refrigerator and air-conditioner coils and utensils. Another important use is in alloys such as brass, gun metal, money metal, and German silver. In recent years copper prices have fluctuated wildly, throwing the economies of those countries dependent on copper exports into a cycle of boom and bust.

Number of Countries: 54
Midpoint: 0.1658%
Period Covered: 1976
Type of Ranking: Production of Copper; Share of World Total and Total in Metric Tons; Highest to Lowest

Highlights & Findings: The total world production of copper is 7,840,000 tons, up from 5,030,000 in 1967. The top five nations account for 66% of world production.

Regions	Africa	Asia & Oceania	Europe	Western Hemisphere
Most	Zambia (4)	Philippines (9)	Soviet Union (2)	United States (1)
Least	Kenya (54)	South Korea (44)	France (53)	Ecuador (52)

Rank	Country	Production of Copper Share of World Total (%)	Total (000 tons)
		TOP 10	
1	United States	18.5790	1,456.6
2	Soviet Union	14.4132	1,130.0
3	Chile	12.7691	1,001.1
4	Zambia	10.8367	849.6
5	Canada	9.5293	747.1
6	Zaire	5.6619	443.9
7	Poland	3.4056	267.0
8	Peru	3.0803	241.5
9	Philippines	3.0306	237.6
10	Australia	2.7844	218.3
		UPPER MIDDLE	
11	South Africa	2.5114	196.9
12	Papua New Guinea	2.2512	176.5
13	Yugoslavia	1.5318	120.1
14	China	1.2755	100.0
15	Mexico	1.1352	89.0
16	Japan	1.0408	81.6
17	Bulgaria	0.7270	57.0
18	Rhodesia (Zimbabwe)	0.6377	50.0

Rank	Country	Production of Copper Share of World Total (%)	Total (000 tons)
19	Sweden	0.5727	44.9
20	Finland	0.5612	44.0
21	Namibia	0.5012	39.3
22	Spain	0.4528	35.5
23	Norway	0.4017	31.5
24	Turkey	0.3890	30.5
25	India	0.3673	28.8
26	East Germany	0.2040	16.0
27	North Korea	0.1658	13.0
		LOWER MIDDLE	
28	Botswana	0.1594	12.5
29	Czechoslovakia	0.1288	10.1
30	Albania	0.1275	10.0
31	Mauritania	0.1198	9.4
32	Cyprus	0.0969	7.6
33	Uganda	0.0892	7.0
34	Bolivia	0.0599	4.7
35	Morocco	0.0586	4.6
36	Portugal	0.0586	4.6
37	Ireland	0.0522	4.1

Rank	Country	Production of Copper Share of World Total (%)	Total (000 tons)
38	Cuba	0.0369	2.9
39	Israel	0.0267	2.1
40	Brazil	0.0255	2.0
41	Mozambique	0.0255	2.0
42	West Germany	0.0204	1.6
43	Iran	0.0191	1.5
44	South Korea	0.0178	1.4
		BOTTOM 10	
45	Austria	0.0153	1.2
46	Italy	0.0127	1.0
47	Nicaragua	0.0076	0.6
48	Algeria	0.0051	0.4
49	Congo	0.0051	0.4
50	Hungary	0.0050	0.4
51	Argentina	0.0038	0.3
52	Ecuador	0.0038	0.3
53	France	0.0025	0.2
54	Kenya	0.0012	0.1

Sources: *World Metal Statistics,* London
U.S. Bureau of Mines

157. Silver Production

Silver is one of the earliest metals to be used by man. Although sometimes found uncombined in nature, most silver is obtained from its ores. The metal is prepared in various ways depending on the nature of its occurrence; the greatest quantity is obtained during the refining of lead and copper by the Parkes process.

Number of Countries: 50
Midpoint: 0.4670%
Period Covered: 1976
Type of Ranking: Production of Silver; Share of World Total and Total in Metric Tons; Highest to Lowest

Highlights & Findings: The total world production of silver is 9,420 tons up from 8,120 tons in 1967. The top five nations account for 65% of world production. Included among the top five are the fabled silver mines of Mexico and Peru, whose output dazzled the Spanish conquistadores over four centuries ago.

Regions	Africa	Asia & Oceania	Europe	Western Hemisphere
Most	South Africa (16)	Australia (6)	Soviet Union (1)	Mexico (2)
Least	Rhodesia (Zimbabwe) (45)	Fiji (47)	Portugal (50)	Haiti (48)

Rank	Country	Production of Silver Share of World Total (%)	Total (tons)
		TOP 10	
1	Soviet Union	14.5435	1,370
2	Mexico	14.0764	1,326
3	Canada	13.5987	1,281
4	Peru	12.4840	1,176
5	United States	11.3375	1,068
6	Australia	7.6640	722
7	Japan	3.0679	289
8	Poland	2.6539	250

Rank	Country	Production of Silver Share of World Total (%)	Total (tons)
9	Chile	2.4097	227
10	Yugoslavia	2.1019	198
		UPPER MIDDLE	
11	Bolivia	1.6772	158
12	Sweden	1.5286	144
13	France	1.2101	114
14	Spain	1.0297	97
15	Honduras	0.9766	92

Rank	Country	Production of Silver Share of World Total (%)	Total (tons)
16	South Africa	0.9341	88
17	Zaire	0.8174	77
18	South Korea	0.6050	57
19	Argentina	0.5732	54
20	East Germany	0.5307	50
21	North Korea	0.5307	50
22	Italy	0.5095	48
23	Philippines	0.4883	46
24	Papua New Guinea	0.4777	45

Rank	Country	Production of Silver Share of World Total (%)	Total (tons)
25	Namibia	0.4670	44
	LOWER MIDDLE		
26	Czechoslovakia	0.4246	40
27	Rumania	0.4246	40
28	West Germany	0.3503	33
29	Zambia	0.3503	33
30	Ireland	0.2760	26
31	China	0.2653	25

Rank	Country	Production of Silver Share of World Total (%)	Total (tons)
32	Finland	0.2547	24
33	Bulgaria	0.2441	23
34	Burma	0.2441	23
35	Morocco	0.2229	21
36	Greece	0.1592	15
37	Brazil	0.0849	8
38	Tunisia	0.0849	8
39	Nicaragua	0.0636	6
40	Algeria	0.0530	5
41	El Salvador	0.0530	5

Rank	Country	Production of Silver Share of World Total (%)	Total (tons)
	BOTTOM 9		
42	Colombia	0.0318	3
43	India	0.0318	3
44	Indonesia	0.0318	3
45	Rhodesia (Zimbabwe)	0.0318	3
46	Ecuador	0.0212	2
47	Fiji	0.0106	1
48	Haiti	0.0106	1
49	Hungary	0.0106	1
50	Portugal	0.0106	1

Source: U. S. Bureau of Mines.

158. Gold Production

Gold is possibly the first metal used by man. Known as the king of metals (because it is unaffected by moisture, oxygen and ordinary acids), gold is widely distributed on land and large amounts are also present in the sea. Most gold is found in the form of dust, grains, flakes and nuggets and usually in association with silver and other metals. In many countries, including until recently the United States, gold formed the basis of the monetary system; from 1900 to 1933 the U.S. currency was fully backed by gold. In many countries it is still illegal for private persons or firms to own gold bullion. Until the special drawing rights were created by the International Monetary Fund, all international payments were settled by central bank gold movements. Gold is also one of the most widely smuggled articles in the world. Because Indian women have an inordinate fondness for gold ornaments, India since time immemorial has been one of the major countries to which the gold-smuggling trade is directed. Kuwait and the United Arab Emirates serve as staging areas for transshipment of gold into India in small sailing vessels.

Number of Countries: 46
Midpoint: 0.1589%
Period Covered: 1976
Type of Ranking: Production of Gold; Share of World Total and Total in Kg and Lb; Highest to Lowest

Highlights & Findings: The world production of gold is 998,000 kg (2,200,590 lb), down from 1,282,200 kg (2,827,251 lb) in 1965. Gold has been steadily declining in production as it has been gaining in value; how much of this decline is attributable to smuggling is not clear. Because South Africa alone accounts for 71% of total production, no other country exerts any influence on supply or prices.

Although the Soviet Union is one of the world's major producers of gold its production figures are only infrequently released. In 1975 the United States Bureau of Mines (as cited in *Europa Yearbook*) estimated its production figures at 283,500 kg (625,000 lb). In the following table this output would have placed the Soviet Union second.

Regions	Africa	Asia & Oceania	Europe	Western Hemisphere
Most	South Africa (1)	Japan (4)	West Germany (11)	Canada (2)
Least	Kenya (45)	New Zealand (39)	Portugal (34)	Surinam (46)

Rank	Country	Production of Gold Share of World Total (%)	Kg	Total Lb
	TOP 10			
1	South Africa	71.2925	711,500	1,568,857.5
2	Canada	5.2561	52,456	115,665.5

Rank	Country	Production of Gold Share of World Total (%)	Kg	Total lb
3	United States	3.2663	32,598	71,878.6
4	Japan	3.2527	32,462	71,578.7
5	Rhodesia (Zimbabwe)	2.5050	25,000	55,125.0

Rank	Country	Production of Gold Share of World Total (%)	Kg	Total Lb
6	Papua New Guinea	2.0811	20,770	45,797.8
7	Ghana	1.6652	16,619	36,664.8
8	Philippines	1.5557	15,526	34,234.8

Rank	Country	Production of Gold Share of World Total (%)	Kg	Total Lb
9	Australia	1.5492	15,462	34,093.7
10	Dominican Republic	1.2895	12,870	28,378.3
	UPPER MIDDLE			
11	West Germany	1.0810	10,789	23,789.7
12	Colombia	0.9472	9,454	20,846.0
13	Mexico	0.5074	5,064	11,166.1
14	Brazil	0.4931	4,922	10,853.0
15	Yugoslavia	0.4895	4,886	10,773.6
16	Chile	0.4070	4,062	8,956.7
17	Sweden	0.3669	3,662	8,074.7
18	Zaire	0.2691	2,686	5,922.6
19	Peru	0.2516	2,511	5,536.7
20	India	0.2215	2,211	4,875.2
21	Fiji	0.2026	2,022	4,458.5

Rank	Country	Production of Gold Share of World Total (%)	Kg	Total Lb
22	Nicaragua	0.1954	1,951	4,301.9
23	France	0.1589	1,586	3,497.1
	LOWER MIDDLE			
24	Ethiopia	0.0934	933	2,057.2
25	Bolivia	0.0897	896	1,975.6
26	Finland	0.0819	818	1,803.7
27	South Korea	0.0516	515	1,133.0
28	Venezuela	0.0515	514	1,130.8
29	Guyana	0.0487	487	1,073.8
30	Argentina	0.0369	369	813.6
31	Indonesia	0.0355	355	782.7
32	Ecuador	0.0343	343	756.3
33	Zambia	0.0341	341	751.9
34	Portugal	0.0247	247	544.6

Rank	Country	Production of Gold Share of World Total (%)	Kg	Total Lb
35	Malaysia	0.0141	141	310.9
36	Liberia	0.0140	140	308.7
	BOTTOM 10			
37	Gabon	0.0096	96	211.7
38	French Guyana	0.0087	87	191.8
39	New Zealand	0.0076	76	167.6
40	Honduras	0.0041	41	90.4
41	Cameroon	0.0030	30	66.1
42	Congo	0.0015	15	33.0
43	Madagascar	0.0005	5	11.0
44	Tanzania	0.0002	2	4.4
45	Kenya	0.0001	1	2.2
46	Surinam	0.0001	1	2.2

Source: International Monetary Fund.

159. Iron Ore Production

Until the 20th century the production of iron ore was one of the most important indices of industrial power: the term Iron Age has been applied to the period of recorded history beginning with the general use of iron as early as 1900 B.C. and continuing into modern times. Although iron ore has lost its strategic preeminence, its availability is an important element in industrial development.

Number of Countries: 54
Midpoint: 0.1850%
Period Covered: 1976
Type of Ranking: Production of Iron Ore; Share of World Total and Total in Metric Tons; Highest to Lowest

Highlights & Findings: The total world production of iron ore is 512,700,000 tons, up from 338,200,000 tons in 1967. The top five countries account for 55% of the world total.

Regions	Africa	Asia & Oceania	Europe	Western Hemisphere
Most	Liberia (9)	Australia (3)	Soviet Union (1)	Brazil (2)
Least	Morocco (45)	Thailand (53)	Denmark (54)	Argentina (47)

Rank	Country	Production of Iron Ore Share of World Total (%)	Total (000 tons)
	TOP 10		
1	Soviet Union	25.5295	130,890
2	Brazil	11.8189	60,596
3	Australia	11.3639	58,263
4	United States	9.7819	50,152
5	Canada	6.8252	34,993
6	China	6.3389	32,500
7	India	5.2984	27,165
8	Sweden	3.7271	19,109
9	Liberia	2.7325	14,010
10	France	2.6900	13,792
	UPPER MIDDLE		
11	Venezuela	2.2596	11,585
12	South Africa	1.9114	9,800
13	Mauritania	1.2157	6,233
14	Chile	1.2065	6,186

Rank	Country	Production of Iron Ore Share of World Total (%)	Total (000 tons)
15	Spain	0.7733	3,965
16	North Korea	0.7411	3,800
17	Mexico	0.7107	3,644
18	Peru	0.6024	3,089
19	Norway	0.4956	2,541
20	Turkey	0.3696	1,895
21	Angola	0.3245	1,664
22	Algeria	0.2906	1,490
23	Yugoslavia	0.2806	1,439
24	Swaziland	0.2397	1,229
25	Austria	0.2272	1,165
26	United Kingdom	0.2145	1,100
27	Greece	0.1850	949
	LOWER MIDDLE		
28	Sierra Leone	0.1786	916
29	Finland	0.1497	768

Rank	Country	Production of Iron Ore Share of World Total (%)	Total (000 tons)
30	West Germany	0.1462	750
31	Bulgaria	0.1458	748
32	Rumania	0.1417	727
33	Iran	0.1306	670
34	Egypt	0.1211	621
35	Luxembourg	0.1199	615
36	Czechoslovakia	0.0994	510
37	Colombia	0.0971	498
38	Japan	0.0877	450
39	Rhodesia (Zimbabwe)	0.0748	384
40	Philippines	0.0690	354
41	South Korea	0.0678	348
42	Tunisia	0.0497	255
43	Italy	0.0421	216
44	Poland	0.0419	215
	BOTTOM 10		
45	Morocco	0.0393	202

Rank	Country	Production of Iron Ore Share of World Total (%)	Total (000 tons)	Rank	Country	Production of Iron Ore Share of World Total (%)	Total (000 tons)	Rank	Country	Production of Iron Ore Share of World Total (%)	Total (000 tons)
46	Malaysia	0.0335	172	49	Portugal	0.0054	28	52	Hong Kong	0.0038	19
47	Argentina	0.0312	160	50	East Germany	0.0040	21	53	Thailand	0.0027	14
48	Hungary	0.0276	142	51	Belgium	0.0039	20	54	Denmark	0.0005	3

Source: U.S. Bureau of Mines.

160. Diamond Production

The data in this ranking relate to mine and alluvial production of uncut diamonds and cover both gem and industrial stones. Industrial diamonds are small and impure diamonds, such as bort and carbonado, suitable only for industrial uses as abrasives.

Number of Countries: 19
Midpoint: 1.1306%
Period Covered: 1976
Type of Ranking: Production of Diamonds; Share of World Total and Total in Metric Carats; Highest to Lowest

Highlights & Findings: The total world production of diamonds is 39.8 million carats, comprising 28,850,000 metric carats of industrial diamonds and 10,950,000 metric carats of gems. Production has not risen significantly since 1967, when the output was 36,150,000 carats. Obviously the data refer only to legally recorded production; there is vast illegal trade in smuggled diamonds, estimated at over 50% of actual production. Most of the producers in the free world belong to a cartel formed to maintain the artificially high level of diamond prices. The power behind this cartel is the legendary firm of De Beers Consolidated Mines, controlled by the South African financier Harry Oppenheimer.

Regions	Africa	Asia & Oceania	Europe	Western Hemisphere
Most	Zaire (1)	India (16)	Soviet Union (2)	Venezuela (8)
Least	Lesotho (19)	Indonesia (17)	N.A.	Guyana (18)

Rank	Country	Production of Diamonds Share of World Total (%)	Total (000 metric carats)	Rank	Country	Production of Diamonds Share of World Total (%)	Total (000 metric carats)	Rank	Country	Production of Diamonds Share of World Total (%)	Total (000 metric carats)
	TOP 5			7	Sierra Leone	3.7688	1,500		*BOTTOM 5*		
1	Zaire	29.6984	11,820	8	Venezuela	2.0929	833	15	Ivory Coast	0.1507	60
2	Soviet Union	24.8743	9,900	9	Angola	1.6582	660	16	India	0.0502	20
3	South Africa	17.6432	7,022	10	Tanzania	1.1306	450	17	Indonesia	0.0376	15
4	Botswana	5.9321	2,361	11	Central African Empire	1.0175	405	18	Guyana	0.0351	14
5	Ghana	5.8869	2,343	12	Liberia	1.0050	400	19	Lesotho	0.0075	3
				13	Brazil	0.6783	270				
	MIDDLE			14	Guinea	0.2010	80				
6	Namibia	4.2562	1,694								

Source: U.S. Bureau of Mines.

ENERGY

Energy may be described as a doomsday indicator —one that is bound to get worse before it gets worse! It therefore needs to be looked at closely, even if with quiet desperation. Energy is bound up with the whole mythology of industrial civilization; it is inconceivable that civilization as we know it can exist without energy, certainly not its marvels, its conveniences, its extravagances, and its 1,001 useless luxuries. What is wrong with energy is that both its production and consumption are lopsided. The production is monopolized by the Arabs whose main use for the black gold is for blackmail; the consumption is monopolized by the Americans, many of whom believe they have a constitutional right to a third of the world's energy supplies. The energy shortage, the first phase of which we are now in, has been triggered by two phenomena that will soon converge: the first is the finite supply of the nonrenewable fossil fuels that generate most of the energy presently consumed; the second is the soaring demand caused by a growing population, the greater number and variety of technological goods available and the increased affluence that has brought these goods within the reach of a larger proportion of the population.

The principal objective of this section is to present a global framework of data on energy supply and demand. The first group of rankings is an overview presenting production of energy in terms of total production, annual growth rate of production and consumption per capita. The share of fuel in imports is examined in another ranking. The next five groups of rankings deal with the principal sources of energy: nuclear (including production of uranium), coal, petroleum, natural gas and electricity. For coal and natural gas there are rankings on production and reserves; for petroleum, rankings on production, reserves and refinery capacity. A related ranking on gasoline consumption appears under "Consumption."

161. Energy Production

Energy statistics have assumed critical importance and, next to food, are perhaps the most alarming indicators to watch in the future. While the world's insatiable energy requirements are climbing relentlessly year by year, the finite supplies are being depleted at a faster rate; surely one day the oil wells and the coal pits will be empty holes, and man will be faced with the dreadful task of sustaining an industrial civilization without the natural resources that he had squandered so recklessly within a century. This could well become the ultimate future shock that could destroy the complacency on which technological society is based.

Number of Countries: 122
Midpoint: 5.04 Million Metric Tons of Coal Equivalent
Period Covered: 1976
Type of Ranking: Total Production of Energy in Million Metric Tons of Coal Equivalent; Highest to Lowest

Highlights & Findings: Total world production of energy is 8.951 billion metric tons of coal equivalent, up from 8.447 billion metric tons of coal equivalent in 1973. The regional distribution is as follows (in million metric tons of coal equivalent): Africa, 536.69; North America, 2,308.50; South America, 100.59; Central America, 328.46; Middle East, 1,688.49; Asia excluding the Middle East, 350.54; Europe, 680.13; Oceania, 125.95; and the Soviet Union, 2,831.27. (The disparity between production and consumption of energy is revealed by comparing this ranking with the "Energy Consumption Per Capita" ranking).

Regions	Africa	Asia & Oceania	Europe	Western Hemisphere
Most	Nigeria (13)	Saudi Arabia (3)	Soviet Union (2)	United States (1)
Least	Mauritius (121)	Nepal (113)	Faroe Islands (118)	Panama (122)

Rank	Country	Production of Energy (million metric tons of coal equivalent)	Rank	Country	Production of Energy (million metric tons of coal equivalent)	Rank	Country	Production of Energy (million metric tons of coal equivalent)
	TOP 10		41	Trinidad & Tobago	18.42	82	Cuba	0.25
1	United States	2,049.70	42	Gabon	16.69	83	Costa Rica	0.18
2	Soviet Union	1,674.10	43	South Korea	16.65	84	Cameroon	0.16
3	Saudi Arabia	643.99	44	Syria	14.94	85	Surinam	0.15
4	China	614.78	45	Ecuador	14.10	86	Uruguay	0.15
5	Iran	467.36	46	Bulgaria	14.08	87	Sri Lanka	0.14
6	Canada	258.80	47	Turkey	12.20	88	Israel	0.13
7	Poland	200.35	48	Malaysia	12.06	89	Uganda	0.11
8	Venezuela	199.00	49	Austria	9.96	90	Lebanon	0.10
9	United Kingdom	198.18	50	Belgium	8.81	91	El Salvador	0.09
10	Kuwait	169.10	51	Sweden	8.73	92	Kenya	0.09
			52	Pakistan	8.33	93	Paraguay	0.08
	UPPER MIDDLE		53	Greece	7.68	94	Honduras	0.06
11	Iraq	167.70	54	Bahrain	7.17	95	Luxembourg	0.06
12	West Germany	165.88	55	Peru	7.06	96	Tanzania	0.06
13	Nigeria	153.58	56	Angola	6.75	97	Guatemala	0.05
14	Libya	145.58	57	New Zealand	6.00	98	Ivory Coast	0.05
15	United Arab Emirates	141.21	58	Tunisia	5.80	99	New Caledonia	0.05
16	India	121.09	59	Chile	5.73	100	Nicaragua	0.05
17	Australia	119.86	60	Vietnam	5.07	101	Sudan	0.05
18	Netherlands	118.06	61	Bolivia	5.04	102	Barbados	0.04
19	Indonesia	113.84				103	Ethiopia	0.04
20	Algeria	91.62		*LOWER MIDDLE*		104	Liberia	0.04
21	Mexico	91.44	62	Albania	4.55	105	Malawi	0.04
22	Rumania	83.90	63	Switzerland	4.21	106	Puerto Rico	0.04
23	Czechoslovakia	83.84	64	Afghanistan	3.62	107	Laos	0.03
24	East Germany	79.25	65	Rhodesia (Zimbabwe)	3.42	108	Papua New Guinea	0.03
25	South Africa	76.32	66	Congo	3.00			
26	North Korea	48.10	67	Ireland	2.41		*BOTTOM 14*	
27	France	45.10	68	Zaire	2.37	109	Dominican Republic	0.02
28	Argentina	41.82	69	Burma	1.78	110	Haiti	0.02
29	Japan	38.21	70	Zambia	1.62	111	Jamaica	0.02
30	Qatar	37.71	71	Finland	1.41	112	Madagascar	0.02
31	Norway	31.41	72	Bangladesh	1.14	113	Nepal	0.02
32	Yugoslavia	29.42	73	Mongolia	1.10	114	Reunion	0.02
33	Italy	28.43	74	Morocco	0.95	115	Rwanda	0.02
34	Egypt	27.26	75	Portugal	0.79	116	Burundi	0.01
35	Oman	26.89	76	Philippines	0.76	117	Central African Empire	0.01
36	Brazil	26.47	77	Thailand	0.68	118	Faroe Islands	0.01
37	Brunei	25.96	78	Mozambique	0.56	119	Guinea	0.01
38	Hungary	22.21	79	Ghana	0.51	120	Mali	0.01
39	Spain	19.00	80	Denmark	0.29	121	Mauritius	0.01
40	Colombia	18.73	81	Iceland	0.29	122	Panama	0.01

Source: *World Energy Supplies.*

162. Annual Growth Rate of Energy Production

No natural resource is being exploited so thoroughly as energy, especially fossil fuels. All commercial forms of primary energy are included under this rubric: coal and lignite, crude petroleum, natural gas and natural gas liquids, and hydro and nuclear electricity. This ranking covers a long period, emphasizing long-range patterns at the expense of recent developments.

Number of Countries: 103	Highlights & Findings: The growth rate was highest in oil-exporting countries with 12.8% and
Midpoint: 7.1%	lowest in industrialized countries with 3.0%. In between, low-income countries had a growth rate
Period Covered: 1960-75	of 9.4%, middle-income countries 8.5% and Communist countries 4.6%. Thirty-five countries had
Type of Ranking: Average Annual Growth Rate of Energy Production; Highest to Lowest	a growth rate exceeding 10% and nine countries—most of them industrialized—had negative growth rates.

Regions	Africa	Asia	Europe	Western Hemisphere
Most	Zambia (5)	Syria (1)	Greece (26)	Paraguay (2)
Least	Rhodesia (Zimbabwe) (91)	Japan (101)	Denmark (103)	Chile (98)

Rank	Country	Annual Growth Rate of Energy Production (%)	Rank	Country	Annual Growth Rate of Energy Production (%)	Rank	Country	Annual Growth Rate of Energy Production (%)
	TOP 10		35	Algeria	10.1	70	Sweden	3.5
1	Syria	70.9	36	Guatemala	9.9	71	Kuwait	3.4
2	Paraguay	44.0	37	Kenya	9.9	72	Mozambique	3.3
3	Malaysia	34.6	38	Mongolia	9.8	73	Philippines	3.3
4	Afghanistan	34.1	39	Sri Lanka	9.8	74	Finland	3.2
5	Zambia	34.1	40	North Korea	9.5	75	Italy	3.1
6	Israel	32.8	41	Albania	9.2	76	Bulgaria	3.0
7	Angola	30.0	42	Ivory Coast	9.0	77	Uruguay	3.0
8	Nigeria	29.5	43	Tanzania	9.0	78	Trinidad & Tobago	2.9
9	Malawi	28.2	44	Costa Rica	8.9	79	United States	2.9
10	Ghana	27.3	45	Pakistan	8.9	80	New Zealand	2.8
			46	Norway	8.7	81	Zaire	2.8
	UPPER MIDDLE		47	Canada	8.6	82	Colombia	2.6
11	Liberia	26.3	48	Indonesia	8.5	83	Peru	2.0
12	Honduras	23.9	49	Dominican Republic	8.0	84	Hungary	1.9
13	Libya	21.7	50	Egypt	7.4	85	Morocco	1.6
14	Rwanda	21.4	51	Brazil	7.1	86	Czechoslovakia	1.3
15	Nicaragua	20.9				87	Portugal	1.3
16	Ecuador	20.3		*LOWER MIDDLE*		88	Cameroon	1.1
17	Nepal	20.1	52	Turkey	6.8	89	Spain	1.1
18	Cuba	18.5	53	South Korea	6.2	90	East Germany	0.6
19	Congo	17.9	54	Mexico	6.0	91	Rhodesia (Zimbabwe)	0.6
20	Thailand	17.2	55	Argentina	5.8	92	Vietnam	0.5
21	Bolivia	16.1	56	Soviet Union	5.7			
22	Mali	15.8	57	Madagascar	5.5		*BOTTOM 11*	
23	Netherlands	15.3	58	Tunisia	5.5	93	Austria	0.3
24	Panama	13.6	59	Iraq	5.2	94	Venezuela	0.3
25	Central African Empire	13.3	60	Uganda	5.1	95	Ireland	−0.1
26	Greece	13.2	61	El Salvador	5.0	96	Jamaica	−0.6
27	Iran	13.0	62	China	4.6	97	West Germany	−0.8
28	Saudi Arabia	12.8	63	Burma	4.5	98	Chile	−1.0
29	Ethiopia	12.5	64	Switzerland	4.3	99	United Kingdom	−1.3
30	Sudan	11.7	65	Rumania	4.2	100	France	−2.8
31	Lebanon	11.1	66	India	4.1	101	Japan	−3.9
32	Papua New Guinea	11.0	67	Yugoslavia	4.0	102	Belgium	−7.6
33	Australia	10.4	68	Poland	3.9	103	Denmark	−20.5
34	Guinea	10.4	69	South Africa	3.8			

Source: *World Energy Supplies.*

163. Energy Consumption per Capita

Energy is consumed in many forms and obtained from a variety of sources, such as coal and lignite, gasoline, kerosene, fuel oils, natural gas, and hydro-electric power and also derivatives, such as bri-quettes, refinery gases, coke, manufactured gas, thermal electric power, liquefied petroleum gases and benzols. The total world consumption of energy in 1975 was 8 billion tons of coal equivalent or 2,028 kg (4,471 lb) per capita. The figures by region are:

Region	Total (in million metric tons of coal equivalent)	Per Capita Kg	Lb
Africa	157.28	393	866
North America	2,575.61	10,888	24,008
Central America	166.26	1,174	2,588
South America	144.59	813	1,792
Middle East	126.58	1,055	2,326
Asia (excluding Middle East)	673.68	545	1,201
Europe	1,467.52	4,023	8,870
Oceania	100.74	4,782	10,544

Number of Countries: 178
Midpoint: 671 kg (1,479 lb)
Period Covered: 1975
Type of Ranking: Per Capita Consumption of Energy in Kg and Lb; Highest to Lowest

Highlights & Findings: Qatar, which leads the list, consumed more than 3,500 times as much energy as Nepal, which ranks last. Qatar's position is a result of its vast petrochemical industry, which consumes enormous quantities of energy. Twenty-five of the 31 bottom countries are in Africa. Contrary to popular notions, the United States consumes less energy per capita than six smaller countries.

Regions	Africa	Asia & Oceania	Europe	Western Hemisphere
Most	South Africa (44)	Qatar (1)	Luxembourg (3)	Netherlands Antilles (5)
Least	Burundi (177)	Nepal (178)	Albania (84)	Haiti (170)

Rank	Country	Per Capita Consumption of Energy in Kg	Lb
	TOP 10		
1	Qatar	35,328	77,898
2	Christmas Island	20,537	45,284
3	Luxembourg	15,504	34,186
4	United Arab Emirates	13,699	30,206
5	Netherlands Antilles	12,231	26,969
6	Bahrain	12,079	26,634
7	United States	10,999	24,252
8	New Caledonia	9,933	21,902
9	Canada	9,880	21,785
10	Brunei	9,628	21,229
	UPPER MIDDLE		
11	Kuwait	8,718	19,223
12	Czechoslovakia	7,151	15,768
13	East Germany	6,835	15,071
14	Nauru	6,626	14,610
15	Australia	6,485	14,229
16	Bahamas	6,279	13,845
17	Sweden	6,178	13,622
18	Netherlands	5,784	12,753
19	Belgium	5,584	12,312
20	Soviet Union	5,546	12,229
21	Greenland	5,465	12,050
22	West Germany	5,345	11,785
23	Denmark	5,268	11,616
24	United Kingdom	5,265	11,609
25	Poland	5,007	11,040
26	Bulgaria	4,781	10,542
27	Finland	4,766	10,509
28	Iceland	4,720	10,407
29	Norway	4,607	10,158
30	Faroe Islands	4,325	9,536
31	St. Pierre & Miquelon	4,122	9,089
32	France	3,944	8,696
33	Rumania	3,803	8,385
34	Austria	3,700	8,158
35	Switzerland	3,642	8,031
36	Hungary	3,624	7,991
37	Japan	3,622	7,986
38	Puerto Rico	3,203	7,062
39	Trinidad & Tobago	3,132	6,906
40	New Zealand	3,111	6,859
41	Ireland	3,097	6,829
42	Bermuda	3,090	6,813
43	Italy	3,012	6,641
44	South Africa	2,953	6,511
45	Cayman Islands	2,838	6,257

Rank	Country	Per Capita Consumption of Energy in Kg	Lb
46	North Korea	2,808	6,191
47	Israel	2,806	6,187
48	Venezuela	2,639	5,819
49	Antigua	2,184	4,815
50	Singapore	2,151	4,742
51	Spain	2,147	4,734
52	Greece	2,090	4,608
53	Surinam	2,063	4,549
54	Yugoslavia	1,930	4,255
55	Argentina	1,754	3,867
56	Jamaica	1,427	3,146
57	Saudi Arabia	1,398	3,082
58	Iran	1,353	2,983
59	Libya	1,299	2,864
60	Cyprus	1,278	2,818
61	Gibraltar	1,267	2,793
62	Mexico	1,221	2,692
62	Cuba	1,157	2,551
64	British Virgin Islands	1,121	2,472
65	Hong Kong	1,119	2,467
66	Guyana	1,114	2,456
67	Mongolia	1,091	2,405
68	Barbados	1,078	2,377
69	Martinique	1,062	2,341
70	South Korea	1,038	2,289
71	Malta	1,032	2,275
72	Gabon	1,026	2,262
73	Portugal	983	2,167
74	French Guyana	953	2,101
75	Uruguay	942	2,077
76	Lebanon	928	2,046
77	Pacific Islands	909	2,004
78	French Polynesia	877	1,933
79	Panama	865	1,907
80	Chile	765	1,687
81	Rhodesia (Zimbabwe)	764	1,684
82	Algeria	754	1,662
83	Falkland Islands	750	1,653
84	Albania	741	1,634
85	Montserrat	716	1,578
86	Iraq	713	1,572
87	China	693	1,528
88	Peru	682	1,504
89	Colombia	671	1,479
	LOWER MIDDLE		
90	Brazil	670	1,477
91	Turkey	630	1,389

Rank	Country	Per Capita Consumption of Energy in Kg	Lb
92	Fiji	582	1,283
93	Guadeloupe	564	1,243
94	New Hebrides	561	1,237
95	Malaysia	552	1,217
96	Costa Rica	544	1,199
97	Belize	520	1,146
98	Zambia	504	1,111
99	Seychelles	481	1,060
100	Nicaragua	479	1,056
101	Syria	477	1,051
102	Dominican Republic	458	1,010
103	Djibouti	450	992
104	Tunisia	447	985
105	Ecuador	442	974
106	Reunion	434	957
107	Jordan	408	899
108	Egypt	405	893
109	Liberia	404	890
110	Ivory Coast	366	807
111	Gilbert Islands	346	763
112	St. Lucia	345	760
113	Oman	334	736
114	South Yemen	328	723
115	Philippines	326	719
116	Grenada	323	712
117	Bolivia	303	668
118	Thailand	284	626
119	St. Kitts-Nevis-Anguilla	280	617
120	Mauritius	279	615
121	Papua New Guinea	278	613
122	Morocco	274	604
123	Macao	264	582
124	El Salvador	248	546
125	Solomon Islands	241	531
126	Guatemala	237	522
127	Honduras	232	511
128	India	221	487
129	Congo	209	461
130	Dominica	208	458
131	Senegal	195	430
132	Mozambique	186	410
133	Vietnam	186	410
134	Pakistan	183	403
135	Ghana	182	401
136	Indonesia	178	392
137	Angola	174	383
138	Kenya	174	383
139	Western Samoa	160	353

Rank	Country	Per Capita Consumption of Energy in Kg	Lb
140	Paraguay	153	337
141	St. Vincent	152	335
142	Sudan	140	308
143	Sri Lanka	127	280
144	Sierra Leone	116	255
145	Mauritania	108	238
146	Cameroon	104	229
147	Sao Tome & Principe	102	225
148	Equatorial Guinea	101	222
149	Guinea	92	203
150	Nigeria	90	198
151	Guinea-Bissau	82	181
152	Zaire	78	172
153	Madagascar	71	156

Rank	Country	Per Capita Consumption of Energy in Kg	Lb
154	Tanzania	70	154
155	Gambia	66	145
156	Togo	65	143
157	Laos	63	139
158	Cape Verde Islands	61	134
159	Malawi	56	123
160	Uganda	55	121
161	Afghanistan	52	114
161	Benin	52	114
163	Burma	51	112
164	Comoros	51	112
165	Yemen Arab Republic	49	108
166	Chad	39	86
167	Somalia	36	79

Rank	Country	Per Capita Consumption of Energy in Kg	Lb
168	Niger	35	77
	BOTTOM 10		
169	Central African Empire	34	75
170	Haiti	30	66
171	Ethiopia	29	64
172	Bangladesh	28	61
173	Mali	25	55
174	Upper Volta	20	44
175	Cambodia	16	35
176	Rwanda	14	30
177	Burundi	13	28
178	Nepal	10	22

Source: *World Energy Supplies.*

164. Share of Fuel in Imports

The plight of oil-consuming countries and nonoil-producing developing countries is nowhere more dramatically highlighted than in the growing share of fuel in their import bills. The crippling costs of importing fuel for domestic needs has also served to widen the gap between the rich and the poor nations and to create a new class of rich nations. The severe economic imbalances and dislocations that this division of the world into oil producers and oil consumers has caused will become fully apparent only during the 1980s and 1990s.

Number of Countries: 120
Midpoint: 9.6%
Period Covered: Latest Available Year, 1974-76
Type of Ranking: Share of Fuel in Imports; Highest to Lowest

Highlights & Findings: The figures include fuel imported by refineries and intended for exports. This explains the presence of small countries with large refineries, such as the Bahamas, the Netherlands Antilles and Trinidad and Tobago at the top of the list. Most countries in the upper and lower middle have no internal energy resources and are thus totally dependent on oil imports.

Regions	Africa	Asia & Oceania	Europe	Western Hemisphere
Most	Senegal (6)	Japan (4)	Spain (7)	Bahamas (1)
Least	Uganda (118)	Iran (120)	Soviet Union (107)	Venezuela (116)

Rank	Country	Share of Fuel in Imports (%)
	TOP 10	
1	Bahamas	92.2
2	Netherlands Antilles	86.1
3	Trinidad & Tobago	50.6
4	Japan	43.9
5	Bahrain	42.4
6	Senegal	29.5
7	Spain	29.5
8	United States	27.9
9	Singapore	27.4
10	Kenya	26.4
	UPPER MIDDLE	
11	Italy	25.8
12	India	25.7
13	Philippines	23.5

Rank	Country	Share of Fuel in Imports (%)
14	France	22.4
15	Finland	21.5
16	Greece	20.4
17	Panama	20.3
18	South Korea	19.9
19	Netherlands	19.5
20	Jamaica	19.2
21	Tanzania	18.2
22	United Kingdom	18.1
23	West Germany	18.0
24	Argentina	17.7
25	Sweden	17.6
26	Turkey	17.5
27	Honduras	16.9
28	Ghana	16.6
29	Israel	16.5

Rank	Country	Share of Fuel in Imports (%)
30	Denmark	16.4
31	Fiji	16.0
32	Portugal	16.0
33	Chad	15.9
34	Cyprus	15.2
35	Brazil	15.1
36	New Zealand	14.7
37	Yugoslavia	14.7
38	Belgium-Luxembourg	14.2
39	Uruguay	14.1
40	Zambia	13.6
41	Hungary	13.5
42	Ireland	13.4
43	Guyana	13.0
44	Ivory Coast	12.8
45	Niger	12.6

Rank	Country	Share of Fuel in Imports (%)	Rank	Country	Share of Fuel in Imports (%)	Rank	Country	Share of Fuel in Imports (%)
46	Bangladesh	12.5	71	Mozambique	8.4	98	Benin	5.7
47	Iceland	12.3	72	Pakistan	8.1	99	Egypt	5.7
48	Austria	12.2	73	Congo	7.9	100	South Africa	5.0
49	Malaysia	12.0	74	Sri Lanka	7.9	101	Yemen Arab Republic	5.0
50	Tunisia	11.7	75	Indonesia	7.8	102	Papua New Guinea	4.9
51	Thailand	11.3	76	Afghanistan	7.7	103	Lebanon	4.8
52	Norway	11.2	77	Mauritania	7.7	104	Syria	4.6
53	Cuba	11.1	78	Liberia	7.6	105	Angola	4.5
54	Canada	10.8	79	Togo	7.5	106	Somalia	4.3
55	Switzerland	10.7	80	Chile	7.4	107	Soviet Union	3.9
56	Costa Rica	10.6	81	Guatemala	7.4	108	Ecuador	3.1
57	Jordan	10.6	82	El Salvador	7.3	109	Brunei	2.3
58	Zaire	9.8	83	Nicaragua	7.3	110	Libya	2.0
59	Czechoslovakia	9.7	84	Reunion	7.3			
			85	Mexico	7.1		_BOTTOM 10_	
	LOWER MIDDLE		86	Dominican Republic	6.9	111	Algeria	1.6
60	Australia	9.6	87	Mauritius	6.9	112	Nigeria	1.1
61	Madagascar	9.6	88	Rumania	6.9	113	Colombia	1.0
62	Ethiopia	9.4	89	Barbados	6.6	114	Kuwait	0.9
63	Bulgaria	9.1	90	Morocco	6.5	115	Gabon	0.8
64	Haiti	9.1	91	Hong Kong	6.2	116	Venezuela	0.8
65	Cameroon	8.9	92	Burma	6.0	117	Saudi Arabia	0.7
66	Malawi	8.9	93	Burundi	6.0	118	Uganda	0.7
67	Mali	8.9	94	Peru	6.0	119	Iraq	0.3
68	Malta	8.8	95	Sudan	6.0	120	Iran	0.2
69	Upper Volta	8.8	96	Sierra Leone	5.9			
70	Rwanda	8.7	97	Poland	5.8			

Source: _World Energy Supplies._

165. Nuclear Energy Production

The total world production of nuclear energy in the mid-1970s was 397 billion kwh, less than one-twentieth of the world production of electric energy. However, while electric energy production grew only by 76% during the 10-year period between 1966 and 1975, nuclear energy grew by over 1,000%. This growth has been achieved despite the continuing opposition of environmentalists and formidable technological problems.

Number of Countries: 19
Midpoint: 7.561 million kwh
Period Covered: 1976
Type of Ranking: Total Production in Million Kwh: Highest to Lowest

Highlights & Findings: In 1966 there were only 12 nations producing nuclear energy. Of these, Puerto Rico suspended production in 1968. New nuclear plants were established in eight other countries: Argentina, Bulgaria, Czechoslovakia, India, the Netherlands, Pakistan, Spain and Switzerland. The United Kingdom was the leading producer until 1970, when it was overtaken by the United States. Nuclear energy is not produced in Africa.

Regions	Asia & Oceania	Europe	Western Hemisphere
Most	Japan(3)	United Kingdom(2)	United States(1)
Least	Pakistan(18)	Czechoslovakia(19)	Argentina(17)

Rank	Country	Total in Million Kwh	Rank	Country	Total in Million Kwh	Rank	Country	Total in Million Kwh
	TOP 5		7	France	15,100		_BOTTOM 5_	
1	United States	191,108	8	Soviet Union	14,000	15	Italy	3,807
2	United Kingdom	36,155	9	Belgium	10,037	16	India	3,253
3	Japan	34,079	10	Switzerland	7,561	17	Argentina	2,572
4	West Germany	24,262	11	Spain	7,555	18	Pakistan	600
5	Canada	16,430	12	East Germany	5,271	19	Czechoslovakia	442
			13	Bulgaria	4,989			
	MIDDLE		14	Netherlands	3,872			
6	Sweden	15,993						

Source: _World Energy Supplies._

166. Uranium Reserves

Uranium was discovered by M. H. Klaproth in 1789 and named after the planet Uranus; it was isolated in 1841. Uranium-235 is the only naturally-occurring fission fuel, but this isotope is only about one part in 140 of natural uranium. Because the supply of uranium-235 is so limited, the use of fast breeder reactors that convert nonfissionable uranium-238 to fissionable plutonium-239 is becoming increasingly popular. Uranium is found most widely dispersed in nature, although rarely found uncombined with other minerals. It is about 40 times as abundant as silver in the earth's crust. The most important mineral in which uranium is found is pitchblende, mined in Zaire and Canada. No figures are available for the Soviet Union.

Number of Countries: 27
Midpoint: 0.4353%
Period Covered: 1976
Type of Ranking: Reserves of Uranium; Share of World Total and Total in Metric Tons; Highest to Lowest

Highlights & Findings: The total world reserves of uranium are estimated at 1,562,000 tons; the total production in 1976 was 22,293 tons; based on this rate of production, the reserves are expected to last for 70 years.

Regions	Africa	Asia & Oceania	Europe	Western Hemisphere
Most	South Africa (2)	Australia (3)	France (6)	United States (1)
Least	Zaire (24)	South Korea (20)	Sweden (27)	Mexico (17)

Rank	Country	Reserves of Uranium Share of World Total (%)	Total (tons)	Rank	Country	Reserves of Uranium Share of World Total (%)	Total (tons)	Rank	Country	Reserves of Uranium Share of World Total (%)	Total (tons)
	TOP 5			9	Gabon	1.2804	20,000	20	South Korea	0.1920	3,000
1	United States	33.4827	523,000	10	Brazil	1.1650	18,200	21	Finland	0.1216	1,900
2	South Africa	19.5902	306,000	11	Argentina	1.1395	17,800				
3	Australia	18.5019	289,000	12	Central African Empire	0.5121	8,000		*BOTTOM 6*		
4	Canada	10.6914	167,000	13	Japan	0.4929	7,700	22	Austria	0.1152	1,800
5	Niger	4.7375	74,000	14	Portugal	0.4353	6,800	23	United Kingdom	0.1152	1,800
				15	Spain	0.4353	6,800	24	Zaire	0.1152	1,800
	MIDDLE			16	Greenland	0.3713	5,800	25	West Germany	0.0960	1,500
6	France	2.3687	37,000	17	Mexico	0.3008	4,700	26	Italy	0.0768	1,200
7	India	1.9078	29,800	18	Yugoslavia	0.2880	4,500	27	Sweden	0.0640	1,000
8	Algeria	1:7925	28,000	19	Turkey	0.2624	4,100				

Source: International Atomic Energy Agency.

167. Coal Production

Coal is the least efficient and the most ecologically harmful of all fossil fuels. Its production, especially through strip mining, often disfigures the landscape and leaves permanent scars. Its burning adds to air pollution. Nevertheless, it is the most plentiful of all fossil fuels and as such may be the most significant source of energy after other sources have been depleted. Because it is providentially located in consuming countries coal offers these countries a viable alternative to overdependence on petroleum-exporting nations.

Number of Countries: 52
Midpoint: 0.0956%
Period Covered: 1976
Type of Ranking: Production of Coal: Share of World Total and Total in Metric Tons; Highest to Lowest

Highlights & Findings: Total annual world production of coal is 2,419,993,000 metric tons, up only slightly from 2,143,189,000 in 1970. However, coal production has actually declined in a number of countries such as the United Kingdom and Japan, reflecting the switchover from coal to oil in the 1950s and 1960s. Coal production is expected to snap back in all those countries where the uncertainties of oil supplies are beginning to be felt. The top five countries together account for 86% of world coal production.

Regions	Africa	Asia & Oceania	Europe	Western Hemisphere
Most	South Africa (8)	China (3)	Soviet Union (2)	United States (1)
Least	Tanzania (52)	Burma (49)	Italy (51)	Venezuela (47)

Rank	Country	Coal Production Share of World Total (%)	Total (000 tons)
		TOP 10	
1	United States	24.2018	585,684
2	Soviet Union	20.4288	494,377
3	China	19.8347	480,000
4	Poland	7.4092	179,303
5	United Kingdom	5.1166	123,822
6	India	4.1681	100,870
7	West Germany	3.9629	95,902
8	South Africa	3.1293	75,730
9	Australia	2.8024	67,820
10	North Korea	1.6528	40,000
		UPPER MIDDLE	
11	Czechoslovakia	1.1802	28,652
12	France	0.9628	23,300
13	Canada	0.8594	20.798
14	Japan	0.7601	18,396
15	South Korea	0.6788	16,428
16	Spain	0.4419	10,696
17	Belgium	0.3166	7,662
18	Rumania	0.2938	7,111
19	Mexico	0.2334	5,650
20	Vietnam	0.2231	5,400
21	Turkey	0.1914	4,632
22	Colombia	0.1495	3,620
23	Brazil	0.1345	3,256
24	Honduras	0.1212	2,934
25	Rhodesia (Zimbabwe)	0.1165	2,820
26	New Zealand	0.0956	2,315
		LOWER MIDDLE	
27	Pakistan	0.0557	1,349
28	Chile	0.0514	1,245
29	Iran	0.0371	900
30	Zambia	0.0323	784
31	Morocco	0.0290	702
32	Argentina	0.0254	615
33	Yugoslavia	0.0242	587
34	Norway	0.0214	519
35	East Germany	0.0189	458
36	Mozambique	0.0153	371
37	Nigeria	0.0128	310
38	Bulgaria	0.0121	295
39	Botswana	0.0092	224
40	Mongolia	0.0084	205
41	Indonesia	0.0079	193
42	Portugal	0.0079	193
		BOTTOM 10	
43	Afghanistan	0.0066	160
44	Philippines	0.0065	158
45	Swaziland	0.0052	126
46	Zaire	0.0045	109
47	Venezuela	0.0036	89
48	Ireland	0.0020	49
49	Burma	0.0005	13
50	Sweden	0.0004	12
51	Italy	0.00008	2
52	Tanzania	0.00004	1

Source: *World Energy Supplies.*

168. Coal Reserves

Coal is a general term applied to a whole series of carbon-containing fuels each of which differ in the amount of fixed carbon they contain. These are in descending order of usefulness: anthracite, semianthracite, semibituminous coal, bituminous coal and subbituminous coal or black lignite. Bituminous coal is used extensively by industries, by railroads and in making coke. Anthracite, which is nearly pure carbon, is mainly used as domestic fuel.

Number of Countries: 59
Midpoint: 0.0083%
Period Covered: 1976
Type of Ranking: Reserves of Coal; Share of World Total and Total in Metric Tons; Highest to Lowest

Highlights & Findings: World coal reserves are estimated at 8.134 trillion tons, or enough to last for 3,362 years at the 1976 production figure of 2.4 billion tons. The total includes both proved recoverable reserves and additional resources based on information gained from geological information; these comprise undiscovered deposits in fuel-bearing areas and unexplored extensions of known deposits. Coal reserves are virtually monopolized by the top five countries, which account for a staggering 95% of the total. The pattern of distribution here is more unequal than that of any other mineral.

Regions	Africa	Asia & Oceania	Europe	Western Hemisphere
Most	South Africa (10)	China (3)	Soviet Union (1)	United States (2)
Least	Egypt (54)	New Caledonia (53)	Italy (58)	Honduras (59)

| Rank Country | Reserves of Coal | | Rank Country | Reserves of Coal | | Rank Country | Reserves of Coal | |
	Share of World Total (%)	Total (million tons)		Share of World Total (%)	Total (million tons)		Share of World Total (%)	Total (million tons)
TOP 10			20 Peru	0.0286	2,334	40 Pakistan	0.0023	190
1 Soviet Union	49.0923	3,993,357	21 Brazil	0.0220	1,790	41 Nigeria	0.0022	180
2 United States	28.1000	2,285,763	22 Bangladesh	0.0180	1,471	42 Norway	0.0018	152
3 China	12.4287	1,011,000	23 South Korea	0.0178	1,450	43 Yugoslavia	0.0012	104
4 West Germany	2.8279	230,034	24 Turkey	0.0158	1,291	44 Morocco	0.0011	96
5 United Kingdom	2.0015	162.814	25 Vietnam	0.0122	1,000	45 Sweden	0.0011	90
6 Australia	1.3752	111,865	26 Venezuela	0.0103	845	46 Afghanistan	0.0010	85
7 Canada	1.1929	97,041	27 Zaire	0.0088	720	47 Zambia	0.00098	80
8 India	0.9951	80,953	28 Hungary	0.0087	714	48 Ireland	0.0005	48
9 Poland	0.5623	45,741	29 Mozambique	0.0086	700	49 Bulgaria	0.0004	34
10 South Africa	0.5450	44,339	30 New Zealand	0.0083	678			
						BOTTOM 10		
UPPER MIDDLE			**LOWER MIDDLE**			50 Madagascar	0.0003	30
11 Mexico	0.1475	12,000	31 Rumania	0.0072	590	51 Burma	0.0002	21
12 Czechoslovakia	0.1422	11,573	32 Indonesia	0.0070	573	52 Algeria	0.0002	20
13 Japan	0.0915	7,443	33 Argentina	0.0068	555	53 New Caledonia	0.0001	15
14 Rhodesia (Zimbabwe)	0.0812	6,613	34 Botswana	0.0062	506	54 Egypt	0.0001	13
15 Swaziland	0.0617	5,022	35 France	0.0054	443	55 Portugal	0.00009	8
16 Colombia	0.0504	4,100	36 Iran	0.0047	385	56 Austria	0.00004	4
17 Chile	0.0484	3,945	37 Tanzania	0.0045	370	57 Greenland	0.00002	2
18 Netherlands	0.0455	3,705	38 Belgium	0.0031	253	58 Italy	0.00001	1
19 Spain	0.0291	2,370	39 East Germany	0.0024	200	59 Honduras	0.00001	1

Source: *World Energy Supplies.*

169. Crude Petroleum Production

Petroleum production is the world's largest industry in terms of the value of output, estimated at between $500 and $600 billion annually (based on pre-1979 OPEC prices). Of this amount close to one-fifth is estimated to go into OPEC coffers and the rest is accounted for by tankerage, refineries, distribution markups, and oil company profits. It is significant that of the top *Fortune* 40 companies in the world 17 are in the petroleum sector and each of these companies has an annual revenue that exceeds the GNP of over half the nations of the world.

The production figures are given in metric tons following U. N. usage although barrels and gallons are the more popular units. Because of differences in the specific gravity of crude petroleum tons can be converted into barrels only approximately. Middle East crude petroleum has an average conversion rate of about 7.5 barrels to a metric ton.

Number of Countries: 65
Midpoint: 0.1929%
Period Covered: 1976
Type of Ranking: Production of Crude Petroleum; Share of World Total and Total in Metric Tons; Highest to Lowest

Highlights & Findings: The total world production of crude petroleum is 2,863,518,000 tons, up from 2,276,868,000 in 1970, representing a 25% growth in six years. The top five nations account for 63% of world production. On a scale of exporters, however, Saudi Arabia is the leader followed by Iran, Venezuela and Iraq.

Regions	Africa	Asia & Oceania	Europe	Western Hemisphere
Most	Nigeria (8)	Saudi Arabia (2)	Soviet Union (1)	United States (3)
Least	Morocco (63)	Thailand (64)	East Germany (60)	Guatemala (65)

| Rank Country | Production of Crude Petroleum | | Rank Country | Production of Crude Petroleum | | Rank Country | Production of Crude Petroleum | |
	Share of World Total (%)	Total in (000 tons)		Share of World Total (%)	Total in (000 tons)		Share of World Total (%)	Total in (000 tons)
TOP 10			7 Kuwait	3.7731	108,046	12 Indonesia	2.5910	74,195
1 Soviet Union	18.1482	519,677	8 Nigeria	3.6137	103,479	13 Canada	2.1704	62,152
2 Saudi Arabia	15.8128	425,804	9 United Arab Emirates	3.3268	95,265	14 Algeria	1.7608	50,423
3 United States	14.0111	401,211	10 Libya	3.2635	93,452	15 Mexico	1.4435	41,336
4 Iran	10.3049	295,084				16 Qatar	0.8387	24,018
5 Venezuela	4.1959	120,153	**UPPER MIDDLE**			17 Argentina	0.7263	20,800
6 Iraq	3.9211	112,284	11 China	2.9683	85,000	18 Australia	0.7164	20,515

Rank Country	Production of Crude Petroleum Share of World Total (%)	Total in (000 tons)	Rank Country	Production of Crude Petroleum Share of World Total (%)	Total in (000 tons)	Rank Country	Production of Crude Petroleum Share of World Total (%)	Total in (000 tons)
19 Oman	0.6387	18,290	35 Yugoslavia	0.1354	3,880	53 New Zealand	0.0166	477
20 Egypt	0.5851	16,756	36 Peru	0.1318	3,775	54 Poland	0.0158	455
21 Rumania	0.5133	14,700	37 Tunisia	0.1295	3,710	55 Pakistan	0.0106	305
22 Norway	0.4829	13,828	38 Bahrain	0.1013	2,902			
23 United Kingdom	0.4061	11,630	39 Turkey	0.0906	2,595	*BOTTOM 10*		
24 Gabon	0.3947	11,305	40 Albania	0.0873	2,500	56 Denmark	0.0068	195
25 Trinidad & Tobago	0.3837	10,990	41 Hungary	0.0748	2,142	57 Cuba	0.0050	144
26 Brunei	0.3527	10,100	42 Congo	0.0699	2,002	58 Czechoslovakia	0.0045	131
27 Syria	0.3506	10,041	43 Austria	0.0674	1,931	59 Bulgaria	0.0040	117
28 Ecuador	0.3313	9,488	44 Bolivia	0.0660	1,890	60 East Germany	0.0020	60
29 India	0.3023	8,659	45 Spain	0.0618	1,772	61 Israel	0.0012	36
30 Brazil	0.2836	8,121	46 Netherlands	0.0478	1,371	62 Barbados	0.0006	20
31 Malaysia	0.2802	8,026	47 Zaire	0.0436	1,251	63 Morocco	0.0003	9
32 Colombia	0.2637	7,553	48 Burma	0.0406	1,163	64 Thailand	0.0002	8
33 West Germany	0.1929	5,524	49 Italy	0.0384	1,102	65 Guatemala	0.0002	7
			50 France	0.0369	1,057			
LOWER MIDDLE			51 Chile	0.0327	938			
34 Angola	0.1569	4,494	52 Japan	0.0202	580			

Sources: *World Energy Supplies;* World Oil, Houston.

170. Petroleum Reserves

Industrial civilization is heavily dependent on petroleum for motive power, lubrication, fuel, dyes, drugs and many synthetics. Estimates of the total petroleum reserves have been revised upward almost every year since its exploitation began on a commercial basis in the 1860s. Yet the demand is so great that oil companies have been unable to recover and refine sufficient quantities to meet all needs. Petroleum has also acquired in recent years a political and strategic dimension conferring on the few nations with disproportionately vast reserves a degree of leverage and clout that they could never possess otherwise. Oil-exporting nations have also learned to manipulate their oil wealth as a bargaining chip in international negotiations, thus converting oil into a sword of Damocles hanging over the industrialized West. On the other hand, the widespread use of petroleum has also caused serious environmental problems and in many cases perhaps irreversible damage to air, land and water resources.

Number of Countries: 61
Midpoint: 0.1726%
Period Covered: 1976
Type of Ranking: Reserves of Petroleum; Share of World Total and Total in Metric Tons; Highest to Lowest.

Highlights & Findings: The total world reserves of petroleum are estimated at 74.713 billion metric tons, enough to last for 26 years at the 1976 rate of production (see previous ranking). The top five nations account for 60% of world reserves. Because exploration is being conducted throughout the world constantly, the picture might change dramatically with a few discoveries. For example, new reserves have been reported recently in Mexico that may bring that country into the top five class.

Regions	Africa	Asia & Oceania	Europe	Western Hemisphere
Most	Libya (8)	Saudi Arabia (1)	Soviet Union (3)	United States (6)
Least	Zaire (49)	Japan (57)	Czechoslovakia (61)	Guatemala (59)

Rank Country	Reserves of Petroleum Share of World Total (%)	Total (million tons)	Rank Country	Reserves of Petroleum Share of World Total (%)	Total (million tons)	Rank Country	Reserves of Petroleum Share of World Total (%)	Total (million tons)
TOP 10			9 Venezuela	3.4906	2,608	16 Canada	1.1269	842
1 Saudi Arabia	20.6858	15,455	10 China	3.2939	2,461	17 Norway	1.0506	785
2 Kuwait	13.4233	10,029				18 Qatar	0.9021	674
3 Soviet Union	10.9110	8,152	*UPPER MIDDLE*			19 Oman	0.5782	432
4 Iran	8.8284	6,596	11 Nigeria	2.2245	1,662	20 India	0.5300	396
5 Iraq	6.3375	4,735	12 Indonesia	2.0705	1,547	21 Syria	0.5112	382
6 United States	5.5960	4,181	13 United Kingdom	1.8376	1,373	22 Argentina	0.4845	362
7 United Arab Emirates	4.7274	3,532	14 Algeria	1.6476	1,231	23 Australia	0.4109	307
8 Libya	4.3419	3,244	15 Mexico	1.5084	1,127	24 Tunisia	0.4001	299

Rank	Country	Reserves of Petroleum Share of World Total (%)	Total (million tons)
25	Brunei	0.3399	254
26	Egypt	0.2917	218
27	Malaysia	0.2623	196
28	Denmark	0.2449	183
29	Angola	0.2395	179
30	Rumania	0.2141	160
31	Colombia	0.1726	129
	LOWER MIDDLE		
32	Brazil	0.1472	110
33	Peru	0.1311	98
34	Trinidad & Tobago	0.1231	92
35	Gabon	0.1017	76
36	New Zealand	0.1003	75

Rank	Country	Reserves of Petroleum Share of World Total (%)	Total (million tons)
37	Congo	0.0856	64
38	Chile	0.0682	51
39	Italy	0.0642	48
40	Yugoslavia	0.0629	47
41	West Germany	0.0588	44
42	Bahrain	0.0481	36
43	Spain	0.0441	33
44	Hungary	0.0401	30
45	Austria	0.0307	23
46	Albania	0.0254	19
47	Bolivia	0.0254	19
48	Greece	0.0254	19
49	Zaire	0.0254	19
50	Netherlands	0.0173	13

Rank	Country	Reserves of Petroleum Share of World Total (%)	Total (million tons)
51	Pakistan	0.0160	12
52	Turkey	0.0160	12
	BOTTOM 9		
53	Burma	0.0120	9
54	Denmark	0.0093	7
55	France	0.0093	7
56	Poland	0.0066	5
57	Japan	0.0053	4
58	East Germany	0.0040	3
59	Guatemala	0.0040	3
60	Bulgaria	0.0026	2
61	Czechoslovakia	0.0026	2

Source: *World Energy Supplies.*

171. Petroleum Refinery Capacity

Petroleum refinery capacity is the theoretical maximum capability of crude oil distillation plants. The actual capacity may vary depending on the density of the crude oil and may be less than the theoretical by 2 to 3% on the average.

Number of Countries: 109
Midpoint: 6,000,000 Metric Tons
Period Covered: 1976
Type of Ranking: Petroleum Refinery Capacity in Metric Tons; Highest to Lowest

Highlights & Findings: World petroleum refinery distillation capacity is estimated at 3,170,593,000 metric tons (excluding the Soviet Union and China, for which no figures are available). Nearly 70% of this capacity is concentrated in Europe and North America with 1,117,690,000 tons and 1,098,340,000 tons respectively. The other 30% is distributed among other continents as follows: Africa 72,854,000 tons; South America 198,710,000 tons; Asia 642,299,000 tons; and Oceania 40,700,000 tons.

Regions	Africa	Asia & Oceania	Europe	Western Hemisphere
Most	South Africa (26)	Japan (2)	Italy (3)	United States (1)
Least	Sierra Leone (101)	Mongolia (109)	Cyprus (92)	Barbados (107)

Rank	Country	Petroleum Refinery Capacity (000 tons)
	TOP 10	
1	United States	779,320
2	Japan	287,000
3	Italy	207,510
4	France	169,500
5	West Germany	153,900
6	United Kingdom	145,600
7	Canada	103,950
8	Netherlands	102,130
9	Venezuela	77,750
10	Spain	74,050
	UPPER MIDDLE	
11	Belgium	55,955
12	Brazil	51,300
13	Mexico	47,870
14	Singapore	46,260
15	Iran	40,260
16	Netherlands Antilles	40,100
17	Argentina	39,500
18	Australia	35,500
19	Saudi Arabia	35,000

Rank	Country	Petroleum Refinery Capacity (000 tons)
20	India	31,960
21	Kuwait	30,450
22	Bahamas	26,750
23	Indonesia	25,140
24	Rumania	23,500
25	Trinidad & Tobago	23,050
26	South Africa	22,000
27	South Korea	21,750
28	East Germany	18,800
29	Czechoslovakia	17,000
30	Puerto Rico	16,580
31	Poland	16,000
32	Bahrain	15,550
33	Finland	15,000
34	Austria	14,300
35	Sweden	14,000
36	Turkey	14,000
37	Philippines	13,570
38	Greece	12,900
39	Norway	12,800
40	Bulgaria	12,000
41	Yugoslavia	12,000

Rank	Country	Petroleum Refinery Capacity (000 tons)
42	Denmark	11,225
43	Egypt	11,100
44	Israel	11,000
45	Hungary	10,200
46	Panama	10,000
47	Iraq	9,175
48	Peru	9,060
49	South Yemen	8,900
50	Colombia	8,670
51	Thailand	8,410
52	Switzerland	6,850
53	Portugal	6,500
54	Cuba	6,350
55	Chile	6,000
	LOWER MIDDLE	
56	Algeria	5,790
57	Libya	5,624
58	Kenya	4,750
59	Syria	4,520
60	Malaysia (West)	3,900
61	Morocco	3,900

Rank	Country	Petroleum Refinery Capacity (000 tons)
62	Pakistan	3,690
63	New Zealand	3,500
64	Sarawak	3,500
65	Albania	3,000
66	Nigeria	3,000
67	Ireland	2,970
68	Lebanon	2,500
69	Uruguay	2,450
70	Ecuador	2,190
71	Jamaica	1,850
72	Sri Lanka	1,850
73	Angola	1,750
74	Guam	1,700
75	Bangladesh	1,680
76	Dominican Republic	1,500
77	Ivory Coast	1,500
78	Ghana	1,450

Rank	Country	Petroleum Refinery Capacity (000 tons)
79	Burma	1,320
80	Sudan	1,300
81	Bolivia	1,290
82	Guatemala	1,250
83	Gabon	1,200
84	Tunisia	1,200
85	Jordan	1,145
86	Zambia	1,100
87	Rhodesia (Zimbabwe)	1,000
88	Antigua	900
89	Tanzania	850
90	Zaire	850
91	Mozambique	800
92	Cyprus	750
93	El Salvador	750
94	Liberia	750
95	Madagascar	750

Rank	Country	Petroleum Refinery Capacity (000 tons)
96	Nicaragua	750
97	Senegal	750
98	United Arab Emirates	750
99	Ethiopia	740
	BOTTOM 10	
100	Honduras	700
101	Sierra Leone	700
102	Cambodia	600
103	Martinique	550
104	Paraguay	500
105	Costa Rica	470
106	Qatar	369
107	Barbados	150
108	Brunei	90
109	Mongolia	70

Source: *World Energy Supplies.*

172. Natural Gas Production

The production of natural gas has become critical in industrial countries, where it is being used extensively as an illuminant and a fuel. The main constraint is that the construction of pipelines—until recently the only means of transporting natural gas—involves enormous engineering problems and expense. Because of the short life span of proved resources, the construction of new pipelines is not commercially viable. Since its boiling point is very low, natural gas is not easy to liquefy or maintain in its liquid state. Although cryogenic technology has now advanced to the point where such liquefaction is technologically possible, the weight of the containers (made of stainless steel) necessary to contain liquefied natural gas (LNG) limits its usefulness.

Number of Countries: 62
Midpoint: 0.1465%
Period Covered: 1976
Type of Ranking: Production of Natural Gas; Share of World Total and Total in Teracalories; Highest to Lowest

Highlights & Findings: The total production of natural gas worldwide is 11,681,458 teracalories, up from 9,257,825 in 1970. The top five nations account for 80% of world production.

Regions:	Africa	Asia & Oceania	Europe	Western Hemisphere
Most	Algeria (12)	Iran (7)	Soviet Union (2)	United States (1)
Least	Congo (59)	Burma (62)	Spain (61)	Barbados (60)

Rank	Country	Production of Natural Gas Share of World Total (%)	Total (teracalories)
	TOP 10		
1	United States	42.7758	4,996,843
2	Soviet Union	22.8422	2,668,307
3	Netherlands	6.9059	806,711
4	Canada	5.7622	673,111
5	United Kingdom	3.1018	362,347
6	Rumania	2.8292	330,499
7	Iran	1.8087	211,284
8	West Germany	1.3823	161,473
9	Italy	1.2268	143,318
10	Mexico	1.0297	120,286

Rank	Country	Production of Natural Gas Share of World Total (%)	Total (teracalories)
	UPPER MIDDLE		
11	Venezuela	1.0124	118,270
12	Algeria	0.8035	93,867
13	Indonesia	0.7052	82,379
14	Brunei	0.6601	77,110
15	France	0.5694	66,524
16	Argentina	0.5478	63,995
17	Poland	0.4963	57,981
18	Saudi Arabia	0.4708	55,000
19	Australia	0.4516	52,759
20	Kuwait	0.4496	51,978

Rank	Country	Production of Natural Gas Share of World Total (%)	Total (teracalories)
21	Hungary	0.4148	48,457
22	Pakistan	0.3748	43,783
23	China	0.3127	36,530
24	Libya	0.3037	35,488
25	East Germany	0.2303	26,904
26	Japan	0.2270	26,525
27	Afghanistan	0.2026	23,678
28	Austria	0.1793	20,950
29	Bahrain	0.1738	20,303
30	Iraq	0.1583	18,497
31	Yugoslavia	0.1465	17,124

Rank	Country	Production of Natural Gas Share of World Total (%)	Total (teracalories)
	LOWER MIDDLE		
32	Colombia	0.1424	16,645
33	Trinidad & Tobago	0.1350	15,774
34	Bolivia	0.1256	14,681
35	Qatar	0.1177	13,756
36	Chile	0.0949	11,090
37	Egypt	0.0941	11,000
38	India	0.0909	10,625
39	New Zealand	0.0762	8,903
40	United Arab Emirates	0.0700	8,181
41	Bangladesh	0.0643	7,513

Rank	Country	Production of Natural Gas Share of World Total (%)	Total (teracalories)
42	Czechoslovakia	0.0623	7,287
43	Brazil	0.0581	6,787
44	Nigeria	0.0504	5,890
45	Peru	0.0362	4,240
46	Norway	0.0276	3,234
47	Tunisia	0.0205	2,401
48	Albania	0.0128	1,500
49	Syria	0.0092	1,081
50	Malaysia	0.0071	836
51	Morocco	0.0068	798
52	Israel	0.0045	535

Rank	Country	Production of Natural Gas Share of World Total (%)	Total (teracalories)
	BOTTOM 10		
53	Gabon	0.0039	466
54	Ecuador	0.0027	326
55	Bulgaria	0.0026	312
56	Belgium	0.0024	282
57	Angola	0.0017	200
58	Cuba	0.0016	196
59	Congo	0.0012	149
60	Barbados	0.0003	37
61	Spain	0.0001	12
62	Burma	0.000008	1

Sources: *World Energy Supplies*.

173. Natural Gas Reserves

Because of its flammability and its high high caloric value, natural gas is used widely as a fuel and as an illuminant. Although generally believed to be a by-product of petroleum, it is found sometimes at a distance from petroleum fields, leading some geologists to conclude that it has a separate origin. Until recently it was flared off in many countries, but the construction of natural gas pipelines has enabled the maximum utilization of this important source of energy.

Number of Countries: 60
Midpoint: 0.2859%
Period Covered: 1976
Type of Ranking: Reserves of Natural Gas; Share of World Total and Total in Cubic Meters; Highest to Lowest

Highlights & Findings: The total world reserves of natural gas are estimated at 63.301 trillion cubic meters. The caloric value of gas varies from one country to another. It is highest in Ecuador (11,570 kilocalories per cubic meter) and lowest in East Germany (3,120 kilocalories per cubic meter). The top five nations account for 68% of the world's natural gas reserves. Technology has now advanced to the point where liquefaction of natural gas is commercially feasible (although it requires special and expensive containers), and this is bound to affect transnational trade in natural gas.

Regions	Africa	Asia & Oceania	Europe	Western Hemisphere
Most	Algeria (4)	Iran (2)	Soviet Union (1)	United States (3)
Least	Guinea (59)	Turkey (60)	Spain (56)	Brazil (50)

Rank	Country	Reserves of Natural Gas Share of World Total (%)	Total (billion cubic meters)
	TOP 10		
1	Soviet Union	34.9378	22,116
2	Iran	16.7750	10,619
3	United States	9.6633	6,117
4	Algeria	5.1673	3,271
5	Saudi Arabia	3.2779	2,075
6	Netherlands	2.7787	1,759
7	Canada	2.6060	1,650
8	Nigeria	2.3001	1,456
9	Kuwait	2.0994	1,329
10	Qatar	2.0678	1,309
	UPPER MIDDLE		
11	Venezuela	1.9272	1,220
12	Australia	1.2843	813

Rank	Country	Reserves of Natural Gas Share of World Total (%)	Total (billion cubic meters)
13	United Kingdom	1.2780	809
14	Libya	1.2685	803
15	Iraq	1.2195	772
16	Norway	1.1453	725
17	China	0.9399	595
18	United Arab Emirates	0.9273	587
19	Mexico	0.9178	581
20	Indonesia	0.8056	510
21	Pakistan	0.6650	421
22	Malaysia	0.5371	340
23	West Germany	0.4676	296
24	Bahrain	0.3933	249
25	Trinidad & Tobago	0.3586	227
26	Argentina	0.3191	202
27	Italy	0.3127	198

Rank	Country	Reserves of Natural Gas Share of World Total (%)	Total (billion cubic meters)
28	Tunisia	0.2954	187
29	Brunei	0.2859	181
30	Colombia	0.2859	181
	LOWER MIDDLE		
31	New Zealand	0.2685	170
32	Rumania	0.2574	163
33	Poland	0.2195	139
34	Hungary	0.1895	120
35	France	0.1848	117
36	Bolivia	0.1737	110
37	India	0.1563	99
38	East Germany	0.1405	89
39	Syria	0.1184	75
40	Chile	0.1090	69

Rank	Country	Reserves of Natural Gas Share of World Total (%)	Total (billion cubic meters)	Rank	Country	Reserves of Natural Gas Share of World Total (%)	Total (billion cubic meters)	Rank	Country	Reserves of Natural Gas Share of World Total (%)	Total (billion cubic meters)
41	Oman	0.1011	64	49	Congo	0.0442	28	55	Albania	0.0189	12
42	Egypt	0.0979	62	50	Brazil	0.0426	27	56	Spain	0.0173	11
43	Denmark	0.0900	57	51	Japan	0.0379	24	57	Burma	0.0078	5
44	Gabon	0.0805	51					58	Zaire	0.0031	2
45	Ecuador	0.0695	44		*BOTTOM 10*			59	Guinea	0.0015	1
46	Angola	0.0663	42	52	Czechoslovakia	0.0252	16	60	Turkey	0.0015	1
47	Yugoslavia	0.0631	40	53	Austria	0.0236	15				
48	Peru	0.0568	36	54	Bulgaria	0.0221	14				

Sources: *World Energy Supplies*

174. Electrical Energy Consumption

The total production of electric energy in the world in mid-1975 was 6.439 trillion kwh, distributed as follows:

Region	Kwh million
Africa	129,700
North America	2,355,700
South America	167,300
Asia	874,800
Europe	1,774,100
Oceania	98,700
Soviet Union	1,038,600

It will be seen from the above that developed countries consume 80% of the world's production of electric energy.

Number of Countries: 188
Midpiont: 420 kwh
Period Covered: 1975
Type of Ranking: Per Capita Consumption of Electric Energy in Kwh; Total Consumption in Million Kwh; Highest to Lowest

Highlights & Findings: Disparities in per capita consumption of electric energy are striking and in some cases startling. An average Norwegian consumes 3,465 times as much electric energy as an average Burundian and more than twice as much as an average American. It may also be noted that colder countries consume more electric energy than warm countries. Oil-rich Arab countries are also found near the top of the list because of the need for year-round air conditioning.

Regions	Africa	Asia & Oceania	Europe	Western Hemisphere
Most	South Africa (34)	New Caledonia (3)	Norway (1)	Canada (2)
Least	Burundi (188)	Nepal (183)	Albania (75)	Haiti (173)

Rank	Country	Electric Consumption per Capita (kwh)	Total Electric Consumption (million kwh)	Rank	Country	Electric Consumption per Capita (kwh)	Total Electric Consumption (million kwh)	Rank	Country	Electric Consumption per Capita (kwh)	Total Electric Consumption (million kwh)
	TOP 10			14	Switzerland	5,670	36,000	30	Nauru	3,710	26
1	Norway	20,790	83,000	15	East Germany	5,290	89,100	31	Bahamas	3,320	680
2	Canada	12,460	298,000	16	Andorra	5,260	100	32	Bulgaria	3,150	27,700
3	New Caledonia	11,890	1,700	17	Belgium	5,190	50,900	33	Israel	3,140	11,000
4	Iceland	11,740	2,500	18	United Kingdom	4,934	277,000	34	South Africa	3,060	80,300
5	Sweden	9,970	82,000	19	Austria	4,860	36,600	35	Poland	3,030	104,100
6	United States	9,456	2,000,000	20	Denmark	4,710	23,900	36	Ireland	2,930	9,000
7	United Arab Emirates	7,860	1,400	21	Netherlands	4,590	63,000	37	Italy	2,865	163,000
8	Bahrain	7,690	1,900	22	Luxembourg	4,480	1,548	38	Gibraltar	2,760	80
9	New Zealand	7,270	22,900	23	Japan	4,470	504,500	39	Rumania	2,720	58,200
10	Netherlands Antilles	7,000	1,700	24	Soviet Union	4,320	1,109,000	40	Spain	2,640	94,000
				25	Kuwait	4,230	4,500	41	Greenland	2,290	117
	UPPER MIDDLE			26	Czechoslovakia	4,200	62,700	42	Greece	2,250	20,400
11	Finland	6,190	29,300	27	Qatar	3,980	600	43	Faroe Islands	2,150	88
12	Australia	5,970	81,800	28	France	3,900	206,000	44	Hungary	2,080	22,000
13	West Germany	5,710	353,100	29	Surinam	3,760	1,600	45	Liechtenstein	2,040	56

Rank	Country	Electric Consumption per Capita (kwh)	Total Electric Consumption (million kwh)
46	Yugoslavia	2,020	43,600
47	Singapore	2,000	4,600
48	Hong Kong	1,630	7,300
49	Venezuela	1,620	20,000
50	Taiwan	1,580	26,000
51	Panama	1,450	2,500
52	Brunei	1,440	230
53	Zambia	1,410	7,000
54	Trinidad & Tobago	1,280	1,300
55	Cyprus	1,220	792
56	North Korea	1,200	21,000
57	Argentina	1,170	30,000
58	Falkland Islands	1,150	2.5
59	Malta	1,130	380
60	French Guiana	1,111	60
61	Jamaica	1,110	2,300
62	Portugal	1,105	9,600
63	Uruguay	1,079	3,000
64	Rhodesia (Zimbabwe)	1,000	6,900
65	Chile	960	10,000
66	Barbados	920	220
67	French Polynesia	883	105
68	Gilbert Islands	820	45
69	Libya	750	1,900
70	Costa Rica	740	1,500
71	Cuba	740	7,000
72	Mexico	740	46,000
73	Brazil	730	80,000
74	Saudi Arabia	720	4,500
75	Albania	710	1,700
76	Macao	700	175
77	South Korea	650	23,000
78	Namibia	630	578
79	Colombia	600	13,700
80	Gabon	590	328
81	Iran	590	20,000
82	Liberia	580	880
83	Guadeloupe	570	200
84	Mongolia	560	840
85	Cook Islands	530	10
86	Peru	510	8,000
87	Malaysia	503	6,495
88	Turkey	470	19,000
89	Guyana	460	370
90	Oman	460	240
91	St.Kitts-Nevis-Anguilla	460	32

Rank	Country	Electric Consumption per Capita (kwh)	Total Electric Consumption (million kwh)
92	Fiji	450	270
93	Nicaragua	450	1,000
94	Martinique	420	150

LOWER MIDDLE

Rank	Country	Electric Consumption per Capita (kwh)	Total Electric Consumption (million kwh)
95	Iraq	400	4,500
96	Lebanon	400	1,000
97	Reunion	370	185
98	St. Lucia	360	40
99	Dominican Republic	350	1,700
100	Ghana	350	3,600
101	Djibouti	310	55
102	Philippines	310	13,500
103	Mauritius	280	248
104	South Yemen	277	190
105	El Salvador	270	1,100
106	Swaziland	270	125
107	Dominica	260	7
108	Papua New Guinea	250	700
109	Egypt	240	9,000
110	Algeria	230	4,000
111	Belize	230	32
112	Ecuador	230	1,600
113	Grenada	230	25
114	Guatemala	230	1,400
115	Angola	220	1,300
116	Tunisia	220	1,300
117	Paraguay	210	550
118	Thailand	210	9,200
119	Syria	200	1,500
120	Cameroon	190	1,265
121	St. Vincent	190	18
122	Bolivia	180	1,000
123	Jordan	180	500
124	Pakistan	180	12,700
125	Ivory Coast	170	1,200
126	Morocco	170	3,100
127	Honduras	160	450
128	Zaire	152	3,900
129	India	150	93,500
130	China	135	138,000
131	New Hebrides	130	13
132	Botswana	120	85
133	Senegal	110	474
134	Guinea	100	450
135	Sri Lanka	100	1,400

Rank	Country	Electric Consumption per Capita (kwh)	Total Electric Consumption (million kwh)
136	Congo	90	120
137	Laos	80	270
138	Seychelles	80	5
139	Sierra Leone	80	235
140	Tonga	80	8
141	Kenya	70	1,000
142	Mauritania	70	100
143	Sao Tome & Principe	70	5
144	Uganda	70	788
145	Solomon Islands	67	13
146	Vietnam	65	3,000
147	Madagascar	60	465
148	Mozambique	60	588
149	Nigeria	60	3,600
150	Tanzania	60	913
151	Equatorial Guinea	50	17
152	Malawi	50	263
153	Maldives	50	6
164	Central African Empire	45	82
165	Indonesia	40	5,600
166	Sudan	40	655
167	Togo	40	100
168	Afghanistan	30	580
169	Cambodia	30	260
170	Burma	30	850
171	Gambia	30	16
172	Guinea-Bissau	30	17
173	Haiti	30	135
174	Bangladesh	20	1,500
175	Benin	20	55
176	Chad	20	60
177	Cape Verde	20	7
178	Ethiopia	20	500
179	Mali	20	90

BOTTOM 9

Rank	Country	Electric Consumption per Capita (kwh)	Total Electric Consumption (million kwh)
180	Lesotho	18	20
181	Yemen Arab Republic	12	80
182	Bhutan	10	8
183	Nepal	10	140
184	Niger	10	55
185	Rwanda	10	35
186	Somalia	10	45
187	Upper Volta	9	57
188	Burundi	6	25

Source: *World Energy Supplies.*

LABOR

The employed segment of the population is usually called the work force, labor force or economically active population, although these terms are not strictly interchangeable. The term labor is not used in these rankings in the conventional Marxian sense of workers as opposed to capitalists but rather in the sense of persons engaged in any form of gainful activity, as distinguished from children and senior citizens who may not be so engaged. On any given working day, about 2 billion persons may be working (including housewives, whose work, of course, is never done) to make the world go round. This equals about 16 billion man-hours a day—a staggering thought in itself. In the following rankings we are trying to describe this 16-billion-man-hour figure.

The 22 rankings in this section are grouped into seven areas: The first presents an overview: the total size of the economically active population, the annual growth rate of the labor force, and the employment index and total wage bill as a percentage of national income.

The second group deals with the structure of the labor force, the percentage of women in the labor force, the percentage of children in the labor force and the dependency rate.

The third group deals with wages and working hours.

The fourth group deals with the occupational sectors of the labor force: the share of agriculture and manufacturing with annual growth rates for each. Then it examines the share of the principal occupational categories: administrative and managerial workers; and professional and technical workers.

The fifth group deals with the unemployment rate and unemployed professional and technical workers.

The sixth group deals with industrial relations, organized labor as a percentage of total labor force, and mandays lost through strikes.

The seventh group deals with the productivity index and value added per worker.

What are the emerging trends and prospects in the labor field? First, the median age of the labor force has been rising along with a downswing in the growth of the economically active population; secondly, there has been increased participation by women in the labor force leading to a proportionate reduction in the dependency rate; thirdly, there has been a universal reduction in working hours and improvement in working conditions; and lastly, there has been an increase in measured unemployment, but much of this increase is accounted for by those seeking work for the first time, disadvantaged minorities and women.

175. Economically Active Population

The economically active population refers to the total population between 15 and 64 years of age. It should be distinguished from the labor force, because the latter term excludes housewives, students and other economically unproductive groups.

Number of Countries: 125	**Highlights & Findings:** The spread between the highest and the lowest in this ranking is only 20 percentage points. Generally, countries with a higher birth rate tend to have a lower percentage of economically active inhabitants. Industrialized countries, therefore, have a larger segment of persons in the economically active age bracket, close to 64%. Communist countries have a slightly lower percentage at 61%. Low-income countries have an average of 54%, which is 1% more than that of middle-income and oil-producing countries.
Midpoint: 54%	
Period Covered: 1975	
Type of Ranking: Percentage of Population of Working Age, 15 to 64; Highest to Lowest	

Regions	Africa	Asia & Oceania	Europe	Western Hemisphere
Most	Cameroon (39)	Japan (1)	Bulgaria (2)	Canada (6)
Least	Morocco (123)	Bangladesh (121)	Albania (48)	Jamaica (125)

Rank	Country	Economically Active Population as Percentage of Total		Rank	Country	Economically Active Population as Percentage of Total		Rank	Country	Economically Active Population as Percentage of Total
	TOP 10			42	Burma	56		84	Rwanda	53
1	Japan	68		43	Cuba	56		85	Saudi Arabia	53
2	Bulgaria	67		44	Egypt	56		86	Somalia	53
3	Finland	67		45	Haiti	56		87	Uganda	53
4	Hungary	67		46	Lesotho	56		88	Venezuela	53
5	Poland	67		47	Trinidad & Tobago	56		89	Yemen Arab Republic	53
6	Yugoslavia	66		48	Albania	55		90	South Yemen	53
7	Canada	65		49	Angola	55		91	Zaire	53
8	Czechoslovakia	65		50	Bhutan	55		92	Benin	52
9	Rumania	65		51	Brazil	55		93	Cambodia	52
10	Soviet Union	65		52	Central African Empire	55		94	Colombia	52
				53	Costa Rica	55		95	Lebanon	52
	UPPER MIDDLE			54	India	55		96	Madagascar	52
11	Switzerland	65		55	North Korea	55		97	Niger	52
12	Argentina	64		56	Laos	55		98	Paraguay	52
13	Denmark	64		57	Liberia	55		99	Sudan	52
14	West Germany	64		58	Mauritania	55		100	Togo	52
15	Greece	64		59	Nepal	55		101	Tunisia	52
16	Hong Kong	64		60	Papua New Guinea	55		102	Ecuador	51
17	Italy	64		61	South Africa	55		103	Iran	51
18	Netherlands	64		62	Vietnam	55		104	Iraq	51
19	Sweden	64						105	Jordan	51
20	United States	64			**LOWER MIDDLE**			106	Kenya	51
21	Australia	63		63	Bolivia	54		107	Kuwait	51
22	Belgium	63		64	Burundi	54		108	Malawi	51
23	France	63		65	Congo	54		109	Mexico	51
24	Singapore	63		66	Ethiopia	54		110	Pakistan	51
25	Uruguay	63		67	Guinea	54		111	Philippines	51
26	Norway	62		68	Indonesia	54		112	Rhodesia (Zimbabwe)	51
27	Portugal	62		69	Ivory Coast	54		113	Tanzania	51
28	Spain	62		70	Mozambique	54		114	Thailand	51
29	United Kingdom	62		71	Senegal	54				
30	Austria	61		72	Sierra Leone	54			**BOTTOM 11**	
31	China	61		73	Turkey	54		115	El Salvador	50
32	Taiwan	61		74	Upper Volta	54		116	Ghana	50
33	East Germany	61		75	Afghanistan	53		117	Honduras	50
34	New Zealand	61		76	Guatemala	53		118	Syria	50
35	Israel	60		77	Libya	53		119	Zambia	50
36	South Korea	60		78	Malaysia	53		120	Algeria	49
37	Chile	59		79	Mali	53		121	Bangladesh	49
38	Ireland	59		80	Mongolia	53		122	Dominican Republic	49
39	Cameroon	57		81	Nigeria	53		123	Morocco	49
40	Chad	57		82	Panama	53		124	Nicaragua	49
41	Sri Lanka	57		83	Peru	53		125	Jamaica	48

Source: United Nations Population Division

176. Annual Growth Rate of Labor Force

The labor force growth rates are projections derived by the International Labor Organization from the 1960-70 census information but adjusted to ensure uniformity. The projections do not take into account international migration.

Number of Countries: 125
Midpoint: 2.1%
Period Covered: 1970-75
Type of Ranking: Labor Force Annual
Growth Rate; Highest to Lowest

Highlights & Findings: The highest growth rates are experienced in oil-exporting countries, reflecting the new-found economic affluence in these countries. They also enjoy ideal conditions for labor growth: expanding employment opportunities, a limited native labor force, liberal immigration laws and relatively high wages. Middle-income countries also are projected to have high growth rates as a result of rising birth rates. The lowest rates are recorded for industrialized countries. By categories, low-income countries have a growth rate of 2.0%, middle-income countries 2.7%, oil-exporting countries 2.4%, Communist countries 1.5% and industrialized countries 1.0%.

Regions	Africa	Asia & Oceania	Europe	Western Hemisphere
Most	Algeria (26)	Taiwan (1)	Albania (25)	Costa Rica (3)
Least	Lesotho (100)	Japan (99)	Greece (125)	Uruguay (110)

Rank	Country	Labor Force Annual Growth Rate (%)	Rank	Country	Labor Force Annual Growth Rate (%)	Rank	Country	Labor Force Annual Growth Rate (%)
	TOP 11		42	Rwanda	2.5	84	Burundi	1.7
1	Taiwan	5.0	43	Sri Lanka	2.5	85	Guinea	1.7
2	Kuwait	4.7	44	Bolivia	2.4	86	Senegal	1.7
3	Costa Rica	3.8	45	Cambodia	2.4	87	United States	1.7
4	Venezuela	3.7	46	Libya	2.4	88	Bangladesh	1.6
5	El Salvador	3.3	47	Mongolia	2.4	89	Burma	1.6
6	Mexico	3.3	48	Saudi Arabia	2.4	90	Laos	1.6
7	Colombia	3.2	49	Tanzania	2.4	91	Vietnam	1.6
8	Ecuador	3.2	50	Trinidad & Tobago	2.4	92	Chad	1.5
9	Malaysia	3.2	51	Uganda	2.4	93	China	1.5
10	Nicaragua	3.2	52	Yemen Arab Republic	2.4	94	Liberia	1.5
11	Singapore	3.2	53	Zambia	2.4	95	Mozambique	1.5
			54	Madagascar	2.3	96	Soviet Union	1.5
	UPPER MIDDLE		55	Tunisia	2.3	97	Cameroon	1.4
12	Dominican Republic	3.1	56	South Yemen	2.3	98	Haiti	1.4
13	Honduras	3.0	57	Indonesia	2.2	99	Japan	1.4
14	Iraq	3.0	58	Afghanistan	2.1	100	Lesotho	1.4
15	North Korea	3.0	59	Australia	2.1	101	France	1.3
16	Lebanon	3.0	60	Canada	2.1	102	Ireland	1.3
17	Paraguay	3.0	61	Ghana	2.1	103	Yugoslavia	1.3
18	Peru	3.0	62	Nepal	2.1	104	Argentina	1.2
19	Brazil	2.9	63	Nigeria	2.1	105	Netherlands	1.2
20	Guatemala	2.9	64	Togo	2.1	106	Czechoslovakia	1.1
21	Hong Kong	2.9				107	Jamaica	1.1
22	Jordan	2.9				108	Spain	1.0
23	South Korea	2.9		*LOWER MIDDLE*		109	Switzerland	1.0
24	Thailand	2.9	65	Angola	2.0	110	Uruguay	1.0
25	Albania	2.8	66	Benin	2.0	111	Finland	0.9
26	Algeria	2.8	67	Bhutan	2.0	112	West Germany	0.9
27	Israel	2.8	68	Congo	2.0	113	Belgium	0.8
28	Morocco	2.8	69	Ethiopia	2.0	114	Hungary	0.8
29	Panama	2.7	70	India	2.0			
30	Philippines	2.7	71	Mali	2.0		*BOTTOM 11*	
31	Rhodesia (Zimbabwe)	2.7	72	Ivory Coast	1.9	115	Austria	0.7
32	Somalia	2.7	73	Malawi	1.9	116	Bulgaria	0.7
33	Sudan	2.7	74	New Zealand	1.9	117	Norway	0.7
34	Iran	2.6	75	Papua New Guinea	1.9	118	Denmark	0.6
35	Kenya	2.6	76	Zaire	1.9	119	Italy	0.6
36	Pakistan	2.6	77	Central African Empire	1.8	120	Rumania	0.6
37	South Africa	2.6	78	Cuba	1.8	121	Sweden	0.5
38	Syria	2.6	79	Mauritania	1.8	122	East Germany	0.4
39	Chile	2.5	80	Poland	1.8	123	United Kingdom	0.3
40	Egypt	2.5	81	Sierra Leone	1.8	124	Portugal	0.2
41	Niger	2.5	82	Turkey	1.8	125	Greece	0.1
			83	Upper Volta	1.8			

Source: International Labor Organization.

177. Employment Index

One measure of the health of an economy is its ability to create jobs and to absorb able-bodied youths into the workforce. In a vigorous economy the number of jobs created every year must be at least equal to the number of people reaching productive age. Since employment potentials are limited in agriculture (and in a mechanized environment actually decline), the growth rate in employment is directly related to the growth of the nonagricultural sector. The employment index, therefore, measures the growth of employment outside of agriculture with 1970 as the base year.

Number of Countries: 65
Midpoint: 113
Period Covered: 1976
Type of Ranking: Employment (Excluding Agriculture) Index, 1970=100; Highest to Lowest

Highlights & Findings: The Employment Index is subject to certain distortions because its coverage is restricted to wage earners and salaried employees in mining, manufacturing, construction, transport, commerce and personal and public services. Furthermore, nations experiencing short but rapid spurts of growth during the period of reference may rank higher in the index than those nations that have a steady record of growth.

Regions	Africa	Asia & Oceania	Europe	Western Hemisphere
Most	Mauritius (1)	Jordan (2)	Yugoslavia (12)	Canada (15)
Least	Sierra Leone (65)	Thailand (55)	West Germany (64)	Puerto Rico (46)

Rank	Country	Employment Index, 1970=100	Rank	Country	Employment Index, 1970=100	Rank	Country	Employment Index, 1970=100
	TOP 10		22	Egypt	119	44	Zambia	110
1	Mauritius	188	23	Trinidad & Tobago	119	45	East Germany	109
2	Jordan	166	24	Cameroon	117	46	Puerto Rico	109
3	Malaysia	162	25	Panama	117	47	Sweden	108
4	Swaziland	157	26	South Africa	117	48	Austria	107
5	Malawi	149	27	El Salvador	116	49	Hungary	107
6	Kenya	146	28	India	116	50	Italy	107
7	South Korea	144	29	Jamaica	116	51	France	106
8	Turkey	139	30	Soviet Union	116	52	Malta	106
9	Fiji	138	31	Sri Lanka	115	53	Philippines	106
10	Syria	136	32	Gibraltar	114	54	Singapore	106
			33	Brunei	113	55	Thailand	105
	UPPER MIDDLE		34	Finland	113			
11	Pakistan	130	35	New Zealand	113		*BOTTOM 10*	
12	Yugoslavia	130	36	Gambia	112	56	Belgium	103
13	Rumania	129	37	Norway	112	57	Luxembourg	103
14	Tunisia	129	38	Uganda	112	58	Denmark	102
15	Canada	123	39	United States	112	59	Ireland	102
16	Israel	123				60	Portugal	101
17	Spain	123		*LOWER MIDDLE*		61	United Kingdom	101
18	Iceland	122	40	Australia	111	62	Cyprus	100
19	Poland	120	41	Cuba	111	63	Netherlands	100
20	Albania	119	42	Czechoslovakia	110	64	West Germany	95
21	Bulgaria	119	43	Japan	110	65	Sierra Leone	92

Source: International Labor Organization.

178. Total Wage Bill

How much of the national income is being spent on employee compensation as salaries and other benefits? Much of public expenditures are actually administrative costs, and by separating these costs it may be possible to determine their cost-benefits. It is interesting to note here that administrative costs or salaries rarely exceed 8% of income in industrial enterprises.

Number of Countries: 72
Midpoint: 48.2%
Period Covered: 1976
Type of Ranking: Compensation of Employees as Percentage of National Income; Total Wage Bill in Millions of National Currency; Highest to Lowest

Highlights & Findings: The wage bill, as percentage of national income, is high in all Western countries, perhaps because of higher wage levels but also because of expanding state services requiring more intensive staffing and the recruitment of more highly paid specialists. Furthermore, it is nearly impossible to tie salaries of public employees with specific standards of performance or production quotas. In developing countries the percentage is low but, unfortunately, so also is the quality of public administration services.

Regions	Africa	Asia & Oceania	Europe	Western Hemisphere
Most	Zambia (10)	New Zealand (13)	Luxembourg (1)	Netherlands Antilles (2)
Least	Niger (70)	Kuwait (71)	Greece (55)	Haiti (72)

Rank	Country	Compensation of Employee's as Percentage of National Income	Total Wage Bill (in million national currency)		Rank	Country	Compensation of Employees as Percentage of National Income	Total Wage Bill (in million national currency)		Rank	Country	Compensation of Employees as Percentage of National Income	Total Wage Bill (in million national currency)	
		TOP 10			25	France	59.9	764,271	franc	50	Colombia	38.1	142,659	peso
1	Luxembourg	77.9	56,080	franc	26	Japan	59.8	79,184,700	yen	51	Chile	37.7	3,180.8	peso
2	Netherlands Antilles	77.8	536	guilder	27	Nicaragua	59.1	5,925	cordoba	52	Ivory Coast	37.2	285,403	CFA franc
3	Panama	75.3	1,210.9	balboa	28	Spain	58.6	2,659,200	peseta	53	Paraguay	36.4	65,260	guarani
4	Puerto Rico	74.8	5,128	dollar	29	Togo	57.4	45,677	CFA franc	54	Malaysia	36.3	3,726	ringgit
5	United Kingdom	73.7	68,354	pound	30	Papua New Guinea	52.9	476.1	kina	55	Greece	35.1	226,378	drachma
6	Sweden	71.5	183,894	krona	31	Sudan	51.3	708	pound	56	Jordan	34.5	125.4	dinar
7	United States	70.2	935,560	dollar	32	Israel	50.1	35,797	pound	57	South Korea	33.8	2,817,600	won
8	Norway	68.9	85,667	krone	33	Costa Rica	49.8	7,563	colon	58	Madagascar	32.7	80,000	franc
9	Netherlands	68.3	126,020	guilder	34	Surinam	49.7	354	guilder	59	Tanzania	32.3	5,701	shilling
10	Zambia	68.3	855	kwacha	35	Swaziland	49.1	59.8	emalangeni	60	Iraq	31.0	363.5	dinar
					36	Vietnam	48.2	450,300	piastre	61	Ecuador	30.1	29,240	sucre
		UPPER MIDDLE								62	India	29.8	192,770	rupee
11	Jamaica	66.7	1,567.8	dollar										
12	Switzerland	65.9	84,985	franc			*LOWER MIDDLE*					*BOTTOM 10*		
13	New Zealand	65.7	6,590	dollar	37	Malta	46.8	83	pound	63	Libya	28.7	968.5	dinar
14	Italy	64.7	65,053,000	lire	38	Mauritius	46.1	1,582	rupee	64	Benin	28.6	16,344	CFAF franc
15	Canada	64.6	91,912	dollar	39	Fiji	45.0	129.1	dollar	65	Cameroon	26.9	78,296	CFAF franc
16	Denmark	64.1	105,803	krone	40	Argentina	44.9	579,370	peso	66	Thailand	26.8	72,538	baht
17	South Africa	63.0	14,241	rand	41	Egypt	44.7	1,765	pound	67	Malawi	25.5	102.7	kwacha
18	Australia	62.6	40,672	dollar	42	Guyana	43.9	480	dollar	68	Sierra Leone	24.4	78	Leone
19	West Germany	62.6	568,560	mark	43	Uruguay	43.3	1,846.9	nuevo peso	69	Uganda	22.8	2,325	shilling
20	Finland	61.8	54,018	markkaa	44	Venezuela	43.2	45,160	bolivar	70	Niger	14.8	13,800	CFA franc
21	Portugal	61.8	221,563	escudo	45	Peru	43.0	227,291	sole	71	Kuwait	14.2	433	dinar
22	Austria	61.1	355,150	schilling	46	Honduras	42.8	769	lempira	72	Haiti	12.7	455	gourd
23	Belgium	60.9	1,284,915	franc	47	Kenya	41.0	401.1	pound					
24	Ireland	60.2	1,975	pound	48	Bolivia	40.4	4,143	peso					
					49	Sri Lanka	39.4	8,942	rupee					

Source: *Yearbook of Labor Statistics.*

179. Women in the Labor Force

Historically, women have been part of the labor force only since the Industrial Revolution, and the struggle to ensure their fair share of jobs and equal rights in the labor market continues even today in most countries. Not only are women openly and often legally discriminated against, but they receive unequal wages and unequal treatment under existing labor laws. Female labor, therefore, has always been cheaper. It has also been confined to certain sectors, dressmaking for example, where women may have certain physiological advantages.

Number of Countries: 109
Midpoint: 29%
Period Covered: Mid-1970s
Type of Ranking: Percentage of Women in the Labor Force: Highest to Lowest

Highlights & Findings: Although women form the majority of the population in over 60 countries, they form the majority of the labor force in only two countries, Upper Volta and the Soviet Union. The percentage is naturally lowest in the Middle East (religious taboos against the employment of women persist there, and at least until quite recently, women were considered chattel) where it is 8.7% and highest in industrialized countries where it is 34.8%. In between, the percentage is 24.8% in Africa, 25.4% in Southern Europe, 27.9% in South Asia, 32.2% in East Asia and 21.0% in the Western Hemisphere. However, these percentages do not include the unpaid domestic labor that women perform in most countries.

Regions	Africa	Asia & Oceania	Europe	Western Hemisphere
Most	Upper Volta (1)	Thailand (6)	Soviet Union (2)	Haiti (11)
Least	Mauritania (107)	Iraq (109)	Spain (88)	Honduras (97)

Rank	Country	Percentage of Women in the Labor Force	Rank	Country	Percentage of Women in the Labor Force	Rank	Country	Percentage of Women in the Labor Force
	TOP 9		37	United Kingdom	36.0	74	Tunisia	24.0
1	Upper Volta	53.0	38	Yugoslavia	36.0	75	Malta	23.0
2	Soviet Union	50.4	39	Algeria	35.0	76	Paraguay	23.0
3	Botswana	49.0	40	Ethiopia	35.0	77	Peru	23.0
4	Madagascar	49.0	41	Israel	35.0	78	Argentina	22.0
5	Rwanda	48.0	42	South Korea	35.0	79	Nicaragua	22.0
6	Thailand	48.0	43	Sweden	35.0	80	Papua New Guinea	22.0
7	Ivory Coast	47.0	44	Kenya	34.0	81	Sri Lanka	22.0
8	Lesotho	47.0	45	Switzerland	34.0	82	Brazil	21.0
9	Mali	47.0	46	Belgium	33.0	83	Venezuela	21.0
			47	Indonesia	33.0	84	Bolivia	20.0
	UPPER MIDDLE		48	Liberia	33.0	85	Colombia	20.0
10	Burundi	45.0	49	Australia	32.0	86	Ecuador	20.0
11	Haiti	45.0	50	Canada	32.0	87	Portugal	20.0
12	Rumania	45.0	51	Philippines	32.0	88	Spain	20.0
13	Gambia	44.0	52	India	31.0	89	Mexico	19.0
14	Togo	44.0	53	Somalia	30.0	90	Afghanistan	18.0
15	Zaire	44.0	54	Zambia	30.0	91	Mauritius	18.0
16	Cameroon	43.0				92	Costa Rica	17.0
17	Gabon	43.0		*LOWER MIDDLE*		93	Lebanon	17.0
18	Finland	42.0	55	Cyprus	29.0	94	Bangladesh	15.0
19	Senegal	41.0	56	El Salvador	29.0	95	Morocco	15.0
20	Nepal	40.0	57	New Zealand	29.0	96	Guatemala	13.0
21	Bahamas	40.0	58	Greece	28.0	97	Honduras	13.0
22	Austria	39.0	59	Iceland	28.0	98	Iran	13.0
23	Burma	39.0	60	Norway	28.0	99	Syria	11.0
24	Jamaica	39.0	61	Trinidad & Tobago	28.0			
25	Japan	39.0	62	Guyana	27.0		*BOTTOM 10*	
26	Nigeria	39.0	63	Italy	27.0	100	Niger	10.0
27	Ghana	38.0	64	Malaysia	27.0	101	Sudan	10.0
28	Malawi	38.0	65	Chile	26.0	102	Pakistan	9.0
29	Turkey	38.0	66	Ireland	26.0	103	Egypt	8.0
30	Congo	37.0	67	Netherlands	26.0	104	Kuwait	7.0
31	Denmark	37.0	68	Panama	26.0	105	Jordan	5.0
32	Tanzania	37.0	69	Singapore	26.0	106	Libya	5.0
33	United States	37.0	70	Uruguay	26.0	107	Mauritania	4.0
34	France	36.0	71	Chad	25.0	108	South Yemen	4.0
35	West Germany	36.0	72	Taiwan	25.0	109	Iraq	3.0
36	Sierra Leone	36.0	73	Dominican Republic	25.0			

Source: World Bank.

180. Children in the Labor Force

There is hardly a country in the world where child labor is not illegal, according to the statute books; yet, in one guise or another child labor, like many other social evils, continues to exist and few governments have made concerted efforts to eradicate the practice completely. The paradox is that child labor is most prevalent in countries where manpower is abundant and actually coexists with adult unemployment. There is no doubt that in any form child labor is degrading; it overtaxes the physical and mental abilities of the child and may stunt the growth processes permanently. Yet, it has one economic advantage that may explain the persistence of the practice: it is cheap.

Number of Countries: 142
Midpoint: 11.4 per 1,000 Inhabitants
Period Covered: 1978
Type of Ranking: Children in the Labor Force per 1,000 Population; Total Number of Children in the Labor Force; Highest to Lowest

Highlights & Findings: Africa, with 27.6 children in the labor force per 1,000 population, has the largest juvenile component of the labor force in the world; Europe has the least with 1.3 per 1,000. In between, Asia has 14.2 per 1,000 and the Americas 6.5 per 1,000. The percentage is expected to drop in all regions by the year 2000: to 13.3 in Africa, 5.4 in Asia, 2.5 in South America, 1.9 in North and Central America and 0.8 in Europe.

Regions	Africa	Asia & Oceania	Europe	Western Hemisphere
Most	Rwanda (1)	Bhutan (4)	Portugal (74)	Haiti (19)
Least	Reunion (120)	Australia (125)	Switzerland (142)	Surinam (133)

Rank	Country	Children in Labor Force per 1,000 Inhabitants	Total (000)	Rank	Country	Children in Labor Force per 1,000 Inhabitants	Total (000)	Rank	Country	Children in Labor Force per 1,000 Inhabitants	Total (000)
	TOP 10			47	Liberia	20.5	32	95	North Korea	5.6	88
1	Rwanda	55.6	230	48	Namibia	19.8	17	96	Peru	5.5	84
2	Botswana	53.8	36	49	Pakistan	19.6	1,358	97	Uruguay	5.4	15
3	Mali	52.3	298	50	Comoros	19.3	6	98	Sri Lanka	5.3	72
4	Bhutan	51.2	60	51	Honduras	19.3	56	99	Cyprus	5.1	3
5	Upper Volta	50.0	302	52	Bolivia	18.7	105	100	Barbados	4.9	1
6	Nepal	49.5	624	53	Mongolia	18.4	27	101	Spain	4.0	143
7	Madagascar	48.1	425	54	Nigeria	18.3	1,370	102	South Korea	3.7	132
8	Central African Empire	46.3	83	55	Indonesia	18.2	2,401	103	Singapore	3.5	8
9	Ivory Coast	42.8	287	56	Rhodesia (Zimbabwe)	18.2	115	104	Yugoslavia	3.0	65
10	Bangladesh	41.7	3,623	57	Guatemala	18.0	113	105	Guyana	2.9	2
				58	Philippines	17.7	748	106	Soviet Union	2.9	616
	UPPER MIDDLE			59	Nicaragua	17.0	36	107	Austria	2.7	21
11	Papua New Guinea	41.4	114	60	El Salvador	16.6	66	108	Kuwait	2.6	3
12	Togo	40.8	91	61	Guinea	15.2	8	109	South Africa	2.6	67
13	Burundi	39.8	148	62	Ecuador	14.5	102	110	Rumania	2.3	49
14	Malawi	39.3	200	63	Syria	14.3	106	111	Canada	2.2	51
15	Guinea	37.1	205	64	Saudi Arabia	14.1	127	112	Italy	2.1	116
16	Benin	36.5	113	65	Egypt	14.0	523	113	Albania	1.9	18
17	Tanzania	36.2	534	66	Equatorial Guinea	13.8	4	114	Chile	1.8	18
18	Ethiopia	36.0	1,008	67	South Yemen	13.6	23	115	France	1.8	96
19	Haiti	35.9	164	68	Morocco	13.3	222	116	Ireland	1.6	5
20	Somalia	35.9	114	69	Brazil	13.1	1,403	117	Trinidad & Tobago	1.6	2
21	Uganda	35.4	410	70	Ghana	12.7	126	118	United States	1.5	326
22	Niger	33.8	155	71	Taiwan	11.4	182	119	Netherlands	1.4	19
23	Mozambique	32.1	297					120	Reunion	1.4	1
24	Thailand	32.1	1,346		*LOWER MIDDLE*			121	Israel	1.3	5
25	Chad	31.9	129	72	Costa Rica	10.8	21	122	Czechoslovakia	1.2	18
26	Laos	31.7	105	73	Paraguay	10.8	28	123	Japan	1.2	136
27	Cameroon	31.6	236	74	Portugal	10.3	99	124	West Germany	1.1	68
28	Vietnam	31.0	648	75	Iraq	9.6	106	125	Australia	1.0	14
29	Kenya	29.5	396	76	Libya	9.2	23	126	Iceland	0.9	–
30	Senegal	29.0	145	77	Malaysia	9.0	111	127	Malta	0.9	–
31	Swaziland	29.0	14	78	Fiji	8.8	5	128	Jamaica	0.9	2
32	Gambia	28.7	15	79	Tunisia	8.8	49	129	Cuba	0.8	7
33	Afghanistan	28.6	392	80	Colombia	8.7	205	130	Guadeloupe	0.8	–
34	Sudan	28.4	442	81	Algeria	8.5	134	131	Martinique	0.8	–
35	Turkey	28.1	1,130	82	Cape Verde	8.2	2	132	Puerto Rico	0.7	2
36	Mauritania	27.7	37	83	Dominican Republic	8.2	39	133	Surinam	0.7	–
37	Lesotho	27.4	33	84	Greece	8.1	74				
38	Zambia	25.5	126	85	Mexico	8.1	487		*BOTTOM 9*		
39	Burma	24.7	747	86	Hong Kong	8.0	35	134	Hungary	0.6	8
40	India	24.7	15,030	87	Panama	8.0	13	135	Luxembourg	0.6	–
41	Zaire	24.5	607	88	Angola	7.7	42	136	Belgium	0.5	5
42	Cambodia	23.7	193	89	Lebanon	7.7	24	137	Denmark	0.5	3
43	Gabon	22.1	12	90	Congo	7.4	10	138	Bulgaria	0.4	3
44	Sierra Leone	21.8	65	91	Argentina	6.6	167	139	Finland	0.4	2
45	Iran	21.7	724	92	Venezuela	6.4	77	140	Poland	0.4	13
46	Yemen Arab Republic	21.7	142	93	Jordan	6.1	17	141	Sweden	0.3	2
				94	Mauritius	6.1	5	142	Switzerland	0.2	1

Source: World Bank.

181. Dependency Ratio

Dependency ratio is defined as the number of persons aged under 15 and aged 65 and over divided by the number of persons aged 15 to 64. In other words, it measures the economically active population in terms of the population which it has to support as dependents. The ratio neutralizes some of the differences between developed and developing countries, because in the latter higher proportions of younger persons are somewhat offset by the lower proportions of older persons and the reverse is true in the case of developed countries. A possible source of error in the data—this applies to a number of other indicators as well—is the use of censuses of varying vintage, but demographers generally find this acceptable because of the high inertia of age structures. There are no figures available for the USSR or for most Communist countries.

Number of Countries: 112
Midpoint: 1.2
Period Covered: Mid-1970s
Type of Ranking: Dependency Ratio; Highest to Lowest

Highlights & Findings: In industrialized countries each economically active person has to support 0.9 dependent, while in the Middle East such a person has to support 1.8 dependents. The figures are 1.4 persons in Africa, 1.0 person in Southern Europe, 1.5 persons in South Asia, 1.4 persons in East Asia and 1.6 persons in the Western Hemisphere. This finding confirms the opinion of many economists that one of the keys to the economic prosperity of developed countries is the greater proportion of economically active persons, each of whom has to support fewer dependents.

Regions	Africa	Asia & Oceania	Europe	Western Hemisphere
Most	Algeria (1)	Jordan (2)	Portugal (58)	Nicaragua (5)
Least	Gabon (109)	Japan (112)	Rumania (111)	United States (108)

Rank	Country	Dependency Ratio	Rank	Country	Dependency Ratio	Rank	Country	Dependency Ratio
	TOP 10		34	Mauritius	1.5	70	Malta	1.1
1	Algeria	2.3	36	Peru	1.5	71	Netherlands	1.1
2	Jordan	2.3	37	Somalia	1.5	72	New Zealand	1.1
3	Syria	2.3	38	Chad	1.4	73	Thailand	1.1
4	Morocco	2.2	39	Taiwan	1.4	74	Turkey	1.1
5	Nicaragua	2.1	40	Ghana	1.4	75	Zaire	1.1
6	Mexico	2.0	41	Kenya	1.4	76	Austria	1.0
7	Paraguay	2.0	42	South Korea	1.4	77	Belgium	1.0
8	Guatemala	1.9	43	Kuwait	1.4	78	Bolivia	1.0
9	Libya	1.9	44	Sri Lanka	1.4	79	Botswana	1.0
10	Oman	1.9	45	Dominican Republic	1.3	80	Burundi	1.0
			46	Jamaica	1.3	81	Cameroon	1.0
	UPPER MIDDLE		47	Nigeria	1.3	82	Canada	1.0
11	Ecuador	1.8	48	Philippines	1.3	83	Cyprus	1.0
12	Egypt	1.8	49	Sierra Leone	1.3	84	Greece	1.0
13	Iraq	1.8	50	Singapore	1.3	85	Haiti	1.0
14	Lebanon	1.8	51	Togo	1.3	86	Iceland	1.0
15	Tunisia	1.8	52	Trinidad & Tobago	1.3	87	Italy	1.0
16	Venezuela	1.8	53	Barbados	1.2	88	Ivory Coast	1.0
17	South Yemen	1.8	54	Ethiopia	1.2	89	Lesotho	1.0
18	Zambia	1.8	55	India	1.2	90	Mauritania	1.0
19	Colombia	1.7	56	Liberia	1.2	91	Niger	1.0
20	Costa Rica	1.7	57	Nepal	1.2	92	Spain	1.0
21	Guyana	1.7	58	Portugal	1.2	93	Rwanda	1.0
22	Iran	1.7	59	Senegal	1.2	94	Uruguay	1.0
23	Sudan	1.7	60	Swaziland	1.2	95	Australia	0.9
24	Brazil	1.6	61	Tanzania	1.2	96	France	0.9
25	Chile	1.6				97	West Germany	0.9
26	El Salvador	1.6		*LOWER MIDDLE*		98	Luxembourg	0.9
27	Fiji	1.6	62	Argentina	1.1	99	Malawi	0.9
28	Malaysia	1.6	63	Bahamas	1.1	100	Norway	0.9
29	Pakistan	1.6	64	Benin	1.1	101	Sweden	0.9
30	Afghanistan	1.5	65	Burma	1.1	102	United Kingdom	0.9
31	Bangladesh	1.5	66	Ireland	1.1	103	Upper Volta	0.9
32	Honduras	1.5	67	Israel	1.1	104	Yugoslavia	0.9
33	Indonesia	1.5	68	Madagascar	1.1			
35	Panama	1.5	69	Mali	1.1			

Rank	Country	Dependency Ratio	Rank	Country	Dependency Ratio	Rank	Country	Dependency Ratio
	BOTTOM 8		107	Switzerland	0.8	110	Finland	0.7
105	Papua New Guinea	0.8	108	United States	0.8	111	Rumania	0.7
106	Denmark	0.8	109	Gabon	0.7	112	Japan	0.6

Source: World Bank.

182. Workweek

The length of the workweek (outside of agriculture) is regulated by law in almost all countries of the world that adhere to International Labor Organization (ILO) conventions. Since this length has historically tended to decline in direct relation to improvements in living conditions, wages and productivity, the workweek can be used as a multipurpose and versatile indicator. It determines the amount of leisure time available to workers, the amount of overtime and per capita productivity, among other things.

Number of Countries: 55
Midpoint: 41.9 hours
Period Covered: 1976
Type of Ranking: Average Number of Hours per Week in Manufacturing; Lowest to Highest

Highlights & Findings: Since the end of World War II, the 40-hour workweek has been accepted as more or less the norm, and countries with a higher legal maximum have been under pressure from labor organizations (including the ILO) to bring down the maximum to this limit. Evidently, progress in this direction has been erratic and slow because the majority of the reporting countries in the ranking have a legal workweek exceeding 40 hours. The Scandinavian countries are exceptions and have reduced the length of the workweek to phenomenally low levels. Such reductions have been combined with other innovations in work scheduling and working conditions, not all of which have been reported to be uniformly successful. It is important to stress here the differences between average workweek, legal workweek and the conventional workweek for white-collar workers. For example, the workweek in a standard U.S. office is only 35 hours, although both the legal workweek and the average workweek are more.

Regions	Africa	Asia & Oceania	Europe	Western Hemisphere
Most	Algeria (19)	Israel (12)	Sweden (1)	Barbados (6)
Least	Egypt (55)	South Korea (54)	Gibraltar (42)	Ecuador (53)

Rank	Country	Average Number of Hours of Work per Week in Manufacturing	Rank	Country	Average Number of Hours of Work per Week in Manufacturing	Rank	Country	Average Number of Hours of Work per Week in Manufacturing
	TOP 10		19	Algeria	40.8	38	Philippines	44.9
1	Sweden	30.2	20	Portugal	41.2	39	Cyprus	45.0
2	Norway	32.6	21	Netherlands	41.3	40	Fiji	45.1
3	Denmark	33.6	22	Japan	41.4	41	Burma	45.6
4	Austria	34.4	23	France	41.4	42	Gibraltar	45.6
5	Belgium	35.8	24	Australia	41.4	43	Mexico	45.6
6	Barbados	36.0	25	Sierra Leone	41.5	44	South Africa	46.1
7	Poland	36.8	26	Spain	41.6	45	Panama	47.1
8	Puerto Rico	37.9	27	West Germany	41.7	46	Syria	47.1
9	Hungary	38.0	28	Greece	41.9			
10	Finland	38.2					*BOTTOM 9*	
				LOWER MIDDLE		47	Guatemala	47.2
	UPPER MIDDLE		29	Ireland	42.1	48	Peru	48.1
11	Italy	38.7	30	Malta	42.4	49	Thailand	48.1
12	Israel	38.7	31	Czechoslovakia	43.5	50	Singapore	48.4
13	Canada	38.8	32	Switzerland	43.5	51	Guyana	48.8
14	New Zealand	39.0	33	United Kingdom	43.5	52	Brunei	50.7
15	Luxembourg	39.5	34	Venezuela	43.6	53	Ecuador	51.0
16	Yugoslavia	40.4	35	Sri Lanka	44.0	54	South Korea	52.5
17	Soviet Union	40.7	36	El Salvador	44.1	55	Egypt	57.0
18	United States	40.8	37	Mali	44.6			

Source: International Labor Organization, *Yearbook of Labor Statistics.*

183. Percentage of Labor Force in Agriculture

Traditionally, agricultural labor is the least skilled and the least productive segment of the labor force. In most countries agricultural laborers are excluded from the purview of labor laws, have no guaranteed minimum wage and receive no social security. Because of their diffusion, they are rarely organized and play only a marginal role in social or labor union movements. Agricultural labor is also characterized by the greater proportion of women, most of whom serve as unpaid family workers. They are often required to work for longer hours each day than workers in industrial or service establishments. Work may be seasonal, resulting in serious underemployment or long periods of inactivity.

Number of Countries: 125
Midpoint: 53%
Period Covered: 1976
Type of Ranking: Agricultural Manpower as a Percentage of Total Manpower; Highest to Lowest

Highlights & Findings: Because mechanization has made little headway in the developing world and because labor is so cheap in many countries where agriculture is the mainstay of the economy, agricultural labor constitutes over 50% of the labor force in the majority of the countries of the world. The disparity is most dramatically demonstrated by the ratios of low-income countries and industrialized countries, 85% and 11% respectively. Even middle-income countries employ 51% of their labor force in agriculture. The comparable ratio is 39% in Communist countries and 32% in oil-exporting countries (which are net importers of food and have only a negligible proportion of their land area under crops).

Regions	Africa	Asia & Oceania	Europe	Western Hemisphere
Most	Niger (3)	Bhutan (1)	Malta (6)	Haiti (34)
Least	South Africa (91)	Kuwait (125)	United Kingdom (124)	United States (122)

Rank	Country	Percentage of Labor Force in Agriculture
	TOP 9	
1	Bhutan	94
2	Nepal	94
3	Niger	93
4	Rwanda	93
5	Central African Empire	91
6	Malta	91
7	Chad	90
8	Lesotho	90
9	Madagascar	89
	UPPER MIDDLE	
10	Malawi	88
11	Mauritania	88
12	Burundi	87
13	Upper Volta	87
14	Bangladesh	86
15	Papua New Guinea	86
16	Tanzania	86
17	Uganda	86
18	Cameroon	85
19	Ivory Coast	85
20	Guinea	85
21	Somalia	85
22	Ethiopia	84
23	Afghanistan	82
24	Kenya	82
25	Sudan	82
26	Senegal	80
27	Thailand	80
28	Laos	79
29	Yemen Arab Republic	79
30	Zaire	79
31	Cambodia	78
32	Liberia	76

Rank	Country	Percentage of Labor Force in Agriculture
33	Vietnam	76
34	Haiti	74
35	Mozambique	74
36	Togo	73
37	Zambia	73
38	Sierra Leone	72
39	Turkey	71
40	India	69
41	China	68
42	Burma	67
43	Honduras	67
44	Albania	66
45	Indonesia	66
46	Saudi Arabia	66
47	South Yemen	65
48	Angola	64
49	Rhodesia (Zimbabwe)	64
50	Mongolia	62
51	Niger	62
52	Algeria	61
53	Dominican Republic	61
54	Guatemala	61
55	Pakistan	59
56	Ghana	58
57	Morocco	57
58	Bolivia	56
59	El Salvador	56
60	North Korea	55
61	Sri Lanka	55
62	Egypt	54
	LOWER MIDDLE	
63	Paraguay	53
64	Philippines	53
65	Ecuador	51

Rank	Country	Percentage of Labor Force in Agriculture
66	South Korea	51
67	Nicaragua	51
68	Syria	51
69	Benin	50
70	Malaysia	50
71	Tunisia	50
72	Yugoslavia	50
73	Rumania	49
74	Bulgaria	47
75	Iraq	47
76	Brazil	46
77	Iran	46
78	Mexico	45
79	Peru	45
80	Congo	42
81	Costa Rica	42
82	Panama	42
83	Greece	41
84	Poland	39
85	Colombia	38
86	China	37
87	Jordan	34
88	Portugal	33
89	Libya	32
90	Cuba	31
91	South Africa	31
92	Jamaica	30
93	Ireland	27
94	Soviet Union	26
95	Spain	26
96	Venezuela	26
97	Hungary	25
98	Chile	24
99	Finland	21
100	Japan	20

Rank	Country	Percentage of Labor Force in Agriculture	Rank	Country	Percentage of Labor Force in Agriculture	Rank	Country	Percentage of Labor Force in Agriculture
101	Lebanon	20	110	New Zealand	12	117	Netherlands	8
102	Italy	19	111	Norway	12	118	Sweden	8
103	Trinidad & Tobago	19	112	Denmark	11	119	Switzerland	8
104	Czechoslovakia	17	113	Israel	10	120	Belgium	5
105	Argentina	16				121	Hong Kong	4
106	Austria	15		*BOTTOM 12*		122	United States	4
107	Uruguay	15				123	Singapore	3
108	France	14	114	Australia	8	124	United Kingdom	3
109	East Germany	13	115	Canada	8	125	Kuwait	2
			116	West Germany	8			

Source: International Labor Organization.

184. Industrial Labor Force

The structure of the economically active population has been shifting in favor of industry in most countries of the world, although in no country does industrial labor constitute more than 46% of the total labor force. This trend is more marked in developed countries because of the ability of the industrial sector to absorb and train workers. Unlike agricultural workers, industrial workers require special-ized skills, are more intensively unionized, and are covered by an array of regulations and laws governing wages, work periods, occupational health and fringe benefits. The industrial work force constitutes the core of the organized labor movement in many countries and therefore wields a disproportionately large influence in national affairs.

Number of Countries: 111
Midpoint: 13.6
Period Covered: 1976
Type of Ranking: Workers Employed in Manufacturing Industries as Percentage of the Economically Active Population; Total Number of Industrial Workers; Highest to Lowest

Highlights & Findings: Industrial classifications employed in different countries present many points of divergence. In the Soviet Union (which ranks first) for example, construction, transport and communications workers are included in the total, and many other countries include mining workers in the industrial category. In all such cases, the rank order may be seriously affected by this variation in definition. The top of the list is dominated by European countries, the majority of which have more than one-quarter of their work force employed in the industrial sector.

Regions	Africa	Asia & Oceania	Europe	Western Hemisphere
Most	Tunisia (50)	Hong Kong (2)	Soviet Union (1)	United States (29)
Least	Tanzania (110)	Nepal (111)	Monaco (53)	British Virgin Islands (101)

Rank	Country	Percentage of Labor Force in Industry	Total	Rank	Country	Percentage of Labor Force in Industry	Total	Rank	Country	Percentage of Labor Force in Industry	Total
	TOP 10			13	Poland	30.2	5,295,361	28	Gibralter	22.6	2,650
1	Soviet Union*	45.1	52,771,253	14	Malta	27.8	31,287	29	United States	22.4	21,732,000
2	Hong Kong	44.4	867,310	15	Belgium	26.8	1,082,582	30	Portugal	21.7	236,765
3	Switzerland	37.7	1,129,763	16	France	26.5	5,784,800	31	South Korea	20.5	2,678,000
4	East Germany	37.6	3,093,689	17	Sweden	26.5	1,100,400	32	Ireland	20.1	224,790
5	Czechoslovakia	35.3	2,464,599	18	Finland**	25.7	584,000	33	Puerto Rico	20.0	183,300
6	Hungary**	35.2	1,794,000	19	Spain	25.7	3,428,562	34	Faroe Islands	19.8	2,993
7	West Germany	34.8	9,347,000	20	Singapore	25.6	233,954	35	Argentina	19.7	1,771,250
8	Luxembourg***	33.6	43,526	21	Japan	25.1	13,450,000	36	Cuba	19.4	510,402
9	United Kingdom	32.6	8,135,790	22	Australia****	24.8	1,442,000	37	Rumania***	19.4	2,013,525
10	Bulgaria	32.3	1,438,242	23	Norway	24.4	449,000	38	Trinidad & Tobago***	19.2	75,150
				24	New Zealand	24.2	308,490	39	Uruguay	18.8	205,300
	UPPER MIDDLE			25	Netherlands	24.1	1,151,000	40	Iran	18.4	1,420,000
11	Italy	30.6	6,221,000	26	Israel***	23.9	279,000	41	Canada	18.0	1,915,000
12	Austria	30.4	901,000	27	Denmark	23.1	576,372	42	Mexico	17.8	2,961,171

Rank	Country	Percentage of Labor Force in Industry	Total
43	Yugoslavia***	17.7	1,574,512
44	Greece	17.1	554,380
45	Lebanon	16.5	94,620
46	Cyprus	16.0	32,668
47	Chile	15.9	415,440
48	Venezuela	15.4	573,197
49	Guyana	15.1	26,372
50	Tunisia	14.9	240,640
51	Barbados	14.6	12,256
52	Netherlands Antilles	14.4	10,549
53	Monaco	14.2	1,470
54	Bahrain	13.9	8,372
55	Guatemala	13.7	211,631
56	Paraguay	13.6	102,441
	LOWER MIDDLE		
57	Pakistan	13.4	2,819,000
58	Egypt	12.9	1,071,288
59	South Africa	12.8	1,023,720
60	Greenland	12.7	2,371
61	Peru	12.5	485,234
62	Nicaragua	12.4	62,509
63	Costa Rica	11.9	69,917
64	Sri Lanka	11.9	181,066
65	Ecuador	11.7	226,265

Rank	Country	Percentage of Labor Force in Industry	Total
66	Mauritius	11.5	30,093
67	Colombia	11.4	678,322
68	Philippines	11.3	1,720,000
69	Syria	11.2	205,771
70	Brazil	11.0	3,241,861
71	Honduras	11.0	84,284
72	Thailand	10.9	1,514,050
73	Jamaica	10.8	96,500
74	New Caledonia	10.8	5,469
75	Guadeloupe	10.4	9,326
76	El Salvador	9.8	113,983
77	India	9.5	17,067,500
78	Morocco	9.3	329,264
79	Bolivia	9.0	135,280
80	St. Pierre & Miquelon	8.9	167
81	Malaysia (West)	8.8	251,939
82	Martinique	8.8	7,910
83	Dominican Republic	8.1	100,989
84	Kuwait	8.0	24,467
85	Panama	8.0	38,847
86	Reunion	7.6	14,125
87	Turkey	7.6	1,243,567
88	Fiji	7.4	13,039
89	Antigua	7.3	1,680
90	Burma	7.3	872,000

Rank	Country	Percentage of Labor Force in Industry	Total
92	Bermuda	6.5	1,765
92	Indonesia	6.5	2,681,952
93	Algeria	6.4	163,002
94	French Guyana	6.1	1,030
95	Bahamas	5.5	3,824
96	Mozambique	5.4	155,996
97	Haiti	5.1	119,564
98	Montserrat	5.1	204
99	Sarawak	4.9	18,318
100	Seychelles	4.9	969
101	British Virgin Islands	4.7	187
	BOTTOM 10		
102	Brunei	4.3	1,751
103	Tanzania (Zanzibar)	4.3	7,423
104	Libya	4.1	22,173
105	Sudan	4.0	179,000
106	Sabah	3.3	7,079
107	Tonga***	2.6	502
108	Zambia	2.6	30,674
109	Western Samoa***	2.2	819
110	Tanzania (Tanganyika)	1.6	91,441
111	Nepal	1.1	51,902

* Including construction, transportation, communications.
** Including mining and electricity.
*** Including mining.
**** Including electricity.

Source: International Labor Organization, *Yearbook of Labor Statistics.*

185. Administrative & Managerial Workers

In the postfeudal age the class that most closely approximates the nobility is that composed of administrators and managers. In both government and business, this elite group is concerned with planning, organization, direction, coordination and control; it makes decisions, sets goals and priorities and determines policy. No group is better trained or educated, is more visible in public affairs, or plays a more crucial role in national development.

Number of Countries: 96
Midpoint: 1.4%
Period Covered: 1976
Type of Ranking: Administrative and Managerial Workers as Percentage of Economically Active Population; Total Number of Administrator and Managers; Highest to Lowest

Highlights & Findings: The percentage of administrative and managerial workers is highest in developed countries and lowest in developing countries. In 35 countries this group constitutes less than 1% of the total labor force. Since the definition of this category of workers is not uniform in every country, reasonable caution must be used in drawing conclusions from that ranking.

Regions	Africa	Asia & Oceania	Europe	Western Hemisphere
Most	Morocco (22)	Australia (8)	Gibralter (1)	Trinidad & Tobago (2)
Least	Tunisia (92)	Nepal (96)	Portugal (89)	Greenland (93)

Rank	Country	Administrators & Managers as Percentage of Economically Active Population	Total Number	Rank	Country	Administrators & Managers as Percentage of Economically Active Population	Total Number	Rank	Country	Administrators & Managers as Percentage of Economically Active Population	Total Number
	TOP 10			33	Bolivia	1.9	29,031	65	Algeria	0.8	19,861
1	Gibraltar*	20.1	2,362	34	Chile	1.9	49,860	66	Libya	0.8	4,131
2	Trinidad & Tobago*	10.1	39,300	35	Lebanon	1.9	10,590	67	Sabah	0.8	1,697
3	United States	9.9	9,611,000	36	Sweden	1.9	80,600	68	Colombia	0.7	39,277
4	Puerto Rico	9.0	82,200	37	Martinique	1.8	1,648	69	India	0.7	1,208,600
5	Jamaica**	7.8	70,200	38	Bahrain	1.7	1,035	70	Malaysia (West)	0.7	20,308
6	Bulgaria	7.6	324,096	39	Brazil	1.7	497,097	71	Pakistan	0.7	146,000
7	Malta	7.1	7,242	40	Costa Rica	1.7	9,671	72	Spain	0.7	80,547
8	Australia	6.5	348,874	41	Denmark	1.6	38,001	73	Samoa	0.7	256
9	Canada	6.4	685,000	42	Egypt	1.6	137,315	74	Zambia	0.7	8,603
10	Bahamas	5.2	3,608	43	Ireland	1.6	17,916	75	Austria	0.6	19,948
				44	Argentina	1.5	137,850	76	Greece	0.6	19,880
	UPPER MIDDLE			45	Brunei	1.5	606	77	Hungary	0.6	28,491
11	Belgium	4.6	166,208	46	Netherlands Antilles	1.5	1,115	78	Italy	0.6	122,028
12	Cuba	4.3	112,745	47	Uruguay	1.5	16,100	79	South Korea	0.6	82,000
13	Norway	4.2	76,000					80	Paraguay	0.6	4,640
14	Japan	4.0	2,150,000		*LOWER MIDDLE*			81	Belize	0.5	169
15	Israel	3.8	44,100	48	Barbados	1.4	1,158	82	Indonesia	0.5	189,467
16	United Kingdom	3.7	924,420	49	New Caledonia	1.4	709	83	Sarawak	0.5	1,827
17	Bermuda	3.6	982	50	Montserrat	1.3	50	84	Mauritius	0.5	1,211
18	Venezuela	3.6	134,035	51	Finland	1.2	28,000	85	Peru	0.4	16,095
19	New Zealand	3.4	43,320	52	Guatemala	1.1	16,663				
20	Rumania*	3.1	322,245	53	Thailand	1.1	156,240		*BOTTOM 11*		
21	British Virgin Islands	3.0	121	54	Antigua	1.0	229	86	Dominican Republic	0.3	3,797
22	Morocco	3.0	119,169	55	Ecuador	1.0	19,344	87	El Salvador	0.3	3,161
23	Singapore	3.0	27,699	56	Faroe Islands	1.0	143	88	Ghana	0.3	11,530
24	France	2.7	555,380	57	Luxembourg	1.0	1,304	89	Portugal	0.3	11,725
25	Mexico	2.6	432,141	58	Philippines	1.0	148,000	90	Sri Lanka	0.3	13,917
26	Seychelles	2.6	522	59	Poland	1.0	163,135	91	Sudan	0.3	13,000
27	Czechoslovakia	2.4	165,363	60	South Africa	1.0	75,880	92	Tunisia	0.3	4,700
28	West Germany	2.2	585,500	61	Yugoslavia	1.0	92,136	93	Greenland	0.2	35
29	Netherlands	2.2	107,000	62	Honduras	0.9	7,012	94	Iran	0.2	14,000
30	Hong Kong	2.1	40,160	63	Kuwait	0.9	2,854	95	Syria	0.1	2,014
31	Panama	2.1	10,330	64	Nicaragua	0.9	4,750	96	Nepal	0.02	1,095
32	Switzerland	2.1	61,623								

* Includes clerical workers.
** Includes professional, technical and clerical workers.

Source: ILO, *Yearbook of Labor Statistics.*

186. Professional and Technical Workers

The following list ranks countries by their total stock of scientific and technical manpower. This is an important factor ensuring technological capability in both basic and applied research and industry. Without a large skilled manpower base, no country can hope to make any significant gains in productivity. The demand for professional and technical workers is so great in developed countries that it has given rise to the phenomenon commonly known as brain drain, in which the developing countries serve as the drainage area and the Western world, especially the United States, as the catchment area. By depleting the reservoir or skills, the brain drain serves to keep developing countries at the bottom of the technological ladder.

Number of Countries: 96
Midpoint: 7.8%
Period Covered: 1976
Type of Ranking: Professional and Technical Workers as Percentage of Economically Active Population; Total Number of Professional and Technical Workers; Highest to Lowest

Highlights & Findings: The percentage of professional and technical workers is high in all developed countries. When developing countries appear at the top, it is as a result of importing skilled workers. Kuwait, Brunei and Libya are examples of such importation of skills. It is significant that professional and technical workers constitute more than 10% of the economically active population (the optimum according to manpower experts) in only 22 countries. Caution should be used with this ranking, since the definition of professional and technical workers is not uniform throughout the world.

Regions	Africa	Asia & Oceania	Europe	Western Hemisphere
Most	Libya (23)	Israel (3)	Sweden (1)	United States (7)
Least	Sudan (94)	Nepal (96)	Portugal (84)	Dominican Republic (90)

Rank	Country	Professional & Technical Workers as Percentage of Economically Active Population	Total Number	Rank	Country	Professional & Technical Workers as Percentage of Economically Active Population	Total Number	Rank	Country	Professional & Technical Workers as Percentage of Economically Active Population	Total Number
	TOP 10			33	New Caledonia	9.1	4,568	66	Faroe Islands	5.2	778
1	Sweden	22.9	951,600	34	Bahamas	8.9	6,179	67	Mauritius	5.2	13,535
2	Czechoslovakia	19.4	1,356,120	35	Montserrat	8.9	353	68	Nicaragua	5.2	26,040
3	Israel	19.1	223,500	36	Austria	8.7	269,316	69	Brazil	4.8	1,410,746
4	Finland	17.0	391,000	37	Samoa	8.6	3,250	70	Colombia	4.5	269,740
5	Norway	15.8	287,000	38	Venezuela	8.6	321,084	71	Malaysia	4.5	129,436
6	New Zealand	14.4	183,930	39	Cuba	8.4	220,298	72	Sabah	4.5	9,578
7	United States	14.2	13,769,000	40	Bulgaria	8.3	354,299	73	Syria	4.5	82,768
8	Canada	14.0	1,489,000	41	Gibraltar	8.2	961	74	Egypt	4.4	366,994
9	Kuwait	13.7	41,836	42	Antigua	8.1	1,865	75	Tunisia	4.4	72,090
10	Netherlands	13.3	636,000	43	Martinique	8.1	7,283	76	Paraguay	4.2	31,370
				44	Bahrain	8.0	4,824	77	Honduras	4.1	30,982
	UPPER MIDDLE			45	Belize	8.0	2,644	78	South Africa	4.1	330,060
11	Bermuda	13.2	3,603	46	Costa Rica	8.0	46,622	79	Morocco	4.0	158,007
12	Denmark	12.2	282,452	47	Trinidad & Tobago	8.0	31,100	80	Sri Lanka	4.0	178,488
13	Switzerland	12.1	363,177	48	Jamaica*	7.8	70,200	81	Zambia	4.0	46,859
14	Brunei	11.9	4,892	49	Poland	7.8	1,325,900	82	Ghana	3.7	122,465
15	France	11.4	2,330,540					83	Guatemala	3.6	56,374
16	Belgium	11.1	402,929		*LOWER MIDDLE*			84	Portugal	3.6	121,060
17	United Kingdom	11.1	2,787,070	50	Yugoslavia	7.6	678,653	85	El Salvador	3.5	40,388
18	Puerto Rico	11.0	100,400	51	Argentina	7.5	677,500	86	Iran	3.5	269,000
19	Hungary	10.9	544,797	52	Peru	7.4	288,004				
20	Malta	10.7	10,907	53	Italy	7.3	1,443,757		*BOTTOM 10*		
21	British Virgin Islands	10.6	420	54	Uruguay	7.2	79,100	87	Algeria	3.4	86,707
22	Australia	10.1	536,508	55	Chile	7.1	185,060	88	Pakistan	3.0	622,000
23	Libya	9.9	53,812	56	Japan	7.1	3,800,000	89	Sarawak	3.0	11,044
24	West Germany	9.8	2,608,000	57	Panama	6.8	33,129	90	Dominican Republic	2.7	34,060
25	Singapore	9.5	86,864	58	Seychelles	6.7	1,319	91	India	2.7	4,834,300
26	Ireland	9.3	104,341	59	Mexico	6.2	1,029,220	92	South Korea	2.6	346,000
27	Netherlands Antilles	9.3	6,792	60	Bolivia	5.9	88,401	93	Thailand	2.6	363,020
28	Barbados	9.2	7,760	61	Greece	5.7	183,480	94	Sudan	2.5	112,000
29	Greenland	9.2	1,716	62	Spain	5.5	657,517	95	Indonesia	2.1	883,537
30	Lebanon	9.2	52,875	63	Hong Kong	5.3	103,370	96	Nepal	0.5	25,317
31	Luxembourg	9.2	11,847	64	Philippines	5.3	811,000				
32	Rumania	9.2	949,845	65	Ecuador	5.2	100,510				

* Includes administrative and clerical workers.

Source: International Labor Organization, *Yearbook of Labor Statistics.*

187. Unemployment Rate

Unemployment results, as U.S. President Calvin Coolidge sagely observed, when people are out of work. Because of its social costs and political implications, unemployment is perhaps the most widely underestimated of all economic indicators. Many governments deliberately manipulate unemployment figures because of possible repercussions on their own domestic popularity. Others include only those who are registered with labor exchanges and ignore those who seek employment through other means. Another source of error with percentage rates, as in this ranking, is the uncertainty regarding the total labor force on which the percentage is based. In any event, unemployment figures and rates must be accepted with reservations regarding both their validity and their scope.

Number of Countries: 36
Midpoint: 5.5%
Period Covered: 1976
Type of Ranking: Percentage of Unemployed; Number of Unemployed; Highest to Lowest

Highlights & Findings: Because of the limited number of countries in this ranking, it is difficult to establish valid conclusions. Those countries at the top of the table possibly may have a better reporting system than others.

Regions	Africa	Asia & Oceania	Europe	Western Hemisphere
Most	Egypt (29)	Guam (8)	Ireland (6)	Jamaica (1)
Least	N.A.	Brunei (34)	Iceland (36)	Argentina (30)

Rank	Country	Unemployment Rate (%)	Total Unemployed
	TOP 10		
1	Jamaica	22.4	197,800
2	Puerto Rico	19.6	179,000
3	Trinidad & Tobago	15.0	58,600
4	Chile	14.7	467,600
5	Uruguay	12.7	68,700
6	Ireland	12.3	83,500
7	Yugoslavia	11.4	635,300
8	Guam	9.7	2,640
9	Belgium	8.6	266,600
10	United States	7.7	7,288,000
	MIDDLE		
11	Nicaragua	7.3	45,900

Rank	Country	Unemployment Rate (%)	Total Unemployed
12	Canada	7.1	736,000
13	Cyprus	7.1	14,500
14	Panama	6.5	33,000
15	Syria	6.2	113,400
16	Denmark	6.1	126,100
17	United Kingdom	5.8	1,358,800
18	Netherlands	5.5	210,900
19	Peru	5.2	258,300
20	West Germany	4.6	1,060,300
21	Australia	4.4	267,700
22	Finland	4.0	90,000
23	South Korea	3.9	505,000
24	Philippines	3.9	581,000
25	Italy	3.7	732,000

Rank	Country	Unemployment Rate (%)	Total Unemployed
26	Israel	3.6	42,500
	BOTTOM 10		
27	Bolivia	3.2	63,000
28	Spain	2.8	376,400
29	Egypt	2.5	233,400
30	Argentina	2.3	88,000
31	Austria	2.0	55,300
32	Japan	2.0	1,080,000
33	Norway	1.8	32,000
34	Brunei	1.6	. . .
35	Sweden	1.6	66,000
36	Iceland	0.5	510

Source: International Labor Organization.

188. Unemployment Among Professional and Technical Workers

Bureaucrats and social scientists often talk of "acceptable" levels of unemployment. But, of course, unemployment is always unacceptable for the person who is unemployed. In the case of unemployed professionals and scientists, unemployment represents not only a grievous waste of scarce skills (on which the individual and the nation have invested time and money) but also a failure of a nation's manpower policy. The aggregate figures are presented in the following ranking rather than percentages because the latter may only be small arithmetical fractions, quite unimpressive in themselves.

Number of Countries: 40
Midpoint: 3,070
Period Covered: 1976
Type of Ranking: Total Number of Unemployed Professionals and Technical Workers; Highest to Lowest

Highlights & Findings: The problem of unemployment among professionals and scientists has been most acute in the Indian subcontinent as well as in the developed countries of the West. Outside of these countries such unemployment is not significant. On a per capita basis, Sri Lanka leads the list.

Regions	Africa	Asia & Oceania	Europe	Western Hemisphere
Most	Egypt (29)	India (1)	West Germany (4)	United States (2)
Least	Sierra Leone (40)	Syria (30)	Cyprus (32)	Trinidad & Tobago (28)

Rank Country	Total Number of Unemployed Professionals & Technical Workers	Rank Country	Total Number of Unemployed Professionals & Technical Workers	Rank Country	Total Number of Unemployed Professionals & Technical Workers
TOP 10		13 Sweden	7,000	28 Trinidad & Tobago	1,200
1 India	544,672	14 South Korea	6,000	29 Egypt	1,100
2 United States	440,000	15 Puerto Rico	5,000	30 Syria	1,088
3 Canada	247,000	16 Malaysia (West)	4,950		
4 West Germany	115,539	17 Jamaica	4,400	**BOTTOM 10**	
5 Sri Lanka	103,993	18 Indonesia	3,325	31 Greece	973
6 France	84,755	19 Switzerland	3,160	32 Cyprus	629
7 Pakistan	31,109	20 Thailand	3,070	33 Liberia	275
8 Yugoslavia	25,513	21 Finland	3,000	34 Ghana	172
9 Australia	13,600	22 Uruguay	2,900	35 South Africa	172
10 Venezuela	9,947	23 Austria	2,698	36 Mauritius	142
		24 Singapore	2,600	37 Tunisia	58
MIDDLE		25 Israel	2,400	38 Nigeria	53
11 Spain	9,846	26 Chile	1,700	39 Malawi	9
12 Philippines	9,000	27 Norway	1,201	40 Sierra Leone	5

Source: ILO, *Yearbook of Labor Statistics.*

189. Organized Labor as Percentage of Labor Force

The strength of the organized labor movement varies from country to country and from sector to sector within a country. The political power of organized labor is greatest in democratic countries, such as United States and United Kingdom, where it operates either as a pressure group or overt political party and where it influences legislation through intensive lobbying; labor is weakest, ironically, in Communist countries, where it has been incorporated into the ruling political apparatus and has virtually no independent existence of its own. However, the political power of organized labor can be measured only very imprecisely; on the other hand, the strength of unionization within the labor force can be measured rather accurately and expressed as a percentage of dues-paying members in relation to the wage-earning workforce.

Number of Countries: 107
Midpoint: 20%
Period Covered: 1977
Type of Ranking: Organized Labor as a Percentage of the Labor Force; Highest to Lowest

Highlights & Findings: In some countries, such as Guinea and Burundi, all workers are compelled to be members of the officially sponsored labor union, and those governments report a 100% membership. Such countries have been excluded from this ranking because of the obvious improbability of a 100% membership. In other cases only voluntary dues-paying membership has been considered acceptable for the purpose of this ranking. Unionization is highest in countries with moderate socialist governments. In 15 countries more than 50% of the labor force is unionized.

Regions	Africa	Asia & Oceania	Europe	Western Hemisphere
Most	Benin (5)	Israel (1)	East Germany (2)	Netherlands Antilles (6)
Least	Central African Empire (106)	India (102)	Spain (79)	Haiti (107)

Rank Country	Organized Labor as Percentage of Labor Force	Rank Country	Organized Labor as Percentage of Labor Force	Rank Country	Organized Labor as Percentage of Labor Force
TOP 9		7 Austria	66.6	12 Norway	60.0
1 Israel	90.0	8 Denmark	65.0	13 New Zealand	52.0
2 East Germany	87.7	9 San Marino	65.0	14 Brazil	50.0
3 Portugal	85.0			15 Fiji	50.0
4 Sweden	80.0	**UPPER MIDDLE**		16 Mauritania	49.0
5 Benin	75.0	10 Finland	60.0	17 Belgium	48.0
6 Netherlands Antilles	70.0	11 Iceland	60.0	18 Cuba	46.0

Rank	Country	Organized Labor as Percentage of Labor Force	Rank	Country	Organized Labor as Percentage of Labor Force	Rank	Country	Organized Labor as Percentage of Labor Force
19	Luxembourg	45.0	50	United States	24.2	80	Tunisia	10.0
20	Venezuela	45.0	51	Singapore	24.0	81	Turkey	10.0
21	Australia	44.0		*LOWER MIDDLE*		82	Jordan	9.8
22	Sri Lanka	43.0	52	Chad	20.0	83	Honduras	9.0
23	Gibraltar	40.5	53	Greece	20.0	84	Kenya	8.6
24	Malta	40.0	54	Italy	20.0	85	Brunei	8.4
25	United Kingdom	40.0	55	Ivory Coast	20.0	86	Panama	8.4
26	Peru	37.1	56	Mexico	20.0	87	Belize	8.0
27	Ireland	36.0	57	St. Lucia	20.0	88	Bolivia	8.0
28	Mauritius	35.0	58	Switzerland	20.0	89	French Guyana	7.0
29	Sierra Leone	35.0	59	Algeria	17.0	90	South Africa (whites only)	7.0
30	St. Kitts-Nevis-Anguilla	34.1	60	France	17.0	91	Lebanon	6.5
31	Guyana	34.0	61	Congo	16.0	92	Guatemala	6.4
32	Japan	33.7	62	Ecuador	15.0	93	Nicaragua	5.6
33	Grenada	33.0	63	Malaysia	15.0	94	El Salvador	5.0
34	Netherlands	33.0	64	Swaziland	15.0	95	Morocco	5.0
35	Surinam	33.0	65	Tanzania	15.0	96	Pakistan	5.0
36	West Germany	32.6	66	Colombia	13.0	97	Paraguay	5.0
37	Barbados	32.0	67	Angola	12.2	98	Syria	5.0
38	Canada	30.0	68	Taiwan	12.0		*BOTTOM 9*	
39	Gabon	30.0	69	Dominican Republic	12.0	99	Cameroon	4.5
40	Trinidad & Tobago	30.0	70	Hong Kong	12.0	100	Madagascar	4.0
41	Gambia	27.0	71	Costa Rica	11.5	101	Uganda	2.7
42	Argentina	25.0	72	Guadeloupe	11.0	102	India	2.5
43	Bahamas	25.0	73	Iraq	11.0	103	Nigeria	2.4
44	Chile	25.0	74	Martinique	11.0	104	Botswana	2.3
45	Dominica	25.0	75	Ghana	10.0	105	Liberia	2.0
46	Egypt	25.0	76	Indonesia	10.0	106	Central African Empire	1.0
47	Jamaica	25.0	77	South Korea	10.0	107	Haiti	1.0
48	Uruguay	25.0	78	St. Vincent	10.0			
49	Zambia	25.0	79	Spain	10.0			

Source: U.S. Central Intelligence Agency.

190. Strike Days Lost

This ranking lists countries by the number of man-days lost through industrial disputes. No differentiation has been possible between strikes and lockouts, since such a distinction is not observed by most countries when compiling statistics. The data also do not include disputes of small importance, political strikes or the lost man-days of workers who are only indirectly affected, i.e., those who do not participate in a strike by their coworkers.

Number of Countries: 87
Midpoint: 27,674 man-days
Period Covered: 1976
Type of Ranking: Number of Man-Days Lost Through Industrial Disputes; Total Number of Disputes; Man-Days Lost per Industrial Dispute; Highest to lowest

Highlights & Findings: Because of the limited number of countries covered by the data no general pattern of strike-proneness is evident. If the leading countries in the ranking are all democracies, it is because strikes are banned in Communist countries and most one-party dictatorships. In these countries there are no legitimate labor union movements functioning independently of the government or party in power. Although lost man-days are the best available yardstick of industrial unrest, they fail to reveal the degree of violence involved in these disputes or their impact on the national economy. A strike in certain vital sectors could paralyze the economy, while one in another less important industry may scarcely be noticed.

Regions	Africa	Asia & Oceania	Europe	Western Hemisphere
Most	Morocco (22)	India (4)	Italy (2)	United States (1)
Least	Seychelles (87)	Solomon Islands (84)	Austria (79)	Barbados (86)

Rank	Country	Man-Days Lost	Number of Industrial Disputes	Man-days Lost Per dispute	Rank	Country	Man-Days Lost	Number of Industrial Disputes	Man-Days Lost Per dispute	Rank	Country	Man-Days Lost	Number of Industrial Disputes	Man-Days Lost Per dispute
	TOP 10				30	Niger	160,822	107	1,503	60	Kenya	8,755	26	337
1	United States	37,960,300	5,649	6,720	31	Jamaica	138,655	142	976	61	French Guyana	5,666	11	515
2	Italy	25,377,571	2,706	9,378	32	Norway	137,651	35	3,933	62	South Yemen	5,589	4	1397
3	Spain	12,593,100	N.A.	N.A.	33	Guyana	135,199	175	772	63	Algeria	5,321	99	54
4	India	11,473,949	1,355	8,468	34	Trinidad & Tobago	133,826	44	3,041	64	Hong Kong	4,751	15	317
5	Canada	10,768,870	1,039	10,365	35	Mauritius	114,716	86	1,334	65	Singapore	3,193	4	798
6	France	5,010,687	4,348	1,152	36	Greece	113,891	89	1,280	66	Gibraltar	3,040	8	380
7	Australia	3,799,200	2,055	1,849	37	Malaysia (West)	108,562	70	1,551	67	Tanzania	3,026	3	1,008
8	United Kingdom	3,284,000	2,016	1,629	38	Venezuela	91,267	171	534	68	Vietnam	2,893	8	362
9	Japan	3,253,715	2,720	1,196	39	Burma	76,364	37	2,064	69	Cyprus	2,683	9	298
10	Chile	2,503,356	2,050	1,221	40	Tunisia	65,572	131	500	70	Upper Volta	1,890	2	945
					41	Zambia	51,003	78	654	71	Bermuda	1,260	1	1,260
	UPPER MIDDLE				42	Ghana	39,410	33	1,194	72	Bahamas	1,224	1	1,224
11	Finland	1,237,830	3,199	387	43	Burundi	27,674	5	5,535	73	Indonesia	1,148	6	191
12	Philippines	1,003,646	69	14,545						74	Sudan	1,014	2	507
13	Peru	852,778	440	1,938		**LOWER MIDDLE**				75	Egypt	921	10	92
14	Pakistan	798,183	260	3,070	44	Bangladesh	27,118	5	5,424	76	Malawi	865	13	66
15	Ireland	776,949	134	5,798	45	Sweden	24,744	73	339	77	Sabah	695	5	139
16	Argentina	651,555	543	1,120	46	Martinique	24,645	15	1,643					
17	Belgium	610,186	243	2,511	47	Guadeloupe	20,295	4	5,074		**BOTTOM 10**			
18	El Salvador	601,800	2	300,900	48	Switzerland	19,586	19	1,031	78	St. Lucia	600	1	600
19	West Germany	533,696	N.A.	N.A.	49	South Africa	19,209	276	70	79	Austria	589	N.A.	N.A.
20	Thailand	495,619	133	3,726	50	Panama	18,939	15	1,262	80	New Caledonia	466	3	155
21	New Zealand	488,165	485	1,006	51	South Korea	17,046	49	348	81	Sarawak	410	5	82
22	Morocco	479,863	521	921	52	Fiji	15,669	46	341	82	Belize	240	4	60
23	Turkey	395,245	56	7,058	53	Uganda	15,031	34	442	83	Jordan	240	2	120
24	Puerto Rico	365,380	65	5,621	54	Malta	14,677	42	349	84	Solomon Islands	197	61	3
25	Israel	308,214	123	2,506	55	Iraq	14,000	7	2,000	85	Antigua	188	102	2
26	Iceland	306,621	123	2,493	56	Netherlands	13,984	11	1,271	86	Barbados	129	2	64
27	Denmark	210,300	204	1,031	57	Cameroon	13,778	3	4,593	87	Seychelles	3	1	3
28	Guatemala	167,831	16	1,049	58	Sierra Leone	9,770	8	1,221					
29	Sri Lanka	161,092	157	1,026	59	Surinam	9,091	24	379					

Source: International Labor Organization, *Yearbook of Labor Statistics.*

191. Labor Productivity Index

The index of labor productivity (with 1970=100) measures the GNP per employed person or wage-earner in 1976. It shows what countries have achieved the most growth in labor productivity in the six-year period.

Number of Countries: 37
Midpoint: 117
Period Covered: 1976
Type of Ranking: Index of Labor Productivity (1970=100); Highest to Lowest

Highlights & Findings: Very few of the reporting countries have made significant gains in labor productivity. Except for the four Communist countries at the top (the measurement of productivity in Communist systems may not correspond to that used in the West and, in all probability, is self-serving), only four countries have an annual growth rate of over 4%.

Regions	Africa	Asia & Oceania	Europe	Western Hemisphere
Most	Malawi (26)	Japan (5)	Rumania (1)	Bolivia (3)
Least	Zambia (35)	Philippines (32)	Luxembourg (34)	Chile (37)

Rank	Country	Index of Labor Productivity	Rank	Country	Index of Labor Productivity	Rank	Country	Index of Labor Productivity
	TOP 9		12	West Germany	123	26	Malawi	109
1	Rumania	168	13	Turkey	123	27	Belgium	108
2	Poland	154	14	Finland	121	28	Mexico	108
3	Bolivia	137	15	Ireland	121	29	United Kingdom	108
4	Honduras	136	16	Israel	118	30	United States	108
5	Japan	134	17	Netherlands	118			
6	Singapore	130	18	Panama	118		*BOTTOM 7*	
7	Czechoslovakia	129	19	Ecuador	117	31	Sweden	107
8	Soviet Union	129	20	Italy	117	32	Philippines	105
9	Norway	126	21	Denmark	115	33	Cyprus	104
			22	Canada	114	34	Luxembourg	103
	MIDDLE		23	Switzerland	112	35	Zambia	97
10	Austria	124	24	New Zealand	110	36	El Salvador	85
11	France	124	25	Nicaragua	110	37	Chile	83

Source: International Labor Organization, *Yearbook of Labor Statistics.*

192. Value-Added per Worker

Value-added per worker is derived by dividing the gross domestic product by the total labor force. Used as an indicator, it measures the contribution each worker makes to the national wealth, the monetary value of his input and his general productivity. The concept is, however, subject to serious limitations in service-oriented economies. Obviously, the contribution that a scholar, writer or clergyman makes to the economy can be measured only very imperfectly, if at all. But it has real validity when confined to the gross material product of an economy. It is also useful in estimating the human resources of a country in terms of productive capability. Communist countries do not report value-added data.

Number of Countries: 119
Midpoint: $1,122.50
Period Covered: Early 1970s
Type of Ranking: Value-Added per Worker in Dollars; Highest to Lowest

Highlights & Findings: Value-added per worker provides conclusive proof that the economic strength of the industrialized world is closely linked to its superior productivity. With a value-added per worker of $2,296.90, higher-income countries have a productivity nearly nine times greater than low-income countries, where the figure is $266.00, and three times greater than middle-income countries, where the figure is $760.40. Middle Eastern countries have a value-added per worker of $5,667.20, an unrealistic figure reflecting their oil-generated booms. Countries in the Western Hemisphere and Southern Europe have a reasonably high value-added per worker of $2,043.70 and $2,014.80 respectively. The lowest figures are reported in Africa with $458.00, East Asia with $440.80 and South Asia with $324.40.

Regions	Africa	Asia & Oceania	Europe	Western Hemisphere
Most	South Africa (30)	New Zealand (12)	Sweden (3)	United States (1)
Least	Rwanda (119)	Nepal (115)	Luxembourg (54)	Bolivia (78)

Rank	Country	Value-Added per Worker ($)	Rank	Country	Value-Added per Worker ($)	Rank	Country	Value-Added per Worker ($)
	TOP 10			*UPPER MIDDLE*		21	Venezuela	4,346.10
1	United States	14,374.00	11	Iceland	7,958.00	22	Greece	4,140.30
2	Canada	11,950.00	12	New Zealand	7,877.00	23	Singapore	3,911.10
3	Sweden	9,894.00	13	Australia	7,483.00	24	Argentina	3,733.50
4	France	9,569.00	14	Saudi Arabia	6,958.70	25	Lebanon	3,574.00
5	Netherlands	8,696.00	15	Finland	6,786.00	26	Spain	3,429.20
6	West Germany	8,684.00	16	Italy	6,303.00	27	Panama	3,054.30
7	Switzerland	8,678.00	17	United Kingdom	6,275.00	28	Chile	3,020.70
8	Belgium	8,667.00	18	Austria	6,021.00	29	Trinidad & Tobago	2,915.10
9	Denmark	8,357.00	19	Japan	5,529.00	30	South Africa	2,815.00
10	Norway	8,203.00	20	Ireland	4,742.00	31	Cyprus	2,807.00

Rank	Country	Value-Added per Worker ($)	Rank	Country	Value-Added per Worker ($)	Rank	Country	Value-Added per Worker ($)
32	Mexico	2,802.50	62	Paraguay	1,083.20	94	Cambodia	315.50
33	Malta	2,786.40	63	Mauritius	1,074.10	95	Uganda	311.90
34	Portugal	2,763.40	64	Honduras	1,061.30	96	Central African Empire	296.00
35	Solomon Islands	2,626.80	65	Morocco	1,037.80	97	India	280.70
36	Costa Rica	2,602.60	66	South Korea	999.50	98	Niger	273.50
37	Costa Rica	2,324.60	67	Zambia	983.70	99	Tanzania	271.70
38	Hong Kong	2,305.80	68	Egypt	882.30	100	Madagascar	260.90
39	Barbados	2,145.00	69	Liberia	857.20	101	Indonesia	257.00
40	Gabon	2,099.20	70	Turkey	852.20	102	Zaire	246.10
41	Iran	2,041.60	71	Israel	819.40	103	Laos	237.00
42	Uruguay	2,023.30	72	Libya	739.00	104	Malawi	232.70
43	Algeria	2,016.90	73	Ivory Coast	700.10	105	Guinea	232.50
44	Dominican Republic	1,949.60	74	Ghana	690.30	106	Burma	220.70
45	Yugoslavia	1,922.80	75	Congo	688.40	107	Benin	211.10
46	Peru	1,901.60	76	Philippines	683.80	108	Afghanistan	209.40
47	Fiji	1,877.50	77	Swaziland	673.90	109	Somalia	206.90
48	Guatemala	1,839.30	78	Bolivia	659.30			
49	Brazil	1,816.00	79	Papua New Guinea	642.50		**BOTTOM 10**	
50	Iraq	1,763.10	80	Angola	591.40	110	Chad	204.80
51	Malaysia	1,610.80	81	Mauritania	591.00	111	Gambia	199.20
52	Taiwan	1,574.80	82	Senegal	580.10	112	Ethiopia	193.90
53	Nicaragua	1,557.20	83	Botswana	490.50	113	Bangladesh	185.50
54	Luxembourg	1,511.10	84	Pakistan	479.20	114	Lesotho	184.90
55	Colombia	1,425.00	85	Thailand	476.50	115	Nepal	171.20
56	Tunisia	1,414.80	86	Sierra Leone	455.30	116	Burundi	143.30
57	Guyana	1,330.60	87	Kenya	450.90	117	Upper Volta	141.60
58	Ecuador	1,208.40	88	Cameroon	442.30	118	Mali	134.60
59	Syria	1,196.20	89	Nigeria	436.50	119	Rwanda	120.20
60	El Salvador	1,122.50	90	Sudan	378.50			
	LOWER MIDDLE		91	Togo	374.20			
61	Jordan	1,105.40	92	Vietnam	339.30			
			93	Sri Lanka	332.40			

Source: World Bank.

TRANSPORTATION & COMMUNICATIONS

Scene 1: The Concorde leaves Heathrow Airport, London, at 9 A.M. and arrives at Kennedy Airport, New York, at 7 A.M. local time the same day.

Scene II: A man from Koro Toro in Ennedi Province in Chad walks hundreds of miles of pathless wild to D'jamena, then sails down the Lagone River to the Cameroon border town of Yagoua from where he travels by cart, if he is lucky, to the railhead at Betare Oya and then takes the train to the port of Douala. The distance: over 2,500 km (1,550 mi); the time taken: over three weeks.

Between these two extremes the world of transportation presents a picture of contrasts. It is not often realized that a good transportation system is not merely a convenience or facility; it is a prerequisite for industrial development and military power. A nation is only as efficient as its transportation system. Even in developed countries transportation is the weakest sector in the economy. The trains that break down, the black star airports and the potholed roads are symptoms of arterial weakening; it can impair mobility and slow more than the traffic. The plight of the railroads in the United States is as good an illustration as any of the deterioration of a once-proud system through nothing more than simple neglect.

The situation is less encouraging in many developing countries where the transportation policies are directed toward the creation of showcase projects rather than an integrated national grid. There are countries with only a few kilometers of paved roads spending a good part of their GNP on flag-carrier airlines; in others four-lane concrete highways end at the city limits.

The following section focuses on the five main arms of transportation: there are four rankings on railways, two on roads (another four on motor vehicles), one on inland waterways, two on ocean shipping and four on airlines. There are also two rankings on tourism, the number of tourist arrivals and receipts per tourist.

We have followed conventional practice in bunching transportation and communications, although the latter is a field that is bound to outstrip the former in importance in coming decades with the emergence of satellite communications and other technological breakthroughs. There are three rankings in this subsection dealing with mail, telephones and telegrams, all presented in per capita terms.

193. Railway Trackage

The following listing ranks countries by rail trackage in relation to the national territory. It should be borne in mind that length is only one element in determining adequacy of trackage; nevertheless, it is the most widely used and the most important. Other elements include the gauge; proportion of double tracks, electrified tracks, etc; the type of beds; and regular maintenance and upgrading.

Number of Countries: 122
Midpoint: 120.85 Sq Km (46.66 Sq Mi)
Period Covered: 1977
Type of Ranking: Sq Km/Sq Mi of National Territory per Km/0.621 Mi of Railroad; Total Length of Railroad in Km; Lowest to Highest

Highlights & Findings: Europe maintains its historic lead in railroads; of the top 17 countries, 13 are European. The first African country ranks only 32nd on the scale, and Asia, other than Japan, fares almost as badly. In terms of absolute length, the United States has the largest rail network in the world; to no one's surprise, the Soviet Union follows. Because of the uncertain future facing railroads, total worldwide trackage has remained more or less stable for a number of years and very few new rail lines are being constructed.

Region	Africa	Asia & Oceania	Europe	Western Hemisphere
Most	Ghana (32)	Taiwan (5)	Monaco (1)	Antigua (2)
Least	Mali (117)	Afghanistan (122)	Soviet Union (67)	French Guyana (120)

Rank	Country	National Territory per Km/0.621 Mi of Track Sq Km	Mi	Total Km
	TOP 10			
1	Monaco	0.93	0.35	1.6
2	Antigua	3.58	1.38	78
3	St.Kitts-Nevis-Anguilla	6.82	2.63	57
4	Belgium	6.95	2.68	4,394
5	Taiwan	7.16	2.76	4,500
6	West Germany	7.43	2.86	33,453
7	East Germany	7.57	2.92	14,298
8	Norway	7.60	2.93	4,257
9	Cuba	7.81	3.01	14,640
10	Switzerland	8.12	3.13	5,098
	UPPER MIDDLE			
11	Luxembourg	9.59	3.70	270
12	Czechoslovakia	9.68	3.73	13,215
13	Liechtenstein	10.50	4.05	16
14	Hungary	11.07	4.27	8,392
15	Netherlands	11.38	4.39	2,979
16	Poland	11.74	4.53	26,597
17	Japan	12.81	4.94	28,912
18	Austria	12.87	4.96	6,517
19	United Kingdom	13.10	5.05	18,614
20	Italy	14.55	5.61	20,690
21	France	15.02	5.79	36,720
22	Singapore	15.34	5.92	38
23	Denmark	16.67	6.43	2,578
24	Rumania	19.71	7.61	12,048
25	North Korea	21.69	8.37	4,345
26	Yugoslavia	24.79	9.57	10,319
27	Bulgaria	25.92	10.00	4,314
28	Portugal	26.23	10.12	3,593
29	Israel	27.01	10.42	767
30	Lebanon	27.04	10.44	383
31	Hong Kong	29.60	11.42	35
32	Ghana	29.67	11.45	953
33	Dominican Republic	30.43	11.74	1,600
34	South Korea	31.29	12.08	3,144
35	Ireland	31.47	12.15	2,189
36	Spain	31.61	12.20	15,975
37	United States	33.71	13.01	277,686
38	Jamaica	35.03	13.52	326
39	El Salvador	35.66	13.76	600
40	Sweden	37.51	14.48	11,943

Rank	Country	National Territory per Km/0.621 Mi of Track Sq Km	Mi	Total Km
41	Bangladesh	41.06	15.85	3,470
42	Sri Lanka	42.67	16.47	1,535
43	Greece	50.86	19.63	2,607
44	India	51.15	19.74	61,313
45	South Africa	54.49	21.03	22,432
46	Finland	55.76	21.52	6,038
47	New Zealand	55.90	21.58	4,799
48	Uruguay	66.90	25.83	2,795
49	Argentina	69.73	26.92	39,738
50	Swaziland	78.21	30.19	222
51	Tunisia	78.60	30.34	2,089
52	Philippines	85.76	33.11	3,503
53	Costa Rica	90.58	34.97	563
54	Turkey	92.89	35.86	8,253
55	Mexico	100.54	38.81	19,680
56	Albania	103.78	40.06	277
57	Pakistan	107.22	41.39	7,489
58	Guatemala	114.97	44.38	947
59	Chile	116.45	44.96	6,361
60	Jordan	117.61	45.40	817
61	Syria	120.85	46.66	1,543
	LOWER MIDDLE			
62	Togo	128.91	49.77	442
63	Thailand	133.79	51.65	3,833
64	Canada	139.45	53.84	71.503
65	Rhodesia (Zimbabwe)	142.57	55.04	2,743
66	Panama	155.02	59.85	488
67	Soviet Union	160.50	61.96	138,776
68	Malawi	167.93	64.83	566
69	China	175.50	67.76	54,700
70	Malaysia	182.82	70.58	1,819
71	Egypt	185.06	71.45	5,405
72	Australia	189.29	73.08	40,636
73	Senegal	190.55	73.57	1,033
74	Uganda	193.82	74.83	1,216
75	Honduras	195.38	75.43	574
76	Benin	199.95	77.20	579
77	Burma	206.57	79.75	3,285
78	Liberia	221.85	85.65	502
79	Morocco	233.02	89.96	1,756
80	Upper Volta	234.04	90.36	1,173
81	Djibouti	240.30	92.77	97
82	Indonesia	242.43	93.60	7,863

Rank	Country	National Territory per Km/0.621 Mi of Track Sq Km	Sq Mi	Total Km
83	Ecuador	244.90	94.55	1,121
84	Mozambique	248.81	96.06	3,162
85	Iraq	262.04	101.17	1,700
86	Nigeria	263.57	101.76	3,508
87	Tanzania	264.31	102.05	3,555
88	Brazil	267.15	103.14	31,896
89	Kenya	285.66	110.29	2,040
90	Cambodia	296.24	114.37	612
91	Guinea	305.65	118.01	805
92	Bolivia	307.43	118.69	3,572
93	Colombia	331.66	128.05	3,436
94	Haiti	346.41	133.74	80
95	Namibia	354.09	136.71	2,326
96	Iran	365.32	141.05	4,509
97	Zambia	370.36	142.99	2,014
98	Paraguay	389.86	150.52	1,043
99	Angola	405.92	156.72	3,069
100	Congo	437.06	168.74	800
101	Zaire	455.22	175.76	5,149
102	Sudan	458.20	176.91	5,466
103	Nicaragua	465.09	179.57	318
104	Cameroon	473.97	182.99	1,003
105	Ivory Coast	492.77	190.25	657
106	Peru	598.06	230.91	2,148
107	Brunei	601.66	232.30	10
108	Algeria	622.91	240.50	3,950
109	Madagascar	673.86	260.17	884
110	Botswana	824.60	318.17	691
111	Nepal	836.68	323.04	169
112	Surinam	859.69	331.92	166
	BOTTOM 10			
113	Sierra Leone	860.25	332.14	84
114	Mongolia	1,032.07	398.48	1,516
115	Ethiopia	1,162.17	448.71	1,014
116	Mauritania	1,669.55	644.61	650
117	Mali	1,875.93	724.29	642
118	Guyana	1,972.20	761.46	109
119	Venezuela	2,444.18	943.69	373
120	French Guyana	2,840.90	1,096.87	32
121	Saudi Arabia	4,053.91	1,565.21	575
122	Afghanistan	1,079,166.60	416,665.99	0.6

Source: International Union of Railways, Paris.

194. Railway Passenger Traffic

Railway passenger traffic has been steadily declining over the years until it has ceased to be economically viable in many countries requiring state intervention and subsidies on a large scale. Where state support has not been forthcoming, the systems have been rationalized—or Beechingized, as it is called in the United Kingdom—involving the closing of unprofitable lines and reduction in other facilities.

Number of Countries: 84
Midpoint: 112 passenger-Km
Period Covered: 1976
Type of Ranking: Passenger-Km per Capita; Total Passenger-Km in Million Km; Highest to Lowest

Highlights & Findings: Although railways have ceased to be as commercially attractive as they were in the days of the robber barons in 19th century America—the Vanderbilts, the Jay Goulds and the Herrimans—they can be operated successfully as a state-owned public utility, as evidenced by the presence of six Communist countries in the top 10. Nowhere has rail passenger traffic declined so sharply as in the United States, which appears in the bottom half of the ranking. European railways are still healthy, and most European countries rank high on this list.

Region	Africa	Asia & Oceania	Europe	Western Hemisphere
Most	Egypt (29)	Japan (1)	East Germany (2)	Argentina (21)
Least	Ethiopia (81)	Lebanon (84)	Greece (36)	Venezuela (82)

Rank	Country	Passenger-Km per Capita	Total (million)	Rank	Country	Passenger-Km per Capita	Total (million)	Rank	Country	Passenger-Km per Capita	Total (million)
		TOP 10		29	Egypt	237	8,831	58	Bangladesh	45	3,331
1	Japan	2,872	322,911	30	Chile	236	2,464	59	Mozambique	45	396
2	East Germany	1,308	21,955	31	Sri Lanka	214	2,898	60	Cameroon	40	264
3	Switzerland	1,279	8,124	32	Ivory Coast	192	918	61	Costa Rica	40	81
4	Hungary	1,261	13,365	33	New Zealand	187	589	62	Madagascar	35	289
5	Poland	1,245	42,799	34	Congo	179	249	63	Senegal	35	180
6	Soviet Union	1,227	315,061	35	Pakistan	179	12,957	64	Jamaica	33	69
7	Czechoslovakia	1,200	17,910	36	Greece	173	1,583	65	Benin	30	97
8	Rumania	1,053	22,380	37	Mongolia	147	219	66	Peru	29	455
9	France	967	51,168	38	Thailand	135	5,640	67	Indonesia	23	3,258
10	Austria	894	6,712	39	Canada	133	3,090	68	Syria	22	166
				40	Uruguay	133	372	69	Colombia	21	511
		UPPER MIDDLE		41	Turkey	115	4,615	70	Mali	21	121
11	Bulgaria	856	7,499	42	Tunisia	112	641	71	Zaire	19	447
12	Luxembourg	830	299	43	Brazil	106	11,638	72	Philippines	18	780
13	Belgium	828	8,191	44	Malaysia	95	1,173	73	Nigeria	13	785
14	Italy	696	39,118					74	Malawi	12	62
15	Denmark	675	3,415					75	Nicaragua	12	28
16	Sweden	675	5,548			*LOWER MIDDLE*					
17	United Kingdom	658	36,840	45	Burma	94	2,912				
18	Finland	631	2,985	46	Cuba	81	767			*BOTTOM 9*	
19	Netherlands	597	8,218	47	Israel	81	280	76	Paraguay	10	26
20	West Germany	593	36,451	48	United States	73	15,688	77	Ecuador	9	65
21	Argentina	563	14,480	49	Angola	72	418	78	Guyana	8	6
22	Portugal	554	5,235	50	Algeria	69	1,369	79	Saudi Arabia	8	72
23	Norway	495	1,997	51	Iran	66	2,126	80	Cambodia	7	54
24	Spain	464	16,686	52	Mexico	65	4,058	81	Ethiopia	5	132
25	Yugoslavia	461	9,941	53	Bolivia	63	366	82	Venezuela	4	42
26	South Korea	399	14,305	54	Iraq	63	704	83	Vietnam	4	170
27	India	249	148,916	55	Hong Kong	57	251	84	Lebanon	0.7	2
28	Ireland	249	788	56	Ghana	47	431				
				57	Morocco	46	828				

Source: International Union of Railways, Paris.

195. Railway Freight Traffic

In all but a few countries, freight traffic is not only the principal source of railway revenues but also the only cause for its continued existence. Recent developments in streamlining the capability of rail systems to carry more freight faster have given them a slight competitive edge over trucking and inland waterways. Particularly, raw materials such as pig iron and coal, depend largely on railways for movement from the pits to the factories.

Number of Countries: 92
Midpoint: 185 net-ton-km
Period Covered: 1976
Type of Ranking: Net-Ton-Km of Freight per Capita; Total Net-Ton-Km of Freight in Million Metric Tons; Highest to Lowest

Highlights & Findings: Rail is the principal mode of freight transport in all developed countries. The presence of Mauritania in the top 10 needs an explanation; the iron ore from the mines of F'Derik is transported to the ports entirely by rail. The same distortion may appear in the case of all countries with a small population but a relatively large mineral production.

Region	Africa	Asia & Oceania	Europe	Western Hemisphere
Most	Mauritania (3)	Australia (10)	Soviet Union (1)	Canada (2)
Least	Ethiopia (82)	Vietnam (92)	Portugal (58)	Venezuela (90)

Rank	Country	Freight Net-Ton-Km Per Capita	Total (million)	Rank	Country	Freight Net-Ton-Km Per Capita	Total (million)	Rank	Country	Freight Net-Ton-Km Per Capita	Total (million)
	TOP 10			31	Japan	423	47,550	62	Jamaica	77	159
1	Soviet Union	12,839	3,295,399	32	Mozambique	385	3,400	63	Egypt	61	2,260
2	Canada	8,454	195,642	33	China	383	301,000	64	Thailand	56	2,353
3	Mauritania	5,403	6,808	34	United Kingdom	364	20,400	65	Colombia	47	1,157
4	United States	5,329	1,146,492	35	Congo	360	501	66	Peru	45	707
5	Czechoslovakia	4,741	70,748	36	Denmark	357	1,805	67	Syria	40	305
6	Poland	3,808	130,857	37	Italy	291	16,376	68	Benin	39	127
7	East Germany	3,465	58,181	38	Spain	274	9,842	69	Malawi	39	204
8	Rumania	3,149	67,560	39	South Korea	271	9,728	70	Ghana	33	305
9	South Africa	2,653	69,336	40	India	225	134,874	71	Senegal	32	164
10	Australia	2,259	30,816	41	Tunisia	222	1,277	72	Mali	25	148
				42	Chile	207	2,165	73	Madagascar	24	200
	UPPER MIDDLE			43	Iraq	202	2,252	74	Sri Lanka	20	282
11	Austria	2,222	10,685	44	Netherlands	196	2,700	75	Guatemala	19	117
12	Hungary	2,127	22,552	45	Cuba	195	1,848	76	Nigeria	16	972
13	Sweden	1,981	16,283	46	Ireland	185	585	77	Lebanon	12	15
14	Bulgaria	1,947	17,055	47	Turkey	181	7,278	78	Burma	12	382
15	Mongolia	1,824	2,718					79	Paraguay	12	30
16	Botswana	1,739	1,200		*LOWER MIDDLE*			80	Hong Kong	11	47
17	Luxembourg	1,739	626	48	Morocco	176	3,143	81	Bangladesh	9	639
18	Finland	1,384	6,547	49	Iran	153	4,917	82	Ethiopia	9	260
19	France	1,294	68,508	50	Sudan	152	2,288				
20	New Zealand	1,162	3,649	51	Malaysia	134	1,653		*BOTTOM 10*		
21	Yugoslavia	974	21,017	52	Uruguay	133	372	83	Costa Rica	7	14
22	West Germany	963	59,219	53	Israel	129	449	84	Saudi Arabia	7	66
23	Angola	941	5,461	54	Zaire	128	3,017	85	Ecuador	6	46
24	Switzerland	890	5,652	55	Pakistan	120	8,677	86	Nicaragua	6	14
25	Rhodesia (Zimbabwe)	790	5,158	56	Ivory Coast	111	529	87	Indonesia	5	717
26	Norway	672	2,709	57	Greece	92	844	88	Cambodia	1	10
27	Belgium	671	6,637	58	Portugal	90	854	89	Guyana	1	1
28	Brazil	579	63,246	59	Bolivia	89	518	90	Venezuela	1	15
29	Mexico	559	34,821	60	Algeria	87	1,727	91	Philippines	0.9	40
30	Argentina	429	11,038	61	Cameroon	82	534	92	Vietnam	0.02	1

Source: International Union of Railways, Paris.

196. Total Locomotives

Railway systems may be ranked not only by the length of the track in relation to land area, the passengers carried and the net-ton-km of freight but also according to their rolling stock, especially by the number and horsepower of locomotives. The term locomotives includes electric locomotives. The tractive force is usually expressed in horsepower but in some countries in metric tons.

Number of Countries: 73
Midpoint: 306
Period Covered: 1976
Type of Ranking: Number of Locomotives Along with Their Tractive Force in Thousand Horsepower (or Thousand Metric Tons, as Noted); Highest to Lowest

Highlights & Findings: This ranking is subject to certain qualifications. The number and horsepower of the locomotives are only two of many elements that determine the efficiency of a rail system. Others include the age of the locomotives, the type of motive power (i.e., diesel, electric, coal), repair and maintenance facilities, and availability of parts and supplies. Nevertheless, the top countries in this ranking may be safely accepted as having the most developed rail systems in the world outside the Soviet Union, for which no statistics are available.

Regions	Africa	Asia & Oceania	Europe	Western Hemisphere
Most	South Africa (5)	India (2)	West Germany (3)	United States (1)
Least	Mali (70)	Hong Kong (72)	Luxembourg (56)	Dominican Republic (73)

Rank	Country	Number of Locomotives	Horsepower (000)	Rank	Country	Number of Locomotives	Horsepower (000)	Rank	Country	Number of Locomotives	Horsepower (000)
		TOP 10		24	South Korea	774	N.A.	49	Malaysia	132	N.A.
1	United States	27,573	59,500	25	Finland	674	768	50	Tunisia	124	93.9
2	India	11,095	170	26	Chile	672	N.A.	51	Madagascar	112	47
			(000 metric tons)	27	Netherlands	589	600	52	Vietnam	109	N.A.
3	West Germany	7,987	16,771	28	Indonesia	527	616	53	Philippines	101	103.4
4	France	5,964	11,424	29	Bangladesh	516	5.9	54	Costa Rica	94	N.A.
5	South Africa	4,519	81				(000 metric tons)	55	Cameroon	91	N.A.
			(000 metric tons)	30	Thailand	507	N.A.	56	Luxembourg	84	134
6	Japan	4,270	6,861	31	New Zealand	504	560	57	Zambia	84	N.A.
7	Canada	4,008	7,818	32	Kenya	418	7.5	58	Congo	80	108.5
8	United Kingdom	3,731	5,815				(000 metric tons)	59	Israel	57	67
9	Italy	3,441	6,518	33	Burma	393	N.A.	60	Senegal	56	41.5
10	Argentina	3,104	N.A.	34	Greece	384	597	61	Lebanon	39	28.6
				35	Portugal	342	454	62	Malawi	39	38.3
		UPPER MIDDLE		36	Nigeria	338	N.A.	63	Ethiopia	36	25.7
11	Brazil	1,970	3,062	37	Algeria	308	274				
12	Australia	1,928	N.A.	38	Sri Lanka	306	N.A.			*BOTTOM 10*	
13	Yugoslavia	1,605	3,128					64	Jamaica	31	N.A.
14	Sweden	1,500	2,693			*LOWER MIDDLE*		65	Jordan	29	N.A.
15	Switzerland	1,424	N.A.	39	Mozambique	301	N.A.	66	Cambodia	28	N.A.
16	Austria	1,417	2,677	40	Sudan	289	N.A.	67	Saudi Arabia	26	32.2
17	Mexico	1,293	28.4	41	Norway	247	612	68	Togo	23	11.1
			(000 metric tons)	42	Angola	234	N.A.	69	Guyana	19	7.6
18	Spain	1,174	2,455	43	Ireland	215	143	70	Mali	18	18.9
19	Belgium	1,145	1,542	44	Colombia	208	N.A.	71	Paraguay	17	N.A.
20	Egypt	1,139	N.A.	45	Morocco	197	N.A.	72	Hong Kong	10	15.4
21	Pakistan	1,024	N.A.	46	Iraq	184	N.A.	73	Dominican Republic	2	0.3
22	Turkey	956	1,746	47	Syria	168	N.A.				
23	Denmark	815	770	48	Uruguay	157	127				

Source: *International Railway Statistics,* International Union of Railways, Paris.

197. Length of Roads

In terms of length and intensity of use, roads dwarf both railroads and inland waterways. Ranging from the great national highways of the world, which are engineering marvels to small dusty paths, they form arterial networks for almost every conceivable kind of vehicular traffic. To be meaningful, the length of roads has to be presented in relation to the size of the national territory, and this relationship is what has been attempted in the following ranking.

Number of Countries: 175
Midpoint: 6.91 Sq Km (2.66 Sq Mi)
Period Covered: 1977
Type of Ranking: National Territory in Sq Km and Sq Mi per Km/0.621 Mi of Roads; Total length of Roads in Km; Lowest to Highest

Highlights & Findings: Differences in the rank order between this and the following ranking on paved roads are significant only in the lower half because developing countries have a greater percentage of unpaved roads. There is also a strong correlation between the type and level of traffic and the length and condition of the roads. In other words, it seems logical to conclude that the road system is more closely related to the volume of traffic than to the size of the national territory. A country, such as Sudan, with few motor vehicles per capita has little incentive to construct or maintain a modern road network.

Region	Africa	Asia & Oceania	Europe	Western Hemisphere
Most	Mauritius (31)	Singapore (3)	Gibraltar (1)	Bermuda (4)
Least	Namibia (174)	Saudi Arabia (169)	Portugal (146)	Falkland Islands (175)

Rank	Country	Nat'l Terr per Km/0.621 Mi of Road Sq Km	Sq Mi	Total Length of Roads (Km)	Rank	Country	Nat'l Terr per Km/0.621 Mi of Road Sq Km	Sq Mi	Total Length of Roads (Km)	Rank	Country	Nat'l Terr per Km/0.621 Mi of Road Sq Km	Sq Mi	Total Length of Roads (Km)
	TOP 10				50	East Germany	2.27	0.87	47,573	100	Chile	9.85	3.80	75,200
1	Gibraltar	0.11	0.04	56	51	India	2.36	0.91	1,327,450	101	Mexico	9.89	3.81	200,060
2	Malta	0.25	0.09	1,239	52	Austria	2.49	0.96	33,600	102	Equatorial Guinea	10.13	3.91	2,760
3	Singapore	0.26	0.10	2,200	53	Yugoslavia	2.55	0.98	100,300	103	Tunisia	10.20	3.93	16.093
4	Bermuda	0.28	0.10	190	54	Phillipines	2.73	1.05	109.690	104	Sierra Leone	10.21	3.94	7,073
5	Belgium	0.29	0.11	104,000	55	Rwanda	2.83	1.09	9,120	105	Nigeria	10.35	3.99	89,318
6	Barbados	0.31	0.11	1,370	56	New Zealand	2.90	1.11	92,374	106	Guinea-Bissau	11.26	4.34	3,218
7	Netherlands	0.33	0.12	100,960	57	El Salvador	2.95	1.13	7,250	107	China	11.49	4.43	835,000
8	Grenada	0.34	0.13	1,000	58	Rumania	3.04	1.17	77,949	108	Kenya	11.58	4.47	50,290
9	Japan	0.34	0.13	1,066,028	59	Bangladesh	3.17	1.22	44,930	109	Uruguay	11.91	4.59	15,700
10	Macao	0.36	0.13	42	60	Tuvalu	3.25	1.25	8	110	Canada	12.02	4.64	829,325
					61	Bulgaria	3.55	1.37	31.454	111	Ecuador	12.33	4.76	22,250
	UPPER MIDDLE				62	Greece	3.61	1.39	36,714	112	Argentina	12.61	4.86	219,700
11	Luxembourg	0.57	0.22	4,528	63	Western Samoa	3.63	1.40	784	113	Pakistan	12.63	4.87	63,567
12	San Marino	0.59	0.22	104	64	Spain	3.64	1.40	138,560	114	Turkey	12.77	4.93	60,000
13	West Germany	0.62	0.23	398,720	65	Burundi	3.65	1.40	7,800	115	Qatar	12.86	4.96	805
14	Denmark	0.66	0.25	64,480	66	Tonga	4.00	1.54	249	116	Honduras	12.89	4.97	8,700
15	Switzerland	0.68	0.26	60,512	67	New Caledonia	4.23	1.63	5,200	117	Laos	13.15	5.07	18,000
16	France	0.69	0.26	795,520	68	Dominican Republic	4.27	1.64	11,400	118	Malaysia	13.68	5.28	24,297
17	St. Vincent	0.70	0.27	550	69	Norway	4.39	1.69	73,600	119	Cambodia	13.90	5.36	13,036
18	United Kingdom	0.71	0.27	343,315	70	Finland	4.62	1.78	72,800	120	Liberia	14.00	5.40	7,952
19	Antigua	0.73	0.28	380	71	Sweden	4.63	1.78	96,640	121	Soviet Union	14.24	5.49	1,564,000
20	Martinique	0.75	0.28	1,450	72	Israel	4.76	1.83	4,348	122	Jordan	14.39	5.55	6,677
21	Guadeloupe	0.77	0.29	2,300	73	Brunei	4.78	1.84	1,207	123	Senegal	14.48	5.59	13,589
22	Czechoslovakia	0.78	0.30	73,600	74	Andorra	4.85	1.87	96	124	Venezuela	15.55	6.00	58,600
23	Ireland	0.78	0.30	88,302	75	North Korea	4.85	1.87	20,278	125	Cameroon	15.91	6.14	29,866
24	Nauru	0.78	0.30	27	76	Rhodesia (Zimbabwe)	4.98	1.92	78,428	126	Zaire	16.16	6.23	145,000
25	St. Lucia	0.82	0.31	750	77	Bahamas	5.42	2.09	2,100	127	Syria	16.21	6.25	11,500
26	Cook Islands	0.92	0.35	260	78	Cuba	5.50	2.12	20,700	128	Upper Volta	16.82	6.49	16,320
27	Hungary	0.93	0.35	99,595	79	Gambia	5.57	2.15	1,858	129	Angola	16.87	6.51	73,828
28	Cyprus	0.98	0.37	9,358	80	Fiji	5.70	2.20	3,205	130	Thailand	17.80	6.87	28,806
29	Jamaica	1.01	0.38	11,250	81	Brazil	5.72	2.20	1,489,000	131	Indonesia	20.05	7.74	93,053
30	Poland	1.02	0.39	305,863	82	Albania	5.76	2.22	4,989	132	Colombia	20.11	7.76	56,650
31	Mauritius	1.04	0.40	1,770	83	South Africa	5.84	2.25	209,244	133	Egypt	21.15	8.16	47,276
32	Dominica	1.05	0.40	750	84	Malawi	6.37	2.45	14,913	134	Zambia	21.39	8.25	34,869
33	Italy	1.05	0.40	286,400	85	Kuwait	6.43	2.48	2,494	135	Iraq	21.42	8.27	20,791
34	Hong Kong	1.07	0.41	966	86	Swaziland	6.54	2.52	2,653	136	Madagascar	22.06	8.51	26,992
35	Netherlands Antilles	1.07	0.41	950						137	Peru	24.51	9.46	52,400
36	French Polynesia	1.08	0.41	3,700		*LOWER MIDDLE*				138	Papua New Guinea	24.75	9.55	19,200
37	Sri Lanka	1.25	0.48	52,200	87	Ghana	6.91	2.66	34,449	139	Burma	25.13	9.70	27,000
38	Reunion	1.26	0.48	1,983	88	Ivory Coast	6.93	2.67	46,675	140	Central African Empire	28.16	10.87	22,250
39	St. Kitts-Nevis-Anguilla	1.29	0.49	300	89	Lesotho	7.73	2.98	3,916	141	Bolivia	29.44	11.36	37,300
40	Lebanon	1.40	0.54	7,370	90	Morocco	7.82	3.01	52,304	142	Mozambique	29.71	11.47	26,477
41	Gilbert Islands	1.41	0.54	483	91	Guatemala	7.94	3.06	13,700	143	Afghanistan	31.00	11.96	20,885
42	United States	1.54	0.59	6,059,200	92	Vietnam	8.00	3.08	41,190	146	Djibouti	31.08	11.99	750
43	Trinidad & Tobago	1.65	0.63	3,100	93	Togo	8.17	3.15	6,974	145	Algeria	31.37	12.11	78,410
44	Seychelles	1.87	0.72	215	94	Haiti	8.66	3.34	3,200	146	Portugal	31.85	12.29	29,600
45	Taiwan	1.90	0.73	16,900	95	Nicaragua	8.75	3.37	16,900	147	Guinea	32.35	12.49	7,604
46	Costa Rica	1.99	0.76	25,600	96	Australia	9.18	3.54	837,866	148	Uganda	34.84	13.45	6,763
47	Wallis & Futuna	2.07	0.79	100	97	Iceland	9.24	3.56	11,137	149	Benin	35.05	13.53	3,303
48	South Korea	2.10	0.81	46,664	98	Belize	9.37	3.61	2,450	150	Solomon Islands	35.71	13.78	834
49	Comoros	2.17	0.83	999	99	Panama	9.69	3.74	7,800	151	Bhutan	35.73	13.79	1,304

Rank	Country	National Territory per Km/0.621 Mi of Road Sq Km	Sq Mi	Total Length of Roads (Km)	Rank	Country	National Territory per Km/0.621 Mi of Road Sq Km	Sq Mi	Total Length of Roads (Km)	Rank	Country	National Territory per Km/0.621 Mi of Road Sq Km	Sq Mi	Total Length of Roads (Km)
152	Iran	37.91	14.63	43,442	161	Tanzania	55.24	21.32	17,010	168	Libya	108.47	41.88	16,212
153	Nepal	38.21	14.75	3,700	162	Botswana	55.75	21.52	10,219	169	Saudi Arabia	130.58	50.41	17,850
154	Gabon	38.40	14.82	6,878	163	Yemen Arab Republic	55.86	21.56	3,477	170	Niger	177.83	68.66	7,122
155	Congo	42.40	16.37	8,246	164	Surinam	57.08	22.03	2,500	171	Mauritania	178.19	68.79	6,090
156	Chad	46.70	18.03	27,505						172	French Guyana	181.81	70.19	500
157	Somalia	47.05	18.16	13,541		*BOTTOM 11*				173	Sudan	237.17	91.57	10,560
158	Guyana	52.43	20.24	4,100	165	Oman	75.41	29.11	2,816	174	Namibia	242.24	93.52	3,400
159	South Yemen	54.13	20.89	5,311	166	Mali	76.71	29.61	15,699	175	Falkland Islands	347.65	134.22	35
160	Paraguay	54.21	20.93	7,500	167	Ethiopia	108.16	41.76	10,895					

Source: International Road Federation.

198. Length of Paved Roads

Roads are paved with a variety of materials, including cobblestones, but the most common substances are bitumen and concrete. Because only paved roads are designed to carry heavy traffic, their length is an important indicator of a nation's transportation capacity. Included in the category of paved roads are all arterial roads such as national, state and municipal highways or throughways and toll roads or turnpikes.

Number of Countries: 171
Midpoint: 42.69 Sq Km (16.48 Sq Mi)
Period Covered: 1977
Type of Ranking: National Territory in Sq Km and Sq Mi per Km/0.621 Mi of Paved Road; Total Length of Paved Roads in Km; Lowest to Highest

Highlights & Findings: Mininations have an advantage in this respect and naturally dominate the top of the ranking. Among the larger nations the United Kingdom, Japan, France and Italy have the best paved road systems. In those countries with over 100 sq km of land per km of paved road, it may be assumed that paved roads are limited to cities and that there are no national highways in the conventional sense.

Region	Africa	Asia & Oceania	Europe	Western Hemisphere
Most	Mauritius (18)	Singapore (6)	Gibraltar (1)	Bermuda (3)
Least	Sudan (170)	Oman (171)	Soviet Union (106)	Bolivia (164)

Rank	Country	National Territory per Km/0.621 Mi of Paved Road Sq Km	Sq Mi	Total Length of Paved Roads (Km)	Rank	Country	National Territory per Km/0.621 Mi of Paved Road Sq Km	Sq Mi	Total Length of Paved Roads (Km)	Rank	Country	National Territory per Km/0.621 Mi of Paved Road Sq Km	Sq Mi	Total Length of Paved Roads (Km)
	TOP 11				15	Japan	1.09	0.42	336,733	32	Czechoslovakia	2.23	0.86	57,200
1	Gibraltar	0.11	0.04	56	16	Martinique	1.10	0.42	1,000	33	Sri Lanka	2.69	1.03	24,300
2	Malta	0.27	0.10	1,128	17	Antigua	1.16	0.44	240	34	Seychelles	2.78	1.07	145
3	Bermuda	0.28	0.10	190	18	Mauritius	1.16	0.44	1,593	35	Hungary	2.85	1.10	32,583
4	Belgium	0.32	0.12	93,809	19	France	1.17	0.45	468,160	36	United States	3.08	1.18	3,036,525
5	Barbados	0.33	0.12	1,290	20	Guadeloupe	1.18	0.45	1,500	37	Netherlands Antilles	3.40	1.31	300
6	Singapore	0.34	0.13	1,700	21	Italy	1.18	0.45	254,400	38	St. Kitts-Nevis-Anguilla	3.89	1.50	100
7	Macao	0.36	0.13	42	22	St. Lucia	1.36	0.52	450	39	Austria	4.03	1.55	20,800
8	Grenada	0.57	0.22	600	23	Reunion	1.49	0.57	1,683	40	Taiwan	4.26	1.64	7,564
9	Luxembourg	0.57	0.22	4,528	24	Jamaica	1.50	0.57	7,600	41	Israel	4.76	1.83	4,348
10	Denmark	0.68	0.26	62,400	25	West Germany	1.54	0.59	161,400	42	Poland	4.80	1.85	65,000
11	Switzerland	0.68	0.26	60,512	26	Hong Kong	1.56	0.60	660	43	Portugal	5.35	2.06	17,600
					27	Dominica	1.58	0.61	500	44	Spain	5.91	2.28	85,400
	UPPER MIDDLE				28	Lebanon	1.65	0.63	6,270	45	New Zealand	5.96	2.30	44,940
12	United Kingdom	0.70	0.27	345,600	29	Trinidad & Tobago	1.83	0.70	2,800	46	Bahrain	6.40	2.47	93
13	Ireland	0.87	0.33	78,616	30	St. Vincent	1.94	0.74	200	47	Yugoslavia	6.61	2.55	38,700
14	Nauru	1.00	0.38	21	31	Cyprus	2.20	0.84	4,203	48	Greece	7.27	2.80	18,223

Rank	Country	National Territory per Km/0.621 Mi of Paved Road Sq Km	Sq Mi	Total Length of Paved Roads (Km)
49	Kuwait	7.31	2.82	2,195
50	Comoros	7.35	2.83	295
51	India	7.55	2.91	415,250
52	Western Samoa	7.59	2.93	375
53	South Korea	8.13	3.13	12,097
54	East Germany	8.34	3.22	12,978
55	Dominican Republic	8.39	3.23	5,800
56	Finland	11.37	4.38	29,600
57	Cook Islands	12.63	4.87	19
58	Iceland	12.93	4.99	7,959
59	Cuba	13.00	5.01	8,800
60	Bahamas	13.40	5.17	850
61	El Salvador	14.26	5.50	1,500
62	Philippines	14.66	5.66	20,483
63	Brunei	15.36	5.93	376
64	Tunisia	15.42	5.95	10,646
65	Sweden	15.47	5.97	28,960
66	Bulgaria	16.73	6.45	6,683
67	Rumania	18.10	6.98	13,117
68	Uruguay	18.69	7.21	10,000
69	Malaysia	19.89	7.67	16,719
70	Albania	22.33	8.62	1,287
71	Morocco	22.36	8.63	18,299
72	Norway	22.48	8.67	14,400
73	Qatar	23.43	9.04	442
74	Netherlands	23.56	9.09	1,440
75	Costa Rica	26.15	10.09	1,950
76	Syria	26.90	10.38	6,930
77	Panama	30.26	11.68	2,500
78	Mexico	31.91	12.32	62,005
79	Thailand	34.71	13.40	14,773
80	Bangladesh	35.23	13.60	4,044
81	Turkey	36.50	14.09	21,000
82	New Caledonia	36.69	14.16	600
83	China	36.92	14.25	260,000
84	Australia	37.04	14.30	207,644
85	Jordan	39.82	15.37	2,413
86	Guatemala	42.69	16.48	2,550
	LOWER MIDDLE			
87	Venezuela	43.00	16.60	21,200
88	Ghana	45.30	17.49	5,260
89	Haiti	46.18	17.83	600
90	Togo	47.16	18.20	1,208
91	Rhodesia (Zimbabwe)	48.91	18.88	7,995
92	Guinea	49.71	19.19	4,949
93	Pakistan	49.94	19.28	16,077
94	Canada	52.53	20.28	189,800
95	Gambia	54.52	21.05	190
96	Algeria	54.59	21.07	45,070
97	South Africa	56.26	21.72	21,726
98	Fiji	59.51	22.97	307
99	Vietnam	60.26	23.26	5,471
100	Nigeria	60.43	23.33	15,300
101	New Hebrides	61.51	23.74	240
102	Sierra Leone	62.94	24.30	1,148
103	Argentina	64.37	24.85	43,050
104	Malawi	68.63	26.49	1,385
105	Iraq	68.64	26.50	6,490
106	Soviet Union	69.17	26.70	322,000
107	Indonesia	71.73	27.69	26,573
108	Cambodia	74.60	28.80	2,430
109	Belize	76.57	29.56	300
110	Senegal	77.22	29.81	2,549
111	Swaziland	77.51	29.92	224
112	Chile	82.30	31.77	9,000
113	Ecuador	83.19	32.11	3,300
114	Equatorial Guinea	84.50	32.62	331
115	Nepal	84.87	32.76	1,666
116	Guinea-Bissau	86.74	33.49	418
117	Burundi	94.96	34.66	300
118	Honduras	97.52	37.65	1,150
119	Nicaragua	98.60	38.06	1,500
120	Egypt	105.02	40.54	9,524
121	United Arab Emirates	106.25	41.02	780
122	Bhutan	111.48	43.04	418
123	Brazil	119.67	46.20	71,200
124	Uganda	121.86	47.05	1,934
125	Solomon Islands	123.58	47.71	241
126	Ivory Coast	135.57	52.34	2,388
127	Iran	136.58	52.73	12,060
128	Colombia	138.97	53.65	8,200
129	Lesotho	139.00	53.66	218
130	Madagascar	139.01	53.67	4,285
131	Angola	145.24	56.07	8,577
132	Kenya	155.40	59.99	3,750
133	Benin	165.21	63.78	705
134	Zambia	167.39	64.62	4,456
135	Mozambique	182.03	70.28	4,322
136	Laos	182.15	70.32	1,300
137	Liberia	184.69	71.30	603
138	Burma	212.06	81.87	3,200
139	French Guyana	213.90	82.58	425
140	Rwanda	215.83	83.33	120
141	Saudi Arabia	216.83	83.71	10,750
142	Cameroon	220.60	85.17	2,155
143	Guyana	226.28	87.36	950
144	Libya	228.03	88.04	7,712
145	Djibouti	233.10	89.99	100
146	Peru	237.89	91.84	5,400
147	Afghanistan	263.21	101.62	2,460
148	Surinam	285.41	110.19	500
149	Namibia	307.32	118.65	2,680
150	Tanzania	364.06	140.56	2,581
151	Ethiopia	364.95	140.90	3,229
152	North Korea	400.42	154.60	304
153	Yemen Arab Republic	415.95	160.59	467
154	Paraguay	451.81	174.44	900
155	Upper Volta	527.96	203.84	520
156	Congo	653.55	252.33	535
157	Niger	670.46	258.86	1,889
158	Somali	680.70	262.81	936
159	Mali	721.59	278.60	1,669
160.	Papua New Guinea	742.76	286.77	640
161	Falkland Islands	760.50	293.62	16
	BOTTOM 10			
162	Gabon	772.45	298.24	342
163	South Yemen	892.82	344.71	322
164	Bolivia	954.92	368.69	1,150
165	Zaire	1,171.97	452.49	2,000
166	Botswana	1,300.91	502.28	438
167	Mauritania	1,944.82	750.89	558
168	Central African Empire	2,161.31	834.48	290
169	Chad	5,308.42	2,049.58	242
170	Sudan	8,079.12	3,119.34	310
171	Oman	42,476.00	16,399.98	5

Source: International Road Federation.

199. Passenger Cars

Passenger cars are defined as vehicles seating not more than nine persons (counting the driver) and include taxis, jeeps and station wagons. The data are based on registration figures as reported by national motor vehicle departments.

Number of Countries: 156
Midpoint: 21.9 per 1,000 inhabitants
Period Covered: 1976
Type of Ranking: Registered Passenger Cars per 1,000 Inhabitants; Total Number of Passenger Cars in Use; Highest to Lowest

Highlights & Findings: Worldwide (excluding the Soviet Union, China and North Korea) there are 271.59 million passenger cars in use. The regional distribution is as follows: Africa, 5.23 million; North America, 122.4 million; South America, 10.43 million; Asia, 24.36 million; Europe, 96.91 million; and Oceania, 6.67 million. North America accounts for 45% of the world total.

Regions	Africa	Asia & Oceania	Europe	Western Hemisphere
Most	Libya (40)	New Caledonia (2)	Luxembourg (6)	United States (1)
Least	Chad (152)	Nepal (156)	Poland (65)	Bolivia (148)

Rank	Country	Passenger Cars per 1,000 Inhabitants	Total Number (000)
	TOP 10		
1	United States	506.7	109,003.0
2	New Caledonia	403.0	52.5
3	Canada	388.5	8,870.3
4	New Zealand	383.0	1,205.4
5	Australia	375.6	5,124.0
6	Luxembourg	363.0	130.7
7	Sweden	350.4	2,881.6
8	West Germany	307.5	18,919.7
9	France	300.4	15,900.0
10	Iceland	298.6	65.7
	UPPER MIDDLE		
11	Italy	283.5	15,925.3
12	Belgium	276.8	2,738.0
13	Netherlands	273.6	3,768.0
14	Switzerland	271.3	1,723.0
15	Denmark	265.1	1,344.2
16	United Kingdom	260.0	14,562.4
17	Norway	253.5	1,022.0
18	Austria	243.4	1,828.1
19	Kuwait	230.1	237.1
20	Finland	218.3	1,032.9
21	Bermuda	211.6	12.7
22	Puerto Rico	200.5	607.8
23	Malta	188.0	56.4
24	Gibraltar	183.3	5.5
25	Ireland	176.0	556.4
26	Bahamas	173.8	36.5
27	Netherlands Antilles	169.0	39.0
28	Japan	164.3	18,475.0
29	Spain	148.7	5,351.4
30	French Polynesia	143.3	17.2
31	Brunei	136.0	24.6
32	French Guyana	128.3	7.7
33	East Germany	122.2	2,052.2
34	British Virgin Islands	116.6	1.4
35	Martinique	116.4	39.6
36	Guadeloupe	112.9	38.4
37	Czechoslovakia	112.4	1,677.5
38	Portugal	109.4	1,034.0
39	Cyprus	107.9	69.1
40	Libya	107.8	263.1
41	Djibouti	101.8	11.0
42	Barbados	96.0	24.0
43	Trinidad & Tobago	93.7	101.3
44	Reunion	91.8	45.0
45	Bahrain	89.6	23.3
46	Israel	85.9	297.3
47	South Africa	83.0	2,169.0
48	Argentina	80.9	2,027.5
49	Yugoslavia	80.3	1,732.1
50	Venezuela	79.6	955.2
51	Lebanon	79.2	220.2
52	Surinam	65.4	28.8

Rank	Country	Passenger Cars per 1,000 Inhabitants	Total Number (000)
53	Singapore	62.3	142.1
54	Hungary	61.7	654.8
55	Greece	55.6	510.0
56	Jamaica	55.6	109.6
57	Uruguay	54.7	151.6
58	Seychelles	46.6	2.8
59	Brazil	44.9	4,907.8
60	Grenada	42.2	3.8
61	Malaysia	42.1	518.2
62	Mexico	41.3	2,580.4
63	Belize	40.0	5.6
64	Panama	39.6	66.2
65	Poland	37.5	1,290.1
66	Guyana	35.2	27.5
67	St. Vincent	35.0	3.5
68	St. Lucia	33.6	3.7
69	Fiji	31.2	18.1
70	Costa Rica	30.3	59.8
71	St. Kitts-Nevis-Anguilla	30.0	2.1
72	Rhodesia (Zimbabwe)	29.5	180.0
73	Hong Kong	27.3	120.0
74	New Hebrides	26.0	2.6
75	Macao	25.0	6.5
76	Chile	24.9	255.7
77	Mauritius	23.7	20.7
78	Angola	21.9	127.3
	LOWER MIDDLE		
79	Sao Tome & Principe	20.0	1.6
80	Ivory Coast	19.9	90.5
81	Gabon	19.4	10.1
82	Morocco	19.4	347.4
83	Tunisia	18.2	102.6
84	Zambia	18.0	85.8
85	Iran	17.8	589.2
86	Peru	17.6	266.9
87	Algeria	17.0	286.1
88	Colombia	16.4	401.3
89	Greenland	16.0	0.8
90	Dominican Republic	15.9	77.3
91	Nicaragua	15.9	32.0
92	Swaziland	15.8	7.9
93	Jordan	14.9	41.5
94	Congo	14.3	20.0
95	Guatemala	13.2	82.7
96	Turkey	11.7	471.5
97	Senegal	11.3	44.8
98	El Salvador	10.5	41.0
99	Mozambique	10.4	89.3
100	Tonga	10.0	1.0
101	Cape Verde	9.6	2.9
102	Cameroon	9.1	59.5
103	Iraq	8.8	98.6
104	Philippines	8.8	386.2
105	Samoa	8.6	1.3

Rank	Country	Passenger Cars per 1,000 Inhabitants	Total Number (000)
106	Cuba	8.4	80.0
107	Syria	8.2	62.8
108	Honduras	7.2	20.5
109	Liberia	7.2	12.1
110	Kenya	7.0	98.3
111	Madagascar	7.0	55.0
112	Saudi Arabia	6.8	59.4
113	Sri Lanka	6.8	93.8
114	South Yemen	6.8	11.9
115	Paraguay	6.7	16.0
116	Egypt	6.4	245.6
117	Ecuador	6.3	43.6
118	Thailand	6.3	266.1
119	Ghana	6.2	64.0
120	Papua New Guinea	6.2	17.7
121	Gambia	6.1	3.0
122	Sierra Leone	6.0	18.9
123	Bostwana	5.9	4.1
124	Togo	5.9	13.0
125	Benin	5.3	17.0
126	Central African Empire	4.8	9.1
127	Lesotho	4.4	4.6
128	Laos	4.3	14.1
129	Cambodia	3.6	27.2
130	Mauritania	3.6	4.4
131	Zaire	3.5	84.8
132	Haiti	3.4	15.7
133	Indonesia	3.0	420.9
134	Pakistan	2.7	196.1
135	Somalia	2.7	8.0
136	Tanzania	2.7	42.0
137	South Korea	2.6	96.1
138	Nigeria	2.5	150.0
139	Guinea	2.4	10.2
140	Uganda	2.4	27.0
141	Afghanistan	2.1	38.4
142	Mali	2.1	11.9
143	Niger	2.0	9.9
144	Malawi	1.9	10.2
145	Ethiopia	1.8	52.5
	BOTTOM 11		
146	Burundi	1.7	5.1
147	Sudan	1.7	29.2
148	Bolivia	1.6	9.1
149	Upper Volta	1.6	9.5
150	Vietnam	1.5	70.0
151	Rwanda	1.5	6.5
152	Chad	1.4	5.8
153	Burma	1.2	37.7
154	India	1.2	769.2
155	Bangladesh	0.4	31.7
156	Nepal	0.3	4.0

Source: International Motor Vehicle Association, Detroit, U.S.

200. Commercial Vehicles

Commercial vehicles include vans, trucks, buses, tractor and semitrailer combinations. The data are based on registration figures as reported by national motor vehicle departments. This ranking has more relevance than the passenger car ranking as an indication of the relative economic strength of road transportation systems in the countries listed.

Number of Countries: 157
Midpoint: 10.2 per 1,000 Inhabitants
Period Covered: 1976
Type of Ranking: Registered Commercial Vehicles per 1,000 Persons; Total Number of Commerical Vehicles in Use; Highest to Lowest

Highlights & Findings: Worldwide (excluding the Soviet Union, China and North Korea) there are 69.29 million commercial vehicles in use, distributed as follows: Africa, 2.43 million; North America, 29.94 million; Asia, 14.11 million; South America, 3.27 million; Europe, 12.63 million; and Oceania, 1.6 million. North America accounts for 43% of the world total.

Regions	Africa	Asia & Oceania	Europe	Western Hemisphere
Most	Libya (10)	New Caldeonia (1)	Austria (9)	United States (2)
Least	Ethiopia (154)	Nepal (157)	Rumania (133)	Haiti (156)

Rank	Country	Commercial Vehicles per 1,000 Inhabitants	Total Number (000)	Rank	Country	Commercial Vehicles per 1,000 Inhabitants	Total Number (000)	Rank	Country	Commercial Vehicles per 1,000 Inhabitants	Total Number (000)
	TOP 10			44	Trinidad & Tobago	23.7	25.7	88	Lebanon	8.4	23.4
1	New Caledonia	152.3	19.8	45	Surinam	23.1	10.2	89	Dominican Republic	8.1	39.4
2	United States	121.5	26,152.0	46	Belize	22.8	3.2	90	Morocco	8.1	145.7
3	Japan	97.9	11,011.0	47	Singapore	22.3	51.0	91	Guatemala	8.0	50.1
4	Canada	94.5	2,157.8	48	West Germany	22.0	1,353.9	92	New Hebrides	8.0	0.8
5	Australia	88.3	1,204.6	49	Costa Rica	21.6	42.7	93	St. Vincent	8.0	0.8
6	Kuwait	81.2	83.7	50	Gibraltar	20.0	0.6	94	Cameroon	7.8	51.2
7	New Zealand	70.6	221.7	51	Greenland	20.0	1.0	95	Syria	7.3	55.9
8	French Guyana	66.6	4.0	52	Hungary	19.9	211.4	96	Papua New Guinea	6.7	19.2
9	Austria	61.1	459.1	53	Sweden	19.7	162.7	97	Madagascar	6.5	51.0
10	Libya	53.8	131.3	54	Ireland	18.6	58.9	98	Philippines	6.4	281.0
				55	Czechoslovakia	18.4	275.4	99	Senegal	6.3	25.0
	UPPER MIDDLE			56	Guyana	17.8	13.9	100	Thailand	6.3	266.7
11	Denmark	51.6	262.0	57	Fiji	17.5	10.2	101	Angola	6.1	35.7
12	Martinique	51.1	17.4	58	British Virgin Islands	16.6	0.2	102	Saudi Arabia	6.0	52.6
13	French Polynesia	48.3	5.8	59	Chile	16.4	168.7	103	South Yemen	6.0	10.5
14	Guadeloupe	47.0	16.0	60	St. Lucia	16.3	1.8	104	Liberia	5.9	10.0
15	France	45.5	2,410.0	61	Mexico	15.8	988.0	105	Paraguay	5.9	14.0
16	Malta	44.0	13.2	62	Barbados	15.2	3.8	106	Gambia	5.1	2.5
17	Bermuda	41.6	2.5	63	Jamaica	14.5	28.6	107	Kenya	5.1	69.2
18	Puerto Rico	41.0	124.5	64	Malaysia	14.5	178.7	108	Sao Tome & Principe	5.0	0.4
19	Reunion	37.7	18.5	65	Swaziland	14.2	7.1	109	El Salvador	4.9	19.1
20	Norway	36.6	147.6	66	Gabon	14.0	7.3	110	Jordan	4.7	13.2
21	Bahrain	36.5	9.5	67	Poland	13.5	467.1	111	Macao	4.6	1.2
22	Argentina	35.1	879.8	68	Botswana	13.3	9.2	112	Ghana	4.4	46.0
23	Iceland	35.0	7.7	69	Seychelles	13.3	0.8	113	Turkey	4.4	179.9
24	Netherlands Antilles	34.7	8.0	70	Zambia	13.0	62.0	114	Cuba	4.2	40.0
25	United Kingdom	33.9	1,897.6	71	Mauritius	12.8	11.2	115	St. Kitts-Nevis-Anguilla	4.2	0.3
26	East Germany	32.6	548.1	72	Ivory Coast	12.6	57.4	116	Mauritius	4.0	5.0
27	South Africa	31.4	821.0	73	Samoa	12.6	1.9	117	Tonga	4.0	0.4
28	Uruguay	30.9	85.7	74	Tunisia	11.9	67.0	118	Colombia	3.8	93.4
29	Venezuela	30.8	369.4	75	Panama	11.7	19.6	119	Sri Lanka	3.5	49.2
30	Portugal	30.4	288.0	76	Rhodesia (Zimbabwe)	11.4	70.0	120	Iran	3.3	111.2
31	Spain	30.3	1,091.6	77	Honduras	10.6	30.2	121	Bolivia	3.2	18.4
32	Israel	30.0	104.0	78	Hong Kong	10.5	46.6	122	South Korea	3.2	117.5
33	Finland	29.9	141.5	79	India	10.2	628.1	123	Togo	3.2	7.0
34	Italy	29.9	1,682.0	80	Brazil	10.1	1,076.0	124	Zaire	3.1	76.4
35	Belgium	29.6	293.6					125	Lesotho	3.0	3.2
36	Luxembourg	28.6	10.3		**LOWER MIDDLE**			126	Benin	2.9	9.5
37	Djibouti	27.7	3.0	81	Ecuador	10.0	68.4	127	Somalia	2.7	8.0
38	Switzerland	27.4	176.5	82	Nicaragua	9.9	20.0	128	Tanzania	2.7	41.8
39	Cyprus	26.8	17.2	83	Congo	9.3	13.0	129	Cape Verde	2.6	0.8
40	Greece	25.8	237.4	84	Algeria	9.2	154.7	130	Guinea	2.6	10.8
41	Netherlands	25.4	350.0	85	Peru	9.2	139.9	131	Mozambique	2.5	21.5
42	Bahamas	25.2	5.3	86	Iraq	8.8	61.8	132	Niger	2.4	11.8
43	Brunei	23.8	4.3	87	Yugoslavia	8.8	190.7	133	Rumania	2.2	45.1

Rank	Country	Commercial Vehicles per 1,000 Inhabitants	Total Number (000)	Rank	Country	Commercial Vehicles per 1,000 Inhabitants	Total Number (000)	Rank	Country	Commercial Vehicles per 1,000 Inhabitants	Total Number (000)
134	Vietnam	2.2	100.0	144	Mali	1.3	7.6	151	Laos	0.7	2.5
135	Central African Empire	2.0	3.9	145	Nigeria	1.3	82.0	152	Uganda	0.7	8.9
136	Malawi	2.0	10.6	146	Pakistan	1.3	91.7	153	Burundi	0.5	2.2
137	Sierra Leone	2.0	6.3	147	Sudan	1.2	21.2	154	Ethiopia	0.4	13.1
138	Indonesia	1.8	263.1					155	Bangladesh	0.3	24.8
139	Upper Volta	1.7	10.1		*BOTTOM 10*			156	Haiti	0.3	1.5
140	Chad	1.6	6.3	148	Grenada	1.1	0.1	157	Nepal	0.2	3.0
141	Egypt	1.5	57.4	149	Rwanda	1.1	4.8				
142	Afghanistan	1.4	26.1	150	Cambodia	0.9	11.0				
143	Burma	1.3	40.5								

Source: International Motor Vehicle Association, Detroit, U.S.

201. Motorcycles

Almost all types of transportation data emphasize automobiles at the expense of humbler vehicles such as motorcycles and bicycles. Since modes of transportation may change rapidly in the coming decades as the energy crunch begins to take effect, it might be sensible to take a closer look at existing alternatives to the automobile. Although its use in the United States seems to be linked to the counterculture, the motorcycle is a vehicle that combines speed and economy and as such has great appeal to those who think of vehicles primarily in terms of utility rather than as status symbols. The great names in personal transportation in the future may not be Ford or Chevrolet but rather Yamaha or Kawasaki.

Number of Countries: 139
Midpoint: 41 per 10,000 inhabitants
Period Covered: 1975
Type of Ranking: Number of Motorcycles (Including Mopeds and Motorbikes) per 10,000 Inhabitants; Total Number of Motorcycles; Highest to Lowest

Highlights & Findings: Motorcycle ownership is naturally highest in countries like Japan and Italy, but, for reasons that are not clear, it is also very high in a number of smaller countries such as Singapore and Bermuda. Obviously, the motorcycle is better suited to short-distance travel or commuting; it also requires better roads with less sharp inclines and curves.

Region	Africa	Asia & Oceania	Europe	Western Hemisphere
Most	Seychelles (31)	Japan (6)	Netherlands (3)	Bermuda (1)
Least	Ethiopia (139)	South Korea (137)	Iceland (95)	Haiti (135)

Rank	Country	Motor Cycles per 10,000 Inhabitants	Total Number of Motorcycles	Rank	Country	Motor Cycles per 10,000 Inhabitants	Total Number of Motorcycles	Rank	Country	Motor Cycles per 10,000 Inhabitants	Total Number of Motorcycles
	TOP 10			14	Belgium	524	510,000	31	Seychelles	161	964
1	Bermuda	3,900	19,500	15	Surinam	504	20,170	32	Argentina	159	393,200
2	Falkland Islands	1,500	300	16	Taiwan	483	749,188	33	Cambodia	143	110,118
3	Netherlands	1,480	1,990,000	17	Guadeloupe	441	15,000	34	Central African Empire	137	24,000
4	France	1,173	6,115,000	18	Malaysia	436	493,847	35	Reunion	128	6,036
5	Switzerland	1,114	716,538	19	Norway	417	165,091	36	Ireland	128	39,080
6	Japan	785	8,536,000	20	Spain	352	1,226,392	37	Israel	126	40,540
7	Austria	778	586,218	21	New Zealand	260	76,674	38	Canada	112	248,501
8	Cook Islands	726	1,452	22	Bahamas	253	4,816	39	Gibraltar	110	331
9	Italy	722	3,965,000	23	Cyprus	240	14,900	40	Malta	110	3,525
10	St. Pierre & Miquelon	642	321	24	Luxembourg	228	8,000	41	Thailand	106	419,400
				25	New Caledonia	224	5,160	42	Yugoslavia	105	220,589
				26	Guyana	212	16,097	43	Martinique	103	3,500
	UPPER MIDDLE			27	Vietnam	207	885,202	44	Barbados	101	2,422
11	Poland	569	1,900,000	28	United States	207	4,354,196	45	French Guyana	100	500
12	Singapore	558	122,274	29	United Kingdom	205	1,146,958	46	Finland	97	45,304
13	Monaco	525	1,050	30	Australia	200	262,700	47	Greece	88	78,765

Rank	Country	Motor Cycles per 10,000 Inhabitants	Total Number of Motorcycles	Rank	Country	Motor Cycles per 10,000 Inhabitants	Total Number of Motorcycles	Rank	Country	Motor Cycles per 10,000 Inhabitants	Total Number of Motorcycles
48	Portugal	84	72,000	78	Mali	27	14,360	110	Sierra Leone	6	1,710
49	Grenada	83	832	79	El Salvador	26	10,000	111	Madagascar	6	4,800
50	Liberia	79	13,000	80	Jamaica	26	5,126	112	St. Lucia	6	69
51	Denmark	75	37,679	81	Fiji	25	1,418	113	Benin	6	1,824
52	Costa Rica	74	13,903	82	Peru	24	35,746	114	St. Kitts-Nevis-Anguilla	6	40
53	St. Vincent	74	742	83	Belize	23	305	115	Cameroon	5	3,174
54	Iran	70	219,279	84	Pakistan	23	154,953	116	Congo	5	1,512
55	Mauritius	66	5,515	85	Turkey	23	85,000	117	Somalia	5	1,512
56	Venezuela	64	72,543	86	Guatemala	22	13,002	118	Uganda	5	5,398
57	Dominican Republic	63	27,773	87	Trinidad & Tobago	22	2,299	119	Ghana	5	4,600
58	South Africa	60	145,000	88	Panama	21	3,330	120	Malawi	4	2,000
59	Hong Kong	58	24,184	89	Tunisia	21	11,500	121	Senegal	4	1,400
60	Uruguay	57	17,000	90	Philippines	16	108,781	122	Botswana	3	228
61	Indonesia	56	719,405	91	Montserrat	16	16	123	Jordan	3	830
62	Puerto Rico	55	16,250	92	Zambia	16	7,422	124	Guinea	3	1,350
63	Djibouti	53	960	93	Rhodesia (Zimbabwe)	15	9,230	125	Zaire	3	7,383
64	Egypt	50	17,795	94	Sri Lanka	15	20,014	126	Upper Volta	3	1,550
65	Netherlands Antilles	48	1,100	95	Iceland	14	296	127	Algeria	2	3,770
66	Paraguay	47	11,830	96	Nigeria	13	80,400	128	Burundi	2	845
67	Sweden	45	37,000	97	Swaziland	12	561	129	Burma	2	6,168
68	Lebanon	45	12,100	98	Papua New Guinea	12	3,047	130	Afghanistan	2	3,300
69	Togo	43	9,126	99	Bolivia	11	5,806	131	Niger	2	766
70	Laos	41	13,162	100	India	11	617,132		**BOTTOM 8**		
	LOWER MIDDLE			101	Brazil	10	99,773	132	Lesotho	1	153
71	Mexico	36	201,974	102	Dominica	10	67	133	Sudan	1	2,300
72	Angola	35	20,200	103	Syria	9	6,400	134	Chad	1	471
73	Nicaragua	33	6,679	104	Kenya	9	11,349	135	Haiti	1	450
74	West Germany	32	200,000	105	Morocco	9	14,240	136	Rwanda	0.7	300
75	Gambia	30	1,488	106	Tanzania	8	11,640	137	South Korea	0.5	1,818
76	Iraq	29	30,000	107	Greenland	8	40	138	Mauritania	0.4	56
77	Chile	28	27,500	108	Ecuador	7	5,000	139	Ethiopia	0.4	1,056
				109	Ivory Coast	7	3,500				

Source: International Road Federation.

202. Length of Inland Waterways

One of a nation's most important natural resources is its waterways, but, as in other things, nations are not equally endowed. They differ not only in the length of the waterways but also in their quality. Some, like the Amazon in Brazil, are so deep that giant steamers can sail up the river for thousands of miles, while others may be so shallow that even canoes and similar craft navigate with difficulty.

Some are navigable year round, while others dry up in the summer and are subject to floods in the rainy season. The usefulness of many of the largest rivers, such as the Nile and the Zaire, is diminished by intervening rapids. Therefore in interpreting the following ranking, it must be remembered that length is only of the many attributes of a usable inland waterway system.

Number of Countries: 106
Midpoint: 1,770 Km (1,099 Mi)
Period Covered: 1976
Type of Ranking: Length of Inland Waterways in Km and Mi; Highest to Lowest

Highlights & Findings: This ranking is presented in terms of length rather than per sq km of land surface because the benefits of inland waterways are limited to the immediate riverine areas. In fact, in earlier ages rivers served as magnets helping, as in Egypt, to create urban settlements along their banks. Of the total length of inland waterways of 598,850 km, 58% is accounted for by the top 10—24.4% by the Soviet Union alone. Brazil accounts for another 8.3%.

Regions	Africa	Asia & Oceania	Europe	Western Hemisphere
Most	Zaire (6)	Indonesia (4)	Soviet Union (1)	Brazil (2)
Least	Togo (103)	Gilbert Islands (106)	Luxembourg (105)	Haiti (100)

Rank	Country	Length of Inland Waterways Km	Mi	Rank	Country	Length of Inland Waterways Km	Mi	Rank	Country	Length of Inland Waterways Km	Mi
		TOP 10		36	Angola	3,220	1,999	72	Ireland	1,000	621
1	Soviet Union	146,400	90,914	37	Philippines	3,219	1,999	73	Guatemala	990	614
2	Brazil	50,000	31,050	38	Paraguay	3,100	1,925	74	Iran	904	561
3	United States	40,416	25,098	39	Canada	3,000	1,863	75	Portugal	820	509
4	Indonesia	21,579	13,400	40	Mexico	2,900	1,801	76	Belize	800	497
5	Vietnam	17,072	10,601	41	East Germany	2,520	1,565	77	Mauritania	800	497
6	Zaire	15,000	9,315	42	Italy	2,500	1,552	78	Panama	800	497
7	France	14,912	9,260	43	North Korea	2,253	1,399	79	Sierra Leone	800	497
8	Colombia	14,300	8,880	44	Nicaragua	2,220	1,378	80	Ivory Coast	740	459
9	India	14,300	8,880	45	Cameroon	2,090	1,298	81	Costa Rica	730	453
10	Burma	12,800	7,949	46	Chad	2,090	1,298	82	Chile	725	450
				47	Sweden	2,052	1,274	83	Zambia	724	449
		UPPER MIDDLE		48	Belgium	2,043	1,268	84	Syria	672	417
11	Argentina	11,000	6,831	49	Yugoslavia	2,001	1,242	85	Benin	645	400
12	Papua New Guinea	10,940	6,793	50	Pakistan	1,850	1,149	86	Gambia	605	375
13	Uganda	10,280	6,383	51	Mali	1,815	1,127	87	Czechoslovakia	483	300
14	Bolivia	10,000	6,210	52	Guinea	1,795	1,114	88	Bulgaria	471	292
15	Peru	8,600	5,340					89	Sri Lanka	430	267
16	Nigeria	8,575	5,325			*LOWER MIDDLE*		90	Austria	427	265
17	Australia	8,368	5,196	52	Japan	1,770	1,099	91	Denmark	417	259
18	Malaysia	8,001	4,968	54	United Kingdom	1,770	1,099	92	Liberia	370	229
19	Laos	7,484	4,647	55	Rumania	1,691	1,050	93	Niger	300	186
20	Venezuela	7,100	4,409	56	Turkey	1,689	1,048	94	Rhodesia (Zambabwe)	280	174
21	Central African Empire	7,080	4,396	57	Hungary	1,688	1,048	95	Ethiopia	266	165
22	Bangladesh	7,000	4,347	58	New Zealand	1,609	999	96	Cuba	240	149
23	Finland	6,597	4,097	59	Gabon	1,600	993				
24	Congo	6,485	4,027	60	Guinea-Bissau	1,600	993			*BOTTOM 10*	
25	Netherlands	6,340	3,937	61	Uruguay	1,600	993	97	Brunei	209	129
26	Guyana	5,900	3,664	62	Norway	1,577	979	98	Fiji	203	126
27	Sudan	5,310	3,297	63	Senegal	1,505	934	99	Equatorial Guinea	167	103
28	West Germany	5,106	3,170	64	Ecuador	1,500	931	100	Haiti	100	62
29	Surinam	4,500	2,794	65	Malawi	1,434	890	101	Greece	80	49
30	Thailand	3,999	2,483	66	Ghana	1,350	838	102	Switzerland	65	40
31	French Guyana	3,760	2,335	67	Afghanistan	1,200	745	103	Togo	50	31
32	Poland	3,759	2,576	68	Honduras	1,200	745	104	Albania	43	26
33	Mozambique	3,750	2,328	69	Tanzania	1,168	725	105	Luxembourg	37	23
34	Cambodia	3,700	2,298	70	Spain	1,045	649	106	Gilbert Islands	5	3
35	Egypt	3,360	2,086	71	Iraq	1,015	630				

Source: U.S. Central Intelligence Agency.

203. Size of Merchant Marine

The data in this table rank merchant fleets registered in each country in terms of gross registered tons (GRT)—100 cubic feet or 2.83 cubic meters. Vessels without mechanical means of propulsion are excluded, but sailing vessels with auxiliary power are included. Because of the existence of flags of convenience, the data must be interpreted with caution, at least as far as countries such as Liberia and Panama are concerned. The figures, however, are extremely precise because of the care with which Lloyd's of London compile its shipping register.

Number of Countries: 79	Highlights & Findings: The total GRT of all merchant fleets in the world is 393.678 million

Number of Countries: 79
Midpoint: 1,002,000 GRT
Period Covered: 1977
Type of Ranking: Gross Registered Tonnage of Merchant Marine with GRT of Oil Tankers and Ore and Bulk Carriers Shown Separately; Highest to Lowest

Highlights & Findings: The total GRT of all merchant fleets in the world is 393.678 million (140,000,000 steam vessels and 253,578,000 motor vessels). Of this, oil tanker fleets have a GRT of 174.124 million and ore and bulk carriers a GRT of 100.922 million. Liberia, the top nation and also the most popular flag of convenience, accounts for 20% of the world total. The top five nations together account for over 50% of the world total; the top 10 nations account for 70%.

Regions	Africa	Asia & Oceania	Europe	Western Hemisphere
Most	Liberia (1)	Japan (2)	United Kingdom (3)	Panama (7)
Least	Ethiopia (79)	Nauru (77)	Czechoslovakia (69)	Honduras (73)

Rank	Country	GRT of Merchant Marine (000)	Of Which Oil Tankers (000)	GRT of Ore & Bulk Carriers (000)
	TOP 10			
1	Liberia	79,983	50,772	23,243
2	Japan	40,036	17,117	13,478
3	United Kingdom	31,646	14,834	8,260
4	Greece	29,517	9,725	10,580
5	Norway	27,801	14,401	9,613
6	Soviet Union	21,438	4,385	1,229
7	Panama	19,458	6,524	4,289
8	United States	15,300	5,976	1,841
9	France	11,614	7,513	1,631
10	Italy	11,111	4,685	3,987
	UPPER MIDDLE			
11	West Germany	9,592	3,534	2,152
12	Sweden	7,429	3,713	2,225
13	Spain	7,186	4,217	1,116
14	Singapore	6,791	3,104	1,298
15	India	5,482	1,147	2,341
16	Denmark	5,331	2,683	638
17	Netherlands	5,290	2,286	601
18	China	4,245	996	747
19	Poland	3,448	572	204
20	Brazil	3,330	1,202	827
21	Canada	2,823	275	1,619
22	Cyprus	2,788	302	211
23	South Korea	2,495	1,054	399
24	Yugoslavia	2,285	234	590
25	Finland	2,262	1,167	401
26	Kuwait	1,831	1,079	...
27	Bermuda	1,752	1,009	594
28	Argentina	1,677	563	251
29	Belgium	1,595	292	675
20	East Germany	1,487	275	238
31	Australia	1,374	284	591
32	Turkey	1,288	367	333
33	Portugal	1,281	653	73
34	Rumania	1,218	247	464
35	Indonesia	1,163	101	–
36	Philippines	1,147	295	188
37	Iraq	1,135	979	–
38	Algeria	1,056	623	–
39	Saudi Arabia	1,019	859	–
40	Iran	1,002	617	–
	LOWER MIDDLE			
41	Bulgaria	964	290	233
42	Libya	674	–	–
43	Mexico	674	336	–
44	Cuba	668	64	–
45	Venezuela	639	268	
46	Hong Kong	610	26	388
47	Malaysia	564		301
48	Peru	555	80	148
49	Pakistan	476		
50	South Africa	476		40
51	Egypt	408	127	
52	Chile	406	61	67
53	Israel	405		206
54	Nigeria	336		
55	Morocco	270		
56	Thailand	261	144	
57	Switzerland	253		125
58	Colombia	247	5	
59	Bangladesh	244		
60	Lebanon	227		
61	Ireland	212		206
62	New Zealand	199		
63	Ecuador	197	114	
64	Uruguay	193	134	
65	Ghana	183		
66	Iceland	167		
67	Somalia	158	25	
68	United Arab Emirates	152		
69	Czechoslovakia	149	103	
	BOTTOM 10			
70	Ivory Coast	116		
71	Zaire	110		
72	Bahamas	106	15	56
73	Honduras	105		
74	Gabon	99		
75	Sri Lanka	93		
76	North Korea	89		
77	Nauru	48		
78	Sudan	43		
79	Ethiopia	2		

Source: *Lloyd's Register of Shipping.*

204. Cargo Handled by Ports

Much of international trade is seaborne, and a nation's share of this traffic is represented by the cargo handled by its ports. The figures include the total weight of cargo unloaded and loaded from sea-going vessels of all flags at the ports of a country, but exclude ballast, bunkers, ships' stores and transshipment goods.

Number of Countries: 141
Midpoint: 6,050,000 metric tons
Period Covered: 1976
Type of Ranking: Total Cargo Handled by Ports in Metric Tons; Highest to Lowest

Highlights & Findings: The world's busiest ports are found in North America (the United States), Japan, Europe (the Netherlands, the United Kingdom and France), oil-exporting countries (Saudi Arabia, Iran and Venezuela) and Australia. However, the ratio of goods loaded and goods unloaded varies sharply among countries. It is 20:1 in Liberia, 53:1 in Kuwait, 118:1 in Saudi Arabia, 2:5 in the United States, 1:4 in the Netherlands and 1:3 in the United Kingdom.

Regions	Africa	Asia & Oceania	Europe	Western Hemisphere
Most	Nigeria (19)	Japan (2)	Netherlands (3)	United States (1)
Least	St. Helena (141)	Tonga (139)	Gibraltar (123)	St. Pierre & Miquelon (137)

Rank	Country	Cargo Handled by Ports (000 metric tons)
	TOP 10	
1	United States	746,389
2	Japan	652,112
3	Netherlands	338,315
4	Saudi Arabia	337,700
5	Iran	287,593
6	Italy	248,941
7	United Kingdom	237,117
8	France	221,191
9	Venezuela	195,372
10	Australia	194,063
	UPPER MIDDLE	
11	Soviet Union	175,814
12	Canada	171,290
13	Brazil	151,188
14	West Germany	139,964
15	Kuwait	109,765
16	Spain	108,019
17	Indonesia	95,756
18	Belgium	93,865
19	Nigeria	92,315
20	Sweden	87,429
21	United Arab Emirates	82,891
22	Libya	82,613
23	India	62,273
24	Poland	59,374
25	Singapore	57,976
26	Netherlands Antilles	56,380
27	Norway	56,184
28	Algeria	56,032
29	South Korea	55,758
30	Greece	39,194
31	Denmark	38,062
32	Malaysia	35,960
33	Finland	35,313
34	South Africa	33,379
35	Trinidad & Tobago	33,313
36	Syria	32,065
37	Lebanon	30,167
38	Philippines	27,631
39	Thailand	25,752
40	Qatar	25,730
41	Morocco	25,244
42	Bulgaria	25,228
43	Argentina	24,453
44	Hong Kong	23,341
45	Liberia	21,747
46	Turkey	21,525

Rank	Country	Cargo Handled by Ports (000 metric tons)
47	Brunei	21,505
48	Mexico	21,444
49	Yugoslavia	20,187
50	Oman	19,585
51	Iraq	19,372
52	Cuba	19,222
53	Portugal	18,800
54	New Zealand	18,257
55	Egypt	17,141
56	Peru	16,143
57	Chile	15,342
58	East Germany	14,838
59	Angola	14,028
60	Ecuador	12,697
61	Mozambique	12,259
62	Jamaica	10,254
63	Pakistan	10,063
64	Bahrain	9,751
65	Tunisia	9,713
66	Rumania	9,116
67	Mauritania	8,880
68	Israel	8,789
69	Ivory Coast	6,672
70	Panama	6,561
71	Gabon	6,050
	LOWER MIDDLE	
72	Sri Lanka	5,885
73	Kenya	5,745
74	Dominican Republic	5,508
75	Ghana	5,003
76	Vietnam	4,973
77	Bangladesh	4,884
78	Surinam	4,650
79	Senegal	4,615
80	Colombia	4,524
81	Tanzania	4,257
82	Guyana	4,238
83	New Caledonia	3,918
84	Congo	3,777
85	South Yemen	3,630
86	Cyprus	3,409
87	Albania	3,320
88	Sudan	3,081
89	Uruguay	3,066
90	Jordan	3,001
91	Togo	2,988
92	Costa Rica	2,664
93	Sierra Leone	2,491
94	Cameroon	2,468

Rank	Country	Cargo Handled by Ports (000 metric tons)
95	Papua New Guinea	2,332
96	Honduras	2,248
97	Nicaragua	2,240
98	Nauru	2,210
99	El Salvador	2,189
100	Madagascar	2,115
101	Guatemala	2,075
102	Guinea	1,850
103	Christmas Islands	1,739
104	Ethiopia	1,621
105	Iceland	1,552
106	Mauritius	1,527
107	Martinique	1,400
108	Haiti	1,247
109	Zaire	1,180
110	Burma	1,172
111	Fiji	1,170
112	Malta	1,148
113	Reunion	1,108
114	Benin	912
115	Somalia	912
116	Djibouti	870
117	Macao	741
118	Cambodia	633
119	Gilbert Islands	555
120	French Polynesia	476
121	Equatorial Guinea	445
122	Guadeloupe	423
123	Gibraltar	366
124	Belize	258
125	New Hebrides	248
126	Gambia	236
127	St. Lucia	216
128	Solomon Islands	216
129	Guinea-Bissau	212
130	Cape Verde	179
131	French Guyana	139
	Bottom 10	
132	Grenada	130
133	Seychelles	124
134	St. Vincent	107
135	Bermuda	96
136	St. Kitts-Nevis-Anguilla	90
137	St. Pierre & Miquelon	85
138	Samoa	81
139	Tonga	67
140	Comoros	63
141	St. Helena	10

Source: International Maritime Organization.

205. International Aviation Passengers

The data in this table rank countries according to the number of passengers carried annually by domestic and international scheduled services operated by airlines registered in the respective countries. In 1976 world airlines carried 633 million passengers, up from 382 million in 1970. Of these, 116 million passengers were on international flights. The regional distribution of passenger traffic was as follows:

Africa	13.249 million
North America	253.117 million
South America	22.138 million
Asia	71.707 million
Europe	102.400 million
Oceania	12.535 million
Soviet Union	100.859 million

Number of Countries: 103
Midpoint: 400,000
Period Covered: 1976
Type of Ranking: Number of International Passengers Carried Annually; Highest to Lowest

Highlights & Findings: The rankings reveal the heavy concentration of air passenger traffic in the large countries. The United States alone accounts for 35% of all those who travel by air and the combined share of the Soviet Union and the U.S. together is over 50%. Asia, Africa and South America together claim a share of only 17%, less than half that of the United States.

Regions	Africa	Asia & Oceania	Europe	Western Hemisphere
Most	Algeria (31)	Japan (10)	United Kingdom (2)	United States (1)
Least	Somalia (101)	Cambodia (103)	Malta (66)	Nicaragua (88)

Rank	Country	Air Passengers Carried (000) International	Air Passengers Carried (000) Domestic & International
	TOP 10		
1	United States	17,655	223,923
2	United Kingdom	13,403	19,473
3	France	7,815	14,302
4	West Germany	5,752	10,419
5	Switzerland	4,497	5,085
6	Canada	4,132	16,833
7	Spain	4,082	11,801
8	Italy	3,743	8,238
9	Netherlands	3,736	4,081
10	Japan	2,751	29,566
	UPPER MIDDLE		
11	Singapore	2,132	2,132
12	Soviet Union	2,043	100,859
13	Sweden	1,763	3,909
14	Belgium	1,682	1,682
15	Australia	1,564	8,809
16	Ireland	1,436	1,578
17	Mexico	1,434	7,676
18	Thailand	1,337	1,634
19	South Korea	1,291	2,075
20	Denmark	1,175	2,796
21	Norway	1,175	3,853
22	Greece	1,159	3,541
23	Yugoslavia	1,098	2,647
24	Lebanon	1,050	1,050
25	Austria	1,041	1,061
26	Saudi Arabia	1,040	3,268
27	Malaysia	973	2,671
28	Brazil	948	8,799
29	India	923	4,640
30	Israel	902	1,300
31	Algeria	863	1,682
32	Egypt	812	1,113
33	Pakistan	786	1,947
34	New Zealand	766	3,023

Rank	Country	Air Passengers Carried (000) International	Air Passengers Carried (000) Domestic & International
35	Portugal	754	1,650
36	Iran	741	2,499
37	Kuwait	739	737
38	Poland	729	1,472
39	Tunisia	725	809
40	Finland	698	2,040
41	Morocco	695	809
42	Argentina	639	3,294
43	Venezuela	629	2,708
44	Jamaica	621	643
45	South Africa	603	2,999
46	Turkey	584	2,427
47	Colombia	550	3,730
48	Indonesia	524	3,103
49	Czechoslovakia	490	1,657
50	Hungary	427	427
51	Iceland	402	601
	LOWER MIDDLE		
52	Bulgaria	400	1,370
53	Jordan	400	417
54	Philippines	400	2,900
55	Kenya	399	450
56	Trinidad & Tobago	384	384
57	Iraq	367	568
58	Syria	352	381
59	Libya	334	670
60	Uruguay	263	327
61	Rumania	258	913
62	Luxembourg	250	250
63	Honduras	233	289
64	Cyprus	225	225
65	Costa Rica	222	390
66	Malta	221	221
67	Chile	218	490
68	Tanzania	207	310
69	Sudan	165	265

Rank	Country	Air Passengers Carried (000) International	Air Passengers Carried (000) Domestic & International
70	Ethiopia	145	288
71	Bolivia	139	745
72	Peru	138	1,439
73	Guatemala	119	119
74	Nigeria	105	485
75	Ecuador	103	463
76	Ghana	101	215
77	Sri Lanka	101	128
78	Gabon	90	190
79	Zaire	87	463
80	Zambia	87	260
81	Afghanistan	81	102
82	Cuba	77	717
83	Senegal	77	120
84	Uganda	69	74
85	Cameroon	68	248
86	Malawi	65	94
87	Madagascar	63	262
88	Nicaragua	49	89
89	Mauritania	47	94
90	Burma	46	396
91	Togo	44	44
	BOTTOM 12		
92	Benin	40	40
93	Central African Empire	40	98
94	Chad	40	72
95	Congo	40	77
96	Ivory Coast	40	114
97	Mali	40	55
98	Niger	40	75
99	Upper Volta	40	42
100	Guinea	20	65
101	Somalia	19	38
102	Laos	15	45
103	Cambodia	13	113

Source: International Civil Aviation Organization.

206. Distances Flown by Airlines

Airline traffic is generally measured by many indicators, but the two most reliable are the distances flown and the number of passengers carried. Figures for distances flown cover both domestic and international scheduled services operated by airlines registered in each country. Scheduled services include supplementary services that handle overflow traffic on regularly scheduled trips. Worldwide, (excluding the Soviet Union) airlines flew 7.85 billion km (4.87 billion mi) in 1976, of which 3.05 billion km (1.89 billion mi) were accounted for by international services. The percentage of international air traffic was 38% in 1976 as compared to 36% in 1970. The regional distribution of airline distances flown is as follows:

	(million km)	(million mi)	(% of growth since 1970)
Africa	294	182	47
North America	4,222	2,621	−1
South America	404	250	39
Asia	999	620	67
Europe	1,683	1,045	16
Oceania	250	155	12

Note: The Soviet Union does not release the figures relating to distances flown by its airlines, although it is a member of the International Civil Aviation Organization.

Number of Countries: 102
Midpoint: 11.8 million km (7.3 million mi)
Period Covered: 1976
Type of Ranking: Distances Flown by National Airlines in Km and Mi; Highest to Lowest

Highlights & Findings: As expected, the developed nations of North America and Europe as well as Japan dominate the top of the rankings. The United States alone accounts for 6% of all airline traffic in terms of distances flown. In the upper middle are large countries, such as Brazil and India, where air traffic performs a vital function in bridging vast distances. Aviation is still more important in countries with undeveloped jungle terrain, where it may be the most cost-effective means of reaching otherwise inaccessible areas.

Regions	Africa	Asia & Oceania	Europe	Western Hemisphere
Most	South Africa (22)	Japan (5)	United Kingdom (2)	United States (1)
Least	Guinea (100)	Cambodia (102)	Malta (78)	Uruguay (89)

Rank	Country	Distances Flown in Million Km	Mi	Rank	Country	Distances Flown in Million Km	Mi	Rank	Country	Distances Flown in Million Km	Mi
	TOP 10			30	New Zealand	24.1	14.9	60	Syria	9.5	5.9
1	United States	471.9	293.0	31	Pakistan	24.0	14.9	61	Peru	9.3	5.7
2	United Kingdom	283.6	176.1	32	Yugoslavia	21.9	13.6	62	Costa Rica	5.7	3.5
3	France	198.7	123.3	33	Venezuela	20.9	12.9	63	Zaire	5.6	3.4
4	West Germany	153.6	95.3	34	Saudi Arabia	20.2	12.5	64	Bulgaria	5.5	3.4
5	Japan	108.7	67.5	35	Finland	19.5	12.1	65	Cuba	5.3	3.3
6	Canada	103.5	64.2	36	Ireland	19.0	11.8	66	Libya	5.0	3.1
7	Netherlands	93.6	58.1	37	Egypt	18.6	11.5	67	Nigeria	5.0	3.1
8	Italy	93.5	58.0	38	Philippines	18.5	11.4	68	Cyprus	4.9	3.0
9	Switzerland	85.3	52.9	39	Morocco	18.0	11.1	69	Sudan	4.7	2.9
10	Spain	81.7	50.7	40	Poland	17.4	10.8	70	Honduras	4.5	2.8
				41	Austria	16.6	10.3	71	Guatemala	4.2	2.6
	UPPER MIDDLE			42	Jamaica	16.3	10.1	72	Sri Lanka	4.1	2.5
11	Australia	63.0	39.1	43	Czechoslovakia	15.9	9.8	73	Ecuador	4.0	2.4
12	Brazil	53.8	33.4	44	Indonesia	15.4	9.5	74	Luxembourg	3.7	2.3
13	Lebanon	48.5	30.1	45	Algeria	15.0	9.3	75	Tanzania	3.6	2.2
14	Belgium	47.8	29.6	46	Malaysia	14.2	8.8	76	Bolivia	3.5	2.1
15	Mexico	45.3	28.1	47	Chile	14.0	8.6	77	Afghanistan	3.4	2.1
16	Singapore	40.8	25.3	48	Trinidad & Tobago	12.5	7.7	78	Malta	3.4	2.1
17	Sweden	40.3	25.0	49	Kenya	12.3	7.6	79	Gabon	3.3	2.0
18	India	36.8	22.8	50	Kuwait	12.3	7.6	80	Uganda	3.3	2.0
19	Greece	34.1	21.1	51	Iceland	11.8	7.3	81	Ghana	2.9	1.8
20	South Korea	33.1	20.5					82	Madagascar	2.9	1.8
21	Thailand	31.7	19.6		**LOWER MIDDLE**			83	Malawi	2.7	1.6
22	South Africa	29.2	18.1	52	Tunisia	11.1	6.8	84	Cameroon	2.5	1.5
23	Israel	29.0	18.0	53	Turkey	10.9	6.7	85	Senegal	2.2	1.3
24	Argentina	28.0	17.3	54	Hungary	10.7	6.6	86	Mauritania	2.0	1.2
25	Portugal	27.8	17.2	55	Jordan	10.5	6.5	87	Nicaragua	2.0	1.2
26	Denmark	26.8	16.6	56	Rumania	10.5	6.5	88	Togo	1.9	1.1
27	Norway	26.8	16.6	57	Ethiopia	10.4	6.4	89	Uruguay	1.9	1.1
28	Colombia	26.3	16.3	58	Iraq	10.4	6.4	90	Benin	1.8	1.1
29	Iran	25.0	15.5	59	Zambia	10.1	6.2	91	Central African Empire	1.8	1.1

Rank	Country	Distances Flown in Million		Rank	Country	Distances Flown in Million		Rank	Country	Distances Flown in Million	
		Km	Mi			Km	Mi			Km	Mi
92	Chad	1.8	1.1		*BOTTOM 6*			100	Guinea	0.4	0.2
93	Congo	1.8	1.1	97	Mali	1.3	0.8	101	Laos	0.4	0.2
94	Ivory Coast	1.8	1.1	98	Burma	1.0	0.6	102	Cambodia	0.3	0.1
95	Niger	1.8	1.1	99	Somalia	0.6	0.3				
96	Upper Volta	1.8	1.1								

Source: International Civil Aviation Organization.

207. Civil Aircraft

Of the 10,634 civil (commercial) aircraft reported in the non-Communist world (few Communist countries reveal any information relating to aviation that may have potential strategic value), the United States accounts for 51.4%, an impressive lead which may be explained partly by the U.S. aircraft manufacturing technology and capacity. The next nine countries account for another 23%.

Number of Countries: 141
Midpoint: 13
Period Covered: 1977
Type of Ranking: Total Number of Registered Civil Aircraft; Highest to Lowest

Highlights & Findings: In no field does the developed world, particularly the United States, the United Kingdom, France and West Germany, dominate so completely as in aviation. Not only do they supply almost all the civil aircraft used by the world's airlines but they also maintain and service them.

Regions	Africa	Asia & Oceania	Europe	Western Hemisphere
Most	South Africa (15)	Japan (5)	United Kingdom (3)	United States (1)
Least	Sierra Leone (140)	Qatar (136)	Gibraltar (134)	Surinam (141)

Rank	Country	Number of Civil Aircraft	Rank	Country	Number of Civil Aircraft	Rank	Country	Number of Civil Aircraft
	TOP 10		27	Zaire	42	56	Burma	20
1	United States	5,480	28	Argentina	41	57	Egypt	20
2	Canada	609	29	Finland	39	58	Ethiopia	20
3	United Kingdom	503	30	Algeria	38	59	Morocco	20
4	France	297	31	Chile	37	60	Singapore	20
5	Japan	230	32	Ecuador	37	61	Austria	19
6	West Germany	180	33	Libya	35	62	Papua New Guinea	19
7	Spain	171	34	Nigeria	35	63	Ivory Coast	18
8	Brazil	149	35	Israël	34	64	Panama	18
9	Indonesia	130	36	Peru	33	65	Hong Kong	17
10	Italy	129	37	Cuba	32	66	Bahamas	15
			38	Greece	32	67	Kuwait	15
	UPPER MIDDLE		39	Dominican Republic	31	68	Rhodesia (Zimbabwe)	15
11	Australia	120	40	Lebanon	31	69	Jamaica	14
12	Mexico	110	41	Bolivia	30	70	Mozambique	14
13	Netherlands	106	42	Ireland	30	71	Yemen Arab Republic	14
14	India	93	43	Gabon	29			
15	South Africa	89	44	South Korea	28		*LOWER MIDDLE*	
16	Colombia	87	45	Portugal	28	72	Syria	13
17	Denmark	85	46	Malaysia	27	73	Jordan	12
18	Switzerland	83	47	Pakistan	27	74	Tunisia	12
19	Venezuela	70	48	Iraq	26	75	Uruguay	12
20	Sweden	66	49	Oman	25	76	Ghana	11
21	Saudi Arabia	62	50	Thailand	25	77	Guatemala	11
22	Philippines	60	51	Iceland	24	78	Kenya	11
23	Iran	55	52	Honduras	23	79	Nicaragua	11
24	New Zealand	50	53	Turkey	23	80	Angola	10
25	Norway	49	54	Bahrain	21	81	Netherlands Antilles	10
26	Belgium	45	55	Costa Rica	21	82	Sudan	10

Rank	Country	Number of Civil Aircraft	Rank	Country	Number of Civil Aircraft	Rank	Country	Number of Civil Aircraft
83	Trinidad & Tobago	10	104	Central African Empire	5		*BOTTOM 18*	
84	Zambia	10	105	Cyprus	5	124	Belize	2
85	Bangladesh	9	106	Fiji	5	125	Brunei	2
86	Cameroon	9	107	Madagascar	5	126	Cape Verde	2
87	El Salvador	9	108	Namibia	5	127	Equatorial Guinea	2
88	Tanzania	9	109	Nepal	5	128	Greenland	2
89	Sri Lanka	8	110	Senegal	5	129	Guadeloupe	2
90	Antigua	8	111	Barbados	4	130	Maldives	2
91	Botswana	8	112	Burundi	4	131	Mali	2
92	Luxembourg	8	113	Chad	4	132	Mauritius	2
93	Mauritania	8	114	Comoros	4	133	Western Samoa	2
94	Guinea	7	115	Nauru	4	134	Gibraltar	1
95	Paraguay	7	116	Niger	4	135	Liberia	1
96	Afghanistan	6	117	Uganda	4	136	Qatar	1
97	Congo	6	118	United Arab Emirates	4	137	Rwanda	1
98	Guyana	6	119	Bermuda	3	138	St. Kitts-Nevis-Anguilla	1
99	Haiti	6	120	French Polynesia	3	139	St. Lucia	1
100	Malawi	6	121	Liechtenstein	3	140	Sierra Leona	1
101	Somalia	6	122	Malta	3	141	Surinam	1
102	Swaziland	6	123	Togo	3			
103	South Yemen	6						

Source: International Civil Aviation Organization.

208. Usable Airfields

One of the principal indicators of development is accessibility by air. The inherent advantages of air travel are demonstrated most dramatically not in urban areas but in remote jungles and deserts inaccessible by road, rail or river. During the post-World War II period, thousands of airfields and airstrips have been built even in countries without a civil air fleet. Many of them are not properly maintained and do not have air traffic control systems. The following ranking therefore includes only usable airfields and airstrips with or without permanent surface runways. Since the Soviet Union and many other Communist countries treat the number of airfields as classified information, they are therefore not represented in this ranking.

Number of Countries: 167
Midpoint: 50
Period Covered: 1976
Type of Ranking Number of Usable Airfields and Airstrips; Highest to Lowest

Highlights & Findings: Eight of the top 10 countries are in the Western Hemisphere, but African countries are well represented in the upper and lower middle, reflecting the difficulty of surface travel in those countries.

Regions	Africa	Asia & Oceania	Europe	Western Hemisphere
Highest	South Africa (10)	Australia (5)	France (13)	United States (1)
Lowest	Gambia (162)	Tuvalu (167)	Luxembourg (164)	Falkland Islands (160)

Rank	Country	Number of Usable Airfields	Rank	Country	Number of Usable Airfields	Rank	Country	Number of Usable Airfields
	TOP 10					17	Guatemala	358
1	United States	15,257	10	South Africa	523	18	Chile	351
2	Brazil	4,261				19	India	344
3	Argentina	2,153		*UPPER MIDDLE*		20	Rhodesia (Zimbabwe)	342
4	Mexico	1,718	11	Angola	504	21	Zaire	332
5	Australia	1,662	12	Papua New Guinea	473	22	Mozambique	321
6	Canada	1,440	13	France	433	23	Philippines	302
7	Paraguay	801	14	Nicaragua	405	24	Peru	301
8	Colombia	680	15	West Germany	386	25	Venezuela	260
9	Bolivia	535	16	Indonesia	362			

Rank	Country	Number of Usable Airfields	Rank	Country	Number of Usable Airfields	Rank	Country	Number of Usable Airfields
26	China	247	75	Uruguay	63	122	Benin	10
27	Sweden	240	76	Cameroon	60	123	French Guyana	10
28	Honduras	224	77	Guinea-Bissau	59	124	Sri Lanka	10
29	Kenya	220	78	United Arab Emirates	56	125	Rwanda	9
30	United Kingdom	200	79	South Yemen	56	126	Guadeloupe	8
31	New Zealand	184	80	Upper Volta	54	127	Djibouti	7
32	Cuba	182	81	Nepal	52	128	Netherlands Antilles	7
33	Algeria	176	82	Austria	51	129	Reunion	7
34	Ethiopia	176	83	Bahamas	51	130	Trinidad & Tobago	7
35	Japan	175	84	Congo	51	131	Cape Verde	6
36	Ecuador	173	85	Somalia	50	132	Greenland	6
37	Iran	166				133	Kuwait	6
38	Zambia	165		**LOWER MIDDLE**		134	Lebanon	6
39	El Salvador	153	86	Portugal	49	135	Comoros	5
40	Thailand	153	87	Central African Empire	48	136	Mauritius	5
41	Panama	151	88	Uganda	48	137	Singapore	5
42	Italy	149	89	Ivory Coast	48	138	St. Vincent	4
43	Costa Rica	146	90	Dominican Republic	46	139	Sao Tome & Principe	4
44	Vietnam	142	91	Israel	46	140	Seychelles	4
45	Oman	140	92	Malawi	46	141	Tonga	4
46	Malaysia	139	93	Belgium	45	142	Western Samoa	4
47	Denmark	135	94	Mali	42	143	Antigua	3
48	Madagascar	121	95	Ireland	38	144	Brunei	3
49	South Korea	114	96	Afghanistan	36	145	Cook Islands	3
50	Finland	111	97	Belize	36	146	Equatorial Guinea	3
51	Gabon	105	98	Taiwan	36	147	Grenada	3
52	Norway	105	99	New Caledonia	31	148	Martinique	3
53	Pakistan	105	100	Mauritania	29	149	St. Kitts-Nevis-Anguilla	3
54	Iceland	101	101	Surinam	29	150	St. Lucia	3
55	Turkey	101	102	Tunisia	29	151	Bahrain	2
56	Syria	97	103	Senegal	27	152	Bhutan	2
57	Saudi Arabia	89	104	Yemen Arab Republic	27	153	Hong Kong	2
58	Guyana	88	105	Netherlands	26	154	Maldives	2
59	Spain	87	106	Swaziland	26	155	Malta	2
60	Namibia	85	107	Cambodia	25	156	Wallis & Futuna	2
61	Egypt	81	108	French Polynesia	25			
62	Burma	79	109	Jamaica	22		**BOTTOM 11**	
63	Laos	78	110	Solomon Islands	21	157	Barbados	1
64	Liberia	78	111	Lesotho	20	158	Bermuda	1
65	Morocco	78	112	Ghana	18	159	Dominica	1
66	Libya	77	113	Guinea	17	160	Falkland Islands	1
67	Botswana	76	114	Bangladesh	16	161	Faroe Islands	1
68	Nigeria	76	115	Jordan	16	162	Gambia	1
69	Switzerland	73	116	Sierra Leone	16	163	Gibraltar	1
70	Sudan	72	117	Fiji	15	164	Luxembourg	1
71	Iraq	67	118	Haiti	13	165	Nauru	1
72	Chad	63	119	Burundi	12	166	Qatar	1
73	Greece	63	120	Cyprus	12	167	Tuvalu	1
74	Niger	63	121	Togo	11			

Source: U.S. Central Intelligence Agency.

209. Length of Pipelines

There are three types of pipelines: those carrying crude petroleum, those carrying refined products and those carrying natural gas. The construction and maintenance of pipelines have become strategic and key industries, although pipelines remain the least studied form of transportation.

Number of Countries: 84	**Highlights & Findings:** The total length of pipelines in the world is estimated at 875,443 km (543,650 mi). Of this total, the United States alone accounts for 32% and the top 10 countries for 85.6%.
Midpoint: 1,087 km (675 mi)	
Period Covered: 1976	
Type of Ranking: Combined Length of Crude Petroleum, Natural Gas and Refined Products Pipelines in Km and Mi; Highest to Lowest	

Regions	Africa	Asia & Oceania	Europe	Western Hemisphere
Most	Algeria (14)	Iran (11)	Soviet Union (2)	United States (1)
Least	Ghana (84)	South Yemen (79)	Portugal (81)	Jamaica (82)

Rank	Country	Total Length of Pipelines Km	Mi	Rank	Country	Total Length of Pipelines Km	Mi	Rank	Country	Total Length of Pipelines Km	Mi
		TOP 10		29	Pakistan	2,161	1,341.9	58	Mozambique	306	190.0
1	United States	279,966	173,858	30	Brazil	2,087	1,296.0	59	United Arab Emirates	282	175.1
2	Soviet Union	183,000	113,643	31	Japan	1,956	1,214.6	60	Qatar	266	165.1
3	West Germany	98,954	61,450.4	32	Chile	1,860	1,155.0	61	Philippines	251	155.8
4	Canada	96,723	60,064.9	33	Syria	1,819	1,129.5	62	Jordan	209	129.7
5	France	28,744	17,850.0	34	East Germany	1,529	949.5	63	Albania	181	112.4
6	Italy	17,028	10,574.3	35	Spain	1,514	940.1	64	Angola	179	111.1
7	Argentina	14,410	8,948.6	36	Switzerland	1,360	844.5	65	Finland	161	99.9
8	Mexico	12,820	7,961.2	37	Nigeria	1,307	811.6	66	Bangladesh	150	93.1
9	Rumania	9,313	5,783.3	38	Egypt	1,255	779.3	67	Gabon	129	80.1
10	Venezuela	9,005	5,592.0	39	Yugoslavia	1,214	753.8	68	Costa Rica	125	77.6
				40	Ecuador	1,096	680.6	69	Malaysia	125	77.6
		UPPER MIDDLE		41	Morocco	1,094	679.3	70	Bahrain	104	64.5
11	Iran	8,553	5,311.4	42	Israel	1,087	675.0	71	Panama	96	59.6
12	Australia	8,027	4,984.7	43	Kuwait	1,038	644.5	72	Cuba	80	49.6
13	Czechoslovakia	7,910	4,912.0	44	Tanzania	982	609.8	73	Lebanon	72	44.7
14	Algeria	7,250	4,502.0	45	Tunisia	879	545.8				
15	Netherlands	5,872	3,646.5							**BOTTOM 11**	
16	Iraq	5,766	3,580.0			**LOWER MIDDLE**		74	Dominican Republic	69	42.8
17	Poland	5,270	3,272.6	46	Sudan	800	496.8	75	Nicaragua	56	34.7
18	Colombia	5,265	3,269.5	47	New Zealand	785	487.4	76	Norway	53	32.9
19	United Kingdom	4,610	2,862.8	48	Trinidad & Tobago	758	470.7	77	Guatemala	48	29.8
20	Hungary	4,473	2,777.7	49	Zaire	740	459.5	78	Luxembourg	48	29.8
21	Belgium	4,344	2,697.6	50	Zambia	724	449.0	79	South Yemen	32	19.8
22	Libya	3,976	2,469.0	51	China	712	442.1	80	Congo	25	15.5
23	India	3,811	2,366.6	52	Greece	573	355.8	81	Portugal	11	6.8
24	Bolivia	3,725	2,313.0	53	Peru	535	332.2	82	Jamaica	10	6.2
25	Turkey	3,343	2,076.0	54	South Korea	515	319.8	83	Rhodesia (Zimbabwe)	8	4.9
26	Austria	3,336	2,071.6	55	Brunei	488	303.0	84	Ghana	3	1.8
27	Saudi Arabia	2,914	1,809.5	56	Denmark	418	259.5				
28	South Africa	2,206	1,370.0	57	Oman	370	229.7				

Source: U.S. Central Intelligence Agency.

210. Annual Tourist Arrivals

Tourists are defined as persons traveling for pleasure, domestic reasons, health, meetings, business and study and stopping for a period of 24 hours or more in a country other than that in which they usually reside. These figures do not include immigrants, transport crews or troops passing through a country. The data are generally based on frontier checks. In the absence of such checks, hotel registration figures are used. These two sources are not strictly comparable because some tourists stay in private houses and others move from one hotel to another.

Number of Countries: 112
Midpoint: 339,500
Period Covered: 1976
Type of Ranking: Annual Number of
Reported Tourist Arrivals; Highest to Lowest

Highlights & Findings: Because travel and tourism are related to—and indeed are the products of—national affluence tourism is concentrated in North America and Europe. The top 22 countries in this ranking belong to these regions. Africa remains the least traveled continent and Southeast Asia and the Arabian Peninsula do only slightly better.

Regions	Africa	Asia & Oceania	Europe	Western Hemisphere
Most	Morocco (32)	Turkey (23)	Spain (1)	United States (2)
Least	Central African Empire (112)	Cambodia (108)	Gibraltar (98)	Grenada (99)

Rank	Country	Number of Tourist Arrivals (000) Total	Per 1,000 Inhabitants
	TOP 10		
1	Spain	30,014.1	834
2	United States	17,523.0	81
3	Scandinavia (undistributed)	16,440.1	746
4	Italy	13,929.8	248
5	Czechoslovakia	13,863.3	930
6	France	13,470.0	254
7	Canada	13,002.0	562
8	Austria	11,598.3	1,544
9	United Kingdom	10,089.0	180
10	Poland	9,623.2	280
	UPPER MIDDLE		
11	Belgium	7,914.5	800
12	West Germany	7,889.6	128
13	Switzerland	7,609.1	1,198
14	Yugoslavia	5,572.3	258
15	Hungary	5,551.0	524
16	Bulgaria	4,033.4	460
17	Soviet Union	3,879.3	15
18	Greece	3,845.2	419
19	Mexico	3,217.9	52
20	Rumania	3,168.7	148
21	Netherlands	2,910.5	211
22	San Marino	2,435.5	121,750
23	Turkey	1,675.8	42
24	Hong Kong	1,560.0	356
25	Lebanon	1,554.9	525
26	Singapore	1,492.2	654
27	Syria	1,392.6	183
28	Puerto Rico	1,298.7	405
29	Ireland	1,291.0	408
30	Malaysia	1,224.8	99
31	Argentina	1,200.0	47
32	Morocco	1,107.7	62
33	Thailand	1,098.4	25
34	East Germany	1,085.3	65
35	Egypt	984.0	26
36	Tunisia	977.8	170
37	Portugal	958.2	101

Rank	Country	Number of Tourist Arrivals (000) Total	Per 1,000 Inhabitants
38	Bahamas	939.9	4,476
39	South Korea	834.2	23
40	Japan	795.2	7
41	Israel	732.7	212
42	Jordan	707.6	255
43	Iraq	630.2	55
44	Iran	628.2	19
45	Philippines	615.2	14
46	Bermuda	558.9	9,316
47	Brazil	556.0	5
48	India	534.0	0.8
49	Australia	531.9	39
50	Colombia	522.1	21
51	Venezuela	491.7	35
52	Uruguay	436.7	176
53	Guatemala	407.9	65
54	Kenya	407.4	29
55	New Zealand	384.0	122
56	Malta	339.5	1,131
	LOWER MIDDLE		
57	Jamaica	327.7	159
58	Indonesia	313.5	2
59	Panama	307.0	178
60	Costa Rica	299.8	148
61	Chile	279.1	27
62	El Salvador	277.9	67
63	Peru	264.0	16
64	Dominican Republic	259.8	54
65	Barbados	224.3	897
66	Nicaragua	207.0	93
67	Pakistan	197.3	3
68	Algeria	184.8	11
69	Monaco	181.0	6,033
70	Cyprus	180.2	281
71	Ecuador	171.8	23
72	Fiji	168.7	291
73	Trinidad & Tobago	156.7	145
74	Libya	144.8	59
75	Senegal	136.2	27

Rank	Country	Number of Tourist Arrivals (000) Total	Per 1,000 Inhabitants
76	Ivory Coast	122.2	24
77	Tanzania	120.0	8
78	Sri Lanka	119.0	9
79	Nepal	105.1	8
80	Cameroon	96.1	15
81	French Polynesia	92.0	708
82	Afghanistan	91.0	4
83	Guyana	85.9	110
84	Mauritius	74.6	86
85	Iceland	70.2	319
86	Zambia	56.2	11
87	Ghana	55.8	5
88	Surinam	54.7	124
89	Cayman Islands	54.1	5,410
90	Gabon	52.5	99
91	Seychelles	49.5	825
92	Malawi	40.5	8
93	Bangladesh	37.4	0.5
94	Madagascar	33.1	4
95	Burundi	31.4	8
96	Sudan	30.7	2
97	Ethiopia	30.6	1
98	Gibraltar	29.2	973
99	Grenada	24.6	246
100	Laos	23.1	7
101	Samoa	22.9	153
102	Mauritania	20.7	17
	BOTTOM 10		
103	Mali	19.9	3
104	Benin	18.9	6
105	Zaire	18.9	0.7
106	South Yemen	18.6	11
107	Chad	16.7	4
108	Cambodia	16.5	2
109	Upper Volta	14.6	2
110	Uganda	10.3	0.9
111	Sierra Leone	7.8	2
112	Central African Empire	4.1	2

Source: World Tourism Organization, Madrid.

211. Tourist Receipts

Data on tourist receipts are derived from two sources: the International Monetary Fund (IMF) and the World Tourism Organization (WTO) in Madrid.

The IMF includes tourist receipts in its balance of payments reports on the basis of information supplied by member countries. It covers receipts for goods and services provided to foreigners and also transportation expenses. In other countries the WTO estimates travel receipts by applying an average per diem expenditure to the number of days spent by foreigners. Per diem expenditures are based on inquiries made of travel agents, banks, hotels and shops. Many countries keep systematic records of the number of nights spent in their hotels by foreign tourists.

Number of Countries: 99
Midpoint: $203.25
Period Covered: 1976
Type of Ranking: Tourist Receipts per Tourist in Dollars; Total Tourist Receipts in Dollars; Highest to Lowest

Highlights & Findings: Certain types of tourists and visitors spend more money than others; businessmen with expense accounts, for example, are more uninhibited in their spending. Tourist receipts per tourist are greater in countries where the business content of tourist activities is greater. Also, of course, the cost of living index has an enormous impact on per capita tourist expenditures.

Regions	Africa	Asia & Oceania	Europe	Western Hemisphere
Most	Central African Empire (4)	Iran (1)	West Germany (12)	Mexico (2)
Least	Burundi (98)	Malaysia (94)	Poland (99)	El Salvador (90)

Rank	Country	Tourist Expenditures per Tourist ($)	Total Tourist Expenditures ($ million)	Rank	Country	Tourist Expenditures per Tourist ($)	Total Tourist Expenditures ($ million)	Rank	Country	Tourist Expenditures per Tourist ($)	Total Tourist Expenditures ($ million)
	TOP 10			33	Haiti	291.03	25	66	Gabon	152.38	12
1	Iran	686.08	431	34	Mauritania	289.85	7	67	Canada	151.59	1,971
2	Mexico	674.66	2,192	35	Switzerland	289.25	2,201	68	Philippines	149.54	92
3	Australia	564.01	300	36	United Kingdom	286.84	2,894	69	Zaire	146.69	6
4	Central African Empire	487.80	6	37	Bermuda	283.53	145	70	Yugoslavia	143.90	802
5	Panama	485.34	149	38	Dominican Republic	275.02	61	71	Uruguay	138.29	68
6	Trinidad & Tobago	485.00	76	39	Austria	270.81	3,141	72	Upper Volta	136.98	2
7	Hong Kong	475.00	741	40	France	269.33	3,628	73	Tanzania	133.33	10
8	India	468.16	250	41	Libya	269.33	39	74	Afghanistan	131.86	12
9	Fiji	463.82	75	42	Senegal	264.38	34	75	Nicaragua	130.43	27
10	Chad	419.16	7	43	Samoa	256.41	5	76	Sudan	130.29	7
				44	Morocco	247.35	274	77	Laos	129.87	3
	UPPER MIDDLE			45	Singapore	241.25	360	78	Argentina	128.33	154
11	Venezuela	412.80	219	46	Ethiopia	228.75	6	79	Cameroon	124.86	24
12	West Germany	406.35	3,206	47	Kenya	228.27	102	80	Malawi	123.45	5
13	New Zealand	406.25	156	48	Italy	227.56	3,170	81	Belgium	108.40	858
14	Israel	398.52	292	49	Greece	215.07	827	82	Turkey	107.41	180
15	Colombia	398.39	208	50	Ireland	203.25	262	83	Scandinavia (undistributed)	107.29	1,764
16	Japan	393.61	313					84	Bangladesh	106.95	4
17	Bahamas	386.21	363		*LOWER MIDDLE*			85	Spain	103.11	3,095
18	Sierra Leone	384.61	3	51	Malta	203.24	69	86	Brazil	102.51	57
19	Barbados	374.49	84	52	Pakistan	197.66	39	87	Nepal	100.22	9
20	Netherlands	365.22	1,063	53	Sri Lanka	193.27	23	88	Indonesia	89.31	34
21	Peru	355.19	91	54	Ecuador	186.26	32	89	Syria	71.80	100
22	Ivory Coast	348.94	38	55	Lebanon	183.48	415				
23	Portugal	345.43	331	56	Surinam	182.81	10		*BOTTOM 10*		
24	United States	331.45	5,808	57	Thailand	179.35	197	90	El Salvador	67.66	18
25	South Korea	329.65	275	58	Zambia	177.93	10	91	Madagascar	67.11	2
26	Grenada	325.20	8	59	Costa Rica	174.96	52	92	Bulgaria	56.79	230
27	Jamaica	323.46	106	60	Iraq	174.23	84	93	Mali	50.25	1
28	Chile	322.46	90	61	Algeria	172.00	51	94	Malaysia	49.02	58
29	Tunisia	301.80	306	62	Iceland	167.36	12	95	Hungary	47.37	263
30	Cyprus	299.66	54	63	Benin	164.83	3	96	Ghana	35.84	2
31	Mauritius	294.90	22	64	Guatemala	161.80	66	97	Rumania	35.34	112
32	Uganda	291.26	2	65	Jordan	158.28	208	98	Burundi	34.84	1
								99	Poland	16.31	157

Sources: World Tourism Organization. International Monetary Fund.

212. Domestic Mail per Capita

The mail is perhaps the most universal form of communication and also the cheapest and the most convenient. Because the post office is a state monopoly in all countries of the world, it has acquired some of the characteristics of a public service, which despite many shortcomings is generally acknowledged as the smoothest and the most efficient public service everywhere in the world. It is also one operation where the methods and techniques do not vary greatly among countries. Mail gets stamped, collected, transported and delivered in more or less the same way in the United States as it is in Western Samoa or Botswana.

Number of Countries: 155
Midpoint: 9 per capita
Period Covered: 1976
Type of Ranking: Domestic Mail per Capita; Total Domestic Mail; Highest to Lowest

Highlights & Findings: Total domestic mail traffic worldwide is estimated at 203 billion pieces, or 50.7 pieces per capita. Of this, the United States alone accounts for 43%, although the bulk of the U.S. mail is generated by business. This fact may also explain the dominance of industrialized Western countries at the top of the ranking.

Regions	Africa	Asia & Oceania	Europe	Western Hemisphere
Most	South Africa (35)	New Zealand (11)	Switzerland (2)	Turks & Caicos (1)
Least	Chad (152)	Laos (155)	Norway (53)	Bolivia (148)

Rank	Country	Domestic Mail per Capita	Total Domestic Mail (000)	Rank	Country	Domestic Mail per Capita	Total Domestic Mail (000)	Rank	Country	Domestic Mail per Capita	Total Domestic Mail (000)
	TOP 10			39	Portugal	41.0	387,840	80	Gabon	8.5	4,526
1	Turks & Caicos	750.6	4,504	40	Barbados	40.1	9,642	81	Angola	7.9	46,072
2	Switzerland	429.7	2,729,000	41	Malta	39.0	12,880	82	Solomon Islands	7.6	1,533
3	United States	416.6	87,661,000	42	Jamaica	37.3	76,930	83	Brunei	7.1	1,288
4	Liechtenstein	371.6	7,433	43	Hong Kong	33.9	148,656	84	Belize	7.0	910
5	Sweden	309.6	2,545,000	44	Rumania	32.2	686,262	85	Pakistan	6.9	501,863
6	Netherlands	261.5	3,602,000	45	Soviet Union	30.8	7,923,000	86	St. Lucia	6.4	708
7	Canada	241.7	5,594,000	46	Iran	28.8	858,077	87	Kenya	6.1	82,371
8	Denmark	240.6	1,220,000	47	Greece	28.1	264,094	88	Nicaragua	5.9	12,028
9	Belgium	231.7	2,229,000	48	Cyprus	27.6	17,697	89	Honduras	5.5	15,179
10	France	215.0	11,382,000	49	Netherlands Antilles	26.7	6,427	90	Ghana	5.3	54,730
				50	Malaysia	25.6	315,427	91	Colombia	5.1	118,953
	UPPER MIDDLE			51	French Polynesia	24.1	3,145	92	Ivory Coast	5.0	25,454
11	New Zealand	200.1	628,521	52	Argentina	24.0	619,849	93	El Salvador	5.0	20,875
12	West Germany	193.5	11,908,000	53	Norway	22.6	914,440	94	Swaziland	4.7	2,373
13	Austria	185.1	1,394,000	54	Sierra Leone	21.5	56,760	95	Gilbert Islands	4.7	284
14	United Kingdom	157.2	8,795,000	55	Trinidad & Tobago	20.2	21,278	96	Samoa	4.7	718
15	Australia	151.4	2,044,000	56	Fiji	19.0	10,297	97	Panama	4.6	7,356
16	United Arab Emirates (including foreign mail)	148.8	32,378	57	South Korea	17.9	642,909	98	Central African Empire	4.6	8,732
17	Czechoslovakia	148.5	2,216,000	58	Philippines	17.6	630,248	99	Cuba	4.4	41,663
18	Bermuda	145.8	8,750	59	Venezuela	17.4	202,428	100	Morocco	4.4	79,405
19	Hungary	144.6	1,533,000	60	Montserrat	17.3	173	101	Kuwait	4.4	4,548
20	Guyana	139.1	109,900	61	Mexico	17.1	1,068,000	102	Guatemala	4.2	26,709
21	Finland	131.3	621,257	62	Rhodesia (Zimbabwe)	15.8	103,222	103	Saudi Arabia	4.1	31,341
22	Luxembourg	126.8	45,649	63	Brazil	15.4	1,683,000	104	Cameroon	3.7	22,935
23	Japan	108.3	12,186,000	64	Cayman Islands	15.3	153	105	Malawi	3.7	19,530
24	Spain	107.9	3,882,000	65	Libya	14.5	34,205	106	Egypt	3.5	132,585
25	Italy	103.5	5,781,000	66	Costa Rica	14.2	28,155	107	Thailand	3.5	151,158
26	Ireland	99.7	308,131	67	Chile	13.6	142,703	108	St. Helena	3.4	17
27	Norfolk Island	93.2	157	68	Seychelles	13.5	677	109	Tanzania	3.3	50,748
28	Israel	89.2	308,941	69	Nigeria	13.2	857,697	110	Syria	3.2	22,546
29	Iceland	78.5	17,273	70	Bahamas	12.9	2,726	111	Comoros	3.2	934
30	Gibraltar	69.6	2,090	71	Mauritius	12.5	10,961	112	Congo	3.0	4,238
31	Sri Lanka	62.6	846,641	72	Algeria	12.2	211,094	113	Bangladesh	2.9	238,070
32	East Germany	55.7	935,763	73	Turkey	12.0	471,444	114	Iraq	2.8	33,069
33	New Caledonia	54.0	7,029	74	Tunisia	11.9	68,456	115	Djibouti	2.8	305
34	Yugoslavia	52.2	1,096,000	75	India	11.6	7,109,000	116	Madagascar	2.7	22,438
35	South Africa	51.8	1,355,000	76	Zambia	10.8	55,907	117	Macao	2.5	654
36	Singapore	50.9	116,090	77	Lebanon	10.8	26,072	118	Burma	2.4	75,214
37	Poland	50.3	1,730,000	78	Bahrain	9.0	2,450	119	Sudan	2.4	39.764
38	Falkland Islands	48.2	92					120	Lesotho	2.4	2,302
					LOWER MIDDLE			121	New Hebrides	2.3	230
				79	Antigua	8.7	613				

Rank	Country	Domestic Mail per Capita	Total Domestic Mail (000)	Rank	Country	Domestic Mail per Capita	Total Domestic Mail (000)	Rank	Country	Domestic Mail per Capita	Total Domestic Mail (000)
122	Togo	2.2	5,192	134	Ecuador	0.9	6,871	146	Afghanistan	0.3	6,269
123	Cape Verde	1.8	544	135	Mozambique	0.9	8,756				
124	Jordan	1.8	5,031	136	Somalia	0.9	2,580		*BOTTOM 9*		
125	Uganda	1.8	21,172	137	Sao Tome & Principe	0.8	67	147	Guinea-Bissau	0.2	123
126	Zaire	1.7	42,036	138	Bhutan	0.7	1,172	148	Bolivia	0.2	1,403
127	South Yemen	1.7	2,529	139	Ethiopia	0.7	20,977	149	Yemen Arab Republic	0.2	1,556
128	St. Kitts-Nevis-Anguilla	1.6	113	140	Niger	0.7	3,042	150	Burundi	0.2	809
129	Vietnam	1.3	59.230	141	Liberia	0.6	1,045	151	Cambodia	0.1	1,402
130	Rwanda	1.2	5,496	142	Mauritania	0.5	708	152	Chad	0.1	571
131	Dominican Republic	1.2	5,906	143	Guinea	0.4	1,874	153	Maldives	0.1	17
132	Indonesia	1.2	172,452	144	Botswana	0.4	282	154	Wallis & Futuna	0.1	1
133	Senegal	1.1	4,171	145	Mali	0.3	1,873	155	Laos	0.1	391

Source: Universal Postal Union.

213. Telephones per Capita

Telephones per capita has been cited (K. Finster-busch and T. Caplow in *A Matrix of Modernization*) as the most reliable index of economic development. According to the International Telecommunications Union, there were 379,524,000 telephones in use (in 1975), or 9.6 per 100 inhabitants. By major regions, there were 4,616,000 telephones in Africa (1.1 per 100 inhabitants); 166,861,000 telephones in North America (47.1 per 100 inhabitants); 9,172,000 telephones in South America (4.1 per 100 inhabitants); 57,432,000 telephones in Asia (2.6 per 100 inhabitants); 118,199,000 telephones in Europe 24.6 per 100 inhabitants) and 7,115,000 telephones in Oceania (35.1 per 100 inhabitants).

Number of Countries: 169
Midpoint: 3.2 per 100 inhabitants
Period Covered: 1975
Type of Ranking: Telephones per 100 Inhabitants and Total; Highest and Lowest

Highlights & Findings: The United States, where the telephone was invented, accounts for nearly 40% of the world's telephones. The bottom 10 countries account for only 0.05% of the world's telephones.

Regions	Africa	Asia & Oceania	Europe	Western Hemisphere
Most	South Africa (56)	New Zealand (8)	Monaco (1)	United States (2)
Least	Upper Volta (168)	Yemen Arab Republic (169)	Rumania (72)	Haiti (155)

Rank	Country	Telephones (per 100 inhabitants)	Total (000)	Rank	Country	Telephones (per 100 inhabitants	Total (000)	Rank	Country	Telephones (per 100 inhabitants	Total (000)
	TOP 10			16	Netherlands	36.8	5,047	34	Barbados	17.2	42
1	Monaco	84.0	21	17	Cayman Islands	36.6	4	35	Malta	16.3	49
2	United States	69.5	149,012	18	Norway	35.0	1,407	36	New Caledonia	16.0	19
3	Sweden	66.1	5,423	19	Hong Kong	33.6	1,034	37	East Germany	15.2	2,570
4	Liechtenstein	64.0	15	20	West Germany	31.7	19.603	38	Puerto Rico	15.2	474
5	Bermuda	63.5	37	21	Belgium	28.5	2,798	39	French Guyana	14.9	8
6	Switzerland	61.1	3,913	22	Austria	28.1	2,133	40	Ireland	14.1	444
7	Canada	57.2	13,142	23	Bahamas	28.0	57	41	Montserrat	13.6	2
8	New Zealand	50.2	1,571	24	France	26.2	13,833	42	Singapore	12.9	290
9	Denmark	45.4	2,295	25	San Marino	26.1	5	43	Kuwait	12.3	128
10	Iceland	41.7	91	26	Gibraltar	26.0	8	44	Qatar	11.4	18
				27	Italy	25.9	14,496	45	Portugal	11.3	1,066
	UPPER MIDDLE			28	Israel	23.1	813	46	Cambodia	11.2	71
11	Luxembourg	41.1	147	29	British Virgin Islands	22.2	2	47	Cyprus	10.7	68
12	Japan	40.5	45,515	30	Greece	22.1	2,009	48	French Polynesia	10.7	13
13	Australia	39.0	5,267	31	Spain	22.0	7,836	49	Bahrain	10.0	26
14	Finland	38.9	1,834	32	Netherlands Antilles	19.7	47	50	Hungary	9.9	1,048
15	United Kingdom	37.9	21,244	33	Czechoslovakia	17.6	2,616	51	Martinique	9.0	31

Rank	Country	Telephones (per 100 inhabitants)	Total (000)
52	Uruguay	9.0	250
53	Bulgaria	8.9	777
54	Panama	8.5	142
55	Argentina	7.8	1,996
56	South Africa	7.8	1,936
57	Lebanon	7.7	227
58	Poland	7.5	2,578
59	United Arab Emirates	7.3	44
60	Guadeloupe	6.7	24
61	Soviet Union	6.6	16,949
62	Namibia	6.2	46
63	Yugoslavia	6.1	1,301
64	Trinidad & Tobago	6.0	67
65	Brunei	5.8	10
66	Reunion	5.8	28
67	St. Lucia	5.7	7
68	Costa Rica	5.6	112
69	Seychelles	5.6	3
70	Colombia	5.5	1,280
71	Venezuela	5.3	650
72	Rumania	5.1	1,076
73	Fiji	5.0	29
74	Jamaica	5.0	100
75	St. Vincent	4.8	5
76	Chile	4.5	437
77	Grenada	4.5	5
78	Antigua	4.4	3
79	Surinam	4.2	18
80	Dominica	4.1	3
81	Belize	4.0	5
82	South Korea	4.0	1,400
83	Macao	3.9	10
84	Cuba	3.2	289
85	Brazil	3.1	3,371
86	St. Kitts-Nevis-Anguilla	3.0	2

LOWER MIDDLE

87	Mauritius	2.9	25
88	Mexico	2.8	2,915
89	Rhodesia (Zimbabwe)	2.8	183
90	Ecuador	2.7	182

Rank	Country	Telephones (per 100 inhabitants)	Total (000)
91	Guyana	2.6	21
92	Malaysia	2.5	292
93	Turkey	2.5	1,012
94	Dominican Republic	2.4	108
95	Tunisia	2.3	129
96	Libya	2.1	4
97	Mongolia	2.1	31
98	Peru	2.1	333
99	Syria	2.1	152
100	Western Samoa	2.1	3
101	Iran	2.0	688
102	Iraq	1.7	185
103	Zambia	1.7	77
104	Jordan	1.6	40
105	Swaziland	1.5	7
106	Algeria	1.4	250
107	Djibouti	1.4	4
108	Egypt	1.4	503
109	El Salvador	1.4	56
110	Paraguay	1.4	37
111	Papua New Guinea	1.3	36
112	Botswana	1.2	8
113	Gabon	1.2	11
114	Philippines	1.2	490
115	Cape Verde	1.0	2
116	Guatemala	1.0	53
117	Morocco	1.0	168
118	Nicaragua	1.0	22
119	Saudi Arabia	1.0	85
120	Bolivia	0.9	49
121	Ivory Coast	0.9	59
122	Kenya	0.9	122
123	Senegal	0.9	38
124	Congo	0.8	10
125	Honduras	0.7	20
126	Thailand	0.7	312
127	Angola	0.6	38
128	Ghana	0.6	60
129	Mozambique	0.6	56
130	South Yemen	0.6	10
131	Comoros	0.5	2

Rank	Country	Telephones (per 100 inhabitants)	Total (000)
132	Gambia	0.5	2
133	Guinea-Bissau	0.5	3
134	Sri Lanka	0.5	72
135	Cameroon	0.4	22
136	Madagascar	0.4	31
137	Malawi	0.4	20
138	Sierra Leone	0.4	11
139	Tanzania	0.4	63
140	Uganda	0.4	45
141	Benin	0.3	8
142	Ethiopia	0.3	69
143	India	0.3	1,817
144	Lesotho	0.3	4
145	Liberia	0.3	0.7
146	Oman	0.3	5
147	Pakistan	0.3	240
148	Sudan	0.3	56
149	Togo	0.3	8
150	Vietnam	0.3	47
151	Afghanistan	0.2	25
152	Central African Empire	0.2	5
153	Chad	0.2	5
154	Guinea	0.2	10
155	Haiti	0.2	9
156	Indonesia	0.2	305
157	Laos	0.2	5
158	Nigeria	0.2	111
159	Somalia	0.2	5
160	Zaire	0.2	48

BOTTOM 9

161	Bangladesh	0.1	80
162	Burma	0.1	31
163	Burundi	0.1	4
164	Mali	0.1	5
165	Nepal	0.1	8
166	Niger	0.1	5
167	Rwanda	0.1	3
168	Upper Volta	0.1	6
169	Yemen Arab Republic	0.1	4

Sources: International Telecommunications Union, *Telecommunications Statistics*
American Telephone & Telegraph Company, *The World's Telephones*

214. Telegrams per Capita

Until electronic transmission of facsimile documents becomes more widely accepted, telegrams will remain the fastest means of transmitting documents. However, its use has been declining in many countries—particularly those with a high ratio of telephones per capita—in relation to other means of communication.

Number of Countries: 101
Midpoint: 11 per 100 inhabitants
Period Covered: 1976
Type of Ranking: Domestic Telegrams per 100 Inhabitants; Highest to Lowest

Highlights & Findings: The presence of many Communist countries in the top 10 is noteworthy. As evidenced in the rankings, telegraphic communication has limited use in developing countries.

Regions	Africa	Asia & Oceania	Europe	Western Hemisphere
Most	South Africa (25)	New Zealand (5)	Monaco (1)	Cuba (2)
Least	Ethiopia (100)	Singapore (101)	Netherlands (74)	Surinam (90)

Rank	Country	Domestic Telegrams per 100 Inhabitants	Domestic Telegrams Total (000)	Rank	Country	Domestic Telegrams per 100 Inhabitants	Domestic Telegrams Total (000)	Rank	Country	Domestic Telegrams per 100 Inhabitants	Domestic Telegrams Total (000)
	TOP 10			35	Norway	24	1,002	69	United Kingdom	6	3,378
1	Monaco	303	91	36	France	23	12,196	70	Chad	5	223
2	Cuba	178	16,413	37	Cape Verde	20	58	71	Ghana	5	548
3	Soviet Union	178	458,607	38	Austria	18	1,355	72	Malaysia	5	593
4	Iceland	159	350	39	Belgium	18	1,785	73	Mozambique	5	468
5	New Zealand	137	4,320	40	Egypt	18	6,433	74	Netherlands	5	696
7	Bulgaria	115	10,064	41	Portugal	18	1,757	75	Pakistan	5	3,983
8	Hungary	100	10,699	42	Congo	17	242	76	Paraguay	5	151
9	Australia	94	12,930	43	Brazil	16	18,027	77	Tunisia	5	293
10	Czechoslovakia	93	13,984	44	Finland	14	667	78	Burma	4	1,289
				45	Israel	13	452	79	Central African Empire	4	83
	UPPER MIDDLE			46	Bangladesh	12	9,200	80	Iraq	4	446
11	Colombia	86	20,530	47	Ecuador	12	778	81	Tanzania	4	720
12	Mexico	70	43,800	48	Thailand	12	5,368	82	Cameroon	3	225
13	East Germany	65	10,950	49	United States	12	35,002	83	Jordan	3	76
14	South Korea	64	23,107					84	Kenya	3	427
15	Argentina	57	14,758		*LOWER MIDDLE*			85	Zaire	3	776
16	Costa Rica	56	1,031	50	Canada	11	2,747	86	Indonesia	2	3,623
17	Greece	54	5,014	51	Ireland	11	372	87	Malawi	2	109
18	French Polynesia	52	68	52	Switzerland	11	740	88	Morocco	2	527
19	Yugoslavia	52	11,327	53	Algeria	10	1,777	89	Nigeria	2	1,472
20	Chile	51	5,403	54	Angola	10	627	90	Surinam	2	12
21	Jamaica	48	982	55	Ivory Coast	10	538	91	Syria	2	183
22	Rumania	46	9,805	56	Denmark	9	478	92	Vietnam	2	1,024
23	Poland	44	15,206	57	Guinea	9	419				
24	Netherlands Antilles	43	105	58	India	9	57,665		*BOTTOM 9*		
25	South Africa	42	10,980	59	West Germany	8	5,247	93	Benin	1	43
26	Spain	42	15,125	60	Madagascar	8	696	94	Guinea-Bissau	1	7
27	Italy	40	22,556	61	New Caledonia	8	11	95	Togo	1	37
28	Japan	37	41,891	62	Sudan	8	1,421	96	Uganda	1	197
29	Sri Lanka	37	5,128	63	Cyprus	7	48	97	Upper Volta	1	74
30	Peru	34	5,607	64	Lebanon	7	185	98	Kuwait	0.5	6
31	Uruguay	34	979	65	Senegal	7	286	99	Laos	0.5	17
32	Turkey	33	13,491	66	Zambia	7	364	100	Ethiopia	0.4	133
33	El Salvador	28	1,167	67	Niger	6	282	101	Singapore	0.1	4
34	Luxembourg	28	102	68	Sweden	6	570				

Source: International Telecommunications Union.

CONSUMPTION

Consumption is important in a consumer-oriented economy because consumption generates demand and demand in turn governs supply. Unfortunately, few consumption statistics are published, although they are collected regularly by market research organizations for their own confidential use. The U.N. data that are available relate to what is called apparent consumption, which is based on a simple formula: production minus exports plus imports. It is logical to assume that the resulting figure represents actual consumption in a broad sense; however, in the case of perishables it does not tell how much was wasted and in the case of consumer durables how much was held in stock. But this should not cause undue concern so long as the usual precautions are adopted.

The key ranking in this section is the per capita consumption index, which provides a clue to the overall personal consumption expenditures. There are 19 other rankings, of which 11 are food items.

215. Per Capita Consumption Index

The per capita consumption index is perhaps one of the most useful in the vast arsenal of economic indexes. It measures the growth in total private and public expenditures in a nation as compared to a base year. Because it does not distinguish between various types of expenditures (such as food, durables, etc.), it presents a more reliable guide to a country's total spending. Needs and spending patterns vary in individual areas; some spend more on clothing, some more on leisure; some more on food. The question this index answers is a broader one: is the nation on a spending spree, or is it exercising some kind of spending restraint?

Number of Countries: 115 **Midpoint:** 106.5 **Period Covered:** 1973 **Type of Ranking:** Per Capita Consumption Index, 1970=100; Highest to Lowest	**Highlights and Findings:** The index reveals that the growth rate in consumption for industrialized and developing countries varies by less than three index points: 114.3 for the former and 111.6 for the latter. The largest spread is between Middle Eastern Countries (123.0) and South Asian countries (99.0). In between are African countries (100.8), Southern European countries (116.2), East Asian countries (109.1) and the Western Hemisphere (109.7). Per capita consumption has declined in 26 countries.

Regions	Africa	Asia & Oceania	Europe	Western Hemisphere
Most	Gabon (3)	Iraq (1)	Iceland (4)	Brazil (10)
Least	Niger (115)	Bangladesh (110)	Malta (80)	Venezuela (106)

Rank	Country	Per Capita Consumption Index	Rank	Country	Per Capita Consumption Index	Rank	Country	Per Capita Consumption Index
	TOP 10		12	Cyprus	120.7	26	Finland	115.7
1	Iraq	140.9	13	Fiji	120.6	27	Singapore	115.7
2	Saudi Arabia	131.6	14	Israel	120.0	28	Austria	115.6
3	Gabon	131.5	15	South Korea	120.0	29	Taiwan	115.6
4	Iceland	127.2	16	Congo	119.6	30	France	115.3
5	Greece	126.8	17	Nigeria	119.4	31	Denmark	114.8
6	Iran	123.3	18	Portugal	118.7	32	Dominican Republic	114.7
7	Japan	123.1	19	Mauritius	118.5	33	Rhodesia (Zimbabwe)	114.5
8	Tunisia	122.6	20	New Zealand	117.8	34	Switzerland	114.4
9	Malawi	122.1	21	Guinea	117.7	35	Spain	114.0
10	Brazil	121.5	22	Belgium	117.2	36	Ireland	113.8
			23	Lebanon	117.0	37	Turkey	113.0
	UPPER MIDDLE		24	Canada	116.7	38	Bolivia	112.6
11	Yugoslavia	120.9	25	Jamaica	116.4	39	United Kingdom	112.5

Rank	Country	Per Capita Consumption Index	Rank	Country	Per Capita Consumption Index	Rank	Country	Per Capita Consumption Index
40	West Germany	112.3	65	Morocco	105.0	92	Honduras	99.2
41	Somalia	110.9	66	Sudan	104.9	93	Burundi	99.0
42	Guyana	110.7	67	Syria	104.9	94	Pakistan	98.7
43	Peru	110.7	68	Togo	104.8	95	Mauritania	98.2
44	Guatemala	110.2	69	Libya	104.7	96	Gambia	97.8
45	Thailand	110.2	70	Sierra Leone	104.6	97	Ivory Coast	97.3
46	Argentina	109.7	71	Trinidad & Tobago	104.5	98	Ghana	97.0
47	United States	109.6	72	South Africa	104.4	99	Sri Lanka	96.8
48	Kenya	109.1	73	Egypt	104.3	100	Upper Volta	96.4
49	Indonesia	109.0	74	Paraguay	104.0	101	Rwanda	96.1
50	Colombia	108.6	75	Mozambique	103.4	102	Uruguay	96.0
51	Norway	108.5	76	Sweden	103.3	103	Benin	95.7
52	Australia	108.4	77	Costa Rica	103.2	104	India	95.7
53	Hong Kong	108.3	78	Panama	102.8	105	Vietnam	95.2
54	Zaire	107.5	79	Botswana	102.6			
55	Swaziland	107.3	80	Malta	102.1		*BOTTOM 10*	
56	Malaysia	107.0	81	Tanzania	102.0	106	Venezuela	95.1
57	Mexico	107.0	82	Ethiopia	101.6	107	Uganda	94.1
58	Netherlands	106.5	83	Afghanistan	100.9	108	Jordan	92.3
			84	Burma	100.9	109	Lesotho	92.2
	LOWER MIDDLE		85	Mali	100.9	110	Bangladesh	92.1
59	Ecuador	106.3	86	Nicaragua	100.4	111	Liberia	91.8
60	Algeria	106.2	87	Angola	100.3	112	Central African Empire	90.5
61	Zambia	106.2	88	El Salvador	100.3	113	Madagascar	83.8
62	Barbados	105.5	89	Senegal	100.2	114	Chad	82.9
63	Philippines	105.5	90	Chile	99.6	115	Niger	78.3
64	Italy	105.1	91	Cameroon	99.2			

Source: World Bank.

216. Cereal Consumption

This ranking compares the national consumption of cereals, including wheat, rice, corn, oats, barley and other basic food crops of the world. The production of each of these crops is dealt with in the chapter on agriculture.

Number of Countries: 64
Midpoint: 115.8 kg (255.33 lb)
Period Covered: Early 1970s
Type of Ranking: Per Capita Consumption of Cereals in Kg and Lb; Highest to Lowest

Highlights & Findings: The rank order in this ranking is significantly different with developing countries reporting vastly greater consumption of cereals than developed countries.
Cereals—typically in the form of bread or rice—constitute the staple food in those countries in the upper half of the ranking.

Region	Africa	Asia & Oceania	Europe	Western Hemisphere
Most	Egypt (2)	Turkey (1)	Rumania (3)	Guatemala (16)
Least	Uganda (63)	Australia (50)	Sweden (58)	Dominican Republic (64)

Rank	Country	Annual per Capita Consumption of Cereals in Kg	Lb	Rank	Country	Annual per Capita Consumption of Cereals in Kg	Lb	Rank	Country	Annual per Capita Consumption of Cereals in Kg	Lb
	TOP 10			7	Taiwan	160.5	353.90	12	Japan	149.2	328.98
1	Turkey	223.0	491.71	8	Madagascar	160.4	353.68	13	Ethiopia	148.5	327.44
2	Egypt	198.6	437.91	9	Syria	157.6	347.50	14	Poland	146.4	322.81
3	Rumania	196.3	432.84	10	Greece	157.1	346.05	15	Iran	143.8	317.07
4	Yugoslavia	189.3	417.40					16	Guatemala	141.2	311.34
5	Afghanistan	173.8	383.22		*UPPER MIDDLE*			17	India	139.5	307.59
6	South Africa	166.4	366.91	11	Pakistan	154.7	341.11	18	Jordan	135.9	299.65

Rank Country	Annual per Capita Consumption of Cereals in Kg	Lb	Rank Country	Annual per Capita Consumption of Cereals in Kg	Lb	Rank Country	Annual per Capita Consumption of Cereals in Kg	Lb
19 Hungary	134.9	297.45	34 Sudan	113.3	249.82	51 United Kingdom	81.4	179.48
20 Italy	134.2	295.91	35 Ireland	109.4	241.22	52 Jamaica	81.3	179.26
21 Mauritius	130.2	287.09	36 Brazil	108.9	240.12	53 Netherlands	80.4	177.28
22 Iraq	129.6	285.76	37 Finland	106.9	235.71	54 West Germany	79.2	174.63
23 El Salvador	129.1	284.66	38 Honduras	106.8	235.49			
24 Mexico	127.5	281.13	39 Austria	103.9	229.09			
25 Sri Lanka	127.3	280.69	40 Panama	102.7	226.45	*BOTTOM 10*		
26 Portugal	126.1	278.05	41 France	98.0	216.09	55 Norway	78.2	172.43
27 Lebanon	121.6	268.12	42 Switzerland	96.0	211.68	56 Denmark	77.9	171.76
28 Chile	119.8	264.15	43 Bolivia	95.8	211.23	57 Paraguay	75.4	166.25
29 Surinam	119.8	264.15	44 Peru	95.7	211.01	58 Sweden	71.9	158.53
30 Philippines	118.3	260.85	45 Argentina	91.3	201.31	59 Ecuador	69.1	152.36
31 Israel	116.1	256.00	46 Belgium-Luxembourg	89.7	197.78	60 Canada	66.3	146.19
32 Spain	115.8	255.33	47 Uruguay	89.7	197.78	61 United States	66.0	145.53
			48 Venezuela	87.5	192.93	62 Colombia	64.6	142.44
LOWER MIDDLE			49 New Zealand	86.6	190.95	63 Uganda	61.1	134.72
33 Libya	114.7	252.91	50 Australia	83.6	184.33	64 Dominican Republic	56.5	124.58

Source: *Compendium of Social Statistics.*

217. Coffee Consumption

Of the total 4.4 million tons of coffee produced in 1975, 3.35 million tons were consumed in 34 countries ranked below and the remainder in over 150 countries where the per capita consumption is insignificant. Because coffee is used principally in affluent countries, its demand and popularity have not been seriously affected by the steep rise in prices in recent years.

Number of Countries: 34
Midpoint: 1.89 kg (4.16 lb)
Period Covered: 1975
Type of Table: Per Capita Consumption in Kg and Lb and Total Consumption in Tons; Highest to Lowest

Highlights & Findings: On the assumption that each kilogram of coffee is equivalent to 150 cups, Swedes, who lead the world in coffee consumption, drink nearly 2,031 cups a year, or 5.7 cups per day per capita. Of the top 10 consuming nations, nine are European.

Region	Africa	Asia & Oceania	Europe	Western Hemisphere
Most	South Africa (28)	New Zealand (16)	Sweden (1)	United States (9)
Least	Egypt (34)	Turkey (32)	Soviet Union (33)	Chile (27)

Rank Country	Cups of Coffee per Capita per year	Per Capita Consumption in kg	lb	Total (000 metric tons)	Rank Country	Cups of Coffee per Capita per year	Per Capita Consumption in kg	lb	Total (000 metric tons)	Rank Country	Cups of Coffee per Capita per year	Per Capita Consumption in kg	lb	Total (000 metric tons)
TOP 10					11 Austria	742	4.95	10.91	37.20	22 Yugoslavia	202	1.35	2.97	28.92
1 Sweden	2,031	13.54	29.85	67.14	12 Italy	548	3.65	8.04	203.88	23 Cyprus	196	1.31	2.88	0.84
2 Denmark	1,981	13.27	29.26	67.14	13 Canada	546	3.64	8.02	83.16	24 Japan	149	0.99	2.18	109.38
3 Finland	1,882	12.55	27.67	59.10	14 Spain	328	2.19	4.82	77.76					
4 Netherlands	1,650	11.00	24.25	150.12	15 East Germany	314	2.09	4.60	35.28	*BOTTOM 10*				
5 Switzerland	1,537	10.25	22.60	65.58	16 New Zealand	294	1.96	4.32	5.94	25 Poland	138	0.92	2.02	31.20
6 Norway	1,455	9.70	21.38	38.88	17 Australia	283	1.89	4.16	25.50	26 Israel	110	0.73	1.60	2.46
7 Belgium & Luxembourg										27 Chile	96	0.64	1.41	6.60
	1,263	8.42	18.56	85.56	*LOWER MIDDLE*					28 South Africa	88	0.59	1.30	15.00
8 France	900	6.00	13.23	317.70	18 Greece	280	1.87	4.12	16.92	29 Jordan	80	0.53	1.16	1.38
9 United States	860	5.73	12.63	1,217.34	19 United Kingdom	248	1.65	3.63	92.10	30 Portugal	58	0.39	0.85	3.42
10 West Germany	830	5.53	12.19	342.12	20 Argentina	245	1.63	3.59	41.40	31 Morocco	54	0.36	0.79	6.18
					21 Czechsoslovakia	216	1.44	3.17	21.24	32 Turkey	39	0.26	0.57	10.02
										33 Soviet Union	28	0.19	0.41	48.06
										34 Egypt	21	0.14	0.30	5.10

Source: Pan-American Coffee Bureau.

218. Egg Consumption

This ranking compares the consumption of eggs in each country. Despite inflation, the egg remains one of the cheapest sources of protein in the world, and there are few known ritual restrictions against its consumption. Eggs are consumed directly as well as mixed in other items of food such as cakes and biscuits.

Number of Countries: 64	Highlights & Findings: Because dietary patterns in the West place so much emphasis on eggs,
Midpoint: 4.1 kg (9.04 lb)	consumption is highest in Western countries. Conversion of eggs by weight as presented here
Period Covered: Early 1970s	into number of eggs may be nothing more than an educated guess; even so, back-of-an-envelope
Type of Ranking: Per Capita Consumption	calculation reveals that the top ranking Israelis consume five eggs per capita per week while the
of Eggs in Kg and Lb; Highest to Lowest	Malagasy at the bottom only two eggs per capita per year.

Region	Africa	Asia & Oceania	Europe	Western Hemisphere
Most	South Africa (40)	Israel (1)	Ireland (3)	United States (2)
Least	Madagascar (64)	India (63)	Yugoslavia (41)	Paraguay (61)

Rank	Country	Annual per Capita Consumption of Eggs in Kg	Lb		Rank	Country	Annual per Capita Consumption of Eggs in Kg	Lb		Rank	Country	Annual per Capita Consumption of Eggs in Kg	Lb
	TOP 10				22	Spain	7.3	16.09		44	Ecuador	2.2	4.85
1	Israel	20.2	44.54		23	Greece	6.8	14.99		45	Ethiopia	2.2	4.85
2	United States	18.8	41.45		24	Uruguay	6.6	14.55		46	Guatemala	1.9	4.18
3	Ireland	16.5	36.38		25	Japan	6.0	13.23		47	Sudan	1.9	4.18
4	New Zealand	15.9	35.05		26	Mexico	5.4	11.90		48	Jordan	1.8	3.96
5	Canada	15.4	33.95		27	Rumania	5.2	11.46		49	Libya	1.8	3.96
6	United Kingdom	15.2	33.51		28	El Salvador	4.7	10.36		50	Turkey	1.8	3.96
7	Belgium & Luxembourg	13.3	29.32		29	Panama	4.4	9.70		51	Iran	1.7	3.74
8	West Germany	13.1	28.88		30	Chile	4.2	9.26		52	China	1.6	3.52
9	Netherlands	12.0	26.46		31	Jamaica	4.2	9.26		53	Mauritius	1.5	3.30
10	Sweden	12.0	26.46		32	Honduras	4.1	9.04		54	Syria	1.5	3.30
	UPPER MIDDLE					*LOWER MIDDLE*					*BOTTOM 10*		
11	Australia	11.9	26.23		33	Peru	3.7	8.15		55	Egypt	1.1	2.42
12	Austria	11.9	26.23		34	Dominican Republic	3.6	7.93		56	Iraq	1.1	2.42
13	France	11.4	25.13		35	Portugal	3.6	7.93		57	Sri Lanka	1.1	2.42
14	Denmark	11.1	24.47		36	Brazil	3.4	7.49		58	Bolivia	1.0	2.20
15	Switzerland	9.9	21.82		37	Colombia	3.4	7.49		59	Uganda	1.0	2.20
16	Italy	9.3	20.50		38	Philippines	3.3	7.27		60	Afghanistan	0.7	1.54
17	Hungary	8.9	19.62		39	Venezuela	3.3	7.27		61	Paraguay	0.6	1.32
18	Norway	8.8	19.40		40	South Africa	3.2	7.05		62	Pakistan	0.3	0.66
19	Argentina	8.1	17.86		41	Yugoslavia	3.2	7.05		63	India	0.2	0.44
20	Finland	8.0	17.64		42	Lebanon	2.7	5.95		64	Madagascar	0.2	0.44
21	Poland	7.7	16.97		43	Surinam	2.6	5.73					

Source: *Compendium of Social Statistics.*

219. Fish Consumption

This ranking compares the national consumption of fish in any form. The 73 million tons of fish that are caught in the world annually represent a worldwide per capita consumption of 17.82 kg (39.29 lb) per year. The most popular types of fish are cod, herring, haddock, mackerel, shrimp, tuna and salmon.

<table>
<tr><td colspan="2">Number of Countries: 63
Midpoint: 4.5 kg (9.92 lb)
Period Covered: Early 1970s
Type of Ranking: Per Capita Consumption of Fish in Kg and Lb; Highest to Lowest</td><td colspan="6">Highlights & Findings: Logically, consumption is highest in maritime countries and in Scandinavia. Even though there are few food taboos against fish in any society (fish being acceptable even in Lent), fish ranks low in food preferences compared to meat as reflected in this ranking.</td></tr>
</table>

Region	Africa	Asia & Oceania	Europe	Western Hemisphere
Most	South Africa (14)	Japan (1)	Portugal (2)	Jamaica (8)
Least	Ethiopia (61)	Syria (63)	Hungary (53)	Guatemala (62)

Rank	Country	Annual per Capita Fish Consumption in Kg	Lb	Rank	Country	Annual per Capita Fish Consumption in Kg	Lb	Rank	Country	Annual per Capita Fish Consumption in Kg	Lb
	TOP 10			22	Sri Lanka	6.0	13.23	44	Rumania	2.0	4.41
1	Japan	26.6	58.65	23	Canada	5.6	12.34	45	Lebanon	1.9	4.18
2	Portugal	20.8	45.80	24	Netherlands	5.6	12.34	46	Pakistan	1.6	3.52
3	Norway	20.2	44.54	25	Mauritius	5.5	12.12	47	Uruguay	1.5	3.30
4	Sweden	19.6	43.21	26	Belgium & Luxembourg	5.3	11.68	48	Colombia	1.2	2.64
5	Denmark	16.1	35.50	27	Australia	5.2	11.46	49	El Salvador	1.2	2.64
6	Spain	13.2	29.10	28	Italy	5.1	11.24	50	Libya	1.2	2.64
7	Taiwan	12.2	26.90	29	Egypt	4.8	10.58	51	Yugoslavia	1.2	2.64
8	Jamaica	11.4	25.13	30	Panama	4.8	10.58	52	India	1.0	2.20
9	Philippines	10.8	23.81	31	United States	4.8	10.58				
10	Finland	10.5	23.15						**BOTTOM 11**		
					LOWER MIDDLE			53	Hungary	0.8	1.76
	UPPER MIDDLE			32	Ecuador	4.5	9.92	54	Iran	0.8	1.76
11	Surinam	9.6	21.16	33	Uganda	4.4	9.70	55	Iraq	0.8	1.76
12	United Kingdom	9.6	21.16	34	Iceland	4.2	9.26	56	Jordan	0.8	1.76
13	Greece	9.2	20.28	35	Poland	4.1	9.04	57	Honduras	0.7	1.54
14	South Africa	8.8	19.40	36	Madagascar	3.8	8.37	58	Sudan	0.7	1.54
15	France	7.2	15.87	37	Switzerland	3.7	8.10	59	Paraguay	0.3	0.66
16	West Germany	6.7	14.77	38	Austria	3.6	7.93	60	Bolivia	0.2	0.44
17	Israel	6.7	14.77	39	Dominican Republic	3.5	7.71	61	Ethiopia	0.2	0.44
18	Peru	6.7	14.77	40	Brazil	2.6	5.73	62	Guatemala	0.2	0.44
19	Venezuela	6.7	14.77	41	Mexico	2.5	5.51	63	Syria	0.1	0.22
20	New Zealand	6.6	14.55	42	Turkey	2.5	5.51				
21	Chile	6.2	13.67	43	Argentina	2.1	4.63				

Source: *Compendium of Social Statistics*

220. Fruit Consumption

The following ranking compares the consumption of fruits in each country as an indicator of the quality of food available to its citizens. The name fruit is often loosely applied to all edible plant products but in this ranking is restricted to the juicy or fleshy product of a tree, bush, vine or plant that is good to eat.

<table>
<tr><td colspan="2">Number of Countries: 64
Midpoint: 65.2 kg (143.76 lb)
Period Covered: Early 1970s
Type of Ranking: Per Capita Consumption of Fruits in Kg and Lb; Highest to Lowest</td><td colspan="6">Highlights & Findings: Fruit consumption per capita is highest in Latin American, European and Middle Eastern countries. Relative to other foods, fruit consumption is high in all reporting countries. In developing countries the bulk of the fruit production is consumed directly, but in developed countries the proportion favors canned fruits and preserves. Not surprisingly, tropical and semitropical countries are especially well represented at the top of the list.</td></tr>
</table>

Region	Africa	Asia & Oceania	Europe	Western Hemisphere
Most	Egypt (24)	Lebanon (4)	Switzerland (3)	Honduras (1)
Least	Ethiopia (64)	Sri Lanka (61)	Poland (60)	Bolivia (57)

Rank	Country	Per Capita Consumption of Fruits in		Rank	Country	Per Capita Consumption of Fruits in		Rank	Country	Per Capita Consumption of Fruits in	
		Kg	Lb			Kg	Lb			Kg	Lb
	TOP 10			22	Portugal	83.8	184.77	44	Finland	43.7	96.35
1	Honduras	244.5	539.12	23	Argentina	79.9	176.17	45	South Africa	39.6	87.31
2	Dominican Republic	219.5	483.99	24	Egypt	78.4	172.87	46	Iran	38.1	84.01
3	Switzerland	162.0	357.21	25	Jamaica	77.6	171.10	47	Philippines	35.8	78.93
4	Lebanon	160.4	353.68	26	Venezuela	75.6	166.69	48	Iceland	32.0	70.56
5	Syria	158.8	350.15	27	Sweden	74.0	163.17	49	Surinam	31.0	68.35
6	Paraguay	143.0	315.31	28	Iraq	71.7	158.09	50	Pakistan	29.0	63.94
7	Israel	141.8	312.66	29	Netherlands	71.7	158.09	51	Guatemala	28.4	62.62
8	Austria	118.0	260.19	30	Denmark	68.6	151.26	52	Sudan	27.8	61.29
9	Jordan	118.0	260.19	31	Libya	67.9	149.71	53	Afghanistan	27.3	60.19
10	Panama	116.0	255.78	32	New Zealand	65.2	143.76	54	Japan	26.4	58.21
	UPPER MIDDLE				*LOWER MIDDLE*				*BOTTOM 10*		
11	Brazil	111.5	245.85	33	France	64.0	141.12	55	Madagascar	24.3	53.58
12	Greece	107.1	236.15	34	Norway	62.9	138.69	56	El Salvador	22.4	49.39
13	West Germany	105.1	231.74	35	Mexico	62.8	138.47	57	Bolivia	21.2	46.74
14	Australia	104.1	229.54	36	Hungary	61.2	134.94	58	Taiwan	21.2	46.74
15	United States	101.1	222.92	37	Chile	58.2	128.33	59	India	17.5	38.58
16	Italy	91.0	200.65	38	United Kingdom	55.3	121.93	60	Poland	16.0	35.28
17	Peru	90.8	200.21	39	Uruguay	55.2	121.71	61	Sri Lanka	8.8	19.40
18	Ecuador	90.1	198.67	40	Belgium	52.1	114.88	62	Uganda	7.3	16.09
19	Turkey	88.6	195.36	41	Yugoslavia	46.8	103.19	63	Mauritius	5.1	11.24
20	Spain	87.7	193.37	42	Colombia	44.9	99.00	64	Ethiopia	1.7	3.74
21	Canada	85.6	188.74	43	Rumania	44.1	97.24				

Source: *Compendium of Social Statistics.*

221. Meat Consumption

The consumption of meat is critical in any nutritional system because it is an incomparable source of protein. There is therefore a strong correlation between this ranking and the ranking by per capita protein consumption. Meat itself is a broad term that includes beef, mutton and lamb and pork but generally excludes poultry.

Number of Countries: 64
Midpoint: 26.8 kg (59.09 lb)
Period Covered: Early 1970s
Type of Ranking: Per Capita Consumption of Meat in Kg and Lb; Highest to Lowest

Highlights & Findings: Australia and New Zealand lead in lamb and mutton consumption and Uruguay and Argentina in beef consumption. Meat prices are the pacemakers of all food prices, and even in producing countries meat has become expensive beyond the reach of the poorer consumers. This, in turn, may affect consumption patterns adversely.

Region	Africa	Asia & Oceania	Europe	Western Hemisphere
Most	South Africa (20)	New Zealand (1)	France (6)	Uruguay (3)
Least	Mauritius (61)	India (64)	Portugal (41)	Surinam (59)

Rank	Country	Per Capita Consumption of Meat in		Rank	Country	Per Capita Consumption of Meat in		Rank	Country	Per Capita Consumption of Meat in	
		Kg	Lb			Kg	Lb			Kg	Lb
	TOP 10			7	Canada	77.6	171.10	12	Belgium-Luxembourg	60.4	133.18
1	New Zealand	110.2	242.99	8	United Kingdom	74.1	163.39	13	Switzerland	59.9	132.07
2	Australia	108.7	239.68	9	Denmark	66.3	146.19	14	Austria	59.8	131.85
3	Uruguay	101.0	222.70	10	Ireland	63.4	139.79	15	Poland	54.3	119.73
4	Argentina	99.8	220.05					16	Sweden	51.2	112.89
5	United States	95.5	210.57		*UPPER MIDDLE*			17	Hungary	48.6	107.16
6	France	77.8	171.54	11	West Germany	60.5	133.40	18	Netherlands	45.9	101.20

Rank	Country	Per Capita Consumption of Meat in Kg	Lb
19	Paraguay	44.9	99.00
20	South Africa	44.5	98.12
21	Israel	39.7	87.53
22	Norway	39.6	87.31
23	Colombia	35.9	79.15
24	Rumania	34.8	76.73
25	Panama	34.4	75.85
26	Finland	34.3	75.63
27	Chile	33.3	73.42
28	Lebanon	31.5	69.45
29	Italy	30.7	67.69
30	Yugoslavia	28.4	62.62
31	Brazil	27.5	60.63
32	Ethiopia	26.8	59.09
	LOWER MIDDLE		
33	Greece	26.3	57.99

Rank	Country	Per Capita Consumption of Meat in Kg	Lb
34	Peru	26.3	57.99
35	Venezuela	25.3	55.78
36	Sudan	25.1	55.34
37	Mexico	22.7	50.05
38	Spain	20.9	46.08
39	Ecuador	20.8	45.86
40	Iraq	20.1	44.32
41	Portugal	19.7	43.43
42	Dominican Republic	18.5	40.79
43	Bolivia	18.4	40.57
44	Jamaica	17.1	37.70
45	Taiwan	16.0	35.28
46	Iran	15.9	35.05
47	Madagascar	15.3	33.73
48	Philippines	14.9	32.85
49	Syria	13.8	30.42
50	Turkey	13.5	29.76

Rank	Country	Per Capita Consumption of Meat in Kg	Lb
51	Afghanistan	13.4	29.54
52	El Salvador	12.8	28.22
53	Guatemala	12.4	27.34
54	Jordan	12.2	26.90
	BOTTOM 10		
55	Egypt	12.1	26.68
56	Honduras	10.8	23.81
57	Libya	10.0	22.06
58	Uganda	10.0	22.05
59	Surinam	9.1	20.06
60	Japan	7.7	15.43
61	Mauritius	5.8	12.78
62	Pakistan	3.5	7.71
63	Sri Lanka	2.1	4.63
64	India	1.5	3.30

Source: *Compendium of Social Statistics.*

222. Potato Consumption

This ranking compares the national consumption of potatoes, one of the most widely used articles of food. For its historical importance see the introduction to the production of potatoes in the chapter on agriculture.

Number of Countries: 65
Midpoint: 67.3 kg (148.39 lb)
Period Covered: Early 1970s
Type of Ranking: Per Capita Consumption of Potatoes and Other Starchy Foods in Kg and Lb; Highest to Lowest

Highlights & Findings: Of the 10 top countries, only three are European and these include, predictably, Ireland. In the main potato-consuming countries, per capita consumption is high relative to other foods; in Uganda it is nearly 1.3 kg (2.8 lb) per day and even in middle-ranking Spain consumption is 2.2 kg (4.8 lb) per week. There is a sharp drop-off toward the bottom and consumption is not significant in any Asian country.

Region	Africa	Asia & Oceania	Europe	Western Hemisphere
Most	Uganda (1)	Japan (29)	Poland (3)	Paraguay (2)
Least	Egypt (56)	Afghanistan (65)	Greece (44)	EL Salvador (64)

Rank	Country	Annual Per Capita Consumption of Potatoes in Kg	Lb
	TOP 10		
1	Uganda	475.7	1,048.91
2	Paraguay	262.1	577.93
3	Poland	220.9	487.08
4	Colombia	205.6	453.34
5	Bolivia	166.9	368.01
6	Brazil	149.3	329.20
7	Ireland	141.2	311.34
8	Ecuador	133.1	293.48
9	West Germany	130.9	288.63
10	Peru	126.7	279.37
	UPPER MIDDLE		
11	Dominican Republic	124.0	273.42

Rank	Country	Annual Per Capita Consumption of Potatoes in Kg	Lb
12	Madagascar	123.3	271.87
13	Denmark	119.0	262.39
14	Belgium-Luxembourg	118.2	260.63
15	Spain	115.2	254.01
16	Finland	111.2	245.19
17	Venezuela	100.0	220.50
18	Norway	99.3	218.95
19	Portugal	99.3	218.95
20	France	99.2	218.73
21	Netherlands	98.7	217.63
22	United Kingdom	98.2	216.53
23	Hungary	95.6	210.79
24	Sweden	90.8	200.21
25	Argentina	87.9	193.81

Rank	Country	Annual Per Capita Consumption of Potatoes in Kg	Lb
26	Austria	84.1	185.44
27	Chile	70.3	155.01
28	Uruguay	70.0	154.35
29	Japan	68.9	151.92
30	Panama	68.6	151.26
31	Switzerland	68.5	151.04
32	Yugoslavia	67.3	148.39
	LOWER MIDDLE		
33	Rumania	66.1	145.75
34	Canada	64.4	141.12
35	Taiwan	63.8	140.67
36	Jamaica	63.6	140.23
37	New Zealand	59.3	130.75

Rank	Country	Annual Per Capita Consumption of Potatoes in Kg	Lb	Rank	Country	Annual Per Capita Consumption of Potatoes in Kg	Lb	Rank	Country	Annual Per Capita Consumption of Potatoes in Kg	Lb
38	Italy	52.3	115.32	49	Ethiopia	19.1	42.11	58	Jordan	10.4	22.93
39	United States	47.6	104.95	50	Mexico	17.2	37.92	59	Syria	8.9	19.62
40	Australia	47.1	103.85	51	Sudan	17.1	37.70	60	Guatemala	7.8	17.19
41	Honduras	44.4	97.90	52	Libya	17.0	37.48	61	Iraq	5.4	11.90
42	Philippines	42.8	94.37	53	Lebanon	15.6	34.39	62	Pakistan	4.6	10.14
43	Iraq	41.2	90.84	54	South Africa	14.4	31.75	63	Iran	3.5	7.71
44	Greece	39.4	86.87	55	Mauritius	13.0	28.66	64	El Salvador	2.9	6.39
45	Turkey	38.5	84.89					65	Afghanistan	0.2	0.44
46	Israel	37.6	82.90		**BOTTOM 10**						
47	Sri Lanka	34.7	76.51	56	Egypt	10.7	23.59				
48	Surinam	27.2	59.97	57	India	10.6	23.37				

Source: *Compendium of Social Statistics.*

223. Pulse and Nut Consumption

The following ranking compares the consumption of pulses and nuts in each country. Pulses—also called peas or legumes—provide valuable and nutritive foods, and in areas where meat is scarce or expensive, they are the staples of diet, especially peas, beans, lentils, peanuts, carob and soybeans. The term nut is used not in the strict botanical sense—according to which acorns, hazelnuts, and chestnuts are among the true nuts—but in the marketplace sense, thus including cashewnuts, pistachios and walnuts.

Number of Countries: 64
Midpoint: 8.5 kg (18.74 lb)
Period Covered: Early 1970s
Type of Ranking: Per Capita Consumption of Pulses & Nuts in Kg and Lb; Highest to Lowest

Highlights & Findings: Consumption of pulses and nuts is highest in developing countries, where they supply some of the protein requirements that in developed countries are derived from meat and meat products. Consumption is also determined by dietary preferences for foods made from pulses and nuts. Such preferences are most marked in Asia, Africa and Latin America.

Region	Africa	Asia & Oceania	Europe	Western Hemisphere
Most	Uganda (3)	Sri Lanka (2)	Spain (12)	Brazil (1)
Least	South Africa (49)	Afghanistan (64)	Finland (63)	Bolivia (61)

Rank	Country	Annual Per Capita Consumption of Pulses & Nuts in Kg	Lb	Rank	Country	Annual Per Capita Consumption of Pulses & Nuts in Kg	Lb	Rank	Country	Annual Per Capita Consumption of Pulses & Nuts in Kg	Lb
	TOP 10			15	Greece	14.2	31.31	32	Guatemala	8.5	18.74
1	Brazil	29.6	65.26	16	Turkey	13.2	29.10	33	Surinam	8.3	18.30
2	Sri Lanka	29.6	65.26	17	Lebanon	11.8	26.02	34	United States	7.9	17.42
3	Uganda	27.1	59.75	18	El Salvador	11.6	25.57	35	Switzerland	7.8	17.19
4	India	22.9	50.49	19	Syria	11.5	25.35	36	Italy	7.6	16.75
5	Mexico	22.7	50.05	20	Mauritius	11.3	24.90				
6	Ethiopia	19.4	42.77	21	Honduras	11.0	24.25		**LOWER MIDDLE**		
7	Sudan	17.6	38.80	22	Ecuador	10.8	23.81	37	Libya	6.6	14.55
8	Venezuela	16.7	36.82	23	Jamaica	10.8	23.81	38	Philippines	6.5	14.33
9	Dominican Republic	16.6	36.60	24	Taiwan	10.1	22.27	39	Denmark	6.3	13.89
10	Japan	16.4	36.16	25	Jordan	9.9	21.82	40	France	5.8	12.78
				26	Yugoslavia	9.9	21.82	41	Sweden	5.8	12.78
	UPPER MIDDLE			27	Chile	9.8	21.60	42	Iraq	5.7	12.56
11	Panama	15.8	34.83	28	Peru	9.8	21.60	43	Canada	5.4	11.90
12	Spain	14.7	32.41	29	Israel	9.5	20.94	44	Colombia	5.3	11.68
13	Egypt	14.5	31.97	30	Rumania	9.3	20.50	45	Pakistan	5.3	11.68
14	Paraguay	14.5	31.97	31	Portugal	9.1	20.06	46	Madagascar	4.8	10.58

Rank	Country	Annual Per Capita Consumption of Pulses & Nuts in Kg	Lb		Rank	Country	Annual Per Capita Consumption of Pulses & Nuts in Kg	Lb		Rank	Country	Annual Per Capita Consumption of Pulses & Nuts in Kg	Lb
47	Australia	4.4	9.70		54	New Zealand	3.8	8.37		59	Ireland	2.8	6.17
48	Netherlands	4.2	9.26							60	Argentina	2.6	5.73
49	South Africa	4.1	9.04			*BOTTOM 10*				61	Bolivia	2.4	5.29
50	Uruguay	4.0	8.82		55	West Germany	3.7	8.15		62	Poland	1.8	3.96
51	Iran	3.9	8.59		56	Norway	3.7	8.15		63	Finland	1.6	3.52
52	Austria	3.8	8.37		57	Sweden	3.4	7.49		64	Afghanistan	0.3	0.66
53	Belgium-Luxembourg	3.8	8.37		58	Hungary	3.1	6.83					

Source: *Compendium of Social Statistics.*

224. Sugar Consumption

The data in this table rank countries by their consumption of sugar, including both sugar consumed directly and used in the manufacture of soft drinks, candies and other products. World consumption of sugar in 1976 was 81.9 million tons, up by 13% from 72.1 million tons in 1970. In per capita terms the consumption was 20.4 kg (44.9 lb), up by only 2% since 1970. The regional distribution of sugar consumption was as follows:

	Total (000 metric tons)	Per Capita (kg)	(lb)
Africa	5,276	12.8	28.2
North America	15,230	44.0	97.0
South America	8,991	40.6	89.5
Asia	20,237	8.9	19.6
Europe	19,115	40.1	88.4
Oceania	1,048	48.7	107.3
Soviet Union	12,000	46.8	103.1

Number of Countries: 71
Midpoint: 31.6 kg (69.6 lb)
Period Covered: 1976
Type of Ranking: Per Capita Consumption of Sugar in Kg and Lb; Total Consumption of Sugar; Highest to Lowest

Highlights & Findings: The data do not reveal any discernible pattern; nevertheless, ethnic preferences and dietary traditions play a large part in determining the level of sugar consumption. Also, because of the substantial contribution sugar makes to calorie intake, the consumption is higher in countries with above-average per capita food consumption.

Regions	Africa	Asia & Oceania	Europe	Western Hemisphere
Most	South Africa (8)	Australia (2)	Bulgaria (1)	Costa Rica (3)
Least	Uganda (71)	Bangladesh (70)	Yugoslavia (41)	Bolivia (49)

Rank	Country	Per Capita Sugar Consumption in Kg	Lb	Total Consumption (000 metric tons)		Rank	Country	Per Capita Sugar Consumption in Kg	Lb	Total Consumption (000 metric tons)		Rank	Country	Per Capita Sugar Consumption in Kg	Lb	Total Consumption (000 metric tons)
	TOP 10					15	Nicaragua	44.8	98.7	100		31	Iraq	33.6	74.0	387
1	Bulgaria	63.9	140.8	560		16	Venezuela	43.7	96.3	540		32	Dominican			
2	Australia	57.3	126.3	781		17	Switzerland	43.0	94.8	275			Republic	32.7	72.1	167
3	Costa Rica	56.8	125.2	114		18	Mexico	42.9	94.5	2,675		33	Ecuador	32.5	71.6	245
4	Cuba	56.6	124.8	532		19	Hungary	42.5	93.7	451		34	Colombia	32.2	71.0	844
5	New Zealand	54.2	119.5	170		20	East Germany	42.3	93.2	710		35	Chile	31.6	69.6	330
6	Israel	53.1	117.0	188		21	Czechoslovakia	42.2	93.0	630		36	Greece	31.6	69.6	277
7	Jamaica	50.5	111.3	104		22	Canada	41.7	91.9	964		37	Malaysia	30.9	68.1	380
8	South Africa	47.6	104.9	1,305		23	European Eco. Com.					38	Spain	30.8	67.9	1,077
9	Poland	47.1	103.8	1,619			(Undistributed)	41.6	91.7	10,751		39	Rumania	30.3	66.8	650
10	United States	47.0	103.6	9,843		24	Finland	41.3	91.0	195						
						25	Norway	41.2	90.8	166			*LOWER MIDDLE*			
	UPPER MIDDLE					26	Argentina	39.8	87.7	1,023		40	Portugal	28.7	63.2	254
11	Soviet Union	46.8	103.1	12,000		27	Singapore	39.6	87.3	90		41	Yugoslavia	28.4	62.6	610
12	Sweden	46.3	102.0	380		28	Uruguay	37.1	81.8	115		42	El Salvador	28.0	61.7	123
13	Brazil	46.2	101.8	5,091		29	Guatemala	36.5	80.4	204		43	Iran	28.0	61.7	950
14	Austria	45.9	101.2	352		30	Peru	35.7	78.7	574		44	Morocco	28.0	61.7	500

Rank	Country	Per Capita Sugar Consumption in		Total Consumption (000 metric tons)	Rank	Country	Per Capita Sugar Consumption in		Total Consumption (000 metric tons)	Rank	Country	Per Capita Sugar Consumption in		Total Consumption (000 metric tons)
		Kg	Lb				Kg	Lb				Kg	Lb	
45	Japan	27.9	61.5	3,182	54	Sudan	15.7	34.6	285	62	South Korea	6.6	14.5	235
46	Syria	26.8	59.0	203	55	Kenya	14.4	31.7	200	63	Tanzania	6.1	13.4	95
47	Tunisia	26.1	57.5	150	56	Mozambique	13.8	30.4	130	64	China	5.5	12.1	4,600
48	Turkey	24.8	54.6	1,021	57	Thailand	13.3	29.3	569	65	Sri Lanka	5.3	11.6	72
49	Bolivia	22.6	49.8	131	58	Indonesia	9.9	21.8	1,387	66	Vietnam	5.1	11.2	240
50	Algeria	20.8	45.8	360	59	Pakistan	8.3	18.3	652	67	Ethiopia	5.0	11.0	124
51	Rhodesia (Zimbabwe)	19.9	43.8	130	60	North Korea	8.0	17.6	130	68	Nigeria	3.1	6.8	200
52	Egypt	19.8	43.6	754						69	Burma	2.6	5.7	80
53	Philippines	19.5	42.9	841		*BOTTOM 11*				70	Bangladesh	1.4	3.0	103
					61	India	6.6	14.5	4,016	71	Uganda	1.2	2.6	14

Source: International Sugar Organization, London.

225. Tea Consumption

Although not as universally popular as coffee, tea is a staple drink in most Middle Eastern and Anglo-Saxon countries. Its overall consumption in the 1970s has shown only a small increase and has actually declined in many countries.

Number of Countries: 38 **Midpoint:** 564 gr (19.9 oz) **Period Covered:** 1974-76 **Type of Ranking:** Per Capita Consumption of Tea in Gr and Oz; Total Consumption of Tea; Highest to Lowest	**Highlights & Findings:** Tea is the preferred drink in most countries with an Anglo-Saxon and Middle Eastern population. Strangely, the major producing countries, such as India and Sri Lanka, rank lower in per capita consumption.

Regions	Africa	Asia & Oceania	Europe	Western Hemisphere
Most	Tunisia (8)	New Zealand (3)	Ireland (1)	Canada (13)
Least	Uganda (33)	Thailand (38)	Italy (37)	Argentina (27)

Rank	Country	Per Capita Consumption of Tea in		Total Consumption (000 metric tons)	Rank	Country	Per Capita Consumption of Tea in		Total Consumption (000 metric tons)	Rank	Country	Per Capita Consumption of Tea in		Total Consumption (000 metric tons)
		Gr	Oz				Gr	Oz				Gr	Oz	
	TOP 10				13	Canada	944	33.3	21,570	26	United States	366	12.9	78,220
1	Ireland	3,713	131.0	11,620	14	Sudan	824	29.0	12,960	27	Argentina	332	11.7	8,440
2	United Kingdom	3,552	125.3	199,160	15	Morocco	766	27.0	13,260	28	Sweden	329	11.6	2,700
3	New Zealand	2,377	83.9	7,300	16	South Africa	750	26.4	20,790					
4	Iraq	2,045	72.1	22,030	17	Pakistan	692	24.4	48,630		*BOTTOM 10*			
5	Australia	1,939	68.4	26,180	18	Netherlands	660	23.2	9,010	29	Algeria	283	9.9	4,610
6	Hong Kong	1,518	53.5	6,630	19	Egypt	564	19.9	20,990	30	Switzerland	249	8.7	1,600
7	Sri Lanka	1,494	52.7	20,900						31	West Germany	171	6.0	10,580
8	Tunisia	1,186	41.8	6,690		*LOWER MIDDLE*				32	Tanzania	169	5.9	2,590
9	Japan	1,019	35.9	11,370	20	Kenya	562	19.8	7,530	33	Uganda	140	4.9	1,610
10	Jordan	1,003	35.4	2,630	21	Syria	497	17.5	3,540	34	Czechoslovakia	118	4.1	1,770
					22	Soviet Union	465	16.4	117,260	35	East Germany	118	4.1	2,000
	UPPER MIDDLE				23	India	443	15.6	260,000	36	France	104	3.6	5,490
11	Iran	979	34.5	31,460	24	Denmark	424	14.9	2,150	37	Italy	57	2.0	3,190
12	Turkey	969	34.2	37,080	25	Poland	392	13.8	13,220	38	Thailand	21	0.7	860

Source: International Tea Committee, London.

226. Vegetable Consumption

The following ranking compares the consumption of vegetables in each country. There is no clear distinction between vegetables and fruits. Many vegetables, especially those with green and yellow coloring, are valuable as sources of vitamins; some contain a large proportion of proteins and can be used as meat substitutes.

Number of Countries: 64
Midpoint: 49.5 kg (109.14 lb)
Period Covered: Early 1970s
Type of Ranking: Per Capita Consumption of Vegetables in Kg and Lb; Highest to Lowest

Highlights & Findings: Of the top 15 countries, seven are European, five are Middle Eastern, two are American and one is Asian. This pattern continues throughout the top half of the ranking. Vegetables are essentially a truck crop, i.e., raised on truck farms, and statistics about production in many countries may be incomplete.

Region	Africa	Asia & Oceania	Europe	Western Hemisphere
Most	Egypt (13)	Jordan (5)	France (1)	United States (10)
Least	Ethiopia (55)	India (64)	Finland (53)	El Salvador (63)

Rank	Country	Kg	Lb	Rank	Country	Kg	Lb	Rank	Country	Kg	Lb
	TOP 10			22	Denmark	66.4	146.41	44	Sudan	29.7	65.48
1	France	141.5	312.00	23	Ireland	65.4	144.20	45	Philippines	29.6	65.26
2	Italy	138.6	305.61	24	Australia	63.5	140.01	46	Madagascar	28.1	61.96
3	Greece	134.8	297.23	25	Austria	61.9	136.48	47	Afghanistan	23.3	51.37
4	Spain	130.0	286.65	26	Rumania	61.5	135.60	48	Uganda	23.1	50.93
5	Jordan	117.8	259.74	27	United Kingdom	58.3	128.55	49	Dominican Republic	22.5	49.61
6	Portugal	117.2	258.42	28	Taiwan	58.1	128.11	50	Pakistan	18.5	40.79
7	Israel	111.9	246.73	29	Libya	57.1	125.90	51	Jamaica	17.3	38.14
8	Turkey	105.0	231.52	30	Iraq	56.8	125.24	52	Paraguay	16.2	35.72
9	Lebanon	103.2	227.55	31	Yugoslavia	55.1	121.49	53	Finland	15.3	33.73
10	United States	98.6	217.41	32	West Germany	49.5	109.14	54	Venezuela	13.5	29.76
	UPPER MIDDLE				*LOWER MIDDLE*				*BOTTOM 10*		
11	Poland	92.1	203.08	33	Argentina	47.7	105.17	55	Ethiopia	12.6	27.78
12	Japan	89.6	197.56	34	Ecuador	46.1	101.65	56	Mexico	12.5	27.56
13	Egypt	88.9	196.02	35	Sri Lanka	42.1	92.83	57	Panama	12.4	27.34
14	Chile	80.5	177.50	36	Uruguay	39.3	86.65	58	Colombia	12.3	27.12
15	Hungary	80.3	177.06	37	Guatemala	38.7	85.33	59	Surinam	11.3	24.91
16	New Zealand	79.4	175.07	38	South Africa	36.3	80.04	60	Brazil	8.1	17.86
17	Canada	76.7	169.12	39	Norway	33.4	73.64	61	Iran	7.9	17.41
18	Belgium	76.3	168.24	40	Syria	33.4	73.64	62	Honduras	5.2	11.46
19	Peru	76.3	168.24	41	Bolivia	32.6	71.88	63	El Salvador	4.8	10.58
20	Switzerland	75.2	165.81	42	Mauritius	31.9	70.33	64	India	2.8	6.17
21	Netherlands	69.9	154.12	43	Sweden	29.9	65.92				

Source: *Compendium of Social Statistics.*

227. Cotton Consumption

The data in this ranking relate to cotton consumed as a commodity in spinning mills and other factories plus estimates of noncommercial and household consumption. They do not necessarily represent the final domestic consumption of cotton, since the figures include exports.

Number of Countries: 85
Midpoint: 2.38 kg (5.24 lb)
Period Covered: 1976
Type of Ranking: Per capita Consumption of Cotton in Kg and Lb; Total Consumption of Cotton in metric tons; Highest to Lowest

Highlights & Findings: Total world consumption of cotton is 13,320,000 tons, of which four countries account for 54%: China, the Soviet Union, the United States and India. Thanks to the increasing use of synthetic fabrics, cotton consumption has grown only slightly in the past decade (by a little over 1% annually) and in fact has declined from a high of 13,600,000 tons in 1975.

Regions	Africa	Asia & Oceania	Europe	Western Hemisphere
Most	Egypt (12)	Hong Kong (1)	Greece (2)	United States (11)
Least	Sudan (85)	Vietnam (81)	Norway (83)	Haiti (84)

Rank	Country	Per Capita Consumption of Cotton Kg	Lb	Total Consumption (000 tons)	Rank	Country	Per Capita Consumption of Cotton Kg	Lb	Total Consumption (000 tons)	Rank	Country	Per Capita Consumption of Cotton Kg	Lb	Total Consumption (000 tons)
	TOP 10				29	Spain	3.46	7.62	124.7	57	Tunisia	1.32	2.91	7.6
1	Hong Kong	46.27	102.02	202.7	30	West Germany	3.41	7.51	210.3	58	Uruguay	1.32	2.91	3.7
2	Greece	13.59	29.96	124.7	31	Austria	3.18	7.01	23.9	59	Ecuador	1.19	2.62	8.7
3	Portugal	11.23	24.76	106.2	32	Albania	3.13	6.90	8.0	60	Lebanon	1.11	2.44	2.44
4	Bulgaria	9.28	20.46	81.3	33	China	3.05	6.72	2,601.8	61	Senegal	0.94	2.07	4.8
5	Turkey	7.77	17.13	312.2	34	Colombia	2.89	6.37	70.5	62	Afghanistan	0.92	2.02	18.4
6	Czechoslovakia	7.55	16.64	112.7	35	Cuba	2.86	6.30	27.1	63	Nigeria	0.87	1.91	56.4
7	Hungary	7.46	16.44	79.1	36	Venezuela	2.80	6.17	34.7	64	Sri Lanka	0.86	1.89	11.9
8	Soviet Union	7.43	16.38	1,908.0	37	Finland	2.79	6.15	13.2	65	Kenya	0.85	1.87	11.9
9	Switzerland	7.33	16.16	46.6	38	Mexico	2.64	5.82	164.8	66	Costa Rica	0.84	1.85	1.7
10	Israel	7.19	15.85	24.9	39	Ivory Coast	2.58	5.68	13.0	67	Mozambique	0.80	1.76	7.6
					40	Nicaragua	2.51	5.53	5.6	68	Sweden	0.79	1.74	6.5
	UPPER MIDDLE				41	Netherlands	2.45	5.40	33.8	69	Tanzania	0.76	1.67	11.9
11	United States	6.75	14.88	1,453.1	42	Iran	2.43	5.35	81.3	70	Bolivia	0.74	1.63	4.3
12	Egypt	6.26	13.80	238.5	43	Canada	2.38	5.24	55.3	71	Ethiopia	0.67	1.47	19.5
13	South Korea	6.04	13.31	126.8						72	Philippines	0.61	1.34	27.1
14	Japan	5.97	13.16	672.1						73	Morocco	0.60	1.32	10.8
15	Pakistan	5.43	11.97	393.5		*LOWER MIDDLE*				74	Zaire	0.59	1.30	15.2
16	Yugoslavia	5.02	11.06	108.4	44	Thailand	2.27	5.00	97.6	75	Algeria	0.56	1.23	9.8
17	East Germany	4.96	10.93	83.4	45	Chile	2.18	4.80	22.8					
18	Syria	4.85	10.69	36.9	46	Ireland	2.18	4.80	6.9		*BOTTOM 10*			
19	Rumania	4.75	10.47	101.9	47	Peru	2.15	4.74	34.7	76	Uganda	0.54	1.19	6.5
20	Argentina	4.55	10.03	117.1	48	Guatemala	2.07	4.56	13.0	77	Jamaica	0.53	1.16	1.1
21	Poland	4.41	9.72	151.8	49	India	1.99	4.38	1,214.2	78	Angola	0.51	1.12	3.3
22	El Salvador	4.19	9.23	17.3	50	South Africa	1.99	4.38	52.0	79	Indonesia	0.46	1.01	65.0
23	Belgium	4.16	9.17	41.2	51	Australia	1.90	4.18	26.0	80	Burma	0.45	0.99	14.1
24	Brazil	3.97	8.75	433.6	52	United Kingdom	1.90	4.18	106.5	81	Vietnam	0.35	0.77	16.3
25	France	3.93	8.66	208.1	53	Paraguay	1.76	3.88	4.8	82	Denmark	0.33	0.72	1.7
26	Malta	3.66	8.07	1.1	54	Iraq	1.69	3.72	19.5	83	Norway	0.32	0.70	1.3
27	Italy	3.58	7.89	201.6	55	Madagascar	1.43	3.15	11.9	84	Haiti	0.14	0.30	0.7
28	Rhodesia (Zimbabwe)	3.46	7.62	18.4	56	Ghana	1.36	2.99	14.1	85	Sudan	0.10	0.22	17.3

Source: International Cotton Advisory Committee.

228. Wool Consumption

The data in this ranking refer to the consumption of virgin wool, but do not necessarily represent the final consumption of wool in countries such as Uruguay where the bulk of the production is exported. The figures are presented in terms of clean wool by converting the production figures of greasy wool. This conversion factor varies from country to country, from 0.72 in New Zealand to 0.47 in the United States.

Number of Countries: 32
Midpoint: 0.92 kg (2.02 lb) per capita
Period Covered: 1976
Type of Ranking: Per Capita Consumption of Wool in Kg and Lb; Total Consumption in Metric Tons; Highest to Lowest

Highlights & Findings: The total world consumption of wool is 1,533,000 tons, up only slightly from 1,478,000 tons in 1967. The top five consuming nations—the Soviet Union, Japan, France, the United Kingdom and Italy—account for 57% of total consumption.

Regions	Africa	Asia & Oceania	Europe	Western Hemisphere
Most	South Africa (21)	New Zealand (2)	Belgium (3)	Uruguay (1)
Least	N.A.	India (32)	Sweden (29)	Mexico (31)

Rank	Country	Consumption of Wool per Capita Kg	Lb	Total (000 tons)	Rank	Country	Consumption of Wool per Capita Kg	Lb	Total (000 tons)	Rank	Country	Consumption of Wool per Capita Kg	Lb	Total (000 tons)
		TOP 5			11	Soviet Union	1.35	2.97	348.0	24	Netherlands	0.47	1.03	6.5
1	Uruguay	8.32	18.34	23.3	12	Argentina	1.25	2.75	32.3	25	South Korea	0.32	0.70	11.7
2	New Zealand	5.63	12.41	17.7	13	Canada	1.19	2.62	4.6	26	Austria	0.27	0.59	2.1
3	Belgium	3.16	6.96	31.3	14	West Germany	1.09	2.40	67.3	27	Finland	0.25	0.55	1.2
4	France	2.37	5.22	125.2	15	Yugoslavia	1.02	2.24	22.2					
5	United Kingdom	2.14	4.71	119.8	16	Portugal	0.92	2.02	8.7			*BOTTOM 5*		
					17	Israel	0.89	1.96	3.1	28	United States	0.24	0.52	52.9
		MIDDLE			18	Turkey	0.81	1.78	32.8	29	Sweden	0.23	0.50	1.9
6	Italy	2.11	4.65	118.7	19	Switzerland	0.77	1.69	4.9	30	Pakistan	0.12	0.26	9.1
7	Australia	2.01	4.43	27.5	20	Denmark	0.67	1.47	3.4	31	Mexico	0.06	0.13	4.2
8	Greece	1.84	4.05	16.9	21	South Africa	0.65	1.43	17.2	32	India	0.03	0.06	22.1
9	Ireland	1.39	3.06	4.4	22	Spain	0.65	1.43	23.5					
10	Japan	1.39	3.06	156.8	23	Norway	0.54	1.19	2.2					

Source: Commonwealth Secretariat.

229. Paper Consumption

In the mid-1970s the annual consumption of paper worldwide was 28.5 million metric tons, or 7.2 kg (15.8 lb) per capita. By regions, North America consumed 10.3 million metric tons (43.7 kg, 96.3 lb, per capita); Latin America 1.2 million metric tons (3.6 kg, 7.9 lb, per capita); Africa 0.4 million metric tons (1 kg, 2.205 lb, per capita); Asia 5.6 million metric tons (2.5 kg, 5.5 lb, per capita); Europe 9.4 million metric tons (19.9 kg, 43.8 lb, per capita); Oceania 0.4 million metric tons (16.8 kg, 37 lb per capita); and the Soviet Union 1.2 million metric tons (4.6 kg, 10.1 lb, per capita).

Number of Countries: 115
Midpoint: 1,966 kg (4,335 lb)
Period Covered: 1975
Type of Ranking: Consumption of Cultural Paper, i.e., Paper Other than Newsprint, per 1,000 Inhabitants in Kg and Lb; Highest to Lowest

Highlights & Findings: The consumption of paper follows closely the curve of cultural development and is highest in culturally developed nations. The consumption of paper is also a dependable indicator of the growth of knowledge-related industries, such as book publishing.

Regions	Africa	Asia & Oceania	Europe	Western Hemisphere
Most	South Africa (38)	Japan (12)	Sweden (2)	United States (1)
Least	Mali (115)	Afghanistan (113)	Cyprus (51)	Haiti (114)

Rank	Country	Consumption of Paper per 1,000 Inhabitants Kg	Lb	Rank	Country	Consumption of Paper per 1,000 Inhabitants Kg	Lb	Rank	Country	Consumption of Paper per 1,000 Inhabitants Kg	Lb
		TOP 10		5	West Germany	33,128	73,047	10	Denmark	26,805	59,105
1	United States	45,315	99,919	6	Netherlands	32,820	72,368				
2	Sweden	44,695	98,552	7	Canada	28,231	62,249			*UPPER MIDDLE*	
3	Norway	36,115	79,633	8	Belgium	27,846	61,400	11	Finland	25,954	57,228
4	Switzerland	35,761	78,853	9	France	27,092	59,737	12	Japan	23,417	51,634

Rank	Country	Consumption of Paper per 1,000 Inhabitants Kg	Lb	Rank	Country	Consumption of Paper per 1,000 Inhabitants Kg	Lb	Rank	Country	Consumption of Paper per 1,000 Inhabitants Kg	Lb
13	United Kingdom	23,318	51,416	49	Jamaica	3,105	6,846	83	Angola	897	1,978
14	Australia	22,135	48,807	50	Cuba	2,837	6,255	84	Nicaragua	863	1,903
15	Spain	18,198	40,126	51	Cyprus	2,823	6,225	85	Ivory Coast	860	1,896
16	Italy	17,558	38,715	52	Netherlands Antilles	2,479	5,466	86	Honduras	856	1,887
17	New Zealand	17,324	38,199	53	Egypt	2,368	5,221	87	Zambia	796	1,755
18	Austria	16,622	36,651	54	Costa Rica	2,156	4,754	88	India	749	1,651
19	Hong Kong	14,462	31,889	55	China	2,120	4,675	89	Jordan	744	1,640
20	Singapore	14,368	31,681	56	Mauritius	2,002	4,414	90	Bolivia	721	1,587
21	Israel	14,311	31,556	57	Turkey	1,966	4,335	91	Madagascar	648	1,429
22	Hungary	11,819	26,061					92	Nigeria	639	1,409
23	Kuwait	9,954	21,948		**LOWER MIDDLE**			93	Morocco	628	1,385
24	East Germany	9,447	20,830					94	Malawi	590	1,301
25	Yugoslavia	9,056	19,968	58	Algeria	1,894	4,176	95	Tunisia	574	1,266
26	Lebanon	8,818	19,444	59	Ecuador	1,862	4,105	96	Burma	573	1,263
27	Iceland	8,333	18,374	60	Western Samoa	1,829	4,033	97	Paraguay	529	1,166
28	Ireland	8,240	18,169	61	Peru	1,742	3,841	98	Pakistan	512	1,129
29	Greece	8,175	18,026	62	Iran	1,701	3,751	99	Papua New Guinea	479	1,056
30	Poland	7,801	17,201	63	Colombia	1,653	3,645	100	Indonesia	454	1,001
31	Czechoslovakia	7,571	16,694	64	Guyana	1,643	3,623	101	Sudan	378	873
32	Belgium	6,681	14,731	65	Rhodesia (Zimbabwe)	1,641	3,618	102	Tanzania	324	714
33	Malta	6,383	14,074	66	Fiji	1,560	3,440	103	Uganda	282	622
34	Argentina	5,421	11,953	67	Syria	1,557	3,433	104	Bangladesh	258	569
35	Mexico	5,337	11,768	68	Panama	1,549	3,415	105	South Yemen	241	531
36	Uruguay	5,084	11,210	69	Bahamas	1,471	3,243				
37	Portugal	4,782	10,544	70	El Salvador	1,461	3,221		**BOTTOM 10**		
38	South Africa	4,699	10,361	71	Thailand	1,418	3,127				
39	Soviet Union	4,621	10,189	72	Brunei	1,361	3,001	106	Liberia	234	516
40	Venezuela	4,585	10,110	73	Kenya	1,343	2,961	107	Ethiopia	164	362
41	Brazil	4,126	9,120	74	Iraq	1,229	2,710	108	Somalia	158	348
42	Rumania	3,976	8,767	75	Saudi Arabia	1,227	2,705	109	Laos	151	333
43	Trinidad & Tobago	3,865	8,522	76	Surinam	1,185	2,613	110	North Korea	132	291
44	Libya	3,858	8,506	77	Dominican Republic	1,153	2,542	111	Zaire	127	280
45	Chile	3,823	8,430	78	Sri Lanka	1,089	2,401	112	Sierra Leone	101	223
46	Malaysia	3,774	8,322	79	Philippines	1,080	2,381	113	Afghanistan	83	183
47	South Korea	3,497	7,711	80	Guatemala	1,012	2,231	114	Haiti	66	145
48	Barbados	3,265	7,199	81	Ghana	962	2,121	115	Mali	35	77
				82	Senegal	905	1,995				

Source: *UNESCO Statistical Yearbook.*

230. Gasoline Consumption

Gasoline is the weakest link in the energy chain, and it is the resource that is being depleted at the fastest pace and the one that will be exhausted first. Consumption of gasoline has become critical in world economy for a number of reasons. The first is that consumption rates are lopsidedly in favor of developed countries. The United States, for example, consumes 1,346 times more gasoline per capita than Nepal. Much of this consumption is undoubtedly squandered; it is acknowledged that even simple conservation measures can help to reduce per capita consumption in the United States by one-quarter to one-third. The second reason is that because the gasoline deficit has grown so rapidly in developed countries (and is bound to grow more in the future), they are being subjected to a variety of threats and measures that can only be described as energy blackmail by the oil-producing countries, especially the Arabs. It is this political dimension of the oil shortage that is even more alarming than the economic one. This ranking tells us which nations will be hurting most when the Arabs and the Iranians decide to turn off the spigot.

Number of Countries: 183
Midpoint: 69 Kg (152 Lb)
Period Covered: 1976
Type of Ranking: Per Capita Consumption of Gasoline in Kg and Lb; Total in Million Metric Tons; Highest to Lowest

Highlights & Findings: Worldwide consumption of gasoline in 1975 was 599.997 million metric tons and the per capita consumption was 152 kg (335.16 lb) The distribution by categories is as follows:

	Total Million Metric Tons	Per Capita Kg	Lb
Developed Countries	442.927	582	1,283
Developing Countries	63.217	33	73
Communist Countries	93.853	75	165
Africa	10.554	26	57
North America	313.127	1,324	2,919
Other Western Hemisphere	18.155	102	225
Middle East	8.909	74	163
Far East & South Asia	30.037	24	53
Western Europe	93.057	255	562
Eastern Europe	83.943	231	509
Oceania	11.486	543	1,197

Regions	Africa	Asia & Oceania	Europe	Western Hemisphere
Most	Libya (51)	Wake Island (1)	Sweden (14)	United States (2)
Least	Rwanda (181)	Nepal (183)	Albania (111)	Haiti (170)

Rank	Country	Per Capita Consumption of Gasoline Kg	Lb	Total Consumption (million metric tons)	Rank	Country	Per Capita Consumption of Gasoline Kg	Lb	Total Consumption (million metric tons)	Rank	Country	Per Capita Consumption of Gasoline Kg	Lb	Total Consumption (million metric tons)
	TOP 10				38	Martinique	262	578	0.095	78	Poland	93	205	3.157
1	Wake Island	5,000	11,025	0.010	39	Gibraltar	259	571	0.007	79	Portugal	93	205	0.814
2	United States	1,346	2,968	287.503	40	Ireland	259	571	0.809	80	Chile	89	196	0.909
3	Greenland	1,204	2,655	0.065	41	Israel	242	533	0.816	81	Iran	88	194	2.916
4	Canada	1,118	2,465	24.520	42	Barbados	233	514	0.057	82	Fiji	87	192	0.050
5	Guam	1,087	2,397	0.113	43	Faroe Islands	220	485	0.009	83	Sabah	87	192	0.070
6	Qatar	750	1,654	0.069	44	French Guyana	217	478	0.013	84	Oman	85	187	0.066
7	Australia	701	1,546	9.470	45	Italy	206	454	11.505	85	St. Lucia	83	183	0.009
8	Antigua	686	1,512	0.048	46	St. Pierre & Miquelon	200	441	0.001	86	Yugoslavia	83	183	1.768
9	Bermuda	679	1,497	0.038	47	Brunei	197	434	0.029	87	Cook Islands	80	176	0.002
10	Cayman Islands	636	1,402	0.007	48	Bulgaria	193	425	1.680	88	Grenada	73	161	0.007
					49	Japan	192	423	21.257	89	Costa Rica	71	156	0.139
	UPPER MIDDLE				50	Trinidad & Tobago	192	423	0.207	90	Nicaragua	70	154	0.150
11	Puerto Rico	566	1,248	1.747	51	Libya	182	401	0.446	91	Dominican Republic	69	152	0.324
12	Kuwait	525	1,157	0.523	52	Lebanon	179	394	0.513	92	Seychelles	69	152	0.004
13	New Zealand	520	1,146	1.606	53	Argentina	155	342	3.945					
14	Sweden	513	1,131	4.205	54	Montserrat	154	339	0.002		**LOWER MIDDLE**			
15	Luxembourg	507	1,118	0.181	55	East Germany	145	320	2.449	93	Dominica	67	148	0.005
16	New Caledonia	496	1,094	0.062	56	Panama	143	315	0.238	94	Uruguay	67	148	0.205
17	United Arab Emirates	473	1,043	0.105	57	Mexico	140	309	8.392	95	South Yemen	67	148	0.113
18	Denmark	410	904	2.076	58	Guadeloupe	136	300	0.048	96	Djibouti	66	145	0.077
19	Switzerland	402	886	2.582	59	Jamaica	136	300	0.276	97	Gabon	65	143	0.034
20	Bahamas	392	864	0.080	60	Malta	133	293	0.040	98	New Hebrides	63	139	0.006
21	Iceland	390	860	0.085	61	Singapore	133	293	0.299	99	Jordan	59	130	0.159
22	Venezuela	377	831	4.524	62	Spain	130	286	4.599	100	Surinam	59	130	0.025
23	Nauru	375	827	0.003	63	Saudi Arabia	127	280	1.140	101	Bolivia	58	128	0.326
24	Netherlands Antilles	335	739	0.081	64	Cyprus	124	273	0.079	102	Guyana	57	126	0.045
25	Christmas Island	333	734	0.001	65	Reunion	120	264	0.060	103	Ivory Coast	56	123	0.276
26	West Germany	333	734	20.607	66	Hungary	115	253	1.213	104	Sarawak	55	121	0.061
27	Bahrain	309	681	00.079	67	Rumania	114	251	2.416	105	Mauritius	53	117	0.045
28	France	299	659	15.853	68	Pacific Islands	108	238	0.013	106	Syria	47	104	0.346
29	Austria	297	655	2.234	69	Colombia	107	236	2.508	107	Malaysia (West)	45	99	0.452
30	Finland	287	633	1.350	70	Czechoslovakia	106	234	1.575	108	Philippines	45	99	1.922
31	Norway	287	633	1.150	71	Cuba	105	231	0.980	109	St. Kitts-Nevis-Anguilla	45	99	0.003
32	Belgium	282	622	2.761	72	Greece	105	231	0.954	110	Iraq	44	97	0.492
33	United Kingdom	282	622	15.833	73	Mongolia	104	229	0.150	111	Albania	40	88	0.100
34	French Polynesia	281	620	0.036	74	Ecuador	102	225	0.685	112	St. Vincent	40	88	0.004
35	Soviet Union	280	617	71.353	75	Peru	101	223	1.574	113	Samoa	39	86	0.006
36	British Virgin Islands	273	602	0.003	76	Belize	100	220	0.014	114	Guatemala	37	81	0.225
37	Netherlands	266	586	3.635	77	Brazil	97	214	10.348	115	Liberia	37	81	0.064

Rank	Country	Per Capita Consumption of Gasoline Kg	Lb	Total Consumption (million metric tons)	Rank	Country	Per Capita Consumption of Gasoline Kg	Lb	Total Consumption (million metric tons)	Rank	Country	Per Capita Consumption of Gasoline Kg	Lb	Total Consumption (million metric tons)
116	Turkey	37	81	1.446	140	Congo	18	40	0.024	164	Central African Empire	7	15	0.013
117	Algeria	34	75	0.570	141	Cameroon	17	37	0.111	165	Malawi	7	15	0.036
118	Egypt	34	75	1.267	142	Chad	17	37	0.070	166	Tanzania (Tanganyika)	7	15	0.103
119	Papua New Guinea	33	73	0.092	143	Nigeria	17	37	1.046	167	Yemen Arab Republic	7	15	0.047
120	Zambia	33	73	0.164	144	Thailand	17	37	0.704	168	Zaire	7	15	0.179
121	North Korea	31	68	0.490	145	Equatorial Guinea	16	35	0.005	169	Burma	6	13	0.178
122	El Salvador	30	66	0.119	146	Angola	15	33	0.095	170	Haiti	6	13	0.0128
123	Gilbert Islands	30	66	0.002	147	Sierra Leone	15	33	0.042	171	Mali	6	13	0.036
124	Honduras	30	66	0.092	148	Tanzania (Zanzibar)	14	31	0.006	172	Sri Lanka	6	13	0.088
125	Mexico	30	66	0.008	149	Indonesia	13	29	1.765					
126	Paraguay	30	66	0.080	150	Guinea-Bissau	13	29	0.007		*BOTTOM 11*			
127	Rhodesia (Zimbabwe)	29	64	0.180	151	Mozambique	13	29	0.116	173	Niger	5	13	0.023
128	Tonga	29	64	0.003	152	Sudan	13	29	0.228	174	Pakistan	5	11	0.327
129	Ghana	26	57	0.253	153	Togo	13	29	0.029	175	Somalia	5	11	0.017
130	Senegal	26	57	0.106	154	South Korea	11	24	0.391	176	Upper Volta	5	11	0.028
131	Hong Kong	25	55	0.108	155	Madagascar	11	24	0.087	177	Burundi	3	7	0.012
132	Sao Tome & Principe	25	55	0.002	156	Uganda	11	24	0.122	178	Ethiopia	3	7	0.077
133	Tunisia	23	51	0.132	157	Benin	10	22	0.030	179	Cambodia	2	4	0.015
134	Gambia	21	46	0.011	158	China	10	22	8.370	180	India	2	4	1.217
135	Laos	21	46	0.070	159	Comoros	10	22	0.003	181	Rwanda	2	4	0.009
136	Morocco	21	46	0.372	160	Guinea	9	20	0.040	182	Bangladesh	1	2	0.052
137	Solomon Islands	21	46	0.004	161	Mauritania	9	20	0.012	183	Nepal	1	2	0.018
138	Vietnam	21	46	0.900	162	Afghanistan	8	18	0.145					
139	Kenya	19	42	0.255	163	Cape Verde	7	15	0.002					

Source: *World Energy Supplies.*

231. Rubber Consumption

The data in this table rank countries by their consumption of raw rubber, both natural and synthetic. Worldwide the consumption of rubber in 1976 was 8,550,000 tons of which 2,835,000 tons were natural and 5,715,000 tons synthetic.

Number of Countries: 18
Period Covered: 1976
Type of Ranking: Per Capita Consumption of Rubber in Kg and Lb; Total Consumption of Rubber; Highest to Lowest

Highlights & Findings: Because the ranking is limited to the largest consumers who are also members of the International Rubber Study Group in London, its value is rather limited. However, the United States alone accounts for 34% of world consumption; when synthetic rubber is considered separately, its share is even higher at 38%.

Rank	Country	Per Capita Consumption Kg	Lb	Total consumption (000 metric tons)	Rank	Country	Per Capita Consumption Kg	Lb	Total Consumption (000 metric tons)	Rank	Country	Per Capita Consumption Kg	Lb	Total Consumption (000 metric tons)
1	United States	13.5	29.7	2,906.0	7	Japan	8.5	18.7	960.0	14	South Africa	2.2	4.8	58.1
2	Canada	12.5	27.5	2,288.6	8	Australia	7.9	17.4	107.1	15	Soviet Union & Eastern Europe (undistributed)	1.9	4.1	720.0
3	Belgium & Luxembourg	10.8	23.8	109.4	9	Italy	7.1	15.6	400.0					
4	West Germany	10.3	22.7	633.5	10	Sweden	6.0	13.2	49.6	16	Argentina	1.7	3.7	43.5
5	United Kingdom	8.9	19.6	495.7	11	Netherlands	5.5	12.1	75.2	17	China	0.3	0.6	232.0
6	France	8.6	18.9	452.9	12	Spain	3.2	7.0	149.3	18	India	0.1	0.2	166.9
					13	Brazil	2.4	5.2	267.7					

Source: International Rubber Study Group, London.

232. Steel Consumption

The consumption of steel is one of the most reliable indices of the pace of industrial growth because it is directly proportionate to the degree of industrialization. On the basis of U.N. Standard International Trade Classification, steel is defined as including ingots and semis, rolled products, steel tubes and fittings, steel tires, railway tires, wheels and axles but excluding pig-iron, ferroalloys, cast-iron pipes and iron foundry products.

Number of Countries: 110
Midpoint: 56 kg (123.4 lb)
Period Covered: 1975
Type of Table: Per Capita Consumption of Steel in Kg and Lb and Total Consumption in Metric Tons; Highest to Lowest

Highlights & Findings: Of the total 1975 world production of 643 million tons of steel, the top 10 countries consumed 383.76 million tons or 60%. The bottom 10 countries consumed 259,000 tons or 0.04%.

Region	Africa	Asia & Oceania	Europe	Western Hemisphere
Most	Libya (21)	Singapore (3)	Sweden (1)	Canada (5)
Least	Uganda (110)	Laos (107)	Albania (57)	Haiti (92)

Rank	Country	Kg	Lb	Total Consumption in Metric tons (000)
	TOP 10			
1	Sweden	772	1,702.2	6,328
2	Czechoslovakia	733	1,616.2	10,812
3	Singapore	636	1,402.3	1,432
4	Japan	583	1,285.5	64,736
5	Canada	577	1,272.2	13,178
6	East Germany	566	1,248.0	9,530
7	Soviet Union	554	1,221.5	141,031
8	United States	549	1,210.5	116,821
9	Poland	524	1,155.4	17,833
10	Norway	514	1,133.3	2,062
	UPPER MIDDLE			
11	West Germany	490	1,080.4	30,282
12	Australia	467	1,029.7	6,298
13	Rumania	464	1,023.1	9,831
14	Finland	430	948.1	2,027
15	United Kingdom	385	848.9	21,540
16	Hungary	361	796.0	3,806
17	Denmark	358	789.3	1,814
18	Kuwait	354	780.5	354
19	France	350	771.7	18,538
20	Netherlands	330	727.6	4,509
21	Libya	321	707.8	738
22	Italy	319	703.3	17,778
23	Belgium & Luxembourg	314	692.3	3,185
24	New Zealand	300	661.5	925
25	Austria	286	630.6	2,153
26	Spain	284	626.2	10,057
27	Bahrain	281	619.6	73
28	South Africa	263	579.9	7,518
29	Bulgaria	252	555.6	2,197
30	North Korea	251	553.4	3,978
31	Switzerland	232	511.5	1,482
32	Israel	221	487.3	744
33	Gabon	208	458.6	111
34	Yugoslavia	205	452.0	4,379
35	Venezuela	194	427.7	2,327
36	Iceland	191	421.1	42

Rank	Country	Kg	Lb	Total Consumption in Metric tons (000)
37	Iraq	181	399.1	2,010
38	Argentina	172	379.2	4,357
39	Iran	163	359.4	5,382
40	Saudi Arabia	159	350.5	1,410
41	Trinidad & Tobago	144	317.5	154
42	Greece	143	315.3	1,290
43	Hong Kong	138	304.2	605
44	Portugal	118	260.1	1,036
45	Ireland	106	233.7	333
46	Brazil	105	231.5	11,239
47	Mexico	103	227.1	6,189
48	Lebanon	101	222.7	291
49	Cuba	85	187.4	786
50	South Korea	85	187.4	2,952
51	Algeria	73	160.9	1,233
	LOWER MIDDLE			
52	Turkey	69	152.1	2,709
53	Syria	64	141.1	469
54	Peru	61	134.5	969
55	Tunisia	56	123.4	322
56	Chile	55	121.2	563
57	Albania	48	105.8	120
58	Malaysia	46	101.4	549
59	Rhodesia (Zimbabwe)	45	99.2	285
60	Jamaica	43	94.8	87
61	China	42	92.6	35,184
62	Egypt	42	92.6	1,582
63	Costa Rica	41	90.4	80
64	Jordan	34	74.9	92
65	Panama	33	72.7	55
66	Dominican Republic	29	63.9	137
67	Morocco	28	61.7	488
68	Colombia	27	59.5	637
69	Ecuador	27	59.5	183
70	Congo	24	52.9	32
71	Ivory Coast	23	50.7	114
72	Nigeria	22	48.5	1,380
73	Philippines	22	48.5	950

Rank	Country	Kg	Lb	Total Consumption in Metric tons (000)
74	Bolivia	21	46.3	118
75	Uruguay	21	46.3	63
76	Thailand	20	44.1	845
77	Nicaragua	18	39.6	38
78	Guatemala	14	30.8	81
79	India	14	30.8	8,413
80	Senegal	14	30.8	60
81	Zambia	14	30.8	68
82	El Salvador	11	24.2	44
83	Honduras	11	24.2	32
84	Indonesia	10	22.0	1,348
85	Liberia	10	22.0	17
86	Angola	9	19.8	52
87	Ghana	9	19.8	93
88	Kenya	9	19.8	122
89	Togo	9	19.8	20
90	Pakistan	7	15.4	537
91	Paraguay	7	15.4	19
92	Haiti	5	11.0	23
93	Madagascar	5	11.0	39
94	Sudan	5	11.0	82
95	Tanzania	5	11.0	72
96	Vietnam	5	11.0	206
97	Guinea	4	8.8	18
98	Sierra Leone	4	8.8	11
99	Sri Lanka	4	8.8	62
100	Zaire	4	8.8	97
	BOTTOM 10			
101	Malawi	3	6.6	15
102	Burma	2	4.4	75
103	Afghanistan	1	2.2	21
104	Bangladesh	1	2.2	93
105	Cambodia	1	2.2	4
106	Ethiopia	1	2.2	30
107	Laos	1	2.2	3
108	Mozambique	1	2.2	8
109	Rwanda	1	2.2	4
110	Uganda	1	2.2	6

Source: U.N. Economic Commission for Europe.

HOUSING

Housing censuses have been carried out under U.N. auspices in 152 countries and have yielded a wealth of data on the quality of housing in each country, particularly with reference to minimum standards of what may be described as habitability. These include the provision of the 5Cs (to coin a term), that is the five basic conveniences or facilities: piped water, electric light, kitchen, toilet and bath. The censuses also dealt with new homes built per 1,000 inhabitants, tenure, i.e., whether the homes are rented or owned, the number of persons per room and the number of rooms per house. Unfortunately, no effort was made to determine what might have

been considered an important and interesting fact: the condition of the roof and the nature of the construction materials used.

The general trend in these rankings is toward more and better housing. In almost all countries the 5Cs have become the norm rather than the exception and the number of countries reporting 100% of homes with these facilities has doubled since 1960. Subsidized housing is now almost universal for industrial workers. Mortgages, financed partly by state funds, have made home construction and ownership practicable even for the less well-to-do. Please also see the "Rent Index" in the chapter on economy.

233. Construction Index

The construction index is designed to measure the growth in expenditures on construction and their contribution to GDP. The index is most useful in locating countries that have experienced a sudden spurt in the construction of both residential buildings and public offices.

Number of Countries: 86 **Midpoint:** 130 **Period Covered:** 1976 or Latest Available Year **Type of Ranking:** Index Numbers of Construction Activity, 1970=100; Highest to Lowest	**Highlights & Findings:** Construction activities are most intensive in developing countries—part of what may be described as a catching-up process. Five of the top 10 are oil-producers, and in these countries construction is a priority item in capital expenditures.

Regions	Africa	Asia & Oceania	Europe	Western Hemisphere
Most	Nigeria (7)	Saudi Arabia (1)	Poland (13)	Guatemala (4)
Least	Uganda (82)	Thailand (77)	Cyprus (84)	Jamaica (86)

Rank Country	Construction Index	Rank Country	Construction Index	Rank Country	Construction Index
TOP 10		18 Tunisia	197	38 Turkey	137
1 Saudi Arabia	305	19 Peru	195	39 Austria	134
2 Syria	296	20 El Salvador	192	40 Soviet Union	134
3 Philippines	294	21 Iraq	176	41 Norway	132
4 Guatemala	291	22 Singapore	167	42 New Zealand	131
5 Indonesia	270	23 Brazil	163	43 Hungary	130
6 Hong Kong	268	24 Czechoslovakia	161		
7 Nigeria	258	25 United States	161		
8 Haiti	251	26 Iceland	158	*LOWER MIDDLE*	
9 Iran	241	27 East Germany	152	44 Zambia	128
10 Mauritius	238	28 Pakistan	151	45 Canada	127
		29 South Korea	149	46 Spain	125
UPPER MIDDLE		30 Ghana	147	47 Bangladesh	124
11 Ecuador	235	31 Honduras	147	48 Portugal	122
12 Paraguay	222	32 Rumania	147	49 Sri Lanka	121
13 Poland	221	33 Mexico	146	50 Bulgaria	120
14 Dominican Republic	214	34 Bolivia	144	51 Colombia	120
15 Venezuela	207	35 Zaire	141	52 Uruguay	118
16 Morocco	199	36 Israel	138	53 Costa Rica	113
17 Nicaragua	198	37 Trinidad & Tobago	137	54 Switzerland	112
				55 Ethiopia	111

Rank	Country	Construction Index	Rank	Country	Construction Index	Rank	Country	Construction Index
56	Panama	111	68	Belize	100	78	Egypt	90
57	Yugoslavia	111	69	Italy	99	79	United Kingdom	89
58	France	110	70	Denmark	98	80	Argentina	84
59	Kenya	110	71	Liberia	98	81	Greenland	80
60	Tanzania	110	72	Sweden	98	82	Uganda	66
61	Finland	107	73	Belgium	95	83	Puerto Rico	64
62	Mongolia	107	74	Burma	94	84	Cyprus	62
63	Fiji	106	75	Netherlands	94	85	Chile	61
64	Greece	105	76	Sierra Leone	92	86	Jamaica	50
65	Australia	103						
66	India	103		**BOTTOM 10**				
67	West Germany	101	77	Thailand	91			

Source: *U.N. Statistical Yearbook.*

234. New Houses Built per 1,000 Inhabitants

Construction statistics are frequently of poor quality. Much of the information in this ranking is based on building permits issued. Only a few countries conduct special surveys to determine to what extent such permits have been translated into actual houses. In other cases data refer only to a part of the country or area or some of the larger cities.

Number of Countries: 57
Midpoint: 6.3 per 1,000
Period Covered: 1971-73
Type of Ranking: New Houses Built During 1971-73 per 1,000 Inhabitants; Total Number of New Houses; Highest to Lowest

Highlights & Findings: On the basis of available data, not only are more homes being built in developed countries but they are invariably more spacious and better constructed. The rate of construction in developed countries is up to 16 times higher than that in developing countries.

Regions	Africa	Asia & Oceania	Europe	Western Hemisphere
Most	Reunion (32)	Japan (1)	Finland (4)	Canada (11)
Least	Mozambique (57)	Papua New Guinea (56)	Malta (44)	Dominican Republic (55)

Rank	Country	New Houses per 1,000	Total New Houses	Rank	Country	New Houses per 1,000	Total New Houses	Rank	Country	New Houses per 1,000	Total New Houses
	TOP 10			20	Czechoslovakia	8.9	129,063	40	Western Samoa	3.3	502
1	Japan	18.7	2,030,314	21	Puerto Rico	8.5	24,955	41	Mauritius	3.2	2,623
2	Israel	16.1	51,070	22	Hungary	8.2	85,211	42	Albania	3.1	6,696
3	New Caledonia	15.7	1,879	23	Ireland	7.9	24,012	43	Martinique	2.8	951
4	Finland	13.2	61,572	24	Rumania	7.4	154,896	44	Malta	2.7	865
5	Switzerland	12.9	83,300	25	Greenland	7.2	360	45	Trinidad & Tobago	2.6	2,645
6	Sweden	12.0	97,484	26	Cyprus	6.9	4,530	46	Djibouti	2.2	221
7	Netherlands	11.7	157,246	27	Poland	6.8	227,088	47	Colombia	1.8	40,846
8	West Germany	11.5	714,226	28	Yugoslavia	6.4	134,819				
9	Australia	11.4	149,144								
10	Norway	11.3	44,756		**LOWER MIDDLE**						
				29	Belgium	6.3	61,116		**BOTTOM 10**		
	UPPER MIDDLE			30	Bulgaria	6.3	54,200	48	Iraq	1.6	17,040
11	Canada	11.2	248,873	31	Kuwait	6.1	5,411	49	Tunisia	1.5	7,863
12	Singapore	11.1	24,320	32	Reunion	6.0	2,817	50	Morocco	1.2	19,822
13	Denmark	11.0	55,566	33	Austria	5.9	44,200	51	Algeria	0.9	13,487
14	Iceland	10.6	2,220	34	United Kingdom	5.6	315,400	52	Ecuador	0.9	8,967
15	Spain	10.0	348,500	35	Portugal	5.2	44,581	53	Egypt	0.8	27,812
16	France	9.9	517,600	36	Guadeloupe	4.6	1,555	54	Mongolia	0.8	1,100
17	United States	9.4	1,980,800	37	Guyana	3.9	2,853	55	Dominican Republic	0.5	1,979
18	Soviet Union	9.2	2,300,000	38	Italy	3.3	181,290	56	Papua New Guinea	0.5	1,313
19	New Zealand	9.0	26,505	39	French Guyana	3.3	164	57	Mozambique	0.4	3,383

Source: *Compendium of Housing Statistics.*

235. Households Owning Their Dwellings

The extent to which households own or rent accommodation is of special significance for housing programs. It provides an indication of the adequacy and quality of housing and also provides a basis for estimating housing needs. The ranking is restricted to households occupying conventional dwellings, but in a few countries mobile units or semi-permanent units are considered acceptable as places of habitation. Data are tabulated in terms of conventional dwellings by tenure of households; the percentage of renters is not shown separately because it may be safely assumed that those who do not own buildings either rent them or use them under some comparable arrangements. The Soviet Union does not report household ownership figures.

Number of Countries: 115
Midpoint: 58.2%
Period Covered: 1973 or Latest Available Year
Type of Ranking: Percentage of Households Owning Their Dwellings; Highest to Lowest

Highlights & Findings: Interestingly, the percentage of home ownership is not necessarily related to the level of economic development. In some of the most advanced countries as well as in some of the largest cities, apartment rentals are considered, irrespective of the economic status of the occupant, normal and even convenient. On the other hand, in rural areas and in many developing countries where there is little occupational mobility the only way to occupy a dwelling is to own it.

Regions	Africa	Asia & Oceania	Europe	Western Hemisphere
Most	Tunisia (23)	Tokelau Islands (1)	Cyprus (5)	Cayman Islands (11)
Least	Nigeria (113)	Christmas Island (115)	Gibraltar (114)	Bermuda (94)

Rank	Country	Percentage of Households Owning their Dwellings	Rank	Country	Percentage of Households Owning their Dwellings	Rank	Country	Percentage of Households Owning Their Dwellings
	TOP 10		37	Mexico	66.0	74	Austria	49.4
1	Tokelau Islands	97.7	38	Norfolk Island	66.0	75	Sabah	48.8
2	Pacific Islands	96.5	39	Guadeloupe	65.9	76	Jordan	48.5
3	Niue Island	90.8	40	Israel	64.6	77	Mauritius	48.5
4	Philippines	89.4	41	Sri Lanka	63.3	78	Rhodesia (Zimbabwe)	48.0
5	Cyprus	86.3	42	Hungary	62.9	79	El Salvador	47.9
6	Thailand	85.9	43	Panama	62.9	80	Greenland	47.4
7	Pakistan	85.5	44	United States	62.9	81	Zaire	47.4
8	Faroe Islands	84.3	45	Reunion	62.8	82	Denmark	47.0
9	India	84.0	46	Colombia	61.3	83	Costa Rica	46.8
10	Iraq	83.0	47	Martinique	61.2	84	St. Helena	46.6
			48	Ecuador	60.8	85	Northern Ireland	45.6
	UPPER MIDDLE		49	Bahrain	60.6	86	Portugal	44.5
11	Cayman Islands	82.0	50	Brazil	60.4	87	Surinam	44.0
12	St. Pierre & Miquelon	81.4	51	Canada	60.0	88	French Guyana	43.5
13	Turkey	81.4	52	Antigua	59.8	89	France	43.3
14	San Marino	78.0	53	Sudan	59.2	90	England & Wales	43.0
15	Turks & Caicos	77.3	54	Argentina	58.7	91	Egypt	43.0
16	Nepal	75.3	55	Netherlands Antilles	58.6	92	Malawi	39.6
17	Bolivia	74.2	56	Finland	58.5	93	Uruguay	39.4
18	Barbados	73.5	57	Trinidad & Tobago	58.3	94	Bermuda	39.1
19	Honduras	72.5	58	Japan	58.2	95	Seychelles	37.2
20	Iran	71.6	59	Congo	57.8	96	Sweden	35.2
21	Puerto Rico	71.5	60	Belize	57.6	97	West Germany	33.5
22	Bulgaria	71.0	61	St. Kitts-Nevis-Anguilla	57.2	98	Malta	32.6
23	Tunisia	70.7				99	Morocco	28.9
24	Yugoslavia	70.7		*LOWER MIDDLE*		100	Switzerland	28.5
25	Greece	70.6	62	Peru	56.0	101	Ethiopia	28.1
26	Dominican Republic	70.5	63	Belgium	55.9	102	Scotland	27.4
27	Iceland	70.3	64	Bahamas	55.1	103	New Zealand	26.5
28	Guatemala	69.3	65	Luxembourg	54.7	104	Monaco	26.3
29	Montserrat	69.2	66	British Virgin Islands	54.5	105	Netherlands	25.7
30	Paraguay	69.2	67	Chile	53.3	106	Tanzania	25.7
31	South Korea	69.0	68	Norway	52.9			
32	Ireland	68.8	69	Jamaica	52.1		*BOTTOM 9*	
33	Venezuela	68.7	70	Italy	50.9	107	East Germany	23.0
34	Vietnam	68.4	71	New Caledonia	50.8	108	Singapore	22.0
35	Australia	67.3	72	Czechoslovakia	50.4	109	Brunei	20.6
36	Nicaragua	66.1	73	Sarawak	49.8	110	Papua New Guinea	20.6

Rank	Country	Percentage of Households Owning their Dwellings	Rank	Country	Percentage of Households Owning their Dwellings	Rank	Country	Percentage of Households Owning their Dwellings
111	Hong Kong	18.1	113	Nigeria	8.0	115	Christmas Island	0.5
112	Nauru	11.0	114	Gibraltar	4.1			

Source: *Compendium of Housing Statistics.*

236. Number of Rooms per Dwelling

The size of a dwelling in terms of the number of rooms has an important bearing not only on levels of density but also on construction costs. Although no statistics are available on the size of the rooms themselves, it is assumed that they conform to normal building codes and regulations in force in each country or city. The data are also assumed to include rooms used for business and professional purposes, although only a few countries specifically state that this is the case. Figures for the Soviet Union and some other Communist countries were not reported. However, extremely crowded housing conditions are reported in almost all Russian cities by the Soviet press itself.

Number of Countries: 129
Midpoint: 3 Rooms
Period Covered: 1973 or Latest Available Year
Type of Ranking: Average Number of Rooms per Dwelling; Highest to Lowest

Highlights & Findings: Although the size of a family is the factor that determines its requirements in terms of space or number of rooms, the minimum would appear to be 2.5 rooms (a living room cum dining room, a bedroom and a kitchen). On this basis, 35 countries in the ranking have substandard housing. All averages must be treated with caution because they undoubtedly conceal the wide disparities that exist between the houses of the rich and the middle class, on the one hand, and those of the poor on the other.

	Africa	Asia & Oceania	Europe	Western Hemisphere
Most	Rhodesia (Zimbabwe) (20)	Australia (8)	Faroe Islands (3)	Falkland Islands (1)
Least	Central African Empire (128)	Wallis & Fortuna Islands (129)	Rumania (86)	El Salvador (123)

Rank	Country	Average Number of Rooms Per Dwelling	Rank	Country	Average Number of Rooms Per Dwelling	Rank	Country	Average Number of Rooms Per Dwelling
	TOP 10		20	Rhodesia (Zimbabwe)	4.6	42	South Africa	3.7
1	Falkland Islands	7.1	21	Brazil	4.5	43	Egypt	3.6
2	St. Pierre & Miquelon	5.7	22	Norfolk Island	4.5	44	Nauru	3.6
3	Faroe Islands	5.4	23	Cyprus	4.4	45	Portugal	3.6
4	Canada	5.3	24	Cayman Islands	4.3	46	Bahamas	3.5
5	Luxembourg	5.1	25	West Germany	4.2	47	Denmark	3.5
6	Netherlands	5.1	26	Scotland	4.2	48	Greece	3.5
7	United States	5.1	27	Spain	4.2	49	Kuwait	3.5
8	Australia	5.0	28	Austria	4.1	50	Norway	3.5
9	Bermuda	5.0	29	Costa Rica	4.0	51	France	3.4
10	Northern Ireland	5.0	30	Venezuela	3.9	52	British Virgin Islands	3.2
			31	Barbados	3.8	53	Seychelles	3.2
			32	Japan	3.8	54	Bulgaria	3.2
	UPPER MIDDLE		33	Malta	3.8	55	Macao	3.2
11	England & Wales	4.9	34	Netherlands Antilles	3.8	56	Argentina	3.1
12	Pitcairn Island	4.9	35	Niue Island	3.8	57	Czechoslovakia	3.1
13	Iceland	4.8	36	Sweden	3.8	58	Finland	3.1
14	New Zealand	4.8	37	Turks & Caicos	3.8	59	Gibraltar	3.1
15	Ireland	4.7	38	Cocos (Keeling) Islands	3.7	60	Hong Kong	3.1
16	Puerto Rico	4.7	39	Italy	3.7	61	Martinique	3.1
17	San Marino	4.7	40	Nepal	3.7	62	New Caledonia	3.1
18	Switzerland	4.7	41	St. Helena	3.7	63	Reunion	3.1
19	Papua New Guinea	4.6						

Rank	Country	Average Number of Rooms Per Dwelling	Rank	Country	Average Number of Rooms Per Dwelling	Rank	Country	Average Number of Rooms Per Dwelling
64	Sabah	3.1	86	Rumania	2.6	110	Ecuador	2.1
			87	Belize	2.5	111	Malawi	2.1
	LOWER MIDDLE		88	Guyana	2.5	112	Morocco	2.1
65	Bahrain	3.0	89	Israel	2.5	113	Tanzania	2.1
66	Guadeloupe	3.0	90	St. Kitts-Nevis-Anguilla	2.5	114	Western Samoa	2.1
67	Iran	3.0	91	St. Vincent	2.5	115	Guatemala	2.0
68	South Korea	3.0	92	Syria	2.5	116	India	2.0
69	Surinam	3.0	93	Trinidad & Tobago	2.5	117	Paraguay	2.0
70	Belgium	2.9	94	Uruguay	2.5	118	Singapore	2.0
71	Chile	2.9	95	Antigua	2.4			
72	Colombia	2.9	96	Jamaica	2.4		*BOTTOM 11*	
73	Mauritius	2.9	97	Brunei	2.3	119	Ivory Coast	1.9
74	Poland	2.9	98	Dominica	2.3	120	Kenya	1.9
75	Sarawak	2.9	99	Honduras	2.3	121	United Arab Emirates	1.9
76	Hungary	2.8	100	Malaysia (West)	2.3	122	Zambia	1.9
77	Monaco	2.8	101	Mexico	2.3	123	El Salvador	1.7
78	Montserrat	2.8	102	Peru	2.3	124	Pakistan	1.7
79	Yugoslavia	2.8	103	St. Lucia	2.3	125	Tunisia	1.6
80	Christmas Island	2.7	104	Senegal	2.3	126	Nigeria	1.4
81	Dominican Republic	2.7	105	Algeria	2.2	127	Congo	1.3
82	East Germany	2.7	106	French Guyana	2.2	128	Central African Empire	1.1
83	Grenada	2.7	107	Nicaragua	2.2	129	Wallis & Futuna Islands	1.1
84	Turkey	2.7	108	Panama	2.2			
85	Greenland	2.6	109	Sri Lanka	2.2			

Source: *Compendium of Housing Statistics.*

237. Number of Persons per Room

Density of occupation in terms of number of persons per room is a measure of the adequacy of housing conditions. Although national standards may vary, dwellings with densities of three or more persons per room are considered overcrowded and unhealthy under all circumstances. (However, outdoor spaces in rural areas in tropical and semitropical countries may be considered as offsetting, to some extent, high densities prevailing within the dwellings). Excluded from the data are rooms used exclusively for business and professional purposes and improvised housing units that do not conform to the conventional characteristics of a dwelling.

Number of Countries: 132
Midpoint: 1.5 Persons per Room
Period Covered: 1973 or Latest Available Year
Type of Ranking: Average Number of Persons per Room; Highest to Lowest

Highlights & Findings: At least eight countries report overcrowded housing conditions with three or more persons per room. However, it should be noted that low national averages may mask high levels of densities in urban areas, particularly in ghettos and inner cities. Almost all industrialized countries have comfortable levels of densities per room.

Regions	Africa	Asia & Oceania	Europe	Western Hemisphere
Most	Central African Empire (2)	Wallis & Fortuna Islands (1)	Poland (77)	El Salvador (5)
Least	St. Helena (87)	Pitcairn Island (129)	Switzerland (130)	Falkland Islands (132)

Rank	Country	Average Number of Persons per Room	Rank	Country	Average Number of Persons per Room	Rank	Country	Average Number of Persons per Room
	TOP 9		7	Nigeria	3.0	12	Nicaragua	2.8
1	Wallis & Futuna Islands	6.1	8	Sarawak	3.0	13	Congo	2.7
2	Central African Empire	3.4	9	Singapore	2.9	14	Ethiopia	2.7
3	Western Samoa	3.4				15	Guatemala	2.6
4	Tunisia	3.2		*UPPER MIDDLE*		16	Malaysia (West)	2.6
5	El Salvador	3.1	10	Algeria	2.8	17	Paraguay	2.6
6	Pakistan	3.1	11	India	2.8	18	Zambia	2.6

Rank	Country	Average Number of Persons per Room	Rank	Country	Average Number of Persons per Room	Rank	Country	Average Number of Persons per Room
19	Ecuador	2.5	59	Cocos (Keeling) Islands	1.6	97	Christmas Island	1.0
20	Kenya	2.5	60	Egypt	1.6	98	Barbados	1.0
21	Macao	2.5	61	Nauru	1.6	99	Finland	1.0
22	Mexico	2.5	62	Reunion	1.6	100	Japan	1.0
23	Sri Lanka	2.5	63	St. Kitts-Nevis-Anguilla	1.6	101	Austria	0.9
24	Sudan	2.5	64	Seychelles	1.6	102	Cyprus	0.9
25	Honduras	2.4				103	France	0.9
26	Morocco	2.4		**LOWER MIDDLE**		104	Greece	0.9
27	Bahrain	2.3	65	British Virgin Islands	1.5	105	Iceland	0.9
28	Brunei	2.3	66	Guadeloupe	1.5	106	Ireland	0.9
29	Iran	2.3	67	Israel	1.5	107	Italy	0.9
30	South Korea	2.3	68	Senegal	1.5	108	Monaco	0.9
31	Peru	2.3	69	Uruguay	1.5	109	Puerto Rico	0.9
32	Sabah	2.3	70	Venezuela	1.5	110	Spain	0.9
33	Syria	2.3	71	Argentina	1.4	111	Bermuda	0.8
34	Panama	2.2	72	Chile	1.4	112	Denmark	0.8
35	Turkey	2.2	73	French Guyana	1.4	113	Faroe Islands	0.8
36	Guyana	2.1	74	Martinique	1.4	114	Netherlands	0.8
37	Kuwait	2.1	75	Montserrat	1.4	115	Norway	0.8
38	Dominican Republic	2.0	76	New Caledonia	1.4	116	San Marino	0.8
39	Nepal	2.0	77	Poland	1.4	117	Australia	0.7
40	Rhodesia (Zimbabwe)	2.0	78	Rumania	1.4	118	West Germany	0.7
41	Belize	1.9	79	Yugoslavia	1.4	119	New Zealand	0.7
42	Hong Kong	1.9	80	Finland	1.3	120	Northern Ireland	0.7
43	Jamaica	1.9	81	South Africa	1.3	121	Papua New Guinea	0.7
44	Mauritius	1.9	82	Soviet Union	1.3	122	St. Pierre & Miquelon	0.7
45	St. Vincent	1.9	83	Bahamas	1.2	123	Scotland	0.7
46	United Arab Emirates	1.9	84	Belgium	1.2	124	Sweden	0.7
47	Dominica	1.8	85	Gibraltar	1.2			
48	Ivory Coast	1.8	86	Netherlands Antilles	1.2		**BOTTOM 8**	
49	Norfolk Island	1.8	87	St. Helena	1.2	125	Belgium	0.6
50	St. Lucia	1.8	88	Turks & Caicos	1.2	126	Canada	0.6
51	Tanzania	1.8	89	Brazil	1.1	127	England & Wales	0.6
52	Trinidad & Tobago	1.8	90	Cayman Islands	1.1	128	Luxembourg	0.6
53	Greenland	1.7	91	Costa Rica	1.1	129	Pitcairn Island	0.6
54	Grenada	1.7	92	Czechoslovakia	1.1	130	Switzerland	0.6
55	Liberia	1.7	93	East Germany	1.1	131	United States	0.6
56	Malawi	1.7	94	Hungary	1.1	132	Falkland Islands	0.5
57	Niue Island	1.7	95	Malta	1.1			
58	Surinam	1.7	96	Portugal	1.1			

Source: *Compendium of Housing Statistics.*

238. Dwellings with Piped Water

The data in this table rank countries by availability in occupied dwellings of safe water piped inside or within 100 meters.

Number of Countries: 122
Midpoint: 41.9%
Period Covered: 1976 or Latest Available Year
Type of Ranking: Percentage of Occupied Dwellings with Safe Water Piped Inside (Availability Within 100 Meters Noted Separately); Highest to Lowest

Highlights & Findings: In many of the developing countries, one of the principal chores of the female household members of the household is the bringing of water from a well or a river, the nearest of which may be many miles off. In the majority of countries in this ranking, less than 50% of dwellings have piped water, and there are 38 countries where less than 25% of the dwellings have piped water. Figures for the USSR are not available.

Regions	Africa	Asia & Oceania	Europe	Western Hemisphere
Most	Senegal (30)	Christmas Island (1)	San Marino (2)	United States (9)
Least	Zambia (103)	Mongolia (122)	Rumania (105)	British Virgin Islands (118)

Rank	Country	Percentage of Dwellings with Piped Water	Rank	Country	Percentage of Dwellings with Piped Water	Rank	Country	Percentage of Dwellings with Piped Water
	TOP 10		41	Czechoslovakia	75.4	82	Panama	26.1
1	Christmas Island	100.0	42	Ethiopia*	74.3	83	El Salvador	26.0
2	San Marino	100.0	43	Ireland	73.2	84	St. Vincent*	25.0
3	West Germany*	99.2	44	Venezuela	72.4	85	Vietnam*	23.7
4	Luxembourg*	98.8	45	Finland*	72.1	86	Seychelles	23.2
5	Denmark*	98.7	46	New Caledonia*	70.3	87	Algeria	22.7
6	England & Wales	98.7	47	Greece	65.0	88	Surinam	21.9
7	Iceland	98.7	48	Morocco*	64.8	89	Nauru	21.8
8	Monaco	97.6	49	Sudan*	63.9	90	Jamaica	21.6
9	United States*	97.5	50	Sarawak	63.4	91	Malawi	21.6
10	Sweden	97.3	51	Puerto Rico*	62.7	92	Jordan	21.3
			52	Chile	59.6	93	Iraq*	20.8
	UPPER MIDDLE		53	Uruguay	59.4	94	South Korea	19.6
11	Israel*	96.5	54	Nepal*	47.7	95	Guadeloupe	18.6
12	St. Pierre & Miquelon	96.5	55	Gibraltar	47.5	96	Montserrat	18.0
13	Switzerland	96.1	56	Argentina*	47.3	97	Tunisia*	14.8
14	Canada*	96.1	57	Poland	47.3	98	Peru	14.6
15	Faroe Islands	95.0	58	Spain	45.0	99	Cayman Islands	14.4
16	Japan*	94.9	59	Hungary	44.0	100	Pacific Islands	13.8
17	Bermuda	94.6	60	St. Helena	43.9	101	Bolivia*	13.6
18	Scotland	94.6	61	Syria*	41.9	102	Iran	13.1
19	Falkland Islands*	94.5				103	Zambia	12.4
20	Norway	94.4		**LOWER MIDDLE**		104	Ecuador	12.3
21	Hong Kong*	94.3	62	Colombia	41.3	105	Rumania	12.3
22	Malta*	93.0	63	Barbados	40.0	106	Honduras	12.1
23	Bahrain*	92.8	64	Egypt*	39.5	107	Guatemala	11.3
24	New Zealand	92.7	65	Mexico	38.7	108	St. Kitts-Nevis-Anguilla	9.8
25	Northern Ireland	92.6	66	French Guyana	36.1	109	Thailand	8.6
26	France	90.8	67	Turkey*	35.9	110	Dominican Republic	8.1
27	Netherlands*	89.6	68	West Malaysia	34.6	111	Antigua	7.4
28	Brunei*	88.1	69	Philippines	34.4	112	Belize	6.2
29	Austria	87.8	70	Yugoslavia	34.0			
30	Senegal	87.7	71	Martinique	33.9		**BOTTOM 10**	
31	Macao*	87.1	72	Brazil	33.0	113	Paraguay	5.9
32	Belgium*	86.6	73	Greenland	32.8	114	Turks & Caicos	4.6
33	Italy	86.1	74	Trinidad & Tobago	32.3	115	Niue Island	4.5
34	Netherlands Antilles*	84.1	75	United Arab Emirates*	30.9	116	Sri Lanka	4.4
35	East Germany	82.1	76	Bahamas	30.8	117	Indonesia	3.3
36	Singapore	79.7	77	Portugal	28.9	118	British Virgin Islands	2.4
37	Sabah	79.4	78	Bulgaria	28.2	119	Tokelau Islands	2.3
38	Australia	78.8	79	Nicaragua	27.9	120	Wallis & Futuna Islands	2.3
39	Costa Rica*	78.2	80	Reunion	27.3	121	Western Samoa	2.3
40	Cyprus	77.3	81	Mauritius	27.1	122	Mongolia	0.3

*Including water within 100 meters.

Source: *Compendium of Housing Statistics.*

239. Dwellings with Electric Lights

The data in this table rank countries by percentage of occupied buildings with access to electricity. Access to electricity refers to electric lights only in all countries; however, in developed countries it also refers to the whole range of electric appliances, such as refrigerators, air conditioners, washing machines, and even electric toothbrushes and hairdryers.

Number of Countries: 111	Highlights & Findings: Although electricity is almost universally available in most developed

Number of Countries: 111
Midpoint: 59.3%
Period Covered: Latest Available Year, 1970-76
Type of Ranking: Percentage of Occupied Buildings with Access to Electricity; Highest to Lowest

Highlights & Findings: Although electricity is almost universally available in most developed countries, its availability in many developing nations is restricted to urban areas. There are 45 countries on the list where 50% of the dwellings have no electricity and 19 countries where 75% of the dwellings have no electricity.

Regions	Africa	Asia & Oceania	Europe	Western Hemisphere
Most	Senegal (25)	Christmas Island (1)	East Germany (2)	United States (14)
Least	Ivory Coast (111)	Wallis & Fortuna Island (110)	Portugal (76)	Montserrat (107)

Rank	Country	Percentage of Dwellings with Electricity	Rank	Country	Percentage of Dwellings with Electricity	Rank	Country	Percentage of Dwellings with Electricity
	TOP 9		38	Netherlands Antilles	87.4	76	Portugal	40.5
1	Christmas Island	100.0	39	Singapore	87.0	77	Guadeloupe	39.8
2	East Germany	100.0	40	Sabah	82.9	78	Syria	38.0
3	Gibraltar	100.0	41	Papua New Guinea	82.5	79	Egypt	37.8
4	San Marino	100.0	42	Morocco	81.5	80	El Salvador	34.1
5	Czechoslovakia	99.7	43	Nigeria	81.3	81	Algeria	33.7
6	West Germany	99.7	44	Puerto Rico	79.9	82	Ecuador	32.3
7	Belgium	99.6	45	Uruguay	78.4	83	Martinique	31.8
8	Luxembourg	99.5	46	Venezuela	78.4	84	Nepal	30.2
9	New Zealand	99.5	47	Norfolk Island	72.7	85	Reunion	29.3
			48	Chile	70.6	86	Zambia	27.5
	UPPER MIDDLE		49	Mauritius	70.1	87	Seychelles	27.4
10	Cocos (Keeling) Islands	99.0	50	Sarawak	69.5	88	Sudan	26.4
11	Cyprus	99.0	51	Argentina	69.2	89	Peru	26.0
12	Itayl	99.0	52	Costa Rica	68.8	90	Iran	25.4
13	United Kingdom	99.0	53	Trinidad & Tobago	66.0	91	Antigua	25.1
14	United States	99.0	54	French Guyana	64.2	92	United Arab Emirates	24.2
15	St. Pierre & Miquelon	98.8	55	Indonesia	63.5	93	St. Kitts-Nevis-Anguilla	23.9
16	France	98.8	56	Western Samoa	62.4	94	Tunisia	23.9
17	Australia	98.4	57	Nauru	59.3	95	Philippines	22.9
18	Netherlands	98.1				96	Guatemala	22.0
19	Macao	97.9		*LOWER MIDDLE*		97	Bolivia	21.9
20	Guam	97.7	58	Barbados	59.1	98	Dominican Republic	20.0
21	Monaco	97.2	59	Mexico	58.9	99	Niue Island	19.1
22	Israel	96.5	60	Ethiopia	58.2	100	Iraq	17.1
23	Poland	96.2	61	Bahamas	57.7	101	Jordan	17.0
24	Bahrain	95.9	62	Falkland Island	55.0			
25	Senegal	95.9	63	New Caledonia	54.9		*BOTTOM 10*	
26	Finland	95.6	64	Brazil	53.3	102	Malawi	15.7
27	Bulgaria	94.8	65	Panama	52.4	103	Turks & Caicos	15.4
28	Ireland	94.7	66	South Korea	49.7	104	Honduras	14.6
29	Iceland	94.6	67	Surinam	49.0	105	British Virgin Islands	13.8
30	Soviet Union*	95.5	68	Rumania	48.6	106	Paraguay	13.2
31	Hungary	94.3	69	Mongolia	47.5	107	Montserrat	11.0
32	Malta	92.9	70	Colombia	47.4	108	Sri Lanka	9.0
33	Rhodesia (Zimbabwe)	91.6	71	St. Helena	45.1	109	Congo	3.6
34	Brunei	90.1	72	Malaysia (West)	43.4	110	Wallis & Futuna	2.0
35	Spain	89.3	73	Belize	42.9	111	Ivory Coast	0.7
36	Greece	88.3	74	Turkey	41.1			
37	Yugoslavia	87.9	75	Nicaragua	40.9			

*This is an estimate.

Source: *Compendium of Housing Statistics.*

240. Dwellings with Kitchens

This table ranks countries by availability of kitchens or kitchenettes per 100 occupied conventional dwellings. It is assumed that these kitchens would have at least the most primitive facilities, such as an earthen stove for burning firewood or charcoal and a place for washing utensils, grinding corn, etc. Needless to say, kitchens in developed countries would have more elaborate devices and labor-saving appliances.

Number of Countries: 67
Midpoint: 92.5 per 100 Houses
Period Covered: 1973 or Latest Available Year
Type of Ranking: Percentage of Kitchen or Kitchenette per 100 Houses; Highest to Lowest

Highlights & Findings: Most nations rank better on this table than they do with regard to other facilities such as piped water or fixed baths. There are only four nations where the majority of the houses do not have attached kitchens or kitchenettes, and these, obviously, are in rural areas.

Regions	Africa	Asia & Oceania	Europe	Western Hemisphere
Most	Reunion (37)	Australia (14)	San Marino (3)	Falkland Islands (1)
Least	Sudan (63)	Wallis & Fortuna Islands (67)	Rumania (59)	Peru (64)

Rank	Country	Percentage of Kitchen & Kitchenette per 100 Houses	Rank	Country	Percentage of Kitchen & Kitchenette per 100 Houses	Rank	Country	Percentage of Kitchen & Kitchenette per 100 Houses
	TOP 10		23	Faroe Islands	95.8	46	Dominican Republic	73.9
1	Falkland Islands	100.0	24	East Germany	95.8	47	Mexico	73.7
2	St. Pierre & Miquelon	100.0	25	United States	95.6	48	Greece	73.5
3	San Marino	100.0	26	Poland	95.3	49	Sri Lanka	73.5
4	Greenland	99.8	27	Western Samoa	95.2	50	Paraguay	72.1
5	Denmark	99.7	28	Netherlands	95.0	51	Nauru	71.4
6	Norway	99.3	29	Austria	94.9	52	Venezuela	70.4
7	Hungary	99.2	30	Puerto Rico	94.6	53	Morocco	70.1
8	Nicaragua	99.1	31	New Caledonia	93.9	54	Malaysia (West)	70.0
9	Switzerland	99.0	32	Finland	93.1	55	Hong Kong	68.6
10	Guatemala	98.7	33	Malta	92.6	56	Martinique	65.2
			34	South Korea	92.5	57	Guadeloupe	63.2
	UPPER MIDDLE		35	Yugoslavia	92.5	58	Tanzania	63.2
11	Sweden	98.5	36	Brazil	92.4	59	Rumania	62.2
12	Costa Rica	98.4	37	Reunion	91.4			
13	West Germany	98.4	38	Mauritius	91.2		*BOTTOM 8*	
14	Australia	98.3	39	Niue Island	90.8	60	Turkey	59.0
15	France	98.0				61	Panama	56.5
16	Northern Ireland	97.7				62	Malawi	53.9
17	Iceland	97.6		*LOWER MIDDLE*		63	Sudan	53.8
18	Japan	97.5	40	Cyprus	89.6	64	Peru	37.0
19	Israel	97.2	41	Chile	89.0	65	Jordan	35.4
20	Czechoslovakia	97.1	42	Bulgaria	88.6	66	Christmas Island	33.3
21	Portugal	97.0	43	Netherlands Antilles	87.0	67	Wallis & Futuna Islands	2.3
22	Guatemala	96.4	44	Algeria	80.2			
			45	French Guyana	79.7			

Source: *Compendium of Housing Statistics.*

241. Dwellings with Toilets

A primary indicator of public health and sanitation is the extent to which dwellings, especially in urban areas, are equipped with or connected to satisfactory means of disposing of human waste. The ideal means is the flush toilet, although in rural and sparsely populated areas other, less satisfactory, means may be commonly and safely used, even if they do not always come up to the standards considered acceptable by public health authorities. In the following ranking both flush and other types of toilets are combined unless otherwise indicated.

Number of Countries: 114
Midpoint: 86.5%
Period Covered: 1973 or Latest Available Year
Type of Ranking: Percentage of Dwellings with Toilet, Flush or Other; Highest to Lowest

Highlights & Findings: There are only 18 reporting countries where the majority of the dwellings have no toilet facilities. More than half the number of reporting countries have over 85% of their dwellings equipped with toilets.

Regions	Africa	Asia & Oceania	Europe	Western Hemisphere
Most	St. Helena (17)	Christmas Island (2)	Bulgaria (1)	Falkland Islands (4)
Least	Algeria (98)	Tokelau Islands (114)	Poland (109)	Honduras (112)

Rank	Country	Percentage of Dwellings with Toilet	Rank	Country	Percentage of Dwellings with Toilet	Rank	Country	Percentage of Dwellings with Toilet
	TOP 12		39	Israel	95.0	78	Philippines	66.6
1	Bulgaria	100.0	40	South Korea	94.9	79	Spain	66.1
2	Christmas Island	100.0	41	Canada	94.3	80	Indonesia	65.9
3	Denmark	100.0	42	Uruguay	94.3	81	Brazil	64.8
4	Falkland Islands	100.0	43	Switzerland (flush only)	93.3	82	Sri Lanka	64.5
5	East Germany	100.0	44	Malta	93.1	83	Belize	64.2
6	West Germany	100.0	45	Morocco	92.6	84	Antigua	63.5
7	Hungary	100.0	46	Greece	92.5	85	Vietnam	62.8
8	Japan	100.0	47	Yugoslavia	91.8	86	Chile	61.5
9	Nauru	100.0	48	Puerto Rico	91.4	87	Finland (flush only)	61.4
10	Norway	100.0	49	Bahamas	90.7	88	Syria	58.4
11	Rumania	100.0	50	Monaco	90.3	89	Pacific Islands	58.1
12	Western Samoa	100.0	51	Sweden (flush only)	90.1	90	Colombia	56.0
			52	Turks & Caicos	89.5	91	Jordan	55.4
	UPPER MIDDLE		53	Costa Rica	88.9	92	France	54.8
13	Belgium	99.9	54	Singapore	88.7	93	Nicaragua	53.9
14	Liechtenstein	99.9	55	Paraguay	88.3	94	Venezuela	53.5
15	Netherlands	99.9	56	Argentina	87.0	95	Cyprus	52.7
16	Czechoslovakia	99.8	57	Iceland	86.5	96	Tanzania	50.0
17	St. Helena	99.8				97	Zambia	49.6
18	Bermuda	99.5				98	Algeria	49.1
19	Brunei	99.5		**LOWER MIDDLE**		99	Montserrat	48.4
20	Luxembourg	99.5	58	Dominican Republic	86.2	100	British Virgin Islands	45.0
21	Australia	98.9	59	Surinam	85.2	101	Peru	44.3
22	England & Wales (flush only)	98.9	60	Greenland	84.3	102	Portugal (flush only)	41.8
23	San Marino	98.4	61	Netherlands Antilles	80.4	103	Mexico	41.5
24	Niue Island	98.0	62	Ireland	80.2	104	El Salvador	41.3
25	Thailand	97.9	63	Faroe Islands	79.5			
26	Trinidad & Tobago	97.9	64	Malaysia (West)	79.0		**BOTTOM 10**	
27	Barbados	97.7	65	New Caledonia	77.8	105	Guadeloupe	38.5
28	Seychelles	97.7	66	St. Vincent	77.3	106	Nepal	37.2
29	Mauritius	97.2	67	French Guyana	76.8	107	Martinique	37.0
30	Sabah	97.2	68	Cayman Islands	74.0	108	Iraq	33.4
31	New Zealand (flush only)	97.1	69	Reunion	74.0	109	Poland	33.4
32	Sarawak	97.0	70	Turkey	73.8	110	Ecuador	32.8
33	Jamaica	96.7	71	Austria	72.8	111	Guatemala	30.6
34	St. Pierre & Miquelon	96.5	72	Northern Ireland	72.8	112	Honduras	19.7
35	United States	96.0	73	St. Kitts-Nevis-Anguilla	72.1	113	Wallis & Futuna	5.5
36	Gibraltar	95.8	74	Panama	72.0	114	Tokelau Islands	0.0
37	Scotland (flush only)	95.7	75	Sudan	70.3			
38	Italy	95.7	76	Hong Kong (flush only)	69.2			
			77	Malawi	67.7			

Source: *Compendium of Housing Statistics.*

242. Dwellings with Fixed Baths or Showers

This table ranks countries by availability of fixed bath or showers per 100 occupied conventional dwellings. Because it is conducive to good sanitation, most modern buildings in urban areas have fixed baths or showers even in developing countries, but they are a luxury in rural areas. In developing countries villagers may be seen taking their baths in nearby pools or streams, and communal baths are not uncommon in the Middle East and North Africa.

Number of Countries: 79
Midpoint: 45.6 per 100 Houses
Period Covered: 1973 or Latest Available Year
Type of Ranking: Percentage of Fixed Baths per 100 Occupied Conventional Dwellings; Highest to Lowest

Highlights & Findings: The majority of dwellings do not have fixed baths or showers in 44 countries in this ranking. While the presence of Turkey or Sri Lanka on this list may not be surprising, the presence of France, Belgium, the Netherlands, and Eastern European countries is. However, the data are subject to so many qualifications that they may be regarded as only broad approximations.

Regions	Africa	Asia & Oceania	Europe	Western Hemisphere
Most	Mauritius (45)	New Zealand (2)	Liechtenstein (1)	United States (4)
Least	Algeria (69)	South Korea (79)	Bulgaria (74)	Guatemala (71)

Rank	Country	Percentage of Fixed Baths or Showers per 100 Houses	Rank	Country	Percentage of Fixed Baths or Showers per 100 Houses	Rank	Country	Percentage of Fixed Baths or Showers per 100 Houses
	TOP 10		27	Japan	65.6	54	Greece	35.6
1	Liechtenstein	99.0	28	Macao	65.0	55	Christmas Island	33.3
2	New Zealand	98.1	29	Italy	64.5	56	Mexico	31.8
3	Australia	98.0	30	Austria	59.5	57	El Salvador	28.2
4	United States	95.2	31	Uruguay	58.7	58	Netherlands	26.8
5	Canada	92.6	32	Czechoslovakia	58.6	59	Tanzania	24.6
6	Israel	91.0	33	Ireland	55.4	60	Yugoslavia	24.6
7	Singapore	87.3	34	Panama	53.1	61	Morocco	24.3
8	Falkland Islands	85.6	35	Malaysia	51.3	62	Spain	24.0
9	Western Samoa	85.2	36	France	48.9	63	Paraguay	22.6
10	England & Wales	85.1	37	Faroe Islands	48.2	64	Surinam	21.7
			38	Belgium	48.0	65	Malawi	20.1
	UPPER MIDDLE		39	Chile	46.0	66	Portugal	18.6
11	West Germany	81.8	40	Cyprus	45.6	67	Honduras	16.7
12	Switzerland	80.8	41	Luxembourg	45.6	68	Peru	16.4
13	Netherlands Antilles	79.4				69	Algeria	12.3
14	Sweden	78.3		*LOWER MIDDLE*				
15	Scotland	77.4	42	Turkey	44.5		*BOTTOM 10*	
16	Denmark	76.8	43	Malta	44.4	70	Dominican Republic	12.0
17	Puerto Rico	76.1	44	Colombia	42.6	71	Guatemala	11.5
18	San Marino	75.3	45	Mauritius	42.6	72	Iraq	10.3
19	Nauru	73.3	46	Greenland	41.8	73	Rumania	9.6
20	Norway	73.2	47	Nicaragua	41.3	74	Bulgaria	8.7
21	Northern Ireland	72.6	48	Hong Kong	40.9	75	Jordan	8.7
22	Costa Rica	72.4	49	Poland	40.4	76	Sri Lanka	7.0
23	Monaco	72.1	50	Hungary	39.7	77	Niue Island	4.5
24	Iceland	69.7	51	Finland	39.1	78	Wallis & Futuna Islands	2.3
25	Gibraltar	67.5	52	East Germany	38.7	79	South Korea	1.8
26	St. Pierre & Miquelon	65.9	53	Venezuela	37.2			

Source: *Compendium of Housing Statistics.*

HEALTH AND FOOD

Health is one area where measurable and undeniable progress has been achieved in *every* country since the end of World War II. Not only is the incidence of major epidemic diseases and once-dreaded killers, such as plague, smallpox and malaria, down in almost all countries, but there are more hospitals and more trained professionals to staff them, more medical research and more transfer of medical technology, and more people covered by medical insurance today than at any time in history. Much of this improvement has been the direct result of better nutrition, sanitation and water supply and better monitoring procedures.

It is against this background that the following rankings should be considered. But there are a number of negative factors that the rankings may conceal or reveal rather imperfectly. One is the scandalous and prohibitive cost of medical care, especially in developing countries, restricting its availability to the well-to-do. Medical insurance, originally designed to enlarge the reach of health care and delivery services, has been, paradoxically, a contributory factor in these spiraling costs. Medical care in almost all countries remains very much of an urban phenomenon with little or no penetration of rural areas. Even the per capita rankings of medical personnel in this section do not reveal the heavy concentration of health services in towns and cities.

The rankings are grouped into four categories. The first presents the classic health indicators: life expectancy for males and females, infant mortality rate (the abortion rate is presented separately) and the physical quality of life index. (Devised by the Overseas Development Council, this is a composite index that correlates the first two indicators as well as literacy.) The second group deals with the quality of health care in terms of personnel and beds: inhabitants per bed in general and mental hospitals, and inhabitants per physician, dentist, nursing person and pharmacist. The third group deals with health expenditures. The last group presents a series of rankings on mortality by cause: heart diseases, syphilis, tuberculosis, cirrhosis of the liver, diabetes and influenza. Also in this group are rankings on traffic accidents, fatal industrial accidents and suicide rates.

The subsection on food ranks countries by protein intake and calorie intake.

243. Male Life Expectancy

Expectation of life is defined as the average number of years that males and females could hope to live on the basis of the mortality rates prevailing during the period 1970-75. However, in many cases this understates the expectation of life because mortality rates are decreasing almost universally. This limitation apart, the figures are considered to be very reliable because of the ability of actuaries to build computerized model life tables. Expectation of life is presented for males and females separately. A comparison of the two rankings proves the traditional assumption that females have a greater expectation of life than males in most countries of the world.

Number of Countries: 162
Midpoint: 55.80 years
Period Covered: 1970-75
Type of Ranking: Expectation of Life for Males: Highest to lowest

Highlights & Findings: Of the 10 top countries, eight are European and three of these are Scandinavian. Of the bottom 12 countries, 11 are African. The pattern closely reflects the physical quality of life and is determined by such factors as nutrition, medical care, sanitation, weather, environmental conditions and also, according to some authorities, race.

Regions	Africa	Asia & Oceania	Europe	Western Hemisphere
Most	Seychelles (57)	Japan (5)	Sweden (1)	Canada (11)
Least	Gabon (162)	Bangladesh (157)	Soviet Union (47)	Belize (116)

Rank	Country	Expectation of Life (years)	Rank	Country	Expectation of Life (years)	Rank	Country	Expectation of Life (years)
	TOP 10		55	Jamaica	62.65	110	Indonesia	47.50
1	Sweden	72.07	56	Surinam	62.50	111	Namibia	47.50
2	Iceland	71.60	57	Seychelles	61.90	112	Sudan	47.30
3	Norway	71.50	58	Costa Rica	61.87	113	Kenya	46.90
4	Netherlands	71.20	59	Lebanon	61.40	114	Liberia	45.80
5	Japan	71.16	60	Western Samoa	60.80	115	Bolivia	45.70
6	Denmark	70.80	61	Mauritius	60.68	116	Belize	44.99
7	Israel	70.30	62	Antiqua	60.48	117	Lesotho	44.40
8	Switzerland	70.29	63	Chile	60.48	118	Saudi Arabia	44.20
9	Cyprus	70.00	64	Paraguay	60.30	119	Cambodia	44.00
10	Spain	69.69	65	Grenada	60.14	120	South Yemen	43.70
			66	China	59.90	121	Yemen Arab Republic	43.70
	UPPER MIDDLE		67	Colombia	59.20	122	Vietnam	43.20
11	Canada	69.34	68	Mongolia	59.10	123	Zambia	42.90
12	Italy	68.97	69	Guyana	59.03	124	Bhutan	42.20
13	Puerto Rico	68.92	70	Greenland	58.90	125	Nepal	42.20
14	East Germany	68.85	71	Netherlands Antilles	58.90	126	Botswana	41.90
15	United States	68.70	72	North Korea	58.80	127	Congo	41.90
16	France	68.60	73	St. Vincent	58.46	128	Equatorial Guinea	41.90
17	Bulgaria	68.58	74	St. Kitts-Nevis-Anguilla	57.97	129	Ghana	41.90
18	Ireland	68.58	75	Brazil	57.61	130	Ivory Coast	41.90
19	New Zealand	68.55	76	Dominican Republic	57.15	131	Mozambique	41.90
20	Cuba	68.50	77	Dominica	56.97	132	Sierra Leone	41.90
21	Fiji	68.50	78	Gilbert Islands	56.90	133	Swaziland	41.90
22	Malta	68.10	79	Philippines	56.90	134	Zaire	41.90
23	West Germany	68.04	80	El Salvador	56.56	135	India	41.89
24	United Kingdom	67.80	81	Reunion	55.80	136	Comoros	40.90
25	Belgium	67.79				137	Malawi	40.90
26	Austria	67.70		**LOWER MIDDLE**		138	Burundi	40.00
27	Australia	67.63	82	St. Lucia	55.13	139	Tanzania	40.00
28	Greece	67.46	83	Syria	54.49	140	Afghanistan	39.90
29	Hong Kong	67.36	84	Pakistan	53.72	141	Benin	39.40
30	Rumania	67.29	85	Turkey	53.70	142	Cameroon	39.40
31	Poland	67.02	86	Thailand	53.60	143	Guinea	39.40
32	Luxembourg	67.00	87	Jordan	52.60	144	Rwanda	39.40
33	Finland	66.90	88	Peru	52.59	145	Somalia	39.40
34	Hungary	66.54	89	Guadeloupe	52.50	146	Laos	39.10
35	Czechoslovakia	66.53	90	Tunisia	52.50	147	Gambia	38.50
36	Venezuela	66.41	91	Honduras	52.10	148	Senegal	38.50
37	Kuwait	66.14	92	Algeria	51.70	149	Madagascar	37.50
38	Bermuda	65.61	93	Egypt	51.60	150	Nigeria	37.20
39	Uruguay	65.51	94	Libya	51.40	151	Angola	37.00
40	Yugoslavia	65.42	95	Morocco	51.40	152	Guinea-Bissau	37.00
41	Portugal	65.29	96	Iraq	51.20	153	Mauritania	37.00
42	Argentina	65.16	97	Nicaragua	51.20	154	Niger	37.00
43	Singapore	65.10	98	Ecuador	51.04			
44	Malaysia	65.03	99	Iran	50.70		**BOTTOM 8**	
45	Albania	64.90	100	Rhodesia (Zimbabwe)	49.80	155	Ethiopia	36.50
46	Sri Lanka	64.80	101	South Africa	49.80	156	Mali	36.50
47	Panama	64.26	102	British Virgin Islands	49.53	157	Bangladesh	35.80
48	Trinidad & Tobago	64.08	103	Montserrat	49.53	158	Central African Empire	33.00
49	Soviet Union	64.00	104	Haiti	49.00	159	Upper Volta	32.10
50	Bahamas	64.00	105	Burma	48.60	160	Togo	31.60
51	Martinique	63.30	106	Cape Verde	48.30	161	Chad	29.00
52	South Korea	63.00	107	Uganda	48.30	162	Gabon	25.00
53	Mexico	62.76	108	Guatemala	48.29			
54	Barbados	62.74	109	Papua New Guinea	47.70			

Source: *U.N. Demographic Yearbook.*

244. Female Life Expectancy

Number of Countries: 162
Midpoint: 59 years
Period Covered: 1970-75
Type of Ranking: Expectation of Life for Females: Highest to Lowest

Highlights & Findings: There are significant differences in the rankings of life expectancy for males and females. In the female ranking the United States, France and Canada appear among the top 10, whereas in the male ranking they do not. The highest as well as the lowest life expectancy for females are five years more than the corresponding rates for men.

Regions	Africa	Asia & Oceania	Europe	Western Hemisphere
Most	Seychelles (46)	Japan (8)	Norway (1)	United States (5)
Least	Upper Volta (162)	Bangladesh (160)	Albania (52)	Bolivia (113)

Rank	Country	Expectation of Life (years)	Rank	Country	Expectation of Life (years)	Rank	Country	Expectation of Life (years)
	TOP 10		52	Albania	67.00	104	Burma	51.50
1	Norway	77.83	53	South Korea	67.00	105	Iran	51.30
2	Sweden	77.65	54	Sri Lanka	66.90	106	Kenya	51.20
3	Iceland	77.50	55	Surinam	66.70	107	Haiti	51.00
4	Netherlands	77.20	56	Jamaica	66.63	108	Namibia	50.00
5	United States	76.50	57	Mexico	66.57	109	Sudan	49.90
6	France	76.40	58	Venezuela	66.41	110	Guatemala	49.74
7	Canada	76.36	59	Chile	66.01	111	Belize	48.97
8	Japan	76.31	60	Greenland	65.70	112	Pakistan	48.80
9	Denmark	76.30	61	Netherlands Antilles	65.70	113	Bolivia	47.90
10	Switzerland	76.22	62	Grenada	65.60	114	Lesotho	47.60
			63	Mauritius	65.31	115	Papua New Guinea	47.60
	UPPER MIDDLE		64	Western Samoa	65.20	116	Indonesia	47.50
11	Puerto Rico	76.05	65	Lebanon	65.10	117	Cambodia	46.90
12	New Zealand	75.60	66	Costa Rica	64.83	118	Saudi Arabia	46.50
13	Finland	75.41	67	Antigua	64.32	119	Zambia	46.10
14	Hong Kong	75.01	68	Paraguay	63.60	120	Vietnam	46.00
15	Spain	74.96	69	China	63.30	121	Yemen Arab Republic	45.90
16	Austria	74.90	70	Guyana	63.01	122	South Yemen	45.90
17	Italy	74.88	71	Colombia	62.70	123	Botswana	45.10
18	West Germany	74.54	72	North Korea	62.50	124	Congo	45.10
19	Poland	74.26	73	Reunion	62.40	125	Equatorial Guinea	45.10
20	Belgium	74.21	74	Mongolia	62.30	126	Ghana	45.10
21	East Germany	74.19	75	St. Kitts-Nevis-Anguilla	61.90	127	Ivory Coast	45.10
22	Australia	74.15	76	Brazil	61.10	128	Mozambique	45.10
23	Soviet Union	74.00	77	El Salvador	60.42	129	Sierra Leone	45.10
24	Israel	73.90	78	Philippines	60.00	130	Swaziland	45.10
25	Luxembourg	73.90	79	St. Vincent	59.70	131	Zaire	45.10
26	Bulgaria	73.86	80	Dominica	59.18	132	Bhutan	45.00
27	United Kingdom	73.80	81	Gilbert Islands	59.00	133	Gabon	45.00
28	Czechoslovakia	73.49				134	Nepal	45.00
29	Cyprus	72.90		*LOWER MIDDLE*		135	Malawi	44.20
30	Ireland	72.85	82	Syria	58.73	136	Comoros	44.10
31	Hungary	72.42	83	Thailand	58.70	137	Liberia	44.00
32	Bermuda	72.35	84	Dominican Republic	58.59	138	Burundi	43.00
33	Portugal	72.03	85	St. Lucia	58.47	139	Benin	42.60
34	Malta	72.02	86	Tunisia	55.70	140	Cameroon	42.60
35	Kuwait	71.82	87	Peru	55.48	141	Rwanda	42.60
36	Rumania	71.82	88	Honduras	55.00	142	Somalia	42.60
37	Cuba	71.80	89	Algeria	54.80	143	Guinea	42.00
38	Fiji	71.70	90	British Virgin Islands	54.76	144	Laos	41.80
39	Uruguay	71.56	91	Montserrat	54.76	145	Gambia	41.60
40	Argentina	71.38	92	Nicaragua	54.60	146	Senegal	41.60
41	Greece	70.70	93	Libya	54.50	147	Afghanistan	40.70
42	Malaysia	70.30	94	Morocco	54.50	148	India	40.55
43	Yugoslavia	70.22	95	Iraq	54.30	149	Angola	40.10
44	Singapore	70.00	96	Egypt	53.80	150	Guinea-Bissau	40.10
45	Trinidad & Tobago	68.11	97	Turkey	53.70	151	Mauritania	40.10
46	Seychelles	68.00	98	Ecuador	53.67	152	Niger	40.10
47	Panama	67.50	99	Rhodesia (Zimbabwe)	53.30			
48	Barbados	67.43	100	South Africa	53.30		*BOTTOM 10*	
49	Martinique	67.40	101	Jordan	52.00	153	Tanzania	40.00
50	Bahamas	67.30	102	Cape Verde	51.70	154	Ethiopia	39.60
51	Guadeloupe	67.30	103	Uganda	51.70	155	Mali	39.60

Rank Country	Expectation of Life (years)	Rank Country	Expectation of Life (years)	Rank Country	Expectation of Life (years)
156 Togo	38.50	159 Central African Empire	36.00	162 Upper Volta	31.10
157 Madagascar	38.30	160 Bangladesh	35.80		
158 Nigeria	36.70	161 Chad	35.00		

Source: *U.N. Demographic Yearbook.*

245. Infant Mortality Rate

Infant mortality, or the number of deaths of infants under one year of age per 1,000 live births, is a direct measure of the physical quality of life. Infant mortality rates are sensitive to even small improvements in national health care, and rates have been declining in all parts of the world. The problem, however, is still severe in many countries of Asia and Africa as the spread between the highest and lowest rates indicates. The reliability of the figures is affected by the requirements and means provided for registration. Even the definition of an infant varies from country to country. Some countries require breathing to establish a live birth but others recognize any signs of life. Some countries do not register as a live birth any infant dying within 24 hours or before registration. A few countries report births and deaths not by year of occurrence but by year of registration. A few others do not report infant deaths. However, none of these limitations is serious enough to significantly distort the data or make them incomparable.

Number of Countries: 158
Midpoint: 38.2 per 1,000
Period Covered: 1970-75
Type of Ranking: Number of Deaths of Infants under One Year of Age per 1,000 Live Births; Highest to Lowest

Highlights & Findings: Infant mortality is becoming an African phenomenon; 14 of the top 15 countries are in Africa, the other being Burma. Contributing to such high rates are the lack of medical care during pregnancy, malnutrition resulting from ritual dietary taboos and poor environmental conditions.

Regions	Africa	Asia & Oceania	Europe	Western Hemisphere
Most	Zambia (2)	Burma (1)	Albania (37)	St. Vincent (33)
Least	St. Helena (135)	Japan (153)	Faroe Islands (158)	Canada (139)

Rank Country	Infant Mortality Rate per 1,000	Rank Country	Infant Mortality Rate per 1,000	Rank Country	Infant Mortality Rate per 1,000
TOP 10		20 Ivory Coast	138.0	42 Guatemala	75.4
1 Burma	300	21 Rwanda	132.8	43 Ecuador	70.2
2 Zambia	259	22 Togo	127.0	44 San Tome & Principe	64.3
3 Gabon	229	23 Indonesia	125.0	45 St. Lucia	60.0
4 Guinea	216	24 Tunisia	125.0	46 Argentina	59.0
5 Nigeria	200	25 Pakistan	124.0	47 Philippines	58.9
6 Central African Empire	190	26 India	122.0	48 Dominica	58.3
7 Mauritania	187	27 Rhodesia (Zimbabwe)	122.0	49 El Salvador	58.3
8 Upper Volta	182	28 Mali	120.0	50 Peru	58.2
9 Lesotho	181	29 Benin	109.6	51 Chile	55.6
10 Congo	180	30 Zaire	104.0	52 Wallis & Futuna Islands	53.8
		31 Madagascar	102.0	53 Equatorial Guinea	53.2
UPPER MIDDLE		32 Egypt	100.4	54 Solomon Islands	52.4
11 Tanzania	165	33 St. Vincent	99.6	55 Nauru	51.8
12 Chad	160	34 Colombia	97.1	56 Comoros	51.7
13 Uganda	160	35 Sudan	93.6	57 Kenya	51.4
14 Liberia	159	36 Senegal	92.9	58 Mexico	49.7
15 Ghana	156	37 Albania	86.8	59 Gilbert Islands	48.9
16 Turkey	153	38 Algeria	86.3	60 Uruguay	48.1
17 Burundi	150	39 Ethiopia	84.2	61 Guinea-Bissau	47.1
18 Morocco	149	40 Cape Verde	78.9	62 Turks & Caicos	46.9
19 Malawi	142.1	41 Bolivia	77.3	63 Nicaragua	46.0

Rank	Country	Infant Mortality Rate per 1,000	Rank	Country	Infant Mortality Rate per 1,000	Rank	Country	Infant Mortality Rate per 1,000
64	Venezuela	46.0	95	Martinique	31.6	128	Austria	18.3
65	Sri Lanka	45.1	96	Niue Island	31.6	129	Luxembourg	17.9
66	Kuwait	44.3	97	Antigua	31.4	130	Cayman Islands	17.8
67	Dominican Republic	43.4	98	Pacific Islands	31.0	131	Belgium	17.4
68	French Guiana	43.1	99	Surinam	30.4	132	Ireland	17.1
69	St. Kitts-Nevis-Anguilla	42.8	100	Hungary	29.7	133	Malta	16.9
70	Guyana	42.3	101	Macao	29.5	134	New Zealand	16.0
71	New Caledonia	41.2	102	Soviet Union	27.7	135	St. Helena	15.9
72	Fiji	40.9	103	Iraq	27.5	136	East Germany	15.8
73	Tokelau Islands	40.8	104	Cuba	27.3	137	Bermuda	15.7
74	Mauritius	40.4	105	Cyprus	26.9	138	United States	15.1
75	Samoa	40.0	106	Montserrat	26.3	139	Canada	15.0
			107	Thailand	26.3	140	Hong Kong	14.9
	LOWER MIDDLE		108	Falkland Islands	25.6	141	Australia	14.3
76	Greenland	39.2	109	Puerto Rico	24.2	142	United Kingdom	14.3
77	Paraguay	38.6	110	Angola	24.1	143	Lebanon	13.6
78	French Polynesia	38.3	111	Greece	24.0	144	Iceland	12.5
79	Costa Rica	38.2	112	Poland	23.8	145	Spain	12.0
80	Portugal	37.9	113	Grenada	23.5	146	Singapore	11.6
81	Barbados	37.7	114	Bulgaria	23.2	147	France	11.3
82	Yugoslavia	36.3	115	Jamaica	23.2	148	Norway	11.1
83	Reunion	36.2	116	Israel	22.9			
84	Panama	35.6	117	Brunei	22.7		**BOTTOM 10**	
85	Bahamas	34.7	118	Jordan	21.9	149	Switzerland	10.7
86	Rumania	34.7	119	Syria	21.7	150	Finland	10.5
87	Seychelles	34.7	120	Czechoslovakia	20.9	151	Netherlands	10.5
88	Guadeloupe	34.6	121	Italy	20.7	152	Denmark	10.4
89	Honduras	34.1	122	Tonga	20.5	153	Japan	10.1
90	Trinidad & Tobago	33.9	123	West Germany	19.8	154	Monaco	9.3
91	Belize	33.7	124	Netherlands Antilles	19.8	155	San Marino	9.2
92	Malaysia	33.2	125	Mozambique	19.1	156	Sweden	8.7
93	Cook Islands	32.6	126	Gibraltar	19.0	157	Liechtenstein	6.5
94	St. Pierre & Miquelon	32.1	127	British Virgin Islands	18.6	158	Faroe Islands	6.3

Source: *U.N. Demographic Yearbook.*

246. Maternal Mortality Rate

Maternal deaths are defined as deaths caused by deliveries and complications of childbirth and pregnancy. They include maternal deaths caused by the death of the fetus and induced abortion. The data are compiled from civil registers and are thus subject to the same limitations as other vital statistics.

Number of Countries: 69
Midpoint: 30.3 per 100,000 live births
Period Covered: 1970-75
Type of Ranking: Number of Maternal Deaths per 100,000 Live Births; Highest to Lowest

Highlights & Findings: The spread between the highest rate (647.4) and the lowest (2.5) is an indication that maternal mortality rates are closely tied to variations in the quality of medical care. In fact, maternal mortality has ceased to be a major medical concern in advanced countries, but it continues to be a major health problem in Third World countries. Figures for the USSR are not available.

Regions	Africa	Asia & Oceania	Europe	Western Hemisphere
Most	Mozambique (1)	Sri Lanka (7)	Italy (30)	Bolivia (2)
Least	Rhodesia (Zimbabwe) (43)	Hong Kong (69)	Denmark (68)	Canada (63)

Rank	Country	Maternal Mortality per 100,000 Live Births	Rank	Country	Maternal Mortality per 100,000 Live Births	Rank	Country	Maternal Mortality per 100,000 Live Births
	TOP 10		3	Colombia	212.7	6	Ecuador	187.3
1	Mozambique	647.4	4	Reunion	198.0	7	Sri Lanka	179.3
2	Bolivia	316.2	5	Kenya	188.1	8	Peru	177.6

Rank	Country	Maternal Mortality per 100,000 Live Births	Rank	Country	Maternal Mortality per 100,000 Live Births	Rank	Country	Maternal Mortality per 100,000 Live Births
9	Argentina	159.1	30	Italy	41.2	51	New Zealand	15.2
10	Guadeloupe	144.0	31	Portugal	40.1	52	Poland	14.3
			32	Macao	37.5	53	Netherlands	13.4
	UPPER MIDDLE		33	Mauritius	37.2	54	Czechoslovakia	12.7
11	Philippines	137.8	34	Rumania	30.9	55	Switzerland	12.7
12	Guatemala	136.6	35	West Germany	30.3	56	Kuwait	12.2
13	Jamaica	128.3				57	United States	12.0
14	Paraguay	125.6		**LOWER MIDDLE**		58	Israel	11.7
15	Angola	108.9	36	Japan	27.6	59	Australia	11.4
16	Mexico	107.6	37	Luxembourg	25.0			
17	Panama	83.1	38	East Germany	23.3		**BOTTOM 10**	
18	Equatorial Guinea	80.1	39	Spain	23.2	60	Belgium	10.8
19	Chile	78.1	40	Iceland	22.8	61	United Kingdom	10.7
20	South Africa	71.2	41	Hungary	22.1	62	Puerto Rico	10.2
21	Trinidad & Tobago	68.9	42	France	21.8	63	Canada	9.3
22	Nigeria	67.3	43	Rhodesia (Zimbabwe)	21.1	64	Ireland	8.8
23	Guyana	63.3	44	Bulgaria	20.1	65	Sweden	7.7
24	Costa Rica	59.9	45	Jordan	19.6	66	Norway	3.3
25	Cuba	59.4	46	Barbados	18.7	67	Finland	3.2
26	Bahamas	49.6	47	Malta	18.4	68	Denmark	2.8
27	Venezuela	49.4	48	Greece	18.3	69	Hong Kong	2.5
28	Guinea-Bissau	45.3	49	Singapore	17.5			
29	Uruguay	44.6	50	Austria	16.0			

Source: *U.N. Demographic Yearbook.*

247. Physical Quality of Life Index (PQLI)

The physical quality of life index (PQLI) is a concept developed by the Overseas Development Council. It is a composite index calculated by averaging three indices—life expectancy, infant mortality and literacy—giving equal weight to each of the three indicators. Each is rated on a scale from 1 to 100. For the life expectancy index, the upper limit of 100 is assigned to Sweden and the lower limit of 1 to Guinea-Bissau. For infant mortality, Sweden is rated 100 and Gabon 1. The PQLI is free of many of the biases and distortions that affect other measures of human progress. Because it is not weighted by the level of the GNP, this index avoids problems of monetary measurement. Moreover, it is not dependent on absolute technical standards (such as a fixed calorie requirement) about which there may be no genuine agreement. Because it is concerned with basic and universal human needs rather than with technological growth (such as the number of telephones or number of homes with piped water), the PQLI may be applied to developing and developed countries with equal validity.

Number of Countries: 151
Midpoint: 59
Period Covered: 1973
Type of Ranking: Physical Quality of Life Index; Highest to Lowest

Highlights & Findings: Of the 10 top countries, eight are in Europe, while of the 10 bottom countries nine are in Africa. This establishes that there is some correlation between economic development and the PQLI, but there are significant divergences. The oil-rich Arab states have high per capita GNPs but low PQLIs, while the island of Sri Lanka with a low per capita GNP has a very high PQLI.

Regions	Africa	Asia & Oceania	Europe	Western Hemisphere
High	Mauritius (62)	Japan (6)	Sweden (1)	Canada (8)
Low	Guinea-Bissau (151)	Afghanistan (142)	Albania (60)	Haiti (116)

Rank	Country	Physical Quality of Life Index	Rank	Country	Physical Quality of Life Index	Rank	Country	Physical Quality of Life Index
	TOP 10		51	Fiji	83	102	Morocco	40
1	Sweden	100	52	Sri Lanka	83	103	Botswana	38
2	Iceland	99	53	Panama	81	104	Iran	38
3	Netherlands	99	54	Grenada	80	105	Pakistan	37
4	Norway	99	55	South Korea	80	106	Swaziland	36
5	Denmark	98	56	Lebanon	80	107	Papua New Guinea	34
6	Japan	98	57	Venezuela	80	108	United Arab Emirates	34
7	Switzerland	98	58	Portugal	79	109	Bangladesh	33
8	Canada	97	59	Chile	77	110	Sudan	33
9	France	97	60	Albania	76	111	Tanzania	33
10	United Kingdom	97	61	Kuwait	76	112	Uganda	33
			62	Mauritius	75	113	Laos	32
	UPPER MIDDLE		63	Mexico	75	114	Qatar	32
11	Australia	96	64	Paraguay	74	115	Ghana	31
12	East Germany	96	65	Reunion	74	116	Haiti	31
13	Ireland	96	66	Philippines	73	117	Malawi	29
14	Luxembourg	96	67	Colombia	71	118	Saudi Arabia	29
15	New Zealand	96	68	Thailand	70	119	Sierra Leone	29
16	United States	96	69	Tonga	70	120	Cameroon	28
17	Austria	95	70	Brazil	68	121	Equatorial Guinea	28
18	Belgium	95	71	Ecuador	68	122	Ivory Coast	28
19	Czechoslovakia	95	72	El Salvador	67	123	Tanzania	28
20	Finland	95	73	Dominican Republic	64	124	Togo	28
21	West Germany	95	74	Bahrain	60	125	Zaire	28
22	Bulgaria	94	75	Vietnam	60	126	Zambia	28
23	Italy	94	76	China	59	127	Rwanda	27
24	Poland	94	77	Malaysia	59	128	Yemen Arab Republic	27
25	Soviet Union	94				129	South Yemen	27
26	Spain	94		**LOWER MIDDLE**		130	Liberia	26
27	Hungary	92	78	Peru	58	131	Congo	25
28	Puerto Rico	92	79	Turkey	54	132	Nepal	25
29	Rumania	92	80	Guatemala	53	133	Nigeria	25
30	Greece	91	81	Nicaragua	53	134	Benin	23
31	Israel	90	82	Syria	52	135	Burundi	23
32	Malta	89	83	Burma	51	136	Mozambique	23
33	Barbados	88	84	Honduras	50	137	Gambia	22
34	Taiwan	88	85	Indonesia	50	138	Senegal	22
35	Hong Kong	88	86	Lesotho	50	139	Gabon	21
36	Martinique	88	87	Jordan	48	140	Chad	20
37	Trinidad & Tobago	88	88	South Africa	48	141	Guinea	20
38	Uruguay	88	89	Cape Verde	46			
39	Bahamas	87	90	Egypt	46		**BOTTOM 10**	
40	Costa Rica	87	91	Iraq	46	142	Afghanistan	19
41	Cyprus	87	92	Bolivia	45	143	Somalia	19
42	Jamaica	87	93	Madagascar	44	144	Central African Empire	18
43	Cuba	86	94	Tunisia	44	145	Upper Volta	17
44	Western Samoa	86	95	Algeria	42	146	Ethiopia	16
45	Guadeloupe	85	96	Libya	42	147	Angola	15
46	Singapore	85	97	Rhodesia (Zimbabwe)	42	148	Mali	15
47	Surinam	85	98	Cambodia	41	149	Mauritania	15
48	Yugoslavia	85	99	India	41	150	Niger	14
49	Argentina	84	100	Comoros	40	151	Guinea-Bissau	10
50	Guyana	84	101	Kenya	40			

Source: Overseas Development Council, Washington, D.C.

248. Hospital Beds

Hospital establishments include general and specialized hospitals, as well as other medical establishments with beds, such as medical centers, bedded dispensaries, leprosaria, rehabilitation and physiotherapy centers, establishments for alcoholics and convalescent homes. Care should be taken in interpreting the data in this ranking because in almost all countries of the world hospitals are unduly concentrated in urban areas so that the rural population does not receive the medical advantages their urban counterparts enjoy. Also, it must be kept in mind that the very definition of what constitutes a hospital can vary widely.

Number of Countries: 189
Midpoint: 257
Period Covered: Mid-1970s
Type of Ranking: Population per Hospital Bed; Total Number of Hospital Beds; Lowest to Highest

Highlights & Findings: The presence in the top ranks of small island territories that were or are dependencies may be surprising, but in many cases these facilities were built by the former or present colonial masters, often in excess of local requirements. The other four countries in the top 10 are the Scandinavian countries, where the provision of medical care is a prime component of the perceived philosophy of state welfarism. The fact that the last country on the list has 315 times more inhabitants per hospital bed as the top nation is an indication of the unevenness of health care around the world.

Regions	Africa	Asia & Oceania	Europe	Western Hemisphere
Most	St. Helena (1)	Wallis & Futuna (2)	Monaco (5)	St. Pierre & Miquelon (6)
Least	Ethiopia (186)	Nepal (189)	Cyprus (78)	Haiti (174)

Rank	Country	Population per Hospital Bed	Total Number of Beds	Rank	Country	Population per Hospital Bed	Total Number of Beds	Rank	Country	Population per Hospital Bed	Total Number of Beds
	TOP 10			47	Montserrat	116	86	96	Bahrain	257	1,012
1	St. Helena	21	57	48	Hungary	116	90,104				
2	Wallis & Futuna Islands	33	108	49	Bulgaria	116	75,037		*LOWER MIDDLE*		
3	Sao Tome & Principe	33	1,997	50	England & Wales	117	420,943	97	Lebanon	260	10,727
4	Nauru	34	207	51	Gibraltar	119	252	98	Costa Rica	261	7,549
5	Monaco	63	318	52	Solomon Islands	120	1,413	99	Mauritius	266	3,230
6	St. Pierre & Miquelon	64	78	53	Reunion	121	3,886	100	Brazil	266	382,952
7	Sweden	66	124,350	54	Poland	129	264,103	101	Malaysia	273	35,150
8	Finland	66	71,115	55	Qatar	130	661	102	Cayman Islands	275	40
9	Iceland	69	3,209	56	French Polynesia	132	961	103	Singapore	281	8,005
10	Norway	71	56,636	57	Grenada	144	692	104	Panama	284	5,880
				58	Seychelles	147	3,481	105	Swaziland	285	1,717
	UPPER MIDDLE			59	United States	152	1,401,624	106	British Virgin Islands	294	34
11	Falkland Islands	74	27	60	South Africa	152	156,245	107	Turks & Caicos	300	20
12	Greenland	75	666	61	Bermuda	153	392	108	Brunei	302	529
13	Australia	81	160,552	62	Antigua	154	454	109	Tonga	303	330
14	Soviet Union	85	3,009,200	63	Greece	155	58,501	110	Rhodesia (Zimbabwe)	316	19,285
15	Scotland	85	61,339	64	Albania	164	12,715	111	Angola	322	18,011
16	West Germany	85	729,791	65	Yugoslavia	167	127,646	112	Zaire	327	72,090
17	Switzerland	86	72,268	66	Niue Island	167	30	113	Botswana	332	2,074
18	New Caledonia	87	1,501	67	Faroe Islands	167	240	114	Sri Lanka	333	39,732
19	Austria	88	85,461	68	Papua New Guinea	169	15,255	115	Venezuela	334	35,867
20	Northern Ireland	89	17,299	69	St. Vincent	170	529	116	Fiji	350	1,513
21	Guadeloupe	92	3,566	70	Equatorial Guinea	171	1,637	117	Dominican Republic	351	12,618
22	East Germany	92	184,214	71	Israel	174	19,501	118	Algeria	356	39,053
23	New Zealand	93	31,959	72	Argentina	176	133,847	119	Chile	362	38,319
24	Ireland	93	33,772	73	Portugal	181	52,268	120	Guam	370	243
25	Luxembourg	94	3,848	74	St. Kitts-Nevis-Anguilla	182	385	121	Cameroon	390	16,734
26	Italy	95	575,162	75	Surinam	184	2,288	122	Laos	401	3,232
27	Malta	96	3,431	76	Spain	190	185,218	123	Madagascar	405	19,781
28	Japan	96	1,163,726	77	Congo	195	6,912	124	Tunisia	427	13,145
29	Namibia	97	6,905	78	Cyprus	195	3,286	125	Turkey	456	85,872
30	Gabon	98	4,995	79	Guyana	199	3,969	126	Guatemala	457	12,115
31	France	98	534,023	80	St. Lucia	202	545	127	Comoros	458	612
32	Netherlands	99	136,216	81	Macao	209	1,275	128	Nicaragua	462	4,675
33	Czechoslovakia	99	149,976	82	Belize	218	642	129	Egypt	469	79,399
34	Martinique	101	3,281	83	Puerto Rico	219	13,354	130	Lesotho	482	2,114
35	New Hebrides	102	924	84	Pacific Islands	223	538	131	Iraq	485	22,942
36	Mongolia	103	13,648	85	Trinidad & Tobago	224	4,815	132	Ecuador	495	13,594
37	Denmark	103	47,709	86	Samoa	229	655	133	Peru	497	29,086
38	Djibouti	107	1,028	87	Bahamas	229	874	134	Central African Empire	522	3,161
39	Netherlands Antilles	109	1,969	88	Dominica	234	312	135	Bolivia	522	9,451
40	Canada	109	206,763	89	Cuba	234	39,863	136	Colombia	530	44,642
41	Rumania	110	191,910	90	Uruguay	235	11,812	137	United Arab Emirates	550	34,750
42	Gilbert Islands	110	634	91	Kuwait	235	4,255	138	El Salvador	563	7,127
43	Barbados	111	2,161	92	Hong Kong	241	18,156	139	Somalia	569	5,163
44	Cook Islands	112	179	93	Libya	242	10,080	140	Rwanda	583	7,201
45	Belgium	112	87,164	94	Zambia	250	19,901	141	Guinea Bissau	596	889
46	French Guyana	115	523	95	Jamaica	257	7,780	142	Honduras	598	4,602

Rank	Country	Population per Hospital Bed	Total Number of Beds	Rank	Country	Population per Hospital Bed	Total Number of Beds	Rank	Country	Population per Hospital Bed	Total Number of Beds
143	Guinea	599	6,858	160	Tanzania	775	16,640	177	Niger	1,200	3,734
144	Ghana	599	16,476	161	Benin	781	3,984	178	Mali	1,347	4,129
145	Uganda	636	18,156	162	Oman	783	984	179	Yemen Arab Republic	1,443	4,200
146	Philippines	639	62,939	163	Thailand	796	51,215				
147	Malawi	639	6,951	164	Burundi	806	4,221		*BOTTOM 10*		
148	Iran	650	49,194	165	Mexico	863	67,363	180	South Korea	1,515	22,089
149	South Yemen	665	2,340	166	Cambodia	893	7,500	181	India	1,590	331,633
150	Cape Verde	665	376	167	Sierra Leone	927	2,837	182	Indonesia	1,625	83,696
151	Togo	680	3,075	168	Jordan	937	1,986	183	Pakistan	2,070	33,948
152	Liberia	682	2,184	169	Saudi Arabia	968	9,270	184	Mauritania	2,328	567
153	Paraguay	694	3,816	170	Sudan	982	16,020	185	Maldives	2,600	45
154	Gambia	697	488	171	Syria	1,071	6,865	186	Ethiopia	3,081	8,415
155	Ivory Coast	730	6,701	172	Chad	1,140	3,464	187	Bangladesh	5,644	13,610
156	Senegal	735	5,635	173	Nigeria	1,168	53,889	188	Afghanistan	6,592	2,852
157	Morocco	748	23,140	174	Haiti	1,169	3,917	189	Nepal	6,630	1,858
158	Kenya	759	15,904	175	Upper Volta	1,174	4,675				
159	Mozambique	772	11,041	176	Burma	1,180	25,567				

Source: World Health Organization.

249. Mental Hospital Beds

A major dimension of mental health care is the availability of hospital beds and related facilities for mental patients. Some of these beds are in full-fledged mental hospitals; others are in psychiatric wards of general hospitals.

Number of Countries: 113
Midpoint: 5.3 Beds per 10,000 Inhabitants
Period Covered: 1975
Type of Ranking: Number of Beds for Mental Patients per 10,000 Inhabitants; Highest to Lowest

Highlights & Findings: As the ranking reveals, adequate facilities for mental patients exist in very few countries. The concept that mental patients need institutionalization is only slowly gaining ground outside of the Western world. However, in the industrialized countries institutionalization is losing favor to treatment based on outpatient care. In the majority of the reporting countries, less than one bed is available for every 1,000 inhabitants.

Region	Africa	Asia & Oceania	Europe	Western Hemisphere
Most	Reunion (41)	Australia (19)	Finland (1)	Bermuda (8)
Least	Sudan (113)	Bangladesh (112)	Yugoslavia (56)	Haiti (103)

Rank	Country	Mental Hospital Beds per 10,000 Inhabitants	Rank	Country	Mental Hospital Beds per 10,000 Inhabitants	Rank	Country	Mental Hospital Beds per 10,000 Inhabitants
	TOP 10		12	Barbados	25.8	26	Guadeloupe	16.6
1	Finland	52.3	13	Iceland	24.8	27	New Caledonia	16.0
2	Ireland	49.1	14	Canada	23.9	28	St. Lucia	15.7
3	Scotland	48.9	15	Netherlands Antilles	23.3	29	Jamaica	15.0
4	Sweden	41.5	16	Gibraltar	22.2	30	United States	14.2
5	Luxembourg	38.2	17	Antigua	21.6	31	Greece	13.7
6	Malta	38.1	18	Denmark	21.1	32	Trinidad & Tobago	13.5
7	England	31.9	19	Australia	20.7	33	Surinam	13.4
8	Bermuda	31.8	20	Netherlands	20.5	34	Bahamas	13.0
9	Norway	31.1	21	Israel	20.1	35	Spain	12.3
10	Switzerland	28.9	22	East Germany	18.9	36	Poland	12.1
			23	Japan	18.4	37	Portugal	12.0
	UPPER MIDDLE		24	West Germany	17.8	38	Singapore	11.5
11	Belgium	26.9	25	Cyprus	16.9	39	Czechoslovakia	11.3

Rank	Country	Mental Hospital Beds per 10,000 Inhabitants	Rank	Country	Mental Hospital Beds per 10,000 Inhabitants	Rank	Country	Mental Hospital Beds per 10,000 Inhabitants
40	Martinique	11.0	64	Hong Kong	3.4	90	Peru	1.1
41	Reunion	10.5	65	Botswana	2.9	91	Bolivia	0.9
42	Belize	9.9	66	Colombia	2.8	92	Taiwan	0.9
43	Mauritius	9.8	67	Ecuador	2.8	93	Syria	0.9
44	Seychelles	9.2	68	Sarawak	2.8	94	Tanzania (Tanganyika)	0.9
45	Argentina	8.7	69	Dominica	2.6	95	Uganda	0.9
46	St. Vincent	7.7	70	Fiji	2.6	96	Honduras	0.7
47	Costa Rica	7.6	71	Nicaragua	2.2	97	South Yemen	0.7
48	Cuba	7.2	72	Sri Lanka	2.2	98	Indonesia	0.6
49	Rumania	7.0	73	El Salvador	2.0	99	Ivory Coast	0.6
50	Bahrain	6.9	74	Paraguay	2.0	100	Madagascar	0.6
51	Malaysia (West)	6.9	75	Tunisia	1.9	101	Malawi	0.6
52	Guyana	5.9	76	Guatemala	1.8	102	Liberia	0.5
53	Libya	5.7	77	Thailand	1.8	103	Haiti	0.4
54	Panama	5.7	78	Egypt	1.7	104	Papua New Guinea	0.4
55	Puerto Rico	5.6	79	Philippines	1.7			
56	Yugoslavia	5.3	80	Dominican Republic	1.6		**BOTTOM 9**	
			81	Rhodesia	1.6	105	South Korea	0.3
	LOWER MIDDLE		82	Ghana	1.5	106	Nigeria	0.3
57	Tanzania (Zanzibar)	5.2	83	Iraq	1.4	107	Pakistan	0.3
58	Kuwait	5.0	84	Turkey	1.4	108	Zaire	0.3
59	Swaziland	4.9	85	Mozambique	1.3	109	Benin	0.2
60	Chile	4.6	86	Lesotho	1.2	110	Burma	0.2
61	Mongolia	4.3	87	Somalia	1.2	111	Rwanda	0.2
62	Sabah	4.2	88	Iran	1.1	112	Bangladesh	0.1
63	Venezuela	4.1	89	Mexico	1.1	113	Sudan	0.1

Source: World Health Organization.

250. Physicians per Capita

Physicians per capita is a usually reliable index of the quality of national medical and health care. Because all countries require physicians to be licensed, the number of licensed and practicing physicians is in most cases reported accurately. The index is, however, weak in two respects. It does not reflect the continuing and deplorable drain of physicians from developing countries (where they are so badly needed) to developed countries such as the United States. It also does not reflect the concentration of physicians in urban centers and the resulting disparity between urban and rural health care.

Medical statistics, especially those relating to physicians, are subject to numerous qualifications.

Although virtually every country requires physicians to be licensed, the terms of such license and the quality of education that precedes the license are likely to vary substantially from one country to another. These variations result not merely because of available educational resources but also as a consequence of public policy. Maintenance of high standards may drastically limit the total number of physicians entering the medical marketplace every year, and therefore many developing and Communist countries, such as Albania, have relaxed the standards of medical education. In other countries paraprofessionals are included in the data.

Number of Countries: 184 **Midpoint:** One Physician per 2,341 Inhabitants **Period Covered:** Mid-1970s **Type of Ranking:** Number of Inhabitants per Physician and Total Number of Physicians; Highest to Lowest	**Highlights & Findings:** Of the 10 top countries, five are Communist. Even counting aliens, who constitute 25% of its stock of physicians, the United States ranks only 21st on the list. All the 10 bottom countries are African.

Regions	Africa	Asia & Oceania	Europe	Western Hemisphere
Most	Libya (52)	Israel (3)	Albania (1)	Argentina (7)
Least	Ethiopia (184)	Nepal (176)	Gibraltar (69)	Haiti (146)

Rank	Country	Inhabitants per Physician	Total Number of Physicians
	TOP 10		
1	Albania	159	14,371
2	Monaco	351	57
3	Israel	351	9,143
4	Soviet Union	363	697,400
5	Czechoslovakia	432	33,996
6	Hungary	459	22,835
7	Argentina	460	53,684
8	Bulgaria	476	18,238
9	Austria	498	15,168
10	Greece	499	17,942
	UPPER MIDDLE		
11	Italy	502	109,166
12	West Germany	516	120,260
13	Mongolia	538	2,604
14	East Germany	557	30,798
15	Belgium	566	17,272
16	Switzerland	591	10,904
17	Poland	592	56,949
18	Canada	603	37,277
19	Norway	605	6,590
20	Falkland Islands	606	3
21	United States	622	338,111
22	Denmark	624	8,000
23	Sweden	645	12,610
24	Iceland	654	321
25	Netherlands	670	20,200
26	Spain	673	51,743
27	France	681	77,143
28	Nauru	700	10
29	Australia	721	17,972
30	Finland	752	6,234
31	United Kingdom	761	64,600
32	Kuwait	800	1,050
33	Rumania	805	25,870
34	Ireland	836	3,565
35	New Zealand	846	3,426
36	Puerto Rico	848	3,479
37	Yugoslavia	849	24,920
38	Portugal	851	10,312
39	Venezuela	866	13,017
40	Japan	868	124,684
41	Cayman Islands	874	13
42	Cook Islands	909	22
43	Uruguay	911	3,250
44	Qatar	938	96
45	Luxembourg	978	368
46	Malta	988	334
47	United Arab Emirates	995	211
48	Niue Island	1,000	5
49	Bermuda	1,034	58
50	St. Pierre & Miquelon	1,064	5
51	Cyprus	1,131	557
52	Libya	1,139	2,063
53	Cuba	1,153	7,000
54	New Caledonia	1,161	112
55	Greenland	1,190	42
56	Panama	1,234	1,313
57	Faroe Islands	1,250	32
58	Lebanon	1,330	2,300
59	Bahrain	1,348	178
60	Mexico	1,385	38,000
61	Singapore	1,400	1,586
62	British Virgin Islands	1,428	7
63	Bahamas	1,449	138
64	French Guyana	1,463	41
65	Martinique	1,481	243
66	Macao	1,492	181
67	Barbados	1,500	160
68	Hong Kong	1,561	2,723
69	Gibraltar	1,579	19
70	Costa Rica	1,582	1,213
71	Guadeloupe	1,613	217
72	St. Helena	1,666	3
73	Montserrat	1,667	6
74	Nicaragua	1,713	1,214
75	Netherlands Antilles	1,783	120
76	Peru	1,802	8,023
77	Turkey	1,834	20,868
78	Dominican Republic	1,866	2,374
79	Paraguay	1,875	1,370
80	Reunion	1,983	237
81	Djibouti	2,000	52
82	Turks & Caicos	2,000	3
83	South Africa	2,016	12,060
84	Brazil	2,025	48,726
85	Surinam	2,030	202
86	Fiji	2,070	256
87	French Polynesia	2,097	62
88	Bolivia	2,117	2,583
89	Trinidad & Tobago	2,157	494
90	Pacific Islands	2,182	55
91	Colombia	2,184	10,625
92	Chile	2,341	4,306
93	Iraq	2,369	4,545
94	Jordan	2,438	763
95	South Korea	2,571	13,013
96	Philippines	2,632	14,000
97	Gilbert Islands	2,727	22
98	Iran	2,752	11,373
99	Antigua	2,800	25
100	Syria	2,905	2,371
101	Ecuador	2,928	2,080
102	Western Samoa	3,076	52
	LOWER MIDDLE		
103	Seychelles	3,125	16
104	Belize	3,171	41
105	New Hebrides	3,200	25
106	Guyana	3,249	237
107	St.Kitts-Nevis-Anguilla	3,250	20
108	Tonga	3,333	30
109	Wallis Futuna Islands	3,333	3
110	Honduras	3,352	874
111	Jamaica	3,509	570
112	Mauritius	3,617	235
113	Brunei	3,659	41
114	Pakistan	3,967	17,194
115	Grenada	4,000	25
116	Sri Lanka	4,007	3,251
117	El Salvador	4,063	950
118	India	4,162	138,000
119	Guatemala	4,338	1,208
120	Solomon Islands	4,474	38
121	St. Lucia	4,583	24
122	Egypt	4,859	7,495
123	Saudi Arabia	4,995	2,000
124	Oman	5,034	147
125	Gabon	5,208	96
126	Tunisia	5,219	1,004
127	St. Vincent	5,263	19
128	Dominica	5,385	13
129	Rhodesia (Zimbabwe)	5,700	1,035
130	Congo	6,173	162
131	Sao Tome & Principe	6,666	12
132	Burma	6,906	4,280
133	Malaysia	7,487	1,556
134	Zambia	8,159	527
135	Algeria	8,192	1,698
136	Thailand	8,513	4,662
137	Swaziland	8,888	54
138	Bangladesh	9,345	7,663
139	Vietnam	10,143	1,883
140	Botswana	10,476	63
141	Madagascar	11,018	687
142	Ghana	11,227	856
143	Equatorial Guinea	11,600	25
144	Sudan	12,371	1,400
145	Liberia	12,576	132
146	Haiti	13,034	346
147	Morocco	13,802	1,223
148	Comoros	13,810	21
149	Senegal	14,092	281
150	Cambodia	15,297	438
151	Angola	15,404	383
152	Somalia	15,544	193
153	Kenya	16,292	766
154	Mozambique	16,392	510
155	Sierra Leone	17,114	149
156	Guinea-Bissau	17,667	30
157	Mauritania	17,746	71
158	Indonesia	18,863	7,027
159	Gambia	18,947	19
160	Cape Verde	19,230	13
161	Lesotho	20,400	50
162	Uganda	20,685	225
163	Togo	21,200	100
164	Laos	21,589	151
165	Guinea	22,394	188
166	Maldives	24,000	5
167	Nigeria	25,463	2,343
168	Cameroon	25,956	225
169	Afghanistan	26,091	701
170	Yemen Arab Republic	26,449	245
171	Central African Empire	27,097	59
172	Tanzania	27,572	494
173	Zaire	28,802	818
174	South Yemen	32,380	42
	BOTTOM 10		
175	Benin	36,071	84
176	Nepal	36,450	338
177	Malawi	37,982	114
178	Mali	38,963	135
179	Niger	41,101	109
180	Chad	44,382	89
181	Burundi	48,649	74
182	Rwanda	53,506	77
183	Upper Volta	59,595	99
184	Ethiopia	73,314	350

Source: World Health Organization.

251. Nurses per Capita

Nursing personnel include graduate, practical and assistant nurses. Because definitions of nursing personnel vary widely from country to country the data may be not strictly comparable.

Number of Countries: 96
Midpoint: One nurse per 1,570 Inhabitants
Period Covered: 1974
Type of Ranking: Number of Inhabitants per Nursing Person; Highest to Lowest

Highlights & Findings: As a group, Communist countries appear to have the highest level of nursing care with one nurse for every 245 inhabitants and low-income countries the lowest with only one nurse for every 6,710 inhabitants. In between, industrialized countries as a group have one nurse for every 230 inhabitants, oil-producing countries one nurse for every 1,570 inhabitants and middle-income countries one nurse for every 1,570 inhabitants. Because low-income countries have a greater incidence of disease, the paucity of nurses becomes critical in health care delivery.

Regions	Africa	Asia & Oceania	Europe	Western Hemisphere
Most	Libya (22)	New Zealand (7)	Denmark (1)	Canada (3)
Least	Zaire (93)	Bangladesh (96)	Greece (41)	Haiti (85)

Rank	Country	Inhabitants per Nurse
	TOP 10	
1	Denmark	120
2	Finland	130
3	Canada	140
4	Sweden	150
5	Norway	150
6	United States	160
7	New Zealand	160
8	Czechoslovakia	170
9	Rumania	180
10	France	190
	UPPER MIDDLE	
11	Soviet Union	210
12	Hungary	220
13	United Kingdom	270
14	Poland	270
15	Bulgaria	270
16	West Germany	280
17	Kuwait	290
18	Switzerland	300
19	Austria	300
20	Netherlands	320
21	Japan	330
22	Libya	340
23	Singapore	390
24	Italy	390
25	South Africa	440
26	Yugoslavia	450
27	Venezuela	470
28	Chile	470
29	Albania	520
30	Jamaica	540
31	Costa Rica	640
32	Congo	640

Rank	Country	Inhabitants per Nurse
33	Nicaragua	760
34	Portugal	810
35	Ghana	870
36	Tunisia	980
37	Jordan	1,020
38	Argentina	1,040
39	El Salvador	1,140
40	Turkey	1,240
41	Greece	1,280
42	Kenya	1,300
43	Panama	1,440
44	South Korea	1,500
45	Honduras	1,540
46	Sudan	1,550
47	Hong Kong	1,550
48	Malaysia	1,570
49	Angola	1,870
50	Iran	1,910
	LOWER MIDDLE	
51	Senegal	1,920
52	Colombia	1,920
53	Ivory Coast	2,220
54	Central African Empire	2,260
55	Cameroon	2,270
56	Papua New Guinea	2,290
57	Paraguay	2,340
58	Zambia	2,430
59	Mali	2,480
60	Togo	2,490
61	Sri Lanka	2,532
62	Syria	2,620
63	Peru	2,870
64	Ecuador	2,880
65	Lesotho	2,970

Rank	Country	Inhabitants per Nurse
66	Tanzania	3,180
67	Benin	3,220
68	Iraq	3,310
69	Bolivia	3,520
70	Madagascar	3,580
71	Lebanon	3,670
72	Taiwan	3,740
73	Mauritania	3,790
74	Guinea	4,230
75	Thailand	4,330
76	Egypt	4,420
77	Liberia	4,500
78	Upper Volta	4,520
79	Niger	4,840
80	Saudi Arabia	5,510
81	Nigeria	6,230
82	India	6,530
83	Malawi	6,550
84	Uganda	6,870
85	Haiti	6,920
86	Chad	6,990
	BOTTOM 10	
87	Burma	7,040
88	Burundi	7,090
89	Indonesia	8,630
90	Pakistan	11,350
91	Yemen Arab Republic	11,400
92	Rwanda	11,480
93	Zaire	11,770
94	Afghanistan	28,410
95	Nepal	36,770
96	Bangladesh	75,460

Source: World Health Organization.

252. Dentists per Capita

The quality of dental care is best measured by the number of practicing dentists per capita. Other factors influencing dental care delivery are the availability of dental instruments and prosthetic devices as well as fluoridation of water. Dental service appears to be the most neglected of all medical services in most parts of the world.

Number of Countries: 179
Midpoint: One Dentist per 12,710 Inhabitants
Period Covered: 1975
Type of Ranking: Number of Inhabitants per Dentist; Highest to Lowest

Highlights & Findings: Dental authorities have suggested that there should be at least one dentist per 4,000 inhabitants to ensure reasonably good dental care. Only 41 countries meet this standard. The amount of time that each dentist could devote, theoretically, to one patient varies from 2.47 hours per year in top-ranking Monaco to four seconds in Rwanda.

Region	Africa	Asia & Oceania	Europe	Western Hemisphere
Most	St. Helena (52)	Israel (4)	Monaco (1)	United States (10)
Least	Rwanda (179)	Nepal (177)	Spain (79)	St. Vincent (121)

Rank	Country	Inhabitants per Dentist	Rank	Country	Inhabitants per Dentist	Rank	Country	Inhabitants per Dentist
	TOP 10		46	Guam	4,550	92	South Africa	13,430
1	Monaco	970	47	Belgium	4,550	93	Seychelles	13,750
2	Norway	1,090	48	Ireland	4,570	94	St. Kitts	13,750
3	Sweden	1,160	49	Bolivia	4,630	95	South Korea	13,930
4	Israel	1,280	50	Austria	4,950	96	Jordan	15,130
5	Denmark	1,310	51	St. Pierre & Miquelon	5,000	97	Barbados	15,250
6	Finland	1,490	52	St. Helena	5,000	98	Gilbert Islands & Tuvalu	15,750
7	Niue Island	1,670	53	Pacific Islands	5,000	99	Iran	16,410
8	Greece	1,700	54	Lebanon	5,240	100	Brunei	16,670
9	West Germany	1,960	55	Singapore	5,260	101	Iraq	17,060
10	United States	1,970	56	French Polynesia	5,520	102	Libya	17,250
			57	French Guyana	5,560	103	Djibouti	17,330
	UPPER MIDDLE		58	Peru	5,690	104	Egypt	17,480
11	Falkland Islands	2,000	59	Kuwait	5,710	105	Antigua	18,500
12	Iceland	2,020	60	Turks & Caicos	6,000	106	Jamaica	18,670
13	France	2,090	61	Montserrat	6,000	107	Trinidad & Tobago	19,810
14	Poland	2,150	62	Malta	6,130	108	Honduras	21,250
15	Uruguay	2,200	63	Bahamas	6,160	109	Guatemala	21,920
16	East Germany	2,260	64	American Samoa	6,200	110	Grenada	24,000
17	Bermuda	2,290	65	Reunion	6,320	111	Ecuador	24,010
18	Cook Island	2,330	66	Gibraltar	6,750	112	Trinidad & Tobago	27,400
19	Czechoslovakia	2,360	67	Nicaragua	6,950	113	Belize	33,000
20	Greenland	2,380	68	Costa Rica	7,170	114	Guyana	35,180
21	Bulgaria	2,410	69	Colombia	7,370	115	Dominica	35,500
22	Australia	2,460	70	Chile	7,400	116	St. Lucia	35,670
23	Soviet Union	2,480	71	Netherlands Antilles	7,410	117	Rhodesia (Zimbabwe)	36,420
24	Switzerland	2,510	72	Albania	7,570	118	Malaysia (West)	38,880
25	Canada	2,650	73	Panama	7,770	119	Sri Lanka	46,550
26	Japan	2,740	74	Guadeloupe	7,780	120	Haiti	47,020
27	New Zealand	2,890	75	Turkey	8,060	121	St. Vincent	47,500
28	Cyprus	2,890	76	Hong Kong	8,190	122	Vietnam	51,620
29	New Caldonia	2,980	77	Dominican Republic	8,590	123	Solomon Islands	55,330
30	Luxembourg	3,030	78	Mexico	9,620	124	Tunisia	58,450
31	Northern Ireland	3,090	79	Spain	9,650	125	Algeria	60,140
32	Scotland	3,100	80	Philippines	9,750	126	Mauritius	62,290
33	Brazil	3,120	81	Anguilla	10,000	127	India	65,620
34	Netherlands	3,290	82	Samoa	10,860	128	Thailand	66,760
35	Hungary	3,380	83	Sarawak	10,990	129	Indonesia	67,150
36	England & Wales	3,460	84	El Salvador	11,200	130	Sabah	70,000
37	Nauru	3,500	85	British Virgin Islands	12,000	131	Swaziland	79,670
38	Venezuela	3,650	86	Mongolia	12,090	132	New Hebrides	90,000
39	Cayman Islands	3,670	87	Bahrain	12,150	133	Cambodia	98,140
40	Faroe Islands	3,800	88	Tonga	12,250	134	Madagascar	99,700
41	Rumania	3,940	89	Syria	12,280	135	Congo	100,400
42	Paraguay	4,040	90	Qatar	12,710	136	Pakistan	114,260
43	Puerto Rico	4,380				137	Botswana	115,000
44	Yugoslavia	4,410		*LOWER MIDDLE*		138	Sudan	116,270
45	Martinique	4,530	91	Fiji	13,280	139	Zambia	122,140

Rank	Country	Inhabitants per Dentist	Rank	Country	Inhabitants per Dentist	Rank	Country	Inhabitants per Dentist
140	Gabon	125,000	154	Ivory Coast	226,900	168	Cameroon	590,000
141	Liberia	127,620	155	Guinea	233,780	169	Malawi	649,860
142	Oman	128,330	156	Mauritania	251,400			
143	Macao	133,000	157	South Yemen	272,000		*BOTTOM 10*	
144	Comoros	145,500	158	Cape Verde	285,000	170	Upper Volta	655,220
145	Morocco	148,070	159	Central African Empire	330,000	171	Zaire	714,380
146	Senegal	148,790	160	Lesotho	338,670	172	Niger	746,000
147	Papua New Guinea	156,000	161	Gambia	360,000	173	Somalia	750,750
148	Tanzania	177,000	162	Benin	378,630	174	Mali	777,670
149	Kenya	192,030	163	Togo	529,250	175	Ethiopia	1,080,540
150	Burma	202,470	164	Mozambique	531,750	176	Burundi	1,134,330
151	Laos	203,560	165	Nigeria	578,710	177	Nepal	1,539,880
152	Sierra Leone	212,500	166	Uganda	588,000	178	Chad	1,974,500
153	Ghana	218,340	167	Yemen Arab Republic	588,820	179	Rwanda	2,061,500

Source: World Health Organization.

253. Pharmacists per Capita

Pharmacists constitute an important link in the chain of health care and delivery services, but their role is often ignored or obscured by the greater visibility of other medical personnel. In only a few countries do pharmacists undergo rigorous training, but in almost all countries they are licensed and also subject to penalties for dispensing illegal drugs or improper prescriptions.

Number of Countries: 160
Midpoint: One Pharmacist per 12,697 Inhabitants
Period Covered: 1976
Type of Ranking: Number of Inhabitants per Pharmacist and Total Number of Pharmacists; Highest to Lowest

Highlights & Findings: Small countries dominate the top of the list, a peculiarity that this ranking shares with many similar rankings. Even in highly developed countries, there is only one pharmacist for a good-sized neighborhood or suburb; descending down the scale there is only one pharmacist for whole cities or towns and toward the bottom only a handful of pharmacists for an entire country.

Region	Africa	Asia & Oceania	Europe	Western Hemisphere
Most	Reunion (42)	Cook Islands (8)	Monaco (1)	French Guyana (2)
Least	Zaire (160)	South Yemen (156)	Sweden (76)	Mexico (153)

Rank	Country	Inhabitants per Pharmacist	Total Number of Pharmacists	Rank	Country	Inhabitants per Pharmacist	Total Number of Pharmacists	Rank	Country	Inhabitants per Pharmacist	Total Number of Pharmacists
	TOP 10			16	Israel	1,685	2,012	34	Bulgaria	2,854	3,055
1	Monaco	43	46	17	South Korea	1,852	18,729	35	St. Pierre & Miquelon	2,920	2
2	French Guyana	545	11	18	Spain	1,894	18,592	36	Bermuda	3,000	2
3	Grenada	600	15	19	France	2,062	25,272	37	Costa Rica	3,088	638
4	St. Kitts-Nevis-Anguilla	636	11	20	Iceland	2,100	100	38	Netherlands	3,089	4,350
5	Gibraltar	750	4	21	Luxembourg	2,155	167	39	Portugal	3,105	3,043
6	Albania	766	2,714	22	Poland	2,347	14,496	40	Martinique	3,142	105
7	Finland	959	4,912	23	Czechoslovakia	2,431	6,089	41	United Kingdom	3,255	17,194
8	Cook Islands	1,000	2	24	Hungary	2,443	4,289	42	Reunion	3,286	143
9	Malta	1,126	293	25	Denmark	2,465	2,000	43	New Caledonia	3,611	36
10	New Zealand	1,242	2,374	26	United Arab Emirates	2,488	72	44	Venezuela	3,617	3,315
				27	West Germany	2,494	24,787	45	Trinidad & Tobago	3,913	276
	UPPER MIDDLE			28	Bolivia	2,592	1,902	46	Lebanon	4,036	612
11	Belgium	1,271	7,688	29	Austria	2,600	2,892	47	Rumania	4,113	5,113
12	Italy	1,443	37,689	30	Puerto Rico	2,734	1,079	48	Antigua	4,117	17
13	Japan	1,499	74,431	31	Kuwait	2,747	364	49	Dominican Republic	4,159	1,065
14	Ireland	1,584	1,976	32	Norway	2,794	1,435	50	Guadeloupe	4,177	79
15	United States	1,606	132,899	33	Cyprus	2,844	225	51	Nicaragua	4,490	481

Rank	Country	Inhabitants per Pharmacist	Total Number of Pharmacists	Rank	Country	Inhabitants per Pharmacist	Total Number of Pharmacists	Rank	Country	Inhabitants per Pharmacist	Total Number of Pharmacists
52	Yugoslavia	5,095	4,190	88	Rhodesia (Zimbabwe)	18,885	323	126	Comoros	93,333	3
53	South Africa	5,106	4,761	89	Colombia	19,700	1,200	127	Ivory Coast	98,222	45
54	Cayman Islands	5,230	2	90	Bahrain	20,000	13	128	Botswana	98,571	7
55	Libya	5,351	456	91	Tunisia	20,326	276	129	New Hebrides	100,000	1
56	East Germany	5,540	3,054	92	Thailand	21,317	1,913	130	Guyana	112,857	7
57	Turkey	5,595	7,002	93	Ghana	21,456	460	131	Guinea	128,437	32
58	Syria	5,856	1,255	94	Saudi Arabia	22,258	403	132	Central African Empire	135,071	14
59	Peru	5,892	2,422	95	Surinam	28,000	15	133	Belize	140,000	1
60	Nauru	6,057	1	96	Sri Lanka	28,791	455	134	Somalia	140,000	21
61	Jamaica	6,590	305	97	Djibouti	30,000	6	135	Oman	154,000	5
62	Dominica	7,000	1	98	Qatar	30,000	3	136	Guinea-Bissau	163,333	3
63	Gilbert Islands	7,000	1	99	Sudan	31,087	506	137	Lesotho	204,000	5
64	Singapore	7,812	288	100	Cape Verde	32,500	8	138	Liberia	204,285	7
65	India	7,944	66,360	101	Gabon	32,666	15	139	Laos	206,250	16
66	Iraq	8,011	1,388	102	Chile	32,747	313	140	Malaysia	217,500	52
67	Mongolia	8,139	172	103	Morocco	34,620	500	141	Gambia	220,000	2
68	Philippines	8,563	4,685	104	Argentina	36,033	668	142	Mauritania	264,000	5
69	Iran	8,829	3,640	105	Zambia	39,524	126	143	Ethiopia	272,526	95
70	St. Lucia	9,166	12	106	Nigeria	42,462	1,482	144	Yemen Arab Republic	303,000	20
71	Jordan	9,193	285	107	Senegal	44,516	93	145	Burundi	319,090	11
72	Honduras	9,615	286	108	Ecuador	45,205	146	146	Tanzania	340,256	29
73	British Virgin Islands	9,825	1	109	Seychelles	50,000	1	147	Afghanistan	354,716	53
74	El Salvador	10,388	386	110	Algeria	52,490	265	148	Mali	370,666	15
75	Paraguay	10,519	231	111	Solomon Islands	56,666	3	149	Sierra Leone	375,714	7
76	Sweden	11,219	730	112	Pacific Islands	60,000	2	150	Bangladesh	393,948	195
77	Netherlands Antilles	11,666	18	113	Mozambique	60,857	140				
78	French Polynesia	12,000	10	114	Swaziland	61,250	8		**BOTTOM 10**		
79	Samoa	12,500	12	115	Macao	65,000	4	151	Burma	443,676	68
80	Brazil	12,697	7,918	116	Cameroon	66,632	98	152	Upper Volta	499,090	11
				117	Angola	66,666	87	153	Mexico	518,928	112
	LOWER MIDDLE			118	Bahamas	66,666	3	154	Rwanda	700,000	6
81	Cuba	13,328	700	119	Benin	74,047	42	155	Niger	746,666	6
82	Fiji	13,589	39	120	Kenya	74,049	163	156	South Yemen	780,000	2
83	Egypt	15,480	2,405	121	Indonesia	81,754	1,664	157	Chad	790,000	5
84	Vietnam	17,299	2,399	122	Togo	87,083	24	158	Uganda	825,000	14
85	Brunei	17,777	9	123	Madagascar	88,131	91	159	Malawi	1,110,000	4
86	Hong Kong	18,675	234	124	Cambodia	91,898	79	160	Zaire	1,812,307	13
87	Mauritius	18,695	46	125	Papua New Guinea	92,142	28				

Source: World Health Organization, *World Health Statistics Annual.*

254. Public Health Expenditures

Public health expenditures represent current and capital expenditures by governments for medical care and other health services. They include national health insurance, public health, health expenditures under workmen's compensation, and in some countries public expenditures for family planning. Health expenditures are understated for some countries because of imcomplete reporting at intermediate and local levels of government.

Number of Countries: 140
Midpoint: $8
Period Covered: 1976
Type of Ranking: Health Expenditures per Capita in Dollars; Highest to Lowest

Highlights & Findings: Per capita spending on health worldwide is $51, but there are sharp variations among countries and regions. Developed countries, with average per capita expenditures of $188, spend nearly 38 times as much per person as developing countries for which the comparable figure is only $5. Per capita spending is highest in North America with $236, Oceania with $234 and Western Europe with $237. It is lowest in South Asia with $1, Africa with $4, Latin America with $11, the Far East with $16 and the Middle East with $19. In between, South European countries spend $152 and the Soviet Union and Eastern Europe $72.

Regions	Africa	Asia & Oceania	Europe	Western Hemisphere
Most	Libya (29)	Australia (11)	Sweden (1)	Canada (4)
Least	Zaire (140)	Yemen Arab Republic (139)	Albania (70)	Haiti (125)

Rank	Country	Health Expenditures per Capita ($)	Rank	Country	Health Expenditures per Capita ($)	Rank	Country	Health Expenditures per Capita ($)
	TOP 10		47	Taiwan	22	94	Kenya	4
1	Sweden	582	48	Fiji	22	95	Madagascar	4
2	Denmark	470	49	Panama	22	96	Sri Lanka	4
3	West Germany	424	50	Chile	21	97	Benin	3
4	Canada	413	51	Cuba	20	98	Central African Empire	3
5	Norway	389	52	Cyprus	20	99	China	3
6	France	340	53	Uruguay	16	100	Equatorial Guinea	3
7	Netherlands	336	54	Costa Rica	15	101	Guinea	3
8	Switzerland	318	55	Guyana	15	102	Lesotho	3
9	Finland	315	56	Argentina	14	103	Mauritania	3
10	Belgium	301	57	Dominican Republic	14	104	Philippines	3
			58	Malaysia	14	105	Sierra Leone	3
	UPPER MIDDLE		59	Tunisia	14	106	Somalia	3
11	Australia	293	60	Algeria	12	107	Tanzania	3
12	Austria	220	61	Ivory Coast	12	108	Togo	3
13	United States	218	62	Mauritius	12	109	Gambia	2
14	New Zealand	217	63	Yugoslavia	11	110	Malawi	2
15	United Kingdom	193	64	Mongolia	10	111	Mozambique	2
16	Japan	173	65	Nicaragua	10	112	Paraguay	2
17	Ireland	148	66	Papua New Guinea	10	113	Sudan	2
18	Italy	137	67	Swaziland	10	114	Syria	2
19	Czechoslovakia	133	68	Brazil	9	115	Thailand	2
20	Kuwait	133	69	Congo	9	116	Uganda	2
21	Qatar	120				117	South Yemen	2
22	Luxembourg	112		*LOWER MIDDLE*				
23	East Germany	110	70	Albania	8		*BOTTOM 23*	
24	Israel	101	71	Botswana	8	118	Afghanistan	1
25	Spain	83	72	Mexico	8	119	Bangladesh	1
26	Poland	75	73	Peru	8	120	Burma	1
27	Bahrain	70	74	Rhodesia (Zimbabwe)	8	121	Burundi	1
28	Soviet Union	70	75	Zambia	8	122	Cambodia	1
29	Libya	66	76	Colombia	7	123	Chad	1
30	Hungary	63	77	Egypt	7	124	Ethiopia	1
31	Saudi Arabia	61	78	Lebanon	7	125	Haiti	1
32	Venezuela	58	79	El Salvador	6	126	India	1
33	United Arab Emirates	54	80	Ghana	6	127	Indonesia	1
34	Oman	50	81	Iraq	6	128	North Korea	1
35	Bulgaria	49	82	Liberia	6	129	South Korea	1
36	Malta	49	83	Senegal	6	130	Laos	1
37	Greece	47	84	Turkey	6	131	Mali	1
38	Ireland	46	85	Angola	5	132	Nepal	1
39	Gabon	44	86	Bolivia	5	133	Niger	1
40	Barbados	41	87	Ecuador	5	134	Nigeria	1
41	Rumania	40	88	Guatemala	5	135	Pakistan	1
42	Portugal	39	89	Honduras	5	136	Rwanda	1
43	Trinidad & Tobago	39	90	Jordan	5	137	Upper Volta	1
44	Jamaica	38	91	Morocco	5	138	Vietnam	1
45	Singapore	35	92	South Africa	5	139	Yemen Arab Republic	1
46	Iran	24	93	Cameroon	4	140	Zaire	1

Source: *World Military and Social Expenditures.*

255. Death Rate from Cancer

The most widely available and uniformly compiled statistics relating to cancer are mortality rates. Such data cover about 36% of the world population; in the case of developed countries the data are virtually complete, but in the case of developing countries the coverage is below 5%. In the 39 reporting countries, death from cancer was more common in males than in females in all but two countries: Mexico and El Salvador. Furthermore, an upward trend in the proportion of male to female deaths from cancer is reported in 32 of the countries for which data are available. These trends are accompanied by a decreasing incidence of cancer in the principal female site, the breast, and an increasing incidence in the principal male site, the lung.

Number of Countries: 39
Midpoint: 81%
Period Covered: 1976
Type of Ranking: Deaths from Cancer as Percentage of All Deaths of Persons Aged 55 and over; Number of Male Deaths per 100 Female Deaths; Highest to Lowest

Highlights & Findings: Because of the limited number of reporting countries, no conclusions can be drawn other than the obvious one that in all countries in the ranking except one cancer is the principal cause of death in persons aged 55 and over.

Region	Africa	Asia & Oceania	Europe	Western Hemisphere
Most	Egypt (39)	New Zealand (19)	Austria (1)	United States (20)
Least	N.A.	Hong Kong (37)	Rumania (34)	El Salvador (38)

Rank	Country	Cancer Deaths as Percentage of Deaths of Persons Aged 55 and Over	Male Deaths per 100 Female Deaths	Rank	Country	Cancer Deaths as Percentage of Deaths of Persons Aged 55 and Over	Deaths per 100 Female Deaths	Rank	Country	Cancer Deaths as Percentage of Deaths of Persons Aged 55 and Over	Male Deaths per 100 Female Deaths
		TOP 10		13	Ireland	84	128	28	Argentina	77	160
1	Austria	88	153	14	Scotland	84	161	29	Bulgaria	77	159
2	Sweden	88	127	15	Czechoslovakia	83	172	30	Japan	77	156
3	Belgium	87	165	16	Northern Ireland	83	140	31	Poland	77	154
4	West Germany	87	146	17	Greece	82	169				
5	Norway	86	135	18	Italy	82	168			*BOTTOM 8*	
6	Switzerland	86	162	19	New Zealand	81	144	32	Chile	75	116
7	Denmark	85	126	20	United States	81	148	33	Yugoslavia	75	153
8	England & Wales	85	157	21	Australia	80	154	34	Rumania	74	142
9	France	85	189	22	Canada	80	143	35	Costa Rica	69	113
10	Netherlands	85	161	23	Spain	80	157	36	Mexico	65	77
				24	Uruguay	80	155	37	Hong Kong	62	177
		MIDDLE		25	Puerto Rico	79	146	38	El Salvador	58	61
11	Finland	84	189	26	Israel	78	104	39	Egypt	39	205
12	Hungary	84	146	27	Portugal	78	140				

Source: World Health Organization.

---

256. Death Rate from Cirrhosis of the Liver

Cirrhosis of the liver is significant as a cause of death because the disease is believed to be a consequence of excessive consumption of alcoholic beverages and may therefore reflect the incidence of alcoholism in a country.

Number of Countries: 71
Midpoint: 8.1 per 100,000
Period Covered: Early 1970s
Type of Ranking: Number of Deaths Caused by Cirrhosis of the Liver per 100,000 Inhabitants; Highest to Lowest

Highlights & Findings: The highest incidence is found among Western nations; among the top 10 are eight European nations.

Regions	Africa	Asia & Oceania	Europe	Western Hemisphere
Most	Reunion (13)	Japan (21)	France (2)	Chile (1)
Least	Mozambique (69)	Kuwait (62)	Iceland (71)	Paraguay (70)

Rank	Country	Deaths from Cirrhosis of the Liver per 100,000	Rank	Country	Deaths from Cirrhosis of the Liver per 100,000	Rank	Country	Deaths from Cirrhosis of the Liver per 100,000
	TOP 10		24	Rhodesia (Zimbabwe)	13.0	48	Ecuador	5.6
1	Chile	48.5	25	Switzerland	12.7	49	Finland	5.5
2	France	33.4	26	East Germany	12.5	50	New Zealand	5.3
3	Austria	32.5	27	Canada	11.7	51	St. Lucia	5.3
4	Italy	31.8	28	Trinidad & Tobago	11.0	52	Angola	5.1
5	Portugal	31.3	29	Denmark	10.9	53	Barbados	5.0
6	West Germany	26.9	30	Mauritius	10.7	54	Norway	5.0
7	Puerto Rico	26.2	31	Sweden	10.5	55	Sri Lanka	4.9
8	Luxembourg	24.6	32	Guinea-Bissau	10.3	56	Cape Verde	4.8
9	Spain	22.5	33	Poland	10.2	57	Costa Rica	4.8
10	Rumania	21.3	34	Malta	9.6	58	Netherlands	4.5
			35	Australia	8.3	59	Northern Ireland	4.2
	UPPER MIDDLE		36	Uruguay	8.1	60	Kenya	4.1
11	Guadeloupe	20.1				61	Philippines	4.1
12	Mexico	19.4		*LOWER MIDDLE*				
13	Reunion	19.0	37	Guatemala	7.9		*BOTTOM 10*	
14	Argentina	18.7	38	Hong Kong	7.9	62	Kuwait	4.0
15	Hungary	18.2	39	Bulgaria	7.2	63	Nicaragua	4.0
16	Equatorial Guinea	18.1	40	Cuba	6.9	64	Guyana	3.9
17	Czechoslovakia	16.9	41	Venezuela	6.7	65	Colombia	3.7
18	Bahamas	15.2	42	Jamaica	6.4	66	England & Wales	3.6
19	United States	14.8	43	Singapore	6.4	67	Ireland	3.5
20	South Africa	13.8	44	Bolivia	6.3	68	Panama	3.2
21	Japan	13.7	45	Peru	6.2	69	Mozambique	2.8
22	Greece	13.5	46	Israel	6.0	70	Paraguay	2.7
23	Belgium	13.2	47	Scotland	5.9	71	Iceland	0.9

Source: World Health Organization.

257. Death Rate from Diabetes

Although diabetes is a medically controllable disease, it continues to be a major cause of death in many countries, including advanced countries.

Number of Countries: 71	Highlights & Findings: No strict geographical pattern emerges from this ranking, but inhabitants
Midpoint: 10.5 per 100,000	of Eastern Europe and the West Indies seem to be particularly susceptible to this disease.

Period Covered: Early 1970s				
Type of Ranking: Number of Deaths	**Regions**	**Africa**	**Asia & Oceania**	**Europe**	**Western Hemisphere**
Caused by Diabetes per 100,000 Inhabitants;	**Most**	Mauritius (12)	New Zealand (25)	Malta (1)	Trinidad & Tobago (3)
Highest to Lowest	**Least**	Mozambique (71)	Philippines (61)	Iceland (66)	Bolivia (68)

Rank	Country	Deaths from Diabetes per 100,000	Rank	Country	Deaths from Diabetes per 100,000	Rank	Country	Deaths from Diabetes per 100,000
	TOP 10			*UPPER MIDDLE*		21	Austria	16.4
1	Malta	84.7	11	Uruguay	22.6	22	Finland	16.4
2	Luxembourg	46.3	12	Mauritius	22.0	23	Guyana	16.3
3	Trinidad & Tobago	41.7	13	Argentina	21.4	24	France	15.8
4	Rumania	40.0	14	Italy	21.3	25	New Zealand	15.3
5	Barbados	38.6	15	East Germany	20.6	26	Australia	14.7
6	West Germany	33.6	16	Switzerland	19.1	27	Mexico	14.5
7	Belgium	32.5	17	Spain	18.8	28	Canada	14.1
8	Jamaica	31.0	18	Sweden	18.8	29	Bahamas	13.7
9	Greece	29.5	19	Czechoslovakia	16.7	30	Costa Rica	12.7
10	Puerto Rico	25.2	20	United States	16.5	31	Denmark	12.6

Rank Country	Deaths from Diabetes per 100,000	Rank Country	Deaths from Diabetes per 100,000	Rank Country	Deaths from Diabetes per 100,000
32 Ireland	12.1	45 St. Lucia	8.5	60 Peru	3.9
33 Singapore	11.5	46 Guadeloupe	8.4	61 Philippines	2.7
34 Cuba	10.6	47 Bulgaria	8.2		
35 Chile	10.5	48 Japan	8.2	*BOTTOM 10*	
36 England & Wales	10.5	49 South Africa (whites only)	7.7	62 Equatorial Guinea	2.5
		50 Hungary	7.2	63 Scotland	2.2
LOWER MIDDLE		51 Norway	7.2	64 Rhodesia (Zimbabwe)	1.9
37 Netherlands	10.4	52 Colombia	6.5	65 Cape Verde	1.7
38 Sri Lanka	10.3	53 Paraguay	6.5	66 Iceland	1.4
39 Poland	10.1	54 Northern Ireland	6.3	67 Kenya	1.0
40 Venezuela	9.7	55 Ecuador	5.2	68 Bolivia	0.9
41 Reunion	9.6	56 Hong Kong	5.1	69 Angola	0.8
42 Panama	9.4	57 Kuwait	5.0	70 Guinea-Bissau	0.2
43 Portugal	9.3	58 Nicaragua	4.7	71 Mozambique	0.1
44 Israel	9.1	59 Guatemala	4.5		

Source: World Health Organization.

258. Death Rate from Heart Disease

Next to cancer, heart diseases claim the most lives and have become, therefore, one of the major areas of medical research. Statistics relating to heart disease distinguish among various forms, such as chronic rheumatic heart disease, hypertensive heart disease, ischaemic heart disease, and so on, but for the purpose of this ranking all of them have been combined. In most of the countries women are more liable to die of heart disease than men, but in the 45-to-64 age group the percentages are reversed and the risk of heart disease is greater for men. For both sexes deaths from heart disease are highest in the 65-plus group.

Number of Countries: 73
Midpoint: 178.5 per 100,000
Period Covered: 1976
Type of Ranking: Number of Deaths from Heart Disease per 100,000 Inhabitants; Highest to Lowest

Highlights & Findings: The ranking seems to confirm the popular and widely held notion that there is a causal relation between heart disease and certain types of lifestyles. Not only are urbanites more prone to heart disease, but in certain professions, such as business executives, policemen and bus drivers, heart disease has become an accepted occupational hazard. Significantly, the first non-Western, non-Caucasian country in the list ranks only 35th. There is overwhelming evidence that heart disease is indeed a malady of civilization.

Region	Africa	Asia & Oceania	Europe	Western Hemisphere
Most	South Africa (26)	Australia (20)	Scotland (1)	United States (12)
Least	Mozambique (73)	Sri Lanka (63)	Portugal (39)	Bolivia (69)

Rank Country	Deaths from Heart Disease per 100,000	Rank Country	Death from Heart Disease per 100,000	Rank Country	Death from Heart Disease per 100,000
TOP 10		*UPPER MIDDLE*		21 Italy	276.8
1 Scotland	423.5	11 West Germany	349.9	22 Bulgaria	264.4
2 Sweden	414.2	12 United States	338.2	23 New Zealand	263.4
3 Northern Ireland	403.1	13 Luxembourg	331.1	24 Netherlands	263.3
4 England & Wales	401.6	14 Norway	324.9	25 Canada	260.9
5 Austria	396.5	15 Belgium	319.3	26 South Africa (whites only)	257.3
6 East Germany	394.0	16 Czechoslovakia	313.0	27 Yogoslavia	236.5
7 Denmark	379.1	17 Malta	302.6	28 Israel	225.3
8 Ireland	366.4	18 Rumania	291.4	29 Uruguay	224.7
9 Hungary	358.4	19 Switzerland	290.0	30 Poland	214.1
10 Finland	354.2	20 Australia	285.7	31 Rhodesia (Zimbabwe)	209.8

Rank	Country	Death from Heart Disease per 100,000
32	France	208.7
33	Iceland	208.6
34	Spain	184.9
35	Barbados	182.9
36	Greece	178.7
	LOWER MIDDLE	
37	Argentina	178.5
38	Puerto Rico	161.6
39	Portugal	157.5
40	Trinidad & Tobago	156.8
41	Cuba	144.8
42	Mauritius	144.0
43	Jamaica	130.4
44	Guyana	130.2
45	Reunion	128.9

Rank	Country	Death from Heart Disease per 100,000
46	Egypt	119.0
47	Japan	109.1
48	Chile	103.4
49	Singapore	100.3
50	Colombia	89.1
51	Hong Kong	86.5
52	Bahamas	82.4
53	Venezuela	82.0
54	Guadeloupe	75.0
55	Kuwait	73.5
56	Mexico	73.3
57	Philippines	72.9
58	Costa Rica	68.0
59	Cape Verde	67.6
60	St. Lucia	66.0
61	Panama	65.3

Rank	Country	Death from Heart Disease per 100,000
62	Ecuador	64.9
63	Sri Lanka	56.3
	BOTTOM 10	
64	Paraguay	50.2
65	Nicaragua	48.6
66	Peru	33.3
67	Equatorial Guinea	32.6
68	Guatemala	27.7
69	Bolivia	26.3
70	Guinea-Bissau	9.8
71	Angola	9.5
72	Kenya	5.6
73	Mozambique	2.8

Source: World Health Organization.

259. Death Rate from Influenza

Influenza is one of the most universal causes of death, and its incidence is not directly related to specific environmental conditions, as is the case with many other killers. However, with the development of vaccines and antibiotics, many of the developed countries have been dropping to the bottom of the scale in recent years.

Number of Countries: 67
Midpoint: 3 per 100,000
Period Covered: Early 1970s
Type of Ranking: Number of Deaths Caused by Influenza per 100,000 Inhabitants; Highest to Lowest

Highlights & Findings: Scientists have recently established that the viruses that cause influenza are capable of mutation resulting in new types emerging every few years. Since these mutant viruses move from country to country, influenza epidemics may affect any one region more severely than other areas at a given time. Annual statistics, such as those presented in these rankings, may not reflect the actual incidence of the disease or the ratio of fatalities caused by it as accurately as statistics covering a five- or 10-year period.

Regions	Africa	Asia & Oceania	Europe	Western Hemisphere
Most	Reunion (7)	Philippines (21)	Hungary (4)	Guatemala (1)
Least	Angola (62)	Kuwait (67)	Rumania (64)	Cuba (60)

Rank	Country	Deaths from Influenza per 100,000
	TOP 10	
1	Guatemala	99.7
2	Ecuador	25.7
3	Peru	21.3
4	Hungary	14.5
5	France	14.3
6	Spain	12.9
7	Reunion	10.8
8	Chile	10.5
9	Belgium	10.1
10	Norway	9.5
	UPPER MIDDLE	
11	Greece	9.3

Rank	Country	Deaths from Influenza per 100,000
12	Bolivia	9.2
13	Ireland	8.7
14	Uruguay	8.4
15	Austria	8.2
16	Colombia	8.0
17	Switzerland	8.0
18	Panama	7.7
19	Portugal	7.4
20	Mexico	7.2
21	Philippines	7.1
22	Czechoslovakia	6.9
23	East Germany	5.3
24	Mozambique	4.6
25	Paraguay	4.2

Rank	Country	Deaths from Influenza per 100,000
26	Rhodesia (Zimbabwe)	4.2
27	Scotland	4.2
28	Poland	4.1
29	Australia	3.9
30	Costa Rica	3.9
31	Equatorial Guinea	3.6
32	Finland	3.3
33	Italy	3.3
34	Argentina	3.0
	LOWER MIDDLE	
35	Sweden	2.9
36	Venezuela	2.9
37	Bulgaria	2.8

Rank	Country	Deaths from Influenza per 100,000
38	Iceland	2.8
39	Jamaica	2.7
40	Netherlands	2.6
41	England & Wales	2.5
42	Luxembourg	2.5
43	Guadeloupe	2.2
44	Mauritius	2.1
45	Canada	2.0
46	Denmark	2.0
47	West Germany	2.0
48	Northern Ireland	2.0
49	Sri Lanka	2.0

Rank	Country	Deaths from Influenza per 100,000
50	United States	2.0
51	New Zealand	1.9
52	Cape Verde	1.7
53	Guyana	1.6
54	Japan	1.3
55	Puerto Rico	1.3
56	Bahamas	1.0
57	South Africa	1.0
	BOTTOM 10	
58	Trinidad & Tobago	0.9
59	Barbados	0.8

Rank	Country	Deaths from Influenza per 100,000
60	Cuba	0.8
61	Guinea-Bissau	0.8
62	Angola	0.7
63	Israel	0.7
64	Rumania	0.7
65	Singapore	0.5
66	Hong Kong	0.2
67	Kuwait	0.1

Source: World Health Organization.

260. Death Rate from Syphilis

Syphilis is a universal disease and, although it is controllable in its early stages, can lead to progressive degeneration and death. Traditionally, some societies have a greater incidence of the disease than others and, for reasons that may require more investigation, it is more prevalent in times of war and civil unrest.

Number of Countries: 58
Midpoint: 0.3 per 100,000
Period Covered: Early 1970s
Type of Ranking: Number of Deaths from Syphilis per 100,000 Inhabitants; Highest to Lowest

Highlights & Findings: No geographical pattern emerges from these rankings, but the incidence is higher in those countries where there are residual social taboos against reporting and receiving treatment for the disease.

Regions	Africa	Asia & Oceania	Europe	Western Hemisphere
Most	Mozambique (4)	Hong Kong (18)	Luxembourg (6)	St. Lucia (1)
Least	Angola (48)	Sri Lanka (56)	Sweden (57)	United States (58)

Rank	Country	Deaths from Syphilis per 100,000
	TOP 11	
1	St. Lucia	5.3
2	Barbados	3.3
3	Jamaica	3.2
4	Mozambique	1.8
5	Argentina	1.6
6	Luxembourg	1.1
7	Uruguay	0.9
8	Austria	0.6
9	Costa Rica	0.6
10	Guadeloupe	0.6
11	Spain	0.6
	UPPER MIDDLE	
12	Colombia	0.5
13	Hungary	0.5
14	Paraguay	0.5
15	Peru	0.5
16	Reunion	0.5
17	Finland	0.4
18	Hong Kong	0.4
19	Italy	0.4

Rank	Country	Death from Syphilis per 100,000
20	Panama	0.4
21	Venezuela	0.4
22	Belgium	0.3
23	Czechoslovakia	0.3
24	England & Wales	0.3
25	France	0.3
26	East Germany	0.3
27	West Germany	0.3
28	Guatemala	0.3
29	Guyana	0.3
30	Japan	0.3
31	Mexico	0.3
32	New Zealand	0.3
33	Portugal	0.3
34	Switzerland	0.3
	LOWER MIDDLE	
35	Bolivia	0.2
36	Ecuador	0.2
37	Greece	0.2
38	Israel	0.2
39	Kenya	0.2

Rank	Country	Death from Syphilis per 100,000
40	Netherlands	0.2
41	Norway	0.2
42	Poland	0.2
43	Puerto Rico	0.2
44	Rumania	0.2
45	Singapore	0.2
46	South Africa (whites only)	0.2
47	Trinidad & Tobago	0.2
	BOTTOM 11	
48	Angola	0.1
49	Australia	0.1
50	Canada	0.1
51	Chile	0.1
52	Cuba	0.1
53	Denmark	0.1
54	Kuwait	0.1
55	Northern Ireland	0.1
56	Sri Lanka	0.1
57	Sweden	0.1
58	United States	0.1

Source: World Health Organization.

261. Death Rate from Tuberculosis

Historically, tuberculosis has been one of the most widespread diseases, and although it has ceased to be a major health problem in countries with effective health care systems, it continues to rank high among the major causes of death in many countries of the world.

Number of Countries: 70
Midpoint: 5.5 per 100,000
Period Covered: Early 1970s
Type of Ranking: Number of Deaths Caused by Tuberculosis per 100,000 Inhabitants; Highest to Lowest

Highlights & Findings: The incidence of tuberculosis is highest in Latin America and Asia and is directly related to a number of factors, particularly malnutrition, nonavailability of proper drugs and the inadequate reach of BCG vaccination campaigns.

Regions	Africa	Asia & Oceania	Europe	Western Hemisphere
Most	Guinea-Bissau (2)	Philippines (1)	Poland (16)	Bolivia (3)
Least	Mozambique (67)	Australia (68)	Norway (70)	Canada (62)

Rank	Country	Deaths from Tuberculosis per 100,000
	TOP 10	
1	Philippines	69.3
2	Guinea-Bissau	42.9
3	Bolivia	28.8
4	Peru	25.1
5	Chile	21.0
6	Ecuador	16.0
7	Singapore	15.2
8	Cape Verde	15.1
9	Guatemala	14.4
10	Reunion	14.0
	UPPER MIDDLE	
11	Colombia	13.7
12	Argentina	13.6
13	Mexico	13.2
14	Sri Lanka	12.9
15	Hong Kong	12.7
16	Poland	12.1
17	Panama	11.4
18	Hungary	10.2
19	Paraguay	10.0
20	Portugal	9.5
21	Japan	9.2
22	Guadeloupe	9.0
23	St. Lucia	8.5

Rank	Country	Deaths from Tuberculosis per 100,000
24	Puerto Rico	8.4
25	Kuwait	7.4
26	Venezuela	7.4
27	France	7.1
28	Rumania	7.1
29	Austria	6.8
30	Spain	6.8
31	Czechoslovakia	6.5
32	Nicaragua	6.4
33	Mauritius	6.3
34	Bulgaria	6.0
35	Italy	5.5
36	Uruguay	5.5
	LOWER MIDDLE	
37	Angola	5.4
38	Cuba	5.3
39	Equatorial Guinea	5.1
40	Costa Rica	4.9
41	West Germany	4.6
42	Ireland	4.6
43	Kenya	4.6
44	Bahamas	4.4
45	Greece	4.4
46	Belgium	4.3
47	East Germany	3.7

Rank	Country	Deaths from Tuberculosis per 100,000
48	Switzerland	3.7
49	Guyana	3.6
50	Trinidad & Tobago	3.6
51	Finland	3.5
52	Jamaica	3.2
53	South Africa (whites only)	2.6
54	Sweden	2.6
55	Barbados	2.5
56	Scotland	2.2
57	England & Wales	1.6
58	Rhodesia (Zimbabwe)	1.5
59	Denmark	1.2
60	United States	1.2
	BOTTOM 10	
61	Luxembourg	1.1
62	Canada	1.0
63	Iceland	0.9
64	Northern Ireland	0.9
65	New Zealand	0.8
66	Israel	0.7
67	Mozambique	0.7
68	Australia	0.6
69	Netherlands	0.6
70	Norway	0.3

Source: World Health Organization.

262. Suicides

Suicide has been described as a disease of civilization. Paradoxically, as the figures in this ranking bear out, it is more prevalent in affluent societies, where the struggle for existence is intensified and where the individual finds himself adrift in a hostile, or at best indifferent, environment. Traditional societies, on the other hand, seem to have built-in life support mechanisms that serve as umbilical cords in times of emotional crises.

Number of Countries: 65
Midpoint: 8.6 per 100,000
Period Covered: Mid-1970s
Type of Ranking: Number of Suicides per 100,000 Inhabitants; Highest to Lowest

Highlights & Findings: Scandinavian countries, which have been hailed as welfare societies in the true sense of the term, have the highest rates of suicides. Switzerland is the only industrially advanced country that finds a place among nations with a low rate of suicide. In a tragic coincidence, Guyana was the site of the 1978 mass suicide of American religious cultists and has the highest suicide rate in the Western Hemisphere.

Regions	Africa	Asia & Oceania	Europe	Western Hemisphere
Most	Guinea-Bissau(18)	Japan(10)	Rumania(1)	Guyana(3)
Least	Kenya(65)	Kuwait(63)	Switzerland(56)	Bahamas(64)

Rank	Country	Suicides per 100,000	Rank	Country	Suicides per 100,000	Rank	Country	Suicides per 100,000
	TOP 10		22	Poland	11.4	44	Ireland	3.5
1	Rumania	59.9	23	Singapore	11.2	45	Guadeloupe	3.4
2	Hungary	38.4	24	Hong Kong	10.9	46	Guatemala	3.4
3	Guyana	37.2	25	Luxembourg	10.6	47	Panama	3.0
4	Finland	25.1	26	Argentina	10.4	48	Colombia	2.9
5	Austria	24.1	27	Uruguay	10.4	49	Cape Verde	2.8
6	Denmark	23.8	28	Iceland	10.1	50	Greece	2.8
7	Czechoslovakia	22.4	29	Norway	9.9	51	Ecuador	2.6
8	West Germany	21.0	30	Netherlands	9.2	52	Mexico	2.1
9	Sweden	20.0	31	Puerto Rico	9.1	53	Peru	1.8
10	Japan	18.1	32	New Zealand	8.8	54	Barbados	1.7
			33	Portugal	8.6	55	Paraguay	1.6
	UPPER MIDDLE							
11	Sri Lanka	17.2		*LOWER MIDDLE*			*BOTTOM 10*	
12	France	15.4	34	United Kingdom	7.9	56	Switzerland	1.5
13	Cuba	15.0	35	Mauritius	7.8	57	Boliva	1.4
14	Belgium	14.9	36	Trinidad & Tobago	7.0	58	Nicaragua	1.2
15	South Africa (whites only; blacks 5.6)	14.5	37	Reunion	6.9	59	Mozambique	1.1
16	Canada	12.9	38	Italy	5.8	60	Philippines	1.1
17	Bulgaria	12.7	39	Chile	5.4	61	Angola	1.0
18	Guinea-Bissau	12.7	40	Israel	4.9	62	Jamaica	1.0
19	United States	12.7	41	Venezuela	4.7	63	Kuwait	0.8
20	Rhodesia (Zimbabwe)	12.2	42	Costa Rica	4.1	64	Bahamas	0.5
21	Australia	11.7	43	Spain	4.0	65	Kenya	0.2

Source: *U.N. Demographic Yearbook.*

263. Deaths from Motor Vehicle Accidents

Motor vehicle accidents have become a leading cause of fatalities in many countries of the world. Such accidents are due not only to the number of motor vehicles on the road but are also affected by the condition of the roads, national driving habits, lack of driver education, pedestrian habits and the type of cars (smaller cars result in fewer accidents but in a larger proportion of fatalities). Other factors include the effectiveness of the traffic police and the availability of medical and ambulance services.

Number of Countries: 65
Midpoint: 17.2 per 100,000
Period Covered: 1975
Type of Ranking: Number of Deaths from Motor Vehicle Accidents per 100,000 Inhabitants; Highest to Lowest

Highlights & Findings: Although the United States leads the world in annual total of deaths due to traffic accidents, it does not rank among the top 10 nations proporationately. In fact, in terms of the miles driven each year, the United States is among the safest nations in the world.

Regions	Africa	Asia & Oceania	Europe	Western Hemisphere
Most	Rhodesia (Zimbabwe)(1)	Kuwait(6)	Luxembourg(3)	Guadeloupe(4)
Least	Kenya(65)	Sri Lanka(63)	Malta(59)	Bolivia(62)

Rank	Country	Traffic Fatalities per 100,000	Rank	Country	Traffic Fatalities per 100,000	Rank	Country	Traffic Fatalities per 100,000
	TOP 10		22	Trinidad & Tobago	20.3	46	Cuba	12.1
1	Rhodesia (Zimbabwe)	55.0	23	Ireland	20.2	47	Belgium	11.5
2	South Africa	45.5	24	Israel	20.0	48	Singapore	11.3
3	Luxembourg	36.0	25	Ecuador	19.4	49	Bahamas	10.8
4	Guadeloupe	33.8	26	Switzerland	19.3	50	Colombia	9.5
5	Austria	33.0	27	Reunion	18.8	51	Jamaica	8.0
6	Kuwait	32.2	28	Netherlands	18.7	52	Guatemala	7.8
7	Portugal	28.9	29	Finland	18.0	53	Angola	5.8
8	Australia	28.6	30	Hungary	18.0	54	Paraguay	5.8
9	Belgium	28.5	31	Chile	17.9			
10	Canada	28.1	32	Iceland	17.9		**BOTTOM 11**	
			33	Nicaragua	17.2	55	Hong Kong	5.5
	UPPER MIDDLE		34	Greece	16.8	56	Uruguay	5.5
11	Guinea-Bissau	26.3	35	Argentina	16.7	57	Mozambique	5.4
12	Italy	25.9	36	Costa Rica	16.6	58	Peru	5.1
13	Venezuela	25.6	37	Panama	15.4	59	Malta	3.4
14	Denmark	24.0	38	East Germany	15.3	60	Philippines	3.2
15	New Zealand	23.6	39	Mexico	15.3	61	St. Lucia	3.2
16	France	23.5	40	Sweden	15.2	62	Bolivia	2.5
17	West Germany	23.0	41	Barbados	14.9	63	Sri Lanka	1.5
18	Puerto Rico	22.0	42	Norway	14.0	64	Cape Verde	1.4
19	United States	21.5	43	Spain	13.6	65	Kenya	1.0
20	Mauritius	21.1	44	United Kingdom	13.0			
21	Czechoslovakia	20.3	45	Japan	12.9			

Source: *U.N. Demographic Yearbook.*

264. Fatal Industrial Accidents

Industry is a high-accident risk sector. The following list ranks countries by frequency or incidence rates of fatal industrial accidents. The ranking is limited to fatal accidents because although the number is relatively high, minor accidents do not lend themselves to international comparisons; furthermore, the way minor accidents are reported is unsatisfactory in most countries. Deaths resulting from occupational diseases and accidents on the way to and from work (called commuting accidents) are also excluded. The data are based generally on industrial accident compensation claims, which may be accepted as fairly reliable. The incidence rates are calculated for most countries per 1,000 persons employed; for a few countries they are calculated per one million man-hours (A) or per 1,000 man-years (B).

Number of Countries: 67
Midpoint: 0.11%
Period Covered: 1976
Type of Ranking: Fatal Industrial Accident Rates in Manufacturing per 1,000 Persons Employed or as Indicated; Highest to Lowest

Highlights & Findings: The ranking is instructive because it shows that fatal accident rates in industry are lower in industrialized countries. Although overregulation by state agencies (such as the Occupational Safety and Health Administration [OSHA] in the United States) can sometimes be counterproductive, industrial accidents are preventable through properly enforced guidelines and built-in safety features in machinery.

Region	Africa	Asia & Oceania	Europe	Western Hemisphere
Most	Morocco (2)	French Polynesia (1)	Austria (22)	Mexico (11)
Least	Ghana (66)	Japan (67)	United Kingdom (64)	United States (65)

Rank	Country	Fatal Industrial Accident Rate in Manufacturing per 1,000 Persons Employed	Rank	Country	Fatal Industrial Accident Rate in Manufacturing per 1,000 Persons Employed	Rank	Country	Fatal Industrial Accident Rate in Manufacturing per 1,000 Persons Employed
	TOP 10		3	Sri Lanka	1.68	6	Vietnam	0.41
1	French Polynesia	1.78	4	Papua New Guinea	0.90	7	Syria	0.38
2	Morocco	1.70	5	Sarawak	0.70	8	Cameroon	0.34

Rank	Country	Fatal Industrial Accident Rate in Manufacturing per 1,000 Persons Employed	Rank	Country	Fatal Industrial Accident Rate in Manufacturing per 1,000 Persons Employed	Rank	Country	Fatal Industrial Accident Rate in Manufacturing per 1,000 Persons Employed
9	Mali	0.30	29	Tanzania	0.15	49	Zambia	0.08
10	Pakistan	0.29	30	India	0.14	50	Libya	0.07
			31	Israel	0.13	51	Singapore (A)	0.07
	UPPER MIDDLE		32	Switzerland (B)	0.13	52	Tunisia (A)	0.07
11	Mexico	0.26	33	Barbados	0.11	53	Yugoslavia	0.07
12	Panama	0.26	34	Burma	0.11	54	Norway	0.06
13	Guadeloupe	0.25	35	Hong Kong	0.11	55	East Germany	0.05
14	El Salvador	0.24	36	Malta	0.11	56	Ireland	0.05
15	Nigeria	0.24						
16	Fiji	0.23		*LOWER MIDDLE*			*BOTTOM 11*	
17	Egypt	0.22	37	Canada	0.10	57	Bangladesh	0.04
18	Jordan	0.22	38	France	0.10	58	Cyprus	0.04
19	Malaysia (West)	0.21	39	Hungary (B)	0.10	59	Netherlands (B)	0.04
20	Kenya	0.20	40	Puerto Rico (B)	0.10	60	Thailand	0.04
21	New Caledonia	0.19	41	Surinam (B)	0.10	61	Trinidad & Tobago	0.04
22	Austria	0.18	42	Uganda	0.10	62	Malawi	0.03
23	Luxembourg	0.18	43	Jamaica	0.09	63	Sweden (A)	0.03
24	Rumania	0.18	44	Czechoslovakia	0.08	64	United Kingdom	0.03
25	Turkey (B)	0.18	45	Finland	0.08	65	United States (A)	0.03
26	Guatemala	0.17	46	Italy (B)	0.08	66	Ghana	0.02
27	West Germany (B)	0.16	47	Mauritius (A)	0.08	67	Japan (A)	0.01
28	South Korea	0.15	48	Spain (A)	0.08			

(A) Per 1 Million Man-Hours
(B) Per 1,000 Man-years

Source: *ILO, Yearbook of Labor Statistics.*

265. Daily Protein Consumption

The FAO and WHO recommendation for per capita daily consumption of protein is 65 grams, subject to variations because of age, climate, occupation and other factors. This requirement is exceeded in most industrialized countries, which have an average of 94.4 grams and in Southern Europe with an average of 85 grams. Protein supply is lowest in South Asia with an average of 53.5 grams and in East Asia with an average of 55.1 grams. The African diet fares better in terms of protein than calories, and its average of 60.5 grams provides 93% of the recommended minimum requirements. In the Western Hemisphere the protein supply falls fractionally behind Africa with 60.4 grams. The Middle Eastern diet is closer to standard with 62.6 grams.

Number of Countries: 107 **Midpoint:** 64 grams **Period Covered:** Early 1970s **Type of Ranking:** Protein Supply in Grams; Protein Supply from Animals and/or Pulses in Grams; Highest to Lowest	**Highlights & Findings:** Forty-eight countries exceed the recommended minimum requirements. In all these countries the proportion of protein obtained from animals and/or pulses is high. Six of these nations are in Asia and nine in Africa.

Regions	Africa	Asia & Oceania	Europe	Western Hemisphere
Most	Mauritania (32)	New Zealand (1)	France (2)	Canada (9)
Least	Zaire (107)	Indonesia (102)	Cyprus (29)	Haiti (105)

Rank	Country	Protein Supply in Grams	Protein Supply from Animals/Pulses in Grams	Rank	Country	Protein Supply in Grams	Protein Supply from Animals/Pulses in Grams	Rank	Country	Protein Supply in Grams	Protein Supply from Animals/Pulses in Grams
		TOP 10		36	Niger	72	24	72	Afghanistan	58	11
1	New Zealand	107	77	37	Chile	71	32	73	Honduras	58	25
2	France	104	66	38	Kenya	71	29	74	Somalia	57	27
3	Ireland	103	66	39	Lebanon	70	11	75	Algeria	56	9
4	Australia	101	71	40	Nicaragua	70	33	76	Gabon	56	30
5	Italy	100	42	41	Syria	70	16	77	Jamaica	56	29
6	Argentina	99	64	42	Ethiopia	69	25	78	Saudi Arabia	56	13
7	Greece	99	52	43	Mali	69	23	79	South Yemen	56	27
8	Iceland	99	73	44	Taiwan	68	31	80	Benin	55	18
9	Canada	98	67	45	Egypt	66	16	81	Malawi	54	9
10	United States	97	76	46	Upper Volta	66	22	82	Tunisia	54	14
				47	Botswana	65	33	83	India	53	16
		UPPER MIDDLE		48	South Korea	65	19	84	Iran	53	14
11	Uruguay	96	64	49	Mexico	65	28	85	Madagascar	53	17
12	Belgium	94	56	50	Brazil	64	39	86	Nepal	52	11
13	Israel	92	49	51	Morocco	64	14	87	Thailand	52	17
14	Rumania	92	28	52	Senegal	64	28	88	Colombia	51	29
15	Yugoslavia	92	29	53	Trinidad & Tobago	64	34	89	El Salvador	51	18
16	Denmark	91	62	54	Zambia	64	25	90	Togo	51	19
17	Finland	91	60					91	Dominican Republic	50	29
18	Switzerland	91	55			LOWER MIDDLE		92	Mauritius	50	19
19	United Kingdom	90	57	55	Costa Rica	63	35	93	Sri Lanka	50	16
20	Austria	89	51	56	Gambia	63	20	94	Burma	49	13
21	Netherlands	89	55	57	Singapore	63	34	95	Ecuador	49	22
22	West Germany	88	56	58	Sudan	63	24	96	Malaysia	49	20
23	Bahamas	87	45	59	Iraq	62	17	97	Sierra Leone	49	16
24	Norway	87	53	60	Peru	62	24				
25	Malta	86	50	61	Rwanda	62	35			BOTTOM 10	
26	Portugal	85	40	62	Venezuela	62	32	98	Guyana	47	22
27	Sweden	84	56	63	Burundi	61	40	99	Bolivia	46	14
28	Spain	81	40	64	Libya	61	24	100	Ghana	46	10
29	Cyprus	78	33	65	Panama	61	31	101	Philippines	45	22
30	Turkey	78	22	66	Ivory Coast	60	18	102	Indonesia	43	14
31	Japan	76	45	67	Jordan	60	18	103	Tanzania	43	23
32	Mauritania	75	44	68	Nigeria	60	16	104	Congo	40	23
33	Paraguay	74	41	69	Cameroon	59	23	105	Haiti	39	18
34	Barbados	73	47	70	Guatemala	59	19	106	Liberia	36	10
35	Chad	73	33	71	Pakistan	59	14	107	Zaire	33	16

Source: World Bank.

266. Daily Caloric Consumption

The FAO and WHO recommendation of per capita daily consumption of calories is 2,600, but there are considerable variations in requirements because of age, climate, occupation and other factors. The recommended minimum is exceeded only in industrialized countries, where the average is 3,150 calories per capita per day, and in Southern Europe where the relative figure is 2,998. It is lowest in Africa (2,207.1 calories) and only slightly higher in East Asia (2,219.2 calories) and South Asia (2,231.2 calories). People in the Middle East consume more food energy with 2,358 calories, and the average in the Western Hemisphere is only slightly less than the WHO and FAO minimum (2,523 calories). On the whole, the consumption of calories in developing countries is 2,322.5.

Number of Countries: 118
Midpoint: 2,350 Calories
Period Covered: Early 1970s
Type of Ranking: Consumption of Calories per Capita per Day; Highest to Lowest

Highlights & Findings: Only 34 countries exceed the FAO and WHO recommended minimum. Almost all these countries are in Europe and the Western Hemisphere; there are only three Asian countries, and black Africa is not represented in the top bracket at all.

Regions	Africa	Asia & Oceania	Europe	Western Hemisphere
Most	South Africa (28)	Australia (6)	Ireland (1)	United States (4)
Least	Algeria (117)	Yemen Arab Republic (108)	Spain (35)	Haiti (118)

Rank	Country	Calories per Capita per Day	Rank	Country	Calories per Capita per Day	Rank	Country	Calories per Capita per Day
	TOP 10		40	Surinam	2,550	80	India	2,210
1	Ireland	3,410	41	Madagascar	2,530	81	Malawi	2,210
2	Belgium	3,380	42	Japan	2,510	82	Nepal	2,210
3	Luxembourg	3,380	43	Egypt	2,500	83	Colombia	2,200
4	United States	3,330	44	Ivory Coast	2,490	84	Ghana	2,200
5	Austria	3,310	45	Nicaragua	2,450	85	Niger	2,180
6	Australia	3,280	46	Afghanistan	2,440	86	Central African Empire	2,170
7	Turkey	3,250	47	Jordan	2,430	87	Mali	2,170
8	Denmark	3,240	48	Singapore	2,430	88	Burma	2,160
9	West Germany	3,220	49	Venezuela	2,430	89	Congo	2,160
10	Netherlands	3,220	50	Iran	2,400	90	Ethiopia	2,160
			51	Guyana	2,390	91	Indonesia	2,160
	UPPER MIDDLE		52	Trinidad & Tobago	2,380	92	Iraq	2,160
11	France	3,210	53	Gambia	2,370	93	Sudan	2,160
12	New Zealand	3,200	54	Hong Kong	2,370	94	Togo	2,160
13	Greece	3,190	55	Taiwan	2,360	95	Vietnam	2,160
14	Switzerland	3,190	56	Jamaica	2,360	96	Honduras	2,140
15	United Kingdom	3,190	57	Kenya	2,360	97	Guatemala	2,130
16	Yugoslavia	3,190	58	Mauritius	2,360	98	Uganda	2,130
17	Canada	3,180	59	South Korea	2,350	99	Dominican Republic	2,120
18	Italy	3,180				100	South Yemen	2,070
19	Argentina	3,060		*LOWER MIDDLE*		101	Chad	2,060
20	Finland	3,050	60	Peru	2,320	102	Zaire	2,060
21	Israel	2,960	61	Bangladesh	2,310	103	Mozambique	2,050
22	Norway	2,900	62	Pakistan	2,310	104	Botswana	2,040
23	Portugal	2,900	63	Senegal	2,300	105	Burundi	2,040
24	Uruguay	2,880	64	Nigeria	2,290	106	Guinea	2,040
25	Malta	2,820	65	Lebanon	2,280	107	Liberia	2,040
26	Sweden	2,810	66	Saudi Arabia	2,270	108	Yemen Arab Republic	2,040
27	Paraguay	2,740	67	Philippines	2,260			
28	South Africa	2,740	68	Tanzania	2,260		*BOTTOM 10*	
29	Chile	2,670	69	Benin	2,250	109	Ecuador	2,010
30	Cyprus	2,670	70	Tunisia	2,250	110	Angola	2,000
31	Rhodesia (Zimbabwe)	2,660	71	Malaysia	2,240	111	Mauritania	1,970
32	Syria	2,650	72	Sierra Leone	2,240	112	Rwanda	1,960
33	Brazil	2,620	73	Cameroon	2,230	113	Upper Volta	1,940
34	Costa Rica	2,610	74	Cambodia	2,220	114	El Salvador	1,930
35	Spain	2,600	75	Laos	2,220	115	Bolivia	1,900
36	Zambia	2,590	76	Morocco	2,220	116	Somalia	1,830
37	Mexico	2,580	77	Sri Lanka	2,220	117	Algeria	1,730
38	Panama	2,580	78	Thailand	2,220	118	Haiti	1,730
39	Libya	2,570	79	Gabon	2,210			

Source: World Bank.

EDUCATION

Consider the size of the world's educational system: a total enrollment of 542.761 million (fully one-fourth of the world's population), a teaching staff of 23.85 million and a gross public expenditure of $295 billion. The regional distribution is as follows:

Region	Enrollment (million)	Teaching Staff (000)	Public Expenditures ($ million)	% of GNP
Africa	50,032	1,412	5,890	5.5
North America	62,945	3,218	102,310	6.6
Latin America	69,952	3,026	12,020	4.3
Asia	212,789	7,816	30,540	4.0
Europe	90,160	5,221	102,260	4.9
Oceania	4,562	222	6,370	6.3
Soviet Union	52,321	2,935	35,610	7.6

What these figures do not tell is the quality of education achieved at such enormous cost and effort. There are a number of intangibles in any educational system: the training of the teaching staff, the quality of the textbooks, the pedagogical techniques, the examination system, to mention a few. These intangibles are, of course, very difficult to define and cannot be evaluated by fixed or objective criteria.

The rankings begin appropriately with the literacy rate and the total school enrollment rate and then proceed level by level. At the first level the rankings deal with the number of primary schools, the primary school enrollment ratio, cost per pupil, educational expenditures per pupil, the teacher-pupil ratio, grade repetition, and percentage of private enrollment. At the secondary level they deal with the school enrollment ratio and vocational education and at the third level with the graduate population, university enrollment per 10,000, percentage of women in university enrollment, total stock of university professors, foreign students in domestic universities and native students in foreign universities. Another ranking covers educational expenditures as a percentage of GNP.

The subsection on science and technology is designed to measure the size of the pool of scientific manpower, both overall and in basic research, and expenditures on scientific research as a percentage of GNP. There is also an interesting scientific authorship index, which measures national share of scientific authorship; it could tell who is publishing and who is perishing.

A related ranking on unemployment among professionals and scientists appears in the chapter on labor.

267. Literacy Rate

Literacy has conflicting definitions in different countries. UNESCO defines literacy as the ability to read and write a simple sentence. In some countries, such as Japan, Sudan, Uganda and Zambia, illiteracy is defined as never having attended school. In Tunisia literacy is defined as the ability to read but not necessarily to write. In developed countries literacy is defined in functional terms as the ability to fill out a simple application form. Literacy figures are also qualified by the age groups to which they refer. Data for most countries relate to populations aged 15 and over; but in the case of others, such as Italy, the figures are based on the population over age six. Other kinds of error and bias include the exclusion of segments of the population, such as nomads in the Middle East and Africa and Indians in South America. Furthermore, because of the great prestige attached to literacy, governments in developing countries have shown a tendency to inflate, distort or even fabricate literacy ratios. Caution must therefore be exercised in evaluating literacy figures at their face value.

Number of Countries: 178
Midpoint: 60%
Period Covered: 1977
Type of Ranking: Percentage of Literate Population; Highest to Lowest

Highlights & Findings: Literacy is one area where measurable progress has been achieved in almost every country in the world during the last 30 years. At least 20 countries have reported total or near total literacy. All countries at the bottom of the list are either in Africa or Asia. The top eight countries in this ranking are generally ascribed 100% literacy rate by UNESCO and other sources. But because of the statistical improbability of 100%, literacy the figure has been changed to 99.5%.

Regions	Africa	Asia & Oceania	Europe	Western Hemisphere
Highest	South Africa (6)	Macao (3)	Czechoslovakia (2)	Bermuda (1)
Lowest	Maldives (178)	Bhutan (176)	Portugal (87)	Haiti (155)

Rank	Country	Percentage	Rank	Country	Percentage	Rank	Country	Percentage
	TOP 8		50	Chile	89	105	Honduras	47
1	Bermuda	99.5	51	Israel	88	106	Brunei	45
2	Czechoslovakia	99.5	52	Guyana	86	107	Madagascar	45
3	Macao	99.5	53	Lebanon	86	108	Peru	45
4	Monaco	99.5	54	Argentina	85	109	Malaysia	44
5	Nauru	99.5	55	Western Samoa	85	110	Jamaica	41
6	South Africa*	99.5	56	Malta	83	111	Bahrain	40
7	United States	99.5	57	Philippines	83	112	Cameroon	40
8	Vatican	99.5	58	Cyprus	82	113	Egypt	40
			59	Greece	82	114	Lesotho	40
	UPPER MIDDLE		60	Panama	82	115	Syria	40
9	Canada	99	61	Sri Lanka	82	116	Iran	37
10	Denmark	99	62	Antigua	80	117	Bolivia	35
11	Faroe Islands	99	63	Dominica	80	118	Libya	35
12	Finland	99	64	Fiji	80	119	Zaire	35
13	East Germany	99	65	Mongolia	80	120	Tunisia	32
14	West Germany	99	66	Reunion	80	121	Guatemala	30
15	Gibraltar	99	67	St. Kitts-Nevis-Anguilla	80	122	India	29
16	Greenland	99	68	St. Lucia	80	123	Zambia	28
17	Iceland	99	69	St. Vincent	80	124	Kenya	27
18	Norway	99	70	Surinam	80	125	Algeria	25
19	Sweden	99	71	Yugoslavia	80	126	Bangladesh	25
20	United Kingdom	99	72	Hong Kong	75	127	China	25
21	Australia	98	73	Paraguay	74	128	Ghana	25
22	Austria	98	74	Venezuela	74	129	Nigeria	25
23	Ireland	98	75	French Guyana	73	130	Rhodesia (Zimbabwe)	25
24	Japan	98	76	Albania	70	131	Swaziland	25
25	Liechtenstein	98	77	Belize	70	132	United Arab Emirates	25
26	Luxembourg	98	78	Burma**	70	133	Liberia	24
27	Netherlands	98	79	Guadeloupe	70	134	Botswana	22
28	New Zealand	98	80	Martinique	70	135	Benin	20
29	Poland	98	81	Singapore	70	136	Congo	20
30	Rumania	98	82	Thailand	70	137	Iraq	20
31	Soviet Union	98	83	Dominican Republic	68	138	Morocco	20
32	Switzerland	98	84	Brazil	67	139	Uganda	20
33	Belgium	97	85	Ivory Coast	65	140	Pakistan	17
34	France	97	86	Mexico	65	141	Burundi	15
35	Hungary	97	87	Portugal	65	142	Malawi	15
36	San Marino	97	88	Vietnam	65	143	Papua New Guinea	15
37	Spain	97	89	Solomon Islands	60	144	Saudi Arabia	15
38	Cuba	96	90	Indonesia	60	145	Tanzania	15
39	Bulgaria	95	91	Kuwait	60	146	Yemen Arab Republic	15
40	Italy	95	92	Mauritius	60	147	Cape Verde	14
41	Netherlands Antilles	95	93	Seychelles	60	148	Equatorial Guinea	12
42	Trinidad & Tobago	95				149	Gabon	12
43	Barbados	90		*LOWER MIDDLE*		150	Laos	12
44	Taiwan	90	94	Ecuador	57	151	Nepal	12
45	Costa Rica	90	95	Oman	56	152	Angola	11
46	North Korea	90	96	Cambodia	55	153	Afghanistan***	10
47	South Korea	90	97	Togo	55	154	Gambia	10
48	Tonga	90	98	Turkey	55	155	Haiti	10
49	Uruguay	90	99	Nicaragua	52	156	Mauritania	10
			100	El Salvador	50	157	New Hebrides	10
			101	Gilbert Islands	50	158	Qatar	10
			102	Jordan	50	159	Rwanda	10
			103	Tuvalu	50	160	Sierra Leone	10
			104	Colombia	47	161	South Yemen	10

Notes: *Whites only. Estimated literacy for blacks ranges from 50 to 80%.
**Official estimate: questionable.
***Estimate only.

Rank	Country	Percentage	Rank	Country	Percentage	Rank	Country	Percentage
162	Mozambique	7	167	Ethiopia	5	173	Somalia	5
163	Niger	6	168	Guinea	5	174	Upper Volta	5
			169	Mali	5	175	Guinea-Bissau	3
	BOTTOM 15		170	Sao Tome & Principe	5	176	Bhutan	2
164	Central African Empire	5	171	Senegal	5	177	Comoros	2
165	Chad	5	172	Sudan	5	178	Maldives	1
166	Djibouti	5						

Sources: *UNESCO Statistical Yearbook.*

268. School Enrollment

A number of indicators have been developed by UNESCO in order to measure current national efforts to educate the young. The three most important of these are the proportion of school-going population to the total population, the adjusted school enrollment ratio in relation to specific age groups and literacy. Because all these indicators are subject to error and distortion, it has been found necessary to present all of them; it also might be necessary to read them together to determine the degree of success each nation has achieved in this field. School enrollment in relation to total population (presented below) is an effective indicator of the quantitative levels and reach of current educational programs but suffers from a serious inadequacy in that it is biased in favor of countries with a high birthrate. A country, such as Belgium, with a low birthrate and a mature age profile, therefore, suffers in comparison with countries that have unrestrained population growth and a greater proportion of the population in the low age groups.

Number of Countries: 155
Midpoint: 1,715
Period Covered: 1975
Type of Ranking: School-going Population per 10,000 Inhabitants; Highest to Lowest

Highlights & Findings: Of the 10 top countries, nine are developing countries. However, a number of developing countries also rank low on this scale and in the lower middle, where they appear beside developed countries.

Regions	Africa	Asia & Oceania	Europe	Western Hemisphere
Highest	Congo (3)	Qatar (2)	Albania (6)	Grenada (1)
Lowest	Upper Volta (153)	Maldives (155)	Belgium (137)	Haiti (127)

Rank	Country	School Enrollment per 10,000 Inhabitants	Rank	Country	School Enrollment per 10,000 Inhabitants	Rank	Country	School Enrollment per 10,000 Inhabitants
	TOP 10		16	Jamaica	2,542	34	Dominican Republic	2,288
1	Grenada	3,750	17	Trinidad & Tobago	2,523	35	Singapore	2,253
2	Qatar	3,528	18	Chile	2,509	36	Venezuela	2,228
3	Congo	2,939	19	Mauritius	2,465	37	Mexico	2,193
4	Fiji	2,875	20	Syria	2,444	38	Iceland	2,186
5	Bahamas	2,791	21	New Zealand	2,438	39	Kuwait	2,185
6	Albania	2,764	22	United Arab Emirates	2,418	40	Australia	2,167
7	Tonga	2,755	23	Costa Rica	2,415	41	Canada	2,134
8	Libya	2,719	24	South Korea	2,414	42	Barbados	2,131
9	Brunei	2,716	25	Taiwan	2,407	43	Swaziland	2,092
10	United States	2,612	26	Cape Verde	2,396	44	Ecuador	2,068
			27	Cuba	2,369	45	Paraguay	2,052
	UPPER MIDDLE		28	Ireland	2,359	46	South Africa	2,010
11	Lebanon	2,611	29	Philippines	2,358	47	Sri Lanka	1,970
12	Panama	2,581	30	Malaysia	2,347	48	United Kingdom	1,966
13	Western Samoa	2,580	31	Bahrain	2,345	49	El Salvador	1,924
14	Gabon	2,576	32	Seychelles	2,345	50	Mongolia	1,924
15	Guyana	2,545	32	Peru	2,305	51	Zambia	1,919

Rank	Country	School Enrollment per 10,000 Inhabitants	Rank	Country	School Enrollment per 10,000 Inhabitants	Rank	Country	School Enrollment per 10,000 Inhabitants
52	Brazil	1,912	86	Ghana	1,612	122	Benin	1,033
53	Jordan	1,908	87	Zaire	1,597	123	Laos	991
54	Tunisia	1,896	88	Greece	1,595	124	Pakistan	977
55	Israel	1,870	89	Argentina	1,575	125	Rwanda	965
56	Nicaragua	1,842	90	Austria	1,574	126	Sierra Leone	938
57	Malta	1,826	91	Japan	1,568	127	Haiti	906
58	Thailand	1,824	92	East Germany	1,544	128	Nigeria	905
59	Cameroon	1,808	93	West Germany	1,544	129	Angola	889
60	Honduras	1,807	94	Ivory Coast	1,540	130	Saudi Arabia	883
61	Algeria	1,805	95	Sweden	1,540	131	Comoros	872
62	Lesotho	1,801	96	Liechtenstein	1,527	132	Tanzania	846
63	Iran	1,792	97	Italy	1,494	133	Senegal	829
64	Iraq	1,791	98	India	1,462	134	Sudan	827
65	Sao Tome & Principe	1,784	99	Poland	1,460	135	Uganda	804
66	Turkey	1,754	100	Yugoslavia	1,454	136	Guinea-Bissau	735
67	Spain	1,747	101	South Yemen	1,439	137	Belgium	693
68	Madagascar	1,739	102	Nauru	1,428	138	Guinea	619
69	Soviet Union	1,727	103	Central African Empire	1,426	139	Chad	552
70	Botswana	1,724	104	San Marino	1,421	140	Mozambique	552
71	China	1,721	105	Burma	1,403	141	Gambia	549
72	Togo	1,718	106	Monaco	1,400	142	Mali	508
73	Colombia	1,715	107	Bangladesh	1,396	143	Nepal	507
			108	Switzerland	1,376	144	Oman	497
	LOWER MIDDLE		109	Guatemala	1,361	145	Burundi	473
74	Bolivia	1,714	110	Czechoslovakia	1,355			
75	Finland	1,706	111	Andorra	1,327		**BOTTOM 10**	
76	France	1,703	112	Rumania	1,324	146	Cambodia	463
77	Cyprus	1,684	113	Equatorial Guinea	1,278	147	Afghanistan	438
78	Uruguay	1,680	114	Luxembourg	1,257	148	Ethiopia	414
79	Egypt	1,667	115	Malawi	1,248	149	Somalia	398
80	Rhodesia (Zimbabwe)	1,659	116	Bulgaria	1,228	150	Mauritania	379
81	Kenya	1,654	117	Indonesia	1,135	151	Yemen Arab Republic	336
82	Netherlands	1,646	118	Liberia	1,108	152	Niger	285
83	Norway	1,635	119	Hungary	1,055	153	Upper Volta	244
84	Portugal	1,633	120	Papua New Guinea	1,038	154	Bhutan	113
85	Denmark	1,629	121	Morocco	1,036	155	Maldives	78

Source: *UNESCO Statistical Yearbook.*

269. Number of Primary Schools

One of the most important educational indicators is the number of primary, or first-level, schools. Because the duration of each level of schooling varies from country to country, the number of grades in these schools fluctuates; furthermore, in many developing countries, primary schools, especially in rural areas, tend to be one-room and one-teacher institutions providing only the most rudimentary education. This ranking is therefore a quantitative and not a qualitative measurement. It includes all institutions and structures officially accredited as first-level schools but excludes schools for adults and handicapped persons.

Number of Countries: 177
Midpoint: 1,938
Period Covered: Mid-1970s
Type of Ranking: Total Number of First-Level (Primary) Schools; Highest to Lowest

Highlights & Findings: Of the world total of 1,929,255 first-level schools, the top 10 nations account for 60%. The proportion of new school construction follows the same pattern.

Regions	Africa	Asia & Oceania	Europe	Western Hemisphere
Most	South Africa (24)	India (1)	Soviet Union (3)	Brazil (2)
Least	St. Helena (175)	Maldives (177)	Monaco (173)	St. Pierre & Miquelon (176)

Rank	Country	Number of Primary Schools

TOP 10

1	India	443,461
2	Brazil	180,915
3	Soviet Union	147,083
4	United States	79,070
5	Indonesia	72,760
6	France	57,084
7	Pakistan	51,568
8	Mexico	48,848
9	Turkey	41,060
10	Iran	35,796

UPPER MIDDLE

11	Philippines	35,067
12	Italy	33,534
13	Colombia	32,230
14	Spain	30,720
15	Bangladesh	29,869
16	Thailand	29,713
17	United Kingdom	29,337
18	Japan	24,652
19	Argentina	20,646
20	Peru	19,701
21	Burma	18,670
22	West Germany	18,094
23	Portugal	16,147
24	South Africa	15,615
25	Cuba	15,561
26	Poland	14,738
27	Rumania	14,695
28	Nigeria	14,502
29	Yugoslavia	13,540
30	Venezuela	11,098
31	Czechoslovakia	9,840
32	Egypt	9,782
33	Ecuador	9,777
34	Greece	9,736
35	Belgium	9,007
36	Sri Lanka	8,649
37	Netherlands	8,486
38	Chile	8,461
39	Malaysia	8,322
40	Nepal	8,314
41	Kenya	8,161
42	Australia	8,076
43	Algeria	7,798
44	Iraq	7,664
45	Bolivia	6,920
46	Ghana	6,886
47	Syria	6,760
48	South Korea	6,405
49	Guatemala	5,912
50	Madagascar	5,845
51	Tanzania	5,804
52	Zaire	5,324
53	Dominican Republic	5,245
54	Angola	5,208
55	East Germany	5,067
56	Hungary	4,978
57	Sweden	4,819
58	Honduras	4,602

59	Cameroon	4,319
60	Finland	4,236
61	Sudan	4,088
62	Mozambique	3,947
63	Rhodesia (Zimbabwe)	3,723
64	Austria	3,711
65	Ireland	3,659
66	Bulgaria	3,444
67	Afghanistan	3,428
68	Uganda	3,417
69	Laos	3,413
70	Paraguay	3,366
71	Saudi Arabia	3,028
72	El Salvador	3,018
73	Norway	2,960
74	Costa Rica	2,790
75	Ethiopia	2,759
76	Ivory Coast	2,700
77	New Zealand	2,685
78	Zambia	2,669
79	Uruguay	2,324
80	Tunisia	2,319
81	Denmark	2,215
82	Panama	2,190
83	Malawi	2,091
84	Haiti	2,083
85	Nicaragua	2,068
86	Guinea	1,984
87	Yemen Arab Republic	1,952
88	Libya	1,940
89	Puerto Rico	1,938

LOWER MIDDLE

90	Morocco	1,928
91	Papua New Guinea	1,815
92	Israel	1,685
93	Rwanda	1,668
94	Luxembourg	1,667
95	Cambodia	1,534
96	Albania	1,429
97	Togo	1,362
98	Benin	1,325
99	Senegal	1,215
100	Jordan	1,132
101	Sierra Leone	1,132
102	Hong Kong	1,126
103	Mali	1,100
104	Lesotho	1,079
105	Liberia	1,059
106	Congo	1,033
107	Niger	990
108	Jamaica	981
109	Burundi	970
110	South Yemen	963
111	Chad	806
112	Lebanon	735
113	Gabon	734
114	Somalia	730
115	Central African Empire	717
116	Upper Volta	688
117	Fiji	641

118	Equatorial Guinea	559
119	Trinidad & Tobago	473
120	Cape Verde	420
121	Swaziland	412
122	Singapore	396
123	Guyana	395
124	Cyprus	393
125	Reunion	369
126	Mauritius	347
127	Botswana	323
128	Solomon Islands	323
129	Guinea-Bissau	261
130	Guadeloupe	253
131	Pacific Islands	244
132	Martinique	237
133	New Caledonia	235
134	Bahamas	196
135	Belize	186
136	Western Samoa	173
137	Kuwait	171
138	French Polynesia	166
139	Oman	163
140	Barbados	159
141	Malta	140
142	Brunei	136
143	Comoros	130
144	Tonga	126
145	Iceland	124
146	Gilbert Islands	111
147	Bahrain	107
148	Gambia	103
149	New Hebrides	95
150	Qatar	92
151	Bhutan	89
152	Macao	84
153	St. Lucia	74
154	St. Vincent	60
155	Grenada	58
156	Antigua	57
157	Dominica	57
158	French Guyana	45
159	Sao Tome & Principe	45
160	Falkland Islands	42
161	St. Kitts-Nevis-Anguilla	39
162	Seychelles	36
163	Djibouti	34
164	Cook Islands	33
165	Bermuda	22
166	British Virgin Islands	18
167	Montserrat	17

BOTTOM 10

168	San Marino	16
169	Turks & Caicos	16
170	Gibraltar	14
171	Nauru	10
172	Cayman Islands	9
173	Monaco	8
174	Niue Island	8
175	St. Helena	8
176	St. Pierre & Miquelon	6
177	Maldives	2

Source: *UNESCO Statistical Yearbook.*

270. Primary School Enrollment Ratio

In all countries of the world the first level of education (also called primary or elementary education) is the most important and, in nations where compulsory education laws are in force, the most universal. Although primary school age is generally considered six to 11 years, each educational system follows its own definition. Differences among countries in the age and duration of schooling are reflected in the ratios. Enrollment ratios may be either gross or net;

for the purpose of this ranking, the former has been adopted. Gross enrollment ratio is derived by dividing total enrollment by the national population within the specified age group. In the case of countries with differing educational systems (particularly federal countries, such as the United States and West Germany), the age group of the most representative system has been used.

Number of Countries: 140
Midpoint: 96%
Period Covered: 1975 or Latest Available Year
Type of Ranking: Gross Primary School Enrollment Ratio; Gross Female Primary School Enrollment Ratio; Primary School Age Group; Highest to Lowest

Highlights & Findings: The most striking fact about enrollment ratios at the first level is the apparent anomaly of ratios over 100%, as reported by 54 countries in the following ranking. The peculiarity results from the mode of calculating the ratio. Whereas the total enrollment includes actual enrollment of pupils of all ages, the divisor, or the figure used for dividing, is the population within the range of the official school ages. Therefore, for countries with almost universal education the gross enrollment ratio will exceed 100% if: (1) the actual age distribution of pupils spills over the official school ages; (2) there is a significant proportion of alien children in the school-going population; or (3) there is abnormal grade repetition as a result of which overaged children remain enrolled in lower grades. It is interesting to note the presence of many developing, particularly African, countries in the top 20. In all these cases a high enrollment ratio has been accompanied by a dramatic rise in literacy.

Regions	Africa	Asia & Oceania	Europe	Western Hemisphere
Most	Gabon (1)	Lebanon (4)	West Germany (6)	Guadeloupe (7)
Least	Upper Volta (139)	Bhutan (140)	Cyprus (103)	Haiti (121)

Rank	Country	Gross First-Level Enrollment Ratio (%)	Female First-Level Enrollment Ratio (%)	Age Group	Rank	Country	Gross First-Level Enrollment Ratio (%)	Female First-Level Enrollment Ratio (%)	Age Group	Rank	Country	Gross First-Level Enrollment Ratio (%)	Female First-Level Enrollment Ratio (%)	Age Group
	TOP 10				28	Costa Rica	109	109	6-11	58	Poland	100	98	7-14
1	Gabon	193	190	6-11	29	France	109	109	6-10	59	Hungary	99	99	6-13
2	Congo	153	140	6-11	30	Kenya	109	101	5-11	60	Rhodesia (Zimbabwe)	99	87	7-11
3	Libya	145	135	6-11	31	South Korea	109	109	6-11	61	Soviet Union	99	99	7-14
4	Lebanon	132	125	5-9	32	Rumania	109	109	6-13	62	Australia	98	98	5-11
5	Reunion	132	132	6-10	33	Argentina	108	109	5-11	63	Togo	98	68	6-11
6	West Germany	129	128	6-10	34	Ireland	108	108	6-11	64	Sweden	97	98	7-12
7	Guadeloupe	129	132	6-10	35	Italy	107	106	6-10	65	Yugoslavia	97	93	7-14
8	Israel	128	129	6-11	36	South Africa	107	107	6-12	66	Bulgaria	96	96	7-14
9	Cuba	126	123	6-11	37	Albania	106	103	6-13	67	Czechoslovakia	96	97	6-14
10	Martinique	125	125	6-10	38	Greece	106	N.A.	5-10	68	Portugal	96	94	6-11
					39	Paraguay	106	102	7-12	69	Venezuela	96	96	7-12
	UPPER MIDDLE				40	Belgium	105	105	6-11	70	Zambia	96	86	7-13
11	Panama	124	120	6-11	41	Colombia	105	108	7-11					
12	Lesotho	121	144	6-12	42	Philippines	105	103	7-12		*LOWER MIDDLE*			
13	Hong Kong	120	119	6-11	43	Canada	104	103	6-11	71	East Germany	95	96	7-16
14	Chile	119	118	6-13	44	Iceland	104	102	7-12	72	Tunisia	95	75	6-11
15	Barbados	117	116	5-10	45	Turkey	104	94	6-10	73	Uruguay	95	94	6-11
16	United Kingdom	116	116	5-10	46	United States	104	N.A.	5-12	74	Iraq	93	63	6-11
17	Luxembourg	115	120	6-11	47	Swaziland	103	102	6-11	75	Malaysia	93	91	6-11
18	Spain	115	115	6-10	48	Austria	102	102	6-9	76	Switzerland	92	93	6-11
19	Guyana	114	114	6-10	49	Denmark	102	102	6-12	77	Brazil	90	90	7-14
20	Mexico	112	109	6-11	50	Ecuador	102	100	6-11	78	Iran	90	67	6-10
21	Trinidad & Tobago	112	111	5-11	51	Norway	102	102	7-12	79	Kuwait	90	84	6-9
22	Cameroon	111	97	6-11	52	Syria	102	81	6-11	80	Zaire	90	66	6-11
23	Fiji	111	110	6-13	53	Dominican Republic	101	102	7-12	81	Algeria	89	72	6-11
24	Jamaica	111	112	6-10	54	Malta	101	106	5-10	82	Honduras	89	88	6-11
25	New Zealand	111	110	5-10	55	Equatorial Guinea	100	89	6-10	83	Finland	87	84	7-12
26	Peru	111	106	6-11	56	Japan	100	100	6-11	84	Puerto Rico	87	86	5-12
27	Singapore	111	108	6-11	57	Netherlands	100	100	6-11	85	Ivory Coast	86	64	6-11

Rank	Country	Gross First-Level Enrollment Ratio (%)	Female First-Level Enrollment Ratio (%)	Age Group	Rank	Country	Gross First-Level Enrollment Ratio (%)	Female First-Level Enrollment Ratio (%)	Age Group	Rank	Country	Gross First-Level Enrollment Ratio (%)	Female First-Level Enrollment Ratio (%)	Age Group
86	Botswana	85	93	6-12	105	India	65	52	5-10	124	Saudi Arabia	44	32	6-11
87	Burma	85	81	5-9	106	Liberia	62	44	6-11	125	Sudan	40	27	7-12
88	Mongolia	85	85	8-11	107	Malawi	61	48	7-11	126	Cambodia	38	32	6-11
89	Nicaragua	85	87	7-12	108	Morocco	61	44	6-10	127	Chad	37	20	6-11
90	Jordan	83	77	6-11	109	Ghana	60	53	6-11	128	Sierra Leone	35	28	5-11
91	Madagascar	83	77	6-11	110	Papua New Guinea	59	44	5-10	129	Gambia	32	21	6-11
92	Indonesia	81	75	6-11	111	Guatemala	58	52	7-12	130	Guinea	28	18	7-12
93	Mauritius	80	78	5-11	112	Rwanda	58	54	7-12					
94	Angola	79	57	5-9	113	Somalia	58	41	6-9			*BOTTOM 10*			
95	Central African Empire	79	53	6-11	114	Tanzania	57	46	7-13	131	Nepal	27	10	6-10
96	Guinea-Bissau	78	51	6-11	115	Comoros	55	34	8-13	132	Yemen Arab Republic	25	6	7-12
97	Thailand	78	75	5-11	116	Laos	54	40	6-11	133	Afghanistan	23	7	7-12
98	South Yemen	78	48	7-12	117	Senegal	53	42	6-10	134	Burundi	23	17	6-12
99	Sri Lanka	77	77	6-10	118	Uganda	53	43	6-12	135	Ethiopia	23	14	6-13
100	Bolivia	75	65	6-13	119	Mozambique	52	35	6-10	136	Mali	22	16	6-14
101	Bangladesh	73	51	5-9	120	Pakistan	51	31	5-9	137	Mauritania	17	9	6-11
102	Egypt	72	55	6-11	121	Haiti	50	44	7-12	138	Niger	17	12	6-11
103	Cyprus	71	72	6-11	122	Nigeria	49	39	6-12	139	Upper Volta	14	11	6-11
104	El Salvador	71	69	6-14	123	Benin	44	28	5-11	140	Bhutan	8	4	6-10

Source: *UNESCO Statistical Yearbook.*

271. Educational Expenditure per Pupil

Educational expenditure per pupil is an indicator of the educational priorities of each state in relation to each level of education. The first level (or the primary) is universally the most important segment of the educational system because of its impact on functional literacy. The data, where available, are for various years and thus are only roughly compar-

able. The figures, however, are comprehensive and include central or federal, state, provincial and local expenditures and cover both private and public education. The rankings should be interpreted with great caution because the distribution of students by levels of education varies from country to country.

Number of Countries: 121
Midpoint: $81.2 per Pupil
Period Covered: Latest Available Year Since 1965
Type of Ranking: Cost per Pupil at the First Level in U.S. Dollars; Highest to Lowest

Highlights & Findings: Since educational expenditures reflect the social philosophy of the governments, they are highest in welfare states. They are also highest in those states where the state provides not only free tuition but free textbooks, free transportation, free midday lunches and other facilities.

Regions	Africa	Asia & Oceania	Europe	Western Hemisphere
Most	Djibouti (24)	Kuwait (8)	Sweden (1)	United States (3)
Least	Lesotho (119)	Bangladesh (121)	Greece (49)	Colombia (111)

Rank	Country	Educational Expenditure per Pupil ($)	Rank	Country	Educational Expenditure per Pupil ($)	Rank	Country	Educational Expenditure per Pupil ($)
	TOP 10			*UPPER MIDDLE*		21	French Polynesia	455.1
1	Sweden	2,024.4	11	Japan	647.9	22	Italy	419.6
2	Denmark	1,579.4	12	West Germany	637.6	23	Belgium	406.4
3	United States	1,090.8	13	Austria	617.4	24	Djibouti	406.4
4	Canada	1,050.0	14	Czechoslovakia	612.2	25	Rumania	392.4
5	Finland	971.0	15	Hungary	603.4	26	Israel	359.2
6	Switzerland	930.2	16	Luxembourg	582.8	27	France	330.0
7	Poland	888.1	17	San Marino	562.0	28	England & Wales	313.5
8	Kuwait	848.7	18	New Zealand	560.8	29	Gibraltar	285.6
9	East Germany	741.3	19	Netherlands	546.6	30	New Caledonia	276.4
10	Puerto Rico	671.0	20	Bermuda	462.0	31	Qatar	247.4

Rank	Country	Eductional Expenditure per Pupil ($)
32	Bulgaria	244.2
33	Yugoslavia	209.4
34	Cyprus	209.0
35	Pacific Islands	196.1
36	Brunei	178.6
37	Bahrain	172.6
38	Ireland	162.1
39	Barbados	154.1
40	Singapore	144.6
41	Mongolia	141.9
42	Venezuela	141.2
43	Malta	133.8
44	Spain	130.9
45	British Virgin Islands	130.6
46	Portugal	130.5
47	Argentina	124.4
48	Hong Kong	124.4
49	Greece	110.5
50	Malaysia (West)	106.8
51	Iraq	102.7
52	Uruguay	102.7
53	Panama	98.1
54	Jamaica	96.0
55	New Hebrides	88.5
56	Fiji	87.3
57	Ivory Coast	86.5
58	Iran	85.1
59	Mexico	84.8
60	Antigua	83.4
61	Seychelles	81.2
62	Montserrat	77.5

Rank	Country	Educational Expenditure per Pupil ($)
63	Morocco	73.5
64	Senegal	71.0
	LOWER MIDDLE	
65	Costa Rica	68.9
66	Chile	67.7
67	Tunisia	66.9
68	Guyana	66.7
69	Mauritius	66.3
70	Peru	63.0
71	Trinidad & Tobago	61.9
72	Algeria	60.3
73	Egypt	59.7
74	Belize	57.6
75	Zambia	56.6
76	Comoros	56.4
77	Gilbert Islands	53.6
78	Grenada	53.2
79	Cambodia	49.7
80	Ghana	48.9
81	St. Lucia	45.9
82	Niger	44.5
83	Botswana	42.4
84	Somalia	39.5
85	Congo	38.9
86	Guatomala	38.5
87	Jordan	37.7
88	Upper Volta	37.5
89	South Korea	36.6
90	Papua New Guinea	36.3
91	Kenya	34.9

Rank	Country	Educational Expenditure per Pupil ($)
92	Honduras	34.2
93	Nicaragua	33.9
94	El Salvador	30.4
95	Bolivia	29.5
96	Tonga	29.3
97	Benin	26.4
98	Swaziland	25.8
99	Ecuador	24.8
100	Thailand	24.3
101	Nigeria	24.1
102	Tanzania	24.1
103	Ethiopia	22.1
104	Madagascar	20.7
105	Sri Lanka	20.3
106	Cameroon	19.3
107	Dominican Republic	18.8
108	Uganda	18.4
109	Togo	17.3
110	Paraguay	16.8
111	Colombia	16.3
	BOTTOM 10	
112	Afghanistan	14.9
113	Laos	14.9
114	Burundi	13.6
115	India	13.6
116	Rwanda	12.5
117	Malawi	9.9
118	Pakistan	9.8
119	Lesotho	9.6
120	Burma	6.2
121	Bangladesh	4.2

Source: *UNESCO Statistical Yearbook.*

272. Primary School Teacher-Pupil Ratio

One indicator of the quality of education is the number of pupils per teacher. This ratio is particularly significant in the primary grades, where children need individual attention. The number of teachers on which the ratio is based generally includes part-time teachers but excludes other instructional personnel without teaching functions, such as principals and librarians.

Number of Countries: 184
Midpoint: 1:29
Period Covered: 1974
Type of Ranking: Teacher-Pupil Ratio in Primary Schools; Highest to Lowest

Highlights & Findings: Individual country ratios should be interpreted in the light of world and regional ratios. The world teacher-pupil ratio is 1:28; the ratio is 1:21 in developed countries, 1:34 in developing countries, 1:40 in Africa, 1:35 in Asia, 1:22 in Europe, 1:25 in Oceania, 1:28 in Latin America and 1:22 in North America. The ratio in many developing countries would be even more unsatisfactory had it not been for the fact that their teaching staffs are augmented by alien teachers on contract as well as volunteers, such as Peace Corps members and Christian missionaries.

Regions	Africa	Asia & Oceania	Europe	Western Hemisphere
Most	St. Helena (26)	Israel (1)	Soviet Union (2)	Argentina (9)
Least	Chad (184)	South Korea (170)	Greece (107)	Dominican Republic (174)

Rank	Country	Number of Pupils per Teacher in Primary School	Rank	Country	Number of Pupils per Teacher in Primary School	Rank	Country	Number of Pupils per Teacher in Primary School
	TOP 8		62	Antigua	25	124	Mali	35
1	Israel	14	63	Canada	25	125	Syria	35
2	Soviet Union	15	64	Japan	25	126	Thailand	35
3	Denmark	16	65	Martinique	25	127	Afghanistan	36
4	Hungary	16	66	Solomon Islands	25	128	Guinea	36
5	San Marino	16	67	Tonga	25	129	Jordan	36
6	Sweden	16	68	Gambia	26	130	Bahamas	37
7	Nauru	17	69	Iraq	26	131	Djibouti	37
8	Norway	17	70	Maldives	26	132	Laos	37
			71	Montserrat	26	133	Sarawak	37
	UPPER MIDDLE		72	Panama	26	134	Dominica	38
9	Argentina	18	73	Sabah	26	135	Swaziland	38
10	Falkland Islands	18	74	St. Pierre & Miquelon	26	136	Ecuador	39
11	Gibraltar	18	75	United Arab Emirates	26	137	Jamaica	39
12	Kuwait	18	76	Andorra	27	138	Nicaragua	39
13	Niue Island	18	77	Bahrain	27	139	Rhodesia (Zimbabwe)	39
14	Turks & Caicos	18	78	Belize	27	140	South Africa	39
15	Brunei	19	79	Cyprus	27	141	Sudan	39
16	Finland	19	80	Mauritius	27	142	Egypt	40
17	Italy	19	81	Northern Ireland	27	143	India	40
18	Luxembourg	19	82	Portugal	27	144	Morocco	40
19	Malta	19	83	Reunion	27	145	Peru	40
20	New Zealand	19	84	Western Samoa	27	146	Tunisia	40
21	Belgium	20	85	Costa Rica	28	147	Yemen Arab Republic	40
22	British Virgin Islands	20	86	Netherlands	28	148	Algeria	41
23	Czechoslovakia	20	87	Paraguay	28	149	Angola	41
24	Iceland	20	88	Bhutan	29	150	Liberia	41
25	Qatar	20	89	Guadeloupe	29	151	Niger	41
26	St. Helena	20	90	Macao	29	152	St. Kitts-Nevis-Anguilla	41
27	St. Vincent	20	91	Philippines	29	153	Zaire	41
28	United States	20	92	Spain	29	154	Comoros	42
29	Austria	21	93	Ghana	30	155	Pakistan	42
30	Bermuda	21	94	Indonesia	30	156	El Salvador	43
31	Bulgaria	21	95	Ireland	30	157	Guinea-Bissau	45
32	Monaco	21	96	Mongolia	30	158	Haiti	45
33	Pacific Islands	21	97	Papua New Guinea	30	159	Ivory Coast	45
34	Poland	21	98	Sri Lanka	30	160	Ethiopia	46
35	Puerto Rico	21	99	South Yemen	30	161	Mexico	46
36	Rumania	21				162	Upper Volta	46
37	Saudi Arabia	21		**LOWER MIDDLE**		163	Burma	47
38	Brazil	22	100	Burundi	31	164	Zambia	48
39	Cook Islands	22	101	Gilbert Islands	31	165	Bangladesh	49
40	England & Wales	22	102	Iran	31	166	Senegal	49
41	Mauritania	22	103	St. Lucia	31	167	Gabon	50
42	New Caledonia	22	104	Singapore	31	168	Rwanda	50
43	New Hebrides	22	105	Venezuela	31	169	Cameroon	51
44	Scotland	22	106	Fiji	32	170	South Korea	52
45	Yugoslavia	22	107	Greece	32	171	Benin	53
46	Bolivia	23	108	Guyana	32	172	Lesotho	53
47	Cayman Islands	23	109	Hong Kong	32	173	Tanzania	53
48	Cuba	23	110	Malaysia (West)	32	174	Dominican Republic	55
49	France	23	111	Sierra Leone	32			
50	French Guyana	23	112	Botswana	33		**BOTTOM 10**	
51	West Germany	23	113	Colombia	33	175	Equatorial Guinea	57
52	Lebanon	23	114	Kenya	33	176	Somalia	57
53	Libya	23	115	Trinidad & Tobago	33	177	Malawi	58
54	Uruguay	23	116	Grenada	34	178	Cape Verde	60
55	Australia	24	117	Nigeria	34	179	Togo	60
56	Cambodia	24	118	Sao Tome & Principe	34	180	Congo	61
57	French Polynesia	24	119	Turkey	34	181	Madagascar	63
58	Nepal	24	120	Uganda	34	182	Central African Empire	69
59	Oman	24	121	Chile	35	183	Mozambique	69
60	Seychelles	24	122	Guatemala	35	184	Chad	75
61	Albania	25	123	Honduras	35			

Source: *UNESCO Statistical Yearbook.*

273. Percentage of Repeaters: First-Level Last Grade

One measure of the academic success of a country's school population is the percentage of repeaters in each grade, particularly in the final or transitional grades of each level. Where the percentage of repeaters is high, it indicates that either the curriculum is too difficult or too unsuited for the general run of children, the level of teaching is too low, or the assimilative powers of the children are too underdeveloped in relation to the language or content of instruction. Combined with the dropout or attrition rate, this ranking reflects one aspect of the quality of education.

Number of Countries: 83
Midpoint: 13%
Period Covered: Mid-1970s
Type of Ranking: Percentage of Repeaters in the Last Grade of the First Level; Highest to Lowest

Highlights & Findings: The top 17 countries are all in Africa, confirming the opinion of many observers that much of African education has no relevance to conditions on the continent and is not rooted in African traditions. In most of these countries the language of instruction is a foreign language. Furthermore, the curricula are modeled on those of the West, teachers are poorly trained, the classrooms are crowded and ill-equipped. The percentage of grade repeaters was insignificant in the United States, the Soviet Union, the United Kingdom, West Germany and other highly developed countries.

Regions	Africa	Asia & Oceania	Europe	Western Hemisphere
Most	Chad (1)	Singapore (21)	Belgium (19)	Martinique (4)
Least	Ghana (79)	Papua New Guinea (74)	Yugoslavia (83)	El Salvador (78)

Rank	Country	Percentage of Repeaters	Rank	Country	Percentage of Repeaters	Rank	Country	Percentage of Repeaters
	TOP 9		28	Iraq	18	56	Tanzania	6
1	Chad	57	29	Lesotho	18	57	Chile	5
2	Ivory Coast	46	30	Sri Lanka	18	58	Portugal	5
3	Morocco	44	31	Swaziland	18	59	Jordan	4
4	Martinique	43	32	Zaire	18	60	Malta	4
5	Tunisia	41	33	India	16	61	Oman	4
6	Benin	40	34	Kenya	16	62	Peru	4
7	Burundi	39	35	Libya	16	63	Seychelles	4
8	Malawi	37	36	Madagascar	16	64	Costa Rica	3
9	Mali	37	37	Burma	15	65	Cuba	3
			38	Guyana	14	66	Italy	3
	UPPER MIDDLE		39	Cameroon	13	67	Nicaragua	3
10	Central African Empire	36	40	Egypt	13	68	Panama	3
11	Niger	36	41	Fiji	13	69	Paraguay	3
12	Upper Volta	36	42	France	13	70	Rumania	3
13	Djibouti	35						
14	Gambia	35		**LOWER MIDDLE**			**BOTTOM 13**	
15	Congo	34	43	Kuwait	12	71	Guatemala	2
16	Senegal	34	44	New Caledonia	10	72	Indonesia	2
17	Togo	34	45	Ecuador	9	73	Thailand	2
18	French Guyana	29	46	Iran	9	74	Papua New Guinea	2
19	Belgium	28	47	Saudi Arabia	9	75	Antigua	1
20	Guadeloupe	28	48	Sudan	9	76	Argentina	1
21	Singapore	27	49	Venezuela	9	77	Bulgaria	1
22	Rwanda	24	50	Zambia	9	78	El Salvador	1
23	French Polynesia	23	51	Colombia	8	79	Ghana	1
24	Gabon	23	52	Syria	8	80	Greece	1
25	Algeria	22	53	Uruguay	7	81	Netherlands	1
26	Mozambique	22	54	Brazil	6	82	Poland	1
27	Botswana	21	55	Dominican Republic	6	83	Yugoslavia	1

Source: *UNESCO Statistical Yearbook.*

274. Private Primary-Level Education

In all countries of the world, education is a state responsibility, and the educational system is operated and/or supervised by the state. But within most of these educational systems, private schools function with varying degrees of freedom. Many of these schools are run by Christian missionaries and local Catholic and Protestant churches. Others are sponsored by ethnic groups and philanthropic organiza-

tions. In many countries these schools enjoy greater prestige than public schools and maintain better educational standards. Nevertheless, in many countries they are subject to government supervision, receive government subsidies, and are required to recruit only accredited teachers and to conform to state curricula.

Number of Countries: 126		
Midpoint 14%		
Period Covered: Mid-1970s		
Type of Ranking: Percentage of First-Level Enrollment in Private Schools; Highest to Lowest		

	Africa	**Asia & Oceania**	**Europe**	**Western Hemisphere**
Most	Lesotho (2)	Solomon Islands (4)	Ireland (1)	Belize (3)
Least	Tunisia (126)	South Korea (124)	Iceland (120)	Canada (110)

Rank	Country	Percentage of First-Level Enrollment in Private Schools	Rank	Country	Percentage of First-Level Enrollment in Private Schools	Rank	Country	Percentage of First-Level Enrollment in Private Schools
	TOP 10		42	Malta	22	84	Italy	7
1	Ireland	100	43	Madagascar	21	85	Qatar	7
2	Lesotho	100	44	Tonga	21	86	Reunion	7
3	Belize	99	45	Australia	20	87	St. Kitts-Nevis-Anguilla	7
4	Solomon Islands	97	46	Ivory Coast	20	88	Chad	6
5	Fiji	94	47	Kuwait	20	89	Guadeloupe	6
6	Burundi	93	48	Uruguay	20	90	Honduras	6
7	Hong Kong	92	49	Angola	19	91	Mali	6
8	Seychelles	89	50	Chile	19	92	Niger	6
9	Netherlands Antilles	83	51	Bahamas	18	93	Portugal	6
10	Swaziland	81	52	Djibouti	18	94	Sri Lanka	6
			53	French Guyana	18	95	Botswana	5
	UPPER MIDDLE		54	Argentina	17	96	Denmark	5
11	Grenada	79	55	Bermuda	17	97	Mexico	5
12	New Hebrides	77	56	Ecuador	17	98	Morocco	5
13	Netherlands	71	57	Gambia	16	99	Panama	5
14	Gilbert Islands	63	58	Colombia	15	100	Philippines	5
15	Lebanon	62	59	Indonesia	15	101	Syria	5
16	Papua New Guinea	62	60	Montserrat	15	102	Upper Volta	5
17	St. Pierre & Miquelon	57	61	Nicaragua	15	103	Costa Rica	4
18	Belgium	51	62	United States	15	104	England	4
19	Northern Ireland	48				105	Austria	3
20	Cameroon	47		*LOWER MIDDLE*		106	Martinique	3
21	Gabon	46	63	British Virgin Islands	14	107	Sudan	3
22	New Caledonia	43	64	France	14	108	Turks & Caicos	3
23	Sabah	43	65	Guatemala	14	109	Cambodia	2
24	Sarawak	40	66	Thailand	14	110	Canada	2
25	Spain	36	67	Dominican Republic	13	111	Ghana	2
26	Singapore	35	68	Paraguay	13	112	Luxembourg	2
27	Haiti	33	69	Peru	13	113	Saudi Arabia	2
28	Nigeria	31	70	Western Samoa	13	114	Scotland	2
29	Jordan	30	71	Dominica	12	115	Tanzania	2
30	Liberia	30	72	Senegal	12			
31	Togo	30	73	Egypt	11		*BOTTOM 11*	
32	Mauritius	28	74	Venezuela	11	116	Algeria	1
33	Antigua	27	75	Bolivia	10	117	Comoros	1
34	Benin	27	76	New Zealand	10	118	Cyprus	1
35	French Polynesia	26	77	Pacific Islands	10	119	West Germany	1
36	Monaco	26	78	Brazil	8	120	Iceland	1
37	Zambia	26	79	El Salvador	8	121	Iraq	1
38	Ethiopia	25	80	Greece	8	122	Japan	1
39	Brunei	24	81	Puerto Rico	8	123	Kenya	1
40	Equatorial Guinea	24	82	Bahrain	7	124	South Korea	1
41	Bangladesh	23	83	Iran	7	125	Libya	1
						126	Tunisia	1

Source: *UNESCO Statistical Yearbook.*

275. Secondary School Enrollment Ratio

Secondary schools provide general or specialized instruction based upon at least four years previous instruction at the first level but do not aim at preparing pupils directly for a given trade or occupation. Such schools are called by various names—high schools, middle schools, lyceums, etc.—and offer courses of study the completion of which is a minimum condition for admission to a university. Secondary school enrollment ratios are expressed as percentages calculated by dividing the actual enrollment by the population of the specific age group to which secondary education is directed according to

official sources. Because these age groups vary and because the duration of primary and middle schooling varies among countries, the data may not be strictly comparable. One peculiarity of the enrollment data is that some countries have a ratio of over 100%. This happens when the actual age distribution of pupils spreads above the school ages, when there is a significant percentage of foreign students and when the ratio is distorted by the presence of higher age groups in lower grades because of grade-repetition.

Number of Countries: 140	**Highlights & Findings:** The ranking follows the general pattern of other enrollment ratios with
Midpoint: 28%	developed countries dominating the top of the list.
Period Covered: 1975	
Type of Ranking: Secondary School Enrollment Ratio; Highest to Lowest	

Regions	Africa	Asia & Oceania	Europe	Western Hemisphere
Most	Reunion (25)	Japan (2)	Finland (1)	Canada (4)
Least	Chad (139)	Bhutan (140)	Albania (59)	Haiti (122)

Rank	Country	Secondary School Enrollment Ratio	Rank	Country	Secondary School Enrollment Ratio	Rank	Country	Secondary School Enrollment Ratio
	TOP 10		36	Argentina	59	72	Libya	28
1	Finland	113	37	Cyprus	59	73	Iran	27
2	Japan	96	38	Denmark	59	74	Gabon	23
3	Mongolia	96	39	Rumania	59	75	Burma	22
4	Canada	94	40	Jamaica	58	76	Dominican Republic	22
5	Norway	90	41	Hungary	57	77	Thailand	21
6	France	88	42	Panama	57	78	Brazil	20
7	Bulgaria	87	43	Philippines	57	79	Iraq	20
8	East Germany	86	44	Kuwait	56	80	Nicaragua	20
9	United States	86	45	Costa Rica	55	81	Paraguay	20
10	Martinique	85	46	Sri Lanka	55	82	Bolivia	18
			47	Guyana	54	83	India	18
	UPPER MIDDLE		48	Luxembourg	54	84	Turkey	18
11	Belgium	84	49	Fiji	52	85	Botswana	17
12	New Zealand	83	50	Chile	51	86	El Salvador	17
13	Netherlands	81	51	Yugoslavia	51	87	South Africa	17
14	Portugal	80	52	South Korea	50	88	Lesotho	15
15	Soviet Union	80	53	Mauritius	46	89	Algeria	13
16	Greece	79	54	Venezuela	46	90	Honduras	13
17	Guadeloupe	79	55	Singapore	45	91	Indonesia	13
18	Austria	76	56	Czechoslovakia	44	92	Tunisia	13
19	Spain	76	57	Trinidad & Tobago	43	93	Bangladesh	11
20	United Kingdom	76	58	Israel	42	94	Morocco	11
21	Iceland	74	59	Albania	37	95	Angola	10
22	Australia	71	60	Colombia	36	96	Kenya	10
23	West Germany	70	61	Ecuador	36	97	Guatemala	9
24	Sweden	70	62	Malaysia	36	98	Saudi Arabia	9
25	Reunion	68	63	Cuba	35	99	Togo	9
26	Uruguay	68	64	Jordan	34	100	Zambia	9
27	Hong Kong	67	65	Lebanon	33	101	Cameroon	8
28	Italy	67	66	Congo	32	102	Equatorial Guinea	8
29	Malta	67	67	Swaziland	31	103	Ivory Coast	8
30	Puerto Rico	66	68	Syria	30	104	Liberia	8
31	Ireland	65	69	Mexico	29	105	Madagascar	8
32	Peru	65				106	South Yemen	8
33	Barbados	61		*LOWER MIDDLE*		107	Nigeria	7
34	Poland	60	70	Egypt	28	108	Pakistan	7
35	Switzerland	60	71	Ghana	28	109	Papua New Guinea	7

Rank	Country	Secondary School Enrollment Ratio	Rank	Country	Secondary School Enrollment Ratio	Rank	Country	Secondary School Enrollment Ratio
110	Rhodesia (Zimbabwe)	7	121	Mozambique	5		*BOTTOM 9*	
111	Sierra Leone	7	122	Haiti	4	132	Afghanistan	1
112	Sudan	7	123	Uganda	4	133	Mali	1
113	Benin	6	124	Central African Empire	3	134	Mauritania	1
114	Comoros	6	125	Ethiopia	3	135	Niger	1
115	Guinea	6	126	Guinea-Bissau	3	136	Rwanda	1
116	Senegal	6	127	Burundi	2	137	Upper Volta	1
117	Nepal	6	128	Laos	2	138	Yemen Arab Republic	1
118	Zaire	6	129	Malawi	2	139	Chad	0.48
119	Cambodia	5	130	Somalia	2	140	Bhutan	0.23
120	Gambia	5	131	Tanzania	2			

Source: *UNESCO Statistical Yearbook.*

276. Vocational Secondary Education

Manual work and blue-collar jobs are still looked down upon in many societies and nowhere is this prejudice more clearly reflected than in enrollments in vocational courses and programs. Poor enrollments at this level are a matter of concern for all governments because they result in a dearth of skilled manpower in every branch of industry. Despite official efforts vocational courses attract only the second-best students and inferior teachers in many countries of the world. Vocational education, therefore, suffers not only in enrollment numbers but also in the quality of students and instruction.

Number of Countries: 141
Midpoint: 10.65%
Period Covered: 1976
Type of Ranking: Vocational Enrollment as Percentage of Total Secondary School Enrollment; Total Vocational Enrollment; Highest to Lowest

Highlights & Findings: It is no mere coincidence that the top countries are all Communist. Communist ideology places great emphasis on vocational training, and their educational system is designed to produce more mechanics than generalists. Technology has long been so glorified in Communist systems that a technical career is regarded as superior to all other vocations. After the top 10 there is a sharp drop-off in the percentages and the average even in Western Europe is only around 16. However, because of different definitions of vocational education, comparisons among countries should be handled with caution.

Region	Africa	Asia & Oceania	Europe	Western Hemisphere
Most	Mozambique (18)	Israel (13)	East Germany (1)	Argentina (7)
Least	St. Helena (138)	Sri Lanka (141)	Gibraltar (116)	Grenada (127)

Rank	Country	Vocational Enrollment as Percentage of Secondary School Enrollment	Total Vocational Enrollment	Rank	Country	Vocational Enrollment as Percentage of Secondary School Enrollment	Total Vocational Enrollment	Rank	Country	Vocational Enrollment as Percentage of Secondary School Enrollment	Total Vocational Enrollment
	TOP 10			12	El Salvador	43.60	25,762	25	Greece	24.24	161.269
1	East Germany	89.61	412,785	13	Israel	43.21	170,168	26	New Caledonia	23.91	2,316
2	Yugoslavia	72.65	601,485	14	Netherlands	39.44	506,364	27	Finland	22.68	115,000
3	Hungary	71.88	267,329	15	Soviet Union	39.24	4,214,413	28	Cameroon	22.45	27,524
4	Bulgaria	70 58	242,809	16	Bhutan	39.09	699	29	Papua New Guinea	22.14	9,031
5	Rumania	69.95	560,712	17	Chile	33.90	157.989	30	Indonesia	21.48	722,193
6	Poland	65.87	949,113	18	Mozambique	31.50	17,216	31	Peru	21.40	190,559
7	Argentina	65.28	837,659	19	Philippines	29.40	662,949	32	Angola	21.16	16,735
8	Belgium	61.88	488,114	20	Djibouti	28.08	560	33	Norway	19.99	66,224
9	Czechoslovakia	59.42	190,462	21	French Guyana	27.75	1,536	34	Iceland	19.88	4,977
10	Brazil	46.54	782,827	22	Italy	27.29	1,321,209	35	Costa Rica	19.28	22,423
	UPPER MIDDLE			23	Honduras	24.92	12,936	36	French Polynesia	18.86	1,719
11	Luxembourg	46.10	7,042	24	Portugal	24.92	166,561	37	St. Pierre & Miquelon	18.84	95

Rank	Country	Vocational Enrollment as Percentage of Secondary School Enrollment	Total Vocational Enrollment	Rank	Country	Vocational Enrollment as Percentage of Secondary School Enrollment	Total Vocational Enrollment	Rank	Country	Vocational Enrollment as Percentage of Secondary School Enrollment	Total Vocational Enrollment
38	Uruguay	18.47	35,842	73	Botswana	10.58	1,722	110	Dominican Republic	3.38	5,100
39	Cuba	18.03	99,974	74	Montserrat	10.57	57	111	Cambodia	3.36	3,483
40	Macao	17.98	458	75	Burundi	9.07	1,250	112	Swaziland	3.34	613
41	Japan	17.94	1,637,141	76	Cape Verde	8.20	336	113	Sudan	3.19	8,996
42	Egypt	17.90	377,495	77	Dominica	7.95	548	114	Libya	2.94	4,888
43	France	17.63	5,025,609	78	Togo	7.92	5,118	115	Ethiopia	2.89	5,533
44	Tunisia	17.01	34,352	79	New Hebrides	7.66	137	116	Gibraltar	2.57	42
45	Colombia	16.84	216,395	80	Central African Empire	7.41	1,771	117	Algeria	2.49	12,801
46	West Germany	16.74	638,720	81	Malawi	7.22	1,208	118	Liberia	2.49	851
47	Singapore	16.54	30,335	82	Switzerland	7.06	26,279	119	Belize	2.41	117
48	Upper Volta	16.44	2,669	83	Iran	6.89	150,509	120	Yemen Arab Republic	2.33	566
49	Guinea-Bissau	16.03	343	84	Barbados	6.66	1,700	121	Jamaica	2.31	4,939
50	Austria	15.81	119,535	85	Nepal	6.39	16,815	122	Lebanon	2.23	3,898
51	South Korea	15.71	533,695	86	Fiji	6.34	1,938	123	Kuwait	2.17	2,375
52	Spain	15.65	456,816	87	Somalia	6.32	1,824	124	Saudi Arabia	2.16	4,832
53	Solomon Islands	15.61	313	88	Oman	6.09	84	125	Brunei	2.14	314
54	Guadeloupe	15.51	6,796	89	Uganda	5.96	3,296	126	St. Vincent	2.12	108
55	Rwanda	14.85	1,790	90	Mongolia	5.92	10,936	127	Grenada	1.99	101
56	Sao Tome & Principe	14.72	1,901	91	Hong Kong	5.83	21,509	128	Ghana	1.99	10,964
57	Turkey	14.61	221,627	92	Nicaragua	5.69	3,900	129	Samoa	1.71	284
58	Gilbert Islands	14.57	183	93	Venezuela	5.42	34,240	130	South Yemen	1.70	676
59	Zaire	14.19	47,579	94	Guyana	5.21	3,539	131	Niger	1.61	233
60	Malta	13.56	4,405	95	Paraguay	5.16	3,700				
61	Martinique	13.31	6,026	96	Mali	5.13	2,605		**BOTTOM 10**		
62	Ivory Coast	13.18	15,758	97	Senegal	5.03	3,240	132	Sierra Leone	1.58	799
63	Denmark	13.04	37,973	98	Gambia	4.97	329	133	Singapore	1.58	799
64	Mauritania	12.46	554	99	Tonga	4.83	549	134	Mauritius	1.53	1,032
65	Cyprus	12.37	6,112	100	United Kingdom	4.82	204,081	135	West Malayasia	1.46	12,488
66	Reunion	11.77	5,943	101	Lesotho	4.65	836	136	Pakistan	1.43	29,234
67	Mexico	10.93	321,456	102	Iraq	4.54	23,791	137	Antigua	1.40	96
68	Laos	10.91	2,273	103	St. Lucia	4.53	190	138	St. Helena	0.73	4
69	Gabon	10.86	2,450	104	United Arab Emirates	4.10	625	139	Macao	0.59	61
70	Bahrain	10.73	1,941	105	Jordan	3.92	6,441	140	Sabah	0.57	300
71	Equatorial Guinea	10.65	586	106	Ireland	3.67	9,957	141	Sri Lanka	0.43	4,778
				107	Qatar	3.65	369				
	LOWER MIDDLE			108	Nigeria	3.59	20,423				
72	Afghanistan	10.61	11,269	109	Benin	3.56	1,687				

Source: *UNESCO Statistical Yearbook.*

277. Graduate Population

In every country graduates or those who have attended or completed postsecondary studies constitute the elite of the population. The percentage of the population that has reached the highest level of educational attainment is therefore an important indicator of the country's intellectual resources. The data are derived from national censuses or sample surveys and are expressed as a percentage of the over-25 population with a postsecondary degree, including those who have undertaken postsecondary studies without completing them.

Number of Countries: 116
Midpoint: 1.7%
Period Covered: Latest Available Year 1950-75
Type of Ranking: Percentage of Total Population with a Graduate Degree or Postsecondary Training; Highest to Lowest

Highlights & Findings: The United States leads the world in this ranking, and most other developed countries are far behind. However, because of differing base periods the data are not strictly comparable. Underdeveloped countries are predictably at the bottom of the scale. There are 40 countries where those who have attended or completed postsecondary studies constitute less than 1% of the population.

Regions	Africa	Asia & Oceania	Europe	Western Hemisphere
Most	Namibia (52)	Israel (3)	East Germany (6)	United States (1)
Least	Uganda (116)	Nepal (114)	Albania (101)	St. Vincent (110)

Rank	Country	Percentage of Those Who Have Attended or Completed Postsecondary Studies
		TOP 10
1	United States	21.1
2	Puerto Rico	12.1
3	Israel	9.9
4	Philippines	9.6
5	Canada	8.8
6	East Germany	8.5
7	Sweden	8.3
8	St. Pierre & Miquelon	7.5
9	Monaco	6.8
10	Norway	6.6
		UPPER MIDDLE
11	Pacific Islands	6.4
12	Finland	6.1
13	Costa Rica	5.8
14	South Korea	5.6
15	Japan	5.5
16	Poland	5.4
17	Bulgaria	5.2
18	Hungary	5.1
19	Hong Kong	4.9
20	New Zealand	4.9
21	Australia	4.7
22	Kuwait	4.6
23	Bermuda	4.5
24	Ireland	4.5
25	Peru	4.5
26	Western Samoa	4.5
27	West Germany	4.3
28	Panama	4.2
29	Soviet Union	4.2
30	Czechoslovakia	4.1
31	Argentina	4.0
32	Greece	3.9
33	Yugoslavia	3.9
34	Bahrain	3.8
35	Chile	3.8
36	Iceland	3.7
37	Spain	3.7
38	Brunei	3.1

Rank	Country	Percentage of Those Who Have Attended or Completed Postsecondary Studies
39	Barbados	3.0
40	Switzerland	2.9
41	Ecuador	2.8
42	France	2.7
43	Rumania	2.7
44	Austria	2.6
45	Belgium	2.6
46	Italy	2.6
47	Mexico	2.6
48	Seychelles	2.6
49	British Virgin Islands	2.4
50	Malta	2.4
51	Sri Lanka	2.3
52	Namibia	2.1
53	Paraguay	2.1
54	Brazil	2.0
55	Singapore	2.0
56	Dominican Republic	1.9
57	Cuba	1.7
58	Mongolia	1.7
		LOWER MIDDLE
59	United Kingdom	1.6
60	Fiji	1.5
61	Malaysia	1.5
62	Venezuela	1.5
63	Cyprus	1.4
64	Macao	1.4
65	Netherlands	1.3
66	Syria	1.3
67	Colombia	1.2
68	Guatemala	1.2
69	Mauritius	1.2
70	Trinidad & Tobago	1.2
71	French Guyana	1.1
72	India	1.1
73	Portugal	1.1
74	Thailand	1.1
75	Turkey	1.1
76	Liberia	1.0
77	El Salvador	0.9

Rank	Country	Percentage of Those Who Have Attended or Completed Postsecondary Studies
78	Iran	0.9
79	Iraq	0.9
80	Jordan	0.8
81	Guadeloupe	0.8
82	Martinique	0.8
83	Netherlands Antilles	0.8
84	Burma	0.7
85	Ghana	0.7
86	Tunisia	0.7
87	Antigua	0.6
88	Bolivia	0.6
89	Botswana	0.6
90	Honduras	0.6
91	Nicaragua	0.6
92	Rhodesia (Zimbabwe)	0.6
93	St. Kitts-Nevis-Anguilla	0.6
94	Zambia	0.6
95	Dominica	0.5
96	Grenada	0.5
97	Indonesia	0.5
98	Jamaica	0.5
99	Montserrat	0.5
100	Reunion	0.5
101	Albania	0.4
102	Algeria	0.4
103	Guyana	0.4
104	Swaziland	0.4
		BOTTOM 12
105	Haiti	0.3
106	Kenya	0.3
107	Pakistan	0.3
108	Papua New Guinea	0.3
109	St. Lucia	0.3
110	St. Vincent	0.3
111	Sierra Leone	0.3
112	Libya	0.2
113	Lesotho	0.1
114	Nepal	0.1
115	Togo	0.1
116	Uganda	0.1

Source: *UNESCO Statistical Yearbook.*

278. Postsecondary Enrollment Ratio

Postsecondary enrollment ratio is presented as a percentage of students attending institutions of higher learning out of the population aged 20 to 24.

Number of Countries: 131
Midpoint: 2.87%
Period Covered: 1975
Type of Ranking: Postsecondary
Enrollment Ratio; Highest to Lowest

Highlights & Findings: Individual country ratios should be interpreted in the light of world and regional ratios. The world ratio is estimated at 16.1% of the relative age group (18.8% for males and 13.4% for females). Developed countries have a ratio of 29.6% and developing countries of 9%. The highest ratios are reported in North America (48.1%) and Europe (25.5%) and the lowest in Latin America (19.7%), Oceania (17.4%), Asia (8.2%) and Africa (5.8%). The enrollment of students from developing countries in institutions of higher learning in developed countries seems to have only a marginal impact on these ratios.

Regions	Africa	Asia & Oceania	Europe	Western Hemisphere
Most	Egypt (47)	Israel (8)	East Germany (5)	United States (1)
Least	Niger (131)	Yemen Arab Republic (122)	Cyprus (89)	Haiti (117)

Rank	Country	Postsecondary Enrollment Ratio
	TOP 10	
1	United States	48.73
2	Puerto Rico	35.76
3	Canada	30.62
4	Argentina	27.23
5	East Germany	26.35
6	Denmark	25.30
7	Soviet Union	23.32
8	Israel	22.13
9	Bulgaria	21.74
10	Sweden	20.43
	UPPER MIDDLE	
11	New Zealand	20.03
12	Philippines	20.00
13	Italy	19.05
14	Venezuela	18.96
15	Panama	17.96
16	Australia	17.80
17	Belgium	17.63
18	Finland	17.46
19	France	17.33
20	Costa Rica	17.15
21	Poland	16.99
22	Japan	16.08
23	Norway	15.81
24	Yugoslavia	15.64
25	Netherlands	14.95
26	Chile	14.94
27	West Germany	14.09
28	Austria	12.52
29	Spain	12.06
30	Uruguay	12.03
31	Lebanon	11.83
32	Ireland	11.42
33	United Kingdom	11.39
34	Hungary	10.88
35	Albania	10.80
36	Greece	10.68
37	Bolivia	10.13
38	Iceland	10.10
39	Peru	9.35
40	Kuwait	9.23
41	Brazil	9.22
42	Czechoslovakia	9.17
43	Portugal	8.49
44	Dominican Republic	8.37
45	Switzerland	7.86
46	Rumania	7.73
47	Egypt	7.40
48	Cuba	6.64
49	Barbados	6.24
50	Jamaica	5.45
51	South Korea	5.45
52	Hong Kong	5.23
53	Iraq	5.06
54	Singapore	4.96
55	Paraguay	4.68
56	Syria	4.68
57	El Salvador	4.67
58	Ecuador	4.65
59	Mexico	3.97
60	Malta	3.69
61	Nicaragua	3.64
62	Colombia	3.60
63	Mongolia	3.32
64	Algeria	3.04
65	Jordan	3.00
	LOWER MIDDLE	
66	Turkey	2.87
67	Honduras	2.77
68	Iran	2.69
69	Trinidad & Tobago	2.59
70	South Africa	2.44
71	Indonesia	2.42
72	India	2.34
73	Guyana	2.27
74	Malaysia	2.25
75	Libya	2.17
76	Thailand	2.10
77	Swaziland	2.06
78	Nepal	2.04
79	Tunisia	2.00
80	Guatemala	1.98
81	Burma	1.90
82	Luxembourg	1.88
83	Fiji	1.65
84	Madagascar	1.21
85	Pakistan	1.11
86	Sri Lanka	0.96
87	Morocco	0.94
88	Papua New Guinea	0.90
89	Cyprus	0.80
90	Saudi Arabia	0.79
91	Senegal	0.74
92	Liberia	0.72
93	Bangladesh	0.62
94	Cambodia	0.62
95	Ivory Coast	0.59
96	Gabon	0.53
97	Zambia	0.51
98	Lesotho	0.50
99	Sudan	0.50
100	Mauritius	0.45
101	Ghana	0.44
102	Angola	0.43
103	Congo	0.43
104	Togo	0.33
105	Kenya	0.32
106	Mozambique	0.32
107	Botswana	0.31
108	Cameroon	0.27
109	South Yemen	0.25
110	Sierra Leone	0.23
111	Benin	0.22
112	Uganda	0.20
113	Zaire	0.19
114	Afghanistan	0.18
115	Laos	0.17
116	Nigeria	0.15
117	Haiti	0.12
118	Somalia	0.12
119	Rhodesia (Zimbabwe)	0.11
120	Guinea	0.09
121	Mali	0.09
122	Yemen Arab Republic	0.09
	BOTTOM 9	
123	Malawi	0.07
124	Rwanda	0.07
125	Upper Volta	0.07
126	Tanzania	0.06
127	Ethiopia	0.05
128	Burundi	0.04
129	Central African Empire	0.03
130	Chad	0.02
131	Niger	0.02

Source: *UNESCO Statistical Yearbook.*

279. Women in University Enrollment

Traditionally female enrollment has lagged at all levels of education but particularly in higher education. The reasons vary from society to society, but generally an enrollment ratio of less than 25% indicates that the doors of educational achievement are open only partially, at best, to women and may even argue that there is widespread discrimination and prejudice against women in public life. This is particularly true in Islamic and African countries, where women have little motivation to seek and very little to gain from education.

Number of Countries: 133
Midpoint: 30%
Period Covered: 1976
Type of Ranking: Percentage of Women in University Enrollment; Highest to Lowest

Highlights & Findings: Female enrollment in higher education is highest in the Soviet Union and East European Countries, where it is 49%, and lowest in South Asia where it is 24%. In between, the ratio is 33% in Africa, 35% in Oceania, 37% in Eastern Asia, 28% in the Middle East, 38% in Western Europe, 39% in Latin America and 44% in North America. It is 42% in developed countries, 35% in developing countries and 40% worldwide. In five countries it is over 50%, and in seven countries it is less than 10%.

Regions	Africa	Asia & Oceania	Europe	Western Hemisphere
Most	Swaziland (4)	Kuwait (1)	Bulgaria (3)	Panama (5)
Least	Chad (133)	Afghanistan (129)	Netherlands (76)	Haiti (120)

Rank	Country	Percentage of Women in University Enrollment
	TOP 11	
1	Kuwait	58
2	Philippines	55
3	Bulgaria	53
4	Swaziland	53
5	Panama	51
6	Bahrain	50
7	China	49
8	Finland	49
9	Hungary	49
10	Portugal	49
11	Soviet Union	49
	UPPER MIDDLE	
12	Jamaica	48
13	Mozambique	48
14	Poland	48
15	Brazil	47
16	France	47
17	East Germany	46
18	Costa Rica	45
19	Dominican Republic	45
20	Paraguay	45
21	Singapore	45
22	Israel	44
23	Rumania	44
24	Uruguay	44
25	United States	44
26	Thailand	43
27	Angola	42
28	Canada	42
29	Cuba	42
30	Lesotho	42
31	Argentina	40
32	Czechoslovakia	40
33	North Korea	40
34	Madagascar	40
35	Mongolia	40
36	Yugoslavia	40
37	Burma	39
38	Italy	39
39	Sweden	39
40	Venezuela	39
41	Cyprus	38
42	Ireland	38
43	New Zealand	38
44	Sri Lanka	37
45	Barbados	36
46	Denmark	36
47	West Germany	36
48	Australia	35
49	Chile	35
50	Fiji	35
51	Greece	35
52	Norway	35
53	Malaysia	34
54	Nicaragua	34
55	Spain	34
56	Trinidad & Tobago	34
57	Botswana	33
58	Colombia	33
59	Luxembourg	33
60	Peru	33
61	Austria	32
62	Belgium	32
63	Ecuador	32
64	Iceland	32
65	Taiwan	32
66	United Kingdom	32
	LOWER MIDDLE	
67	Bolivia	30
68	El Salvador	30
69	Honduras	30
70	Albania	29
71	Egypt	29
72	Jordan	29
73	Malta	29
74	Indonesia	28
75	Laos	28
76	Netherlands	28
77	Iraq	27
78	Guyana	26
79	India	26
80	Iran	26
81	South Korea	26
82	Switzerland	26
83	Tunisia	26
84	Lebanon	25
85	Mexico	25
86	South Africa	25
87	Nepal	24
88	Pakistan	24
89	Algeria	23
90	Guatemala	23
91	Upper Volta	23
92	Japan	22
93	Liberia	22
94	Rhodesia (Zimbabwe)	21
95	Syria	21
96	Turkey	21
97	Cambodia	20
98	Ghana	20
99	Kenya	20
100	Morocco	20
101	Papua New Guinea	20
102	Sierra Leone	18
103	South Yemen	18
104	Ivory Coast	17
105	Senegal	17
106	Zambia	17
107	Libya	16
108	Mauritius	16
109	Nigeria	16
110	Sudan	16
111	Uganda	16
112	Benin	15
113	Saudi Arabia	15
114	Togo	14
115	Malawi	13
116	Rwanda	12
117	Burundi	11
118	Cameroon	11
119	Gabon	11
120	Haiti	11
121	Niger	11

Rank	Country	Percentage of Women in University Enrollment	Rank	Country	Percentage of Women in University Enrollment	Rank	Country	Percentage of Women in University Enrollment
122	Yemen Arab Republic	11	125	Tanzania	10	130	Congo	8
			126	Zaire	10	131	Guinea	8
	BOTTOM 11		127	Ethiopia	9	132	Central African Empire	6
123	Bangladesh	10	128	Mali	9	133	Chad	4
124	Somalia	10	129	Afghanistan	8			

Source: International Association of Universities.

280. University Professors

There are 2.352 million university professors of all grades in the world distributed as follows:

Africa	51,000
North America	677,000
Latin America	253,000
Asia	458,000
Europe	581,000
Oceania	24,000
Soviet Union	308,000

The annual average increase in the stock of uni-

versity professors worldwide during 1965-74 was 6%. The rate of growth was highest in Africa (9.8%), followed by Oceania (9.1%), Latin America (8.6%), Asia (7.2%), Europe (6.6%), North America (4.6%), and the Soviet Union (4.4%). The rate of growth in developing countries reflects the surge in educational enrollment in these countries following independence.

Number of Countries: 121
Midpoint: 1,796
Period Covered: Mid-1970s
Type of Ranking: Total Stock of University Professors; Highest to Lowest

Highlights & Findings: The United States accounts or 27% of all the university professors in the world. The top 10 countries account for 64% of university professors. Because figures are not available for certain large countries, such as India, this ranking should be interpreted with caution.

In terms of university teachers per capita, Israel leads the world (if we limit ourselves to conventional nations) with the United States and Iceland as runners up. The position of Vatican City needs an explanation because mathematically it has more professors than citizens. The population of Vatican City is variously reported, but 1,000 is the most commonly cited figure; at the same time, the number of professors in the pontifical colleges and the various colleges attached to the sacred congregations is 1,192. This might seem an anomaly to some but most of these teachers are foreigners and the turnover is very large.

Another note of caution to be sounded is regarding the nationality of university teachers in developed as well as developing countries. One result of the brain drain is that developed countries have a large percentage of foreign-born teaching in their colleges and universities, but there is a reverse brain drain that is little noticed and that is the employment of citizens of developed countries as teachers in developing countries such as Saudi Arabia and Iran and even in smaller and poorer African countries. Of course the real drain is much larger than the reverse one but it points to the interesting configuration of academic exchange in the world.

Regions	Africa	Asia & Oceania	Europe	Western Hemisphere
Most	Egypt (19)	Japan (3)	Soviet Union (2)	United States (1)
Least	Seychelles (121)	New Caledonia (120)	Luxembourg (101)	Belize (119)

Rank	Country	University Professors	Per 1 million Inhabitants	Rank	Country	University Professors	Per 1 million Inhabitants	Rank	Country	University Professors	Per 1 million Inhabitants
	TOP 10			8	Canada	44,994	1,944	14	East Germany	33,570	1,999
1	United States	633,000	2,942	9	Indonesia	43,720	313	15	Philippines	31,783	726
2	Soviet Union	317,152	1,236	10	Italy	42,639	759	16	Spain	28,499	792
3	Japan	180,446	1,605					17	Czechoslovakia	21,194	1,420
4	West Germany	99,383	1,616		*UPPER MIDDLE*			18	Yugoslavia	19,197	890
5	Brazil	64,479	590	11	France	37,857	715	19	Egypt	19,119	502
6	Poland	46,144	1,343	12	United Kingdom	37,069	663	20	Australia	18,461	1,353
7	Argentina	45,204	1,757	13	Mexico	34,869	559	21	Colombia	17,655	726

Rank	Country	University Professors	Per 1 million Inhabitants
22	Venezuela	15,792	1,278
23	South Korea	15,317	427
24	Israel	13,981	4,040
25	Rumania	13,931	649
26	Turkey	13,778	343
27	Netherlands	13,000	944
28	Iran	12,310	368
29	Hungary	11,604	1,094
30	Peru	11,598	721
31	Chile	11,419	1,093
32	Bulgaria	10,805	1,233
33	Austria	10,487	1,396
34	Thailand	10,010	233
35	Norway	5,975	1,483
36	Greece	5,744	626
37	Cuba	5,725	605
38	Switzerland	5,413	852
39	Pakistan	5,054	70
40	Denmark	4,526	893
41	Finland	4,420	934
42	Portugal	4,220	446
43	Ireland	4,142	1,310
44	Burma	3,989	129
45	New Zealand	3,787	1,206
46	Nigeria	3,459	53
47	Iraq	3,270	284
48	Algeria	2,881	166
49	Hong Kong	2,817	643
50	Lebanon	2,759	932
51	Malaysia	2,682	218
52	Uruguay	2,332	833
53	Zaire	2,083	81
54	Dominican Republic	2,000	413
55	Costa Rica	1,967	974
56	El Salvador	1,951	423
57	Morocco	1,921	108

Rank	Country	University Professors	Per 1 million Inhabitants
58	Sri Lanka	1,860	135
59	Saudi Arabia	1,818	197
60	Bangladesh	1,796	22
	LOWER MIDDLE		
61	Singapore	1,750	767
62	Paraguay	1,529	562
63	Nepal	1,516	118
64	Tunisia	1,427	249
65	Guatemala	1,411	225
66	Sudan	1,320	82
67	Vatican	1,192	1,192,000
68	Cambodia	1,164	139
69	Albania	1,153	452
70	Panama	999	581
71	Syria	989	130
72	Afghanistan	982	49
73	Ghana	952	92
74	Libya	824	337
75	Mongolia	710	476
76	Honduras	642	227
77	Jamaica	638	310
78	Jordan	637	229
79	Uganda	604	50
80	Kuwait	497	482
81	Iceland	447	2032
82	Ethiopia	434	15
83	Tanzania	434	28
84	Madagascar	411	50
85	Senegal	374	73
86	Ivory Coast	368	73
87	Cameroon	328	50
88	Mali	327	56
89	Mozambique	326	34
90	Angola	324	56

Rank	Country	University Professors	Per 1 million Inhabitants
91	Sierra Leone	322	103
92	Somalia	286	88
93	Zambia	256	50
94	Malta	252	840
95	Togo	236	103
96	Guyana	231	296
97	Congo	225	162
98	Papua New Guinea	201	71
99	Malawi	179	34
100	Mauritius	171	196
101	Luxembourg	169	469
102	Fiji	166	286
103	Liberia	164	94
104	Laos	152	45
105	Rwanda	148	34
106	Benin	143	45
107	Burundi	133	34
108	Barbados	111	444
109	Swaziland	106	212
110	Upper Volta	102	16
111	Chad	94	23
	BOTTOM 10		
112	South Yemen	92	52
113	Lesotho	74	71
114	Cyprus	69	108
115	Bahrain	67	248
116	Yemen Arab Republic	58	8
117	Niger	47	10
118	Botswana	30	43
119	Belize	23	164
120	New Caledonia	23	177
121	Seychelles	8	133

Source: *UNESCO Statistical Yearbook.*

281. Study Abroad

In the mid-1970s a total of 665,942 students were attending institutions of higher learning abroad. Of these, 94,481 were from Africa, 66,503 were from North America, 29,281 were from Latin America, 231,084 were from Asia, 122,863 were from Europe and 6,615 were from Oceania. A substantial number of these students, especially those attending universities in Europe and North America, failed to return home after completion of studies, thus intensifying the brain drain.

Number of Countries: 161
Midpoint: 1,474
Period Covered: 1974
Type of Ranking: Total Number of Students Attending Institutions of Higher Learning Abroad; Students Abroad per 1,000 Students in Total Third Level; Highest to Lowest

Highlights & Findings: Although the spread between the highest and the lowest is large (27,623 to 11), study abroad is a significant educational phenomenon in every country. It is more so in underdeveloped countries, where there is a compelling reason for students to seek advanced training in Western countries. Even though scholarships are declining in number and value and college tuition costs are rising, the number of foreign students admitted to North American and European universities has risen every year since the end of World War II.

Regions	Africa	Asia & Oceania	Europe	Western Hemisphere
Most	Nigeria (14)	Iran (2)	Greece (3)	United States (1)
Least	Mozambique (159)	Maldives (161)	Andorra (142)	Dominica (156)

162. Foreign Students in National Countries

Rank	Country	Total Number of Students Attending Institutions of Higher Learning Abroad	per 1,000 Students Abroad of Domestic Third-Level Enrollment
	TOP 10		
1	United States	27,623	2.4
2	Iran	24,384	180.2
3	Greece	22,587	202.7
4	Vietnam (pre-war)	17,198	214.9
5	Hong Kong	16,899	384.0
6	United Kingdom	16,027	25.1
7	Taiwan	15,174	223.1
8	India	13,899	6.2
9	Malaysia	12,038	343.9
10	Canada	11,548	14.1
	UPPER MIDDLE		
11	Jordan	10,972	1,219.1
12	Cyprus	10,961	18,268.3
13	Italy	10,629	10.8
14	Nigeria	10,194	308.9
15	West Germany	9,585	11.4
16	Japan	9,091	4.0
17	France	9,019	11.6
18	Morocco	8,472	188.2
19	Turkey	8,292	37.8
20	Thailand	8,281	106.1
21	Egypt	8,090	19.8
22	Tunisia	7,724	335.8
23	Syria	6,546	102.2
24	Lebanon	6,468	147.0
25	Algeria	6,368	151.6
26	Indonesia	6,025	21.6
27	Spain	5,372	11.8
28	Mexico	5,350	10.2
29	Israel	5,238	69.8
30	Pakistan	4,955	44.2
31	Brazil	4,951	5.1
32	Venezuela	4,815	22.6
33	South Korea	4,462	13.7
34	East Germany	4,177	13.6
35	Colombia	3,921	26.3
36	Netherlands	3,859	13.3
37	Kenya	3,516	319.6
38	Iraq	3,356	42.4
39	Peru	3,257	17.0
40	Belgium	3,246	21.7
41	Czechoslovakia	3,241	20.9
42	Yugoslavia	3,131	7.9
43	Switzerland	3,065	47.1
44	Cuba	3,018	44.3
45	Chile	2,969	19.7
46	Austria	2,959	30.5
47	Norway	2,929	45.7
48	Ethiopia	2,900	483.3
49	Trinidad & Tobago	2,884	961.3
50	Australia	2,811	10.2
51	Finland	2,735	38.5
52	Philippines	2,678	3.5
53	Jamaica	2,614	326.7
54	Poland	2,595	4.5
55	Ghana	2,478	275.3
56	Cameroon	2,463	351.8
57	Hungary	2,419	22.6
58	Saudi Arabia	2,255	86.7
59	Luxembourg	2,199	4,398.0
60	Sudan	2,187	104.1
61	Ivory Coast	2,185	242.7
62	Tanzania	2,172	724.0
63	Argentina	2,081	3.4
64	Belgium	2,015	13.5
65	Panama	1,991	82.9
66	Mongolia	1,966	196.6
67	Cambodia	1,927	192.7
68	South Africa	1,899	19.3
69	Guyana	1,761	880.5
70	Sri Lanka	1,749	124.9
71	Uganda	1,746	349.2
72	Benin	1,742	871.0
73	Pacific Islands	1,697	——*
74	Sweden	1,683	10.3
75	Zaire	1,680	80.0
76	Singapore	1,675	72.8
77	Nicaragua	1,674	139.5
78	Libya	1,665	138.7
79	Portugal	1,641	27.3
80	Bolivia	1,544	30.2
81	Senegal	1,474	184.2
	LOWER MIDDLE		
82	Mauritius	1,452	1,452.0
83	Ireland	1,389	34.7
84	Congo	1,359	453.0
85	El Salvador	1,333	51.2
86	Sierra Leone	1,293	646.5
87	Upper Volta	1,278	1,278.0
88	Ecuador	1,263	21.7
89	Haiti	1,263	——*
90	Togo	1,229	614.5
91	Bahrain	1,218	1,740.0
92	Nepal	1,213	52.7
93	Soviet Union	1,213	0.2
94	Kuwait	1,191	148.8
95	Mali	1,115	557.5
96	New Zealand	1,077	16.0
97	Madagascar	1,054	131.7
98	Costa Rica	995	30.1
99	Afghanistan	952	79.3
100	Honduras	947	78.9
101	Bahamas	917	——*
102	Dominican Republic	904	22.0
103	Gabon	867	867.0
104	Laos	865	1,081.2
105	Denmark	861	7.8
106	Yemen Arab Republic	809	404.5
107	Liberia	785	392.5
108	Bangladesh	750	4.0
109	Rumania	727	4.4
110	South Yemen	656	728.8
111	Rhodesia (Zimbabwe)	627	——*
112	Guinea	621	——*
113	Iceland	610	203.3
114	Barbados	526	375.7
115	Guatemala	512	22.2
116	Uruguay	473	14.3
117	Fiji	470	235.0
118	Chad	445	890.0
119	Mauritania	443	——*
120	Niger	434	868.0
121	Somalia	431	239.4
122	Rwanda	428	428.0
123	Zambia	426	53.2
124	Central African Empire	423	1,410.0
125	Bermuda	371	——*
126	Burma	325	5.8
127	Burundi	302	302.0
128	Paraguay	294	24.5
129	Papua New Guinea	289	52.5
130	Albania	251	8.6
131	San Marino	229	——*
132	Gambia	220	——*
133	Malawi	213	193.6
134	United Arab Emirates	196	——*
135	Qatar	176	251.4
136	North Korea	161	10.0
137	Grenada	159	——*
138	Malta	154	77.0
139	Liechtenstein	152	——*
140	Belize	150	1,500.0
141	Monaco	140	——*
142	Andorra	137	——*
143	Brunei	127	——*
144	Antigua	125	——*
145	Tonga	115	——*
146	Netherlands Antilles	108	——*
147	St. Vincent	94	——*
148	Puerto Rico	90	0.9
149	Oman	84	——*
150	St. Kitts-Nevis-Anguilla	84	——*
151	St. Lucia	82	——*
	BOTTOM 10		
152	Swaziland	76	76.0
153	Lesotho	75	150.0
154	Botswana	65	162.5
155	Equatorial Guinea	65	——*
156	Dominica	63	——*
157	Bhutan	55	——*
158	Angola	54	20.7
159	Mozambique	53	20.3
160	Western Samoa	50	——*
161	Maldives	11	——*

* No third level.

Source: *UNESCO Statistical Yearbook.*

282. Foreign Students in National Universities

In 1974 a total of 755,755 students were engaged in study abroad. Of these 37,067 were studying in Africa, 274,110 in North America, 47,820 in Latin America, 79,506 in Asia, 306,312 in Europe (including the Soviet Union) and 10,950 in Oceania. During the period 1960-74 the enrollment of foreign students increased by 316% worldwide. The greatest increase took place in North America, where the enrollment jumped from 60,358 to 274,110, a gain of 454%.

Number of Countries: 101
Midpoint: 985
Period Covered: 1974
Type of Ranking: Foreign Students Enrolled in Domestic Universities; Highest to Lowest

Highlights & Findings: The pattern of flow of foreign students from low-technology countries to high-technology countries, established soon after World War II, has not changed appreciably over the years. As a result the dominance of the United States, Canada, the United Kingdom, West Germany, France and other industrialized countries of the West has never been challenged. In the case of the Soviet Union there is an added ideological element that makes the enrollment highly selective and even suspect as politically motivated. The only other determinant is language; which means that students from former British colonies tend to gravitate toward the United Kingdom, the United States, or Canada, while students from former French colonies tend to prefer France. The high position of Lebanon in the rankings is principally caused by the presence of the American University of Beirut, an institution whose enrollment has since been drastically reduced because of the civil war in that country.

Regions	Africa	Asia & Oceania	Europe	Western Hemisphere
Highest	Egypt (10)	Lebanon (8)	France (3)	United States (1)
Lowest	Malawi (100)	Sri Lanka (97)	Cyprus (101)	Paraguay (85)

Rank	Country	Foreign Students Enrolled In Domestic Universities
	TOP 10	
1	United States	154,580
2	Canada	119,530
3	France	77,382
4	West Germany	47,096
5	Soviet Union	30,563
6	United Kingdom	29,946
7	Brazil	25,642
8	Lebanon	22,184
9	Italy	20,803
10	Egypt	19,655
	UPPER MIDDLE	
11	Japan	13,564
12	Switzerland	10,038
13	Greece	9,929
14	Austria	9,716
15	Belgium	9,369
16	Argentina	8,862
17	Spain	8,417
18	Vatican	7,910
19	India	7,804
20	Australia	7,635
21	Syria	6,403
22	Turkey	6,385
23	Mexico	6,250
24	East Germany	4,864
25	Iraq	3,862
26	Rumania	3,833
27	Sudan	3,772
28	Singapore	3,599
29	Czechoslovakia	3,400
30	Saudi Arabia	2,716
31	New Zealand	2,688
32	Philippines	2,628
33	Poland	2,624

Rank	Country	Foreign Students Enrolled In Domestic Universities
34	Hungary	2,557
35	Bulgaria	2,484
36	Kuwait	2,401
37	Sweden	2,365
38	Senegal	2,079
39	Netherlands	1,721
40	Denmark	1,644
41	Algeria	1,518
42	Ivory Coast	1,465
43	Pakistan	1,297
44	Uruguay	1,198
45	Colombia	1,195
46	Madagascar	1,119
47	Chile	1,043
48	Libya	1,002
49	Portugal	994
50	Jamaica	992
51	Guatemala	985
	LOWER MIDDLE	
52	Morocco	929
53	Costa Rica	835
54	Cuba	796
55	Norway	741
56	Uganda	705
57	Kenya	702
58	Israel	677
59	Ecuador	671
60	Zaire	501
61	Iran	465
62	Finland	461
63	Sierra Leone	416
64	Trinidad & Tobago	370
65	Zambia	341
66	El Salvador	336
67	South Korea	314

Rank	Country	Foreign Students Enrolled In Domestic Universities
68	Tanzania	282
69	Tunisia	272
70	Togo	269
71	Ghana	242
72	Nigeria	238
73	Lesotho	213
74	Cameroon	211
75	Yemen Arab Republic	200
76	Barbados	193
77	Panama	192
78	Fiji	177
79	Burundi	167
80	Congo	153
81	Hong Kong	150
82	Niger	146
83	Upper Volta	136
84	Thailand	132
85	Paraguay	125
86	Luxembourg	117
87	Jordan	113
88	Iceland	107
89	Afghanistan	99
90	Gabon	99
91	Ethiopia	97
	BOTTOM 10	
92	Malaysia	59
93	Rwanda	51
94	Bahrain	48
95	Chad	46
96	Botswana	42
97	Sri Lanka	42
98	Malta	33
99	Benin	20
100	Malawi	18
101	Cyprus	15

Source: *UNESCO Statistical Yearbook.*

283. Educational Expenditure as Percentage of GNP

Aggregate world expenditure on education in 1974 was $295 billion, an increase of 286% over 1965 yielding an annual average growth rate of 12.4%, compared to the annual average GNP growth rate of 11% for the whole world. Total worldwide public expenditure on education constituted 5.5% of gross global product (GGP) or $98 per capita. The regional distribution was as follows:

Region	Educational Expenditure ($ million)	Annual Growth Rate (%) 1965-74	As % of GNP 1974	Per Capita 1974 (%)
Africa	5,890	16.9	4.2	15
North America	102,310	11.0	6.6	436
Latin America	12,020	15.6	4.3	38
Asia	30,540	17.1	4.0	23
Europe	102,260	12.9	4.9	218
Oceania	6,370	21.9	6.3	305
Soviet Union	35,610	9.6	7.6	141

The figures for Asia do not include China, North Korea and Vietnam. In all regions the expenditure on education as a percentage of GNP is higher than the UNESCO recommended minimum of 4%.

Number of Countries: 109
Midpoint: 4.4%
Period Covered: 1975
Type of Ranking: Total Educational Expenditure (Public and Private) as Percentage of GNP (In the Case of Communist countries as percentage of the Net Material Product or NMP); Highest to Lowest

Highlights & Findings: In most countries and regions of the world, educational expenditures are outpacing the GNP. In oil-rich countries much of this expenditure is on construction of new schools and other capital projects. In other countries it is the result of the introduction of universal, free and compulsory education. In advanced countries it reflects the higher price of textbooks and higher salaries for teachers. The same caution should be used in interpreting this ranking as in other rankings based on GNP. Particularly, there is a lack of comparability between the GNP used for non-Communist countries and the NMP used for Communist countries.

Regions	Africa	Asia & Oceania	Europe	Western Hemisphere
Most	Comoros (2)	Saudi Arabia (1)	Denmark (3)	Canada (5)
Least	Guinea-Bissau (106)	Yemen Arab Republic (109)	Yugoslavia (107)	Haiti (108)

Rank	Country	Educational Expenditure as Percentage of GNP
	TOP 10	
1	Saudi Arabia	11.1
2	Comoros	8.7
3	Denmark	8.3
4	Sudan	8.0
5	Canada	7.9
6	Netherlands	7.9
7	Soviet Union	7.6
8	Sweden	7.5
9	Benin	7.4
10	Israel	7.3
	UPPER MIDDLE	
11	New Caledonia	7.2
12	Jamaica	7.1
13	Norway	7.1
14	Papua New Guinea	6.8
15	Finland	6.7
16	Ireland	6.5
17	Australia	6.3
18	Guyana	6.3
19	United States	6.2
20	Guinea	5.9
21	Ivory Coast	5.9
22	Kenya	5.9
23	Panama	5.9

Rank	Country	Educational Expenditures as Percentage of GNP
24	Puerto Rico	5.9
25	Egypt	5.8
26	Austria	5.7
27	Costa Rica	5.7
28	Antigua	5.6
29	East Germany	5.6
30	New Zealand	5.6
31	Turkey	5.6
32	Bulgaria	5.5
33	Japan	5.5
34	Bahamas	5.4
35	Samoa	5.4
36	Morocco	5.3
37	Togo	5.3
38	Venezuela	5.3
39	British Virgin Islands	5.2
40	Luxembourg	5.2
41	Belgium	5.1
42	Fiji	5.1
43	Switzerland	5.1
44	Italy	5.0
45	Swaziland	5.0
46	Yugoslavia	5.0
47	Hungary	4.8
48	Czechoslovakia	4.7
49	France	4.7

Rank	Country	Educational Expenditures as Percentage of GNP
50	Mali	4.7
51	West Germany	4.5
52	Malta	4.5
53	Jordan	4.4
54	Lesotho	4.4
	LOWER MIDDLE	
55	Cyprus	4.3
56	Trinidad & Tobago	4.3
57	Iceland	4.2
58	Peru	4.2
59	South Korea	4.1
60	Mauritania	4.1
61	Argentina	4.0
62	Madagascar	4.0
63	Chile	3.8
64	Solomon Islands	3.7
65	Bhutan	3.6
66	El Salvador	3.6
67	Rhodesia (Zimbabwe)	3.6
68	Gambia	3.5
69	South Yemen	3.5
70	Burma	3.4
71	Gabon	3.4
72	Poland	3.4

Rank	Country	Educational Expenditures as Percentage of GNP	Rank	Country	Educational Expenditures as Percentage of GNP	Rank	Country	Educational Expenditures as Percentage of GNP
73	Cambodia	3.3	87	Sri Lanka	2.7	100	Spain	1.7
74	Colombia	3.3	88	Dominican Republic	2.6			
75	Honduras	3.3	89	Ethiopia	2.5		**BOTTOM 9**	
76	Hong Kong	3.3	90	Burundi	2.4	101	Philippines	1.6
77	Senegal	3.3	91	Malawi	2.4	102	Cape Verde	1.5
78	Sierra Leone	3.3	92	Portugal	2.4	103	Paraguay	1.4
79	Ecuador	3.2	93	Pakistan	2.3	104	Afghanistan	1.3
80	Rwanda	3.2	94	Angola	2.2	105	Bangladesh	1.2
81	Indonesia	3.1	95	Chad	2.2	106	Guinea-Bissau	1.2
82	Mauritius	3.1	96	Sao Tome & Principe	2.2	107	Yugoslavia	1.0
83	Central African Empire	3.0	97	Qatar	2.0	108	Haiti	0.7
84	Lebanon	3.0	98	Greece	1.7	109	Yemen Arab Republic	0.7
85	Singapore	2.9	99	Guatemala	1.7			
86	Somalia	2.7						

Source: *UNESCO Statistical Yearbook.*

284. Teachers' Salaries as Percentage of Educational Expenditures

One of the most widely used measures of the quality of education is the percentage of teachers' salaries in current educational expenditures. In less developed educational systems, teachers' salaries constitute not only the principal charge on the educational budget but also the lion's share of expenditures. The other vital elements of an educational system—textbooks, classroom facilities, and instructional tools and materials—are scrimped when there is little left over after meeting the salaries of teachers. In one sense this imposes an additional burden on the teaching staff because they have to make up the deficiencies in support facilities and services. The allotment of funds between teachers' salaries and other services, therefore, reflects the underlying priorities and philosophies of national educational systems.

Number of Countries: 100
Midpoint: 67.8%
Period Covered: 1976
Type of Ranking: Teachers' Salaries as Percentage Of Current Educational Expenditures; Highest to Lowest

Highlights & Findings: In most developing countries teachers' salaries make up the bulk of current educational expenditures. But in the case of some advanced countries, such as the Netherlands, Austria and Luxembourg, that also appear near the top, it should be noted that the percentages include the pensions of retired teachers.

Region	Africa	Asia & Oceania	Europe	Western Hemisphere
Most	Djibouti (3)	French Polynesia (1)	Austria (10)	Ecuador (13)
Least	St. Helena (95)	Mongolia (100)	Hungary (99)	Barbados (92)

Rank	Country	Teachers' Salaries as Percentage of Educational Expenditures	Rank	Country	Teachers' Salaries as Percentage of Educational Expenditures	Rank	Country	Teachers' Salaries as Percentage of Educational Expenditures
	TOP 10		8	Niue Island	85.7	14	South Yemen	80.3
			9	Norfolk Island	83.2	15	Netherlands Antilles	79.9
1	French Polynesia	93.8	10	Austria	83.1	16	Jordan	79.8
2	Tokelau	90.3				17	Greece	79.6
3	Djibouti	89.9		**UPPER MIDDLE**		18	Hong Kong	79.4
4	Sri Lanka	88.0	11	Lesotho	82.8	19	Cyprus	79.1
5	Morocco	87.6	12	Luxembourg	82.6	20	Mexico	78.3
6	Philippines	87.0	13	Ecuador	82.3	21	Ethiopia	78.2
7	Afghanistan	86.6						

Rank	Country	Teachers' Salaries as Percentage of Educational Expenditures
22	Seychelles	77.7
23	Netherlands	77.2
24	Thailand	77.2
25	Central African Empire	76.4
26	France	75.6
27	Madagascar	75.3
28	San Marino	75.0
29	Bermuda	73.5
30	Italy	73.4
31	Mauritius	73.4
32	Swaziland	73.3
33	Tonga	73.2
34	South Korea	72.6
35	Zambia	71.4
36	Norway	71.3
37	Monaco	70.9
38	Ireland	70.7
39	Grenada	70.6
40	Argentina	70.5
41	Spain	70.5
42	West Germany	70.4
43	Burma	70.2
44	Jamaica	68.9
45	Malaysia	68.6
46	St. Lucia	68.2
47	Malta	68.1
48	British Virgin Islands	68.0
49	Guatemala	67.8

Rank	Country	Teachers' Salaries as Percentage of Educational Expenditures
50	Singapore	67.8
	LOWER MIDDLE	
51	Japan	67.7
52	Peru	67.4
53	Bahrain	67.3
54	Oman	67.2
55	Gambia	66.3
56	Portugal	66.2
57	Guyana	65.3
58	Yugoslavia	64.9
59	Belize	64.7
60	Colombia	63.7
61	Malawi	62.6
62	New Caledonia	62.2
63	Ghana	62.0
64	Finland	61.9
65	Canada	61.6
66	Switzerland	61.5
67	Uganda	60.8
68	Papua New Guinea	60.4
69	Turks & Caicos	60.3
70	Niger	60.2
71	Ivory Coast	59.6
72	Chad	59.2
73	Fiji	58.3
74	New Zealand	58.3
75	Venezuela	58.3

Rank	Country	Teachers' Salaries as Percentage of Educational Expenditures
76	Angola	57.9
77	Antigua	57.9
78	Somalia	57.2
79	Comoros	57.1
80	Falkland Islands	57.1
81	Botswana	56.8
82	Congo	56.5
83	Czechoslovakia	53.8
84	Kuwait	53.8
85	Yemen Arab Republic	53.8
86	Nepal	52.5
87	Gibraltar	52.4
88	Northern Ireland	52.4
89	New Hebrides	52.3
90	Saudi Arabia	52.2
	BOTTOM 10	
91	Qatar	51.8
92	Barbados	51.5
93	Scotland	51.4
94	England & Wales	51.1
95	St. Helena	49.4
96	Israel	48.7
97	Bulgaria	47.6
98	Sweden	46.4
99	Hungary	44.4
100	Mongolia	38.5

Source: *UNESCO Statistical Yearbook.*

285. Scientific & Engineering Manpower

Scientific and engineering manpower is a major indicator of a country's technological orientation and capability. This indicator is presented both in terms of scientists and engineers per 10,000 inhabitants and total stock. Statistics on technical personnel are subject to a number of limitations, one of which is the problem of definition. However, in the countries ranked below, technicians and related categories have been excluded.

Number of Countries: 79
Midpoint: 43.3 per 10,000
Period Covered: 1976
Type of Ranking: Number of Scientists and Engineers per 10,000 Inhabitants; Total Stock of Scientists and Engineers; Highest to Lowest

Highlights & Findings: The most surprising conclusion in the ranking is the relatively low standing of the United States in scientists and engineers per capita. Even in terms of total stock the United States falls behind the Soviet Union and Japan. It is certain that problems of definition are involved here. In most countries the criterion for inclusion is completion of third level of scientific or technical training whether or not leading to a degree and/or the holding of a professional license or certificate. In the Soviet Union the definition includes all specialists employed in the national economy.

Regions	Africa	Asia & Oceania	Europe	Western Hemisphere
Most	Egypt (16)	Japan (3)	Finland (1)	Bermuda (5)
Least	Togo (77)	Yemen Arab Republic (79)	Gibraltar (59)	Panama (78)

Rank	Country	Number of Scientists & Engineers per 10,000	Total Number of Scientists & Engineers	Rank	Country	Number of Scientists & Engineers per 10,000	Total Number of Scientists & Engineers	Rank	Country	Number of Scientists & Engineers per 10,000	Total Number of Scientists & Engineers
	TOP 10			27	Hong Kong	102.3	41,420	54	Belize	16.8	201
1	Finland	446.5	109,035	28	British Virgin Islands	100.0	120	55	Pakistan	16.8	111,000
2	Soviet Union	372.5	9,477,000	29	Cook Islands	82.0	164	56	Pacific Islands	14.6	161
3	Japan	372.0	4,127,200	30	United States	75.2	1,594,000	57	Mongolia	14.5	1,908
4	Netherlands	335.1	442,000	31	Ireland	73.4	21,886	58	El Salvador	13.8	5,489
5	Bermuda	325.2	1,626	32	Uruguay	69.4	20,069	59	Gibraltar	13.7	41
6	Hungary	322.3	336,143	33	Antigua	68.6	480	60	Botswana	12.5	786
7	Philippines	294.1	1,083,742	34	Brazil	58.5	541,328	61	Papua New Guinea	10.3	2,646
8	Israel	291.9	96,300	35	Peru	57.0	84,923	62	Guatemala	9.8	5,551
9	Canada	280.9	621,645	36	Seychelles	51.2	300	63	Sudan	8.6	13,792
10	Poland	238.3	803,000	37	Libya	51.0	8,319	64	Ghana	8.0	6,897
				38	Singapore	47.6	N.A.	65	French Polynesia	7.9	95
	UPPER MIDDLE			39	Syria	43.7	27,369	66	Solomon Islands	7.6	129
11	Bulgaria	230.3	199,839	40	Iraq	43.3	43,465	67	Cameroon	6.0	N.A.
12	Czechoslovakia	225.1	327,772					68	Burma	5.9	18,500
13	Cayman Islands	200.0	200		**LOWER MIDDLE**			69	New Caledonia	5.3	69
14	Norway	193.2	77,400	41	Brunei	42.1	589				
15	West Germany	178.6	1,083,000	42	Iran	41.8	127,793		**BOTTOM 10**		
16	Egypt	178.0	593,254	43	Saudi Arabia	38.4	33,376	70	Sri Lanka	5.2	6,845
17	Bahamas	176.5	3,000	44	Jordan	36.2	9,787	71	Thailand	4.8	20,288
18	Austria	158.6	118,294	45	New Zealand	27.4	8,120	72	Niue Island	4.0	2
19	Iceland	158.4	3,169	46	Turks & Caicos	26.7	16	73	Nigeria	3.6	19,885
20	Argentina	155.7	390,000	47	Kuwait	24.2	2,151	74	Djibouti	3.5	35
21	Qatar	150.2	1,352	48	Zambia	23.7	11,000	75	Kenya	3.3	3,955
22	South Korea	132.7	460,037	49	India	21.3	N.A.	76	Bangladesh	3.2	23,500
23	Australia	115.8	147,758	50	Western Samoa	21.0	323	77	Togo	2.3	461
24	San Marino	114.0	228	51	Gilbert Islands	18.7	112	78	Panama	2.2	359
25	Yugoslavia	113.3	239,770	52	New Hebrides	17.9	161	79	Yemen Arab Republic	2.2	1,394
26	Norfolk Island	110.0	22	53	Bolivia	17.7	9,674				

Source: *UNESCO Statistical Yearbook.*

286. Scientists in Basic Research

Basic research may be defined as creative and systematic scientific research directed toward enlarging the stock of human knowledge in science and technology. It includes fundamental research, applied research in certain fields such as medicine, agriculture and chemistry, and experimental development work that may eventually lead to practical applications. The criterion that distinguishes research and development (R & D) (a term here used synonymously with basic research) from non-R & D work is the element of innovation. Because the collection of scientific statistics has not reached the same stage in all countries, the data on which the following ranking is based have limited comparability and accuracy. In most countries only those scientists working in recognized research institutes are included in the survey; in some countries social scientists are omitted, yet other nations have included those engaged in research in the humanities, arts and law.

Number of Countries: 90
Midpoint: 2%
Period Covered: Mid-1970s
Type of Ranking: Percentage of Scientists Engaged in Basic Research; Total Number of Scientists Engaged in Basic Research; Highest to Lowest

Highlights & Findings: This ranking yields no surprises. Predictably, the Soviet Union leads the list and Japan and the Eastern European nations find a place in the top 10 along with the United States.

Regions	Africa	Asia & Oceania	Europe	Western Hemisphere
Most	Ghana (31)	Japan (2)	Soviet Union (1)	United States (6)
Least	Tunisia (89)	Yemen Arab Republic (90)	Malta (58)	Guatemala (76)

Rank	Country	Percentage of Scientists in Basic Research	Total Number of Scientists in Basic Research
	TOP 10		
1	Soviet Union	48.1	1,223,400
2	Japan	35.7	395,898
3	Bulgaria	35.5	30,963
4	Czechoslovakia	30.1	44,508
5	Poland	29.7	101,000
6	United States	24.8	525,900
7	Switzerland	23.1	14,396
8	Hungary	21.4	22,588
9	Australia	19.6	25,746
10	Netherlands	16.9	22,920
	UPPER MIDDLE		
11	West Germany	16.1	100,005
12	Norway	14.8	5,930
13	Sweden	14.4	11,762
14	United Kingdom	13.8	77,086
15	Rumania	12.5	26,107
16	France	12.4	65,069
17	St. Pierre & Miquelon	11.7	7,000
18	Israel	10.2	3,350
19	New Zealand	10.0	2,948
20	Denmark	9.4	4,717
21	Western Samoa	8.8	135
22	Yugoslavia	8.2	17,434
23	Canada	6.9	15,244
24	Ireland	6.7	2,065
25	Iceland	6.3	126
26	Italy	6.2	34,308
27	Mongolia	6.2	797
28	Chile	5.8	5,948
29	Turks & Caicos	5.0	3

Rank	Country	Percentage of Scientists in Basic Research	Total Number of Scientists in Basic Research
30	Cook Islands	4.5	9
31	Ghana	3.9	3,559
32	Uruguay	3.9	1,150
33	Trinidad & Tobago	3.7	380
34	Argentina	3.2	8,100
35	Egypt	3.2	10,665
36	Cayman Islands	3.0	3
37	Singapore	2.8	635
38	Sri Lanka	2.7	3,611
39	Portugal	2.6	2,216
40	Venezuela	2.6	2,720
41	Austria	2.5	1,870
42	Kuwait	2.3	205
43	Spain	2.2	7,924
44	Pacific Islands	2.1	23
45	El Salvador	2.0	802
	LOWER MIDDLE		
46	South Korea	1.9	6,314
47	Cyprus	1.8	117
48	India	1.7	NA
49	Iran	1.6	4,896
50	Sudan	1.6	2,731
51	Brunei	1.5	22
52	Mauritius	1.5	135
53	Thailand	1.5	6,097
54	Iraq	1.4	1,486
55	Nigeria	1.4	2,083
56	Belize	1.2	15
57	Laos	1.2	364
58	Malta	1.2	39
59	Panama	1.2	204

Rank	Country	Percentage of Scientists in Basic Research	Total Number of Scientists in Basic Research
60	Peru	1.2	1,686
61	Bahamas	1.1	19
62	Ecuador	1.0	595
63	Mexico	1.0	5,896
64	Senegal	1.0	392
65	French Polynesia	0.9	11
66	Jordan	0.9	235
67	Bermuda	0.8	4
68	Brazil	0.8	7,725
69	Ivory Coast	0.7	319
70	Burma	0.6	1,720
71	Cameroon	0.6	329
72	Pakistan	0.6	4,164
73	Togo	0.6	118
74	Zambia	0.6	260
75	Colombia	0.5	1,140
76	Guatemala	0.5	310
77	Kenya	0.5	569
78	Papua New Guinea	0.5	131
79	Botswana	0.4	24
80	New Hebrides	0.4	4
	BOTTOM 10		
81	Central African Empire	0.3	76
82	Libya	0.3	50
83	Madagascar	0.3	201
84	Algeria	0.2	242
85	Bangladesh	0.2	1,649
86	Chad	0.2	85
87	Gabon	0.2	8
88	Seychelles	0.2	1
89	Tunisia	0.2	818
90	Yemen Arab Republic	0.1	60

Source: *UNESCO Statistical Yearbook.*

287. Expenditure on Scientific Research

Research and development (R & D) is defined as systematic activity undertaken to increase the stock of scientific and technical knowledge and to devise new applications. It includes fundamental research, applied research and experimental development resulting in the introduction of new materials, products and processes or the improvement of existing ones. Expenditure on scientific research and development includes both current and capital spending.

Number of Countries: 69
Midpoint: 0.6%
Period Covered: Mid-1970s
Type of Ranking: Expenditure on Scientific R & D as Percentage of GNP; Highest to Lowest

Highlights & Findings: The Soviet Union spends more than twice as much as the United States on Scientific R & D in relation to GNP, but there are significant differences in comparability because the USSR includes related scientific and technological activities that are not classified as R & D in the United States. Only 20 countries spend more than 1% of their GNP on scientific research and, with the exception of Western Samoa and Togo, they include the most industrially advanced countries in the world.

Region	Africa	Asia & Oceania	Europe	Western Hemisphere
Most	Togo (17)	Western Samoa (2)	Soviet Union (1)	United States (7)
Least	Botswana (56)	Burma (65)	Malta (68)	Nicaragua (69)

Rank	Country	Expenditure on Scientific R & D as Percentage of GNP	Rank	Country	Expenditure on Scientific R & D as Percentage of GNP	Rank	Country	Expenditure on Scientific R & D as Percentage of GNP
	TOP 12		24	Jordan	0.9	48	Algeria	0.3
1	Soviet Union	4.8	25	Egypt	0.8	49	Ecuador	0.3
2	Western Samoa	4.4	26	El Salvador	0.8	50	Iran	0.3
3	Czechoslovakia	3.9	27	Ireland	0.8	51	Philippines	0.3
4	Hungary	3.4	28	Kenya	0.8	52	Portugal	0.3
5	Spain	3.0	29	Madagascar	0.8	53	Trinidad & Tobago	0.3
6	Poland	2.7	30	New Zealand	0.8	54	Turkey	0.3
7	United States	2.3	31	Senegal	0.8			
8	West Germany	2.1	32	Yugoslavia	0.7			
9	Japan	2.1	33	Cameroon	0.6		*BOTTOM 15*	
10	Netherlands	2.0	34	Mauritius	0.6	55	Bangladesh	0.2
11	Switzerland	2.0	35	Zambia	0.6	56	Botswana	0.2
12	United Kingdom	2.0				57	Brazil	0.2
						58	Guatemala	0.2
				LOWER MIDDLE		59	Iraq	0.2
	UPPER MIDDLE		36	Argentina	0.5	60	Mexico	0.2
13	France	1.7	37	Austria	0.4	61	Pakistan	0.2
14	Australia	1.6	38	Chad	0.4	62	Panama	0.2
15	Sweden	1.6	39	Cyprus	0.4	63	Uruguay	0.2
16	Norway	1.5	40	Iceland	0.4	64	Venezuela	0.2
17	Togo	1.5	41	India	0.4	65	Burma	0.1
18	Canada	1.2	42	Ivory Coast	0.4	66	Colombia	0.1
19	Denmark	1.0	43	South Korea	0.4	67	Jamaica	0.1
20	Finland	1.0	44	Nigeria	0.4	68	Malta	0.1
21	Israel	1.0	45	Peru	0.4	69	Nicaragua	0.1
22	Ghana	0.9	46	Sudan	0.4			
23	Italy	0.9	47	Upper Volta	0.4			

Source: *UNESCO Statistical Yearbook.*

288. Scientific Authorship Index

A country's contribution to scientific authorship is an indicator of its technological potential. The scope and investment of a country in scientific research is best evaluated by the output of its scientists in terms of published articles. Although the quality of the articles and the prestige of the journals in which they are published may vary, such differences are not serious enough to affect a broad judgment. In the following ranking the term scientific is restricted to the natural sciences.

Number of Countries: 112
Midpoint: 0.022%
Period Covered: Early 1970s
Type of Ranking: Proportion of Authors of Scientific Papers Living in Each Country out of a Total of 100; Highest to Lowest

Highlights & Findings: The United States is so far ahead in these rankings with close to 42% of the total that the other nine countries in the top 10 together only add up to the U.S. share. All the other countries in the table together contribute only 14% of world scientific authorship.

Regions	Africa	Asia & Oceania	Europe	Western Hemisphere
Most	South Africa (25)	Japan (6)	United Kingdom (2)	United States (1)
Least	Niger (112)	Laos (111)	Cyprus (93)	Guyana (110)

Rank	Country	Percentage of Contribution to World Scientific Authorship	Rank	Country	Percentage of Contribution to World Scientific Authorship	Rank	Country	Percentage of Contribution to World Scientific Authorship
	TOP 10		7	Canada	3.37	12	Czechoslovakia	1.29
1	United States	41.70	8	India	2.26	13	Sweden	1.28
2	United Kingdom	10.17	9	Italy	1.98	14	Netherlands	1.08
3	Soviet Union	8.20	10	Australia	1.80	15	Poland	0.95
4	West Germany	6.89				16	Israel	0.86
5	France	5.44		*UPPER MIDDLE*		17	Hungary	0.76
6	Japan	4.22	11	Switzerland	1.35	18	Belgium	0.73

Rank	Country	Percentage of Contribution to World Scientific Authorship		Rank	Country	Percentage of Contribution to World Scientific Authorship		Rank	Country	Percentage of Contribution to World Scientific Authorship
19	Denmark	0.57		52	Philippines	0.025		83	Sierra Leone	0.003
20	Austria	0.53		53	Sudan	0.025		84	Afghanistan	0.002
21	Rumania	0.44		54	Uruguay	0.023		85	Bolivia	0.002
22	Norway	0.37		55	Colombia	0.022		86	Ecuador	0.002
23	Finland	0.36		56	Iraq	0.022		87	Honduras	0.002
24	Belgium	0.27						88	Liberia	0.002
25	South Africa	0.26			*LOWER MIDDLE*			89	Libya	0.002
26	Spain	0.26		57	Peru	0.020		90	Luxembourg	0.002
27	Argentina	0.24		58	Ghana	0.019		91	Malawi	0.002
28	New Zealand	0.23		59	Algeria	0.018		92	Cambodia	0.001
29	Yugoslavia	0.23		60	South Korea	0.018		93	Cyprus	0.001
30	Egypt	0.21		61	Rhodesia (Zimbabwe)	0.017		94	Ivory Coast	0.001
31	Brazil	0.16		62	Sri Lanka	0.015		95	Jordan	0.001
32	Ireland	0.13		63	Senegal	0.013		96	Papau New Guinea	0.001
33	Greece	0.11		64	Trinidad & Tobago	0.012		97	Paraguay	0.001
34	Mexico	0.11		65	Ethiopia	0.011		98	Syria	0.001
35	Chile	0.096		66	Tanzania	0.011		99	Nepal	0.0009
36	Nigeria	0.074		67	Morocco	0.009		100	El Salvador	0.0006
37	Venezuela	0.061		68	Iceland	0.008		101	Gambia	0.0006
38	Taiwan	0.058		69	Indonesia	0.008		102	Kuwait	0.0006
39	Pakistan	0.055		70	Madagascar	0.008				
40	Turkey	0.045		71	Malta	0.008			*BOTTOM 10*	
41	Iran	0.043		72	Saudi Arabia	0.008		103	Congo	0.0005
42	Lebanon	0.043		73	Costa Rica	0.007		104	Barbados	0.0004
43	Uganda	0.042		74	Zaire	0.007		105	Mali	0.0004
44	Malaysia	0.038		75	Tunisia	0.006		106	Mozambique	0.0004
45	Jamaica	0.037		76	Vietnam	0.006		107	Nicaragua	0.0004
46	Portugal	0.037		77	Zambia	0.006		108	Angola	0.0002
47	Singapore	0.033		78	Guatemala	0.005		109	Chad	0.0002
48	Thailand	0.033		79	Cameroon	0.004		110	Guyana	0.0002
49	Kenya	0.032		80	Cuba	0.004		111	Laos	0.0002
50	Hong Kong	0.030		81	Gabon	0.004		112	Niger	0.0002
51	China	0.029		82	Burma	0.003				

Source: Derek J. de Solla Price, "The Distribution of Scientific Papers by Country and Subject," (mimeographed) based on *The International Directory of Research and Development Scientists.*

289. Scientific Book Production

One need not search too far to see the relationship between the output of scientific books and technological capability. The reason is that publication and dissemination of scientific knowledge is closely linked with research; one cannot exist without the other. Scientific publishing is dominated by the academies of science and other professional bodies as well as university presses and a few private publishers. Before World War II, German was the principal medium of scientific communication, a position occupied today by English.

Number of Countries: 84
Midpoint: 195
Period Covered: 1976
Type of Ranking: Annual Output of Titles in Applied and Pure Sciences; Highest to Lowest

Highlights & Findings: Of the total world output of 139,009 titles in all scientific disciplines, the Soviet Union alone accounts for 28.6% and the top 11 countries account for 72.1%. It is significant that although the United States leads the world in total book output, in the world it ranks only fourth in the output of scientific books. Translations and reprints are included in the totals, but it is not possible to determine whether the rank order is affected by their inclusion. On the other hand, pirated books are excluded, and this may affect those Asian countries where pirating is a major activity.

Region	Africa	Asia & Oceania	Europe	Western Hemisphere
Most	South Africa (29)	Japan (2)	Soviet Union (1)	United States (4)
Least	Mali (75)	Brunei (83)	Malta (78)	Honduras (84)

Rank	Country	Annual Output of Scientific Titles
	TOP 10	
1	Soviet Union	39,846
2	Japan	10,113
3	United Kingdom	9,356
4	United States	8,849
5	West Germany	7,760
6	France	6,457
7	Poland	4,647
8	Hungary	3,510
9	Czechoslovakia	3,429
10	Rumania	3,406
	UPPER MIDDLE	
11	Spain	2,982
12	Switzerland	2,712
13	Sweden	2,691
14	South Korea	2,622
15	Mexico	2,473
16	Netherlands	2,216
17	Denmark	1,940
18	Yugoslavia	1,908
19	Austria	1,775
20	Italy	1,568
21	India	1,406
22	Belgium	1,317
23	East Germany	1,277
24	Bulgaria	1,273
25	Portugal	1,269
26	Finland	1,261
27	Norway	1,233

Rank	Country	Annual Output of Scientific Titles
28	Canada	1,175
29	South Africa	1,060
30	Philippines	924
31	New Zealand	553
32	Indonesia	540
33	Malaysia	462
34	Argentina	392
35	Australia	369
36	Nigeria	320
37	Syria	303
38	Egypt	296
39	Thailand	284
40	Israel	229
41	Peru	206
42	Greece	195
	LOWER MIDDLE	
43	Colombia	173
44	Sri Lanka	161
45	Hong Kong	152
46	Cuba	150
47	Mongolia	144
48	Uganda	143
49	Iceland	133
50	Pakistan	128
51	Ireland	101
52	Chile	88
53	Singapore	81
54	Uruguay	80
55	Bangladesh	77

Rank	Country	Annual Output of Scientific Titles
56	Burma	73
57	Costa Rica	65
58	Jordan	60
59	Malawi	60
60	Saudi Arabia	59
61	Cyprus	55
62	Bolivia	51
63	Nepal	42
64	Qatar	40
65	Iraq	38
66	Luxembourg	37
67	Sudan	36
68	Barbados	30
69	Libya	23
70	Panama	17
71	Madagascar	16
72	Ghana	15
73	Netherlands Antilles	13
74	Mauritius	11
	BOTTOM 10	
75	Mali	10
76	Guyana	7
77	Laos	7
78	Malta	7
79	Kuwait	6
80	Guatemala	5
81	Dominica	4
82	Fiji	3
83	Brunei	2
84	Honduras	2

Source: *UNESCO Statistical Yearbook.*

CRIME

This section presents 10 rankings on crime based on the resources of the INTERPOL, which is currently the only organization engaged in the collection of international crime statistics. Because of the limited number of governments cooperating with INTERPOL in its data collection efforts, the rankings are not conclusive and have only limited use for analyses or interpretation. Criminal statistics also suffer from another grave deficiency built into the reporting system. It is well known that only a certain percentage of crimes are reported, and of these only a certain percentage are recorded on the police blotter. Only in a few countries is a copy of this record transmitted regularly to the national headquarters, and in even fewer countries are these criminal statistics published.

There is no way of verifying whether a greater crime rate is simply the result of better law enforcement or a better reporting system. A country could have a low crime rate as the result of inefficient law enforcement or a poor reporting system. It is not clear whether INTERPOL has grappled with this problem. In any case many countries are reluctant to publish criminal statistics or admit law enforcement problems because of fear that it might hurt their image or cause an adverse public reaction.

INTERPOL statistics present two very useful indicators: reported criminal offenses per 10,000 and the criminal ratio, which is essentially a measure of the criminal component of the population. Next it deals with six major crimes: homicides, rapes, burglaries, fraud, counterfeit, and drug-related offenses, of which the first three are what are known as index crimes in the FBI lexicon. The final group relates to two special classes of criminals, juveniles and females, both of which have begun to attract attention as emerging law enforcement problems.

290. Crime Rate

This ranking presents the general crime rate per 100,000 inhabitants. The figures are only for reported crimes, and they probably constitute the tip of the iceberg in many countries. There may be many reasons why crimes are not reported by victims or why they are not recorded on the police blotter. Nevertheless, these crime rates are fairly valid within limits because the ratio of reported to unreported crimes remains stable in most countries.

Number of Countries: 59 **Midpoint:** 989.44 per 100,000 **Period Covered:** Mid-1970s **Type of Ranking:** Crime Rate per 100,000 and Total Number of Reported Crimes; Highest to Lowest	**Highlights & Findings:** The most common word of caution regarding crime statistics is that countries with greater crime rates may simply have better law enforcement and better reporting systems. It would certainly be unwise to jump to the conclusion that countries at the bottom of the ranking are crime-free havens.

Region	Africa	Asia & Oceania	Europe	Western Hemisphere
Most	Lesotho (28)	Lebanon (1)	Finland (4)	Guyana (2)
Least	Zaire (56)	Jordan (59)	Greece (50)	Peru (42)

Rank	Country	Crime Rate per 100,000	Total	Rank	Country	Crime Rate per 100,000	Total	Rank	Country	Crime Rate per 100,000	Total
	TOP 10			5	Sweden	8,258.55	675,276	10	Trinidad & Tobago	4,916.70	53,388
1	Lebanon	37,384.77	1,121,543	6	New Zealand	7,112.40	216,416				
2	Guyana	15,663.34	119,872	7	Denmark	6,467.65	325,723		*UPPER MIDDLE*		
3	St. Kitts-Nevis-Anguilla	12,638.33	7,583	8	Fiji	6,296.37	35,499	11	United States	4,890.77	10,520,952
4	Finland	11,037.79	517,783	9	Monaco	5,659.96	1,286	12	Bahamas	4,887.96	9.615

Rank	Country	Crime Rate per 100,000	Total	Rank	Country	Crime Rate per 100,000	Total	Rank	Country	Crime Rate per 100,000	Total
13	West Germany	4,419.23	2,741,728	30	Tanzania	989.44	142,667	45	Libya	373.51	8,404
14	Austria	4,096.48	306,253	31	South Korea	988.43	342,906	46	Burma	314.23	89,870
15	England & Wales	3,990.97	1,963,360					47	Egypt	227.92	82,052
16	Scotland	3,687.57	192,233		*LOWER MIDDLE*			48	Ivory Coast	210.00	12,180
17	France	3,462.24	1,827,373	32	Kuwait	978.47	8,317	49	India	187.87	1,077,181
18	Australia	3,364.24	506,081	33	Venezuela	867.17	100,592				
19	Netherlands	3,114.63	420,113	34	Singapore	862.92	19,295		*BOTTOM 10*		
20	Italy	2,742.23	1,525,891	35	Chile	808.40	84,837	50	Greece	162.11	14,214
21	Netherlands Antilles	2,576.11	5,992	36	Uganda	790.38	79,038	51	Nigeria	144.36	79,400
22	Norway	2,305.14	91,583	37	Cyprus	574.33	3,670	52	Mali	107.30	5,365
23	Jamaica	1,959.25	39,185	38	Kenya	541.21	65,378	53	Madagascar	105.34	8,954
24	Hong Kong	1,746.25	74,198	39	Spain	456.14	160,949	54	Iraq	103.04	10,729
25	Solomon Islands	1,372.36	2,532	40	Morocco	439.60	79,128	55	Indonesia	87.15	112,425
26	Luxembourg	1,228.00	4,912	41	Malaysia	437.39	52,312	56	Zaire	70.34	16,882
27	Japan	1,204.75	1,325,811	42	Peru	435.42	66,969	57	Philippines	32.01	13,218
28	Losotho	1,140.61	12,889	43	Sri Lanka	430.45	57,638	58	Syria	22.86	1,372
29	Malawi	1,116.40	44,656	44	Sierra Leone	404.53	12,136	59	Jordan	10.82	1,841

Sources: INTERPOL, *International Crime Statistics*.
For U.S.: U.S. Department of Justice, "Criminal Victimization in the United States"

291. Criminal Ratio

The data in this ranking present the percentage of criminals in the population, or what INTERPOL calls the coefficient of offenders.

Number of Countries: 51
Midpoint: 558.62 per 100,000
Period Covered: Mid-1970s
Type of Ranking: Percentage of Criminals in the Population Expressed as Ratio per 100,000 Inhabitants; Total Number of Criminal Offenders; Highest to Lowest

Highlights & Findings: Because the figures refer to those actually charged with offenses, we are on firm ground. There are 18 countries in the ranking where criminals constitute more than 1% of the population. Seven of these countries are developed countries.

Regions	Africa	Asia & Oceania	Europe	Western Hemisphere
Most	Uganda (21)	Fiji (2)	Finland (1)	Guyana (4)
Least	Egypt (51)	Philippines (49)	Spain (43)	El Salvador (50)

Rank	Country	Criminals per 100,000	Total	Rank	Country	Criminals per 100,000	Total	Rank	Country	Criminals per 100,000	Total
	TOP 10			18	South Korea	1,135.44	393,906	36	Cyprus	293.89	1,878
1	Finland	8,378.62	393,041	19	Netherlands Antilles	974.17	131,400	37	Chile	281.29	29,520
2	Fiji	5,731.63	32,315	20	Hong Kong	876.44	37,240	38	Ivory Coast	264.81	15,359
3	Sweden	5,088.10	329,890	21	Uganda	844.19	84,419	39	Singapore	247.54	5,535
4	Guyana	4,872.71	37,291	22	Solomon Islands	833.60	1,538	40	Denmark	233.17	11,743
5	United States	4,583.80	6,146,043	23	England & Wales	762.10	374,918	41	India	216.69	1,242,502
6	St. Kitts-Nevis-Anguilla	4,251.67	2,551	24	Scotland	687.18	35,823				
7	New Zealand	3,855.66	117,320	25	Australia	628.74	94,622		*BOTTOM 10*		
8	Austria	2,566.69	191,886	26	Malawi	558.62	22,345	42	Greece	184.58	16,184
9	Netherlands Antilles	2,454.44	5,709					43	Spain	171.05	60,354
10	Monaco	2,350.25	534		*LOWER MIDDLE*			44	Sierra Leone	105.63	3,169
				27	Luxembourg	534.00	2,136	45	Mali	100.04	5,002
	UPPER MIDDLE			28	Lesotho	523.00	5,753	46	Nigeria	79.98	43,992
11	Kuwait	1,938.82	16,480	29	Japan	519.01	571,170	47	Madagascar	73.30	6,231
12	Burma	1,817.18	519,713	30	Morocco	441.72	79,509	48	Malaysia	54.26	6,490
13	West Germany	1,597.64	991.188	31	Libya	415.50	9,141	49	Philippines	42.01	17,350
14	Trinidad & Tobago	1,573.05	17,081	32	Venezuela	410.99	47,675	50	El Salvador	25.36	–
15	Jamaica	1,506.40	30,128	33	Sri Lanka	336.16	45,013	51	Egypt	19.31	6,952
16	Bahamas	1,399.54	2,753	34	Norway	335.74	13,339				
17	France	1,358.68	717,116	35	Peru	303.06	58,916				

Sources: INTERPOL, *International Crime Statistics*
For U.S.: U.S. Department of Justice, "Criminal Victimization in the United States"

292. Murder Rate

Murder in the first degree is a calculated act of slaying and generally receives the severest penalty under law, including capital punishment. Most nations distinguish between criminal homicide and manslaughter, the difference being deliberate cold-blooded intent.

Number of Countries: 59
Midpoint: 3.82 per 100,000
Period Covered: Mid-1970s
Type of Ranking: Number of Murders per 100,000 and Total Number of Murders; Highest to Lowest

Highlights & Findings: Although Western societies are generally pictured as violent, the statistics do not bear out this assumption. Many developing and traditional societies are just as violent, even if they do not have as many psychologists and sociologists analyzing the roots of criminal behavior. The data also do not substantiate the theory often propounded in the West that crime rates bear a direct relation to the pressures created by urban life, such as overcrowding, unemployment and the breakup of family ties. Many of the countries at the top of the list are rural societies exempt from several of these problems. Lesotho's extraordinary murder rate is related to inter-tribal tensions and rivalries, particularly expressed by stealing livestock with many murders committed in the process or in retaliation for such thefts.

Regions	Africa	Asia & Oceania	Europe	Western Hemisphere
Most	Lesotho (1)	Lebanon (4)	Cyprus (8)	Bahamas (2)
Least	Uganda (56)	Fiji (57)	Norway (59)	Peru (44)

Rank	Country	Murder Rate per 100,000	Total	Rank	Country	Murder Rate per 100,000	Total	Rank	Country	Murder Rate per 100,000	Total
	TOP 10			20	St. Kitts-Nevis-Anguilla	6.67	4	40	France	2.70	1,429
1	Lesotho	140.81	1,592	21	Jordan	6.06	103	41	Philippines	2.68	1,106
2	Bahamas	22.88	45	22	Syria	5.52	331	42	Hong Kong	2.59	110
3	Guyana	22.21	170	23	Luxembourg	5.25	21	43	Malaysia	2.49	298
4	Lebanon	20.33	610	24	Mali	5.02	251	44	Peru	2.44	376
5	Netherlands Antilles	12.47	29	25	Finland	4.88	229	45	England & Wales	2.24	1,102
6	Iraq	11.94	1,243	26	Malawi	4.57	183	46	Denmark	2.03	102
7	Sri Lanka	11.92	1,597	27	West Germany	4.47	2,771	47	Japan	1.74	1,912
8	Cyprus	11.11	71	28	Monaco	4.40	1	48	New Zealand	1.51	46
9	Trinidad & Tobago	10.41	113	29	Sierra Leone	4.00	120	49	South Korea	1.33	460
10	Jamaica	10.25	205	30	Scotland	3.82	199				
	UPPER MIDDLE				*LOWER MIDDLE*				*BOTTOM 10*		
11	United States	9.60	18,155	31	Libya	3.77	85	50	Zaire	1.19	286
12	Kuwait	9.18	78	32	Egypt	3.45	1,241	51	Morocco	1.11	199
13	Tanzania	8.98	1,295	33	India	3.40	19,480	52	Ivory Coast	1.09	63
14	Kenya	8.66	1,047	34	Sweden	3.36	275	53	Solomon Islands	1.08	2
15	Madagascar	8.14	692	35	Austria	3.06	229	54	Greece	0.87	77
16	Burma	8.06	2,304	36	Italy	2.95	1,643	55	Indonesia	0.87	1,120
17	Venezuela	7.19	834	37	Singapore	2.77	62	56	Uganda	0.83	83
18	Netherlands	7.15	964	38	Nigeria	2.75	1,510	57	Fiji	0.71	4
19	Chile	6.89	723	39	Australia & Papua New Guinea	2.73	411	58	Spain	0.67	233
								59	Norway	0.50	20

Source: INTERPOL, *International Crime Statistics.*

293. Rape and Sex Offense Rate

A variety of offenses are generally grouped together under the rubric "sex offenses," but the most prominent of these is rape. Rape has been described as the most underreported offense in the world. In its psychological consequences it is also perhaps the most traumatic. Even today in many countries rape is equated with murder and is punishable by death.

Number of Countries: 59
Midpoint: 16.48 per 100,000
Period Covered: Mid-1970s
Type of Ranking: Rape and Sex Offenses per 100,000; Total Offenses; Highest to Lowest

Highlights & Findings: The definition of sex offenses varies widely and the data are therefore not strictly comparable. In the United States only rape is included, while in other countries molestation, traffic in women and related crimes are also tabulated. The rankings reveal no pattern that could enable a sociologist to improvise a new theory on why some people are more prone to sex offenses than others. At the top of the ranking is as heterogeneous a group as one could think of: the almost puritanical Libya is placed cheek by jowl with the "liberated" West Germans and the primitive Solomon Islanders. Some rankings may illuminate and explain; others, such as this, only serve to deepen the mystery.

Region	Africa	Asia & Oceania	Europe	Western Hemisphere
Most	Libya (7)	Australia (1)	West Germany (2)	Venezuela (4)
Least	Ivory Coast (59)	India (57)	Cyprus (55)	Chile (29)

Rank	Country	Rape & Sex Offenses per 100,000	Total	Rank	Country	Rape & Sex Offenses per 100,000	Total	Rank	Country	Rape & Sex Offenses per 100,000	Total
	TOP 10			20	St. Kitts-Nevis-Anguilla	26.67	16	40	Luxembourg	9.25	37
1	Australia	90.82	13,674	21	Monaco	26.41	6	41	Jordan	7.71	131
2	West Germany	77.49	48,075	22	United States	26.30	40,168	42	Sierra Leone	7.47	224
3	Solomon Islands	76.96	142	23	France	26.19	13,828	43	Zaire	5.85	1,404
4	Venezuela	66.84	7,754	24	Fiji	26.07	147	44	Mali	5.60	280
5	New Zealand	65.73	2,000	25	Lebanon	25.93	778	45	Malaysia	4.72	564
6	Bahamas	62.02	122	26	Trinidad & Tobago	25.23	274	46	Burma	3.79	1,085
7	Libya	56.58	1,277	27	Jamaica	24.95	499	47	Singapore	3.67	82
8	Netherlands	56.00	7,554	28	Norway	23.43	931	48	Iraq	3.65	380
9	England & Wales	50.20	24,698	29	Chile	22.51	2,362	49	Madagascar	3.25	276
10	Lesotho	49.53	560	30	Uganda	16.48	1,648				
	UPPER MIDDLE				*LOWER MIDDLE*				*BOTTOM 10*		
11	Kuwait	48.35	411	31	South Korea	13.99	4,854	50	Nigeria	2.60	1,428
12	Netherlands Antilles	46.96	109	32	Morocco	12.69	2,284	51	Greece	2.31	203
13	Scotland	44.69	2,330	33	Spain	12.21	4,310	52	Sri Lanka	1.53	205
14	Denmark	41.06	2,068	34	Italy	11.87	6,605	53	Philippines	1.08	447
15	Sweden	40.52	3,313	35	Malawi	11.45	458	54	Indonesia	0.90	1,162
16	Guyana	34.50	264	36	Tanzania	10.31	1,487	55	Cyprus	0.63	40
17	Hong Kong	32.97	1,401	37	Japan	10.30	11,338	56	Syria	0.52	31
18	Austria	30.42	2,274	38	Kenya	9.76	1,180	57	India	0.51	2,919
19	Peru	29.14	4,482	39	Finland	9.44	443	58	Egypt	0.34	122
								59	Ivory Coast	0.17	10

Source: INTERPOL, *International Crime Statistics.*

294. Larceny Rate

Larceny generally includes both grand larceny, which is a felony, and petty larceny, which is a misdemeanor. The ranking is limited to grand, or major, larceny comprising robbery and burglary. Historically, grand larceny and petty larceny have led all other crimes since the days of Hammurabi. In almost all countries these offenses outnumber those of every other kind combined.

Number of Countries: 58
Midpoint: 199.41 per 100,000
Period Covered: Mid-1970s
Type of Ranking: Grand Larceny per 100,000 and Total Offenses; Highest to Lowest

Highlights & Findings: Developed countries appear prominently at the top of the ranking, perhaps because there are more things to rob and steal and more rich people to steal them from.

Region	Africa	Asia & Oceania	Europe	Western Hemisphere
Most	Lesotho (14)	New Zealand (3)	Italy (1)	Bahamas (2)
Lowest	Uganda (53)	Japan (57)	Greece (58)	Venezuela (29)

Rank	Country	Grand Larceny per 100,000	Total
	TOP 10		
1	Italy	2,355.68	1,310,798
2	Bahamas	2,267.83	4,461
3	New Zealand	2,193.93	66,757
4	United States	1,744.00	2,641,000
5	Denmark	1,723.71	86,809
6	West Germany	1,611.12	999.861
7	Guyana	1,555.07	11,901
8	Scotland	1,486.65	77,499
9	Sweden	1,427.51	116,723
10	Austria	1,214.16	90,771
	UPPER MIDDLE		
11	England & Wales	1,001.11	492,498
12	Australia & Papua New Guinea	888.63	133,795
13	Netherlands Antilles	863.72	2,009
14	Lesotho	861.05	9,735
15	Norway	815.00	32,380
16	Netherlands Antilles	802.19	108,190
17	Luxembourg	493.00	1,972
18	Hong Kong	450.18	19,128
19	Trinidad & Tobago	428.14	4,649
20	Jamaica	402.75	8,055
21	France	387.70	204,630
22	Spain	360.54	127.215
23	Peru	333.89	51,362
24	Fiji	275.27	1,552
25	St. Kitts-Nevis-Anguilla	256.67	154
26	Chile	231.85	24,331
27	South Korea	231.60	80,348
28	Monaco	215.66	49
29	Venezuela	199.41	23,131
	LOWER MIDDLE		
30	Malawi	197.42	7,897
31	Tanzania	155.24	22,384
32	Cyprus	149.61	956
33	Lebanon	145.30	4,359
34	Kenya	133.28	16,101
35	Finland	131.38	6,163
36	Nigeria	126.86	69,775
37	Kuwait	101.76	865
38	Sierra Leone	96.67	2,900
39	Solomon Islands	91.06	168
40	Singapore	78.04	1,745
41	India	66.19	379,412
42	Libya	50.15	1,132
43	Sri Lanka	31.68	4,243
44	Madagascar	27.25	2,316
45	Jordan	22.71	386
46	Morocco	21.10	3,798
47	Zaire	21.07	5,058
48	Malaysia	20.84	2,493
	BOTTOM 10		
49	Mali	19.08	954
50	Burma	14.95	4,275
51	Syria	12.00	720
52	Ivory Coast	10.96	636
53	Uganda	5.36	536
54	Indonesia	2.95	3,802
55	Iraq	2.79	290
56	Philippines	2.09	865
57	Japan	1.94	2,140
58	Greece	1.18	104

Source: INTERPOL, *International Crime Statistics.*

295. Counterfeiting Rate

Counterfeiting of coins, paper money, or bonds of one's own government or of a foreign government is punishable as a felony under the U.S. Constitution, and it is a crime in nearly every other country in the world. Under some foreign legal systems the offense is considered as treason and is punishable by death. It is also illegal to retain counterfeit money and to pass such money.

Number of Countries: 46
Midpoint: 0.30 per 100,000
Period Covered: Mid-1970s
Type of Ranking: Counterfeiting Offenses per 100,000 Inhabitants; Total Offenses; Highest to Lowest

Highlights & Findings: Because of the technical requirements and the professional skills involved, counterfeiting flourishes only in the more advanced countries. But where it prevails, counterfeiters generally operate as a ring with international connections. Two Western European countries are notable for their low counterfeiting rates: Spain and France.

Comparable figures are not available for the United States. However, $21,401,788 worth of counterfeit notes and coins were seized in the U.S. during 1974, of which $18,962,501 worth of counterfeit notes and coins were seized before circulation. Fifty-six counterfeit plant operations were suppressed during that year.

Regions	Africa	Asia & Oceania	Europe	Western Hemisphere
Most	Ivory Coast (12)	Lebanon (11)	England & Wales (1)	Guyana (3)
Least	Mali (45)	South Korea (44)	Spain (46)	Jamaica (40)

Rank	Country	Counterfeiting Rate per 100,000	Total
	TOP 10		
1	England & Wales	33.31	16,385
2	Scotland	28.35	1,478
3	Guyana	13.59	104
4	Italy	13.56	7,548
5	Monaco	8.80	2
6	Austria	2.23	167
7	Sweden	2.32	190
8	Denmark	1.79	90
9	Netherlands	1.45	195
10	Netherlands Antilles	0.86	2
	UPPER MIDDLE		
11	Lebanon	0.80	24
12	Ivory Coast	0.71	41

Rank	Country	Counterfeiting Rate per 100,000	Total	Rank	Country	Counterfeiting Rate per 100,000	Total	Rank	Country	Counterfeiting Rate per 100,000	Total
13	Singapore	0.63	14		*LOWER MIDDLE*			36	Libya	0.09	2
14	West Germany	0.53	326	25	Luxembourg	0.25	1	37	Malaysia	0.09	11
15	Kuwait	0.47	4	26	Morocco	0.25	46	38	Trinidad & Tobago	0.09	1
16	Finland	0.46	22	27	Iraq	0.23	24				
17	Tanzania	0.42	61	28	Australia	0.21	32		*BOTTOM 8*		
18	Peru	0.40	62	29	Norway	0.18	7	39	Zaire	0.08	19
19	Burma	0.36	102	30	Uganda	0.16	16	40	Jamaica	0.05	1
20	Jordan	0.35	6	31	Greece	0.15	13	41	Sri Lanka	0.05	7
21	Nigeria	0.33	179	32	Kenya	0.12	15	42	Egypt	0.04	16
22	Syria	0.33	20	33	India	0.10	582	43	France	0.04	23
23	New Zealand	0.30	9	34	Indonesia	0.09	122	44	South Korea	0.03	11
24	Madagascar	0.27	23	35	Japan	0.09	101	45	Mali	0.03	22
								46	Spain	0.01	4

Source: INTERPOL, *International Crime Statistics.*

296. Fraud Rate

The data in this ranking refer to crimes of fraud, which generally includes swindling, misappropriation, forgery and willful misrepresentation, or false pretenses.

Number of Countries: 58 **Midpoint:** 54.05 per 100,000 **Period Covered:** Mid-1970s **Type of Ranking:** Crimes of Fraud per 100,000 Inhabitants and Total Offenses; Highest to Lowest	**Highlights & Findings:** In the highest ranking country, Sweden, nearly 158 crimes of fraud are perpetrated every day, while in the lowest, Syria, fraud occurs only once in over 10 days.

Regions	Africa	Asia & Oceania	Europe	Western Hemisphere
Most	Egypt (14)	New Zealand (6)	Sweden (1)	Bahamas (9)
Least	Tanzania (55)	Syria (59)	Greece (57)	St. Kitts-Nevis-Anguilla (48)

Rank	Country	Fraud per 100,000	Total	Rank	Country	Fraud per 100,000	Total	Rank	Country	Fraud per 100,000	Total
	TOP 10			20	United States	68.04	91,176	40	Zaire	19.01	4,653
1	Sweden	705.48	57,685	21	Peru	65.13	10,019	41	Madagascar	18.88	1,605
2	France	625.05	329,905	22	Chile	65.07	6,829	42	Uganda	18.66	1,866
3	Monaco	611.77	139	23	Trinidad & Tobago	63.18	686	43	Lebanon	16.33	490
4	Denmark	454.41	22,885	24	Japan	60.59	66,682	44	Cyprus	12.99	83
5	West Germany	410.70	254,804	25	Kuwait	59.53	506	45	Burma	12.57	3,596
6	New Zealand	295.06	8,978	26	Netherlands Antilles	59.33	138	46	Jordan	12.53	213
7	Finland	292.43	13,718	27	Ivory Coast	58.69	3,404	47	Malawi	11.82	473
8	Australia & Papua New Guinea	223.55	33,659	28	Solomon Islands	58.54	108	48	St. Kitts-Nevis-Anguilla	11.67	7
9	Bahamas	220.12	433	29	Sierra Leone	56.93	1,708				
10	England & Wales	202.76	99,747	30	Jamaica	54.05	1,081				
	UPPER MIDDLE				*LOWER MIDDLE*				*BOTTOM 10*		
11	Scotland	156.34	8,150	31	Hong Kong	53.14	2,258	49	Kenya	10.67	1,290
12	Austria	135.43	10,125	32	Morocco	43.68	7,862	50	Iraq	10.55	1,099
13	Norway	134.00	5,324	33	Venezuela	41.95	4,866	51	Malaysia	10.30	1,232
14	Egypt	120.04	43,235	34	Lesotho	40.69	460	52	Nigeria	10.03	5,517
15	South Korea	111.66	38,736	35	Libya	37.53	847	53	Indonesia	9.11	11,759
16	Netherlands	87.27	11,771	36	Mali	34.76	1,738	54	Tanzania	7.50	1,081
17	Fiji	78.75	444	37	Italy	31.20	17,364	55	India	6.32	36,229
18	Guyana	72.65	556	38	Singapore	29.79	666	56	Greece	4.15	364
19	Luxembourg	68.50	274	39	Sri Lanka	28.04	3,756	57	Philippines	1.12	463
								58	Syria	0.70	42

Sources: Interpol, *International Criminal Statistics.*
For U.S.: *Uniform Crime Reports.*

297. Drug-Related Offenses

Most nations have laws on their statute books that make it a criminal offense to sell, obtain and use drugs, such as heroin, LSD, marijuana and similar psychoactive substances. The severity and effectiveness of these laws vary from country to country. In technologically advanced countries the social implications of drug abuse are more severe. Much of this social concern is not merely related to the pharmacological effects of drug addiction but also to the role of drugs as symbols of a deviant subculture that is generally antagonistic to the prevailing moral climate. Drug addiction has also a criminological significance because it feeds and generates other crimes such as shoplifting, prostitution and burglary by addicts who are unable to hold regular jobs and need to obtain several hundreds of dollars a day to support their habits.

Number of Countries: 54
Midpoint: 8.80 per 100,000 Inhabitants
Period Covered: Mid-1970s
Type of Ranking: Drug-Related Offenses per 100,000 Inhabitants and Total Offenses; Highest to Lowest

Highlights & Findings: Because the definition of drug offenses varies from country to country, the rates are not strictly comparable. Some countries consider addiction as a medical problem. The impact of the drug subculture also varies sharply; in traditional societies, such as Ireland and Spain, the problem never reached the epidemic proportions that it has in the Western Hemisphere.

Region	Africa	Asia & Oceania	Europe	Western Hemisphere
Most	Lesotho (13)	Hong Kong (1)	Finland (2)	United States (4)
Least	Ivory Coast (50)	India (54)	Italy (44)	Guyana (47)

Rank	Country	Drug-Related Offenses per 100,000	Total
		TOP 10	
1	Hong Kong	463.52	19,695
2	Finland	431.35	21,173
3	Sweden	296.90	24,277
4	United States	281.00	601,400
5	Bahamas	230.80	454
6	Jamaica	173.05	3,461
7	Trinidad & Tobago	113.83	1,236
8	New Zealand	77.40	2,355
9	Netherlands Antilles	65.77	153
10	Australia	64.10	9,651
		UPPER MIDDLE	
11	Burma	59.80	17,104
12	Singapore	54.34	1,215
13	Lesotho	47.94	542
14	Norway	44.10	1,752
15	Kenya	43.57	5,264
16	West Germany	43.37	26,909
17	Austria	32.08	2,398
18	Sri Lanka	29.25	3,918

Rank	Country	Drug-Related Offenses per 100,000	Total
19	St. Kitts-Nevis-Anguilla	28.33	17
20	Luxembourg	23.75	95
21	Venezuela	19.37	2,247
22	Malawi	17.67	707
23	Netherlands	12.91	1,741
24	Egypt	11.38	4,099
25	Malaysia	10.42	1,247
26	Lebanon	9.87	296
27	Monaco	8.80	2
		LOWER MIDDLE	
28	France	6.14	3,241
29	Tanzania	5.80	837
30	Sierra Leone	5.50	165
31	Chile	5.44	571
32	Kuwait	5.29	45
33	Peru	4.34	668
34	Morocco	4.16	749
35	Madagascar	3.84	326
36	Libya	3.63	82
37	Syria	3.30	198

Rank	Country	Drug-Related Offenses per 100,000	Total
38	Cyprus	2.35	15
39	Zaire	2.15	275
40	Uganda	2.02	202
41	Nigeria	1.80	991
42	Greece	1.79	157
43	Philippines	1.72	692
44	Italy	1.51	843
		BOTTOM 10	
45	Fiji	0.89	5
46	Mali	0.74	37
47	Guyana	0.65	5
48	Solomon Islands	0.54	1
49	South Korea	0.53	185
50	Ivory Coast	0.41	24
51	Indonesia	0.39	504
52	Iraq	0.36	38
53	Japan	0.32	355
54	India	0.12	711

Source: INTERPOL, *International Crime Statistics.*

298. Female Criminal Ratio

Women throughout the world are moving toward equality in every field of endeavor, including crime. There has been a sharp reported increase in the female share of the crime pie. If these reports indicate a trend, it would reverse the traditional assumptions regarding the relative criminal drives in men and women. In fact, in the past criminologists have regarded several areas of crime, including terrorism and kidnapping, as preserves of the male species.

Number of Countries: 45
Midpoint: 9.66%
Period Covered: Mid-1970s
Type of Ranking: Percentage of Female Criminals in the Criminal Population; Total Number of Female Criminals: Highest to Lowest

Highlights & Findings: Despite the reported increase in female crime, female criminals still constitute a small minority in every country. The highest percentage is only 21.52 and the lowest less than 1%. The countries at the top of the list are almost equally divided between developed and developing.

Region	Africa	Asia & Oceania	Europe	Western Hemisphere
Most	Morocco (1)	Australia (5)	West Germany (3)	Chile (2)
Least	Sierra Leone (41)	Solomon Islands (45)	Cyprus (37)	Trinidad & Tobago (35)

Rank	Country	Percentage of Female Offenders (%)	Total Number of Female Offenders	Rank	Country	Percentage of Female Offenders (%)	Total Number of Female Offenders	Rank	Country	Percentage of Female Offenders (%)	Total Number of Female Offenders
	TOP 10			16	Austria	13.85	26,584	32	Denmark	7.50	881
1	Morocco	21.52	17,117	17	Finland	13.36	15,854	33	Philippines	7.15	1,241
2	Chile	20.41	6,026	18	France	13.36	95,854	34	Libya	5.90	540
3	West Germany	17.56	174,116	19	Guyana	11.46	4,275	35	Trinidad & Tobago	5.49	939
4	Lesotho	17.33	997	20	Monaco	11.23	60				
5	Australia	17.03	16,121	21	Sweden	11.17	36,852		*BOTTOM 10*		
6	Ivory Coast	16.32	2,507	22	Norway	10.11	1,349	36	Mali	4.09	205
7	United States	16.10	994,296	23	Jamaica	9.66	2,912	37	Cyprus	3.83	72
8	Bahamas	15.65	431					38	Hong Kong	3.66	1,363
9	New Zealand	15.00	17,604		*LOWER MIDDLE*			39	Egypt	3.36	234
10	Scotland	14.67	5,257	24	South Korea	9.48	37,368	40	Kuwait	2.70	445
				25	Nigeria	9.28	4,084	41	Sierra Leone	2.61	83
	UPPER MIDDLE			26	Netherlands	9.25	12,163	42	India	2.46	30,677
11	England & Wales	14.23	53,352	27	Burma	9.06	47,105	43	Fiji	2.34	758
12	El Salvador	14.20	137	28	Greece	8.85	1,433	44	Malaysia	1.24	81
13	Madagascar	14.04	875	29	Malawi	8.32	1,861	45	Solomon Islands	0.19	3
14	Japan	13.97	79,797	30	Peru	7.74	4,561				
15	Luxembourg	13.95	298	31	Netherlands Antilles	7.58	433				

Sources: INTERPOL, *International Crime Statistics.*
For U.S.: *Uniform Crime Reports.*

299. Juvenile Criminal Ratio

Although definitions and age limits of juveniles vary (the upper limit being as low as 14 in some countries and as high as 21 in others), this age group has one of the highest incidences of crime. A high proportion of adult criminals have a background of juvenile delinquency. Generally delinquents begin with theft and later graduate to serious property crimes and rape. The causes of such behavior are complex; some studies point to individual emotional maladjustments, while others have uncovered persisting patterns of delinquency in inner cities regardless of changing occupants. One corollary of delinquency is the street gang, which serves as the core magnet of crime in each neighborhood. Juvenile courts and correctional institutions have been separated from those of adults since the 19th century and now emphasize intensive rehabilitation, vocational training and psychiatric treatment. The English Borstal system is perhaps the most notable of such programs. Although communist countries do not reveal crime data, it was recently estimated that some 60% of the crimes in China are commited by juveniles.

Number of Countries: 46
Midpoint: 12.57%
Period Covered: Mid-1970s
Type of Ranking: Percentage of Juvenile Offenders in the Criminal Population; Total Number of Juvenile Offenders: Highest to Lowest

Highlights & Findings: One phenomenon that has baffled sociologists is confirmed by these rankings: delinquency rates are highest in economically and technologically advanced countries where the welfare policies and the prevailing affluence should presumably, if only men were rational, diminish such crimes. It is interesting to note that all countries in the bottom 10 are the so-called developing countries.

Region	Africa	Asia & Oceania	Europe	Western Hemisphere
Most	Madagascar (9)	Australia (2)	Norway (1)	Bahamas (3)
Least	Egypt (46)	Burma (45)	Monaco (41)	El Salvador (43)

Rank	Country	Percentage of Juvenile Offenders (%)	Total Number of Juvenile Offenders	Rank	Country	Percentage of Juvenile Offenders (%)	Total Number of Juvenile Offenders	Rank	Country	Percentage of Juvenile Offenders (%)	Total Number of Juvenile Offenders
	TOP 10			16	Libya	21.32	1,949	32	Solomon Islands	5.91	91
1	Norway	56.45	7,531	17	Luxembourg	20.13	430	33	Morocco	5.31	4,225
2	Australia	39.75	37,618	18	Malaysia	17.71	1,150	34	Jamaica	5.25	1,582
3	Bahamas	37.23	1,025	19	Peru	17.36	10,229	35	Hong Kong	4.72	1,758
4	United States	31.30	1,343,773	20	Chile	14.62	4,316	36	Kenya	4.39	1,210
5	Denmark	30.31	3,560	21	Cyprus	12.93	243				
6	New Zealand	29.88	35,065	22	Lesotho	12.89	742		*BOTTOM 10*		
7	West Germany	27.50	272,639	23	Ivory Coast	12.57	1,932	37	India	4.28	52,227
8	Finland	25.76	101,280	24	South Korea	12.57	49,523	38	Kuwait	3.93	649
9	Madagascar	24.97	1,556	25	Philippines	11.63	2,018	39	Malawi	3.11	695
10	Netherlands	24.80	32,598					40	Nigeria	2.82	1,243
					LOWER MIDDLE			41	Monaco	2.62	14
	UPPER MIDDLE			26	France	10.57	75,845	42	Guyana	2.36	883
11	England & Wales	24.77	92,879	27	St. Kitts-Nevis-Anguilla	10.07	257	43	El Salvador	2.08	201
12	Venezuela	23.74	11,320	28	Mali	8.97	449	44	Fiji	1.45	471
13	Austria	23.60	45,290	29	Sierra Leone	8.96	284	45	Burma	1.09	5,682
14	Japan	22.90	130,805	30	Greece	7.60	1,228	46	Egypt	0.28	20
15	Netherlands Antilles	21.56	1,231	31	Trinidad & Tobago	6.99	1,195				

Sources: INTERPOL, *International Crime Statistics.*
For U.S., U.S. Department of Justice, "Criminal Victimization in the United States"

MEDIA

The Japanese call it *johoka,* the information explosion, a word that best describes the deluge of information and ideas that is being transmitted through the print and electronic media throughout the world. Peter Drucker has defined information as a form of energy, and its production is as important as that of other forms of energy. The media function not only as transmission belts conveying information to their ultimate consumers but also, as Lewis A. Coser defines them, as gatekeepers of ideas or sluice gates that determine what will be and will not be published or broadcast. It is this power that makes the media such a terror to errant governments. Marshall McLuhan notwithstanding, the printed word remains the key means of access to the complex world of information and ideas, but the economic status of the print media has been steadily declining over a number of years. Some newspapers may claim larger circulations, but in almost all countries of the world, the daily press stands more or less where it did 20 years ago. Because of the astronomical speed with which news is transmitted, the newspaper has become an obsolescent means of reporting current news. Even the best newspapers—the prestigious *Times* of London, for example—find themselves constantly in financial difficulties and losing advertising revenue to electronic media.

Particularly critical is the short supply of newsprint. It is produced in only 36 countries and only six—Canada, Finland, Sweden, Norway, the Soviet Union and New Zealand—produce enough for export. The United States consumes more than three times its own annual production, while Africa produces no newsprint at all. In terms of circulation the contrasts among regions is striking. In Africa, nine countries and territories have no newspapers and in only 15 of the others does the daily circulation exceed 10 per 1,000 and in none does it exceed 100 per 1,000. Circulation rates are highest in Europe, reaching up to 400 per 1,000. While overall circulation figures have increased in North America, circulation per 1,000 has dropped to around 300 in the United States and 220 in Canada. In Latin America the median circulation is around 100 per 1,000, and the number of newspapers have declined in Brazil, Argentina and Colombia. Asia presents great contrasts. Only Japan with a circulation of 511 per 1,000 approaches Western standards. In most of the others,

including India, the ratio is less than 20 per 1,000. The relative figure is 300 for Oceania and 336 for the Soviet Union.

Over 90 countries have national news agencies, but some 40 have none. Fifty of the news agencies are directly controlled or operated by the state, while the other 40 are either autonomous public corporations or are cooperative organizations controlled by the press and electronic media. The scale, scope and effectiveness of these agencies vary; some are only government information offices under other names. Worldwide, the collection and dissemination of news is dominated by five multinational agencies: Agence France-Presse (AFP), Associated Press (AP), Reuters, Tass and United Press International. Most of the other news agencies depend on these five for foreign news. Each of the Big Five has between 100 and 200 offices in as many cities or countries.

Broadcasting, unlike the press, is subject to strict state control and legislation in almost all countries of the world. Originally, such control was necessary for technical reasons, particularly the allocation of frequencies; but later, as the impact of broadcasting became more clearly understood, it became a matter of political convenience. The majority of the states operate or directly control radio and television services, which are financed either by state funds or through license fees. In other countries the services are operated by autonomous corporations, which enjoy some freedom in day-to-day operations. In still others the pattern is mixed with private commercial companies, universities, religious organizations and private foundations operating services side by side or in competition with state or autonomous services. In only a few countries, such as the United States, are the services operated almost entirely by private commercial companies and financed solely by advertising revenues.

The number of radio receivers is less than 100 per 1,000 in 40 African countries, 17 Asian countries, and in all but 15 of the Latin American countries. Television has spread to many more countries in the 1970s, but there are still no television services in 20 African countries and 10 Asian countries. In no African country does the number of television receivers exceed 30 per 1,000. The number of television receivers is less than 100 per 1,000 in 19 Asian countries and 10 Latin American countries. In countries where television has been introduced, it has had an adverse effect on both radio and print media.

Film stands out from other types of media because although its production is, outside of Communist countries, almost entirely in private hands, it is subject to strict surveillance and monitoring by censorship boards that are invariably official bodies. Around 4,000 feature-length entertainment films are produced annually in some 50 countries. More than half of this total are produced by 17 Asian countries, including the two giants, India and Japan; the Soviet Union and Eastern Europe account for about a third and the rest is divided among the other countries of the world. The number of cinemas, cinema seats, and annual movie attendance figures are increasing in Asia in contrast to the rest of the world, where they are slipping or have remained stable for a number of years. It is noteworthy that the Soviet Union is among the more advanced countries to buck the trend and report better attendance in movie theaters. Film imports and exports are affected by linguistic, ethnic and cultural affinities as well as political and commercial ties. Dubbing and subtitling, although expensive, are now obligatory in almost all countries for foreign-language films.

On the assumption that the average household consists of four or five persons, the rate of over 200 to 250 per 1,000 inhabitants for both print and electronic media would indicate that the whole population of a country is being reached by that medium. On this basis the saturation point has been reached for daily newspapers in 30 countries (including 19 in Europe), for radio in 48 (including 26 in Europe) and for television in 22 (including 15 in Europe). In 21 countries (including 14 in Europe, Australia, Canada, Cuba, Japan, New Zealand, the United States and the Soviet Union) this point has been reached for all the three media. In developed countries the coming decades will witness remarkable breakthroughs in electronic media; these will include the electronic transmission of facsimiles, communication satellites, video-cassettes and cable TV.

The section presents two rankings on radio, two on TV, four on cinema, two on daily newspapers, one on media ad expenditures and one on book publishing. There is also an interesting freedom of the press index devised by the University of Missouri School of Journalism, which, although dated, examines one of the key concerns in communications.

300. Radio Receivers

David Lerner in *The Passing of Traditional Society: Modernizing the Middle East* has described the radio as the principal instrument of political and economic modernization in developing societies.

Other scholars have drawn attention to the relation between radios per capita and mass participation and competitiveness.

Number of Countries: 182
Midpoint: 144 per 1,000
Period Covered: 1975
Type of Ranking: Number of Radios per 1,000 and Total Number of Radios; Highest to Lowest

Highlights & Findings: In 1975, 938.2 million radio receivers were in use around the world. Of this figure, the United States alone accounted for 401.6 million or 42.8%. The United States is also among the few countries that does not require licenses or charge license fees for radios. The top 10 nations account for 60% of the total number of radios and the bottom 10 nations for 0.2%. South Yemen's extraordinarily high ranking for a poor country is apparently due to the fact that Aden, its capital, is a center for smugglers of electronic goods.

Regions	Asia & Oceania	Africa	Europe	Western Hemisphere
Most	New Zealand (4)	Algeria (76)	United Kingdom (7)	United States (1)
Least	Nepal (182)	Ethiopia (180)	Albania (123)	Dominican Republic (142)

Rank	Country	Radios per 1,000	Total Number of Radios (000)
	TOP 10		
1	United States	1,895	401,600
2	Bermuda	909	50
3	Canada	894	20,252
4	New Zealand	892	2,700
5	Argentina	838	21,000
6	British Virgin Islands	750	9
7	United Kingdom	750	42,000
8	St. Lucia	748	81
9	Japan	658	70,794
10	Pacific Islands	632	72
	UPPER MIDDLE		
11	Belize	588	80
12	St. Pierre & Miquelon	583	3.5
13	Puerto Rico	572	1,755
14	French Polynesia	565	70
15	Faroe Islands	563	23
16	Netherlands Antilles	550	131
17	Norfolk Island	550	1.1
18	Fiji	532	300
19	Luxembourg	515	176
20	Nauru	514	3.6
21	Turks & Caicos	500	3
22	Uruguay	495	1,500
23	Barbados	477	116
24	Lebanon	474	1,321
25	Falkland Islands	467	0.9
26	Soviet Union	461	116,110
27	Bahamas	457	14
28	Finland	427	1,997
29	Bahrain	412	100
30	South Yemen	407	600
31	Malta	401	129
32	Belgium	384	3,769
33	Sweden	378	3,086
34	Syria	374	2,500
35	East Germany	356	6,114
36	Guyana	346	268
37	West Germany	337	20,909
38	Denmark	336	1,693
39	Western Samoa	329	50
40	France	324	17,000
41	Cayman Islands	321	3.5
42	Cyprus	321	206
43	Jamaica	320	633
44	Norway	320	1,277
45	Switzerland	314	2,036
46	Monaco	313	7.5
47	New Caledonia	303	36
48	Mexico	301	17,514
49	St. Vincent	300	30
50	Chile	298	3,100
51	Andorra	295	6.5
52	Iceland	295	64
53	Austria	288	2,170
54	Ireland	287	886
55	Netherlands	284	3,846
56	Ecuador	279	1,700
57	Greece	279	2,500
58	Czechoslovakia	266	3,910
59	Surinam	264	109
60	Bulgaria	262	2,273

Rank	Country	Radios per 1,000	Total Number of Radios (000)
61	Iran	249	8,000
62	Hungary	243	2,541
63	Poland	237	7,988
64	United Arab Emirates	237	51
65	Hong Kong	235	1,000
66	Trinadad & Tobago	235	250
67	Kuwait	231	215
68	Spain	229	8,050
69	Italy	228	12,641
70	Greenland	224	11
71	Israel	221	680
72	Grenada	219	21
73	Gilbert Islands	214	12
74	Australia	214	2,815
75	Cuba	199	1,805
76	Algeria	198	3,220
77	Jordan	198	529
78	Antigua	193	14
79	Yugoslavia	193	4,081
80	Reunion	185	91
81	San Marino	181	3.4
82	St. Helena	180	0.9
83	Niue Island	175	0.7
84	Portugal	174	1,516
85	Gabon	173	90
86	Seychelles	161	9.0
87	Panama	159	260
88	Liberia	156	261
89	Venezuela	147	1,709
90	Rumania	146	3,066
91	South Korea	144	4,812
92	Singapore	142	320
93	Egypt	140	5,115
94	Brunei	133	20
95	Peru	131	2,010
96	Mongolia	129	166
97	Gibraltar	126	3.4
98	Mauritius	125	107
99	Thailand	125	5,111
100	Comoros	121	36
101	Gambia	118	60
102	Colombia	117	2,805
103	Iraq	116	1,250
104	Djibouti	115	12
	LOWER MIDDLE		
105	Madagascar	112	855
106	Ghana	110	1,060
107	Swaziland	110	53
108	New Hebrides	108	10
109	Turkey	107	4,096
110	Tonga	102	10
111	Zaire	101	2,448
112	Cameroon	96	603
113	Sao Tome & Principe	95	7.5
114	South Africa	94	2,335
115	Martinique	90	31
116	El Salvador	85	300
117	Botswana	83	55
118	Cook Islands	83	2.0
119	Sudan	80	1,310
120	Bolivia	78	425
121	Morocco	77	1,300

Rank	Country	Radios per 1,000	Total Number of Radios (000)
122	Costa Rica	74	142
123	Albania	72	173
124	Nigeria	69	5,000
125	Paraguay	68	176
126	Senegal	66	286
127	Mauritania	64	82
128	Congo	61	80
129	Brazil	60	6,275
130	Guadeloupe	60	21
131	Nicaragua	60	126
132	Vietnam	60	2,550
133	Honduras	54	158
134	Benin	52	150
135	Tunisia	49	277
136	French Guyana	48	2.8
137	Guatemala	47	261
138	Libya	45	105
139	Philippines	43	1,825
140	Solomon Islands	42	7.7
141	Central African Empire	41	70
142	Dominican Republic	41	185
143	Kenya	40	510
144	Indonesia	39	5,000
145	Laos	38	125
146	Rhodesia (Zimbabwe)	37	225
147	Sri Lanka	37	505
148	Niger	36	145
149	Rwanda	32	133
150	Malaysia	31	365
151	Macao	29	9
152	Burundi	27	100
153	Equatorial Guinea	26	7.5
154	Malawi	26	125
155	India	25	14,848
156	Guinea	24	105
157	Togo	23	50
158	Burma	22	659
159	Sierra Leone	22	61
160	Somalia	22	67
161	Uganda	22	250
162	Maldives	21	2.4
163	Zambia	21	100
164	Angola	20	116
165	Haiti	20	91
166	Cape Verde	19	5.2
167	Mozambique	19	176
168	Chad	18	70
169	Guinea-Bissau	17	9
170	Ivory Coast	17	75
171	Upper Volta	17	100
	BOTTOM 11		
172	China	16	12,000
173	Tanzania	16	231
174	Pakistan	15	1,015
175	Cambodia	14	112
176	Mali	13	75
177	Yemen Arab Republic	13	86
178	Lesotho	11	11
179	Saudi Arabia	11	85
180	Ethiopia	7	200
181	Afghanistan	6	111
182	Nepal	6	76

Source: *UNESCO Statistical Yearbook.*

301. Radio Transmitters

The number of radio transmitters operating worldwide on a regular basis is 25,510 distributed as follows:

Africa	700
North America	8,470
Latin America	4,270
Asia	2,730
Europe	5,980
Soviet Union	3,030
Oceania	330

In all countries radio is either operated by the government or is subject to government licensing. These figures are therefore extremely reliable.

Number of Countries: 148
Midpoint: 11
Period Covered: 1976
Type of Ranking: Total Number of Radio Transmitters and Total Transmitting Power in Kw; Highest to Lowest

Highlights & Findings: The degree of concentration in the top 10 bracket is less than that for TV; the 10 leading countries account for 68% of the world total. The top three nations operate half of all radio transmitters. It is interesting to note that many of the more industrially advanced countries such as Japan, France and West Germany have fewer radio transmitters than television transmitters.

Regions	Africa	Asia & Oceania	Europe	Western Hemisphere
Most	Mozambique (44)	Japan (5)	Soviet Union (2)	United States (1)
Least	Seychelles (138)	Western Samoa (148)	Malta (135)	Turks & Caicos (147)

Rank	Country	Total Number of Radio Transmitters	Total Transmitting Power (kw)	Rank	Country	Total Number of Radio Transmitters	Total Transmitting Power (kw)	Rank	Country	Total Number of Radio Transmitters	Total Transmitting Power (kw)
	TOP 10			38	East Germany	66	3,260.5	76	Syria	11	1,340.0
1	United States	7,785	N.A.	39	El Salvador	65	N.A.	77	Brunei	10	74.0
2	Soviet Union	3,034	N.A.	40	Rumania	62	N.A.	78	Congo	10	65.10
3	Italy	1,964	2,939.09	41	New Zealand	61	484.0	79	Gabon	10	157.1
4	Brazil	999	2,640.99	42	Iran	53	6,460.0	80	Ghana	10	108.0
5	Japan	944	3,996.9	43	Greece	51	762.0	81	Pacific Islands	10	29.5
6	Mexico	668	4,218.1	44	Mozambique	49	N.A.	82	Trinidad & Tobago	9	32.45
7	Indonesia	586	N.A.	45	Belgium	48	1,574.5	83	Ethiopia	8	651
8	Canada	531	N.A.	46	Nigeria	46	1,190.75	84	Kuwait	8	2,476.0
9	Yugoslavia	487	6,879.0	47	Egypt	43	4,886.0	85	Tunisia	8	1,053.0
10	Spain	406	4,870.0	48	Bolivia	39	N.A.	86	Guyana	7	44.1
				49	Israel	39	2,667.3	87	Sudan	7	490.0
				50	Hungary	37	1,689.0	88	Swaziland	7	130.49
	UPPER MIDDLE			51	Morocco	33	1,779.5	89	Afghanistan	6	305.05
11	Austria	399	3,507.7	52	Bulgaria	32	2,095.0	90	Bahamas	6	21.35
12	United Kingdom	364	6,903.3	53	Netherlands	30	1,125.5	91	Burundi	6	38.75
13	West Germany	346	21,079.0	54	Iceland	29	132.8	92	Belize	6	24.0
14	Norway	343	2,006.0	55	Sri Lanka	24	335.6	93	Central African Empire	6	135.56
15	Philippines	333	11,408.55	56	Pakistan	22	1,256.0	94	French Guyana	6	9.1
16	France	290	5,911.40	57	Zaire	22	1,044.0	95	Lebanon	6	237.0
17	Sweden	282	1,120.0	58	Jamaica	21	47.57	96	Monaco	6	1,035.0
18	Peru	279	875.32	59	Turkey	21	4,834.25	97	Qatar	6	161.05
19	Colombia	244	1,925.0	60	Angola	19	N.A.	98	Bahrain	5	23.01
20	Venezuela	235	1,686.25	61	Denmark	19	752.41	99	Bermuda	5	5.25
21	Ecuador	232	371.0	62	Ireland	18	975.0	100	Burma	5	250.0
22	Chile	229	873.1	63	Algeria	17	4,000.0	101	French Polynesia	5	68.0
23	Australia	219	2,646.0	64	Ivory Coast	17	N.A.	102	Maldives	5	73.0
24	Thailand	217	3,211.15	65	Vatican	17	1,105.25	103	Nepal	5	120.25
25	Switzerland	211	3,011.0	66	Madagascar	16	203	104	Somalia	5	71.0
26	Portugal	180	4,736.34	67	Singapore	16	1,140.0	105	Togo	5	126.0
27	Argentina	163	2,716.98	68	Liberia	15	123.3	106	Benin	4	35.1
28	Dominican Republic	146	262.7	69	Malawi	15	149.0	107	Botswana	4	21.05
29	India	146	5,739.90	70	Senegal	14	321.1	108	Cameroon	4	22.0
30	Czechoslovakia	123	N.A.	71	Greenland	13	62.35	109	Cape Verde	4	. . .
31	Panama	117	172.6	72	Niger	13	40.75	110	Cyprus	4	42.5
32	Uruguay	101	N.A.	73	Iraq	12	910.0	111	Djibouti	4	12.05
33	Finland	96	2,458.0					112	Faroe Islands	4	12.0
34	Guatemala	95	355		*LOWER MIDDLE*			113	Gambia	4	4.56
35	Puerto Rico	95	218	74	Hong Kong	11	90.0	114	Macao	4	. . .
36	South Korea	94	2,488.0	75	Fiji	11	40.5	115	Martinique	4	62.0
37	Malaysia	92	3,557.5								

Rank	Country	Total Number of Radio Transmitters	Total Transmitting Power (kw)	Rank	Country	Total Number of Radio Transmitters	Total Transmitting Power (kw)	Rank	Country	Total Number of Radio Transmitters	Total Transmitting Power (kw)
116	Mauritania	4	55.0	128	St. Helena	3	N.A.		*BOTTOM 9*		
117	New Caledonia	4	64.0	129	Antigua	2	6.0	140	Cayman Islands	1	0.1
118	New Hebrides	4	6.0	130	British Virgin Islands	2	10.0	141	Cook Islands	1	10.0
119	Reunion	4	20.0	131	Falkland Islands	2	6.5	142	Gilbert Islands	1	10.0
120	Rwanda	4	58.05	132	Guadeloupe	2	24.0	143	Nauru	1	0.13
121	Sao Tome & Principe	4	N.A.	133	Guam	2	12.5	144	Niue Island	1	0.25
122	Yemen Arab Republic	4	170.0	134	Guinea-Bissau	2	N.A.	145	Norfolk Island	1	0.05
123	South Yemen	4	63.5	135	Malta	2	6.0	146	St. Vincent	1	0.25
124	Barbados	3	11.02	136	St. Lucia	2	10.25	147	Turks & Caicos	1	1.5
125	Comoros	3	N.A.	137	St. Pierre & Miquelon	2	5.0	148	Western Samoa	1	10.0
126	Gibraltar	3	3.0	138	Seychelles	2	11.0				
127	Mauritius	3	30.0	139	Tonga	2	20.0				

Source: *UNESCO Statistical Yearbook.*

302. Television Sets

In the mid-1970s there were 357 million television sets in use in 123 countries around the world. Compared to radio, television has made only modest gains in recent years in the developing countries, where a television set is still a luxury. However, the growth of satellite communications augurs a breakthrough in making television a truly universal medium. Another area in which there has been considerable progress is color television. Although no separate statistics are available for color television sets, the proportion of black-and-white sets has been steadily decreasing in all industrially advanced countries.

Number of Countries: 124
Midpoint: 61 per 1,000
Period Covered: 1974
Type of Ranking: Per Capita Television Sets and Total; Highest to Lowest

Highlights & Findings: The United States accounts for nearly 34% of the world total; the United States and the Soviet Union together account for nearly 49%. Fifty-six countries require licenses for the use of television sets, while others, including the United States, impose no fees.

Regions	Africa	Asia & Oceania	Europe	Western Hemisphere
Most	Reunion (62)	New Zealand (13)	Monaco (1)	United States (2)
Least	Mozambique (124)	India (122)	Albania (115)	Haiti (110)

Rank	Country	Television Sets per 1,000	Total (000)	Rank	Country	Television Sets per 1,000	Total (000)	Rank	Country	Television Sets per 1,000	Total (000)
	TOP 10			14	Netherlands	259	3,510	30	Barbados	203	40
1	Monaco	667	16	15	Luxembourg	257	88	31	Kuwait	196	182
2	United States	571	121,100	16	Norway	256	1,021	32	Hong Kong	185	785
3	Canada	366	8,232	17	Belgium	252	2,464	33	Poland	181	6,100
4	Bermuda	354	20	18	Austria	247	1,856	34	Argentina	180	4,500
5	Sweden	348	2,841	19	Czechoslovakia	245	3,602	35	Ireland	178	550
6	St. Pierre & Miquelon	340	1.7	20	France	235	12,335	36	San Marino	174	3.3
7	United Kingdom	315	17,641	21	Japan	233	25,564	37	Spain	174	6,125
8	Denmark	308	1,556	22	Malta	232	75	38	Antigua	171	12
9	West Germany	305	18,920	23	Gibraltar	230	6.2	39	Bulgaria	168	1,457
10	East Germany	297	5,096	24	Iceland	230	50	40	Netherlands Antilles	143	34
				25	Australia	226	3,013	41	Lebanon	135	375
	UPPER MIDDLE			26	Hungary	219	2,296	42	Israel	134	441
11	Finland	269	1,261	27	Italy	213	11,817	43	Cyprus	133	85
12	Switzerland	264	1,714	28	Soviet Union	208	52,500	44	Yugoslavia	132	2,784
13	New Zealand	261	791	29	Puerto Rico	206	625	45	Bahrain	123	30

Rank	Country	Television Sets per 1,000	Total (000)	Rank	Country	Television Sets per 1,000	Total (000)	Rank	Country	Television Sets per 1,000	Total (000)
46	Uruguay	116	350	72	Guadeloupe	37	13	100	Senegal	8	35
47	Rumania	114	2,405	73	Ecuador	36	250	101	St. Vincent	7	0.6
48	Singapore	114	252	74	Nicaragua	36	75	102	Sudan	6	100
49	Panama	112	183	75	Dominican Republic	34	156	103	Liberia	5	8.5
50	Greece	106	950	76	Brunei	33	5	104	Zambia	5	22
51	New Caledonia	106	14	77	Malaysia	33	390	105	Congo	3.8	3.8
52	French Polynesia	105	13	78	Jordan	32	85	106	Cambodia	3.3	26
53	Venezuela	103	1,200	79	Syria	31	224	107	Libya	3	6
54	Trinidad & Tobago	94	100	80	El Salvador	28	111	108	Kenya	3	37
55	Mexico	84	4,885	81	Peru	28	425	109	Ghana	3	33
56	Brazil	83	8,650	82	Tunisia	27	147	110	Haiti	2.9	13
57	Surinam	80	33	83	Vietnam	26	500	111	Sierra Leone	2.2	6
58	Costa Rica	78	150	84	Algeria	25	410	112	Mongolia	2.1	3
59	Chile	72	750	85	Djibouti	23	2.3	113	Nigeria	1.8	110
60	Portugal	66	572	86	Morocco	23	382	114	Pakistan	1.8	125
61	Cuba	65	595	87	Paraguay	21	53				
62	Reunion	61	30	88	Guatemala	19	106		**BOTTOM 10**		
				89	South Yemen	18	30	115	Albania	1.7	4
	LOWER MIDDLE			90	Egypt	17	610	116	Uganda	1.4	15
63	Greenland	55	2.7	91	Philippines	17	711	117	Madagascar	1.0	7.5
64	French Guyana	52	3.0	92	Thailand	17	715	118	Upper Volta	1.0	5.5
65	Iraq	50	520	93	Honduras	16	46	119	Ethiopia	0.8	20
66	Jamaica	49	97	94	St. Lucia	16	1.7	120	Indonesia	0.7	275
67	South Korea	48	1,619	95	Saudi Arabia	14	122	121	China	0.6	500
68	Iran	47	1,500	96	Turkey	12	458	122	India	0.5	275
69	Martinique	45	16	97	Rhodesia (Zimbabwe)	10	57	123	Zaire	0.3	7
70	Mauritius	44	38	98	Gabon	10	5.1	124	Mozambique	0.1	1
71	Colombia	43	971	99	Ivory Coast	9	40				

Source: *World Communications.*

303. Television Transmitters

The number of television transmitters operating worldwide on a regular basis is 24,980 distributed as follows:

Africa	200
North America	4,360
Asia (excluding China, Vietnam and North Korea)	6,610
Europe	11,250
Latin America	450
Soviet Union	1,750
Oceania	360

Because television in all countries is either operated by the government or is subject to government licensing, these figures are extremely reliable.

Number of Countries: 99
Midpoint: 17
Period Covered: 1976
Type of Ranking: Total Number of Television Transmitters; Highest to Lowest

Highlights & Findings: The degree of concentration in the top 10 bracket is unusually high; the 10 leading countries account for 79.1% of all transmitters. More than half of all transmitters are operated by the top three nations: Japan, the United States and France.

Regions	Africa	Asia & Oceania	Europe	Western Hemisphere
Most	Algeria (25)	Japan (1)	France (3)	United States (2)
Least	Djibouti (97)	Singapore (99)	Malta (98)	St. Vincent (93)

Rank	Country	Number of Transmitters	Rank	Country	Number of Transmitters	Rank	Country	Number of Transmitters
	TOP 10		3	France	3,001	6	West Germany	1,153
1	Japan	6,117	4	Soviet Union	1,749	7	Czechoslovakia	788
2	United States	3,695	5	Italy	1,199	8	Spain	741

Rank	Country	Number of Transmitters	Rank	Country	Number of Transmitters	Rank	Country	Number of Transmitters
9	Norway	665	40	Ireland	28	71	Ghana	4
10	Canada	661	41	Israel	28	72	Liberia	4
			42	Chile	27	73	Mauritius	4
	UPPER MIDDLE		43	Hong Kong	26	74	Antigua	3
11	United Kingdom	596	44	Morocco	23	75	Colombia	3
12	Switzerland	583	45	Hungary	22	76	El Salvador	3
13	Austria	461	46	Philippines	22	77	French Guyana	3
14	East Germany	461	47	Netherlands	21	78	Gabon	3
15	Yugoslavia	430	48	Ecuador	19	79	Guadeloupe	3
16	Sweden	358	49	French Guyana	19	80	Qatar	3
17	Australia	198	50	Puerto Rico	17	81	Monaco	3
18	Rumania	194	51	Jamaica	13	82	Pacific Islands	3
19	Iran	157	52	Reunion	13	83	St. Pierre & Miquelon	3
20	Bulgaria	154				84	Sudan	3
21	New Zealand	144		*LOWER MIDDLE*		85	Trinidad & Tobago	3
22	Finland	83	53	Guatemala	12	86	Zaire	3
23	Argentina	82	54	Nigeria	10			
24	Iceland	80	55	Panama	10		*BOTTOM 13*	
25	Algeria	75	56	Saudi Arabia	10	87	Barbados	2
26	Mexico	71	57	Tunisia	10	88	Bermuda	2
27	Poland	69	58	Ethiopia	8	89	Bolivia	2
28	Brazil	66	59	Lebanon	8	90	Gibraltar	2
29	South Korea	59	60	Dominican Republic	7	91	Guam	2
30	Greece	54	61	Kuwait	7	92	Jordan	2
31	Peru	52	62	New Caledonia	7	93	St. Vincent	2
32	Thailand	48	63	Pakistan	7	94	Senegal	2
33	Portugal	41	64	Syria	7	95	Bahrain	1
34	Venezuela	39	65	Iraq	6	96	Congo	1
35	Malaysia	38	66	Martinque	6	97	Djibouti	1
36	Turkey	38	67	Cyprus	5	98	Malta	1
37	Denmark	30	68	India	5	99	Singapore	1
38	Belgium	28	69	Madagascar	5			
39	Egypt	28	70	South Yemen	5			

Source: *UNESCO Statistical Yearbook.*

304. Movie Attendance

Movie attendance statistics are comparatively reliable because they are based on the number of tickets sold and almost all countries charge sales or entertainment tax on these tickets. Wherever possible these statistics include drive-ins and mobile units. Annual movie attendance worldwide in the mid-1970s was 13.261 billion, or 3.3 per capita. Because of the rapid growth of television as a rival form of entertainment, per capita movie attendance has actually declined in the 1970s.

Number of Countries: 134
Midpoint: 3.3
Period Covered: Mid-1970s
Type of Ranking: Per Capita Movie Attendance and Total Attendance per Year; Highest to Lowest

Highlights & Findings: The Soviet Union is currently the largest movie-going nation in the world, contributing over 33% of total movie attendance. The top 10 nations do not include a single Western industrialized country. African nations are at the bottom of the scale, reflecting the minimal impact of the cinema on African culture.

Regions	Africa	Asia & Oceania	Europe	Western Hemisphere
Most	Mauritius (2)	Macao (1)	Soviet Union (4)	Cuba (6)
Least	Burundi (134)	Pakistan (125)	West Germany (87)	St. Vincent (106)

Rank	Country	Movie Attendance per Capita per Year	Total Movie Attendance (Million) (... Negligible)
	TOP 10		
1	Macao	81.0	21.2
2	Mauritius	18.9	17.0
3	Singapore	18.7	42.0
4	Soviet Union	17.7	4,497.3
5	Brunei	17.0	2.5
6	Cuba	14.2	124.3
7	Bulgaria	13.1	114.3
8	Hong Kong	12.4	54.1
9	Grenada	11.5	1.1
10	Guyana	11.2	8.7
	UPPER MIDDLE		
11	Gibraltar	11.1	0.3
12	Iceland	10.8	2.3
13	San Marino	10.5	0.2
14	Guam	10.3	1.0
15	Nauru	10.0	0.1
16	Malta	9.7	3.1
17	Falkland Islands	9.5	...
18	Libya	9.4	23.0
19	Italy	9.2	515.5
20	Malaysia	9.1	108.8
21	Cyprus	9.0	6.0
22	Rumania	8.7	185.7
23	Seychelles	8.6	0.5
24	Bahrain	8.2	2.0
25	Burma	8.1	222.5
26	Trinidad & Tobago	8.0	8.4
27	Israel	7.8	27.0
28	Gilbert Islands	7.8	0.5
29	Philippines	7.6	318.0
30	Faroe Islands	7.5	0.3
31	Barbados	7.4	1.8
32	Greenland	7.4	0.4
33	Spain	7.2	255.8
34	Hungary	7.0	74.4
35	Colombia	6.8	163.6
36	Turkey	6.7	246.7
37	Czechoslovakia	5.8	85.9
38	Djibouti	5.8	0.6
39	Ecuador	5.6	38.7
40	Syria	5.5	42.0
41	New Caledonia	5.1	0.7
42	Chile	5.0	44.6
43	United States	5.0	920.6
44	Panama	4.8	7.1
45	Kuwait	4.7	4.7
46	British Virgin Islands	4.6	0.1
47	East Germany	4.6	76.9
48	Norway	4.6	18.5
49	Canada	4.3	97.5
50	Mexico	4.2	251.2
51	Poland	4.1	140.8
52	Portugal	4.1	35.7
53	Belize	4.0	0.5
54	Cook Islands	4.0	0.1
55	Monaco	4.0	0.1
56	Sri Lanka	4.0	55.5
57	India	3.8	2,260.0
58	New Zealand	3.8	11.9
59	Turks & Caicos	3.8	...
60	Yugoslavia	3.8	81.6
61	Denmark	3.7	19.0
62	French Polynesia	3.7	0.5
63	Iran	3.7	123.1
64	Switzerland	3.6	23.0
65	El Salvador	3.5	14.1
66	France	3.4	178.5
67	Liechtenstein	3.3	0.1
68	St. Pierre & Miquelon	3.3	...
	LOWER MIDDLE		
69	Argentina	3.2	82.2
70	Luxembourg	3.2	1.1
71	Sweden	3.1	25.4
72	Venezuela	3.1	36.1
73	Australia	3.0	36.0
74	Jamaica	3.0	6.4
75	Austria	2.8	20.8
76	Guatemala	2.8	15.4
77	Algeria	2.7	45.0
78	Belgium	2.6	25.7
79	Brazil	2.6	275.4
80	South Yemen	2.4	3.5
81	Tunisia	2.3	12.5
82	South Korea	2.2	75.6
83	Puerto Rico	2.2	6.8
84	Netherlands	2.1	28.3
85	United Kingdom	2.1	116.3
86	Finland	2.0	9.6
87	West Germany	2.0	121.0
88	Egypt	1.9	65.0
89	Samoa	1.9	0.3
90	Lebanon	1.8	49.7
91	Japan	1.7	185.7
92	Somalia	1.7	4.7
93	Thailand	1.7	71.0
94	Morocco	1.6	26.1
95	Ivory Coast	1.5	10.0
96	Sudan	1.4	24.0
97	Sao Tome & Principe	1.3	0.1
98	Dominican Republic	1.2	5.2
99	Niue Island	1.2	...
100	Senegal	1.2	5.2
101	Afghanistan	1.1	19.2
102	Cape Verde	1.1	0.3
103	Cameroon	1.0	6.5
104	Nigeria	1.0	68.7
105	Oman	1.0	0.8
106	St. Vincent	1.0	0.1
107	Tonga	1.0	0.1
108	Congo	0.9	0.9
109	Indonesia	0.9	112.5
110	Gabon	0.8	0.4
111	Jordan	0.8	2.0
112	Qatar	0.8	0.1
113	Angola	0.6	3.7
114	Bhutan	0.6	0.5
115	Guinea-Bissau	0.6	0.3
116	Liberia	0.6	1.0
117	St. Helena	0.6	...
118	Benin	0.4	1.2
119	Ethiopia	0.4	9.5
120	Kenya	0.4	5.7
121	Madagascar	0.4	2.9
122	Malawi	0.4	2.0
123	Mozambique	0.4	3.2
124	Central African Empire	0.3	0.5
125	Pakistan	0.3	18.3
	BOTTOM 9		
126	Comoros	0.2	0.2
127	Niger	0.2	0.8
128	Swaziland	0.2	0.1
129	Tanzania	0.2	3.5
130	Botswana	0.1	0.1
131	Ghana	0.1	1.1
132	Uganda	0.1	1.3
133	Zaire	0.1	1.7
134	Burundi	0.04	0.1

Source: *UNESCO Statistical Yearbook.*

305. Fixed Cinemas

The term fixed cinema refers to an indoor cinema with a permanent fixed roof as distinguished from mobile units and drive-ins. Only cinemas regularly used for showing films of 16 or 35 mm and over are included in the data. In the mid-1970s there were 265,500 such cinemas in the world distributed as follows: Soviet Union 154,000; North America 16,500; Latin America 11,000; Asia 20,500; Europe 59,000; Africa 3,100 and Oceania 1,400. The figures for Asia exclude China, North Korea and Vietnam.

Number of Countries: 157
Midpoint: 42
Period Covered: Mid-1970s
Type of Ranking: Total Number of Fixed Cinemas: Highest to Lowest

Highlights & Findings: The Soviet Union has 58% of the world's cinemas, which would be incredible were it not for the fact that the film is not only a medium of entertainment in the USSR but also a principal instrument of ideology and indoctrination. This is also the principal factor that lifts almost all the Eastern European countries to the top ranks. The number of cinemas has been declining in almost all countries and furthermore the new cinemas are much more smaller in size, reflecting the economic uncertainties of the film industry and shrinking audiences.

Regions	Africa	Asia & Oceania	Europe	Western Hemisphere
Most	South Africa (26)	India (6)	Soviet Union (1)	United States (2)
Least	Sao Tome & Principe (157)	Norfolk Island (151)	Monaco (148)	British Virgin Islands (156)

Rank	Country	Number of Fixed Cinemas
	TOP 10	
1	Soviet Union	154,100
2	United States	11,110
3	Rumania	6,084
4	Italy	5,920
5	France	5,844
6	India	5,650
7	Spain	5,076
8	Bulgaria	3,597
9	Hungary	3,528
10	Czechoslovakia	3,390
	UPPER MIDDLE	
11	Brazil	3,096
12	West Germany	2,655
13	Japan	2,468
14	Turkey	2,424
15	Mexico	2,395
16	Poland	2,145
17	United Kingdom	1,530
18	Yugoslavia	1,303
19	Sweden	1,253
20	Argentina	1,183
21	East Germany	1,181
22	Canada	1,042
23	Australia	976
24	Indonesia	960
25	Philippines	716
26	South Africa	686
27	Thailand	658
28	South Korea	584
29	Belgium	568
30	Pakistan	550
31	Switzerland	519
32	Portugal	459
33	Norway	451
34	Cuba	439
35	Venezuela	431
36	Burma	418
37	Malaysia	410
38	Iran	403
39	Netherlands	387
40	Denmark	375
41	Colombia	352
42	Sri Lanka	350
43	Finland	319
44	Algeria	317
45	Chile	291
46	Peru	276
47	Austria	243
48	Israel	228
49	New Zealand	228
50	Morocco	196
51	Ecuador	185
52	Ireland	184

Rank	Country	Number of Fixed Cinemas
53	Lebanon	170
54	Egypt	152
55	Cyprus	150
56	Nigeria	120
57	Guatemala	106
58	Puerto Rico	105
59	Tunisia	105
60	Syria	100
61	Zaire	91
62	Hong Kong	87
63	Dominican Republic	80
64	Ivory Coast	78
65	Senegal	77
66	Greenland	73
67	El Salvador	72
68	Rhodesia (Zimbabwe)	72
69	Singapore	71
70	Trinidad & Tobago	66
71	Sudan	52
72	Guyana	50
73	Libya	50
74	Angola	48
75	Kenya	48
76	Mauritius	48
77	Panama	45
78	Jamaica	44
79	Iceland	42
	LOWER MIDDLE	
80	Cameroon	40
81	Jordan	40
82	Malta	36
83	Ethiopia	31
84	Madagascar	31
85	Tanzania	31
86	Mozambique	28
87	Papua New Guinea	28
88	Uganda	28
89	Zambia	28
90	Iraq	27
91	Luxembourg	27
92	Liberia	26
93	Somalia	26
94	Afghanistan	24
95	Pacific Islands	23
96	Yemen Arab Republic	20
97	South Yemen	19
98	Namibia	18
99	Mongolia	17
100	New Caledonia	17
101	United Arab Emirates	17
102	New Hebrides	12
103	Oman	12
104	Botswana	11
105	Bahrain	10

Rank	Country	Number of Fixed Cinemas
106	Cook Islands	10
107	Mauritania	10
108	Samoa	10
109	Brunei	9
110	Faroe Islands	9
111	Gambia	9
112	Ghana	9
113	Macao	9
114	St. Lucia	9
115	Belize	8
116	Central African Empire	8
117	Kuwait	8
118	Qatar	8
119	San Marino	8
120	Congo	7
121	Guam	7
122	Guinea-Bissau	7
123	Tonga	7
124	Barbados	6
125	Benin	6
126	Cape Verde	6
127	French Polynesia	6
128	Grenada	6
129	Bahamas	5
130	Burundi	5
131	Gilbert Islands	5
132	Malawi	5
133	Bermuda	4
134	Djibouti	4
135	Gibraltar	4
136	Niger	4
137	Swaziland	4
138	Bhutan	3
139	Cayman Islands	3
140	Dominica	3
141	Liechtenstein	3
142	Rwanda	3
143	St. Vincent	3
	BOTTOM 14	
144	Comoros	2
145	Falkland Islands	2
146	Gabon	2
147	Lesotho	2
148	Monaco	2
149	Nauru	2
150	Niue Island	2
151	Norfolk Island	2
152	St. Helena	2
153	St. Pierre & Miquelon	2
154	Seychelles	2
155	Turks & Caicos Islands	2
156	British Virgin Islands	1
157	Sao Tome & Principe	1

Source: *UNESCO Statistical Yearbook.*

306. Cinema Seats

In the mid-1970s it was estimated that there were 77 million cinema seats worldwide, or 25 per 1,000 inhabitants. Asia and Africa have less than the world average with nine and five per 1,000 inhabitants respectively, while the Western Hemisphere has 33, Europe 40, Oceania 34 and the Soviet Union 100 per 1,000 inhabitants. In terms of total number of cinema seats, the Soviet Union leads the world with 25 million seats or nearly one-third of the world total; Europe has 19 million, North America 11 million, Latin America 7 million, Asia 12 million and Africa 2 million. The figures for Asia do not include China, North Korea and Vietnam. The rankings also do not include drive-ins or mobile units.

Number of Countries: 141
Midpoint: 19.2 per 1,000
Period Covered: 1975
Type of Ranking: Number of Seats in Fixed Commercial Cinemas per 1,000 Inhabitants; Highest to Lowest

Highlights & Findings: Because the film has been declining as a medium of entertainment in almost all large or industrialized countries, this ranking is led by smaller countries.

Regions	Africa	Asia & Oceania	Europe	Western Hemisphere
Most	St. Helena (6)	Cook Islands (2)	Cyprus (3)	Falkland Islands (1)
Least	Malawi (140)	Afghanistan (138)	Rumania (92)	Cayman Islands (141)

Rank	Country	Cinema Seats per 1,000	Total Seating Capacity (000)	Rank	Country	Cinema Seats per 1,000	Total Seating Capacity (000)	Rank	Country	Cinema Seats per 1,000	Total Seating Capacity (000)
	TOP 10			43	Turks & Caicos	33.0	0.3	86	Colombia	13.0	291.7
1	Falkland Islands	250.0	0.5	44	Faroe Islands	32.5	1.3	87	South Korea	12.8	359.5
2	Cook Islands	156.0	3.9	45	Turkey	31.5	1,164.8	88	Kuwait	12.5	11.0
3	Cyprus	136.0	88.0	46	Gilbert Islands	31.3	2.0	89	Algeria	12.0	190.0
4	St. Pierre & Miquelon	133.3	0.8	47	New Caledonia	30.3	3.7	90	Namibia	12.0	7.1
5	San Marino	121.0	2.3	48	Switzerland	30.1	188.4	91	Burma	11.0	302.6
6	St. Helena	120.0	1.2	49	Portugal	29.9	260.9	92	Rumania	10.4	218.8
7	Nauru	114.3	0.8	50	Canada	28.7	608.8	93	Western Samoa	10.3	1.6
8	Norfolk Islands	100.0	0.5	51	Malaysia	27.8	250.0	94	Japan	10.1	1,107.0
9	Soviet Union	100.0	25,000.0	52	Argentina	27.7	704.6	95	Cape Verde	9.8	2.8
10	Gibraltar	88.9	2.4	53	British Virgin Islands	27.3	0.3	96	Dominican Republic	9.7	40.7
				54	Chile	27.3	185.5	97	Liberia	9.5	14.9
	UPPER MIDDLE			55	Singapore	27.3	60.2	98	Rhodesia (Zimbabwe)	9.3	51.0
11	Bulgaria	84.8	736.7	56	Mexico	27.0	1,575.9	99	Thailand	9.2	389.0
12	Qatar	83.3	7.0	57	Panama	26.9	39.8	100	Tunisia	9.0	49.8
13	Malta	76.0	29.1	58	Denmark	25.4	138.2	101	Seychelles	8.6	0.8
14	Spain	73.8	2,550.0	59	Rwanda	24.3	1.0	102	Jordan	8.4	22.5
15	Czechoslovakia	66.6	958.7	60	St. Vincent	24.0	2.4	103	St. Lucia	8.3	9.5
16	Austria	64.0	94.5	61	Hong Kong	23.7	105.7	104	Somalia	8.2	23.0
17	Brunei	59.2	8.3	62	Jamaica	22.8	45.0	105	Iran	8.1	272.3
18	Djibouti	55.8	5.8	63	South Africa	22.5	498.0	106	Senegal	7.8	33.5
19	Mauritius	55.0	48.0	64	Bahamas	22.0	4.1	107	Morocco	7.7	129.2
20	Guam	53.6	5.2	65	Yugoslavia	21.4	451.0	108	Papua New Guinea	7.3	18.8
21	Hungary	53.3	561.7	66	Finland	20.1	95.2	109	India	6.5	3,955.0
22	Israel	52.0	154.0	67	Dominica	20.0	1.5	110	Guinea-Bissau	6.3	3.0
23	Guyana	48.4	37.5	68	Niue Island	20.0	0.1	111	Angola	6.1	35.7
24	United States	48.0	10,000.0	69	East Germany	19.8	345.0	112	Congo	5.0	5.1
25	New Hebrides	46.7	4.2	70	Barbados	19.3	4.7	113	Iraq	5.0	54.0
26	Pacific Islands	45.5	5.0	71	West Germany	19.2	894.5	114	Vietnam	5.0	91.0
27	Iceland	43.3	9.5					115	Pakistan	4.6	300.0
28	Bahrain	43.2	10.5		*LOWER MIDDLE*			116	Botswana	4.5	3.0
29	Liechtenstein	43.0	0.9	72	Brazil	18.1	1,026.9	117	Egypt	4.1	140.9
30	New Zealand	41.0	125.2	73	Ivory Coast	17.1	69.0	118	Cameroon	3.6	22.8
31	Trinidad & Tobago	40.9	42.7	74	United Kingdom	17.4	879.0	119	Gabon	3.3	1.7
32	Bermuda	40.0	2.2	75	Ecuador	16.5	114.6	120	Benin	3.1	9.0
33	Luxembourg	39.4	13.7	76	Poland	16.3	532.8	121	Zambia	3.1	13.4
34	Belgium	37.0	267.7	77	El Salvador	16.0	57.0	122	Comoros	2.8	0.8
35	Macau	36.9	9.9	78	Venezuela	15.2	177.0	123	Sudan	2.8	47.3
36	Australia	36.9	478.4	79	French Polynesia	15.0	3.2	124	Swaziland	2.7	1.3
37	Norway	35.5	143.3	80	Netherlands	14.0	169.2	125	Mozambique	2.3	19.5
38	Belize	35.0	4.5	81	South Yemen	14.0	20.0	126	Madagascar	1.9	12.5
39	France	34.6	1,817.0	82	Guatemala	13.6	75.2	127	Bhutan	1.9	1.5
40	Cuba	33.6	294.3	83	Philippines	13.5	569.8	128	Kenya	1.6	24.0
41	Monaco	33.3	0.8	84	Sao Tome & Principe	13.3	1.0	129	Central African Empire	1.0	2.0
42	Lebanon	33.0	86.6	85	Sri Lanka	13.3	183.8	130	Tanzania	1.0	14.5

Rank	Country	Cinema Seats per 1,000	Total Seating Capacity (000)	Rank	Country	Cinema Seats per 1,000	Total Seating Capacity (000)	Rank	Country	Cinema Seats per 1,000	Total Seating Capacity (000)
131	Zaire	1.0	23.3	134	Niger	0.9	3.8	139	Burundi	0.4	1.5
				135	Mauritania	0.8	1.0	140	Malawi	0.4	1.8
	BOTTOM 10			136	Nigeria	0.8	60.0	141	Cayman Islands	0.1	1.0
132	Ethiopia	0.9	25.6	137	Uganda	0.8	9.1				
133	Lesotho	0.9	0.8	138	Afghanistan	0.7	12.0				

Source: *UNESCO Statistical Yearbook.*

307. Film Production

Average annual production of long films (including coproductions but excluding films produced exclusively for television) was about 3,600, of which about 14% were produced by the leading film-making nation, India. The minimum length of films classified as long films varies considerably from country to country, ranging from 1,000 meters to 3,000 meters, but the standard in most countries is closer to 2,000 meters.

Number of Countries: 60
Midpoint: 21
Period Covered: Mid-1970s
Type of Ranking: Number of Long (or Feature) Films Produced Annually; Highest to Lowest

Highlights & Findings: The most significant statistics to emerge from this ranking is the decline of the United States from its position as the top film-producing nation in the world during the Thirties and Forties to eighth place. Even in the Western Hemisphere it takes second place to Mexico. Five of the top film-producing nations are Asian, but in almost all countries outside India the total number of films produced domestically has been falling.

Regions	Africa	Asia & Oceania	Europe	Western Hemisphere
Most	Egypt (21)	India (1)	France (3)	Mexico (7)
Least	Tanzania (60)	Qatar (59)	Ireland (53)	Colombia (52)

Rank	Country	Number of Long Films Produced Annually	Rank	Country	Number of Long Films Produced Annually	Rank	Country	Number of Long Films Produced Annually
	TOP 10		21	Egypt	45	42	Austria	6
1	India	475	22	Canada	41	43	Brunei	6
2	Japan	405	23	Indonesia	41	44	Cuba	6
3	France	234	24	Poland	36	45	Finland	6
4	Philippines	208	25	Argentina	34	46	Lebanon	6
5	Italy	203	26	Sri Lanka	31	47	Malaysia	5
6	Soviet Union	184	27	Bulgaria	25	48	Guyana	4
7	Mexico	162	28	Rumania	23	49	Singapore	4
8	United States	156	29	Denmark	22			
9	Pakistan	120	30	Yugoslavia	21		*BOTTOM 11*	
10	Hong Kong	112				50	Afghanistan	3
						51	Algeria	3
	UPPER MIDDLE			*LOWER MIDDLE*		52	Colombia	2
11	Spain	105	31	Hungary	19	53	Ireland	2
12	South Korea	99	32	Belgium	17	54	Libya	2
13	Thailand	95	33	East Germany	16	55	Ghana	1
14	Brazil	90	34	Netherlands	16	56	Jordan	1
15	West Germany	81	35	Switzerland	15	57	Mauritius	1
16	Greece	70	36	Norway	14	58	Morocco	1
17	United Kingdom	70	37	Sweden	14	59	Qatar	1
18	Iran	68	38	Australia	11	60	Tanzania	1
19	Czechoslovakia	62	39	Venezuela	9			
20	Burma	49	40	Israel	8			
			41	Tunisia	8			

Source: *UNESCO Statistical Yearbook.*

308. Daily Newspapers

A daily general-interest newspaper is defined as a publication devoted primarily to recording events of current public affairs, international affairs, politics, etc., and one that is published at least four times a week. National statistics on daily newspapers (unlike those relating to periodicals) are fairly accurate. In the mid-1970s, 7,900 newspapers were being published in the world. The regional distribution is as follows:

Asia	2,230	(excluding China, Vietnam and North Korea)
North America	1,935	
Europe	1,660	
Latin America	1,075	
Africa	190	
Oceania	120	
Soviet Union	690	

Number of Countries: 156
Midpoint: 7
Period Covered: Mid-1970s
Type of Ranking: Number of Daily General Interest Newspapers; Highest to Lowest

Highlights & Findings: Nearly 23% of all newspapers in the world are published in the United States. The top 10 nations account for 65% of the total. The number of daily newspapers is related to a number of factors, such as the extent of freedom of the press, literacy, the number of languages spoken in the country and historical traditions of free communications.

Regions	Africa	Asia & Oceania	Europe	Western Hemisphere
Most	Mauritius (61)	India (2)	Soviet Union (3)	United States (1)
Least	Upper Volta (155)	Papua New Guinea (151)	Vatican (156)	St. Kitts-Nevis-Anguilla (153)

Rank	Country	Number of Daily Newspapers	Rank	Country	Number of Daily Newspapers	Rank	Country	Number of Daily Newspapers
	TOP 10		39	Belgium	30	80	Surinam	7
1	United States	1,815	40	Portugal	30			
2	India	835	41	Uruguay	30		*LOWER MIDDLE*	
3	Soviet Union	691	42	Czechoslovakia	29	81	Costa Rica	6
4	Turkey	437	43	Ecuador	29	82	Kuwait	6
5	West Germany	334	44	Nepal	29	83	Macao	6
6	Brazil	280	45	Hungary	27	84	Malta	6
7	Mexico	256	46	Yugoslavia	26	85	Panama	6
8	Japan	180	47	South Africa	24	86	Syria	6
9	Indonesia	172	48	Israel	23	87	Yemen Arab Republic	6
10	Argentina	164	49	Iran	20	88	Iceland	5
			50	Rumania	20	89	Mozambique	5
	UPPER MIDDLE		51	Sri Lanka	18	90	Netherlands Antilles	5
11	Sweden	135	52	Afghanistan	17	91	Puerto Rico	5
12	Canada	121	53	Cambodia	16	92	Algeria	4
13	Spain	115	54	Cuba	15	93	Chad	4
14	United Kingdom	111	55	Philippines	15	94	French Polynesia	4
15	Greece	106	56	Bolivia	14	95	Ghana	4
16	Pakistan	102	57	Egypt	14	96	Jordan	4
17	France	98	58	Bulgaria	13	97	Sudan	4
18	Netherlands	95	59	Cyprus	12	98	Tunisia	4
19	Switzerland	95	60	El Salvador	12	99	Uganda	4
20	Hong Kong	82	61	Mauritius	12	100	Congo	3
21	Norway	80	62	Nigeria	12	101	Guyana	3
22	Italy	78	63	Guatemala	11	102	Ivory Coast	3
23	Australia	70	64	Saudi Arabia	11	103	Jamaica	3
24	Finland	60	65	Zaire	11	104	Kenya	3
25	Thailand	56	66	Dominican Republic	10	105	Liberia	3
26	Denmark	49	67	Singapore	10	106	Rhodesia (Zimbabwe)	3
27	Venezuela	49	68	Madagascar	9	107	Trinidad & Tobago	3
28	Chile	47	69	Morocco	9	108	Tanzania	3
29	Poland	44	70	Ethiopia	8	109	South Yemen	3
30	Columbia	40	71	Honduras	8	110	Albania	2
31	East Germany	40	72	Laos	8	111	Bahamas	2
32	New Zealand	39	73	Paraguay	8	112	Burundi	2
33	South Korea	36	74	Burma	7	113	Cameroon	2
34	Peru	35	75	Haiti	7	114	Guadeloupe	2
35	Lebanon	33	76	Iraq	7	115	Libya	2
36	Malaysia	31	77	Ireland	7	116	Malawi	2
37	Australia	30	78	Luxembourg	7	117	Martinique	2
38	Bangladesh	30	79	Nicaragua	7	118	Namibia	2

Rank	Country	Number of Daily Newspapers	Rank	Country	Number of Daily Newspapers	Rank	Country	Number of Daily Newspapers
119	New Caledonia	2	131	Belize	1	145	Lesotho	1
120	Niger	2	132	Benin	1	146	Liechtenstein	1
121	Reunion	2	133	Bermuda	1	147	Maldives	1
122	Senegal	2	134	Botswana	1	148	Mali	1
123	Seychelles	2	135	Cook Islands	1	149	Mauritania	1
124	Sierra Leone	2	136	Faroe Islands	1	150	Mongolia	1
125	Somalia	2	137	Fiji	1	151	Papua New Guinea	1
126	United Arab Emirates	2	138	French Guyana	1	152	Rwanda	1
127	Zambia	2	139	Gabon	1	153	St. Kitts-Nevis-Anguilla	1
			140	Gibraltar	1	154	Togo	1
	BOTTOM 29		141	Grenada	1	155	Upper Volta	1
128	Angola	1	142	Guam	1	156	Vatican	1
129	Antigua	1	143	Guinea	1			
130	Barbados	1	144	Guinea-Bissau	1			

Source: *Editor & Publisher International Yearbook.*

309. Daily Newspaper Circulation

Because the circulation of daily newspapers is in most countries certified by audit bureaus, statistics relating to the circulation of dailies are fairly reliable. (For the definition of a daily newspaper see the ranking of countries by number of daily newspapers published). The total circulation of daily newspapers worldwide in the mid-1970s was 408 million, equal to 130 per 1,000 inhabitants and 175 per 1,000 inhabitants aged 10 years and older. The regional distribution is as follows:

Region	Total (million)	Per 1,000 Inhabitants	Per 1,000 Inhabitants 10 Years and Older
Africa	6	14	21
North America	66	281	334
Latin America	23	70	100
Asia	90	64	90
Europe	115	243	289
Oceania	7	305	389
Soviet Union	101	396	473

(The figure for Asia does not include China, North Korea and Vietnam.)

Number of Countries: 142
Midpoint: 51 per 1,000
Period Covered: Mid-1970s
Type of Ranking: Circulation of Daily Newspapers per 1,000 Inhabitants; Total Circulation of Daily Newspapers; Highest to Lowest

Highlights & Findings: Since newspaper readership is directly related to rates of literacy, circulation of daily newspapers is highest in countries with near total literacy. Of the top 10, eight are in Europe. Of the bottom 10 countries, eight are in Africa. However, in poorer countries each copy of a daily tends to be read by more people as it is passed around. The ratio of readership to circulation may be therefore higher in countries lower down this scale.

Regions	Africa	Asia & Oceania	Europe	Western Hemisphere
Most	Mauritius (51)	Japan (2)	Sweden (1)	United States (20)
Least	Rwanda (142)	South Yemen (134)	Faroe Islands (141)	Cuba (121)

Rank	Country	Daily Newspapers Circulation per 1,000	Total Circulation (000)	Rank	Country	Daily Newspapers Circulation per 1,000	Total Circulation (000)	Rank	Country	Daily Newspapers Circulation per 1,000	Total Circulation (000)
	TOP 11			10	Israel	394	1,337	18	West Germany	312	19,298
1	Sweden	572	4,678	11	Australia	394	5,320	19	Czechoslovakia	300	4,436
2	Japan	526	57,820					20	United States	287	61,222
3	East Germany	472	7,946		*UPER MIDDLE*			21	Liechtenstein	277	61
4	Luxembourg	447	161	12	United Kingdom	388	21,700	22	Poland	248	8,429
5	Iceland	431	94	13	New Zealand	376	1,058	23	Belgium	239	2,340
6	Finland	425	1,970	14	Hong Kong	349	1,325	24	Hungary	233	2,454
7	Norway	412	1,657	15	Denmark	341	1,723	25	Bulgaria	232	2,023
8	Switzerland	402	2,573	16	Austria	320	2,405	26	Uruguay	229	637
9	Soviet Union	397	100,928	17	Netherlands	315	4,100	27	Netherlands Antilles	223	54

Rank	Country	Daily Newspapers Circulation per 1,000	Total Circulation (000)
28	Ireland	222	693
29	France	214	11,341
30	Canada	213	4,872
31	Singapore	201	412
32	Bermuda	196	11
33	Guam	173	18
34	South Korea	173	6,010
35	Guyana	155	120
36	Bahamas	152	31
37	New Caledonia	144	18
38	Puerto Rico	132	405
39	Rumania	129	2,716
40	Cyprus	121	78
41	Mexico	116	4,763
42	Italy	113	6,296
43	Gibraltar	111	3
44	Argentina	108	2,773
45	Greece	107	162
46	Lebanon	98.6	283
47	Barbados	98	24
48	Spain	98	3,491
49	Trinidad & Tobago	92.6	100
50	Peru	91.9	1,436
51	Mauritius	91	82
52	Venezuela	89	1,067
53	Yugoslavia	89	1,896
54	Costa Rica	88	174
55	Malaysia	87	1,038
56	French Polynesia	86	11
57	Kuwait	86	80
58	Panama	79	131
59	Surinam	78.5	33
60	Mongolia	78	112
61	Martinique	74	27
62	Portugal	70	612
63	South Africa	70	1,776
64	Guadeloupe	68	24
65	Jamaica	64.2	131
66	Seychelles	60	3.5
67	El Salvador	58.5	234

Rank	Country	Daily Newspapers Circulation per 1,000	Total Circulation (000)
68	Antigua	57	4
69	Reunion	54	27
70	Colombia	52.8	1,248
71	Ghana	51	500
LOWER MIDDLE			
72	Ecuador	49	331
73	Sri Lanka	49	612
74	Albania	46	115
75	Bangladesh	46	356
76	Nicaragua	42.1	91
77	Dominican Republic	42	197
78	Brazil	39	4,050
79	Honduras	36	99
80	Bolivia	35	199
81	Fiji	35	20
82	Tunisia	33	190
83	Cook Islands	32	8
84	Togo	32	7
85	Macao	30	171
86	Belize	29	4
87	Paraguay	27.5	73
88	Guatemala	27.1	165
89	French Guyana	25	1.5
90	Thailand	24	849
91	St. Kitts-Nevis-Anguilla	23	1.5
92	Zambia	22	106
93	Egypt	21	773
94	Morocco	21	360
95	Botswana	20	14
96	Haiti	20	93
97	Jordan	18	49
98	Rhodesia (Zimbabwe)	18	116
99	Iraq	17.2	192
100	Algeria	17	285
101	Libya	17	41
102	Philippines	16.1	686
103	India	16	9,383
104	Indonesia	15.9	2,171
105	Iran	15	484

Rank	Country	Daily Newspapers Circulation per 1,000	Total Circulation (000)
106	Guinea-Bissau	11	6
107	Saudi Arabia	11	96
108	Burma	10	319
109	Kenya	10	134
110	Sierra Leone	10	30
111	Yemen Arab Republic	10	56
112	Nigeria	9.7	613
113	Madagascar	9	59
114	Mozambique	9	79
115	United Arab Emirates	9	2
116	Syria	8.7	64
117	Liberia	7.6	13
118	Ivory Coast	7.2	35
119	Papua New Guinea	7	18
120	Senegal	6	25
121	Cuba	5.6	53
122	Pakistan	5	358
123	Uganda	5	58
124	Tanzania	4.5	70
125	Cameroon	3.9	25
126	Ethiopia	2.5	70
127	Angola	2	14
128	Malawi	1.8	9
129	Zaire	1.8	45
130	Laos	1.5	5
131	Lesotho	1.2	1
BOTTOM 11			
132	Guinea	1	5
133	Somalia	1	4
134	South Yemen	1	2
135	Mali	0.5	3
136	Chad	0.4	1.5
137	Niger	0.4	1.3
138	Benin	0.3	1
139	Upper Volta	0.3	2
140	Mauritania	0.2	3
141	Faroe Islands	0.1	3.7
142	Rwanda	0.04	0.2

Source: *UNESCO Statistical Yearbook; World Communications.*

310. Advertising Expenditures

Advertising performs several critical functions in a free-enterprise economy: it creates and sustains demand for consumer and industrial goods; it virtually finances the media, both print and electronic; and it serves as the link between the industrial and communications sectors. Advertising expeditures may be therefore accepted as one reliable index of the state of the economy. Because of the element of risk in advertising, it reflects the business community's confidence in the future and in its own ability to control that future.

Number of Countries: 86
Midpoint: $7.47
Period Covered: 1976
Type of Ranking: Advertising Expenditures per Capita in Dollars; Advertising Expenditures as Percentage of GNP; Total Advertising Expenditures in Dollars; Highest to Lowest

Highlights & Findings: Total advertising expenditures in the non-Communist world exceeded $59 billion in 1976. This amount exceeds the GNP of all but 15 countries in the world. Nearly 57% of the total was spent in the United States. The top 10 countries—the United States, Australia, Brazil, Canada, France, Japan, the Netherlands, Spain, the United Kingdom and West Germany—account for 88% of the total. Print continues to be the most important media category in all regions of the world except Latin America, where television is the principal medium.

Regions	Africa	Asia & Oceania	Europe	Western Hemisphere
Most	South Africa (33)	Australia (8)	Switzerland (3)	United States (1)
Least	Ethiopia (86)	Nepal (85)	Cyprus (54)	Honduras (73)

Rank	Country	Per Capita $	Advertising Expenditures as Percentage of GNP	Total ($million)	Rank	Country	Per Capita $	Advertising Expenditures as Percentage of GNP	Total ($ million)	Rank	Country	Per Capita $	Advertising Expenditures as Percentage of GNP	Total ($ million)
	TOP 10				29	Jamaica	17.24	1.03	36.2	58	Thailand	3.04	0.82	130.8
1	United States	156.69	1.98	33,720.0	30	Bahamas	17.00	0.68	3.4	59	Rhodesia (Zimbabwe)	2.79	0.52	18.1
2	Bermuda	110.00	1.65	6.6	31	Argentina	16.80	1.40	431.8	60	Syria	2.72	0.32	20.7
3	Switzerland	109.59	1.23	701.4	32	Israel	16.74	0.42	58.6	61	Nicaragua	2.50	0.31	5.5
4	Canada	103.40	1.20	2,378.1	33	South Africa	13.11	1.09	342.1	62	Jordan	2.46	0.53	6.9
5	Denmark	99.41	1.30	507.0	34	Lebanon	11.63	0.94	34.9	63	Zambia	2.24	0.41	11.4
6	Sweden	91.81	1.03	752.8	35	Brazil	11.54	1.40	1,260.0	64	Guatemala	1.95	0.28	12.3
7	Finland	82.19	1.38	386.3	36	Italy	10.69	0.42	601.0	65	Mauritius	1.89	0.28	1.7
8	Australia	82.06	1.07	1,116.0	37	Taiwan	10.36	1.00	168.9	66	Bolivia	1.79	0.36	10.4
9	Netherlands	81.28	1.30	1,121.7	38	Costa Rica	9.95	0.83	19.9	67	Iraq	1.70	0.11	19.6
10	Norway	72.73	0.95	290.9	39	Trinidad & Tobago	9.91	0.44	10.9	68	Iran	1.58	0.08	53.7
					40	Saudi Arabia	9.63	0.16	88.6	69	Egypt	1.52	0.44	57.9
	UPPER MIDDLE				41	Malta	8.00	0.48	2.4	70	Philippines	1.35	0.32	59.0
11	Austria	56.13	1.18	421.0	42	Mexico	7.71	0.46	480.6	71	Paraguay	1.30	0.21	3.5
12	West Germany	48.56	0.68	2,986.3	43	Panama	7.47	0.64	12.7	72	El Salvador	1.20	0.22	4.9
13	France	47.31	0.72	2,502.5						73	Honduras	1.03	0.27	3.2
14	Netherlands Antilles	44.50	0.69	8.9		*LOWER MIDDLE*				74	Sudan	0.95	0.24	15.3
15	Japan	43.05	0.88	4,856.0	44	Portugal	7.24	0.52	68.8	75	Kenya	0.93	0.59	12.9
16	Bahrain	41.00	0.65	12.3	45	Greece	6.70	0.26	61.6	76	Nigeria	0.82	0.21	52.8
17	United Kingdom	40.25	1.04	2,249.9	46	Dominican Republic	6.38	0.77	30.6					
18	New Zealand	39.52	1.02	122.5	47	Turkey	6.32	0.62	254.0		*BOTTOM 10*			
19	Spain	36.73	1.25	1,322.3	48	Peru	5.89	0.65	94.8	77	Morocco	0.71	0.15	12.6
20	Iceland	35.50	0.39	7.1	49	Chile	5.44	0.46	57.1	78	Indonesia	0.45	0.20	63.4
21	Puerto Rico	30.09	0.99	96.3	50	South Korea	5.21	0.69	187.0	79	Liberia	0.39	0.18	0.7
22	Belgium	29.73	0.47	294.3	51	Uruguay	5.07	0.39	15.7	80	Sri Lanka	0.33	0.15	4.7
23	Luxembourg	28.25	0.47	11.3	52	Ecuador	4.78	0.68	34.9	81	Ghana	0.25	0.08	2.6
24	Singapore	22.04	0.85	50.7	53	Libya	4.36	0.06	10.9	82	India	0.23	0.15	138.3
25	Hong Kong	20.00	0.92	88.0	54	Cyprus	4.00	0.24	2.4	83	Pakistan	0.20	0.10	14.5
26	Venezuela	19.36	0.77	240.1	55	Colombia	3.79	0.69	92.5	84	Bangladesh	0.13	0.12	10.8
27	Ireland	18.69	0.92	59.8	56	Surinam	3.75	0.25	1.5	85	Nepal	0.05	0.05	0.6
28	Kuwait	17.70	0.13	17.7	57	Malaysia	3.42	0.57	42.1	86	Ethiopia	0.03	0.03	0.9

Source: *World Advertising Expenditures*, 1978, © Starch INRA Hooper by permission

311. Book Production

National book production statistics are governed by the definitions and classifications set forth in the International Standardization of Statistics Relating to Book Production and Periodicals adopted in 1964 by the General Conference of UNESCO. According to this recommendation, a book is defined as a printed nonperiodical publication of at least 49 pages, exclusive of the cover pages, published in the country and made available to the public. Book production statistics cover publications included in the national bibliographies of their respective countries and also government publications, school textbooks, offprints, publications that form part of a series and illustrated works. However, it excludes publications issued for advertising purposes, publications of a transitory character, such as timetables, price lists and telephone directories, and publications in which the text is not the most important part, such as musical scores.

In 1975 the annual output of titles worldwide was 568,000 distributed as follows:

Region	Number of Titles 1975	1955	Number of Titles per 1 Million Inhabitants 1975	1955	Share of World Total 1975	1955
World	568,000	269,000	182	129	100.0	100.0
Africa	11,000	3,000	27	13	1.9	1.1
North America	92,000	14,000	389	77	16.2	5.2
Latin America	29,000	11,000	89	60	5.1	4.1
Asia	88,000	54,000	62	61	15.5	20.1
Europe	264,000	131,000	558	320	46.5	48.7
Oceania	5,000	1,000	235	68	0.9	0.4
Soviet Union	79,000	55,000	310	279	13.9	20.4

In the 20-year period from 1955 to 1975, Asia, Europe and the Soviet Union have reduced their share of the world book market, while North America has more than tripled its share and Africa, Latin America and Oceania have made significant gains.

Number of Countries: 91
Midpoint: 1,090 titles
Period Covered: 1975
Type of Ranking: Annual Output of Book Titles; Highest to Lowest

Highlights & Findings: Of the top 10 countries, seven are in Europe. For a number of years the rank order of the United States at the top and the Soviet Union second has remained stable. Although publishing is characterized by relative ease of entry and small investment in terms of individual publishers, the overall national production tends to remain stable in most countries because a glut in titles is almost invariably offset by a fall in unit sales.

Regions	Africa	Asia & Oceania	Europe	Western Hemisphere
Most	Nigeria (41)	Japan (6)	Soviet Union (2)	United States (1)
Least	Mali (84)	Bhutan (90)	Malta (71)	Trinidad & Tobago (91)

Rank	Country	Annual Book Title Output
	TOP 10	
1	United States	85,287
2	Soviet Union	78,697
3	West Germany	40,616
4	United Kingdom	35,526
6	Japan	34,590
7	France	28,245
8	Spain	23,527
9	India	12,708
10	Netherlands	12,028
	UPPER MIDDLE	
11	Yugoslavia	11,239
12	South Korea	10,921
13	Czechoslovakia	10,372
14	Poland	10,227
15	Switzerland	9,928
16	Italy	9,187
17	Sweden	9,012
18	Hungary	8,603
19	Rumania	7,860
20	Denmark	7,068
21	Canada	6,735
22	Portugal	5,943
23	Belgium	5,848
24	Mexico	5,822
25	East Germany	5,800
26	Austria	5,636
27	Argentina	5,141
28	Norway	4,855
29	Finland	4,558
30	South Africa	3,849
31	Bulgaria	3,669

Rank	Country	Annual Book Title Output
32	Greece	2,613
33	Thailand	2,419
34	Philippines	2,247
35	Indonesia	2,187
36	Israel	1,907
37	New Zealand	1,887
38	Egypt	1,765
39	Australia	1,761
40	Malaysia	1,445
41	Nigeria	1,324
42	Colombia	1,272
43	Burma	1,164
44	Sri Lanka	1,153
45	Pakistan	1,143
46	Peru	1,090
47	Hong Kong	880
48	Cuba	851
49	Iceland	753
50	Chile	628
	LOWER MIDDLE	
51	Iraq	595
52	Singapore	577
53	Mongolia	490
54	Uruguay	481
55	Bangladesh	457
56	Jordan	418
57	Luxembourg	387
58	Cyprus	373
59	Uganda	373
60	Ghana	366
61	Ireland	345
62	Bolivia	339

Rank	Country	Annual Book Title Output
63	Malawi	234
64	Panama	226
65	Vatican	207
66	Madagascar	190
67	Costa Rica	186
68	Nepal	180
69	Syria	177
70	Qatar	152
71	Malta	135
72	Libya	130
73	Saudi Arabia	125
74	Fiji	117
75	Tunisia	107
76	Sudan	106
77	Barbados	87
78	Guatemala	84
79	Netherlands Antilles	63
80	Guyana	56
81	Mauritius	49
	BOTTOM 10	
82	Kuwait	48
83	Laos	48
84	Mali	42
85	Ecuador	31
86	Honduras	30
87	Brunei	29
88	Dominica	20
89	El Salvador	14
90	Bhutan	10
91	Trinidad & Tobago	7

Source: *UNESCO Statistical Yearbook.*

312. Press Freedom Index

The press freedom index was created by the University of Missouri School of Journalism in order to measure the freedom of a country's media to criticize their own local and national governments. Two native and two nonnative judges were asked to rate each country on fixed scales for 23 items, such as legal controls, favoritism in the release of government news and censorship. If there was disagreement between the native and nonnative judges by more than 6%, judgments of the nonnatives only were used. The index consists of the averages of the scores and ranges from −4.00 for the least to +4.00 for the most.

A cautionary note is in order. The index ratings reflect the status of the press freedom around the early 1970s. While there is no reason to believe that the condition of the press in democratic countries has been affected adversely by the political changes since then, at least two exceptions stand out: Peru and the Philippines, both of which have become dictatorships where the press has been muzzled, if not suppressed. By the same token, there has been some amelioration in the condition of the Spanish press since the death of Franco, which these rankings do not reflect.

Number of Countries: 91
Midpoint: 1.00
Period Covered: Early 1970s
Type of Ranking: Index of Press Freedom on Scale from +4.00 to −4.00; Highest to Lowest.

Highlights & Findings: Since freedom of the press is an essential ingredient of political freedom, traditional democracies have the highest scores. On the other hand, a free press is virtually nonexistent in all dictatorships, both on the right and the left. In the twilight zone between these two categories are the emerging nations of the Third World, where a moderately free press may maintain a precarious existence.

Regions	Africa	Asia & Oceania	Europe	Western Hemisphere
Most	Kenya (38)	Philippines (10)	Norway (1)	Canada (5)
Least	Algeria (89)	North Korea (90)	Albania (91)	Cuba (82)

Rank	Country	Index	Rank	Country	Index	Rank	Country	Index
	TOP 10		31	Israel	1.75	62	Zaire	−0.45
1	Norway	3.06	32	Panama	1.69	63	Laos	−0.46
2	Switzerland	3.06	33	Malaysia	1.66	64	Jordan	−0.51
3	Netherlands	3.02	34	Turkey	1.66	65	Nepal	−0.59
4	Sweden	2.83	35	Mexico	1.46	66	Tunisia	−0.66
5	Canada	2.78	36	Greece	1.37	67	Spain	−0.99
6	Peru	2.76	37	Brazil	1.25	68	Iran	−1.02
7	Finland	2.72	38	Kenya	1.20	69	Cambodia	−1.14
8	United States	2.72	39	Chile	1.19	70	Afghanistan	−1.29
9	Costa Rica	2.68	40	Lebanon	1.18	71	Iraq	−1.35
10	Philippines	2.66	41	Dominican Republic	1.16	72	Portugal	−1.42
			42	Rhodesia (Zimbabwe)	1.16	73	Hungary	−1.57
			43	Sri Lanka	1.14	74	Senegal	−1.98
	UPPER MIDDLE		44	South Africa	1.07	75	Syria	−1.99
11	Denmark	2.65	45	Zambia	1.05	76	Egypt	−2.31
12	Uruguay	2.61	46	Morocco	1.00	77	Cameroon	−2.41
13	Venezuela	2.54				78	Czechoslovakia	−2.50
14	Australia	2.53				79	Poland	−2.53
15	Belgium	2.53		*LOWER MIDDLE*		80	Bulgaria	−2.70
16	Japan	2.44	47	India	0.98	81	Chad	−2.71
17	West Germany	2.43	48	Argentina	0.92			
18	Bolivia	2.39	49	Tanzania	0.87			
19	Ireland	2.37	50	Uganda	0.77		*BOTTOM 10*	
20	United Kingdom	2.37	51	Taiwan	0.61	82	Cuba	−3.01
21	El Salvador	2.26	52	Thailand	0.70	83	Soviet Union	−3.07
22	New Zealand	2.24	53	Malawi	0.62	84	Upper Volta	−3.08
23	Colombia	2.21	54	Nigeria	0.45	85	Ethiopia	−3.15
24	Jamaica	2.16	55	South Korea	0.42	86	China	−3.15
25	Ecuador	2.12	56	Burma	0.38	87	East Germany	−3.19
26	Austria	2.10	57	Ghana	0.34	88	Rumania	−3.19
27	Italy	1.98	58	Yugoslavia	0.08	89	Algeria	−3.25
28	Cyprus	1.96	59	Pakistan	−0.01	90	North Korea	−3.38
29	France	1.92	60	Indonesia	−0.39	91	Albania	−3.50
30	Singapore	1.81	61	Vietnam	−0.44			

Source: Freedom of Information Center, School of Journalism, University of Missouri.

THE WORLD'S CITIES

The following rankings explore the world of cities. Large cities are virtually ministates; if the ranking of the most populous cities were to be superimposed on the ranking of the most populous countries, Mexico City would rank 64th, ahead of the majority of the countries of the world. Another ranking presents the highest cities. The economics of living in cities are dealt with in three rankings devised by the *Financial Times* of London as well as the U.N. Cost of Living Allowances.

It is unfortunate that neither the United Nations nor any of the other international organizations has been interested in collecting data about cities; the International Statistical Institute at The Hague, the only body that ever tried to do so, never made much progress after the 1960s. The result is that interesting and reliable statistics about cities are sparse. The inclusion of this section is an effort to highlight the importance of cities as independent entities. Because of the nature of the data, there may be some structural dissimilarities between rankings in this section and those in the sections relating to countries. For climatic factors, see the rankings on the hottest, coldest and wettest places in the chapter on geography.

313. Population

The following table ranks 287 cities in the world with populations of over 500,000 in the mid-1970s. Except in a few cases where only the figures for the combined populations of the cities and the suburbs (variously called metropolitan areas or urban agglomerations) are available, the figures relate to the cities proper. Because of the nature of this ranking, the usual categories of top 10, upper and lower middle, and bottom 10 have been substituted by nine specific divisions beginning with "over 3 Million" and closing with "from 400,000 to 500,000."

What is most significant about urban size is the vulnerability of larger units to disaster. At some stage every city reaches a critical mass making it more efficient than any rural settlement; but when it begins to grow beyond this optimal stage, it begins to slowly implode, creating massive economic problems, such as overcrowding and unemployment and also psychological problems, often leading to the breakup of the family and even of the human personality. Urbanologists have called this process Calcuttaization, after the Indian city, cited as the classic case of a city disintegrating as a result of overgrowth.

A further element of vulnerability is introduced in the West and the Soviet Union, where the larger the city the greater its vulnerability to military attack. In almost every scenario of nuclear war, the cities are destroyed first. Between implosion through overgrowth and explosion as a result of nuclear attack, each city has to devise an intelligent strategy for survival.

Number of Cities: 287
Midpoint: 832,392
Period Covered: 1976 or Latest Available Year
Type of Ranking: Population of Cities; Highest to Lowest

Highlights & Findings: Mexico City has within the last few years edged out Tokyo, Peking and New York to become the world's most populous city. It is noteworthy that Mexico City's population exceeds those of all but 64 countries of the world. Its rank is surprising because it enjoys few of the natural advantages that its competitors possess. It is not a port and its altitude is higher than that of any comparable city. There are 14 other cities in the over 4 million league, and 106 other cities with over one million population. Given the present growth rate of these cities, it is not inconceivable that by the year 2000 there will be at least eight cities with a population of over 10 million and 50 cities with a population of over 5 million.

Region	Africa	Asia & Oceania	Europe	Western Hemisphere
Most	Cairo (8)	Tokyo (2)	London (5)	Mexico City (1)
Least	Luluabourg (284)	Higashiosaka (287)	Tuha (285)	Fortaleza (272)

Rank	City	Population
	OVER 3 MILLION	
1	Mexico City	8,628,024
2	Tokyo	8,442,634
3	Shanghai	8,072,000
4	Peking	7,570,000
5	New York	7,481,613
6	London	7,167,600
7	Moscow	6,941,961
8	Bombay	5,970,575
9	Cairo	5,715,000
10	Jakarta	5,476,009
11	Seoul	5,433,198
12	Sao Paulo	5,186,752
13	Tientsin, China	4,280,000
14	Rio de Janeiro	4,252,009
15	Berlin (East & West)	4,085,960
16	Teheran	4,002,000
17	Madrid	3,520,320
18	Leningrad	3,512,974
19	Karachi	3,498,634
20	Delhi	3,287,883
21	Santiago de Chile	3,273,600
22	Calcutta	3,148,746
23	Chicago	3,099,391
	2 MILLION TO 3 MILLION	
24	Buenos Aires	2,972,453
25	Sydney	2,898,330
26	Rome	2,868,248
27	Bogota	2,855,065
28	Lima, Peru	2,833,609
29	Los Angeles	2,727,399
30	Osaka, Japan	2,714,642
31	Melbourne, Australia	2,620,400
32	Yokohama, Japan	2,610,124
33	Bangkok-Thonburi, Thailand	2,495,286
34	Madras, India	2,469,449
35	Shenyang (Mukden), China	2,411,000
36	Istanbul	2,376,296
37	Paris	2,290,000
38	Alexandria, Egypt	2,259,000
39	Singapore	2,249,900
40	Lahore, Pakistan	2,165,372
41	Wuhan, China	2,146,000
42	Chungking, China	2,121,000
43	Nagoya, Japan	2,083,111
44	Budapest	2,063,306
45	Kiev, Soviet Union	2,103,000
46	Kinshasa, Zaire	2,008,352
	1 MILLION TO 2 MILLION	
47	Pusan, South Korea	1,842,259
48	Canton, China	1,840,000
49	Ho Chi Minh City, Vietnam	1,825,297
50	Philadelphia, Pa.	1,815,808
51	Barcelona, Spain	1,809,722
52	Taipei, Taiwan	1,769,568
53	Milan, Italy	1,731,281
54	Dacca*	1,730,253
55	Hamburg, West Germany	1,717,383
56	Caracas, Venezuela	1,662,627
57	Tashkent, Soviet Union	1,643,000
58	Guadalajara, Mexico	1,640,902
59	Vienna	1,614,841
60	Hyderabad, India	1,607,396
61	*Rangoon, Burma	1,586,422
62	Ahmedabad, India	1,585,544
63	Bucharest, Rumania	1,565,872
64	Surabaja, Indonesia	1,556,255

Rank	City	Population
65	Harbin, China	1,552,000
66	Bangalore, India	1,540,741
67	Port Arthur-Dairen, China	1,508,000
68	Baghdad, Iraq	1,490,759
69	Ankara, Turkey	1,461,345
70	Kyoto, Japan	1,458,675
71	Warsaw, Poland	1,448,900
72	Manila, Philippines	1,438,252
73	Nanking, China	1,419,000
74	Kharkov, Soviet Union	1,385,000
75	Casablanca, Morocco	1,371,330
76	Houston, Texas	1,357,394
77	Kobe, Japan	1,337,557
78	Detroit, Mich.	1,335,085
79	Munich, West Germany	1,314,865
80	Sian, China	1,310,000
81	Gorky, Soviet Union	1,305,000
82	Novosibirsk, Soviet Union	1,286,000
83	Addis Ababa, Ethiopia	1,242,555
84	Naples, italy	1,223,785
85	Sapporo, Japan	1,215,615
86	Montreal, Canada	1,214,355
87	Turin, Italy	1,202,215
88	Bandung, Indonesia	1,201,730
89	Kuibyshev, Soviet Union	1,186,000
90	Sverdlovsk, Soviet Union	1,171,000
91	Kanpur, India	1,154,388
92	Tsingtao, China	1,121,000
93	Chengtu, China	1,107,000
94	Belo Horizonte, Brazil	1,106,722
95	Prague, Czechoslovakia	1,095,615
96	Monterey, Mexico	1,090,226
97	Birmingham, United Kingdom	1,086,500
98	Medellin, Colombia	1,070,924
99	Taegu, South Korea	1,063,553
100	Kitakyushu, Japan	1,061,221
101	Lagos, Nigeria	1,060,848
102	Recife, Brazil	1,046,454
103	Damascus, Syria	1,042,245
104	Tbilisi, Soviet Union	1,030,000
105	Odessa, Soviet Union	1,023,000
106	Taiyuan, China	1,020,000
107	Koln, West Germany	1,013,771
108	Havana, Cuba	1,008,500
109	Omsk, Soviet Union	1,002,000
	900,000 to 1,000,000	
110	Salvador, Brazil	998,258
111	Quezon City, Philippines	994,679
112	Kawasaki, Japan	989,041
113	Chelyabinsk, Soviet Union	989,000
114	Fushun, China	985,000
115	Dnepropetrovsk, Soviet Union	976,000
116	Changchun, China	975,000
117	Donetsk, Soviet Union	967,000
118	Fukuoka, Japan	964,755
119	Sofia, Bulgaria	962,500
120	Kazan, Soviet Union	958,000
121	Perm, Soviet Union	957,000
122	Erevan, Soviet Union	928,000
123	Ufa, Soviet Union	923,000
124	Volgograd, Soviet Union	918,000
125	Minsk, Soviet Union	907,104
126	Rostov on Don, Soviet Union	907,000
127	Algiers, Algeria	903,530
	800,000 to 900,000	
128	Cali, Colombia	898,253
129	Chittagong, Bangladesh*	889,760

Rank	City	Population
130	Marseilles, France	889,029
131	Adelaide, Australia	885,400
132	Glasgow, Scotland	880,617
133	Kunming, China	880,000
134	Porto Alegre, Brazil	869,795
135	Athens, Greece	867,023
136	Nagpur, India	866,076
137	Tsinan, China	862,000
138	Pune, India	856,105
139	Giza, Egypt	853,700
140	Baltimore, Md.	851,698
141	Baku, Soviet Union	851,547
142	Alma-Ata, Soviet Union	851,000
143	Saratov, Soviet Union	848,000
144	Ibadan, Nigera	847,000
145	Hiroshima, Japan	832,392
146	Kaohsiung, China	828,191
147	Guayaquil, Ecuador	823,219
148	Dallas, Texas	822,451
149	Lyallpur, Pakistan	822,263
150	Riga, Soviet Union	806,000
151	Tzepo, China	806,000
152	Genoa, Italy	805,855
153	Anshan, China	805,000
154	Lodz, Poland	804,300
155	Tangshan, China	800,000
	700,000 to 800,000	
156	Hangchow, China	784,000
157	Cordoba, Argentina	781,565
158	Aleppo, Syria	778,523
159	Lisbon, Portugal	774,500
160	San Diego, Calif.	773,996
161	San Antonio, Texas	773,248
162	Chengchow, China	766,000
163	Vozonezh, Soviet Union	764,000
164	Zaporozhye, Soviet Union	760,000
165	Krasnoyarsk, Soviet Union	758,000
166	Amsterdam, Netherlands	754,557
167	Rosario, Argentina	750,455
168	Lucknow, India	749,239
169	Leeds, United Kingdom	748,300
170	Belgrade, Yugoslavia	746,105
171	Auckland, New Zealand*	742,786
172	Sakai, Japan	739,618
173	Howrah, India	737,877
174	Copenhagen, Denmark	736,951
175	Nairobi, Kenya*	736,000
176	Indianapolis, Ind.	735,077
177	Krivoi Rog, Soviet Union	734,000
178	Durban, South Africa	729,857
179	Valencia, Spain	713,026
180	Toronto, Canada	712,785
181	Brisbane, Australia	712,500
182	Washington, D.C.	711,518
183	Changsha, China	703,000
184	Guatemala City, Guatemala	700,504
	600,000 to 700,000	
185	Lanchow, China	699,000
186	Krakow, Poland	693,800
187	Cape Town, South Africa	691,296
188	Essen, West Germany	677,508
189	Suchow, China	676,000
190	Santo Domingo, Dominican Republic	673,470
191	Tsitsihar, China	668,000
192	Riyadh, Saudi Arabia	666,840
193	Milwaukee, Wisc.	665,796
194	Stockholm, Sweden	665,202

Rank City	Population	Rank City	Population	Rank City	Population
195 Phoenix, Ariz.	664,721	227 Shinkiachwang, China	598,000	261 Krasnodar, Soviet Union	543,000
196 San Francisco, Calif.	664,520	228 Rabat-Sale, Morocco	596,600	262 Multan, Pakistan	542,195
197 Dusseldorf, West Germany	664,338	229 Mashhad, Iran	592,000	263 Amagasaki, Japan	537,171
198 Palermo, Italy	662,567	230 Agra, India	591,917	264 Columbus, Ohio	535,610
199 Barranguilla, Colombia	661,920	231 Duisburg, West Germany	591,685	265 Novokaznetsk, Soviet Union	530,000
200 Memphis, Tenn.	661,319	232 Izmir, Turkey	590,997	266 Lyon, France	527,800
201 La Paz, Bolivia	654,713	233 Seville, Spain	588,784	267 Vladivostok, Soviet Union	526,000
202 Johannesburg, South Africa	654,682	234 Sendai, Japan	586,092	268 Leon, Mexico	525,947
203 Chiba, Japan	653,872	235 Varanasi, India	583,856	269 St. Louis, Mo.	524,964
204 Maracaibo, Venezuela	651,574	236 Palembang, Indonesia	582,961	270 Izhevsk, Soviet Union	522,000
205 Semarang, Indonesia	646,590	237 Dakar, Senegal*	581,000	271 Poznan, Poland	521,600
206 Cleveland, Ohio	638,793	238 Wroclaw, Poland	579,600	272 Fortaleza, Brazil	520,175
207 Boston, Mass.	636,725	239 Yaroslavl, Soviet Union	577,000	273 Irkutsk, Soviet Union	519,000
208 Frankfurt am Main, West Germany	636,197	240 Bremen, West Germany	572,969	274 Dar es Salaam, Tanzania	517,000
209 Medan, Indonesia	635,562	241 Karaganda, Soviet Union	570,000	275 Okayama, Japan	516,821
210 Inchon, South Korea	634,046	242 Kirin, China	568,000	276 Manchester, United Kingdom	516,100
211 Amman, Jordan	634,000	243 Salisbury, Rhodesia*	568,000	277 Davao, Philippines	515,520
212 Hong Kong	633,138	244 Zagreb, Yugoslavia	566,224	278 Barnaul, Soviet Union	514,000
213 Soochow, China	633,000	245 Dublin, Ireland	566,034	279 Khabarovsk, Soviet Union	513,000
214 Dortmund, West Germany	630,309	246 Leipzig, East Germany	565,392	280 Tabriz, Iran	510,000
215 Lvov, Soviet Union	629,000	247 Belem, Brazil	565,097	281 Dresden, West Germany	509,253
216 Hyderabad, Pakistan	628,310	248 Accra, Ghana	564,194	282 Nanchang, China	508,000
217 Colombo, Sri Lanka	618,000	249 Jacksonville, Fla.	562,283	283 Helsinki, Finland	506,657
218 Rotterdam, Netherlands	617,817	250 Sheffield, United Kingdom	561,500	284 Luluabourg, Zaire	506,033
219 Foochow, China	616,000	251 Jeddah, Saudi Arabia	561,104	285 Tula, Soviet Union	506,000
220 Rawalpindi, Pakistan	615,392	252 Liverpool, United Kingdom	561,100	286 Kweiyang, China	504,000
221 Jaipur, India	615,258	253 New Orleans, La.	559,700	287 Higashiosaka, Japan	501,223
222 Wusih, China	613,000	254 San Jose, Costa Rica	555,707		
223 Isphahan, Iran	605,000	255 Hanover, West Germany	552,956		
224 Kananga, Zaire	601,239	256 Madurai, India	549,114		
225 Stuttgart, West Germany	600,421	257 Zarazoga, Spain	547,317		
		258 Ciudad Juarez, Mexico	544,900		
500,000 to 600,000		259 Pretoria, South Africa	543,950		
226 Quito, Ecuador	599,828	260 Indore, India	543,381		

*Includes urban agglomerations.

Source: *U.N. Demographic Yearbook.*

314. Highest Cities

The following ranking lists cities by their elevation. Historically, human settlements were commonly established in the plains near rivers and sea outlets. These cities—all over 3,000 ft—therefore represent exceptions, and their origins and locations were generally determined by strategic rather than trade considerations.

Number of Cities: 133
Midpoint: 1,411 meters (4,629 ft)
Period Covered: 1977
Type of Ranking: Cities by Elevation in Meters and Feet; Highest to Lowest

Highlights & Findings: Latin American cities figure prominently in the top half of the ranking because of the general topography of the land and also because of Indian capacity to survive in high altitudes. A number of capitals are also found in the ranking: Lhasa, La Paz, Quito, Bogota, Addis Ababa, Sana and Mexico City being the most prominent.

Region	Africa	Asia & Oceania	Europe	Western Hemisphere
Most	Addis Ababa (16)	Lhasa (1)	Leninakan (57)	La Paz (2)
Least	Zomba (127)	Bangalore (132)	Les Escaldes (106)	Tepic (133)

Rank	Country	Elevation Meters	Feet
	TOP 10		
1	Lhasa, Tibet	3,658	12,002
2	La Paz, Bolivia	3,658	12,001
3	Le Quiaca, Argentina	3,458	11,345
4	Cusco, Peru	3,312	10,866
5	Eismitte, Greenland	3,000	9,843
6	Ipiales, Colombia	2,950	9,680
7	Potervillos, Chile	2,850	9,350
8	Sucre, Bolivia	2,848	9,344
9	Quito, Ecuador	2,811	9,222
10	Toluca, Mexico	2,680	8,793
	UPPER MIDDLE		
11	Cajamarca, Peru	2,640	8,662
12	Arequipa, Peru	2,579	8,460
13	Cochabamba, Bolivia	2,557	8,390
14	Bogota, Colombia	2,546	8,355
15	Cuenca, Ecuador	2,530	8,301
16	Addis Ababa, Ethiopia	2,450	8,038
17	Asmara, Ethiopia	2,325	7,628
18	Netzahualcoyotl, Mexico	2,278	7,474
19	Sining, China	2,244	7,363
20	Sana, Yemen Arab Republic	2,242	7,360
21	Mexico City, Mexico	2,237	7,340
22	Puebla, Mexico	2,162	7,094
23	Maniazales, Colombia	2,140	7,021
24	Santa Fe, N.M.	2,118	6,950
25	Erzurum, Turkey	1,951	6,402
26	Morelia, Mexico	1,941	6,368
27	Kunming, China	1,893	6,211
28	Durango, Mexico	1,889	6,198
29	Aguascalientes, Mexico	1,888	6,195
30	Leon, Mexico	1,888	6,195
31	San Luis Potosi, Mexico	1,877	6,158
32	Cheyenne, Wyo.	1,867	6,126
33	Colorado Springs, Colo.	1,823	5,980
34	Kabul, Afghanistan	1,815	5,955
35	Hamadan, Iran	1,775	5,824
36	Johannesburg, South Africa	1,753	5,750
37	Kokiu, China	1,740	5,709
38	Windhoek, Namibia	1,728	5,669
39	Irapuato, Mexico	1,724	5,656
40	Nova Lisboa, Angola	1,700	5,577
41	Queretaro, Mexico	1,685	5,528
42	Srinagar, India	1,663	5,458
43	Nairobi, Kenya	1,662	5,453
44	Germiston, South Africa	1,661	5,450

Rank	Country	Elevation Meters	Feet
45	Boulder, Colo.	1,655	5,450
46	Lakewood, Colo.	1,632	5,355
47	Iringa, Tanzania	1,624	5,330
48	Albuquerque, N.M.	1,619	5,311
49	Merida, Venezuela	1,613	5,293
50	Denver, Colo.	1,609	5,280
51	Saltillo, Mexico	1,599	5,246
52	Isphahan, Iran	1,596	5,238
53	Guadalajara, Mexico	1,583	5,194
54	Casper, Wyo.	1,561	5,123
55	Siakwan, China	1,560	5,118
56	Lanchow, China	1,556	5,105
57	Leninakan, Soviet Union	1,556	5,105
58	Oaxaca, Mexico	1,550	5,086
59	Cuerna Vaca, Mexico	1,542	5,059
60	Medellin, Colombia	1,541	5,056
61	Shiraz, Iran	1,539	5,049
62	Guatemala City, Guatemala	1,480	4,855
63	Salisbury, Rhodesia (Zimbabwe)	1,472	4,831
64	Vereeniging, South Africa	1,440	4,725
65	Pueblo, Colo.	1,430	4,690
66	Jalapa, Mexico	1,427	4,682
	LOWER MIDDLE		
67	Bloemfontein, South Africa	1,426	4,678
68	Pereira, Colombia	1,424	4,672
69	Kashgar, China	1,411	4,629
70	Tamanrasset, Algeria	1,400	4,593
71	Provo, Utah	1,387	4,549
72	Kasama, Zambia	1,385	4,544
73	Antananarive, Madagascar	1,372	4,500
74	Pretoria, South Africa	1,369	4,491
75	Tabriz, Iran	1,362	4,469
76	Pocatello, Idaho	1,361	4,464
77	Chihuahua, Mexico	1,350	4,429
78	Katmandu, Nepal	1,348	4,423
79	Bulawayo, Rhodesia (Zimbabwe)	1,343	4,405
80	Reno, Nev.	1,342	4,404
81	Rezaiyah, Iran	1,330	4,364
82	Cangamba, Angola	1,320	4,331
83	Kermanshah, Iran	1,320	4,331
84	Kampala, Uganda	1,312	4,304
85	Ulan Bator, Mongolia	1,307	4,287
86	Salt Lake City, Utah	1,286	4,220
87	Orizaba, Mexico	1,284	4,213
88	Lusaka, Zambia	1,277	4,191

Rank	Country	Elevation Meters	Feet
90	Ibague, Colombia	1,249	4,098
91	Lubumbashi, Zaire	1,230	4,035
92	Sheridan, Wyo.	1,208	3,964
93	Diredawa, Ethiopia	1,200	3,937
94	Teheran, Iran	1,200	3,937
95	Kimberley, South Africa	1,197	3,927
96	El Paso, Texas	1,194	3,918
97	Salta, Argentina	1,182	3,878
98	San Jose, Costa Rica	1,146	3,760
99	Torreon, Mexico	1,130	3,708
100	Amarillo, Texas	1,123	3,685
101	Yinchwan, China	1,111	3,645
102	Ngaoundere, Cameroon	1,097	3,601
103	Guarapuava, Brazil	1,095	3,592
104	Balovale, Zambia	1,090	3,577
105	Lira, Uganda	1,085	3,560
106	Les Escaldes, Andorra	1,080	3,543
107	Calgary, Canada	1,079	3,540
108	Kayseri, Turkey	1,071	3,514
109	Kweiyang, China	1,071	3,514
110	Blantyre, Malawi	1,067	3,501
111	Huhehot, China	1,062	3,484
112	Brasilia, Brazil	1,061	3,481
113	Kandahar, Afghanistan	1,055	3,462
114	Tatung, China	1,049	3,442
115	Cali, Colombia	1,046	3,432
116	Paotow, China	1,044	3,425
117	Caracas, Venezuela	1,042	3,418
118	Yenan, China	1,036	3,400
119	Konya, Turkey	1,026	3,366
120	Great Falls, Mont.	1,015	3,330
121	Tegucigalpa, Honduras	1,007	3,304
122	Keetmanshoop, Namibia	1,004	3,295
123	Meshed, Iran	985	3,232
124	Rapid City, S.D.	985	3,232
	BOTTOM 9		
125	Lubbock, Texas	974	3,195
126	Missoula, Mont.	972	3,190
127	Zomba, Malawi	957	3,141
128	Billings, Mont.	951	3,120
129	Curitiba, Brazil	950	3,117
130	Bucaramanga, Colombia	925	3,035
131	Herat, Afghanistan	922	3,025
132	Bangalore, India	921	3,021
133	Tepic, Mexico	915	3,002

Source: Library of Congress.

315. Cities: Land Area

The conventional distinction between cities and rural areas is eroding under the homogenizing influences of modern life. The whole world is becoming, in Marshall McLuhan's oft-quoted phrase, a global village. Nevertheless the fiction of city limits is maintained for administrative convenience, and urbanologists sometimes talk of an inner city, a central city and suburbs as if they were separate worlds. Yet there is no way of determining where a city ends and where its suburbs begin. In urbanized countries like the United Kingdom, the entire nation is a vast city-state, and in the United States the Northeastern seaboard is similarly defined as a single megalopolis.

The continuum of urban environment and the fluid nature of city limits pose a problem when trying to rank cities by land area. Furthermore, some cities, such as New York, are vertical (one even talks of vertical suburbs). The architectural intensity and share of streets in city areas vary so greatly that square kilometers are among the least reliable gauges of a city's importance. Yet the following ranking provides certain insights even though limited to some 40 selected cities.

Number of Cities: 41
Midpoint: 415 sq km (160 sq mi)
Period Covered: 1978
Type of Ranking: Land Area of Cities in Sq Km and Sq Mi; Highest to Lowest

Highlights & Findings: It is interesting to note that there are at least 11 countries that are smaller than the largest city in this ranking. The areas are not strictly comparable because some cities jealously hold on to the "ancient" city limits while others (Sydney is a prime example) report only the current metropolitan limits.

Regions	Africa	Asia & Oceania	Europe	Western Hemisphere
Most	Cairo (30)	Sydney (1)	London (3)	Sao Paulo (2)
Least	—	Calcutta (40)	Lisbon (41)	Toronto (38)

Rank	City	Physical Size in Sq Km	Sq Mi	Rank	City	Physical Size in Sq Km	Sq Mi	Rank	City	Physical Size in Sq Km	Sq Mi
		Top 10		14	Manila	628	242	30	Cairo	215	83
1	Sydney	1,740	670	15	Madrid	607	234	31	Osaka	206	80
2	Sao Paulo	1,624	627	16	Chicago	591	228				
3	London	1,580	610	17	Singapore	581	224			*BOTTOM 10*	
4	Rome	1,508	582	18	Tokyo	578	223	32	Buenos Aires	200	77
5	Mexico City	1,500	579	19	Budapest	525	203	33	Montreal	176	68
6	Houston	1,401	541	20	Warsaw	450	174	34	Washington, D.C.	176	68
7	Los Angeles	1,202	464	21	Vienna	415	160	35	Minneapolis	153	59
8	New York	945	365	22	Philadelphia	373	144	36	Pittsburgh	150	58
9	New Orleans	943	364	23	Detroit	370	143	37	Vancouver	114	44
10	Berlin	853	341	24	San Francisco	337	130	38	Toronto	111	43
				25	Santiago	302	117	39	Paris	106	41
		MIDDLE		26	Kansas City	287	111	40	Calcutta	100	40
11	Moscow	849	339	27	Baghdad	272	105	41	Lisbon	84	32
12	Hamburg	754	291	28	Istanbul	238	92				
13	Havana	740	286	29	Birmingham	233	90				

Source: *World Book Encyclopedia.*

316. Bus Service

Buses are perhaps the most important of the many modes of public transportation that are bound to grow in the future. Bus ratio yields some general relationships when compared with density, per capita income, mobility and other factors; no such conclusions can be derived and no patterns can be discerned when intercity comparisons made. The reason may be that while in some cities buses are the only regulated public transport system, they are supplemented by rapid transit, trams and other modes in other cities. The number of buses may also depend on official public transport policies, with some countries deliberately encouraging their citizens to use buses as a viable alternative to cars.

Number of Cities: 29
Midpoint: 5.5 per 10,000
Period Covered: Mid-1970s
Type of Ranking: Buses per 10,000 Inhabitants and Total Number of Buses; Highest to Lowest

Highlights & Findings: By continents African cities lead the world in buses as percentage of commercial vehicles with 8.0%; they are followed by South American cities (6.6%), Asian cities (5.4%), European cities (3.9%), and North and Central American cities (2.0%).

Regions	Africa	Asia	Europe	Western Hemisphere
Most	Addis Ababa (23)	Tel Aviv (2)	Athens (3)	Montreal (1)
Least	Casablanca (29)	Tokyo (27)	East Berlin (26)	Los Angeles (28)

Rank City	Buses per 10,000	Total Number of Buses	Rank City	Buses per 10,000	Total Number of Buses	Rank City	Buses per 10,000	Total Number of Buses
TOP 9			11 Soviet Union (Leningrad)	6.5	2,148	22 United States (New York)	3.0	2,310
1 Montreal, Canada	11.0	2,000	12 Soviet Union (Moscow)	6.4	4,081	23 Ethiopia (Addis Ababa)	2.7	135
2 Tel Aviv, Israel	10.3	775	13 Japan (Osaka)	5.8	1,846	24 Switzerland (Zurich)	2.6	142
3 Greece (Athens)	8.9	1,782	14 United States (Cleveland)	5.5	959	25 Turkey (Istanbul)	2.5	498
4 Poland (Warsaw)	8.0	1,002	15 United States (Detroit)	5.5	1,163	26 Germany, East (East Berlin)	2.4	270
5 United States (Washington, D.C.)	7.9	1,192	16 United States (Philadelphia)	4.9	1,342	27 Japan (Tokyo)	1.7	1,816
6 United States (Chicago)	7.9	2,799	17 France (Paris)	4.6	3,508	28 United States (Los Angeles)	1.5	1,477
7 United Kingdom (London)	7.7	7,917	18 Spain (Madrid)	4.1	1,073	29 Morocco (Casablanca)	1.3	169
8 Northern Ireland (Belfast)	7.6	456	19 United States (Atlanta)	3.9	472			
9 Italy (Milan)	7.2	1,241						
MIDDLE			**BOTTOM 10**					
10 West Germany (West Berlin)	6.5	1,429	20 Rotterdam (Netherlands)	3.4	305			
			21 India (Bombay)	3.0	1,338			

Source: World Bank, *Travel Characteristics.*

317. Visitor Index

A regular survey of the cost of living in or visiting 65 business centers around the world is carried out annually by the London *Financial Times*. The visitor index is based on a three-night stopover and includes cost of room and breakfast in a first-class or international hotel with dinners, snacks, drinks and cab fares also thrown in for good measure. The index, however, is only a comparative guide and the prices quoted are only ballpark figures based on the experiences of a limited number of people.

Number of Cities: 65
Midpoint: 73
Period Covered: 1977
Type of Ranking: Visitor Index with New York as 100; Highest to Lowest

Highlights & Findings: There are 15 cities in the world that are more expensive on this scale than New York. Within a few years, Tokyo has soared to be the most expensive city in the world; London, considered by many in the most expensive league, now ranks below many other European capitals.

Region	Africa	Asia & Oceania	Europe	Western Hemisphere
Most	Lagos (18)	Tokyo (1)	Paris (2)	Nassau (13)
Least	Salisbury (64)	Peking (65)	Nicosia (63)	Mexico City (58)

Rank Country	Visitor Index (New York = 100)	Rank Country	Visitor Index (New York = 100)	Rank Country	Visitor Index (New York = 100)
TOP 10		8 Copenhagen, Denmark	118	14 Amsterdam, Netherlands	103
1 Tokyo, Japan	145	9 Geneva, Switzerland	112	15 Stockholm, Sweden	101
2 Paris, France	143	10 Jeddah, Saudi Arabia	111	16 New York, New York	100
3 Dubai, United Arab Emirates	130			17 Oslo, Norway	99
4 Brussels, Belgium	128	**UPPER MIDDLE**		18 Lagos, Nigeria	98
5 Abu Dhabi, United Arab Emirates	126	11 London, England	109	19 Houston, Texas	96
6 Frankfurt, West Germany	126	12 Kuwait	107	20 Rio de Janeiro, Brazil	95
7 Manama, Bahrain	120	13 Nassau, Bahamas	105	21 Vienna, Austria	90

Rank	Country	Visitor Index (New York=100)	Rank	Country	Visitor Index (New York=100)	Rank	Country	Visitor Index (New York=100)
22	Luxembourg	86	36	Algiers, Algeria	70	52	Tunis, Tunisia	59
23	Taipei, Taiwan	85	37	Budapest, Hungary	70	53	Cairo, Egypt	57
24	Los Angeles, Calif.	84	38	Tel Aviv, Israel	70	54	Dar es Salaam, Tanzania	52
25	Chicago, Ill.	83	39	Dublin, Ireland	68	55	Johannesburg, South Africa	52
26	Helsinki, Finland	83	40	Singapore	67	56	Rabat, Morocco	52
27	Khartoum, Sudan	83	41	Warsaw, Poland	67	57	Wellington, New Zealand	52
28	Atlanta, Ga.	80	42	Panama City, Panama	66			
29	Amman, Jordan	78	43	Jakarta, Indonesia	65		**BOTTOM 8**	
30	Sydney, Australia	78	44	Nairobi, Kenya	64	58	Mexico City, Mexico	47
31	Montreal, Canada	74	45	Damascus, Syria	63	59	Karachi, Pakistan	46
32	Moscow, Soviet Union	74	46	Kuala Lumpur, Malaysia	63	60	Belgrade, Yugoslavia	38
33	Hong Kong	73	47	Rome, Italy	63	61	Colombo, Sri Lanka	37
			48	Madrid, Spain	62	62	Lisbon, Portugal	37
	LOWER MIDDLE		49	Toronto, Canada	61	63	Nicosia, Cyprus	37
34	Athens, Greece	72	50	Vancouver, Canada	61	64	Salisbury, Rhodesia (Zimbabwe)	36
35	New Delhi, India	71	51	Port of Spain, Trinidad	59	65	Peking, China	35

Source: Living Costs Overseas © *Financial Times* By Permission.

318. Cities: Cost of Living

The International Civil Service Commission regularly compiles index numbers that approximately measure the relative cost of living in various cities of the world with New York as 100. It should be borne in mind that these indices are intended for the guidance of U. N. officials, whose consumption patterns may differ from those of the native population. The index includes housing, utilities and domestic service.

Number of Countries: 130
Midpoint: 99
Period Covered: March 1979
Type of Ranking: Cost of Living Index Relating to Living Expenditures of U.N. Officials with New York = 100; Highest to Lowest

Highlights & Findings: The principal conclusion is that New York City, once considered very expensive, is actually cheaper than 60 major cities in the world. Forty-six of these cities are located in developing countries where the per capita income bears no apparent relation to such high living costs.

Region	Africa	Asia & Oceania	Europe	Western Hemisphere
Most	Kinshasa (2)	Tokyo (1)	Geneva (3)	Buenos Aires (10)
Least	Maseru (124)	Colombo (130)	Valetta (127)	Kingston (129)

Rank	Country	Cost of Living Index (New York=100)	Rank	Country	Cost of Living Index (New York=100)	Rank	Country	Cost of Living Index (New York=100)
	TOP 9		14	Paris, France	140	30	Nouakchott, Mauritania	119
1	Tokyo, Japan	199	15	Dakar, Senegal	137	31	Sanaa, Yemen Arab Republic	118
2	Kinshasa, Zaire	189	16	Conakry, Guinea	136	32	Moroni, Comoros	117
3	Geneva, Switzerland	182	17	Libreville, Gabon	135	33	Brazzaville, Congo	114
4	Kampala, Uganda	153	18	Ouagadougou, Upper Volta	131	34	Rabat, Morocco	113
5	Bonn, West Germany	148	19	Abidjan, Ivory Coast	130	35	Algiers, Algeria	112
6	Brussels, Belgium	147	20	Ndjamena, Chad	130	36	Kigali, Rwanda	110
7	Manama, Bahrain	147	21	Bamako, Mali	128	37	Monrovia, Liberia	110
8	Copenhagen, Denmark	146	22	Teheran, Iran	126	38	Madrid, Spain	109
9	Bangui, Central African Empire	145	23	Tripoli, Libya	126	39	Seoul, South Korea	109
			24	Niamey, Niger	125	40	Freetown, Sierra Leone	108
	UPPER MIDDLE		25	Tunis, Tunisia	125	41	Nassau, Bahamas	108
10	Buenos Aires, Argentina	143	26	Caracas, Venezuela	123	42	Accra, Ghana	106
11	The Hague, Netherlands	143	27	Amman, Jordan	124	43	Athens, Greece	106
12	Vienna, Austria	141	28	Doha, Qatar	120	44	London, United Kingdom	106
13	Muscat, Oman	140	29	Kuwait	119	45	Lome, Togo	105

Rank	Country	Cost of Living Index (New York=100)
46	Port Moresby, Papua New Guinea	105
47	Brasilia, Brazil	104
48	Bujumbura, Burundi	104
49	Cotonou, Benin	104
50	Damascus, Syria	104
51	Mogadiscio, Somalia	104
52	Rio de Janeiro, Brazil	104
53	Antananarivo, Madagascar	103
54	Yaounde, Cameroon	103
55	Lagos, Nigeria	102
56	Sydney, Australia	102
57	Banjul, Gambia	101
58	Budapest, Hungary	101
59	Guatemala City, Guatemala	101
60	Khartoum, Sudan	101
61	Beirut, Lebanon	100
62	Sofia, Bulgaria	100
63	Belgrade, Yugoslavia	99
64	Nairobi, Kenya	99
65	Port au Prince, Haiti	99
	LOWER MIDDLE	
66	Santiago, Chile	97
67	San Salvador, El Salvador	96
68	Singapore	96
69	Bridgetown, Barbados	95
70	Kuala Lumpur, Malaysia	95
71	Luanda, Angola	95
72	Praia, Cape Verde	95
73	Rome, Italy	95

Rank	Country	Cost of Living Index (New York=100)
74	Addis Ababa, Ethiopia	94
75	Curacao, Netherlands Antilles	94
76	Lusaka, Zambia	94
77	Manila, Philippines	94
78	Port of Spain, Trinidad & Tobago	94
79	Washington, D.C., United States	94
80	Ankara, Turkey	93
81	Baghdad, Iraq	93
82	Jakarta, Indonesia	93
83	La Paz, Bolivia	93
84	Georgetown, Guyana	92
85	Kabul, Afghanistan	91
86	Dar es Salaam, Tanzania	91
87	Lilongwe, Malawi	91
88	Managua, Nicaragua	91
89	Paramaribo, Surinam	91
90	Port Louis, Mauritius	91
91	Aden, Southern Yemen	90
92	Dacca, Bangladesh	90
93	Panama City, Panama	90
94	Santo Domingo, Dominican Republic	90
95	Tegucigalpa, Honduras	89
96	Ulan Bator, Mongolia	89
97	Asuncion, Paraguay	88
98	Bissau, Guinea-Bissau	88
99	Bucharest, Rumania	88
100	Suva, Fiji	88
101	Apia, Samoa	87
102	Quito, Ecuador	86
103	San Jose, Costa Rica	86

Rank	Country	Cost of Living Index (New York=100)
104	Bogota, Colombia	84
105	Islamabad, Pakistan	84
106	Havana, Cuba	83
107	St. John's, Antigua	83
108	Bangkok, Thailand	82
109	New Delhi, India	82
110	St. George's, Grenada	82
111	Montevideo, Uruguay	81
112	Gaborone, Botswana	80
113	Mbabane, Swaziland	80
114	Montreal, Canada	80
115	Nicosia, Cyprus	80
116	Vientiane, Laos	80
117	Mexico City, Mexico	79
118	Maputo, Mozambique	78
119	Rangoon, Burma	78
120	Roseau, Dominica	77
	BOTTOM 10	
121	Bratislava, Czechoslovakia	76
122	Cairo, Egypt	76
123	Katmandu, Nepal	76
124	Maseru, Lesotho	75
125	Warsaw, Poland	73
126	Lima, Peru	72
127	Valetta, Malta	70
128	Belmopan, Belize	66
129	Kingston, Jamaica	63
130	Colombo, Sri Lanka	58

Source: United Nations.

319. Hotel Expenses

This ranking compares hotel expenses in 65 business centers around the world. Only first-class hotel accommodations are considered but quality is relative and is colored by the lifestyles and preferences of the resident. In every case the costs include breakfast but no other amenities.

Number of Cities: 65
Midpoint: $53.15
Period Covered: 1977
Type of Ranking: Cost of One-Day First-Class Hotel Accommodation (Including Breakfast) in Dollars; Highest to Lowest

Highlights & Findings: It is interesting to note that five of the top 10 are the oil-rich Middle Eastern cities that might be considered arrivé by any standard. Hotel costs may be related not only to the quality of service provided but also to the status and number of transients as well as to occupancy rates.

Region	Africa	Asia & Oceania	Europe	Western Hemisphere
Most	Lagos (23)	Dubai (2)	Paris (1)	Nassau (7)
Least	Salisbury (65)	Colombo (62)	Belgrade (64)	Port of Spain (59)

Rank	Country	Cost of One-Day First-Class Hotel Accommodation ($)
	TOP 10	
1	Paris, France	110.63
2	Dubai, United Arab Emirates	97.69
3	Kuwait	96.19
4	Manama, Bahrain	95.33

Rank	Country	Cost of One-Day First-Class Hotel Accommodation ($)
5	Abu Dhabi, United Arab Emirates	94.02
6	London, United Kingdom	91.70
7	Nassau, Bahamas	88.37
8	Jeddha, Saudi Arabia	86.02
9	Frankfurt, West Germany	85.64

Rank	Country	Cost of One-Day First-Class Hotel Accommodation ($)
10	Copenhagen, Denmark	85.21
	UPPER MIDDLE	
11	Brussels, Belgium	84.76
12	Tokyo, Japan	80.87

Rank	Country	Cost of One-Day First-Class Hotel Accommodation ($)
13	Geneva, Switzerland	80.10
14	Amsterdam, Netherlands	79.27
15	Houston, Texas	74.68
16	New York, New York	74.38
17	Los Angeles, Calif.	71.94
18	Moscow, Soviet Union	68.27
19	Stockholm, Sweden	68.13
20	Vienna, Austria	66.71
21	Amman, Jordan	66.42
22	Chicago, Ill.	65.67
23	Lagos, Nigeria	65.35
24	Athens, Greece	63.34
25	Atlanta, Ga.	62.87
26	Oslo, Norway	62.00
27	Sydney, Australia	58.96
28	Damascus, Syria	55.14
29	Tel Aviv, Israel	54.74
30	Hong Kong	54.70
31	Dublin, Ireland	53.24

Rank	Country	Cost of One-Day First-Class Hotel Accommodation ($)
32	Budapest, Hungary	53.18
33	Warsaw, Poland	53.15
34	Rio de Janeiro, Brazil	52.68
35	Helsinki, Finland	51.51
36	Khartoum, Sudan	51.23
	LOWER MIDDLE	
37	Montreal, Canada	49.79
38	Rome, Italy	49.62
39	Singapore	49.30
40	Luxembourg	49.26
41	Nairobi, Kenya	48.16
42	Taipei, Taiwan	47.74
43	Panama City, Panama	47.11
44	Cairo, Egypt	46.84
45	New Delhi, India	46.02
46	Madrid, Spain	45.97
47	Jakarta, Indonesia	45.67
48	Vancouver, Canada	45.32

Rank	Country	Cost of One-Day First-Class Hotel Accommodation ($)
49	Toronto, Canada	44.03
50	Algiers, Algeria	43.46
51	Karachi, Pakistan	43.15
52	Tunis, Tunisia	41.61
53	Kuala Lumpur, Malaysia	40.88
54	Johannesburg, South Africa	39.76
55	Mexico City, Mexico	38.18
	BOTTOM 10	
56	Wellington, New Zealand	36.42
57	Rabat, Morocco	36.36
58	Dar es Salaam, Tanzania	34.98
59	Port of Spain, Trinidad	34.98
60	Peking, China	31.41
61	Nicosia, Cyprus	28.64
62	Colombo, Sri Lanka	26.84
63	Lisbon, Portugal	25.62
64	Belgrade, Yugoslavia	25.34
65	Salisbury, Rhodesia (Zimbabwe)	21.10

Source: Living Costs Overseas © *Financial Times* By Permission.

320. Taxi Fares

The following ranking rates cities by the cost of a 5 km (3 mi) taxi ride within city limits. In most cities the tariff is regulated by ordinance; nevertheless, these regulations are not always strictly enforced. So-called gypsy cabs flourish and more often than not unwary tourists may be taken for a ride, literally and figuratively.

Number of Cities: 65
Midpoint: $2.66
Period Covered: 1977
Type of Ranking: Cost of a 5 Km (3 Mi) Taxi Ride in Dollars; Highest to Lowest

Highlights & Conclusions: In Frankfurt the cost is 12 times higher than in Warsaw, and the disparity is not explained by the cost of gasoline or related factors. It seems to be based more on the principle of charging what the traffic will bear. Most European cities rank high on the lists; this is understandable in light of their general living expenses. But Lagos, ranking second, provides a real surprise.

Region	Africa	Asia & Oceania	Europe	Western Hemisphere
Most	Lagos (2)	Tokyo (6)	Frankfurt (1)	Montreal (7)
Least	Khartoum (62)	Kuala Lumpur (64)	Warsaw (65)	Rio de Janeiro (58)

Rank	Country	Cost of a 5 km (3 Mi) Taxi Ride ($)
	TOP 11	
1	Frankfurt, West Germany	7.99
2	Lagos, Nigeria	6.23
3	Geneva, Switzerland	6.17
4	Oslo, Norway	5.99
5	Copenhagen, Denmark	5.76
6	Tokyo, Japan	5.32
7	Montreal, Canada	5.13
8	Stockholm, Sweden	5.09
9	Amsterdam, Netherlands	4.93
10	Helsinki, Finland	4.93
11	London, United Kingdom	4.93
	UPPER MIDDLE	
12	Brussels, Belgium	4.75

Rank	Country	Cost of a 5 km (3 mi) Taxi Ride ($)
13	Paris, France	4.65
14	Vienna, Austria	4.36
15	Houston, Texas	4.00
16	Nassau, Bahamas	4.00
17	New York, New York	4.00
18	Panama City, Panama	4.00
19	Vancouver, Canada	3.85
20	Toronto, Canada	3.41
21	Belgrade, Yugoslavia	3.19
22	Wellington, New Zealand	3.19
23	Chicago, Ill.	3.02
24	Damascus, Syria	3.02
25	Los Angeles, Calif.	3.01
26	Port of Spain, Trinidad	2.92
27	Salisbury, Rhodesia (Zimbabwe)	2.90

Rank	Country	Cost of a 5 km (3 mi) Taxi Ride ($)
28	Johannesburg, South Africa	2.88
29	Kuwait	2.78
30	Luxembourg	2.72
31	Dar es Salaam, Tanzania	2.68
32	Atlanta, Ga.	2.67
33	Tel Aviv, Israel	2.66
	LOWER MIDDLE	
34	Algiers, Algeria	2.62
35	Dubai, United Arab Emirates	2.60
36	Manana, Bahrain	2.60
37	Sydney, Australia	2.54
38	Dublin, Ireland	2.37
39	Moscow, Soviet Union	2.35
40	Budapest, Hungary	2.17

Rank	Country	Cost of a 5 km (3 mi) Taxi Ride ($)
41	Nairobi, Kenya	2.15
42	Rome, Italy	2.15
43	Madrid, Spain	2.13
44	Rabat, Morocco	2.05
45	Jakarta, Indonesia	2.01
46	Tunis, Tunisia	1.97
47	Taipei, Taiwan	1.91
48	Abu Dhabi, United Arab Emirates	1.83
49	Nicosia, Cyprus	1.68
50	Athens, Greece	1.64

Rank	Country	Cost of a 5 km (3 mi) Taxi Ride ($)
51	Colombo, Sri Lanka	1.62
52	Jeddah, Saudi Arabia	1.57
53	Lisbon, Portugal	1.52
54	Peking, China	1.52
55	Amman, Jordan	1.38
56	Singapore	1.38
	BOTTOM 9	
57	Mexico City, Mexico	1.32
58	Rio de Janeiro, Brazil	1.28

Rank	Country	Cost of a 5 km (3 mi) Taxi Ride ($)
59	Cairo, Egypt	1.08
60	Hong Kong	1.05
61	Karachi, Pakistan	1.03
62	Khartoum, Sudan	1.01
63	New Delhi, India	0.97
64	Kuala Lumpur, Malaysia	0.93
65	Warsaw, Poland	0.63

Source: Living Costs Overseas © *Financial Times* By Permission.

321. Cities: Air Pollution

The following ranking is based on the WHO Air Quality Monitoring Project implemented in cooperation with a number of national centers and laboratories. The project provides input to the Global Environmental Monitoring System (GEMS). In each of the 13 participating cities, three sampling locations are identified; one in an industrial area, one in a commercial area and one in a residential area. This ranking is based on data relating to the central-city commercial areas. The principal goal of the project is to determine levels and trends in air pollution. Although data are gathered on many different kinds of air pollution, only suspended particulate matter and sulfur dioxide are included in the survey. Because participating stations use a number of different methods to sample and analyze air pollutants, they may not be strictly comparable. Great care should be exercised in interpreting or comparing the results because current techniques do not distinguish between natural and man-made pollutants. For example, in tropical countries naturally occurring concentrations may reach high levels during the dry season and may, in fact, mask man-made emissions.

Number of Cities: 13
Midpoint: 93.9 micrograms per cubic meter of sulfur dioxide
Period Covered: 1974
Type of Ranking: Micrograms per Cubic Meter in 24 Hours (Arithmetic Mean) of Suspended Particulate Matter and Sulfur Dioxide; Highest to Lowest

Highlights & Findings: Because of the limited nature of the survey, no conclusions have been attempted. It is, however, interesting to note the low standing of cities in developed countries, normally considered the worst offenders of air quality.

Rank	City	Sulfur Dioxide Micrograms per Cubic Meter (arithmetic mean)	Suspended Particulates Micrograms per Cubic Meter (arithmetic mean)
	TOP 6		
1	Zagreb, Yugoslavia	172.9	166.6
2	Madrid	161.2	190.2
3	London	150.0	25.8
4	Prague	125.9	239.1
5	Brussels	106.6	36.7

Rank	City	Sulfur Dioxide Micrograms per Cubic Meter (arithmetic mean)	Suspended Particulates Micrograms per Cubic Meter (arithmetic mean)
6	Frankfurt	93.9	N.A.
	BOTTOM 7		
7	Tokyo	69.4	44.5
8	Calcutta	64.0	519.0
9	Tel Aviv	59.7	65.0

Rank	City	Sulfur Dioxide Micrograms per Cubic Meter (arithmetic mean)	Suspended Particulates Micrograms per Cubic Meter (arithmetic mean)
10	Vancouver	49.1	63.8
11	Rome	42.5	46.4
12	Nykoping, Sweden	31.8	N.A.
13	Amsterdam	27.3	N.A.

Source: World Health Organization.

CULTURE AND SPORTS

This chapter is a mixed grab bag but its emphasis is on culture—an appropriate upbeat note on which to end this great feast of numbers. Nobel Prize winners and Olympic medal winners form the subject of two rankings, which could have been titled "Mind and Body." Museum attendance is dealt with in another ranking. There are two rankings on public libraries, one on total number of volumes and another on volumes borrowed per capita.

322. Nobel Prizes

During the almost 80 years of its existence, the Nobel Prize has been acknowledged as the most prestigious and sought-after of all awards for human achievement. It is not only the ultimate accolade but also the most publicized. The following list ranks countries by the number of Nobel laureates. Nationality is determined by domicile at the time of receipt of the award.

Number of Countries: 35
Midpoint: 3
Period Covered: 1900-78
Type of Ranking: Total Number of Nobel Laureates; Highest to Lowest

Highlights & Findings: Of the 475 Nobel Prizes awarded since 1900, the United States alone accounts for 30%. Asia, Africa and Latin America are poorly represented on the list, together accounting for only 20 prizes.

Region	Africa	Asia & Oceania	Europe	Western Hemisphere
Most	South Africa (33)	Japan (14)	United Kingdom (2)	United States (1)
Least	N.A.	Vietnam (34)	Yugoslavia (35)	Puerto Rico (32)

Rank	Country	Total Number of Nobel Laureates	Rank	Country	Total Number of Nobel Laureates	Rank	Country	Total Number of Nobel Laureates
	TOP 9		12	Belgium	7		*BOTTOM 10*	
1	United States	153	13	Norway	7	26	Czechoslovakia	1
2	United Kingdom	74	14	Japan	4	27	Egypt	1
3	Germany (undistributed)	55	15	Spain	4	28	Greece	1
4	France	44	16	Canada	4	29	Guatemala	1
5	Sweden	24	17	Argentina	3	30	Iceland	1
6	Switzerland	14	18	Australia	3	31	Portugal	1
7	Soviet Union	14	19	Ireland	3	32	Puerto Rico	1
8	Netherlands	11	20	Chile	2	33	South Africa	1
9	Denmark	11	21	Finland	2	34	Vietnam	1
	MIDDLE		22	Hungary	2	35	Yugoslavia	1
10	Austria	9	23	India	2			
11	Italy	9	24	Israel	2			
			25	Poland	2			

Source: *World Almanac.*

323. Olympic Medals

The Olympic Games are not intended to provide a forum for international rivalry; nonetheless, they have increasingly become a showcase of national athletic skills, and the number of medals won by each nation is sometimes viewed as an index of the importance attached in each country to athletic prowess and training. The following chart ranks countries by the number of medals (gold, silver and bronze) won in the 1976 Summer Olympics at Montreal per one million inhabitants.

Number of Countries: 40
Midpoint: 0.4753 per one million
Period Covered: 1976
Type of Ranking: Number of Medals (Gold, Silver and Bronze) won in the 1976 Summer Olympics per One Million Inhabitants; Total Number of Medals; Highest to Lowest

Highlights & Findings: Bermuda at the top of the ranking may be a surprise for many, but of course its ranking is a result of winning a single medal. There are two West Indian countries in the top 10. The presence of so many Communist countries in the top 10 is less surprising because physical fitness is one of the ideals of a Communist society.

Regions	Africa	Asia & Oceania	Europe	Western Hemisphere
Most	N.A.	New Zealand (6)	East Germany (2)	Bermuda (1)
Least	N.A.	Pakistan (39)	Spain (35)	Venezuela (40)

Rank	Country	Olympic Medals per 1 Million Inhabitants	Total	Rank	Country	Olympic Medals per 1 Million Inhabitants	Total	Rank	Country	Olympic Medals per 1 Million Inhabitants	Total
		TOP 10		13	Switzerland	0.6299	4	28	Portugal	0.2116	2
1	Bermuda	16.6666	1	14	Sweden	0.6082	5	29	Puerto Rico	0.2066	1
2	East Germany	5.3603	90	15	Belgium	0.6066	6	30	France	0.1700	9
3	Bulgaria	2.7397	24	16	Denmark	0.5917	3				
4	Hungary	1.9811	21	17	Czechoslovakia	0.5361	8			*BOTTOM 10*	
5	Cuba	1.3742	13	18	Norway	0.4962	2	31	South Korea	0.1673	6
6	New Zealand	1.2738	4	19	Soviet Union	0.4870	125	32	Austria	0.1331	1
7	Finland	1.2684	6	20	Canada	0.4753	11	33	North Korea	0.1230	2
8	Rumania	1.2587	27	21	United States	0.4369	94	34	Iran	0.0598	2
9	Jamaica	0.9708	2	22	Yugoslavia	0.3710	8	35	Spain	0.0556	2
10	Trinidad & Tobago	0.9259	1	23	Australia	0.3665	5	36	Mexico	0.0320	2
				24	Netherlands	0.3631	5	37	Thailand	0.0232	1
		MIDDLE		25	United Kingdom	0.2324	13	38	Brazil	0.0182	2
11	Mongolia	0.6711	1	26	Italy	0.2314	13	39	Pakistan	0.0138	1
12	West Germany	0.6340	39	27	Japan	0.2223	25	40	Venezuela	0.0080	1

Source: *New York Times.*

324. Museum Attendance

Museums serve as vast reservoirs of culture but in another sense they also serve as transmission belts for communicating artistic values to the people. Museum attendance figures may be an imperfect index of the cultural roots of a people, but at least they indicate to some extent the awareness of the heritage of the past and the aesthetic dimension of human history.

Number of Countries: 114
Midpoint: 98 per 1,000
Period Covered: Early 1970s
Type of Ranking: Per 1,000 Museum Attendance and Total Museum Attendance; Highest to Lowest

Highlights & Findings: One would have expected countries like Italy and France, with their vast museums and rich hoards of art, to lead the list, but surprisingly they do not. Evidently, there is little relation between artistic wealth and museum attendance. On the other hand, it was to be expected that developing countries would rank poorly on this scale. After all, most of their artifacts and historical treasures have been either plundered or removed and are to be found now in Western collections. In some smaller countries—Monaco, for one—the figures reflect a very high ratio of tourists to the resident population.

Region	Africa	Asia & Oceania	Europe	Western Hemisphere
Most	Equatorial Guinea (37)	Israel (11)	Monaco (1)	Bermuda (3)
Least	St. Helena (114)	Afghanistan (109)	Finland (72)	Haiti (111)

Rank	Country	Museum Attendance per 1,000 Inhabitants	Total (000)	Rank	Country	Museum Attendance per 1,000 Inhabitants	Total (000)	Rank	Country	Museum Attendance per 1,000 Inhabitants	Total (000)
		TOP 10		39	Japan	258	28,023	78	Jamaica	36	71
1	Monaco	51,450	1,029	40	Mauritius	252	209	79	Mongolia	35	48
2	San Marino	22,250	445	41	French Guyana	240	12	80	Nepal	34	397
3	Bermuda	7,000	350	42	South Korea	220	7,503	81	Algeria	32	443
4	Canada	2,579	54,999	43	Tunisia	220	1,108	82	Vietnam	32	1,362
5	Denmark	1,529	7,585	44	Greece	214	1,889	83	Thailand	31	1,185
6	East Germany	1,485	25,214	45	France	212	11,054	84	India	29	15,500
7	United States	1,450	312,000	46	Sri Lanka	206	1,817	85	Pakistan	23	1,460
8	Sweden	1,376	11,202	47	Egypt	187	6,533	86	Uganda	18	170
9	Vatican	1,349	1,349	48	Mexico	169	9,510	87	Mauritania	14	18
10	Bulgaria	1,335	11,507	49	Martinique	167	57	88	Dominican Republic	12	53
				50	El Salvador	160	162	89	Gabon	12	6
		UPPER MIDDLE		51	Turkey	144	5,399	90	Panama	12	18
11	Israel	1,072	3,217	52	Cyprus	137	85	91	Papua New Guinea	12	30
12	Switzerland	923	5,672	53	Venezuela	128	1,385	92	Sudan	11	164
13	Hungary	894	9,322	54	Peru	126	1,748	93	Benin	8	21
14	Czechoslovakia	885	12,897	55	Argentina	119	2,938	94	Somalia	7	20
15	Singapore	875	1,917	56	Trinidad & Tobago	110	113	95	Tanzania	7	95
16	Norway	769	3,047	57	Brazil	98	9,572	96	Cambodia	6	44
17	Netherlands	707	9,429	58	Guyana	96	73	97	Ethiopia	6	162
18	Australia	635	8,106	59	Fiji	94	52	98	Kenya	7	84
19	Malta	584	187	60	Spain	88	3,090	99	Bangladesh	5	395
20	Rumania	583	12,164	61	Togo	88	8	100	Chad	5	19
21	Italy	575	31,600					101	Bhutan	4	5
22	Poland	564	18,810			*LOWER MIDDLE*		102	Philippines	4	178
23	Iceland	562	118	62	Hong Kong	77	322	103	Nigeria	3	200
24	Ireland	506	1,508	63	Belize	75	9	104	Cameroon	3	15
25	Austria	476	3,588	64	Guatemala	75	405				
26	Soviet Union	470	117,562	65	Kuwait	71	63			*BOTTOM 10*	
27	French Polynesia	458	55	66	Bahrain	69	16	105	Guinea	2	7
28	Cuba	435	3,782	67	Iraq	69	722	106	Jordan	2	5
29	Belgium	432	4,173	68	Niger	69	300	107	Senegal	2	9
30	New Zealand	350	998	69	Zambia	64	300	108	Yemen Arab Republic	2	10
31	Seychelles	350	21	70	Reunion	57	25	109	Afghanistan	1	23
32	Brunei	340	51	71	Barbados	54	13	110	Malawi	1	6
33	Gibraltar	333	10	72	Finland	54	2,818	111	Haiti	0.9	4
34	Portugal	326	2,790	73	Costa Rica	53	100	112	Burundi	0.8	3
35	West Germany	284	17,509	74	Iran	52	1,643	113	Central African Empire	0.5	1
36	United Kingdom	283	15,675	75	Lebanon	44	118	114	St. Helena	0.1	0.5
37	Equatorial Guinea	276	83	76	Madagascar	38	288				
38	Yugoslavia	259	5,314	77	Syria	38	262				

Source: *UNESCO Statistical Yearbook.*

325. Public Library Volumes

Public libraries act as vast storehouses of human knowledge, just as books serve as transmission belts of knowledge. Globally, the number of titles is growing by around half a million titles per year. In addition, an enormous number of periodical titles are being published. Librarians serve as gatekeepers of knowledge in so far as they decide which books and periodicals, out of this vast output, will find a place on their shelves. The number of volumes in a public library, therefore, may be used as an indicator of a country's commitment to making the best of human knowledge, as selected by professionals, available to all its citizens. The definition of what constitutes a public library, however, varies considerably from country to country.

Number of Countries: 93
Midpoint: 134,000 volumes
Period Covered: 1974
Type of Ranking: Number of Volumes in Public Libraries and Number of Public Libraries; Highest to Lowest

Highlights & Findings: Both the industrialized West and the Communist East have strong library systems financed by public funds and fed by equally vigorous publishing programs. The total number of volumes in all the libraries of the world is estimated at close to 4 billion, or one per capita. Of this, the Soviet Union accounts for around 37% and the United States for 10%.

Regions	Africa	Asia & Oceania	Europe	Western Hemisphere
Most	Egypt (30)	Japan (7)	Soviet Union (1)	United States (2)
Least	Senegal (89)	Solomon Islands (92)	San Marino (93)	St. Pierre & Miquelon (80)

Rank	Country	Volumes in Public Libraries (000)	Number of Libraries
	TOP 10		
1	Soviet Union	1,507,836	130,653
2	United States	387,565	8,337
3	Poland	70,478	8,950
4	Rumania	52,882	6,575
5	West Germany	43,000	2,500
6	Czechoslovakia	39,764	10,861
7	Japan	38,849	895
8	East Germany	33,660	9,775
9	Denmark	32,713	251
10	Canada	31,282	780
	UPPER MIDDLE		
11	Hungary	30,583	8,279
12	Sweden	30,534	416
13	Netherlands	17,941	411
14	Yugoslavia	17,245	1,826
15	Italy	16,979	8,686
16	Finland	14,890	484
17	Panama	14,269	46
18	Australia	11,476	847
19	Norway	9,361	445
20	Brazil	9,278	1,717
21	Spain	8,745	1,435
22	Argentina	8,535	1,513
23	Portugal	7,039	77
24	Ireland	5,124	31
25	New Zealand	4,902	191
26	Austria	4,364	426
27	Mexico	1,530	423
28	Peru	1,894	213
29	Iceland	1,033	251
30	Egypt	1,029	156
31	Cuba	850	53
32	Philippines	802	2

Rank	Country	Volumes in Public Libraries (000)	Number of Libraries
33	South Korea	759	104
34	Ghana	700	1
35	Sri Lanka	652	324
36	Thailand	586	526
37	Malaysia	469	8
38	Sierra Leone	392	11
39	Trinidad & Tobago	343	2
40	Burma	305	43
41	Cyprus	253	116
42	Hong Kong	230	8
43	Malta	206	1
44	Iraq	195	24
45	Kuwait	178	1
46	Kenya	150	3
47	Madagascar	134	20
	LOWER MIDDLE		
48	Nigeria	132	75
49	Guyana	126	1
50	Bermuda	122	1
51	Malawi	122	2
52	Fiji	121	6
53	Belize	101	1
54	Bahrain	100	1
55	Bahamas	95	25
56	Greenland	93	1
57	Netherlands Antilles	92	1
58	Uganda	90	1
59	Gibraltar	81	3
60	Jordan	81	11
61	Guatemala	54	3
62	Qatar	53	1
63	St. Vincent	53	1

Rank	Country	Volumes in Public Libraries (000)	Number of Libraries
64	St. Lucia	46	1
65	Laos	38	3
66	Western Samoa	36	1
67	New Caledonia	34	1
68	Dominica	26	1
69	Gambia	25	2
70	Ivory Coast	23	2
71	Antigua	22	2
72	British Virgin Islands	21	1
73	Gilbert Islands	20	1
74	Pacific Islands	20	4
75	French Polynesia	18	1
76	Equatorial Guinea	17	1
77	Seychelles	16	1
78	Cook Islands	15	1
79	Grenada	15	1
80	St. Pierre & Miquelon	15	3
81	Montserrat	14	1
82	St. Helena	14	1
83	Singapore	14	2
84	Sudan	14	2
	BOTTOM 9		
85	Burundi	10	1
86	Comoros	8	2
87	Niue Island	6	1
88	Djibouti	5	1
89	Senegal	3	1
90	New Hebrides	3	1
91	Norfolk Island	3	1
92	Solomon Islands	2	2
93	San Marino	1	1

Source: *UNESCO Statistical Yearbook.*

326. PUBLIC LIBRARY USE INDEX

How well are public libraries being used? What is the extent of readership in public libraries? The following ranking attempts to answer these questions by presenting the number of volumes borrowed annually per 1,000 inhabitants.

Number of Countries: 75
Midpoint: 458.2 volumes per 1,000
Period Covered: 1974 or Latest Available Year
Type of Ranking: Number of Volumes Borrowed from Public Libraries per 1,000 Inhabitants; Total Number of Volumes Borrowed from (and Hopefully Returned to) Public Libraries Annually; Highest to Lowest

Highlights & Findings: This is one of the many rankings where the distance between the top and the bottom is phenomenally large. An average library patron in Denmark borrows over 33,000 times more books than his counterpart in Sudan. Borrowing is high in almost all industrialized countries but falls precipitously as developing countries crowd the bottom of the scale.

Regions	Africa	Asia & Oceania	Europe	Western Hemisphere
Most	Seychelles (24)	New Zealand (5)	Denmark (1)	United States (12)
Least	Sudan (75)	Sri Lanka (71)	San Marino (64)	Brazil (61)

Rank	Country	Number of Volumes Borrowed from Public Libraries Per 1,000 Inhabitants	Total Number of Volumes Borrowed from Public Libraries Annually	Rank	Country	Number of Volumes Borrowed from Public Libraries Per 1,000 Inhabitants	Total Number of Volumes Borrowed from Public Libraries Annually	Rank	Country	Number of Volumes Borrowed from Public Libraries Per 1,000 Inhabitants	Total Number of Volumes Borrowed from Public Libraries Annually
		TOP 10		25	Soviet Union	958.9	47,082,700	51	Ghana	93.6	830,000
1	Denmark	16,568.9	83,673,128	26	Belize	864.2	121,000	52	Malawi	73.8	363,481
2	Finland	9,220.4	43,059,626	27	Guyana	807.9	589,780	53	Costa Rica	66.4	119,570
3	Sweden	8,712.5	71,094,274	28	St. Vincent	794.8	71,535	54	Qatar	63.7	5,739
4	Czechoslovakia	7,999.7	63,118,100	29	Dominica	750.8	52,561	55	Malaysia	58.5	681,699
5	New Zealand	7,681.3	23,120,926	30	French Polynesia	739.9	88,797	56	Guatemala	55.2	326,392
6	Iceland	7,296.2	1,605,170	31	Netherlands Antilles	690.9	165,828	57	South Korea	55.1	1,912,568
7	Netherlands	6,975.4	94,447,434	32	Bahamas	644.2	128,841	58	Cyprus	53.4	32,600
8	Ireland	6,846.4	21,155,594	33	St. Lucia	610.1	67,120	59	Sierra Leona	51.3	139,167
9	Hungary	5,389.3	56,479,978	34	New Caledonia	559.8	72,786	60	Gambia	41.4	21,140
10	East Germany	4,669.5	79,009,122	35	Pacific Islands	540.0	64,800	61	Brazil	40.2	3,820,950
				36	Japan	536.1	59,065,700	62	Philippines	32.6	1,347,724
		UPPER MIDDLE		37	Grenada	503.9	45,355	63	Singapore	26.2	55,400
11	Poland	4,212.8	141,932,400	38	Trinidad & Tobago	458.2	490,313	64	San Marino	25.0	500
12	United States	4,150.4	892,854,268					65	Djibouti	23.1	2,500
13	Canada	4,081.9	90,333,866			**LOWER MIDDLE**					
14	Bermuda	3,641.2	218,476	39	Fiji	365.7	204,800			**BOTTOM 10**	
15	Norway	3,197.3	12,661,316	40	Antigua	288.3	20,183	66	Burma	22.6	625,002
16	Montserrat	2,840.7	28,407	41	Western Samoa	226.6	34,000	67	Kuwait	20.5	19,285
17	Greenland	2,321.4	116,071	42	Egypt	194.6	6,780,000	68	Madagascar	17.3	135,328
18	British Virgin Islands	2,123.9	20,815	43	Argentina	192.1	4,625,000	69	Uganda	9.6	107,583
19	West Germany	2,095.4	130,000,000	44	Italy	183.1	9,967,004	70	Laos	5.2	15,870
20	Malta	1,611.4	515,655	45	Cuba	180.7	1,570,952	71	Sri Lanka	4.6	61,723
21	Yugoslavia	1,551.3	32,810,609	46	Peru	165.8	2,439,098	72	Equatorial Guinea	3.1	909
22	Austria	1,325.2	9,979,062	47	Chile	161.2	1,625,657	73	Ivory Coast	2.7	12,413
23	Norfolk Island	1,301.2	2,190	48	Spain	148.0	5,215,499	74	Kenya	1.7	22,200
24	Seychelles	1,033.3	62,000	49	Bahrain	125.0	30,000	75	Sudan	0.5	9,435
				50	Hong Kong	111.8	475,501				

Source: *UNESCO Statistical Yearbook.*

COUNTRY SUMMARIES

AFGHANISTAN

Afghanistan, a landlocked country in central Asia, ranks 34th in the world in land area and 38th in population. Although less than 10% of the land is cultivated, the country ranks fourth in the world in agriculture's share of the GDP. The country appears in the top 10 only in three rankings and fares poorly in all others, particularly in physical quality of life, where it is among the bottom 10. The discovery of natural gas fields in the north has led to a spurt in the production of energy, making the country fourth in the world in the annual growth rate of energy ranking. The most notable feature of the transportation system is that it has the shortest rail track in the world (0.6 km), a government-owned spur of the Soviet line.

ALBANIA

Albania, located on the Adriatic Sea coast of the Balkan Peninsula, ranks 124th in the world in land area and 112th in the world in size of population. With a centrally planned economy and a per capita GNP of $540, it is officially classified as a lower middle-income country. It ranks lowest in Europe on the combined economic and social indicators scale and the physical quality of life index; nevertheless, it ranks high in at least two health indicators: pharmacists per capita (6th) and physicians per capita (1st). It is possible that these rankings are based on a rather loose definition of the terms pharmacist and physician. Albania also ranks sixth in the world in school enrollment per capita. Although about two-thirds of the population is still engaged in agriculture, mining provides the largest percentage of the national income and employs the highest percentage of the industrial labor force. The country's rugged terrain has isolated Albania from its neighbors and helped it to preserve its homogeneity; about 97% of the population is ethnic Albanian.

ALGERIA

Located midway along the Maghrebian littoral and extending southward into the heart of the Sahara, Algeria is the 10th largest country in the world but ranks only 37th in population. With a per capita GNP of $990, Algeria is officially classified as an upper middle-income country. It ranks 71st in the world on the combined social and economic indicators scale and 95th on the physical quality of life index. Its GNP is growing at a faster rate than its population (4.3% and 3.2% respectively). The state-controlled economy is based on the production of petroleum and natural gas; Algeria ranks first in Africa in production of natural gas and fourth in the world in natural gas reserves. The country also ranks eighth in uranium production. Petroleum revenues have enabled Algeria to embark on a massive and ambitious program of rapid industrialization. Algeria ranks fifth in the world in annual industrial growth rate and seventh in industry's share of the GDP. As a corollary, it has managed to achieve very favorable terms of trade, in which it ranks eighth. Besides petroleum, Algeria's principal export is wine, in the production of which it ranks first in Africa.

ANGOLA

Located on the west coast of southern Africa, Angola ranks 20th in the world in land area and 71st in population. With a per capita GNP of $330, Angola is officially classified as an upper middle-income country. Its population growth rate of 3.3%, however, exceeds the GNP growth rate of 3.2%. It ranks poorly on both the combined social and economic indicators scale, on which it ranks 102nd, and the physical quality of life index, on which it ranks 147th. Angola is one of the richest countries in southern Africa in mineral resources, notably diamonds (in the production of which Angola ranks ninth in the world), iron ore and copper. The country is also one of the world's major producers of coffee. Large-scale exploitation of oil reserves began in 1968, enabling Angola to achieve the seventh rank in the annual growth rate of energy production and 10th in the annual growth rate of exports.

ARGENTINA

Argentina is the second largest country in Latin America and the eighth largest in the world. Because of its low population density (less than 9 per sq km; 23 per sq mi), Argentina ranks only 30th in the world in size of population. Classified as an upper middle-income country with a per capita income of $1,550 (the third highest in Latin America), Argentina has a GNP growth rate (2.9%) that is more than double its population growth rate of 1.3%. However, in recent years the country has been subject to the third highest inflation rate in the world. It ranks second in the wholesale price index and the consumer price index for both food and all items. The Argentine economy is based on agriculture with grains and livestock forming the bulwark of its wealth. The pampa, with its deep rich soil, is the granary of South America. Argentine cattle herds are among the world's finest, and Argentina is one of the world's largest exporters of livestock products. The agricultural indicators are uniformly good: the country ranks seventh in meat production, 10th in peanut production, fourth in soybean production, fourth in wool production, ninth in wheat production, 10th in corn production, ninth in cheese production, fifth in horses per capita and fifth in cattle per capita. With such an impressive productive capacity in agriculture, it is not surprising that the country ranks fifth in consumption of proteins and fourth in consumption of meat. In the average size of farms, Argentina leads the world. Despite erosion through inflation, the Argentine standard of living is higher than that of most countries in Latin America. Argentina ranks 40th on the combined economic and social indicators scale and 49th on the physical quality of life index. The country ranks among the top 10 in five educational and health indicators: number of university professors, teacher-pupil ratio in primary schools, post-secondary enrollment ratio, physicians per capita and vocational enrollment ratio. Argentina is near the top in a number of other rankings: production of uranium (10th), length of pipelines (7th), radios per capita (5th), number of daily newspapers (10th), usable airfields (3rd) and percentage of population in cities over 50,000 (8th).

AUSTRALIA

The world's smallest continent and the sixth largest country, Australia is the driest of the inhabited continents, with the inner third of its territory a desert ringed by another third of marginal agricultural lands. As a result, the country is highly urbanized; more than three-fifths of the people live in cities of more than 100,000 and the country ranks seventh in urbanization. Relative to Australia's physical size, the population is small. Although replenished by over 100,000 immigrants annually, Australia ranks only 46th in size of population. With a per capita GNP of $6,100, Australia is officially classified as a high-income country; the annual GNP growth rate of 2.4% exceeds the population growth rate of 1.5%. Australia ranks 10th on the combined economic and social indicators scale and 11th on the physical quality of life index. By virtue of its enormous natural resources, Australia ranks among the top 10 on a number of agricultural, manufacturing and mining rankings. Although the agricultural sector has been declining, the country ranks second in meat production, seventh in sugar production, first in wool production, eighth in wheat production, fourth in cattle per capita, 10th in oats production and third in sheep per capita. The dominance in agricultural and livestock production is related to the availability of agricultural land; in per capita terms Australia ranks third in this respect. The mineral sector has gained in importance as a result of new mineral discoveries, and iron ore has replaced wool as the single leading export. Australia ranks third in uranium production, fourth in salt production, ninth in coal production, ninth in gold production, sixth in coal reserves, sixth in silver production, third in iron ore production, 10th in copper production and seventh in beer production. Manufactured goods account for about two-thirds of the total value of production, but Australia does not appear among the top 10 in any industrial indicator because of the small size of its domestic market. However, when translated into per capita consumption terms, the country places among the top 10 in a number of rankings: seventh in wool consumption, fifth in newsprint consumption, eighth in consumption of rubber, second in sugar consumption, fifth in tea consumption, fourth in protein consumption, sixth in calorie consumption, fourth in tin consumption, seventh in gasoline consumption, second in meat consumption, fifth in passenger cars per capita and fifth in commercial vehicles per capita.

Australia's other distinctions include the third rank in tourist receipts per tourist, the eighth rank in telegrams per capita, the 10th rank in cargo handled by ports, the ninth rank in scientists in basic research, the fifth rank in usable airfields, the ninth rank in new houses per 1,000, the second rank in net private investment and the eighth rank in advertising expenditures. On the negative side the country ranks ninth in abortions as a percentage of live births, seventh in mandays lost through industrial disputes, 10th in drug-related offenses, and eighth in motor vehicle fatalities. On the whole, Australia appears 49 times in the top 10 of the rankings.

AUSTRIA

Located at the crossroads of central Europe, Austria ranks 106th in land area and 69th in population. With a per capita GNP of $5,330, Austria is officially classified as a high-income country. Compared to a GNP growth rate of 4%, the population growth rate is only 0.3%, the sixth lowest in the world. As a result, the Austrians have a mature age profile and Austria ranks first in the world in percentage of senior citizens in the population. Austria is one of the major tourist centers of Europe and ranks eighth in the number of tourists. Austria ranks 14th on the combined economic and social indicators scale and 17th on the physical quality of life index. The rankings also reveal a strange dichotomy: on the one hand Austria ranks ninth in the world in the number of Nobel Prize recipients, and on the other it ranks seventh in the criminal ratio and fifth in the number of suicides. Austria's economic track record is healthy, as revealed in these rankings: third in strength of currency, seventh in currency per capita, ninth in stock market performance of industrial shares, 10th in aluminum production and ninth in industry's share of the GDP. Austria's other distinctions include ranking seventh in public expenditures on social welfare, eighth in pigs per capita, ninth in physicians per capita, eighth in balance of trade, ninth in commercial vehicles per capita, fifth in consumption of calories, fourth in tractors per hectare, seventh in percentage of unionized labor, 10th on the labor productivity index, seventh in motor cycles per capita and seventh in farm ownership. On the whole, Austria appears in the top ten 24 times.

BAHAMAS

The Bahamas, a group of over 700 coral islands stretching from the western Atlantic near Florida almost to Haiti, ranks 137th in land area and 152nd in population. With a per capita GNP of $2,490, the Bahamas is officially classified as a high-income country and ranks 37th on the physical quality of life index. Tourism is by far the most important industry and foreign exchange earner. Most of the population is concentrated on a few islands, placing the Bahamas sixth in population density in agricultural areas. The country's liberal tax laws and banking regulations have attracted considerable foreign investment. Petroleum refining and transshipment account for the country's first rank in both exports and imports per capita, first rank in share of fuel in imports, third rank in annual growth rate in exports and fifth rank in annual growth rate in imports. Inagua is one of the world's largest solar salt complexes, and the Bahamas ranks first in salt production per capita. The islands' prosperity has attracted immigrants from all over the West Indies, and the country ranks sixth in annual population growth rate. On the negative side, the islands rank fifth in drug-related offenses and eighth in mental hospital admissions.

BAHRAIN

A sheikhdom and archipelago in the Persian Gulf, Bahrain ranks 157th in land area and 150th in population. With a per capita GNP of $2,430, generated almost entirely by oil production and exports, Bahrain is officially classified as a high-income country. It ranks 34th on the combined economic and social indicators scale and 74th on the physical quality of life index. Bahrain is expected to be the first Persian Gulf nation to run out of oil, and therefore the country is diversifying the nonagricultural sector, plowing back its oil revenues into refineries, shipbuilding and aluminum. This development is reflected in Bahrain's fifth rank in exports per capita, third rank in imports per capita, sixth rank in energy consumption per capita and eighth rank in production of electric energy. As in other Persian Gulf states, Bahrain's new prosperity has been accompanied by an influx of immigrants particularly from the Indian subcontinent, and the country ranks ninth in annual growth rate of population.

BANGLADESH

Located on the Indian subcontinent in the great combined delta of the Ganges, the Brahmaputra and the Meghna rivers, Bangladesh ranks 87th in size of land area but eighth in size of population. The result is that Bangladesh has the highest density of any nation on earth other than small city-states; it also has the 12th highest birthrate, the sixth highest fertility rate and the third highest death rate. Uncontrolled population growth has consigned Bangladesh to the bottom of the majority of the rankings. Although it ranks fourth in percentage of land area under cultivation and also fourth in rice production, it ranks first in share of food in imports and in population living in absolute poverty. With a per capita GNP of only $110, Bangladesh is officially classified as a low-income country, one of the 29 least-developed countries and one of the 45 countries most affected by recent adverse economic conditions. It ranks 126th on a combined economic and social indicators scale and 109th on the physical quality of life index.

BARBADOS

Barbados is an island state in the West Indies ranking 160th in size of land area and 151st in size of population. The island is densely populated and intensely cultivated; it ranks sixth in the world in both respects. Tourism is the country's largest source of foreign exchange. With a per capita GNP of $1,660, Barbados is officially classified as an upper middle-income country. It ranks 33rd on the combined economic and social indicators scale and on the physical quality of life index.

BELGIUM

Belgium comprises two ethnic and cultural regions generally called Flanders and Wallony. The country ranks 122nd in land area and 58th in population. With a per capita GNP of $6,780, Belgium is officially classified as a high-income country. The GNP is growing at an annual rate of 3.9%, compared to a population growth rate of 0.2%, the fifth lowest in the world. Belgium ranks 12th on the combined economic and social indicators scale and 18th on the physical quality of life index. The population density is the second highest in Europe after the Netherlands, and population density in agricultural areas is the ninth highest in the world. Belgium also ranks fourth in the percentage of senior citizens in the population. The country is one of the most industrialized in Europe with an emphasis on heavy industry. It stands out in a number of economic indicators: third in wool production, 10th in meat production, third in production of cigars, fifth in beer production, sixth in production of cigarettes, ninth in production of radio receivers and eighth in value added per worker. In the consumption rankings, Belgium is also among the top 10 in rubber, coffee, paper and calories. Agriculture employs only about 6% of the work force, but supplies three-fourths of the agricultural requirements. Belgium ranks ninth in tractors per hectare and pigs per capita. The largest single export item is steel. Because of its role as a processor and importer of raw materials and exporter of finished and semi-finished goods, Belgium ranks fifth in the world in imports per capita and eighth in the world in exports per capita. The strength of the economy is reflected in a number of financial rankings: the sixth strongest currency in the world, seventh in gold holdings, 10th in SDR quotas, fifth in net direct private investments, second in foreign aid as percentage of GNP and second in currency per capita. Belgium's other distinctions include ranking eighth in vocational enrollment, 10th in public expenditures per capita, 10th in health expenditures per capita and ninth in domestic mail per capita. On the negative side, Belgium ranks ninth in unemployment rate and motor vehicle fatalities. Overall, Belgium is among the top 10 in 33 rankings.

BENIN

A republic in West Africa between Nigeria and Togo, Benin ranks 95th in land area and 103rd in population. With a per capita GNP of $130, Benin is officially classified as a low-income country; it is also one of the least-developed countries and one of the countries most seriously affected by recent adverse economic conditions. Benin ranks 126th on the combined economic and social indicators scale and 134th on the physical quality of life index. While the population grows annually by 2.7%, the GNP per capita has a negative annual growth rate of −1.1%. Benin's economic problems are compounded by a high birth rate, in which it ranks eighth, and a high urban growth rate, in which it ranks 10th. Over 75% Beninese live in absolute poverty. The economy is overwhelmingly agricultural, and the majority of the workers are engaged in subsistence farming. Industrial activity is almost entirely limited to the processing of agricultural goods, and Benin ranks first in the percentage of primary products in exports.

BERMUDA

An archipelago of some 300 coral rocks, islets and islands (of which 20 are inhabited), Bermuda is so small that despite a population of only 58,000, it has an average density of over 1,158 per sq km (3,000 per sq mi). Bermuda is a fashionable year-round resort, and most of Bermuda's inhabitants owe their livelihood, directly or indirectly, to the tourist industry. The island's remarkable prosperity, stemming partly from the presence of over 2,000 "exempted" foreign companies and partly from a U.S. naval base and tourism, is reflected in a number of rankings: fourth in television sets per capita, fifth in telephones per capita, second in radios per capita, first in literacy, fifth in scientific and engineering manpower per 10,000, ninth in consumption of gasoline, first in motor cycles per capita, third in museum attendance and second in advertising expenditures. On the negative side, Bermuda ranks sixth in divorce rates and second in mental hospital admissions. On the whole, Bermuda is among the top 10 in 14 rankings.

BHUTAN

Bhutan, nestling in the East Himalayas, ranks 115th in land area and 129th in population. With a per capita GNP of only $70, Bhutan is one of the poorest and least developed of the low-income countries. Because of a paucity of data, Bhutan appears only in a few rankings but in two it ranks among the top 10: it ranks first in percentage of labor force in agriculture and eighth in percentage of land under forests. With one of the most primitive economies in the world, Bhutan has only a rudimentary banking and currency system. Nevertheless, the country is self-sufficient in food and there is significant potential for lumber-based industries.

BOLIVIA

One of the two landlocked countries in South America, Bolivia ranks 25th in land area and 76th in population. It also has one of the highest concentrations of native Indians in Latin America, with Indians constituting 62% of the population. Bolivia is at once one of the richest as well as one of the poorest of Latin American countries. It is endowed with immense mineral resources, remarkable both for the size of the deposits and the variety of the ores. It is the largest tin producer in the Western Hemisphere and the second largest in the world. Bolivia is the world's largest producer of bismuth and the second largest producer of antimony. On the other hand, with a per capita GNP of only $390, it is officially classified as a low-income country. It ranks 83rd on the combined social and economic indicators scale and 92nd on the physical quality of life index. Its GNP is growing at a faster rate than its population (3.4% as against 2.7%). The low population growth rate is partly explained by a high maternal

mortality rate, in which it ranks second in the world. Agriculture accounts for about one-third of the GNP and employs about two-thirds of the population, mostly on a subsistence level. Although racked by a high rate of inflation (eighth highest in the world), at least two economic indicators look healthy: a third rank on the labor productivity index and a first rank on the manufacturing index. It also ranks ninth in usable airfields.

BOTSWANA

A landlocked country in southern Africa, Botswana ranks 41st in land area and 134th in size of population. With a per capita GNP of $330, Botswana is officially classified as one of the least developed of the low-income countries. It ranks 91st on the combined economic and social indicators scale and 103rd on the physical quality of life index. The annual growth rate of the population at 3.7% is the seventh highest in the world; yet it is easily outpaced by the GNP annual growth rate of 6.2%. Although the country ranks second in agricultural land per capita, water shortage has hampered agriculture and only a small percentage of potentially arable land is under cultivation. Most of the inhabitants are pastoralists, and with 2.2 million head of cattle Botswana ranks third in cattle per capita. In the 1960s several mineral deposits were discovered, particularly diamonds, in the production of which the country now ranks fourth. Botswana also ranks third in percentage of women in the labor force and percentage of divorced persons; both may be explained by the fact that large numbers of males are employed in South Africa and Rhodesia.

BRAZIL

The fifth largest country in the world (occupying 5.68% of the earth's land surface), Brazil occupies nearly half the continent of South America and also accounts for half the population. In population, Brazil ranks seventh in the world. Its international borders, the third longest in the world, touch every South American country except Ecuador and Chile. With a per capita GNP of $1,140, Brazil is officially classified as an upper middle-income country. On the combined economic and social indicators scale, Brazil ranks 54th and on the physical quality of life index it ranks 70th. While the population grows annually by around 3%, the urban population grows by over 4.5%, creating serious economic and social problems. Brazil's GNP, the 10th highest in the world, has grown steadily since 1968 averaging above 10% annually. Brazil also ranks 10th in the annual growth rate of per capita GNP. But its prosperity is being eroded by the seventh highest rate of inflation in the world. From 1970 to 1976 the rate reached 26.1% annually, reflecting demand pressure on an industrial sector working at capacity as well as a sharp rise in petroleum prices. During this period Brazil developed the system of "monetary correction" (periodic adjustment of key prices, wages and interest roughly in proportion to the increases in the overall price index). Despite these measures, Brazil still has the third weakest currency and the fifth highest wholesale price index. The economy is in a transitional phase moving from an agricultural to an industrial base. The agricultural sector employs 45% of the population, and accounts for 15% of the GNP and about 60% of the exports. Except for wheat, the country is largely self-sufficient in food. With a cattle population of 80 million, Brazil ranks third in the world in livestock. It also ranks 10th in horses per capita. The country appears among the top 10 in 13 agricultural rankings: eighth in rice production, milk production and average size of farms; second in production of coffee and sugar; third in production of soybean and corn; fourth in production of roundwood; sixth in production of tobacco; ninth in production of peanuts; and 10th in production of wool and eggs. The industrial sector accounts for about one-third of the GNP and employs 18% of the work force. In addition to ranking third on the manufacturing index, Brazil also ranks fourth in production of radios, eighth in production of television sets, and 10th in production of passenger cars and cement. Known mineral reserves are extensive, and Brazil ranks second in production of iron ore. The country places high in three transportation rankings: second in inland navigation and usable airfields and eighth in number of civil aircraft. The educational system, one of the largest in the world, is most notable for the number of primary schools (in which it ranks second), the number of foreign students in domestic universities (in which it ranks seventh) and the vocational enrollment ratio (in which it ranks 10th). Brazil also ranks sixth in number of daily newspapers. But what should hearten Brazil's present rulers most is the country's position as the 10th most powerful nation in the world. Overall, Brazil appears among the top 10 in 45 rankings.

BULGARIA

Located on the Balkan Peninsula, Bulgaria ranks 98th in land area and 61st in population. With a per capita GNP of $2,310, Bulgaria is officially classified as an upper middle-income country. It ranks 29th on the combined economic and social indicators scale and 22nd on the physical quality of life index. The annual population growth rate is the 13th lowest in the world at 0.5%, while the annual growth rate of GNP is a healthy 3.9%. The economic system, highly centralized after the Soviet pattern, is directed through the five-year development plans. The largest industrial sector is machine building, which accounts for 25% of industrial production. About 62% of the labor force is employed outside of agriculture, and Bulgaria ranks 10th in industrial work force. Although only about 40% of the land area is arable, Bulgaria has one of the highest ratios of arable land to population in Eastern Europe. A number of rankings confirm the importance of agricultural products in both production and consumption: fourth in cotton consumption, first in sugar consumption, eighth in tobacco production, and seventh in wine production. The country also ranks first in production of cigarettes per capita and is the fourth largest exporter of tobacco in the world and the largest exporter of cigarettes, mainly to the Soviet Union. Other rankings reveal a strong educational system: ninth in post-secondary enrollment ratio, seventh in secondary school enrollment ratio, third in scientists in basic research and percentage of women in university enrollment, fourth in vocational enrollment and 10th in museum attendance. Bulgarians must be avid cinema-goers; Bulgaria is among the top 10 in all three film-related rankings: 10th in cinema seats, seventh in movie attendance per capita and eighth in number of cinemas. Bulgaria also ranks eighth in physicians per capita.

BURMA

Burma, the largest country in Mainland Southeast Asia, is also the 37th largest in the world and the 25th most populous. With a per capita GNP of $120, Burma is officially classified as a low-income country and it is also considered by the U.N. as one of the 45 countries most seriously affected by recent adverse economic conditions. It ranks 109th on the combined economic and social indicators scale and

83rd on the physical quality of life index. Compared to a population growth rate of 2.5% annually, the GNP per capita growth rate is only 0.9%. The economy is primarily agricultural and is dependent on rice cultivation, which accounts for 60% of the nation's export earnings. Until 1946 Burma was the world's largest rice exporter and even today it ranks ninth in rice production. Another important crop is peanuts, in the production of which Burma ranks eighth. The Irrawaddy River, the country's lifeline and major transportation artery, is also responsible for placing Burma in the 10th rank in inland navigation. Burma has the world's highest infant mortality rate.

BURUNDI

A landlocked country in Central Africa, Burundi ranks 127th in land area and 92nd in population. With a per capita GNP of $120, Burundi is officially classified as one of the least-developed low-income countries, and it is also considered by the U.N. to be one of the 45 countries most seriously affected by recent adverse economic conditions. Burundi ranks 135th on the combined economic and social indicators scale and 134th on the physical quality of life index; both ranks underline the fact that Burundi is one of the poorest countries in the world with less than 25% of its GNP in the cash economy. While the average annual population growth rate is 2.4%, the per capita GNP annual growth rate is −1.1%. Burundi's density of population is one of the highest in sub-Saharan Africa. The economy is almost entirely agricultural and Burundi ranks second in agriculture's share of the GDP. Industry accounts for only 5 to 6% of the GNP. The country's only cash crop is coffee, of which 80% is purchased by the United States. Over 75% of Burundians are believed to subsist in absolute poverty.

CAMBODIA

Cambodia, the second smallest state in Southeast Asia, ranks 81st in land area and 64th in population. The severe disruptions following the Vietnamese takeover of 1978/79 have dried up even the small trickle of information about the country that reached the West through unofficial channels. At the present time, there is no means of determining the social conditions or economic status of the country. Even at the time of takeover, Cambodia had the weakest currency in the world, the second highest rate of inflation, the third highest rank on the consumer price index for food and was fourth on the consumer price index for all items. Cambodia is officially classified as a low-income country and among the most seriously affected by recent adverse economic conditions. It ranks 122nd on the combined economic and social indicators scale and 98th on the physical quality of life index. Its annual population growth rate is a moderate 2.8%, but large-scale and forced relocation of urban populations under the Khmer Rouge regime is believed to have retarded the growth profile significantly.

CAMEROON

Cameroon is located in the western part of Africa and ranks 47th in land area and 73rd in population. With a per capita GNP of $290, Cameroon is officially classified as a lower middle-income country and as one of the 45 countries most seriously affected by recent adverse economic conditions. It ranks 105th on the combined economic and social indicators scale and 120th on the physical quality of life index. As in many other developing nations, the annual growth rate of population exceeds that of the GNP; the former is 1.9% while the latter is only 0.5%. Cameroon has a very diverse ethnic configuration even by African standards, with over 200 tribes speaking 24 major African languages. It is also the only African country where both French and English are accorded official status. The mainstay of the economy is agriculture, which employs 80% of the labor force and accounts for 70% of export earnings. The main cash crop is cocoa.

CANADA

The largest country in the Western Hemisphere and the second largest in the world, Canada ranks only 31st in population. More than two-thirds of the population live within 160 km (100 mi) of the U.S. border and more than half in the southeast near the Great Lakes and the St. Lawrence River. Ranked as the eighth most powerful nation in the world, Canada has the eighth highest GNP, and its per capita GNP of $7,510 ranks seventh, not far behind its powerful neighbor to the south. Its performance is even better in terms of real income per capita, in which it ranks fourth. It ranks fourth on the combined economic and social indicators scale and eighth on the physical quality of life index, in both cases ahead of the United States. Its GNP per capita annual growth rate of 3.3% is more than double its population growth rate of 1.4%.

Canada appears among the top 10 in 92 of these rankings and is surpassed in this respect only by the United States. This track record is all the more impressive because of Canada's smaller population. Looking just among the top five countries on each ranking, there are nine areas in which Canada stands out. The first is mineral wealth, which plays a large part in Canada's economic success. It ranks fifth in salt production per capita, fourth in uranium, second in gold production, fifth in iron ore and copper production, third in silver production, and first in asbestos, nickel and zinc production. In the energy sector it ranks fourth in natural gas production, fourth in length of pipelines, and second in production of electric energy. In the agricultural sector it ranks third in production of barley, fifth in production of wheat and third in production of oats. In the industrial sector it ranks second in value added per worker, third in production of television sets and fifth in aluminum production. Among the consumption rankings, it ranks fourth in gasoline consumption per capita, second in consumption of rubber and fifth in consumption of steel. In the communications sector it ranks third in television sets per capita, third in radios per capita, second in number of civil aircraft, fourth in commercial vehicles per capita and third in passenger cars per capita. In the field of education it ranks fourth in educational expenditures per pupil, fifth in educational expenditures as percentage of GNP, second in foreign students in domestic universities, second in literacy, fourth in museum attendance, fifth in university professors, fourth in secondary school enrollment ratio, third in post-secondary enrollment ratio and fifth in graduate population. In the financial sector it ranks fifth in foreign aid as percentage of GNP. In the health sector it ranks fourth in health expenditures per capita and third in inhabitants per nursing person. In the media sector it ranks fourth in advertising expenditures and fifth in press freedom. On the negative side, Canada also ranks 10th in motor vehicle fatalities and fifth in mandays lost through industrial disputes.

CENTRAL AFRICAN EMPIRE

A landlocked country in the heart of Africa, the Central African Empire ranks 40th in land area and 120th in population. With a per capita GNP of $230, the Central African Empire is one of the least developed among low-income countries and is also among the 45 countries considered most seriously affected by recent adverse economic conditions. It ranks 119th on the combined economic and social indicators scale and 144th on the physical quality of life index. While the population grows annually by 2.3%, the per capita GNP has a negative growth rate of −0.7%. Diamonds account for about 35% of the nation's foreign exchange receipts. Although only about 2% of the land area is under cultivation, the nation ranks fifth in percentage of labor force in agriculture. For reasons that are not clear, the nation also ranks fourth in tourist receipts per tourist.

CHAD

Chad, the largest among the countries of former French Equatorial Africa, ranks 18th in land area and 91st in population. With a per capita GNP of $120, Chad is one of the least developed of low-income countries and is also among the 45 countries considered by the U.N. to be most seriously affected by recent adverse economic conditions. It ranks 138th on the combined economic and social indicators scale and 141st on the physical quality of life index. While the population grows annually by 2.1%, the per capita GNP has a negative growth rate of −2.1%. More than 75% of Chad's inhabitants subsist in absolute poverty. The economy is almost exclusively agricultural, and about 96% of the people are engaged in subsistence agriculture. As a result Chad ranks sixth in agriculture's share of the GDP and agricultural land per capita and seventh in percentage of the labor force in agriculture.

CHILE

Chile ranks 35th in land area and 54th in population. With a per capita GNP of $1,050, Chile is one of the 35 upper middle-income countries. It ranks 52nd on the combined economic and social indicators scale and 59th on the physical quality of life index. While the population growth rate is relatively low at 1.8%, the per capita GNP growth rate of −2.7% lags far behind. Chile ranks eighth in urbanization. Over 70% of the population live in urban centers, and more than one-third of the inhabitants are concentrated in and around Santiago and Valparaiso. Compared to other Latin American countries, Chile enjoys many significant advantages. Because of its geographical and cultural isolation, the population is extremely homogeneous. The country has one of the highest literacy rates in South America at 85%. It is endowed with a variety of minerals, which account for more than 85% of the total value of exports. It ranks ninth in silver production and third in copper production. Despite these advantages, the Chilean economy has been reeling for years under the highest rate of inflation in the world. Chile has the world's fifth weakest currency, fourth highest unemployment rate, and the highest consumer price index (both food and all items), wholesale price index, and rent index. Based on 1970-100, the wholesale price is a staggering 258,663. One of the main reasons for Chile's poor economic performance is the decline in agricultural output and the consequent increases in food imports. Although agriculture employs a third of the population, it only produces about 10% of the national wealth and less than half of domestic food requirements. On the positive side, Chile is the world's ninth ranking wine producer (as well as Latin America's second largest) and consumes the largest amount of fish of any South American nation.

CHINA

As is often said, China is the most populous country in the world (accounting for nearly one in every four human beings) and also the third largest in size. Dr. Ray Cline also ranks it the third most powerful nation in the world both in military power and total power. It has the sixth highest GNP, but because its per capita GNP is only $410, it is generally ranked as a lower middle-income country. It ranks 79th on a combined social and economic indicators scale and 76th on the physical quality of life index. Despite its large size, China has the second highest population density in agricultural areas. One encouraging feature is the fact that while the government has managed to bring down the birthrate to 1.7%, the per capita GNP has grown at a healthy 5.3%. China exhibits all the characteristics of a developing country. Once the superlatives that are merely a function

of size are exhausted, China's economic track record is neither impressive nor extraordinary in relation to its enormous potential. It appears among the top 10 only in 13 agricultural rankings, six mining rankings and four industrial rankings. In the agricultural sector it ranks first in rice production and tobacco production; second in peanut, barley, soybean, egg and corn production and irrigated lands; third in potato production, fish catch and wheat production; and sixth in oats production. In the energy sector it ranks fourth in energy production, third in coal production and reserves, 10th in petroleum reserves and 22nd in production of natural gas. In the industrial sector it ranks sixth in sugar production and fifth in production of pig iron, steel and cement. It also ranks third in production of roundwood. As might be expected it has the highest annual growth rate of the labor force. In the mining sector it ranks sixth in production of iron ore, second in the production of salt, seventh in manganese, eighth in lead ore, first in tungsten, and is among the three top producers of tin, antimony, and magnesite. Although China has an agricultural economy, only about 11% of the land is suited for agricultural purposes. Because all arable land is used for crops, there is only limited animal husbandry. However, China is the world's largest pork producer. China's military prowess is underlined in two rankings: in total defense expenditures where it ranks third and men under arms where it ranks second. Perhaps the most unsurprising ranking is that Peking has the largest cabinet in the world.

COLOMBIA

Colombia ranks 24th in land area and 27th in population. It is the fourth most populous as well as the fourth largest country in Latin America. With a per capita GNP of $630, Colombia is officially classified as a lower middle-income country. It ranks 74th on the combined economic and social indicators scale and 67th on the physical quality of life index. Colombia's prospects for growth are good in view of the fact that while the population growth rate is 2.8%, the per capita GNP growth rate is 3.9%. As all coffee-lovers know, Colombia is, after Brazil, the world's largest producer and exporter of coffee. The economy is still predominantly agricultural; agriculture contributes 30% of the GDP and employs one-half of the labor force. Colombia is also an important producer of cocoa and ranks seventh in percentage of land under forests. The country is rich in minerals. Its 18 billion tons of known coal reserves are the largest in Latin America. Colombia also produces 90% of the world's supply of emeralds. The country appears among the top 10 in three communications rankings: eighth in usable airfields and inland navigation and 10th in telegrams per capita. Like many other Latin American countries, Colombia is racked by inflation, as reflected in its sixth rank on the wholesale price index. Colombia ranks third in the maternal mortality rate.

CONGO

Located on the Equator in west-central Africa, Congo ranks 121st in land area and 126th in population. With a per capita GNP of $520, Congo is one of the few African countries that has reached the lower middle-income level. It ranks 85th on the combined economic and social indicators scale and 131st on the physical quality of life index. The most encouraging prognosis is that Congo's per capita GNP growth rate of 4.3% easily outpaces its population growth rate of 2.5%. In fact, Congo ranks first in the world in the annual growth rate of industry and fifth in the annual growth rate of exports. Agriculture and forestry remain important, and Congo ranks fifth in agricultural land per capita. Congo also stands out in school enrollment per capita, in which it ranks third. Congo's central geographic location at the crossroads of the transit trade to and from Zaire, the Central African Empire, Chad and Gabon and Brazzaville's former status as administrative capital of French Equatorial Africa have both had a beneficial impact on the economy.

COSTA RICA

The second smallest Central American republic, Costa Rica ranks 113th in land area and 117th in population. With a per capita GNP of $1,040, Costa Rica is one of the 35 upper middle-income countries. It ranks 49th on the combined social and economic indicators scale and 39th on the physical quality of life index. Its per capita GNP annual growth rate of 3.7% has managed to keep ahead of the population growth rate of 2.6%. Politically one of the most stable countries in Latin America, Costa Rica's main distinctions include a literacy rate of over 90% and the absence of a standing army. Not only does Costa Rica have the highest per capita GNP in the region,

but the national income is more evenly distributed than among its neighbors. Although industry is becoming increasingly important, agriculture employs more than half the labor force and the country ranks high in three agricultural rankings: third in sugar consumption, ninth in average size of farms and seventh in per capita food production.

CUBA

The largest and the westernmost of the West Indies, Cuba ranks 94th in land area and 56th in population. With a per capita GNP of $860, Cuba is officially designated a lower middle-income country. It ranks 46th on the combined social and economic indicators scale and 43rd on the physical quality of life index. Its per capita GNP annual growth rate of 1.0% is not enough to keep pace with the population growth rate of 1.6%. Historically, Cuba has been a one-crop economy based on sugar, and it remains so despite attempts at diversification by the government of Fidel Castro; sugar and its derivatives still account for 85% of the value of all exports. Cuba ranks fourth in both the production and consumption of sugar. The country imports approximately 40% of its food requirements; the resulting balance of payments deficits are covered by Soviet credits, which are believed to exceed $4.1 billion. Although Cuba's nickel deposits are among the largest in the world, extraction presents serious technical problems; however, production has increased substantially and nickel is now the country's second most valuable export item. Cuba ranks seventh in the annual growth rate of exports. Since the Bay of Pigs, Cuba has remained in a state of constant military alert and has the highest civilian-soldier ratio in the Western Hemisphere. Cuba's other distinctions include ranking sixth in movie attendance per capita and second in telegrams per capita.

CYPRUS

Cyprus, the third largest island in the Mediterranean Sea, ranks 142nd in land area and 135th in population. With a per capita GNP of $1,220, Cyprus is officially classified as one of 35 upper middle-income countries. It ranks 50th on the combined economic and social indicators scale and 39th on the physical quality of life index. Its per capita GNP annual growth rate of 5.1% is more than six times its population growth rate of 0.8%. This is all the more remarkable because of the continued economic strains of the communal strife between Greek Cypriots and Turks and the occupation of the northern half of the island by Turkey. The country's favorable climate may explain its ninth ranking in the life expectancy (males) table. The economy is predominantly agricultural, and over 40% of the economically active population is engaged in farming. The principal crops include grapes, and Cyprus ranks fifth in wine production. Light manufacturing contributes approximately 20% of the GDP and is oriented toward consumer goods such as cigarettes, in the production of which Cyprus ranks fifth. The country also ranks third in cinema seats per capita.

CZECHOSLOVAKIA

A landlocked nation in central Europe, Czechoslovakia ranks 91st in land area and 135th in size of population. With a per capita GNP of $3,840, Czechoslovakia is considered to be a high-income developed country. It ranks 20th on the combined social and economic indicators scale and 19th on the physical quality of life index. Its per capita GNP annual growth rate of 3.0% is five times higher than its population growth rate of 0.6%. Communist Czechoslovakia has managed to retain, although not improve upon, the leading industrial position it enjoyed before World War II. Czechoslovakia ranks 10th in steel production and coal production, third in beer production, fifth in industrial work force as well as second in steel consumption and sixth in cotton consumption. Its industrial leadership is also attested by its seventh rank on the labor productivity index. Even more impressive are its rankings in the field of education, culture and health: ninth in university professors, vocational enrollment, and production of scientific books, fourth in volumes borrowed from public libraries and scientists in basic research, sixth in volumes in public libraries, third in expenditures on scientific research, eighth in nurses per capita, fifth in physicians per capita and 10th in number of cinemas. In the communications sector, it ranks fifth in the number of tourists and ninth in telegrams per capita. On the negative side, it ranks eighth in abortions and seventh in suicides. On the whole, Czechoslovakia appears among the top 10 in 27 of the rankings.

DENMARK

Denmark ranks 116th in land area and 85th in population. With a per capita GNP of $7,450, Denmark is one of the 37 high-income developed countries. It ranks second on the combined economic and social indicators scale and fifth on the physical quality of life index. Although the per capita GNP growth rate is only 1.7% (the same as for Italy and South Africa), it is still over three times its population growth rate of 0.5%. Denmark appears among the top 10 in 55 rankings spread over a number of key areas. The country ranks ninth in female life expectancy and sixth in male life expectancy, second in health expenditures per capita, eighth in calorie consumption, second in literacy, third in educational expenditures as a percentage of the GNP, second in educational expenditures per pupil, fifth in public expenditures on social welfare, sixth in post-secondary enrollment ratio, third in teacher-pupil ratio in primary schools, first in volumes borrowed from public libraries, ninth in volumes in public libraries, first in nurses per capita, fifth in dentists per capita, fifth lowest in infant mortality, and seventh lowest in dependency rate. Although agriculture contributes only 10% of the GNP, more than 70% of the land area is cultivated, and Denmark ranks fifth in this respect. Despite the country's small size, the agricultural sector is third in the world in meat production, 10th in barley production, first in pigs per capita, ninth in fish catch and second in farm ownership. The leading industrial manufactures include cigars (fifth), merchant vessels (eighth) and beer (second). The Danes are among the top-ranking consumers of three items: paper, meat and coffee. The nation is ranked ninth in press freedom, foreign aid per capita, telephones per capita, imports per capita, value added per worker, and domestic mail per capita; fifth in museum attendance, advertising expenditures, and stock market performance of industrial shares; eighth in television sets per capita and percentage of unionized labor, and 10th in number of Nobel laureates. On the negative side, Denmark ranks seventh in crime rate, ninth in divorce rates, sixth in suicide rate and fifth in mental hospital admissions.

DOMINICAN REPUBLIC

The Dominican Republic, which occupies the eastern two-thirds of the island of Hispaniola in the Caribbean Sea, ranks 114th in land area and 79th in size of population. With a per capita GNP of $780, the Dominican Republic is officially designated one of the lower middle-income countries of the world. It ranks 66th on the combined economic and social indicators scale and 73rd on the physical quality of life index. Its per capita GNP annual growth rate of 6.6% is more than double the annual growth rate of the population at 3.0%. In fact, the Dominican Republic ranks ninth in per capita GNP annual growth rate. The economy is predominantly agricultural with sugar and cocoa as the principal products. The country ranks 10th in gold production.

EAST GERMANY

East Germany ranks 100th in land area and 42nd in population. With a per capita GNP of $4,220, East Germany is officially classified as a developed high-income country. It ranks 13th on the combined economic and social indicators scale and 12th on the physical quality of life index. East Germany is one of two countries in the world with a negative annual population growth rate (−0.2%); despite this advantage, its per capita GNP growth rate is only a modest 3.7%. East Germany appears among the top 10 in 27 rankings, of which 12 are educational, cultural and media rankings: fourth in university professors, 10th in volumes borrowed from public libraries, eighth in volumes in public libraries, fifth in post-secondary enrollment ratio, eighth in secondary school enrollment ratio, third in Nobel laureates (combined with West Germany), sixth in graduate population, ninth in educational expenditures per pupil, second in literacy, third in circulation of daily newspapers, first in educational enrollment and sixth in museum attendance. East Germany is the most highly industrialized country in Eastern Europe and has the world's fourth highest percentage of population in the industrial work force, but it does not appear among the top 10 in any strictly industrial rankings. Its performance is better in agricultural production rankings: ninth in meat production and beer production, fourth in production of cigars, seventh in production of potatoes, and sixth in production of butter. East Germany's other distinctions include ranking 10th in television sets per capita and second in pigs per capita. As in many other countries with low birth rates, the divorce rate is high, and East Germany ranks 10th in this respect.

ECUADOR

Straddling the equator on the Pacific coast of South America, Ecuador is the third smallest South American country, the world's 63rd largest and 65th most populous. With a per capita GNP of $640, Ecuador is one of the 39 lower middle-income countries of the world. It ranks 69th on the combined social and economic indicators scale and 70th on the physical quality of life index. Recent increases in oil production have enabled Ecuador to achieve a per capita GNP annual growth rate of 6.1% (the 11th highest in the world), while the population growth rate has been held to 3.4% (slightly excessive according to demographers). Agriculture is the mainstay of the economy, employing over one-half of the labor force and contributing more than one-quarter of the GDP. The most important crops are bananas, of which Ecuador is the world's largest exporter, and cocoa. Petroleum revenues have spurred industries producing a broad range of goods; Ecuador ranks seventh in annual growth rate of industry and second on the manufacturing index. Ecuador ranks second only to Venezuela in oil production among South American countries. Ecuador ranks second in the world in horses per capita. On the negative side, the nation ranks sixth in maternal mortality rate.

EGYPT

Egypt is the most populous country in the Arab world, the second most populous in Africa and the 20th most populous in the world. Nearly 99% of the population is compressed into 3.5% of the land area, one of the most skewed population distributions in the world. In the valley of the Nile, the population density is the fifth highest in the world. With a per capita GNP of $280, Egypt is officially classified as a low-income country. It ranks 88th on the combined economic and social indicators scale and 89th on the physical quality of life index. Efforts to control the growth of population are only sporadic, but have brought the growth rate down to 2.2% ahead of the GNP annual growth rate of 1.3%. The Egyptian economy remains agriculture-based, as it has been for centuries, and the most encouraging rankings are found in this sector: first in irrigated lands (100% of the cultivated area is irrigated), 10th in cheese production, and eighth in the production of cotton fiber. The country's farmland is intensively cultivated with usually two and sometimes three crops annually, and yields per acre are extremely high. Nevertheless, Egypt is not self-sufficient in food and ranks fourth in share of food in imports. The 30-year hostilities with Israel (to which the 1979 peace treaty has brought about an end or at least a pause) have been ruinous for the Egyptian economy. The country ranks first in the world in defense expenditures as percentage of GNP and eighth in total defense expenditures, a burden out of all proportion to its internal resources. Chronic balance of payments difficulties have forced Egypt to borrow heavily and thus add to its already substantial debt service ratio. Egypt ranks 10th in external public debt as percentage of GNP. Despite restrictions, imports have grown every year since the 1960s, and Egypt ranks seventh in annual import growth rate. There are a few bright spots, however, in the educational field. The country ranks 10th in foreign students in domestic universities. Within Africa, it has the highest post-secondary enrollment ratio and the largest stock of scientific and engineering manpower.

EL SALVADOR

El Salvador, the smallest mainland American republic, ranks 131st in land area and 89th in size of population. With a per capita GNP of $490, El Salvador is one of 39 lower middle-income countries and one of the most seriously affected by recent adverse economic conditions. It ranks 82nd on the combined social and economic indicators scale and 72nd on the physical quality of life index. Its per capita GNP growth rate of 1.9% trails behind the annual population growth rate of 3.0%. Although more industrialized than that of its neighbors, the Salvadoran economy is still agricultural. Coffee, in the production of which El Salvador ranks eighth in the world, accounts for 41% of the exports. The country's basic problems include heavy population pressure on available land, a high birth rate (a significant proportion of births are illegitimate; El Salvador ranks ninth in illegitimate births), a high illiteracy rate and a very uneven distribution of income.

EQUATORIAL GUINEA

The least populous nation in black Africa, Equatorial Guinea ranks 126th in land area and 147th in population. With a per capita GNP of $240, it is one of the 49 low-income countries. It ranks 103rd on the combined social and economic indicators scale and 120th on the physical quality of life index. Its population growth rate, a low 1.7%, must be considered excessive in relation to the negative annual growth rate of per capita GNP at −3.7%. Equatorial Guinea appears among the top 10 only in one ranking: in percentage of land under forests, where it ranks ninth.

ETHIOPIA

The oldest nation in the world according to the Age of Nations ranking, Ethiopia ranks 22nd in land area and 26th in population. With a per capita GNP of $100, the fourth lowest in the world, Ethiopia is officially classified as one of the least-developed, low-income countries. More than 75% of the population subsist in absolute poverty. It ranks 140th on a combined social and economic indicators scale and 146th on the physical quality of life index. Because of a high death rate (in which it ranks sixth), the annual population growth is only 2.6%, but the GNP per capita grows at a much slower pace of 0.4%. The great majority of the economically active population is engaged in the most inefficient type of subsistence farming; nevertheless, Ethiopia is nearly self-sufficient in agricultural produce and ranks eighth in agriculture's share of the GDP. The principal export is coffee, which is believed to have been grown first in the Ethiopian highlands, and in coffee production the nation ranks seventh. The nation's recent domestic troubles are reflected in its seventh ranking in civil disorders.

FIJI

A group of some 320 islands (of which 105 are inhabited) in the Melanesian island chain, Fiji ranks 133rd in land area and 137th in population. With a per capita GNP of $1,130, Fiji is officially classified as one of the upper middle-income countries. It ranks 50th on a combined social and economic indicators scale and 51st on the physical quality of life index. The per capita GNP annual growth rate of 5.5% is impressive for a small country with limited resources; at the same time its population growth rate is a modest 2.0%. The sugar industry is the mainstay of the Fijian economy, accounting for over two-thirds of Fiji's exports, one-fifth of its GNP and one-fourth of the wage-earning labor force. Tourism is the second most important sector and largest foreign exchange earner. Fiji ranks ninth in tourist revenues per tourist. It has also a well-developed educational system and ranks fourth in school enrollment per capita. On the negative side, Fiji ranks second in the criminal ratio and eighth in crime rate.

FINLAND

The second northernmost country in Europe, Finland ranks 55th in land area and 90th in population.

With a per capita GNP of $5,620, Finland is a high-income developed country. It ranks sixth on a combined social and economic indicators scale and 19th on the physical quality of life index. Its per capita GNP annual growth rate of 4.1% is 10 times its annual population growth rate of 0.4%. Finland appears among the top 10 in 36 rankings. It makes its best showing in educational, cultural and health-related rankings. In the educational sector it ranks first in secondary school enrollment ratio, fifth in educational expenditures per pupil, first in scientific and engineering manpower, second in literacy and eighth in percentage of women in university enrollment. In the health sector it ranks first in mental hospital beds, sixth in dentists per capita, ninth in health expenditures per capita, eighth in inhabitants per hospital bed and second in nurses per capita. In the media field it ranks seventh in advertising expenditures, sixth in circulation of daily newspapers and press freedom, and second in volumes borrowed from public libraries. The Finns are the third highest consumers of coffee. Although agriculture employs only 20% of the labor force, Finland is virtually self-sufficient in grains, meat and dairy products. Most farms are small, but the country ranks fifth in farm ownership. The leading agricultural product is oats, in whose production Finland ranks seventh. The economy is essentially based on forestry and wood processing, and forest products account for about 50% of the exports. Finland's other interesting rankings include: fourth in percentage of professional and technical workers, 10th in unionized labor, fourth in new houses per 1,000, seventh in stock market performance of industrial shares, and first in both registered voters and on the political opposition index. On the negative side, Finland ranks second in abortions, fourth in suicides, first in mental hospital admissions and criminal ratio, fourth in crime ratio and second in drug-related offenses.

FRANCE

The largest country in Europe (excluding the Soviet Union), France ranks 44th in land area and 15th in population. With the fifth highest GNP and a per capita GNP of $6,550, France is the fifth leading economic power in the world. It ranks fourth on the combined economic and social indicators scale and ninth on the physical quality of life index. Like other industrialized oil-consuming countries, its per capita GNP annual growth rate has slowed down to 3.4% but is nevertheless comfortably ahead of its population growth rate of 0.8%. France appears among the top 10 in 75 rankings spread over a broad spectrum. It is one of the few industrial powers where agriculture continues to play a key role in the economy. France stands out in nine agricultural rankings: it is third in butter production, fourth in cheese production, third in milk production, eighth in oats production, seventh in wheat production, fourth in barley production, 10th in sugar production, fourth in wool production, and, of course, first in wine production. Frenchmen are also among the top 10 consumers of wine (second), proteins (second), coffee (eighth), rubber (sixth), paper (ninth) and meat (sixth). France's highly developed and diversified industrial sector generates almost one-half of the GNP and employs 40% of the work force. It ranks seventh in cement production, eighth in aluminum production, seventh in steel production, 10th in sugar production, seventh in production of television sets, fourth in production of passenger cars and sixth in production of pig iron. In the communications sector, France ranks third in aviation (distance flown), sixth in number of tourists, 10th in domestic mail per capita, eighth in cargo handled by ports, fifth in length of pipelines, ninth in merchant marine, third in aviation (passengers carried), seventh in radio receivers per capita, ninth in passenger cars per capita, seventh in inland navigation and fourth in civil aircraft and motorcycles. In the fields of education and culture, France ranks sixth in number of primary schools, secondary school enrollment ratio and production of scientific books, seventh in book production, fourth in Nobel laureates, fifth in contribution to scientific authorship, third in foreign students in domestic universities, third in production of films and fifth in number of cinemas. As the sixth most powerful military nation, France ranks high in a number of military rankings: sixth in men and women under arms, fifth in total defense expenditures and ninth in defense expenditures per capita. Although France has virtually no domestic oil production, it appears among the top 10 in three energy rankings: fifth in nuclear energy production, fourth in petroleum refinery capacity, and sixth in uranium production. In the financial sector, France ranks fifth in currency per capita, fourth in foreign aid per capita, fourth in SDR quotas and third in gold holdings. In the health sector France is 10th in nurses per capita and sixth in health expenditures per capita.

FRENCH GUYANA

Located on the northern coast of South America, French Guyana is best known as a former penal colony. With a GNP per capita of $800, it is officially classified as a lower middle-income country. It appears among the top 10 in six rankings: 10th in annual population growth rate, second in pharmacists per capita, eighth in commercial vehicles per capita, and first in land under forests. It is also first in fatal industrial accidents.

GABON

Spanning the equator on the west coast of Africa, Gabon ranks 48th in land area and 141st in population. A small population and enormous mineral resources have combined to make Gabon one of the wealthiest nations in black Africa, with a per capita GNP of $2,960, and one of the four African nations in the upper middle-income group. Gabon ranks 57th on the combined economic and social indicators scale and 139th on the physical quality of life index, which reveals that the benefits of national wealth have not reached the people. While the annual population growth rate is only 1.0% (the lowest in Africa), the per capita GNP is climbing at a healthy clip of 6.4%. Gabon is also one of the most Christian countries in Africa with over 50% of the population professing the Christian faith. Gabon's inhabitants are heavily concentrated in urban areas, and Gabon ranks second in percentage of population in cities over 50,000. Agricultural land is abundant; Gabon ranks ninth in agricultural land per capita. It also ranks fourth in land under forests. It is the world's leading exporter of manganese and ninth leading producer of uranium. Its reserves of iron ore are believed to exceed 1 billion tons of 65% purity. Its last and most important source of wealth is oil, which, however, may be exhausted by 1985. Gabon ranks ninth in annual export growth rate. Despite apparent prosperity, the educational and health indicators are uniformly negative. It ranks among the bottom countries in life expectancy, literacy and infant mortality.

GAMBIA

The Gambia, the smallest country in Africa, ranks 138th in land area and 140th in size of population. With a per capita GNP of $200, the Gambia is officially classified as one of the least-developed, low-income countries. It ranks 126th on a combined economic and social indicators scale and 137th on the physical quality of life index. Its population growth rate and its per capita GNP growth rate are remarkably close: 2.7% and 2.6% respectively. The Gambia has a classic one-crop economy based on peanuts, which account for 90% of the value of all exports. Because almost all available land is cultivated, the Gambia ranks eighth in land under cultivation. Nevertheless, because of the precarious economic base, the dalasi, the Gambia's monetary unit, is the second weakest currency in the world.

GHANA

Located on the west coast of Africa, Ghana ranks 71st in land area and 53rd in population. With a per capita GNP of $580, Ghana is officially classified as a lower middle-income country and is also one of the 45 countries most seriously affected by recent adverse economic conditions. It ranks 96th on the combined social and economic indicators scale and 115th on the physical quality of life index. Its per capita GNP annual growth rate, declining for many years, is now negative (-0.3%); this decline is compounded by a high population annual growth rate of 2.7% that has not responded to family planning measures. The major crop and exchange earner is cocao and the country's economic health falls and rises with the wildly fluctuating price of cocao on world markets. Ghana ranks seventh in gold production and fifth in diamond production. Thanks to a vast hydroelectric project on the Volta River, Ghana ranks 10th in energy production annual growth rate and first in Africa in aluminum production. At the same time, Ghana suffers from the highest inflation rate in Africa; it is among the top 10 in the world on the consumer price index (both food and general) and the wholesale price index.

GREECE

Greece ranks 89th in land area and 60th in population. With a per capita GNP of $2,590, Greece is officially classified as a high-income developed country. It ranks 35th on the combined social and economic indicators scale and 30th on the physical quality of life index. As in other developed countries, the per capita GNP annual growth rate exceeds the population growth rate, by 4.2% to 0.6%. About 75% of Greece is mountainous and only the balance is arable. Even with such a constraint, Greece produces a variety of crops and ranks sixth on the per capita agricultural production index, seventh in production of proteins and eighth in wine production. It ranks ninth in tobacco production and eighth in cigarette production. Sheep raising is important, and the nation ranks eighth in wool production. Because of its easy accessibility to the sea, Greece has a large merchant fleet, ranking fourth in the world in gross registered tonnage. Greece suffers from a chronic trade deficit, which is partially covered by invisible receipts from shipping, tourism and Greek workers' remittances from abroad. In the fields of education and health Greece ranks high three times: third in study abroad, eighth in dentists per capita and 10th in physicians per capita.

GUATEMALA

The northernmost and the most populous of the Central American republics, Guatemala ranks 99th in land area and 72nd in population. With a per capita GNP of $630, Guatemala is officially classified as a lower middle-income country and also as one of the 45 countries most seriously affected by recent adverse economic conditions. It ranks 85th on the combined economic and social indicators scale and 80th in the physical quality of life index. Its per capita GNP annual growth rate of 2.8% is only slightly less than its population growth rate of 2.9%. The economy is primarily agricultural with coffee, in the production of which the country ranks ninth, as the single most important source of foreign exchange. Wide disparities characterize the social and income distribution structure. The political system is noted for its proliferation of political parties, and the nation ranks third in the political opposition index.

GUINEA

Located on the bulge of West Africa, Guinea ranks 69th in land area and 81st in population. With a per capita GNP of $150, Guinea is officially classified as one of the least-developed, low-income countries and as one of the 45 countries most seriously affected by recent adverse economic conditions. It ranks 123rd on the combined social and economic indicators scale and 140th on the physical quality of life index. The population grows annually by 2.4% despite the fourth highest infant mortality rate in the world; the growth rate is sustained by a high fertility rate, in which Guinea ranks eighth. As a result Guinea's

economy has never really taken off and its per capita GNP growth rate hovers around an anemic 1.3%. Although mining is the key sector of the economy, the bulk of the work force is employed in agriculture, and Guinea ranks second in annual growth rate of agriculture. The country claims the third largest deposits of bauxite. Little of this enormous mineral wealth has been translated into improvements in living standards, however, and over 75% of the population subsist in absolute poverty. Guinea has also recklessly incurred an insupportable burden of foreign debt and ranks first in the world in external public debt as a percentage of GNP.

GUINEA-BISSAU

Located on the West African coast, Guinea-Bissau ranks 120th in land area and 139th in population. With a per capita GNP of $230, Guinea-Bissau is officially classified as one of the least-developed, low-income countries. Until its independence Guinea-Bissau had a per capita GNP annual growth rate of 5.4%. The annual population growth rate of 1.3% is the second lowest in Africa and is a most hopeful sign for this comparatively young nation. Guinea-Bissau appears among the top 10 in only two rankings, both negative: first in illegitimate births and ninth in the death rate.

GUYANA

Located on the northern Atlantic coast of South America, Guyana ranks 75th in land area and 133rd in population. With a per capita GNP of $530, Guyana is officially designated a lower middle-income country and is considered one of the 45 countries most seriously affected by recent adverse economic conditions. It ranks 59th on the combined social and economic indicators scale and 49th on the physical quality of life index. While the population growth rate remains high at 2.2% (reflecting the high fertility rate of the East Indian segment of the population), the per capita GNP has actually declined. Traditionally an agrarian economy based on sugar and rice, the exploitation of bauxite and the production of alumina have provided the stimulus for industrialization. Because most of the land lies below the high tide mark of the sea and because the rivers' cultivation is dependent on a system of dikes and dams, Guyana ranks fourth in irrigation. As in other countries with an East Indian majority, movie attendance is high and the country ranks 10th in this respect. On the negative side, Guyana ranks second in crime rate, third in suicides, and fourth in criminal ratio.

HAITI

Haiti occupies the western third of the island of Hispaniola in the Caribbean, and ranks 128th in land area and 87th in population. The sixth most densely populated country in the Western Hemisphere, Haiti is also one of the poorest with a per capita GNP of $200. It is officially classified as one of the least-developed, low-income countries and is one of the 45 countries most seriously affected by recent adverse economic conditions. It ranks 121st on the combined social and economic indicators scale and 115th on the physical quality of life index. Its annual growth rates of population and per capita GNP are remarkably close: 1.6% and 1.5% respectively. Apart from its poverty, Haiti is best known as the only republic in the Western Hemisphere where French is the official language and where voodoo is widely practiced. Haiti appears among the top 10 only in two key rankings: it ranks sixth in share of food in imports and in linguistic and ethnic homogeneity. Within the Western Hemisphere it ranks first in percentage of women in the labor force and in the percentage of the total labor force in agriculture.

HONDURAS

One of the "banana republics" of Central America, Honduras ranks 96th in land area and 109th in population. With a per capita GNP of $390, Honduras is officially classified as a lower middle-income country and also one of the 45 countries most seriously affected by recent adverse economic conditions. It ranks 94th on the combined social and economic indicators scale and 84th on the physical quality of life index. While the country's annual population growth rate of 3.9% is the fifth highest in the world, the per capita GNP growth rate is a discouraging 0.8%. The poor economic growth rate is blamed on the disruptions that followed the Soccer War with neighboring El Salvador. Although the U.S.-owned banana companies no longer wield the influence they once did, bananas remain the staple crop, but coffee, timber and beef are growing in importance. Horse raising is a major economic activity and the country ranks eighth in horses per capita. The country also ranks fourth in gains in labor productivity.

HONG KONG

The British crown colony of Hong Kong is located on the southeastern coast of the China mainland and consists of two large islands, 200 smaller islands and a portion of the mainland. It ranks 155th in land area and 91st in population. Hong Kong is the most populous nonself-governing territory in the world. Since 1949 when the Communists took over the mainland, thousands of refugees have crossed the border making Hong Kong the second most densely populated area in the world, with densities of over 38,610 per sq km (100,000 per sq mi). With a per capita GNP of $1,570, Hong Kong is classified as an upper middle-income country and it ranks 33rd on the physical quality of life index. Its per capita GNP growth rate is more than double its annual population growth rate of 2.0%. Hong Kong has virtually no natural resources, but it is one of the greatest banking, trading and transshipment centers in the world. Utilizing its abundant supply of cheap labor, Hong Kong has become a leading manufacturer of textiles, garments, plastics, electrical and electronic equipment, rubber products, machinery, chemicals and ceramics. It ranks second in percentage of work force employed in industry and first in the production of radio receivers. With over 146,000 registered vehicles, the colony has the third highest vehicle density per mile of roadway in the world. Tourism is becoming a major source of revenue, and the colony ranks seventh in tourist receipts per tourist. Hong Kong leads the world in per capita consumption of cotton and ranks sixth in the consumption of tea. Operating on pay-as-you-go budgets, Hong Kong has shown a surplus of revenues over expenditures every year but three since World War II. Hong Kong is also noted as one of the most important Asian centers of motion picture production, banking and insurance, and printing and publishing. It ranks 10th in film production and eighth in movie attendance per capita. The colony also ranks sixth on the construction index and fourth in students studying abroad. On the negative side, Hong Kong leads the world in drug-related offenses, a throwback to the days of the Opium War which led to the initial British occupation of the island.

HUNGARY

Hungary ranks 104th in land area and 55th in size of population. With a per capita GNP of $2,280, Hungary is classified as a high-income developed country. It ranks 26th on the combined social and economic indicators scale and 27th on the physical quality of life index. Since 1960 the annual population growth rate has been less than 0.5% and is now close to zero. On the other hand, the per capita GNP annual growth rate is fairly stable at 3.2%. Hungary's prewar agricultural economy has been transformed under the Communist government into an industrialized one; nevertheless, Hungary is self-sufficient in food crops and even exports some to Western Europe. Hungary's strong export capacity and favorable balance of trade have combined to make the forint the world's eighth strongest currency. Hungary ranks high in two agricultural rankings: fifth in per capita food production and seventh in land under cultivation. Despite growing industrial strength, Hungary does not appear among the top 10 in any strictly industrial ranking except percentage of work force in industry, in which it ranks sixth. The country makes its strongest showing in educational and cultural rankings: it ranks third in vocational enrollment, ninth in percentage of women in university enrollment, fourth in expenditures on scientific research, eighth in scientists in basic research, sixth in scientific and engineering manpower, fourth in teacher-pupil ratio in primary schools, ninth in volumes borrowed from public libraries and eighth in the production of scientific books. In the related media and communications rankings, it ranks ninth in the number of cinemas and seventh in telegrams per capita. The high quality of health care is reflected in the country's sixth rank in physicians per capita. On the negative side, Hungary ranks first in abortions per live births, second in suicides and 11th in divorce rates.

ICELAND

Iceland, the westernmost country in Europe, ranks 101st in the world in land area and 152nd in population. Historically a democracy, its parliament, the Althing, is the oldest representative assembly in the world, founded in 930. With a per capita GNP of $6,100 Iceland is classified as a high-income developed country. It ranks 11th on the combined social and economic indicators scale and second on the physical quality of life index. The per capita GNP annual growth rate seems to have leveled off at 1.9%; so has the population growth rate at 1.1%. Iceland has the highest book readership per capita and not surprisingly is also first in school enrollment ratio, ranks second in literacy, third in

number of university teachers and sixth in volumes borrowed from public libraries. Although only 11% of the population is employed in agriculture (as compared to 14% in fishing and 30% in manufacturing and construction), Iceland ranks high in five agricultural rankings: first in tractors per hectare, third in horses per capita, seventh in sheep per capita, and eighth in agricultural land per capita and consumption of proteins. Iceland's near perfect rating on the physical quality of life index is based partly on its third rank in life expectancy for females and second rank in life expectancy for males. In a number of areas it fares better than larger developed countries: it ranks 10th in passenger cars per capita, fourth in electric energy per capita, ninth in population per hospital bed, 10th in telephones per capita, fourth in telegrams per capita, eighth in spacious houses and fifth in circulation of dailies per capita. The Icelandic economy, which is dependent on a broad range of exports, has been hard hit by world prices. Its rate of inflation is the highest in Western Europe and has necessitated two devaluations of the krona since 1974, making it the seventh weakest currency in the world. Iceland's economic plight has been intensified by a drop in the world prices for fish, its major export. The country ranks seventh on the consumer food index (food and all items) and fifth on the rent index. Another negative ranking is mental hospital admissions in which Iceland ranks sixth.

INDIA

The largest country on the Indian subcontinent, India is the second most populous country in the world and the seventh largest. Although it occupies only 2.09% of the world's land area, it supports 14% of the world's population. More languages are spoken and more religions professed in India than in any other country. Ray Cline ranks India as the ninth most powerful nation in the world. With a per capita GNP of $150, India is classified as a low-income country and as one of the 45 countries most seriously affected by recent adverse economic conditions. It ranks 111th on the combined social and economic indicators scale and 98th on the physical quality of life index. Although the birth rate has been reduced from 43 per 1,000 in 1963 to 38 per 1,000, the annual population growth rate is still 2.1%, a cause of alarm particularly because the per capita GNP growth rate is only 0.5%. Agriculture is the mainstay of the economy supporting 90% of the economically active population, and India ranks among the top 10 in 14 agricultural rankings: second in rice production, fifth in sugar production, first in peanut production, fourth in cotton fiber production, fifth in rubber production, fourth in wheat production, third in tobacco production, seventh in fish catch, sixth in production of roundwood, fourth in production of milk, ninth in production of corn, sixth in production of potatoes, second in production of cheese and fourth in production of butter. India also ranks first in Asia in average size of farms. Despite such productive capacity, India is not self-sufficient in food products and suffers periodically from food shortages and even famine. Industry has been greatly expanded in recent years but still employs less than 10% of the work force and the country appears among the top 10 only in one industrial ranking: 10th in production of pig iron. The principal mineral resources are mica, manganese and ilmenite, which are all fully exploited. In addition India ranks sixth in coal production and seventh in production of iron ore and uranium. With one of the largest educational systems in the world, India leads in the number of primary schools and also places seventh in the number of students attending foreign universities. The most encouraging rankings are those relating to transportation, communications and media. India ranks eighth in tourist receipts per tourist, 10th in radio receivers per capita, second in number of locomotives and ninth in length of inland navigation. It has the ninth largest book industry in the world in terms of annual output of titles and second largest press in terms of circulation per capita. It is the world's top producer of full-length films (mostly of indifferent quality) and ranks sixth in number of cinemas. Cline regards India as the seventh most powerful military nation and it ranks fourth in men under arms.

INDONESIA

An archipelago of some 13,500 islands extending along the Equator for over 4,800 km (3,000 mi), Indonesia is the fifth most populous nation in the world and the 16th largest in size. Although overall density is moderate, Java is one of the most densely populated areas of the world with over 75 million inhabitants compressed into an area the size of New York state. With a per capita GNP of $240, Indonesia is classified as a low-income country and it is the only oil-producing country in this category. It ranks 110th on the combined economic and social indica-

tors scale and 84th on the physical quality of life index. Its per capita GNP annual growth rate and annual population growth rate are extremely close: 3.5% and 3.6%. Despite being one of the largest and most populous countries of the world and one richly endowed in natural resources, it appears among the top 10 in only 17 positive rankings, highlighting its underdevelopment. In the agricultural sector it ranks third in rice production, seventh in peanut production, second in rubber production, fifth in soybean production and fifth in roundwood production. The country's geography necessitates an extensive communications and transportation network as reflected in at least six rankings: fourth rank in inland navigation, second rank in coastlines, first rank in usable airfields, ninth rank in number of civil aircraft and seventh rank in radio transmitters. The impact of inflation may be measured by Indonesia's 10th rank in consumer price index (food) and eighth rank in wholesale price index. As a supplier of raw materials, Indonesia invariably has a favorable balance of trade in which it ranks ninth in terms of trade. In addition to petroleum, it is the sixth ranking producer of nickel. Other significant rankings include fifth in number of primary schools and fifth on the construction index and ninth in number of daily newspapers.

IRAN

Located in southwestern Asia, Iran is larger than all countries of the European Economic Community; it ranks 14th in land area and 21st in population. With a per capita GNP of $1,930, Iran is classified as one of the 35 upper middle-income countries of the world. It ranks 65th on the combined economic and social indicators scale and 103rd on the physical quality of life index. Iran leads the world in annual growth rate of per capita GNP. With such a rate it can obviously tolerate its high population growth rate of 2.9%. Oil is the lifeblood of the Iranian economy and it ranks high in all the key energy rankings: fifth in energy production, seventh in natural gas production, fourth in production of crude petroleum, second in petroleum exports, fourth in petroleum reserves and second in natural gas reserves. Oil revenues have enabled Iran to achieve a commanding position in international trade. It ranks second in annual export growth rate, seventh in ratio of international reserves to imports, third in balance of trade, ninth in ratio of exports to imports and fourth in terms of trade. Oil revenues are also used in a two-pronged effort to industralize and militarize the country. Total defense expenditures have soared to seventh highest in the world, and as a percentage of GNP they rank fourth. Although Iran ranks fourth in industrial share of GDP, agriculture supports 75% of the population, and modernization and mechanization programs have pushed Iran to the seventh rank in agricultural production index. The principal product is cotton fiber, in the production of which Iran ranks 10th. About one-third of the cultivated land is irrigated and Iran ranks ninth in this respect. Other distinctions include ninth rank on the construction index, sixth rank on the consumption index, second in native students attending foreign universities, 10th in number of primary schools, first in tourist receipts per tourist, sixth in cargo handled by ports and fifth in index of mineral production. Recently, the strains of rapid growth have become apparent in Iran's rising inflation, the ninth highest in the world. Even before the establishment of the Islamic Republic, Iran ranked fourth in civil disorder.

IRAQ

Known as Mesopotamia or the land between the rivers (i.e., the Tigris and the Euphrates), Iraq ranks 51st in land area and 52nd in population. With a per capita GNP of $1,390, Iraq is classified as an upper middle-income country. It ranks 67th on the combined social and economic indicators scale and 89th on the physical quality of life index. Its per capita GNP, fueled by oil revenues, soars annually by 6.7% (the eighth highest rate in the world); in comparison, its population growth rate of 3.3% (high by normal standards) appears acceptable. Iraq is the sixth largest oil producer in the world (and the fourth largest in the Middle East), and its potential reserves are considered second only to Saudi Arabia's. The impact of oil revenues is most clearly visible in trade indicators where it ranks first in both export and import growth rates. It had the sixth highest balance of trade in 1976. Iraq's hard-line belligerency against Israel is reflected in its fifth rank in defense expenditures as a percentage of GNP. There is very little rainfall and agriculture depends upon irrigation, as a result of which Iraq ranks sixth in irrigated lands. Tea is the national drink: the Iraqis rank fourth in its consumption.

IRELAND

Ireland ranks 110th in land area and 105th in population. Its per capita GNP of $2,560, although low by European standards, nevertheless places it in the category of a high-income developed country. It ranks 21st on the combined social and economic indicators scale and 13th on the physical quality of life index (in the same league as the United States). Its population growth rate, historically among the lowest because of a large proportion of unmarrieds, is currently 1.2%; its per capita GNP growth rate is only slightly higher at 1.3%. Because of its modest economic resources, Ireland appears among the top 10 in only 18 rankings; eight of them relate to the production or consumption of agricultural products. It ranks ninth in wool production, fifth in meat production, sixth in beer (or stout) production and eighth in per capita food production. Irishmen consume the most tea per capita in the world as well as the most calories per capita. They also rank third in consumption of proteins and 10th in consumption of meat. Ireland also stands out in two other agricultural rankings: sixth in cattle per capita and 10th in tractors per hectare.

ISRAEL

Israel, the embattled republic at the eastern end of the Mediterranean Sea, is also one of the most remarkable countries in the world. Estranged from all of its neighbors since its creation, Israel's borders have never been defined except through a hodge podge of armistice agreements and cease-fire lines. A highly developed country with a per capita GNP of $3,920, it has never been considered, in spite of its location, as part of the Third World; on the other hand, Israel has always regarded itself as a bastion of Western values and culture. One of the smallest nations in the world (132nd in land area and 100th in population), it is nevertheless considered by Ray Cline as the fifth most powerful military force. In fact Israel dominates military rankings; it ranks first in both soldier-civilian ratio and defense expenditures per capita and third in U.S. military aid received and defense expenditures as percentage of GNP. And its track record in health, education and welfare is as impressive. It ranks 22nd on the combined social and economic indicators scale and 31st on the physical quality of life index. It ranks among the top 10 in 11 rankings relating to education and health: first in stock of university professors, teacher-pupil ratio in primary schools, third in graduate population and percentage of professional and technical workers, fourth in dentists and physicians per capita, eighth in post-secondary enrollment ratio and scientific and engineering manpower, and 10th in educational expenditures as percentage of GNP. Despite adverse conditions, agriculture has developed to a degree that compares favorably with advanced countries and meets all domestic needs other than grains. It ranks sixth in annual growth rate of agriculture and agricultural production index and 10th in irrigated lands. Because of the need to provide homes for immigrants, building construction has boomed and Israel ranks second in new houses per 1,000. For security and other reasons, Israelis prefer to live in urban settlements and the country ranks ninth in urbanization. Along with an 88% literacy rate, Israel has the 10th highest daily newspaper circulation per capita. There is a dark side to this picture. The crushing burden of defense, chronic trade deficits and declining foreign exchange reserves have led to a weakening of the Israeli pound, now the world's fourth weakest currency. Israel ranks seventh in external public debt as percentage of GNP. Its rate of inflation is the 10th highest in the world, and it ranks among the top 10 on both the wholesale price index and consumer price index (food and all items). Israel also ranks 10th in mental hospital admissions.

ITALY

A peninsula extending from the Alps to within 145 km (90 mi) of Africa, Italy ranks 60th in land area and 14th in population. Italy has the fifth highest density in Europe. With a per capita GNP of $3,050, Italy is classified as a high-income developed country. It ranks 24th on the combined social and economic indicators scale and 23rd on the physical quality of life index. The annual population growth rate is only 0.8%—the same as for the United States—but the battered Italian economy is limping along at a rate of 1.7%—slightly better than that of the United States. By comparison with other European countries, Italy is poorly endowed in natural resources. It has neither coal nor iron ore but some natural gas and petroleum. Nevertheless it is the fourth largest industrial power in Europe; it ranks sixth in the production of steel, ninth in aluminum production, eighth in pig iron production, fifth in passenger car production, ninth in television set production, fourth in cement production, sixth in wool production and third in petroleum refinery capacity. Its rankings are equally impressive in the transportation and communications sector: eighth in aviation (distances flown), ninth in motor cycles and in number of locomotives, 10th in merchant marine

and civil aircraft, fifth in television transmitters and third in radio transmitters, sixth in cargo handled by ports and pipelines, and fourth in tourists. Agriculture contributes only 11% of the GNP but Italy claims second rank in wine production, sixth in cheese production, 10th in milk production, seventh in egg production and 10th in wheat production. Despite its periodic bouts with near bankruptcy, Italy ranks fifth in gold holdings and seventh in SDR quotas. As a senior partner of the North Atlantic Treaty Organization (NATO), Italy ranks ninth in defense expenditures. Racked by terrorism, the country ranks second in civil disorder. Since the 1960s Rome has partially supplanted Hollywood in the production of certain types of films and Italy ranks fifth in film production as well as fourth in the number of cinemas. Italian universities are the ninth favorite destination of foreign students. Italian scientists rank ninth in their contribution to scientific authorship.

IVORY COAST

The Ivory Coast ranks 58th in land area and 83rd in population. With a per capita GNP of $610, it is one of the richest and economically most self-sufficient of African states; nevertheless, it is classified as a lower middle-income country and as one of the 45 countries most seriously affected by recent adverse economic conditions. It ranks 92nd on the combined social and economic indicators scale and 122nd on the physical quality of life index. Its per capita GNP annual growth rate of 1.9% does not match its population growth rate of 2.5%. The country's principal distinction is its rank as the world's third largest coffee producer.

JAMAICA

The largest island in the Caribbean after Cuba and Hispaniola, Jamaica ranks 140th in size and 119th in population. With a per capita GNP of $1,430, Jamaica is classified as an upper middle-income country. It ranks 43rd on the combined social and economic indicators scale and 42nd on the physical quality of life index. The annual per capita GNP growth rate is a healthy 4.0% and its growth is no doubt helped by the low population growth rate of 1.7%. Jamaica's principal distinction is that it is the world's largest bauxite producer. Tourism is the second largest foreign exchange earner. However, cutbacks in bauxite production and a decline in tourism following racial riots have led to extensive unemployment, in which the island ranks first in the world.

JAPAN

An arc of mountainous islands off the east coast of Asia, Japan ranks 54th in land area and seventh in size of population. Although less than 20% of the land is arable, density is third highest in the world in the arable areas. A population growth rate that fell to 0.8% in the 1950s has stabilized at about 1.2% and Japan is expected to reach a stationary population by 2045. The population is remarkably homogeneous and also physically healthy; in life expectancy Japanese men rank fifth and Japanese women eighth. The capital, Tokyo, is the second most populous city in the world, and Japan ranks fourth in percentage of population in cities over 50,000. Japan is the third most powerful economic nation, outranked only by the United States and the Soviet Union. Japan's phenomenal economic growth is the result of a unique ability to blend two opposing economic tendencies: government activism with free enterprise and private ownership with public-spirited management. Japan is also the world's second largest foreign aid donor. The per capita GNP, currently $4,910, is the highest in Asia and is growing at an annual rate of 4.0%. Japan ranks 24th on the combined social and economic indicators scale and sixth on the physical quality of life index with a rating of 98. The key element of Japanese economic power is manufacturing; Japan surpasses all non-Communist countries in the rate of growth in this sector. Japanese industry is also characterized by diversity, efficiency and technological skill. Japan is the third largest producer of steel and the world's largest producer of television sets. It is by far the world's biggest shipbuilder, with the gross tonnage of its output exceeding that of its four closest competitors combined. It ranks second in production of passenger cars, radio receivers, cement and pig iron; ninth in the production of tobacco and cigarettes and 10th in the production of wool. It is the world's sixth largest exporter and ranks second only to Canada as a U.S. trading partner. All arable land is intensively cultivated and per-acre crop yields are among the highest in the world. Japan is the sixth largest rice producer, supplying all domestic requirements, and the fourth largest egg producer. As the world's largest fishing nation, Japan claims nearly 15% of the world's fish catch and the Japanese consume more fish per capita than any other people. Japan ranks fourth in the consumption of steel, seventh in the consumption of rubber and ninth in the consumption of tea. In the transportation and communications sector, Japan ranks fifth in aviation (distances flown), 10th in cargo handled by ports, second in merchant marine, sixth in motorcycles, sixth in number of locomotives, third in commercial vehicles, fifth in civil aircraft, fifth in radio transmitters, first in television transmitters, ninth in radios per capita, and 10th in aviation (passengers carried). Japan ranks among the top 10 in seven educational and scientific rankings: sixth in contribution to scientific authorship, ninth in expenditures on scientific research, second in scientists in basic research, third in scientific and engineering manpower, second in secondary school enrollment ratio, eighth in students attending universities abroad and eighth in university professors. The yen, Japan's monetary unit, is the fifth strongest currency and Japan's financial vigor is reflected in a number of other rankings as well: 10th rank in gold holdings, fifth in SDR quotas, fourth in stock market performance of industrial shares and seventh lowest in discount rate of central bank. Another area of strength is media and culture; the country ranks second in production of scientific books and films, seventh in volumes borrowed from public libraries, second in circulation of daily newspapers, eighth in number of daily newspapers and sixth in book production. Because Japan has no oil, it ranks fourth in share of fuel in imports; however, it ranks second in petroleum refinery capacity and third in the production of nuclear energy. The only two mineral rankings in which it appears among the top 10 are gold (fourth rank) and silver (seventh rank). As the sixth most powerful nation, it ranks 10th in total defense expenditures. The construction rate for new housing is the highest in the world and Japan's goal is "one house for each family." On the negative side, Japan ranks third in abortions and 10th in suicides.

JORDAN

A nearly landlocked nation in the heart of the Arab world, Jordan ranks 103rd in land area and 108th in population. With a per capita GNP of $610, Jordan is classified as a lower middle-income country. It ranks 87th on the combined social and economic indicators scale and the physical quality of life index, a remarkable coincidence in itself. Its annual population growth rate of 3.3% is almost double that of its per capita GNP (1.9%). Jordan is one of the many countries that have managed to pull themselves up by U.S. bootstraps. Through effective use of U.S. aid, Jordan has achieved the sixth highest annual industrial growth rate and export growth rate in the world. The economic revival has created a record demand for imports, in the growth rate of which Jordan ranks 10th. The burden of hostilities with Israel is reflected in two rankings: ninth in defense expenditures as percentage of GNP and third in civilian-soldier ratio.

KENYA

A country of striking topographical and climatic variety located on the equator, Kenya ranks 43rd in land area and population. With a per capita GNP of $240, Kenya is classified as a low-income country and as one of the 45 countries most seriously affected by recent adverse economic conditions. It ranks 101st on the combined social and economic indicators scale and 100th on the physical quality of life index. Its annual population growth rate of 3.6% is the eighth highest in the world, way ahead of its per capita GNP growth rate of 2.4%. Kenya ranks among the top 10 in seven rankings but almost all of them are discouraging, particularly its fifth rank in maternal mortality rate.

KUWAIT

Kuwait, a hereditary emirate located on the Persian Gulf, is a comparatively young nation. It ranks 138th in land area and 124th in size of population. Kuwait's principal distinction is that it has the highest per capita GNP in the world, estimated at $15,-480 and growing. Its wealth is based almost entirely on oil, in the production of which it currently ranks seventh. It also ranks 10th in the production of energy. Its natural gas reserves are the ninth highest and the petroleum reserves the second highest. With its coffers bursting at the seams with petrodollars, Kuwait ranks second in public revenues per capita, fourth in public expenditures per capita and ninth in currency per capita. Prosperity and growth have brought a flood of immigrants who now constitute the majority of the population. In fact Kuwait leads the world in the proportion of aliens among its residents. The impact of oil wealth is felt across the board in educational and health rankings. It ranks 19th on the combined social and economic indicators scale and 60th on the physical quality of life index. It ranks ninth in percentage of professional and technical workers, first in percentage of women in university enrollment, eighth in educational expenditures per pupil and first in Asia in inhabitants per nursing person. Kuwait's population dynamics are buoyant and all indicators are up: the country ranks first in annual population growth rate, fifth in urbanization, second in urban annual growth rate and second in fertility. Oil wealth has also spawned myriad social welfare and public works projects. Kuwait's broad range of state-run social services surpass even that of Scandinavian countries in scope and paternalism. Both education and health-care services are universal and free and the government bears the expenses of Kuwaiti students and medical patients going abroad. Kuwait ranks among the top 10 in all the key trade indicators: it ranks fourth in balance of trade, second in exports per capita, sixth in imports per capita, first in terms of trade, and fourth in ratio of exports to imports. Defense-spending levels have climbed every year until Kuwait now ranks sixth in defense expenditures per capita and per soldier. Growth has not been without problems, however, and Kuwait has the fifth highest rate of inflation in the world.

LAOS

One of five landlocked countries in Asia, Laos ranks 73rd in land area and 101st in population. With a per capita GNP of less than $90, Laos is one of the poorest and least developed of low-income countries and also one of the 45 countries most seriously affected by recent adverse economic conditions. It ranks 129th on the combined social and economic indicators scale and 113th on the physical quality of life index. The per capita GNP growth rate is the lowest in the world, a frightful −15.9%; yet every year there are 2.2% more Laotian mouths to feed. The Laotian monetary unit, the kip, is the weakest currency in the world. The country appears in three other rankings among the top 10 but all are negative.

LEBANON

Once known as the "Switzerland of Asia," strife-torn Lebanon ranks 141st in land area and 114th in population. With a per capita GNP of $1,070 (based on pre-civil war figures; all statistical activities have been suspended in the country). Lebanon is classified as an upper middle-income country. It ranks 48th on the combined social and economic indicators scale and 56th on the physical quality of life index. Its annual population growth rate is estimated to be around 3.0%; it is doubtful that its per capita GNP has grown at all in recent years. Until the civil war Beirut was the focal point for trading activity in the Middle East, and the most important economic sector was service, including transit trade, banking, insurance, tourism and shipping. Lebanese universities attracted students from all over the Middle East, and the country ranked eighth in foreign students in domestic universities. Lebanon also ranked seventh in population density in agricultural areas.

LESOTHO

An enclave located in the east-central part of South Africa, Lesotho ranks 123rd in land area and 130th in size of population. With a per capita GNP of $170, Lesotho is classified as one of the least-developed, low-income countries and it is also one of the 45 countries most seriously affected by recent adverse economic conditions. It ranks 97th on the combined social and economic indicators scale and 86th on the physical quality of life index. It ranks fourth in the world in per capita GNP annual growth rate (7.3%), and its population growth rate of 2.2% is the ninth lowest in Africa. The literacy rate of 40% is among the highest in Africa. Lesotho's economy is based on subsistence agriculture and livestock raising, and the country ranks eighth in percentage of labor force in agriculture and percentage of women in the labor force. As in all transitional societies, the urban growth rate is high and Lesotho ranks ninth in this respect.

LIBERIA

The oldest black republic in Africa, Liberia ranks 97th in land area and 121st in population. With a per capita GNP of $450, Liberia is classified as a lower middle-income country. It ranks 104th on the combined social and economic indicators scale and 130th on the physical quality of life index. Its per capita GNP annual growth rate of 0.9% is outdistanced by the population growth rate of 2.3%. The vital statistics point to even greater population growth; the country ranks first in marriage rate and ninth in birth rate. Liberia is identified most closely with two things; ships and rubber. In terms of gross registered tonnage, the Liberian merchant marine is the world's largest because the Liberian flag is the most popular flag of convenience. Rubber plantations, initiated by the U.S. tire manufacturer Firestone, have made Liberia the world's sixth ranking rubber producer. More recently, rubber has been superseded by iron ore, which accounts for approximately 75% of Liberian exports and in the production of which Liberia ranks ninth.

LIBYA

Libya ranks 13th in land area and 113th in population, the disparity explained by the fact that Libya is mostly desert. With a per capita GNP of $6,310, the highest in Africa, Libya is classified as a high-income but developing country. It ranks 41st on the combined social and economic indicators scale and 96th on the physical quality of life index. Its population growth rate of 4.2% is the highest in Africa and is slightly ahead of its per capita GNP growth rate of 3.9%. With the eighth largest petroleum reserves in the world, Libya ranks 10th in crude oil production. Oil wealth has helped Libya to achieve a commanding position in international trade: it ranks fifth in balance of trade and terms of trade, sixth in ratio of exports to imports and ninth in ratio of international reserves to imports. It has been less successful in translating wealth into standard-of-living improvements, although it ranks eighth in school enrollment per capita and first in Africa in both health expenditures per capita and inhabitants per nursing person. Agriculture is the second largest economic sector and claims the world's highest annual growth rate and second rank in agricultural production index. Nevertheless, Libya is not self-sufficient in food, 60% of which has to be imported. Libya's military ambitions are reflected in its first rank in Africa in soldier-civilian ratio.

LUXEMBOURG

A landlocked country in Western Europe, Luxembourg ranks 149th in land area and 146th in population. With a per capita GNP of $6,390, Luxembourg is a high-income developed country. It ranks 13th on the combined social and economic indicators scale and 14th on the physical quality of life index (on the same rung as the United States). Its annual population growth rate of 1.0% and its per capita GNP growth rate of 2.7% are very close to the European average. Despite its tiny size Luxembourg is highly industrialized; in per capita terms it is the largest steel producer in the world. The steel industry accounts for 47% of industrial production and employs

45% of the industrial labor force. Also in per capita terms Luxembourg is the world's leading beer producer. Due to favorable fiscal policies, the country has become one of Europe's major financial centers with over 80 banks, and banking activity contributes 10% of public revenues. The same reason may explain why Luxembourg has the highest per capita investment by U.S. business in any country outside North America. The Luxembourg franc is the seventh strongest currency in the world. The country ranks fifth in both public revenues and public expenditures per capita. Luxembourg's high standard of living is reflected in a number of rankings: third in energy consumption per capita, fourth in circulation of daily newspapers, sixth in passenger cars per capita, third in consumption of calories, fifth in mental hospital beds and second in spacious houses.

MADAGASCAR

The world's fourth largest island, Madagascar ranks 42nd in land area and 59th in population. With a per capita GNP of $200, Madagascar is a low-income country and one of the nations most seriously affected by recent adverse economic conditions. It ranks 100th on the combined social and economic indicators scale and 93rd on the physical quality of life index. The economy has suffered from a negative per capita GNP growth rate of −2.2%, while the population grows by almost the same rate (2.3%) despite the 10th highest death rate in the world. The Malagasy economy is almost entirely agricultural and the country ranks ninth in the percentage of labor force in agriculture. The principal crop is coffee, in the production of which the country ranks 10th.

MALAWI

Malawi, a landlocked nation on the western side of Lake Malawi, ranks 93rd in land area and 82nd in size of population. With a per capita GNP of $140, Malawi is one of the least-developed, low-income countries. It ranks 124th on the combined social and economic indicators scale and 117th on the physical quality of life index. Malawi has the sixth highest per capita GNP growth rate (7.0%), reflecting a recent sharp spurt in light manufacturing. Population growth rate, on the other hand, is 2.6%, not much higher than the African average. Malawi ranks fourth in birth rate and in death rate. A number of rankings indicate that the Malawian economy is on

the move: ninth rank on the consumption index, fifth on the agricultural production index and employment index and ninth in energy production annual growth rate. Since 1975 Malawi's external reserves have been dwindling, and the kwacha, the monetary unit, is the 10th weakest currency in the world.

MALAYSIA

Located partly on the southern half of the Malay Peninsula and partly on the northern quarter of Borneo, Malaysia ranks 56th in land area and 50th in population. With a per capita GNP of $860, Malaysia is classified as a lower middle-income country. It ranks 61st on the combined social and economic indicators scale and 76th on the physical quality of life index. The country's economic development is determined by two rankings: a healthy per capita GNP growth rate of 5.3% and a population growth rate of 2.8%. The federation is largely a producer of raw materials and is the world's leading supplier of tin and rubber. Agriculture is the staple economic activity and the country enjoys second rank on the per capita food production index, third on the agricultural production index and seventh in agricultural growth rate. Another favorable ranking is energy production growth rate in which it ranks third, largely as a result of increased petroleum exploitation in East Malaysia.

MALI

A landlocked country in the interior of West Africa, Mali ranks 21st in land area and 78th in size of population. With a per capita GNP of less than $100, Mali is one of the poorest and least developed of low-income countries, and it is also one of the 45 countries most seriously affected by recent adverse economic conditions. Over 75% of the population subsists in absolute poverty. It ranks 137th on the combined social and economic indicators scale and 148th on the physical quality of life index. While its per capita GNP is declining by 0.1% annually, the population is growing by 2.5%, helped by a fertility rate in which it ranks first and a birth rate in which it ranks sixth. Were it not for a high death rate, in which Mali ranks fifth, its annual population growth rate would have been even more disastrous. Mali appears among the top 10 in at least two more negative rankings: external public debt as percentage of GNP and fatal industrial accident rate.

MAURITANIA

Mauritania ranks 26th in land area and 128th in size of population, a disparity characteristic of all desert countries. With a per capita GNP of $340, Mauritania is classified as a low-income country and one of the nations most seriously affected by recent adverse economic conditions. It ranks 118th on the combined social and economic indicators scale and 149th on the physical quality of life index. Its population growth rate of 2.5% conforms to the African average, but its per capita GNP growth rate of 2.6% is above average by African standards. About 90% of Mauritanians live in rural areas as nomadic herdsmen. With over 7 million sheep and goats, Mauritania ranks eighth in the world in sheep per capita and also first in Africa in protein consumption. The most important natural resource is the large deposits of high-grade iron ore in the F'Derick region, exports of which account for 70% of the country's foreign exchange earnings.

MAURITIUS

An island in the southwest Indian Ocean, Mauritius ranks 152nd in land area and 132nd in population. With a per capita GNP of $550, the island is classified as a lower middle-income country. It ranks 64th on the combined social and economic indicators scale and 62nd on the physical quality of life index. The population explosion that followed the eradication of malaria during World War II has been more or less brought under control and the birth rate is now 2.6%, but the per capita GNP growth rate is lagging at 1.6%. The island is one of the most overpopulated in the world and ranks ninth in overall density. Exposed to both French and English cultural values, Mauritians display a natural affinity to the media. The country ranks second in movie attendance per capita and first in Africa in circulation of dailies.

MEXICO

Mexico is the third largest country in Latin America, the 12th largest in the world, the 11th most populous and the largest Spanish-speaking country in the world. Mexico's per capita GNP of $1,090 is the sixth highest in Latin America, placing it in the upper middle-income category. It ranks 56th on the combined social and economic indicators scale and 63rd on the physical quality of life index. Its per capita GNP annual growth rate of 2.3% compares unfavorably with the population growth rate of 3.5%, the fourth highest in Latin America. With its immense natural resources one would expect Mexico to appear among the top 10 in a broad array of indicators but surprisingly it does not. It ranks among the top 10 in 23 rankings with no solid strength in any particular area and it does not lead in any field except perhaps in the production of hormones. Two of the rankings relate to energy (10th rank in crude oil production and natural gas production), seven relate to agriculture (fourth in average size of farms, coffee production and farm ownership; seventh in the production of soybean and corn; and ninth in the production of cotton fiber), three relate to transportation (fourth rank in usable airfields, eighth in pipelines and second in tourist receipts per tourist), three relate to media and communications (seventh rank in output of films and number of daily newspapers and sixth in radio transmitters), one relates to mining (second rank in silver production), one relates to education (eighth rank in number of primary schools) and two relate to finance (sixth rank in stock market performance of industrial shares and fourth in net direct private investment).

MONACO

Monaco is the second smallest independent principality in the world (after the Vatican) and also the second least populous. Although it may thus seem eminently ignorable, it appears among the top 10 in 15 rankings and actually heads 10 of those rankings: first rank in pharmacists per capita, telegrams per capita, television sets per capita, telephones per capita, literacy, density of population, urbanization, dentists per capita and museum attendance. It also ranks ninth in graduate population and fifth in inhabitants per hospital bed.

MONGOLIA

Located in the heart of central Asia, Mongolia ranks 15th in land area and 125th in population. With a per capita GNP of $860 (equal to that of Cuba), Mongolia is classified as a lower middle-income country. It ranks 53rd on the combined social and economic indicators scale and its rank on the physical quality of life index has not been determined. With Albania it has the highest population growth rate of any Communist country (3.0%). Historically, the economy has been pastoral, and the national herd of some 18 to 24 million cattle, sheep and horses account for half of the GDP and 90% of the exports. The country ranks first in horses per capita, fourth in sheep per capita and sixth in meat production. Under Soviet tutelage, defense and education have assumed greater importance and the country ranks eighth in soldier-civilian ratio and third in secondary school enrollment ratio.

MOROCCO

Located in the northwest corner of Africa facing both the Atlantic Ocean and the Mediterranean Sea, Morocco ranks 50th in land area and 36th in population. With a per capita GNP of $540, the country is classified as a lower middle-income country. It ranks 99th on the combined social and economic indicators scale and 102nd on the physical quality of life index. Both its population growth rate and per capita GNP growth rate are balanced at 3.0%. Morocco appears among the top 10 only in three rankings, two of them negative. The only distinction that Morocco can claim is that of being the third largest producer of phosphate. In Africa it is the favorite destination of foreign tourists.

MOZAMBIQUE

Mozambique ranks 33rd in land area and 66th in population. With a per capita GNP of $170, Mozambique is classified as a lower middle-income country and one of the nations most seriously affected by recent adverse economic conditions. It ranks 112th on the combined social and economic indicators scale and 134th on the physical quality of life index. Its per capita GNP is declining by 2.6% annually, while its population is growing by 2.3% despite the highest maternal mortality rate in the world. Mozambique is heavily urbanized, a legacy of Portuguese rule and ranks first in Africa in this respect. Mozambique's economy, shattered in the wake of the Portuguese departure, stands out only on the index of mineral production where it ranks 10th. Nevertheless, the country is relatively well endowed with minerals and has immense economic potential. The giant Cabora Bassa hydroelectric project, the fourth largest in the world and the largest in Africa, is bound to facilitate the expansion of industry and to enhance Mozambique's productive capacity.

NAURU

Nauru, an oval-shaped island in the west-central Pacific, is so tiny that it does not appear worthy of notice. Its land area is only 21 sq km (8 sq mi) and its population slightly over 7,000, making it little more than a good-sized village. It has no capital city and no currency of its own. Yet, Nauru has the highest per capita GNP in the world, $17,140, almost one-third higher than that of the United States, derived entirely from the island's phosphate deposits estimated at 50 to 55 million tons. This distinction has enabled Nauru to come out on the top in several rankings; first rank in literacy, third rank in public expenditures and revenues per capita, second rank in urbanization, fourth rank in inhabitants per hospital bed, seventh rank in teacher-pupil ratio in primary schools and seventh rank in cinema seats per capita.

NEPAL

Located on the southern slopes of the Himalayas, Nepal ranks 88th in land area and 47th in population. With a per capita GNP of $120, Nepal is classified as one of the least-developed, low-income countries and one of the 45 countries most seriously affected by recent adverse economic conditions. It ranks 132nd on both the combined social and economic indicators scale and on the physical quality of life index. Its population growth rate of 2.3% is three times its per capita GNP growth rate. The two rankings in which Nepal appears among the top 10 confirm the primarily agricultural nature of the economy: second rank in percentage of labor force in agriculture and first rank in agriculture's share of the GDP.

NETHERLANDS

The Netherlands ranks 118th in land area and 49th in population. With a per capita GNP of $6,300, the Netherlands is classified as a high-income developed country. It ranks 15th on the combined social and economic indicators scale and third on the physical quality of life index. Its population growth rate of 0.8% is the same as that of the United States, yet its per capita GNP growth rate of 2.2% is much higher, although Dutch economic growth has been constrained in recent years by the general economic slowdown in the West. The Netherlands appears among the top 10 in 60 rankings and reveals unsuspected strengths in many areas. As a nation with the 10th highest density of population, productivity is critical not merely for prosperity but for survival, and the Netherlands ranks fifth in value added per worker. Agriculture is important because more than one-third of the agricultural production is exported. In the agricultural sector the Netherlands ranks third in land under cultivation and on the per capita food production index, ninth in production of milk and butter, seventh in cheese production and pigs per capita and eighth in meat production. The energy sector received a boost when the largest proved natural gas deposits in the West were discovered at Groningen in the 1950s. The Netherlands now ranks third in gas production, sixth in gas reserves and eighth in petroleum refinery capacity. Amsterdam is one of the world's great financial centers and the country ranks high in many financial rankings: sixth in gold holdings, ninth in SDR quotas, fourth lowest in the discount rate of the central bank, first in foreign aid as percentage of GNP, eighth in currency per capita, and ninth in public revenues and expenditures per capita. The Dutch guilder is also the fourth strongest currency in the world. The Dutch also make a strong showing in transportation and communications. Royal Dutch Airlines (KLM) is the world's oldest airline in continuous service, and Rotterdam is one of the world's busiest ports. The nation ranks seventh in aviation (distances flown), third in cargo handled by ports, sixth in domestic mail per capita, ninth in aviation (passengers carried) and third in motorcycles. Because the economy is based on the export of finished goods and import of raw materials, the nation ranks seventh in imports per capita and ninth in exports per capita. The standard of living is reflected in the country's sixth rank in the consumption of paper, fourth in the consumption of coffee and 10th in the consumption of calories. Not only are Dutch houses the third most spacious but the country ranks seventh in new houses per 1,000. Dutch democratic traditions are brought out in their fourth rank on the political opposition index and eighth rank in registered voters. The Dutch are also long-lived; both the men and women have the fourth highest life expectancy, a phenomenon that may be related to the country's seventh rank in health expenditures per capita. Finally, six rankings relating to education, media and culture include the Netherlands among the top 10;

third in press freedom, seventh in volumes borrowed from public libraries, fourth in scientific and engineering manpower, 10th in book production and scientists in basic research, sixth in educational expenditures as percentage of GNP and ninth in advertising expenditures.

NEW ZEALAND

New Zealand ranks 65th in land area and 106th in population. With a per capita GNP of $4,250, New Zealand is classified as a high-income developed country. It ranks 17th on the combined social and economic indicators scale and 15th on the physical quality of life index. Since overpopulation is not a problem, the country can afford to grow at a comfortable rate of 1.9%, a rate that is almost matched by its per capita GNP growth rate of 1.5%. What is most impressive about New Zealand is its standard of living. It ranks second in wool consumption, ninth in spacious houses and consumption of electric power, eighth in telephones per capita, fourth in radios per capita, third in the consumption of tea, fifth in sugar consumption, seventh in commercial vehicles per capita and fourth in passenger cars per capita, and first in the consumption of proteins and meat. Supporting this consumption pattern is one of the most productive agricultural systems in the world. New Zealand is the world's largest exporter of lamb, mutton and butter and the second largest exporter of wool. It ranks first in meat production, eighth in beer production, third in wool production, eighth in butter production, second in sheep per capita and eighth in tractors per hectare. As a welfare state great emphasis is placed on public health and the country ranks 10th in pharmacists per capita and inhabitants per nursing person. On the negative side it ranks sixth in criminal ratio and crime rate and eighth in drug-related offenses.

NICARAGUA

The largest of the Central American republics, Nicaragua ranks 90th in land area and 116th in population. With a per capita GNP of $750, Nicaragua is classified as a lower middle-income country. It ranks 73rd on the combined social and economic indicators scale and 81st on the physical quality of life index. Its per capita GNP annual growth rate of 2.5% is the third highest among Central American republics, and its population growth rate of 3.3% is the second highest in the region. The Nicaraguan economy is essentially agricultural, with livestock raising and the production of cotton, coffee and sugar cane as the main activities. The country ranks 10th in cattle per capita and seventh in horses per capita; in average size its farms are the 10th largest in the world. Nicaragua's economic development took a sharp downswing as a result of the disastrous earthquake that struck Managua in 1972 and the 1979 civil war. The country is recovering slowly from these catastrophes.

NIGER

Landlocked Niger, located on the southern fringe of the Sahara Desert, ranks 19th in land area and 84th in population. With a per capita GNP of $160, Niger is classified as a least-developed, low-income country and as one of the 45 countries most seriously affected by recent adverse economic conditions. It ranks 134th on the combined social and economic indicators scale and next to last on the physical quality of life index. Its per capita GNP growth rate is declining by 2.8% annually, while the population is gaining by almost the same rate (2.7%) with a birthrate that is the highest in the world. The population growth rate could conceivably be higher but for Niger's death rate, which is the eighth highest in the world. Niger ranks third in the world in percentage of the labor force in agriculture—over 95%. The only hopeful economic indicator is uranium, in the production of which Niger ranks fifth.

NIGERIA

Located on the west coast of Africa, Nigeria ranks 29th in land area and 10th in population. The most populous country in Africa, Nigeria accounts for 25% of black Africa's population. Its population density is about twice as high as that for Africa as a whole. It is also, according to Ray Cline, the most powerful nation in Africa with the highest GNP. Nevertheless, its per capita GNP is only $380 and it is therefore still classified as a low-income country. It ranks 139th on the combined social and economic indicators scale and 133rd on the physical quality of life index. Its population growth rate of 2.7% is not markedly worse than that of comparable African nations and is perhaps redeemed by a per capita GNP growth rate of 5.3%. Although less than 20% of the inhabitants are urban dwellers, the country ranks sixth in annual urban growth rate. The most influential growth factor in Nigerian economy is energy; the country ranks eighth in the annual growth

rate of energy production, in natural gas reserves and in the production of crude petroleum. Nigeria is also the fifth largest exporter of oil. The impact of oil is felt in terms of trade, in which Nigeria ranks seventh, in the annual industrial growth rate, in which it ranks 10th; on the construction index, in which it ranks seventh; and in net direct private investment, in which it ranks sixth. Despite petroleum's growing importance, agriculture employs 70% of the labor force and Nigeria claims sixth rank in peanut production and eighth in rubber and roundwood production. Nigeria also leads African nations in the number of students attending foreign universities.

NORTH KOREA

North Korea ranks 92nd in land area and 39th in population. With a per capita GNP of $470 (slightly over two-thirds of South Korea's per capita GNP), North Korea is classified as a lower middle-income country. It ranks 84th on the combined social and economic indicators scale; its physical quality of life rank has not been determined. Its per capita GNP annual growth rate is 0.9%, in comparison with South Korea's 8.2%, and its population growth rate of 2.7% is higher than that of South Korea at 2.1%. Like its southern neighbor North Korea has 100% ethnic and linguistic homogeneity. However, it ranks higher in percentage of population in cities over 50,000 and in land under forests. Although rice and corn are the principal crops, the country appears among the top 10 only in soybean production. The Korean peninsula is believed to be the most militarized region in the world, and North Korea shares with South Korea the spotlight in military rankings. It ranks fourth in civilian-soldier ratio and 10th in men under arms.

NORWAY

Norway ranks 57th in land area and 93rd in population. It is the fifth largest country in Europe, yet it has the lowest population density of any European nation barring Iceland. With a per capita GNP of $7,420, Norway is classified as a high-income developed country. It ranks third on the combined social and economic indicators scale and fourth on the physical quality of life index. With a population growth rate of 0.7%, it is expected to reach a stationary population in 2045. Its per capita GNP growth rate, buoyed by the discoveries of North Sea oil and gas deposits, is a healthy 3.3%. Some pundits predict that Norway will be one of the richest developed countries in the world within a few decades. Even without oil, the Norwegian economy is prosperous and diversified and claims sixth rank in aluminum production, ninth in the production of merchant vessels and 10th in value added per worker. Norway's merchant fleet is the fifth largest in gross tonnage and is the country's largest foreign exchange earner. Less than 4% of the land area is under cultivation and over 50% of domestic grain requirements have to be imported; yet farming is heavily mechanized and the country ranks seventh in tractors per hectare. The Norwegian fishing industry is one of the most developed in Europe and claims the sixth largest catch. With vast water power resources, Norway ranks first in the production of electric energy. Consumption is high in three items: sixth in coffee, 10th in steel and third in paper. The krone is the ninth strongest currency in the world, and Norway ranks fourth in currency per capita, seventh in net direct private investment and eighth in foreign aid as percentage of GNP. As in other Scandinavian countries, the most encouraging rankings are those that deal with health, education and the media. Norwegian women have the longest life spans of any women in the world and Norwegian men have the third longest life spans of any men in the world. Norway ranks 10th in inhabitants per hospital bed and ninth in inhabitants per mental hospital bed, second in dentists per capita and fifth in health expenditures per capita. In the educational sector Norway holds the 10th rank in graduate population, the second rank in literacy, the fifth rank in secondary school enrollment ratio and the eighth rank in teacher-pupil ratio in primary schools. In the field of media the country ranks first in press freedom, 10th in advertising expenditures, seventh in circulation of daily newspapers and ninth in television transmitters.

OMAN

Located on the southeastern part of the Arabian Peninsula, Oman ranks 77th in land area and 138th in population. With a per capita GNP of $2,710, Oman is classified as a high-income developing country. It ranks 71st on the combined social and economic indicators scale. Its population growth rate is an unrestrained 3.1% combined with a negative per capita GNP growth rate of −1.0%. The most interesting fact about Oman is that it appears among the top 10 in all the key defense rankings: second in defense expenditures as percentage of GNP and per

capita, third in defense expenditures per soldier and 10th in soldier-civilian ratio.

PAKISTAN

The third largest country on the Indian subcontinent, Pakistan ranks 32nd in land area and ninth in size of population. With a per capita GNP of $170, Pakistan is classified as a low-income country and one of the nations most seriously affected by recent adverse economic conditions. It ranks 112th on the combined economic and social indicators scale (immediately below India) and 105th on the physical quality of life index. As in other countries of the Indian subcontinent, the per capita GNP growth rate crawls at 0.8% while the population rate gallops at 3.0%. Pakistan displays all the negative characteristics of an underdeveloped economy: unrestrained population growth; a rigid, highly stratified and largely illiterate society, overdependence on agriculture, inadequate infrastructure and limited natural resources. The country boasts of the seventh largest irrigation system in the world yet ranks ninth in share of food in imports. Apart from cotton fiber in which it ranks sixth and butter in which it ranks 10th, agricultural production falls short of the top 10. One of the most unstable political systems in Asia, Pakistan ranks ninth in civil disorders. Like its neighbor India, it is among the world's leading film producers, ranking ninth. It is the fifth largest recipient of U.S. aid and seventh largest recipient of aid from international organizations.

PANAMA

Panama is the least populous mainland republic in Latin America, the 122nd most populous in the world and the 108th largest in size. With a per capita GNP of $1,310, Panama is an upper middle-income country. It ranks 42nd on the combined social and economic indicators scale and 53rd on the physical quality of life index. Because the population density is moderate, the annual growth rate of 3.1% may be considered acceptable, and the per capita GNP growth rate of 2.2% is close to the Latin American average. Panama's population dynamics reveal at least two abnormalities: a high percentage of divorced persons (in which it ranks first) and a high percentage of illegitimate births (in which it ranks eighth). Since 1968, Panama has developed into a major international banking and financial center capitalizing on its location, absence of exchange regulations, liberal banking laws and use of the dollar as Panamanian currency. With one of the most popular flags of convenience in the world, Panama ranks seventh in merchant marine. Tourism, helped by good communications and transportation facilities, claims fifth rank in receipts per tourist. Panama is also noted for its horses and ranks ninth in horses per capita.

PAPUA NEW GUINEA

Located on the eastern half of the island of New Guinea and including a number of island groups, Papua New Guinea ranks 48th in land area and 110th in size of population. With a per capita GNP of $490, Papua New Guinea is classified as a lower middle-income country. It ranks 95th on the combined social and economic indicators scale and 107th on the physical quality of life index. Its per capita GNP grows faster than its population (2.3% and 2.0% respectively). Covered by luxuriant rain forests, Papua New Guinea ranks 10th in percentage of land area under forests. As in other countries in the threshold of development, considerable urban drift has occurred in the past decade; the country ranks first in annual urban growth rate. Papua New Guinea is moving from a plantation-type economy into one based on the exploitation of minerals, yet it ranks among the top 10 in rubber production. The principal mineral deposits are gold, copper and silver. Although its gold reserves are steadily declining, the country still ranks sixth in gold production.

PARAGUAY

A landlocked country in the heart of South America, Paraguay ranks 52nd in land area and 111th in population. With a per capita GNP of $640, Paraguay is classified as a lower middle-income country. It ranks 68th on the combined social and economic indicators scale and 64th on the physical quality of life index. Its per capita GNP growth rate of 3.3% has overtaken its population growth rate of 2.8%. Paraguay's population is unevenly distributed with 96% of the population living in 40% of the territory. Cattle raising, agriculture and lumbering, roughly in that order, constitute the bases of the economy. Paraguay ranks among the top 10 in three agricultural and three livestock rankings: 10th in agricultural growth rate and production of soybeans, sixth in average size of farms, seventh in horses per capita and in cattle per capita and first in the Western Hemisphere in pigs per capita. Two other rankings in which Paraguay stands out are usable airfields (seventh rank) and energy production growth rate (second rank).

PERU

Located on the western coast of South America, Peru is the third largest country in South America, 17th largest in the world and 40th most populous. With a per capita GNP of $800, Peru is classified as an upper middle-income country. It ranks 60th on the combined social and economic indicators scale and 78th on the physical quality of life index. Although the population growth rate is high at 3.0%, its impact is cushioned by a relatively high per capita GNP growth rate of 3.4%. Peru has always been noted for its rich and varied mineral resources and the economy continues to be based on the exploitation of minerals, particularly lead, zinc and iron, as well as silver in which it ranks fourth and copper in which it ranks eighth. Since 1950, Peru has built up a large fishing industry that ranks fourth in fish catch and first in export of fish meal. Despite these favorable trends, Peru faces serious economic problems primarily because of the runaway growth rate of its imports, in which it ranks fourth. As a result the Peruvian monetary unit, the sol, is the eighth weakest currency in the world.

PHILIPPINES

An archipelago of some 7,100 islands and islets with the sixth longest coastline in the world (twice as long as that of the continental United States), the Philippines ranks 61st in land area and 16th in population. With a per capita GNP of $410, the Philippines is classified as a lower middle-income country. It ranks 77th on the combined social and economic indicators scale and 66th on the physical quality of life index. Its traditionally high population growth rate has dipped slightly to 2.9% and is now less than its per capita GNP growth rate of 3.7%. Agriculture is the largest economic sector, contributing 38% of the GDP, employing more than half of the labor force and accounting for 58% of the exports. The Philippines is the eighth largest producer of sugar. With extensive mineral deposits, the country ranks eighth on the index of mineral production and production of gold and ninth in the production of copper. Its chromite and nickel deposits are among the largest in the world. The production of feature films has received considerable impetus from the Marcos regime, and the Philippines ranks fourth in annual film output. It ranks among the top 10 in three educational rankings: fourth in graduate population, seventh in scientific and engineering manpower and second in percentage of women in university enrollment.

POLAND

Poland ranks 59th in land area and 24th in population. In both area and population, it is the largest country in Europe after the Soviet Union. With a per capita GNP of $2,860, Poland is classified as a high-income developed country. It ranks 28th on the combined social and economic indicators scale and 24th on the physical quality of life index, immediately above the Soviet Union. As in all developed countries, the birth rate is low at 0.9%, but at the same time Poland has managed to achieve a high per capita GNP growth rate of 5.8%. Poland is considered the 11th largest industrial power in the world, ranking seventh in steel production, second on the labor productivity index, 10th in the production of television sets, fourth in coal production, seventh in energy production, ninth in cement production, sixth in sulfur production, eighth in cigarette production and 10th in tobacco production. Although the agricultural sector has been declining and per hectare yields are low (because of the acidity and infertility of the soil), Poland ranks second in the production of potatoes, sixth in the production of milk, seventh in the production of butter, eighth in the production of cheese, fourth in the production of oats, and sixth in pigs per capita. Poland is preeminent in educational rankings, placing 10th in university professors, seventh in the production of scientific books, third in volumes in public libraries, seventh in educational expenditures per pupil, sixth in expenditures on scientific research, sixth in vocational enrollment, and 10th in scientific and engineering manpower. The Poles rank ninth in the consumption of steel and sugar. Poland is also the 10th favorite destination of tourists.

PORTUGAL

The westernmost country of mainland Europe, Portugal ranks 105th in land area and 57th in population. With a per capita GNP of $1,690, Portugal is classified as an upper middle-income country. It ranks 38th on the combined social and economic in-

dicators scale and 58th on the physical quality of life index. The country has suffered a significant decline in population (about 2%) since 1960, and the current growth rate of 0.2% is close to the zero population growth level. More encouragingly the per capita GNP growth rate of 4.5% is higher than that of most developed countries. Although Portugal appears among the top 10 in 13 rankings, they do not reveal what might be called any areas of dominance. Financially, the country ranks eighth in gold holdings; militarily, fifth in soldier-civilian ratio; agriculturally, fourth in wine production; and educationally, 10th in percentage of women in university enrollment. The nation also ranks third in cotton consumption and percentage of unionized labor. On the negative side, it ranks seventh in motor vehicle fatalities.

QATAR

A hereditary oil-rich sheikhdom located on the Persian Gulf, Qatar ranks 139th in land area and 155th in population. With the third ranking per capita GNP of $12,660, Qatar is classified as a high-income developing country. It ranks 30th on the combined social and economic indicators scale and 114th on the physical quality of life index. Its per capita GNP growth rate has slowed down to 2.4%, but its population growth rate remains high at 3.1%. Qatar ranks first in energy consumption per capita, and fifth in gasoline consumption and 10th in natural gas reserves. With so much wealth to go around, Qatar ranks first in both public revenues and public expenditures per capita and sixth in currency per capita. A large share of Qatar's public expenditures is obviously being diverted to defense; the country ranks fourth in defense expenditures per capita and second in defense expenditures per soldier. With most of the inhabitants concentrated in Doha and Umm Said, the nation ranks sixth in urbanization. Affluence has also led to a jump in school enrollment per capita, in which Qatar ranks second.

RHODESIA (Zimbabwe)

A landlocked country located in south-central Africa, Rhodesia (Zimbabwe) ranks 53rd in land area and 70th in population. With a per capita GNP of $550, the country is classified as a lower middle-income country. It ranks 89th on the combined social and economic indicators scale, and 97th on the physical quality of life index. Its population growth rate of 3.5% is the 12th highest in the world, while the per capita GNP growth rate of 2.8% is close to the world mean. Prior to the Unilateral Declaration of Independence in 1965, Rhodesia was, next to South Africa, the most economically developed country in sub-Saharan Africa, but U.N. economic sanctions and the burden of anti-guerrilla operations have combined to depress the economy, which nevertheless continues to show consistent, if limited, gains. The country ranks fifth in gold production and first in Africa in tobacco production.

RUMANIA

Occupying the northeastern quarter of the Balkan Peninsula, Rumania ranks 72nd in land area and 33rd in population. With a per capita GNP of $1,450, Rumania is classified as an upper middle-income country. It ranks 32nd on the combined social and economic indicators scale and 29th on the physical quality of life index. Its population growth rate of 1.0% is not significantly different from other Eastern European countries; where it differs is in its per capita GNP growth rate in which it ranks second in the world, with a 10.2% rate, reflecting the impact of oil price hikes on Europe's largest oil producer. But Rumania still remains one of the least-developed countries in Europe, and places among the top 10 in only two energy rankings: sixth in natural gas production and ninth in length of pipelines. Although Rumania ranks fourth in industry's share of GDP, sixth on the manufacturing index, and first in Europe in industrial growth rate as well as first on the labor productivity index, it does not rank prominently in any industrial production ratings. On the other hand, agriculture, long neglected, claims the fourth highest growth rate, eighth rank on the agricultural production index, 10th in the production of potatoes and wine and fourth in corn production. Stressing economic nationalism, maverick Rumania also conducts more than half of its trade with non-Communist countries. The cultural profile of the country is reflected in four rankings: third rank in number of cinemas, fifth rank in vocational enrollment, fourth rank in volumes in public libraries and 10th rank in output of scientific books. On the negative side, Rumania has the highest suicide rate in the world.

RWANDA

A landlocked country in central Africa, Rwanda ranks 129th in land area and 88th in population. As the disparity suggests, Rwanda is one of the most densely populated countries in sub-Saharan Africa. With a per capita GNP of $110, Rwanda is classified as one of the poorest and least developed of low-income countries and also one of the nations most seriously affected by recent adverse economic conditions. It ranks 131st on the combined social and economic indicators scale and 127th on the physical quality of life index. With the seventh highest birth rate in the world, Rwanda has an annual population growth rate of 2.7%, yet it has a per capita GNP growth rate of only 0.2%. Over 75% of Rwandians live in absolute poverty. The economy, overwhelmingly agricultural, operates at a subsistence level; the nation ranks seventh in agriculture's share of the GDP and fourth in percentage of the labor force in agriculture. One of the bright spots in the otherwise bleak picture is the fact that Rwanda produces about 0.5% of the world's coffee.

SAUDI ARABIA

The home of Islam and oil, Saudi Arabia occupies about four-fifths of the Arabian Peninsula, roughly the size of the eastern United States. It ranks 75th in land area and 67th in population. With a per capita GNP of $4,480 (growing by 4.1% annually), Saudi Arabia is classified as one of the high-income developed countries. It ranks 63rd on the combined social and economic indicators scale and 118th on the physical quality of life index. Unrestrained by any control measures, the population has been gaining by 3.0% annually. However, it must be borne in mind that a true census has never been held in the country (the 1974 census may not qualify as one in the proper sense because the enumeration of women is frowned upon and nomads are more often than not left out). All rankings in which Saudi Arabia appears among the top 10 are related in some way or other to energy and oil wealth. It ranks third in energy production, second in production of crude petroleum, fifth in natural gas reserves, first in petroleum reserves, first in balance of trade, and third in ratio of exports to imports and terms of trade. Saudi Arabia's military ambitions are reflected in its sixth rank in defense expenditures as percentage of GNP, third rank in defense expenditures per capita and first rank in defense expenditures per soldier. The ripple effect of oil wealth is felt in all other sectors, pushing the country to the fourth rank in industrial growth rate, first rank on the construction index and educational expenditures as percentage of GNP, fourth rank in cargo handled by ports, first rank in industry's share of GDP and second rank on the consumption index. Saudi Arabia's foreign exchange reserves are expected to exceed $100 billion by 1980, and it is perhaps the only country whose very prosperity may pose a threat to the stability of the world economic system.

SENEGAL

Located on the bulge of West Africa, Senegal ranks 78th in land area and 86th in population. With a per capita GNP of $390, Senegal is classified as a lower middle-income country and one of the nations most seriously affected by recent adverse economic conditions. It ranks 100th on the combined social and economic indicators scale and 138th on the physical quality of life index. Its population growth rate is estimated at approximately 2.5%, which, coupled with periodic droughts and poor harvests, has led to a decline in the per capita GNP by 1.1% annually. The export of peanuts (the principal crop, in the production of which Senegal ranks fourth) provides about 80% of total export earnings. At the same time, Senegal is one of the most industrialized states of West Africa and ranks 10th on the manufacturing index and fourth on the mineral production index.

SIERRA LEONE

Located in West Africa, Sierra Leone ranks 109th in land area and 104th in population. With a per capita GNP of $200, Sierra Leone is classified as a low-income country most seriously affected by recent adverse economic conditions. It ranks 114th on the combined social and economic indicators scale and 119th on the physical quality of life index. Sierra Leone has Africa's sixth highest growth rate in population and 10th lowest per capita GNP growth rate (−0.5%). The major economic activity is mining; the principal minerals are diamonds (in the production of which Sierra Leone ranks seventh), iron ore, bauxite and titanium, which together account for 80% of the country's exports by value. (The world's third largest diamond, the 969.8 carat "Star of Sierra Leone," was discovered here in 1972). The country also claims the third largest deposit of rutile, a form of titanium oxide.

SINGAPORE

One of the world's great commercial centers and ports, Singapore ranks 159th in land area and 115th in population. With a per capita GNP of $2,700, Singapore is classified as a high-income country and, since 1977, as a developed nation. It ranks 36th on the combined social and economic indicators scale and 46th on the quality of life index. Its per capita GNP growth (7.3%) is the fifth highest in the world, while its population growth rate has been successfully brought down to 1.6%, the lowest in Asia outside of Japan. Singapore is the third most densely populated and urbanized country in the world and is a remarkable amalgam of three important Asian races, Chinese, Malayan and Indian. Relative to its size, it excels in several economic indicators. Its currency is the 10th strongest in the world, and it enjoys one of the highest standards of living in Asia. Traditionally geared to the entrepot trade, it ranks fourth in imports per capita and exports per capita, and the port of Singapore is the fourth largest in the world in cargo handled. However, in recent years the government has shifted its economic strategy placing greater emphasis on industrialization. The result has been to make Singapore a regional leader in shipbuilding, electronics and oil-refining industries, with the sixth highest labor productivity index. There has been a dramatic increase in foreign and local investment as reflected in its third rank in net direct private investment. The most surprising fact about Singapore is that although agriculture, limited to 25% of the land area, is a marginal economic activity, the island ranks first on both the agricultural and per capita food production indexes and 10th in pigs per capita. Both the Chinese and the Indians are avid movie-goers and the country ranks third in movie attendance per capita.

SOMALIA

Located on the horn of Africa, Somalia ranks 39th in land area and 102nd in population. With a per capita GNP of $110, Somalia is classified as one of the least-developed, low-income countries and as one of the nations most seriously affected by recent adverse economic conditions. It ranks 132nd on the combined social and economic indicators scale and 143rd on the physical quality of life index. Its population growth rate of 2.6% is close to the world average, and it is one of the 13 African nations reporting a decline in per capita GNP growth rate. Over 75% of the population subsist in absolute poverty. The principal economic activity is the nomadic and sedentary herding of camels, sheep, goats and cattle; the country ranks ninth in sheep per capita. The crushing burden of its recent war with Ethiopia is reflected in its third rank in external public debt as percentage of GNP.

SOUTH AFRICA

South Africa ranks 23rd in land area and 29th in population. With a per capita GNP of $1,340, South Africa is classified as an upper middle-income country. It ranks 62nd on the combined social and economic indicators scale and 88th on the physical quality of life index. Its per capita GNP growth rate of 1.7% is on the same rung as that of Italy and Denmark, while its population growth rate of 2.5% may be influenced by the higher birth rate of its nonwhite inhabitants. South Africa appears among the top 10 in 11 rankings, the principal one being production of gold, in which it ranks first (accounting for about 67% of the world total), production of diamonds, in which it ranks third, and production of coal, in which it ranks eighth. In addition, nearly every useful mineral is found within the country, particularly copper, uranium (in which it ranks second), asbestos, iron ore, platinum, chrome, antimony and manganese. Coal reserves, in which it ranks 10th, are expected to last for half a century. As the most industrialized country in Africa, South Africa has a rapidly growing industrial sector (contributing over 22% to the GDP) that leads Africa in production of steel, pig iron, cement, radio receivers, and steel and in petroleum refining capacity. Agriculturally, South Africa is self-sufficient in most foods and ranks eighth in production of corn, fifth in wool production and first in Africa in wheat production. Consumption of sugar is the eighth highest and that of calories, paper, and wool first in Africa. In the transportation sector, South Africa ranks 10th in usable airfields and first in Africa in aviation (distances flown).

SOUTH KOREA

Located on the southern half of the Korean penin-

sula, South Korea ranks 102nd in land area and 22nd in population. Although it has less natural resources than North Korea, its per capita GNP is much higher at $670, and it is officially classified as a lower middle-income country. It ranks 77th on the combined social and economic indicators scale and 54th on the physical quality of life index. The per capita GNP annual growth rate of 8.2%, the third highest in the world, has been achieved despite a moderately high population growth rate of 2.1%. The South Korean population is ethnically and linguistically the most homogeneous in the world. The most impressive rankings are those that relate to the industrial sector in the growth rate of which South Korea ranks third. It ranks fifth in the production of radio receivers and television sets and 10th in the production of merchant vessels. Although agriculture accounts for one-fourth of the GNP and employs one-half of the work force, South Korea runs a net deficit in food grains every year. Rice makes up 40% of all farm production by value. South Korea is the 10th ranking producer of rice and the ninth ranking producer of soybeans. As the ninth most powerful military nation in the world, South Korea ranks fifth in men under arms and ninth in soldier-civilian ratio. Fish is the chief source of protein in the Korean diet and fishing waters off Korea are among the best in the world. Deep-sea fishing is expanding and Korean ships compete with the Japanese on every ocean. The annual fish catch is the eighth largest in the world. South Korea's development is in no small measure due to the fact that it ranks second in both U.S. military and economic aid. It also ranks ninth in net direct private investment from abroad and fifth in aid from international organizations. The booming economy has pushed South Korea to the seventh rank on the employment index.

SOUTHERN YEMEN

Located on the southern coast of the Arabian Peninsula, Southern Yemen ranks 62nd in land area and 124th in population. With a per capita GNP of $280, Southern Yemen is classified as one of the least-developed, low-income countries and as one of the nations most seriously affected by recent adverse economic conditions. It ranks 108th on the combined social and economic indicators scale and 129th on the physical quality of life index. Like the neighboring Yemen Arab Republic, it has a high population growth of 3.1%, but unlike it the per capita GNP is declining by an alarming 5.8% annually. The decline may be partly explained by the burden of defense expenditures, in which, in terms of GNP, it ranks eighth.

SPAIN

Spain is the 46th largest country in the world, the third largest nation in Europe and the 23rd most populous. With a per capita GNP of $2,920 (the third lowest in Western Europe), Spain is classified as a high-income developed country. It ranks 31st on the combined social and economic indicators scale and 26th on the physical quality of life index. Its population growth rate of 1.0% is higher than that of the majority of Western European countries but so is its per capita GNP growth rate of 5.1%. Since 1960, Spain has been engaged in a effort to shed its reputation as one of the least prosperous nations in Europe. Encouraged by a variety of government incentives, Spanish industry has achieved an excellent long-term growth record and joined the top 10 in a number of areas: ninth in passenger car production, sixth in wine production, ninth in nuclear energy, eighth in cement production, fourth in production of merchant vessels and 10th in petroleum refinery capacity. Although agriculture's share of GDP has fallen from one-fourth to one-seventh, Spain is still primarily an agricultural country and ranks sixth in wine production, eighth in barley production, ninth in egg production and 10th in per capita food production. Spain also ranks first in Europe in average size of farms and 10th in annual fish catch. Acknowledged as the leading tourist country in the world, Spain attracts over 35 million tourists each year. Contributing to its supremacy in tourism is an excellent transportation and communications network that ranks 10th in aviation (distances flown), seventh in aviation (passengers carried) and number of civil aircraft, 10th in radio transmitters and eighth in television transmitters. Spain also stands out in three educational and media rankings: eighth in book production, fifth in expenditures on scientific research and seventh in number of cinemas. Almost as an anticlimax, Spain leads the world in civil disorders.

SRI LANKA

A pear-shaped island in the Indian Ocean south-east of India, Sri Lanka (also known as the Resplendent Isle or the Isle of Delight) ranks 111th in land area and 44th in population. With a per capita GNP of $200, Sri Lanka is officially classified (as are all countries in the Indian subcontinent) a low-income country and one of the nations most seriously affected by recent adverse economic conditions. It ranks 81st on the combined social and economic indicators scale and 52nd on the physical quality of life index. Family-planning programs have managed to bring down population growth rate to 2.2%, high enough to double the population every 25 years. The per capita GNP growth rate is exactly half of the population growth rate. The staple products of the island's predominantly agricultural economy are tea, rubber and coconut, which bring in 90% of foreign exchange and 30% of national income. The country ranks fourth in rubber production, seventh in tea consumption and first in production of amorphous graphite.

SUDAN

The largest country in Africa, Sudan ranks ninth in land area (covering 1.66% of the earth's land surface) and 35th in population. With a per capita GNP of $290, Sudan is classified as one of the least developed of low-income countries and as one of the nations most seriously affected by recent adverse economic conditions. It ranks 115th on the combined social and economic indicators scale and 110th on the physical quality of life index. Sudan's population growth rate of 2.5% is close to the African average, but its per capita GNP of 3.8% is definitely higher. The country's principal distinction is that it is the world's largest producer of gum arabic, supplying 90% of the total. The other leading products are cotton, durra, sugarcane and peanuts, in the production of which it ranks fifth. The agricultural sector has on the whole experienced rapid growth and ranks fifth.

SWAZILAND

A landlocked country surrounded on three sides by South Africa, Swaziland ranks 135th in land area and 136th in population. With a per capita GNP of $420, Swaziland is classified as a lower middle-income country. It ranks 79th on the combined social and economic indicators scale and 106th on the physical quality of life index. The country's high population growth rate of 3.2% is partly offset by a per capita GNP growth rate of 7.9%, the highest in Africa. The economic boom that has made Swaziland one of the more prosperous countries in Africa is stimulated by British and South African investments particularly in iron ore, sugar, asbestos and tourism. A growing percentage of the labor force are wage earners and the country ranks fourth in the employment index. Cattle, status symbols of Swazi wealth, are raised in large numbers and the country ranks ninth in cattle per capita.

SWEDEN

The largest, the most populous and the wealthiest of Scandinavian states, Sweden ranks 49th in land area and 62nd in population. With its fifth ranking GNP per capita of $8,670, Sweden is classified as a high-income developed country. It ranks first in the world on the combined social and economic indicators scale and on physical quality of life index (the latter with a perfect rating of 100). Evidence of this perfect rating in the physical quality of life is found in Sweden's lowest infant mortality rate, highest ranking in life expectancy for males and second highest for females, and near-total literacy. With one of the lowest birthrates, population grows by only 0.4% annually and Sweden is expected to achieve a stationary population by 2015. Per capita GNP growth of 2.3% is close to the world mean. Although one of the world's leading industrial nations with strengths in iron and steel, machinery, construction materials, motor vehicles and ships, Sweden ranks among the top 10 in only two industrial rankings: 10th in cigar production and second in production of merchant vessels. The productivity of the Swedish worker in value-added terms is the third highest in the world. Swedish agriculture does not fare much better, ranking ninth in only two products: roundwood and oats. In fact, the rankings reveal that Sweden has passed into what has been called the post-industrial society in which the key and most sensitive indicators are those that relate to education, health and welfare and consumption, in all of which the country has a solid track record. It ranks first in educational expenditures per pupil, third in volumes borrowed from public libraries, fifth in Nobel laureates, sixth in teacher-pupil ratio in primary schools, seventh in graduate population, eighth in educational expenditures as percentage of GNP and museum attendance and 10th in post-secondary enrollment. As one of the oldest welfare states, Sweden ranks second in public expenditures on social welfare and first in health expenditures per capita, fourth in mental hospital beds and inhabitants per nursing person, third in dentists per capita and seventh in inhabitants per hospital bed. The welfare state extends to industry, and Swedish industrial relations are among the most stable in the world and mandays lost through strikes are among the lowest. Unemployment is virtually nonexistent in many regions. Because welfare costs are paid from taxes, income tax rates are among the world's highest and range up to 85%. Housing is a major priority and Sweden ranks sixth in new houses per 1,000. Consumption is highest in coffee and steel (both first rank), paper (second rank), rubber (10th rank) and gasoline (first rank in Europe). In the transportation and communications sector, Sweden ranks seventh in passenger cars per capita, third in telephones per capita, fifth in television sets per capita and domestic mail per capita. Sweden leads in circulation of daily newspapers and ranks fourth in press freedom and fifth in advertising expenditures. It is the sixth ranking foreign aid donor, devoting 1% of its GNP to assist developing countries achieve better economic and social justice. In the field of energy, Sweden ranks sixth in the production of nuclear energy and fifth in electricity production. As the most powerful neutral country in the world, Sweden ranks eighth in defense expenditures per capita and seventh in defense expenditures per soldier. However, Sweden appears among the top 10 in more negative rankings than any country of comparable size: seventh in abortions and divorce rate, third in mental hospital admissions and drug-related offenses, second in criminal ratio, fifth in crime rate and ninth in suicides. On the whole, Sweden ranks among the top 10 in 70 rankings.

SWITZERLAND

Switzerland ranks 117th in land area and 74th in population. With a per capita GNP of $8,880, the fourth highest in the world, Switzerland is classified as a high-income developed country. It ranks eighth on the combined social and economic indicators scale and seventh on the physical quality of life index. Its per capita GNP, after growing uninterruptedly for over 20 years, began to decelerate in the early 1970s in response to a double-digit inflation and is currently only 0.7%, the same rate as its population growth. Nevertheless, Switzerland still retains its place as the world's most important banking center, and the Swiss franc is the strongest currency in the world. It appears among the top 10 in at least four more financial rankings: first rank in currency per capita, third rank in foreign aid as percentage of GNP, fourth rank in gold holdings, and the lowest discount rate of any central bank. But what is most significant is Switzerland's strength in social welfare, health and educational rankings. It has the second lowest mortality rate, and ranks fourth in public expenditures on social welfare, sixth in Nobel laureates, 10th rank in life expectancy for females and eigth in life expectancy for males, sixth in educational expenditures per pupil, seventh in scientists in basic research, eighth in health expenditures per capita and 10th in mental hospital beds. Because of its geographical position, Switzerland has developed an efficient transportation and communications system; it ranks ninth in aviation for distance flown and fifth in aviation for passengers carried, second in domestic mail per capita, sixth in telephones per capita and fifth in motorcycles. Swiss consumption rates are fifth highest in the world in coffee and fourth highest in paper. The Swiss press is ranked second in press freedom and has the eighth largest circulation per capita. In a related field, the country ranks third in advertising expenditures. Historically a bastion of democracy, the Swiss political system is noteworthy for its second rank on the political opposition index. With such an excellent showing it may not seem important that Switzerland is the second largest per capita producer of cigars and cigarettes, and ranks 10th in the production of nuclear energy.

SYRIA

Syria ranks 80th in land area and 63rd in population. With a per capita GNP of $780, Syria is classified as a lower middle-income country. It ranks 76th on the combined social and economic indicators scale and 82nd on the physical quality of life index. The population growth rate of 3.3%, the fifth highest in the Islamic world, is almost double the per capita GNP growth rate. Nevertheless, there are many encouraging signs among the rankings, such as second place on the construction index, first on the mineral production index, fourth on the manufacturing index, first in annual growth rate of energy production, 10th on the employment index and eighth in annual growth rate of agriculture. As the arch-foe of Israel, Syria has built up a well-equipped defense force. Its military impact is calibrated in two rankings: seventh in defense expenditures as percentage of GNP and sixth in soldier-civilian ratio.

TAIWAN

The Republic of China, commonly known as Taiwan, ranks 119th in land area and 41st in population. With a per capita GNP of $1,050 (more than double that of mainland China), Taiwan is classified as an upper middle-income country. It ranks 55th on the combined economic and social indicators scale and 33rd on the physical quality of life index. The per capita GNP growth rate of 5.7% is nearly three times the annual population growth rate of 2.0%. Ray Cline ranks Taiwan as the 10th most powerful military nation, and it ranks high in three military rankings: second in soldier-civilian ratio, ninth in men and women under arms and sixth in U.S. military aid. During the past two decades, Taiwan has changed dramatically from an agricultural to an industrialized economy. The island ranks eighth in annual industrial growth rate. Taiwan's transportation facilities are reputed to be among the best in Asia.

TANZANIA

Located in East Africa, Tanzania ranks 28th in land area and 38th in population. With a per capita GNP of $180, Tanzania is classified as one of the least-developed, low-income countries and also as one of the most seriously affected by recent adverse economic conditions. It ranks 120th on the combined social and economic indicators scale and 123rd on the physical quality of life index. Its population growth rate and per capita GNP growth rate are balanced at 2.9%. Although 90% of the population is rural, the rate of urban growth is the fifth highest in the world. The economy is overwhelmingly agricultural, with cotton, coffee and sisal representing 40% of all exports. However, the country reaches the top 10 only in the production of roundwood and diamonds.

THAILAND

Thailand, the world's largest Buddhist nation, ranks 45th in land area and 17th in population. With a per capita GNP of $380, Thailand is classified as a lower middle-income country. It ranks 89th on the combined social and economic indicators scale and 68th on the physical quality of life index. Its population growth rate of 2.9% is about the Southeast Asian norm and is partially redeemed by a slightly higher per capita GNP growth rate of 3.6%. Thailand is prominent in three areas: it ranks fifth in rice production and second to the United States in rice exports, and places third in natural rubber production.

TOGO

Located on the Guinea coast of West Africa, Togo ranks 112th in land area and 118th in population. With a per capita GNP of $260, Togo is classified as a low-income country. It ranks 107th on the combined social and economic indicators scale and 124th on the physical quality of life index. The growth rates are 2.5% for population and 2.0% for per capita GNP, both at the less-desirable ends of the scales. It is surprising that Togo's population growth rate is not higher considering it ranks third in birth rate and seventh in fertility rate. Apart from subsistence agriculture, the major economic activity is the mining of phosphates, in the production of which Togo ranks seventh.

TRINIDAD AND TOBAGO

The southernmost islands in the Lesser Antilles chain in the Caribbean, the independent state of Trinidad and Tobago ranks 146th in land area and 131st in population. With a per capita GNP of $2,240, Trinidad and Tobago is classified as an upper middle-income country. It ranks 37th on the combined social and economic indicators scale and 37th on the physical quality of life index. The islands' prosperity has been accompanied by a reduction in the population growth rate to 1.3%. Largely because of its oil wealth, the country's per capita GNP, exceeded only by Venezuela and Argentina, is growing at a steady pace of 2.5%. The three key elements in its economy are oil, agriculture and tourism. Although domestic oil reserves are approaching exhaustion, imports and new discoveries are expected to sustain the islands' high refinery capacity. Trinidad claims the world's largest natural asphalt bog. Despite these favorable indicators, the islands are plagued with the third highest unemployment rate and rank seventh in drug-related offenses and 10th in crime rate.

TUNISIA

Located on the northern coast of Africa, Tunisia ranks 85th in land area and 77th in population. With a per capita GNP of $840, Tunisia is classified as a lower middle-income country. It ranks 75th on the combined social and economic indicators scale and 93rd on the physical quality of life index. After a long spell of indifferent economic performance, the country has rallied and the per capita GNP growth rate has surged to 6.9%, the seventh highest in the world. The population is growing by about 2.5% annually, a high but not alarming rate by North African standards. Although petroleum and tourism are the mainstays of the economy, it is in agricultural rankings that Tunisia stands out. The country has the third highest agricultural growth rate, ranks fourth on the agricultural production index and per capita food production index, and first in Africa in average size of farms. Tunisian women are perhaps the most liberated in the Muslim world, and the country ranks first in abortions in Africa. In the consumption of tea, the national drink, Tunisia ranks eighth.

TURKEY

Occupying the southwest corner of Asia and the southeast corner of Europe, Turkey ranks 34th in land area and 19th in population. With a per capita GNP of $990, Turkey is classified as an upper middle-income country. It ranks 70th on the combined social and economic indicators scale and 79th on the physical quality of life index. Its growth rates are 4.9% in per capita GNP and 2.4% in population. During the 1960s, Turkey experienced sustained and rapid economic growth, and although inflation and adverse balance of payments have slowed this growth in the 1970s, its impetus was sufficient to push the country to the eighth rank on the manufacturing and employment indexes and the sixth rank on the mineral production index. Agriculture, the backbone of the economy, is the most productive sector in terms of top 10 rankings: seventh in wool production, sixth in wheat production, fourth in tobacco production, 10th in cotton fiber production and ninth in barley production. As one of seven countries permitted to export opium, Turkey ranks next to India as the world's largest opium-exporter with about 20% of the market. Turkey has received substantial economic and military aid from abroad and ranks eighth in aid from international organizations and fourth in U.S. military aid. Despite this aid, the Turkish lira is the ninth weakest currency in the world, and the country's wholesale price index is the 10th highest. Turkish economic problems have been compounded by political instability and civil disorders, in which Turkey ranks seventh. The Turks are generally well fed and rank seventh in calorie consumption. There are only two noneconomic rankings in which Turkey appears among the top 10: fourth rank in number of daily newspapers and ninth rank in number of primary schools.

UGANDA

Located in central Africa, Uganda ranks 74th in land area and 51st in population. With a per capita GNP of $240, Uganda is classified as one of the least developed of low-income countries and as one of the nations most seriously affected by recent adverse economic conditions. It ranks 116th on the combined social and economic indicators scale and 112th on the physical quality of life index. Its per capita GNP growth rate of −4.5% is the third lowest in the world, its population growth rate of 3.3% is the 21st highest. Uganda displays most of the characteristics of the typical African economy: overdependence on agriculture (fifth rank in agriculture's share of GDP), a one-crop export market (fifth rank in percentage of primary products in exports) and an above average urban growth rate (seventh rank). The principal cash crop is coffee, in the production of which Uganda ranks fifth. Idi Amin's eight-year rule has pushed Uganda to the verge of bankruptcy and the country has the world's sixth highest consumer price index. Until 1979 it had the highest criminal ratio in Africa and the highest incidence of police brutality.

UNION OF SOVIET SOCIALIST REPUBLICS

Stretching from the Baltic Sea to the Pacific Ocean, the Soviet Union is a superpower in every sense of the term. The largest country in the world (occupying 14.84% of the earth's land surface), it ranks second in length of international borders and third in length of coastlines. It is the third most populous country after China and India. Because Communist states use a different system of national accounting and because the Soviet Union withholds certain types of statistics, it is difficult to estimate the GNP accurately; However, Western economists estimate the Soviet GNP at half that of the United States and its per capita GNP at $2,760 or one-third that of the United States. According to Ray Cline, it is the second most powerful nation in the world, a judgment few would dispute. The Soviet Union ap-

pears among the top 10 in 83 rankings spread over at least 10 areas. It comes out strongest in agriculture, industry, education, energy, transportation and communications, media and culture, mining, defense and labor and weakest in consumption, finance, health, trade and housing. In agriculture, it is less dominant that its size would indicate. It has relatively little suitable farming area; the growing season is brief and variable; many parts of the country are too infertile or too inaccessible; and over 5 million sq km get inadequate rainfall each year. As a result Soviet agriculture suffers from periodic shortages and a few years of disastrous grain harvests (as in 1972 and 1975). Nevertheless, the agricultural sector claims first rank in the production of barley, cotton fiber, wheat, roundwood, oats, milk, rye, butter, lard, honey, raw sugar and potatoes; second rank in wool, fish catch, beef, veal, pork, mutton, lamb and goat meat; third rank in eggs and cheese, fifth rank in tea, tobacco and corn; and sixth rank in soybeans. In industry, its dominance is also far from decisive or complete. Although the Soviet Union has taken the lead in steel production from the United States, it ranks first in only three other products: sugar, cement and pig iron. It ranks second in aluminum production, third in the production of television sets and seventh in passenger car production. Two sectors where the Soviet Union dominates are mining and energy, because its natural resources are so enormous and its proved reserves are but the tip of the iceberg. It is believed to possess every mineral known to man except uranium. It ranks first in coal and lignite, silver, iron ore, copper, chromite, manganese ore, platinum, pyrite, potash and tungsten; second in diamonds, asbestos, gold, lead, mercury, nickel, phosphate rock and zinc ore; third in cobalt, fluorite, molybdenum; and fourth in antimony, bauxite and sulfur. Its energy rankings are equally impressive. It ranks second in energy production, gas production and coal production; first in production of crude petroleum and coal and gas reserves; third in coal production and petroleum reserves; second in the production of electric energy and eighth in nuclear power. Soviet emphasis on education has paid off in a number of rankings: third in the number of primary schools and scientific authorship; second in teacher-pupil ratio in primary schools; seventh in Nobel laureates, educational expenditures as percentage of GNP and post-secondary enrollment; fifth in foreign students in domestic universities; second in scientific and engineering manpower; and first in scientists in basic research and expenditures on scientific research. Although tendentious and steeped in ideology, the Soviet media outranks other countries by sheer numbers: it ranks first in the production of scientific books, volumes in public libraries and the number of fixed cinemas; second in annual output of books, third in the number of dailies; fourth in movie attendance; sixth in annual output of films, and ninth in circulation of daily newspapers. Similarly in transportation and communications, the sheer size of the country has enabled the Soviet Union to claim the first rank in inland navigation, second in pipelines and radio transmitters, third in telegrams per capita, fourth in television transmitters and radio receivers, and sixth in merchant marine. As the most powerful military nation (again according to Ray Cline), the Soviet Union ranks first in men under arms and total defense expenditures, seventh in defense expenditures per capita, eighth in defense expenditures per soldier, and 10th in defense expenditures as percentage of GNP. In consumption the Soviet Union fares badly, appearing only twice in the top 10: eighth in cotton and seventh in steel. The Soviet Union has the highest percentage of industrial work force and ranks second in percentage of women in the work force. Finally, it ranks 17th on the combined social and economic indicators scale and 25th on the physical quality of life index.

UNITED ARAB EMIRATES

A federation of seven emirates, the United Arab Emirates (UAE) ranks 107th in land area and 154th in population. With its second ranking per capita GNP of $11,710, the United Arab Emirates is classified as a high-income developing country. It ranks 27th on the combined social and economic indicators scale and 108th on the physical quality of life index. Its population growth rate is 3.2% and its per capita GNP growth rate, spurred by exploitation of its vast oil riches, an incredible 24%. Not surprisingly, the UAE ranks ninth in the production of crude petroleum, seventh in petroleum reserves and fourth in energy consumption per capita. Its public revenues and expenditures are the sixth highest in per capita terms. It also has possibly more soldiers than it needs and ranks seventh in soldier-civilian ratio.

UNITED KINGDOM

The United Kingdom ranks 70th in land area and 13th in population. Ray Cline considers it the seventh most powerful nation in the world. It ranks seventh in GNP, although its per capita GNP of $4,020 is about half that of the United States level. It ranks 16th on the combined social and economic indicators scale and 10th on the physical quality of life index. Its population growth rate of 0.2% is the third lowest in the world, only barely above zero population growth, and despite its economic vicissitudes the per capita GNP grows annually by 2.0%. The United Kingdom appears among the top 10 in 66 rankings with measurable strength in agriculture, industry, consumption, education, energy, and transportation and communications. It is weakest in health, mining, media and culture, and housing. The United Kingdom is one of the most highly industrialized countries. While the relative importance of traditional industries such as cotton textiles and locomotives has declined, their place has been taken by others such as aluminum (seventh rank); steel (eighth rank); television sets, passenger cars and cigars (sixth rank); pig iron (seventh rank); beer (10th rank); and merchant vessels (fifth rank). Even without the North Sea deposits, the British energy picture is promising. It ranks second in nuclear power, ninth in energy production, fifth in coal reserves and coal and gas production and sixth in petroleum refinery capacity. But the driving force behind British industry is its export orientation. The United Kingdom is the third most active trading nation in the world, accounting for 7% of world trade. Its standard of living is reflected in its fifth rank in the consumption of wool, tin and second rank in the consumption of tea. Agriculture contributes only 3% of GDP yet supplies half the nation's food requirements, and Britain ranks sixth in the production of eggs and barley and ninth in the production of potatoes. British contributions to the intellectual heritage of the Western world are measured, if partly, by the nation's second rank in Nobel laureates and scientific authorship. The United Kingdom remains the sixth most popular destination of foreign students and the seventh favorite destination of foreign tourists. Britain's traditional leadership in transportation and communications is borne out in a number of rankings. The London transport system is believed to be the largest of its kind in any city in the world. The country ranks third in merchant marine (by gross tonnage) and civil aircraft (by number), second in aviation (both distance and passengers), seventh in cargo handled by ports and eighth in the number of locomotives. The country's telephone system is the largest in Europe and the third largest in the world. Per capita the British rank seventh in ownership of radios and television sets. In book production the country ranks fourth in annual output and third in output of scientific books. Although London is no longer the financial hub of a vast empire, Britain is still the seventh largest foreign aid donor relative to GNP. Similarly, although no longer a major military power (ranking below West Germany, France, Israel, China, India, Vietnam and South Korea among conventional powers), it ranks sixth in total defense expenditures. Finally, as the headlines remind us, the United Kingdom is the eighth most strike-prone nation in the world in terms of mandays lost.

UNITED STATES

Acknowledged to be the richest and most powerful nation on earth, the United States ranks fourth in both size and population with the seventh longest coastline and fifth longest international border. Its GNP, which passed the one trillion dollar mark in 1972, is now 1.5 trillion and is expected to nudge the 2 trillion mark within the next decade. Thus the United States with just 5% of the world's population and 6.24% of the land surface produces one-fourth of the gross world product (GWP). If it seems surprising that the United States ranks only sixth in its per capita GNP of $7,890, it should be remembered that the law of averages favors the smaller countries. It ranks sixth on the combined social and economic indicators scale and 16th on the physical quality of life index. Because its population growth rate is only 0.8%, the 21st lowest in the world, it is expected to reach a stationary population of 276 million in 2035. On the other hand, its per capita GNP growth rate, battered by inflation, has dipped to 1.6% and may in all probability recede even further.

The United States appears 144 times among the top 10 in these rankings, 50 times in the first rank. Its leadership is not only versatile and pervasive but also well balanced so that there is no sector where its influence and presence is not felt, with the probable exception of health, where it ranks among the top 10 in only two rankings: sixth in dentists per capita and 10th in inhabitants per nursing person. (This is not surprising because the United States has undoubtedly the most expensive and money-oriented rather than patient-oriented medical delivery system in the world). U.S. dominance in agriculture is so great that it could be called the bread basket of the world. It produces 42% of the world's corn, 52% of the soy-

beans and sorghum, 55% of the tallow and greases, 13% of the wheat, 17% of the tobacco, and 20% of the cotton, meat and barley. U.S. agricultural exports account for more than one-fifth of total U.S. exports and about one-fifth of the total world trade in agricultural products. It leads in the production of corn, eggs and soybean; ranks second in the production of roundwood, oats, milk, and wheat and in average size of farms; and ranks third in peanuts, fourth in potatoes, and fifth in barley and annual fish catch. The United States is the world's leading industrial nation, a position that it owes to a unique interface of technology and business. In terms of total assets of industrial corporations, currently exceeding $4 trillion, the United States is far ahead of all countries. It ranks first in value added per worker, and in the production of passenger cars, aluminium, computers and cheese; second in the production of steel, television sets and tobacco; third in the production of pig iron, radio receivers, cement, cotton fiber and sugar; fourth in the production of cigarettes; fifth in the production of butter; seventh in the production of merchant vessels and eighth in the production of wool. U.S. consumption levels have been the subject of much recent concern and criticism because, at least in some areas, they are characterized by wasteful extravagance and profligacy. Americans rank first in the consumption of paper and rubber, and first in the Western Hemisphere in the consumption of cotton, second in the consumption of gasoline, fourth in the consumption of calories, fifth in the consumption of meat, seventh in the consumption of tin, eighth in the consumption of steel, ninth in the consumption of coffee, and 10th in the consumption of protein and sugar. The United States appears in practically all the energy-related rankings: first in the production of energy, coal, natural gas, nuclear energy and electric energy and in reserves of natural gas and petroleum refinery capacity; third in the consumption of energy and in the production of crude petroleum and sixth in petroleum reserves. However, because of increasing dependence on petroleum from abroad, it ranks eighth in share of fuel in imports. Two bright spots in the energy picture are U.S. reserves of coal, in which it ranks third, and reserves of uranium, in the production of which it ranks first. Among nonfuel minerals the pattern of leadership is not different. The United States ranks first in the production of lead, sulfur, salt, and copper; second in zinc; third in gold; fourth in iron ore and fifth in silver. It produces 69% of the world's mica, 68% of its molybdenum and 46% of its magnesium. The United States appears among the top 10 in 15 educational rankings; it leads in graduate population, Nobel laureates, study abroad, foreign students in domestic universities, scientific authorship, literacy and post-secondary enrollment ratio; and it places second in the number of university professors, fourth in the number of primary schools, third in educational expenditures per pupil, sixth in scientists in basic research, seventh in expenditures on scientific research, ninth in secondary school enrollment ratio and 10th in school enrollment per capita. The United States is one of the few countries where the media are completely under private ownership and are shaped entirely by private initiative and the laws of the marketplace. The latter, however, are not favorable to certain types of media, such as films, with the result that the United States ranks only second in the number of cinemas and eighth in output of films. On the other hand, it leads in the number of daily newspapers, advertising expenditures, and book production and ranks fourth in the production of scientific books. It also ranks seventh in museum attendance and second in volumes in public libraries. The U.S. press ranks seventh in press freedom in the world. In transportation and communications, the United States leads in aviation (both distance and passengers), radios per capita, radio transmitters, length of pipelines, cargo handled by ports, passenger cars per capita, and the number of locomotives, useful airfields and civil aircraft; ranks second in tourism, telephones per capita, television transmitters, and commercial vehicles per capita; ranks third in domestic mail per capita and inland navigation; and ranks eighth in merchant marine. As the second most powerful military nation (according to Ray Cline), it ranks second in total defense expenditures, fourth in defense expenditures per soldier, and fifth in defense expenditures per capita and men under arms. Its financial power is measured in its first rank in gold holdings and SDR quotas and 10th rank in currency per capita. Some of its negative rankings deserve to be noticed. It ranks fourth in drug-related offenses, second in divorce rate, 10th in unemployment rate and civil disorders, and first in mandays lost through industrial disputes.

UPPER VOLTA

A landlocked country in West Africa, Upper Volta ranks 64th in land area and 75th in population. With a per capita GNP of $110, Upper Volta is classified as one of the least-developed, low-income countries and as one of the nations most seriously affected by recent adverse economic conditions. It ranks 136th on the combined social and economic indicators scale and seventh lowest on the physical quality of life index. Its growth rates are 1.1% in per capita GNP and 2.3% in population, the latter despite the eighth highest infant mortality rate and seventh highest death rate in the world. Over 75% of the population subsists in absolute poverty. Upper Volta ranks first in percentage of women in the work force.

URUGUAY

The smallest country in South America, Uruguay ranks 82nd in land area and 107th in population. With a per capita GNP of $1,390, Uruguay is classified as an upper middle-income country. It ranks 45th on the combined social and economic indicators scale and 38th on the physical quality of life index. Hard hit by the fourth highest rate of inflation, its per capita GNP is declining by 0.3% annually, and it ranks third in all three gauges of inflation: the wholesale price index, the consumer price index and the rent index. It places fifth in unemployment rate. Its traditional low population growth rate remains unaffected at 1.2%. Uruguay's richest resource is its livestock, raised on 70% of its agricultural land. The country ranks among the top 10 in all livestock-related rankings: first in cattle per capita and wool production, third in meat consumption, fourth in meat production and horses per capita, and fifth in sheep per capita. As a welfare state with one of the most comprehensive social welfare systems in the world, Uruguay ranks first in social welfare expenditures.

VENEZUELA

Venezuela ranks 30th in land area and 48th in population. With a per capita GNP of $2,570, the highest in Latin America, Venezuela is classified as an upper middle-income country. It ranks 47th on the combined social and economic indicators scale and 57th on the physical quality of life index. Venezuela is one of the least densely populated countries of the Western Hemisphere; the population growth rate of 2.9% (down from 3.4% in the 1950s) is therefore considered acceptable. The per capita GNP growth rate of 1.5% is less than the Latin American average. All of Venezuela's indicators converge on petroleum; the nation ranks eighth in energy production, ninth in petroleum refinery capacity and petroleum reserves, fifth in crude petroleum production, and 10th in length of pipelines. It is also the world's third leading oil exporter. Oil accounts for 90% of export income, 70% of government revenues and 20% of GNP. Closely related is Venezuela's strong performance in trade. It ranks sixth in terms of trade, 10th in ratio of exports to imports, seventh in balance of trade in 1976, and third in ratio of international reserves to imports and in international reserves per capita. Other significant rankings include eighth in diamond production, third in stock market performance, ninth in cargo handled by ports and 10th in press freedom.

VIETNAM

The only country in the world engaged in almost continuous hostilities since the end of World War II, Vietnam ranks 57th in land area and 18th in population. With an estimated per capita GNP of $140, Vietnam is classified as a low-income country, and it ranks 97th on the combined social and economic indicators scale. Population growth rate is estimated at 2.9% (the same as for Thailand), and per capita GNP growth rate at 2.0%. Ray Cline ranks Vietnam as the eighth leading military power in the world, and the Vietnamese have not lost a war since 1945. The quality of their military forces is unsurpassed in the world, and in number of troops the country ranks seventh. Vietnam ranks seventh in rice production and ninth in rubber production, but it is doubtful if these rankings still hold true.

YEMEN ARAB REPUBLIC

A country out of the Middle Ages, the Yemen Arab Republic ranks 79th in land area and 68th in population. With a per capita GNP of $250, Yemen is one of the least-developed, low-income countries and also one of the nations most seriously affected by recent adverse economic conditions. It ranks 130th on the combined social and economic indicators scale and 128th on the physical quality of life index. Its per capita GNP growth rate of 5.8% is inexplicably high; its population growth rate of 2.9% conforms to Middle Eastern levels and is helped by the 10th highest birth rate in the world. Once self-sufficient, Yemen is now the third most dependent on food imports.

WEST GERMANY

West Germany ranks 68th in land area and 12th in population. With a per capita GNP of $7,380, West Germany is the fourth ranking economic power in the world. It ranks ninth on the combined social and economic indicators scale and 21st on the physical quality of life index. With a population annual growth rate of 0.4% (seventh lowest in the world), West Germany is expected to reach zero population growth by 2005. Its GNP per capita annual growth rate, long the marvel of economists, also seems to have stabilized at around 1.9%. West Germany appears among the top 10 in 81 rankings. Its strength is spread over a number of areas. In addition to being the strongest industrial power in Europe (outside the Soviet Union), it is also the world's second most important trading nation after the United States, and the deutsche mark is the second strongest currency in the world. West Germany ranks sixth highest in value added per worker; eighth in industrial share of GDP; ninth in production of salt and sugar; fourth in production of steel, aluminum, beer, television sets and pig iron; third in the production of passenger cars and merchant vessels; sixth in the production of cement and radio receivers; and seventh in the production of cigars. The agricultural sector, although eclipsed by West Germany's industrial might, is still significant and ranks seventh in barley production; fifth in production of eggs, oats, milk, potatoes and cheese; and second in production of butter. West Germany also ranks third in tractors per hectare. Consumption is high in coffee (10th), rubber (fourth) and paper (fifth). West Germans also rank ninth in consumption of calories. Although deficient in oil, West Germany ranks seventh in coal production, eighth in natural gas production and fourth in the production of nuclear power. In the field of transportation and communications, West Germany ranks fourth in aviation (both distances flown and passengers carried), third in the number of locomotives and length of pipelines, sixth in the number of civil aircraft and eighth in passenger cars per capita. West Germany ranks third in total book production and fifth in production of scientific books; its public libraries hold more volumes than all but four nations. Its daily newspapers rank fifth in circulation per capita. West German universities are the fourth favorite destination of foreign students. It ranks third in stock of university professors, eighth in expenditures on scientific research, fourth in contribution to scientific authorship, and third in Nobel laureates (along with East Germany). West Germany ranks second in gold holdings and third in SDR quotas; the discount rate of its central bank is the fifth lowest in the world. In the area health and welfare, West Germany ranks third in health expenditures per capita, ninth in dentists per capita and third in public expenditures on social welfare. On the negative side, it has the eighth highest suicide rate. As the fourth most powerful military nation in the world, according to Ray Cline, West Germany ranks eighth in men and women under arms, 10th in defense expenditures per capita and defense expenditures per soldier and fourth in total defense expenditures.

YUGOSLAVIA

Located in southeastern Europe, Yugoslavia ranks 67th in land area and 32nd in population. With a per capita GNP of $1,680, Yugoslavia is classified as an upper middle-income country. It ranks 43rd on the combined social and economic indicators scale and 48th on the physical quality of life index. Its per capita GNP growth rate of 5.9% is the second highest in Europe (and the 12th highest in the world), while its population growth rate is 0.9% is among the lowest. Although endowed with considerable agricultural and mineral resources, Yugoslavia places among the top 10 in only three rankings: sixth in corn production, 10th in silver production and ninth in the production of radio transmitters. Yugoslavia's performance is significant because it represents one of the most successful efforts to blend a centralized command economy with some elements of a free-market economy. At the same time, the country has suffered from the seventh highest unemployment rate and the highest rate of inflation in Europe.

ZAIRE

Located in south-central Africa, Zaire ranks 11th in land area and 28th in population. With a per capita GNP of $140, Zaire is classified as a low-income country. It ranks 117th on the combined social and economic indicators scale and 125th on the physical quality of life index. Its population growth rate of 2.8% is almost double that of its per capita GNP (1.5%). Drained by one of the longest rivers in Africa, Zaire ranks sixth in inland navigation, and its enormous hydroelectric potential is estimated at 13% of the world total. Zaire is by far the world's largest source of cobalt and industrial diamonds, and it also ranks sixth in the production of copper.

ZAMBIA

A landlocked country in central Africa, Zambia ranks 36th in land area and 80th in population. With a per capita GNP of $440, Zambia is classified as a lower middle-income country, a status that it owes solely to the fact that it is the world's fourth largest copper producer. It ranks 93rd on the combined social and economic indicators scale and 126th on the physical quality of life index. Its population growth rate of 3.2% is high even by African standards. Zambia has the second highest birth rate in the world and also the second highest infant mortality rate. Its per capita GNP growth rate fluctuates widely with copper prices and currently is 0.9%. Zambia appears prominently in three rankings: fifth in energy production growth rate, eighth in urban growth rate and 10th in agricultural land per capita.

BIBLIOGRAPHY

Agency for International Development. *Economic Growth Trends: Africa, Asia, Latin America.* Washington, D.C. 1978.

American Telephone & Telegraph Co. *The World's Telephones.* New York, 1977.

Banks, Arthur. *Cross-National Time Series 1815-1973.* Ann Arbor, 1976.

_____. *Political Handbook of the World.* New York, Annual.

British Steel Corporation. *International Steel Statistics.* London, 1976.

CBD Research. *Subject Index to Sources of Comparative International Statistics.* London, 1978.

Central Intelligence Agency. *National Basic Intelligence Factbook.* Washington, D.C. Biannual.

_____. *Communist Aid to Less Developed Countries of the Free World.* Washington, D.C. 1977.

Cline, Ray, *World Power Assessment.* Boulder, 1977.

Dupuy, Trevor N.; Hayes, Grace P.; and Andrews, John A.C. *The Almanac of World Military Power.* New York, 1974.

Euromonitor Publications. *European Marketing Data & Statistics.* London, 1978.

_____. *International Marketing Data & Statistics.* London, 1978.

Europa Publications. *Europa Yearbook: A World Survey.* London, Annual.

Food and Agriculture Organization. *Production Yearbook.* Rome, Annual.

_____. *Trade Yearbook.* Rome, Annual.

_____. *Yearbook of Fishery Statistics.* Rome, Annual.

_____. *Yearbook of Forest Products.* Rome, Annual.

Gulf Publishing Company. *World Oil.* Houston, 1977.

_____. *World Petroleum Report.* Houston, 1977.

Heron House. *The Book of Numbers.* New York, 1978.

Hoover Institution Press. *Yearbook on International Communist Affairs.* Stanford, Annual.

Institute for Strategic Studies. *The Military Balance.* London, Annual.

International Civil Aviation Organization. *Digest of Statistics-Airline Traffic.* Montreal, Annual.

International Labor Office. *Yearbook of Labor Statistics.* Geneva, Annual.

International Monetary Fund. *Balance of Payments Yearbook.* Washington, D.C. Annual.

_____. *Direction of Trade.* Washington, D.C. Annual.

_____. *International Financial Statistics.* Washington, D.C. Annual.

International Motor Vehicle Association. *World Motor Vehicle Annual.* Detroit, Annual.

International Population and Urban Research Institute. *World Urbanization: Basic Data for City, Country and Region.* Berkeley, 1969.

International Road Federation. *World Road and Motor Vehicle Statistics.* Washington, D.C. Annual.

_____. *World Road Statistics.* Washington, D.C. Annual.

International Statistical Institute. *International Statistics of Large Towns.* The Hague, Series: Latest Available Year, 1969.

International Telecommunication Union. *Telecommunications Statistics.* Geneva, Annual.

INTERPOL. *International Crime Statistics, 1973-75.* Paris, 1975.

Johnson, Hugh. *The World Atlas of Wine.* London, 1977.

Lloyd's. *Lloyd's Register of Shipping.* London, Annual.

Organization for Economic Cooperation and Development. *General Statistical Bulletin.* Paris, Bimonthly.

_____. *Main Economic Indicators.* Paris, Bimonthly.

Overseas Development Council. *Disparity Reduction Rates in Social Indicators.* Washington, D.C. 1978.

_____. *Physical Quality of Life Index.* Washington, D.C. 1977.

Paxton, John. *Statesman's Yearbook.* New York, Annual.

Showers, Victor. *The World in Figures.* New York, 1973.

Sivard, Ruth Leger. *World Military & Social Expenditures.* Leesburg, Va., 1978.

Starch INRA Hooper. *World Advertising Expenditures.* New York, 1978.

Taylor, Charles Lewis, and Hudson, Michael C. *World Handbook of Political and Social Indicators.* New Haven, 1976.

Union Bank of Switzerland. *Prices and Earnings Around the Globe.* Zurich, 1977.

United Nations. *Compendium of Housing Statistics.* New York, 1976.

——————. *Compendium of Social Statistics.* New York, 1972.

——————. *Directory of International Statistics.* New York, 1976.

——————. *Demographic Yearbook.* New York, Annual.

——————. *Monthly Bulletin of Statistics.* New York, Monthly.

——————. *Population & Vital Statistics Report.* New York, Monthly.

——————. *Selected World Demographic Indicators by Countries, 1950-2000.* New York, 1975.

——————. *Statistical Yearbook.* New York, Annual.

——————. *World Energy Supplies, 1971-75.* New York, 1977.

——————. *Yearbook of Industrial Statistics.* New York, Annual.

——————. *Yearbook of International Trade Statistics.* New York, Annual.

——————. *Yearbook of National Accounts Statistics.* New York, Annual.

U.N. Conference on Trade and Development. *Handbook of International Trade & Development Statistics.* New York, 1977.

United Nations Educational, Scientific and Cultural Organization. *Current Social Indicators in the Field of Education.* Paris, 1976.

——————. *Statistical Yearbook.* Paris, Annual.

——————. *World Communications.* London, 1975.

U.S. Bureau of the Census. *World Population, 1977.* Washington, D.C. 1978.

U.S. Bureau of Mines. *Minerals Yearbook.* Washington, D.C. Annual.

U.S. Arms Control and Disarmament Agency. *Worldwide Military Expenditures & Related Data.* Washington, D.C. Annual.

U.S. Government Printing Office. *Social Security Systems of the World.* Washington, D.C. 1978.

Water Information Center. *Water Resources of the World.* Port Washington, N.Y., 1977.

World Bank, *World Bank Atlas.* Washington, D.C. Monthly.

——————. *World Development Report, 1978.* Washington, D.C. 1978.

——————. *World Tables.* Washington, D.C. 1976.

World Health Organization. *World Health Statistics Annual.* Geneva, Annual.

World Tourism Organization. *World Travel Statistics.* Madrid, Annual.

INDEX